Dictionary of Literary Biography

1 *The American Renaissance in New England*, edited by Joel Myerson (1978)

2 *American Novelists Since World War II*, edited by Jeffrey Helterman and Richard Layman (1978)

3 *Antebellum Writers in New York and the South*, edited by Joel Myerson (1979)

4 *American Writers in Paris, 1920-1939*, edited by Karen Lane Rood (1980)

5 *American Poets Since World War II*, 2 parts, edited by Donald J. Greiner (1980)

6 *American Novelists Since World War II, Second Series*, edited by James E. Kibler Jr. (1980)

7 *Twentieth-Century American Dramatists*, 2 parts, edited by John MacNicholas (1981)

8 *Twentieth-Century American Science-Fiction Writers*, 2 parts, edited by David Cowart and Thomas L. Wymer (1981)

9 *American Novelists, 1910-1945*, 3 parts, edited by James J. Martine (1981)

10 *Modern British Dramatists, 1900-1945*, 2 parts, edited by Stanley Weintraub (1982)

11 *American Humorists, 1800-1950*, 2 parts, edited by Stanley Trachtenberg (1982)

12 *American Realists and Naturalists*, edited by Donald Pizer and Earl N. Harbert (1982)

13 *British Dramatists Since World War II*, 2 parts, edited by Stanley Weintraub (1982)

14 *British Novelists Since 1960*, 2 parts, edited by Jay L. Halio (1983)

15 *British Novelists, 1930-1959*, 2 parts, edited by Bernard Oldsey (1983)

16 *The Beats: Literary Bohemians in Postwar America*, 2 parts, edited by Ann Charters (1983)

17 *Twentieth-Century American Historians*, edited by Clyde N. Wilson (1983)

18 *Victorian Novelists After 1885*, edited by Ira B. Nadel and William E. Fredeman (1983)

19 *British Poets, 1880-1914*, edited by Donald E. Stanford (1983)

20 *British Poets, 1914-1945*, edited by Donald E. Stanford (1983)

21 *Victorian Novelists Before 1885*, edited by Ira B. Nadel and William E. Fredeman (1983)

22 *American Writers for Children, 1900-1960*, edited by John Cech (1983)

23 *American Newspaper Journalists, 1873-1900*, edited by Perry J. Ashley (1983)

24 *American Colonial Writers, 1606-1734*, edited by Emory Elliott (1984)

25 *American Newspaper Journalists, 1901-1925*, edited by Perry J. Ashley (1984)

26 *American Screenwriters*, edited by Robert E. Morsberger, Stephen O. Lesser, and Randall Clark (1984)

27 *Poets of Great Britain and Ireland, 1945-1960*, edited by Vincent B. Sherry Jr. (1984)

28 *Twentieth-Century American-Jewish Fiction Writers*, edited by Daniel Walden (1984)

29 *American Newspaper Journalists, 1926-1950*, edited by Perry J. Ashley (1984)

30 *American Historians, 1607-1865*, edited by Clyde N. Wilson (1984)

31 *American Colonial Writers, 1735-1781*, edited by Emory Elliott (1984)

32 *Victorian Poets Before 1850*, edited by William E. Fredeman and Ira B. Nadel (1984)

33 *Afro-American Fiction Writers After 1955*, edited by Thadious M. Davis and Trudier Harris (1984)

34 *British Novelists, 1890-1929: Traditionalists*, edited by Thomas F Staley (1985)

35 *Victorian Poets After 1850*, edited by William E. Fredeman and Ira B. Nadel (1985)

36 *British Novelists, 1890-1929: Modernists*, edited by Thomas F. Staley (1985)

37 *American Writers of the Early Republic*, edited by Emory Elliott (1985)

38 *Afro-American Writers After 1955: Dramatists and Prose Writers*, edited by Thadious M. Davis and Trudier Harris (1985)

39 *British Novelists, 1660-1800*, 2 parts, edited by Martin C. Battestin (1985)

40 *Poets of Great Britain and Ireland Since 1960*, 2 parts, edited by Vincent B. Sherry Jr. (1985)

41 *Afro-American Poets Since 1955*, edited by Trudier Harris and Thadious M. Davis (1985)

42 *American Writers for Children Before 1900*, edited by Glenn E. Estes (1985)

43 *American Newspaper Journalists, 1690-1872*, edited by Perry J. Ashley (1986)

44 *American Screenwriters, Second Series*, edited by Randall Clark, Robert E. Morsberger, and Stephen O. Lesser (1986)

45 *American Poets, 1880-1945, First Series*, edited by Peter Quartermain (1986)

46 *American Literary Publishing Houses, 1900-1980: Trade and Paperback*, edited by Peter Dzwonkoski (1986)

47 *American Historians, 1866-1912*, edited by Clyde N. Wilson (1986)

48 *American Poets, 1880-1945, Second Series*, edited by Peter Quartermain (1986)

49 *American Literary Publishing Houses, 1638-1899*, 2 parts, edited by Peter Dzwonkoski (1986)

50 *Afro-American Writers Before the Harlem Renaissance*, edited by Trudier Harris (1986)

51 *Afro-American Writers from the Harlem Renaissance to 1940*, edited by Trudier Harris (1987)

52 *American Writers for Children Since 1960: Fiction*, edited by Glenn E. Estes (1986)

53 *Canadian Writers Since 1960, First Series*, edited by W. H. New (1986)

54 *American Poets, 1880-1945, Third Series*, 2 parts, edited by Peter Quartermain (1987)

55 *Victorian Prose Writers Before 1867*, edited by William B. Thesing (1987)

56 *German Fiction Writers, 1914-1945*, edited by James Hardin (1987)

57 *Victorian Prose Writers After 1867*, edited by William B. Thesing (1987)

58 *Jacobean and Caroline Dramatists*, edited by Fredson Bowers (1987)

59 *American Literary Critics and Scholars, 1800-1850*, edited by John W. Rathbun and Monica M. Grecu (1987)

60 *Canadian Writers Since 1960, Second Series*, edited by W. H. New (1987)

61 *American Writers for Children Since 1960: Poets, Illustrators, and Nonfiction Authors*, edited by Glenn E. Estes (1987)

62 *Elizabethan Dramatists*, edited by Fredson Bowers (1987)

63 *Modern American Critics, 1920-1955*, edited by Gregory S. Jay (1988)

64 *American Literary Critics and Scholars, 1850-1880*, edited by John W. Rathbun and Monica M. Grecu (1988)

65 *French Novelists, 1900-1930*, edited by Catharine Savage Brosman (1988)

66 *German Fiction Writers, 1885-1913*, 2 parts, edited by James Hardin (1988)

67 *Modern American Critics Since 1955*, edited by Gregory S. Jay (1988)

68 *Canadian Writers, 1920-1959, First Series*, edited by W. H. New (1988)

69 *Contemporary German Fiction Writers, First Series*, edited by Wolfgang D. Elfe and James Hardin (1988)

70 *British Mystery Writers, 1860-1919*, edited by Bernard Benstock and Thomas F. Staley (1988)

71 *American Literary Critics and Scholars, 1880-1900*, edited by John W. Rathbun and Monica M. Grecu (1988)

72 *French Novelists, 1930-1960*, edited by Catharine Savage Brosman (1988)

73 *American Magazine Journalists, 1741-1850*, edited by Sam G. Riley (1988)

74 *American Short-Story Writers Before 1880*, edited by Bobby Ellen Kimbel, with the assistance of William E. Grant (1988)

75 *Contemporary German Fiction Writers, Second Series,* edited by Wolfgang D. Elfe and James Hardin (1988)

76 *Afro-American Writers, 1940–1955,* edited by Trudier Harris (1988)

77 *British Mystery Writers, 1920–1939,* edited by Bernard Benstock and Thomas F. Staley (1988)

78 *American Short-Story Writers, 1880–1910,* edited by Bobby Ellen Kimbel, with the assistance of William E. Grant (1988)

79 *American Magazine Journalists, 1850–1900,* edited by Sam G. Riley (1988)

80 *Restoration and Eighteenth-Century Dramatists, First Series,* edited by Paula R. Backscheider (1989)

81 *Austrian Fiction Writers, 1875–1913,* edited by James Hardin and Donald G. Daviau (1989)

82 *Chicano Writers, First Series,* edited by Francisco A. Lomelí and Carl R. Shirley (1989)

83 *French Novelists Since 1960,* edited by Catharine Savage Brosman (1989)

84 *Restoration and Eighteenth-Century Dramatists, Second Series,* edited by Paula R. Backscheider (1989)

85 *Austrian Fiction Writers After 1914,* edited by James Hardin and Donald G. Daviau (1989)

86 *American Short-Story Writers, 1910–1945, First Series,* edited by Bobby Ellen Kimbel (1989)

87 *British Mystery and Thriller Writers Since 1940, First Series,* edited by Bernard Benstock and Thomas F. Staley (1989)

88 *Canadian Writers, 1920–1959, Second Series,* edited by W. H. New (1989)

89 *Restoration and Eighteenth-Century Dramatists, Third Series,* edited by Paula R. Backscheider (1989)

90 *German Writers in the Age of Goethe, 1789–1832,* edited by James Hardin and Christoph E. Schweitzer (1989)

91 *American Magazine Journalists, 1900–1960, First Series,* edited by Sam G. Riley (1990)

92 *Canadian Writers, 1890–1920,* edited by W. H. New (1990)

93 *British Romantic Poets, 1789–1832, First Series,* edited by John R. Greenfield (1990)

94 *German Writers in the Age of Goethe: Sturm und Drang to Classicism,* edited by James Hardin and Christoph E. Schweitzer (1990)

95 *Eighteenth-Century British Poets, First Series,* edited by John Sitter (1990)

96 *British Romantic Poets, 1789–1832, Second Series,* edited by John R. Greenfield (1990)

97 *German Writers from the Enlightenment to Sturm und Drang, 1720–1764,* edited by James Hardin and Christoph E. Schweitzer (1990)

98 *Modern British Essayists, First Series,* edited by Robert Beum (1990)

99 *Canadian Writers Before 1890,* edited by W. H. New (1990)

100 *Modern British Essayists, Second Series,* edited by Robert Beum (1990)

101 *British Prose Writers, 1660–1800, First Series,* edited by Donald T. Siebert (1991)

102 *American Short-Story Writers, 1910–1945, Second Series,* edited by Bobby Ellen Kimbel (1991)

103 *American Literary Biographers, First Series,* edited by Steven Serafin (1991)

104 *British Prose Writers, 1660–1800, Second Series,* edited by Donald T. Siebert (1991)

105 *American Poets Since World War II, Second Series,* edited by R. S. Gwynn (1991)

106 *British Literary Publishing Houses, 1820–1880,* edited by Patricia J. Anderson and Jonathan Rose (1991)

107 *British Romantic Prose Writers, 1789–1832, First Series,* edited by John R. Greenfield (1991)

108 *Twentieth-Century Spanish Poets, First Series,* edited by Michael L. Perna (1991)

109 *Eighteenth-Century British Poets, Second Series,* edited by John Sitter (1991)

110 *British Romantic Prose Writers, 1789–1832, Second Series,* edited by John R. Greenfield (1991)

111 *American Literary Biographers, Second Series,* edited by Steven Serafin (1991)

112 *British Literary Publishing Houses, 1881–1965,* edited by Jonathan Rose and Patricia J. Anderson (1991)

113 *Modern Latin-American Fiction Writers, First Series,* edited by William Luis (1992)

114 *Twentieth-Century Italian Poets, First Series,* edited by Giovanna Wedel De Stasio, Glauco Cambon, and Antonio Illiano (1992)

115 *Medieval Philosophers,* edited by Jeremiah Hackett (1992)

116 *British Romantic Novelists, 1789–1832,* edited by Bradford K. Mudge (1992)

117 *Twentieth-Century Caribbean and Black African Writers, First Series,* edited by Bernth Lindfors and Reinhard Sander (1992)

118 *Twentieth-Century German Dramatists, 1889–1918,* edited by Wolfgang D. Elfe and James Hardin (1992)

119 *Nineteenth-Century French Fiction Writers: Romanticism and Realism, 1800–1860,* edited by Catharine Savage Brosman (1992)

120 *American Poets Since World War II, Third Series,* edited by R. S. Gwynn (1992)

121 *Seventeenth-Century British Nondramatic Poets, First Series,* edited by M. Thomas Hester (1992)

122 *Chicano Writers, Second Series,* edited by Francisco A. Lomelí and Carl R. Shirley (1992)

123 *Nineteenth-Century French Fiction Writers: Naturalism and Beyond, 1860–1900,* edited by Catharine Savage Brosman (1992)

124 *Twentieth-Century German Dramatists, 1919–1992,* edited by Wolfgang D. Elfe and James Hardin (1992)

125 *Twentieth-Century Caribbean and Black African Writers, Second Series,* edited by Bernth Lindfors and Reinhard Sander (1993)

126 *Seventeenth-Century British Nondramatic Poets, Second Series,* edited by M. Thomas Hester (1993)

127 *American Newspaper Publishers, 1950–1990,* edited by Perry J. Ashley (1993)

128 *Twentieth-Century Italian Poets, Second Series,* edited by Giovanna Wedel De Stasio, Glauco Cambon, and Antonio Illiano (1993)

129 *Nineteenth-Century German Writers, 1841–1900,* edited by James Hardin and Siegfried Mews (1993)

130 *American Short-Story Writers Since World War II,* edited by Patrick Meanor (1993)

131 *Seventeenth-Century British Nondramatic Poets, Third Series,* edited by M. Thomas Hester (1993)

132 *Sixteenth-Century British Nondramatic Writers, First Series,* edited by David A. Richardson (1993)

133 *Nineteenth-Century German Writers to 1840,* edited by James Hardin and Siegfried Mews (1993)

134 *Twentieth-Century Spanish Poets, Second Series,* edited by Jerry Phillips Winfield (1994)

135 *British Short-Fiction Writers, 1880–1914: The Realist Tradition,* edited by William B. Thesing (1994)

136 *Sixteenth-Century British Nondramatic Writers, Second Series,* edited by David A. Richardson (1994)

137 *American Magazine Journalists, 1900–1960, Second Series,* edited by Sam G. Riley (1994)

138 *German Writers and Works of the High Middle Ages: 1170–1280,* edited by James Hardin and Will Hasty (1994)

139 *British Short-Fiction Writers, 1945–1980,* edited by Dean Baldwin (1994)

140 *American Book-Collectors and Bibliographers, First Series,* edited by Joseph Rosenblum (1994)

141 *British Children's Writers, 1880–1914,* edited by Laura M. Zaidman (1994)

142 *Eighteenth-Century British Literary Biographers,* edited by Steven Serafin (1994)

143 *American Novelists Since World War II, Third Series,* edited by James R. Giles and Wanda H. Giles (1994)

144 *Nineteenth-Century British Literary Biographers,* edited by Steven Serafin (1994)

145 *Modern Latin-American Fiction Writers, Second Series,* edited by William Luis and Ann González (1994)

146 *Old and Middle English Literature,* edited by Jeffrey Helterman and Jerome Mitchell (1994)

147 *South Slavic Writers Before World War II,* edited by Vasa D. Mihailovich (1994)

148 *German Writers and Works of the Early Middle Ages: 800–1170,* edited by Will Hasty and James Hardin (1994)

149 *Late Nineteenth- and Early Twentieth-Century British Literary Biographers,* edited by Steven Serafin (1995)

150 *Early Modern Russian Writers, Late Seventeenth and Eighteenth Centuries,* edited by Marcus C. Levitt (1995)

151 *British Prose Writers of the Early Seventeenth Century*, edited by Clayton D. Lein (1995)
152 *American Novelists Since World War II, Fourth Series*, edited by James R. Giles and Wanda H. Giles (1995)
153 *Late-Victorian and Edwardian British Novelists, First Series*, edited by George M. Johnson (1995)
154 *The British Literary Book Trade, 1700–1820*, edited by James K. Bracken and Joel Silver (1995)
155 *Twentieth-Century British Literary Biographers*, edited by Steven Serafin (1995)
156 *British Short-Fiction Writers, 1880–1914: The Romantic Tradition*, edited by William F. Naufftus (1995)
157 *Twentieth-Century Caribbean and Black African Writers, Third Series*, edited by Bernth Lindfors and Reinhard Sander (1995)
158 *British Reform Writers, 1789–1832*, edited by Gary Kelly and Edd Applegate (1995)
159 *British Short-Fiction Writers, 1800–1880*, edited by John R. Greenfield (1996)
160 *British Children's Writers, 1914–1960*, edited by Donald R. Hettinga and Gary D. Schmidt (1996)
161 *British Children's Writers Since 1960, First Series*, edited by Caroline Hunt (1996)
162 *British Short-Fiction Writers, 1915–1945*, edited by John H. Rogers (1996)
163 *British Children's Writers, 1800–1880*, edited by Meena Khorana (1996)
164 *German Baroque Writers, 1580–1660*, edited by James Hardin (1996)
165 *American Poets Since World War II, Fourth Series*, edited by Joseph Conte (1996)
166 *British Travel Writers, 1837–1875*, edited by Barbara Brothers and Julia Gergits (1996)
167 *Sixteenth-Century British Nondramatic Writers, Third Series*, edited by David A. Richardson (1996)
168 *German Baroque Writers, 1661–1730*, edited by James Hardin (1996)
169 *American Poets Since World War II, Fifth Series*, edited by Joseph Conte (1996)
170 *The British Literary Book Trade, 1475–1700*, edited by James K. Bracken and Joel Silver (1996)
171 *Twentieth-Century American Sportswriters*, edited by Richard Orodenker (1996)
172 *Sixteenth-Century British Nondramatic Writers, Fourth Series*, edited by David A. Richardson (1996)
173 *American Novelists Since World War II, Fifth Series*, edited by James R. Giles and Wanda H. Giles (1996)
174 *British Travel Writers, 1876–1909*, edited by Barbara Brothers and Julia Gergits (1997)
175 *Native American Writers of the United States*, edited by Kenneth M. Roemer (1997)
176 *Ancient Greek Authors*, edited by Ward W. Briggs (1997)
177 *Italian Novelists Since World War II, 1945–1965*, edited by Augustus Pallotta (1997)

178 *British Fantasy and Science-Fiction Writers Before World War I*, edited by Darren Harris-Fain (1997)
179 *German Writers of the Renaissance and Reformation, 1280–1580*, edited by James Hardin and Max Reinhart (1997)
180 *Japanese Fiction Writers, 1868–1945*, edited by Van C. Gessel (1997)
181 *South Slavic Writers Since World War II*, edited by Vasa D. Mihailovich (1997)
182 *Japanese Fiction Writers Since World War II*, edited by Van C. Gessel (1997)
183 *American Travel Writers, 1776–1864*, edited by James J. Schramer and Donald Ross (1997)
184 *Nineteenth-Century British Book-Collectors and Bibliographers*, edited by William Baker and Kenneth Womack (1997)
185 *American Literary Journalists, 1945–1995, First Series*, edited by Arthur J. Kaul (1998)
186 *Nineteenth-Century American Western Writers*, edited by Robert L. Gale (1998)
187 *American Book Collectors and Bibliographers, Second Series*, edited by Joseph Rosenblum (1998)
188 *American Book and Magazine Illustrators to 1920*, edited by Steven E. Smith, Catherine A. Hastedt, and Donald H. Dyal (1998)
189 *American Travel Writers, 1850–1915*, edited by Donald Ross and James J. Schramer (1998)
190 *British Reform Writers, 1832–1914*, edited by Gary Kelly and Edd Applegate (1998)
191 *British Novelists Between the Wars*, edited by George M. Johnson (1998)
192 *French Dramatists, 1789–1914*, edited by Barbara T. Cooper (1998)
193 *American Poets Since World War II, Sixth Series*, edited by Joseph Conte (1998)
194 *British Novelists Since 1960, Second Series*, edited by Merritt Moseley (1998)
195 *British Travel Writers, 1910–1939*, edited by Barbara Brothers and Julia Gergits (1998)
196 *Italian Novelists Since World War II, 1965–1995*, edited by Augustus Pallotta (1999)
197 *Late-Victorian and Edwardian British Novelists, Second Series*, edited by George M. Johnson (1999)
198 *Russian Literature in the Age of Pushkin and Gogol: Prose*, edited by Christine A. Rydel (1999)
199 *Victorian Women Poets*, edited by William B. Thesing (1999)
200 *American Women Prose Writers to 1820*, edited by Carla J. Mulford, with Angela Vietto and Amy E. Winans (1999)
201 *Twentieth-Century British Book Collectors and Bibliographers*, edited by William Baker and Kenneth Womack (1999)
202 *Nineteenth-Century American Fiction Writers*, edited by Kent P. Ljungquist (1999)
203 *Medieval Japanese Writers*, edited by Steven D. Carter (1999)

204 *British Travel Writers, 1940–1997*, edited by Barbara Brothers and Julia M. Gergits (1999)
205 *Russian Literature in the Age of Pushkin and Gogol: Poetry and Drama*, edited by Christine A. Rydel (1999)
206 *Twentieth-Century American Western Writers, First Series*, edited by Richard H. Cracroft (1999)
207 *British Novelists Since 1960, Third Series*, edited by Merritt Moseley (1999)
208 *Literature of the French and Occitan Middle Ages: Eleventh to Fifteenth Centuries*, edited by Deborah Sinnreich-Levi and Ian S. Laurie (1999)
209 *Chicano Writers, Third Series*, edited by Francisco A. Lomelí and Carl R. Shirley (1999)
210 *Ernest Hemingway: A Documentary Volume*, edited by Robert W. Trogdon (1999)
211 *Ancient Roman Writers*, edited by Ward W. Briggs (1999)
212 *Twentieth-Century American Western Writers, Second Series*, edited by Richard H. Cracroft (1999)
213 *Pre-Nineteenth-Century British Book Collectors and Bibliographers*, edited by William Baker and Kenneth Womack (1999)
214 *Twentieth-Century Danish Writers*, edited by Marianne Stecher-Hansen (1999)
215 *Twentieth-Century Eastern European Writers, First Series*, edited by Steven Serafin (1999)
216 *British Poets of the Great War: Brooke, Rosenberg, Thomas. A Documentary Volume*, edited by Patrick Quinn (2000)
217 *Nineteenth-Century French Poets*, edited by Robert Beum (2000)
218 *American Short-Story Writers Since World War II, Second Series*, edited by Patrick Meanor and Gwen Crane (2000)
219 *F. Scott Fitzgerald's* The Great Gatsby: *A Documentary Volume*, edited by Matthew J. Bruccoli (2000)
220 *Twentieth-Century Eastern European Writers, Second Series*, edited by Steven Serafin (2000)
221 *American Women Prose Writers, 1870–1920*, edited by Sharon M. Harris, with the assistance of Heidi L. M. Jacobs and Jennifer Putzi (2000)
222 *H. L. Mencken: A Documentary Volume*, edited by Richard J. Schrader (2000)
223 *The American Renaissance in New England, Second Series*, edited by Wesley T. Mott (2000)
224 *Walt Whitman: A Documentary Volume*, edited by Joel Myerson (2000)
225 *South African Writers*, edited by Paul A. Scanlon (2000)
226 *American Hard-Boiled Crime Writers*, edited by George Parker Anderson and Julie B. Anderson (2000)
227 *American Novelists Since World War II, Sixth Series*, edited by James R. Giles and Wanda H. Giles (2000)
228 *Twentieth-Century American Dramatists, Second Series*, edited by Christopher J. Wheatley (2000)
229 *Thomas Wolfe: A Documentary Volume*, edited by Ted Mitchell (2001)

230 *Australian Literature, 1788–1914*, edited by Selina Samuels (2001)

231 *British Novelists Since 1960, Fourth Series*, edited by Merritt Moseley (2001)

232 *Twentieth-Century Eastern European Writers, Third Series*, edited by Steven Serafin (2001)

233 *British and Irish Dramatists Since World War II, Second Series*, edited by John Bull (2001)

234 *American Short-Story Writers Since World War II, Third Series*, edited by Patrick Meanor and Richard E. Lee (2001)

235 *The American Renaissance in New England, Third Series*, edited by Wesley T. Mott (2001)

236 *British Rhetoricians and Logicians, 1500–1660*, edited by Edward A. Malone (2001)

237 *The Beats: A Documentary Volume*, edited by Matt Theado (2001)

238 *Russian Novelists in the Age of Tolstoy and Dostoevsky*, edited by J. Alexander Ogden and Judith E. Kalb (2001)

239 *American Women Prose Writers: 1820–1870*, edited by Amy E. Hudock and Katharine Rodier (2001)

240 *Late Nineteenth- and Early Twentieth-Century British Women Poets*, edited by William B. Thesing (2001)

241 *American Sportswriters and Writers on Sport*, edited by Richard Orodenker (2001)

242 *Twentieth-Century European Cultural Theorists, First Series*, edited by Paul Hansom (2001)

243 *The American Renaissance in New England, Fourth Series*, edited by Wesley T. Mott (2001)

244 *American Short-Story Writers Since World War II, Fourth Series*, edited by Patrick Meanor and Joseph McNicholas (2001)

245 *British and Irish Dramatists Since World War II, Third Series*, edited by John Bull (2001)

246 *Twentieth-Century American Cultural Theorists*, edited by Paul Hansom (2001)

247 *James Joyce: A Documentary Volume*, edited by A. Nicholas Fargnoli (2001)

248 *Antebellum Writers in the South, Second Series*, edited by Kent Ljungquist (2001)

249 *Twentieth-Century American Dramatists, Third Series*, edited by Christopher Wheatley (2002)

250 *Antebellum Writers in New York, Second Series*, edited by Kent Ljungquist (2002)

251 *Canadian Fantasy and Science-Fiction Writers*, edited by Douglas Ivison (2002)

252 *British Philosophers, 1500–1799*, edited by Philip B. Dematteis and Peter S. Fosl (2002)

253 *Raymond Chandler: A Documentary Volume*, edited by Robert Moss (2002)

254 *The House of Putnam, 1837–1872: A Documentary Volume*, edited by Ezra Greenspan (2002)

255 *British Fantasy and Science-Fiction Writers, 1918–1960*, edited by Darren Harris-Fain (2002)

256 *Twentieth-Century American Western Writers, Third Series*, edited by Richard H. Cracroft (2002)

257 *Twentieth-Century Swedish Writers After World War II*, edited by Ann-Charlotte Gavel Adams (2002)

258 *Modern French Poets*, edited by Jean-François Leroux (2002)

259 *Twentieth-Century Swedish Writers Before World War II*, edited by Ann-Charlotte Gavel Adams (2002)

260 *Australian Writers, 1915–1950*, edited by Selina Samuels (2002)

Dictionary of Literary Biography Documentary Series

1 *Sherwood Anderson, Willa Cather, John Dos Passos, Theodore Dreiser, F. Scott Fitzgerald, Ernest Hemingway, Sinclair Lewis*, edited by Margaret A. Van Antwerp (1982)

2 *James Gould Cozzens, James T. Farrell, William Faulkner, John O'Hara, John Steinbeck, Thomas Wolfe, Richard Wright*, edited by Margaret A. Van Antwerp (1982)

3 *Saul Bellow, Jack Kerouac, Norman Mailer, Vladimir Nabokov, John Updike, Kurt Vonnegut*, edited by Mary Bruccoli (1983)

4 *Tennessee Williams*, edited by Margaret A. Van Antwerp and Sally Johns (1984)

5 *American Transcendentalists*, edited by Joel Myerson (1988)

6 *Hardboiled Mystery Writers: Raymond Chandler, Dashiell Hammett, Ross Macdonald*, edited by Matthew J. Bruccoli and Richard Layman (1989)

7 *Modern American Poets: James Dickey, Robert Frost, Marianne Moore*, edited by Karen L. Rood (1989)

8 *The Black Aesthetic Movement*, edited by Jeffrey Louis Decker (1991)

9 *American Writers of the Vietnam War: W. D. Ehrhart, Larry Heinemann, Tim O'Brien, Walter McDonald, John M. Del Vecchio*, edited by Ronald Baughman (1991)

10 *The Bloomsbury Group*, edited by Edward L. Bishop (1992)

11 *American Proletarian Culture: The Twenties and The Thirties*, edited by Jon Christian Suggs (1993)

12 *Southern Women Writers: Flannery O'Connor, Katherine Anne Porter, Eudora Welty*, edited by Mary Ann Wimsatt and Karen L. Rood (1994)

13 *The House of Scribner, 1846–1904*, edited by John Delaney (1996)

14 *Four Women Writers for Children, 1868–1918*, edited by Caroline C. Hunt (1996)

15 *American Expatriate Writers: Paris in the Twenties*, edited by Matthew J. Bruccoli and Robert W. Trogdon (1997)

16 *The House of Scribner, 1905–1930*, edited by John Delaney (1997)

17 *The House of Scribner, 1931–1984*, edited by John Delaney (1998)

18 *British Poets of The Great War: Sassoon, Graves, Owen*, edited by Patrick Quinn (1999)

19 *James Dickey*, edited by Judith S. Baughman (1999)

See also DLB 210, 216, 219, 222, 224, 229, 237, 247, 253, 254

Dictionary of Literary Biography Yearbooks

1980 edited by Karen L. Rood, Jean W. Ross, and Richard Ziegfeld (1981)
1981 edited by Karen L. Rood, Jean W. Ross, and Richard Ziegfeld (1982)
1982 edited by Richard Ziegfeld; associate editors: Jean W. Ross and Lynne C. Zeigler (1983)
1983 edited by Mary Bruccoli and Jean W. Ross; associate editor Richard Ziegfeld (1984)
1984 edited by Jean W. Ross (1985)
1985 edited by Jean W. Ross (1986)
1986 edited by J. M. Brook (1987)
1987 edited by J. M. Brook (1988)
1988 edited by J. M. Brook (1989)
1989 edited by J. M. Brook (1990)
1990 edited by James W. Hipp (1991)
1991 edited by James W. Hipp (1992)
1992 edited by James W. Hipp (1993)
1993 edited by James W. Hipp, contributing editor George Garrett (1994)
1994 edited by James W. Hipp, contributing editor George Garrett (1995)
1995 edited by James W. Hipp, contributing editor George Garrett (1996)
1996 edited by Samuel W. Bruce and L. Kay Webster, contributing editor George Garrett (1997)
1997 edited by Matthew J. Bruccoli and George Garrett, with the assistance of L. Kay Webster (1998)
1998 edited by Matthew J. Bruccoli, contributing editor George Garrett, with the assistance of D. W. Thomas (1999)
1999 edited by Matthew J. Bruccoli, contributing editor George Garrett, with the assistance of D. W. Thomas (2000)
2000 edited by Matthew J. Bruccoli, contributing editor George Garrett, with the assistance of George Parker Anderson (2001)
2001 edited by Matthew J. Bruccoli, contributing editor George Garrett, with the assistance of George Parker Anderson (2002)

Concise Series

Concise Dictionary of American Literary Biography, 7 volumes (1988–1999): *The New Consciousness, 1941–1968; Colonization to the American Renaissance, 1640–1865; Realism, Naturalism, and Local Color, 1865–1917; The Twenties, 1917–1929; The Age of Maturity, 1929–1941; Broadening Views, 1968–1988; Supplement: Modern Writers, 1900–1998.*

Concise Dictionary of British Literary Biography, 8 volumes (1991–1992): *Writers of the Middle Ages and Renaissance Before 1660; Writers of the Restoration and Eighteenth Century, 1660–1789; Writers of the Romantic Period, 1789–1832; Victorian Writers, 1832–1890; Late Victorian and Edwardian Writers, 1890–1914; Modern Writers, 1914–1945; Writers After World War II, 1945–1960; Contemporary Writers, 1960 to Present.*

Concise Dictionary of World Literary Biography, 10 volumes projected (1999–): *Ancient Greek and Roman Writers; German Writers; African, Caribbean, and Latin American Writers; South Slavic and Eastern European Writers.*

Dictionary of Literary Biography® • Volume Two Hundred Sixty

Australian Writers, 1915–1950

Dictionary of Literary Biography® • Volume Two Hundred Sixty

Australian Writers, 1915–1950

Edited by
Selina Samuels

A Bruccoli Clark Layman Book

GALE

ST. PHILIP'S COLLEGE LIBRARY

THOMSON
GALE

Detroit • New York • San Diego • San Francisco • Cleveland • New Haven, Conn. • Waterville, Maine • London • Munich

THOMSON

GALE

Dictionary of Literary Biography
Australian Writers,
1915–1950

Advisory Board
John Baker
William Cagle
Patrick O'Connor
George Garrett
Trudier Harris
Alvin Kernan
Kenny J. Williams

Editorial Directors
Matthew J. Bruccoli and Richard Layman

Senior Editor
Karen L. Rood

© 2002 by Gale. Gale is an imprint of The Gale Group, Inc., a division of Thomson Learning, Inc.

Gale and Design™ and Thomson Learning™ are trademarks used herein under license.

For more information, contact
The Gale Group, Inc.
27500 Drake Rd.
Farmington Hills, MI 48331-3535
Or you can visit our Internet site at
http://www.gale.com

ALL RIGHTS RESERVED
No part of this work covered by the copyright hereon may be reproduced or used in any form or by any means—graphic, electronic, or mechanical, including photocopying, recording, taping, Web distribution, or information storage retrieval systems—without the written permission of the publisher.

For permission to use material from this product, submit your request via Web at http://www.gale-edit.com/permissions, or you may download our Permissions Request form and submit your request by fax or mail to:

Permissions Department
The Gale Group, Inc.
27500 Drake Rd.
Farmington Hills, MI 48331-3535
Permissions Hotline:
248-699-8006 or 800-877-4253, ext. 8006
Fax: 248-699-8074 or 800-762-4058

While every effort has been made to ensure the reliability of the information presented in this publication, The Gale Group, Inc. does not guarantee the accuracy of the data contained herein. The Gale Group, Inc. accepts no payment for listing; and inclusion in the publication of any organization, agency, institution, publication, service, or individual does not imply endorsement of the editors or publisher. Errors brought to the attention of the publisher and verified to the satisfaction of the publisher will be corrected in future editions.

LIBRARY OF CONGRESS CATALOGING-IN-PUBLICATION DATA

Australian writers, 1915-1950 / edited by Selina Samuels.
  p. cm.—(Dictionary of literary biography; v. 260)
"A Bruccoli Clark Layman book."
  Includes bibliographical references and index.
  ISBN 0-7876-6004-3 (alk. paper)
  1. Australian literature—20th century—Bio-bibliography—Dictionaries. 2. Authors, Australian—20th century—Biography—Dictionaries. 3. Australian—In literature—Bibliography—Dictionaries. 4. Australian literature—20th century—Dictionaries.
  I. Samuels, Selina. II. Series.

PR9609.6 .A97 2002
820.9'994'03—dc21   2002007016

Printed in the United States of America
10 9 8 7 6 5 4 3 2 1

This volume is dedicated to the memories of Judith Wright and A. D. Hope, great Australian poets who died as the commissioning of this volume commenced.

Contents

Plan of the Series xv
Introduction xvii

Marjorie Barnard (1897–1987) and
    Flora Eldershaw (1897–1956)
    (M. Barnard Eldershaw) 3
    Maryanne Dever

Martin Boyd (1893–1972) 14
    Susan Lever

David Campbell (1915–1979) 22
    Philip Mead

Gavin Casey (1907–1964) 30
    Don Grant

Charmian Clift (1923–1969) 37
    Nadia Wheatley

Peter Cowan (1914–   ) 45
    Bruce Bennett

Dymphna Cusack (1902–1981) 52
    Marilla North

Eleanor Dark (1901–1985) 63
    Barbara Brooks

Frank Dalby Davison (1893–1970) 72
    Robert Darby

C. J. Dennis (1876–1938) 81
    Philip Butterss

Jean Devanny (1894–1962) 88
    Carole Ferrier

Rosemary Dobson (1920–   ) 99
    Marie-Louise Ayres

Mary Durack (1913–1994) 106
    Don Grant

Louis Esson (1878–1943) 116
    Peter Fitzpatrick

Robert D. FitzGerald (1902–1987) 124
    Julian Croft

Mary Gilmore (1865–1962) 133
    Jennifer Strauss

Frank Hardy (1917–1994) 143
    Ian Syson

Xavier Herbert (1901–1984) 151
    Frances de Groen

Rex Ingamells (1913–1955) 162
    Robert Sellick

George Johnston (1912–1970) 169
    Josephine Jill Kinnane

Norman Lindsay (1879–1969) 179
    James Packer

Kenneth Mackenzie (Seaforth Mackenzie)
    (1913–1955) 189
    Richard Rossiter

Frederic Manning (1882–1935) 196
    James Packer

Alan Marshall (1902–1984) 204
    Joanne McPherson

David Martin (1915–1997) 212
    John McLaren

James McAuley (1917–1976) 220
    Michael Ackland

Hugh McCrae (1876–1958) 230
    Justin Lucas

John Morrison (1904–1998) 239
    C. A. Cranston

Nettie Palmer (1885–1964) 250
    Deborah Jordan

Vance Palmer (1885–1959) 262
    Vivian Smith

Ruth Park (1923?–   ) 275
    Paul Genoni

Brian Penton (1904–1951) 286
    James Packer

Hal Porter (1911–1984) 295
    David McCooey

Katharine Susannah Prichard (1883–1969) 307
    Delys Bird

Kenneth Slessor (1901–1971) 320
Adrian Caesar

Christina Stead (1902–1983) 331
Brigid Rooney

P. R. Stephensen (1901–1965) 347
James Packer

Douglas Stewart (1913–1985) 355
David McCooey

Harold Stewart (1916–1995) 367
Michael Ackland

Dal Stivens (1911–1997) 375
Harry Heseltine

Randolph Stow (1935–) 382
Anthony Hassall

Francis Webb (1925–1973) 392
Bill Ashcroft

Patrick White (1912–1990) 400
Michael Ackland

Judith Wright (1915–2000) 416
Veronica Brady

Checklist of Further Readings 429
Contributors 435
Cumulative Index 439

Plan of the Series

... Almost the most prodigious asset of a country, and perhaps its most precious possession, is its native literary product—when that product is fine and noble and enduring.

Mark Twain*

The advisory board, the editors, and the publisher of the *Dictionary of Literary Biography* are joined in endorsing Mark Twain's declaration. The literature of a nation provides an inexhaustible resource of permanent worth. Our purpose is to make literature and its creators better understood and more accessible to students and the reading public, while satisfying the needs of teachers and researchers.

To meet these requirements, *literary biography* has been construed in terms of the author's achievement. The most important thing about a writer is his writing. Accordingly, the entries in *DLB* are career biographies, tracing the development of the author's canon and the evolution of his reputation.

The purpose of *DLB* is not only to provide reliable information in a usable format but also to place the figures in the larger perspective of literary history and to offer appraisals of their accomplishments by qualified scholars.

The publication plan for *DLB* resulted from two years of preparation. The project was proposed to Bruccoli Clark by Frederick G. Ruffner, president of the Gale Research Company, in November 1975. After specimen entries were prepared and typeset, an advisory board was formed to refine the entry format and develop the series rationale. In meetings held during 1976, the publisher, series editors, and advisory board approved the scheme for a comprehensive biographical dictionary of persons who contributed to literature. Editorial work on the first volume began in January 1977, and it was published in 1978. In order to make *DLB* more than a dictionary and to compile volumes that individually have claim to status as literary history, it was decided to organize volumes by topic, period, or

*From an unpublished section of Mark Twain's autobiography, copyright by the Mark Twain Company

genre. Each of these freestanding volumes provides a biographical-bibliographical guide and overview for a particular area of literature. We are convinced that this organization—as opposed to a single alphabet method—constitutes a valuable innovation in the presentation of reference material. The volume plan necessarily requires many decisions for the placement and treatment of authors. Certain figures will be included in separate volumes, but with different entries emphasizing the aspect of his career appropriate to each volume. Ernest Hemingway, for example, is represented in *American Writers in Paris, 1920–1939* by an entry focusing on his expatriate apprenticeship; he is also in *American Novelists, 1910–1945* with an entry surveying his entire career, as well as in *American Short-Story Writers, 1910–1945, Second Series* with an entry concentrating on his short fiction. Each volume includes a cumulative index of the subject authors and articles.

Since 1981 the series has been further augmented by the *DLB Yearbooks*, which update published entries, add new entries to keep the *DLB* current with contemporary activity, and provide articles on literary history. There have also been nineteen *DLB Documentary Series* volumes which provide illustrations, facsimiles, and biographical and critical source materials for figures, works, or groups judged to have particular interest for students. In 1999 the *Documentary Series* was incorporated into the *DLB* volume numbering system beginning with *DLB 210: Ernest Hemingway*.

We define literature as the *intellectual commerce of a nation:* not merely as belles lettres but as that ample and complex process by which ideas are generated, shaped, and transmitted. *DLB* entries are not limited to "creative writers" but extend to other figures who in their time and in their way influenced the mind of a people. Thus the series encompasses historians, journalists, publishers, book collectors, and screenwriters. By this means readers of *DLB* may be aided to perceive literature not as cult scripture in the keeping of intellectual high priests but firmly positioned at the center of a nation's life.

DLB includes the major writers appropriate to each volume and those standing in the ranks behind them. Scholarly and critical counsel has been sought in deciding which minor figures to include and how full their entries should be. Wherever possible, useful references are made to figures who do not warrant separate entries.

Each *DLB* volume has an expert volume editor responsible for planning the volume, selecting the figures for inclusion, and assigning the entries. Volume editors are also responsible for preparing, where appropriate, appendices surveying the major periodicals and literary and intellectual movements for their volumes, as well as lists of further readings. Work on the series as a whole is coordinated at the Bruccoli Clark Layman editorial center in Columbia, South Carolina, where the editorial staff is responsible for accuracy and utility of the published volumes.

One feature that distinguishes *DLB* is the illustration policy–its concern with the iconography of literature. Just as an author is influenced by his surroundings, so is the reader's understanding of the author enhanced by a knowledge of his environment. Therefore *DLB* volumes include not only drawings, paintings, and photographs of authors, often depicting them at various stages in their careers, but also illustrations of their families and places where they lived. Title pages are regularly reproduced in facsimile along with dust jackets for modern authors. The dust jackets are a special feature of *DLB* because they often document better than anything else the way in which an author's work was perceived in its own time. Specimens of the writers' manuscripts and letters are included when feasible.

Samuel Johnson rightly decreed that "The chief glory of every people arises from its authors." The purpose of the *Dictionary of Literary Biography* is to compile literary history in the surest way available to us–by accurate and comprehensive treatment of the lives and work of those who contributed to it.

The DLB Advisory Board

Introduction

Dictionary of Literary Biography 260: Australian Literature, 1915–1950 is the second in the *DLB* series on Australian literature and the sequel to *DLB 230: Australian Literature, 1788–1914*. These volumes, and the ones covering the periods 1950–1975 and 1975–2000 to follow, will constitute the first series devoted to the literary historiography of Australia and will provide a thorough overview of the most prominent and influential Australian writers and of the central literary and cultural developments of the nation.

The starting date for this volume is central to Australia's self-definition; it is the year of the most famous battle in Australian military history. On 25 April 1915 the Australia and New Zealand Army Corps (Anzac) landed on the beaches near Gallipoli, Turkey (which was, as it turned out, the wrong place), to fight against the Turkish forces in the Dardanelles Campaign of World War I. The Anzac forces charged over open ground against entrenched Turkish forces and sustained heavy losses. World War I was the first war in which Australians fought as a nation rather than part of the British military, and the Gallipoli campaign has come to signify a legendary image of the Australian character. Contemporary publications, such as C. E. W. Bean's *Official History of Australia in the War of 1914–1918* (1921–1942), a collection of fiction, journalism, and illustrations from soldiers who fought in the war, characterize the archetypal Australian type in terms familiar from the literature of the late nineteenth century—a man who is brave in the face of danger, stoic in adversity, and loyal to his mates (male companions). Indeed, in many ways the Anzac mythology that emerged from Gallipoli is an extension of the nationalistic literature of the 1890s—the desire to distinguish Australian culture from British culture, and the consequent focus on certain characteristics of the landscape and its idealized inhabitants. But the significance of Gallipoli goes further than self-definition; it has come to represent a moment of crisis within the relationship between Australia and Great Britain, a point of postcolonial disaffection. In the popular understanding of the battle, the Australian troops were sacrificed—sent by the British military commanders to charge the Turkish trenches with bayonets against machine-gun fire—in order to distract the enemy from the British troops landing on the beach. The strong sense of rejection and betrayal that emerged from the Australian history of convictism is resurrected in the representations of Gallipoli and the World War I diggers (soldiers), indicated by the schematically evil characterizations of the British participants in more-recent reconstructions of the events. The British, not the Turks, are always the enemies in these reconstructions.

The cult of Anzac was and is deeply paradoxical. On the one hand, contemporary accounts of the Anzac troops, which described them in quasi-spiritual and romantic terms—"They were . . . the finest body of young men ever brought together in modern times"—are reflected in the increasing popularity of Anzac Day celebrations among young Australians, in parades in the Australian cities and at the site of the battle itself. Australian politicians continuously use references to the emotive "Anzac spirit" to generate nationalist feelings and as a shorthand way to conjure a familiar image of what it is to be Australian. Anzac Day provides an opportunity to glorify and romanticize the Australian national past, when men from the colonies were as valorous as those from the imperial centers; moreover, they were all volunteers who freely offered their lives. On the other hand, the Anzac cult is a symbol of Australia as a colony, despite Federation and ostensible independence in 1901. This part of the myth still serves its spiritual aspect; but this interpretation depicts the Anzac troops as innocent victims of the colonizer Britain, who perceived them as expendable.

World War I was only the first war of the period in question to affect international as well as domestic perceptions of the Australian character. The Great War was followed by the Great Depression, originating in the United States but equally devastating to the Australian economy. Then came World War II, which, like the war before it, was not fought on Australian soil, indicating the enormous influence of the outside world on Australian social and cultural development. The conduct of the Australian troops in this war continued the mythology of the Anzacs, but domestic perception of Australian involvement in war was substantially altered by the experience of war in the Asia Pacific region and the internment of many Australian soldiers in Japanese Prisoner of War camps, such as Changi, and slave labor on the Burma railway. For the first time there was also a threat to the security of Australia, with heavy Japanese attacks on Darwin and Broome in the north of Australia and an unsuccessful midget submarine advance into Sydney Harbour.

Winston Churchill's reluctance to return Australian soldiers to protect the country against the threat of invasion continued the domestic perception that the British felt Australians to be expendable and prompted Australian prime minister John Curtin to turn to the United States for protection and support in the Asian Pacific region. The fascination of Australia with the American GIs (soldiers) who began to gather in Australia during leave periods was a continuation of the Australian loss of innocence—the American soldiers were popularly described as "overpaid, oversexed and over here"—and part of the shift from loyalty to the Mother Country to the Stepmother Country, which culminated in the 1960s with the Vietnam War. The cooperation between Australia and the United States during World War II was one of the factors that induced Australian politicians to pledge themselves to join America in support of South Vietnam against the communist North Vietnam, but public opposition to the war resulted, at least in part, from an inevitable disillusionment following Australian involvement in both world wars.

Like Australian foreign and military policy, Australian literary movements during this period were inevitably influenced by international developments, such as European Romanticism and aestheticism (as espoused by Norman Lindsay, for example), modernism (led in Australia by James McAuley and Harold Stewart, and the fictitious Ern Malley), and Nietzschean philosophy (adopted by Brian Penton). The literature of this period is particularly marked by a strong political focus, influenced by Australian involvement in international wars and economic collapse. The politics of the Left is fully represented in this volume—from Mary Gilmore's early utopian Marxism, through the full-fledged communism of writers such as Jean Devanny, Alan Marshall, Frank Hardy, and Katharine Susannah Prichard, to the socialism of Dymphna Cusack and Eleanor Dark. Also represented, with the entries on Xavier Herbert and P. R. Stephensen, are the fascist sympathies and anti-Semitism of the "Australia First" movement. The strong support shown by writers of this period to political ideologies, of whatever character, reflects the idealism of the young nation, influenced by developments elsewhere and yet hopeful that Australia could be a better place, the crucible for testing the future. This political emphasis in the literature and the lives of Australian writers reflects one of the many paradoxes of Australian postcolonial culture—that the influence of the rest of the world, and particularly the high cultural metropolitan centers of London, Paris, Moscow, and New York, is so completely conjoined with the desire for cultural independence.

The strong communist and socialist affiliations of many of the women writers of the period are particularly marked. Their work can be seen as in reaction to the male-focused literary myths of the 1890s and the masculinist construction of Australian character defined by the cult of Anzac. But for many of these women writers the relationship between feminism and communism was not without a certain strain. Mary Gilmore was the editor of the Women's Page of the communist publication *The Worker* from 1908 to 1931. In her journalism the relationship between political radicalism and domesticity is marked; in line with the socialist thinking of the time, she supported the distinction between the roles of the genders, thus suggesting that true female emancipation and politics were not the easiest of allies. Jean Devanny also found that the Communist Party was unsympathetic to her feminist and sexual freedom: she was excommunicated from the party during World War II for "sexual indiscretion."

Despite the increasing numbers of women writing and publishing, women writers were still extremely conscious of their secondary status in the world, and even in the comparatively liberal, even radical, environments in which they lived and worked. During the late 1930s the writer-collaborators Marjorie Barnard and Flora Eldershaw held a literary salon every Wednesday evening, at which writers gathered to discuss literature, philosophy, and politics in the interests of fostering a socially responsible art. Although the hosts and many of the guests were women, Xavier Herbert announced on his first visit that "the women could get together and talk" while he and Frank Dalby Davison took themselves to the other side of the room and got on with the serious conversation. In consequence, women writers felt the need to support one another in their literary endeavors, and the many letters between Barnard, Eldershaw, Dark, Devanny, Miles Franklin, and Prichard—collected by Carole Ferrier in the volume *As Good as a Yarn with You* (1992)—attest to the female literary community that they fostered and nurtured. What is also revealed is the difficulty these women faced as they juggled domestic and familial responsibilities and writing, the difficulty of taking up a responsible public role and being accorded authority and respect, and the expectation that women's careers would always be secondary to those of men. Novels such as Dymphna Cusack and Florence James's iconic *Come In Spinner* (1951), set in Sydney during World War II, and Christina Stead's *The Man Who Loved Children* (1940), interrogate the treatment of women by men. Cusack was particularly scathing about the tolerance offered the man of "genius" by the rest of society, and particularly women. She labeled those women who subsumed themselves in order to nurture parasitic male genius "potato wives," after the slips of potato that sustained willow cuttings on the long sea voyage from England to Australia in early colonial days.

The surviving correspondence indicates the development of a strong community of writers. This literary community first emerged in Sydney during the early days of *The Bulletin* in the 1880s and 1890s, but it developed into a full-fledged Bohemia in the Sydney of the 1920s (called the Golden Decade by its queen, Dulcie Deamer), captured in retrospect most beautifully by Kenneth Slessor's famous and haunting poem "Five Bells." Literary community was reinforced by the founding in 1928 of the Fellowship of Australian Writers by such writers as John Le Gay Brereton, Gilmore, and Steele Rudd, and by thus bringing together Australian literature enthusiasts from the disparate literary societies of Sydney and other sections of the community with literary interests. While the organization's founding members were motivated by a diversity of reasons, the foremost was an overriding desire to promote Australian literature in the face of the quantity of imported writing. The 8 December 1928 *Sydney Morning Herald* report announcing the formation of the society stated,

> The organisation will function in the material as well as the sentimental interests of Australian literature, and among the activities will be a methodical and practical encouragement of local authors, artists and scenario writers. . . . Efforts will be made to ensure Australian creative talent against "the flood of cheap and often morally questionable literature."

The recognition by the writers themselves that they were part of a literary milieu encouraged them to develop literature not just in reference to external models—earlier Australian writers and the English canon—but also in conversation with one another. Literature of this period includes many complex intertextual debates and in-jokes, the most famous of which was the Ern Malley hoax (the creation of a modernist author, complete with works), perpetrated by James McAuley and Harold Stewart to—as they saw it—poke fun at the pomposity of Max Harris and his modernist pretensions, showcased in the magazine Harris edited, *Angry Penguins*. However, the Ern Malley affair, which is one of a series of famous Australian literary hoaxes, highlighted more than just personal rivalry. By attributing their parodies of modernism to "Ern Malley," McAuley and Stewart touched a nerve within Australian cultural self-perception, an anxiety about its capacity as a nation to produce "real literature," which was always at the heart of the efforts to define and create Australian literature and culture in the face of the continued cultural imperialism of Europe and, increasingly, the United States.

This desire for an Australian cultural identity represents the essence of the country that encouraged such literary movements as the South Australian Jindyworobak movement, founded by Rex Ingamells in 1937–1938 to "symbolize distinctive Australian quality in literature" and "to free Australian art from whatever alien influences trammel it—that is, bring it into proper contact with its material." Central to this movement was a desire to turn away from external influence to derive inspiration and aesthetic guidance from Aboriginal legend and language and from the landscape itself. Other writers of the period turned to Aboriginal legend and contemporary culture as a way to represent and to explain Australian society. The work of Mary Durack—while labeled paternalistic and appropriative by more-recent critics—indicates an attempt to legitimize Aboriginal culture as well as to identify Australia according to its defining features. Prichard's controversial novel *Coonardoo* (1929), also dismissed by some critics as reductive and essentialist in its portrait of its Aboriginal female protagonist, is a more blatant attack on the treatment of the Aboriginal community by the European colonizers and points to the emptiness in the midst of the literary self-representation of Australia.

Australian literature was recognized domestically as a legitimate subject within the academy only toward the middle of the twentieth century, greatly influenced by the critical and revisionist work of Vance and Nettie Palmer and P. R. Stephensen. Again, much of the criticism of this period was concerned with defining Australian literature in relation to international movements and the literature of the nineteenth century, and despite the critical dissension between the nationalist (radical nationalists) and internationalist (New Critical) critical schools, both were primarily concerned to find and articulate an essentialist version of Australian cultural identity that could be mapped as a trajectory throughout the history of Australian literature and applied to contemporary and future developments. (For a more detailed discussion of the critical movements within Australian literary scholarship, see the Introduction to *DLB 230: Australian Literature, 1788–1914*.)

In this critical environment, writers such as Patrick White constituted both a blessing and a complex dilemma. On the one hand, his international success—the Nobel Prize awarded in 1973—indicated that Australian literature could place itself confidently within the international literary arena and be placed legitimately within the canon. At the same time, his treatment of the legacy of European realism and modernism, and of Australian social and literary history, is complimentary to no one and still problematic. Because the critics of the 1950s considered White to be the creator of "un-Australian Australian novels," his work is still seen within the context of the development of Australian literature and in comparison with the "dreary dun-coloured . . . journalism" he so decried. His self-appointed position as social critic, cynic, and outsider makes him a strange candidate to be the benchmark of an entire literary tradition, but it is perhaps the mark of Australia's continued lack of cultural self-confidence that such an onerous and unwelcome (and, from a national perspective, limiting) role should be conferred on the only Nobel laureate of Australia. He is the "best" writer Australia has produced, and to many the "only" writer Australia has produced.

White—who lived for the majority of his life in Sydney—unquestionably played a central role in the burgeoning recognition paid to Australian literature both nationally and internationally. Nevertheless, the period covered by this volume is considered by many commentators to be one defined by artistic expatriation and fueled by a national sense of "cultural cringe." This phrase, coined by A. A. Phillips in *The Australian Tradition: Studies in a Colonial Culture* (1958), refers to giving the preference in Australian literature and scholarship to the European, and particularly English, culture over everything produced domestically. Writers and artists felt compelled to travel to the colonial centers of culture in order to be legitimized in their professions—that is, in order to acquire the necessary international experience and cachet. At the same time, there was a strong perception of the parochial character and small-mindedness of Australian society, unsympathetic to aesthetic aspirations and quick to condemn and destroy any intellectual pretensions. Expatriate writers of the period include Martin Boyd, Charmian Clift, George Johnston, Harold Stewart, Frederic Manning, Randolph Stow, Katharine Susannah Prichard, and Christina Stead. Expatriation, in some writers, encouraged literary analysis and reproduction of Australia from a distance. Stow's *The Merry-Go-Round in the Sea* (1965), for example, written while he was in America, is an homage to his childhood and captures a sense of nostalgia made more poignant by the distance—in time and space—of the writer from his subject. On the other hand, the internationalization of Australian writers allowed them to move away from the focus on documenting Australia, away from the obsession with national self-definition. Stead's *The Man Who Loved Children* is an example of a novel transposed from one location to another. On the advice of her American publishers, Stead transported to Baltimore the action of *The Man Who Loved Children*, which was based on her own childhood in Sydney, without losing any of the extraordinary impact of the story or skill of the language. Indeed, Stead's status as an expatriate writer has greatly complicated her critical category and reception; after she left for England in 1928 she was rejected as an Australian writer until her return in 1975, and none of her works were published in Australia until 1965, despite her recognition elsewhere. Stead's treatment is one that other expatriate Australian writers have experienced and is, perhaps, the inevitable corollary of the cultural cringe. The expatriate writer highlights, far too brightly, the anxiety associated with defining the meaning of *Australian*, and particularly of *Australian literature*.

Written in the twenty-first century, the essays in this volume view the writing of the period covered and the writers themselves from a temporal distance. They are inevitably informed by the critical responses that have intervened between the point of the creation of the works and their current reception. The popular perception of Gallipoli has been irretrievably influenced by the successful 1980 Peter Weir movie *Gallipoli*, which glorified the bravery and solidarity of the Anzac troops and condemned British self-interest for the tremendous Australian loss of life: as the Australian troops are preparing to go to their deaths, the British troops are reported to be "drinking tea on the beach." That motion picture, in turn, is a product of the post-Vietnam age; in *Gallipoli*, World War I is presented as completely absurd, quite separate from Australia; moreover, that so many Australians died in such a battle is presented as a tragicomic statement about Australian subservience to the rationale of allegiance to stronger powers. Similarly, the literature of the period is inevitably read through the lens of the feminist revisionism of the 1970s and 1980s, and the debates between political conservatism and radicalism are seen through the centrism and cynicism that are particular features of the fin de siècle temperament. In reading these literary histories, then, one must be aware of the way in which, in historic and literary reconstructions of the past, certain moments collide and coalesce, defined and altered by one another.

There have inevitably been omissions in this volume, attributable to the usual problems of editorial selection and the more unexpected hindrances of scholarly fashion. Some writers who are not represented by a full entry, although their names may appear and reappear, are Dulcie Deamer, Lesbia Harford, Eve Langley, and Kylie Tennant. While the omissions are much regretted, they do indicate that the study of a national literature is not a matter of closure, but a continuous process of discovery and revelation.

—*Selina Samuels*

Acknowledgments

This book was produced by Bruccoli Clark Layman, Inc. Karen L. Rood is senior editor. Penelope M. Hope was the in-house editor.

Production manager is Philip B. Dematteis.

Administrative support was provided by Ann M. Cheschi and Amber L. Coker.

Accountant is Ann-Marie Holland.

Copyediting supervisor is Sally R. Evans. The copyediting staff includes Phyllis A. Avant, Brenda Carol Blanton, Caryl Brown, Melissa D. Hinton, Philip I. Jones, Rebecca Mayo, Nancy E. Smith, and Elizabeth Jo Ann Sumner.

Editorial associates are Michael S. Allen, Michael S. Martin, and Catherine M. Polit.

Permissions editor is Jason Paddock.

Database manager is José A. Juarez.

Layout and graphics supervisor is Janet E. Hill. The graphics staff includes Zoe R. Cook and Sydney E. Hammock.

Office manager is Kathy Lawler Merlette.

Photography supervisor is Paul Talbot. Photography editor is Scott Nemzek.

Digital photographic copy work was performed by Joseph M. Bruccoli.

Systems manager is Marie L. Parker.

Typesetting supervisor is Kathleen M. Flanagan. The typesetting staff includes Patricia Marie Flanagan, Mark J. McEwan, and Pamela D. Norton. Freelance typesetter is Wanda Adams.

Walter W. Ross did library research. He was assisted by Jo Cottingham and the following librarians at the Thomas Cooper Library of the University of South Carolina: circulation department head Tucker Taylor; reference department head Virginia W. Weathers; reference department staff Brette Barron, Marilee Birchfield, Paul Cammarata, Gary Geer, Michael Macan, Tom Marcil, Rose Marshall, and Sharon Verba; interlibrary loan department head John Brunswick; and interlibrary loan staff Robert Arndt, Hayden Battle, Alex Byrne, Jo Cottingham, Bill Fetty, Marna Hostetler, and Nelson Rivera.

Dictionary of Literary Biography® • Volume Two Hundred Sixty

Australian Writers, 1915–1950

Dictionary of Literary Biography

Marjorie Barnard
(16 August 1897 – 8 May 1987)

and

Flora Eldershaw
(16 March 1897 – 20 September 1956)

(M. Barnard Eldershaw)

Maryanne Dever
Monash University

All books, unless otherwise indicated, were written by Marjorie Barnard and Flora Eldershaw as M. Barnard Eldershaw.

BOOKS: *The Ivory Gate,* by Marjorie Barnard (Melbourne: Champion, 1920);

A House Is Built (London & Sydney: Harrap, 1929; New York: Harcourt, Brace, 1929);

Green Memory (London & Sydney: Harrap, 1931; New York: Harcourt, Brace, 1931);

The Glasshouse (London: Harrap, 1936; Sydney: Australasian, 1945);

Plaque with Laurel (London: Harrap, 1937);

Essays in Australian Fiction (Melbourne: Melbourne University Press / London: Oxford University Press, 1938);

Phillip of Australia: An Account of the Settlement at Sydney Cove 1788-1792 (London & Sydney: Harrap, 1938);

The Life and Times of Captain John Piper (Sydney: Australian Limited Editions Society, 1939);

My Australia (London: Jarrolds, 1939; London & New York: Jarrolds, 194?; revised, 1951);

Macquarie's World, by Barnard (Sydney: Australian Limited Editions Society, 1941);

The Persimmon Tree and Other Stories, by Barnard (Sydney: Clarendon Press, 1943; London: Virago, 1985);

Australian Outline, by Barnard (Sydney: Ure Smith, 1943; revised, 1949);

The Sydney Book, by Barnard (Sydney: Ure Smith, 1947);

Tomorrow and Tomorrow (Melbourne: Georgian House, 1947, London: Phoenix House, 1948); republished in full as *Tomorrow and Tomorrow and Tomorrow* (London: Virago, 1983; Garden City, N.Y.: Dial, 1984);

Sydney: The Story of a City, by Barnard (Melbourne: Melbourne University Press, 1956);

Australia's First Architect: Francis Greenway, by Barnard (Croydon, Vic.: Longmans, 1961);

A History of Australia, by Barnard (Sydney: Angus & Robertson, 1962; New York: Praeger, 1963);

Lachlan Macquarie, by Barnard (Melbourne: Oxford University Press, 1964);

Miles Franklin, by Barnard (New York: Twayne, 1967; Melbourne: Hill of Content, 1967);

But Not for Love: Stories of Marjorie Barnard and M. Barnard Eldershaw, edited by Robert Darby (Sydney: Allen & Unwin, 1988);

M. Barnard Eldershaw: Plaque with Laurel, Essays, Reviews and Correspondence, edited by Maryanne

Flora Eldershaw, circa 1915, and Marjorie Barnard, circa 1935 (from Carole Ferrier, ed., As Good as a Yarn with You, *1992)*

Dever (St. Lucia: University of Queensland Press, 1995).

OTHER: *Australian Writers Annual,* edited and with a contribution by Flora Eldershaw (Sydney: Fellowship of Australian Writers, 1936), pp. 11–14;

The Peaceful Army: A Memorial to the Pioneer Women of Australia, edited and with a contribution by Flora Eldershaw (Sydney: Australia's 150th Anniversary Celebrations Council, Women's Executive Committee and Advisory Council, 1938), pp. 86–89.

SELECTED PERIODICAL PUBLICATIONS–UNCOLLECTED: "Contemporary Australian Women Novelists," Australian English Association offprint no. 4, *Union Recorder* (Sydney), 23 April 1931, pp. 2–28;

"History as the Raw Material of Literature," *Royal Australian Historical Society Journal and Proceedings,* 20, Part I (1934): 1–17;

"Australian Literature Society Medallists," Australian English Association offprint no. 20, *Union Recorder* (Sydney), 7 November 1935, pp. 2–12.

The writing partnership of Marjorie Barnard and Flora Eldershaw, who published together under the pseudonym of M. Barnard Eldershaw, is recognized as one of the most successful and enduring collaborations in Australian literary history. In a shared career spanning nearly twenty years, Barnard and Eldershaw cowrote five novels in addition to writing short stories, critical articles, volumes of history, and a significant collection of literary criticism. While their first novel, *A House Is Built,* which appeared in 1929, enjoyed enormous popular success, recent critical attention has focused primarily upon their controversial final novel, *Tomorrow and Tomorrow and Tomorrow,* an ambitious dystopian novel that was subjected to wartime censorship prior to publication as *Tomorrow and Tomorrow* in 1947 and, as a result, was not published in full until 1983. The two authors made few public statements about their shared writing routine; the scarcity of information has led to substantial curiosity and speculation over each author's part in the collaboration. The public's desire to know more was further heightened by Barnard's claims later in life that she alone was responsible for their final novel. That she published fiction and history independently of the collaboration initially lent weight to these claims, although recent scholarship has since pointed to Eldershaw's continued involvement in *Tomorrow and Tomorrow and Tomorrow*.

Active at a time when women dominated the Australian literary scene, Barnard and Eldershaw rapidly became influential figures in the literary circles of the 1930s and 1940s and played significant roles in the Fellowship of Australian Writers (FAW). Eldershaw, the more outgoing of the pair, twice served as president of that organization. Throughout their careers, Barnard and Eldershaw maintained close friendships and professional alliances with the leading writers of the period, including Nettie and Vance Palmer, Frank Dalby Davison, Eleanor Dark, Jean Devanny, and Judah Waten. Barnard and Eldershaw shared with many of these writers a desire to foster a national literature that distinguished itself from English literary traditions through its engagement with the particular cultural, social, economic, and political conditions of life in Australia. In their published criticism and public lectures they celebrated the images of rural, working-class life found in the works of an earlier generation of Australian writers such as Henry Lawson, Joseph Furphy, and Bernard O'Dowd. However, in their own fiction they turned increasingly to the exploration of urban experiences and the dilemmas of the writing process itself. In recent decades, their lives as independent women and their achievements as writers have brought Barnard and Eldershaw to the attention of feminist scholars. Yet, unlike the works of their contemporaries Dark, Dymphna Cusack, and Devanny, the novels of M. Barnard Eldershaw are muted in their treatment of women's issues, although they do offer several compelling studies of single women struggling against family and convention.

Marjorie Faith Barnard and Flora Sydney Patricia Eldershaw were both born in 1897, Eldershaw growing up on a farm in the Riverina district of New South Wales and Barnard in Sydney. The two first met at the University of Sydney in 1916, where their initial encounter was, in Barnard's estimation, less than auspicious:

> I was the greenest of green "freshers." Flora was established in her second year. Chance had given me the locker immediately above hers. Its untidy contents frequently spilled out into her more ordered domain. My then meagre person was continually underfoot, and Flora's brown eyes flashed with indignation more often than they smiled. But within the year we were close friends. She widened my horizons and quickened my mind.

Together they studied history under George Arnold Wood and literature under Sir Mungo MacCallum, both of whom played significant roles in their intellectual development. In the years during which Barnard and Eldershaw attended the University of Sydney (1915–1920), it was for the most part a women's university because of the impact of World War I on the student population. As Eldershaw later observed, the war represented a time when "opportunities opened for women" and "conventional women of ability got for the first time full scope of their ability and were able to make use of it." Their respective academic records indicate the level of success each experienced: Eldershaw is reputed to have achieved the highest mark ever awarded in Latin and would have been awarded first-class honors in history had she not been disqualified under the existing regulations; Barnard was at the top of her class in history throughout her college career and was awarded the University Medal and a place at Oxford. Her father's refusal to allow her to continue her studies at Oxford led Barnard into librarianship. Following a brief stint as secretary of the University of Sydney Women's Union, Eldershaw embarked on a successful career as a schoolteacher, rising to be senior mistress at the Presbyterian Ladies College in Croydon, Sydney, before leaving the profession for government work during World War II.

While they were undergraduate students, Barnard and Eldershaw discovered a mutual interest in writing and first talked of the possibility of collaborating. In 1920 Barnard published a collection of children's stories, *The Ivory Gate,* but not until 1928 when the *Bulletin* magazine advertised its first novel competition did the two writers begin work on *A House Is Built,* the novel that eventually shared first prize with Katharine Susannah Prichard's *Coonardoo* (1929). When Barnard and Eldershaw sought publication in London the following year, a literary agent suggested that readers might be discomfited by the appearance of two names on the spine of the book, and so the authors devised the pen name M. Barnard Eldershaw. Unlike pseudonyms adopted by many nineteenth-century women writers, M. Barnard Eldershaw disguised neither the authors' sex nor their identities. In the words of the critic Nettie Palmer, "there is no mystery about it. You can meet the two writers in Sydney; their photos (separate not composite) have frequently been published; and their compound name is the merest convenience."

A House Is Built proved to be enormously successful: it remained in print for nearly fifty years. The novel was widely reviewed, and the two young authors were gratified to receive an extremely positive endorsement in the London press from Arnold Bennett, who declared it a "very notable novel" and one that had "deeply impressed" him. But as the authors later warned in *Essays in Australian Fiction* (1938), "to write a very successful and critic proof first book is, as a rule, an ill omen. An early and too complete success is likely to arrest growth." The continuing popularity of this initial novel came to haunt them as they moved away from that style of writing to more-contemporary issues and more-experimental forms. Set in early-nineteenth-century Sydney, *A House Is Built* recounts the rise and fall of the Hyde family, successful shipping merchants in the early decades of the colony in New South Wales. Meticulously researched, the novel was praised for its historical accuracy and for this reason remained for many years a standard work in the school curriculum. While primary focus is given to James Hyde, his sons, and his grandsons, the portraits of his capable, unmarried daughter, Fanny, who is refused an active and ongoing role in the family business, and of his frail daughter-in-law, Adela, are striking in their sympathetic rendering of the women's isolated and constrained roles within the Hyde family:

> Fanny's eyes and lips were always contradicting one another. Adela had seen her, sitting at the end of a long quiet evening, suddenly idle, staring at her sewing with something wild and frightened in her eyes, and her mouth twisted in a sort of bitter comprehension.

More than a simple narrative of commerce and male progress, the novel can also be read as a version of the female bildungsroman as it traces Fanny Hyde's struggle between her designated social role as a daughter and prospective wife and her desire for a meaningful vocation. Unlike her brother, who is always uncomfortable in his role in the family's firm, Fanny is represented as her father's true heir, for she shares his love of the business and joy in his life's work. But while James Hyde is willing to consider his sons and sons-in-law as potential business partners, he refuses to look upon daughters in this same light, so Fanny must ultimately be satisfied with the limited freedom and independence she achieves through philanthropy. Her refusal to marry and accept the roles of wife and mother is represented as a small victory that enables her to find more rewarding paths for herself beyond the strictures of bourgeois family life.

Publication of *A House Is Built* brought Barnard and Eldershaw to the attention of Nettie and Vance Palmer, then emerging as influential critics and writers. Nettie Palmer established a correspondence with Barnard that lasted several decades and provided the young authors with their most valuable source of advice, support, and informed criticism. To Nettie Palmer, Barnard confessed the collaborators' unease about the development of their second novel, *Green Memory,* which appeared in 1931. This novel had proven more difficult to produce than the first one, its progress slowed by the problems of combining creative work with paid employment. Both writers worked long hours and lived some distance from one another, circumstances that left them with limited opportunities either to write or to meet. They felt that the book had been marred by their inability to work on it steadily, and they were more disappointed than surprised by its lukewarm reception and mediocre sales. *Green Memory,* set in Sydney in the 1850s and 1860s, is a rather gloomy work that continues the theme of the distorting influence of powerful fathers on the lives of their daughters. However, whereas Fanny Hyde remains a sympathetic figure throughout *A House Is Built,* the progress of the Haven sisters in *Green Memory* becomes increasingly melodramatic. The novel tells of the competition between Lucy and Charlotte Haven to honor the memory of their father, Alfred Haven, a disgraced government official whose suicide in the opening pages of the novel throws his family into disarray. Lucy Haven is consumed by memories of her father's affection and of his death, an incident for which she feels directly responsible. She believes she must take her father's place at the head of the family, dedicating her life and theirs to the continued fulfillment of his plans for them. Lucy's pressure to restore the family prestige finally leads to the destruction of the family when one of her younger brothers repeats his father's crime by cheating on an important exam. Her sister, Charlotte, endeavors to shield the family from Lucy's influence, but she is also dogged by feelings of loss and guilt. Neither sister succeeds in freeing herself from the enduring influence of their father, and their lives and desires remain distorted by their rival efforts to appease his memory.

The interest that Barnard and Eldershaw showed in writing was not confined simply to their own work, and, with the encouragement of the Palmers, in the course of the 1930s they established themselves as critics and became actively involved in the promotion of Australian literature to a wider reading audience. They were both members of the Sydney Branch of the FAW and participated in many of its key initiatives for developing a keen, informed readership for Australian writing. Their activities included reviewing Australian books for magazines and newspapers, presenting lectures on Australian literature for Extension Board classes at the University of Sydney, and judging literary competitions. Barnard and Eldershaw knew from their own experience the particular difficulties Australian authors faced through the lack of informed criticism. They felt the absence of detailed critical feedback made

The house in Sydney where Barnard and Eldershaw held their literary salon during the late 1930s (from Ferrier, ed., As Good As a Yarn with You, *1992)*

it hard for writers to assess their own creative efforts. Some of their initial reviews and criticism were written in direct response to their dissatisfaction with the current standard of newspaper reviewing and with the poor treatment of works written by their contemporaries. Beyond allegiance to their fellow writers, however, in their public critical contributions they were motivated by a sense of broad cultural responsibility and by a genuine desire to promote vigorous debate about developments in Australian literature.

In the years following *Green Memory,* Barnard and Eldershaw moved away from historical fiction to work on a collection of short stories titled "But Not For Love." They had been encouraged in this direction by their London agent, who suggested there was a market for short fiction, but they were then disappointed by the responses the manuscript received. In early 1933, after the stories had been rejected by a series of publishers in England and Australia, the authors sought Nettie Palmer's advice on the collection. They reluctantly agreed with her assessment that the project should be abandoned, and the stories remained unpublished until after their deaths. Short stories proved difficult and elusive for the pair, and it was not until Barnard's superb collection *The Persimmon Tree* appeared in 1943 that either author experienced any success with the form. In 1935 Barnard's writing career received a boost when her father offered to pay her an allowance that would enable her to leave work to write full-time for three years. The offer initially disconcerted Barnard, who drew significant confidence and support from her collaborative relationship with Eldershaw, and for a time she questioned her own ability and wondered whether she might be considered an author in her own right. Freed to devote her time solely to writing, Barnard appears to have taken on a larger role in producing their joint works. But she reported to Nettie Palmer that this change in her circumstances did not alter her harmonious working relations with Eldershaw. She argued that since the real collaboration took place in their lengthy discussions, who then put pen to paper was immaterial.

With Barnard free to write full-time, the later 1930s proved to be a highly productive period for the collaborative publications of M. Barnard Eldershaw. In 1936 their third novel, *The Glasshouse,* appeared. It was the first of three novels centrally concerned with writers and the literary life. *The Glasshouse,* which draws on material from the authors' own recent voyages to Europe, is set among a small group of passengers traveling from Antwerp to Australia on a Norwegian cargo ship. The central character is a novelist, Stirling Armstrong, who is reluctant to become too familiar with the other passengers or to let her identity be discovered. Fearful that people might regale her with their life stories, Stirling preempts them by writing their stories for them. The structural innovation of embedding these stories into the main narrative of the sea voyage introduces into the novel a significant focus on the writing process itself. Readers are permitted glimpses into Stirling's fiction-writing dilemmas as the traditionally invisible or private elements of the creative process are revealed in her thoughts and observations. Stirling's tales of her fellow passengers also offered Barnard and Eldershaw an opportunity to experiment once again with the short-story form, but this time from within the familiar and protective framework of a novel. Through imaginative sleight of hand, Stirling Armstrong, not M. Barnard Eldershaw, must own the success or failure of the individual stories.

The Glasshouse can also be read as an exploration of women's literary careers, and in it one can see Barnard and Eldershaw toying with the same stereotypes of the "lady novelist" with which they were regularly confronted in their careers. While Stirling claims at the outset to be a serious novelist who mocks cheap plot devices and melodrama, these assertions are undermined by the often sentimental and clichéd stories she produces in the course of the novel. Her pose as the aloof and matter-of-fact woman writer is further challenged by her growing attraction to the distant, married captain of the ship. As the reader realizes that Stirling is participating in precisely the kind of stereotypical romance plot she apparently eschews, she ceases to resemble a "serious" literary figure and is reduced instead to the type of "lady writer" whose traditional domain is romance. Her character is redeemed at least partially by her decision to leave the ship early, abandoning her liaison with the captain and confounding the conventional romance plot. At the end of the novel she remains alone and on the move, free to return to the solitude of her writing.

Barnard and Eldershaw's fourth novel, *Plaque with Laurel,* appeared only a year later, in 1937, and continues the exploration of writing and creativity begun in *The Glasshouse*. *Plaque with Laurel* tells of a writer's conference in the relatively newly established Australian capital city of Canberra. In many ways the novel can be read as a reflection of Barnard's and Eldershaw's own personal and professional concerns. The two authors always claimed to be able to write only of what they knew, and their satirical account of the conference provides interesting insights into the issue confronting them as Australian writers in the interwar period—namely, the struggle to establish themselves in an often less-than-encouraging environment. Their particular focus on the relationship between writers and society bears comparison with that of Eleanor Dark in *The Little Company* (1945) and Christina Stead in the posthumous *I'm Dying Laughing* (1987). Dark and Stead were two authors who influenced Barnard and Eldershaw considerably. Indeed, while from time to time Barnard and Eldershaw criticized aspects of both Dark's and Stead's novels, they were clearly impressed by the intellectual power and structural innovation in Dark's and Stead's work. Although not strictly a roman à clef, *Plaque with Laurel* so clearly paralleled the activities of the contemporary Australian literary scene that Barnard and Eldershaw's London publishers, fearing a lawsuit might ensue, insisted on seeking a legal opinion prior to publication. The choice of Canberra as the venue for the conference is an interesting one as Barnard and Eldershaw in their work with the FAW had recently been involved in successfully lobbying politicians in Canberra to develop a program of governmental support for writers, including such initiatives as individual writers' grants and publishing subsidies. In this respect, they perhaps momentarily viewed Canberra, rather than Sydney or Melbourne, as the "cultural" capital of Australia.

Plaque with Laurel departs from convention by focusing on a group of writers rather than a single literary protagonist, reflecting perhaps the extent to which Barnard and Eldershaw considered the development of Australian literature to be a collective endeavor, in which pursuit of the all-too-rare genius might give way to support of the sincere and able writers they saw as the mainstay of any national literature. A mixed crowd of writers is drawn to the conference through their shared desire to commemorate the late Richard Crale, whose memorial plaque gives the novel its title. Crale is the significant absence in the novel, the missing guest of honor who nevertheless provides the focal point for a consideration of the shape taken by individual writing careers. In the course of the narrative, his troubled life and career are reconstructed through the fragmented and conflicting memories of his wife, his lover, his closest friend, and those who would bask momentarily in his reflected glory. The question arises as to what Crale symbolizes for them, individually and collectively, and what they are commemorating in fixing a plaque to the wall of the National Library in Canberra. While at times there seem to be almost too many characters to follow, the satirical treatment of their interrelationships and professional rivalries provides an interesting, if slightly malicious, portrait of contemporary literary societies and of the literary terrain that Barnard and Eldershaw (as M. Barnard Eldershaw) and their contemporaries were endeavoring to negotiate. The novel also charts the hierarchical relationship between journalism and so-called serious literature in Australian culture, posing the question of whether a separate and identifiable "Australian literature" exists.

Many of the issues explored in *Plaque with Laurel* find distinct parallels in *Essays in Australian Fiction*, the volume of critical essays published by M. Barnard Eldershaw in 1938. In a letter to Nettie Palmer, Barnard described the collection as an attempt to clarify their literary position and, considering that it appeared at a time when scholarly appraisals of Australian literature were extremely rare, it represents an extraordinary initiative on the part of the two women. The volume builds on their occasional reviews and public lectures, but rather than attempting an historical survey of Australian literature, it focuses on established and emerging contemporary writers. *Essays in Australian Fiction* did not simply offer a series of critical responses to individual works. More significantly, it provided an opportunity to draw readers' attention to various contemporary authors by providing much-needed attention or publicity for those whose works were otherwise unlikely to gain much attention beyond initial brief reviews. In this way *Essays in Australian Fiction* was instrumental in consolidating the reputations of Vance Palmer, Henry Handel Richardson, Prichard, and Davison, and in establishing those of Stead, Dark, Leonard Mann, and Martin Boyd in the crucial early stages of their careers. Fellow critic H. M. Green suggested that it said "something for Barnard Eldershaw's judgement that she [sic] was able to perceive the worth of Mann and Dark at a time when their best work had not yet appeared." Despite this supportive, publicizing aspect of their literary essays, Barnard and Eldershaw were by no means so broadly propagandist in their appraisals as Nettie Palmer was sometimes inclined to be. They were not afraid to consider Australian writing on its own merits and were always willing to be critical of elements of an individual's work when they felt criticism was warranted. "The function of the critic," Barnard argued, "is to set up standards, to stimulate interest, and to integrate the patterns of contemporary writing." Yet, even in their roles as critics, Barnard and Eldershaw never

Dust jacket for the 1961 edition of Barnard and Eldershaw's 1929 novel, about the rise and fall of a family of shipping merchants (Bruccoli Clark Layman Archives)

lost sight of their identities as writers, and their commentaries clearly demonstrate their indebtedness to insights gained from personal struggles with the creative process.

As an extension of these critical endeavors, in the late 1930s Barnard and Eldershaw conducted an informal Wednesday-evening salon in various small apartments they rented around Kings Cross, the erstwhile center of the literary bohemia of Sydney. As Barnard still resided in her parents' home and Eldershaw held a live-in position at the school where she taught, gatherings such as these represented rare opportunities for them to develop an independent social life as single women. Their guests included at various times such literary figures as Davison, Xavier Herbert, Leslie Rees, Tom Inglis Moore, Louis Esson, Frank Wilmot, Miles Franklin, Vance Palmer, and Kylie Tennant. Discussion ranged from the literary and cultural to the social and political, and it fostered a sense of community among writers, critics, booksellers, and broadcasters alike. During these years Barnard commenced a lengthy and secret love affair with Davison. Barnard, Eldershaw, and Davison–all prominent writers by this time–were often referred to as "the triumvirate" and credited with shaping a heavily politicized cultural agenda for Sydney writers in the years around World War II and for transforming the FAW from a relatively apolitical and amateurish organization into an articulate and informed political lobby group.

Neither the gently ironic tone of *Plaque with Laurel* nor the measured criticism of *Essays in Australian Fiction* readily reveal the depth of concern Barnard and Eldershaw felt across these same years as they confronted the rapidly changing climate of international politics. Recent events in Australia and in Europe had underscored for the two collaborators the politically sensitive role of writers in periods of major upheaval and social change. The furor surrounding the 1934 visit of Czech writer Egon Kisch to Australia and Nettie Palmer's campaigning in support of the Republican government in Spain reinforced for them the notion that being involved in writing at this time necessarily meant being involved in politics. This gradual coming to consciousness appears to have instilled in them a heightened sense of self-scrutiny and the desire to rethink their roles as writers. Across the late 1930s and early 1940s they show a marked shift toward an understanding of writers as enmeshed in a network of tensions—social, political, and cultural—and a perception of fiction writing as a complex and contingent process. They became convinced of the need for Australian writers and intellectuals to assume a higher public profile, to become involved in the cultural and political life of the nation, and to engage with the rapidly shifting international situation. They viewed the growing Fascist movement in Europe as a negative and threatening politicization of culture that challenged fundamental freedoms and against which writers should protest. While neither Barnard nor Eldershaw was directly involved with the Communist Party or any other organized left-wing group, close links with writers such as Davison, Prichard, and Devanny, who were, together with the 1937 amalgamation of the FAW with the more explicitly leftist Writers' League, meant that they were well aware of the debates taking place at that time on the Left. Barnard later reflected "it was a period in which we had to know where we stood and with whom. There was a confusion of ideologies and we sought among them for some sort of intellectual salvation."

Probably the most explicit expression of the nexus between Barnard's and Eldershaw's literary and political ideals can be found in the attempt on the part of the FAW in 1938 to publish a collection of statements and essays titled *Writers in Defence of Freedom*. Eldershaw was one of the nominated editors, and both she and Barnard belonged to the planning committee. The volume represented a collective response to restrictive political and cultural changes both in Australia and in Europe, and it was to be prefaced by a strongly worded condemnation of authoritarianism, militarism, infringements of civil liberties, suppression of free thought and utterance, and the use of violence as an instrument of government. These were all issues Barnard and Eldershaw ultimately explored at length in their final novel, *Tomorrow and Tomorrow and Tomorrow*. Contributors to the collection included fellow writers Miles Franklin, Leonard Mann, Brian Penton, Vance Palmer, Brian Fitzpatrick, Dulcie Deamer, and Dymphna Cusack. That the volume grew out of a genuine sense of cultural and ideological crisis on the part of these writers is evident in Barnard's account of planning their own contribution, titled "Liberty and Violence," while returning by ship from a holiday in Tasmania. Barnard was staunchly pacifist in her outlook and had increasing difficulty reconciling this position with demands for effective action in the face of Fascist aggression. She wrote to Nettie Palmer:

> We had a tortured two days on the ship trying to plan our contribution. Nothing came of it for we could not agree. Everyday reality moves further and further away from my political philosophy, yet I cannot bring myself to abandon the beliefs that are a part of my flesh. My mind is a gulf of black melancholy—but that I know well is a luxury to which I have no right.

The volume was edited in readiness for publication before publishers' delays, the outbreak of war, and, subsequently, wartime paper shortages caused the project to be shelved.

The outbreak of war placed further pressures upon Barnard and Eldershaw as writers and intellectuals. They were at the forefront of the FAW's campaign against the repressive National Security Acts, so-called emergency legislation, which permitted the confiscation of property considered "subversive" and threatened to make unlawful the exercising of the basic freedoms of speech, of the press, and of assembly. While Australia joined in fighting Fascism abroad, at home its wartime legislation targeted those active on the Left. Eldershaw involved herself in documenting cases of property confiscated under the National Security Acts, while Barnard was responsible for drafting the FAW's statement on "Freedom of Speech, the Press and Association," a document calling for the reversal of the government's current policy and outlining the fellowship's position on freedom of speech and censorship. The urgency of Barnard's task was no doubt underscored by the suppression of her own political pamphlet "The Case For the Future" by the censors, as were some historical plays she had written for the Australian Labor Party's Education Committee. The irony of having to defend at home the freedoms Australia was allegedly fighting to preserve abroad was not lost on them. As Barnard reported in a letter to Eleanor Dark, it was "curious that people who have been staunchly democratic all their lives should now come to look upon liberty as some sort of handicap, which OUGHT [sic] to be sacrificed for the time being."

In common with other writers of their circle, Barnard and Eldershaw found reconciling their current creative interests with the world around them increasingly difficult. Following the publication of *Plaque with Laurel,* Barnard and Eldershaw turned their attention to Australian history, producing over the next two years *Phillip of Australia: An Account of the Settlement at Sydney Cove 1788–1792* (1938), *The Life and Times of Captain John Piper* (1939), and *My Australia* (1939). As the first two works suggest, they possessed a particular interest in the colonial past of Australia and the development of the early settlement at Sydney. They were drawn to the wealth of historical documentation on this period, and their writing inevitably reveals the benefit of such primary research. And yet, despite the success of these projects, they were confronted by what they felt was their futility in the face of world events. While working on these books, they toyed with various ideas for another novel, including a fictional account of the life of the colonial painter Conrad Martens. Ultimately, they settled on "an account of the death of civilisation," an idea that grew into *Tomorrow and Tomorrow and Tomorrow*. This book was their last collaborative effort and represented both their greatest achievement and their greatest disappointment. Work on this novel was slower than anticipated as wartime conditions and changed personal circumstances frequently interfered with progress. In 1941, just as the novel was getting under way, Eldershaw left her teaching job for an appointment in the Commonwealth Public Service, moving first to Canberra and then to Melbourne. The following year Barnard returned to full-time work as a librarian. Weekends and rare holidays were often spent retracing their steps, and each collaborator had to snatch brief opportunities to continue working on the novel. Although the novel was completed in 1944, it faced lengthy delays because of wartime paper shortages and was also subjected to clumsy government censorship. Its eventual release in 1947 under the truncated title of *Tomorrow and Tomorrow* was something of an anticlimax. Both writers felt they had put all of themselves into the novel only to have it fall flat: the issues it confronted suddenly seemed dated, and its innovation went largely unnoticed. Only with the publication of the full uncensored text in 1983 did the novel begin to receive the serious critical appraisal it deserved.

Tomorrow and Tomorrow and Tomorrow is the most ambitious, complex, and intellectually challenging of the novels by M. Barnard Eldershaw. Structured as a novel within a novel, the framing narrative tells of Knarf, a novelist living in a futuristic twenty-fourth-century soci-

Dust jacket for Barnard and Eldershaw's best-known novel, about a novelist living in the twenty-fourth century who encounters many of the same political problems current in Australia during the 1930s and 1940s (Bruccoli Clark Layman Archives)

ety. In the course of a single day Knarf reads to a friend the novel he has written about the life of Harry Munster and his family. Harry's story follows the lives of the urban working class in Sydney's inner city from World War I, in which Harry fought, through the Great Depression and World War II to a projected World War III, in which Australian society is effectively destroyed. It is replaced by the technologically advanced society in which Knarf now lives, in which science successfully provides for all human needs, but liberty and choice are limited. The novel alternates between Harry's story of increasing disillusionment and social and economic marginalization and Knarf's world in which his son Ren is leading a dissident youth movement in a campaign for greater public participation in government. The contest of ideologies played out within both narratives focuses largely upon the question of liberty and the possibilities for its realization in any society. *Tomorrow and Tomorrow and Tomorrow* begs the question of whether any of the available ideologies—capitalism, Marxism, or pacifism—can by their nature guarantee individual and collective liberty. As Knarf explains to his son, liberty itself "is always a threat to those who operate the engines of authority," because liberty "cannot help being a courage to resist the demands of power at some point that is decisive." Like George Orwell's *Nineteen Eighty-Four* (1949), *Tomorrow and Tomorrow and Tomorrow* is not a work in which the future is planned or projected so much as one in which the threatening potentialities of the present are analyzed. The novel can be seen to arise directly out of the social and political crises of the 1930s and 1940s, and yet its hybrid combination of fiction with political and social theory challenged and confused many of its initial readers and reviewers. As Barnard later noted, "with the publication of the novel I was involved in a labyrinth of denials. No, I wasn't a Communist or a Trotskyist or a fellow traveller or a reactionary or an intellectual or a prophet."

One of the most memorable aspects of *Tomorrow and Tomorrow and Tomorrow* is its representation of the city of Sydney. Wandering through its streets, Harry Munster provides readers with an intense, fragmentary, and subjective map of its districts and byways, its bloated department stores, sparkling beaches, teeming alleys, parks, memorials, and rundown boardinghouses. Earlier, in *A House Is Built* and *Green Memory*, M. Barnard Eldershaw offered images of the city as a relatively fixed and stable social milieu—the locus of growth and progress where the positive and productive forces of history are enacted. By contrast, in *Tomorrow and Tomorrow and Tomorrow* Sydney becomes the symbolic figure for the conflicting pressures confronting twentieth-century civilization. There are colorful glimpses of the city as the shining emblem of modernity with its glistening glass and chrome shops, neon lights, and humming traffic. Yet, at the same time, through a series of images of dislocation and social alienation reminiscent of John Dos Passos's *Manhattan Transfer* (1925) and Stead's *Seven Poor Men of Sydney* (1934), Sydney emerges as the figure of Western capitalism and of postindustrial society, a world of mindless machine technology governed by profit, competition, and overproduction. Unemployed and cast adrift in its streets, Harry Munster imagines "the city whirring with its own momentum, a strange machine for devouring men." The city is characterized as a monstrous machine that strips individuals of any control over their own lives. In this guise, the previously celebrated symbols of modernity become sinister and threatening, and the city itself a cold, nightmarish place.

In the novel, the critique of technology is confined neither to the twentieth century nor to the capitalist system. The society of the twenty-fourth century, in which a form of scientific socialism is practiced, is revealed, despite its apparently progressive and innovative nature, to have similar limitations. Society is still imaged as a "machine," and the technocratic elite responsible for its running—the "Technical Bureau"—is exposed as repressive, exclusive, and self-perpetuating. While scientific methods have overcome the problems of production, distribution, competition, and profit, they are shown to foster in turn a new set of troubles: an emphasis on material welfare only, the surfeit of leisure that accompanies the lack of genuinely useful labor, and the impulse to perfect human life by eugenic means. This society is one in which the individual remains almost as alienated and enslaved as was Harry Munster in the twentieth century and in which the familiar dialectical oppositions between reason and imagination, the material and the spiritual, and nature and civilization persist. Rather than being offered as a utopian ideal, the society of the twenty-fourth century instead points to the contingent and provisional nature of all forms of social organization and ideology.

After completing *Tomorrow and Tomorrow and Tomorrow* Barnard and Eldershaw contemplated collaborating on a comprehensive literary history of Australia. However, as Eldershaw was now employed permanently in Melbourne and facing increasing ill health, they did not follow through on this project. In the late 1940s, the political crises of the 1930s and the war years, which had lent such urgency to their literary activities, were replaced by a complacency and conservatism in the wider community. These feelings grew under the government of Sir Robert Menzies into an acceptance of the Cold War and its rhetoric. Barnard's and Eldershaw's roles as influential critics centrally involved in creating, promoting, and defending Australian literature were suddenly curtailed in 1952 when conservative members of the federal parliament, influenced by anti-Communist sentiment, attacked Barnard and Eldershaw as "fellow travellers" and labeled *Tomorrow and Tomorrow and Tomorrow* "a trashy, tripey novel with a Marxist slant." Her health failing, Flora Eldershaw withdrew from public life, retiring to her sister's farm, where she died on 20 September 1956. Barnard continued to write but focused on history rather than fiction. Her important study *A History of Australia* appeared in 1962, and in 1967 she published the first full-length critical study of the writer Miles Franklin. In 1983 Marjorie Barnard received the Patrick White Award in recognition of the novels written by M. Barnard Eldershaw, but principally for *Tomorrow and Tomorrow and Tomorrow*, which the judging committee argued had been unjustly neglected. She died on 8 May

1987. Renewed interest in Australian women writers of the 1930s and 1940s has meant that greater attention is being paid to the works of M. Barnard Eldershaw. The cultural activities of Barnard and Eldershaw are now viewed as central to the development of literary and cultural policy in interwar Australia, while their fiction and criticism are acknowledged as shaping forces in the literature of the same period.

Interviews:

Candida Baker, "Marjorie Barnard," in *Yacker 2: Australian Writers Talk About Their Work* (Sydney: Pan/Picador, 1987), pp. 29–41;

Giulia Giuffré, "Marjorie Barnard," in *A Writing Life: Interviews With Australian Women Writers* (Sydney: Allen & Unwin, 1990), pp. 131–167.

References:

Marjorie Barnard, "The Gentle Art of Collaboration," *Ink No. 2* (Sydney: Society of Women Writers, 1977), pp. 126–128;

Barnard, "How 'Tomorrow and Tomorrow' Came to Be Written," *Meanjin*, 3 (1970): 328–330;

Barnard, "Tributes to Flora Eldershaw," *Meanjin*, 4 (1956): 391–392;

David Carter, "Current History Looks Apocalyptic: Barnard Eldershaw, Utopia and the Literary Intellectual," *Australian Literary Studies*, 14, no. 2 (1989): 174–187;

Maryanne Dever, "The Case for Flora Eldershaw," *Hecate*, 15, no. 2 (1989): 38–48;

Dever, "'No Mine and Thine But Ours': Finding 'M. Barnard Eldershaw,'" *Tulsa Studies in Women's Literature*, 14 (Spring 1995): 65–74;

Flora Eldershaw, "The Feminisation of Literature," *All About Books*, 14 (October 1933): 170;

H. M. Green, *A History of Australian Literature*, Volume 2 (Sydney: Angus & Robertson, 1961);

Drusilla Modjeska, *Exiles at Home: Australian Women Writers 1925–1945* (Sydney: Sirius, 1981);

Nettie Palmer, "Writing under a Pen Name: Consistent and Inconsistent Disguises," *Illustrated Tasmanian Mail*, 11 August 1932, p. 61;

Louise Rorabacher, *Marjorie Barnard and M. Barnard Eldershaw* (New York: Twayne, 1973).

Papers:

The principal collection of the papers and manuscripts of "M. Barnard Eldershaw" is held in the Mitchell Library, State Library of New South Wales, Sydney (Marjorie Barnard Papers and Flora Eldershaw Papers). Further items pertaining to Barnard's and Eldershaw's activities in the Fellowship of Australian Writers can be found in the same library (Papers of the Fellowship of Australian Writers). Approximately two hundred letters from Barnard to Nettie and Vance Palmer and a small number from Eldershaw to members of the Palmer family are held in the National Library of Australia, Canberra (Papers of Vance and Nettie Palmer, Papers of Helen Palmer, and Papers of Aileen Palmer). The National Library of Australia also holds further relevant correspondence in the papers of Frank Dalby Davison, Eleanor Dark, and Judah Waten.

Martin Boyd
(10 June 1893 – 3 June 1972)

Susan Lever
University of New South Wales at the
Australian Defence Force Academy

BOOKS: *Retrospect* (Melbourne: H. H. Champion, 1920);

Love Gods, as Martin Mills (London: Constable, 1925);

Brangane: A Memoir, as Mills (London: Constable, 1926); republished as *The Aristocrat: A Memoir* (Indianapolis: Bobbs-Merrill, 1927);

The Madeleine Heritage, as Mills (Indianapolis: Bobbs-Merrill, 1928); revised as *The Montforts* (London: Constable, 1928; revised, Adelaide: Rigby, 1963);

Dearest Idol, as Walter Beckett (Indianapolis: Bobbs-Merrill, 1929);

Scandal of Spring (London: Dent, 1934);

The Lemon Farm (London: Dent, 1935; revised edition, New York: Norton, 1936; revised edition, Melbourne: Macmillan, 1973);

The Painted Princess: A Fairy Story, illustrated by Jocelyn Crowe (London: Constable, 1936);

The Picnic (London: Dent, 1937; New York: Putnam, 1937; Ringwood, Vic.: Penguin, 1985);

Night of the Party (London: Dent, 1938);

A Single Flame (London: Dent, 1939);

Nuns in Jeopardy (London: Dent, 1940; Melbourne: Macmillan, 1973; New York: Harcourt Brace Jovanovich, 1975);

Lucinda Brayford (London: Cresset, 1946; New York: Dutton, 1948; Melbourne: Lansdowne, 1969);

Such Pleasure (New York: Dutton, 1948; London: Cresset, 1949); republished as *Bridget Malwyn* (New York: Dutton, 1949); republished as *Such Pleasure* (Ringwood, Vic.: Penguin, 1985);

The Cardboard Crown (London: Cresset, 1952; New York: Dutton, 1953; revised edition, Harmondsworth, U.K.: Penguin, 1964; Melbourne: Lansdowne, 1971);

A Difficult Young Man (London: Cresset, 1955; New York: Reynal, 1956; Melbourne: Lansdowne, 1965);

Outbreak of Love (London: Murray, 1957; New York: Reynal, 1957; Melbourne: Lansdowne, 1971);

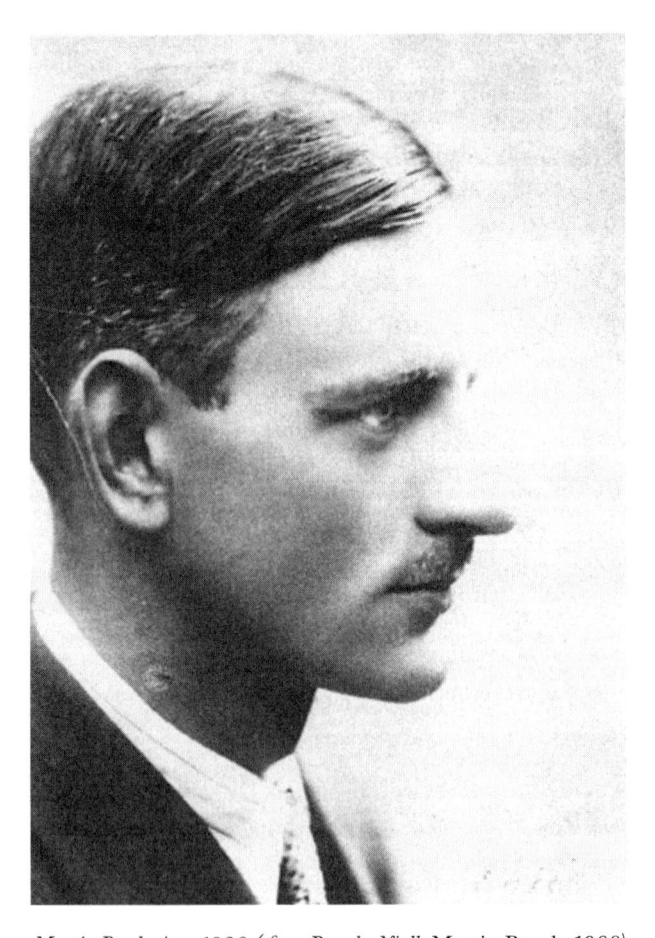

Martin Boyd, circa 1928 (from Brenda Niall, Martin Boyd, *1988)*

Much Else in Italy: A Subjective Travel Book (London: Macmillan / New York: St. Martin's Press, 1958);

When Blackbirds Sing (London & New York: Abelard-Schuman, 1962; Melbourne: Lansdowne, 1971);

Day of My Delight: An Anglo-Australian Memoir (Melbourne: Lansdowne, 1965; revised, 1974);

The Tea-Time of Love: The Clarification of Miss Stilby (London: Bles, 1969);

Why They Walk Out: An Essay in Seven Parts (Rome: Published by the author, 1970).

SELECTED PERIODICAL PUBLICATIONS–UNCOLLECTED: "Their Link with Britain," in *The Sunburnt Country,* edited by Ian Bevan (London: Collins, 1953), pp. 238–247;

Letter in reply to Brenda Niall's article, *Twentieth Century,* 18 (1963): 73;

"Dubious Cartography," *Meanjin,* 23 (1964): 5–13;

Answer to questionnaire in *Authors Take Sides on Vietnam,* edited by Cecil Woolf and John Bagguley (London: Peter Owen, 1967), pp. 94–95;

"Australian Writers in Profile: Preoccupations and Intentions," *Southerly,* 28 (1968): 83–90;

"De Gustibus," *Overland* (1972): 5–9.

Martin Boyd's novels affirm the European heritage of Australians and insist on the role of history and culture in maintaining civilized values. His interest in the relationship of Australians to the culture of Europe and his preoccupation with the twentieth-century decline of aristocratic values stands in opposition to the Australian nationalist literary tradition, which has stressed the distinctive qualities of Australians and their egalitarian ethos. Some Australian readers have dismissed Boyd's novels for their preoccupation with British class values and the social life of the English gentry. For the most part, Boyd wrote stylish social comedy, but he emerged in his later years as a novelist with passionate concerns about the decline of society.

Boyd came from a family with claims to the English landed gentry, though it is now better known for the number of Australian artists it has produced. Family artists include Martin Boyd's brothers, Penleigh and Merric; his nephews, painters Arthur and David Boyd, sculptor Guy Boyd, and architect Robin Boyd; his nieces, potters Lucy Beck and Mary Perceval Nolan; and their children. Martin Boyd's parents, Arthur Merric Boyd and Emma Minnie Boyd, were both painters of some distinction, so Boyd developed as a writer among visual artists. His family provided much of the material for his best-known novels, the Langton sequence—*The Cardboard Crown* (1952), *A Difficult Young Man* (1955), *Outbreak of Love* (1957), and *When Blackbirds Sing* (1962)—but he was too restless to remain in Australia. He lived most of his life in England and Italy, but his finest novels recall with affection his early life in Australia, particularly the social life of Melbourne before World War I.

Martin à Beckett Boyd was born in a *pensione* in Lucerne, Switzerland, on 10 June 1893, while his parents were touring Europe with his maternal grandparents, W. A. C. and Emma à Beckett. These grandparents had acquired such wealth in Melbourne in the 1880s that they returned to England at the end of the decade and bought the family manor house in Wiltshire. Martin was born just as news of the 1890s financial crash reached the family, and while his parents remained wealthy enough to live without working for money, they never again enjoyed the financial security of the years immediately before his birth. The sense of a lost Golden Age associated with his childhood that permeates his writing about the period before World War I may have been strengthened by an awareness that he was born into a family in financial and social, though certainly not artistic, decline.

Boyd always took pride in his family background, even claiming a link to St. Thomas à Beckett, but his biographer, Brenda Niall, has discovered that his maternal grandmother, Emma à Beckett, was the daughter of a convict, John Mills, who had been transported from Gloucestershire to Hobart in 1827 for his involvement in the Wickwar Gang, a group of thieves apparently based in his immediate family. On his release, Mills established a brewery and several public houses in Melbourne, with such success that he left a fortune to his daughter. The social position of the à Becketts, and later the Boyds, was founded on the career of Sir William à Beckett, the first Chief Justice of Victoria, but their wealth came directly from the convict brewer and publican John Mills. W. A. C. à Beckett's marriage to Emma Mills, transformed into the elopement of Austin Langton with Alice Verso in *The Cardboard Crown,* reconciled a more serious difference in social position than Boyd suggests in his novel. In *Martin Boyd: A Life* (1988), Niall argues that Boyd's use of the pseudonym Martin Mills for his first three novels indicates that he knew about the convict background. If so, his neglect of the convict heritage in his autobiographies and novels indicates something of his own sensitivities about the darker elements in his family's past.

After his birth the family returned to Melbourne, where the Boyds settled on a farm at Yarra Glen outside Melbourne. Along with The Grange, Boyd's grandparents' home in the Harkaway hills, this farm became the model for Westhill in the Langton novels, a place of simple living and refuge from trouble. Boyd attended Trinity Grammar School in Melbourne and spent a year at St. John's Theological College, St. Kilda, training for the Anglican priesthood. He then worked in an architect's office in Melbourne until sailing for England in August 1915 to enlist as an officer in the Royal East Kent Regiment

Dust jacket for the 1963 revised edition of Boyd's novel about the European history of his family (Bruccoli Clark Layman Archives)

(the Buffs) of the British army. He served with the army in France before transferring to the Royal Flying Corps at the end of 1917 as a flight observer.

If Boyd's family background was the source of material for his finest novels, World War I provided the moral and social crisis that impelled him to write. His experience of the war made morality and religion central to his understanding of the social changes taking place in the twentieth century. While he is sometimes dismissed as a light social novelist, his undoubted skill in social comedy is complicated by a deeper concern about the ways that human pleasure has been corrupted by the powers of commercialism and nationalism.

After the war Boyd visited his parents in Melbourne. There he published his book of poems, *Retrospect* (1920), which expresses his feelings of loss at the deaths of his comrades; the poems subvert pastoral ideas of the English countryside by reflecting on the battlefields of France. The book also reflects Boyd's dissatisfaction with the society offered to the returned soldier, in which heroes find themselves working as bank clerks. Restless in Australia, in 1921 Boyd returned to England with an allowance from his parents. Once again he tried the religious life,

briefly joining a community of Anglican Franciscan friars in Dorset. This experience provided the material for his first novel, *Love Gods* (1925), which demonstrates his interest in the conflict between a religious life, committed to the highest ideals, and a secular life, ready to enjoy material pleasure. Since the hero decides for the latter, the dominant tone of the novel, appropriately, is comic. While Boyd later wanted the novel forgotten, it retains interest as a novel written immediately after World War I about the choices facing a returned soldier with strong religious and moral convictions.

Boyd's next novel, *Brangane: A Memoir* (1926), republished as *The Aristocrat* (1927), is the first of his studies of pleasure-seeking women who aspire to the British aristocracy. Niall proposes that Boyd based the novel on the life of Australian writer Barbara Baynton, whom he met in London during the war. Baynton made a series of marriages, each increasing her wealth and social position, and Boyd transformed these into the story of a baker's wife who manages to scale the British class system. Brangane never finds the perfect life of pleasure she seeks, and Boyd uses the novel to explore his ideas about the need to reconcile an appreciation of art with spiritualism and morality.

The Madeleine Heritage, or *The Montforts* (1928), presents Boyd's own family history in fiction for the first time. The characters are more directly based on the à Beckett and Boyd families than those in Boyd's later novels. Though it lacks the careful structure of the later family novels, it is written with the wit and ironic observation that distinguish Boyd's best writing. Australian critics greeted the novel with enthusiasm and welcomed its acknowledgment of Australian ties with a European past. In 1929 it won the Australian Literature Society gold medal.

After the success of *The Montforts,* Boyd's career stalled; his only accepted manuscript for several years was *Dearest Idol* (1929), published in the United States under the pseudonym Walter Beckett. During the 1930s Boyd lived frugally in various Sussex villages, usually near the sea, maintaining friendships with other writers and artists and publishing a series of novels set in similar surroundings. While these novels rarely move beyond domestic society, Boyd always wrestles with some moral dilemma, particularly the disparity between "natural" human love and religious or legal prohibitions. In *Scandal of Spring* (1934) an adolescent elopes with his girlfriend only to find himself imprisoned as a result of laws regarding the age of consent. In *The Lemon Farm* (1935) the wife of a wealthy businessman has an illicit affair with a young man more sympathetic with her artistic aspirations. *The Picnic* (1937) introduces a family of Anglo-Australians to country society and explores the kind of relationship between two brothers that Boyd later developed in the Langton novels. In *Night of the Party* (1938) a painter leaves his socially ambitious wife—initially for a more inspiring woman but eventually to pursue his art more seriously. *Nuns in Jeopardy* (1940) is perhaps the most interesting of these novels; in it Boyd departs from any pretense of realism to develop an allegory in which a group of nuns are shipwrecked on an island, where their commitment to religion and humanity are tested. The novel maintains a whimsical lightness of touch while examining the relationship between love of humanity and the restrictions of a self-disciplining religion.

On the basis of these novels, Boyd could be classified as one of the minor English novelists of the interwar years, sharing preoccupations with more distinguished writers such as Evelyn Waugh, Aldous Huxley, and Anthony Powell. In 1936 Boyd published a children's story called *The Painted Princess: A Fairy Story,* and at the end of the 1930s he wrote his first autobiography, *A Single Flame* (1939), which reflects directly on his war experience and family background. This exercise in reflection may have served as preparation for the later novels that made his reputation.

The outbreak of World War II heightened Boyd's sense of the increasing loss of humane values, and all his novels after 1940 explore his preoccupations within the context of a growing twentieth-century destructiveness. In 1942 Boyd moved into rooms in Cambridge, where he regularly attended the services at King's College Chapel and mixed with a range of young people and intellectuals, including pacifists and conscientious objectors to war. There he wrote the novel that transformed him from an entertaining social novelist to a writer with claims to serious consideration.

In *Lucinda Brayford* (1946) Boyd's knowledge of the Anglo-Australian Melbourne elite provides the background for his study of a twentieth-century pleasure seeker. Lucinda's childhood in Australia ensures that her education has not dulled her natural capacity for material and aesthetic pleasure, so that she brings a responsive sensibility to her experiences of Europe in the twentieth century. Lucinda marries the third son of an aristocratic English family, Hugo Brayford, but her enjoyment of an aristocratic life is thwarted when World War I reduces Hugo to a damaged and malevolent presence. Their son, Stephen, grows to maturity as World War II erupts and develops pacifist convictions that lead to his imprisonment and eventually to his death. At the end of the novel, Lucinda, by now a worldly and cynical society matron, confronts his suffering with a universal pity and grasps as consolation the slight possibility of human good, represented by the singing of the choirboys in King's College Chapel.

The novel begins and ends at Cambridge and is clearly influenced by Boyd's friendships with young men there and his participation in discussions about the morality of the war. At the same time, through the character of Hugo's brother Paul, Lucinda learns about the place of art in human understanding. Through Paul, Boyd conveys his own wide knowledge of art and music, and his particular version of the meaning of aristocratic values. Paul, one of many characters in Boyd's later novels who seem to represent the author, cannot fully live out his own precepts, but Lucinda—warm, intelligent, and pleasure-loving—is bound to humanity through her commitment to Stephen. She provides Boyd with a means of counterbalancing Paul's despair at the destruction of civilized society with an optimism about the possibilities for the young.

The novel carries a strong sense of Boyd's keen interest in architecture and the decoration of houses, his passion for certain works of art, and his affection for places, particularly in the scenes set at the beach near Melbourne, the country house in Somerset, and King's College in Cambridge. These enthusiasms inform Lucinda's education and the commitment of the novel to living life in Boyd's "aristocratic" manner as a pleasurable aesthetic and moral devotion. Dorothy Green has discussed, in a 1968 article for *Southerly,* the way this novel uses the passing down of family characteristics as an organizing principle, and Kieran Dolin, in a 1989 article for *Westerly,* has explicated the way Boyd's interest in classical and Christian myth patterns the novel. Dolin argues that myth underpins the realist surface of the novel so that, for example, Lucinda functions not merely as an individual society woman but also as the pietà figure of the archetypal grieving mother. Boyd uses classical and Christian references to depict the decay of the aristocracy while seeking signs of the renewal of the aristocratic tradition in the young.

After the critical and financial success of *Lucinda Brayford,* Boyd visited Ireland for the first time in 1946 and, on his return to England, reworked the material in *Brangane* and *Love Gods* as *Such Pleasure* (1948), this time with an Irish central character. Like Lucinda Brayford, Bridget Malwyn seeks happiness through the aristocratic life, but Bridget mistakes the trappings of aristocracy for that civilized harmony with the natural world that Boyd ascribes to it. A character representing Boyd's point of view explains that aristocracy "is only a dream

Boyd, circa 1946 (from Niall, Martin Boyd, *1988)*

in the mind of the artist, and the actual aristocracy are only the puppets he drapes with his ideas." The novel has none of the breadth or detail of *Lucinda Brayford,* but Boyd experiments for the first time with a first-person narrator to frame his novel, a step toward the Guy Langton figure in the first Langton novels.

Boyd returned to Australia in 1948 and devoted his energies to renovating The Grange at Harkaway, where he intended to settle. In 1951, however, he went to England on a visit and never returned to Australia. He moved to Rome in 1957 and lived there for the rest of his life. The return visit to Australia gave him renewed inspiration, and the first pages of *The Cardboard Crown* describe the narrator's excitement on discovering that his grandmother's diaries might provide a key to understanding the history of his family. The novel begins with Guy Langton's conversation with his artist nephew, Julian Langton–an episode clearly based on a similar conversation with Martin Boyd's nephew, Arthur Boyd, who was painting a fresco in the dining room at The Grange.

The Cardboard Crown reworks the family material first used in *The Montforts,* this time through the amusing and opinionated voice of Guy Langton, who confesses his unreliability: "one must talk a great deal of nonsense to arrive at a little truth. If you go mining you must dig up a great deal of quartz to find a little gold." In this scene Guy explains to Julian his notion of the Left and Right sides of society, in which the Left includes all those who work for material gain in the industrial world–from the international financier to the factory worker–while the Right encompasses those who live in preindustrial harmony with nature, from the Duke to the peasant. This theory, presented by the self-conscious and good-natured Guy, offers an underlying standard for the narrator's versions of the characters introduced in the subsequent novels.

Guy tells the story of his grandmother's married life through speculation, quotation from Alice's diaries, and family anecdotes, especially stories related by Uncle Arthur. The narrative itself is not particularly dramatic—Alice Verso elopes with Austin Langton, bringing a financial lifeline to the aristocratic but impoverished Langton family. She becomes the Langtons's "onion woman," clinging to the onion of financial support while her family drags her down by the skirts. For Arthur, she was a saint who attempted to achieve the balance between the pleasures of cultivated existence and care for humanity, between a Protestant sense of responsibility and a Catholic love of beauty and passion. During their marriage Austin maintained an affair with his cousin Hetty, fathering several illegitimate sons. When Alice discovers this fact, she travels to Italy where she meets a cultivated Englishman and contemplates the possibility of staying with him in Rome. Alice's desire to live out the pattern of perfection she sees in Rome founders on the selfishness and sensuality of the family she supports. Her love of the aesthetic and spiritually enriching pleasures of Europe must be reconciled with her commitment to the warm family life of Australia.

The manner of the telling is as important as the tale. Guy cannot know fully the events, the motivations, or even the personalities of his grandmother's generation; so, as Leonie J. Kramer has noted in an essay for *Southerly* (1968), he builds the novel from small details and his own interpretation. In this way he openly creates a kind of family mythology with Alice as saint, Hetty as grasping materialist, and Austin as sensualist. Cousin Sarah, too, emerges as a representative of the kind of puritanical fundamentalist Christianity that Boyd's mother imposed on her sons, allowing Boyd to give only her warm and creative qualities to Guy's mother, Laura. In *Australian Literary Studies* (1976), Warwick Gould has compared this narrative method to Ford Madox Ford's in *The Good Soldier* (1915), suggesting that these indirect methods of storytelling are "especially appropriate forms, when the novelist wishes to consider the whole decay of a social order."

A Difficult Young Man focuses on Dominic, Guy's moody older brother, and Dominic's inability to conform to the expectations of the changing society around him. Guy's narrative position is stronger in this book, as he can play the part of close observer and witness to Dominic's life—the sensitive younger brother who can see the consequences of Dominic's actions. Both brothers have elements of Martin Boyd's personality—Guy, aesthetic and religious, and Dominic, passionate and instinctively responsive. The action demonstrates Dominic's unthinkingly aristocratic—in Boyd's terms—behavior, while Guy interprets events. As in *The Cardboard Crown,* attitudes and values are ascribed to individual characters: Cousin Sarah persuades Dominic to share her self-punishing religion while Aunt Baba opposes him at every opportunity with her energetic greed and materialism. In this way the family-centered events of the novel—Dominic's expulsion from school, his activities with the maids at Baba's farm, his destruction of a horse, his various heroic physical exploits, and his elopement with his cousin Helena—become emblematic of a battle of values.

In this novel Guy says he is looking for "The Memline in the cellar, the beautiful portrait of the human face, lost in the dissolution of our family and our religion," and Dominic performs not so much as a credible individual character as Guy's means of exploring human possibilities. The confidence of its narration and the way in which Boyd carries the action through minor family squabbles and contretemps while conveying wider implications of a social order on the brink of destruction make *A Difficult Young Man* the most subtle of his novels.

Outbreak of Love leaves the members of Guy's immediate family to follow the pattern of discontent through the experiences of Alice's daughter, Diana Von Flugel. Set in Melbourne immediately before the outbreak of World War I, the novel recounts Diana's flirtation with the urbane traveler Russell Lockwood and her desire to emulate her mother's dreams of a cultured life in Europe. In a comic subplot, her husband, Wolfie, is inspired by his affair with a barmaid to compose his second brilliant musical work. The narrative offers a pale parody of Alice's story in *The Cardboard Crown,* with the eastern suburbs of Melbourne standing in for Florence and Rome and Wolfie's barmaid for the ferocious Cousin Hetty, seductress of Austin. The outbreak of war finally ends the possibility of Diana's dream and leads her to confront the need to defend Wolfie from the anti-German feeling about to erupt in Australia. While *Outbreak of Love* reasserts Boyd's concerns about social decline and the barbarity of the impending war, it has little of the vitality of the two previous novels, and some critics have had difficulty in comprehending its use of Guy's voice to initiate a narrative in which he has little part.

Boyd's next published work was *Much Else in Italy: A Subjective Travel Book* (1958), in which the narrator and his young companion tour Italy, studying various works of art and meditating on the relationship between the classical and Christian worlds. This work gave Boyd the opportunity to express directly some of the responses to art that he gives to characters in his novels, and it provides a rationale for his decision to settle finally in Italy. It also reveals the depth of meaning that Boyd attached to particular works of art, such as Michelangelo's *Pietà*, or Flemish painter Hans Memlinc's portraits, which are reference points for characters such as Paul Brayford and Guy Langton.

Guy Langton disappears completely from the final novel of the series, *When Blackbirds Sing,* which gives a third-person account of Dominic's enlistment in the British army, his experiences at the front, and his relationship with the now-married Sylvia Dilton. Without the witty glaze of Guy's narration, this novel confronts the reader directly with Boyd's passionate hatred of war. Dominic shares Boyd's own war experiences, as detailed in his autobiographies, though Boyd also draws on Robert Graves's and Siegfried Sassoon's experiences of the war. Dominic does not reflect on the meaning of the war, nor does he engage in political analysis. His movement from enthusiastic warrior to disgusted objector follows from his direct engagement in battle and his encounters with the representatives of the new powerful class in Britain, including his recognition of Sylvia's callous materialism. As Patricia Dobrez suggests in a 1996 article in *Kunapipi,* for Dominic the war has been a conflict, not between nations but between the commercial class and those with traditional values, between the Left and Right of Guy Langton's theory. On his return to Australia, Dominic finds that Helena cannot comprehend the nature of his experiences, and his act of throwing his medal into the pond gives her the final words of the Langton series: "'You're not serious?' she said."

The loss of Guy as narrator renders *When Blackbirds Sing* a less complex novel than *A Cardboard Crown* or *A Difficult Young Man*. Boyd uses the mythological and emblematic elements of those earlier novels in a broader and less subtle way, and *When Blackbirds Sing* lacks the level of sophisticated irony or comic sense of the first two novels. At the same time, the novel shows a more somber and more tragic dimension to Boyd's writing, as if the author has cast aside the mask of the witty Guy.

In 1965, with growing Australian interest in his work, Boyd published a second autobiography, *Day of My Delight: An Anglo-Australian Memoir*. Some critics now admire the two autobiographies as the most interesting of Boyd's books, though the relationship between the autobiographies, *Much Else in Italy,* and the novels is strong. Taking up Dolin's point about the mythological foundation of Boyd's later novels, David McCooey has argued in *Artful Histories: Modern Australian Autobiography* (1996) that *Day of My Delight* treats in historical form the same concerns presented in mythofictional form in the novels, revealing the necessary placement of the autobiography in history. McCooey also refers to Boyd's "tragicomic" temperament, noting that Boyd's impulse toward autobiography is also a shift to a more tragic mode than that of his novels.

Boyd's novels have been the subject of critical debate in Australia since the 1950s when Kathleen Fitzpatrick began to lecture on what she saw as Boyd's version of Henry James's complex fate of divided nationality. Her remarks stimulated a debate about Boyd's place in Australian literature, with Niall developing the idea—in her 1963 article for *Twentieth Century,* "The Double Alienation of Martin Boyd"—that Boyd's characters were alienated from both Australia and Europe. Boyd answered Niall's article in a 1963 letter to *Twentieth Century* and later wrote several articles engaging with Australian critics, including "Dubious Cartography," a 1964 article for *Meanjin* in which he objects to being put "on a gilt chair in a pretty drawing-room, as a 'delightful minor novelist' of suburban Melbourne." By the time he had published the last of the Langton novels, Boyd had several critical supporters to argue that nationality was not an issue for him, and that, in his novels, Australia and Britain represented different balances of cultural values rather than separate poles.

Since Kramer's and Green's defenses of Boyd's novels as serious works of art, several critics have explicated the way in which Boyd's values are worked and reworked throughout his oeuvre. One of the most important contributions to Boyd criticism has been Niall's meticulous biography, which has opened up understanding of the way in which Boyd selected, reworked, or suppressed his material.

Boyd's last published novel, *The Tea-Time of Love: The Clarification of Miss Stilby* (1969), offers a comic account of the romantic dreams of an elderly English woman living in Rome, though his last published work was an angry denunciation of the conscription of young Australian men for the Vietnam War. These two strands of lighthearted comedy and political denunciation represent the two elements in all of Boyd's fiction. At his best, as in *Lucinda Brayford* and the first two Langton novels, Boyd manages to bring all his pleasure in art and the natural world to serve his abiding fear that such pleasure might be banished forever by the powers taking over the world.

After years as a Protestant among Catholics, Martin Boyd converted to Catholicism shortly before his death in Rome on 3 June 1972. He was buried, however, in the English Protestant Cemetery in Rome as he had wished.

Interview:

Desmond O'Grady, *Conversation with Martin Boyd,* Sound Recording, National Library of Australia, ORAL DeB 137, 1965.

Bibliography:

Brenda Niall, *Martin Boyd* (Oxford: Oxford University Press, 1977).

Biographies:

Desmond O'Grady, "Those Marvellous Blue Skies: Martin Boyd's Seventeen Years in Rome," *Overland* (1973): 26–33;

Brenda Niall, *Martin Boyd: A Life* (Melbourne: Melbourne University Press, 1988);

Walter Crocker, "Martin Boyd," *Overland,* 114 (May 1989): 9–14.

References:

Patricia Dobrez, "*When Blackbirds Sing:* Martin Boyd and the Reality of Good Friday," *Kunapipi,* 18 (1996): 68–82;

Kieran Dolin, "*Mater Dolorosa:* War and Motherhood in *Lucinda Brayford,*" *Westerly,* 34 (1989): 51–57;

Kathleen Fitzpatrick, *Martin Boyd* (Melbourne: Lansdowne, 1963);

Warwick Gould, "The Family Face: Martin Boyd's Art of Memoir," *Australian Literary Studies,* 7 (1976): 269–278;

Dorothy Green, "The Fragrance of Souls: A Study of *Lucinda Brayford,*" *Southerly,* 28 (1968): 110–126;

Green, "From Yarra Glen to Rome: Martin Boyd, 1893–1972," *Meanjin Quarterly,* 31 (1972): 245–258;

Leonie J. Kramer, "The Seriousness of Martin Boyd," *Southerly,* 28 (1968): 91–109;

David McCooey, *Artful Histories: Modern Australian Autobiography* (Cambridge & Melbourne: Cambridge University Press, 1996);

Susan [Lever] McKernan, "Much Else in Boyd: The Relationship Between Martin Boyd's Non-Fiction Work and His Later Novels," *Southerly,* 38 (1978): 309–330;

Pamela Nase, "Martin Boyd's Langton Novels: Praising Superior People," in *The Australian Experience: Critical Essays on Australian Novels,* edited by W. S. Ramson (Canberra: Australian National University Press, 1974), pp. 229–248;

Brenda Niall, "The Double Alienation of Martin Boyd," *Twentieth Century,* 17 (1963): 32–38;

Ramson, "Lucinda Brayford: A Form of Music," in *The Australian Experience: Critical Essays on Australian Novels,* edited by Ramson (Canberra: Australian National University Press, 1974), pp. 209–228;

G. A. Wilkes, "The Achievement of Martin Boyd," *Southerly,* 19 (1958): 90–98.

Papers:

The major collection of Martin Boyd's manuscripts, diaries, notebooks, and correspondence is held in the National Library of Australia, Canberra. Holdings of other family papers are listed in Brenda Niall's biography.

David Campbell
(16 July 1915 – 29 July 1979)

Philip Mead
University of Tasmania

BOOKS: *Speak with the Sun* (London: Chatto & Windus, 1949; Toronto: Clarke, Irwin, 1949);
The Miracle of Mullion Hill; Poems (Sydney: Angus & Robertson, 1956);
Collected Poems, edited by Leonie J. Kramer (London: Bodley Head, 1956–1957);
Evening under Lamplight: Selected Stories of David Campbell (Sydney: Angus & Robertson, 1959); republished as *Flame and Shadow: Selected Stories of David Campbell* (St. Lucia: University of Queensland Press, 1976); republished as *Evening under Lamplight: Selected Short Stories of David Campbell,* foreword by David Malouf (St. Lucia: University of Queensland Press, 1987);
Cocky's Calendar, Australian Artists and Poets Booklets, no. 2, text by Campbell, illustrations by Russell Drysdale (Adelaide: Australian Letters, 1961);
Poems (Sydney: Edwards & Shaw, 1962);
Selected Poems: 1942–1968 (Sydney: Angus & Robertson, 1968);
The Branch of Dodona and Other Poems: 1969–1970 (Sydney: Angus & Robertson, 1970);
Starting from Central Station: A Sequence of Poems (Canberra: Brindabella, 1973);
Selected Poems (Sydney: Angus & Robertson, 1973);
Devil's Rock and Other Poems: 1970–1972 (Sydney: Angus & Robertson, 1974);
Deaths and Pretty Cousins (Canberra: Australian National University Press, 1975);
The History of Australia, text by Campbell, illustrations by Keith Looby (Sydney: Macleay Museum, 1976);
Words with a Black Orpington (Sydney: Angus & Robertson, 1978; London: Angus & Robertson, 1978);
The Man in the Honeysuckle (Sydney: Angus & Robertson, 1979; London: Angus & Robertson, 1979);
Collected Poems, edited by Kramer (Sydney: Angus & Robertson, 1989).

RECORDINGS: *David Campbell Reads from His Own Work,* Poets on Record Series, read by Campbell, University of Queensland Press, 1975;

David Campbell, 1976 (photograph by Porter/John Felix Group)

Australian Poetry Live Classics from the Hazel de Berg Collection (Canberra: National Library of Australia, 1996).

OTHER: *Modern Australian Poetry,* edited by Campbell (Melbourne: Sun Books, 1970);
Moscow Trefoil: Poems from the Russian of Anna Akhmatova and Osip Mandelstam, by Campbell and Rosemary

Dobson, translated by Natalie Staples, foreword by A. D. Hope (Canberra: Australian National University Press, 1975);

Seven Russian Poets: Imitations, by Campbell and Dobson (St. Lucia: University of Queensland Press, 1979);

A Field Guide to Aboriginal Rock Engravings: With Special Reference to Those around Sydney, by Peter Stanbury and John Clegg, with poems by Campbell (Melbourne & Oxford: Oxford University Press, 1996).

David Campbell was a lyric poet of Australian rural life, and of love and war. Like others of his generation, particularly Judith Wright and Francis Webb, he contributed in distinctive ways to developments in Australian poetry. Born in the year of the Battle of Gallipoli, Turkey, Campbell was descended on both his mother's side and his father's side from long-established grazing families in New South Wales. Critics of Campbell's work have frequently noted the "squatter pastoral" strand in his poetry and its obvious relation to his family's history as pioneer settlers, his childhood on isolated sheep stations, as well as his own farming experience as an adult in the Monaro district of southern New South Wales. In the words of Manning Clark from the eulogy he delivered at Campbell's funeral, Campbell belonged by birth to the "Old Australia."

When he first published poems such as "Harry Pearce" and "The Stockman" in the mid 1940s, Campbell was working from within the native, ballad tradition of Australian poetry, one of the "New *Bulletin*" group of poets. Critic Vincent Buckley—in one of his articles collected in *Essays in Poetry, Mainly Australian* (1957)—laments the return, represented by this group of poets, "to the outback poetry of forty years ago," albeit in "more sophisticated and far more pessimistic terms." While he was right about the nostalgia for rural Australia in the poetry of Judith Wright, Douglas Stewart, Roland Robinson, Nancy Keesing, and Campbell, Buckley underestimated the element of celebration and praise that was already characteristic of Campbell's writing. Also incipient in Campbell's work was a restless impulse to connect with contemporary and international thinking about poetic styles and practice that ushered in remarkable changes to his poetic in the 1970s. His later poetry represents one of the most distinctive attempts in Australian writing of the twentieth century to renew and adapt the lyric tradition.

David Alfred Campbell—name changed to David Watt Ian Campbell in 1939—was born 16 July 1915 on his parents' grazing property, Ellerslie, near the town of Adelong, west of Canberra. His father, Alfred Campbell, trained for and practiced medicine as a young man, receiving his degree from Edinburgh in 1900. At about the time of his marriage, Alfred Campbell returned to pastoral management in partnership with his brothers. Campbell's mother, Edith Madge Watt, was a descendant of the Blackman family, another longstanding New South Wales grazing family. Campbell was educated by a series of governesses at Ellerslie in company with his three sisters—Dorothy, Madge, and Diana. In 1930 he was sent to The King's School in Parramatta, Sydney, where he excelled at sports. Among other outstanding accomplishments at The King's School, he was in both the first XV in rugby and the first VIII in rowing; he was Captain of the School in 1933 and 1934. In 1935 Campbell went up to Jesus College, Cambridge, where he initially studied history but then changed to English. At Cambridge, also, he excelled at sports, playing rugby for Cambridge against Oxford and for England in two tests in 1936 (against Wales and Ireland).

At Cambridge, Campbell began to write poetry, publishing poems in 1937 in both *Chanticlere* (the Jesus College magazine) and the *Cambridge Review*. He was encouraged to do so by his tutor, E. M. W. Tillyard, by Arthur Quiller-Couch, and by his compatriot poet friend at Cambridge, John Manifold. Campbell's two "Out Back" poems date from this time. While these early works hark back to the Australian ballad tradition, Campbell was also absorbing the works of William Butler Yeats, Federico García Lorca, Antonio Machado, and French symbolist poetry, "trying to couple," as he wrote in the preface to his *Selected Poems* (1973), "the bush ballad and my early memories with the traditional ballad and early English lyrics." He completed his B.A. degree with a major in English in 1937.

As a member of the University Air Squadron at Cambridge, Campbell also learned to fly, and shortly after the outbreak of World War II in 1939, he joined the Royal Australian Air Force (RAAF). He married Bonnie Lawrence on 20 January 1940, and the couple subsequently had three children—John, Raina, and Andrew. Campbell spent the war flying bombing, reconnaissance, and supply missions over New Guinea and Timor as Commanding Officer of 1 Squadron, 2 Squadron, and 32 Squadron as well as training RAAF pilots at air force bases in Gippsland and outside Darwin. His poem "Men in Green," first published in the *Bulletin* on 24 February 1943, arose out of Campbell's flying experience in New Guinea.

Ellerslie, Campbell's childhood home near Adelong

Oh, there were fifteen men in green,
Each with a tommy-gun
Who leapt into my plane at dawn;
We rose to meet the sun.
. . . .
They did not fear the ape-like cloud
That climbed the mountain crest
And hung from twisted ropes of air
With thunder in their breast.
. . . .
And when on Dobadura's field
We landed, each man raised
His thumb towards the open sky;
But to their right I gazed.

For fifteen men in jungle green
Rose from the kunai grass
And came towards the plane. My men
In silence watched them pass;

It seemed they looked upon themselves
In Time's prophetic glass.
Oh, there were some leaned on a stick
And some on stretchers lay,
. . . .
And I think still of men in green
On the Soputa track,
With fifteen spitting tommy-guns
To keep the jungle back.

The poem was collected in *Speak with the Sun,* which was published in 1949 simultaneously in London by Chatto & Windus and in Toronto by Clarke, Irwin and included a "Glossary of Australian Terms." It was generally greeted with acclaim by Australian critics, who noticed the distinctive use of language in the poetry: a makeover of the native ballad form—arrived at through Yeats—and a compactness of imagery, with Surrealist or at least symbolist inflections. Campbell's characteristic gestures of delight and celebration of the natural world are also established. In 1983 the critic R. F. Brissenden—in his article "'Speak with the Sun': Energy, Light, and Love in the Poetry of David Campbell" for *Australian Papers: Yugoslavia, Europe and Australia*—noticed the influence of Henry Vaughan, from whom Campbell took the title *Speak with the Sun,* on Campbell's early poetry.

Campbell also wrote short stories, such as "Tumult in the Clouds" and "Zero at Rabaul," about his New Guinea war experience. These short stories were included in an expanded collection of Campbell's short stories, first published as *Evening under Lamplight* in 1959. After the war, Campbell returned to farming on the property Wells, on the outskirts of Canberra. In 1961 he moved to Palerang, near Bundgendore, and by the beginning of the 1970s he was living on a small farm outside Queanbeyan, The Run.

Between 1949 and 1970 Campbell published *The Miracle of Mullion Hill; Poems* (1956), *Poems* (1962), and the collection of short stories, *Evening under Lamplight*. He also edited an annual anthology of Australian poetry in 1966 and the anthology *Modern Australian Poetry* in 1970 and became poetry editor of the *Australian* newspaper in 1964, all of which consolidated his position as a leading Australian writer. Leonie J. Kramer critically surveys this first stage of Campbell's writing life in her article "David Campbell's Early Poems," collected in *A Tribute to David Campbell: A Collection of Essays* (1987), a volume edited by Harry Heseltine.

Campbell won many awards for his writing during his lifetime, including the Henry Lawson Australian Arts Award (1970), the Patrick White Literary Award (1975), the New South Wales Premier's Prize (1980), and the Fellowship of Australian Writers' Christopher Brennan Award (1980). But, as Brissenden points out in his introduction for *A Tribute to David Campbell*, by the early 1970s, Campbell's work "though charming, craftsmanlike and idiosyncratic, [appeared] slightly passé." With the publication in 1970 of *The Branch of Dodona and Other Poems: 1969-1970,* however, Campbell seemed to take a leap into the present at a time when Australian culture and writing were undergoing seismic changes.

All knowledgeable readers of Campbell's work come back to this 1970 collection as crucial in Campbell's development as a poet and in his influence on the lyric tradition generally in Australian poetry. The first poem in *The Branch of Dodona and Other Poems*, "My Lai," was both a powerful response to the violence of the Vietnam War and an announcement of his review of the fundamentals of his poetic language:

> I was milking the cow when a row of tall bamboo
>   Was mowed by rifle fire
> With my wife and child in the one harvest,
> And the blue milk spilt and ruined.
>
> One life, one field, one wife. Now the village burns
> . . . .
> The cow is dead that I lie under,
>   Bodies bloat in the sun.
> Who would have thought that they would lie
> So heavily upon my heart?
>
> The bamboo mowed in lines. Somehow this happened
>   *Here and in my head.—*
>   "Put a rocket in that old cow,
>   Then it's time to line for chow."

Campbell during his years in the Royal Australian Air Force (from Harry Heseltine, ed., A Tribute to David Campbell, *1987)*

Campbell's anti–Vietnam War stance came as a shock to some readers, considering his own history as a decorated combatant in World War II. But Campbell said in an interview quoted by David Headon in "Balancing More Plates on the Tip of a Wand," collected in *A Tribute to David Campbell,* that "one of the reasons I started a change of direction was the Vietnam War. We were suddenly pulled out of a rather insular way of life and had large moral issues to look at. I found myself very much against the Australian involvement there and it made me very much more aware of the general violence in the world." Campbell also became increasingly supportive of the environmental movement, and hand in hand with these new directions in his public stance went an expansion of the lyric scope of his poetry. The "Works and Days" sequence in *The Branch of Dodona and Other Poems,* for example, remakes what

MEN IN GREEN.

Oh there were fifteen men in green
Each with a tommy gun
Who leapt into my plane at dawn;
We rose to meet the sun.

We set our course towards the east
And climbed into the day
Till the ribbed jungle underneath
Like a giant fossil lay.

We climbed towards the distant range
Where two white paws of cloud
Clutched at the shoulders of the pass;
The green men laughed aloud.

They did not heed the ape-like cloud
That climbed the mountain crest
And hung from ropes invisable
With lightening in its breast;

They did not fear the summer's sun
In whose hot centre lie
A hundred hissing cannon shells
For the unwatchful eye.

Typescript for a poem based on Campbell's experiences in the RAAF during World War II (National Library of Australia, MS5028/2/1)

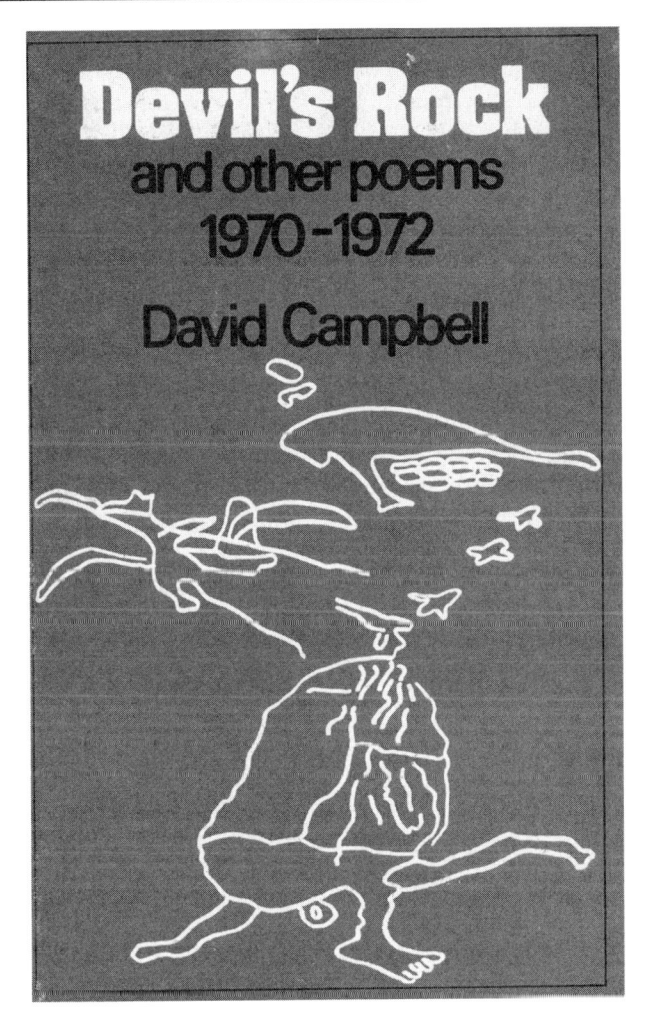

Dust jacket for Campbell's 1974 book, one of four collections of poetry he published during the 1970s (Bruccoli Clark Layman Archives)

Chris Wallace-Crabbe labeled Campbell's earlier "squatter pastoral"–characterized by serenity and lyric plainness–into demythologized depictions of everyday country life and language: "Sheep! They're not dumb, they know every trick in the book." In his preface to his 1973 *Selected Poems,* Campbell remarked that "it was not until 'Works and Days' that I was able to write directly about work on the land and its slow seasonal change. These poems spring from the shop of countrymen." The deliberate conjunction of "My Lai" and the "Works and Days" poems also suggests Campbell's ambition to bring a political dimension to the lyric. The "Ku-ring-gai Rock Carvings" sequence from this collection, part of the same impulse, introduces a serious awareness of Aboriginal culture into Campbell's version of pastoral poetry.

In December 1973 Campbell divorced his first wife; on 18 February 1974 he married Judy Jones, a historian. The four collections of poetry Campbell published after *The Branch of Dodona and Other Poems*–*Devil's Rock and Other Poems: 1970–1972* (1974), *Deaths and Pretty Cousins* (1975), *Words with a Black Orpington* (1978), and *The Man in the Honeysuckle* (1979)–represent an intense burst of creativity that is both an extension and a working-out of the lyric possibilities unleashed by *The Branch of Dodona and Other Poems.* The poems in these volumes share some common preoccupations: the relations of memory and place as inflected by family, the astonishing minutiae of nature, Aboriginal rock art–"Devil's Rock and Other Carvings," "Sydney Sandstone (Rock Carvings)"– and a celebration of the sexual energies and cycles of nature and art. Also characteristic of Campbell's writing in these collections is an eclectic, even promiscuous, reaching after analogous and supportive practices in other art forms, such as the painting of Willem de Kooning, Jean Arp, Paul Klee, Balthus

(Count Balthazar Klossowski de Rola), Jackson Pollock, and Paul Cézanne; in crafts, ceramics, and pottery; in the lessons of line and shape from life-drawing classes; in Chinese calligraphy; and in the paradoxes of modern theoretical science. In the poetry of these four collections, Campbell is never simply relying on the evocative and musical possibilities of the lyric, Australian-style, nor interested much in developing a recognizable and nuanced poetic "voice." Rather, he is continually and obsessively attempting to follow the poetic impulse to its source and to push the lyric form to its logical extreme. Campbell's later poetry always gives the sense of being under pressure to get to the subatomic essence of things, whether in terms of content or form, as in "Lizard and Stone" from *The Man in the Honeysuckle*:

> A bronze lizard
> Is wrapped around a river stone
>
> The lizard is half awake
> The stone has not yet woken
>
> Each preserves an outward stillness
>
> Within the stone
> A dance of atoms
> Warms the basking lizard
> . . . .
> About the stone and lizard
> Where they lie like lovers
> The cosmos dances.

Campbell's particular kind of experimentation in his last four volumes also owes something to his translation of modern Russian poetry, principally in *Moscow Trefoil: Poems from the Russian of Anna Akhmatova and Osip Mandelstam* (1975) but also in the works of Marina Tsvetaeva, Olga Berggolts, Bella Akhmadulina, Natalia Gorbanevskaia, and Yunna Morits in *Seven Russian Poets: Imitations* (1979). These translations were collaborative poetic work with his fellow Canberra poet Rosemary Dobson and with the native Russian speakers and scholars of Russian poetry Natalie Staples, Olga Hassanov, and Robert Dessaix. The influence of Ted Hughes's poetry, including his advocacy of contemporary European poetry in translation, is related to this aspect of Campbell's remaking of his poetic self after 1970. As A. D. Hope discerned in "Variations on a Theme: David Campbell's Translations" for *Poetry Australia: David Campbell* (1981), edited by Kramer, Campbell's work as a translator and collaborator is important because it forms "quite a large part of his work but also because the range of what can be called translation is so wide and various in its intent and its methods and those methods are integral to [Campbell's] whole practice and concept of poetry." At Cambridge, when he was first beginning to write poetry, Campbell had been interested in both the native tradition of Australian poetry and in contemporary European models. His late, collaborative translations of Russian and other European poets is another sense in which Campbell was, late in his creative life, working with the fundamentals of a poetic with which he had begun.

Campbell published two volumes of *Selected Poems* during his lifetime, in 1968 and 1973. The 1968 *Selected Poems* includes a section of translations, "Talking to Strangers," that had not previously been published in a book. These nineteen poems include, in addition to translations, imitations of old and contemporary Spanish and French poems. This collection is also divided into two sections, "Lyrical" and "Satirical." The small "Satirical" section consists of three poems: "The Miracle of Mullion Hill," "The Golden Cow," and "The Australian Dream." For the 1973 *Selected Poems*, Campbell kept the generic groupings of the earlier volume and added a remark in the preface about the "surrealism of the [Australian] landscape" that was designed to complicate the reader's sense of his version of pastoral poetry. Kramer's Angus and Robertson Modern Poets edition of Campbell's *Collected Poems* (1989) departs from the usual practice in its arrangements of the poems in chronological order of first publication rather than in the order in which they appear in individual volumes. This version of *Collected Poems* also omits the translations of *Moscow Trefoil* and *Seven Russian Poets*, the twenty-four uncollected poems published in the David Campbell memorial issue of *Poetry Australia*, and also in some cases, according to the introduction, restores "a sequence of verses to its full form where this was shortened for inclusion in either a single volume or for one of the three *Selected Poems*." Kramer had also edited an earlier version of Campbell's *Collected Poems* for publication in England in 1956.

Critical reception of Campbell's work was summed up in the tributary collection of essays edited by Heseltine in 1987. Since then, one of the most useful readings of Campbell's work and its cultural context is available in Susan McKernan's chapter "The Writer and the Crisis: Judith Wright and David Campbell" in her critical account of postwar Australian literature, *A Question of Commitment: Australian Literature in the Twenty Years after the War* (1989). McKernan judiciously readjusts Buckley's account of the "New *Bulletin*" school and carefully identifies the different aesthetic trajectories and values of Wright, Stewart, and Campbell. But arguably, Campbell remains best known for his poems of the 1940s and 1950s–"Windy Gap" and "Harry Pearce," for instance–and war poems such as "Men in

Green." Critical reading has yet to come to terms with the lyric energies and experiments of Campbell's late poetry, which have important relations to the revisions of the pastoral tradition in Australian poetry represented in the formally innovative work of Robert Adamson and John Kinsella.

Interview:

Kevin Hart, "New Directions: An Interview with David Campbell," *Makar*, 11, no. 1 (1975): 4–10.

References:

R. F. Brissenden, "Remembering David Campbell," *Quadrant*, 24, nos. 1-2 (1980): 16–20;

Brissenden, "'Speak with the Sun': Energy, Light, and Love in the Poetry of David Campbell," *Australian Papers: Yugoslavia, Europe and Australia*, edited by Mirko Jurak (Ljubljana: Edvard Cardelj University, 1983), pp. 203–215;

Vincent Buckley, *Essays in Poetry, Mainly Australian* (Melbourne: Melbourne University Press, 1957);

Manning Clark, *David Campbell 1915–1979: Words Spoken at His Funeral* (Canberra: Brindabella, 1979);

Rosemary Dobson, "A Rare Poet of His Time," *Age* (4 August 1979): 24;

Harry Heseltine, ed., *A Tribute to David Campbell: A Collection of Essays*–includes a bibliography of Campbell's works by Sandra Burchill with notes on the Campbell Manuscript Collection in the National Library, Canberra (Kensington: University of New South Wales Press, 1987);

Graeme Kinross-Smith, "David Campbell–A Profile," *Westerly*, 3 (1973): 31–38;

Kinross-Smith, "The Poetry of David Campbell," *Southerly*, 25, no. 3 (1965): 193–198;

Leonie J. Kramer, "The Surreal Landscape of David Campbell," *Southerly*, 41, no. 1 (1981): 3–16;

Kramer, ed., *Poetry Australia: David Campbell*, 80 (December 1981)–includes an autobiographical sketch by Campbell, letters about Campbell from John Manifold, and other reminiscences;

Susan McKernan, *A Question of Commitment: Australian Literature in the Twenty Years after the War* (Sydney: Allen & Unwin, 1989);

Geoff Page, "David Campbell: The Last Ten Years," *Australian Book Review*, 15 (1979): 21–23;

Dennis Robinson, "David Campbell's Poetic Mind," *Australian Literary Studies*, 11, no. 4 (1984): 480–492;

Chris Wallace-Crabbe, "Squatter Pastoral," in his *Falling into Language* (Melbourne: Oxford University Press, 1990), p. 72–84;

Robin Wallace-Crabbe, "David Campbell: An Appreciation," *Overland*, 79 (1980): 55–59.

Papers:

David Campbell's papers are held in the National Library of Australia, MS5028 (seventeen boxes), index available via the following URL: <http://www.nla.gov.au/ms/findaids/5028.html>.

Gavin Casey

(10 April 1907 – 25 June 1964)

Don Grant
Curtin University of Technology

BOOKS: *It's Harder for Girls; and Other Stories* (Sydney: Angus & Robertson, 1942); republished as *Short-Shift Saturday and Other Stories* (Sydney: Angus & Robertson, 1973);

Birds of a Feather (Perth: Sampson, 1943);

Downhill Is Easier (Sydney: Angus & Robertson, 1945);

The Wits Are Out (Sydney: Angus & Robertson, 1947);

City of Men (London: Davies, 1950);

Walk into Paradise (Sydney: Horwitz, 1956);

Snowball (Sydney: Angus & Robertson, 1958);

Amid the Plenty: A Novel of Today (Sydney: Australasian Book Society, 1962);

The Man Whose Name Was Mud (London: Heinemann, 1963);

The Mile That Midas Touched, by Casey and Ted Mayman (Adelaide: Rigby, 1964);

The Writing of Novels and Short Stories, published with *James McAuley's Recent Poetry* by Vivian Smith (Canberra: Australian National University, 1964).

SELECTED PERIODICAL PUBLICATIONS– UNCOLLECTED: "A Year-Old Infant Still Bellows Lustily," *Bohemia* (January 1940): 5;

"Means and Ends in Writing," *Australian Literary Studies,* 9, no. 2 (October 1979): 225–231.

Gavin Casey's reputation as one of the leading fiction writers of Australia relies heavily upon the brilliance of his short stories, especially those published in his first collection, *It's Harder for Girls; and Other Stories* (1942). Although he also published nine novels and won respect for his journalism and reviewing, Casey will be remembered primarily for the quality and unusual nature of his short stories. Some of these are extremely funny, but many convey a feeling of despondency and a sense that the joys and hopes of the past will not be fulfilled in the future. Casey's world is a male one in which mateship, the quality of the Australian (male) who is loyal to his mates (other males), is paramount and beery bonhomie prevails. The best stories reveal deep understanding of the lives and

Gavin Casey (from John Hetherington, Forty-Two Faces, *1946)*

work of the miners who toil on the "Golden Mile" near Kalgoorlie, the town in which Casey grew up.

Gavin Stodart Casey was born at Kalgoorlie, the major town on the Western Australian goldfields, on 10 April 1907 to Australian-born Frederick Arthur Casey and Scottish-born Jean Allan Stodart. Frederick Casey was town surveyor of Kalgoorlie from 1900, a lover of literature, and a part-time writer. Both parents died young, leaving Gavin and a younger brother, Allan, orphans when Gavin was seventeen. He attended local state schools before being apprenticed as an electrician with the Kalgoorlie Electricity Supply. After studying briefly at the School of Mines, he dropped out when, at age eighteen, he began a relationship with Dorothy Wulff, later to become his wife. In 1927 Casey moved to Perth to work as a motorbike salesman but, like so many others, was unemployed by 1931 when he returned to Kalgoorlie, which had an economic resurgence during the Great Depression. He obtained work in the mines and then in a motorbike shop. He also promoted and participated in various sporting events, mainly bicycle and motorbike racing, but without much financial success. Indeed, despite brief periods of relative affluence, Casey was not a good manager of money and actually died in debt.

On 8 February 1933 he and Wulff married in Kalgoorlie. The following year they moved to Perth, where their only son, Fred, was born in 1936. Although only sketchily educated, Casey was a voracious reader and had writing ambitions from an early age. In the early 1930s he became part-time Goldfields correspondent for two Perth weekly newspapers—*The Sunday Times* and *The Mirror*. He reported the serious race riots of January 1934 for both newspapers. But his journalism experience in Kalgoorlie did not help him after the return to Perth, where his job applications to newspapers were rejected, usually on the grounds of lack of qualifications and education. His first short stories were also rejected by publishers until "Nobody's Goat" was published in 1936 by the *Bulletin* (Sydney), at that time the most famous and significant literary journal of Australia. Casey continued to eke out a living as a car salesman but was having more short stories accepted for publication in the *Australian Journal* and especially in the *Bulletin*. This journal published thirty-seven of his stories between 1936 and 1945 and in successive years awarded him their best short-story prize for "Rich Stew" and "Mail Run East."

In June 1938 a group of eleven Western Australian writers held a dinner to meet American author, journalist, and critic C. Hartley Grattan, who was visiting Australia on a Carnegie Fellowship to pursue his interest in Australian literature. As a result of this meeting, the Western Australian Section of the Fellowship of Australian Writers (FAW) was formed, with Casey as inaugural secretary. A constitution for the FAW was prepared and accepted, but it did not include a whimsical addition written by Casey:

> PROPERTY. All property of the Fellowship, whether land and animals, buildings, slaves, jewels, bullion, stores of foodstuffs, drink, explosives, valuable manuscripts written by members, fishing rights, mining leases, works of art or articles of agreements or concessions of value of any kind, shall be under the control of the Executive.

Casey reflected on the achievements and events of the first year of the FAW in an article published in *Bohemia* (Melbourne) January 1940. His lighthearted, humorous touches and his imbibing tastes are evident in the following extract:

> More threatening to the spirit of fellowship than debate upon the imminence or otherwise of the revolution, was the discovery last winter, of a number of confirmed and incurable coffee-drinkers in the ranks. For a time the clattering of milk-cans and the swishing of sugar-spoons sadly interfered with the meditations of devotees of the Better Beverage, and feeling ran high. Changing weather has solved the difficulty, however, and the clear melody of clinking glass and gurgling beer is no longer interrupted by baser sounds.

Casey was elected president of the FAW for 1941–1942.

Casey joined the *Daily News* (Perth) in 1940 as a full-time journalist and the next year was responsible for the "Home Front" page, which reported World War II as it was seen from within Western Australia. A colleague who worked on the "Home Front" page with him later described Casey as a "tremendous person to work with, afraid of no one or no thing." After a brief period with the Australian Army Education Service, Casey became a publicity censor in Western Australia and in 1944 a journalist with the Commonwealth Department of Information in Canberra. Between 1945 and 1947 he was head of the Australian News and Information Bureau, first in New York and then in London, before returning to Canberra as the Bureau's chief publicity officer. After 1950 he was a freelance journalist in Canberra and Sydney until 1956, when he returned to Perth.

In 1947 Dorothy and Gavin Casey divorced. The following year Gavin married Jessie Lorraine Craigie, who had been his secretary in New York. They eventually had two sons, Gavin and Allan. The last years in Perth were difficult for the Caseys. Gavin struggled to support his new family through journalism and other writing, but his poor health forced him to have lengthy hospital stays.

His first book, *It's Harder for Girls*, which won the S. H. Prior Memorial Prize for the best Australian book of the year in 1942, was republished in 1973 as *Short-Shift Saturday and Other Stories*. This collection of twenty-one short stories, all of which were previously published in the *Bulletin*, is widely acclaimed as Casey's best book and the one that has earned him his reputation as one of the greatest short-story writers of Australia. Some critics have argued that never again did Casey's writing match the artistic achievements of these early stories. Comparisons have been drawn between Casey and Henry Lawson, perhaps the greatest exponent of the short story in Australia. Lawson produced his best work before he turned forty, much of which was published in the *Bulletin* during the depres-

Casey posing for a motorcycle advertisement in 1930 (from Dorothy Casey-Congdon, Casey's Wife, *1982)*

sion of the 1890s. Both men were familiar with hardship and poverty and grew to value Australian mateship. Lawson and Casey both wrote humorous stories, but underlying some of these, and in other stories, there is a prevailing sense of unfulfilled ambition, acceptance of the next best, and even failure.

Although literary recognition came relatively early for Casey through publication of *It's Harder for Girls* in 1942 and for six years before then because of the regular appearance of his stories in the *Bulletin,* that recognition had not been achieved easily. Casey told of his early struggle to master the genre of the short story when, as recipient of a grant, he delivered the Commonwealth Literary Fund Lecture in 1962. The title of the lecture was "The Writing of Novels and Short Stories." He spoke of his early wish to tell tales about the Western Australian goldfields that he knew so well. But he could not create believable characters in his early work.

> What opened my eyes was the depression of the nineteen-thirties.... I saw good men... thrown on the scrap-heap.... What happened moved me to anger rather than to gloom, and it acquainted me with meanings of the traditional Australian mateship.... I am in literature, and in many of my social beliefs and attitudes, a product of the depression.... It was after these experiences and this observation that I began to write stories which editors found publishable.

Not only was Casey, as he says, "a product of the depression," he was also a product of his place. This place, Kalgoorlie, 390 miles northeast of Perth, the capital city of Western Australia, is situated on the edge of the great inland deserts that make up much of Australia. Today the region of the eastern goldfields remains the center of a flourishing mining industry. In the 1890s the region attracted thousands of prospectors to harvest the rich surface gold deposits. Subsequently, the "Golden Mile," the richest gold-bearing concentrate in the world, was pitted with shafts and tunnels blasted through the rock by miners employed by scores of Australian and international companies. This goldfield country forms the backdrop of most of the stories in *It's Harder for Girls.* It is a hard environment. Sometimes, as in "The Thunderstorm," the harshness of nature strikes from above.

> Out of a black, low, seething sky volleys of rain are peppering the sheet-iron roofs and walls of the mine buildings. Over the gables and gutterings the water tumbles in sheets that fold and shatter on the red earth beneath. Streams course down the sides of the lofty grey dumps, and where there is earth that has not been

hoisted from far underground, speckled, muddy torrents eddy between rocks and posts. The sun is shut out, and poppet-legs and buildings a few chains distant are vague and grey behind the screen of lashing water. But there is lightning dancing above the clouds, making flashlight pictures of the workings every few seconds, and there is thunder, gathering force as it rolls, and making the whole sky tremble.

Another story, "Dust," compares the red desert dust stirred by nature on the surface of the ground with the insidious dust that slowly accumulates in the lungs of the miners who work underground. However, sometimes the miners, working up to four thousand feet below ground level, faced more immediate and frightening problems than lung-clogging dust. In "Talking Ground" Casey focuses on the mounting terror of a miner as he listens to the rock above and about him.

> Just then the murmur of the uneasy earth became perceptibly louder. . . . Away in some corner out of sight a staccato noise that was more like straining timber than grating stone joined the weird medley of sound. . . . The grunting of the mile-wide masses of stone was ringing in his ears like the sobbing breath of a giant struggling in bonds. A few tiny flakes dropped off. . . . Over his head a gigantic sharp-fanged lip of stone drooped slowly (like the lower jaw of a titanic, hungry beast) away from the main body. . . .

One of Casey's most acclaimed stories is "Rich Stew." Its farcical, sympathetic, even sad humor evokes comparison with Lawson's "The Loaded Dog." Both stories show compassion for the battler, the Aussie bloke (and in "Rich Stew" the bloke's "missus" also), who averts disaster with a comic triumph. Old Man Thompson in "Rich Stew" has shown his family the grains of gold he has smuggled out of the mine that day. "Well . . . the luck's changed [he tells them]. I ain't seen nothin' but dirt f'r so long I hardly reckernized this when I seen it." Alas, Sergeant O'Malley of the Gold-stealing Investigation staff thunders on the door. Mrs. Thompson tosses the gold into the stew and, after O'Malley's search has unearthed nothing, triumphantly invites him to share the stew with the family. The tension and farce increase as the sleuth eats more and more of the "damn good stoo." The baby and the dog assist in the final discomfiture of the policeman.

In 1982 Casey's first wife, Dorothy, published a frank and generously sympathetic account of her life with Gavin. In this book, *Casey's Wife,* she says she was extremely proud of his success as a short-story writer and "basked a bit in reflected glory."

> There was only one short story I had no wish to see published. It was called "Buck's Party." When Gavin finished it late one night he read it to me. . . . I told him I did not want "Buck's Party" submitted for publication. I said it made our private life public. It was bad enough to have to endure those parties without having them described to the world. But the story was submitted and accepted.

"Buck's Party" extends over about twelve hours as a group of "the boys" say farewell to a mate who is moving to another state. They meet after work and in high spirits drink, drive, eat, and swim at the beach. By dawn they are all drunk, argumentative, and full of self-pity. The first-person narrator—and many of Casey's best stories are written in the first person—eventually arrives home feeling "dirty and stale and shaky" and, although he cannot admit it, rather ashamed of himself.

"Short-Shift Saturday," a long short story, is probably Casey's greatest achievement. The first-person point of view is that of a miner who has been on the goldfields for five years, having come to escape unemployment on the coast. The day seems to start well.

> It was Saturday morning, so there was only half a shift to do, but the bad taste of the underground was in my mouth, and four hours of it seemed a lot too much. . . . It was hard to get out of bed, but it was good to climb into soft white underclothes and a good silk shirt that would only be taken off for four hours out of the next fifty-six.

But his wife, Annie, is irritable and querulous, and he feels hardly treated and misunderstood.

> I wanted to get away, to leave her to her job and come back when I felt like it. I wanted to get out with other men—cobbers who took you as they found you and didn't want to alter your way of life to suit them.

Despite the short shift underground, the men lack their usual ebullience. One of the team, Don Bell, has just been diagnosed with the miner's complaint and will be pensioned off until the congestion and disease in his lungs leads to early death. Back on the surface after the shift, the men drink quickly with their mates before drifting off to their homes. Annie is still irritable, but as usual on Saturday evening they join the crowd walking the main street downtown. Annie is disgusted to see the drunken Don Bell thrown out of a hotel, but Don's mates know the reason for his drunkenness and belligerence, and their hearts go out to him. The gap between Annie and the narrator widens even further. In bed he reflects on the day and especially his relationship with Annie.

> She looked after me and she looked after young Bill, and we were both fond of the kid. I was fond of her,

too, in a way, but it was different. It wasn't like the old times. I wanted the old times back but I couldn't get them. I wanted to touch her, to make some sort of contact with her that might help the words to come. But there was so much time between now and the last time I'd spoken that I knew I could never fill it in. I'd grown new ways of thinking, and so had she.

"Short-Shift Saturday" is a short-story masterpiece in many ways. One of these is its evocation of time and place. Another is the exploration of the fears and uncertainties of the central character. But in this story, as elsewhere, the character seems unable to penetrate beneath the surface discontent and vague unhappiness to discover basic causes and perhaps contemplate alternative actions. He seems bewildered and lost as the people and the world he knew change, not realizing that he more than anything else might be the cause of the change. The closest Casey comes to real introspection in a character is in another of his finest stories, "That Day at Brown Lakes." The main character and a friend he has not seen since they were teenagers have met in a pub. The story describes an idyllic day from childhood when the two boys rode their bikes to the Brown Lakes. The past is recalled with joy and warmth in the mind of the narrator. But things have changed in the intervening years.

> You didn't disappoint me then, but would you now? I must be afraid you would, or I'd have said it aloud, told you all. . . . The years we haven't seen each other, that we've spent chasing the hopes we had that day, have done a lot to us. You don't look my kind now, Dick. . . . I don't know. I only know that you're different. But perhaps I'm wrong. You've been silent for a long time now, just sitting there staring at your beer while I've been remembering all this, and for all I know you might have been thinking about the day we pedalled out to the Brown Lakes too.

R. S. Sampson's United Press in Perth published Casey's second book in 1943, another collection of short stories, all sixteen of which had previously appeared in the *Bulletin*. Before obtaining his full-time job with the *Daily News* in 1940, Casey had worked for Sampson, writing and editing various trade and other journals. The new collection was titled *Birds of a Feather*. As did those in *It's Harder for Girls,* these stories reflect the mateship, speech patterns, and concerns of the ordinary man, but none of them quite reaches the quality of the best stories in the first book.

The years in Perth between 1935 and 1943 have been recalled by Ted Mayman in the introduction to a book he edited, *View from Kalgoorlie: Classic Stories of the Goldfields* (1969), as "those years he [Casey] was at the height of his powers and doing his best work." Mayman had known Casey on the goldfields and had raced motorbikes with him. He himself also published short stories in the *Bulletin*. Mayman recalls the bonhomie and conviviality Casey enjoyed at that time:

> . . . . there were frequent keg parties on Saturday nights with Gavin and Dorothy Casey in Lawler Street, South Perth, crowded with odd bodies we knew and casual blow-ins we didn't know.

Mayman would sometimes sleep overnight after the party.

> But even in those early mornings, no matter how heavy the night before had been, would be heard the tapping of Gavin's typewriter. He seldom rewrote a story.

In his 1962 lecture "The Writing of Novels and Short Stories" Casey confirmed the speed of his writing:

> Fast workers, such as I am, write a short story at one sitting, while gripped by a creative mood. . . . The short story writer . . . must be swift and lucid in the establishment of his characters and situations, and in the action that follows this. . . . The reader can love a novel for its good parts, and forgive and forget the bad ones, but there cannot, of course, be any bad bits in a short story.

Casey then turned to his own experiences as a novelist and, interestingly, confirmed what most of his critics have written about his novels:

> I am one who has found it very hard to write novels after having been successful with short stories. I do not think that my earlier novels were bad books, and I believe that they have been entertaining and worthwhile for some readers. But structurally they have lacked the full form and shape of novels, tending towards the episodic and irregular, and in some cases being in fact short stories joined together to achieve length, rather than long stories really requiring length for their telling.

Casey's first three published novels fit that description well. These were *Downhill Is Easier* (1945), *The Wits Are Out* (1947), and *City of Men* (1950), all published while he was working for the Department of Information and the Australian News and Information Bureau in Sydney, Canberra, New York, and London.

The Wits Are Out is in a category of its own. It is not so much many short stories joined together as an extremely long short story that, although episodic, holds together as a whole. It is probably Casey's best lengthy piece of fiction. The subject is the preparation for and the occurrences at one of those Saturday-night keg parties to which Mayman referred. Some readers might find the

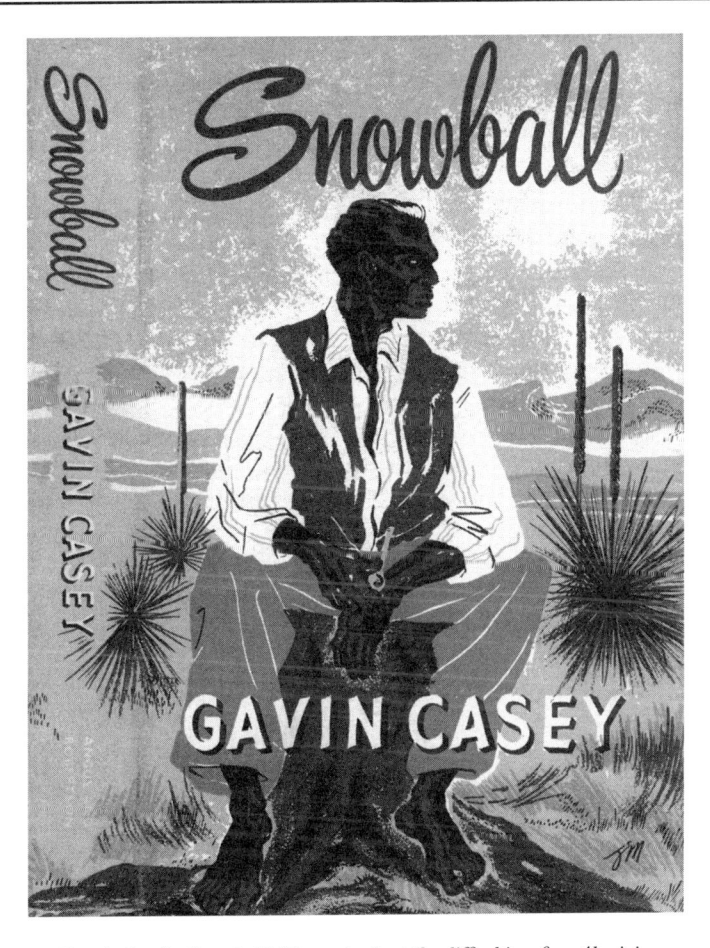

Dust jacket for Casey's 1958 novel, about the difficulties of an Aborigine family living in white society (Bruccoli Clark Layman Archives)

subject—excessive drinking—distasteful, but others, who remember the Australia of the 1930s to 1960s, can vouch for its authenticity and enjoy the humor, rather vulgar though it sometimes is. The main characters, especially Bill, the host, whose point of view prevails throughout, are well developed. Bill's moods and perceptions change as the party progresses and alcohol takes effect. Unusual in Casey's writing is some insight into the feelings of women and a less despondent view of the world than is typical.

> However differently they [Bill and Myra] might look at the moment, it was one of the rare enough ones in which all the sweat and worry of being alive, and marrying, and having children, and seeing the world shrink into a smaller, meaner place than it had once been, seemed worth while to both of them.

Downhill Is Easier and *City of Men* are not bad books, but they are certainly "episodic and irregular." Indeed, both of them include segments that had been published in whole or in part in Casey's short-story collections. *City of Men* also intersperses chapters that describe the goldfields, Perth, outback life, and working underground between the chapters that develop the plot. The novel is a mini family saga that follows the fortunes of the Willard family on the goldfields. Several of the characters are fairly well drawn, but the reader does not empathize much with them. The same is true of the characters in *Downhill Is Easier*, although the novel does produce some drama and suspense as the weak protagonist entangles himself in an ever tightening net of dishonesty and deceit. On the positive side both novels are as successful as the short stories in their realistic portrayal of life on the goldfields.

Snowball (1958) has won praise from critics and is probably Casey's best novel if *The Wits Are Out* is categorized as a long short story. Snowball and his family are Australian Aborigines whose difficulties in a predominantly hostile white society are handled sympathetically by the author. The plot is developed to a peak of racial intolerance and confrontation, but the happy ending seems contrived and unlikely. As usual in Casey's longer fiction, the reader has difficulty in understanding why many of the characters act as they do sometimes.

The two last novels—*Amid the Plenty* (1962) and *The Man Whose Name Was Mud* (1963)—are fairly pedestrian.

Both are interesting period pieces, the first set in the city and the second mainly in the country. In both, the plot plods from incident to incident involving uninteresting and sometimes almost unbelievable characters. They are the work of an author who has lost most of the confidence and deftness that were features of his early writing.

Walk into Paradise (1956) is a piece of journalism rather than a novel. It is an adaptation of a moderately successful Australian film set in Papua, New Guinea, and does not warrant serious analysis. Casey died a few weeks before the personally informed history of Kalgoorlie—*The Mile That Midas Touched* (1964), written in collaboration with Mayman—was published. The book has enjoyed considerable success, but to determine how much of its content was the work of each of its respective authors is not possible now.

Jessie Casey died in January 1964, and Gavin Casey on 25 June 1964, aged fifty-seven, from tuberculosis pulmonary fibrosis. In his introduction to *View from Kalgoorlie*, Mayman wrote of the rich legacy of mateship that Casey bequeathed to his friends and of Casey's ironic sense of humor:

> I was beside his bed a few hours earlier [before he died] and he managed to remove his oxygen mask for a few moments and clumsily reached for an envelope near his pillow. "Wouldn't it?" he whispered with a smile. It was a letter from a well-known correspondence school advising that they had heard that Mr Casey was interested in writing. It suggested he sign up with them for their special course in short story writing.

References:

John Barnes, "Gavin Casey: The View from Kalgoorlie," *Meanjin,* 22, no. 4 (1964): 341–347;

Dorothy Casey-Congdon, *Casey's Wife* (Perth: Artlook Books, 1982);

Henrietta Drake-Brockman, "Gavin Casey," *Westerly,* 4 (1964): 7–10;

Maurice Dunlevy, "Novelist Not Impressed by Canberra's Winter Sunshine," *Canberra Times,* 12 July 1974, p. 10;

Dorothy Hewett, "Literary Obituary," *Critic,* 7 (1964): 61–63;

Peter Kemeny, "Gavin Casey and the Australian Common Man," *Australian Quarterly,* 38, no. 3 (1966): 88–92;

Jean Lang, *At the Toss of a Coin* (Perth: Tom Collins Press, 1987);

Ted Mayman, "Gavin Casey's World," *Australian Literary Studies,* 9, no. 2 (1979): 231–234;

Mayman, *View from Kalgoorlie: Classic Stories of the Goldfields* (Perth: Landfall, 1969);

F. B. Vickers, "Gavin Casey–The Man I Knew," *Overland,* 30 (1964): 25.

Papers:

The Battye Library of West Australian History, Perth, holds manuscripts, notebooks, proof copies of many of Gavin Casey's published works, and manuscripts in various states of completion of ten unpublished works, including novels.

Charmian Clift

(30 August 1923 – 9 July 1969)

Nadia Wheatley

BOOKS: *High Valley,* by Clift and George Johnston (Sydney: Angus & Robertson, 1949; Indianapolis: Bobbs-Merrill, 1950);

The Big Chariot, by Clift and Johnston (Indianapolis: Bobbs-Merrill, 1953; Sydney: Angus & Robertson, 1953; London: Faber & Faber, 1953);

The Sea and the Stone, by Clift and Johnston (Indianapolis: Bobbs-Merrill, 1955); republished as *The Sponge Divers* (London: Collins, 1956; Pymble, N.S.W.: Angus & Robertson, 1992);

Mermaid Singing (Indianapolis: Bobbs-Merrill, 1956; Sydney: Collins, 1988);

Peel Me a Lotus (London: Hutchinson, 1959; Sydney: Collins, 1969);

Walk to the Paradise Gardens (New York: Harper, 1960; London: Hutchinson, 1960; Sydney: Collins, 1989);

Honour's Mimic (London: Hutchinson, 1964; Sydney: Collins, 1989);

Images in Aspic, edited by Johnston (Sydney: Horwitz, 1965);

The World of Charmian Clift, edited by Johnston (Sydney: Ure Smith, 1970);

Strong-Man from Piraeus and Other Stories, by Clift and Johnston, edited by Garry Kinnane (Melbourne: Thomas Nelson, 1983);

Trouble in Lotus Land, Essays 1964–1967, edited by Nadia Wheatley (Sydney: Collins/Angus & Robertson, 1990);

Being Alone with Oneself, Essays 1968–1969, edited by Wheatley (North Ryde, N.S.W.: Angus & Robertson, 1991).

Collection: *The Selected Essays of Charmian Clift,* edited by Wheatley (Sydney: HarperCollins, 2001).

PRODUCED SCRIPTS: "The Edge of Darkness," radio, *Quality Street,* Australian Broadcasting Commission, 14 August 1949;

"Diary of a Modern Woman," radio, *Radio Diary,* Australian Broadcasting Commission, 27 December 1949;

"Diary of an Unhappy Marriage," radio, by Clift and George Johnston, *Radio Diary,* Australian Broadcasting Commission, 28 February 1950;

"Sappho of Lesbos," radio, by Clift and Johnston, *Famous Women,* Australian Broadcasting Commission, 26 March 1950;

"The Lady Bright," radio, *Famous Women,* Australian Broadcasting Commission, 2 May 1950;

"Change Another Pound," radio, Australian Broadcasting Commission, 27 June 1950;

My Brother Jack, television, 10 episodes, Australian Broadcasting Commission, 21 August 1965 – 23 October 1965.

Through the watershed years of the latter half of the 1960s, Charmian Clift was a household name to many Australians. On Thursday mornings, thousands of men as well as women would go straight to the Women's Section when opening their morning newspapers. What they were looking for was the Clift column. Every week from November 1964 until July 1969, Clift produced approximately 1,200 words that challenged Australians to think in a new way. Her column was refreshing after the political climate of the 1950s and early 1960s, in which the country was dominated by the Cold War and the long-running conservative government of Prime Minister Sir Robert Menzies. Clift herself had left that political situation in 1951 and spent a decade and a half in Europe. On her return in 1964 she was able to look at her homeland with a loving but critical eye.

Her concerns covered an extraordinary range of topics—including suburban architecture, military conscription, censorship, the need to develop a local movie industry, Australia's participation in Asia, the changing role of women, the division between the "Haves" and the "Have Nots," the iniquities of the Greek Junta, the right to protest, Australia's relationship with the United States, and the need to extend citizenship to Aborigines. However, while sometimes the columnist felt provoked into politics, on other occasions the column might take

Charmian Clift, circa 1968 (photograph by Lance Nelson)

the form of a classical essay about dreams or moonshine or the sounds of summer.

While many of Clift's opinions were so radical that they could not be found at this time in other Australian newspaper columns, it was particularly surprising to find such ideas tucked away in the Women's Section among "Weddings of Interest" and advertisements for wrinkle cream, domestic appliances, wigs, "serviced ranchettes," and "gear au gogo." Just as astonishing was to find these passionate arguments expressed in a polished prose style.

Clift was born in the township of Kiama, New South Wales, a speck on the east coast of Australia, a hundred kilometers south of Sydney. Set in rich dairy country, the town in the 1920s also had a small but flourishing quarrying industry. On the edge of Kiama, near one of the gravel quarries, was a straggly little coastal settlement of tiny weatherboard cottages where the quarry workers and their families lived. Charmian Clift was born on 30 August 1923 in the last of this row of cottages. She described her birthplace in her unfinished and unpublished autobiographical novel, "The End of the Morning," in which Kiama is represented by the fictional town of Lebanon Bay:

> The center of the world was the last house of five identical wooden cottages at the bottom of the hill, just before the new concrete bridge that spanned the creek....
> The creek looped around the five cottages, separated from their front picket fences by the width of the highway, then trickled through the tall striding silvery legs of the railway bridge and spread out on the beach beyond in a wide brackish bowl which we children dignified with the name of lagoon; all of us had to learn to swim in it first, before our father permitted us the lovely dangerous pleasures of the surf....
> Apart from this terrace of quarry cottages there was not more than a score or so of houses at this end of the town, all variations on the same architectural butterbox theme, their faded corrugated iron roofs straggling down beside the plunging swoop of the gunmetal highway. It was obviously the end, rather than the beginning of somewhere.
> Lebanon Bay proper lay over the hump of Pheasant Point and through the Cutting. It was a pretty place of solid brick bungalows and older, more graceful houses of stone and wood with wide verandahs held by slim cedar posts, set down in pleasant gardens on vertiginous hills and laced together about two wide shopping streets and a small hoop of harbour with the dark stiff serried verticals of Norfolk pines.

On the one hand, there was a sense of freedom and wild beauty, encapsulated by the beach, which the writer described as her "nursery, playground and school too," and the ocean. On the other hand, there was the sense of living on the outside, on the edge–at "the end, rather than the beginning of somewhere." Throughout most of her life, Clift retained a feeling of being an outsider looking in. She also for many years carried a sense of inferiority that had its origin in the snobbery that the residents of the main part of town showed for those who lived in the wrong part. This feeling of being second-rate was increased by her being the youngest of three children and growing up in the shadow of her elder sister, whom the parents openly favored.

If the Clift family did not fit into the middle-class respectability of the town of Kiama, they were also an anomaly in the quarry settlement, for Clift's father, Sydney Clift, held the position of engineer, while all the other neighborhood men were laborers. A self-educated English migrant, he was a bombastic and eccentric figure who had "strong opinions" about every topic under the sun, and whose political ideas were always radical, if sometimes inconsistent. As Clift said in her unpublished autobiographical novel, she learned how to argue from her father: she was in conflict with "the terrible tyrant" from an early age. Her father also developed her mind with the eclectic range of reading that he "force fed" his three young offspring.

> Tristram Shandy, Don Quixote, and the Essays of Montaigne were thrust upon all of us before we had fairly got started on Tanglewood Tales or The Wind in the Willows. We had Balzac's Contes Drollatiques instead of fairy stories and the adventures of Gargantua instead of the adventures of Tarzan.

At the same time, Charmian's mother, Amy Currie Clift, was introducing her children to a love of poetry. She had a habit of quoting long passages from such favorites as Alfred Tennyson; George Gordon, Lord Byron; and William Shakespeare. She also made a practice of scribbling away late at night at her own verse, which she would subsequently poke into the kitchen fire.

Charmian herself began writing poetry and stories at an early age. At school, she excelled at sports but did not make friends easily and was mostly unhappy. She left school in 1938 after receiving her Intermediate Certificate at the age of fourteen. In an interview given for the oral history collection of the National Library of Australia she explained,

> I wanted to get out into the big bad world and do—I didn't know what I wanted to do, but like most kids with any sort of creative ability I wanted it to be big, I wanted it to be enormous, I wanted to see the world, I wanted to do something—I didn't know what—better than anyone else could do.

Her beauty, rather than her brains, won Clift her chance to escape from the small town. In May 1941 a photograph of Clift in a swimsuit won a Beach Girl competition run by *Pix* magazine. With the money, she was able to move to Sydney "on the search for glamour," as she told Hazel De Berg in a 1965 interview. This first foray into the world led to disaster. At the end of 1942, Clift, aged nineteen, gave birth to an illegitimate daughter. Under pressure from family and social values, the young mother offered her child for adoption. This episode left Clift with a burden of secrecy as well as sadness.

Clift as a lieutenant in the Australian Women's Army Service, in which she served from 1943 to 1946 (from Kinnane, George Johnston, *1986)*

In April 1943 Clift made a fresh start by enlisting in the Australian Women's Army Service in which she manned anti-aircraft gun sites. In August 1944 she was made a lieutenant and transferred to Melbourne, where she was given the job of editing a news sheet for the Ordnance Corps. At this time she had her first short story published in a magazine, the *Australia National Journal,* and she attracted the attention of Brigadier Errol Knox, Director General of Army Public Relations, who in civilian life was managing director of *The Melbourne Argus* newspaper. He invited her to join his staff, which she did as soon as she was demobilized, in May 1946.

On one of her first days at her new job Clift met George Johnston, a thirty-three-year-old journalist who had established his reputation as the main war correspondent for the newspaper and had also published many nonfiction war books. Although Clift had a fiancé and George had a wife and young child, the two immediately began an affair that was seen by colleagues as the scandal of the office. Within weeks Clift was summarily dismissed. Johnston resigned in protest. Thus began a partnership that continued through twenty-three years, thirty books (her own and her husband's), and three children.

By 1947 the couple were unemployed and living in squalid circumstances in Sydney; Clift was pregnant. In the hope of making some cash, they began a collaborative novel, *High Valley* (1949), using the exotic setting of a valley in Tibet where George had spent a couple of months of wartime leave and which he had described in his travel book *Journey through Tomorrow* (1947). Johnston obtained a divorce in April 1947, and the couple were married that August, not long before the birth of their first child. Clift decided to spend the months of her pregnancy back at her parents' home in Kiama, while George stayed in Sydney and began work on *The Sun* newspaper. This separation proved beneficial for the collaborative process.

Clift was a painstakingly slow writer, whereas Johnston was accustomed to the speed of the newsroom. Clift also liked to keep her work-in-progress private. Johnston needed to test his work on a sounding board, page by page, idea by idea. It would be hard to find two writers whose methods were less compatible. Yet, for most of their professional lives, they worked in the same room, often even at the same table.

With this particular book, the incompatibility of the collaborators was of little account because Clift was able to work alone during the week, while Johnston was busy with his paid job in Sydney. On weekends he traveled down to the coastal town, where the two writers "exchanged ideas and rewrote each other's work if necessary," Johnston explained in the *Sydney Morning Herald* (8 May 1948). Paying tribute to Clift's vital part in writing this joint text, Johnston later noted, "If there is any quality in this book it is the work of my wife. She is responsible for characterisation and emotional content. I was the journalist who provided the substance, she was the artist who provided the burnish."

By November 1947 the work on this novel was completed, in time for the birth of a son, Martin Clift Johnston. Soon Clift and the baby joined Johnston in a flat in Bondi, a beachside suburb of Sydney. Instead of sending the typescript to a publisher, the authors entered it in a literary competition run by the *Sydney Morning Herald*. In May 1948 the front page of the newspaper declared, "'HERALD' NOVEL PRIZES: Husband And Wife Win £2000."

Since the two writers made their first appearance as novelists together and in such a blaze of publicity, from this time a public image of Charmian Clift and George Johnston as a couple united in love and work began to take on a mythic element. This public perception put a strain on the Clift-Johnston relationship and was particularly problematic for Clift, who was depicted as the junior colleague. In neither the newspaper features about the prize nor in the judges' reports was the surname Clift mentioned. Yet, the qualities praised in the novel were those that she had contributed. Thus the judges noted that "The reader feels . . . the working of a higher imagination. . . . The writing has a real distinction, a sureness and delicacy of touch." Two decades after the award, Clift wryly reminisced, "I was twenty-four and suddenly found myself a literary celebrity except that most people didn't think I'd had much to do with it."

Despite these public misconceptions, winning this competition represented a major breakthrough in the career of Clift as well as that of Johnston. While it brought the novelists to the attention of the reading public of their own country, the award also gave them an opening overseas. In Australia, Angus and Robertson published the first edition of the novel in mid 1949. In early 1950 the prestigious British publishers Faber and Faber brought out another edition, to glowing reviews. At the same time the American publishers Bobbs-Merrill decided to publish a U.S. edition, with a $10,000 promotion campaign.

For Clift, the winning of the prize was soon overshadowed by the discovery that she was pregnant again. She later told the Australian National Library interviewer:

> At this point I should have taken wings and started to fly but at this point also, of course, I was involved in having children. . . . I think those are terribly difficult years for any young woman, and for a young woman who wants to write or paint or anything else, even more so.

As well as looking after her young son and her daughter, Shane, over the next couple of years Clift wrote six radio dramas—two with her husband—and began work with Johnston on another collaborative novel, with the working title "The Piping Cry."

In early 1951 Johnston was posted overseas to run the London office of Associated Newspaper Services, which owned the Sydney *Sun*. Although initially exhilarated at being in London, Clift quickly began to feel that she was losing her identity. "The Piping Cry"—completed in October 1951—was promptly rejected by the couple's American publishers, and not offered elsewhere. In these years Clift collaborated with her husband on a novel titled *The Big Chariot* (1953), set in seventeenth-century China, and on other uncompleted projects, but already it was becoming clear that the couple's work methods were too much at variance for successful collaboration. Unable

Dust jacket for the second book Clift wrote with her husband, a novel set in seventeenth-century China (Bruccoli Clark Layman Archives)

to keep up with Johnston's production speed, Clift's main role was to be, in her words, "a literary hod-carrier"—doing the library research for collaborative projects, as well as acting as sounding board and editorial assistant for her husband's solo work. Clift attempted to work on an autobiographical novel set in her hometown, titled *Walk to the Paradise Gardens*—published much later, in 1960—as well as other autobiographical fragments but was unable to complete anything while she was living cooped up with two small children in a London apartment.

A holiday trip to Greece in the spring of 1954 held out the promise of a new world and a new way of life. If the couple were to move there, away from the rat race of the city, they might be able to survive by writing full time. At the end of that year they rented a house on the island of Kalymnos—a barren and isolated place where sponge diving was the only industry. In order to complete a contract that bound the couple to producing three collaborative novels, Clift and Johnston set to work on a new novel, which was set on an island similar to Kalymnos. This work was titled *The Sea and the Stone* (1955) in the United States and *The Sponge Divers* (1956) in Great Britain. Again, Clift's role was mainly that of researcher and editor, but as she gathered material for her husband, she also began to write up her notes about the people and place of Kalymnos as a sort of travel book. By mid 1955 she was nearly finished revising this journal of the family's life on the island, which she titled *Mermaid Singing* (1956). In this text Clift used for the first time the personal and lyrical voice that became the identifying feature of her unique prose style.

Toward the end of that year—with both Kalymnos books finished—Clift and Johnston moved to the island of Hydra, which was only three hours away from Athens. With her first solo book accepted, Clift was again at a turning point in her career. Again she discovered herself to be pregnant. Her second son, Jason, was born on Hydra in April 1956. Although their finances were precarious, the couple decided to spend their small reserve of cash on a house on the island. The family lived there for the next eight years.

On Hydra, Clift at last felt that she was an insider. Among the small number of resident foreigners, her status and role were acknowledged. She also

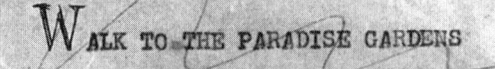

WALK TO THE PARADISE GARDENS

IN THE FIRST PLACE Julia had not really wanted to return to Lebanon Bay.

Although she had loved the town fiercely and possessively in her childhood she had never had any conscious desire to share it with Charles, not even during her first extraordinary rapture of love, when heaven knows, had it occurred to her for a moment that he wanted them, she would have shared with him not only places and possessions, but every happy moment she had ever known, every breath of wonder she had ever breathed, every wildest of the winged thoughts that had come to her so naturally then, and even the still and secret places of her soul.

Perhaps, during that early time, they had been too busy discovering new places, the sort of places which later, in brief moments of tender reminiscence -- briefer and more infrequent as the years had passed -- they would refer to as "our place -- remember, darling?" Or perhaps, even so early, she had been afraid that Charles might laugh.

In any case she had not mentioned -- nor, indeed, even thought of -- Lebanon Bay for years, when Charles had suggested that they should go there for his summer holidays. Julia was even mildly put out; she had been hoping that this year at last they might do the trip through the Northern Territory. Everybody else had done it

First page of the setting-copy for Clift's 1960 novel (National Library of Australia, MS9537)

felt that she was able at last to manage a successful division of her time between her domestic life, her professional life, and her social life. Under these circumstances, Clift's writing developed. By April 1957 she had completed a second personal travel book, this time set on Hydra and titled *Peel Me a Lotus* (1959). The depiction of the aridness of the island and the internecine tensions of the foreign colony were not, however, what American publishers wanted. This book appeared only in Britain and, later, Australia.

Having completed these two nonfiction texts, Clift felt it was time for her to write "THE novel," as she put it in a letter to David Higham, her literary agent in London. Between the spring of 1957 and December 1958 she completed the work titled *Walk to the Paradise Gardens*, which she had set aside in London. This novel contrasts the lives of two women who meet during a summer holiday in a seaside town based closely on Kiama. While themes of infidelity and guilt are evident, a deeper thread is concerned with a kind of fidelity as the two women put up with miserable marriages in order to protect and support their vulnerable and inadequate husbands.

At times the novel reads like a modern rendering of *A Midsummer Night's Dream*, as the two couples chase each other through nights of barbecue and dance. A further influence is that of classical Greek drama. As in a Greek tragedy, the characters seem to have no alternative but to act as they do, and their actions form a kind of ritual that leads to a predestined disaster.

Once again, as Clift's professional life moved forward, her private life and domestic responsibilities blocked her progress. Her husband had for years suffered severe respiratory problems during winter. By October 1959 his weight loss was so extreme that he finally consented to consult a doctor. He was diagnosed as having tuberculosis. This illness, together with emphysema, continued to destroy Johnston's health over the next decade. His poor health also brought about a change in his temperament and in the balance of the marriage. From now on, Clift's main priority became to help and encourage her husband's work.

Through four difficult years, Clift managed to find small spaces of time in which to write her second solo novel, *Honour's Mimic* (1964). The prose reaches a new level as Clift explores the passion that develops between a middle-class Australian woman—convalescing on a Greek island after a failed suicide attempt—and a sponge diver who has lost his courage. The ultimate meaning of the story is that there can be no happy ending for the lovers: they will be forced to endure their separate fates. When the diver goes back to his dangerous work, the heroine silently promises that

The Johnston family—Shane, George, Charmian, Jason, and Martin—on Hydra, 1963 (from Kinnane, George Johnston, *1986)*

He will conquer even the smell of fear because of me. Because I will be with him waking and sleeping, I will crawl with him along the bottom of the sea, I will be the air that he breathes, I will be his lungs and his eyes and the pump of his heart.

It is no coincidence that the imagery in this vow is all of lungs, air, and breathing at a time when the author's husband was struggling with tuberculosis and emphysema.

In the autumn of 1962, with this text nearly completed, Clift was prompted by her mother's death to return to the autobiographical story of childhood and adolescence on which she had been working sporadically for more than a decade. In this revision of "The End of the Morning" she renamed her alter ego Cressida Morley, and she redrafted the text as a first-person narrative. Around the same time, Johnston made a start on a first-person narrative about growing up in Melbourne. Clift put aside her own work so that she could assist her husband. Sitting at his side every day from about September 1962 until March 1963, her input into the text was so great that Johnston described *My Brother Jack* (1964) as "virtually a collaboration."

This novel, which was partly spurred by homesickness, provided a pathway home for Johnston, who returned to Australia for the launch of the book in March 1964. Clift followed six months later, together with the three children. Soon after her return she was invited by the Melbourne *Herald* newspaper to write a short series of "pieces," looking at Australian society from the point of view of a recently returned exile. The Sydney *Morning Herald* also ran the weekly essays. Within a month or so, the Clift column was one of the most popular features of both newspapers, and the columnist had a permanent job.

Clift found the form of the essay perfectly suited to her style, and she enjoyed the regular communication with thousands of readers. Yet, the weekly deadline prevented her from working on her fiction. Although she appeared gregarious, she was in fact a private person, and she found being a public persona increasingly difficult. At the same time, her alter ego character, Cressida Morley–who had appeared in a cameo role in *My Brother Jack*–was being taken over as Johnston developed this character in the sequel to *My Brother Jack, Clean Straw for Nothing* (1969).

Clift could make no headway with her own portrayal of Cressida Morley's life in her novel "The End of the Morning"–not least because she had to keep churning out the column to support the family, as Johnston's health deteriorated and he was hospitalized for long periods (from July 1965 to April 1966 and from May to October 1968). Living with a spouse who was slowly dying was, of course, debilitating in itself.

Meanwhile, the political climate was also distressing Clift. As Australian politicians cemented an alliance with the United States by sending conscripts to the war in Vietnam, Clift's view of the world became darker. She worried also about the gap between the Haves and Have Nots of the world. In April 1967 the democratic government of Greece was overthrown by a military junta. At home, she increasingly found her fellow countrymen and countrywomen to be complacent and selfish.

By 1969 she was becoming profoundly depressed. A particular concern was the imminent publication of her husband's novel, *Clean Straw for Nothing*, which included a portrayal of Cressida Morley as an unfaithful wife whose adultery causes her husband's fatal illness. Other anguish was physical, as she suffered a particularly severe menopause. Though alcohol was an additional problem, neither it nor other troubles ever prevented her from meeting her weekly column deadline. In her writing, the public persona was so strong that few people realized how deeply the columnist was suffering in private. Even close friends were astonished when Clift took an overdose of sleeping tablets on the night of 8 July 1969 and died in her sleep. This action seemed at odds with someone who appeared to epitomize an attitude of exuberant and carefree enthusiasm for life. Over the next week, Clift's newspaper editors received a wave of letters that showed how deeply a variety of Australians had esteemed her.

Overall, Charmian Clift's published literary output was relatively small–3 collaborative novels, 2 travel books, 2 solo novels, and 225 essays. Of her twenty-year career as a published writer, she spent only seven years in her homeland. Yet, her effect on Australian society was far greater than these statistics suggest. As well as recording political change in the volatile years of the 1960s, Clift was also instrumental in helping Australian society discard many of the narrow and xenophobic values that it had held through the Cold War period. To live in advance of one's time is difficult for a writer because it often means that the writing is misunderstood and undervalued. Yet, one of the benefits of writing from the vanguard is that the work tends to remain relevant. Clift continues to win a new readership, both for her travel books and for her essays.

Interview:

Hazel De Berg, "Interview with Charmian Clift," 8 June 1965, National Library of Australia, tape 105 [ten page transcript].

Biographies:

Garry Kinnane, *George Johnston, a Biography* (Melbourne: Nelson, 1986);

Suzanne Chick, *Searching for Charmian* (Sydney: Pan Macmillan, 1994);

Nadia Wheatley, *The Life and Myth of Charmian Clift* (Sydney: HarperCollins, 2001).

Papers:

Collections of Charmian Clift's manuscripts and correspondence are in the National Library of Australia; the State Library of New South Wales (Mitchell Library); the University of Texas at Austin (Harry Ransom Humanities Research Center); and the Lilly Library, Indiana University.

Peter Cowan

(4 November 1914 -   )

Bruce Bennett
University of New South Wales

BOOKS: *Drift: Stories* (Melbourne & Adelaide: Reed & Harris, 1944);
The Unploughed Land: Stories (Sydney: Angus & Robertson, 1958);
Summer (Sydney: Angus & Robertson, 1964);
The Empty Street: Stories (Sydney: Angus & Robertson, 1965);
Seed (Sydney: Angus & Robertson, 1966);
The Tins and Other Stories (St. Lucia: University of Queensland Press, 1973);
A Unique Position: A Biography of Edith Dircksey Cowan, 1861-1932 (Nedlands: University of Western Australia Press, 1978);
Mobiles and Other Stories (Fremantle, W.A.: Fremantle Arts Centre Press, 1979);
A Window in Mrs X's Place (Ringwood, Vic.: Penguin, 1986; New York: Penguin, 1986);
The Color of the Sky: A Novel (Fremantle, W.A.: Fremantle Arts Centre Press, 1986);
Maitland Brown: A View of Nineteenth Century Western Australia (Fremantle, W.A.: Fremantle Arts Centre Press, 1988);
Voices (Fremantle, W.A.: Fremantle Arts Centre Press, 1988);
The Hills of Apollo Bay (Fremantle, W.A.: Fremantle Arts Centre Press, 1989);
The Tenants (Fremantle, W.A.: Fremantle Arts Centre Press, 1994).

SELECTED PERIODICAL PUBLICATIONS–
UNCOLLECTED: "Conservation"–weekly articles on conservation in Western Australia, *Independent* (Perth), September 1969-November 1970;
"Statement," by Cowan, *Australian Literary Studies*–short-story issue, 10, no. 2 (October 1981): 196-198.

OTHER: *Short Story Landscape: The Modern Short Story,* edited by Cowan (Sydney: Longmans, 1964);
Spectrum One: Narrative Short Stories, edited by Bruce Bennett, Cowan, and John Hay (Melbourne: Longman, 1970);

Peter Cowan (from the dust jacket for The Tins and Other Stories, *1973)*

Spectrum Two: Modern Short Stories, edited by Bennett, Cowan, and Hay (Camberwell, Vic.: Longman, 1970);
Today: Short Stories of Our Time, edited by Cowan (Melbourne: Longman, 1971);
New Country: A Selection of Western Australian Short Stories, edited by Bennett (Fremantle, W.A.: Fremantle Arts Centre Press, 1976), pp. 1-31;
A Faithful Picture: The Letters of Eliza and Thomas Brown at York in the Swan River Colony, 1841-1852, edited

by Cowan (Fremantle, W.A.: Fremantle Arts Centre Press, 1977);

A Colonial Experience: Swan River 1839–1888, from the Diary and Reports of Walkinshaw Cowan, edited by Cowan (Perth: Peter Cowan, 1978);

Westerly 21: An Anniversary Selection from Westerly 1956–1977, edited by Bennett and Cowan (Fremantle, W.A.: Fremantle Arts Centre Press, 1978);

Spectrum Three: Experimental Short Stories, edited by Bennett, Cowan, and Hay (Melbourne: Longman Cheshire, 1979);

Perspectives One: Short Stories, edited by Bennett, Cowan, and Hay (Melbourne: Longman Cheshire, 1985);

Perspectives Two, edited by Bennett, Cowan, and Hay (Melbourne: Longman Cheshire, 1987);

Impressions: West Coast Fiction 1829–1988, edited by Cowan (Fremantle, W.A.: Fremantle Arts Centre Press, 1989);

Hungerford: Short Fiction by T. A. G. Hungerford, edited by Cowan (Fremantle, W.A.: Fremantle Arts Centre Press, 1989);

Western Australian Writing: A Bibliography, by Bennett, Cowan, Hay, and Susan Ashford (Fremantle, W.A.: Fremantle Arts Centre Press, 1990).

Peter Cowan is an Australian short-fiction writer, novelist, biographer, and editor whose published work spans a period from the early 1940s to the 1990s. He has established a reputation both as a modernist and as a regional Western Australian author. Cowan's largest contribution in the first half of his career was in short fiction: his first, second, and fourth books were collections of stories. A lifelong fascination with formal experiment in short fiction brought him to publish a total of six collections and a volume of selected stories. Cowan has also published five novels and two biographies. He was an assiduous and influential editor of the literary journal *Westerly* from the 1970s to the early 1990s, and he edited or co-edited colonial diaries and letters together with a variety of anthologies. Although Cowan can be described as a "man of letters," he has never been a socializer, and a major theme in his work is the essential isolation of the individual—whether he or she is set against a vast Australian landscape or in a suburban home.

Peter Walkinshaw Cowan was born on 4 November 1914 in Perth, Western Australia, in the first year of World War I. His father, Norman Walkinshaw Cowan, was a barrister and solicitor who married Marie Emily Johnston in 1913. They built a house in York Street, South Perth, where Cowan spent his early years. However, when his father died suddenly in 1925, Cowan, his two sisters, Mary and Elizabeth, and their mother moved to a smaller house in Karoo Street,

South Perth. Another death that impacted profoundly on Cowan's childhood and youth was that of his sister Elizabeth, a talented musician and a family favorite, who died suddenly when she was fourteen.

These deaths, and the trauma associated with them, may account in part for the relative silence about childhood in Cowan's fiction. By contrast, author Tom Hungerford, who also was born in South Perth, in 1915, and lived there through World War I and the 1920s, presented the semirural life by the river and the Chinese market gardens as an adventure-filled boyhood idyll in his autobiographical *Stories from Suburban Road* (1983). On the rare occasions when Cowan does offer portraits of childhood or adolescence—for example, in "The Red-Backed Spiders" or in *A Window in Mrs X's Place* (1986)—his boys/men are conflicted and isolated, interesting chiefly for their problematic states of mind and emotions. Cowan's fiction steadfastly rejects the sentimental view of childhood and youth.

Cowan's schooling commenced in 1922 at the age of eight when he attended primary school; he entered Wesley College in 1924 when he was ten. His unhappiness at college was exacerbated by the poor teaching he encountered there, but by this time he had established a habit of reading widely beyond institutional requirements. The most memorable events of Cowan's schooling were holidays with an uncle in the karri forests of the southwest of Western Australia at Jardee near Manjimup. A sense of awe at the massive scale of these forests and of indignation at the criminality of subsequent governments devoted to "development" that endorsed the destruction of these forests for woodchipping and other purposes recurs in Cowan's fiction. In an interview with Stuart Reid in 1991–1992, Cowan recalled a vivid image of his uncle's farm from childhood:

> He'd got a small area cut out of that karri forest, and the sense of that enormous wall of karri around you.... Now, even as a child I could feel the enormous power that the land has always had to me. So it was a marvellous sense for a child of a contained world, this property with him and his wife and three kids, contained in this place.

A suspicion—and sometimes a fear—of institutions and the recurrent need to escape from them informs much of Cowan's life and art. When Cowan left school in 1930, he worked for three years for the Commercial Union Assurance Company in Perth, which reminded him of Charles Dickens's offices. In these years he suffered psychosomatic illnesses and migraine headaches. A more formative period for Cowan's writing during the Great Depression was from 1933 to 1935, when he left Perth and was employed at various places in the eastern wheat belt and southwest as a casual agricultural laborer. Cowan enjoyed the physical work, from milking cows to mending fences. The outdoor life appealed to him, and it did not worry him that he was "a sort of social outcast" because he never had "any liking for, or trust or feeling, for social things. . . . I quite enjoyed the isolation," as he told Reid. Cowan temporarily entertained the idea of buying an abandoned Group Settlement Farm near Cowaramup in the coastal southwest with a friend, Roy Brown from Northam. However, they lacked capital and did not proceed with this idea.

Returning to Perth in 1935, Cowan obtained casual jobs around the city and suburbs while he attended night school at Perth Technical College in order to matriculate at the University of Western Australia. He was a full-time student at the university from 1938 to 1940, obtaining a Bachelor of Arts degree, majoring in English and philosophy. Cowan arrived as a student at the university when Walter Murdoch's long tenure as Professor of English, 1913–1939, was on the wane. The two academics in English who enlarged Cowan's view of literature were H. S. Thompson, in his lectures on Thomas Hardy, and Alec King, in his enthusiasm for T. S. Eliot. After his first year of study Cowan was awarded a Hackett studentship, which enabled him to continue as a full-time student. In summer vacations he continued to work on the wheat bins. Literature interacted intermittently with Cowan's thinking and writing: later, he found himself silently reciting Eliot's "The Hollow Men" (1925) on an air force parade ground during World War II. Cowan's eloquent epigraph to *The Hills of Apollo Bay* (1989) is from Eliot's "Rhapsody on a Windy Night" (collected in *Prufrock and Other Observations* [1917]): "Memory! / You have the key, / The little lamp spreads a ring on the stair." But Cowan's self-directed, independent reading was more significant. In retrospect, he was appalled at university academics' willful ignorance of American writers such as Ernest Hemingway and John Dos Passos, who led him toward a sense of relevance to present times and viable literary idioms, techniques, and voices. By 1939 Cowan was writing stories, finding an interest in the form and not simply in writing a story that conformed to the expectations of dominant magazines, such as the *Bulletin*. By 1941 Cowan had written most of the stories that became *Drift* (1944).

After completing his Bachelor of Arts degree, he obtained a position as resident master at Guildford Grammar School, which involved dormitory and house supervision, including leave and financial arrangements, coaching games, and supervising. Guildford was a conservative Anglican boarding school; among its most notable attendees were novelist and poet Kenneth Seaforth Mackenzie and novelist and poet Randolph

Dust jacket for Cowan's first book, stories inspired by modernist writers such as Ernest Hemingway and John Dos Passos (Bruccoli Clark Layman Archives)

Stow. At Guildford, Cowan held the respect of students through his genuine interest in the boys and their problems, his proficiency in the literature he taught, and his quiet, dry sense of humor.

On 18 June 1941 Cowan married Edith Howard, whom he had known since 1935. Some of their experiences as partners before marriage—for example, concealing the fact that they were lovers, in a puritanical provincial setting in prewar Western Australia—provided Cowan with material for his fiction. In February 1943 he applied for a commission in the Royal Australian Air Force Reserve (RAAF) as a trainee technician and wireless assistant. Cowan passed a trainee technical course but was judged more suitable for clerical work, in which he served as a leading aircraftsman and temporarily as acting corporal. From April 1943 he was attached to nine different units, including three service hospitals in Melbourne, before being discharged from the RAAF on 7 May 1945 as "medically unfit for further service." This discharge followed his arrest by military police after he had gone absent without leave.

Cowan's two years with the RAAF in Melbourne from 1943 to 1945 are glossed over in his brief autobiographical statement in *Peter Cowan: New Critical Essays*

(1992); yet, these years and his two post–World War II years in Melbourne form some basic elements of his most praised novel, *The Hills of Apollo Bay.*

While the regulations, rations, identification cards, and other restrictions of the war years on the "home front" in Melbourne presented Cowan with images of a "City of Dreadful Night," the city also provided for him the kind of exhilaration that surfaces in *The Hills of Apollo Bay.* In the darkness, shadows, and mysteries of this metropolis, Cowan found a vitality in art and new possibilities in human relationships. The commitment of some men and women he met to contemporary art and writing seemed a more urgent and real commitment in the context of war. Cowan found its expression in groups that formed around the Contemporary Art Society, Angry Penguins, and John and Sunday Reed. The firm of Reed and Harris published Cowan's first book, *Drift*. These are some of the contexts in which Cowan found his vocation as a modernist writer, influenced and encouraged by artists Albert Tucker and Sidney Nolan, for a time with the Reed and Harris firm, as well as by Max Harris and the Reeds.

Cowan taught in Melbourne after the war but returned to Western Australia in 1946 with Edith and their young son Julian, who had been born in 1944, to a postwar housing shortage. The family lived first at an aunt's house at Rockingham, near the coast some fifty kilometers south of Perth, with only two buses a day to the city. Cowan commuted by motorbike, completing a degree in education and working part-time as a tutor and temporary lecturer in English at the University of Western Australia. In 1950 he began building a house at Alfred Road, Mount Claremont, near a lake called Butler's Swamp, which attracted rare waterbirds. Cowan became an expert ornithologist. He built an aviary behind the house, and he and Julian regularly photographed birds at the lake and recorded their movements. His critical approach to thoughtless "development" that threatened the natural environment was fueled by the construction of a municipal rubbish heap at the lake, which in due course became a golf course. A drive-in movie theater further destroyed the illusion that it was possible to enjoy a semirural life in the rapidly expanding Australian suburbs of the 1950s. Some aspects of these settings appear in his novel *Seed* (1966).

Having completed his university studies, Cowan obtained a full-time job in 1950 as a teacher of English and geography at Scotch College, where he remained until 1962. Although some of Cowan's short fiction touches on the business of school common rooms and suburban encounters, his imagination was nurtured chiefly at this time by summer holidays, which he spent with his wife and son camping in the still largely unspoiled country of the southwest from Cape Naturaliste to the Leeuwin. His second book, *The Unploughed Land* (1958), includes thirteen stories from *Drift*, complemented by six new stories, including the title story and the widely anthologized "The Red-Backed Spiders." Cowan's attraction was to the unsettled parts of the vast state into which he was born–one-third of the Australian landmass. His treatment of human relationships avoids sentimental romanticism and reveals the fears, anxieties, and betrayals of apparently ordinary men and women. The boy in "The Red-Backed Spiders," isolated from others of his age on a farm and caught in the web of his parents' anger, is a murderer. But Cowan's understated narrative typically avoids melodrama, while suggesting the pervasiveness of the dark impulses of the human heart. Such stories hint at psychological depths. The spare prose style and cool narrative manner of Cowan's early stories derives something from Hemingway and Anton Pavlovich Chekhov, but Cowan was creating his own literary voice to convey his vision of the intractability of human affairs, which ultimately leave the individual alone, without emotional or spiritual solace. These were the hard conditions of the world that Cowan saw emerging.

Cowan–nicknamed "Mo" because he was already sporting a trademark moustache–is remembered by former students of Scotch College as a popular and respected teacher. He is also remembered for his International Norton motorbike, which he parked in the college grounds. Motorbike and later race-car competitions became an important bond between father and son, and Julian went on to become a race-car driver and organizer of rallies as well as a professional photographer.

After twelve years at Scotch College, Cowan suffered burnout. He had been publishing stories in *Meanjin* and spending summers working as a tally clerk at wheat bins–jobs which, together with similar jobs in the 1930s, provided him with material for his first novel, *Summer* (1964). But a more decisive break from schoolteaching was required. Cowan applied for and was granted a Commonwealth Literary Fund fellowship in 1963 to write a second novel, *Seed,* which was published in 1966. While it was not autobiographical, *Seed* showed the influence of Cowan's interest in motor vehicles and the use of them by his son's generation. The novel reveals the changing values of a society increasingly dependent on the car: from juvenile theft of cars to secondhand-car sales rackets, a provincial middle-class community is shown in the process of breakup. But Cowan's project is not primarily sociological or judgmental: this writer is chiefly engaged with the psychology of individuals and of relationships between them. The novel ends in a ghostly scene at a drive-in movie theater as a couple, faced with cinematic romance, try to untangle the sources of their impending separation.

Cowan was appointed senior tutor in the English department of the University of Western Australia in 1964. This position was the beginning of a long and fruitful professional career that continued until his retirement in 1979 and then as honorary research fellow until the early 1990s. The change of profession enabled Cowan to teach, read, write about, and edit literature as well as to produce his own short stories, novels, and biographies. His appointment as senior tutor enabled him to avoid the onerous administrative and managerial burdens that can dominate academic life. One duty that he took seriously, though, was editing and production of the quarterly literary journal *Westerly*. He served on the journal's editorial committee from 1966 and then co-edited *Westerly* with Bruce Bennett from 1975 to 1992, joined in 1986 by Dennis Haskell. Cowan was a supporter of John Barnes's attempts to include Australian literature in the curriculum of the English department and of the first full-year course in Australian literature, introduced by Bennett and Veronica Brady in 1973. Cowan's own teaching included the general first-year course (novel, poetry, and drama) and courses on the nineteenth- and twentieth-century novel. Although he tended to be a "loner" in the English department, avoiding staff meetings when he could and seldom socializing, Cowan found there a group of people—including poet and playwright Dorothy Hewett—who supported his attempts to write against the grain of a largely complacent West Australian community.

To suggest that Cowan was uninvolved through the 1960s in the wider West Australian community would be a mistake. Together with his wife, Edith—whose personality was more outgoing than Cowan's and who worked at the Playhouse Theatre as wardrobe mistress—he took part in a regular commercial television word game quiz. More significantly, he took his environmental interests into the popular press with a series of commissioned weekly articles in Perth's Sunday *Independent* newspaper in 1969 and 1970. But his deepest insights and his literary craftsmanship were reserved for his short stories and novels. His third and best-selling collection of stories, *The Empty Street*, was published by Angus and Robertson in 1965. The haunting cover painting, "Boy in a Street" by Robert Dickerson, was a reminder, along with Albert Tucker's picture of unemployed men on the cover of *Drift*, of Cowan's links with leading artists of his time, who overturned realism in favor of surrealistic imagery. The eleven stories in *The Empty Street* shifted the center of gravity in Cowan's work to contemporary concerns of suburban Australians in the postwar years. Cowan's

Dust jacket for Cowan's 1958 book, which includes "The Red-Backed Spiders," one of his most widely anthologized stories (Bruccoli Clark Layman Archives)

image of suburban life at this time is somber. Tenderness and love contend against the pressures of material well-being and respectability. Yet, Cowan does not write of these subjects with lighthearted, or even savage, satiric flourish as Barry Humphries did, from the outside. Cowan writes from within, presenting himself as both implicated and critical. He depicts paralyzed lives and the seldom successful attempts of individuals to escape from stunted conditions, but without the coldness of James Joyce's treatment in *Dubliners* (1914). Cowan's rendition of states of mind in *The Empty Street* leaves room for sympathy and sometimes pity.

In 1971 Cowan traveled to England with his wife on a year of study leave from the University of Western Australia. One of his aims was to understand the background of the English nineteenth-century novel, which he taught, and its relation to the many Australian novels by British writers of the 1890s and after. His interest focused on the romance novel, which was at that time neglected by academics and critics, and subsequently led to published essays on E. L. Grant Watson (*Westerly*, 25, no. 1, 1980) and Hume Nisbet (*Westerly*, 27, no. 4, 1982 and *Westerly*, 28, no. 1, 1983). He visited many bookshops in various parts of the United King-

Dust jacket for Cowan's 1973 book, short fiction exemplifying his prescription that stories should deal with the "here and now" (Thomas Cooper Library, University of South Carolina)

dom and established connections that enabled him to build a substantial collection of nineteenth-century Australiana. When he writes ironically of lobbyists and collectors, he has himself under scrutiny. More significantly for his own writing, he developed an understanding of colonial Australia and its links with Great Britain, which informed his subsequent work on nineteenth-century Australian biography and history in the 1970s and 1980s.

Cowan continued to produce short fiction in the 1970s. *The Tins and Other Stories* (1973) was his only volume published by the University of Queensland Press. *Mobiles and Other Stories* (1979) was published by the Fremantle Arts Centre Press, which was founded in 1975 and became Cowan's main publisher in the second half of his writing career. Both *The Tins* and *Mobiles* include stories that fulfilled Cowan's prescription–via Hemingway and Sherwood Anderson–that the short story should deal with the "here and now." These volumes show Cowan's awareness of a liberalizing of censorship laws in relation to "adult" themes in Australia, but his focus remains on psychological states. Stylistically, his "realist-impressionist" method moves toward an interiorization of dialogue. Some stories in *The Tins* collection retain direct quotation marks, but in *Mobiles* these are dropped altogether. If this method sometimes leads to difficulties in identifying characters and speakers, it also contributes to a sense that words spoken and words thought can interact in surprising ways. In this process the reader is required to work actively to interpret tonal variations and ambiguities. Another feature of these volumes is Cowan's experiments with stories of different lengths. "Love and Affection" in *The Tins*, for example, is a dramatic monologue of one page, while "The Lakes" in *Mobiles* is a story of thirty-eight pages.

The settings of many of the stories in *Mobiles* shifted from the wheat belt or southwest to the inland and northwest with its vast, flat landscapes and occasional iron-ore towns, which Cowan had begun to explore in his four-wheel-drive Toyota "tank." Beyond such replicas of suburbia, Cowan remarked in the introduction to *A Window in Mrs X's Place*, "there are stretches of quite pitiless but utterly attractive landscape. Even here we put down instant towns and suburbs. . . . Yet a few miles outside their air conditioning and supermarts one can die in a couple of days, left alone." His title story in *Mobiles* shows two tough young women from this environment who have learned the tricks of survival; in "Collector," a man and a woman face the hot desert alone, with only their problematic past joining them. Cowan's dialogue simulates their strained, attenuated voices against this landscape.

The literary resources Cowan had discovered in Great Britain in 1971 encouraged him to explore and write about the past. His first excursion into colonial Australia involved transcribing and editing family letters left to him, which were published as *A Faithful Picture: The Letters of Eliza and Thomas Brown at York in the Swan River Colony, 1841–1852* by Fremantle Arts Centre Press in 1977. The letters were mainly by Eliza to her gentleman-farmer father, William Bussey, in Oxfordshire. This work was followed by *A Colonial Experience: Swan River 1839–1888, from the Diary and Reports of Walkinshaw Cowan* (1978); Walkinshaw Cowan was Cowan's great-grandfather who was Secretary to John Hutt, Governor of Western Australia and who became Protector of Aborigines at York. Cowan received a grant from the Literature Board to research and write a biography of his grandmother, Edith Cowan, who was elected to the Legislative Assembly of the Western Australian Parliament from 1921 through 1924, thus making her the first woman to be elected to an Australian Parliament. *A Unique Position: A Biography of Edith Dircksey Cowan, 1861–1932* was published by the University of

Western Australia Press in 1978. The book is in the "life and times" genre, which gives great weight to the location of the individual life in the social and cultural context of Western Australia. Cowan's biographical and historical quartet was completed when he wrote *Maitland Brown: A View of Nineteenth Century Western Australia,* published by the Fremantle Arts Centre Press in 1988, another "life and times" study, which makes scrupulous use of available documents and newspapers.

The deaths of Cowan's mother and his wife in 1980, both of whom had been anchors in his life, led to two kinds of development in his writing. First was a search for anchors of a kind through researching and writing family histories that might locate his identity in relation to place. Arising from this was a recognition of the transience and uncertainty of the human condition. After Edith's death he lived alone and frugally in the house he had built at 149 Alfred Road, Mt. Claremont, with occasional visits to his son Julian and Julian's wife, Diana, at Darlington.

Cowan's third novel, *The Color of the Sky* (1986), was in some respects a fictional spin-off of the documented histories, dramatizing the recognition of a deep need in the narrator and protagonist—Cowan's alter ego Leon—to explore his genealogy, however his forebears may turn out to be. But in consciously seeking to know his past, and hence some sources of his identity, Leon is inevitably frustrated, discovering other stories to complement and complicate his "own" family history. *The Color of the Sky* offers a more ironic treatment of the uses of history and memory than Cowan's fourth novel, *The Hills of Apollo Bay,* his most lyrical novel. The principal sources of lyricism—fragments of remembered relationships during the war years and the excitement of discovery of a vocation—are discovered in shadowy moments.

Voices (1988) was self-consciously designed as Cowan's last collection of stories. The cover is black, but one small corner of a building is spotlit. The mood of the book is similarly dark, with occasional spotlit moments. This book aspires toward an austere minimalism, as does Samuel Beckett's *Endgame* (1958). The voices that arise from the pages of *Voices* testify to the pointlessness and frustration of much of contemporary living, but they do so in memorable ways. The secret, as critic John Barnes remarks in his back-cover endorsement of the book, is in the writing, which through its "subtlety and fineness of phrase and rhythmic intensity . . . re-creates intangible unspoken perceptions and responses of the characters with remarkable precision."

Cowan's fifth novel, *The Tenants* (1994), has a cover picture of the Perth skyline. The novel reveals the transience of individuals who inhabit such cities. Planning and building offices and "homes" are shown to be obsessive pursuits, giving power to developers over ordinary citizens, but some of them elude its grasp. Characterization occurs via vignettes, or fragments. One of Cowan's characters, a young, high-flying architect living in one of his creations, muses on the mysteries of identity with a young woman from an escort agency:

> I thought I had one. I always thought I did. I never questioned it. Now I look around out there and I wouldn't have one at all. . . . Perhaps it is one place is much like another now. Or that no place is like anything.

The dialogue is awkward, revealing a loss of personal and locational anchors in contemporary society and some awareness of this loss. In *The Tenants,* Cowan is a modernist critic of the postmodern condition.

Peter Cowan has always been aware that he is not a popular author, nor has he striven to be one. Rather, he has chosen to extend the boundaries of his craft; and in short fiction especially, he has gained a reputation as a writers' writer. In 1987 he was made a Member of the Order of Australia for services to Australian literature. He was presented with the Patrick White Literary Award in 1992 and was awarded the first honorary doctorate of philosophy at Edith Cowan University in 1996. In 1997 the university opened the Peter Cowan Writers' Centre at its Joondalup Campus. Cowan was elected a life member of the Avicultural Society in 1997 and was chosen in 1999, to his amusement, as one of the Living Treasures of Western Australia.

Interview:

Stuart Reid, "Interview with Peter Walkinshaw Cowan," October 1991–August 1992, National Library of Australia (Oral History Collection), 1992.

Reference:

Bruce Bennett and Susan Miller, eds., *Peter Cowan: New Critical Essays*—includes ten essays by various hands, an "Autobiographical Statement" by Cowan, and a bibliography of Cowan's published writings (Nedlands: University of Western Australia Press, 1992).

Papers:

Manuscripts, correspondence, and documents of Peter Cowan are held by the author. The National Archives of Australia holds Cowan's RAAF Service Records. The J. S. Battye Library of West Australian History and the Oral History Section of the National Library of Australia hold transcripts of recorded interviews by Stuart Reid with Cowan between October 1991 and August 1992.

Dymphna Cusack
(21 September 1902 – 19 October 1981)

Marilla North
University of Queensland

BOOKS: *Jungfrau* (Sydney: Bulletin Press, 1936);

Pioneers on Parade, by Cusack and Miles Franklin (Sydney: Angus & Robertson, 1939);

Red Sky at Morning (Melbourne & London: Melbourne University Press in association with Oxford University Press, 1942);

Morning Sacrifice (Sydney: Mulga Publications, 1943);

Kanga-Bee and Kanga-Bo (Sydney: Botany House, 1945);

Four Winds and a Family, by Cusack and Florence James (Sydney: Shakespeare Head Press, 1947);

Three Australian Three-Act Plays (Sydney: Australasian, 1950)—comprises *Comets Soon Pass, Shoulder the Sky,* and *Morning Sacrifice;*

Come In Spinner, by Cusack and James (London: Heinemann, 1951; New York: Morrow, 1951; Melbourne: Heinemann, 1951; enlarged edition, edited by James, Sydney: Angus & Robertson, 1988);

Say No to Death (London: Heinemann, 1951); republished as *The Sun in My Hands* (New York: Morrow, 1952);

Southern Steel (London: Constable, 1953);

Caddie, A Sydney Barmaid. An Autobiography Written by Herself (London: Constable, 1953; Sydney: Walter Standish, 1953);

The Sun in Exile (London: Constable, 1955);

The Golden Girls (London: F. W. Deane, 1955);

Chinese Women Speak (Sydney: Angus & Robertson, 1958);

Heatwave in Berlin (London: Heinemann, 1961);

Picnic Races (London: Heinemann, 1962; Melbourne: Readers Book Club, 1963);

Holidays among the Russians (London: Heinemann, 1964);

Black Lightning (London: Heinemann, 1964; Richmond, Vic.: Marlin, 1977);

Illyria Reborn (London: Heinemann, 1966);

The Sun Is Not Enough (London: Heinemann, 1967);

The Half-Burnt Tree (London: Heinemann, 1969);

A Bough in Hell (London: Heinemann, 1971);

Dymphna Cusack (from Leslie Rees, The Making of Australian Drama, *1973)*

A Window in the Dark (or Boo to a Goose), edited by Debra Adelaide (Canberra: National Library of Australia, 1991).

PLAY PRODUCTIONS: *Safety First,* Sydney, Players' Club, 21 September 1928;

Shallow Cups, Sydney, Players' Club, 20 September 1933;

Anniversary, Sydney, NSW Conservatorium of Music, 24 April 1935;

Red Sky at Morning, Sydney, Players' Club, 21 September 1935;

Tubbs' Teaching Tabloids, Sydney, Teachers' Federation Players, August 1938;

Morning Sacrifice, Perth, W.A., Repertory Theatre, 8 October 1942;

Comets Soon Pass, Perth, W.A., Repertory Theatre, October 1943;

Call Up Your Ghosts, by Cusack and Miles Franklin, Melbourne, New Theatre, 1945;

The Golden Girls, London, Kidderminster Repertory Theatre, September 1955;

Pacific Paradise, Colchester, England, Colchester Repertory Theatre, December 1958.

PRODUCED SCRIPTS: *His Honour Comes to Tea,* radio, 2UE, 1933;

Second Rhapsody, radio, 1933;

How the Other Half Lives, radio, social documentary series, Australian Broadcasting Commission (ABC), 1939;

Spartacus, radio, ABC, December 1940;

Women Today, radio, social documentary series, ABC, 1940;

Married Women on Unemployment Relief, radio, ABC, 1940;

Calling All Women, radio, social documentary series, ABC, 1944;

Among the Firefighters in Eastern Victoria, radio, ABC, 1944;

The Lost Tribe of Australian Writers, radio, ABC, 1944;

The Lure of the Inland Sea: The Story of Charles Sturt, radio, ABC, 1945;

Shoulder the Sky, radio, ABC, 1945;

Eternal Now (also known as *Stand Still Time*), radio, ABC, 1946;

Blood on the Coal, radio, *Australian Walkabout: Newcastle (NSW),* ABC, 4 September 1947;

From Coal to Steel, radio, *Australian Walkabout: Newcastle (NSW),* ABC, 11 September 1947;

Divorce, by Cusack and John Thompson, radio, ABC, 1947;

Mary Reiby, radio, ABC, 1947;

Caddie, radio, serial, WA–ABC, 1953;

Stand Still Time, BBC-TV, U.K., 24 December 1954;

Come In Spinner, radio, Melbourne, serial, Radio 3UZ, 1954;

The Golden Girls, radio, ABC, 1954;

Pacific Paradise, radio, ABC, December 1955;

Red Sky at Morning, radio, ABC, 1957;

The Stranger on Christmas Eve, radio, ABC, 1957;

Heatwave in Berlin, radio, serial, BBC-UK, 1961;

The Half-Burnt Tree, television, Prague, Czechoslovakia, 1979;

Come In Spinner, by Cusack, Florence James, Nick Enright, and Lisa Benyon, television, two-part miniseries, ABC, Australia, 1990.

OTHER: *Shallow Cups,* in *Eight Plays by Australians* (Melbourne: Melbourne Dramatists' Club, 1934);

"Mary Reiby and Her Times," in *The Peaceful Army,* edited by Flora Eldershaw (Sydney: Women's Executive Committee and Advisory Council of Australia's 150th Anniversary Celebrations, 1938), pp. 37–58;

"You Won't Mind the Ghost," in *Pillar to Post: A Collection of Australian Short Stories Selected at Random,* edited by Harley Matthews (Sydney: Frank Johnson, 1944), pp. 34–39;

Miles Franklin: A Tribute from Her Friends (Melbourne: Bread and Cheese Club, 1955), pp. 25–26;

Mary Gilmore—A Tribute, by Cusack, Tom Inglis Moore, Barrie Ovenden, and Walter Stone (Sydney: Australasian Book Society, 1965);

"The Christmas Tree," in *Women of the Whole World* (1965); reprinted in *The Tracks We Travel: Fourth Collection,* edited by Leslie Haylen (Sydney: Australasian Book Society, 1976), pp. 19–23;

Cusack and Norman Freehill, *Dymphna* (Melbourne: Thomas Nelson, 1975);

"Foreword," in *Fifty Years of Feminist Achievement: A History of the United Association of Women,* by Winifred Mitchell (Sydney: UAW, 1979);

Call Up Your Ghosts, in *The Penguin Anthology of Australian Women's Writing,* edited by Dale Spender (Ringwood, Vic.: Penguin, 1988).

SELECTED PERIODICAL PUBLICATIONS—UNCOLLECTED: "Rupert Brook: War's Tragic Waste," as Ella D. Cusack, *Sydney Morning Herald,* 23 April 1927, p. 11;

"The Gateway: Dympna [sic] Cusack Tells How the Spirit of Peter Came Back on Anzac Day," *Sydney Bulletin,* 23 April 1930, pp. 49–50;

"The Sins of the Fathers," *Illustrated London News,* Christmas supplement, December 1951, a–f;

"How I Write," in *Westerly,* no. 3 (1960), pp. 32–35;

"Pacific Paradise: A Play in 13 Scenes by Dymphna Cusack," *Theatregoer,* 3, no. 1 (March 1963);

"The Cultural Cringe in Australian Universities' Study of Australian Literature," in *Social Alternatives* (St. Lucia, Queensland), 1, no. 5 (1979): 79–93;

"From: An Autobiography That I Shall Never Write," in *Hecate,* 6, no. 2 (1980): 84–87.

Cusack during her time at boarding school in Armidale, 1917–1920 (National Library of Australia)

Dymphna Cusack regarded herself, in Jean-Paul Sartre's phrase, as an "écrivain engagé"—one for whom the pen was mightier than the sword. According to Andrea Lofthouse in *Who's Who of Australian Women* (1982), Cusack said,

> I believe that a writer should be in the vanguard of society, analysing her community, its influence on people, and describing through her characters its benign or malign results. I am a socialist, believing that no country or individual should own less than another. As a humanist, I believe that all persons are equally important in life.

Diminutive in stature, with a fragile constitution frequently ravaged by remitting/relapsing symptoms of multiple sclerosis (MS; her "dog's disease"), she was, nonetheless, a courageous and high-profile antinuclear activist in the World Peace Movement during the Cold War era.

A committed social reformer, she wrote her own interpretation of living history as she dramatized the lives of ordinary people. She dealt with the dominant social and political issues of her times, using the channels of popular culture—the little theaters, the lending-library novel, radio and television drama and documentaries, and the daily press—to entertain, inform, and above all educate, for at heart she was always a teacher.

Many of her plays and novels were translated into more than thirty languages worldwide, and she was a critically acclaimed and best-selling author across Europe from the 1950s to the 1990s. Several of her novels sold in the millions in Russia, Hungary, Germany, and Poland, where she maintains a following. Yet, while Cusack also enjoyed a wide Australian readership, she was not given due critical attention in her own country during her lifetime. Active since the mid 1930s in socialist and social-justice organizations, in 1949 she became the partner of journalist Norman Randolph Freehill (1892–1984), the founding member of the Communist Party of Australia (CPA); they married in 1962. The conservative (largely Sydney) literary establishment during the Cold War era excluded her from the developing canon of Australian literature largely because of her leftist associations. The CPA newspaper *Tribune,* oddly enough, frequently criticized her fiction as being outside its preferred "social realist" framework.

Ellen Dymphna "Nell" Cusack was born on 21 September 1902 in West Wyalong, a gold mining boomtown in the central west of New South Wales. Of southern Irish-Catholic stock, her paternal great-uncle, Timothy Cusack, was transported for sedition in 1827, and her maternal grandfather, Michael Crowley, had been a rebel Fenian, migrating to New South Wales in the 1840s. The third of six (surviving) children born to James and Bridget Beatrice Cusack, Cusack was a frequently ill and fractious infant, and her mother's childless sister, Nell, and husband, Tom Leahy, took over the young child's rearing in 1905. Recognizing their ward as a talented and precocious scholar, her surrogate parents paid for her secondary education at the Ursuline Convent Boarding School in Armidale. At this school Cusack gained the Divinity Prize and her Leaving Certificate in 1920, with honors in English and modern history, winning an Exhibition and Teachers' College Scholarship to Sydney University.

At Sydney (1922–1925) Cusack's principal academic mentors were Foundation Professor of History George Arnold Wood and the pioneer Freudian who became the first professor of psychology in Australia, Henry Tasman Lovell. In her undergraduate years Cusack began lifelong friendships with writer Florence James, Marie Beuzeville Byles—the first practicing female solicitor in New South Wales—and writer Christina Stead; at Manning House, in Women's Union teams, they debated the "Russian experiment," eugenics, birth control, and women's right to a career.

The Sydney University Drama Society took Cusack into the "little theatre" world of the city and the mentorship of Duncan Macdougall, a Scottish thespian who in the 1920s set up The Players' Club in his atelier above Rowe Street, Sydney, haunt of the bohemian literati. Cusack's novice play script, *Safety First* (first performed, 1928)–a feminist drama with themes of illegitimacy, middle-class hypocrisy, and a liberated "New Woman" as heroine–was runner-up in the 1927 *Triad* magazine competition.

In 1929, as the Great Depression gained momentum in Australia, Cusack was posted by the Department of Education to the high school at Broken Hill, a silver, lead, and zinc mining town in the far western desert of New South Wales. Her armchair socialism was radicalized as she witnessed the injustice and inhumanity of industrial exploitation in a remote location where the health and safety of the miners and their families were readily sacrificed for profit. Her unpublished play "Strange Victory" transposed the miners' self-defeating struggle for improved conditions to that of the timber-cutters in the cedar forests of northern New South Wales. With almost–but not quite–melodramatic effect she counterpoints a brutal naturalism to depict the boss versus the worker in the timber camp conflicts with a surrealistic, backlit, ghostly chorus of their predecessors: the enslaved early convicts, the massacred Aborigines, and the old-growth trees themselves. She refined this dramatic contrast of styles–hyperrealism set against hypersurrealism–in her feminist Gothic tragicomedy *Shallow Cups* (1933), which became a "little theatre" classic. Her radio plays from the period–such as *His Honour Comes to Tea* (1933) and *Second Rhapsody* (1933)–while dealing with gender politics, interpersonal ethics, and social critique also effectively exploit this stylized technique.

In Broken Hill (1928-1930) Cusack wrote her first (unpublished) novel, "This Nettle Danger." A rite-of-passage, highly autobiographical work, it was rejected by English publisher Gerald Duckworth for its antireligious tone: the heroine–an idealistic, university-educated young "New Woman"–intellectually and emotionally divests herself of the Roman Catholicism of her upbringing. Cusack returned to drama, convinced it was where her talent lay, and the resultant plays, *Anniversary* (1935) and *Red Sky at Morning* (1935), were immediate and enduring successes.

Back in Sydney in 1935 and teaching at the prestigious Sydney Girls' High School after six years of "country service" in Broken Hill, Goulburn, and Parramatta, Cusack completed a second novel, *Jungfrau*, which was runner-up in 1935 for the Prior Memorial Prize, sponsored by *The Bulletin*, and published in 1936. The dialectic of the novel is that of Cusack's undergraduate debates–God, sex, power, and gender politics. The book gained her widespread critical respect. The plot, however, involving corrupted innocence, adultery, abortion, and suicide, left her vulnerable to the conservative forces in the educational politics of Sydney, and her high profile at Sydney Girls' High School ensured that she was much talked of around the town. She was active in the New South Wales teachers' union, and the Teachers' Federation Players produced her plays, including a burlesque caricature of the Education Ministry and its policies. She was high profile in the Fellowship of Australian Writers (FAW) from 1936; her radio documentary series were provocative and challenged social orthodoxies; and she was a media celebrity who was quoted for her witty one-liners and daring opinions.

By 1939, when Angus and Robertson published Cusack's collaboration with Miles Franklin, a pasquinade on Sydney's sesquicentennial celebrations of British colonial settlement–the novel *Pioneers on Parade* (1939), in which the pair wickedly lampooned the upper echelons of Sydney society, whose key figures were only thinly disguised–she had taken on one too many sacred cows. In mid December 1939 Cusack's lawyers won her a landmark victory in her workers' compensation case against the Education Department. That Christmas Eve she was punitively "transferred" to a supernumerary position at Bathurst High.

Her revenge was the prizewinning "female staffroom bitchiness" play *Morning Sacrifice* (performed, 1942; published, 1943), which has remained in print and is played almost annually by both amateur and professional companies. Cusack spent World War II in Bathurst, Parkes, and Newcastle. As ever, she was an astute and empathetic observer of ordinary people living out their time and place in history; from these years of an all-time low in her teaching career came the rich store of observation and experience that she turned into a spate of postwar radio plays and documentaries and the novel *Southern Steel* (1953), which David Allen adapted for the stage for the successful 1991 season of Newcastle Theatre Company.

Another play written during that period, *Comets Soon Pass* (first performed, 1943; first published, 1950), functioned for Cusack as a vehicle for artistic revenge for the defection of a lover, novelist Xavier Herbert, who, according to the 1998 biography of Herbert by Frances de Groen, had "exploited women to nurture his 'genius' and allay sexual fears." According to Cusack's "Notes for an Autobiography I Will Never Write," *Comets Soon Pass* also served as payback to the "local nabob" of the Bathurst-Parkes district, "aspara-

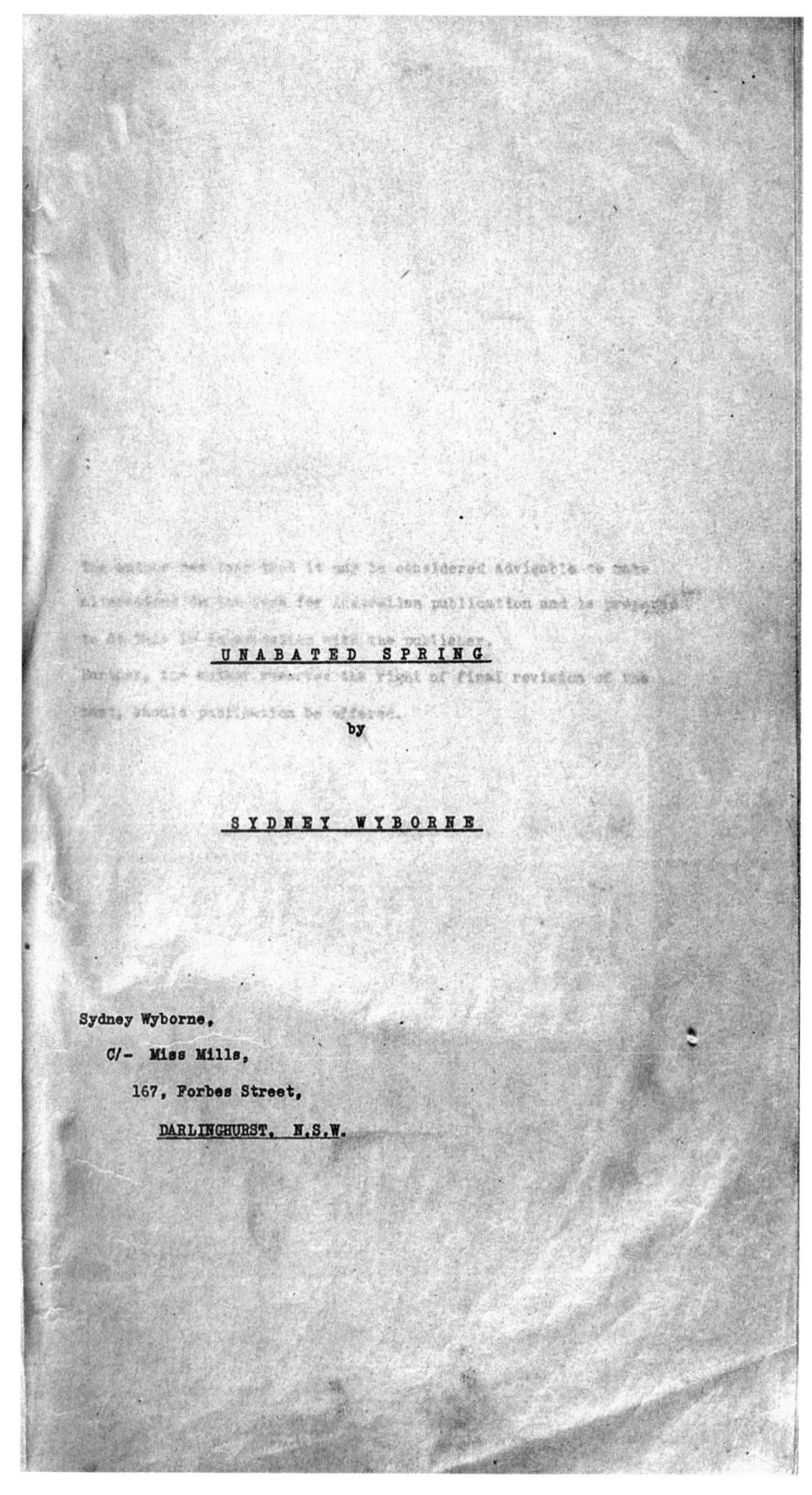

Opening pages of the typescript for the pseudonymous work that won Cusack and co-author Florence James The Daily Telegraph *novel competition in 1948; it was published three years later as* Come In Spinner *(National Library of Australia, MS4621)*

FRIDAY - 1

Blue opened the lift door at the second floor of the South-Pacific hotel. "All aboard," he said cheerfully to the two American officers waiting.

They lifted a finger in friendly greeting. "Just hold it a minute Blue," the Lieutenant looked back along the corridor, "Homer's apparently still round in the Gloucester Room telling his goodbyes. He won't be a minute."

"Good-oh Loot." The lift bell buzzed, Blue looked at the indicator and jerked it. "You can wait," he said amiably to the invisible caller.

"Here he comes."

A lanky sergeant pelted down the corridor and into the lift. "Whew! I w-w-was afraid you'd be g-g-gone," he stuttered.

"Trust us Serg." Blue clapped him affectionately on the shoulder. "Wait all day for you, we would."

"That's real nice B-b-blue," the Sergeant grinned and flicked a cigarette out of a packet of Camels towards him. "Butt?"

"Thanks." Blue opened his maroon tunic and tucked the cigarette away in the pocket of his faded khaki shirt, buttoned up the tunic again and started the lift. "How did the shivoo go off?"

"Swell. Nicest party I've been to since my kid sister graduated. Ellery sure is a lucky guy to get a girl like that."

"And is she easy on the eye," the Loot clicked his tongue admiringly.

"Sure," drawled the young airman, "and sweet as they come."

The sergeant drew a deep sigh. "That's l-l-l-love for you," he said, "C-c-can anyone tell me why no g-g-girl ever looks at me the way Ellery's g-g-girl looks at him?"

gus king" Gordon Edgell–founder of a canned food empire–who had tried to damn Cusack publicly for her social-welfare activism. Edgell himself had financially backed the New Guard, the protofascist, vigilante strikebreakers in the mining and rural industries during the Great Depression.

From January to September 1941 Cusack had taken a leave of absence from teaching while her mother was too ill to take care of the family investment property, "Karoon," a block of bachelor apartments in Orwell Street, Kings Cross. While there Cusack witnessed the United States Army's "occupation" of Sydney during the Pacific War and the none-too-subtle corruption of the naive female citizenry in particular, as they became the recreational objects of the United States troops, "over-paid, over-sexed and over here." Cusack's experiences that year formed the core of the best-selling novel, *Come In Spinner* (1951), which she later wrote in collaboration with Florence James.

Early in 1944 Cusack's always perilous health broke down completely, and she was pensioned out of the Department of Education. For two decades she had been torn between her need to teach and her desire to write, but now she was "unemployed at last." James, who had married Pym Heyting and had returned to Australia with two baby daughters late in 1938, was being eased out of her wartime post as public-relations officer with the Royal Prince Albert Hospital to make way for a returned serviceman. As the year wore on, the two women decided to pool their resources and rent a cottage in the Blue Mountains, where they could recuperate and write. "Pinegrove," in Valley Road, Hazelbrook, became the "sunlit island in Time" where they practiced collaborating on a children's book, *Four Winds and a Family* (1947), before rigorously planning and co-writing the classic wartime epic of Sydney, *Come In Spinner*.

As they worked, Cusack continued with her own radio dramas and documentaries, with the draft of the future novel *Southern Steel,* and on a further satiric collaboration with Franklin, *Call Up Your Ghosts* (first performed, 1945; first published, 1988). In 1946 *The Daily Telegraph* (Sydney) newspaper announced its £1,000 Prize Novel Competition, and so began the saga that–although *Come In Spinner* was awarded the prize in 1948–effectively delayed its publication until 1951. The satirical exposé in the novel of both low-life and high society in wartime Sydney borders on the carnivalesque; however, its potential for libel suits–which lay in the truth of its descriptions of locations and of the vice industries specific to them (including the sale of illicit booze, gambling, prostitution, and abortion) and the caricatures of those who profited by them (including politicians, viceregal candidates, and well-known media personalities)–made for a book that was too hot for *The Daily Telegraph* to handle. The collaborators reclaimed their manuscript with the legal aid of solicitor Marie Byles, eventually publishing it in England with William Heinemann. The review by eminent critic and bibliophile Michael Sadleir in the *Sunday Times* (London) ensured its critical success: according to Sadleir, "To lose oneself in *Come In Spinner* is indeed a stirring and memorable experience." The book was an immediate best-seller and has become a classic.

In 1947–1948, after James and her daughters had returned to Britain, Cusack lost, in quick succession, her surrogate parents, Uncle Tom and Aunt Nell Leahy; several close friends of her Newcastle years; her own mother; and then her younger friend Kay Keen. Keen's courageous and drawn-out battle with tuberculosis provided the inspiration and the impetus for the novel *Say No to Death* (1951). Late in 1948 Cusack took up her long-term, if intermittent, relationship with Norman Freehill. As the Cold War gained momentum, the Australian political scene was becoming dangerous for CPA members: the ultraconservative Menzies government was trying various strategies to render the party illegal while unleashing police persecution and media harassment, thus creating a climate of fear and suspicion bleakly lampooned as the "Reds under the bed" campaign, the equivalent in Australia to McCarthyism in the United States.

In mid May 1949 Cusack sailed for Europe on the *Georgic* via the Panama Canal. Two months later Freehill followed, via the Suez Canal, on the *Esperance Bay*. On the voyage Cusack witnessed the insidious racism of the British colonists when the *Georgic* took on board seven hundred West Indians in the Caribbean bound for the heart of the British Empire. This firsthand experience of racial hatred and her subsequent, enduring friendship with one of the Jamaicans, a chiropractor, and his European wife, triggered the novel *The Sun in Exile* (1955). In what is technically one of her most competent works, Cusack tackles the difficult task of first-person narration in the voice of a conservative, middle-aged, female travel writer whose White-Australian, middle-class assumptions are gradually eroded as she learns, not without difficulty, to empathize with the younger generation and the postcolonial dilemma. Cusack re-creates and transmutes the substance of her own experiences through a cinematic sequence of scenes that culminate in racial violence on the streets of London.

The Sun in Exile received a United Kingdom Book Society recommendation. The reviewer for *The Spectator* (10 June 1955) wrote, "It is an interesting study of the dispossessed. Colored men about London. Australians at odds with Europe. Flotsam of all kinds washed up from the enormous unfriendliness of the world seen through the narrator's own emotional ambiguity." Expatriate Australians in London at the time thought that this diffident narrator must be Cusack's alter ego, but in Cusack's characteristic mode, the middle-aged Alexandra Pendlebury is a blend–according to Cusack's papers held by the National Library of Australia (NLA)–"a composite of three fine women."

From late 1949 in her Belgravia flat, health permitting, Cusack worked to a strictly regimented daily writing routine, and, under Freehill's care and with his expert subediting skills for final drafts and proofing, she nurtured into print the four manuscripts that had arrived with her in London–*Come In Spinner, Say No to Death, Southern Steel,* and *Caddie, A Sydney Barmaid. An Autobiography Written by Herself* (1953)–and wrote *The Sun in Exile*. Dealing initially with Heinemann (who had handled *Come In Spinner*) and with Constable from *Southern Steel* onward until Sadleir's death, Freehill negotiated the publishing and publicity schedules to optimize Cusack's success. From 1951 to 1956 Freehill and Cusack traveled to the south of France for the winter months as the cold in London exacerbated Cusack's MS symptoms.

From his arrival in the United Kingdom, Freehill had been politically active with Lady Jessie Street on both Communist Party and Peace Movement agendas. They were delegates together to the 1950 Warsaw Second World Peace Conference and worked to set up the Authors' World Peace Appeal in the West. Cusack had been too ill to travel to Warsaw; nevertheless, she orchestrated the successful campaign that thwarted the efforts of the Australian government to impound the visas of its citizens traveling to Warsaw or any other Iron Curtain destinations during the Cold War.

Cusack and James reaped their just rewards for patience and tenacity in protecting the integrity of *Come In Spinner*. Cusack's *Say No to Death* was ready to follow the meteoric path of *Come In Spinner,* and Freehill ensured that her established best-seller status gave her negotiating strength for future contracts. James was offered a job as a reader and talent scout for Constable and Company, from which base she helped many Australian writers into print in the United Kingdom.

In 1954, after several months in Middlesex Neurological Hospital paralyzed by her MS symptoms, Cusack dictated the anti-bomb play *Pacific Paradise* (1955), which made her reputation across Asia, Eastern Europe, and the Pacific. Triggered by the United States atomic tests on Bikini Atoll, the theme was timely, the location exotic. It was runner-up to Ray Lawler's *Summer of the Seventeenth Doll* (1955) in the 1955 Playwrights' Advisory Board Competition and adapted for Australian Broadcasting Commission (ABC) radio. It was

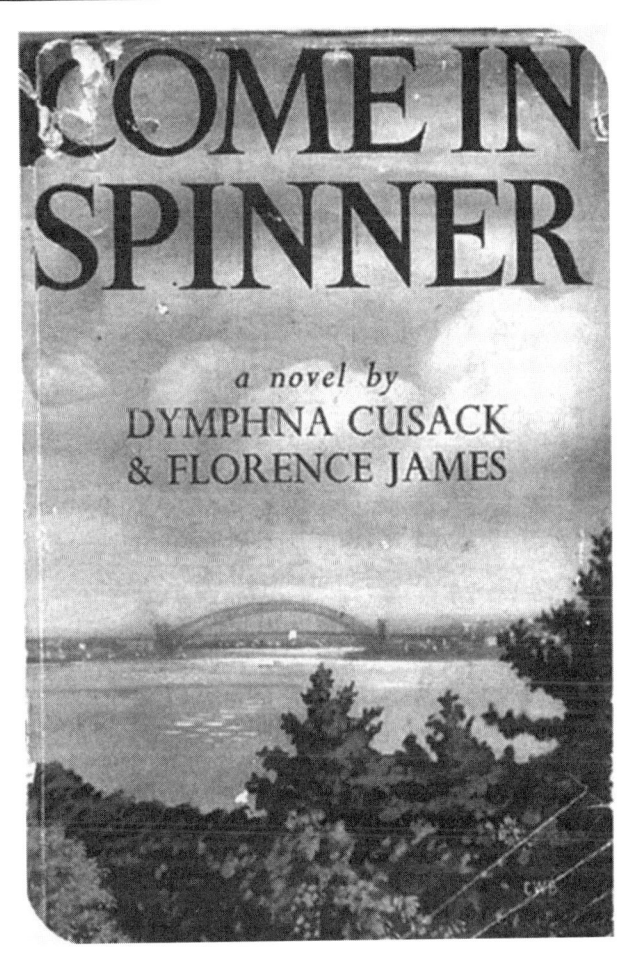

Dust jacket for Cusack's 1951 best-seller, a satirical novel about life in Sydney during World War II (from Marilla North, ed., Yarn Spinners, *2001)*

translated and played worldwide and in 1956 brought Cusack an invitation to its premiere in Peking, where she and Freehill arrived in June 1956 and stayed until December 1958. Freehill ran the Foreign Languages Press in Peking, and Cusack researched and wrote the collection of pen portraits and the sociohistorical documentary *Chinese Women Speak* (1958). She returned briefly to Australia in 1957 and placed it with publishers Angus and Robertson. It was later also published in translation in Russia, Germany, and Albania.

In the winter of 1958–1959, en route to London from Peking, Cusack accidentally witnessed an SS officers' reunion and the beginnings of the neo-Nazi cult in Germany. The result was *Heatwave in Berlin* (1961), which was immediately translated and published in Denmark, Holland, Norway, and France, and in 1962 in Russia and many of the other Soviet republics. From 1959 onward, beginning with *Pacific Paradise,* her works had begun to be published in the Eastern European countries, providing her with royalty payments that were largely untransferable; hence

Dust jacket for Cusack's 1962 novel, a small-town comedy published the year of her marriage and return to Australia (Bruccoli Clark Layman Archives)

she and Freehill began a nomadic annual schedule back and forth from East to West, living on her earnings and writing out of the cultural experiences, including *Holidays among the Russians* (1964), *Illyria Reborn* (1966), newspaper and magazine features, and more serious sociopolitical journalism.

On 21 June 1962 Freehill and Cusack married in the United Kingdom and returned together to Australia for the first time since 1949. Her recently published novel, a small-town comedy dedicated "To [her] pioneering ancestors," *Picnic Races* (1962) was both an atonement for *Pioneers on Parade* and an entrée card for the returning exile. Cusack became associated with Faith and Hans Bandler in the Aboriginal rights movement and over 1963 wrote *Black Lightning* (1964), a book of its time in which she experimented with free indirect style and multiple voices and which became a popular success in France and Eastern Europe, where it was translated, published, serialized in the press, and adapted for television.

Heatwave in Berlin, translated and adapted for the Maly Theatre in Moscow by Irina Golovnya (Nikolay Vasilyevich Gogol's great-niece), was staged and televised across the U.S.S.R. as part of the 1965 celebrations of the Twentieth Anniversary of Victory over Fascism, at which Freehill and Cusack were official guests. During the next few years Cusack researched and wrote *The Sun Is Not Enough* (1967), thematically linked to *Heatwave in Berlin* and equally popular. Family problems brought her back to Australia in 1967, the year of the referendum that belatedly gave citizenship rights to the Aboriginal people in their own land. *The Half-Burnt Tree* (1969) was the result of this period; a book ahead of its time, it incorporates themes of deracination, misguided paternalistic social welfare policies, the Vietnam War, and emotional isolation. It was widely translated, published, and serialized across Europe. In 1968 Cusack was elected president of the FAW and initiated the project of documenting its history that Len Fox completed and published as *Dream at a Graveside* (1989).

Cusack's experiences of her sister Bea's battle with alcoholism resulted in *A Bough in Hell* (1971). The social documentary is realistic and makes for grim reading. Critically it is her most neglected novel.

In 1972 Cusack and Freehill settled on Sydney's lower north shore, living in Balgowlah, Fairy Bower, and eventually in Wesley Heights, Manly. In 1975 Cusack was named Woman of the Year by the Union of Australian Women; in 1976, a lifelong republican, she refused the Order of the British Empire. She wrote several further novels (unpublished) about social justice and environmental issues of the 1970s and about personal issues, including terminal illness and euthanasia. She and Freehill both continued to be active in the local Russian and Chinese cultural and friendship organizations and in civil rights and social justice politics, and Cusack founded a Manly Branch of the FAW, mentoring fledgling writers and especially senior citizens. In 1973 the government awarded Cusack a Literary Pension. In 1975 an International Women's Year grant initiated the production of *Caddie* as a motion picture starring Helen Morse, Jackie Weaver, and Jack Thompson, which premiered in Sydney in 1975 and in London in 1977.

In 1975 Thomas Nelson, Melbourne, published the autobiographical travelogue *Dymphna*, by Freehill with Cusack, based on a series of taped interviews that he had been making with Cusack since the mid 1960s. Although they were both increasingly frail, they traveled to and wrote about Fiji and Noumea (1976), Hong Kong (1977), Southeast Asia (1979), and finally South America for the "Carnivale" in Rio de Janeiro in 1980–by their preferred mode, cargo ship. Since 1978 Cusack had known that her disease was multiple sclerosis, and it was becoming rapidly progressive. From December 1980 she was completely paralyzed. Dymphna Cusack's significant contribution to Australian and world literature was acknowledged with the award of the Order of Australia prior to her death on 19 October 1981.

Manning Clark wrote to her on 23 June 1980:

> I hope by now a whole host of people has told you of their debt to you. I am one of your debtors—and you can think of the work in Australian History as being in part the product of your example.

His comments sum up Cusack's impact on her society and her contribution to human understanding during a period when politically constructed Cold War barriers had created mammoth psychological impediments to travel, cultural exchange, and simple human contact.

Letters:

Yarn Spinners: A Story in Letters between Dymphna Cusack, Miles Franklin and Florence James: 1928–54, edited by Marilla North (St. Lucia: University of Queensland Press, 2001).

Interviews:

Hazel de Berg, "Dymphna Cusack," National Library of Australia Oral Archives, 8 October 1964;

Pamela Barnett, "Norman Freehill and Dymphna Cusack," Sydney, ABC, October 1975;

Lindy Kerr, Tony Joyce, and Company, "Dymphna Cusack at the ABC [Australian Broadcasting Commission]," NLA Oral History Program, 13 September 1979;

Kath Gollan, "Dymphna Cusack at Manly," ABC–RADA, 1979;

Marilla North, group discussion with Cusack and Florence James, Abbotsford, Sydney, October 1980;

Pamela Williams, "Dymphna Cusack," *Coming Out Show,* no. 13, ABC, 1981;

Williams, "A Sense of Worth: Dymphna Cusack on Her Life and Work," in *Coming Out: Women's Voices, Women's Lives,* edited by Julie Rigg and Julie Copeland (Melbourne: Thomas Nelson, 1985);

Bruce Molloy, "Interview with Dymphna Cusack," *Imago,* 1, no. 2 (September 1989): 42–52.

Bibliographies:

Debra Adelaide, *Australian Women Writers: A Bibliographic Guide* (London: Pandora Press, 1988);

Adelaide, "Australian Women's Literature: A Bibliography to 1988. Part II: Special Study of Dymphna Cusack," dissertation, Sydney University, 1990;

Marilla North, ed., "Chronology," in *Yarn Spinners: A Story in Letters between Dymphna Cusack, Miles Franklin and Florence James: 1928–1954* (St. Lucia: University of Queensland Press, 2001).

References:

Jack Beasley, *Socialism and the Novel: A Study of Australian Literature* (Petersham, N.S.W.: J. Beasley, 1957);

Dennis Carroll, *Australian Contemporary Drama 1909–1982, A Critical Introduction* (New York: Peter Lang, 1985);

David Carter, "Journeys in Genre: Australian Literary Travellers to the Soviet Union," in *And What Books Do You Read? New Studies in Australian Literature,* edited by Irmtraud Petersson and Martin Duwell (St. Lucia: University of Queensland Press, 1996);

Clem Christesen, "A Room with a View: Impressions of Germany and the Soviet Union," *Meanjin,* 24, no. 3 (1965): 395;

Susan Dianna Cullen, "Australian War Drama: 1909–1939," dissertation, University of Queensland, 1989;

Frances de Groen, "Dymphna Cusack's 'Comets Soon Pass': The Genius and the Potato Wife," in *Wallflowers and Witches: Women and Culture in Australia;*

1910–1945, edited by Maryanne Dever (St. Lucia: University of Queensland Press, 1989), pp. 91–104;

de Groen, *Xavier Herbert: A Biography* (St. Lucia: University of Queensland Press, 1998);

J. K. Ewers, "Sermons in Steel," *Voice,* 2 (1953): 24;

Len Fox, *Dream at a Graveside: History of the Fellowship of Australian Writers,* (Sydney: FAW, 1989);

Florence James and Marilla North, "*Come In Spinner:* An Addendum," *Meanjin,* 49, no. 1 (Autumn 1990): 178–188;

Joseph Jones and Johanna Jones, "Postwar: Exile and Hope," in *Australian Fiction* (Boston: Twayne, 1983), pp. 63–86;

Victoria Katlyrova, "Romany Dimfna K'uizek: Dymphna Cusack's Place in Australian Literature against the Background of Australian Social Realist Novels of the 1930s," dissertation, Pedagogical Institute Krupskaya (Moscow), 1969;

V. H. Lloyd, "Conscience and Justice: A Study in Conflict in the Novels and Plays of Dymphna Cusack," M.A. thesis, University of Queensland, 1987;

Andrea Lofthouse, ed., *Who's Who of Australian Women* (Sydney: Methuen Australia, 1982);

Susan McKernan, *A Question of Commitment: Australian Literature in the Twenty Years After the War* (Sydney: Allen & Unwin, 1989), pp. 20–49;

Drusilla Modjeska, *Exiles at Home: Australian Women Writers 1925–45* (Sydney: Angus & Robertson, 1981);

North, "The Anatomy of a Best-Seller: The Making of 'Come In Spinner,'" M.A. thesis, University of Wollongong, 1991;

North, "Dymphna Cusack: Beautiful Exile: An Epistolary and Cautionary Tale of What Happens to Tall Poppies When They Take on the Big End of Town," *Hecate,* 25, no. 2 (1999): 135–155;

North, "Tinker, Tailor, Soldier, Sailor: Who Was Norman Randolph Freehill?" *Overland,* 161 (Summer 2000): 36–42;

Susan Pfister-Smith, "Playing with the Past: Towards a Feminist Deconstruction of Australian Theatre Histriography," in *Australasian Drama Studies,* 23 (October 1993): 8–22;

Leslie Rees, *The Making of Australian Drama, a Historical and Critical Survey from the 1830s to the 1970s* (Sydney: Angus & Robertson, 1973);

Rees, *Towards an Australian Drama* (Sydney: Angus & Robertson, 1953);

Jill Roe, ed., *My Congenials: Miles Franklin and Friends in Letters,* 2 volumes (Sydney: State Library of New South Wales in association with Angus & Robertson, 1993);

Susan Sheridan, "Women Writers," *Australian Literary Studies,* 13, no. 4 (October 1988): 319– ;

Monica Stirling, "Dymphna Cusack: A Profile," *Meanjin,* 25 (1965): 317–325;

Helen Thompson, "Dymphna Cusack's Plays," *Australasian Drama Studies,* 32 (April 1998): 63–76;

Mary Wilson, "The Perceptions of the Novelist into Australia and Australian Society: 1920–1939," M.A. thesis, La Trobe University, 1972.

Papers:

Dymphna Cusack's papers are held in the National Library of Australia, Canberra, and her literary executors have added to them since her death. Several other NLA collections include letters from Cusack. Additional material is in the Mitchell Library, Sydney. The Australian Broadcasting Commission Archive holds some of Cusack's radio drama and documentary scripts, and the Campbell Howard Collection at the University of New England Library houses most of her play scripts.

Eleanor Dark

(26 August 1901 – 11 September 1985)

Barbara Brooks

BOOKS: *Slow Dawning* (London: Long, 1932);

Prelude to Christopher (Sydney & Melbourne: Stephensen, 1934; London: Collins, 1936);

Return To Coolami: A Novel (London: Collins, 1936; New York: Macmillan, 1936; London & Sydney: Angus & Robertson, 1981);

Sun across the Sky (London: Collins, 1937; New York: Macmillan, 1937; Sydney: Collins, 1946);

Waterway (London: Collins, 1938; New York: Macmillan, 1938; Sydney: Johnston, 1946);

The Timeless Land (London: Collins, 1941; New York: Macmillan, 1941; Sydney: Collins, 1963);

The Little Company (New York: Macmillan, 1945; Sydney: Collins, 1945);

Storm of Time (London: Collins, 1948; New York: Whittlesey House, 1950; London & Sydney: Angus & Robertson, 1980);

No Barrier (Sydney: Collins, 1953; London: Collins, 1954);

Lantana Lane (London & Sydney: Collins, 1959).

OTHER: "The Leader," in *Australian Writers' Annual*, edited by Flora Eldershaw (Sydney: Fellowship of Australian Writers, 1936), pp. 24–27;

"Caroline Chisholm and Her Times," in *The Peaceful Army*, edited by Eldershaw (Sydney: Women's Executive Committee and Advisory Council of Australia's 150th Anniversary Celebrations, 1938), pp. 55–85;

"Australia and the Australians," in *Australia Weekend Book,* volume 3, edited by Sydney Ure Smith and Gwen Morton Spencer (Sydney: Ure Smith, 1944), pp. 9–19;

This Land of Ours–Australia, edited by George Farwell and F. H. Johnston, introduction by Dark (Sydney: Angus & Robertson, 1949).

SELECTED PERIODICAL PUBLICATIONS–UNCOLLECTED:

POETRY
"My House," as P.O'R., *Triad,* 10 June 1921, p. 27.

Eleanor Dark, 1945 (photograph by Olive Cotton)

FICTION
"Take Your Choice," as P.O'R., *Bulletin,* 7 June 1923, pp. 47–48;

"Wind," as Patricia O'Rane, *Bulletin,* 21 January 1926, pp. 47–48;

"Benevolence," as O'Rane, *Triad,* 1 July 1926, pp. 4–6;

"The Urgent Call," *Home,* 1 August 1935, pp. 44–45;

"Water in Moko Creek," *Australia: National Journal* (March 1946): 17–21;

"A Writer with a Last Story to Write . . . ," *Hecate*, 27, no. 1 (2001): 67–72.

NONFICTION

"Drawing a Line around It," *Writer*, 59 (October 1946): 323–325;

"They All Come Back," *Walkabout*, 17 (1 January 1951): 19–20;

"The Blackall Range Country," *Walkabout*, 21 (1 November 1955): 18–20;

"Balancing the Scales," *Hecate*, 27, no. 1 (2001): 65–66.

Eleanor Dark was one of the most highly regarded and widely read writers in Australia during the 1930s and 1940s, two decades that were crucial in the development of Australian writing and literary culture. She published ten novels, as well as writing essays, poems, stories, plays, and radio scripts. Her work was published in the United Kingdom and the United States as well as in Australia and translated into French, German, Swedish, and Italian. *The Timeless Land* (1941) was a best-seller in Australia and the United States by the standards of the time. Her work was admired by her writer contemporaries at the same time as it was widely read. Her novels combine the influences of European modernism and psychoanalytic insights with elements of the popular genre the romance novel; her work reflects the major social changes and intellectual debates of the time but remains accessible to the general reader. Dark's writer contemporaries, predominantly women, called themselves the first generation of professional writers in Australia. They had a dream of what Australia could be; they wanted to convey in their work not only the country they lived in but also the society they wanted. Australia felt like a new country; it seemed possible to point the way to a more just and democratic society, a community that recognized and valued the arts. Dark's ideas about writing, women, politics, social justice, and sustainable ways to live in Australia seem timely even now.

Born in Sydney on 26 August 1901, Eleanor O'Reilly was the daughter of Dowell Philip O'Reilly—a poet, short-story writer, politician, schoolteacher, and member of an almost exclusively male Bohemian literary set—and Eleanor McCulloch O'Reilly, who died when her daughter was thirteen. Eleanor, known as Pixie to her family and friends, had a difficult childhood: her parents argued; they had no money; her father was absent for long periods; and her mother suffered a kind of nervous collapse. After her mother's death in 1914, Eleanor, her father, and her two brothers were split up; Eleanor went to her maternal grandmother's eccentric household in Mosman, a harborside suburb of Sydney, then to a progressive boarding school for girls. Then she went to secretarial college, which she hated, and worked as a secretary for a firm of lawyers for a short time. On 1 February 1922, at age twenty-one, she married Eric Payten Dark, a doctor who had been a student at the Sydney Grammar School where her father taught. Twelve years older than she and recently returned from the European war, Eric was still devastated by his war experiences and the death of his first wife shortly after the birth of their son, John Oliver. Eleanor and Eric married after a brief—and secret—affair, a trial marriage. She told him she wanted to write and she wanted a child. In 1923 they moved to the Blue Mountains, a wilderness area west of Sydney. She described the area in *Return to Coolami* (1936) as "High cliffs and tangled gullies dwarfed into deceptive flatness by the great expanses round them. Savage country, all but unknown, drowned in its mysterious and ineffable blue." Eric Dark became a general practitioner in Katoomba, the small town where they lived for more than sixty years. He gave Eleanor the financial, emotional, and moral support that had been lacking in her childhood; he was as interested in writing and her writing career as she was. What she achieved as a writer was partly a result of his support and influence.

During Eleanor's childhood, Dowell O'Reilly held court in an eccentric literary household, while his daughter listened to his arguments with friends such as the poet Christopher Brennan and artists such as the Lindsays. She said her father brought her up to question everything; to lead the kind of life she wanted, she had to question some of his ideas. He believed that women were fulfilled by children and would be tormented and unhappy if they tried to lead intellectual lives. Prone to depression—he called himself "a spiritual tempest in a tea-cup"—he was unhappy about his own achievements as a writer.

Dark, also prone to depression, anxiety, and volatile moods, cultivated her privacy. The outward appearance of her life was conventional and bourgeois, but she was independent, tough-minded, and deeply scornful of the merely conventional. When she and Eric Dark set up house in Katoomba, it was as if they were building a life for themselves according to carefully examined and strongly held principles, a life to be lived fully, both physically and mentally. They were generous people, but there was a kind of austerity about their lives. Dark longed for a sense of harmony and calm; her house and large garden were as much expressions of her creativity as her books were. Eric's son, John, came to live with them, and their son, Brian Michael, was born in 1929. Their lives revolved around work, family, their love of books and writing, and exploring the mountain wilderness country.

In the 1920s Dark published poems, stories, and articles in literary and women's magazines under a series of pseudonyms–among them, Patricia O'Rane and P.O'R. She told Kylie Tennant in an interview for the *Sydney Morning Herald* (14 February 1974) that she sold her first poem for the price of a bag of manure for the garden. Her first novels were an autobiographical work, "Pilgrimage," never published, and *Slow Dawning* (1932). Dark disliked *Slow Dawning* and later left it off lists of her novels; she said she wrote it quickly with an eye to publication and money. The story of a young woman doctor in a country town, it has many of the features of a romance-novel plot but is thoughtful and intelligent, challenging ideas about women and their roles. She explores the conflicts in women's lives that Dowell O'Reilly wrote about; she concluded that women have suffered, but the problem is one of social roles, not gender; women can reconcile intellect and emotions.

Her second novel, *Prelude to Christopher* (1934), is one of Dark's most important works and was her favorite. It is an innovative and challenging book a novel of ideas, about madness, utopias, feminism, and eugenics–showing the influences of Freudian psychology and the European novel. Starting with Nigel Hendon, a doctor injured in a car accident, it flashes back over his marriage to Linda and their life in his utopian colony in the South Pacific. Linda is one of the most extraordinary heroines of Australian writing, powerfully intelligent, powerfully sexual, and dangerous because of her refusal to conform–"the sort of woman who made you feel she might indulge in eccentric infidelities–or take drugs–or fly about on a broomstick at Hallowe'en." Nigel refuses her desire for a child on eugenic grounds. Isolation in a narrow-minded country town exacerbates her fear of mental instability. Is she mad or pushed toward madness by the way she is treated? "Mad they called her–mad they made her," and the book ends with her suicide. *Prelude to Christopher* won Dark the respect of the women writers who were her contemporaries and the Australian Literature Society Gold Medal. "Your book will go a long way towards arousing the expectations of sensitive writing here," poet and critic Nettie Palmer wrote; "there is a rare distinction in the texture of your writing." But the book was controversial–it was described in a review for *The Sun* (10 May 1934) as "stark unrelieved tragedy," and the reviewer for *The Bulletin* (30 May 1934) found it "intentionally disjointed." *Slow Dawning* had been published in the United Kingdom; there was almost no publishing industry in Australia. But Dark wanted this novel published in Australia. She sent it to P. R. Stephensen, a passionate advocate of Australian culture, full of ideas but financially reckless. He went bankrupt shortly after her novel was published. The novel disappeared, and

Eleanor O'Reilly with her brother Pat, circa 1905 (from Barbara Brooks, Eleanor Dark, *1998)*

the Darks lost most of the money they had put toward its publication. Meanwhile, through her friendship with Palmer, Dark found a literary agent in the United Kingdom. *Prelude to Christopher* was published in London by Collins in 1936 and received good reviews.

Prelude to Christopher was a controversial book, and Dark thought there was "a Hoodoo" on it. But it brought her into a network of women writers. She exchanged letters with Miles Franklin and Palmer, and later Katherine Susannah Prichard, Jean Devanny, and Marjorie Barnard. They wrote to each other about books and writing, about politics, literary politics, about housework and families and the constant struggle for time to write, about how sometimes what they were doing seemed urgent and important, and sometimes it seemed futile, as if they were working in a vacuum. In her letters and diary, Dark wrote repeatedly about her struggle for time and her doubts and despondency about what she had achieved. The telephone was the worst interruption for her–the doctor's phone that must always be answered. Unlike her contemporaries– Barnard, who held a full-time job much of the time, or Palmer, who wrote reviews and articles to help support her novelist husband and their two children–Dark had

Eleanor O'Reilly and Eric Payten Dark at the time of their engagement, 1921 (from Brooks, Eleanor Dark, *1998)*

her husband's support. She made her contribution to the family finances by writing novels.

Return to Coolami, Sun across the Sky (1937), and *Waterway* (1938) followed in quick succession. Dark called *Return to Coolami* her "Novel with a Happy Ending," which she hoped might make some money. It was the first of her novels to be published in the United States. Like *Prelude to Christopher,* these novels were influenced by European modernism. Dark had achieved her own style and form, breaking out of a linear narrative into ways of exploring a consciousness at a time of crisis. Ranging backward and forward in time, she explored a country suspended between a colonial past and an independent future—"a future coming endlessly upon them that was not quite their future," as she described it in *Return to Coolami*—revealing the intimate relationship of the past to present and future, reflecting on the changing lives of men and women, especially women, in this period between the wars. Her adapted interior monologues give the reader the point of view of several characters, perhaps reflecting Dark's belief that the way to discover the truth about a situation was to listen to all points of view. In these novels she tracks the lives of a group of characters over a short period, a few days or a single day, using the cinematic technique of flashbacks to fill in their lives. The three novels vividly describe Australian landscapes—the "strange loveliness of an ancient land" in *Return to Coolami,* the beaches in *Sun across the Sky,* and in *Waterway,* Sydney's "glittering harbour" and Sydney as an "intimate grey city." "No characters in any books I've read are so distinctively Australian as yours," novelist and friend Eric Lowe wrote to her on 17 August 1938; "the subtle difference between us and our way of moving and seeing and thinking and all other people is coming naturally into character expression."

When *Waterway* was published in 1938, the Great Depression was past, but the Darks were aware of the rise of fascism in Europe and rumors of war. Australian intellectuals were questioning liberalism as an adequate response. "Of course, I'm a Socialist. . . . Everybody of any intelligence is a Socialist nowadays," Dark wrote in

Waterway. Eric Dark had seen what happened to his patients during the Great Depression—the waste of lives, the poverty, and the meanness; reading and reevaluating, he found himself committed to socialism. While he wrote pamphlets about the politics and social aspects of medicine, Eleanor Dark wrote in *Sun across the Sky,* about a doctor concerned with the interdependence of physical, social, and spiritual states of being. Eric became involved in local politics; Eleanor, already calling herself a socialist, questioned the value and meaning of writing. She said in an ABC radio interview on 7 October 1944, "I think that because we live in such times of stress there's an intellectual striving. The writer feels this like everyone else, and his business is to express it. So when people are searching for an understanding of their problems, they naturally turn to their literature, which gives—or ought to give—a reflection, and perhaps an interpretation, of themselves and their community."

Meanwhile, Dark had begun reading Australian history; she had been invited to write an essay on Caroline Chisholm for a book on women pioneers, *The Peaceful Army* (1938). Chisholm was a middle-class Englishwoman who set up housing and a kind of employment agency for single women immigrants in Sydney in the 1850s. History has been the story of men, Dark wrote, but there have been women such as Chisholm, who had the mental vitality to survive the pressures of sex and custom. What Dark saw in Chisholm's story was that history was made by individuals who stood up for what they believed in the face of opposition. Dark identifies in this essay "three black shadows" that fell across the story of the country, themes she took up in *The Timeless Land,* her next novel—the treatment of convicts, the treatment of immigrants, and the treatment of Aboriginal people.

The Darks had found a cave they set up as a weekend retreat, somewhere they often took friends, and there were rumors that Eleanor wrote *The Timeless Land* in a cave. While this rumor was not true, the bush environment influenced her deeply. Her three historical novels tell the story of the country, but they also tell the story of the land and the relationship of the people, white and black, to it. The only way to describe Dark's spiritual beliefs is in terms of the natural world. As she said in *The Timeless Land,* "Silence ruled this land. Out of silence mystery comes, and magic, and the delicate awareness of unreasoning things." The bush was for her, as she said in *Storm of Time* (1948), a place of "Beauty and immensity and silence, so moving to the restless modern mind." She believed that human beings were part of a complex system. She said in an unpublished essay, "The Conquest of Nature," that the idea of "conquering" nature was a mistake; instead, she said, "we need a working agreement with the earth we live on." Aboriginal people had this, while the Europeans who came to Australia suffered, as Dark said in *Storm of Time,* from "the spiritual malaise of humanity uprooted . . . obsessed with this unresponsive land."

In *The Timeless Land,* Dark turned her focus on change at a social rather than an individual level. She told her publisher, William Collins, in a letter dated 26 November 1937, that she started with "the idea of Australia . . . an alarmingly large idea but alluring," and the Aboriginal character Bennilong. It was the first and most successful of three historical novels based on a carefully researched retelling of the history of European settlement; the novel includes fictional characters, convicts, settlers, and Aboriginal people, as well as such historical characters as the early governors. She offered a radical reinterpretation—a history not only of the white arrivals but also of the Aboriginal people, a history that included women and children. The novel begins with Aboriginal people watching the arrival of the Europeans, and she attempts to document their point of view. Her book made Australian history accessible to readers of novels for the first time. History is to the community as memory is to the individual, she said; without history, people do not know who they are. The accuracy of her history made her the darling of historians. Manning Clark said the novel inspired him to write his history of Australia.

Written just before and during World War II, *The Timeless Land* was Dark's response to a time of crisis—looking to the past to understand the present and future—and it was successful. A "novel of towering stature," a reviewer for the *New York Times Book Review* (21 September 1941) called it; a "genuine creative force with here and there a touch of genius," the reviewer for *The Times Literary Supplement* (1 November 1941) said. *The Timeless Land* became a Book-of-the-Month Club choice and sold 120,000 copies immediately. John Manifold, in a July 1959 article in *Overland,* called it the most acclaimed Australian novel of the 1940s, "the nearest thing we have to a national epic." In Australia the novel won Dark a wider and different readership, and she was particularly touched by letters from schoolteachers who used it in their classes and servicemen and women who read it. "It's amazing that such a good book should be so popular. Or . . . extremely fortunate and rare that such a popular book should be so good," Palmer wrote to Dark on 14 October 1942. The American poet Karl Shapiro, who met the Darks when he was in Australia during the war, picked up on the strong sense of the country—it was "acrid, blue, warm as sky, inwoven like tapestry, hung in the space of the Australian atmosphere," he wrote to her on 7 June 1943.

After finishing *The Timeless Land,* Dark complained of writer's block. "Nothing comes—perhaps it's the War, which tends to make all one's thinking restless and chaotic," she wrote to Franklin on 14 April 1941. There are a number of unfinished essays and notes in her papers dat-

Cover for the book-club newsletter that features Dark's 1941 best-seller, the first of three historical novels in which she chronicled the European settlement of Australia (National Library of Australia)

ing from around this time, essays about women, writers and writing, and politics. Meanwhile, she and her husband were involved with local community activities in Katoomba during the war; she helped set up a free library for children. After many false starts, she wrote *The Little Company* (1945), a novel about a family and group of intellectuals in Sydney and the Blue Mountains during the war. Gilbert Massey, a writer, suffers from the same malaise as Dark, questioning the value of writing novels while the world is in turmoil; his wife, Phyllis, is deeply conservative, an example of what fascism does to women: "Instead of being educated like a human being she has been domesticated like a cat." His sister, Marty, is a writer and broadcaster, and his brother, Nick, is an evangelical communist, but an unconvincing character. In the background of the novel Dark documents the progress of the war and reactions to it in Australia, including Japanese bombing raids and the fear of an invasion. *The Little Company* is a kind of fictional intellectual memoir—"a spiritual document of a period and a people," a reviewer called it in *Australian Women's Digest* (December 1945). Some members of the Australian Left were scathing about her politics. Gilbert's writer's block could be seen as the intelligentsia suffering from neurotic guilt, a professional hazard, but Dark saw it as a symptom. She said her book was about the way personal problems are symptoms of social problems, larger problems; Gilbert's writer's block was a symptom of the breakdown in democracy, freedom, and common values. Wartime censorship and propaganda made her acutely aware of the need for freedom of speech and thought, particularly for writers. This book expresses her growing conviction that education was the key to social change and the way for people to prepare themselves to participate in a democracy. She advocated a controversial education that encouraged questioning and independent thought. Education as the attempt to understand society, and writing as the attempt to give a reflection or an interpretation, are at the heart of her politics.

The postwar period of reconstruction brought optimism and a new wave of questions about what it meant to be Australian. In a 1944 essay for *Australia Weekend Book,* volume three, called "Australia and the Australians," Dark described the Australian character as a combination of optimism and melancholy, spiced with a refusal to take authority seriously. Distance and isolation formed the country: "We took root in a country so incredibly isolated as to seem almost mythical. It was not an easy country, and it kept us very busy." Against the achievements of the pioneers, she said, must be set the "ignorance and greed that used the land too recklessly" and "the blunder of our dealings with the black Australians whose land we stole."

Eric Dark had become an outspoken defender of the Communist Party in Australia, though he never joined it. Eleanor believed that the message of organized religion and politics was either to conform or get out; neither she nor Eric would conform. She deplored the gap between theory and practice, but she never joined any political party. In 1947, however, the Darks were named in the Australian Parliament–Eric as a communist and Eleanor as an underground supporter. They were devastated. The charge was untrue, and they put great faith in uncompromising truth telling. Eric Dark received anonymous threatening letters, and his wife believed his life was in danger.

In 1948 Eleanor finished *Storm of Time.* In this second novel in the historical trilogy, she tells the story of the first generation of white Australians and the corruption of the administration and the military. Against the background of the French Revolution, the American War of Independence, and the Irish uprisings, she wrote about the origins of the violence of the convict system, the state as legitimized violence, property as theft, and resistance. Eric had finished his book in defense of the Union of Soviet Socialist Republics (U.S.S.R.), and they set out with their son Michael on a six-month trip around Australia, traveling by bus, train, and plane. When they crossed the Nullarbor Plain between Adelaide and Perth, the train line passed some distance away from the Woomera testing site where the Australian and British governments were testing nuclear weapons. Australian security police had files on many writers sympathetic to left-wing politics, and the security operatives were nervously trying to follow the Darks' movements.

Dark was increasingly depressed by the effects of the changing political climate of the Cold War. In an unpublished essay called "The Peril and the Solitude," she writes about people such as Eric, and by implication herself, who explore the extreme edge of values, the creative thinkers who would fill the spiritual vacuum created by mediocre if not corrupt politicians. But she felt they were being marginalized. Meanwhile, she believed language was being corrupted by propaganda. Reading newspapers made her feel sick; they were full of lies that produced fear, mistrust, and isolation. Her health had never been good: she had suffered from kidney disease

Dust jacket for Dark's 1945 novel, about a writer and his family living in Sydney and the Blue Mountains during World War II (Bruccoli Clark Layman Archives)

as a child and apparently had had a kidney removed. Now she suffered from depression and a series of debilitating minor health problems. Eric Dark's medical practice was affected by rumors about his politics, and in 1951 he decided to sell. Their son, Michael, was working for their friend Eric Lowe on a farm near Montville, in the fertile subtropical southeast of Queensland. Eleanor was enthusiastic about the warmer climate; she bought a farm nearby, and they packed up and moved. Although they would never have said they were driven out of Katoomba because of their politics, Eleanor joked about being "Displaced Persons," like European refugees. For the next seven years they spent winters in Queensland, growing citrus and macadamia nuts, experimenting with sustainable agricultural practices, and returned to Katoomba in the summers. They worked hard but enjoyed the life, and her mood lightened.

She finished the final volume of the trilogy, *No Barrier* (1953), which took the story as far as the building of a

Eric, John, Michael, and Eleanor Dark in 1937 (from Brooks, Eleanor Dark, *1998)*

road through the Blue Mountains in 1814. It was published in Australia and in the United Kingdom. This book did not have the same kind of unified focus on a major event of history as *Timeless Land* and was less successful. But in a review in the *Sydney Morning Herald* (11 July 1953), Sydney Baker said that the trilogy, now complete, might be the long-awaited "Great Australian Novel." *No Barrier* was turned down, however, by several U.S. publishers. The political climate had changed, but Dark's radical interpretation of Australian history had not. *The Bulletin* review of 15 July 1953 described the novel as distinguished, but "tinged with leftism"; this was how Dark's work was regarded in some quarters.

Lantana Lane (1959), Dark's last novel, was based on the family's experiences in the Montville farming community. It is a funny and affectionate book about farmers in a small community with the threat of progress hanging over them. The farmers are caught between the natural and the technological, the anarchic conditions of agriculture and the supposed rationalism of the market. Dark makes analogies between farming and writing: she sees both as occupations that bring in little money, demand hard work, and involve a lot of sitting around watching the grass grow–or, reflection and contemplation of the natural world. This view promotes an independent, if not subversive, state of mind. Arguing about art and propaganda in *The Little Company*, she had speculated about a communist state turning writers into bureaucrats; in *Lantana Lane* she said capitalism would probably replace them with a machine. Reviewers picked up on the humor of the book, but most failed to recognize Dark's lightly and skillfully interwoven thoughts about the Cold War and contemporary social and cultural developments. Although called a novel, *Lantana Lane* is more a series of stories and essays, self-reflexive, meditative, descriptive as well as narrative, moving confidently between different genres and mixing high and popular culture.

In 1957 the Darks returned to Katoomba permanently. Eric Dark took a job as a school medical inspector and worked until he was in his eighties. Eleanor Dark started on another novel, a family saga, "No Room for the Dead," in which she meditates on "time without barriers," and while her narrator reflects on the process of writing a family history, the work can be read as a commentary on the writing of the historical novels. Never completed, the manuscript is among her papers, along with other false starts to stories and novels, her unpublished essays, and the plays that were never performed. A combination of her desire to be a recluse and a change in literary fashion meant Dark's work was almost forgotten, though *The Timeless Land* stayed in print. But with a second wave of feminism in the 1970s and a resurgence of leftist politics under a Labor government, her novels were rediscovered and her concerns recognized as timely. In 1977 she was awarded the Order of Australia, but she said her health was so bad she could not attend the ceremony; in 1978 the Society of Women Writers gave her their Alice Award. In 1980 a televised version of the historical novels, eleven years in the making, finally appeared. Virago Press republished *The Little Company* in 1985 and *Lantana Lane* in 1986. Eleanor Dark died on 11 September 1985. Varuna, her house, is now a residential writers' center.

In *Southerly* in 1951, G. A. Wilkes assessed Dark's work and ranked her among the major Australian novelists, along with Henry Handel Richardson and Katharine Susannah Prichard; Wilkes also praised Dark's craftsmanship but criticized her novels as uneven. In *Meanjin,* also in 1951, Eric Lowe praised Dark's strong sense of place, her technique of building slowly to a climax, and her "stubborn integrity." In 1973 Humphrey McQueen asked why a writer whose work had sold so well for twenty years had been so neglected. American critic A. Grove Day called Dark Australia's foremost historical novelist and a pioneer of modernist narrative methods, with a fine sense of social justice. Drusilla Modjeska wrote sympathetically about the difficulties for Dark of writing as a woman, interweaving public and private, with an emphasis on relationship, dialogue, and interconnection. Australian publishers republished her novels in the 1990s. Barbara Brooks and Judith Clark's biography, *Eleanor Dark: A Writer's Life,* published in 1998, brought about renewed interest in her work.

Interviews:

D. Ingram Smith, "Australian Writers Speak," radio, Australian Broadcasting Commission (ABC), 7 October 1944, transcript in Eleanor Dark Papers, State Library of New South Wales, Mitchell Library;

Jean Devanny, "Writers at Home: Eleanor and Eric Dark," in her *Bird of Paradise* (Sydney: Johnson, 1945), pp. 245–256;

"Interview by Mrs. J. Moore with Eleanor Dark," radio, ABC, National Women's Session, 14 November 1946, transcript in Eleanor Dark Papers, State Library of New South Wales, Mitchell Library;

Kylie Tennant, "*The Little Company* against the Bulldozer Mentality?" *Sydney Morning Herald,* 14 February 1974, Look! p. 3.

Biography:

Barbara Brooks and Judith Clark, *Eleanor Dark: A Writer's Life* (Sydney: Macmillan, 1998).

References:

Barbara Brooks, "Eleanor Dark: Child of the Century," *Varuna–The Writers' House* (July 2000) <http://www.varuna.com.au/essay.html>;

Brooks, "Waterway: The Multi-Layered City," *Hecate,* 27, no. 1 (2001): 11–17;

Susan Carson, "Making the Modern: The Writing of Eleanor Dark," Ph.D. thesis, University of Queensland, 2001;

Carson, "Surveillance and Slander: Eleanor Dark in the 1940s and 1950s," *Hecate,* 27, no. 1 (2001): 32–43;

A. Grove Day, *Eleanor Dark* (Boston: Twayne, 1976);

M. Barnard Eldershaw, "Eleanor Dark," *Bulletin,* 17 November 1937, p. 50;

Eric Lowe, "Novelist with World Audience," *Australasian Book News and Library Journal* (September 1946): 79;

Lowe, "The Novels of Eleanor Dark," *Meanjin,* 4 (1951): 341–349;

John Manifold, "Our Writers: Eleanor Dark," *Overland* (July 1959): 39;

Bernice May, "Patricia O'Rane," *Australian Woman's Mirror,* 23 September 1928, p. 8;

Humphrey McQueen, "The Novels of Eleanor Dark," *Hemisphere,* 17 (January 1973): 38;

Drusilla Modjeska, "Dialogue with Dark," *Age Monthly Review,* 5, no. 11 (1986);

Modjeska, "'A Hoodoo on That Book': The Publishing Misfortunes of an Eleanor Dark Novel," *Southerly,* 57, no. 2 (Winter 1997): 73;

Nicole Moore, "The Rational Natural," *Hecate,* 27, no. 1 (2001): 19–29;

Stephen Murray-Smith, "Murray-Smith's Book of the Month: *Darkness at Dawn,*" *Australian Book Review,* 2, no. 11 (September 1963): 178;

G. M. M., "A Novelist at Home," *Sydney Morning Herald,* Women's Supplement, 23 May 1935, p. 17;

Helen O'Reilly, "The Timeless Eleanor Dark," *Outrider,* 6 (1989): 43–47;

Janet Ryall, "Women's Peacetime World," *Australian Home Budget* (July 1945): 20;

G. A. Wilkes, "The Progress of Eleanor Dark," *Southerly,* 3 (1951): 139.

Papers:

Collections of Eleanor Dark's manuscripts and correspondence are in the State Library of New South Wales (Mitchell Library) in Sydney and the National Library of Australia in Canberra. Other correspondence can be found in the Vance and Nettie Palmer Papers and the A. Grove Day Papers in the National Library of Australia, Canberra; the Evatt Papers, in Flinders University Library; and the Karl Shapiro papers, University of Maryland Libraries (Special Collections). Some letters are held by her son, Michael Dark. Her security files can be found in the Australian Archives, ACT Regional Office.

Frank Dalby Davison

(23 June 1893 – 24 May 1970)

Robert Darby

BOOKS: *Man-Shy: A Story of Men and Cattle* (Sydney: Australian Authors' Publishing, 1931; Sydney: Angus & Robertson, 1932); republished as *Red Heifer, a Story of Men and Cattle* (New York: Coward-McCann, 1934);

Forever Morning: An Australian Romance (Sydney: Australian Authors' Publishing, 1931; Sydney: Angus & Robertson, 1932);

The Wells of Beersheba (Sydney: Angus & Robertson, 1933);

Blue Coast Caravan, by Davison and Brooke Nicholls (Sydney: Angus & Robertson, 1935);

Caribbean Interlude (Sydney: Angus & Robertson, 1936);

Children of the Dark People: An Australian Folk Tale (Sydney: Angus & Robertson, 1936; New York: Coward-McCann, 1937; revised edition, Sydney: Angus & Robertson, 1948);

While Freedom Lives (Sydney: Published by the author, 1938);

The Woman at the Mill (Sydney: Angus & Robertson, 1940);

Dusty: The Story of a Sheepdog (Sydney & London: Angus & Robertson, 1946); republished as *Dusty: A Novel* (New York: Coward-McCann, 1946);

The Road to Yesterday: Collected Stories (Sydney: Angus & Robertson, 1964);

The White Thorntree: A Novel (Melbourne: National Press, 1968);

The Wells of Beersheba and Other Stories (North Ryde, N.S.W.: Angus & Robertson, 1985).

SELECTED PERIODICAL PUBLICATIONS–UNCOLLECTED: "Australian Fiction Today," *Australian Mercury,* no. 1 (July 1935): 57–61;

"Australian Writers Come to Maturity," *Australia, National Journal,* no. 2 (Spring 1939): 68–69;

"What is Literature?" in *Australian Writers Speak: Literature and Life in Australia* (Sydney: Angus & Robertson, 1942), pp. 11–20;

"Vance Palmer in his Writings," *Meanjin,* 7 (Autumn 1948): 10–27;

Frank Dalby Davison (from John Hetherington, Forty-Two Faces, *1946)*

"Focus on Australian Readers," *Adult Education,* 7 (March 1963): 10–18.

Frank Dalby Davison is best known for his sensitive animal fables and sharply observed short stories of life in bush settlements. Starting his career as an author quite late in life–his first novel appeared when he was thirty-eight–Davison quickly became one of the leading writers of the 1930s. He was a regular contributor of stories and reviews to periodicals such as *The Bulletin,* a pivotal figure in the Fellowship of Australian Writers

(FAW) and literary politics generally, and an artist whom novelist M. Barnard Eldershaw–pseudonym of Marjorie Barnard and Flora Eldershaw–described in her *Essays in Australian Fiction* (1938) as "one of the most deeply significant figures in Australian literature today." Subsequent developments did not entirely bear out the optimism of this judgment: at the height of his fame, soon after his novel *Dusty: The Story of a Sheepdog* was published and won a competition in 1946, he left the city and spent the rest of his life on a farm outside Melbourne. The belief that he had retired from writing was dispelled when his vast work *The White Thorntree: A Novel* appeared twenty-two years later, in 1968, but its reception was mixed, and some critics complained that the author of the delightful book *Man-Shy: A Story of Men and Cattle* (1931) had entirely disappeared. Among the many paradoxes surrounding Davison, the deepest is that he is most admired for the work that is least representative of his most heartfelt concerns.

Davison was born at his parents' home in the Melbourne suburb of Hawthorn on 23 June 1893 and christened Frederick Douglas. He was the eldest son of Frederick and Amelia Watterson Davison. His father grew up in central Victoria, ran a printing business in Melbourne in the 1890s, and later became an active member of the Australian Natives Association, whose journal, *Advance Australia,* he produced from 1897 to 1899. Frederick Davison the father was a dynamic and opinionated progressive with a fervent belief in White Australia, the British Empire, national development, and private enterprise. During the 1920s he ran a real-estate business in Sydney and published two short-lived magazines in which he expounded a militantly entrepreneurial ideology more typical of the United States than of Australia at this time, and against which his son reacted sharply during the following decade. Frederick Davison was active in returned soldiers' organizations and instrumental in the construction of the Cenotaph in Martin Place, still the site for the Anzac Day observance in Sydney. Relations with his son were strained in the late 1930s, particularly when the son turned to pacifism, and Sunday dinners at the parental home became argumentative and sometimes rowdy. Davison's father published several didactic novels in the 1930s and died in 1942; there is a satirical though affectionate portrait of him in his son's short story "Meet Darkie Hoskins."

Davison grew up in the outer Melbourne suburbs, attended the local state school, but left at age twelve, after grade six, to work as a farm laborer. In 1909 Frederick Davison took the family to the United States, where his son was apprenticed to the printing trade in Chicago and wrote his first published work in an amateur magazine called *Roo Thuds*. In 1914 the younger Davison took a job as printer on a Caribbean cargo ship–a fictionalized reminiscence of which was published in 1936 as *Caribbean Interlude*–returning to New York shortly after the outbreak of World War I. Traveling to England via Canada, Davison enlisted in the Second Dragoon Guards (mounted infantry) and in October 1915 was shipped to France, where he survived on the Western Front without serious injury until selected for an officer training course in 1918. While training at Aldershot, he met Agnes Harriet Ede, later known as Kay, whom he married on 7 August 1915. They had two children, Doris Mary (born in 1918) and Peter (born in 1922). Like many returned soldiers, Davison never referred to his war experiences, and they did not form the basis of any of his fiction.

In May 1919 Davison and his small family returned to Australia, where he took up a selection, or farm, in a soldier settlement subdivision in wild bush land near Roma, Queensland, under the Discharged Soldiers Settlement Act, 1917. This act was a scheme to return soldiers to civilian life by allowing them to purchase small plots of unimproved land with extended government credit, on the assumption that they would develop it and become successful farmers. Like most of the other selections, Davison's farm failed miserably, and in 1923 he returned penniless to Sydney, where he joined his father's real-estate firm and became advertising manager for his father's latest magazine-publishing venture, *The Australian* (1923-1925). He later established his own real-estate business in the expanding eastern suburbs of Sydney and was prosperous enough to afford a gramophone and a car. At their home in Vaucluse the Davisons enjoyed tennis parties, musical evenings involving songs and recitations, and amateur theatricals in which they and their friends acted plays of their own composition. Davison was always intensely interested in drama, partly because of the opportunities its dialogue offered for airing differing points of view. He wrote at least one play, "When She Came Back" (now lost)–set in the inner Sydney suburbs, with a plot involving adultery and revenge–which was performed publicly in the early 1930s. Although he never became a successful playwright, Davison included in his correspondence much discussion of dramatic issues and critical comments on plays he had seen or read.

While on his selection, Davison had written many poems, sketches, and short stories for an earlier paternal venture, *The Australian Post* (1920-1921), and he produced a torrent of such material for *The Australian,* his contributions sometimes representing more than half the editorial matter of an issue. Most of this work was written to promote his father's ideology of entrepreneurship, national development, and opposition to government interference in business activity, but

Davison with his children, Doris and Peter, during the 1920s
(National Library of Australia)

there were also many fictional pieces. One series of fictional pieces featured a cow that escaped from the herd to live wild in the bush; another focused on the daughter of a successful selector—every soldier settler's dream—and her tribulations in life and love. These two series later became the bases of Davison's first two novels. Despite his considerable journalistic output and forays into short fiction, he did not consider himself a professional author at this time, though he did once attend a meeting of FAW, the only literary organization in Sydney during the 1920s. As he recalled later, however, the most prominent feature of the other writers he met there was their disappointed look, so he gave up writing and turned back to real estate.

When the Great Depression hit in 1929, it destroyed Davison's real-estate business and left him wondering how he was to feed his family; he was so desperate that he thought writing might be a means of survival. He recovered the two sets of related stories he had written for *The Australian*, revised them, and in 1931 published them himself as two novels—*Man-Shy* and *Forever Morning: An Australian Romance*—which he bound in wallpaper and hawked from door to door. The exercise did not raise much cash, but *Man-Shy* met an unexpected literary success, winning praise from critics and the Australian Literature Society Gold Medal for the best novel of 1931. On the basis of these accomplishments the major Australian publisher, Angus and Robertson, republished both books the following year, establishing a relationship with the author that endured until his death. *Man-Shy* entertained both children and adults for several decades. The story of the cow who preferred to starve in the freedom of the bush than feast in the paddocks of captivity works as both a delightful animal adventure and as a meditation on the dialectics of liberty and security. By contrast, *Forever Morning* is a conventional and rather sentimental romance, loaded with clichés and preaching the development ideology of the 1920s.

Encouraged by the award and the flattering contact from the established writers of the day, notably Nettie and Vance Palmer and Barnard, Davison began to consider himself a professional author, even believing that he might make some money. He took the name Frank Dalby—after a town near his selection—and began writing furiously: short stories, plays and a long novel poured from his typewriter, but little of this effort survives today and even less was published. Apart from a few minor short stories, the only significant work to emerge from this period (1931–1934) was *The Wells of Beersheba,* a short "prose epic" commissioned by Angus and Robertson as a Christmas gift book for 1933. The subject of the work was an incident in World War I, a famous charge by the Australian Light Horse during the Palestine campaign in 1917. So vivid was Davison's description of the horses in action that many survivors of the battle assumed that he must have been there. Although it was an artistic success, *The Wells of Beersheba* did not solve Davison's financial problems. During the early 1930s he was extremely poor, working at several odd jobs and accepting unemployment relief before finally achieving precarious security as a regular reviewer for the weekly *Bulletin,* then one of the few Australian publications that paid reasonably well for literary contributions. Davison always had great difficulty writing to order; his children recall him sitting at the typewriter in their small flat with a pile of books on one side and a flagon of marsala wine on the other, desperately trying to get the reviews for the week done on time. Possibly Barnard sometimes helped him with this task or even wrote an occasional piece for him.

The decisive change in Davison's life and outlook began in 1934 when, desperate for cash, he made a trip to Queensland with an amateur naturalist, Brooke Nicholls, planning to write a travel book based on their experiences. The decade of the 1930s was the great age of Australian descriptive and travel writing, and many sought to emulate the success of prolific writers such as Frank Clune and Ion Idriess, who turned out one book after another on the scenic wonders of the nation; they had a selling formula, and Davison intended to copy it. But something went awry; instead of the scenic beauties admired by such writers as Clune, Davison discovered soil erosion, deforestation, unregulated development, and man-made ugliness. He realized at that point that the sort of land settlement he had championed in the 1920s was resulting in the ruin of the Australian environment. He suffered something of a nervous breakdown when he returned to Sydney, and *Blue Coast Caravan* (1935), the book that emerged from the trip, was a scathing critique of national development policies. Davison worked successfully at short stories after this catharsis, but he never recovered his complacency; instead, he regarded his society with increasingly critical eyes. His first mature short story, "The Wasteland" (1935), and his next important published work, *Children of the Dark People: An Australian Folk Tale* (1936), were explicitly conservationist replies to the scenes he had deplored in *Blue Coast Caravan.*

Davison's "political awakening," as he referred to it in a 1968 letter to Ian Reid, was further advanced by his concern over authoritarian trends in Australia and the spread of fascism abroad. He had become active in the increasingly left-wing FAW at the time of the Egon Kisch affair in 1934 and had served as president for 1936–1937. Kisch was a Czech journalist who had been invited to Australia to address a peace conference; acting on advice from British intelligence that he was a communist, the Australian government tried to prevent him from landing. The resulting struggle, in which Kisch jumped from the ship and was given a dictation test in Gaelic under the provisions of the Immigration Act, was crucial in defining left- and right-wing trends in Australian cultural politics and enlisting most significant cultural figures on the side of the left. The incident split the FAW, the old conservative leadership of which was replaced by a younger and more progressive set.

By now quite at home in Sydney literary circles, Davison formed a close working relationship with Barnard and Eldershaw, whose "salon" became a forum in which debates about politics and literature were thrashed out. They worked together to turn the FAW into a trade union of professional writers, differentiate it from a union for journalists, and ensure that it adopted antifascist and, in the context of the adoption of appeasement by the British Empire, often antigovernment, positions on political questions. Davison was one of the judges for the Prior Prize for literature in 1937 sponsored by *The Bulletin* and in 1938 the Sesquicentenary Novel Competition. In 1939 he was part of the delegation that secured an expansion of the Commonwealth Literary Fund to assist living writers. He took strong public stands on many contemporary issues, particularly literary and political censorship; the status of Australian literature, emerging as an effective public controversialist against the patronizing comments of Walter Murdoch in *The London Times;* the policy of appeasing Nazi Germany, Italy, and Japan; and local threats to civil liberties. Despite all his controversial actions and largely through the efforts of his better-connected father, Davison for his services to literature was made a Member of the Order of the British Empire (MBE) in the 1938 Australia Day honors. The most striking result of his labors during this period was his antifascist pamphlet, *While Freedom Lives* (1938), which he wrote in order to clarify his political ideas as a prelude to writing a working-class play. The play did not

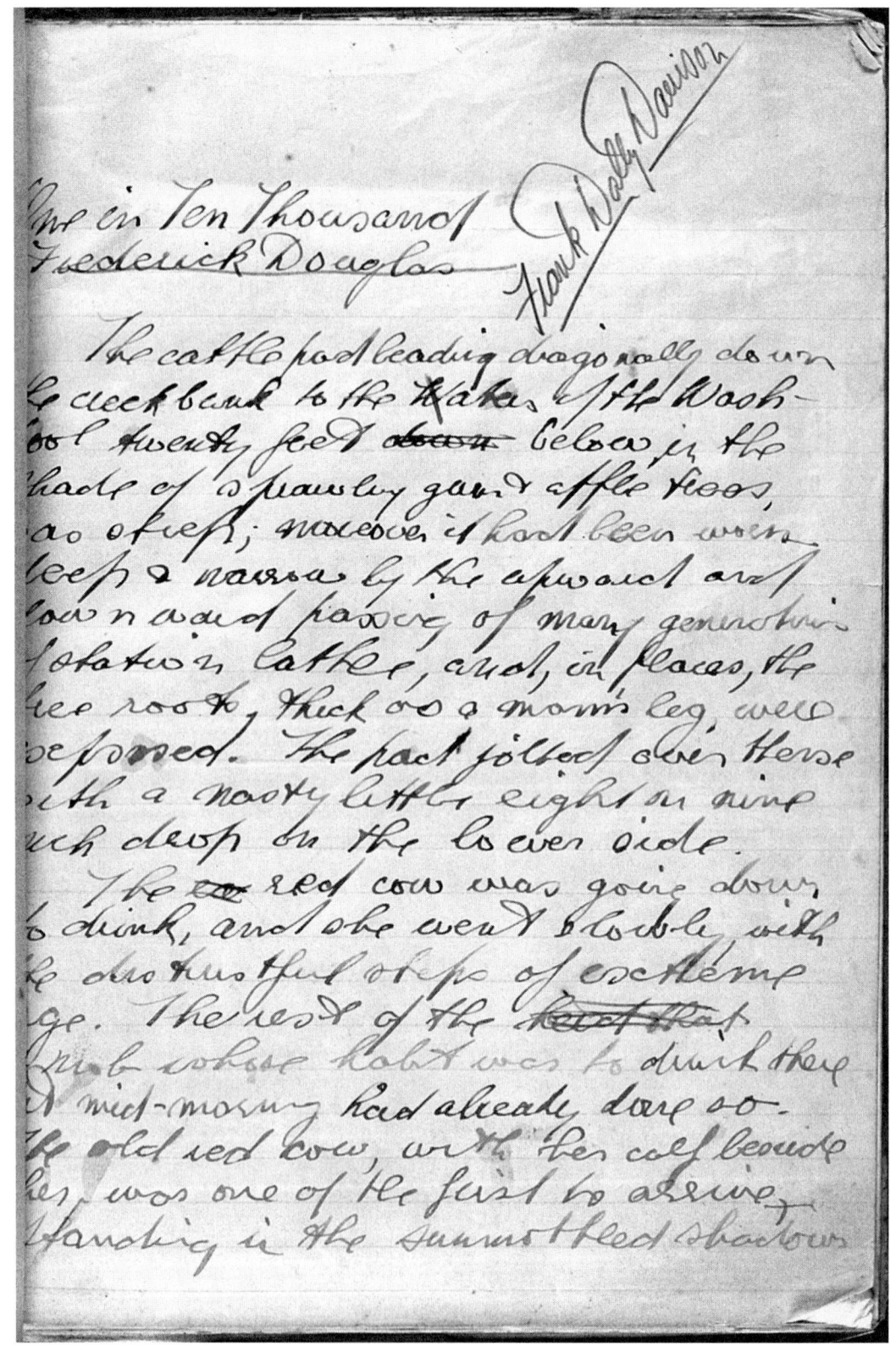

First page of the manuscript for the 1923 story that Davidson revised and published in book form as Man-Shy *in 1931 (National Library of Australia, MS1945/2/32)*

eventuate, but Davison's concern with democratic values may be seen in many of the short stories collected in his next publication, *The Woman at the Mill* (1940), a volume that includes some of his finest work.

At the personal level the 1930s were a difficult time for Davison. His marriage with Kay had been breaking up since the trip to Queensland, which he described cryptically as a "disaster" on the personal-relations side, and it was only lack of financial resources that prevented them from living separately after his return. Davison had brief affairs with several women on the Sydney social and literary scene, but his grand passion was for Pixie O'Harris, a writer and illustrator of children's books and wife of the journalist Bruce Pratt. The sentimental letters and poems he sent her stand in sharp contrast to the severity of his usual prose style and reveal a passionate romantic beneath the stoic realist. O'Harris encouraged Davison at first but later had second thoughts and broke off the romance, a decision that left such a deep mark on him that he returned to it repeatedly in his later fiction. In *Dusty* the episode in which the canine protagonist is conceived involves a chance encounter between a wild dingo bitch and a homestead kelpie. After their mating, the kelpie, "a husbandly dog," anticipates "a repetition of their previous enjoyment of each other," but the dingo wants to get away. He follows her, and she snaps at him; he follows further, and she snaps again, this time inflicting a fatal wound. He bleeds to death, and she returns to the forest. In *The White Thorntree* Davison examines the same situation from many angles in the lives of the many couples whose marital and extramarital liaisons are the substance of the book, but most directly in the affair between Tom Gillespie and Norma Tesdale, which was abruptly halted by the latter just when the former thought the relationship was set.

Better known today, though equally clandestine at the time, was Davison's liaison with Marjorie Barnard, who seems to have fallen in love with the author of *Man-Shy,* a novel she never tired of praising, even before she met Davison. Although they spent most Monday nights together for about six years and cooperated on literary-political projects, he never reciprocated her adoration and did not pretend to. Davison's children believe that Barnard hoped he would divorce his wife and marry her, but he had other obsessions, first O'Harris and then, in the early years of World War II, the Communist Party of Australia, although he never actually joined the party. One factor in his reluctance to commit to the party was Barnard's influence, particularly her pacifism, and they both took a defeatist stance in the early years of the war, principally on the ground that military involvement would be the occasion for an authoritarian crackdown that would destroy civil liber-

Dust jacket for the 1965 edition of Davison's 1946 novel, about a half-dingo sheepdog (Bruccoli Clark Layman Archives)

ties. Davison's short story "Fathers and Sons" (1940) records the feelings of an old soldier who has learned that World War I was neither the war to end war nor one to make the world safe for democracy, as he watches his son march through the streets on his way to yet more old-world battlefields. As in M. Barnard Eldershaw's *Tomorrow and Tomorrow and Tomorrow*—published in censored form in 1947 as *Tomorrow and Tomorrow* but not published in its entirety until 1983—the focus of the story is the Anzac Memorial in Sydney. Davison found himself closely aligned with the Communist Party of Australia at this time, particularly during its period of illegality (1941–1943), and made several public appearances in defense of its right to operate legally. As one of the most prominent literary personalities in the nation, he must have been courted by the party leadership: the frustrated secretary, J. B. Miles, is reported to have once remarked that *Man-Shy* was "an anthropomorphic study of the author evading the discipline of the party." With the entry of Russia, and then Japan, into World War II, Davison's pacifism softened, but he refused to seek work as a war correspondent or publicist for the war effort. After the war he retained his broadly leftist sympathies and was willing to sign most of the petitions circulated by the peace movements of the 1950s.

Earning a living remained a problem for Davison. In 1939–1940 he was the recipient of a fellowship from the Commonwealth Literary Fund, and after that he found work as a clerk at the Commonwealth Aircraft Factory and later as a journalist with the Department of Labour and National Service, a position that removed him to Melbourne in 1943. At an art exhibition in 1942 he had met the beautiful Edna Marie McNab, a woman many years younger than himself, still living with her parents, whose slim lines, youth, and fashion sense made her everything Barnard was not. After a passionate courtship, he proposed; the divorce from Kay was secured; and the two were married on 8 December 1944. Davison changed his name to Frank Dalby at this time, and the couple lived happily until Davison's death. By the time of the wedding Davison was living in Melbourne and hard at work on his next novel, *Dusty,* which won first prize in a novel competition run by the *Argus,* a leading Melbourne newspaper. At one level the story of a half-kelpie, half-dingo sheep dog that becomes a champion worker, then a killer, then a wild dog, *Dusty* can also be read as a meditation on many of the political issues that animated Davison in the early 1940s, particularly his fascination with the rebel and his ambivalent attitude toward the prospect of revolution and the New Social Order promised after victory over fascism.

The rest of Davison's life was outwardly uneventful. He continued to work for the Department of Labour and National Service, but with their savings and the proceeds of the *Argus* prize, he and Marie bought a small farm near Melbourne, which they named Folding Hills and on which they worked during weekends. In 1951 Davison resigned from the department so that they could live there full-time and make a living from mixed farming and the occasional piece of writing. Davison did a column on rural affairs in the *Argus* for a few months during 1950, and he revised many of his short stories for a new collection, *The Road to Yesterday* (1964), but most of his creative energy was reserved for the novel he had been trying to write since the late 1930s—a study of human relationships, and particularly sexual behavior, among the generation he had known in Sydney between the wars. This novel, originally called "Blue Horses" (after a painting by Franz Marc) and then "Separate Lives," was vastly different in style, subject matter, and length from anything Davison had previously attempted. After many false starts and rewrites, it was eventually completed in 1967 and published as *The White Thorntree* in 1968. The novel stimulated widely divergent assessments from critics at the time, and its status remains controversial. One problem was that, although the severe moral censorship of the period meant it could not be published in the 1940s, by the time it was completed the progress of the sexual revolution made it look quaintly old-fashioned. Another was the shock of such a long novel about philandering urbanites emerging from an author who had mainly written short books about animals and hard-working country folk. Yet, the main disappointment was less the lack of sexual explicitness than of dramatic tension. The novel includes little dialogue or action; instead, an omniscient narrator tacks relentlessly to and fro, reporting the events, describing the state of mind of the characters, and analyzing their motivations. Although there are some moving episodes, such an academic approach, oddly like an anthropologist describing the courtship rituals of a remote tribe, creates little scope for drama or characterization. As an extended reflection on what Davison called "the inherent capacity of the sexes for disappointing each other," it has much to offer, but it does not work well as fiction.

By 1961 Davison's health was failing, and his wife had to shoulder an ever-greater burden of the farmwork, but he retained sufficient vigor to complete *The White Thorntree* and an undimmed mental alertness that was evident in the lengthy interviews conducted by Owen Webster for the Australian Broadcasting Commission in 1969. A lifetime of hard drinking and heavy smoking was catching up with him, however; he died at Diamond Valley Hospital on 24 May 1970 and was cremated at a secular funeral, after which his ashes were scattered at Folding Hills.

Davison did not set out to be a writer. Although he had always shown an interest in literature and had written a good deal—mainly ephemeral matter—by the time he made good in real estate, the "accident of the trade depression," as he called it in his 1963 article "Focus on Australian Readers," turned him finally from business to literature. Having arrived on the Sydney literary scene just at the time when writers were organizing themselves professionally, he quickly accepted the prevailing view that quality writing was about realism, or telling the truth as the author saw it, and he decisively rejected his publicist past. That this moment also coincided with the emergence of what was seen as a deadly threat to truth in literature—namely, fascist rule—had a strong influence on the sort of writer and literary activist that he became. In his writings Davison sought to reveal the Australian situation and to promote humane, democratic values. He did not see literature as

*Davison's second wife, Marie, at their farm near Melbourne
(from Graeme Kinross-Smith,* Australia's Writers, *1980)*

a vehicle through which to advocate or advance social change but as a means by which people might be helped to know themselves and their society, a necessary prelude to reform. As a character remarks in "The Yarns Men Tell," a story published in *The Woman at the Mill:* "It does us good to get a glimpse of ourselves occasionally." Like many liberals, Davison was drawn to the Left by the threat of fascism at a time when its only committed opponent seemed to be the communists. Because his dedication to liberal democracy and freedom of speech was stronger than his respect for particular governments, he found himself taking oppositional stances during the antifascist period, and in the postwar years he was sometimes misidentified as a Red.

A man of broad tolerance, Davison was mistrustful of power and particularly hated any kind of authority—whether moral, religious, or political—that blocked or perverted natural human tendencies. In *The White Thorntree* he examined the harmful effects that repression and guilt, especially those arising from a Christian upbringing, could have on sexual and emotional desires. Most unusually for a man of his period, he extended his tolerance to homosexuals: reporting an incident in which a man had made sexual advances to him, he told his family he had been flattered rather than shocked. A lifelong atheist, Davison was married twice and buried without the trappings of religion. He had a mostly genial disposition and enjoyed a few beers with his friends, but he could become easily irritated when drinking.

With four novels, a volume of short stories, and a few miscellaneous works to his credit, Davison is a minor writer, but a significant one, entirely representative of his generation of would-be authors who struggled to make a living in difficult times and to reconcile the demands of art with those of political conviction. His considerable output of literary and other journalism—reviews, descriptive articles, and essays—has never been collected, but a collection would help to correct the misapprehension that he is no more than a homely follower of Henry Lawson's bush realism. Largely for this reason, plus the suspicion of patriarchal attitudes,

Davison is so out of fashion today that not one of his works is in print. A fresh reading of his short stories reveals a sophisticated mind deeply concerned with themes more complex and more modern than the vicissitudes of selection life. In "Further Out" he deals with gender and race on the frontier; in "The Woman at the Mill" he deals with the sadness of unreciprocated desire and the nature of commitment. "Return of the Hunter" is a vivid and effective allegory on the seductive allure of the soldier-settler fantasy; "Nobody's Kelpie" is an exact political fable on the ineffectiveness of submission as a tactic against bullying, with obvious implications for the policy of appeasing the fascist powers of the 1930s. In "Blood Will Tell" Davison rejects the genetic determinism he had espoused in *Forever Morning*, and in "Lady with the Scar" he quietly brings up the burden of the past. His Australian folk tale, *Children of the Dark People*, narrates the adventures of a pair of Aboriginal children, but it is not so much a children's story as an ecological parable on the need to treat the land with tenderness and respect.

Davison was never a propagandist in his fiction, but he saw writing as a political act, with important implications for the life of society, and he agonized over the difference between politically informed and partisan writing. In his most successful stories Davison is able to suggest a political philosophy without appearing to advocate a particular line. In the less effective ones–"Transition," an attempt to fictionalize the experience of moving left, and "Fathers and Sons," a comment on war that relies too heavily on the shaky authority of the narrator–the underlying politics rise to the surface, and he comes close to preaching. But political motivation was vital to Davison's creativity.

At his best Davison wrote prose of rare beauty–simple, clear, precise, yet always sufficiently ambiguous to leave a suggestive aftertaste (the "overtones" as he called it). Like Lawson's sketches, his stories of selection life resemble the pieces of a mosaic that together build up a picture of the whole community. Another power he shares with Lawson is that of evoking the feel of daily routines, and his descriptions of work are often reverent. Tasks such as tree-felling, working on fences, digging a dam, or skinning a possum are brought to life with both the workaday knowledge of the farmer who has done it and the skill of the writer who can find the words. His style is best summed up in his own description of the Crown Lands Ranger's speech: "He had a fine, simple power of words, and a way of talking about commonplace things that put a bloom on them."

References:

Robert Darby, "The Fiction of Frank Dalby Davison," *Overland,* no. 109 (December 1987): 60–66;

Darby, "While Freedom Lives: Political Preoccupations in the Writing of Marjorie Barnard and Frank Dalby Davison, 1935–1947," dissertation, University of New South Wales, 1989;

Hume Dow, *Frank Dalby Davison* (Melbourne: Oxford University Press, 1971);

Harry Heseltine, "The Fellowship of All Flesh: The Fiction of Frank Dalby Davison," *Meanjin,* 27 (Spring 1968): 275–290;

Louise A. Rorabacher, *Frank Dalby Davison* (Boston: Twayne, 1979);

Owen Webster, *The Outward Journey* (Canberra: Australian National University Press, 1978).

Papers:

The papers of Frank Dalby Davison are located at the National Library of Australia, Canberra. Letters may also be found at the National Library of Australia among the papers of Vance and Nettie Palmer, Kay Davison, Owen Webster, and Pixie O'Harris. Papers are also held by the Mitchell Library, Sydney, in the collections of the publishers Angus and Robertson and the Fellowship of Australian Writers. The University of Melbourne also has some papers in the *Meanjin* Archive.

C. J. Dennis
(7 September 1876 – 22 June 1938)

Philip Butterss
University of Adelaide

BOOKS: *Backblock Ballads and Other Verses* (Melbourne: E. W. Cole, 1913);

The Songs of a Sentimental Bloke (Sydney: Angus & Robertson, 1915); republished as *The Sentimental Bloke* (New York: Press of the Woolly Whale, 1932);

The Moods of Ginger Mick (Sydney: Angus & Robertson, 1916; Toronto: S. B. Gundy / New York: John Lane, 1917);

Doreen and the Sentimental Bloke (New York: John Lane / Toronto: S. B. Gundy, 1916); republished as *Doreen* (Sydney: Angus & Robertson, 1917; New York: John Lane, 1918);

The Glugs of Gosh (Sydney: Angus & Robertson, 1917; New York: John Lane, 1917);

Digger Smith (Sydney: Angus & Robertson, 1918);

Jim of the Hills, a Story in Rhyme (Sydney: Angus & Robertson, 1919);

In the Garden of Arden (N.p., 1920);

A Book for Kids (Sydney: Angus & Robertson, 1921);

Rose of Spadgers (Sydney: Cornstalk, 1924);

The Singing Garden (Sydney: Angus & Robertson, 1935);

Selected Verse of C. J. Dennis, edited by Alec H. Chisholm (Sydney: Angus & Robertson, 1950);

Random Verse: A Collection of Verse and Prose by C. J. Dennis (Melbourne: Hallcraft, 1952);

The C. J. Dennis Collection: From His "Forgotten" Writings, edited by Garrie Hutchinson (Melbourne: Lothian, 1987).

C. J. Dennis, circa 1930 (from Alec H. Chisholm, The Making of a Sentimental Bloke, *1946)*

C. J. Dennis was a prolific poet and journalist who made his name with *The Songs of a Sentimental Bloke* (1915) and *The Moods of Ginger Mick* (1916), vernacular verse narratives that celebrated two larrikins (young street rowdies) from inner-city Melbourne. Bill, the sentimental bloke who gave up the ways of a street thug for domestic bliss, and Mick, his mate (close friend), who died as a hero in the Dardanelles, were enormously popular with Australian audiences during World War I, and the former continued to have a strong appeal for more than half a century.

Clarence Michael James Dennis was born to Irish parents in rural South Australia in the District Hotel in Auburn, of which his father was licensee. The family soon moved to a hotel in Watervale, a short distance along the Clare Valley, and then on to hotels in Gladstone and Laura, a little farther away from Adelaide. Although Dennis was later known as "the laureate of the larrikin," much of his verse and prose throughout his life details the beauty and harshness of the Australian bush and the day-to-day events of rural life. In a later poem called "Laura Days" he wrote that "'Twas here his earliest songs were sung / And he won his earliest praise." Also, in *Down the Years,* Dennis's wife, who published under the name Margaret Herron, writes that Dennis told her that it was during a period when he worked for his father as a barman at the Beetaloo Reservoir Hotel in Laura that he "learned to drink," a habit with which he struggled for the rest of his life.

Dennis's earliest political views were formed in the South Australian country towns of his youth as he became aware of the wealth of large landholders and the difficulties faced by others struggling to survive on the land. A concern with such inequalities energized his verse for many years. Some commentators have surmised that Dennis's celebration of the rugged masculinity of the larrikin and the bushman (a person who lives in the Australian bush) may have been a reaction to aspects of his boyhood—his pretentious first name, Clarence, which he never used as an adult, and the cosseting he received from a pair of maiden aunts after the death of his mother in 1890, when he was fourteen.

After leaving school at the age of seventeen, Dennis moved through several jobs, including a couple of stints on the Adelaide newspaper, the *Critic,* ultimately becoming its editor while he was in his late twenties. With A. E. Martin, he founded a lively satirical weekly whose first issue on 14 February 1906 included an editorial by Dennis stating that "*The Gadfly* is run by Australians in the interests of things Australian." Alongside its nationalism, the paper was strong in its support for the Labor Party and for protectionism, attitudes that can sometimes be discerned in the verse that Dennis contributed.

At the end of 1907, after a lengthy period of financial difficulty for *The Gadfly,* Dennis quit the paper and left for Victoria, where he led a hand-to-mouth existence, surviving on sporadic bits of freelancing. He camped with Hal Waugh, an artist, in the mountains northeast of Melbourne and then squatted in a small wooden house formerly occupied by a timber-getter (lumberjack). Here in the peaceful bush of Toolangi, Dennis assembled some of the material that had appeared in various journals over the years and published *Backblock Ballads and Other Verses* (1913), illustrated by his cartoonist friend David Low. Most of the volume is devoted to verse on rural topics, as the first part of the title indicates.

More than a decade earlier, in rejecting one of his bush poems, the editor of *The Sydney Bulletin* wrote in the "Answers to Correspondents" column: "C. J. D. 'Bill' is the old, old familiar Bill, and we yearn for a new Bill." Whether or not he was literally taking the advice in the journal, Dennis published four poems about a larrikin—an urban cousin to the well-worn ballad hero—in *The Bulletin* between 1909 and 1913, and these began the "Other Verses" section of the *Backblock Ballads and Other Verses.* This figure was later identified as "Bill," and the poems formed the basis of *The Songs of a Sentimental Bloke.* Dennis also expressed his frustration with the unquestioning conformism of the Australian public, a theme to which he returned in *The Glugs of Gosh* (1917). He criticized inequality in Australian society and, like other radical nationalists of the period, expressed his fear of Asian invasion.

"A Real Australian Austra-laise," which had been submitted to a competition for an Australian anthem run in 1908 by *The Bulletin,* also made a significant mark. Although Dennis was making fun of the aims of the competition, he did so in a way that balanced nationalist pride with the undercutting of pretense, and the poem was awarded a special prize because the judge felt it would "win its way to every heart in the backblocks." A revised version was published in 1915 as a leaflet titled "A Marching Song, Dedicated to the A.I.F." and became a jingoistic anthem. W. T. Goodge's popular poem "The Great Australian Adjective" had already left no doubt that most of the blanks in Dennis's piece should be filled with the word "bloody." The version in *Backblock Ballads and Other Verses* begins:

> Fellers of Australier,
> Blokes an' coves an' coots,
> Shift yer ——— carcases,
> Move yer ——— boots.
> Gird yer ——— loins up,
> Get yer ——— gun,
> Set the ——— enermy
> An' watch the ——— run.

In spite of some positive reviews, the book did not sell well and brought no improvement to Dennis's financial position. He was, however, moving into a milieu that offered him support and encouragement. A couple of years earlier, he had met R. H. Croll, an educationalist and lover of Australian literature. In 1913 Croll introduced Dennis to J. G. Roberts and his wife, who became Dennis's pseudo-parents; he was soon calling them "Dad" and "Mother." Roberts gave the struggling poet a weekly allowance, conditional on evidence of literary output, and allowed him the use of a deserted tramway bus at their holiday house in the Dandenongs, Sunnyside, which operated as something of an artists' and writers' colony. The Sunnyside circle included the artists Tom Roberts, Harold Herbert, and John Shirlow, the sculptor Web Gilbert, cartoonists David Low and Hal Gye, Guy Innes of *The Melbourne Herald,* and sometimes the novelist Jeannie Gunn, who wrote as Mrs. Aeneas Gunn. At the end of 1913 "Den," as his friends knew him, wrote to Croll of the inspiration that this group provided, saying "I must take a walk around myself, so to speak, and spit on my hands and get a fresh grip."

Early in 1914 Dennis went to Sydney, where he worked on the left-wing papers *The Australian Worker* and *The Call,* publishing radical political verse, drinking heavily, and living the life of a down-and-outer. After the outbreak of war, he returned to Melbourne to be nursed back to health by the Robertses, and in January 1915, through his Labor Party contacts, he found employment as a public servant in the Navy Office and, a year later, for the Federal Attorney-General's Department, learning about the workings of bureaucracy that he later satirized in *The Glugs of Gosh.*

With the encouragement of the Sunnyside circle, Dennis continued to build on the four poems in the "sentimental bloke" series, progressively publishing additions in *The Bulletin.* In 1915 Angus and Robertson brought out the series as a single volume titled *The Songs of a Sentimental Bloke,* with a fourteen-page glossary at the end. Dennis was quickly transformed, as his biographer put it, from "a frayed little wanderer, battered by hard adventure in bush and city" into a household name holding "first place among Australian writers in public esteem."

The humor of the book relies, essentially, on a set of unlikely juxtapositions—literary allusion with larrikin slang, sentimental feeling with tough masculinity, and chivalrous behavior with rough manners. Its larrikin hero's chief entertainments are drinking and gambling, and he has spent time in jail for assaulting policemen. He sees Doreen examining cheap jewelry at the markets and falls in love with her. Then a printer's storeman (stockroom worker) and a girl who pastes labels in a pickle factory carry on a delicate courtship, whose episodes include a formal introduction, an awkward visit to meet her mother, and outings such as in the best-known episode, "The Play." Here the young couple dress up and attend the theater to see *Romeo and Juliet,* which is translated into Dennis's version of larrikin argot. The narrator can see parallels between the action on stage and his own experiences:

> This Romeo 'e's lurkin' wiv a crew—
> A dead tough crowd o' crooks—called Montague.
> 'Is cliner's push wot's nicknamed Capulet—
> They 'as 'em set.
> Fair narks they are, jist like them back-street clicks,
> Ixcep' they fights wiv skewers 'stid o' bricks.

The bloke resolves to mend his ways and give up drinking and gambling for Doreen's sake, and, although he slips up a couple of times—and occasionally longs for masculine freedom—the volume ends with a strong endorsement of domesticity. Bill marries Doreen and leaves the city for the bush, where they take up residence on a berry farm and live in deep happiness with their young son.

Norman Lindsay, the artist and writer, crucified a copy of *The Songs of a Sentimental Bloke* in his front garden, and there were others who agreed with his assessment of its literary worth: no work by Dennis has received much attention from literary critics. But the overwhelming

Bert, Claude, and Clarence Dennis, circa 1889 (from Chisholm, The Making of a Sentimental Bloke, *1946)*

response to the book was positive, with enthusiastic reviews from *The Melbourne Age* to the *London Times* and favorable comment from literary figures such as H. G. Wells, who wrote to the publishers, and even E. V. Lucas, the sophisticated essayist of *Punch.* The book was published in October, and a first printing of almost 2,500 copies sold out in a matter of weeks. A second printing of 5,000 was sold out by December, and three months later a fifth printing was selling well. Today more than 300,000 copies have been produced in some sixty editions.

With the country at war and reports from the battlefields gloomy, the affectionate humor of *The Songs of a Sentimental Bloke* and its happy domestic ending proved to be especially appealing for Australian audiences. Pocket editions were treasured by soldiers, keen for something from home, and the book became known as "the trench bible." But, as Alexander Porteous pointed out in "The Sentimental Bloke and His Critics," published in *Australian Literary Studies* (1964), the sustained success of the volume for half a century cannot be attributed simply to "wartime conditions."

Some readers, such as Henry Lawson, who wrote the foreword to *The Songs of a Sentimental Bloke,* have found eternal human values expressed in Dennis's poem. In explaining his response to the book, Lawson writes,

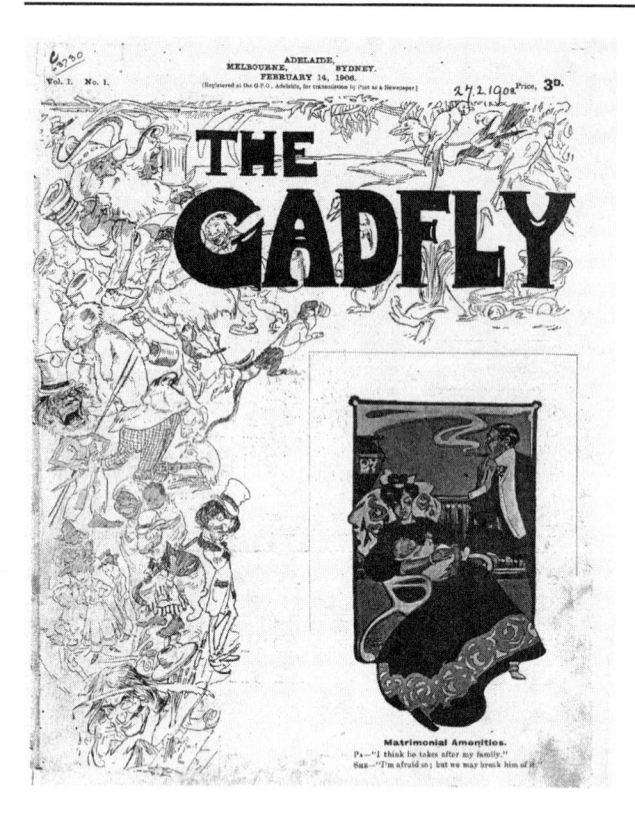

Cover for the first issue of the satirical weekly founded by Dennis and A. E. Martin (from Ian F. McLaren, C. J. Dennis, *1979)*

"Take the first poem for instance, where the Sentimental Bloke gets the hump. How many men, in how many different parts of the world—and of how many different languages—have had the same feeling—the longing for something better—to *be* something better?" Alec H. Chisholm, in *The Making of a Sentimental Bloke: A Sketch of the Remarkable Career of C. J. Dennis* (1946), says that the last poem, "The Mooch o' Life," with its portrait of a happy little family, is "the most moving unit" and "touched the very deeps of human nature."

For audiences both during and after World War I, *The Songs of a Sentimental Bloke* was archetypally Australian, representing antiauthoritarian and egalitarian values and stressing mateship. The book continued the tradition of masculine defiance that Russel Ward in *The Australian Legend* (1958) has traced through convicts, bushrangers, gold miners, and bushmen in the nineteenth century. Australia was already a highly urbanized country, and Dennis's larrikin hero brought that tradition into the city and into the twentieth century. The particular tone with which this Australian hero was represented—a mix of mild self-deprecation, considerable affection, and a certain pride—mirrored many Australians' views of their country and, therefore, worked well for a local readership.

Dennis's letter to Lawson asking him to write the foreword indicates awareness of the potential of the book to help bridge class differences: "I have tried to tell a common but very beautiful story in coarse language, to prove—amongst other things—that life and love can be just as real and splendid to the 'common' bloke as to the 'cultured.'" Instead of the fiercely polemical verse that he had been publishing in *The Australian Worker* and *The Call,* Dennis wanted the book to maintain a tone of "geniality and good humour and optimism." Its juxtaposition of toughness and sentiment—something underlined by Hal Gye's illustrations of cherubic larrikins—also resolves the conflict between different models of masculinity that Marilyn Lake has identified in her discussions of the 1890s; Dennis asserted that tough men could choose love and domesticity.

Following the phenomenal success of *The Songs of a Sentimental Bloke,* Dennis saw another opportunity in developing the minor character, Ginger Mick, who had been Bill's mate and best man. Dedicated to "the boys who took the count" and narrating its hero's career in the army, *The Moods of Ginger Mick* was published in 1916 and, again, was exactly the right book for its time. Even more than "the bloke," Mick had been on the wrong side of the law, having worked for an illegal bookmaker and having done time in jail for fighting and theft. With Australian society deeply divided over conscription, Dennis deftly sidestepped issues that might put off potential readers, in this case by presenting a range of views about the war and leaving vague the reasons for Mick's decision to volunteer—a response to something deep within himself, "the call of stoush [fighting]." His early training in the backstreets proves useful in the fight at Sari Bair, and, as he notes, Mick is now praised for activities that would once have landed him in jail. Even more than in his previous book, Dennis goes out of his way to present a vision of egalitarian mateship and harmony between different classes among the troops in *The Moods of Ginger Mick:*

> So the lumper, an' the lawyer, an' the chap 'oo shifted sand,
> They are cobbers wiv the cove 'oo drove a quill;
> The knut 'oo swung a cane upon the Block, 'e takes the 'and
> Uv the coot 'oo swung a pick on Broken 'Ill;
> An' Privit Clord Augustus drills wiv Privit Snarky Jim—
> They are both Australian soljers, w'ich is good enough fer 'im.

Like "the bloke," Ginger Mick is presented as being "a big, soft-'earted boy" beneath his tough exterior, and one of the themes of the book is his love for Rose, the girlfriend who waits for him back in Spadger's Lane. *The Moods of Ginger Mick* accurately anticipates the mood of the Australian public, presenting a mixture of different aspects of the war experience. At times fighting is boisterous fun—one poem celebrates Australians as "the singing soldiers"—and at times the verse brings out the pathos of war. It also

Dennis as a squatter in the bush of Toolangi, circa 1913 (from Chisholm,
The Making of a Sentimental Bloke, *1946)*

strikes a balance between the sentimental heroizing of the Australian force and Mick's embarrassment at this occurrence. After considering the likely effects on his readership, Dennis decided to have the larrikin soldier die as a hero who had managed "to prove Australia, an' our boastin' uv the breed." In a gesture displaying Australian uncertainty about its position in the world, Dennis puts the most important endorsement of Mick in the mouth of Trent, an English toff, or dandy, who determines that the larrikin soldier was "a gallant gentleman." Like its predecessor, *The Moods of Ginger Mick* proved to be enormously successful, with an initial print run of almost forty thousand copies—unprecedented for a book of verse—that soon sold out. By the end of 1917 another twenty thousand copies had been printed, and its author had been dubbed "the Anzac laureate" to complement his earlier title, "laureate of the larrikin."

Dennis returned to his larrikin material in three further volumes, but none touched the Australian public as deeply as the original two. *Doreen,* a booklet comprised of four sentimental poems, was published for the Christmas gift market at the end of 1917. Lucas's comment was, "It contains more married love to the square inch than anything I have ever read." In 1918 Dennis turned again to the Anzac theme, producing *Digger Smith,* narrated by the "sentimental bloke." Smith had been an acquaintance of Bill and Ginger Mick in inner-city Melbourne, but, when he returns from war, he takes up residence in the bush. *Digger Smith* is essentially a double love story with a vague political message about the just treatment of returned soldiers. The final book from the larrikin subject matter was *Rose of Spadgers,* published in 1924. A sequel to *The Moods of Ginger Mick,* this volume deals with Rose's decline after the death of her beau, and her rescue "From wot base schemes an' wot iniquity / Gawd only knows."

The Glugs of Gosh probably has its origins in some nonsense verse Dennis wrote for the younger son of J. G. Roberts. In July of that year, Dennis married, and the book is dedicated to his wife, Olive (Biddy) Herron. In its final form it is a satire on aspects of Australian society, but it retains clear connections to his verse for children. The poem continues some of Dennis's long-held views, offering a compelling support for protectionism and some sharp criticism of consumerism and of bureaucracy. Its author thought that *The Glugs of Gosh* was his best work, and early on it shows considerable promise as a humorous and apt satire. But the narrative gets bogged down in a complicated plot and loses its satirical focus. Humphrey McQueen points out in "'We are not safe, Clarence; we are not safe': Sentimental Thoughts on 'a moody bloke,'" an essay published in *Meanjin* (1977), that "The picture of the typical Australian to emerge from *The Glugs* totally contradicts the one popularly taken from *The Bloke* and *Ginger Mick,* where we are independent, resourceful, haters

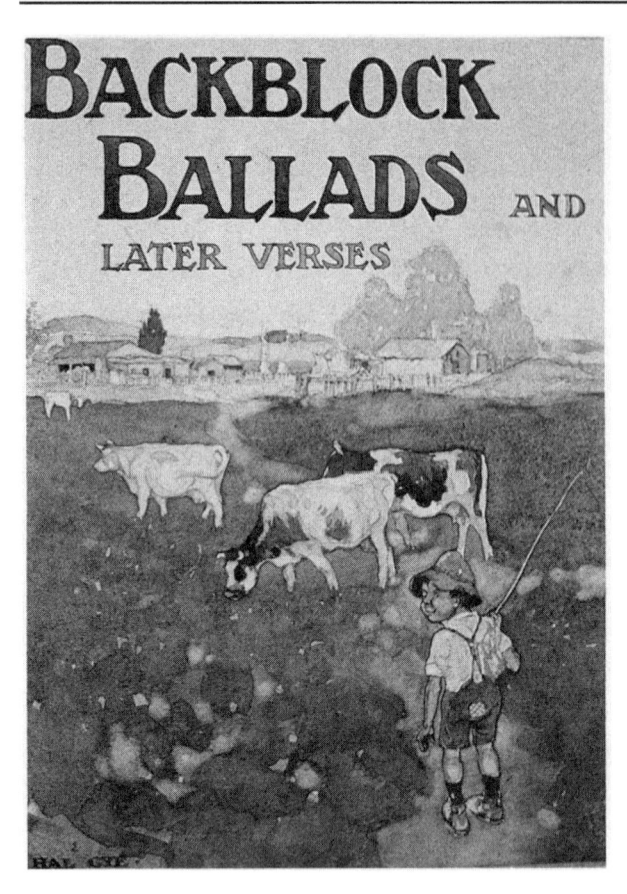

Dust jacket for the 1918 edition, illustrated by Hal Gye, of Dennis's first collection of poems, originally published in 1913 (from McLaren, C. J. Dennis, *1979)*

of authority and good mates. By contrast, Glugs are bound together by mindless conformism."

Neither *The Glugs of Gosh* nor Dennis's next, *Jim of the Hills, a Story in Rhyme* (1919), was a publishing success. Jim is a solitary timber-getter whose romantic development is the focus of attention. The volume is most notable for the marked shift in politics that it reveals. In 1914 Dennis had been working for leftist papers and writing radical verse; five years later, having achieved substantial fame and success, he published a tale in which the boss goes without so that his workers can be paid, and the villain, who wishes to start a strike at the timber mill, is presented as

> crazed by these new creeds that start
> An' grow like mushrooms, overnight;
> An' this strange greed that's spread the more
> Since the great sacrifice of war.

Although his own marriage was childless, Dennis wrote a substantial quantity of verse for children, and in 1921 he published *A Book for Kids,* illustrated with his own suitably childish drawings. His wife recorded that she never knew him happier than when working on this project. The book itself was republished several times, and some of the poems have frequently been anthologized, so that generations of Australian children have grown up with a knowledge of pieces such as "Triantiwontigongolope," "The Swagman," and "The Ant Explorer."

Since the publication of his first larrikin book, there had been some blurring of the distinction between fictional character and author, and this confusion was reinforced by the headline in *The Herald* on 12 May 1922, which read, "'Noted Writer's New Role': 'The Sentimental Bloke' will conduct daily *Herald* column." The job meant Dennis spent most of his time in Melbourne, and he maintained a prodigious output of verse and prose almost continuously until his death. P. I. O'Leary, in *The Catholic Advocate* on 30 June 1938, later commented on the "high gift of verbal dexterity and craft of words" required to produce topical and occasional verses, day in and day out, for many years. The effort took its toll, however, and Dennis's wife later acknowledged that the move to Melbourne was an unwise decision: "Temptations were many, and at times he would give way to his weakness and have to go into hospital." According to Sally Wilkins in "Life Mooches On," Dennis's neighbors reported that sometimes his wife had to hold his head under a tap to sober him up enough to produce his copy.

While at *The Herald,* Dennis invented a number of different characters, often using them for humorous representations of rural life. One of these, Ben Bowyang, was featured by Alex Gurney in a well-known comic strip that began in 1933. Dennis's political attitudes became increasingly conservative: he criticized the union campaign for a forty-four-hour workweek and mocked the Labor Party. The fame achieved by *The Moods of Ginger Mick* meant that he was regularly called on to write nationalistic verse on occasions such as Anzac Day and Armistice Day. Using a series of poems about his garden at Toolangi, Dennis published the last of his books, *The Singing Garden,* in 1935. On 22 June 1938 he died of a heart condition caused by asthma, after a long period of ill health. On his death, the prime minister, Joseph Lyons, described him as "the Robert Burns of Australia."

At the height of its popularity, C. J. Dennis's work had begun to take on a life of its own. A movie called *The Sentimental Bloke*–including a brief appearance of Dennis himself in the act of writing–was directed by Raymond Longford and released in 1919. Today it is recognized as the greatest contribution by Australia to the classic era of silent movies. A version with sound was directed by F. W. Thring and released in 1932. A stage version was produced by E. J. Carroll in 1922, a ballet in 1953, and a musical in 1961. Gramophone and television versions followed. The rest of Dennis's work received much less attention, but a motion picture titled *Ginger Mick* was released in 1920; unfortunately, no print has survived. In

1976 the centenary of Dennis's birth resulted in a revival of interest, and a number of his works were reprinted, while a stage show about his life and work toured the country with considerable success.

Most of Dennis's material was written quickly for newspaper deadlines on items of topical interest, but *The Songs of a Sentimental Bloke* and *The Moods of Ginger Mick* provided a mix of humor and national pride that resonated deeply with Australian audiences during World War I. For more than half a century *The Songs of a Sentimental Bloke* continued to express beliefs about what many regarded as the core values of Australian identity. Today, however, virtually none of C. J. Dennis's work remains in print, partly because contemporary readers find the colloquialisms of the larrikin verse too difficult to understand, partly because the world about which Dennis wrote is long gone, and partly because the values celebrated in these poems are no longer at the center of contemporary views of Australian identity.

Bibliographies:

Ian F. McLaren, *C. J. Dennis: A Comprehensive Bibliography Based on the Collection of the Compiler* (Adelaide: Libraries Board of South Australia, 1979);

McLaren, *C. J. Dennis: A Supplement to a Comprehensive Bibliography Together with a Consolidated Index to the Compiler's Dennis Publications* (Adelaide: Libraries Board of South Australia, 1983).

Biography:

Alec H. Chisholm, *The Making of a Sentimental Bloke: A Sketch of the Remarkable Career of C. J. Dennis* (Melbourne: Georgian House, 1946).

References:

Les Blake, "The Sentimental Bloke on Screen: A Stoush with the Yanks," *Victorian Historical Journal,* 64, no. 1 (1993): 28–45;

Robin Gerster, *Big-Noting: The Heroic Theme in Australian War Writing* (Carlton, Vic.: Melbourne University Press, 1987);

Margaret Herron, *Down the Years* (Melbourne: Hallcraft, 1953);

Geoffrey Hutton, *C. J. Dennis, The Sentimental Bloke: An Appraisal after 100 Years of His Birth* (Melbourne: Premier's Department, 1976);

K. S. Inglis, "The Anzac Tradition," *Meanjin,* 24, no. 1 (1965): 25–44;

Marilyn Lake, "The Politics of Respectability: Identifying the Masculinist Context," *Historical Studies,* 22, no. 8 (1986): 116–131;

Ian McLaren, *Talking about C. J. Dennis* (Melbourne: English Department, Monash University, 1982);

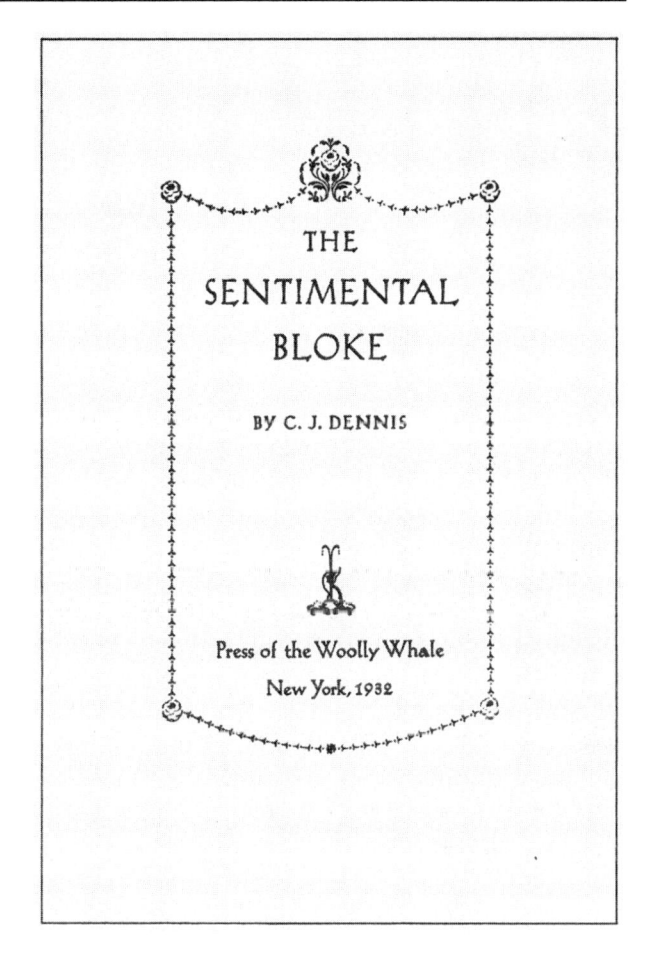

Title page for the American edition of a collection of Dennis's poems originally published in 1915 as The Songs of a Sentimental Bloke *(from McLaren,* C. J. Dennis, *1979)*

Humphrey McQueen, "'We are not safe, Clarence; we are not safe': Sentimental Thoughts on 'a moody bloke,'" *Meanjin,* 36, no. 3 (1977): 343–353;

Alexander Porteous, "The Sentimental Bloke and His Critics," *Australian Literary Studies,* 1 (1964): 260–273;

John Rickard, "Lovable Larrikins and Awful Ockers," *Journal of Australian Studies,* 56 (1998): 78–86;

Russel Ward, *The Australian Legend* (Melbourne: Oxford University Press, 1958);

Sally Wilkins, "Life Mooches On," *The Age* (24 July 1976): 15.

Papers:

The most significant collections of C. J. Dennis's papers are the Ian McLaren Collection in the Baillieu Library, University of Melbourne; Angus & Robertson Papers in the Mitchell Library, State Library of New South Wales; and the Papers of R. H. Croll and the J. G. Roberts Collection in the La Trobe Library, State Library of Victoria.

Jean Devanny
(7 January 1894 – 8 March 1962)

Carole Ferrier
The University of Queensland

BOOKS: *The Butcher Shop* (London: Duckworth, 1926; New York: Macaulay, 1926; Auckland: Auckland University Press, 1981);

Lenore Divine (London: Duckworth, 1926);

Old Savage and Other Stories (London: Duckworth, 1927);

Dawn Beloved (London: Duckworth, 1928; New York: Macaulay, 1928);

Riven (London: Duckworth, 1929); republished as *Unchastened Youth* (New York: Macaulay, 1930);

Bushman Burke (London: Duckworth, 1930; New York: Macaulay, 1930); abridged edition published as *Taipo* (Sydney: Frank Johnson, 1930; New York: Macaulay, 1930);

Devil Made Saint (London: Duckworth, 1930);

Poor Swine (London: Duckworth, 1932); republished as *All for Love* (New York: Macaulay, 1932);

Out of Such Fires (New York: Macaulay, 1934);

The Ghost Wife (London: Duckworth, 1935);

The Virtuous Courtesan (New York: Macaulay, 1935);

Sugar Heaven (Sydney: Modern, 1936; abridged edition, Sydney: Frank Johnson, 1942);

Paradise Flow (London: Duckworth, 1938);

The Killing of Jacqueline Love (Sydney: Frank Johnson, 1942);

By Tropic Sea and Jungle (Sydney & London: Angus & Robertson, 1944);

Bird of Paradise (Sydney: Frank Johnson, 1945);

Roll Back the Night (London: Hale, 1945);

Cindie: A Chronicle of the Canefields (London: Hale, 1949);

Travels in North Queensland (London & New York: Jarrolds, 1951);

Paradise Flow, edited by Carole Ferrier, preface by D. Menghetti (St. Lucia: Hecate Press, 1985);

Point of Departure: The Autobiography of Jean Devanny, edited by Ferrier, with an epilogue by P. Hurd (St. Lucia & New York: University of Queensland Press, 1986).

Editions: *The Butcher Shop,* foreword by Heather Roberts (Auckland: Auckland University Press / Oxford: Oxford University Press, 1981);

Jean Devanny, circa 1920s (James Cook University Library)

Sugar Heaven, foreword by Carole Ferrier (Flemington, Vic.: Redback Press, 1982);

Cindie: A Chronicle of the Canefields, foreword by Ferrier (London: Virago, 1986).

OTHER: "The Worker's Contribution to Australian Literature," *Australian Writers Speak: A Series of Talks Arranged by the Fellowship of Australian Writers for the Australian Broadcasting Commission* (Sydney: Angus & Robertson, 1942), pp. 57–67.

Jean Devanny's radical fiction expresses the contradictory impulses of a socialist libertarian ethic much ahead of its time. She published fifteen novels between 1926 and 1949. Her earlier work includes important examples of the New Woman novel—set first in New Zealand and then in Australia—and of the socialist realist novel. Her *Sugar Heaven* (1936) is one of the most admired Australian industrial fictions. She later began to write historical novels and planned a trilogy about the sugar industry in north Queensland. The focuses and forms of her work changed during her writing career, but a range of persisting concerns continued as they moved through different contexts and different times. Devanny's life and her writing, Kay Ferres suggests in a 1994 article for *Hecate*, "Written on the Body: Jean Devanny, Sexuality and Censorship," show the "exercise of the sometimes ambiguous power available to her as a writer and activist to reform and redefine the political relations of sex, gender, race and class."

Devanny was born Jane Crook on 7 January 1894, the eighth of a family of ten children, in a small coastal settlement at the top of the South Island of New Zealand. Her mother had come from an Irish upper-class background, but the Crook family lived in the mining communities that were the workplaces of her father, a boilermaker from Lancashire, England. When Devanny left school at the age of thirteen, she had already changed her name to Jean, which her schoolteacher preferred—and it was her schoolteacher along with her brothers who initially provided the books for the self-education Jean continued to pursue. In 1911, at the age of seventeen, she married a miner, Hal Devanny, and moved with him to several other mining communities until they settled in Wellington at the beginning of the 1920s. She had by then given birth to three children—Karl, Patricia, and Erin—but the younger of the two girls had died in infancy. In 1929 the family emigrated from New Zealand to Sydney, Australia; the Great Depression had begun, and Sydney was a hotbed of political resistance, agitation, and activity. Jean Devanny joined the Communist Party and was soon put in charge of building its Workers' International Relief organization; in this capacity she was sent to Berlin and Russia in 1931. She separated from her husband soon after her return and, through the 1930s, had a close liaison with the leader of the Australian Communist Party, J. B. Miles. From the middle of that decade she spent increasing amounts of time in north Queensland, the sugarcane country and coral reefs of which became the settings of much of her later fiction. In 1950, following a reconciliation with her husband, Hal, Devanny moved to Townsville and lived there until her death in 1962.

Devanny's literary development demonstrates a constant interest in the plotting of sexuality. Her writing shows varying emphases at different periods on an engagement with the politics of the same large questions: novels such as *Lenore Divine* (1926), about the New Woman, are interwoven with issues of class, race, and ethnicity; novels such as *Sugar Heaven*, about class struggles, are interwoven with sexual politics and ethnicity; novels set in earlier times, such as *Cindie: A Chronicle of the Canefields* (1949), about history, are interwoven with the topics of class, race and ethnicity, and gender. In addition to fifteen novels, Devanny published one book of short stories and three travel books; a play and her autobiography were published after her death, and several more novels remain unpublished.

At the end of the nineteenth century the notion of Australasia had a widespread currency, and there were expectations that New Zealand would federate: the Tasman Sea was seen as not much more of a barrier than the state boundary between New South Wales and Victoria. This unification did not occur, however, and perhaps Devanny's literary reputation has suffered, as probably did that of the much more peripatetic novelist Christina Stead, by her "belonging" to more than one place more profoundly than in the mere settings and contexts of her fiction.

In the early decades of the twentieth century, Australia offered few opportunities for publication. Consequently, authors sought publication in Britain or perhaps the United States. Devanny had a lucky break in finding favor with the firm of Duckworth, which published most of her earlier work. The reviewing reception of her first novels was enthusiastic; changes in the times and changes in her subject matter and implied audience later produced a different story. As Duckworth became less welcoming of her work because of more daring aspects of its content, she began to publish in the United States with Macaulay, but she did not or could not stay with this publishing house either.

Susan Sheridan has suggested in her *Along the Faultlines: Sex, Race and Nation in Australian Women's Writing, 1880s–1930s* (1995) that there emerged in Australia in the early twentieth century "a new narrative of female subjectivity, which might be named 'the romance of experience.'" The "focus on the singularity of the individual female subject" that could be seen as typical of much modernist fiction is, to some extent, counterposed to the material of historical sagas and epics, and "political novels about working class communities" that tended to be "more compatible with current nationalist discourses" and in which the development of the heroine was "more arbitrary and uncertain." The straddling of these two currents in much of Devanny's writing made many readers uncomfortable.

Devanny's work is remarkable for its innovation—the more so because there were few local models to inspire or guide her. Although she had left school

Devanny with sugarcane workers in north Queensland during the 1935 strike on which she based her 1936 novel Sugar Heaven *(James Cook University Library)*

early, her education had been continued through "a book a day" supplied by her schoolteacher, as well as the use of the libraries of her brother and his friends—which included many socialist classics—and, later, by contact with the traveling socialists who visited the mining communities and who habitually had a high regard for culture and its uses. Frank Sargeson, the first New Zealand fiction writer to achieve any substantial recognition, did not begin to be published until the mid 1930s; Iris Wilkinson (Robin Hyde), Sargeson's neighbor in Auckland in the 1930s, knew of Devanny and her work, as did the older Jane Mander, but Devanny does not mention reading their novels. Only in Katherine Mansfield did Devanny find—as she recalled in her autobiography, *Point of Departure* (1986)—"something different, close to me, of my own." P. J. Gibbons in his essay "The Climate of Opinion" in *The Oxford History of New Zealand* (1981) suggests that Mansfield represented for her contemporaries in New Zealand "a symbol of the promise which could be fulfilled in the old world"; the prospects of a brilliant career for a female novelist in the 1920s in New Zealand did not seem promising. Not until 1955 did Janet Frame begin to see the possibility of success in publishing, when she was "adopted" by Sargeson. In 1981 Keri Hulme, in an interview with Sue Kedgley for *Our Own Country: Leading New Zealand Writers Talk about Writing and Their Lives*

(1989), reflected upon the situation of writers such as Devanny, who were "exploring things on the fringes that were very important to women way back then." Hulme considered it "very freeing (and very oppressive at the same time) to realize how completely these women were submerged." In the early years of the twentieth century, women writers continued to experience fringe status in various ways; there were further specificities to their Australasian situation to which Devanny's novels and her writing life gave a voice.

The main early influences on Devanny's literary production were European; she mentions Henrik Ibsen, George Bernard Shaw, and John Galsworthy in particular. Only in the mid 1930s in Australia did she begin to form friendships with writers—many of them women—some of whom became close. In 1930 Miles Franklin, on a visit back to Australia, noticed Devanny's striking figure at the Mitchell Library, but their close association did not develop until some years later. Devanny had visited Katharine Susannah Prichard when she passed through Perth on her way to Europe; when both were living in Sydney in 1934, they developed a close alliance that, a few years later, was largely destroyed by Devanny's conflict with the party. In the later 1930s Marjorie Barnard, whom Devanny had met in the course of work in the Fellowship of Australian Writers (FAW), became a friend and confidante, and Eleanor Dark was another writer whose company and writing came to interest Devanny. Only the work of Prichard, however, really commanded her continuing admiration.

Devanny's earlier novels include many radical and advanced women characters, among whom is Rose Stallard in *Poor Swine* (1932), who responds to her doctor-brother Eddie's agonizings over his affair with a miner's wife, Lilian, with "All this damn rot in the twentieth century!" Rose is an advanced woman who reads "the frankest kind of fiction"; she shares many of the traits of the New Women that she finds depicted in these novels. Frank fiction was where many early twentieth-century women found models of different lives or encouragement to become New Women.

Devanny's first writing in New Zealand was nonfictional "sociological" work about gender and race, and her interest in the politics of such issues persisted throughout her writing life. Much of her work, far ahead of its time, raises issues of racial and sexual politics, and of the notion of the personal as political that the second-wave women's liberation movement of the 1960s found so new and important. Her "Evolution of the Sex Life"—a large and much-revised manuscript that was never published—is a precursor, from a different time and place, to Simone de Beauvoir's *The Second Sex* (1949); Devanny wrote another manuscript that also remained unpublished, called "The Sexlife of the Maoris." The analysis of the woman question and of the interactions of the racially different, embarked upon in her early nonfictional work, is embodied and further worked out throughout her career of fiction writing. Her novels differ from those of many of her contemporaries in the centrality of their intersection with the political—a complicated intellectual engagement that included sexual politics as well as the politics subscribed to by many of her peers.

Devanny began to write fiction when she arrived in Wellington in 1921. "Story after story I turned out, but only a few were sold," she recalls in *Point of Departure*. The encouragement of Jack MacDonald, an organizer for the Socialist Party of Canada, who toured the West Coast coalfields at the end of 1921, led to Devanny's embarking upon a novel: "My first book was a long time in the making. I wrote it in fits and starts. Deep down the proposition seemed chimerical and pretentious," she confesses in *Point of Departure*. For a woman from a working-class background to consider herself a fiction writer constituted a leap of the imagination, even a certain presumption. In addition, Devanny was involved in socialist circles that, even in Wellington, the capital of New Zealand, tended to consider literature and art in general as a luxury for the middle classes; in the wider community there was little developed cultural activity.

Evidence is lacking to establish whether the novel Devanny wrote first was *The Butcher Shop* or *Lenore Divine*, both published in 1926, or *Dawn Beloved*, published in 1928. With no idea of how to find a publisher, she had sent a novel to Robert Gibbings, who, happily for her, forwarded it on to Duckworth, who said that it needed further work but they would consider more manuscripts. When she submitted *The Butcher Shop*, it was accepted, and *Lenore Divine* apparently was accepted soon afterward. She then revised *Dawn Beloved*, which Duckworth published in 1928.

Devanny's first published novel, *The Butcher Shop*, shows an uncomfortable melding of didactic intent—an early form of what is now called materialist feminism—with experimentation with the generic conventions of the romance. In an interview with Nelle M. Scanlan for the *New Zealand Free Lance* (26 May 1926), Devanny commented that she chose the title *The Butcher Shop* "because the woman is butchered in life." She conceived of the socialist problem novel in this way: "Other writers have attacked this subject, but usually they chose a woman who is childless. That problem is simple. It is where there are children that the real problem arises." Devanny later, in *Point of Departure*, described her initial attempt at handling this subject as "terribly confused and foolish," but she had no Friedrich Engels to correspond with, as did Minna Kautsky, about the difficulties of producing the *tendenzroman* (novel with a purpose). The interview categorizes her first published novel as explicitly polemical: "a good deal of the opposition to the book might be political. I cannot disassociate my writing from my Socialistic views, and the book was written with a purpose." *The Butcher Shop*, despite being modified by Duckworth's editors, was banned; its proscription did, of course, curtail its circulation and influence, but it also made Devanny well known: "the censors here have given the book the best advertisement it could have," she explained in a 4 June 1926 article in *The New Zealand Times*. She never found out what the official grounds for the censorship were. "It is possible the reason is that it would have been a bad advertisement for New Zealand," she speculated at one point in the article; at another, that the cause might be "its brutality, but that cannot be helped, for it is a true story of New Zealand country life. I know it is true. I have lived in the country and seen for myself." When she arrived in Australia and began to draw attention with public lectures on literary censorship, the novel was also prohibited there.

The opinion of one reviewer, that Devanny's work was "both weak and strong, artistically and emotionally" (*The London Morning Post*, 26 June 1928), has

Devanny giving a speech in the Sydney Domain during the late 1930s, when she was active as a Communist orator and agitator (James Cook University Library)

some cogency. Discussing her first published novel later, in *Point of Departure,* she placed herself within the tradition of frank fiction and described "its meagre merit" as "sincerity, frankness and a certain power of phrasing." Many of the 1926 reviews of *The Butcher Shop,* while ambivalent about the "crude slabs of distasteful sex stuff," were nonetheless favorable. *The Sydney Daily Telegraph* (15 May 1926) even went so far as to suggest that "With one or two possible exceptions, this book marks the largest stride yet made by an English writer of fiction towards that absolute liberty of thought and expression possessed and exercised by the novelist [sic] of France."

Lenore Divine, also published in 1926, is a novel about urban flappers within the context of bohemian Wellington. It is particularly interesting for the marriage between the heroine and a Maori man with which it concludes. Alcoholism, race, sexuality–especially women's sexual pleasure–mothering, illegitimacy, and parenting are all explored against a background of new labor politics and militant industrial unionism. The New Woman, Lenore, is an urban professional, faced with the largest dilemmas for white women of her class in her age–financial control and economic independence, along with the "personal" issues of the claiming of sexual pleasure, the morality of marriage as ownership, child care and custody, and the illusions and pleasures of romantic love across race and class boundaries. "To the unspoiled woman natural consummation of healthy desire is the strictest morality; the opposite lies in the loveless communion sanctioned by man-made custom." Lenore had refused to marry her lover, Holly Virtue:

> You think you are not my husband because we have not had a few official words said over us. . . . To me, you are my husband, because we love each other. Do not think, Holly, that if I were your legal wife, as well as your legitimate love-mate, that I would be more subservient to you, more thoughtful of you, more devoted or more truly your wife in any sense than I am now.

Marriage, she declares, is only "for children and my protection under the law."

On another occasion, Lenore's political mentor, Lafe Osgood, discusses sexuality with her, declaiming against "conventional" women's attitudes and advocating an informed and scientific understanding of sexuality: "you're a creature of vicious instincts . . . if you can't discuss the plain happenings of your daily life with a man of my type; if you can't, with your knowledge, detach plain physiological facts from pruriency." Lafe asks Lenore if she understands, in the euphemistic phrase from paleobotanist and pioneer birth-control campaigner Marie Stopes's *Married Love* (1918), "how beautiful married love should be." But of course, Lenore and Virtue are not married, and this distinguishes the agenda here from the monogamist arguments of *Married Love* and birth-control sexology, and offers a significant departure from the bourgeois morality of the birth-control movement and its conservative family ideologies. Lenore's authority as a model woman figure is not, however, automatically associated with embracing sexual pleasure. Her new knowledge is about work and economic independence, like that of the heroine—a female doctor, surrounded by other doctors—of Eleanor Dark's first novel, *Slow Dawning*, begun around the same time but not published until 1932. Devanny's use of a man as knowledgeable informant for her New Woman about sex and birth control in this text is not repeated in her later fiction—except to some extent with Dr. Stallard in *Poor Swine*; more often in her later work women's knowledge of these matters is constructed as something opaque to men, as in *Bushman Burke* (1930).

Lenore challenges to some extent the notions of "good" women held by her Maori lover, Kowhatu. When Lenore resists his urgings for her to leave Holly Virtue, with whom she lives, he asserts: "'You are a good woman.... The only right and proper thing is for you to walk right out of this house with me now.'... She went obediently, though she answered as fiercely: 'I am your wife! It is love makes husbands and wives, not ceremonies.'" But her later awakening to true love with her Maori landowning soul mate becomes the proper plot of the novel, and Devanny permits a degree of closure at the end of the novel.

Another feature of these early novels is the discussing and categorizing of different "types" of women. In Devanny's "Evolution of the Sex Life," artists as well as working-class women are "low" in that they share a capacity for sexual pleasure (the "low type" is sexually active, titillated, and ignorant, as embodied, for example, in Margaret's double, Miette, in *The Butcher Shop*). Sex and sexuality function as modalities through which these types are recognizable or not, and as meanings through which classification itself is questioned and negotiated. Devanny's novels use typologies and taxonomies that articulate race and class distinctions in order to focus on the differences among women so that these differences can be discussed. Many of the novels employ doubles—usually white women of different classes. Devanny has a range of attributes attached to the two "types," although her female characters can to some extent go from one type to the other. The two variations of the serious, ethical woman and the butterfly woman correspond to some degree with the earlier New Woman figure and the more modern postwar flapper seeking freedom. The former is usually sexually "unawakened"; both are often unhappily mated. The butterfly never attains substantial ethical responsibility for her actions. The serious, perhaps sexually repressed, woman can move to a sexual "satisfaction" as Lenore does, and Cindie later does—although the latter is "betrayed" in the sequel novel. Pursuit of "the big things of life" done by "big" people comes into conflict with individual fulfillment, mainly sexual—as it does for Eileen in *Sugar Heaven*.

Much of Devanny's short fiction was collected in *Old Savage and Other Stories*, published in 1927. Its reception in reviews was mixed. The reviewer for *The Dundee Courier* (22 March 1927), under the heading "A Colonial Realist," said of the stories: "they are written with a sincerity so absolute that one cannot turn away from them even when they shock and scarify sensibilities. If realism must be, one would desire it to be exercised as it is here." *The Edinburgh Evening News* of 23 March 1927 saw in the stories an extension toward "absolute liberty of thought," perhaps facilitated by their being peopled with characters of "our Dominions," "where life in the great lonely places is in strong contrast to the habits and morals of the civilized world; people whose reason melts before rougher instinct and passion." Devanny here is being taken up in Great Britain in the tradition of what Billie Melman in *Women and the Popular Imagination in the Twenties: Flappers and Nymphs* (1988) calls the Empire romance novel. Melman considers that "the increasing complexity of *real life* after the First World War" produced a shift from the realist to the escapist novel. Apart from the "sex novel" common in the 1920s, the Empire romance, along with the "desert-love" romance, had great appeal.

The setting of the autobiographical *Dawn Beloved* has many resemblances to Devanny's own early life in the mining communities, and the central character, Dawn, has some similarities to Devanny. An article in the 4 August 1928 *Otago Daily Times* considered that the main interest of the book lay in its being "the first attempt to depict in fiction form the home life of the West Coast miner and to analyse the reasons for his communistic tendencies." But it is also a novel about how a young woman such as Dawn gains education, emerges into consciousness, and struggles toward her own liberation.

Lenore Divine is a bridge to a further group of cosmopolitan novels set in Wellington: *Riven* (1929), *Devil Made Saint* (1930), and *Bushman Burke* (in part). With *Riven* the focus shifts from younger flapper freedom-seekers to the mothers to whom it is dedicated, who are also in need of liberation. The usual characterizations of the New Woman paint her as "unmaternal" and motherhood as an unnecessary burden, but this novel shows a mother moving into modernity—able to understand her family but also to free herself from it. *Devil Made*

Dust jacket for Devanny's 1944 book, one of three travel books she published in the 1940s and early 1950s (Bruccoli Clark Layman Archives)

Saint is "a gloomy though powerful story of temperament and genius . . . a harsh repelling story, but written with strength and insight," according to the reviewer in *All About Books* (18 November 1930).

Bushman Burke, which also appeared in 1930, is part cosmopolitan, part bush; its heroine, Flo, goes from Wellington out to the country. The novel forms an interesting comparison with Prichard's *Working Bullocks* (1926), since it involves a triangle that bears some similarities to that of Red Burke, Tessa, and Deb in Prichard's novel. Flo, the urban New Woman, vies with Mary, the country schoolteacher, for Taipo Burke; unlike the outcome in Prichard's book, in this novel the "exotic" woman is the one who gets her man. In *Bushman Burke* Devanny draws a picture of an urban flapper mixing in rather dissolute company; she is very attractive to the man from the bush come into a fortune, but the pair do not have much in common in the city:

All Flo's talk was of dresses and her set's doings and its scandals and the latest erotic novel . . . what he found to say of erotic novels would never keep Flo at his side. All they could do together was dance.

Flo's opposite is a "pure" young country schoolteacher named Mary, who dresses plainly, is at home in the New Zealand bush, and from whom Flo must eventually win Burke. This doubling reverses the Deb/Tessa coupling in Prichard's *Working Bullocks,* in which Deb the rural worker is the heroine and condemns the "town" New Woman as oversexed and corrupt. Flo is also quite blasé about birth control and sees it as a straightforward aspect of managing her own sexuality. She "educates" Mary, largely by introducing her to the delights of frank fiction: she "interested Mary greatly in expounding her knowledge of erotic fiction and of various literary personalities." Isabel Maud Cluett's review of *Bushman Burke* in *All About Books* (17 June 1930) commented that "*Bushman Burke* may be said to be a riotous 'saga of sex.' . . . This writer is–to use a favourite expression of her own–something of an 'exotic' in the field of New Zealand literature."

Devanny's critique of patriarchal sexual politics from the standpoint of the New Woman is complicated by class, generational, and country/city divides, and the implied authorial sympathies are sometimes ambiguous. Flo's response to a boxing match recalls the almost nightmarish dogfight in *Working Bullocks.* She reflects: "This fool Burke thinks me a terribly cold, adroit modern, yet I am sickened by brutality and he loves it. . . . Cock-fights. Bull-fights. Dog-fights. And men-fights." One of Burke's first reactions to Flo is "I just don't understand your class that's all." The country is counterposed to the city: one older character's opinion of modern youth is "what they need is to be dumped down in the bush for a year or two," but this solution is more problematic than perhaps was the retreat to the countryside in the ending to *Lenore Divine.*

Devanny arrived in Sydney in August 1929 with the intention of continuing on to Great Britain, where she felt she had established a market for her fiction. She was welcomed as a novelist of some note in a literary community that included the bohemian group of Sam Rosa and her compatriot, Dulcie Deamer. In the early 1930s there was great interest in committed writing and in "art as a weapon" for the class struggle. In the Soviet Union in 1934 Andrei Aleksandrovich Zhdanov produced his influential account of "revolutionary romanticism" in art, and this and other ideas were much discussed in the leftist circles of the New Theatre and in the Workers' Art Club, in which Devanny played an important organizing role. In addition, when Egon Kisch visited Australia in 1934, she was much influenced by his notions of "reportage" and went on to write *Sugar Heaven,* which she claimed in "The Worker's Contribution to Australian Literature" (1942), was "the first really proletarian novel in Australia."

Another of Devanny's novels had come close to being banned, although Devanny was probably unaware of this incident. In March 1932 the authorities were reading *Poor Swine,* which she had completed during her trip to Europe the previous year. A copy had been intercepted by the South Australian Customs and Excise; they had carefully "enumerate[d] pages on which objectionable matter appears," and official communications suggested that the book had "no literary merit, catering only for the pruriently minded," as well as noting that it was written by the author of another prohibited publication. In June, however, the book was allowed in and was attacked by reviewers in similar terms. The reviewer for *All About Books* (14 June 1932) disliked Devanny's "clever 'modern' portrayals of dissolute characters.... This is the story of a woman who, though married and with children of her own, uses a succession of lovers, firstly, to satisfy a vague 'desire to develop,' and secondly, to assist her to a career . . . her story is nauseating . . . by definitely appealing for the reader's sympathy the author hoists a banner of conscienceless 'freedom.'"

Out of Such Fires (1934), another novel of the bush, came out in New York since Duckworth, Devanny recalls in *Point of Departure,* "on account of an anti-religious bias pervading its main theme, thought it unsuitable for publication in England." The conflict between the city and the countryside that features in several of the novels through the counterposed values and lives of their characters was based on Devanny's own experiences. She wrote in a letter to Frank Ryland dated 2 November 1946 that, despite needing and enjoying what urban environments could offer to an artist, "I never had any feeling of fascination or fineness in connection with work in cities. I belong to the earth, the sea." For Helena Savine, the heroine of *Out of Such Fires,* the issue of birth control, identified by Devanny in other earlier writings as a crucial aspect of women's independence, becomes a central ground of conflict between herself and the station owner, Boy, whom she marries, and her mother-in-law. Boy and his mother are dogmatic Catholics, but Helena reveals to Boy that she has a reason for her refusal to have children—hereditary syphilis.

Devanny had spent much of her time since she arrived in Australia working for the Communist Party; she was considered one of the finest public orators of her time. Throughout her life Devanny struggled with how to prioritize politics and literature—both in terms of the time allotted to either activity and in terms of how,

and how far, her fiction could or should engage with politics. To be a writer of fiction at all required much negotiation: to fend off the demands of the Left and the progressive movements, and then of the Communist Party specifically, for her oratorical abilities and energy as an agitator, she came up with various rationales. Among them were that she was writing to make a living for her family and that she was putting a developed writer's craft at the service of the proletarian novel. Many New Women of the time found comradeship and support in activism and organizing around socialist and feminist issues. Such goals could involve some conflict as well, for those who were associated with the Communist Party did not, as Joyce Stevens comments in *Taking the Revolution Home: Work among Women in the Communist Party of Australia, 1920–1945* (1987), "regard themselves as feminists no matter how actively they were engaged in women's politics."

In Sydney in the early 1930s Devanny completed two more novels, *The Ghost Wife* (1935) and *The Virtuous Courtesan* (1935). In *Point of Departure* Devanny remarks, "Though I had ceased to regard fiction writing as of any importance, there was still the necessity to earn some money." According to Kay Brown, the author of the Mount Isa novel *Knock Ten* (1976), in a 1987 essay for *Hecate,* Devanny still had some intermittent bits of income from royalties and would sometimes ask her to go shopping. Brown also recalled one strategy Devanny would employ in order to get novels completed in the face of all her other commitments: "She'd get two large packets of cigarettes and take a room at the Cross and give no-one her address. And I'd take along food—that was always important."

The Ghost Wife has some similarities of atmosphere and urban setting to J. M. Harcourt's *Upsurge* (1934), and to some extent it re-creates the earlier New Woman embarking upon a quest for freedom. The title character is a person of "purity" but also alcoholic and into "the dope." Her combination of "melting grace" and "formidable tenacity" produces some confusion about how she might be understood. Mona, whose novel of this family is destroyed in the course of the story, asks, "What sort of woman was she? Vampire? Angel? She-devil? Saint?" Devanny's novel suggests that she might have been all of these things—a complex angel in the house that has to be exorcised.

The cover of Devanny's next novel, *The Virtuous Courtesan,* published by the American publisher Macauley, describes Devanny as "the Australian iconoclast." The book is innovative in featuring lesbian and gay couples. Their working-class employees observe the sexual and other habits—including heavy drinking and domestic violence—of this group of artists and bohemians with bemusement. Mrs. Myers, the housekeeper,

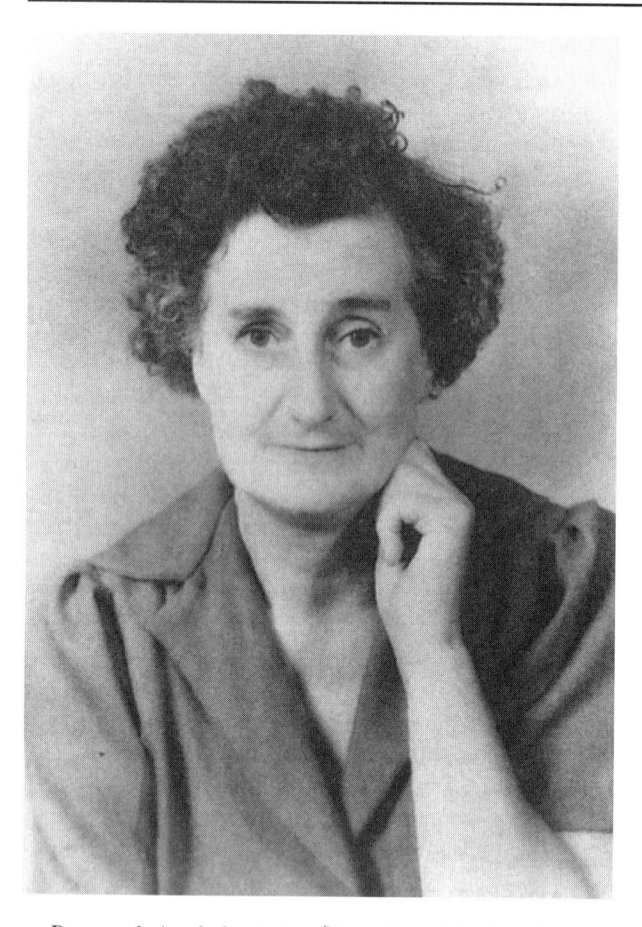

Devanny during the late 1950s (James Cook University Library)

sums up the characters for whom she works as "'Camp' the lot of them." According to the cover blurb the novel focuses upon "the cumulating dilemma of Sharon, a successful dancer and artist's model." She is "married to a worthless sot" but is "reluctantly falling in love with an unemployed labourer." Sharon is described as seeing men as "mere incidents in her life to satisfy a normal hunger"; she "has no inclination to assume the discomfort of what passes for virtue." The novel offers an examination of the situation of working-class women in prostitution at this period; the book focuses on Jo, a prostitute whose "mother sold her out when she was ten." Jo discusses with Poppy, who runs the business, the differences in perceived morality between herself and women such as Sharon. Poppy's opinion is that "they're amateurs and we're professionals. They do it for pleasure and we do it for money." The boundaries are traversed when Sharon visits a brothel and, later, takes Jo to live with her. Poppy describes her entry into sex work as a result of having been betrayed by the man she expected to marry and having aborted her child with a knitting needle: "What put me in the game . . . was the hate, mixed up with the sex." Jo, however, resists being rescued by Sharon. The novel also includes some discussion of the role and purposes of art in society.

Devanny later specifically dismissed these two novels as not "serious," but *The Virtuous Courtesan* deals with some quite radical and confrontational material— indeed, it was banned on publication in 1935. Perhaps the suggestion on the cover that the work dealt with "the manner in which passion, greed and circumstances kick the stuffing out of all the ostensible moral values" encouraged the banning. In this novel the central female character who presented moral problems that confounded the censors was not the older-style New Woman but the freedom-seeking flapper. *The Virtuous Courtesan* is also an interesting precursor to the novel of life in Sydney by Dymphna Cusack and Florence James, *Come in Spinner,* which was heavily censored at its publication in 1951 and only printed in its entirety in 1988.

In the mid 1930s Devanny made a turn to the "industrial novel" and to "reportage." She had begun to spend time in Mount Isa and north Queensland, traveling there initially on speaking tours for the Movement Against War and Fascism. *Sugar Heaven,* the first of her sugar industry novels, was set during the major cane-cutters' strikes over Weil's Disease in the mid 1930s. Apart from being a strike novel, *Sugar Heaven* also sets out to combat prejudices toward migrants and features a relationship between one of the two central female characters, Eileen, and an Italian cane cutter, Tony. Nationalism, often strident, was a strong force in Australian literary life; it included writers of the Left and of the Communist Party. In Bruce Molloy's article "An Interview with Frank Hardy" for *Australian Literary Studies* (1976), Hardy recalled a conversation with Frank Dalby Davison in which they talked of the influence of Prichard's *Working Bullocks:* "Here was a book written by an Australian, written as well as any of the foreign writers. . . . I read *Working Bullocks* and *Sugar Heaven . . .* and I thought, 'These girls are on the right track.'"

Devanny's next sugar novel was *Paradise Flow* (1938). She wrote a letter to Duckworth on 5 August 1937 in relation to it: "Somehow, I think I am only at the beginning of my literary career. The left stuff is coming into its own." But her confidence was greatly misplaced: *Paradise Flow* was the last of her novels that Duckworth published. "The bourgeois publishers, of course," she had commented in a letter to Lily Turner of 8 August 1937, "are scandalised at my work, though the bourgeois press gives me fine reviews," but the reviews never again approached those she had received in her earlier years with Duckworth.

In *Paradise Flow* Devanny returns again to the squatter class. The central female character, Laurel, has some similarities to Elodie in Prichard's *Intimate Strangers,* published in 1937. But while the latter resists the romantic Jerome Hartog, Laurel, by a perhaps too convenient twist of plot, is freed to ally herself with the Lawrencean figure, Muranivich. The landowning "big man," Big Mac, is supplanted–not by his gamekeeper but by his manager. An aged Kanaka briefly appears in the novel, but not until *Cindie,* published in 1949, is there a fuller presentation of South Sea islander and also Aboriginal characters. They were absent in Devanny's earlier pictures of Australian bush life, including *Out of Such Fires,* but she intended in the trilogy to make good this deficit.

Devanny spent most of the period of World War II in Queensland. For much of this time she was under expulsion from the Communist Party. The most widely circulated reason was "sexual immorality" or "sexual indiscretion," but the circumstances of it–detailed in Carole Ferrier's *Jean Devanny: Romantic Revolutionary* (1999)–were complicated and murky. Although Devanny was readmitted to the party at the end of the war, she never really recovered from what many later recognized as a grossly unjust excommunication. Completed in 1942, *Roll Back the Night* (1945) was set in "Pearltown," the north Queensland town of Cairns, in the period of the outbreak of the war. The central characters are German–Hans Gruner and his wife, Greta, and two women, Helen Lorrimer and Eleanor Gold. It deals with the threat of internment that hung indiscriminately over fascist-sympathizing and communist antifascist European migrants. "Gold Is My Heart; or Reconnaissance," which opens in December 1942, was completed as a result of a request Franklin had received for such a novel, but the proposed American publishers did not like it. During the war, Devanny had made a shift to journalism in some of her published literary work with the preparation of *Bird of Paradise* (1945), a rather dull account of the homefront. Another never-published book, set on Magnetic Island, exists in two versions–one a travelogue, the other with an interpolated fictional romance narration that made it a hybrid of fiction and travel writing. Her *By Tropic Sea and Jungle* (1944) is much livelier and better written.

A trilogy on the historical development of the Queensland sugar industry, a similar undertaking to Prichard's planned goldfields novels, was the next major literary task that Devanny had in prospect. *Cindie: A Chronicle of the Canefields* was the first volume; "a long novel around the White Australia policy" she called it in a letter to Frank Ryland of 18 May 1945. Completed in that year, it combines the modes of history, reportage, realism, and romance. The publishers in 1948 expressed a nervousness that "some of the love scenes border on the licentious," but Robert Hale of London published it in 1949.

This was the last novel that Devanny managed to get published, although she persisted throughout the 1950s in writing and in seeking publishing opportunities. She was daunted when the Australasian Book Society did not accept "You Can't Have Everything," the second volume of the trilogy that she had finished by 1947. In 1950 she completed another novel that remains unpublished, set on Thursday Island. "The Divers, the Devil and Pan, or Pearls and Baroque" Devanny described as "built around the pearling industry . . . absolutely authentic . . . in respect of the diving and pearling life in general. I dived myself and lived for some time on Thursday Island to get the material," she told Alan Moyle, editor of *The Australian Post,* in a letter of 6 April 1950. It is an incisive study of endemic alcoholism and highly complex race relations, but all she managed to publish about Thursday Island was a series of articles in the Communist Party's paper, *The Tribune.*

Devanny tried again for Australian publication with Angus and Robertson for another urban novel, "Restaurant," which she described to Beatrice Davis in a letter of 16 May 1957 as "a light novel . . . around a fictional restaurant at Kings Cross . . . unlike anything I have previously written." Davis wrote back on 25 July 1957, "It is just not our kind of book. Though there are several good character studies in it, the novel is of the light, melodramatic, popular type–with everything just a bit overdone . . . there is a great emphasis on sex." Australian publishers were as intransigent about taking her work as those overseas had become, and Devanny encountered endless frustration in relation to the publication of her work throughout the 1950s. Her autobiography, begun in the early 1940s, had undergone several revisions; it was an important book to her because it sought to show the conditions in the Communist Party that had produced the expulsion of someone like herself, and she saw it as likely to have a potentially good effect upon the party. The Cold War climate of the 1950s continued to discourage her from publication, however, since she had no desire to give to the enemies of "Communism" the ammunition that they could have found in its pages.

Jean Devanny died on 8 March 1962. She was a radical figure far ahead of her time. Conflicts persisted throughout her life in relation to political activism and private life, and to political activism and writing. In the latter part of her life she regretted that she had not put more of her time into writing. Given the importance of her activities as agitator, orator, reformer, and political organizer, it is, rather, surprising that she managed to write and publish as much and as interestingly as she did, in a life that she described in her autobiography as "a ridiculously rushed affair." Without her tireless engagement with the life of her times, of course, her writing might well have lacked its inspirational force, its vitality, and its communication of confidence about the ability of human energies to transform the world in small and large ways.

Biography:

Carole Ferrier, *Jean Devanny: Romantic Revolutionary* (Melbourne: Melbourne University Press, 1999).

References:

Ann L. Ardis, *New Women, New Novels: Feminism and Early Modernism* (New Brunswick & London: Rutgers University Press, 1990);

Kay Brown, "Kay Brown Remembers Jean Devanny," *Hecate*, 13, no. 1 (1987): 132–137;

Isabel Maud Cluett, "Exodus of New Zealand Writers," *All About Books* (17 June 1930): 164;

Joy Damousi, *Women Come Rally: Socialism, Communism and Gender in Australia, 1890–1955* (Melbourne: Oxford University Press, 1994);

Maryanne Dever, ed., *Wallflowers and Witches: Women and Culture in Australia, 1910–1945* (St. Lucia: University of Queensland Press, 1994), pp. 73–90, 147–162;

Kay Ferres, "Written on the Body: Jean Devanny, Sexuality and Censorship," *Hecate*, 20, no. 1 (1994): 123–134;

Carole Ferrier, *As Good as a Yarn with You: Letters Between Miles Franklin, Katharine Susannah Prichard, Jean Devanny, Marjorie Barnard, Flora Eldershaw and Eleanor Dark* (Cambridge: Cambridge University Press, 1992);

Ferrier, "*Sugar Heaven* and the Reception of Working Class Texts," *Hecate*, 11, no. 1 (1985): 19–25;

John Hay and Brenda Walker, eds., *Katharine Susannah Prichard: Centenary Essays* (London: University of Western Australia and Australian Studies Centre, 1984), pp. 13–28;

Drusilla Modjeska, *Exiles at Home: Australian Women Writers 1925–1945* (Sydney: Angus & Robertson, 1981);

Nelle M. Scanlan, "Banned by the Censors," *New Zealand Free Lance* (26 May 1926);

Susan Sheridan, *Along the Faultlines: Sex, Race and Nation in Australian Women's Writing, 1880s–1930s* (Sydney: Allen & Unwin, 1995);

Joyce Stevens, *Taking the Revolution Home: Work among Women in the Communist Party of Australia, 1920–1945* (Melbourne: Sybylla, 1987).

Papers:

Jean Devanny's papers, including unpublished manuscripts of novels, and the early treatises on sexuality are in the James Cook University library in Townsville. Extensive correspondence, much published in *As Good as a Yarn with You*, is also in the National Library of Australia and the Mitchell Library, State Library of New South Wales.

Rosemary Dobson
(18 June 1920 -   )

Marie-Louise Ayres
National Library of Australia

BOOKS: *Poems—juvenilia* (Mittagong, N.S.W.: Frensham Press, 1937);
In a Convex Mirror (Sydney: Dymock's Book Arcade, 1944);
The Ship of Ice: With Other Poems (Sydney: Angus & Robertson, 1948);
Child with a Cockatoo and Other Poems (Sydney: Angus & Robertson, 1955);
Poems (Adelaide: Australian Letters, 1960);
Australia: Land of Colour through the Eyes of Australian Painters (Sydney: Ure Smith, 1962);
Rosemary Dobson: Poems (Sydney: Angus & Robertson, 1963);
Cock Crow (Sydney: Angus & Robertson, 1965);
Focus on Ray Crooke (St. Lucia: University of Queensland Press, 1971);
Three Poems on Water-Springs (Canberra: Brindabella Press, 1973);
A World of Difference: Australian Poetry and Painting in the 1940s (Sydney: Wentworth Press, 1973);
Selected Poems (Sydney: Angus & Robertson, 1973; revised, 1980);
Greek Coins: A Sequence of Poems (Canberra: Brindabella Press, 1977);
Over the Frontier (Sydney: Angus & Robertson, 1978);
The Continuance of Poetry: Twelve Poems for David Campbell (Canberra: Brindabella Press, 1981);
The Three Fates and Other Poems (Sydney: Hale & Iremonger, 1984);
Summer Press (St. Lucia & New York: University of Queensland Press, 1987);
Seeing and Believing: Modern Poets, Pamphlet Poets, series 1, no. 3 (Canberra: National Library of Australia, 1990);
Collected Poems (Sydney: Angus & Robertson, 1991);
Untold Lives: A Sequence of Poems (Canberra: Brindabella Press, 1992);
Untold Lives and Later Poems (Rose Bay, N.S.W.: Brandl & Schlesinger, 2000).

Rosemary Dobson (National Library of Australia)

RECORDING: *Rosemary Dobson Reads from Her Own Work,* Poets on Record, St. Lucia, University of Queensland Press, 1970.

OTHER: *Australian Poetry 1949–1950,* selected by Dobson (Sydney: Angus & Robertson, 1950);
Songs for All Seasons: 100 Poems for Young People, selected by Dobson (Sydney: Angus & Robertson, 1967);
Australian Voices: Poetry and Prose of the 1970s, edited by Dobson (Canberra: Australian National University Press, 1975);

Moscow Trefoil: Poems from the Russian of Anna Akhmatova and Osip Mandelstam, translation constituting a new version of the work, by Dobson, David Campbell, and Natalie Staples (Canberra: Australian National University Press, 1975);

Seven Russian Poets: Imitations, translation constituting a new version of the work, by Dobson and Campbell (St. Lucia: University of Queensland Press, 1979);

Sisters Poets, 1, edited by Dobson (Carlton, Vic.: Sisters, 1979);

Journeys: Poems, by Dobson, Judith Wright, Gwen Harwood, Dorothy Hewett, and Fay Zwicky, edited by Zwicky (Carlton South, Vic.: Sisters, 1982), pp. 16–24;

"Statement," in *Poetry and Gender: Statements and Essays in Australian Women's Poetry and Poetics,* edited by David Brooks and Brenda Walker (St. Lucia: University of Queensland Press, 1989), pp. 31–33;

Directions, edited by Dobson (Ryde, N.S.W.: Round Table Publications, 1991).

Rosemary Dobson has been admired as one of the finest and most enduring poets of Australia ever since the appearance of her first volume in 1944. Her long practice of the poetic craft is characterized by a measured cadence, love of the austere, devotion to traditional forms, and a poetic drive that she called in "Statement" (1989) " . . . a search for something only fugitively glimpsed." Dobson's poetic was firmly established early in her writing life and is recognizable in works spanning many years: her aesthetic is one of a continuous reworking of themes and concerns and a deepening artistic apprehension.

Rosemary de Brissac Dobson was born in Sydney, the daughter of Arthur Dobson (son of English poet Austin Dobson) and Marjorie Caldwell Dobson. Her father died when Dobson was five years old and her older sister Ruth seven; their mother was left to raise her daughters in straitened circumstances. Marjorie Dobson accepted a position as housemistress at the prestigious and progressive girls' school Frensham, in Mittagong, New South Wales, in return for scholarships for her daughters. The school served both Dobson sisters well: Rosemary Dobson's successful career in poetry was matched in a different arena by that of her sister Ruth, who became Australia's first female career diplomat to be appointed Australian Ambassador. The school encouraged academic excellence and creative endeavor, in both literary and visual arts. Dobson excelled at both, and her juvenile *Poems* (1937) was written and printed at Frensham when she was only seventeen years old; Dobson produced its linocut cover in addition to printing and binding the volume with the printer Joan Phipson.

After a brief period teaching art at Frensham, Dobson studied English literature at the University of Sydney as a nondegree student and studied drawing with Thea Proctor, a well-known Australian artist. In her early twenties Dobson commenced employment with Australian publishers Angus and Robertson, where she worked with Beatrice Davis, one of the most influential editors of Australian literature during the immediate postwar period. During the 1940s Dobson established friendships and working relationships with many of the most significant Australian writers, including Douglas Stewart, Norman Lindsay, Francis Webb, and Nan McDonald.

Dobson met Alec Bolton in 1950 when he joined Angus and Robertson as an editor, and they married the following year. Their three children–Lissant, Robert, and Ian–were born during the 1950s while the family lived in Sydney. Angus and Robertson appointed Bolton their London editor in 1966, and the family enjoyed a five-year sojourn in England, during which Dobson and Bolton developed their interests in European art, music, and literature, and in fine printing. The family returned to Australia, moving to Canberra in 1971 when Bolton was appointed the first Director of Publications at the National Library of Australia. Dobson undertook some writing and editing while raising their family in the 1950s, 1960s, and 1970s, but her main work besides her family was always her poetry, which flourished in the rich literary atmosphere of Canberra. Bolton's passionate commitment to small-press work, his establishment of the Brindabella Press in 1972, and his eventual retirement from his National Library position in 1987 to work with the Brindabella Press full-time, deepened the couple's ties with Australian literary production and their relationships with the select handful of Australian writers whose works were published by the press, including David Campbell, R. F. Brissenden, A. D. Hope, James McAuley, and Philip Hodgins. Dobson provided editorial advice and proofreading services, and produced illustrations for several of her own works published by the press. After Bolton's death in 1996, Dobson remained in the Canberra home that she and Bolton had shared; she published *Untold Lives and Later Poems* (2000) after her eightieth birthday. Dobson's contribution to Australian literature has been recognized through her receipt of the Patrick White Award in 1984, the Order of Australia in 1987, and an honorary Doctor of Letters from the University of Sydney and Australia Council Writer's Emeritus Award in 1996. In 2000 the National Library of Australia held one of its rare "Celebrations" for Rosemary Dobson–as it had previously done for Alec Bolton in 1993–and published an accompanying tribute volume. She received the *Age* Book of the Year Award in 2001 for *Untold Lives and Later Poems.*

Dobson published her first three volumes—*In a Convex Mirror* (1944), *The Ship of Ice: With Other Poems* (1948), and *Child with a Cockatoo and Other Poems* (1955)—in little more than a decade, with the first establishing her reputation and the following volumes confirming it. The contents of these three early volumes are weighed strongly toward meditations on European painting, cartography, and printing. The earliest critics and reviewers of Dobson's work wrote almost exclusively about these "painting" poems, not always flatteringly. A. D. Hope, for instance, in a 1944 review dismissed her work as "parasitic," but he later repudiated his assessment in 1955 when he called her "the most perfect of our poets." Later critics, such as Elizabeth Lawson and David McCooey, who both contributed articles to *Rosemary Dobson: A Celebration* (2000), edited by Joy Hooton, have concentrated less on what is represented in these poems—often, at first glance, a written "version" of a well known painting—and more on their conscious negotiations of representation.

For the early Dobson, art is the "ampersand"—itself the title of one of her poems—between subject positions and those artists who are peculiarly receptive to this dissolution of ego boundaries. At the extremities of this dissolution, her artists become part of or disappear into their paintings, a device Dobson occasionally employs when writing of her own craft as poet. For Dobson, art—in the form of paintings, poetry, printing, or music—both records a vanishing world and calls that world back into being. In her early and much anthologized "Country Press" (1948), for instance, the use of a printing press transfers the minutiae of country life onto the printed page and returns those histories into the physical world: the premises of the press are progressively covered with print and transformed into one of the worlds within worlds that Dobson explores in much of her early work.

This exchange or transfer is never simple or unproblematic, even in these earliest volumes. There are certainly many moments in which she proposes clear exchanges between artist and viewer, artist and reader, or past and present. In "Paintings" (1955), art transcends boundaries—"What is Time / Since Art has conquered it?"—and is posed as a dialogue—"I speak. . . . You hear"—that collapses subject positions. Even in such poems, however, Dobson retains the sense of a dynamic relationship between presence and absence, speech and silence, and self and other; what principally concerns her is the space between these entities. This space is figured in various ways, most famously in "In a Convex Mirror" (1944), in which neither

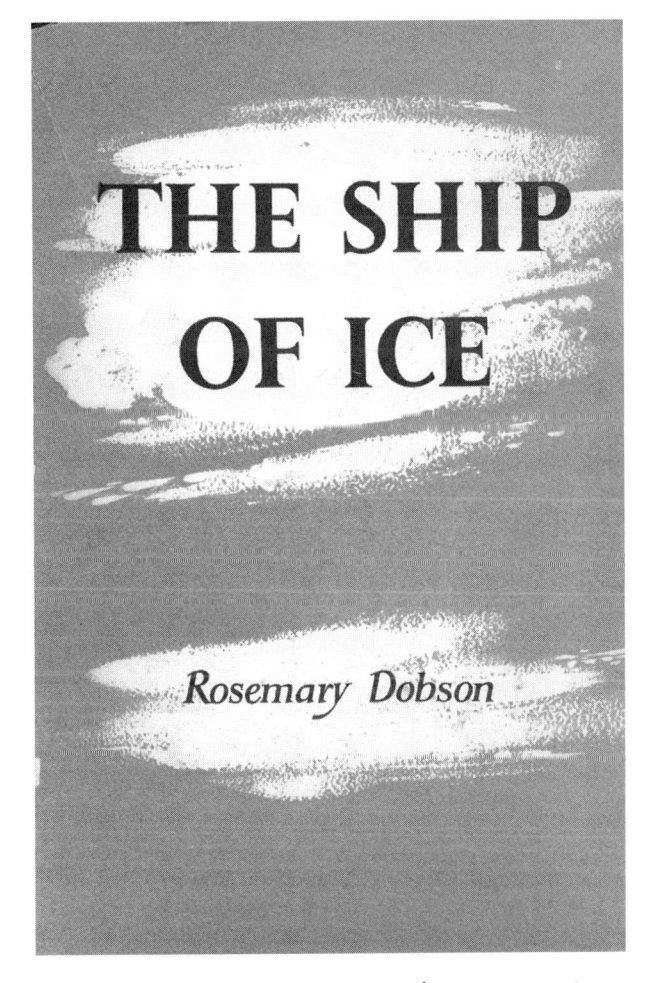

Dust jacket for Dobson's 1948 collection. The title poem won her the Sydney Morning Herald *prize for poetry in 1946 (Bruccoli Clark Layman Archives).*

"selves" or "images" nor presence or absence are opposed neatly on either side of a directly reflecting mirror. In what is a key and continuing aesthetic maneuver in Dobson's work, the mirror changes "images": the convexity of the mirror turns the figures of the poem toward each other, so that they "stand / As pictured angels touching wings."

This sense of the possibilities of images, both artistic and poetic, is figured in many poems as "annunciation," which imbues the last poems of this period—those dealing with the death, just hours after birth, of Dobson and Bolton's first child—with a deep sense of tragedy. In a moving pair of poems, "The Birth" and "The Birth (ii)"—both written in 1955—all the possibilities of connection and coming into being are matched by the grief of connections that do not flower or bear fruit: "So there was light / And human hands, before the tide / Returned you to the oblivious night."

Ten years passed between the publication in 1955 of *Child with a Cockatoo* and Dobson's next volume, *Cock*

Dobson with her husband, Alec Bolton, and their children, Robert, Ian, and Lissant, during a holiday in Moss Vale, circa 1965 (photograph by Alec Bolton)

Crow (1965), years during which Dobson explored and wrote her experiences of grief and then those of pregnancy, childbirth, and motherhood–often figured as countries or territories of which she is explorer and cartographer. In writing of these experiences Dobson neither rejects nor turns away from her earlier visions of paintings and of involvement in the space that they inhabit. In "To Meet the Child," for instance, she becomes a cartographer, traveling alone to map out the unknown country of childbirth, and a painter trying to find the way between "mirage," "focus," and "vision." There is, inevitably, a "return" from this "unmapped country," but the return is not a simple one in which the journey is merely reversed but instead is one that harks back to the convex mirror that translates images inexactly: "And together we shall return to our own country / With word of wonders, by another way."

The "word" itself is not simple or sufficient to describe the "wonders." Indeed, in her poems of maternity, a constant theme is that language is the necessary grief that intrudes upon the undifferentiated and symbiotic relationship between mother and child, a separation that enables agency and subjecthood. In "The Fever" this "doomed, entangled, piercing cry" is also the cry of erotic passion and is intimately connected with edges, extremities, and creative disorder.

Dobson found herself unable to write during her extended stay in England, but her experiences and deeper knowledge of European cultural history provided material for writing following her return to Australia. While she continued to write about paintings and the visual arts, her interests turned increasingly to her own poetic vocation and to her sense of inheriting a long and honorable tradition. During the 1970s, for instance, Dobson and her friend and fellow poet Campbell honed their craft in a long series of "translations" or "imitations" of the great Russian poets of the twentieth century. These translations were published in *Moscow Trefoil: Poems from the Russian of Anna Akhmatova and Osip Mandelstam* (1975) and *Seven Russian Poets: Imitations* (1979). Dobson and Campbell shared an interest in ancient Greek and Chinese poets, in addition to contemporary European, American, and Australian writers.

This sense of a personal poetic heritage–and of obligation to an ancient vocation–informs all of Dobson's work during the 1970s and 1980s. The title poem of her 1978 collection *Over the Frontier* announces that "the poem that exists / will never equal the poem that does not exist." While this statement may appear substantially removed from her earlier certainties about the ability of art to transcend time and separation, the poem reprises earlier themes of annunciation, with the written poem acting as a kind of angel, "bringing news of the poem that does not exist" and the messages of "the possibilities of order / buzzing and humming."

In these meditations on her poetic heritage, Dobson's longing for clarity and order is matched by her passion for the flawed means by which poets will inevitably fail in the search for such order and her understanding that this failure is what defines both her humanity and her aesthetic. In her "Poems from Pausanias," for instance, Dobson marvels at Pausanias's apparently complete and exact translation of the world of which he writes, "kept, by some notation, in his mind," but she reserves most of her praise for the tools he employs to effect this notation, "diligent enquiry" and "reverence."

This theme is repeated many times and in many ways in *Over the Frontier* and her subsequent volume, *The Three Fates and Other Poems* (1984). She praises the painter Giorgio Morandi for spending forty years drawing and painting the same group of pots on a table in "The Artist's Wife" (1973), remembers her early experiences of translation in "Essay for a French Class" (1980), and resolves in her series "On Museums" (1984) to continue with her self-appointed task:

> Learn still; take, reject,
> Choose, use, create,
> Put past to present purpose. Make.

In "The Three Fates" a poem in which the protagonist is condemned to live his life over and over with no possibility of affecting its course—she also recognizes the possible tragic effects of having the desire for transparency, complete knowledge, or exact translation granted. Most of the works in the 1984 volume are concerned with acceptance of loss and the certainty of death, as in "Flute Music":

> We who walk backwards from birth waving and smiling
> Will walk also towards death.
>
> And who can tell when it is time to turn and walk forwards . . .

She is also concerned with celebrating love and friendship—especially literary friendship—in the face of this certainty. This confluence of concerns reaches its highest pitch in *The Continuance of Poetry: Twelve Poems for David Campbell* (1981), published two years after Campbell's death and republished in *The Three Fates*. In these elegies Dobson meditates on the nature of human affection, on the giving and receiving of gifts, and particularly on the nature of exchange between poets:

> Two poets walking together
> May pause suddenly and say,
> Will this be your poem, or mine?

She writes, too, of the transformative power of poetry, as in "2. The Messages":

> But here on the page are your messages.
>
> Here are poems: stones, shells, water.
> This one weighs in the hand. This one is shining.
>
> This one is yellow. And this smooth to the fingers.

While much of the work written in the first forty years of Dobson's career refers to personal experiences—maternity, friendship, and loss—these references are oblique and reticent: Dobson is the antithesis of the "confessional" poet. In her last two volumes, *Seeing and Believing: Modern Poets* (1990) and *Untold Lives and Later Poems,* however, she strips away some of the barriers previously erected between poet and reader, and speaks with a voice that encompasses all her previous aesthetic concerns and disciplines but pursues austerity precisely through stripping disguise from her own lived experience.

Seeing and Believing is inflected throughout by the sudden and devastating deterioration of Dobson's eyesight, as in "One day the dark fell over my eye," and is a sustained meditation on all her loss of sight means, both in the everyday world, in its intimations of mortality, and in its centrality to her poetic:

> If you should come to find me here
> I will look up with one good eye
>
> From these my books, this pen, this chair,
> Table, thin curtained window pane
>
> To greet you. In the other eye
> That edge of light, that shadowy sea.
>   –from "The Eye ii"

While much of Dobson's work is the work of "the other eye"–the world that looks beyond the personal and seeks "fugitive" glimpses of the eternal world–it is as if this bodily experience of doubled sight prompts Dobson to look back clearly with the "eye" that is concerned with the lived world and to resurrect it from the shadows.

Dobson with her husband at the "Celebration of Alec Bolton" held by the Friends of the National Library of Australia in 1993 (photograph by Louis Seselja, National Library of Australia)

Indeed, the project of the *Untold Lives* sequence is a reconciliation between the poetic eye and the eye of personal history, as Dobson herself acknowledges in her preface. The poems are driven by Dobson's need to tell the stories of everyday individuals who remain tantalizingly resistant to the aesthetic habits of recovery that Dobson employs in many of her earlier poems about long-dead painters, poets, or legendary figures. Some, such as the almost forgotten "Aunt Molly" of "Who?" are associated with the innocence and puzzlements of childhood. Others, such as the sinister "Major-General," who presents his wife with a fresh-cut flower each morning "laid on the breakfast-table like a threat," are much darker. But Dobson's "lives" also include those much closer to her, including her dead mother and living daughter. "The Apparition," for instance, laments that the barrier of death means there can be no two-way communication between herself and her mother and the matrilineage that the apparition represents, "My mother, hers, and the long line backwards of women":

Is it grave or swaddling clothes you are after? Tell me.
Can you forgive me, I ask. What should I have done?
Speak to me, turn your face, give me an answer.

The "apparition," however, exists in the silent realm of portents and disturbances, of unease and restlessness, and the longed-for answer does not come. The failure of this communication, the failure of art to conquer time, presses Dobson to write to and for the living, to conduct the exchange while it is still possible:

What can I send that's equal in return?
These words (this gift, this poem) go to my daughter
In Murik village by the Lower Sepik.
                –from "The Anthropologist"

Inevitably, as Dobson has grown older, many of her poems are elegies for parents, friends, and her own youth. All of them honor their subjects and serve as meditations on the nature of love and friendship, gratitude and grief. Some also celebrate intellectual companionship with poets and artists. *Untold Lives* finishes with three elegies for her husband, Alec Bolton, celebrating the fullness of the family and intellectual life they shared. These poems lament the passing of her husband—"And you, oh you / Who were always with me, You, gone, too"—but in doing so, acknowledge what her poetic task has been throughout her career, "Praise taken / From Saxon word-hoard."

Dobson's poetic career, rather like Morandi's painting career, has been one of steady commitment to contemplation, traditional forms, and the discipline of discovering and rendering anew oft-repeated themes and concerns. Unlike the work of her female contemporaries in Australia, such as Judith Wright and Dorothy Hewett, hers has never been overtly political, has invited no controversy, and has eschewed the confessional. Dobson's personal shyness and modesty are reflected in a body of work that honors rather than tries to break with tradition and that "praises" those who have gone before her. Her commitment to classical forms might align her more closely with her male contemporaries, such as Hope, McAuley, Campbell, and Brissenden. Unlike them, however, she has lived no public life as academic and teacher. More importantly, her sustained contemplation of the dualities of life, and more particularly of the texture of the space between those dualities—whether rendered as convex mirror, canvas, or the linen of grave and swaddling clothes—is subtly different from any of her contemporaries, and renders the voice of Rosemary Dobson utterly distinctive and recognizable in twentieth-century Australian poetry.

Biography:
Joy Hooton, "Rosemary Dobson: A Life of Making Poetry," in *Rosemary Dobson: A Celebration,* edited by Hooton (Canberra: Friends of the National Library of Australia, 2000), pp. 1–29.

References:
Marie-Louise Ayres, "'Letting Fall the Folds of Unseen Linen': Rosemary Dobson," in "'Me Is Not a Stable Reality': Negotiations of Identity in the Poetry of Dorothy Auchterlonie, Rosemary Dobson, Dorothy Hewett and J. S. Harry," dissertation, Australian National University, 1994, pp. 80–188;

Ayres, "Rosemary Dobson: The Text and the Textile," *Australian Literary Studies,* 17, no. 1 (May 1995): 3–9;

Veronica Brady, "Over the Frontier: The Poetry of Rosemary Dobson," in *Poetry and Gender: Statements and Essays in Australian Women's Poetry and Poetics,* edited by David Brooks and Brenda Walker (St. Lucia: University of Queensland Press, 1989), pp. 105–127;

Joy Hooton, ed., *Rosemary Dobson: A Celebration* (Canberra: Friends of the National Library of Australia, 2000);

A. D. Hope, "Rosemary Dobson: A Portrait in a Mirror," *Quadrant,* 16, no. 4 (1972): 10–14;

A. Mitchell, "A Frame of Reference: Rosemary Dobson's Grace Notes for Humanity," *Australian Literary Studies,* 10, no. 1 (1981): 3–12;

Fay Zwicky, "Reclusive Grace: The Poetry of Rosemary Dobson," in *The Lyre in the Pawnshop: Essays on Literature & Survival* (Nedlands: University of Western Australia Press, 1986), pp. 112–123.

Papers:
The National Library of Australia holds collections of Rosemary Dobson's papers.

Mary Durack
(20 February 1913 – 16 December 1994)

Don Grant
Curtin University of Technology

BOOKS: *Little Poems of Sunshine* (Perth: Sampson, 1923);

All-About: The Story of a Black Community on Argyle Station, Kimberley, by Durack and Elizabeth Durack (Sydney: Bulletin-Endeavour Press, 1935);

Chunuma, by Durack and Elizabeth Durack (Sydney: Bulletin-Endeavour Press, 1936);

Son of Djaro, by Durack and Elizabeth Durack (Sydney: Bulletin-Endeavour Press, 1938);

Piccaninnies, by Durack and Elizabeth Durack (Sydney: Offset Printing, 1940);

The Way of the Whirlwind, by Durack and Elizabeth Durack (Sydney: Consolidated Press, 1941);

A Book of Picture Stories, by Durack and Elizabeth Durack (Perth: Imperial Printing, 1944);

The Magic Trumpet, by Durack and Elizabeth Durack (London & New York: Cassell, 1946; Melbourne: Cassell, 1946);

Child Artists of the Australian Bush, by Durack and F. Rutter (Sydney: Australasian Publishing, 1952);

Keep Him My Country (London: Constable, 1955; Sydney: Angus & Robertson, 1966);

Kings in Grass Castles (London: Constable, 1959; Hawthorn, Vic.: Lloyd O'Neil, 1974);

To Ride a Fine Horse (London: Macmillan, 1963; Melbourne: Macmillan, 1963; New York: St. Martin's Press, 1963);

Kookanoo and Kangaroo, by Durack and Elizabeth Durack (Adelaide: Rigby, 1963; Minneapolis: Lerner, 1966);

The Courteous Savage: Yagan of Swan River (Edinburgh: Nelson, 1964; Melbourne: Nelson, 1964); republished as *Yagan of the Bibbulmun* (West Melbourne, Vic.: Nelson, 1976);

An Australian Settler (Oxford: Clarendon Press, 1964);

A Pastoral Emigrant (Melbourne & New York: Oxford University Press, 1965);

The Rock and the Sand (London: Constable, 1969; Neutral Bay, N.S.W.: Corgi, 1996);

The End of Dreaming, by Durack and Ingrid Drysdale (Adelaide: Rigby, 1974);

Mary Durack (from John Hetherington, Forty-Two Faces, *1946)*

Swan River Saga: Life of Early Pioneer Eliza Shaw, by Durack and Nita Pannell (Perth: Vanguard Service, 1975);

To Be Heirs Forever (London: Constable, 1976; Sydney: Bantam, 2001);

Tjakamarra: Boy Between Two Worlds (Perth: Vanguard Service, 1977);

The Aborigines in Australian Literature (Perth: Western Australian Institute of Technology, 1978);

Australian Literature: A Voyage of Discovery (Perth: Western Australian Institute of Technology, 1978);

A Legacy of Love, by Durack and B. Mulholland (Perth: Artlook Books, 1981);

Sons in the Saddle (London: Constable / Australia: Hutchinson, 1983);

The Land Beyond Time: A Modern Exploration of Australia's North-West Frontiers, by Durack, John Olsen, Geoffrey Dutton, Vincent Serventy, and Alex Bortignon (Melbourne: Macmillan, 1984);

The Stockman, by Durack, Hugh Sawrey, Marie Mahood, Keith Willey, R. M. Williams, Ron Iddon, and Olaf Buken (Sydney: Landsdowne-Rigby, 1984);

Red Jack, by Durack and Michael Wilkin (Melbourne: Macmillan, 1987).

PLAY PRODUCTIONS: *The Dallying Lama,* Sydney, Australian Broadcasting Commission (ABC), 1959;

Dalgerie, libretto for opera by Durack, music by James Penberthy, Perth, 1966; Sydney, Sydney Opera House, 1973;

The Ship of Dreams, by Durack and music by J. Fitzgerald, Broome, 1968;

The Way of the Whirlwind, Perth, Octagon Theater, 1970;

Swan River Saga, Perth, Hole in the Wall Theater, 1972;

Adam's Rib, Perth, Hole in the Wall Theater, 1975.

SELECTED PERIODICAL PUBLICATIONS–UNCOLLECTED: "Patsy Durack–An Interesting Personality," *Perth Sunday Times,* 1933;

"North Australia Faces a New Phase–Pioneer M. P. Durack Surveys the Past," *Walkabout* (1942);

"Daisy Bates–A Legend in Retrospect," *West Australian,* 1944;

"A Collector in Broome," *Walkabout* (1949);

"Our Native Population," *West Australian,* 1953;

"Writers Don't Spring from the Soil," *West Australian,* 1953;

"Review of Patrick White's *The Tree of Man,*" *Westerly* (1957);

"Afterthoughts on the Adelaide Festival," *Overland* (1963);

"Perth," *Age* (1966);

"Walter Murdoch–Man in the Mirror," *Meanjin Quarterly* (1969);

"WA–A State of Excitement," *Vogue* (1978);

"Ten Best Australian Books," *Age* (1983);

"Call up your Ghosts, Australia," *Northern Perspective* (1986);

"Perth–Cinderella City," *Australian* (1988);

"In Defence of Katharine Susannah Prichard," *West Australian,* 1990.

Mary Durack is remembered as one of Australia's most versatile writers and also as one of the best loved and most highly honored. Her published works number in the hundreds and cover a variety of genres–history, documentary, fiction, poetry, children's stories, drama, radio plays and talks, reviews, articles, lectures, and journalism. Perhaps more than any other white Australian writer she formed deep friendships with and wrote with great understanding and compassion about the indigenous Australians–the Aborigines. She also gave her time unstintingly to literary and artistic causes, writers' groups, and individual writers.

Durack was born in Adelaide, South Australia, on 20 February 1913, the second child and eldest daughter of Michael Patrick Durack and Bessie Ida Muriel Johnstone Durack. Bessie Durack was a third-generation South Australian and the youngest of seven children in the respectable and affluent Anglican Johnstone family. She was eighteen years younger than her husband, who was the eldest son of Irish-born, Catholic pioneer cattleman Patsy Durack. Mary's first few years were spent on the family properties, which comprised nearly six thousand square miles in the Kimberley region spanning the Western Australian-Northern Territory borders in the far north of Australia. Her father purchased a large house in Perth close to the central business district when he was elected member of Parliament for the Kimberley electorate between 1917 and 1924. Mary and her younger sister Elizabeth attended school at the nearby Loreto Convent. During this time Durack's father commuted on the state-owned ships between Perth and the Kimberley pastoral empire, nearly two thousand miles north, while in Perth her mother, with the help of servants, raised the family of six children.

At school Durack excelled in English and history and, to a lesser degree, in music and art. In the absence of her father, Durack's Uncle John guided her reading; he was helped by an English nurse, who came to the home as a companion for Bessie and who read aloud to the Durack children most of the works of Charles Dickens and Sir Walter Scott. At age sixteen, Durack decided she did not want to sit for the school leaving examination but, instead, to return to the Kimberley, the place of her childhood memories. She followed this inclination and said in a recorded interview by Hazel De Berg many years later, on 12 March 1976, that she lost her "heart to the north and more or less lived there from that time on." That living was in her mind, for although her ashes are buried in her "spirit country" at the Argyle Homestead Museum near the huge lake that now covers the old property, she lived most of her years after the age of twenty-six in Perth. She did, however, revisit the Kimberley several times a year, particularly to maintain her

Durack in 1923, the year her parents published her first book, Little Poems of Sunshine *(from Patsy Millett and Naomi Millett, eds.,* Pilgrimage, *2000)*

friendships with the Aboriginal people, whom she loved and respected.

In 1933 her sister Elizabeth, two years younger, joined her at the Ivanhoe cattle station, or ranch, where the two young women became cooks, housekeepers, and general managers. For this work they were paid a small salary between them. The Great Depression of the 1930s had ravaged the fortunes of the Connor, Doherty, and Durack company to the extent that there were few paid white employees. The black stockmen worked for keep and handouts for themselves and their extended families. Thus, Mary and Elizabeth Durack became accustomed to preparing huge quantities of beef and baking twenty or more loaves of bread a day to feed fifty people. In her spare time Mary began to write sketches about station life, which Elizabeth, who later became an acclaimed Australian artist, illustrated. These essays were accepted for publication in Perth newspapers–*The West Australian* and *The Western Mail*–and then in the major literary journal of Australia, *The Bulletin*.

From their savings and from money from maturing insurance policies taken out for them by their father, the two Durack sisters were able to spend a year abroad in Europe and North Africa in 1936. Soon after her return to Perth, Mary Durack obtained work at *The West Australian* newspaper, where she ran a section for country readers under the pseudonym Virgilia. She also became Aunty Mary in the children's section of *The Western Mail*. In 1934 Durack met Horace Clive Miller, the founder of MacRobertson Miller Airlines, whom she married on 2 December 1938. Three children came in quick succession with three more to follow.

Being a wife and a mother was not enough for Durack, however, so she began to write again in a variety of genres–book reviews, radio programs, poetry, short stories, novels, and historical documentaries. In the introduction to *Pilgrimage: A Journey Through the Life and Writings of Mary Durack,* a collection of her poems and stories published posthumously in 2000, Durack wrote,

> I was never aware of having an ambition to write books though I seem to have been a compulsive writer (starting with infantile jingles) from the time I could form words on paper. It is certain, however, that I am fated to continue this habit as long as I am able to push a pen or tap a typewriter. Perhaps this compulsion arose from the genes of Celtic ancestors who were frustrated by lack of opportunity, education or encouragement.

In 1938 Durack became a foundation member of the Fellowship of Australian Writers, Western Australian Section; she later served as president twice and received honorary life membership. She remained an active member until her death and gave much time to encouraging and assisting other writers. She was also active in other writers' organizations, historical and heritage bodies, and an executive member of the Aboriginal Cultural Foundation. She received literary and research grants for many years, beginning in 1973, and many honors and awards, including Dame Commander of the British Empire (1978), Honorary Doctorate of Letters (1978), Honorary Woman of the Year (1985), and Companion of the Order of Australia (1989). Apart from her journalism, Durack's published works number in the hundreds. These include major historical and documentary books, plays and other dramatic works, novels, children's stories, co-authored books, forewords, articles, and contributions to anthologies. Durack indicated her writing preferences in her introduction to *Pilgrimage:*

That the greater part of my literary output has been of a documentary or historical nature was a matter of chance rather than choice. While my inheritance or acquisition of historical documents dictated concentration in this sphere, for preference I would have turned my hand to fiction, short stories, drama and verse. Upon completion of a lengthy non-fiction project, it was a relief to work on a few lighter pieces.

From the age of seven Durack was writing verse. Her parents published, without alteration, a collection of fifty-four poems in 1923 when she was ten years old. Many of the poems in the book, titled *Little Poems of Sunshine*, are about native themes or memories of early childhood, as, for example, "My Day-dream Land":

> As I sat in a patch of clover, I thought of the land far away,
> Where the lakes are covered with lilies, and the bower-birds play,
> I thought of the lovely creatures and the wallabys there,
> And how I played with the little black girls in that fragrant air–
> Sometime, that happy time will come again
> When I may ride with my father, over hill and plain,
> Now I fancy I hear the familiar sound of the old cow bells,
> And listen to the creepy stories the old black man tells....

Throughout 1933–1935 Mary and Elizabeth Durack produced dozens of illustrated stories about life–mainly Aboriginal–on Ivanhoe Station. *The Bulletin* published many of these stories as three books– *All-About: The Story of a Black Community on Argyle Station, Kimberley* (1935), *Chunuma* (1936), and *Son of Djaro* (1938). Perhaps the most delightful of these is *Chunuma*, a collection of sixteen stories about three little Aboriginal children–for example, this extract from the story "Crocodile Eggs." The children are hungry for chicken eggs, and Gwennie suggests they replace the eggs just placed under a broody hen with crocodile eggs from a nest they had discovered. Chunuma and Dingyerri are a little apprehensive about the plan, but Gwennie persuades them to participate.

> "'im sit down longa big mob egg, where Gypsie bin put'm yesterday," Gwennie whispered. "Me an' you sneak up quiet fella now, take away chooky-chooky egg, leave'm sit down longa crocodile egg."
> Chunuma gulped.
> "Alright now," he said cautiously. "Only what about bye an' bye when chooky-chooky fetch'm out crocodile?"
> Gwennie made a scornful sound in her throat. "Silly fella!" she said. "S'pose'm hen sit down longa egg 'im fetch'm out chicken. Spose'm crocodile sit down longa same egg, 'im fetch'm out crocodile!"

In recent times Mary Durack has been mildly criticized for holding a patronizing attitude toward Aboriginal people. This criticism can be disputed, given her deep and lifelong love for many Aborigines and theirs for her, but her writing should be read in the context of the time in which it was written.

Durack's short story "Pilgrimage," first published in 1939, was widely acclaimed for its sensitivity. Its subject is an old station Aborigine named Friday, who is to be sent away to the leprosarium. Instead, Friday leaves the station to travel to his spirit land.

> "How she knows me, my little country!" His heart sang in his breast as he hurried over the last stages of his mountain climb where many younger men would have paused and panted.
> Here, in his own little country, Friday intends to die after singing "the perpetual increase of all things in the whole land."
> He had not meant to sleep, and he felt ashamed that the spirit was forced to wake him by calling first his secret name and then that of his dream totem, the flying fox. Breathlessly he listened, for now at last the Wondjina spoke of his people, spoke of them as they had been, living in thought and deed within the close-knit pattern of the law, rich in a belief that made them a part of all creation. It spoke of them as they were now, the wandering remnants of broken tribes, living on sufferance in the country of their forefathers, the spark of faith too feeble in their hearts for the dreaming of spirit children that became men.
> "Am I not to sing them, then?" the old man asked, tears hot on his shrunken cheeks.
> "Sing them," said the Wondjina. "Sing them the spirit of life with your last strength, and they will dream again."

During the World War II years, Durack's writing consisted mainly of verse–mostly unpublished– some book reviews, talks, radio broadcasts, and more than a dozen articles published in *The West Australian* and the monthly national magazine *Walkabout*. Most of these articles dealt with the pioneering past– in one she tells of journals her father kept over sixty years and with issues relating to Aborigines. But she and Elizabeth did collaborate on three more children's books in the period: *Piccaninnies* (1940), *The Way of the Whirlwind* (1941), and *The Magic Trumpet* (1946). *Piccaninnies* is a simple verse story for young children about an Aboriginal boy and girl who describe their day in the bush. *The Way of the Whirlwind* and *The Magic Trumpet* are beautiful fantasies– one written in prose, one in verse, and both illustrated in colored oils. In *The Way of the Whirlwind* Nungaree and Jungaree and their baby brother, Woogoo, are transported into the country of the dreamtime, where dreams and everyday things are mixed together. With the help of animals, insects, and the rainbow serpent they pursue the elusive

Durack with a crocodile caught at Argyle Station, 1937 (from Millett and Millett, eds., Pilgrimage, *2000)*

Here-and-there through the lands of Somewhere and Nowhere. *The Magic Trumpet* is a didgeridoo—an Aboriginal wind instrument consisting of a wooden pipe—played by an Aboriginal Pied Piper:

> And only children saw him
> Glimpsed a phantom in the bracken
> Heard a music on the morning
> Notes that wove a fairy spell,
> And they knew him for the rebel
> The little brown, elfin rebel,
> Who had piped a fairy music
> That had scorned the school house bell.

Between 1946 and 1955 there is a gap in published monographs, but Durack's output of verse—mainly unpublished—short stories, articles, and radio talks and plays for the Australian Broadcasting Commission (ABC) was considerable. Her father died in 1950, aged eighty-five, and Durack felt free to embark on further researching and writing the saga of her pioneering family, using as her raw material the daily journals kept by her father and the business records and letters of her grandfather Patsy and the firm of Connor, Doherty and Durack. At the same time she worked on her only published novel, *Keep Him My Country* (1955).

While working on what became *Kings in Grass Castles* (1959) and *Keep Him My Country,* Durack was also adapting Aboriginal legends and songs into verse form. One of these appears as an introduction to *Keep Him My Country:*

> I talk to my country in the night,
> I talk of my lover . . .
> I talk to my country for she is a woman
> . . . .
> I cry to my country—
> Keep him that he may come to my side
> For I wait through the burning heat of the day
> And the long quiet cold of the night.
> I wake when the whirlwind scatters my fire to the dry bush
> And its embers die under the falling rain,
> I wait for my lover.

This song is an appropriate introduction to *Keep Him My Country,* for it addresses the two strongest themes that run through the novel. The first of these—one that recurs in much Australian writing about the outback from the 1930s, especially northern Australia—describes the hold that the land comes to exert over often reluctant station proprietors and managers. Stan Rolt, manager and likely inheritor of Trafalgar Station, is one of these people and the main character in *Keep Him My Country*. In 1937, as a young man, Stan had come to the Kimberley domain his grandfather had established. He was always about to get out and start again somewhere else down south, but in 1952, the year in which the novel is set, he is still at Trafalgar. The other theme is also taken up in several post-1930 Australian novels, commencing most notably with Katharine Susannah Prichard's *Coonardoo* (1929). This theme is the white-black sexual relationship, which although widespread in northern Australia, was almost a taboo subject in the south. The young Stan Rolt has a lengthy sexual liaison with the black girl Dalgerie, who is eventually claimed and taken away by the Aborigine to whom she has been promised. Perhaps the most interesting aspect of these two themes is their interrelationship. *Keep Him My Country* and other fiction written about this period challenges the reader to ponder to what degree Aboriginal women exert a hold over the white men who arrive as transients but generally stay to die in this country. At the end of *Keep Him My Country,* Stan is brought to the critically ill Dalgerie, who whispers:

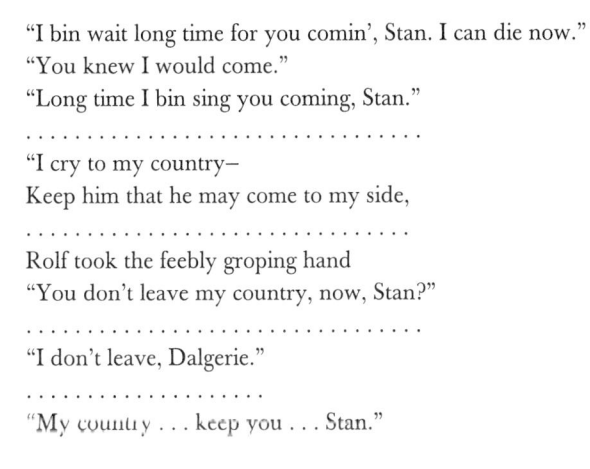

"I bin wait long time for you comin', Stan. I can die now."
"You knew I would come."
"Long time I bin sing you coming, Stan."
. . . .
"I cry to my country–
Keep him that he may come to my side,
. . . .
Rolf took the feebly groping hand
"You don't leave my country, now, Stan?"
. . . .
"I don't leave, Dalgerie."
. . . .
"My country . . . keep you . . . Stan."

Keep Him My Country is a well-constructed novel, moving in places and often lyrical. Characters, both white and black, are drawn sympathetically, but without sentimentality. Its realism re-creates the vigor, the harshness, and also the occasional ennui of cattle-station life through the wet and dry seasons in northwest Australia. Durack helped to convert *Keep Him My Country* to the opera *Dalgerie*, composed by James Penberthy with libretto by Durack. It was performed first in Perth in 1966 and then at the Sydney Opera House in 1973.

Although her next major publication after *Keep Him My Country* was not until 1959, Durack continued to write prolifically during the 1950s: radio plays broadcast on ABC, short stories and verse–once again mainly unpublished, dozens of book reviews for journals and radio, talks on radio and to various groups, and articles for journals and newspapers. The publication that established her reputation was *Kings in Grass Castles,* published in 1959. In the 1976 interview with De Berg, Durack said,

> I suppose I had always had it in my mind that I would do it some day. It was more or less expected of me by the family. They knew they had an interesting story to tell; from the time I was a little girl, when I began scribbling childish verses, my Uncle Pat, one of my father's younger brothers, used to sit down with me, much more than my own father, and he would say, "One day you're going to write the story of your grandfather, whom you never met," and he told me human things about his father.

The grandfather Durack wrote about in *Kings in Grass Castles* was Patrick "Patsy" Durack (1834–1898), a great pioneer of northwestern Australia. Mary was fortunate in that Patsy and her father had retained in black tin trunks the letters, journals, stock books, and check stubs that Patsy had accumulated during his lifetime. Her meticulous research in libraries throughout Australia filled in the details of this family biography, which was reviewed by ABC as "the liveliest and most entertaining history book any secondary school pupil will ever have the good fortune to study."

This beautifully written documentary/history book, which often reads like a novel, has gone through several editions since it first appeared in 1959.

Kings in Grass Castles tells the story of Patsy Durack and his relatives and associates from the time the family arrived in Australia in 1853, when Patsy was eighteen years old. In that same year Patsy's father was killed, and Patsy, the oldest male child, assumed leadership of the family. By 1857 the Duracks had land near Goulburn in New South Wales. After prosperous years they established Thylungra Station in Western Queensland in 1868. This pioneer cattle property prospered also, and the next move was the overlanding (driving) of 7,250 cattle, 200 horses, and 60 working bullocks across northern Australia to the Ord River in the Kimberley, where the Durack pastoral empire of six thousand square miles was established. The first homestead, Argyle, was built by Patsy on the Behn River in 1886. Patsy, at the height of his optimism, had referred to the family's landholdings as principalities, not as properties. However, his perspective had changed just before his death. According to *Kings in Grass Castles,* he said to one of his daughters, "All the little kings in their grass castles, and the wind and the water sweeping them away."

That *Kings in Grass Castles* is far from being a dry history chronicle can be seen from a few observations and pieces of dialogue that are obviously the creations of the author. The first is a reflection on the development of Australians as a distinct people:

> From a medley of people drawn to these shores by crime or poverty, to find living space, adventure, freedom, land or gold or who had come simply for the hell of it, out of many creeds and many races . . . was emerging the Australian people. The land was moulding them already to a certain uniformity shading the raven hair to brown, the flaxen to honey gold, blending dark eyes and blue to a tawny hazel, a smoky grey. Even their voices were losing the distinguishing traits of country, county and class, Australia imposing an intonation and emphasis of her own, abhorrent to the outside ear, inescapable within her frontiers.

One of Patsy's employees was a man named Tom Pethic, who was asked by a traveling companion to get some pepper from the many tins and bottles in their supply wagon. Neither man could read or write, but Tom solved the problem:

> "I've 'eard there's a hell uv a lot of 'P's' in pepper, mate," he said, "and P's the one letter I know on account of it's being at the start of me own name." From this clue the pepper was quickly identified.
>
> This homely old bushman dismissed as hopeless namby-pambies all such as Father and Uncle John who "read books and wore pyjamas."

Dust jacket for Durack's only published novel (1955), about the manager of a cattle station and his relationship with an Aboriginal woman (Bruccoli Clark Layman Archives)

"What did you want 'em learned in a school for?" he asked Grandfather. "That tripe ain't gonna help 'em round up the poddies."

Times were tough in the early 1890s. Indeed, Patsy had lost most of his fortune, and the Durack affairs were being managed by his brothers and sons. Patsy's two daughters were at a convent in Goulburn, and he wanted them to come back to Argyle.

"We'll have them both nuns if we leave them in that convent much longer," Grandfather complained. "There's Mary nineteen already and whatever chance of meeting an eligible man?"
"I don't think much of her chances of meeting one here," Father said, for he had already set an almost impossibly high standard of eligibility for his sisters' suitors. "Besides, what on earth would they do with themselves?"
"What do girls do anywhere?" Grandfather asked. "Help their mother, make pretty clothes, go riding–"
"In this climate? With skins like theirs?"
Father would not hear of it and already it was he who had the last word on family affairs.

Between 1959 and 1969, the publication year of her next major monograph, Mary Durack's output of book reviews, articles, poetry, radio plays, and talks continued to be prolific. She also published four books for young people. Illustrated by Elizabeth Durack, *To Ride a Fine Horse* appeared first in 1963. In a foreword Durack explains that it is a condensation of *Kings in Grass Castles* "for young people who enjoy reading the true life stories of people who have played an important part in history":

I feel he [Patsy Durack] would have wanted his native friends remembered, and because he himself so loved a good tale he would not have minded my telling of a poor Irish boy who came to Australia to ride a fine horse, and rode it so fast and so far. . . .

To Ride a Fine Horse is a rewrite as well as a condensation that uses a tone and language considered appropriate for young teenagers:

Imagine having to ride five hundred miles to the nearest shop! It sounds far-fetched, but in those early years in Western Queensland all stores had to be brought by bullock team from the little town of Bourke, south of the border. The settlers tried to provide for six or nine months at a time, for even if the team was not delayed by bog or flooded rivers it was always a three months' journey there and back.

Mary and Elizabeth Durack published two more children's books, one in 1963 and one in 1964. *Kookanoo and Kangaroo* (1963) is a verse story about a brash, boastful little boy, Kookanoo, who is taught a lesson by "Wise old, cunning old, old man Kangaroo." *The Courteous Savage: Yagan of Swan River* (1964) is a story for older children. It is a sympathetic portrayal of Yagan, a prominent member of the Bibbulmun tribe of Aborigines, whose land was taken by the Europeans for their settlement at Perth and neighboring farmlands—in fact, most of the southwest of Western Australia. Settlement in the Perth area began in 1829, and until 1833 Yagan and other Aborigines were feared by many of the settlers, and not without cause. But other early settlers had a different view:

> To many he had already become a sort of legendary hero, a black Robin Hood of the Australian forest, ruthless in avenging a wrong, quick to defend the rights of the underdogs. Tale after tale was told of his daring, his chivalry, and his disarming simplicity.

Yagan was murdered in 1833 by two teenage boys whom he had befriended, his head severed and sent to England as a curiosity. Publisher Thomas Nelson republished *The Courteous Savage* in 1976, but with a different title, *Yagan of the Bibbulmun,* and a different illustrator, Revel Cooper, himself of Bibbulmun descent. Mary Durack's text remains the same.

Throughout her life Durack returned in her writing to those years in the 1930s when she and Elizabeth were managing Ivanhoe Station. In 1964 she wrote the short story "Jingle Bells and Didgeridoos," which she labeled a 1935 memory.

> Why, of all the Christmases of my life, should it be the one of 1935 that I recall with the greatest clarity? Even the little box-brownie photographs, faded almost to shadows, shine clear to me in every detail.
> There we were, my sister Elizabeth and I with our bush friends, mostly Aboriginal, sundry dogs and cats and a pet wallaby at Ivanhoe Station, a property on which the town of Kununurra was later to spring to life. . . .
> Dave, an ageing bushman arrived to prepare food and make hop beer, the mailman arrived on Christmas Eve with parcels from Perth and also Carl Larsen, a Swede, who had again "yust missed" the ship that was to take him home to visit his old mother. There was fun and excitement on Christmas day.
> Nightfall brought the first big rains of the wet and spirits soared on the "non-alcoholic" brew that Dave had generously distributed. There was singing and laughter in the camp above the drone of the didgeridoos and on the homestead veranda Carl sang "Holy Night" and "Yingle Bells" with tears running down his cheeks for the white Christmas he had missed and, as it happened, was never to see again.

A Pastoral Emigrant, published in 1965, is a short, simply written story for young teenagers, about Tom Kilfoyle, who as a nine-year-old arrived in Australia from Ireland in 1851. He had no formal education, but his acquisition of bush skills and droving experience took him to Thylungra in Queensland and then with the Duracks to the Northern Territory and the Kimberley. An explanation by the author says Tom took two years and nine months to drive his cattle and horses three thousand miles across the Top End. Tom died in 1908, leaving a half million acres of pastoral properties to his son.

After their marriage in 1938 Durack and her husband lived in a large house they had built on a spacious block of land in the western suburbs of Perth. They planted many native eucalyptus trees, which attracted a variety of bird life. In 1968 Mary wrote "To a Crow That Has Nested in My Dalkeith Garden." She remembered the arrival of this crow as a bad omen, for soon after it came, two of her daughters, Robin and Juliana, both died in their twenties.

> Importunate raven,
> Attendant of the dying, guest of the dead.
> When will you learn there is no carrion here
> . . . .
> No friend of yours that tree on which you rest,
>
> Its birds sing songs of cheer
> You do not know.
> . . . .
> You have come to stay!
> Voice of that desert, so hungry-hollow,
> Where then can I go that you will not follow?

In 1961 Durack wrote a series of articles on missionary work among the Aborigines in the Kimberley district. Her research on this topic was expanded through the 1960s and culminated with the publication of *The Rock and the Sand* in 1969. In a foreword to the book she explains that she "did not set out to produce an apology either for Christian missions in general or Catholic missions in particular." She explains that her intention was "to give as honest an account as possible of the circumstances in which missionary work was undertaken and continued in north-western Australia, the people to whom it was directed and those who espoused or opposed the task." She does not comment on the success or failure of the Catholic missions in achieving their aims between 1878 and 1967, but in the conclusion to her foreword she does make one important value judgment, "that the work of the missionaries, sometimes inspired, sometimes blind, was the only evidence the Aborigines had of anything in the nature of consistent altruism within an otherwise ruthless and self-seeking economy."

Mary Durack with her husband and daughters in Broome, 1951 (from Millett and Millett, eds., Pilgrimage, *2000)*

The Rock and the Sand is of interest to historians and sociologists in at least three ways. It provides a detailed history of the building and running of several missions, most notably at Beagle Bay and Lombadina, and the personalities, achievements, and setbacks of the missionaries from various orders—Trappist, Cistercian, Pallottine, Salesian. It also touches on the history and development of the Kimberley district from the earliest years of the pearling industry and pastoral settlement.

Finally, it looks with insight and affection at the Aboriginal people whose conversion to Christianity was the raison d'être for the presence of the missionaries. But the Aborigines in the Kimberley region were no more conducive to conversion to European religions than were any other Aboriginal groups in Australia. Of course, they were attracted to the missions for reasons other than spiritual. As one old man had bluntly explained, it was a case of "no more tobacco, no more 'Allelulia!'" Using a rather startling contrast Durack highlights the unbridgeable gap between black and white cultures in the opening words of *The Rock and the Sand:*

> The people of the dream watched the people of the clock come out of the sea and strike their flagstaff firmly into the sand. . . .
> Both people were mistaken [in their belief that their own culture would subsume the other], for the clock was not a toy but a way of life, as the dreaming was a way of life, the one defining time by an arrow, the other in terms of heavenly bodies and seasonal change. Neither could appreciate the other's logic. . . .

As with *Kings in Glass Castles, The Rock and the Sand* is enlivened by Durack's artistry, her imagination brought to bear on but not to distort the basic facts uncovered by her research, the creativity of her writing. In the following passage she puts herself into the mind of an Italian bishop making his first journey through his 283,000-square-mile vicariate in the early 1920s:

> Although photographs had done less than justice to the wild scenery of plains and ranges, rivers and billabongs, to the European it had a forbidding, almost a frightening quality. Its silence, broken only by the anguished shrieks of cockatoos and the boding utterances of the crows, seemed to defy the settler to impose upon it any pattern of domesticity, any sound but the harsh voices of its own wild progeny.

Durack wrote her most successful play, *Swan River Saga* (first performed in 1972), in collaboration with her good friend Nita Pannell, who was the sole performer in this monodrama that played successfully throughout Australia in the early 1970s. The illustrated script of *Swan River Saga: Life of Early Pioneer Eliza Shaw* was published in 1975. The script is based on the letters and diary of Eliza Shaw, who with her husband, a former captain in a Leicestershire rifle regiment, and their six children migrated to the Swan River colony in 1829, the year of its settlement. Eliza saw and was part of the development of the colony for the next half century.

The following advertisement for the new Swan River Settlement in Australia appeared in London in December 1829: ". . . Settlers will have no purchase money to pay for their lands. . . . Their grants will be conveyed to them in fee simple and will descend to their assignees or heirs for ever. . . ." This advertisement provided the title for Durack's 1976 book, *To Be Heirs Forever*. It had also attracted the attention of Captain Will Shaw, a veteran of the Napoleonic Wars, now living with his family on a military pension that was soon cut by half. Shaw calculated that his investment in migrating to the Swan River Settlement would amount to £1,355.00 when the number of family, servants, animals, and possessions he would bring was determined. This sum would entitle him to 18,466¾ acres of land in the new settlement. So the Shaws left for Australia on the Gravesend in September 1829. Will's wife, Eliza, recorded details of the preparations, the voyage, and life in the colony for the next fifty years in letters that have been preserved. Durack used information from these letters when writing her play, *Swan River Saga*. The success of this play brought her more information about the Shaw family in Western Australia, which with additional research led to the writing of *To Be Heirs Forever*. Durack records in her introduction:

> None of the nine children of Will and Eliza Shaw inherited the coveted Swan or Avon river acres that, according to the alluring notice issued by the Colonial Office in 1828, were to have descended to their heirs forever. . . . it was passed down to children of part Aboriginal blood whose existence, though not unrecognized, remained inevitably obscure.

Tjakamarra: Boy Between Two Worlds (1977) records more history of the Aborigines. It was written to accompany a movie of the same name produced by a German motion-picture company. Durack explains the subject in her introduction. The central figure is Tjakamarra,

> a boy whose background is that of a good many Aborigines who have drifted from the remote western desert into mission centres at Balgo Hills on the Canning stock route and La Grange on the coast south of Broome. The dilemma of Tjakamarra's people, caught between commitment to the customs and beliefs of their ancestors and the problems of survival against the encroachment of western civilization on their hunting grounds, is still that of the few remaining tribal living groups.

In 1978 the Western Australian Institute of Technology, later renamed Curtin University of Technology, published two short monographs originally presented as lectures by Mary Durack. These were *The Aborigines in Australian Literature* and *Australian Literature: A Voyage of Discovery*; both are useful reference books.

The last of Durack's major works was *Sons in the Saddle* (1983), a sequel to *Kings in Grass Castles,* which ended with the death of Patsy Durack in 1898. Durack had written after completing *Kings in Grass Castles* that she had "neither the heart nor the perspective to embark" upon finishing the family saga. However, as she watched the waters of the dammed Ord River rising over the site of the Argyle homestead in the early 1970s, she decided to take up the story again. *Sons in the Saddle* centers on the formidable figure of M. P. Durack, Durack's father, who became the effective head of the Durack clan from the 1890s until his death in 1950. This book, published in 1983, takes the story to 1920. The third and final book in the trilogy was never completed.

On 26 February 1993 a large audience attended a tribute to Dame Mary Durack held at the State Library of Western Australia, at which articles, essays, and critical assessments of her literary achievements were read. Mary Durack died on 16 December 1994, aged eighty-one, and friends, black and white, packed St. Mary's Cathedral in Perth to say their last farewells at her funeral.

Interviews:
Hazel De Berg, National Library of Australia, 1976;
Stuart Reid, J. S. Battye Library of Western Australian History, 1990–1991.

References:
Graeme Kinross-Smith, *Australia's Writers* (Melbourne: Nelson, 1980);
Patsy Millett and Naomi Millett, eds., *Pilgrimage: A Journey Through the Life and Writings of Mary Durack* (Sydney: Bantam, 2000);
Tribute to Dame Mary Durack, program, 26 February 1993 (Library and Information Service of Western Australia, 1993).

Papers:
The Battye Library of West Australian History holds the journals, diaries, letters, and business records of Mary Durack's grandfather, father, and some uncles and brothers. There are as well a few of Durack's own papers. Most of her papers, manuscripts, drafts, unpublished works, notebooks, and letters are in the possession of her daughter Patsy Millett.

Louis Esson
(10 August 1878 – 27 November 1943)

Peter Fitzpatrick
Monash University

BOOKS: *Bells and Bees* (Melbourne: Thomas C. Lothian, 1910);

Three Short Plays (Melbourne: Fraser & Jenkinson, 1912)–comprises *The Woman Tamer, Dead Timber,* and *The Sacred Place;*

Red Gums and Other Verses (Melbourne: Fraser & Jenkinson, 1912);

The Time Is Not Yet Ripe (Melbourne: Fraser & Jenkinson, 1912);

Dead Timber and Other Plays (London: Hendersons, 1920)–comprises *The Woman Tamer, Dead Timber, The Drovers,* and *The Sacred Place;*

The Southern Cross and Other Plays (Melbourne: Robertson & Mullens, 1946)–comprises *The Southern Cross, Mother and Son,* and *The Bride of Gospel Place;*

Ballades of Old Bohemia: An Anthology of Louis Esson, edited by Hugh Anderson (Ascot Vale, Vic.: Red Rooster Press, 1980)–includes verse, prose, and two plays, *Australia Felix* and *Vagabond Camp.*

PLAY PRODUCTIONS: *The Woman Tamer,* Melbourne, Turn Verein Hall, 5 October 1910; Melbourne, Repertory Theatre, 1911;

Dead Timber, Melbourne, St. Patrick's Hall, 13 December 1911;

The Sacred Place, Melbourne, Turn Verein Hall, 15 May 1912;

The Time Is Not Yet Ripe, Melbourne, Athenaeum Hall, 23 July 1912;

The Battler (also known as *Digger's Rest*), Melbourne, Playhouse, 18 May 1922;

Mother and Son, Melbourne, St. Peter's Hall, 7 June 1923;

Mates, adapted as a play by Frank Brown, Melbourne, Playhouse, 16 August 1923;

The Drovers, Melbourne, Playhouse, 13 December 1923;

The Bride of Gospel Place, Melbourne, Playhouse, 9 June 1926;

Louis Esson, 1901 (National Library of Australia, Paterson papers, MS6882)

Australia Felix, Sydney, Stables Theatre, January 1991.

OTHER: *Andeganora,* in *Best Australian One-Act Plays,* edited by William Moore and T. Inglis Moore (Sydney: Angus & Robertson, 1937).

Louis Esson's career as a playwright was, by most estimates, desultory, and his moments of demonstrable success were few and fleeting. But he has been widely regarded, nonetheless, as "the father of Australian drama," and if such a title is to be awarded, there is no other serious competitor; his claims have as much to do with the circumstances of his failures and the boldness of his articulated vision for Australian theater as with the plays themselves.

Thomas Louis Buvelot Esson was born in Edinburgh on 10 August 1878. He was eighteen months old when he sailed with his mother, Mary Jane Esson, to join her eight brothers and sisters in Australia; there is no record of what happened to Thomas Esson, the seaman who was Louis's father, then or thereafter. Mary Jane Esson's family, the Patersons, were already well established in the Melbourne suburb of Carlton when she and the baby immigrated to there. All the sons had achieved success in their fields of art, architecture, and interior design, and they offered the new arrivals not only affluence but also a ready access to some of the liveliest artistic circles in the city. For the young Esson, an easy familiarity with people who understood themselves to be making history and with the sophisticated ideas and cultivated talk that so characterized them came as naturally as childhood games might to other children. In one sense his growing up epitomized cultural privilege; as a preparation for a vocation as the theatrical voice of the people, however, it was not quite so advantageous.

Esson's uncle John Ford Paterson was one of the finest landscape painters of the colonial period, but though Esson shared Paterson's passion for the distinctive light, colors, and textures of the Australian bush, he showed no sign of emulating his uncle's artistic talent. Esson's family assumed that he would excel in one of the arts, but throughout his intermittent and undistinguished studies at Carlton Grammar School and Melbourne University he gave no sign of excellence in any of them. The event that determined the path he would follow took place in 1903–1904, and (in keeping with one of the dominant tendencies of Australian culture) it occurred on a trip overseas.

Esson had become, in the years after he began his perfunctory career at Melbourne University in 1898, a marginal but intensely interested figure in the bohemian groups that met in wine bars and coffee shops around the university fringe in Carlton. This intellectual milieu was extremely different from that in which the Patersons moved. Theirs was respectable, their status and wealth underscored by a formidable Presbyterian probity. The new intelligentsia in which the young Esson found a peripheral place was far more daring—freethinking in matters of art and religion and immensely self-assured at the turn of a new century, and with the establishment of a new federated Commonwealth of Australia, about its capacity to change the world.

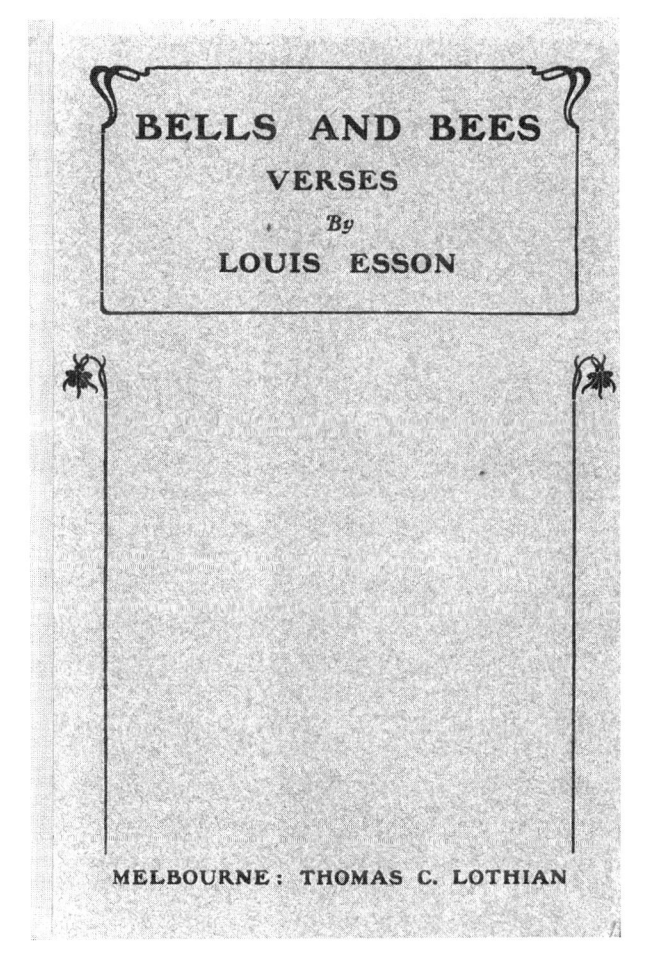

Dust jacket for Esson's first book (1910), a collection of lyrical poetry (Bruccoli Clark Layman Archives)

Esson's friend Leon Brodzky organized for the two of them the bohemian's grand tour of Europe, centered on London and Paris, especially Paris. But Esson went alone and, for all the time he spent on the Left Bank, found his defining moment in Dublin. In a heady few evenings there he visited the Abbey Theatre, met William Butler Yeats and John Millington Synge, and evolved a vision for a distinctively Australian theater.

Many commentators have noted that Esson's program for defiant cultural self-assertion was clearly derivative from a model at the other end of the world and so was dependent initially on the approval and encouragement of its practitioners. For the young Esson, contemptuous of the English mainstream and skeptical about the preciousness of the Paris option, there was no sense that adopting the Irish blueprint might be equally deferential and perhaps just as inappropriate. Certainly he absorbed Yeats's admonition to "Keep within your own borders" in matters of dramatic subject and Synge's rather vague recommendation that the outback was the ideal setting for drama, with "all those shepherds going mad in lonely huts." Esson returned to Melbourne with a new confidence and a new resolve: he was to be a playwright, and his plays would be staged in an unapologetically nationalist context by a company united in its commitment to a greater good, just as was the one he had seen at the Abbey Theatre.

He did not realize his ambition quite as easily as he had hoped. But on his return he quickly established a significant reputation as a prolific contributor of poems and essays to *The Bulletin* magazine of Sydney and as an urbane and talented young man who would surely do great things. He lived mostly on his journalism, writing regularly as a football columnist for *Melbourne Punch* during 1905-1906, traveling widely through Asia in 1907-1908 in order to write a series of commissioned articles for *The Lone Hand* magazine, and spending time in 1908-1909 in Bathurst, New South Wales, as editor of *The Bathurst National Advocate*. He also became for the first time a husband and a father; he married Madeleine Tracy on 22 January 1906, and in the following year their son, James, was born. There was still no sign, however, of the plays that he had meant to write and no indication of any theater in which they might be staged.

This pattern changed with William Moore's Australian Drama Nights, the first of which was staged in 1910. Moore was an enthusiastic man of the theater who shared something of Esson's vision of a distinctively Australian drama. The context was modest enough—one Sunday night in December each year was given over to an amateur performance of local musical works and one-act plays—but it was a beginning. Esson's *The Woman Tamer* (first performed, 1910; first published, 1912), a lively comedy laced with the racy vernacular of the criminals and shady ladies of Melbourne, was the highlight of that opening bill. In the next two seasons, plays by Esson were again on the playbill–in 1911 *Dead Timber* (first published, 1912), an epic story in a single act on the relentlessly grim experience of a family of bush settlers, and in 1912 *The Sacred Place* (first published, 1912), a play about moral comeuppance set in Melbourne's Turkish quarter. During the same period Esson wrote his plays, he achieved modest recognition as a poet, too; moving away from the mostly satirical verse that he had submitted to *The Bulletin* over the previous half-dozen years, he published two slim volumes of lyrical poems, *Bells and Bees* (1910) and *Red Gums and Other Verses* (1912). But the theater was now the arena for his talents. On the relatively small showing of Moore's Sunday nights, Esson was installed as one of the most promising playwrights in the land.

What is striking about those first three short plays is their variety. Each involved a distinctive and colorful part of the local culture and brought to the theater a correspondingly novel style of dialogue. These plays reflected a program, not yet fully articulated by the playwright, to stage those aspects of Australian life that might be thought unique to it. Another striking note is how little connection any of them had with Esson's firsthand experience. He was a shrewd and curious observer, and the distance of these three plays from the social and cultural world he knew best is not necessarily a limitation; but it was the first instance of a problem that reemerged in his later work and of a sense that he was an author conscientiously in search of a subject.

His first full-length play, *The Time Is Not Yet Ripe* (first produced and first published, 1912), staged by Gregan McMahon at his Melbourne Repertory Theatre, was closer to the society Esson actually lived in than his other works. It is a very accomplished Shavian political satire, exposing a gallery of hypocrites and self-deluders to the ridicule of the audience and the flippancy of the central character, Doris Quiverton. In its way, the play is also a significant historical document; its third act, a theatrically daring political rally in which voters are harangued from the roof of a car, gives a vivid impression of the forms and level of contemporary debate. The play was deservedly well received, and it might have seemed to an observer at the time that Esson had now found his métier. However, he never returned to that kind of work and came increasingly to loathe the play. Part of the reason for his dislike presumably lay in an overriding sense of cultural mission that made plays such as *The Time Is Not Yet Ripe* look frivolous and too dependent on familiar English models of the comedy of manners. But part of his feeling may have arisen from the coincidence of his first coming to public prominence as a playwright with the unraveling of his marriage. By 1911 Louis and Madeleine Esson were immersed in a particularly painful and mutually humiliating divorce on the grounds of her adultery with the poet William Mitchell, a member of the bohemian circle in which Esson had once moved. The gaiety and sentimentality of the rather conventional love plot involving Doris and her prickly Socialist Sydney Barrett may well have felt a little false to the solitary man who wrote it.

In 1912, however, Esson met the brilliant young medical graduate Hilda Bull through their mutual friends Vance and Nettie Palmer. Esson and Bull were married on 15 December the following year. Hilda had theatrical ambitions, too, as an actress, and she had been quietly active in bluestocking reformist groups.

But Esson, no doubt seeing many of the causes of the debacle with Madeleine as lying in the decadence of bohemian society, took Hilda off to the bush at Emerald, a village in the foothills of the Dandenongs, and then in 1916 overseas to New York and London. Hilda's hopes of becoming an actress were put to one side in the process, and when she became pregnant in New York with their son, Hugh, her ambitions were decisively shelved. So, it appeared, were Esson's ambitions as a playwright. He published a few short stories in New York and some occasional journalism in London but nothing for performance until Hendersons published a collection of four of Esson's one-act plays in London, *Dead Timber and Other Plays* in 1920–the three that had been produced by William Moore and a fourth, the as yet unstaged *The Drovers* (first published in 1920 but not performed until 1923). There were disturbing signs of writer's block and a related propensity to unspecified illness even in these exciting days of Esson's life. Hilda got work with the army as a doctor, and her salary, almost certainly complemented by some help from the Patersons, created the space for Esson to write. But he produced relatively little.

Esson's sense of purpose was rekindled by another meeting with Yeats in 1920. Esson began writing to Vance Palmer of a new vision for Australian theater. The model was substantially the same that had excited him in 1904–a playwright's theater devoted exclusively to new Australian work and performed by a small, dedicated band of talented amateurs. But this time his enthusiasm was shared and fed by two other aspiring playwrights, Palmer and Melbourne doctor Stewart Macky; Palmer was a disciplined and prolific writer; Macky was a talented man of the theater with strong contacts in the amateur arts community. Esson alone might easily have lost energy. By the time the Essons returned to Melbourne, the Pioneer Players had been named, their initial repertoire and essential character determined, and a myth was about to be formed.

As was implicit in its name, the group saw its mission as the creation of a vital theater where before there had been nothing. The metaphors of exploration, of new growth in a brown dry land, came readily to Esson in those years, especially when he was out of the country. They were always misleading and a little self-serving. In the vigor of local music-hall and vaudeville tradition, and in the rural comedies of Bert Bailey and the melodrama, Australian theater actually was alive and progressing. But those popular traditions were not what the Pioneers had in mind when they talked about theater, and in that fact lay a significant limitation in their work. The heavily scripted "straight" drama was what concerned them, and in

Esson's second wife, Hilda, 1919 (National Library of Australia, Prichard papers, MS6201)

that respect the claims for novelty and adventurousness of vision were well-founded enough.

The Pioneer Players, like their principal playwright, have become in Australia synonymous with heroic failure as well as intrepid cultural enterprise. The myth reinforces the impression of a thanklessly philistine culture, as hostile to art as to dreams, that from the start was implicit in the Pioneers' understanding of the wilderness they were entering; in that sense the collapse of the Pioneers' program was not merely predictable but almost a self-fulfilling prophecy. They staggered through seven seasons–ranging in length from one night to three–in 1922–1923 and one final performance in 1926, producing a total of sixteen plays, eleven of which consisted of only one act. Six of these plays were the work of Esson. Three–*The Battler* in 1922, *Mother and Son* (first published in 1946) in 1923, and *The Bride of Gospel Place* (first published in 1946), which closed the company with what Louis called its "one consecutive performance" in 1926–were full-length plays; the one-act plays were *The Woman Tamer* in 1922, and *The Drovers* and *Mates* in 1923.

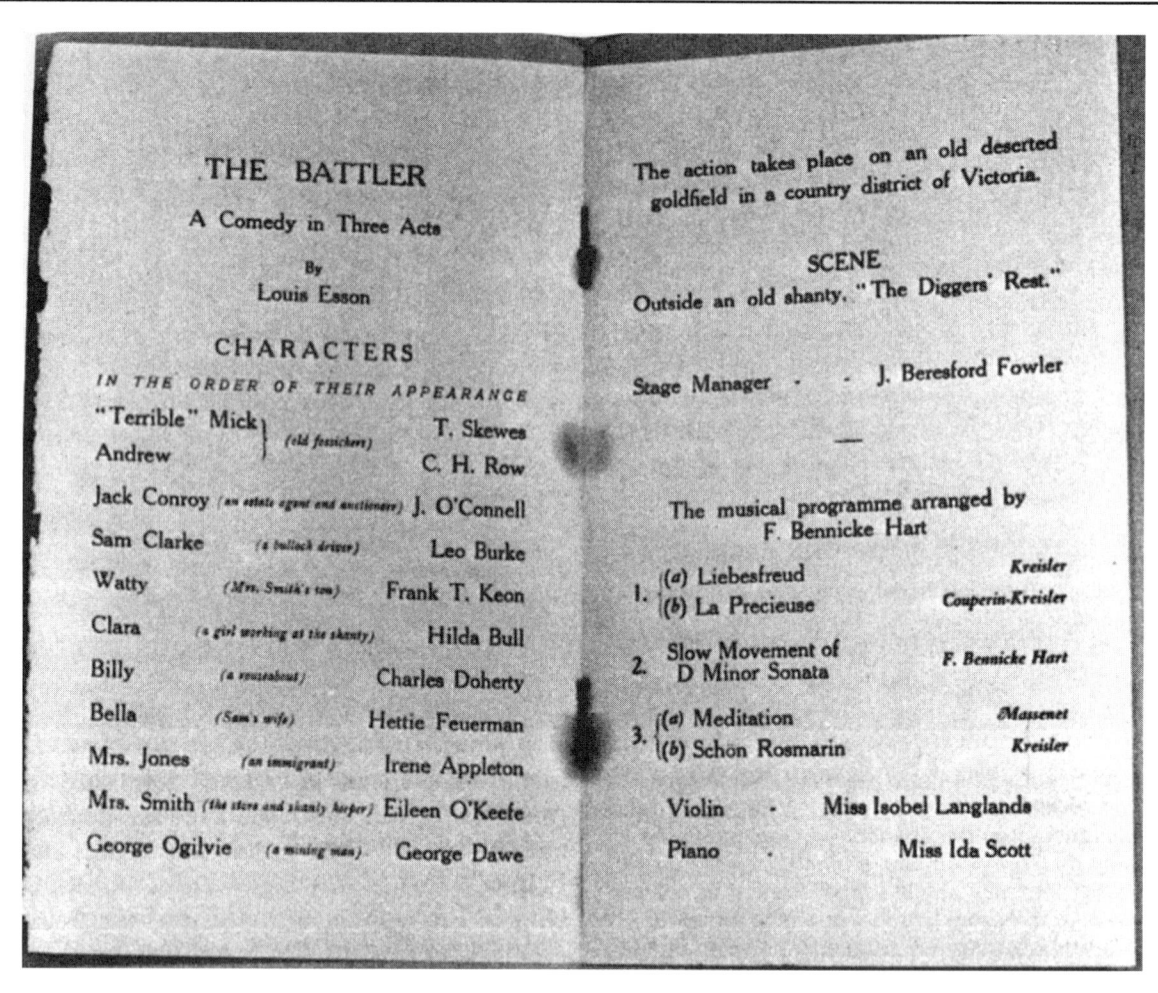

Pages from the program for an unpublished play by Esson, produced in 1922 during the first season of the Pioneer Players of Melbourne (State Library of Victoria, La Trobe Collections)

Certainly, in terms of the grandiose visions that drove the company, the relatively small and spasmodic output might be designated a failure. From another perspective, though, it got astonishingly far; nothing like that concentration of new local work appears again in Australian theater until the late 1960s. The Pioneers' influence, in terms at least of that myth of quixotic aspiration, has been stronger and more resilient than they could have imagined in the amateurish chaos that marked their final days and quite a lot of their earlier ones, too.

Esson's plays for the Pioneers reflected the emphasis, in the project of national mythmaking, on images of outback life. *The Bride of Gospel Place*, like *The Woman Tamer*, was set in the seedy and colorful city, but all the other plays dealt with the heroism or futility of battling an inhospitable land. The outback should, as Synge had suggested, have proved a rich source of stories; but the unevenness of the archetypal conflict between man and nature and the difficulties of realizing the terrifying empty spaces of the interior create real problems for the playwright. *The Drovers* encapsulates the difficulty. It deals with the aftermath of a stampede, in which Briglow Bill, "gun drover" of the North, has been fatally injured after the "New Chum" Jackaroo–a recent arrival from England, and prone therefore to monumental silliness–fired off his pistol in his excitement. The play deals with the leave-taking of Bill's mates, who realize that the cattle drive cannot be delayed and that Bill must be left to die in the care of the Aboriginal "boy" Pidgeon. The plot of the play is a coda to an action; the stampede, like the floods, fires, and famines that are the mighty antagonists in the bush myth, is an offstage catalyst for an essentially unavoidable consequence.

The Drovers is, accordingly, brief. The reactive nature of human choice in this context places great weight on the language that carries it, and Esson's major characters in all the outback plays are people to whom words do not come easily at all. The bushman is a phlegmatic fellow, his heroism expressed in hard-bitten stoicism. His taciturnity is an index of masculine strength; those such as the New Chum, who waste words, or like Pidgeon, who tries to make the Pidgin English he has learned stretch to describe a world of the spirit, are defined as outsiders or "other." The playwright's major resource in dealing with the bushman-hero is the power of understatement. When Bill's best mate, the Boss, bids his final farewell, the monosyllables are heavy with unarticulated feeling:

BOSS: So long, old mate.
BILL: So long, Alec.

The tactic is potent but best suited to the short play. *The Drovers* has the reach and classical outlines of a national epic, but both its strengths and its slightness are symptomatic of the achievements of Esson and the Pioneers, and the peculiar challenges that faced them.

Mother and Son, like *Dead Timber*, deals with family tragedy in the bush. The loss of the doomed son comes more credibly in the three-act play than the drowning of the doomed daughter in the one-act play, but the wider scope puts more pressure on constricted dialogue; this difficulty is true too of *The Battler,* though its loose structure and the genial inconsequentiality of its plot demands yet more whimsy from the author, rather than more passionate revelation. *The Bride of Gospel Place* pushes the boundaries of naturalistic form equally hard in its way, though the contingent nature of city life is in marked contrast, as a plot principle, to the relentless logic of necessity that works itself out in the bush epics. The opening act of the play offers a microcosm of the seedier backstreets of a bustling city; a wide variety of characters come and go in Spiro's fish-and-chips shop, bringing with them a range of idiosyncratic voices and hints of many stories that might be told. That sense of the passing parade is difficult to sustain, however, and disappears from the play as the focus narrows abruptly to the doomed love of Lily, the fading good-time girl, for Bush the boxer.

In general, the dependence on a realist aesthetic proved a significant constraint in the language of Esson's plays for the Pioneers. The vision that underlies them seems often to call for wider resources, poetic or musical perhaps, as well as for a more suggestively symbolic approach to stage design. The Pioneers, for all the largeness of the dreams that created them, had a relatively narrow sense of performance possibilities; they were a company of amateurs largely lacking in direction, not a clearly focused ensemble, and had all the strengths and weaknesses of a writers' theater.

In his work after the Pioneers came to an end in 1926, Esson showed a new readiness to experiment with form. This new interest is evident in the three full-length plays he worked on between 1924 and 1927. In *The Southern Cross* (published in 1946) he dealt with the complexities of the Eureka uprising in a way that reflected the shifting and problematic interpretation of history and national myth; the use of flashbacks, contemporary documents, and folk song anticipated some of the procedures of Brechtian chronicle. "The Quest," a dramatization of the explorations of De Quiros, was similarly innovative; its fragmentary nature is in part a consequence of its never having been quite finished, but it also represents a kaleidoscopic approach to history. In "Shipwreck," a Gothic nightmare in a lighthouse, the action is more conventionally concentrated, but the presentation of evil is verbally and visually moving toward an expressionist mode reminiscent of the works of Eugene O'Neill. Although these plays represent a development in Esson's art, none of these plays was performed in his lifetime.

When the Pioneers formally ceased in 1926, Esson was forty-seven, a man well known not only as a playwright but also as a man of letters. He might reasonably have expected to be at the peak of his career. His letter to Palmer of 15 June 1926, just a few days after the single performance of *The Bride of Gospel Place,* had two emphases: one was relief that the nightmare was over, expressed through a grimly humorous recounting of the shambling amateurism of the process, redeemed only by Hilda's tireless work in every conceivable capacity; the other was how much he had learned and what must be done to ensure that the next production of *The Bride of Gospel Place* was a better one. But that play was not staged again in his lifetime, and Esson's career was effectively finished.

There were the new scripts that never came to production. *The Drovers* had a revival in Sydney, and a new work, *Andeganora* (published 1937), came close to production. There were brief flurries of journalistic activity, with his regular theater reviews for *New Triad* (1927–1928) and the occasional feature on developments in international drama. But he quickly became honored and marginalized as a man of the past. When in 1939 he moved to Sydney, leaving Hilda and Hugh in Melbourne, it was as an elder statesman that he was welcomed to the Fellowship of Australian Writers there; though his time in Sydney was lonely and difficult, it was in many ways richer than the barren years in Melbourne, when there were too many days spent in staring at blank pages. Hilda visited him when she could and was with him when he died there on 27 November 1943.

Several things contributed to Louis Esson's lack of productivity after the last night of the Pioneers. Some related to the lack of opportunity for production

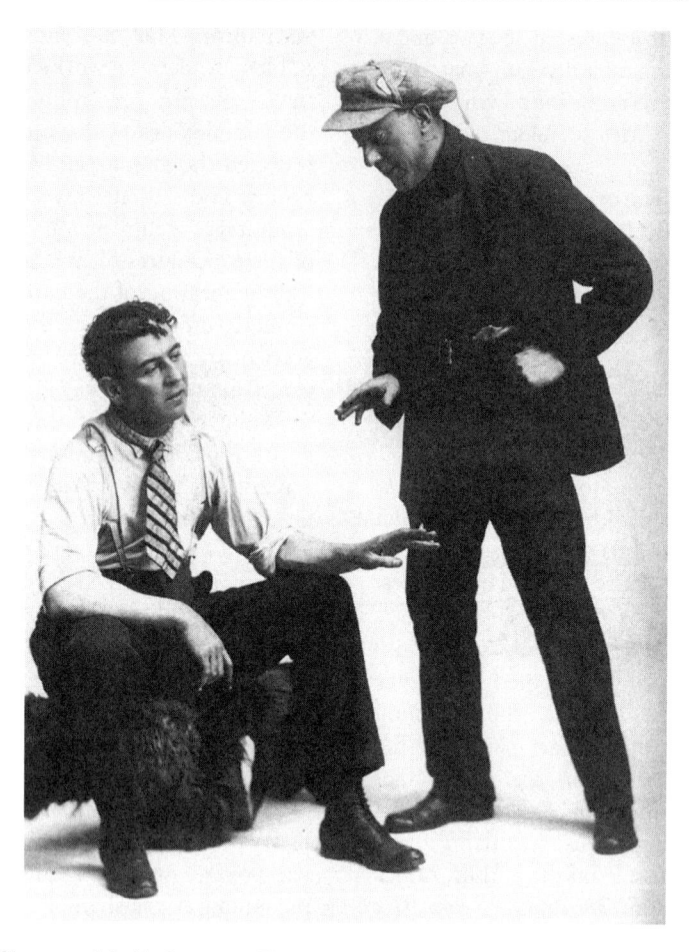

Leo Burke and Frank Keon as Chopsey and Smithy in a 1922 Pioneer Players production of Esson's one-act play The Woman Tamer *(National Library of Australia, Palmer papers, MS1174)*

of the kinds of plays that he wanted to write and the few that he did. Some related to his sudden isolation—Macky went to Sydney and then to London, while the Palmers moved to Queensland before becoming embroiled in the politics of the Spanish Civil War. The rebuffs were more decisive when there was no fellow sufferer to share them; Esson's periods of public theatrical prominence in 1909–1912 and 1922–1926 had been heavily dependent on the initiatives and solidarity of others. Some of those reasons may simply have reflected the lack of a sufficient subject, and perhaps even a lack of vocation. As a playwright, there had always been a slight sense of something willed or overconstructed in his work.

But the major reasons were almost certainly a little closer to home, in the state of his health and the state of his marriage. Esson suffered increasingly from inexplicable pain and a corrosive sense of futility. The official diagnosis of his illness was neuritis, and a regular regimen of morphine-based medication was the only treatment offered to him. The effects of both the disease and the drugs were exacerbated by alcohol. Many of his symptoms, though, look now like signs of acute depression.

Through all this period, Hilda Esson's support was never less than heroic. But insecurities about his marriage may well have been contributing causes to, as well as consequences of, his condition. Hilda had returned to full-time medical practice in 1927, and her work as a medical officer of health for Melbourne in combating smallpox and typhoid epidemics, especially among children, was passionate, important, and took her away from home. Further, she formed a strong friendship during this period with a colleague, John Dale, whom she married five years after Esson's death. In Dale's company Hilda became involved again in theater, working as a director with the left-wing New Theatre Company from 1935; Esson, the playwright, had no association with them. The unhappiness of this last period of his life seems the product of creative, emotional, and physical crises that were mutually reinforcing.

The incongruity between the scale of Esson's hopes and his achievement has led some writers to disparage the significance of his work. That tendency has probably been encouraged by Esson's dependence on the dubious example of Ireland in his vision for an Australian theater and the presumptuous readiness with which he accepted that his task was to create a theater where there had been nothing at all. But no Australian playwright of his time set such ambitious standards or encompassed so much of a past and present Australia in his work. From the beginning his plays included a fascination with two areas of cultural myth that challenged conventional approaches to theater—the epic scale of the outback and the rich miscellaneity of the city streets. In *The Drovers* and *Andeganora* Esson offered the most sophisticated treatments of Aboriginal figures, of their spirituality as well their oppression, which were seen in the Australian theater until the works of indigenous playwrights began to be performed in mainstream theaters in the late 1960s. He was consistently a playwright who refused to rest in repeating the things he did and knew well, and this tendency meant that sometimes his reach exceeded his grasp; in that sense, above all, he was irrefutably a pioneer.

Letters:
Vance Palmer, ed., *Louis Esson and the Australian Theatre* (Melbourne: Meanjin, 1948).

Biography:
Peter Fitzpatrick, *Pioneer Players: The Lives of Louis and Hilda Esson* (Melbourne: Cambridge University Press, 1995).

References:
Dennis Carroll, *Australian Contemporary Drama* (Sydney: Currency Press, 1995);

Hugh Esson, "The Education of a Psychologist," *Melbourne Studies in Education 1985* (Melbourne: Melbourne University Press, 1985);

J. D. Hainsworth, "Some Louis Esson Manuscripts," *Southerly*, 3 September 1983;

John McCallum, "Something with a Cow in It," *Overland*, 108 (September 1987): 6–13;

Leslie Rees, *The Making of Australian Drama* (Sydney: Angus & Robertson, 1973);

David Walker, *Dream and Disillusion* (Canberra: Australian National University Press, 1976).

Papers:
Manuscript copies of Louis Esson's plays are held in the Campbell Howard Library, University of New England (N.S.W.) and the Library of the University of New South Wales. These holdings include several plays which have neither been performed nor published: *Shipwreck, The Quest,* and an untitled MS commonly known as 'Isabel' but clearly 'Lachryma Christi', the last play on which he worked (circa 1936–1937).

Robert D. FitzGerald

(22 February 1902 – 24 May 1987)

Julian Croft
University of New England, Australia

BOOKS: *The Greater Apollo: Seven Metaphysical Songs* (Sydney: Privately printed, 1927);

To Meet the Sun (Sydney: Angus & Robertson, 1929);

Moonlight Acre (Melbourne: Melbourne University Press, 1938);

Heemskerk Shoals (Lower Fern Tree Gully, Vic.: Mountainside Press, 1949);

Between Two Tides (Sydney: Angus & Robertson, 1952);

This Night's Orbit (Melbourne: Melbourne University Press, 1953);

The Wind at Your Door (Cremorne, N.S.W.: Talkarra Press, 1959);

Southmost Twelve (Sydney: Angus & Robertson, 1962);

The Elements of Poetry (St. Lucia: University of Queensland Press, 1963);

Of Some Country (Austin: University of Texas, 1963);

Robert D. FitzGerald: Selection and Introduction by the Author (Sydney: Angus & Robertson, 1963);

Forty Years' Poems (Sydney: Angus & Robertson, 1965);

One Such Morning (Honolulu, Hawaii: White Knight Press, 1974);

Of Places and Poetry (St. Lucia: University of Queensland Press, 1976).

Product: Later Verses (Sydney: Angus & Robertson, 1977);

Robert D. FitzGerald, Australian Authors, edited by Julian Croft (St. Lucia: University of Queensland Press, 1987).

OTHER: Mary Gilmore, *Mary Gilmore,* Australian Authors, edited by FitzGerald (Sydney: Angus & Robertson, 1963);

Hugh McCrae, *The Letters of Hugh McCrae,* edited by FitzGerald (Sydney: Angus & Robertson, 1970).

Robert D. FitzGerald (National Library of Australia)

In his biography of Robert D. FitzGerald, published in 1974, A. Grove Day noted that FitzGerald was "acknowledged during the past quarter of a century to be Australia's most prominent poet." In 1965, when FitzGerald published his collected poems in *Forty Years' Poems* and won the Encyclopædia Britannica Australia prize for literature, that judgment would not have been contested by most literary critics. Today, however, FitzGerald's reputation has been eclipsed by that of his contemporary with a much smaller output, Kenneth Slessor, despite that FitzGerald's poetry is more ambitious and more wide-ranging than Slessor's. These poets are seen as the two most influential early modernist poets in Australia, but FitzGerald's stubborn resistance to the stylistic changes that swept through English poetry in the middle of the century, his uncompromising pursuit of the unfashionable notions of "beauty" and metaphysical ultimates, and the bulk of his output made him seem redundant to the new poets of the 1970s. His achievement in continuing a project in Australian poetry—started by Charles Harpur and Henry Kendall and advanced by Christopher Brennan—to find a metaphysical center to European experience in Australia had faded from sight by the 1980s.

FitzGerald's poetry is important because it is a more strenuous attempt to come to terms with mid-twentieth-century ideas and experiences than Slessor's oeuvre, which came to an end in 1948 when Slessor was forty-seven. FitzGerald's interests moved from late-nineteenth century symbolism to an engagement with the New Physics of the early twentieth century and a metaphysic and an aesthetic that questioned traditional notions of causality and historical necessity. FitzGerald's interest in the evolution of physics in the first half of the century and his meditation on the nature of life and human choice in a world subject to relativity and quantum uncertainty informed his major poems of the 1940s. In short lyrics and major meditative pieces, then during the early 1950s in a long narrative poem of several thousand lines on cultural determinism and the nature of history, set in early-nineteenth-century Tonga, FitzGerald grappled with some of the major philosophical issues of the early twentieth century.

He was also a tireless promoter of poetry and Australian literature. He edited several anthologies and a collection of the poet Hugh McCrae's letters, in addition to lecturing at the University of Texas and giving a series of Commonwealth Literary Fund lectures.

His verse style, though often scrupulously metrical, was never fluent. The impression given to many readers was of a struggle to articulate powerful ideas in which language was wrestled into submission through syntactical and metrical strangleholds; the result was energetic and dynamic but often awkward and difficult to follow. Younger poets and readers found his austere ideas antipathetic at a time of change such as the 1970s. Nevertheless, FitzGerald read and wrote for an anti Vietnam War festival in 1968 and supported Bernadette Devlin in a moving poem in 1969 at the start of the most recent troubles in Ireland.

Although FitzGerald's poetry is still unfashionable, it remains the most comprehensive body of work in Australian poetry from the 1920s to the 1960s in its intellectual scope and in its processing of individual and national preoccupations at midcentury. FitzGerald's concern with the metaphysical ultimates and their intersection with the physical world, together with his fascination with history as a record of human choices determining the present, were peculiarly apt for the Australia of his time, and they rose in part from the intellectual traditions of his family and the city he lived in all his life, Sydney.

Robert David FitzGerald was the child of two prominent colonial Sydney families. His mother, Ida le Gay Brereton, was the sister of the poet, professor of English, and librarian of Sydney University John le Gay Brereton, and her family was prominent in academic and artistic circles through several generations. R. D. FitzGerald's grandfather of the same name, a civil engineer, migrated to Sydney from County Cork in 1856 and became Deputy Surveyor-General of New South Wales. He was also a botanist and in 1882 published the first major book on Australian orchids. FitzGerald's father, also Robert David, was a land surveyor, and his son followed him into that profession after two years studying science at Sydney University. For forty years FitzGerald worked full-time in this demanding profession while also pursuing his successful and highly productive literary career. At the time of his composition of his epic *Between Two Tides* (1952) in his late forties, he did his writing at five in the morning and from nine at night. Having qualified as a licensed surveyor in 1925, he set up in private practice the next year. He followed both his mother's and his father's family traditions of literary activity from the time he was at Sydney Grammar School, and by the age of twenty-five he had acquired some profile as a poet. His poems were published in the Sydney *Bulletin*, the *Triad, Australian University Verse, 1920–22,* and, most notably, *Vision*, an avant-garde magazine published by members of the Lindsay family, dedicated to an aesthetic program dominated by the artist Norman Lindsay. FitzGerald's first collection of poetry, *The Greater Apollo: Seven Metaphysical Songs,* was privately published in 1927 as a tribute to his mother, who had recently died. These poems, together with more recent ones, were republished in his first commercial collection, *To Meet the Sun* (1929), which met with the approval of the poet John Drinkwater in England, who awarded it the bronze medal of the Panton Arts Club Festival of Arts and Letters.

The Great Depression and his freely admitted lack of business enterprise caused FitzGerald to move from the private sector to a government job when he married Marjorie-Claire Harris on 11 March 1931. His new position as a surveyor with the Native Lands Commission in Fiji was a physically demanding but exhilarating challenge. Joined by his wife, who returned to Australia for the births of their two daughters, Jennifer Kerry and Rosaleen Moyra, FitzGerald lived under canvas and in Fijian villages for the next five years. The experience gave him an abiding interest in the traditional societies of the Pacific and also the time for meditation on the philosophical themes that filled his poems of the 1930s and 1940s.

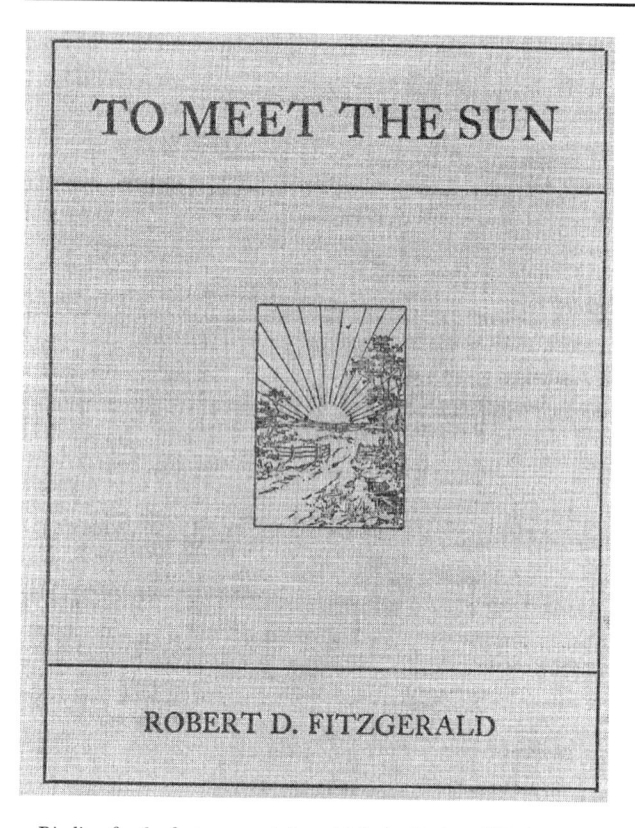

Binding for the first commercially published collection of FitzGerald's poetry, which was praised by British poet John Drinkwater (Bruccoli Clark Layman Archives)

In 1935, while on leave in Sydney recuperating from an appendectomy, FitzGerald completed the first of his major poems, "The Hidden Bole," an extended meditation on art, time, and beauty prompted by a memory of the ballerina Anna Pavlova's tour of Australia in the 1920s and her death in 1931. On his return from Fiji in 1936 FitzGerald picked up the suspended threads of his literary career, reestablishing himself with the major coup of winning the 1938 Sesquicentennial Poetry Prize—celebrating 150 years of European settlement in Australia—with another meditative poem, "Essay on Memory." This poem was an ambitious attempt to develop further his ideas about time, but now in relation to the foundation of European Australia and the function of memory in establishing cultural identity in the form of historical narrative. He expanded some of these ideas later in *Between Two Tides*. Further success followed with the award of the Australian Literature Society's Gold Medal in 1939 for the best book of the year for *Moonlight Acre* (1938). In 1939 a son, Robert Desmond, was born, and in 1942, a third daughter, Phyllida Mary, completed the family.

During World War II FitzGerald worked with the Commonwealth Government's Department of the Interior from 1940 as a surveyor laying out, among other things, airfields in the Northern Territory and the Captain Cook graving dock in Sydney. During this period and around the time of his father's death, FitzGerald wrote his most enigmatic poem, "The Face of the Waters," a profound meditation on process as both a metaphysical and a physical concept. With this philosophical exploration of the meaning of time behind him, he launched into further demonstrations of process at work on the national/cultural level in several poems with historical themes: "Heemskerk Shoals" (first published 1944), *Between Two Tides,* and "The Wind at Your Door" (first published 1958). In 1951 FitzGerald's status as a poet and his contribution to Australian literature were recognized by the award of the Imperial honor, the Order of the British Empire (OBE).

The poems of the 1940s and the 1950s were consolidated into his fourth volume, *Southmost Twelve* (1962), which was followed by his first book of literary criticism, *The Elements of Poetry* (1963), in which he outlined his aesthetic and his view of other poets who had influenced him. In the same year FitzGerald and his wife undertook a world tour—visiting the United States, where he was a visiting lecturer at the University of Texas, and Ireland, where he visited relatives and researched his ancestral roots, work that was to produce some of his best later poetry. In 1965 *Forty Years' Poems* was published, followed in 1977 by *Product: Later Verses,* a collection of poems written in the 1960s and 1970s. Although there was some falling off in productivity, the quality of the verse remained high, with thoughtful and challenging poems such as "Tribute" and the highly regarded "One Such Morning," which is an evocation of life at the turn of the century in Hunter's Hill, the Sydney suburb where several generations of FitzGeralds had lived. A further collection of prose essays, *Of Places and Poetry,* appeared in 1976, and finally in 1987, the year of his death, an anthology of his poetry and prose appeared in the Australian Authors series. FitzGerald died on 24 May 1987 in Glen Innes in northern New South Wales while visiting his son. He had used his theodolite a day before to align a gutter on his son's house, and the previous week he had read his poetry at the University of New England in Armidale.

FitzGerald started writing verse at school, contributed to *Hermes,* the University of Sydney's literary magazine, and published poems in the Australian Universities' anthology of 1920–1922. He was represented in *Poetry in Australia, 1923,* and by the age of twenty-five he had established himself as a prominent younger poet. His early style was seen by contemporary commentators as directly in the line of another Sydney University poet, Christopher Brennan, associate professor in German and Comparative Literature. Brennan's poetry had been profoundly influenced by the French *symboliste* poets during a stay in Europe in the 1890s. Although FitzGerald showed in his later criticism that he was well aware of the deficiencies in some of Brennan's verse, he admired and understood the genius of Brennan's major work in his *Poems* (1913), with its moving search through the images of everyday Sydney for the reassurance of some symbolic meaning or some metaphysical promise of significance beyond empirical reality. Poetry, for Brennan as it was for Stéphane Mallarmé, was the main medium by which this transmutation of reality could be made, a point that FitzGerald returned to in a public lecture, "Poetry and Reality," in 1959. At first, elements of the Georgian diction of the time can be seen in FitzGerald's verse—he was a great admirer of Humbert Wolfe—but during the 1930s his diction becomes less archaic and more direct, though strangely idiosyncratic because of its syntactic complexity. His thoughts on the evolution of diction and stylistic changes in poetry may be found in his collections of essays, *The Elements of Poetry* and *Of Places and Poetry*. By the time he was thirty, FitzGerald's reputation as a major young poet was consolidated, but after five years in Fiji he felt that he had lost contact with the Sydney literary world. Certainly, the scope and nature of his poetry changed noticeably, and the publication of "The Hidden Bole" in 1935 marked the start of his ambitious and mature poetry.

The most striking characteristics of FitzGerald's early verse are its assuredness and focus. The poems include little of the effusion and emotional vagueness of a young man's first intoxication with words. The imagery is precise and concrete, the issues are well-defined, and the strength of the subjective center of the poem anchors its metaphysical concerns in the imagination. In "The Sea Eagles" (1927) he evokes in vivid detail the sea cliffs north of Sydney as the home of the eagles; yet, he can use the physical imagery of the hovering eagles over a changing coastline as the basis for a development of his ideas about the life force as the manifestation of the abstraction Time:

> The eagles wait for ever over the wavering coastline
> because this place,
> being not land nor air nor deep sea-water,
> is still their home in uncreated space;
> and they, still wheeling, still the same untroubled
> warders of chaos, guardians of the dawn,
> watch for the moment when the dark shall swallow
> the crowding worlds that once it sowed like spawn.

The other striking features of FitzGerald's early poems are their celebration of vitalism and their intense commitment to life and optimism. Whereas others in Australia and elsewhere saw little else than a wasteland after World War I, and a state of ennui and spiritual malaise as the Great Depression and the Age of Anxiety arrived in the 1930s, FitzGerald vigorously argued for engagement with life and the heroics of choice. In this respect FitzGerald is the polar opposite of his contemporary Slessor, whose great elegy "Five Bells" (1939) expressed so precisely the sense of nihilism at the end of "a low dishonest decade." Instead, from his earliest verse, life is celebrated, and in "Song V" from *The Greater Apollo*, written in 1926 after his mother's death, he uses a landscape of eroded sea cliffs to point out the new opportunities opened to life by the energy of the sea, not to dwell on the ruin and destruction wrought by change:

> Tomorrow and yesterday are cheated
> while, undefeated, one cliff still stands;
> for the one could speak for all cliffs long vanished
> till Time himself were destroyed or banished
> from the uncompleted work of his hands.

That certainty, expressed with such conviction it is difficult for the stanza form to contain it, remained with the poet all his life. Time, process, and death are the natural order of life and physical reality, and the individual part of a biological life force that is the expression of that reality.

In the enforced solitude of his remote survey camps in Fiji, FitzGerald had time and motivation to think about the ideas he was grappling with in his early poems. He took with him Sir Arthur Eddington's *The Expanding Universe* (1933) and *The Nature of the Physical World* (1928); Alfred North Whitehead's *Science and the Modern World* (1925), a great favorite; and Sir James Jeans's *The Mysterious Universe* (1931). Although he published sixteen poems in the *Bulletin* during his five years in Fiji, FitzGerald admitted that poetry did not come easily in the demanding conditions in remote areas there; not until he was forced to return to Sydney with appendicitis and took leave to recuperate did he have time to develop fully those ideas in a major poem.

"The Hidden Bole" is an extended meditation in the symbolist tradition, using as its central image from which all correspondences radiate outward the Banyan fig tree, famous in Indian mythology for its symbolic integration of earth and sky, body and spirit, through its ability to use aerial roots, which descend from the tree branches to take root in the earth until one cannot tell where the main trunk of the tree is. FitzGerald takes this "hidden bole" as his symbol for the metaphysical center of life, which he sees as the creation of Beauty. Beauty in turn is characterized by the ephemeral art of Pavlova, the famous Russian ballerina who toured Aus-

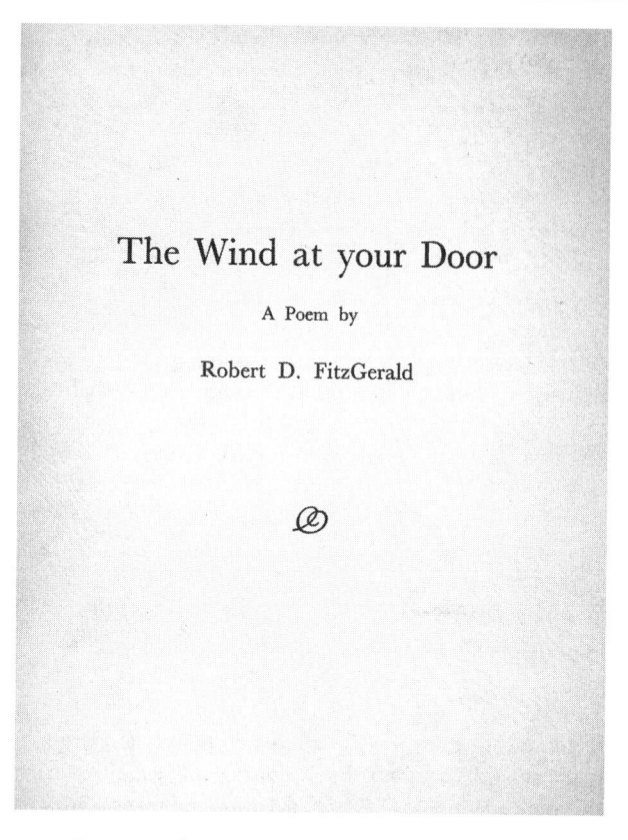

Paper cover for the original, limited edition of FitzGerald's best-known poem, published in 1959 (Bruccoli Clark Layman Archives)

tralia in the 1920s. Time, FitzGerald argues, is the essential component of art as it is of life, and by means of art mankind can transmit through time more than just biological heritage. Art is the hidden bole in the organic structure that makes up human life. Unlike Slessor, who could sense only vacuum and feel despair at the cycles of life and dissolution, FitzGerald celebrates change and the ability of the human mind to use it for positive ends. He illustrates his point by cleverly alluding to Pavlova's starring role as Giselle—the young woman who returns from death to take a living lover—as an example of the process of art itself:

> Death lets her dance on always through my mind—
> is there a grave could close away Giselle
> when music calls her . . .
> She is the prisoned sunshine that became
> delicate contour of escaping fire;
> she is the snowflake blown upon the flame—
> song and the melting wraith of song's desire.

In this verse FitzGerald has thought, language, and metaphoric logic under close control without the sense of strain that was apparent in his attempts at the meditative ode in "The Sea Eagles" eight years earlier.

After his return to Australia in 1936, FitzGerald reestablished his links with Australian literary circles. By 1937 he had not published a major volume of poetry in nearly ten years, and he was in need of a major challenge. That challenge came in 1938, when he sought the poetry prize for the celebration of 150 years of white settlement in Australia. A poem had been gestating in his mind since his time on Fiji, and in 1937 he wrote "Essay on Memory," starting with a memorable Fijian image—the sound of constant rain. The poem, however, was about the foundation of modern Australia and an optimistic account of the national endeavor of the past 150 years and the hope for the future. It is a celebration of FitzGerald's vitalist ethic of action, in which the heroes of the past are the explorers whose vision and endurance founded white Australia. The example they have left is one of energy and purpose, not to give in to nihilism but "to slit gloom's gullet" and "crack great barrels of song in open street." That optimism is based on the poet's analysis of the human condition in the first section of the poem. FitzGerald's view of matter is that of the traditional chemist: nothing is made, it is only changed. The world in the present is only a reconfiguration of what it was in the past—a rearrangement, not a change, of what was already there. This process essentially is what Memory is, the rearrangement of the physical world but also the transmission of thought through individuals, whereby thought is changed by each yet remains the product of the group. FitzGerald's position has evolved more since the one he arrived at in "The Sea Eagles," yet the core notion is still based on vitalism and the cyclical patterns of chemical change:

> And we ourselves are Memory, and retain
> so much of those gone, the little death can gain
> is found a cheat of the senses; change and birth
> convulsive writhings of autophagous earth.

The poem won the Sesquicentenary prize and was printed in *The Sydney Morning Herald,* but it has divided critics ever since. Its length (348 lines), its challenging ideas, its dogged couplets, and its knotty argument have alienated some readers then and now. But others think it one of the great poems of mid-twentieth-century Australia, not only because of its ambition but also because of its success in using poetry as a subtle and necessary part of philosophical enquiry.

FitzGerald's philosophical interest did not stop with this poem. His most ambitious poem, also one of his best meditative poems, followed in 1944. As his mother's death had prompted him to his first meditation of process and ephemerality, his father's death prompted another reflection on time. "The Face of the

Waters," as its title—an allusion to the verse from Genesis "And the Spirit of God moved across the face of the waters"—suggests, is about the moment of creation. FitzGerald's creation is not the same as that in the Bible; his is informed by the New Physics of the twentieth century, and like the Indian creation myths, this creation has happened many times before. What is most disturbing in the beginning of the poem is the sense that there is a deity that takes malevolent pleasure out of the cycle of creation and destruction:

> Once again the scurry of feet—those myriads
> crossing the black granite; and again
> laughter cruelly in pursuit; and then
> the twang like a harpstring or the spring of a trap,
> and the swerve on the polished surface: the soft little pads
> sidling and skidding and avoiding; but soon caught up
> in the hand of laughter and put back.

But as the poem continues, the reader realizes that the system being described is not one with a deity but the physical model of early-twentieth-century science. Drawing on Whitehead's ideas from *Process and Reality*, FitzGerald constructs a system in which reality—the moment—is created endlessly out of nothing. Probably he has in mind the notion of the recurrent collapse of the quantum state into one outcome; these sets of instants then make up Time. Each instant results from the unknowable pool of possibilities in the quantum wave to emerge as one state when it is observed:

> For eternity is not space reaching
> on without end to it; not time without end to it,
> nor infinity working round in a circle;
> but a placeless dot enclosing nothing,
> the pre-time pinpoint of impossible beginning,
> enclosed by nothing, not even by emptiness—
> impossible: so wholly at odds with possibilities
> that, always emergent and wrestling and interlinking
> they shatter it and return to it, are all of it and part of it.

As with "Essay on Memory" the total philosophical system is given a human dimension through the act of will; a hand stretched out to touch a neighbor's produces an instant in time as much as the hand of God across the face of the waters. Stylistically this poem is an advance over "Essay on Memory." It is written in free verse with occasional rhyme, its varying line lengths reflecting the movement of thought within the poem. It reads much more fluently than the earlier poem while still having the muscularity and terseness of FitzGerald's earlier poetry.

If "The Face of the Waters" is an exercise in abstract reasoning through the metaphoric logic of poetry, then another poem from 1944 is an example of this system of ideas put into practice. "Essay on Memory" celebrated the ethic of action in the form of the navigators and explorers who brought European thought to Australia, and *Heemskerk Shoals* is a further development of this theme in the light of the abstract system of "The Face of the Waters." It is significant that both poems were written during World War II, when Japanese occupation of Australia had been a distinct possibility, as both poems exhibit a sense of crisis—one of ontological certainty, the other of national confidence. FitzGerald remained an unapologetic defender of the "white" Australia policy—as supported by the Australian Labor Party from federation until the 1970s—because of opinions he had formed from observing the effect of the importation of Indian labor to Fiji. In the Browning-like monologue of *Heemskerk Shoals*, the Dutch navigator Abel Tasman reviews the choices he has made and the position he is in after nearly being wrecked on shoals in Fiji. Forced to bend his curiosity to fit the commercial ends of the Dutch East Indies company, he turns away from the vision he has of a country to the west where the difficulties of Europe and Asia would be overcome in a new social order based on the best of Europe, which would, in turn, have to remain constantly vigilant to protect itself from the human floods to the north. Despite his dream of the future Australia, Tasman turns away from it, as he turns away from another, the dream of measuring longitude. Because he is driven by commerce, his choices must be practical.

History is a narrative of such choices, which are driven by politics. In 1944 FitzGerald started work on his Tongan epic, *Between Two Tides* (2,414 lines), which took eight years to complete. The poem was to be an extended illustration of the limits of free choice in a determined world through an account of the political struggles in Tonga in the early nineteenth century. The theme is summed up by the Governor of Tola in Peru, whom William Mariner, the protagonist of the poem, visits early in the poem:

> "Every hour holds its choice. We do the choosing;
> but events present the straws. The ends are hidden;
> who knows the short from the long?"

In an undated letter to T. Inglis Moore, FitzGerald himself described the ideas thus: "We determine what we are by choice—limited choice—and the sorting factor (God if you prefer) chooses *us* but with the same limitations" that seem close to Calvinist teaching about choice and election.

The political forces that shape human lives are seen as impersonal forces directed by the simple ethic of eat or be eaten. Possibly reflecting the political situation of the world in the late 1930s and early 1940s, FitzGer-

Dust jacket for FitzGerald's 1962 collection of poems written during the 1940s and 1950s (Bruccoli Clark Layman Archives)

ald memorably makes the case for individual courage and hope in the face of these destructive political forces:

> . . . Nations are not
> men that compose them or even masses of men
> but hungry jelly having no mind save hunger.
> Persons are better than that. Looking at persons
> you can forget nations. . . .

FitzGerald considered *Between Two Tides* his most philosophical poem. As direct exposition it might be, but it does not have the suggestive power of "The Face of the Waters." It is, however, a tour de force of imaginative re-creation of traditional Pacific island life and a forceful illustration of the poet's ideas on history and politics. Stylistically, it is arguably his most accomplished work. The verse is traditional blank verse, and it has an elasticity and directness that must have come from a fluency FitzGerald acquired during the long composition of the poem. The narrative structure is also highly sophisticated, encompassing multiple points of view, and it shows clearly that the poet had learned well from Robert Browning, whose *The Ring and the Book* (November 1868–February 1869) he reread as preparation for writing his epic.

History occupied FitzGerald's mind during the late 1940s and 1950s in his shorter poems. He wrote of a variety of subjects: the trial of Warren Hastings in "Fifth Day," his own family's emigration from Ireland in "Transaction," and the burial ground of a Fijian chief in "Relic at Strength-fled." He concluded the decade with his most famous and widely anthologized poem, "The Wind at Your Door," on convict Australia. The poem treats a major theme in Australian literature–the resistance to authority and the bitterness of the convict legacy.

Written in 1958, "The Wind at Your Door" is perhaps the apotheosis of that generation of Australians that FitzGerald represents–the first to recognize without embarrassment their convict origins. In FitzGerald's case the relationship is paradoxical. The poem recounts a flogging of a convict after the abortive convict rebellion at Castle Hill near Sydney in 1804. The government doctor who supervises the flogging was FitzGerald's direct ancestor on his mother's side, Martin Mason. The convict being flogged, an Irishman named FitzGerald, though not a direct relative, is recognized as kin by the poet both for his name and for his oppressed state. The drama, played out on a windy day when the skin and blood of the near-dead convict are blown onto the onlookers, reaches down the years to the poet himself. It is the wind at his door that poses to him what he would have done if he had been on either side of the equation–rebel or agent of state power. As he concludes at the end of the poem, the convict's courage in refusing to be cowed by the sadistic punishment is a true indication of heroic will; yet, individuals are all part of the larger system with which they make compromises. The foundation of modern Australia is based on such contradictory impulses and compromises:

> It would be well if I could find, removed
> through generations back–who knows how far?–
> more than a surname's thickness as a proved
> bridge with that man's foundations. I need some star
> of courage from his firmament, a bar
> against surrenders: faith. All trials are less
> than rain-blacked wind tells of that old distress.
> Yet I can live with Mason. What is told
> and what my heart knows of his heart, can sort
> much truth from falsehood, much there that I hold
> good clearly or good clouded by report;
> and for things bad, ill grows where ills resort:
> they were bad times. None know what in his place
> they might have done. I've my own faults to face.

The poem is written in Chaucer's favored form, rhyme royal, and shows FitzGerald's mature ability to use such a traditional form in new and surprising ways.

FitzGerald's reputation was at its highest in the 1950s and the 1960s. Even then, however, there were dissenting voices. In a major review of *Forty Years' Poems* in the *Sydney Morning Herald* (7 August 1965), the poet James McAuley was extremely critical of the poetry as "toneless and unmusical," and Evan Jones, in "Australian Poetry since 1920" (published in *The Literaure of Australia*, 1964), and Vincent Buckley, in *Essays in Poetry, Mainly Australian* (1957), were equally negative in their assessments. The attraction of FitzGerald's ideas and the ambition of his vision that gained him readers in this period seems to have declined since 1980. While A. Grove Day could conclude his book in 1974 with "few readers in Australia or elsewhere would deny him the title of foremost living Australian poet," few today would give him precedence over Slessor or A. D. Hope of that generation. On the one hand, this assessment has to do with the great changes in taste that happened after 1970, and on the other hand, with the wider changes in the Anglo Celtic "older" Australia since 1970. As a representative of an Australian sensibility and culture of the early and mid twentieth century FitzGerald has arguably made the most comprehensive and articulate expression of the intellectual currents of that time. While Hope and Macauley responded to the same ideas and pressures, their poetry does not include the struggle and energy of a consciousness actively trying to create the new from the materials at hand. Robert D. FitzGerald is one of the most important mid-century voices in Australian literature because he admirably expressed this struggle to articulate the mystery of thought, as in the short poem "Edge" from 1954, which summarizes cogently the project he undertook in writing and publishing poetry in Australia over seven decades:

> Knife's edge, moon's edge, water's edge,
> graze the throat of the formed shape
> that sense fills where shape vanishes:
> air at the ground limit of steel,
> the thin disc in the moon's curve,
> land gliding out of no land.
> The new image, the freed thought,
> are carved from that inert bulk
> where the known ends and the unknown
> is cut down before it—at the mind's edge,
> the knife-edge at the throat of darkness.

Interviews:

Douglas Stewart, "Interview with FitzGerald," *Australian Book News*, 2 (July 1947): 5-6;

Craig McGregor, "A Kind of Life's Work," *Sydney Morning Herald*, 7 August 1965, p. 13;

John Thompson, "Poetry in Australia," *Southerly*, 27, no. 4 (1967): 233-242.

Bibliographies:

H. Anderson, "A Checklist of the Poems of Robert D. FitzGerald, 1917-1965," *Australian Literary Studies*, 4, no. 3 (1970): 280-286;

Jennifer M. Van Wageningen and P. O'Brien, *R. D. FitzGerald: A Bibliography* (Adelaide: Libraries Board of South Australia, 1970).

Biography:

A. Grove Day, *Robert D. FitzGerald* (New York: Twayne, 1974).

References:

V. Buckley, *Cutting Green Hay* (Melbourne: Allen Lane, 1983), pp. 162-167;

Buckley, *Essays in Poetry, Mainly Australian* (Melbourne: Melbourne University Press, 1957), pp. 70-78, 122-141;

Buckley, "R. D. FitzGerald in 1959," *Nation*, 7 November 1959, p. 21;

K. M. Cantrell, "Some Elusive Passages in 'Essay on Memory,'" *Southerly*, 30, no. 1 (1970): 44-52;

A. R. Chisholm, "Mr. FitzGerald's 'Essay on Memory,'" *Australian Quarterly*, 10, no. 3 (1938): 65-71;

Julian Croft, "R. D. FitzGerald 'The Wind at Your Door,'" in *Australian Poems in Perspective*, edited by P. K. Elkin (St. Lucia: University of Queensland Press, 1978), pp. 89-99;

Croft, "R. D. FitzGerald's 'The Face of the Waters,'" *Australian Literary Studies*, 9, no. 1 (1979): 71-76;

A. Grove Day, "R. D. FitzGerald and Fiji," *Meanjin*, 24, no. 3 (1965): 277-286;

H. M. Green, *A History of Australian Literature*, 2 volumes (Sydney: Angus & Robertson, 1962), II: 868-888;

L. J. Kramer, "R. D. FitzGerald—Philosopher or Poet?" *Overland*, 33 (1965): 15-18;

Jack Lindsay, "Vision of the Twenties," *Southerly*, 13, no. 2 (1952): 62-71;

F. H. Mares, "The Poetry of R. D. FitzGerald," *Southerly*, 26, no. 1 (1966): 3-10;

R. Mezger, "The Poetic Narrative of R. D. FitzGerald's *Between Two Tides*," *Australian Literary Studies*, 8, no. 4 (1978): 457-470;

T. Inglis Moore, *Six Australian Poets* (Melbourne: Robertson & Mullin, 1942), pp. 187-213;

H. J. Oliver, "The Achievement of R. D. FitzGerald," *Meanjin*, 13, no. 1 (1954): 39-48; reprinted in *Australian Literary Criticism*, edited by Grahame

Johnston (Melbourne: Oxford University Press, 1962), pp. 69–78;

A. A. Phillips, "R. D. FitzGerald," in *Responses: Selected Writings* (Kew, Vic.: Australian International Press and Publications, 1979), pp. 131–133;

Phillips, "The Unresented Critic," *Bulletin*, 6 July 1982, pp. 73–74;

J. S. Ryan, "Some Convict Sources in Keneally and FitzGerald," *Australian Literary Studies*, 9, no. 3 (1980): 385–387;

G. Kinross Smith, "R. D. FitzGerald–a Profile," *Australian Literary Studies*, 7, no. 3 (1976): 316–320;

Douglas Stewart, "Introduction," *Voyager Poems* (Brisbane: Jacaranda Press, 1960);

Stewart, ed., "Robert D. FitzGerald, a Background to His Poetry," in *The Literature of Australia,* edited by Geoffrey Dutton (Harmondsworth, U.K.: Penguin, 1964), pp. 332–341;

T. L. Sturm, "The Poetry of R. D. FitzGerald," *Landfall*, 78 (1966): 162–167;

Sturm, "Robert D. FitzGerald's Poetry and A. N. Whitehead," *Southerly*, 29, no. 4 (1969): 288–304;

F. M. Todd, "The Poetry of R. D. FitzGerald," *Twentieth Century*, 9, no. 1 (1954): 20–29;

Val Vallis, *Heart Reasons, These . . . : Commentaries of Five Australian Poets,* (Townsville: Foundation for Australian Literary Studies, 1988);

G. A. Wilkes, "The Poetry of R. D. FitzGerald," *Southerly*, 27, no. 4 (1967): 243–258;

Wilkes, *R. D. FitzGerald* (Melbourne: Oxford University Press, 1981);

Judith Wright, *Preoccupations in Australian Poetry* (Melbourne: Oxford University Press, 1965), pp. 154–169.

Papers:

The manuscripts of Robert D. FitzGerald are found in the R. D. FitzGerald Manuscript Collection, 1904–1960, Australian Defence Force Academy Library, Canberra.

Mary Gilmore

(16 August 1865 – 2 October 1962)

Jennifer Strauss
Monash University

BOOKS: *Marri'd and Other Verses* (Melbourne: George Robertson, 1910);

The Tale of Tiddley Winks, Australian Poetry Books, no. 1 (Sydney: Bookfellow, 1917);

The Passionate Heart (Sydney: Angus & Robertson, 1918);

Hound of the Road, a Collection of Essays and Sketches of Pioneering Days (Sydney: Angus & Robertson, 1922);

The Tilted Cart: A Book of Recitations (Sydney: Workers Trustees, 1925);

The Wild Swan; Poems (Melbourne: Robertson & Mullens, 1930);

The Rue Tree; Poems (Melbourne: Robertson & Mullens, 1931);

Under the Wilgas (Melbourne: Robertson & Mullens, 1932);

Old Days: Old Ways; A Book of Recollections (Sydney: Angus & Robertson, 1934);

More Recollections (Sydney: Angus & Robertson, 1935);

Battlefields (Sydney: Angus & Robertson, 1939);

The Disinherited (Melbourne: Robertson & Mullens, 1941);

Pro Patria Australia and Other Poems (Sydney: W. H. Honey, 1944);

Fourteen Men; Verses (Sydney: Angus & Robertson, 1954).

Editions and Collections: *Selected Verse* (Sydney: Angus & Robertson, 1948); revised and enlarged, edited by R. D. FitzGerald, 1969; republished as *The Passionate Heart and Other Poems* (Sydney: Angus & Robertson, 1979);

Verse for Children (Sydney: Writers' Press, 1955);

Mary Gilmore, selected by R. D. FitzGerald, Australian Poets (Sydney: Angus & Robertson, 1963);

Mary Gilmore: A Tribute, edited by Dymphna Cusack, T. Inglis Moore, and Barrie Ovenden (Sydney: Australasian Book Society, 1965).

OTHER: *The Worker Cook Book*, edited by Gilmore (Australia: Worker Trustees, 1914).

National Library of Australia

SELECTED PERIODICAL PUBLICATION–UNCOLLECTED: "Literature–Our Lost Field," *Sydney Morning Herald*, 8 October, 15 October, 22 October, 29 October, 12 November 1927, p. 13.

When Mary Gilmore, ardent socialist and Dame of the British Empire, died in 1962 at the age of ninety-seven, her standing as a public figure was one rivaled by few Australian writers before or since. If forcefulness of character and the indefatigable prose with which she had championed—in letters, journalism, and essays—the causes of social reform, Australian identity, and Australian writing played a considerable part in that reputation, her poetry was also an essential component. Apart from some six hundred uncollected poems in journals, she had published eight major collections between 1910 and 1954, as well as a *Selected Verse* (1948). Influential critics—H. M. Green, T. Inglis Moore, and Robert D. FitzGerald—had placed her among Australian poets worthy of note, even if giving her preeminence only as "Australia's best woman poet." Yet, by 1988 her biographer, W. H. Wilde, could describe her poetry as virtually unknown apart from a few anthology pieces. Not only had she suffered the common fate of Australian poets in being out of print, but also her "verse" was considered outmoded in form and diction because of the stylistic changes that had overtaken Australian poetics in the 1960s. Her life and its significance for the history of Australian radical movements—including feminism, environmentalism, and Aboriginal rights—continued to draw attention, but only recently, under the aegis of the Academy Editions series, has a collected poems been undertaken, a project that will allow reassessment of a writer whose output has generally been considered both exceptionally prolific and distinctly uneven.

Mary Gilmore was born Mary Jean Cameron on 16 August 1865 at Mary Vale, the property of her maternal grandparents, near the New South Wales township of Goulburn. Hugh and Mary Beattie were Irish Wesleyans who arrived in Australia in 1842. Their daughter, Australian-born Mary Ann, in 1864 married Donald Cameron, born in Scotland to the Presbyterian Highlanders Hugh and Mary Cameron, who arrived in Australia in 1839.

Her maternal grandparents figure benignly in later poems and reminiscences, but her father was more important. Like many a strong-minded oldest daughter in a financially hard-pressed family, Mary Jean Cameron felt that too much was demanded by her mother, and despite the extremely high value she later placed on motherhood, there exists no tribute to her mother to counterbalance the literary idealization of her father. In his daughter's writing, Donald Cameron came to represent not only the morally just pioneer, wise in the ways of nature and the Aborigines, but also an inheritor and transmitter of the heroic traditions of the Highland chieftains. Her Celtic ancestry was a source of intense pride to Cameron. As late as 1930, poems in Scottish idiom remained in her repertoire. Such "dialect" poems, however, were not simply an individualistic quirk. They were part of an established subgenre of early Australian folk poetry, and Cameron's adoption of this mode, like her adoption of the bush ballad, was probably influenced as much by contemporary literary practice as by personal circumstances.

Between 1865 and 1878, six more children were born into the Cameron family, a circumstance that led to a nomadic existence as Donald Cameron switched from station manager to traveling carpenter and building contractor to selector. Mary Cameron's childhood experience of a rural world barely out of pioneering days became a major source of inspiration for her writing and marked indelibly her conceptions of Australian identity. That world afforded her little experience of formal schooling and yet somehow, according to her letters, nurtured a voracious appetite for reading and an enthusiastic if unsystematic pursuit of knowledge. These qualities, which became lifelong attributes, marked her as a likely teacher, and in 1878, just before her thirteenth birthday, she became, under the tutelage of an uncle, a pupil-teacher in a remote bush school. "The Timid Child" (written in 1924) reflects painful memories of the isolation of these pupil-teacher years, but she persevered through the various stages of teacher qualification and in 1887 achieved her first independent posting, a single-teacher school at Silverton. This outback mining town was declining in prosperity as the gold boom ended, and Australia entered a lengthy period of economic difficulty and severe industrial unrest, with emergent labor organizations pitting themselves against industrial and pastoral employers. Although it seems unlikely that Cameron could have spent more than two years in Silverton without developing any awareness of industrial issues, available evidence points more to the budding writer than the incipient socialist. Her earliest surviving verse notebooks date from 1887, and from this period also comes her first recorded publication, "After the Shipwreck," published in *The Bathurst Free Press and Mining Gazette* (12 March 1887).

In 1890 the Education Department granted Cameron's request for a transfer to Sydney. School records suggest she was a conscientious teacher, although much of her energy was spent elsewhere, on literature and politics, the two being combined in the interests of *The Bulletin* literary circle, to which she had gravitated. While acquaintance with A. G. Stephens later proved crucial to her poetic career, a more immediate stylistic influence came from the left-wing satirical and narrative verse of John Farrell. In Cameron's later construction of this period, however, Henry Lawson played a major role. According to the unpublished manuscript "Henry Lawson and I," Lawson opened her eyes to the realities of urban poverty while accepting her advice on literature and education and developing a sentimental attachment for her that was disrupted by his disapproving mother, Louisa Lawson, editor of the feminist journal *The Dawn.*

The full extent of the emotional involvement between Henry Lawson and Cameron remains undetermined. There can be little uncertainty, on the other hand, about her commitment to the ideas of the charismatic Utopian socialist William Lane, who in 1893 led a band of members of the New Australia Co-operative Settlement Association to establish a colony in Paraguay. Arriving in Australia in 1885, Lane rapidly became, as founding editor of *The Boomerang* (Brisbane) and *The Worker* (Brisbane), a major theoretician and spokesman for the union movement. His support for the Maritime Strike of 1890 and the 1891 Queensland Shearers' Strike, which ended disastrously in the trial and imprisonment of twelve union leaders, attracted the attention of Cameron, who had been active in the 1890 Labour Defence Committee. She rallied to Lane's New Australia movement, endorsing wholeheartedly its plan to set up a cooperative commune to demonstrate to the world the principles by which Australian society ought to be regulated.

In 1892 the journal of the New Australia Co-operative Settlement Association, *New Australia,* was established in Sydney, in conjunction with the New South Wales edition of *The Worker.* Cameron—who was already contributing articles and poems under the initials M. J. C., M. C., and M.—became actively involved in the production of *New Australia,* but in 1893 she was not among the first settlers who left for Paraguay, where a government land grant had been negotiated with a country hungry for settlers. A policy decision excluded single women, so Cameron remained in Sydney, teaching and continuing to work—as writer, and for a period as acting editor—for the *New Australia,* giving special attention to the women's issues that William Lane had promoted.

The pattern of her future writing began to emerge in this period. An enthusiast for causes, she worked unstintingly to advance them and was convinced of the propriety and desirability of using whatever language would educate people and goad them into change. For *New Australia* she wrote frankly proselytizing verses such as "The Men of New Australia," whereas poems in *The Worker* and *The Tasmanian Democrat* (later *The Hobart Clipper*) tended to deal more generally with social issues—mateship, rural and urban poverty, prostitution, and infanticide. In *The Tasmanian Democrat* (and in *The Clipper*), however, she also published, as in *The Queenslander* (Brisbane) and the *Albury Banner,* sentimental and quasi-narrative poems indicative of aspirations for a place among more-conventional poets. For these more-literary poems she sometimes employed

William and Mary Gilmore with their son, Billy (National Library of Australia)

the pseudonyms "Emma Jacey" or "Rudione Calvert," the signature for one of her most popular early poems, "A Little Ghost."

Not until 1895 was Cameron summoned as a teacher to Lane's second settlement at Colonia Cosme. Traveling by ship to Montevideo—and thence by paddle steamer, train, and overland—she arrived early in 1896. In 1897 she married the handsome but scantily educated William Gilmore, a former shearer and farm laborer. In 1898 their only child, William Dysart Gilmore, "Billy," was born. A year later the Gilmores witnessed William Lane's departure from Cosme, and, convinced that the Colony could not succeed and that the health of their child was threatened, they made their own plans to leave. To earn money for the return trip to Australia, Will took employment on a Patagonian estancia in the south of Argentina. It was nearly a year before Mary could join him, and then arrangements for them to live together on Killik Aike proved unsustainable. Mary removed to Rio Gallegos, where she supplemented the family income by giving English lessons, reciprocally improving her fluency in Spanish. She long

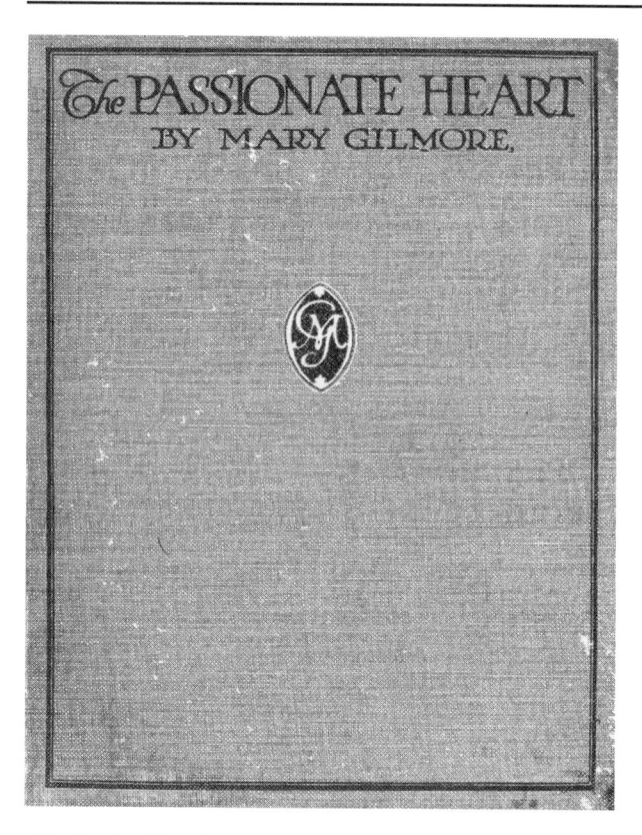

Binding for Gilmore's 1918 collection of poems, which focuses on grief and courage, especially in wartime (University of Virginia Libraries)

retained an interest in Spanish culture, putting time and effort into translating Latin American poetry during 1910–1920 and passionately defending the Republic during the Spanish Civil War.

After returning to Australia in 1902, the family settled near Casterton, on the farm of Will's parents. It was a difficult time for Gilmore. Money was short; Will spent long periods away in search of work; and she was struggling to sustain her commitment to being exclusively a wife and mother. In a letter to Will dated 15 December 1899 she had written:

> People here say I mean to be a writer, and that is why we resigned. They know nothing about it. I wouldn't be a writer in case I should let the love of it grow into my life and perhaps owe to it what I only want to owe to you—or that it might set up another aim or tie in which you would not be the centre.

Back in Australia, however, old literary ties reasserted their strength, notably through correspondence with Stephens, whose persistent perception of Gilmore as a poet must have been hard to resist, especially when he devoted an entire Red Page of *The Bulletin* of 1 October 1903 to her poetry. And if her conscience needed soothing, the family's straitened finances benefited from the modest fees earned by the poems and the journalistic pieces she had begun publishing.

Journalism provided both regular income and a way of reconciling Gilmore's hunger to write and her sense of duty to family obligations. She persuaded the editor of *The Worker* to approve a "Women's Page" so that the wives and mothers of Australia could be educated for socialism. The first issue, in January 1908, established a characteristic mixture of radical political comment and domestic coziness, with household hints and the kind of recipes that were collected in the extremely popular *The Worker Cook Book* (1914). At the same time, Gilmore was working on a collection of poems, and in 1909 Melbourne publisher George Robertson not only agreed to publish it but also offered generous terms. When *Marri'd and Other Verses* appeared in 1910, Gilmore must have hoped for financial as well as critical reward. The book certainly achieved some of the latter. Reviewers—for example, those in *The Bookfellow* and *The Freeman's Journal* (Sydney)—praised its lyricism and its womanliness; Bertram Stevens selected three poems for his 1912 *Golden Treasury of Australian Verse;* and attention was also attracted by musical settings such as G. H. Clutsam's "Six Songs from the South."

In 1911 the divergence of interests between husband and wife crystallized. Will went to North Queensland to attempt to establish a family property; Mary went to Sydney to pursue her literary work. This marital separation, proposed as temporary, became permanent. Gilmore saw her husband, and later her son, only on their rare Sydney visits. Copies of her regular correspondence with Will were destroyed at her request before her death, so no one can know whether, or how, they discussed the issue, or whether there was simply an unspoken acceptance that there was no shared life that could satisfy their divergent interests. Certain poems, notably "Contractual" (*The Passionate Heart*, 1918) and "In Life's Sad School" (*Battlefields*, 1939), tempt autobiographical readings in their depiction of the binding nature of a less-than-satisfactory marriage, but one should remember not only that Gilmore continued to the end of her life to protest her devotion to her husband but also that she criticized the appetite for autobiographical revelation as denying the creativity of poetry. In an unpublished poem dated 9 August 1943 and held in MS 727 at the National Library of Australia, she warns against literal-minded readers: "They will read what you have written," she says, only in order to "find you in a word / made mantle for another's grief."

The grief of others is a dominant note in *The Passionate Heart*. Such grief sounds in poems that speak not only of the horrors and wastefulness of war and the pain of the women left behind but also of the anguish suffered through the failure of love and through social injustice. Yet, grief contends throughout with Gilmore's characteristic vitalism, which celebrates the life force, human courage, and the healing powers of nature. Not surprisingly, therefore, Gilmore's poems display ambivalence toward war—opposing it in principle but giving unqualified support to the heroic Anzacs conducting it. This point of view meant that she was awkwardly placed during the conscription controversy of 1916–1917. Her compromise position, opposing conscription for overseas service but accepting it for the defense of Australia, ran counter to the policy of *The Worker,* which supported the international socialist position that the war was driven by the interests of international capitalism, manipulating imperialist and religious sentiments for its own ends—a position Gilmore herself adopts in "After the Battle" (*The Bulletin,* 23 January 1919).

The difference over conscription reemerged in 1931 as a factor in her final rupture with *The Worker.* In 1918, however, the end of World War I enabled her to enjoy the enhancement of her standing brought about by *The Passionate Heart,* which received wide and almost universally favorable reviews, even if few were as florid as Zora Cross's assertion in *The Lone Hand* (March 1919) that Gilmore's "words are flames; her lines threads of living lightning."

The twenty years after *The Passionate Heart* were extraordinarily productive, the more so because Gilmore's health, never entirely sound, had become so poor that in 1921 she retired to Goulburn, where she spent some four years either in St. John of God's Hospital or living in the Hotel Imperial. Her productivity is highly diversified: rather than a single-minded focusing of her poetic talents, there is an attempt to channel them into discrete collections, each possessing its own thematic and formal logic. Two of these attempts failed to find a publisher. One, preserved in four typed booklets in the Mitchell and National libraries, consisted of about thirty versions of Spanish poems, mostly drawn from *El Parnaso Oriental,* a 1905 anthology of Latin American poetry. The other, which survives in three separate manuscripts—the most substantial comprising forty-one poems—is "The Deil's Chapter," a partly satirical, partly eulogistic phantasmagoria, written in Scots dialect and involving Heaven, Hell, the devil, St. Peter, George Robertson, Henry Lawson, Billy Hughes, and various other less celebrated literary and political figures.

Gilmore had more success with the reminiscences of rural life that were stimulated by her return to the area of her childhood. In 1922 Angus and Robertson published *Hound of the Road, a Collection of Essays and Sketches of Pioneering Days,* and in 1925 *The Worker* trust-

Binding for Gilmore's 1931 book, a collection of religious poems (Northwestern University Library)

ees published *The Tilted Cart: A Book of Recitations.* In this collection Gilmore revisited the bush ballad in order to evoke "*a song of the long ago, / The years that we know no more*" (from "When Myall Creek was Young"). *The Tilted Cart* had popular success but did little to advance Gilmore's claims as a serious poet. This recognition had to wait until the extent to which the Goulburn years had given new directions to her poetry was revealed by the publication of three books in as many years—*The Wild Swan; Poems* (1930), *The Rue Tree; Poems* (1931), and *Under the Wilgas* (1932).

The most surprising of these books was *The Rue Tree,* for its poems were not only explicitly religious but also distinctly churchly and perceptibly Catholic. Until this time, Gilmore's references to religion tended to be either actively anticlerical or, as far as *Marri'd and Other Verses* or *The Passionate Heart* are concerned, emotive and doctrinally unobjectionable to the Protestantism to which Gilmore remained affiliated, if somewhat eclectically, to the end of her life. In 1921–1922, however, Gilmore responded so strongly to the care she received from the nuns of St. John of God's Hospital that she contemplated conversion to the Catholic faith. A retrospective annotation of 27 July 1953 on a Mitchell

Fair copy of the 1940 poem in which Gilmore affirmed her patriotism and British heritage (National Library of Australia) and the poem as it appeared in a 1940 issue of the Australian Women's Weekly

No foe shall gather our harvest

Sons of the mountains of Scotland,
Clansmen from correi and kyle,
Bred of the moors of England,
Children of Erin's green isle,
We stand four-square to the tempest,
Whatever the battering hail—
*No foe shall gather our harvest,
Or sit on our stockyard rail.*

Our women shall walk in honor,
Our children shall know no chain,
This land that is ours forever
The invader shall strike at in vain.
Anzac! . . . Bapaume! . . . and the Marne! . . .
Could ever the old blood fail?
*No foe shall gather our harvest,
Or sit on our stockyard rail.*

So hail-fellow-met we muster,
And hail-fellow-met fall in,
Wherever the guns may thunder,
Or the rocketing "air mail" spin!
Born of the soil and the whirlwind,
Though death itself be the gale—
*No foe shall gather our harvest,
Or sit on our stockyard rail.*

We are the sons of Australia,
Of the men who fashioned the land,
We are the sons of the women
Who walked with them, hand in hand;
And we swear by the dead who bore us,
By the heroes who blazed the trail,
*No foe shall gather our harvest,
Or sit on our stockyard rail.*

—MARY GILMORE.

Library typescript of the title poem reads "written when I was trying to become a Catholic, because my friends, the nuns of the Convent of Mercy so much desired it. But the doctrine defeated me."

The Rue Tree was given an ecumenically favorable reception, but enthusiasm was less universal than that afforded *The Wild Swan,* and Australian culture has maintained more interest in the themes and attitudes of the latter volume than in the kinds of religious experience in *The Rue Tree.*

The Wild Swan showed that Gilmore's renewed affiliation to rural traditions was not unequivocal. Reactivated alongside affectionate memories of pioneer days were darker preoccupations, concerns for environmental destruction and for the fate of Australia's indigenous inhabitants. These intertwined themes dominate Gilmore's work during the 1930s, whether in poetry or in the prose essays and sketches of *Old Days: Old Ways; A Book of Recollections* (1934) and *More Recollections* (1935). *The Wild Swan* is laden with a sense of loss, and while few have quarreled with the phrase "Never again" in such elegiac laments for lost fauna as "A Song of Swans," there have been objections to its use in poems with indigenous subjects. Some argue that Gilmore acceded to nineteenth-century romanticizing of the "dying race," potentially disarming activism on behalf of actual contemporary Aborigines. More distinctive and not always welcome were the moments when Gilmore insisted categorically on white Australia's responsibility for the destructiveness of settlement: "Their blood is black on our hands that nothing can purge" (from "The Aboriginals") was not what most readers wanted to hear.

A less confronting element, one of literary self-interest, is found in the series of articles comprising "Literature: Our Lost Field," published over five weeks during October and November 1927 in *The Sydney Morning Herald*. These essays carried into popular journalism the challenge already offered by anthropologists—that white Australians should acknowledge that the so-called savages of Australia had possessed complex social structures, full-fledged law codes, and a developed oral literature. Gilmore's argument was that a distinctively Australian literature should make use of Aboriginal mythology and language, an anticipation of the Jindyworobak movement of the late 1930s. She was, like them, open to the charge of what today is called cultural appropriation. Most literary critics of the 1940s and 1950s, however, simply berated the theory as producing aesthetically disastrous linguistic hybrids.

A less negative, if cautious, reception greeted the publication of *Under the Wilgas,* Gilmore's most concerted attempt to introduce Aboriginal language into her poems. In general, critics saw this collection as weaker than *The Wild Swan,* in which the Aboriginal poems are less cluttered with explanatory notes and glosses of sometimes dubious authenticity. Some of those who gave glowing tributes to *The Wild Swan,* however, were paying less attention to its Aboriginal poems than to its nature poems or its brief, concentrated lyrics of human experience, such as "Never Admit the Pain" or "Nurse No Long Grief."

The 1930s were a period when Gilmore was secure in her position, not only as a major poet but also as a personage in the literary world, someone fit to be made a Life Member of the Fellowship of Australian Writers (FAW), which she had helped found in 1928, and to become, for her services to literature, a Dame of the British Empire in 1937. Yet, she still found securing publication for her next collection a struggle. The manuscript of *Battlefields* was delivered to Angus and Robertson late in 1937; on 30 June 1939 she wrote to Hugh McCrae that "My poor book promised for Sep. 1938, Oct. Dec. Feb. 1939, Easter is still God knows how far off yet."

Battlefields finally appeared in August 1939, on the day of the announcement of the nonaggression pact between Germany and the Soviet Union. Public attention rapidly became engrossed by World War II, and Gilmore's "poor book" received less notice than might have been expected. *The Sydney Morning Herald* of 26 August 1939 did, however, provide a major review, drawing attention to the "battlefields" as not exclusively those of war. Rather, it claimed, Gilmore could be seen as championing the cause of all those embattled by poverty, oppression, and misfortune, "whether they be families on the dole, Aborigines, or victims of modern warfare and cataclysms of nature." If the reviewer had included those struggling in unhappy personal relationships, the identification of *Battlefields* as gathering together Gilmore's major themes of the past twenty years would have been complete. The collection still reflects the internal contradictions arising when Gilmore's instinctive compassion for victims of misfortune or persecution conflicts with unresolved attachments to ideologies of sexual and racial purity, of eugenics, and of patriotism and the valorization of martial heroism. Conflicting attitudes toward the latter are encapsulated in *Battlefields* in the contrast between the rejection in the title poem of patriot heroics and their celebration in "For Anzac (1939)."

World War II certainly unleashed Gilmore's patriotism, and she earned considerable approval for patriotic poems such as those published in the widely read *Australian Women's Weekly*. The most popular of these was undoubtedly "No Foe Shall Gather Our Harvest," in which British heritage, at least as transformed by Australian bush virtues, was proudly affirmed. The popularity of the poem was both immediate and long lasting. In the ten years after its publication it was frequently read over the radio, recited at concerts, and several times set to music.

In 1942 Gilmore approached the Commonwealth Literary Fund (CLF) for a publishing subsidy for a new collection. Their response was to offer a CLF Scholarship of £200 and the advice that a selection of her previous work would be preferable; her formal application for support for such a selection was made in 1944. In the subsequent negotiations she displayed a terrier-like tenacity, possibly bred of her earlier experiences of publication, but perhaps also in reaction to the enormous sense of loss she suffered in 1945 when her son's death followed within a few months of her husband's.

Selected Verse had the support and advice of influential literary figures in Tom Inglis Moore and Robert D. FitzGerald, although Inglis Moore's account in volume ten of *Southerly* (1949) insists that the choice of poems was Gilmore's. The selection, nonetheless, seems accommodated to the criteria of "high" rather than "popular" culture, giving pride of place to poems from *The Passionate Heart* and *The Wild Swan*, with a small selection from *Marri'd and Other Verses* and *The Tilted Cart* relegated to the closing section, and no representation of previously uncollected poems. This last omission is significant, for Gilmore would not have withheld poems as admired as "No Foe Shall Gather Our Harvest" and "Nationality" if she intended *Selected Verse* to be her farewell appearance. In fact, in the year *Selected Verse* was published, she resumed campaigning for the collection that became *Fourteen Men* (1954), although it was not until several years later that Beatrice Davis, the influential Angus and Robertson editor, agreed, on the recommendation of the board, to print a thousand copies on a guarantee against loss of £75. When *Fourteen Men* finally appeared, Gilmore was in her ninetieth year.

Members of the CLF Board may have felt some relief when Gilmore's "Inscription" declared that "the work is done that I had to do," but *Fourteen Men* was warmly welcomed by a public less involved in its gestation. It received the Gold Medal of the Australian Literature Society as the best book of 1954 and judicious praise in *The Sydney Morning Herald* of 13 November 1954 from A. D. Hope, by no means known for the charity of his reviews. History, however, harbored a time bomb with regard to the title poem. This poem, describing a child's witnessing of the dangling corpses of Chinese killed during the Lambing Flat riots, was accompanied by an authorial note categorically asserting the poem to be autobiographical. On 18 August 1955 readers of *The Sydney Morning Herald* were reminded that the Lambing Flat riots had occurred in 1861, four years before Mary Cameron's birth.

Gilmore at her flat in Sydney (National Library of Australia)

The question of the extent to which Gilmore's copious reminiscences are rendered unreliable by what Wilde calls "Dame Mary's fabrications" is a vexed one, and the possibility of widely divergent critical approaches is usefully rehearsed in Wilde's discussion of the issue in the 1988 *Courage a Grace: A Biography of Dame Mary Gilmore*. Whatever the explanation for the "fabrication," Gilmore's public evidently forgave her, as they forgave her defiant approval of the controversial portrait by William Dobell, commissioned by the Australasian Book Society and first shown in 1957.

In these last years, acknowledgment of Mary Gilmore's place as a public figure came from a wide spectrum of political and cultural opinion: the woman chosen to preside over celebrations of May Day by the union movement could also enjoy the public admiration of Robert Gordon Menzies and Cardinal Gilroy. Her contemporaries may have seen it as a characteristic contradiction that her final published words should appear in the 5 December 1962 issue of the communist newspaper *The Tribune* (Sydney) the day before she was to be accorded the pomp and circumstance of a state funeral, and that they should declare her wish that "no mighty ones" should follow her to the grave, only the poor of whom, and for whom, she had written.

Letters:

W. H. Wilde and T. Inglis Moore, eds., *Letters of Mary Gilmore* (Melbourne: Melbourne University Press, 1980).

Bibliographies:

Hugh Anderson, *A Guide to Ten Australian Poets* (Melbourne: Hawdon-Davison, 1953);

Walter Stone, "Bibliography," in *Mary Gilmore: A Tribute*, edited by Dymphna Cusack, T. Inglis Moore, and Ovenden (Sydney: Australasian Book Society, 1965), pp. 219–223;

The ALS Guide to Australian Writers: A Bibliography 1963–1995, edited by Martin Duwell, Marianne Ehrhardt, and Carol Hetherington (St. Lucia: University of Queensland Press, 1997), pp. 124–126.

Biographies:

Barrie Ovenden, "*Biographical Notes*," in *Mary Gilmore: A Tribute*, edited by Dymphna Cusack, T. Inglis Moore, and Ovenden (Sydney: Australasian Book Society, 1965), pp. 25–51;

Sylvia Lawson, *Mary Gilmore*, Great Australians (Melbourne: Oxford University Press, 1966);

W. H. Wilde, *Three Radicals* (Melbourne: Oxford University Press, 1966);

Wilde, *Courage a Grace: A Biography of Dame Mary Gilmore* (Melbourne: Melbourne University Press, 1988);

Anne Whitehead, *Paradise Mislaid: In Search of the Australian Tribe of Paraguay* (St. Lucia: University of Queensland Press, 1997).

References:

Robert D. FitzGerald, "Mary Gilmore: Poet and Great Australian," *Meanjin,* 19 (1960): 341–356;

F. H. Mares, "Dame Mary Gilmore," *Southerly,* 25 (1965): 234–245;

Drusilla Modjeska, "Love and Independence: The Poems and Letters of Mary Gilmore," *Meanjin,* 41 (1982): 228–235;

T. Inglis Moore, "Mary Gilmore," *Southerly,* 10 (1949): 122–130;

Sharyn Pearce, "Fishing for Women: Mary Gilmore's Journalism in *The Worker*," in *The Time to Write,* edited by Kay Ferres (Ringwood: Penguin, 1993), pp. 88–107;

Susan Sheridan, *Along the Faultlines: Sex, Race and Nation in Australian Women's Writing 1880s–1930s* (St. Leonards, N.S.W.: Allen & Unwin, 1995), pp. 103–152;

Jennifer Strauss, "Australia after all?: Mary Gilmore's Relocation of the Visionary Just Community," in *From a Distance: Australian Writers and Cultural Displacement,* edited by Wenche Ommundsen and Hazel Rowley (Geelong: Deakin University Press, 1996), pp. 21–31;

Strauss, "Stubborn Singers of Their Full Song: Mary Gilmore and Lesbia Harford," in *The Time to Write,* edited by Kay Ferres (Ringwood, Vic.: Penguin, 1993), pp. 108–138;

Strauss, "Un-Australian Activities? Mary Gilmore's Translations from the Spanish," *Australian Literary Studies,* 18 (1997): 156–164;

Shirley Walker, "Mary Gilmore: Constructing the Past," in her *Vanishing Edens: Responses to Australia in the Works of Mary Gilmore, Judith Wright and Dorothy Hewett* (Townsville: Foundation for Australian Studies, 1992), pp. 1–22.

Papers:

Major collections of a range of Mary Gilmore's papers are held in the Mitchell Library (Sydney) and the National Library of Australia (Canberra). Smaller but significant collections of poetry manuscripts and typescripts are held in the Fryer Library (University of Queensland), the Library of the State University of New York at Buffalo, and the Library of the Australian Defence Force Academy (Canberra), which also holds the papers of Gilmore's major biographer, W. H. Wilde.

Frank Hardy

(21 March 1917 – 28 January 1994)

Ian Syson
Victoria University

BOOKS: *Power Without Glory* (Melbourne: Privately printed, 1950);

The Man from Clinkapella and Other Prize-Winning Stories (Auburn, N.S.W.: Capricorn, 1951);

Journey into the Future (Melbourne: Australasian Book Society, 1952);

The Four-Legged Lottery (London: T. Werner Laurie, 1958; Melbourne: Australasian Book Society, 1958);

The Hard Way: The Story Behind Power Without Glory (London: T. Werner Laurie, 1961; Sydney: Australasian Book Society, 1961);

Legends from Benson's Valley (London: T. Werner Laurie, 1963; Sydney: Horwitz, 1967); revised as *It's Moments like These* (Melbourne: Gold Star, 1972);

The Yarns of Billy Borker (Sydney: Reed, 1965);

Billy Borker Yarns Again (Melbourne: Nelson, 1967);

The Unlucky Australians (Melbourne: Nelson, 1968);

The Outcasts of Foolgarah (Melbourne: Allara, 1971);

The Great Australian Lover, and Other Stories (Melbourne: Thomas Nelson, 1972);

But the Dead are Many: A Novel in Fugue Form (London: Bodley Head, 1975; Sydney: Bodley Head in Australia, 1975);

The Needy and the Greedy: Humorous Stories of the Racetrack, by Hardy and Athol Mulley (Canberra: Libra, 1975);

"You Nearly Had Him That Time" and Other Cricket Stories, by Hardy and Fred Trueman (London: Stanley Paul, 1978);

Who Shot George Kirkland? A Novel about the Nature of Truth (Sydney: Pan, 1980);

The Obsession of Oscar Oswald (Carlton, Vic.: Pascoe, 1983);

Warrant of Distress (Carlton, Vic.: Pascoe, 1983);

The Loser Now Will Be Later to Win (Carlton, Vic.: Pascoe, 1985);

Hardy's People. The Stories of Truthful Jones (Fairfield, Vic.: Pascoe, 1986);

Great Australian Legends (Sydney: Hutchinson, 1988);

Frank Hardy during the early 1960s (National Library of Australia, MS4887/156)

Faces in the Street (Westgate, N.S.W.: Stained Wattle, 1990);

Retreat Australia Fair, by Hardy and Truthful Jones (Milson's Point, N.S.W.: Hutchinson, 1990);

Mary Lives! (Sydney: Currency, 1992).

Collection: *A Frank Hardy Swag,* edited by Clement Semmler (Sydney: Harper & Row, 1982).

SELECTED PLAY PRODUCTIONS: *The Nail on the Wall,* Melbourne, New Theatre, 1951;

Faces in the Street, Sydney, Seymour Centre, 16 January 1988;

Mary Lives! Melbourne, Malthouse, 1992.

PRODUCED SCRIPTS: *Jacky-Jacky: Gentleman, Bushranger and Penal Reformer,* as Ross Franklyn, radio, Australian Broadcasting Commission, 1946;

Usual Women, as Franklyn, radio, Australian Broadcasting Commission, 1946;

To Arms! To Arms! as Franklyn, radio, Australian Broadcasting Commission, 1946;

The Yarns of Billy Borker, television, Series 1, ABV2, commenced 14 September 1964; Series 2, ABV2, commenced 20 October 1965;

Daybreak Killers, television, 1972;

Power Without Glory, television, thirteen-part series, ABV2, 1976.

When Frank Hardy died in 1994, Australia lost one of its great larrikins. He was Australia's most famous communist writer: he published six novels, three books of nonfiction, and more than a dozen collections of stories. In the process, he cultivated a reputation as the country's most celebrated working-class writer, yarn spinner, and despiser of authority, debt collectors, and parking police. His first novel, *Power Without Glory,* self-published in 1950, remains his most influential work. It generated an unprecedented level of literary controversy and scandal. Hardy was charged with criminal libel, and the resultant trial was fought in the heady atmosphere of the attempted banning of the Communist Party of Australia (CPA) by Prime Minister Robert Gordon Menzies. The book, the trial, and their aftermath have attained near-mythical status in Australian culture. The Australian Broadcasting Commission (ABC) television series adapted from the novel and broadcast nationally in 1976 contributed to that status by introducing the story to another medium and a younger generation. The book has sold more than one million copies worldwide, and the term "Power Without Glory" has entered the national lexicon as a cliché much-loved and oft-borrowed by newspaper subeditors. Hardy's subsequent publications, while representing important personal and literary-political developments, are remembered in the shadow of such a monumental work as *Power Without Glory.*

Aside from his literary work, Hardy participated in several other aspects of Australian cultural life. He worked in motion picture, radio, and television and wrote several plays, two of them about Henry Lawson, a figure of intense interest to Hardy, and *Mary Lives!* (1992), written after the death of his sister. He contributed to both the mainstream and alternative press and was a public speaker with the ability to hold and move an audience in a variety of contexts.

For all of Hardy's political significance and popularity as a writer and raconteur, he tended to be ignored or dismissed by mainstream and academic Australian literary criticism, especially prior to the 1980s. H. M. Green in *A History of Australian Literature* (1961) captured a general spirit both patronizing and politically loaded when he suggested that *Power Without Glory* was "crude and commonplace, so that it is monotonous and dull; nevertheless, it has sincerity and force, and there is no doubt about its author's talent, if he cared to devote it to literature instead of social propaganda." Of Hardy's works, only *But the Dead are Many: A Novel in Fugue Form* (1975), about the descent to suicide of a CPA apparatchik, achieves anything like positive critical notice from the literary mainstream. Significantly, its reception in the review columns of the Left was generally less than positive. Not until the late 1970s and early 1980s did academic criticism begin to take Hardy seriously. Notably, Peter Williams and John Frow, informed by neo-Marxist and poststructuralist critical perspectives then newly emergent in Australian criticism, examined Hardy's work in depth and without the previous limiting template of aesthetic evaluation.

Critical interest in Hardy strengthened in the late 1990s, drawing on a strong oral history and a consistent, if marginal, leftist written record best exemplified by Jack Beasley's "The Hero of My Own Life" in *Red Letter Days* (1979). Two biographies of Hardy were published at the end of the century—*The Stranger from Melbourne: Frank Hardy—A Literary Biography 1944–1975,* by Paul Adams (1999), and *Frank Hardy and the Making of Power Without Glory,* by Pauline Armstrong (2000). The Association for the Study of Australian Literature devoted a one-day conference to Hardy in 2000.

Francis Joseph Hardy was born on 21 March 1917 in Southern Cross, Victoria, the fifth of Thomas and Winifred Hardy's eight children. The family later moved to Bacchus Marsh (fictionalized in Hardy's work as Benson's Valley) and, following several dislocations through Thomas's changing employment, settled there in 1926. There is some evidence that the memory of this disruption had a lasting influence on Hardy, although virtually all of his schooling was at St. Bernard's Catholic School in Bacchus Marsh. Hardy left school at the age of thirteen and worked in a variety of seasonal jobs until he left for Melbourne in 1938.

His life until this point was typical of the Victorian rural working class. His acculturation was in sporting activities such as football, cricket, billiards, horse racing, and gambling. He participated in local public entertainments and concerts, sometimes reading or speaking. Hardy's Catholicism was also an important aspect of his development, though he came to oppose religious doctrine. Adams stresses the importance of oral culture in Hardy's early life. His father was an extroverted spinner and weaver of yarns, and for Hardy's milieu the general mode of cultural transmission was oral.

Running counter to this oral mode is Hardy's increasing engagement with literacy, facilitated in part by the local Mechanics' Institute and increasing access to the written word. Many of his stories based on his rural life deal with the introduction of literacy to cultures previously dominated by orality. The character of the stranger in "The Stranger from Melbourne" embodies this new transaction. He brings a political newspaper, *The Workers' Voice,* to the narrator's attention. This newspaper instills awareness of "new horizons" outside the "timeless backwater" of Benson's Valley. It also brings organized socialism and Marxism to his notice. Adams argues,

> For the young narrator literacy provides a new, more exciting form of understanding. It is a powerful modernising influence, establishing new forms of knowledge which can be contained outside the human mind. Unconstrained by location or deference to tradition, the stranger's newspaper carries stories from all over the world. It enables the young narrator to locate himself in some relation to the outside world, so offering the young narrator an alternative critical position which promotes "discontent" with a more traditional life. The significance of this moment, as Hardy explains in his autobiographical writings, concerns the capacity of the stranger's literate world to explain things which the oral culture of his father cannot.

This moment renders Hardy's leaving of "Benson's Valley" inevitable and is one of the major themes and dilemmas of his life's work.

Hardy met Rosslyn Couper late in 1939 when they were both employed by the Cavalcade Radio Company, he as a salesman and she as a stenographer. They were married within six months on 27 May 1940. The couple had three children—Frances, Alan, and Shirley. Rosslyn proved an important source of inspiration and practical support for Hardy until they separated in 1970. She died in 1981 at the age of sixty-one.

Later in 1940 Hardy joined the CPA, a decision that had a profound impact on the rest of his life. While it was a plausible and perhaps obvious decision for someone with Hardy's socialist background and leanings to take, it also generated another internal conflict in his life that provided a rich seam for his writing—the psychological, spiritual, and political clash between communism and Catholicism.

Hardy and Rosslyn Couper on their wedding day, 27 May 1940, at St. Patrick's Cathedral, Melbourne (from Pauline Armstrong, Frank Hardy and the Making of Power Without Glory, *2000)*

Unlike many of his party comrades, Hardy did not join the Australian army immediately after the German invasion of the Soviet Union in 1941 but waited to be called up in 1942. Because of a medical condition, Hardy was initially given noncombat stations around Melbourne. During this time he was supplementing his income by drawing cartoons. His first publications were, in fact, cartoons published in *Radio Times* between 1937 and 1939. In 1943 Hardy was stationed in the Northern Territory, where his career as a writer began. He wrote articles, anecdotes, and reports for the unofficial newspaper of his unit, *Troppo Tribune,* of which he became editor in late 1943 and which he continued to edit into 1944. Encouraged by figures such as writer and journalist Frank Ryland and the communist theorist Paul Mortier—presumed to be the model for the central character in *But the Dead are Many*—he began to write down the stories he habitually told, often using the pen name Ross Franklyn.

In late 1944 Hardy returned to Melbourne to work as a graphic artist on the army magazine *Salt*. Here he met and developed links with artists and writers such as Vane Lindesay, Ambrose Dyson, Mungo MacCallum, and Hume Dow. He also had the opportunity to work on his writing, which had already been rewarded with first prize in the School of Modern Writers Competition for "Stranger in the Camp." Hardy left the army at the end of World War II, already a significant figure in leftist literary circles. He was president of the Realist Writers' Group, mixing with such left-wing writers and thinkers as John Morrison, Judah Waten, David Martin, Eric Lambert, Ralph De Boissiere, Ian Turner, and Stephen Murray-Smith. Within the party he was taking on the role of theoretician and lecturer on literature and other cultural and political issues.

Hardy was also beginning to be noticed in literary circles beyond the party. In 1946 his story "A Load of Wood" was selected by Flora Eldershaw to be published in that year's *Coast to Coast* anthology of best Australian stories.

After the war, Hardy worked part-time as a journalist and started work on *Power Without Glory*, "jointly authored" by Hardy and Franklyn. An historical work of epic scale, the novel required a great deal of research into the background of its story. As Armstrong argues, some debate exists over the extent to which the overall project was initiated by Hardy or the CPA and whether the research was performed under the party's auspices or through Hardy's well-developed network. A few critics are even prepared to doubt Hardy's authorship of large sections of the book. What seems easier and more useful to assert is that the research and publication of *Power Without Glory* was a massive enterprise, with Hardy at the center, which required the cooperation and support of many people, some associated with the CPA. Given the refusal of printers and publishers to handle the book, this cooperation extended into the areas of physical production, distribution, and promotion—often in a clandestine way. One method of distribution was via direct sales to workers at lunchtime or stop work meetings held at their workplaces.

Power Without Glory tells the story of a Catholic working-class boy, John West, who grew up in the fictional suburb of Carringbush (Collingwood) in Melbourne toward the end of the nineteenth century. Dissatisfied with the level of opportunity available to him as a bootmaker, West uses his corrupt gambling establishments and the consequent acquisition of power as his means to escape the poverty of his early life. He creates an empire, the influence of which spreads across Australia and reaches into its political parties, especially the Australian Labor Party (ALP). In order to maintain the power of this network, West must resort to criminal activities ranging from bribery to murder. At the end of the book an old John West, wealthy but racked with guilt, lies in bed seeking an elusive forgiveness for his sins.

The novel is a product of political conflict. It is a committed book designed to expose the Catholic Church, the ALP, and the capitalist system to scrutiny. It had some measure of success because it brought stories of corruption and violence, which were circulating orally in limited circles, into print to be forever on the public record. Attempted suppression through the courts served only to assist the promotion of the novel.

Upon the publication of *Power Without Glory* in 1950 Hardy was almost immediately arrested on a charge of criminally libeling Ellen Wren, the wife of leading Catholic John Wren, on the assumption that the West family in the novel is based upon the actual Wren family. In the book, Ellen Wren's fictional counterpart, Nellie West, has an affair with a bricklayer, an episode that leads to her giving birth to an illegitimate child. Despite the charge being made in Ellen Wren's name, the primary insult was felt by John Wren/West. Moreover, Ellen Wren is unidentifiable without the reader first identifying John West as her husband. And this fact underlines the main tactical error of the prosecution. The jury—which on some anecdotal accounts believed Hardy to be technically guilty—saw John Wren's implicit identification with John West and his refusal to be involved as a witness in the case as something akin to an admission of complicity in the criminality and gangsterism represented in the novel. Hardy was eventually acquitted after a sensational and widely publicized court case.

Aside from its "political" impact, the other breakthrough of the book was that it offered a model for left-wing publishing in Australia. It showed that workers would buy and read books targeted at them. It also showed that large-scale distribution and sales were possible, given the right kind of organization, one that used the kind of "underground" and unconventional methods necessary in the distribution of *Power Without Glory*. Indeed, the left-wing publishing company the Australasian Book Society (ABS) was formed in 1952, inspired by the "success" of Hardy's novel. While none of its books had the impact of *Power Without Glory*, the ABS continued to operate for twenty-seven years and published more than eighty Australian books.

Shortly after the acquittal, Hardy and his wife went on their first trip to the Soviet Union to see the "workers' state" in action and to escape the furor and bitterness left over from the criminal trial. They returned to Australia in early 1952, and Hardy com-

MEMBERS of the Defend Hardy Committee signing the petition in support of the author of Power Without Glory. Front row, left to right: Mr. J. O'Connor (Democratic Rights Council); Mr. E. Platz, journalist; Mr. Alan Marshall, author; Miss J. Campbell, secretary, Fellowship of Australian Writers; Mr. "Doc" Doyle, secretary, Ship Painters' and Dockers' Union.

Newspaper clipping about the Frank Hardy Defence Committee, formed during Hardy's nine-month trial on charges of criminal libel in his novel Power Without Glory (from the Guardian [Australia], 23 November 1950)

pleted his travel book *Journey into the Future,* published by ABS later in the same year. In it Stalin's Russia is eulogized. Hardy, however, repudiated the "utopianism" of *Journey into the Future* later in life. He dismissed it as a "dishonest book" of the kind that some visitors to the Soviet Union felt impelled to write.

Back in Australia, Hardy put much of his energies into literary organizations. He contributed to the Realist Writers' new magazine, *Realist Writer*–begun in 1952 and incorporated in 1954 into the new left-wing literary magazine *Overland,* edited by Murray-Smith–and participated in the operations of the ABS. He was also active in the Fellowship of Australian Writers (FAW). He continued to write articles on art and literature, several of which were published in the *Communist Review.* Occasionally he was asked to write for the European communist press. In 1954 Hardy moved to Sydney, where he re-formed the Sydney Realist Writers' Group, which had begun in 1952 only to collapse quickly. He had been a member of the Melbourne group since 1945 and was keen to see the Realist Writers become a strong national network. After the editorship of *Overland* became estranged from significant elements of the party in 1958, Hardy became inaugural editor of the new *Realist Writer* based in Sydney. He remained on the editorial committee until 1966. The magazine lasted until 1970.

The Four-Legged Lottery was published in 1958. Another novel about the destructive effects of gambling, it develops a pattern in Hardy's work, split narration. In this case the narration was intended to achieve what Hardy saw as Brechtian-type effects of estrangement. Yet, like some of his later novels, its reception was particularly muted. Many critics—including Clement Semmler, the compiler of the only collection of Hardy's work, *A Frank Hardy Swag* (1982)—believe that this novel has been particularly underestimated, even by Hardy sympathizers.

In the 1960s Hardy published two significant journalistic works, *The Hard Way: The Story Behind Power Without Glory* (1961) and *The Unlucky Australians* (1968). Presented as novels, they use many fictional devices but in aim and impact obtain the status of nonfiction. The former is an account of the criminal trial from the moment of arrest to the immediate aftermath of the not-guilty verdict. Continuing to use the device of the split author Hardy/Franklyn, *The Hard Way* is a book that the "authors" see as a necessary phase in the process of overcoming the effects of the trial and moving forward as a psychological whole—a whole that Hardy never attains. Two problems of "moving forward," however, were Hardy's growing alienation from the CPA and its Stalinist chiefs and his growing sense of being an outcast from all circles. In 1968 the man who had eulogized the Soviet Union in *Journey into the Future* repudiated that work in a series of pieces for the *Sunday Times* in Britain. Titled "Stalin's Heirs," these articles confirmed for many, especially those in the Communist Party, Hardy's status as a dissident. Judah Waten, Hardy's onetime ally and staunch supporter over *Power Without Glory,* went as far as trying to have Hardy expelled from the CPA.

The Unlucky Australians is one of Hardy's most important and most serious books. Prescient in its genuine interest in and sympathy for radical approaches to the Australian Aboriginal people's struggles, the book is Hardy's attempt to learn from and advocate on behalf of the most outcast of all Australian people. Arriving in Darwin in 1966 to reacquaint himself with the Northern Territory and moviemaker Cecil Holmes, Hardy spent some time with the Gurindji people, and he associated himself with their struggle for land rights. A forerunner to later—and perhaps more sensitive and sophisticated—discussions of Aboriginal politics from a white perspective, *The Unlucky Australians* is nonetheless a landmark in Hardy's career and a significant historical document. While in Darwin, Hardy also maintained his image as a yarn spinner and raconteur. In April 1967 he won the Australian Yarn Spinning Competition in Darwin, a title he retained until 1991.

Hardy's next book, *The Outcasts of Foolgarah,* was published in 1971, though it had been fifteen years in the writing. In 1958 Hardy had challenged fellow Realist Writer Dorothy Hewett to a writing contest to see who could write a novel the fastest. Hewett took up the challenge and produced *Bobbin Up* in eight weeks. It was published by the ABS in 1959. Hardy, working on a book based on a strike action by garbage collectors, took some time longer, even though the first draft of *The Outcasts of Foolgarah,* "Up the Garbos!," had been completed in 1956. Hardy went through several rewrites of a book whose development bridges a significant era in Australian literary-political life. Begun in the Cold War, it was rewritten throughout the late 1950s and the 1960s and published on the cusp of a new age in Australian cultural life. Beginning as an old-left fictional account of a strike, it was published in a new-left atmosphere of sexual and political liberation. It is a satirical and ribald book of Rabelaisian excess. Adams describes it as Hardy's most postmodern work—demotic in tone, vernacular in language, and influenced by a diversity of political and theoretical perspectives from both within and outside the CPA.

But the Dead are Many is Hardy's most "literary" novel. It is self-consciously poetic and structured around a literary version of the musical fugue form. The four contrapuntal voices and the downward spiral to suicide of the central character, John Morel, combine to create this literary effect. It is a brooding, psychological, and deliberately modernist novel exploring political morality and revolutionary disenchantment; it raised Hardy's stock in literary criticism and lowered it perhaps irredeemably in the mind of party functionaries and many on the Marxist left. Some leftist critics, notably John Docker and Jack Beasley, were heavily critical. Max Harris commented dryly that Hardy was now "in the same honours thesis group as Patrick White, Hal Porter and Thomas Kenneally."

Hardy's next novel, *Who Shot George Kirkland? A Novel about the Nature of Truth* (1980), was written when Hardy was living in France in the late 1970s. It failed to build, however, upon the relative success of *But the Dead are Many*. The novel is divided into two sections—one a manuscript written by "Ross Franklyn"; the second by an unnamed researcher essentially trying to work out the truth of Hardy's claim about Ellen Wren's affair in *Power Without Glory. Who Shot George Kirkland?* is an important work in Hardy's oeuvre—one for the true Hardy aficionados because of its continuation, complication, and clarification of many of the themes explored in the earlier work. But the novel fails to stand on its own merits; it is too interlinked with previous works and events to make much sense to readers new to Hardy's writing.

That his later work becomes more inwardly or psychologically focused is some measure of Hardy's increasing isolation from his earlier political support base. Hardy's final published novel, *The Obsession of Oscar Oswald* (1983), is perhaps the end of that process. It tells the story of an embattled, paranoid, and proba-

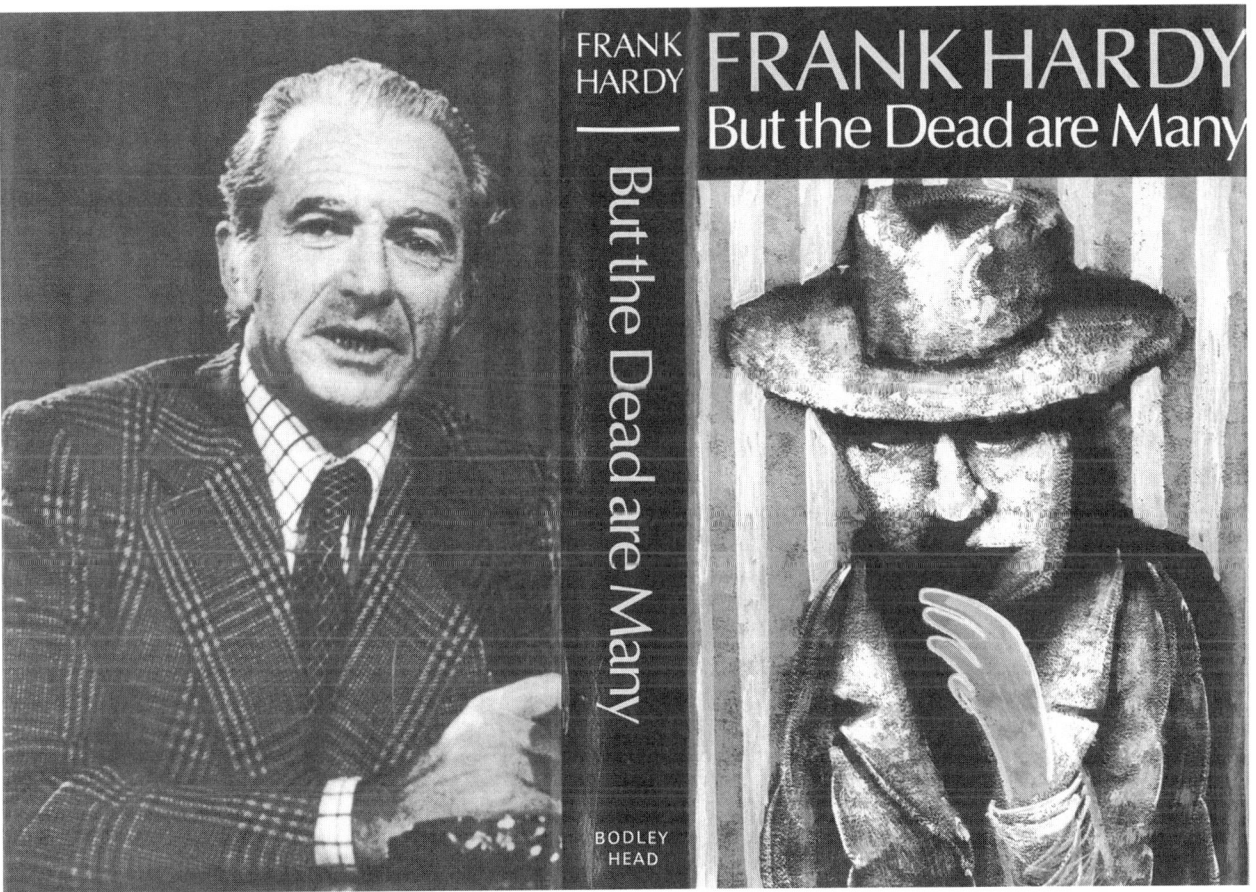

Dust jacket for Hardy's 1975 book, a modernist novel constructed in imitation of a musical fugue (Bruccoli Clark Layman Archives)

bly schizophrenic man fearing all outside his home, especially those he calls the "blue paper men," the members of the conspiracy to rob the poor–big business, repossession men, and government agents. Told by a first-person narrator, an immigrant American writer who lives across the road from Oscar, the book gradually leads the reader to the suggestion that Oscar's paranoia and conspiracy theories might well be justified. When Oscar dies in a hail of bullets at the end of the story, the reader can reach no other conclusion.

In the final ten years of Hardy's life, he published no new full-length works. While he published several story collections, they were new collections of older works or transcriptions of stories told many times over. Between 1985 and 1993 he published regular columns in the populist magazines *People* and *Australasian Post,* appearing sometimes as "the most Australian Australian." During this period Hardy seemed to be mopping up his life, trying to discharge his debts and get his manuscript archives in order. While having no formal political associations, he was active in community campaigns, and he even managed to achieve some *Power Without Glory*–like publicity and notoriety in Sydney at the beginning of the 1990s after his accumulation of thousands of dollars in parking fines caused him once more to be threatened with jail. Hardy was working on two manuscripts at the time of his death–"The Secret Memoirs of F. J. Borky," a novel, and "Voices Off," his autobiography. They remain unpublished.

There is a strong argument to be made that someone who wants to understand Hardy's later works fully needs to read his works sequentially. The reason is that more than most writers, Hardy was openly caught up in social, political, and personal histories. Trajectories in the form and media of Hardy's work reflect the changing nature of social communication in his milieux–from the cartoon and yarn to the written short story, the epic political novel, the involvement in cinema, radio, and television, and the return to shorter fiction and the spoken word. His work also traces the changes in politics and resultant political targets in Australian life–from the naive yarn-spinner telling stories about bush working-class life to the politically tough communist novelist to the disillusioned revolutionary telling tales in a changing political culture. There is also a personal story of growth and disintegration–the stories of expanding horizons, political commitment, disillusion, and growing paranoia and despair.

Frank Hardy died peacefully at his home on 28 January 1994, feet up on the table and the racing form in his hand. He will be remembered as a major literary and radical-political figure of twentieth-century Australian history.

Interview:

Bruce Molloy, "An Interview with Frank Hardy," *Australian Literary Studies,* 7 (1976): 356–374.

Bibliography:

Martin Duwell, Marianne Ehrhardt, and Carol Hetherington, *The ALS Guide to Australian Writers: A Bibliography, 1963–1995* (St. Lucia: University of Queensland Press, 1997).

Biographies:

Paul Adams, *The Stranger from Melbourne: Frank Hardy–A Literary Biography, 1944–1975* (Perth: University of Western Australia Press, 1999);

Pauline Armstrong, *Frank Hardy and the Making of Power Without Glory* (Melbourne: Melbourne University Press, 2000).

References:

Jack Beasley, *Red Letter Days: Notes from Inside an Era* (Sydney: Australasian Book Society, 1979);

John Docker, "A Study in Context: *And the Dead Are Many,*" *Arena,* 41 (1976): 48–61;

John Frow, *Marxism and Literary History* (Cambridge, Mass.: Harvard University Press, 1986);

H. M. Green, *A History of Australian Literature, Volume II: 1923–1950* (Sydney: Angus & Robertson, 1961);

Max Harris, "Browsing," *Australian,* 6 September 1975, p. 20;

John McLaren, *Writing in Hope and Fear: Literature as Politics in Postwar Australia* (Melbourne: Cambridge University Press, 1996);

Peter Williams, "Plagiarism and Rewriting: The Case of Frank Hardy," *New Literature Review,* 10 (1982): 45–53.

Papers:

Collections of Frank Hardy's manuscripts, correspondence, and audio and video recordings are in the National Library of Australia (Manuscript Library and the Oral History Collection) and in the Australian Defence Force Academy (Library Manuscript Collection). Substantial archive material by or relating to Hardy is also in the Australasian Book Society papers at the National Library of Australia and the archive collection in the Mitchell Library, Sydney.

Xavier Herbert

(15 May 1901 – 10 November 1984)

Frances de Groen
University of Western Sydney

BOOKS: *Capricornia* (Sydney: Publicist Press, 1938; New York: Appleton-Century, 1943);
Seven Emus (Sydney: Angus & Robertson, 1959);
Soldiers' Women (Sydney: Angus & Robertson, 1961);
Larger Than Life: 20 Short Stories (Sydney: Angus & Robertson, 1963);
Disturbing Element (Melbourne: Cheshire, 1963);
Poor Fellow My Country (Sydney: Collins, 1975; New York: St. Martin's Press, 1980);
Dream Road [chapter 8, *Poor Fellow My Country*], illustrations by Ray Crooke, foreword by Harry Hesseltine [sic] (Sydney: Collins, 1977).

Editions and Collections: *Xavier Herbert: South of Capricornia: Short Stories 1925–1934,* edited by Russell McDougall (Melbourne: Oxford University Press, 1990);
Xavier Herbert: Episodes from Capricornia, Poor Fellow My Country and Other Fiction, Non-Fiction and Letters, edited by Frances de Groen and Peter Pierce (St. Lucia: University of Queensland Press, 1992).

Aptly nicknamed "Australia Prolix" by a rival in 1938, Xavier Herbert was a controversial visionary novelist and short-story writer whose long career from 1926 to 1984 registered the major social and cultural developments of his generation. Nurtured by 1930s bush-focused, fascist-flavored, anti-British nationalism, his large ambition was to express as vibrantly, capaciously, and accessibly as possible to a wide popular audience the ambivalent significance of what he believed it meant to be Australian. His most important works, *Capricornia* (1938) and *Poor Fellow My Country* (1975), chart the post-invasion history of northern Australia and are exhortatory and polemical in force. Their complicated melodramatic plots celebrate the survival of Aboriginal cultures and castigate Herbert's fellow whites for their failure to shake off the colonial yoke and create a just, fair, and independent nation—a "True Commonwealth." In their prodigious length, profusion of multicultural characters, and epic overland journeys, they suggest the untamed vastness of the far north of

Xavier Herbert, 1939 (Fryer Memorial Library, University of Queensland)

Australia and rhapsodically evoke the beauty and terror of its frontier landscapes.

By 1930 Herbert had reached the radical conclusion that the Australian nation was founded on the theft of the land from its indigenous custodians—a theft masked by the concept of "terra nullius" and the "White Australia Policy" of the 1901 Federal Constitution. He later projected his ambivalent feelings about the community to which he belonged in terms of an idiomatic metaphor uniting both affection and repugnance—a "bastard nation" and a "nation of bastards."

Underpinning his articulation of the primal shame of Australia, however, was the awareness of his own illegitimate status—not only as an alienated child born out of wedlock but also as the adult beneficiary of the neocolonial Australian order. This ambivalent insight permitted him to identify with half-castes and to imagine life from the other side of the frontier. It also authorized him to merge his anomalous personal history with that of the nation and write about it as a national and not merely a personal subject.

Herbert's entire oeuvre exhibits this complex autobiographical impulse. In a log entry of 4 June 1964, he lucidly noted: "I have this self-centred quality that makes me write out of what is symbolic of my own problems." A study of his career reveals an increasingly self-conscious obsession with what he calls in *Disturbing Element* (1963) "the puzzle of all puzzles, the reality of one's own existence." He wrote compulsively—novels, stories, polemical journalism, letters, and literary "logs"—not only to discover, explore, and confirm the "reality" of his existence but also, contradictorily, to project a "larger than life" identity. These contradictory desires, for realism on the one hand and romance on the other, are conflated in the introduction to *Larger Than Life: 20 Short Stories* (1963) as a commitment to communicate, via the mode of excessive melodrama, the "marvellousness of life" that is "all too rarely manifest." Such a commitment energizes, enriches—and at times undermines—Herbert's extensive if uneven literary achievement.

Capricornia, Soldiers' Women (1961) and *Poor Fellow My Country* share a core narrative tracing a misbegotten child's search for identity and creative self-realization. The motive for this quest originated with Herbert's illegitimate birth in the Western Australian coastal port of Geraldton on 15 May 1901, six months after the Commonwealth of Australia was inaugurated. Throughout his life he claimed that his unmarried parents, Welsh-born engine driver Benjamin Herbert and snobbish Anglophile Amy Scammell Herbert, had neglected to register his birth. A birth certificate registered by Amy, nevertheless, does exist. It names him Alfred Jackson and ascribes his paternity to John Jackson, auctioneer, Amy's former de facto partner and father of her two previous illegitimate children. Other evidence, however, suggests that Ben Herbert was Alfred's biological father and that Amy had attempted to disguise her son's illegitimacy and retain her connection with a "gentleman." Amy's deception—if that is what it was—prevented Alfred, or Freddie, as he was known in childhood, from being legitimized when she and Ben Herbert married in 1917. It also created uncertainty and shame. The uncertainty permitted Herbert to adopt in adulthood a range of compensatory personae romanticizing his origins. He boasted, for example, that he was born in Port Hedland and "wet-nursed by a gin" and exaggerated his affiliations with Irish-convict forebears played down by his mother. The shame fed his compulsive need for romantic lies and generated a fearful fascination with sex and a deep distrust, particularly of women. These autobiographical themes, which have links with the masculine bush tradition outlined by Russel Ward in *The Australian Legend* (1958), permeate Herbert's fiction and influence the "selves" he inhabited: in a 1962 Adelaide Arts Festival speech, for example, he identified with Henry Lawson's uncouth, big-talking archmisogynist, the "Bastard from the Bush."

In 1904, three-year-old Alfred moved with his blended family from Geraldton to the little railway township of Midland Junction, sixteen kilometers east of Perth. Here he was baptized as a Herbert at the local Anglican church and attended the local public school, imbibing imperial loyalty through Empire Day rituals, amateur theatricals, British boys' weeklies such as *Gem* and *Magnet,* and popular songs and recitation—especially the verse of Rudyard Kipling and E. G. Sims. In Midland Junction, too, he roamed the countryside with his older half brother, acquiring a love of the bush and coming into contact with the "Beechboro Blacks," fringe-dwelling descendants of the tribes who once had been custodians of the land around Guildford and Midland Junction. *Disturbing Element* recalls the idyllic working-class bush boyhood Herbert enjoyed at Midland Junction during the first decade of the twentieth century. The decline and fall in *Capricornia* of the O'Cannon railway "garrison" at Blackadder Creek, named after a Midland watercourse, delineates the darker forces Herbert encountered in family and community life—the deaths of siblings, parental discord, class tensions, and racial discrimination. His lifelong preference for residing in small, remote bush communities nevertheless stems from his childhood at Midland Junction.

When the family moved in 1912 to the Western Australian main port of Fremantle, a predominantly working-class Irish-Catholic town, Herbert's perceptions of the class and sectarian conflicts beneath apparent community harmony were sharpened. During World War I his family steadily climbed the local social ladder, and his mother encouraged him to pursue the middle-class career of pharmacy. He gained his Preliminary Pharmaceutical Certificate at Christian Brothers College in Fremantle, completing his studies at the Perth Technical School as the apprentice of a colorful dockside pharmacist. Meanwhile, his political affiliations shifted from right to left and back again, depending on the company he was keeping and often in opposition to it. This ambivalence, characteristic of his adult politics in particular and his worldview more generally, reflected the confused and competing class allegiances of his home, where tensions between his Labor-voting, working-class, investment-conscious, upwardly mobile father and his more determinedly upwardly mobile, snobbish, but Industrial Workers of the World (IWW)–approving mother were not atypical of the wider Australian community. The enlistment of his father and half brother in 1917 in a railway unit supplying Australian Imperial Force (AIF) troops in France heightened his awareness of the dual loyalty Australians owed–primarily to the British Empire and only secondly to their own homeland. It also taught him how women, including his mother, welcomed their unaccustomed wartime freedom from patriarchal domination, a theme he returned to in *Soldiers' Women*. The brief postwar euphoria in Fremantle offered him sexual opportunities but also magnified nagging anxieties about the performance of masculinity that his distaste for the local brothels had aroused. As an excited participant in the violent clashes on the Fremantle wharves during the prolonged strikes of 1917 and 1919, he developed an imaginative grasp of the drama of history and his own role in it. Chapters 6 to 11 of *Disturbing Element* vividly portray the public and private turmoil of Herbert's Fremantle years, as he grew from uncertain adolescent to brash, cynical adult.

In mid 1923 Herbert followed his older half siblings to Melbourne, the provisional capital of Australia until 1927. His experiences there as a dispenser in the venereal diseases clinic of a large hospital while studying to matriculate reinforced his cynicism about human nature and confirmed his dislike of cities, which he later labeled "slave camps." He was admitted into medical school at Melbourne University in 1925 but speedily abandoned his studies in favor of a literary career that gave free rein to the romantic yearning for the wilderness his jaundiced response to urban life inspired. He made his debut with "North of Capricorn" in the June number of the *Australian Journal,* the long-running popular magazine that by the 1920s was entertaining its largely female audience with melodramatic and sentimental potboilers, knitting patterns, and cosmetic advertisements. It appeared under his real name, Alfred Herbert.

Set on the far northwest coast of Western Australia, "North of Capricorn" reveals Herbert's fictional models to have been writers of popular frontier romance, notably the American known as "the Victor Hugo of the North"–Rex Beach–an exponent of "the he-man school" of "northwest" writing, which also included Jack London. The hero, who shares Herbert's name, Fred, and his passion for the wilderness, is an engineer on a voyage up the northwest coast of Australia to Darwin. A "big sun-burnt man of the outback,"

Sadie Norden, Herbert's future wife, in 1927 (Fryer Memorial Library, University of Queensland)

Fred is keen to exploit the vast mineral potential of the frontier. Seams of iron ore on coastal cliffs strike him speechless with "a sort of awe, a reverence for something greater than his mind could realise." At an appropriately exotic pearling station and after the obligatory fisticuffs with a conventionally dastardly villain, Fred is rewarded with the heroine's love, plus the pearling station and iron ore deposits bequeathed to her by her father on his deathbed.

"North of Capricorn" was representative of the vogue for imperial romance that drew on but superseded the outworn conventions of the 1890s bush yarn in *The Australian Journal* and other local magazines in the mid 1920s. The awestruck references to the potential for "development" of the "empty" land echoed the call of the conservative Stanley Melbourne Bruce-E. C. G. Page government to "develop the north" with "men, money and markets." It also announced Herbert's enduring preoccupation–the blending of autobiographical concerns with larger national issues that are expressed metaphorically in violent melodramatic action set against the numinous Australian wilderness. Landscapes and seascapes are rendered expressionistically, conveying in their animation the surging energies of the "spirit" of the continent, apprehended by character and author-narrator alike.

Over the next five years, after a stint writing freelance in Sydney while employed as a laboratory assistant at the Sydney Technical College, Herbert traveled widely to several "outposts of empire." In early 1927 he journeyed north to Darwin via Cairns in search of "local color" for his writing. By August he reached Darwin, where he undertook casual dispensing and briefly worked as a fettler on the ill-fated Darwin-Katherine railway. From February 1928, he spent four months as dispenser at the Rue Hospital in Tulagi, the capital of the British Solomon Islands, then recuperated with his family in Sydney before returning to Darwin in 1929 as Government Pharmacist. The insights he accrued into the contrasting worlds of "pukka" colonial bureaucrats, lowly frontier laborers, and exploited natives supplied the raw narrative material he later transformed into *Capricornia*.

During this period he published fifteen short stories, a "thrill-a-minute" novella—"The Sea Vultures"—serialized in a local equivalent of the imperialist *Boy's Own Paper* (*Pals*), an "Autobiographical Letter" romanticizing his frontier exploits, and many paragraphs, mainly on scientific subjects, for popular magazines and newspapers, including *The Bulletin, Truth,* and *Smith's Weekly*. These writings appeared under variants of his own name (Alfred Herbert, A. X. Herbert) or pseudonyms ("Herbert Astor," "Soda," and "Hector Plasm"). Under the tutelage of the editor at *The Australian Journal* and a Sydney journalist acquaintance at *Smith's Weekly,* he extended his range of literary models, learning lessons in terseness, acerbic humor, and an anti-authoritarian tone. Although five stories featured urban or dockside settings, his preferred imaginative world remained the frontier. Two unpublished manuscripts dating from this early phase in his career illustrate his ambition to produce a serious novel about the far north. "Giants of Iron," clearly influenced by American realist Theodore Dreiser's *The Titan* (1914) but in a spirit closer to Beach's Alaskan romances, revisits the numinous landscapes and frontier themes from "North of Capricorn." A crude, untitled "boy's own" narrative traces the contest between two white heroes and Padrona, a vengeful half-caste who wields a megapowerful explosive to dominate the globe from his pirate empire in "Arnheim [sic] Land." As well as expressing contemporary Australian anxieties about the threat that "miscegenation" allegedly posed white racial hegemony, Padrona also represents a first-draft sketch for the sympathetic portrayals of half-castes in *Capricornia*, particularly Charlie Ket. A character who initially describes Padrona as a "half-caste demon," for example, later observes "more reasonably" that he has good cause for hating whites.

By the 1930s a few Australian publishers were beginning to bring out local works with popular appeal, but opportunities for the serious writer aspiring to produce the "Great Australian Novel" were limited. Most Australian writers sailed to London to build their reputations. Herbert was no exception; he stayed in London for two difficult years from 1930 to 1932. His sole publication, "Living Dangerously," a pseudonymous "boys' own" hoax, set in the Arafura Sea, gave little hint that he was reinventing himself as "Xavier" Herbert, avowed republican nationalist and author of the 250,000-word manuscript of *Capricornia*. The circumstances of his transformation are obscure. They appear to have involved the disillusionment of failing to find a publisher for "Black Velvet," the "tough little book" he hoped would launch his international career, and its joyful redrafting as *Capricornia*. A year after his return to Sydney, his association in late 1933 with fellow renegade-expatriate publisher and sometime ghostwriter Percy Reginald "Inky" Stephensen reinforced his belief that he had written the "Great Australian Novel." Author of *The Bushwhackers* (1929), a mediocre collection of iconoclastic outback sketches, Stephensen shared Herbert's nationalist aspirations. His chief goal, however, was to establish an independent publishing house in Australia. His founding of P. R. Stephensen and Company in September 1933 coincided with Herbert's attempt to find an Australian publisher for his vast, unruly, and innovative novel.

In the year before he and Stephensen met, Herbert had been supporting himself and Sadie Norden, a Jewish woman he had teamed up with in London and brought to Australia, by writing stories of trickery and deception featuring frontier characters and settings that link many of them to *Capricornia*. Twelve of these stories appeared in *The Australian Journal* from April 1933 to September 1934; five shorter pieces were published in the *Sunday Sun & Guardian*. Herbert later revised six of the more effective tales for *Larger Than Life,* including "Miss Tanaka" and the comic "Look into My Eyes." When Herbert and Stephensen met, despite being opposite in temperament—Stephensen was gregarious and cosmopolitan, Herbert the reclusive bushman—they found they had much in common. Both were idealists who believed in an Australian tutelary spirit of place and yearned to create a nationalist republic, a "True Commonwealth," free from British colonial domination. Their electrically charged partnership, dedicated to "the Cause" of creating a truly national literature, released Herbert's "genuine satirical, comic and depictive gifts," as Stephensen noted in his initial appraisal of

Herbert as a tantalite miner, 1937 (Fryer Memorial Library, University of Queensland)

the manuscript of *Capricornia* in July 1933. The facts concerning their turbulent relationship and the complicated four-year saga of the publication of *Capricornia*–facts they disputed in *The Observer* (Sydney) and *The Bulletin* in 1961–have been largely clarified by Craig Munro's 1981 article in *Southerly*, "Some Facts about a Long Fiction: The Publication of *Capricornia*." The nature and extent of Stephensen's editorial contribution to *Capricornia*, however, remain vexed questions, answers to which are bedeviled by the sole surviving manuscript of the novel, a collage of drafts, representing widely different stages of development from crude beginnings (possibly "Black Velvet") to ironically sophisticated revisions.

In early 1935, having sabotaged his now bankrupt publisher's production schedule, Herbert retrieved his manuscript and retreated to Darwin, where Norden joined him. His experiences there from 1935 to 1938–as "pox doctor" to Japanese pearl divers, relieving superintendent at the Kahlin Aboriginal Compound, would-be anthropologist, tin and tantalite miner, wharf laborer, and union organizer–provided material for the first two parts of *Poor Fellow My Country*. Failure to find an overseas publisher or obtain a permanent position in the Aboriginal Department, however, led him to renegotiate *Capricornia* with the renascent Stephensen, now editing *The Publicist* (Sydney), a vehemently nationalist monthly funded by the wealthy eccentric W. J. Miles. "The Foundations of Culture in Australia: An Essay in National Self-Respect," Stephensen's 1936 manifesto for his anti-British "Australia-First" movement, sealed their reconciliation. *Capricornia* was scheduled for publication by the press of *The Publicist* on the Aboriginal Day of Mourning and Protest, which Stephensen assisted the Aborigines Progressive Association to organize for 26 January 1938, the 150th birthday of Australia. Advertising the novel vigorously as a fierce exposé of the "plight of Aborigines and Half-castes in Australia's 'Empty North,'" Stephensen guaranteed its reception as a work of social protest. From Darwin, Herbert joined the publicity campaign with "Lynch 'Em," a powerful attack on racial discrimination in the Northern Territory, published in *The Publicist* in May. For the rest of the year Miles and Stephensen promoted *Capricornia* in protofascist Australia-First terms as an emanation of "The Spirit of the Land—depicting in a new and brilliant way the characteristics of Australia and Australians . . . a real Australian book."

The portrait of the nation that it painted was unflattering but too compelling to ignore, and it deservedly won the £250 prize in the Sesquicentenary Novel competition sponsored by the federal government. In 1939 H. G. Wells praised it as "the best written and finest novel that has ever come out of Australia," and in 1940 the Australian Literature Society awarded it their prestigious Gold Medal.

Like Brian Penton's *Landtakers* (1934), Herbert's novel exposed the fissures in the frontier myth of "progress." Its savagely subversive proem, "The Coming of the Dingoes," burlesqued the nineteenth-century Australian "pioneer" novel tradition glorifying the taming and exploitation of the land by worthy immigrants. Viewed from the Aboriginal side of the frontier, the "planting" of British "Civilization" equates to the arrival of dingoes at a waterhole: "the ancient kangaroos, not having teeth or ferocity sharp enough to defend their heritage, must relinquish it or die." Every episode, including the most humorous, reinforces this perspective, highlighting the cruelty and absurdity of a process of colonization that the land itself, with its violent extremes of climate and terrain, resists. The rare characters who display innocence or kindness become victims of the cruelty of "Nature." But if death is the great "leveler," Capricornian funerals (as Jock Driver's and Cho See Kee's obsequies demonstrate) are occasions for savage Lawsonian farce, throwing racial and class discrimination into high relief. Disastrous events, particularly those associated with the erratic Capricornian railway, chief symbol of the folly of Civilization, repeat themselves in a pattern of entropy. So, too, do the fates of characters, most notably the half-castes Norman, Connie Differ, Tocky, Yeller Elbert, Peter Pan, Charlie Ket, and Tocky's baby. Telescoped, duplicated, and multiplied, they recapitulate ever-darkening reflections of the central theme. Myriad side dramas involving some ninety characters are subtly linked by a single narrative thread—the "progress" of little half-caste "bastard" Nawnim, "No-Name," from abandonment in an Aboriginal camp by his wastrel sire, Mark Shillingsworth, to adoption by Mark's brother, Oscar, and ultimately to inheritance of Oscar's cattle ranch. The saga—and the Shillingsworth "line"—nevertheless comes to a bleak and abrupt close with Norman's discovery of the skeletal evidence of the death in childbirth of his Aboriginal concubine and her baby (his heir) in a broken water tank. Arguably the most shocking ending in Australian fiction, the final page underscores Norman's selfish disregard of Tocky and a sudden realization on the part of readers that they, too, have been complicit in forgetting her.

When the *Publicist* edition of *Capricornia* sold out, Angus and Robertson took the novel up as a commercial proposition and brought out a new Australian edition. British and American editions were published in 1939 and 1943 respectively, then translated into several European languages. Despite the warm reception of the book locally and overseas as an Australian "classic," reviewers and critics were, and continued to be, somewhat at a loss to account for its charismatic appeal. They were especially uncertain how to categorize the episodic structure and grotesque characterization or sum up its complex significance. In "The Literary Value of Human Agony" for *The Australian Quarterly* (June 1938) Furnley Maurice commended Herbert's "wall-eyed, pagan vision presented with arresting vividness" but felt overwhelmed by the tragic amplitude of the novel: "it represents so much more than it contains . . . there is too much here for one book to carry. . . . What is its implied message? What does it reveal? I do not know. . . ." Local complaints that the book was "badly constructed" or "written with an axe" persisted into the 1950s. The Red Page of *The Bulletin,* revisiting *Capricornia* on 12 December 1956, decided after much deliberation that the theme was unsuitable. "The Northern Territory" was "not a theme for a novel," indeed was "not a theme at all" but rather "a great slab of land and people" that defeated the reader by its "very richness": "tragedy after tragedy, comedy after comedy, wild spree after wild spree, characters teeming like a shoal of fish, there is too much to take in."

Vincent Buckley's 1961 essay "*Capricornia*" in *Meanjin* (1960) explored the "cosmic" significance of the social protest in the novel, defining Herbert's vision of the universe as that of an "anarchist" but failing to solve the alleged "problem" of the moral ambiguities in Herbert's text and the apparent psychological inconsistencies. The modernist project to disclose the "unity" of the text continued into the 1970s in several sympathetic and illuminating commentaries. These works uncovered psycho-biographical meanings relating to the "father-son relationship" (Harry Heseltine, in *Xavier Herbert,* 1973) and "castration" (Xavier Pons, in "Caste and Castration: The Personal Element in *Capricornia,*" 1977) or offered close readings of the rhetoric of the novel (Laurie Clancy, in *Xavier Herbert,* 1981) and its social, historical, and cultural significance

Dust jacket for Herbert's 1961 novel, focusing on women in wartime Australia (Bruccoli Clark Layman Archives)

(Brian Kiernan, in "Xavier Herbert's *Capricornia*" for *Australian Literary Studies,* 1970; John Joseph Healy, in *Literature and the Aborigine in Australia,* 1978). During the 1980s and 1990s critics were more inclined to read "against the grain" of the text and its existing interpretations, unearthing new layers of meaning rather than celebrating its rich polysemy per se. A feminist deconstruction by Elizabeth Lawson in "'Oh Don't You Remember Black Alice?' or How Many Mothers Had Norman Shillingsworth?" (*Westerly,* 1987) exposed "sexism" in the erasure of "mothers" and an authorial complicity in sexually objectifying female characters as "black velvet"; Frances de Groen and Peter Pierce, in *Xavier Herbert: Episodes from Capricornia, Poor Fellow My Country and Other Fiction, Non-Fiction and Letters* (1992), identified and discussed a metafictional dimension; and Bob Hodge and Vijay Mishra in *Dark Side of the Dream: Australian Literature and the Post-Colonial Mind* (1990) subjected the ideological implications of the romance structure to a postcolonial analysis. A full-scale study of the reception, history, ambivalent discourses, recapitulative structure, historicity, and intertextuality of *Capricornia* is yet to be conducted.

Herbert returned to Sydney in late 1938 to devote himself full-time to an even vaster work than *Capricornia*–provisionally titled at various times "Yellow Fellow," "Rex Versus Dingo Joe," and "True Commonwealth"–which would fully express the Australian ethos. Depressed by writer's block and fleeing an abortive affair with Dymphna Cusack, he abandoned the work in late 1941, unable to imagine a narrative solution to the political issues it raised. His hopes that the Australia-First Movement would deliver an Australian republic had been shouted down by Stephensen's fanatical ambition to spearhead a fascist revolution and build a "New Political Order" after the anticipated defeat of Britain by Germany. When Stephensen and other prominent Australia-First Party members were interned without trial as pro-Japanese traitors in March 1942, Herbert enlisted in the AIF. (Thirty years later in *Poor Fellow My Country* he expressed his rage and disillusion over the failure of Australia-First by pillorying Stephensen as "the Bloke," fanatical leader of the "Australia-Free Party.") By August 1942 he was serving in the North Australia Observer Unit, a mobile reconnaissance force based in the Northern Territory and commanded by anthropologist W. H. Stanner. Herbert's experiences in what has been described as Australia's "most unusual" military force provided plenty of material for part 3 of *Poor Fellow My Country,* including a defamatory portrait of Stanner as the incompetent and cowardly Fabian Cootes.

Between 1938 and 1942 Herbert had produced only three new works, all short stories. "Kaijek the Songman" appeared in *The Bulletin;* "Seven Emus" and "Once a Policeman" were published in *The Australian Journal.* Fragments of the epic he was unable to write, they sketched out characters and themes later resurrected in *Poor Fellow My Country.* "Kaijek the Songman," for example, adopts an Aboriginal persona to explore Herbert's own creative difficulties—Kaijek is suffering the oral equivalent of writer's block. The rhetorical device in the tale of incorporating words from Aboriginal languages was inspired by Herbert's friendship with Jindyworobak poet and vocal Australia-First supporter Ian Mudie, known to him as "Kaijek." In its invention of Aboriginal dreamtime "song," "Kaijek the Songman" anticipates deployment of the indigenous rhapsodists Bob Wirridirridi and his apprentice Prindy in *Poor Fellow My Country* to represent aspects of Herbert's creativity.

While in the army Herbert began drafting "a slick little book" titled "Soldiers' Women," about "women in wartime," a theme also being explored, though from a vastly different angle, by Cusack and Florence James in *Come In Spinner* (1949). Unable to write productively in Sydney after his demobilization in late 1944, Herbert withdrew with Norden to far northern Queensland in search of creative release. In 1953 he and Norden married and settled in Redlynch, a hamlet not far from Cairns. Increasingly self-absorbed and reclusive, Herbert cut cordwood in the rain forests of the Dividing Range to support himself while hammering out the idiosyncratic theory of human eroticism that underpinned all his future work. Drawing on psychosexual and social thinkers—including Friedrich Engels, Friedrich Nietzsche, Sigmund Freud, Havelock Ellis, H. G. Wells, and Sir Julian Sorell Huxley—he appropriated concepts concerning biological and social evolution to address his own sexual anxieties, which focused on the image of the "castrating woman."

Herbert's "slick little book" grew into "Of Mars, the Moon and Destiny," a vast, ponderous, and unpublishable treatise fusing memories of his adolescence during World War I with his experiences of urban Australia during the Pacific campaign. Set in a curiously anachronistic generic Australian coastal city, the work traces the "destinies" of half a dozen women running amok sexually with American enlisted men on leave. Their many lurid affairs result in abortions, venereal disease, violence, prostitution, petty crime, and eventually murder and arson, and they convey the dual image of women as both sexually threatened and sexually uncontrollable, familiar from popular iconography during the Pacific war. The litany of lust lends equivocal support to the anticapitalist arguments for the abolition of bourgeois marriage and its replacement by casual sex during women's "ripe times" propounded by Herbert's alter ego in the novel, the ultramasculine hero Colonel Leon. Leon's dream of a society based on a sexual apartheid system designed to do away with the "monkey house" of the nuclear family and produce "a race of gods" delivers all pleasure and no responsibility to males. Linked in counterpoint to the adult sexual relationships, however, is the more interesting story of Pudsey, the romantic liar and aspiring writer upon whom the plot pivots. In some respects a female version of Herbert himself as a youth, she embodies what he diagnosed in 1963 as "the self-story striving to be told."

Angus and Robertson rejected the manuscript in 1956. Despite being unable to find another publisher, Herbert refused to take the advice of his editor, Beatrice Davis, to cut the narrative ruthlessly by 120,000 words, prune back its pretentious style, change the adulterous ending—which risked prosecution for obscenity—and restore the original title. Instead, he wrote another even less successful work, "I and the Little Widow," to explore related psychosexual themes in a north-Australian sugar town. Homophobic, the work focuses on the contest between the pontificating narrator, Frank—as Herbert was known locally at the time—and his neighbor, a "castrating" widow named Amy, whose domestic tyranny produces effeminate sons. In the opening chapters, Frank discerns compelling parallels between the little widow and his own dominating mother, also named Amy. The first-person account of Frank's life, from oppressed childhood to artistically frustrated adulthood and finally to the metafictional discovery of his vocation as author of the little widow's story, represents Herbert's second and more direct attempt to write autobiography: Pudsey's story is arguably the first. Angus and Robertson rejected this work, too.

In desperation, Herbert returned to "Seven Emus," which Angus and Robertson had been unable to bring out as a book in 1942–1943 because of wartime paper shortages. Expanding it into a novella, Herbert complicated the straightforward style of the story and introduced satirical self-references into the psychological profile and literary aspirations of Appleby Gaunt (chapters 3 and 10) and the passages referring to the "Euraustralian League" (chapters 9 and 10). Most reviews, including Vance Palmer's in the April 1959 number of *Meanjin,* welcomed Herbert's return to his "old vein of ironic comedy" but balked at his "turgid"

Herbert and Beatrice Davis, his editor at Angus and Robertson, at the Adelaide Arts Festival, 1962 (Fryer Memorial Library, University of Queensland)

style. The criticisms helped convince Herbert to take Davis's advice for revising his wartime novel. The revisions he now undertook enhanced its melodramatic energies and bolstered the symbolic structure, based on the lunar cycle, but sanitized the radical—if sexist—social critique: Colonel Leon, for example, unconvincingly renounces his ladylove and advocates chastity. When *Soldiers' Women* was at last published in mid 1961, reviewers generally praised the portrayal of Pudsey but recoiled from Herbert's grotesque style and vehement sexual disgust. Unaware of the alterations to the thesis about sex, Geoffrey Dutton complained in *The Nation* on 29 July of its author's "collapse as a moralist."

Meanwhile, the "self-story" that Herbert had been struggling to articulate for more than a decade now crystalized as the lively if sometimes lurid and unreliable bildungsroman, *Disturbing Element*. He had also resumed publishing short stories with outback themes and settings, some commemorating his recent exploits as the pilot of small aircraft—he gained his license in 1959 and survived a crash in 1960. These found a ready market in local magazines, and in 1963 Angus and Robertson printed them in *Larger Than Life* alongside the best of Herbert's pre-1942 tales, with an introduction defending his preference for "the made-up" or "plotted" story. Several—including "Day of Shame," about the bombing and evacuation of Darwin—were warm-up exercises for the colossal eight-hundred-thousand-word pastoral epic about the Australian ethos that he now began rebuilding from the abandoned "Yellow Fellow."

Poor Fellow My Country represents Herbert's lament for his lost utopian dream of the "true commonwealth." Composed over the decade from 1964 to 1974, it was published by William Collins of Australia during the constitutional crisis preceding the sacking of the Edward Gough Whitlam Labor government in late 1975, evincing an uncanny political relevance that contributed toward its unprecedented commercial success. Its gigantic scope, lyrical delicacy, polemical fervor, vast but intricate "architecture," encyclopedic detail concerning the history of the period 1935–1942, and radical revision of the significance of that period for Australians in the 1970s earned it the acclaim of Randolph Stow, who in a 9 April 1976 review for *TLS: The Times Literary Supplement* identified the novel, despite its flaws, as "an Australian classic," even perhaps "*The* Great Australian Novel." Other reviewers, though generally admiring, were less certain, especially about the pompous, long-winded diatribes of Herbert's mouthpiece, Jeremy Delacy, which include, as Heseltine noted in his reader's report on the novel for Collins, "something to offend everyone." *Poor Fellow My Country* won the prestigious Miles Franklin Award in 1976 but although published by St. Martin's Press in New York in 1980 and translated into Japanese in 1983, remains relatively unread and critically neglected, if widely known in Australia. Sympathetic scholarly discussions by Laurie Hergenhan (1977), John McLaren (1981), and Sean Monahan (1987) have gone some way toward redressing this neglect.

Book 1 (chapters 1–10), "Terra Australis: Blackman's Idyll Sold Out by White Bullies, Thieves and Hypocrites," is set in an imaginary Northern Territory community based on Katherine and dramatizes the despoliation of traditional Aboriginal life indissolubly bound up with the land. Book 2 (chapters 11–20), "Australia Felix: Whiteman's Ideal Sold Out by Rogues and Fools," laments the demise of a republican nationalist movement modeled on Australia-First and satirizes communists and fascists alike as blind ideologues incapable of understanding what constitutes a "true commonwealth," let alone bringing it into being. Book 3 (chapters 21–26), "Day of Shame: A Rabble Fled the Test of Nationhood," treats the inadequate political and military responses to the threat of Japanese invasion.

First and foremost, though, *Poor Fellow My Country* tells the story of Prindy, Herbert's ideal Australian, the youthful half-caste whose failure to achieve full tribal initiation into manhood is an emblem of the defeat of Australian nationhood. The polyphonic plot charting his development from child to adolescent is organized primarily around the seasonal outback ritual of the racing carnival and turns on the contest between the masculine and feminine forces of the universe, Tchamala the Rainbow Serpent and Kunapipi the "Old Woman," respectively. Herbert interprets these mythic figures—associated in Aboriginal cosmology with fertility and increase—in the dualistic Western terms of the Eden myth, identifying Tchamala with Satan. Bob Wirridirridi, wizened old songman and implacable opponent of white hegemony, is Prindy's tribal grandfather, inducting him into secret men's business and firing his zeal to "kill 'im whiteman, kill 'im daid." Prindy's white grandfather, the amateur scientist Jeremy Delacy, provides him with a Western education. The potential reconciliation between Prindy's immigrant and indigenous heritages, however, cannot withstand the destructive interference of "castrating" women. Prindy's mother, Nelyerri, and his child bride, Savitra, both seek to possess and control him, with fatal consequences to all concerned, including Prindy and Delacy. Only Bob Wirridirridi, Tchamala's chief agent, survives the general slaughter. His spirit, united with Prindy's as an emanation of Tchamala's violent "negation," presides over the apocalyptic vision in the epilogue of a uranium-fed holocaust—"the final vengeance of the land." The nuclear motif, inspired by Herbert's rage at the British atomic tests on Australian soil during the 1950s and recapitulated throughout the narrative, lends a chilling contemporary relevance to the tragic conclusion.

In his final years, Herbert gave many interviews and speeches and published a few nonfictional essays on Aboriginal rights and Australian identity. His unfinished quest to solve the "puzzle" of his existence led him to plan a novel, "Billygoat Hill," about the contemporary "Aboriginal industry" and to write a confessional account of his erotic life from 1930 onward. These dual but related final projects illustrate the double focus of his literary achievement, based as it was on the "self-centred" symbolic identification of his own problems with those of the nation. The proposed novel did not progress beyond scattered research notes. In the months before his death on 10 November 1984, however, he completed "Me and My Shadow," a defamatory manuscript justifying his guilt-laden relations with his wife, Sadie, who had died in 1979, and other women. Xavier Herbert's failure in "Me and My Shadow" to dramatize its erotic themes mimics the inadequacies of "The Little Widow" and demonstrates by implied contrast that Herbert's powerful imagination found its most vivid and complete expression in frontier fiction.

Letters:

Xavier Herbert Letters, edited by Frances de Groen and Laurie Hergenhan (St. Lucia: University of Queensland Press, 2002).

Bibliographies:

Marianne Ehrhardt and Lurline Stuart, "Xavier Herbert: A Checklist," *Australian Literary Studies,* 8 (1978): 499–511;

David Sansome, *Xavier Herbert: A Bibliography* (Darwin: Northern Territory Library Service, 1988);

Martin Duwell, Carol Hetherington, and Irmtraud Peterson, *The ALS Guide to Australian Writers. A Bibliography 1963 to 1995* (St. Lucia: University of Queensland Press, 1997).

Biography:

Frances de Groen, *Xavier Herbert: A Biography* (St. Lucia: University of Queensland Press, 1998).

References:

Vincent Buckley, "*Capricornia,*" *Meanjin,* 19 (1960): 13–30;

Laurie Clancy, *Xavier Herbert* (Boston: Twayne, 1981);

Kevin Green, "Xavier Herbert, H. G. Wells and J. S. Huxley: Unexpected British Connections," *Australian Literary Studies*, 15 (1985): 47–64;

John Joseph Healy, *Literature and the Aborigine in Australia* (St. Lucia: University of Queensland Press, 1978);

Laurie Hergenhan, "An Australian Tragedy: Xavier Herbert's *Poor Fellow My Country*," *Quadrant*, 21 (February 1977): 62–70;

Harry Heseltine, *Xavier Herbert* (Melbourne: Oxford University Press, 1973);

John Hetherington, "Xavier Herbert: A Blend of Humility and Assurance as He Faces Life," *Age* (Melbourne), 6 May 1961, p. 18; reprinted as "Xavier Herbert 1901: Cottage at Redlynch," in his *Forty-Two Faces* (Melbourne: Cheshire, 1962), pp. 48–53;

Bob Hodge and Vijay Mishra, *Dark Side of the Dream: Australian Literature and the Post-Colonial Mind* (North Sydney: Allen & Unwin, 1990);

Brian Kiernan, "Xavier Herbert's *Capricornia*," *Australian Literary Studies*, 1 (1970): 360–370; reprinted in his *Images of Society and Nature* (Melbourne: Oxford University Press, 1971);

Elizabeth Lawson, "'Oh Don't You Remember Black Alice?' or How Many Mothers Had Norman Shillingsworth?" *Westerly*, 32 (1987): 29–39;

Furnley Maurice, "The Literary Value of Human Agony," *Australian Quarterly* (June 1938): 65–74;

John McLaren, *Xavier Herbert's Capricornia and Poor Fellow My Country* (Melbourne: Shillington House, 1981);

Sean Monahan, "*Poor Fellow My Country*: A Question of Genre," *Westerly*, 32 (1987): 42–43;

Craig Munro, "Some Facts about a Long Fiction: The Publication of *Capricornia*," *Southerly*, 41 (1981): 82–104;

Munro, *Wild Man of Letters: The Story of P. R. Stephensen* (St. Lucia: University of Queensland Press, 1984);

Xavier Pons, "Caste and Castration: The Personal Element in *Capricornia*," *Caliban*, 14 (1977): 133–147.

Papers:

The principal repository of unpublished and manuscript materials relating to Xavier Herbert is the Fryer Memorial Library (FL: MS) at the University of Queensland. Between 1971 and 1980 Herbert deposited the bulk of his extensive papers here, including manuscripts of *Seven Emus*, "The Little Widow," *Soldiers' Women, Poor Fellow My Country, Disturbing Element,* drafts of many short stories, and journalism, correspondence, literary logs, and other papers. The Manuscript section of the National Library of Australia (ANL: MS), Canberra, holds the surviving manuscript of *Capricornia*, Herbert's correspondence with Arthur Dibley from 1935 to 1938, and other correspondence with Australian writers and literary organizations. The Mitchell Collection of the State Library of New South Wales (ML: MS) holds Herbert's correspondence with P. R. Stephensen, Hal Porter, and Miles Franklin. The Mortlock Library in the State Library of South Australia holds his correspondence with Ian Mudie.

Rex Ingamells
(19 January 1913 – 30 December 1955)

Robert Sellick

BOOKS: *Gumtops* (Adelaide: F. W. Preece, 1935);

Forgotten People (Adelaide: F. W. Preece, 1936);

Conditional Culture (Adelaide: F. W. Preece, 1938; Adelaide: Harman & Jacka, 1938);

Sun-Freedom (Adelaide: F. W. Preece, 1938);

Memory of Hills (Adelaide: F. W. Preece, 1940);

At a Boundary, by Ingamells and John Ingamells (Adelaide: F. W. Preece, 1941);

News of the Sun (Adelaide: F. W. Preece, 1942);

Unknown Land (Adelaide: Jindyworobak, 1943);

Content Are the Quiet Ranges (Adelaide: Jindyworobak, 1943);

Selected Poems (Melbourne: Georgian House, 1944);

Yera: A Verse Narrative (Adelaide: Jindyworobak, 1945);

Come Walkabout (Melbourne: Jindyworobak, 1948);

Handbook of Australian Literature (Melbourne: Jindyworobak, 1949);

From Phillip to McKell: The Story of Australia (Melbourne: Jindyworobak, 1949);

Because Men Went Hungry (Melbourne: Jindyworobak, 1951);

The Great South Land: An Epic Poem (Melbourne: Georgian House, 1951);

The Dunce's Cap: A Critical Essay in Self-Defence (Murrumbeena, Vic.: Privately printed, 1951);

Aranda Boy: An Aboriginal Story (London & New York: Longmans, Green, 1952; Melbourne: Longmans, Green, 1952);

Of Us Now Living: A Novel of Australia (Melbourne: Hallcraft, 1952);

William Gay: Australian Man of Letters (Melbourne: Jindyworobak, 1952);

Royalty and Australia (Melbourne: Hallcraft, 1954);

Australian Aboriginal Words: Aboriginal-English, English-Aboriginal (Melbourne: Hallcraft, 1955);

Platypus and Kookaburra: Poem (Sydney: Collins, 1987).

OTHER: *Jindyworobak Anthology,* edited by Ingamells (Adelaide: F. W. Preece, 1941);

Jindyworobak Review, 1938–1948, edited by Ingamells (Melbourne: Jindyworobak, 1948);

Rex Ingamells (Ingamells Collection, Flinders University of South Australia)

"Novelists of the Pacific," in *The Pacific,* edited by Charles Barrett (Melbourne: N. H. Seward, 1950), pp. 157–166;

"Victor Kennedy," in *Jindyworobak Anthology* (Melbourne: Georgian House, 1951), pp. 69–70;

"Merringek: For Australian Scholarship," in *Merringek,* edited by Ingamells (Melbourne: Jindyworobak, 1953);

"Conditional Culture," in *The Writer in Australia,* edited by John Barnes (Melbourne: Oxford University Press, 1969), pp. 245–265;

"Cheng Ho," in *This World: An Anthology of Poetry for Young People,* edited by M. M. Flynn and J. Groom

(Rushcutters Bay, N.S.W.: Pergamon, 1970), p. 30;

"A Jindyworobak Review," in *Cross Currents: Magazines and Newspapers in Australian Literature,* edited by Bruce Bennett (Melbourne: Longman Cheshire, 1981), pp. 125–133;

"The Word 'Jindyworobak,'" in *The Macmillan Anthology of Australian Literature,* edited by Ken Goodwin and Alan Lawson (South Melbourne, Vic.: Macmillan, 1990), pp. 222–223.

SELECTED PERIODICAL PUBLICATIONS–UNCOLLECTED: "From a High Hill-Road," *Bulletin,* 56 (1935): 47;

"An Exhortation," *Bulletin,* 56 (1935): 45;

"Far-Away Hills," *Bulletin,* 56 (1935): 48;

"Concerning Environmental Values," *Venture: An Australian Quarterly,* 1, no. 1 (July 1937): 1–7;

"Australian Bush," *Bulletin,* 58 (1937): 21;

"Ruins in Mist," *Bulletin,* 58 (1937): 20;

"The Mopoke," *Bulletin,* 59 (1938): 21; 71 (1950): 21;

"Cross-Section," *Angry Penguins* (1941): 21;

"Australianism," *Meanjin Papers,* 1, no. 6 (1941): 3;

"Voice of the Crow," *Meanjin Papers,* 1, no. 8 (1942): 10;

"Australian Outlook," *Meanjin Papers,* 1, no. 8 (1942): 11–12;

"The Tourist Dump," in *Jindyworobak Anthology* (Melbourne: Georgian House, 1944), p. 17; reprinted in *The Jindyworobaks,* edited by Brian Elliott (St. Lucia: University of Queensland Press, 1979), p. 28; reprinted in *My Country: Australian Poetry and Short Stories—Two Hundred Years: Volume 2: 1930s–1980s,* edited by Leonie Kramer (Sydney: Lansdowne, 1985), p. 47;

"Slight Autobiography," in *Jindyworobak Anthology* (Melbourne: Georgian House, 1945), pp. 55–56; reprinted in *The Jindyworobaks,* edited by Elliott (St. Lucia: University of Queensland Press, 1979), pp. 28–29.

"Australian Poets Have a Larger Public Today," *Talk,* 2, no. 6 (1947): 61–63;

"The Exile," *Southerly,* 8, no. 3 (1947): 135; reprinted in *A Book of Australian and New Zealand Verse,* edited by Walter Murdoch and Alan Mulgan (Melbourne: Oxford University Press, 1950), p. 242;

"From Forgotten People," in *A Book of Australian and New Zealand Verse,* edited by Murdoch and Mulgan (Melbourne: Oxford University Press, 1950), p. 240;

[Untitled letter], *Southerly,* 12, no. 2 (1951): 113–114;

"The Golden Bird," *Bulletin,* 73 (1952): 2;

"Kenneth Slessor," *Walkabout,* 18, no. 10 (1952): 41–42;

"John K. Ewers," *Walkabout,* 18, no. 5, (1952): 8;

"The Key Board," *Austrovert,* no. 9 (1952): 4–5;

"In Memory: Victor Kennedy," *Southerly,* 13, no. 2 (1952): 115;

"The Pensioner," in *Jindyworobak Anthology* (Melbourne: Georgian House, 1952), pp. 39–41; reprinted in *The Jindyworobaks,* edited by Elliott (St. Lucia: University of Queensland Press, 1979), pp. 31–33;

"Frank Clune," *Walkabout,* 19, no. 3 (1953): 38–41;

"Fiction Walkabout," *Walkabout,* 19, no. 3 (1953): 10–16;

"Journey to the Rock," *Walkabout,* 19, no. 5 (1953): 20;

"An Apostrophe to Ayers Rock" (from "Uluru"), in *Jindyworobak Anthology* (Melbourne: Jindyworobak, 1953), pp. 31–33; reprinted in *The Jindyworobaks,* edited by Elliott (St. Lucia: University of Queensland Press, 1979), pp. 33–36;

"Australian Books for English School Libraries," *Walkabout,* 20, no. 8 (1954): 36–37;

"Tasmania–A Storied Isle of Rose Beauty!" *Walkabout,* 20, no. 7 (1954): 10–13;

"Sea-Chronicles," in *A Book of Australian Verse,* edited by Judith Wright (Melbourne: Oxford University Press, 1956), p. 140; reprinted in *A Book of Australian Verse,* edited by Wright (Melbourne: Oxford University Press, 1968), pp. 139–140.

Rex Ingamells's name is synonymous with the Jindyworobak movement. Jindyworobak symbolizes the "distinctive Australian quality in literature." He was the founder and chief polemicist of the movement throughout its relatively brief life, which spanned the twenty years from 1935 to 1955. He also produced the manifesto of the movement–although he was later aided in revising it by others–and fought unremittingly to see it applied. Through his enthusiasm he gathered around him a group of like-minded poets, whose work appeared in annual anthologies. How many of these poets shared his passions is difficult to say: many poets who published under the Jindyworobak banner subsequently drifted away from the movement. Although Ingamells continued to promote the movement, by the time the last *Jindyworobak Anthology* appeared in 1955 the heat had dissipated.

Reginald Charles "Rex" Ingamells was born on 19 January 1913 at Orroroo, in the midnorth of South Australia. He was the eldest of the four children of Eric Marfleet and Mabel Gwendolin Ingamells. Since the father was a Methodist minister, the family moved frequently, and Ingamells was educated at many schools in country towns. He was then sent to Prince Alfred College, one of the leading private schools in Adelaide, and he went on to complete a B.A. degree at the University of Adelaide in 1934. His M.A. thesis, "Australian History as a Background to Australian Literature,"

Page from "Aranda Myths," Ingamells's notes on the Arunta (or Aranda) tribe, which were the basis for his 1952 novel Aranda Boy *(Ingamells Collection, Flinders University of South Australia)* was rejected on the grounds that the thesis topic had not been properly approved. On 9 July 1938 Ingamells married Eileen Eva Spensley and, unsuccessful in applications for academic positions, was employed in a variety of teaching jobs. He moved to Melbourne in 1945, where he was employed as a representative and commercial traveler for publishers such as Georgian House and Longmans, Green and Company.

Before he formulated his Jindyworobak thesis, Ingamells published two collections of verse as well as individual poems in such periodicals as *The Bulletin* (Sydney) and *Chapbook* (Adelaide). These early poems—Ingamells was only in his twenties—already show an interest in the Australian Aborigines, landscapes of the outback areas of the Australian continent, and Aboriginal myth. One such poem is "Garrakeen":

> When dawn flamed on the Murray I watched for Garrakeen . . .
> Opaline purple and crimson was the river . . .
> He came from the west with blood on his breast,
> and the colours of the water were sluggish in sheen compared with his fire in the air[.]

Some of Ingamells's trademark touches are already present—the over-reliance on metaphor and the use of Aboriginal vocabulary. The second of these touches was not always in Ingamells's best interests, at least as far as some of his critics were concerned, and the poem "Moorawathimeering" achieved a certain notoriety:

> Into moorawathimeering,
> where atninga dare not tread,
> leaving wurly for a wilban,
> tallabilla, you have fled.

Brian Elliott in *The Jindyworobaks* (1979) provides a helpful paraphrase:

> Into sanctuary in the land of the lost (a place of the dead, whose sacrosanct borders the tribesmen may not safely cross) you have fled. O outcast (victim of a punishment party sent to revenge a murder). But there you shall have no hut to take shelter in, only some comfortless cave.

Poetry requiring such detailed support, such explication, is in danger of collapsing under its own weight.

Ingamells's first two collections of verse, *Gumtops* (1935) and *Forgotten People* (1936), appeared before he had formulated his thesis. *Gumtops* is particularly interesting, not least for its foreword by L. F. Giblin. Giblin is an intriguing intruder on Ingamells's story. One wonders how a friendship between a poet and publisher's representative on the one hand and an economist and adviser to government on the other ever established itself. Of greater relevance, however, is Giblin's foreword. He speaks of Australia's developing "individuality of character and distinction" and laments that these characteristics are not yet "adequately on record in literature or any other art." Giblin continues:

> Our reactions to these things are vague and feeble, because the appropriate language which would define and strengthen them is not ready to our hand. We have neither time nor capacity to hammer it out for ourselves: that is the work of the expert, the poet.

The emphasis on an "appropriate language" became one of the pillars of Ingamells's structure, but at that time only the poetry itself existed, in a poem such as "Boomerang":

> This piece of hardwood, cunningly shaped,
> Was curved so evenly while piccaninnies gaped
> At a warrior who chipped at it with pieces of flint,
> And formed it by meticulous dint upon dint.
> Outside his wurly he sat beside a tree
> And chipped at it patiently for hours—not for me,
> But to kill the wallaby in the rocky pass,
> To kill the fat wild-turkey hiding in the grass.

There is sufficient "individuality" in this poem to locate it indisputably in Australia—"wurly" and "wallaby," for example—although one would perhaps pause over "hardwood" and "piccaninnies" and certainly at "dint upon dint." And the subject itself sets it firmly in a national context. The poem includes hints that Ingamells is celebrating a culture that is already under threat, and this concern emerges frequently even in these early poems, such as "Long Ago":

> Corroboree . . .
> Corroboree . . .
> Red fires all night;
> Men in the firelight,
> Twisting and turning
> Under contorted gums.
>
> Coo-ee . . .
> Coo-ee . . .
> Echoing over
> The calling of the plover.
> And the far-ringing notes
> Of magpies at dawn.
>
> Boomerang . . .
> Swift-hurled boomerang . . .
> Glinting with sun,
> Killing the emu
> On the run;
> Felling the proud old
> Kangaroo,
> In dawn-dim grasses,
> Cold
> With dew.

In 1938 Ingamells published his first hesitant manifesto. He later acknowledged Giblin's foreword as his starting point but mentions other contributions–P. R. Stephensen's *The Foundations of Culture in Australia* (1936) and James Devaney's *The Vanished Tribes* (1929), both of which he read in 1936. In this latter publication he found his defining term, "Jindyworobak," the "symbolic word" for which he had been searching. Early in 1937 Ingamells delivered an address to the Adelaide branch of the English Association. This lecture was subsequently published in *Venture: An Australian Quarterly,* and in 1938 Ingamells expanded on this essay and brought out *Conditional Culture*. *Conditional Culture* was also the first publication to appear under the Jindyworobak imprint, and it explains Ingamells's philosophy:

> "Jindyworobak" is an aboriginal word meaning 'to annex, to join,' and I propose to coin it for a particular use. The Jindyworobaks, I say, are those individuals who are endeavouring to free Australian art from whatever alien influences trammel it, that is, to bring it into proper contact with its material. They are the few who seriously realise that an Australian culture depends on the fulfilment and sublimation of certain definite conditions, namely:
>
> 1. A clear recognition of environmental values.
> 2. A debunking of much nonsense.
> 3. An understanding of Australia's history and traditions, primaeval, colonial and modern.

Ingamells was convinced of the need for the artist–and the writer in particular–to adopt an appropriate language. Again, he went to Giblin for a clear statement and subsequently expanded it in the *Jindyworobak Review 1938-48,* not necessarily with happy results.

> environmental values: the distinctive qualities of an environment which cannot be satisfactorily expressed in conventional terms that suit other environments, scrupulous care being necessary for the indication of their primal essence. The whole of the English vocabulary is ours for appropriate use, but we must discriminate.

Giblin's formulation in the foreword of *Gumtops* was much clearer: "Our fathers, in despair at their strange surroundings, and clutching at some pathetic shred of similarity to familiar things, peopled the bush with a dozen different oaks, ashes, myrtles, pears, cherries. A true story is impossible in these terms."

Ingamells was never noted for his precision or his lucidity, and so he left himself open to attack by unsympathetic critics. This vulnerability was particularly evident in the response of others to his definition of Jindyworobak. What exactly did he mean when he sought "to annex, to join"? He subsequently commented that he had chosen the word, in part, for "its outlandishness to fashionable literary taste." A similar problem arises when one considers his second "definite condition," "The debunking of much nonsense." Nevertheless, Ingamells rarely missed an opportunity to set forth his position: there are statements in various issues of the annual Jindyworobak anthologies, in the *Jindyworobak Review 1938-48,* and elsewhere.

In 1937 and 1938 other South Australian poets were induced to join the campaign, and Ian Tilbrook, Flexmore Hudson, and Max Harris combined with Ingamells to form the Jindyworobak Club. The first Jindyworobak publication was *Conditional Culture,* and circulars were sent out inviting contributions to the first *Jindyworobak Anthology*. The first anthology also appeared in 1938, and annual publication was continued until 1953. Ingamells was the editor for the first four issues; the task was then taken over by a succession of sympathetic poets.

The title poem of Ingamells's next collection, *Sun-Freedom* (1938), together with several others, had appeared previously. Indeed, "Sun-Freedom" had been published twice, once in *The Home* and once in *The Bulletin*. It includes traces of a traditional romanticism–the dislike for cities and the celebration of the natural world.

> I have not known sun-freedom for so long
> that I go carrying hatred in my heart
> for street and trams and limousines ... the song
> of birds about the bush seems so apart ...
> When shall I tread brown bark beneath my feet,
> and, through grey branches, hear the magpie's call
> ring down the valley in the midday heat,
> like the cool, strong voice of a waterfall?
> when shall I walk neck-open to the breeze,
> and know again the friendliness of trees?

Little in the poem connects it to Ingamells's polemics. Some slight touches, perhaps–"grey branches," "brown bark," and the "magpie's call." But the overriding impression is of someone at ease with the landscape and assured in his response to it.

Sun-Freedom also includes poems that treat of Aboriginal people and life–"Ngathungi" and "Boolee," for example. The collection that followed, *Memory of Hills* (1940), however, includes one of Ingamells's earliest elegies for these original inhabitants.

> The sun shall wound with flickering fang
> night-weary ridge and shadowy plain
> and send the blood of evening down
> the western gorges time again.
> Though we depart from camp and soak,

Dust jacket for Ingamells's epic poem about the early history of Australia, published in 1951 (Bruccoli Clark Layman Archives)

from gidgi-shade and waterhole
each night shall speak the desert-oak
in season shall the thunder roll.
Spirits shall haunt this land. O we
shall roam a dim Alcheringa.
Our gods shall show us mystery
and you not know it, Waruntha.

Admittedly the reader, while he does not require such an extensive glossary as he did with "Moorawathimeering," still needs to have some words glossed. Perhaps the most obvious is "Alcheringa." Ingamells had first come across this term in his reading of Baldwin Spencer and Francis Gillen's pioneering work, *The Native Tribes of Central Australia*. This work had first appeared in 1899, but an abridged version, under the title *The Arunta*, had been published in 1927, and possibly Ingamells had encountered it at Adelaide University. He possibly became familiar with the term through his friendship with T. G. H. Strehlow, who had grown up on the Hermannsburg Mission in Arunta (or Aranda) territory in Central Australia, spoke the language, and was even then collecting Aboriginal songs. Elliott provides an accessible definition:

In effect [Alchera or Alcheringa] is a myth of a time outside the limits of history in which whatever exists has the reality of myth, not of fact. It exists in eternal terms as "then" or "now" or "in the future" or "always"; it is the time to which all other time goes back, in which the first things were done, the first creatures came to life, the creation-time.

A later collection by Ingamells, *At a Boundary* (1941), includes an even more strident attack on white-settler treatment of Aboriginal people in "The Gangrened People":

Australia is a land that has no people, for those that were hers we have torn away, we who are not hers nor can be till love shall make us so and fill our hearts with her.

With five collections of poetry to Ingamells's credit, as well as *Conditional Culture* and the editorship of four issues of the *Jindyworobak Anthology*, Australian critics could no longer ignore what was happening in South Australia. The "Red Page" of *The Bulletin*—arguably the foremost critical forum of the country—announced in March 1941 the imminent appearance of a new annual anthology but also mentioned others that were in preparation and went on to include "the customary *Jindyworobak Anthology,* where the young writers have their fling." It further noted that

> the Jindyworobak productions, published in Adelaide but accepting contributions from all over the commonwealth, have let loose some extraordinarily bad verse. But that doesn't say that the movement is without significance. It is proof of a desperate desire to write poetry—and to write a valuable kind of poetry, based in a pantheistic interpretation of the Australian landscape—and it is more likely than not that some genuine poet, in whom the group's feelings coalesce, will emerge.

A subsequent "Red Page" noted that "Movements in poetry are judged not by their theories but by their fruits," and so began a protracted exchange between *The Bulletin* and Ingamells. He continued the battle in the 1941 *Jindyworobak Anthology,* and a certain coolness remained for some considerable time. Ingamells's sense of being under siege was not helped by a review in *Southerly,* also in 1941, by Alec Hope. It covered a selection of recent publications, two directly under the Jindyworobak label but all by members of the movement. Hope's comments were hardly moderate; he described the Jindyworobaks as "the Boy Scout School of Poetry" and commented on their "boyish enthusiasm for playing at being primitive." He identified their chief mistake as their seeing the real Australia as the country untouched by the white man. Hope nevertheless conceded that there was "a core of sound common sense in the Jindyworobak case." Perhaps this final comment explains Hope's submitting a poem, "Meditation Music," to the 1944 *Jindyworobak Anthology.*

Ingamells published three more volumes of poetry in the next two years—*News of the Sun* (1942), *Unknown Land* (1943), and *Content are the Quiet Ranges* (1943). These collections were followed by his *Selected Poems* in 1944. Apart from his attempt at an epic in *The Great South Land* (1951), Ingamells turned his attention to other forms of writing. He wrote a work of criticism, *The Dunce's Cap* (1951), which carried the additional title of *A Critical Essay in Self-Defence;* two novels, *Aranda Boy* (1952) and *Of Us Now Living* (1952); a biography of William Gay (1952); and an Aboriginal-English dictionary (1955).

Rex Ingamells died in a car accident on 30 December 1955; he was survived by his wife and three sons. Although Ingamells produced an extensive body of work, he is remembered less as a poet than as the founder of a literary movement—and one that was not always welcomed. Adelaide acquired something of a reputation for odd or outlandish behavior at this time. There was, after all, the celebrated affair of *Angry Penguins* and the Ern Malley hoax. But this reputation was surely undeserved. However inchoate some of Ingamells's ideas were, they did succeed in making Australian writers more fully aware of their own landscape—their "country"—and their place in it. After Ingamells it was no longer possible to see the land as hostile, a common enough attitude in the nineteenth century. And the Jindyworobak Movement also encouraged a general freeing up of Australian poetic diction, even while poets generally rejected Ingamells's excesses. Elliott, who has published more extensively on the Jindyworobaks than any other critic, was surely justified in adding a final section to his 1979 study, *The Jindyworobaks.* He called it "Jindyworobak Affinities," and he endorsed Les Murray's labeling of himself as "the last of the Jindyworobaks."

> It is for [Les Murray] and others who may respond to his stimulus to define the new Jindyworobak faith on the foundation of principles already laid down. That is, they must make a new harmony out of the old elements of time, territory and eternity, and give it spiritual dimensions equal to the phenomena it is required to celebrate.

References:

John Dally, "The Jindyworobak Movement 1935–1945," dissertation, Flinders University of South Australia, 1978;

Brian Elliott, *The Jindyworobaks* (St. Lucia: University of Queensland Press, 1979);

Elliott, "Jindyworobaks and Aborigines," *Australian Literary Studies,* 8 (1977): 29–50;

Elliott, ed., "Breath of Alchera," in his *Singing to the Cattle, and Other Australian Essays* (Melbourne: Georgian House, 1947), pp. 1–21;

John Healey, "Indignation and Ideology," in his *Literature and the Aborigine in Australia* (St. Lucia: University of Queensland Press, 1989), pp. 154–180;

Humphrey McQueen, "Rex Ingamells and the Quest for Environmental Values," *Meanjin,* 37 (1978): 29–38;

Robert Sellick, "The Jindyworobaks and Aboriginality," in *Southwords: Essays on South Australian Writing,* edited by Philip Butterss (Kent Town, S.A.: Wakefield Press, 1995), pp. 102–115.

Papers:

There are two main repositories of Rex Ingamells's papers. Those kept by Flinders University of South Australia include manuscript material relating to Aborigines; proofs of publications, such as *Aranda Boy;* and books, pamphlets, and periodicals. They also include extensive correspondence with a variety of literary figures and cover the period 1930–1959. The other significant collection is located at the La Trobe Library, State Library of Victoria, and includes correspondence for the years 1933–1952.

George Johnston
(20 July 1912 – 24 July 1970)

Josephine Jill Kinnane

BOOKS: *Grey Gladiator* (Sydney: Angus & Robertson, 1941);

Battle of the Seaways (Sydney: Angus & Robertson, 1941); republished as *Lioness of the Seas* (London: Gollancz, 1941); republished as *Action at Sea* (Boston: Houghton Mifflin, 1942);

Australia at War (Sydney: Angus & Robertson, 1942);

New Guinea Diary (Sydney: Angus & Robertson, 1943; London: Gollancz, 1943);

Pacific Partner (New York: World, 1944);

Skyscrapers in the Mist (Sydney: Angus & Robertson, 1946);

Journey Through Tomorrow (Melbourne: Cheshire, 1947);

Death Takes Small Bites (New York: Dodd, Mead, 1948);

Moon at Perigee (Sydney: Angus & Robertson, 1948); republished as *Monsoon* (New York: Dodd, Mead, 1950; London: Faber & Faber, 1951);

High Valley, by Johnston and Charmian Clift (Sydney & London: Angus & Robertson, 1949; Indianapolis: Bobbs-Merrill, 1950);

The Big Chariot, by Johnston and Clift (Indianapolis: Bobbs-Merrill, 1953; London: Faber & Faber, 1953; Sydney & London: Angus & Robertson, 1953);

The Cyprian Woman (London: Collins, 1955);

The Sea and the Stone, by Johnston and Clift (Indianapolis: Bobbs-Merrill, 1955); republished as *The Sponge Divers* (London: Collins, 1956; Pymble, N.S.W.: Angus & Robertson, 1992);

Twelve Girls in the Garden, as Shane Martin (London: Collins, 1957; New York: Morrow, 1957);

The Saracen Shadow, as Martin (London: Collins, 1957);

The Man Made of Tin, as Martin (London: Collins, 1958);

The Darkness Outside (London: Collins, 1959);

The Myth Is Murder, as Martin (London: Collins, 1959); republished as *The Third Statue, a Professor Challis Adventure* (New York: Morrow, 1959);

Closer to the Sun (London: Collins, 1960; New York: Morrow, 1961);

George Johnston, circa 1952 (from Garry Kinnane, George Johnston, 1986)

The Far Road (London: Collins, 1962; New York: Morrow, 1963; Sydney: Fontana/Collins, 1987);

A Wake for Mourning, as Martin (London: Collins, 1962); republished as *Mourner's Voyage* (Garden City, N.Y.: Doubleday, 1963);

My Brother Jack (London: Collins, 1964; Sydney: Collins, 1964; New York: Morrow, 1964);

The Far Face of the Moon (New York: Morrow, 1964; London: Collins, 1965);

The Australians, by Johnston and Robert Goodman (Adelaide: Rigby, 1966);

Clean Straw for Nothing (London: Collins, 1969; Sydney: Collins, 1969);

The Central Coast: The Shires of Gosford and Wyong, New South Wales, by Johnston, Clifford Tolchard, and Paul Ife Horne (Sydney: Today Publications, 1969?);

A Cartload of Clay (Sydney: Collins, 1971);

Strong Man from Piraeus and Other Stories, by Johnston and Clift, edited by Garry Kinnane (Melbourne: Nelson, 1984).

George Johnston is best remembered for his widely read novel *My Brother Jack,* published in 1964, the first book of a trilogy not quite finished when he died. This novel is a first-person narration by David Meredith of his Australian suburban childhood between the world wars and his eventual attainment of dubious success as a writer and war correspondent. Johnston's earlier writings included fiction and semi-documentary works that grew from his work as a war correspondent, especially in Asia. Three early novels were written in collaboration with his second wife, Charmian Clift. In 1951 Johnston took a post as a newspaper executive in London, but after five years he and Clift decided to take their young family and move to Greece, where they would attempt to live as full-time writers. Their struggle to survive, and the problems that grew from it, prompted Johnston to embark on his Meredith trilogy and to construct the character of David Meredith as his alter ego and means of exploring his life and coming to terms with his profound sense of failure as a man and a writer.

George Henry Johnston was born on 20 July 1912, the third child of John and Minnie Wright Johnston, from Bendigo, Victoria. Just before World War I the family moved to Elsternwick, in Melbourne, where young George grew up with his two sisters and older brother, Jack. His father was a man of strong pro-imperial opinions who spoke of England as the mother country and volunteered to fight in World War I. His mother became a Voluntary Aid Detachment (VAD) nurse at the local hospital. Her mother, Sarah, separated from her husband, came to help with the young family. John Johnston survived Gallipoli and the trenches of France, but after he returned home, he became bitterly disillusioned by the treatment of returning soldiers and considered Irish Catholic criticism of participation in the war to be unpatriotic. In *My Brother Jack,* Johnston writes of growing up in a house replete with war memorabilia and recuperating invalids brought home by his mother, with their crutches and artificial limbs kept behind the door, and of his resentment of his father's irascibility, which stayed with him all his life.

Notwithstanding these circumstances, Johnston's childhood appears to have been a happy one. He did well at school, involving himself in sports and social activities. He started at Caulfield State School, then moved to Brighton Technical School, where he attained the Intermediate Certificate. Because he enjoyed sketching, he became an apprenticed lithographer in a printing firm, a position that required him to attend classes at the National Gallery School in Melbourne. At times intimidated by more middle-class students, he often skipped classes, going instead into the adjoining library to indulge a passion for the history of sailing ships. This interest started him writing, and at sixteen he offered a piece titled "Ill-fated Voyages: Tragic Wrecks on the Australian Coast" to *The Argus* (Melbourne) newspaper, which published it and several subsequent pieces. One student at the gallery who befriended him was Sam Atyeo, a dynamic young modernist, whom Johnston later drew upon for the character of Sam Burlington in *My Brother Jack*.

Johnston was an energetic youth, playing on the local football team alongside his brother, reading keenly, painting, and sketching; much of his reading and artwork was on his favorite subject, sailing ships. In 1930 he helped found the Shiplover's Society and often crewed for members of the Williamstown Yacht Club.

In 1933 he was invited to take up a reporting cadetship on *The Argus* to start on the shipping round. He was an instant success, writing with energy and prodigious speed. His family was proud of him, but his journalism took him away from their working-class interests into a more glamorous, more sophisticated professional world. He married Elsie Taylor on 19 March 1938 and settled in the developing suburb of Glen Iris.

In 1940 his interest in ships led him to write his first book, *Grey Gladiator* (1941), a fast-paced action account of the exploits of HMAS *Sydney,* just returned from six months in the Mediterranean. The success of this book encouraged him to undertake two sequels, *Battle of the Seaways* (1941), detailing the efforts to maintain British trade routes, and *Australia at War* (1942), about the country's defense preparations. The latter was not yet finished when he was made a war correspondent in February 1941. He had arranged to enlist with friends in the army, emulating his brother, but pulled out when he received news of the war correspondent possibility, a decision that caused him some guilt in later years. In October 1941 Elsie gave birth to their daughter, Gae.

Johnston's first posting was to New Guinea, where the Japanese had arrived a month after Pearl

Harbor. He kept a journal as the basis for the book that became *New Guinea Diary* (1943). He spent much of 1943 in the United States and had an open affair there with a young American woman, causing tension in his marriage. His book based on this time, *Skyscrapers in the Mist* (1946), took some time to publish and was not particularly successful. In 1944 he was sent to Asia, where he traveled in Ceylon (Sri Lanka), India, Burma, China, and Tibet, about which he wrote articles of human interest rather than war information; these pieces formed the basis for his next book, *Journey Through Tomorrow* (1947), which is credited with being one of the first and most informative accounts of Tibet by an Australian.

After the war Johnston returned to *The Argus* as an experienced and charismatic figure, with the nickname of "golden boy," denoting the reputation he had achieved for grasping lucky breaks. In 1946 he was appointed editor of a new journal, *The Australasian Post* (Melbourne), though there were soon disagreements between him and his managing director, Sir Errol Knox, over its direction. At the same time, his marriage was showing signs of breaking down, mainly because of his developing interest in Charmian Clift, who had recently joined the secretarial staff of *The Argus*. Clift was beautiful and also passionate in her desire to become a writer, and she and Johnston made no secret of their relationship. When she was dismissed from the paper, Johnston resigned in solidarity. They spent a short time in Sorrento, Victoria, where he completed his first novel, *Moon at Perigee* (1948), which attempts without great success to set a love story in the context of the struggle for independence in India. The novel was published as *Monsoon* in the United States in 1950 and in the United Kingdom in 1951.

The pair set off for Sydney, staying awhile with Clift's family in Kiama, New South Wales, a time that retained fond memories for them. In Sydney and needing money, Johnston completed the thriller *Death Takes Small Bites* (1948), a story of intrigue between corrupt Chinese and American capitalists, which eventually sold modestly well in the United Kingdom, the United States, and France. At the end of 1946, Johnston and Clift started a collaboration on a novel set in Tibet, with Johnston supplying the background and Clift the central love story. *High Valley* (1949) won the biggest literary award in Australia at the time, *The Sydney Morning Herald* prize of £2,000. In April 1947 Elsie Johnston agreed to a divorce, and Johnston and Clift were married the following August, just before the birth of their son Martin. Johnston returned to journalism at *The Sun* in Sydney, and he and Clift became the center of a group of writers, actors, and artists—including William Dobell, Kenneth Slessor, Ruth Park and D'Arcy

Johnston with his daughter Gae, 1945 (from Kinnane, George Johnston, 1986)

Niland, Wilfred Thomas, and Peter Finch—holding regular gatherings at their flat. Like many other Australians at the time, the Johnstons longed to get away from an Australia that offered few possibilities for writers and were eager to experience European life. Their chance came with Johnston's appointment to head the London office of Australian Associated Newspapers, and the couple left for England in February 1951 with Martin and a new daughter, Shane.

Johnston and Clift quickly became part of a glamorous London world, making friends with the talented and the famous, such as actor Finch and painter Sidney Nolan. Another friend was the Australian painter Colin Colahan, who told Johnston of his connection with the notorious Mollie Dean murder in Melbourne in 1930. Johnston used this story in *My Brother Jack* to expose the philistinism of Australian society. At the same time, Johnston and Clift kept up their creative writing, producing stories and doing research for larger projects. In 1952 they embarked on another collaboration, *The Big Chariot* (1953), set in seventeenth-century China, hoping that it might do well enough for Johnston to give up journalism. Despite good reviews, the work was not successful, the readers perhaps put off by its clogged field of characters and confusing narrative. Around 1953 the couple began to dream of getting away from the newspaper world and living somewhere more conducive to writing.

Dissatisfied in his job and feeling the strain from long hours writing, cold winters, and London smogs, Johnston began to experience the first signs of lung disease. On his return from a Greek holiday in April 1954, he wrote *The Cyprian Woman* (1955), but it was not well received. It was time for him and Clift to decide on their future. Johnston resigned from his job, and the family all left for the Greek island of Kalymnos. In their year there, Johnston and Clift produced another collaboration, *The Sea and the Stone* (1955), although it seems to be mostly his book; Clift was at work on a book of her own.

An unexpected sale of the short story "Astypalaian Knife" brought a windfall, enabling them to stay on in Greece; so with a feeling of optimism, and Clift expecting their third child, they moved to Hydra. There they had a second son, Jason, in April 1956. Although still planning to return to Australia eventually, they bought a house and enrolled the children in the local school. Johnston began a series of thrillers under the pseudonym "Shane Martin," and by late 1956 the news from publishers was generally encouraging.

Partly because of the growing Johnston/Clift reputation, Hydra became a fashionable place for tourists and drop-ins to visit, and the couple spent much time and energy on distractions. A steady routine of heavy drinking and smoking, socializing every night, and marital strain between Johnston and Clift began to take its toll. Nevertheless, they both worked steadily at their typewriters every morning, and the books continued to be finished and published.

By 1958 their life on Hydra started to fall apart. Anxiety about money, strained relations in the marriage, and an alarming bout of illness in Johnston were ominous signs. Clift began to look outside the marriage for sexual attention, and her behavior led to bitter fights. Paradoxically, Johnston's writing improved as he became more introspective. His novel *The Darkness Outside* (1959), written in 1958, reflects a new concern to come to grips with his immediate situation. The story is set among a small isolated group of archaeologists in southern Iraq, disintegrated by the arrival of a mysterious, ill visitor. In it Johnston takes up his feelings about being confined in a small group, such as the one on Hydra. The novel was well reviewed, critics noting the influence of Joseph Conrad, but it did not sell well.

At this time Clift was openly having an affair with one of the foreigners who visited in summer. Johnston planned to take revenge on the foreign community in his next novel, *Closer to the Sun* (1960). For this purpose, he created David Meredith, a character whom Johnston later developed into a significant and effective alter ego. This novel dramatizes Meredith's choice to live on Hydra with his wife, Kate, despite his successful brother's criticisms. Kate has an affair that echoes Clift's, and to degrade that affair is central to Johnston's purpose in the novel.

By September, Johnston suspected he had cancer, but tests in Athens proved his disease to be tuberculosis. He stayed with a friend in Athens for six weeks and returned to Hydra under strict medical instructions to stop smoking and drinking, directions that he found impossible to follow.

He returned to his war experience for the next two books. *The Far Face of the Moon* (1964) was rejected for some time, then accepted in the United States. Using as background Johnston's war experience flying the "hump" from Assam over the Himalayas to China, the story centers on the disruption caused among the pilots with the arrival of Hollywood entertainers, including a nymphomaniac singer. Johnston completed *The Far Road* (1962) before leaving for England in October 1960, where they had been offered a cottage in the Cotswolds. Money was again a problem, and Johnston tried to get work in journalism, but no one was interested. A gift of £200 from Nolan helped them. Johnston wrote another "Shane Martin" thriller, *A Wake for Mourning* (1962), but it did not help the financial situation. The cottage proved to be nearly as isolated as Hydra, although the couple made some friends in the local community. Their relationship seemed to improve, but they felt the England experiment had failed. In resignation they returned to Hydra, only to receive news that *Closer to the Sun* had been chosen by The Literary Guild of New York as a selection, earning the useful sum of $12,500. This boost to Johnston's confidence brought them happiness through 1961. *The Far Road* was finally published and received excellent reviews. Based on Johnston's experience in China seeing thousands of starving refugees fleeing the approach of the Japanese, the novel attacks the idea that journalists can be objective observers of suffering by contrasting the values of a morally scrupulous but disillusioned Meredith with an ambitious, amoral younger American journalist. This novel is one of Johnston's most accomplished works.

Clift at this time was happy with life on Hydra, and her work was beginning to attract a following. Johnston, showing no professional jealousy, was proud of her. In fact, they always gave each other unstinting professional support, regardless of the circumstances. But Johnston's illness, their money worries, his general dejection, and the emotional demands

Johnston and Charmian Clift with actor Peter Finch in the studios of 2UE in Sydney, 1947 (from Kinnane, George Johnston, *1986)*

of his writing brought him close to a breakdown. He sought within himself the source of his misery and started to experience a deep nostalgia for Australia. He began to believe that his present despair could be explained in terms of the past. In this situation he began to write *My Brother Jack*.

The theme that runs through this broad and complex novel, binding together the various personal questions that Johnston wished to put to his own formation as a flawed human being, was that of betrayal, which has a number of threads to it—Australian society's betrayal of its artists; Meredith's betrayal of his family, his country, and his wife; and betrayal of heroes by life.

The Sam Burlington episode in the novel focuses on Australian society's suspicion of its artists and intellectuals. The witty enfant terrible Burlington befriends the young Meredith at the art school and introduces him to Melbourne bohemia, including the possibilities of sex, freedom, and a more imaginative grasp of life than his suburban working-class nurturing had hitherto allowed. But when Burlington gets mixed up in the murder of Jessica Wray, who had done some nude modeling, the local press and popular opinion turn savagely on Burlington and artistic lifestyles generally, so that even though he is absolved of any part in the murder, he is devastated and leaves the country to live abroad for the remainder of his life. This outcome is a victory for Australian philistinism, which is shown to be incapable of tolerating difference. The effect of it on Meredith is profound and corrupting: he learns that to succeed in this kind of society one needs to be cunning and duplicitous. "It was after that week of the Jessica Wray case that I became a master of dissimulation," he says, identifying the moment of his lost innocence.

Meredith is contrasted with his brother, Jack, who has all the qualities expected in an Australian hero—unpretentiousness, loyalty, and readiness to try anything. Young Davy wishes he could be like his brother, but Jack ends up envying Davy. In the first two-thirds of the novel, Jack seems destined to take up the warrior tradition of his father, so when World War II breaks out, Jack is, not surprisingly, one of the first to enlist. But an absurd training accident prevents him from ever fulfilling the heroic destiny that seemed inevitable. From that point in the novel, Jack, denied his natural role in life, is a misfit who appears increasingly pathetic. Left with only his ingenuousness, Jack badly misreads his brother's character. There is no sadder moment than Jack's vicarious enjoyment of Meredith's success, which the reader already knows is doubtful and hollow at best, and his unquestioning faith in the final scene that Meredith will join him and his mates at the canteen, despite that Meredith has gone off to try his luck with the beautiful Cressida. Jack's comment "My brother Davy's not the sort of bloke to let anyone down you know" reverberates tellingly with suggestions of betrayal, both by Meredith and by life itself.

Johnston's representation of his betrayals in the character of Meredith are complex. Throughout his narration, Meredith insists that he is a deceiver and is guilty of several "defections," such as his childhood beating of the smaller Harry Meade, his pretense that Steiner's paintings are his own, and his failure to support Sam Burlington. But these failings do not feel important enough to warrant the degree of self-castigation Meredith practices, as when he insists that his image as the "golden boy" of journalism is built on a lie: "my own lie, the lie I *had* to create . . . that I was there in the thin red line of heroes." Indeed, Meredith's confessional mode has the effect of keeping the reader shifting between doubt and sympathy for him. After all, if someone confides his faults to them, people are inclined to admire him more rather than less.

The reasons for this disparity between Meredith's actual transgressions and the intensity of his self-lacerations have much to do with Johnston's situation and state of mind while writing the novel on Hydra. His autobiographical need to make sense of his despair and his knowledge of where Meredith's transgressions are eventually going to lead demand a powerful honesty and self-knowledge in his protagonist. This knowledge reveals itself in Meredith's profound sense of alienation from the values he would most wish to share–those of his brother and those of his country. In chapter 16, Meredith, in a hotel room in Naples, catches sight of his face in a mirror and sees that "what was lacking in it was the truth those other faces had for the passionate regard for the adventure in itself, and I knew then that I was not quite one of them, that I never had been, and never would be." His sense of alienation, Meredith realizes, makes him an expatriate, for expatriation is "in the very soul"; it is existential, not geographical.

There is, however, hope for Meredith at the end of the novel. The exciting Cressida holds a romantic promise for the next phase of his life, and as he takes her to dinner in the final scene, he reflects, "She was more dangerous than a bomb, and more risk than I had ever taken in my life." She is for Meredith the most glittering prize of all, and for her he will risk all the others. Few of the first readers of the novel were in a position to guess what the price of that prize would ultimately be.

From the time he began working on *My Brother Jack*, Johnston knew he wanted to turn it into a trilogy. He started on the second volume in late 1963, while still living on Hydra, but the success of *My Brother Jack* brought on Johnston's sudden decision to return to Australia early in 1964, essentially for a publicity tour, but the trip soon became a repatriation. Clift and their children returned late in the same year. It took Johnston until the middle of 1964 back in Australia to get down to serious work on the second volume, which he had always planned to call *Clean Straw for Nothing* (1969), after a board sign in William Hogarth's print *Gin Lane*. But Johnston's poor health and the emotional difficulties presented by the subject matter made writing the novel tough going, and it took him another four years and many discarded chapter drafts before he could finish the novel. In the meantime, Clift became a successful columnist for *The Sydney Morning Herald* and wrote television scripts, including the Australia Broadcast Commission (ABC) serialization of *My Brother Jack*.

Johnston had a lung operation in July 1965 and remained in the hospital until April 1966. At this time he formed a close friendship with Russell Drysdale and wrote a television script profiling the painter. Relations between Johnston and Clift deteriorated during 1967; their initial optimism about their future had disappeared. Johnston was cheered by a visit from Nolan, and the three of them had a happy reunion on a trip to central Australia.

For the first time in their lives the Johnstons became involved in politics. They spoke publicly against the coup in Greece in 1967; influenced by their son Martin, who was now at Sydney University, they took a prominent stand opposing the role of Australia in Vietnam. But their path toward destruction seemed to be set, and black depression hit them when, in April 1968, Johnston found that the tuberculosis was active again. He was able to continue working on *Clean Straw for Nothing* during five months in the hospital, but for the first time Clift distanced herself from his writing and refused to read the manuscript, convinced it represented an attack on her. She was devastated when a serious relationship ended, and she began drinking heavily. In July 1969 she committed suicide; afterward, tributes poured in from all over the country.

Clean Straw for Nothing came out the next month, to mixed reviews. It proved to be Johnston's most challenging writing task, partly because of the content and partly because the phenomenal success of its predecessor was intimidating; also, Johnston was determined not to repeat the conventional linearity of *My Brother Jack,* preferring to search for a form that was at once more innovative and more appropriate for the tortuous psychological circularities of its subject matter. The subject of the book was the shattering of the romantic promise that the relationship between Meredith and Cressida Morley represents at the end of *My Brother Jack.* In constructing the details of this painful story of disillusion, failure, betrayal, and the breakdown of trust and health, Johnston draws heavily on his own life and relations with Clift and their attempts to establish the good life as expatriate writers in Greece. As Johnston worked through his subject, he found himself writing a penetrating moral and psychological exploration of the self that almost by accident produced a novel with markedly modernist features. The work is frequently self-reflexive, the narrative changes randomly from first to third person, and the chapters are scrambled in time and setting.

The opening pages of the novel are concerned with the question of Meredith's—and by implication Johnston's—difficulties with getting the writing process underway. His solution to the problem of discerning "the difference . . . between the lies and the actualities" is to pretend that it is not a novel he is writing but "a random journal," which will be his more modest means of "trying to work it out, to get it straight before it is too late." But as the work proceeds, this journal method becomes increasingly self-searching and psychologically and morally complex. By "getting it straight," Meredith does not mean ordering his memories into chronological order but rather understanding the truth about himself and giving his memories shape without falsifying them.

Though the chapters are placed out of sequence, identified by place and year, such as "Melbourne, 1945," "London, 1954," and the recurring section "Sydney, 1968," representing the time of Meredith's (and Johnston's) writing of the journal while in the hospital, their randomness is more apparent than actual. The overall narrative has a rough chronology, which covers the period from the end of World War II—corresponding to the closure of *My Brother Jack*—to Meredith's return to Australia after his thirteen years living abroad, and the chapters are frequently connected by thematic association. For instance, the chapter headed "Lebanon Bay, 1946" ends in a depiction of Meredith's and Cressida's honeymoon paradise, and this chapter is immediately followed by the chapter "Central Australia, 1965," in which they discuss with Tom Kiernan the feeling of paradise in the Australian desert.

The theme of betrayal in *My Brother Jack* was placed in the context of family, patriotism, and marriage, whereas the theme of betrayal in *Clean Straw for Nothing* is central and purely personal. As the theme

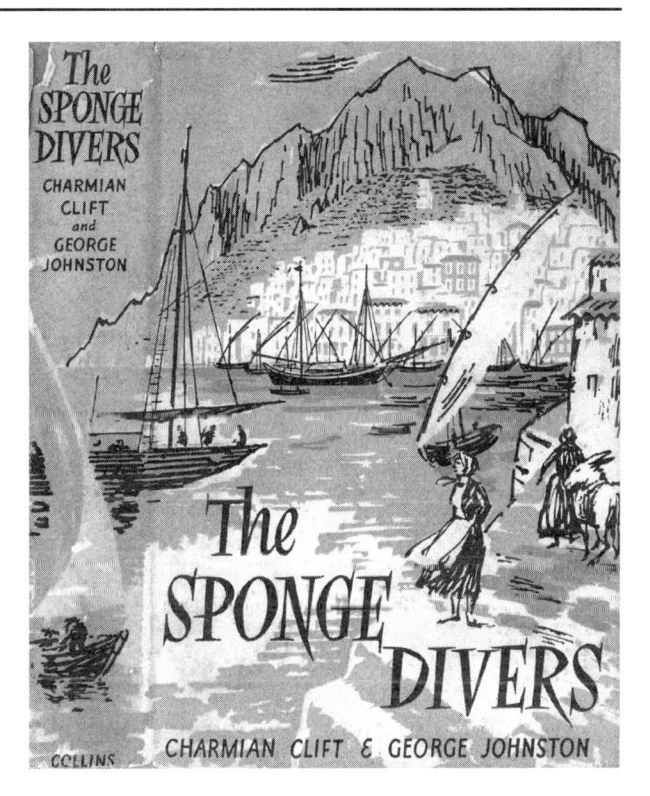

Dust jacket for the British edition of Johnston and Clift's 1955 novel, originally published as The Sea and the Stone
(Bruccoli Clark Layman Archives)

progresses, the reader is presented with a relentless and unforgiving portrayal of Meredith's decline and his transformation from self-critical dissembler in the first novel to a full antihero in the sequel, desperately struggling to justify his worst character failings. The dramatic revelation of this betrayal comes toward the end where, on "the island," there is a sequence of confrontations between the four main players—Meredith, Archie Calverton, Cressida, and her lover, Jim Galloway. The issue is unfaithfulness, with Cressida cast in the role of her literary namesake. Meredith wrings a confession out of her and then confronts Galloway, who is about to leave the island, and bitterly urges him to take Cressida with him, since he has virtually destroyed their marriage. Galloway insists that she would not abandon Meredith and departs from the island alone. He leaves behind a legacy of mistrust between the Merediths that rankles for two years, until David, unable to cope with it any longer, decides that he, too, will quietly slip away to live with a friend in Athens. He fails to get away because Archie Calverton, by a deft combination of trickery and physical force, prevents Meredith from catching the boat. Acting as friend and counselor, Calverton is emphatic that Meredith must try to understand Cressida and recognize his own role in their unhappiness.

Meredith's most serious failure is that he is unable to come to this recognition. Cressida, on the other hand,

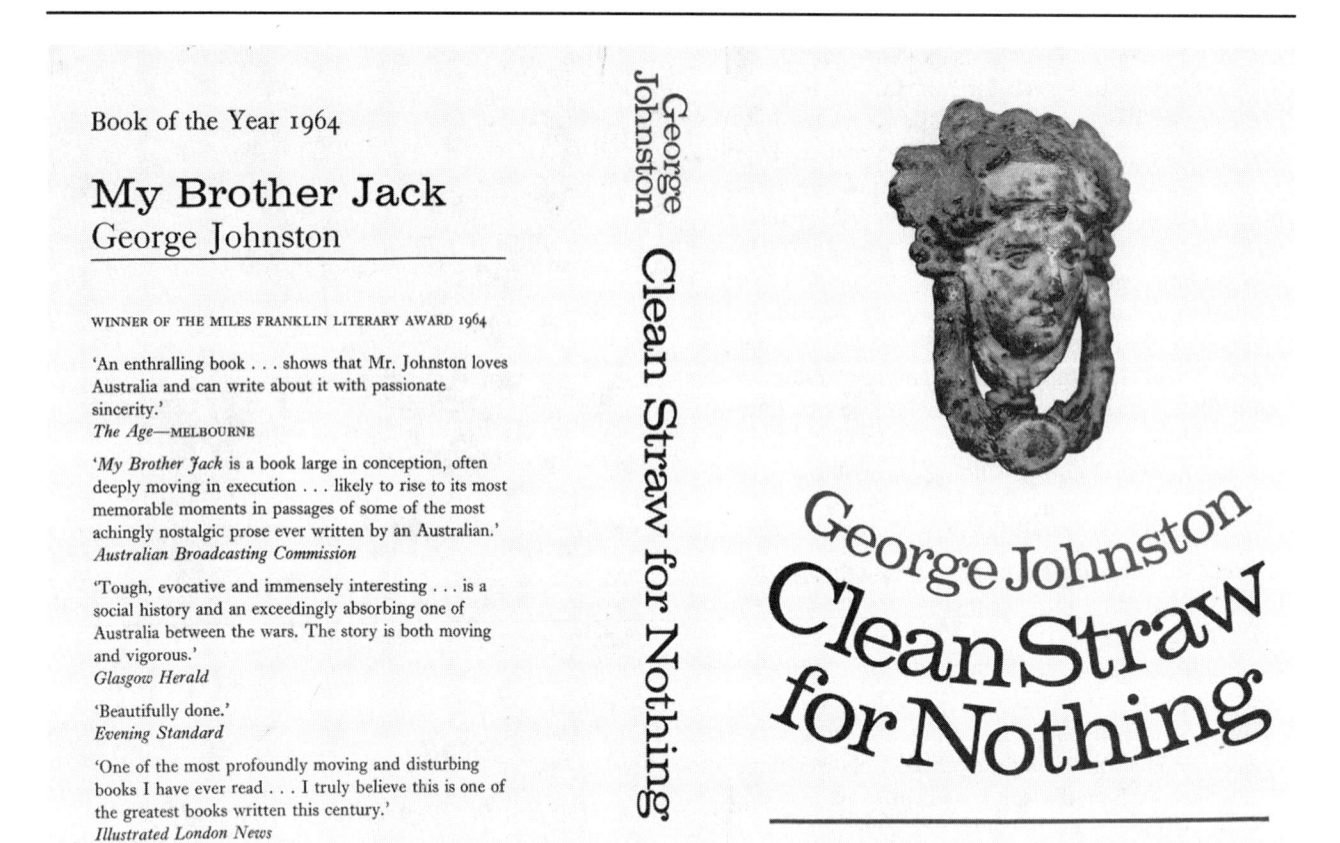

Dust jacket for Johnston's 1969 novel, the second in a trilogy of semi-autobiographical works written toward the end of his life (Bruccoli Clark Layman Archives)

emerges from the fray with her dignity intact and in control of her own sexuality. She insists on her right not to be reduced to a possession of her husband: "I am dreadfully sorry that you have to be hurt," she tells Meredith, "but I can't stand here now and be a liar and say that I'm sorry that it happened. . . . I am not ashamed." Cressida's behavior may be selfish, but her proud honesty and genuine love for Meredith deflect any suggestion of her degradation. Meredith, in comparison, becomes increasingly pathetic. His reactions to her honesty are self-righteous and unforgiving retorts couched in terms of "sin" and "adultery," followed by attempts to cheapen his wife's feelings. He is especially irritated by her determination to keep part of herself inaccessible to others, in particular him. He is equally mean-spirited in his subsequent confrontation with Galloway, who is himself generous-minded and contrite, in contrast to Meredith's hysterical outburst about "the enormity of his adultery" and "moral crime" against "a sick man unable to assert his rights." Meredith's crippling limitations are underscored in the final scene with Archie Calverton, who tells him that Cressida's value is bound up with her independent nature, which listens to its own "music": "it's what makes her Cressida . . . it's her soul if you like, her belief, her poetry . . . Do you ever hear it?" Calverton asks Meredith. "How can I? I told you, I'm barred."

This last comment by an embittered Meredith suggests his surrender to self-pity and despair. *Clean Straw for Nothing* explores the theme of betrayal in order to expose Meredith as a morally unbalanced man, a man so undermined by his own jealousy, insecurity, and resentment that his betrayal is more profound than that of any other character in the novel because it is a betrayal of faith in life itself.

By these very self-implicating tactics, the author of the novel is using his central character in order to face the worst in himself, and he hopes thereby to rise above it. Johnston's own life at the time he was writing *Clean Straw for Nothing*–dogged by ill health, alcoholism, and continuing strain in his marriage–was in such turmoil that the book offered him a way of facing the truth about himself and of conceding that Clift's character, insofar as Cressida represents it, had greater virtue than his own. In this way, this intensely autobiographical second volume had an agenda of self-reconstruction while at the same time Johnston was organizing and designing its material into a psychologically and aesthetically coherent design.

The greatest and most painful difference in Johnston's life when he came to write the third volume of the trilogy was Clift's suicide. Frail, debilitated by tuberculosis and lung surgery, and fighting off depression, he worked heroically toward the completion of *A Cartload of Clay* (1971) in the early months of 1970, no doubt buoyed by his award of the Order of the British Empire (OBE) at this time. He chose yet another structural plan for this novel, using "the journey" as his motif. In his recuperative need for exercise, Johnston took a daily walk along Raglan Street, Mosman, and in the novel he has Meredith undertaking similar walks. Although these physical journeys are short, they serve to stimulate long-range "journeys" of his memory, so that the narrative continually shifts between his immediate experiences as he trudges his suburban street and the soaring flights of his mind as it ranges freely into the past. Often these recollections are of his time in China, where he had experiences that begin to take on an increasing significance for him, such as his meeting with the poet Wen Yi-tuo, his memory of dead babies wedged in trees along the Pan Lung river, and the sight of gum trees that, Meredith speculates, might have been brought back last century by Chinese miners from Bendigo, his hometown. The connectedness of such thoughts prompts a newly meditative Meredith to see his last imaginative task as "To try to plot the arabesque that linked everything together."

In his lonely struggle Meredith also attempts to understand the Australian present, in particular the poles of possibility represented by "Ocker," a coarse-minded conformist he meets in the street, and his son, Julian, who with his "shyness and sensitivity, his bewildered gropings for a place in a society concerned with things and not ideas," has no place in the Ocker's scheme of things. Meredith has the background and experience to understand both sides—the Ocker is in a sense the obverse of his idealization of his brother, Jack—and so he knows that Australian identity is destined to include both its Ockers and its artists and intellectuals.

Johnston's handling of these issues in *A Cartload of Clay* includes some of his most thoughtful and moving prose. His attempt to find unity in his personal journey, with modest prods at the wider society, make this novel a fittingly reflective final volume to the Meredith odyssey. Johnston died at home with only seventeen chapters of the novel finished and little evidence of how he planned to complete it. It was published posthumously and takes its place as a partial but valuable finale to the trilogy.

In tracing the life and times of its central character as he moves through a world marked by the Great Depression, two world wars, expatriation, and the beginnings of radical change in the 1960s, the Meredith trilogy expresses an era in Australian life and identifies many of the stresses, aspirations, and failures of Meredith's, and Johnston's, generation. It represents the pinnacle of Johnston's fictional writing, with the first two volumes winning Miles Franklin Awards. At the same time the trilogy achieved enormous popularity among Australian readers, and the first volume has not been out of print since it was first published.

George Johnston died on 24 July 1970, was cremated at Chatswood, New South Wales, and his ashes buried near Yerinbool. The newspapers carried many fine tributes, and literary historians have recognized that his place in Australian writing is secure.

Biography:

Garry Kinnane, *George Johnston: A Biography* (Carlton South, Vic.: Melbourne University Press, 1996).

References:

Lee Brotherson, "Three-Dimensionality and *My Brother Jack*," *Australian Literary Studies,* 18 (May 1997): 84–89;

Charmian Clift, "Autobiography in the Novel," *The Australia Author,* 1, no. 2 (April 1969): 3–7;

Clift, "On Clean Straw for Nothing," in *Being Alone with Oneself: Essays 1968-1969,* edited by Nadia Wheatley (North Ryde: Angus & Robertson, 1991), pp. 310–316;

Richard E. Coe, "Portrait of the Artist as a Young Australian," *Southerly,* 2 (1981): 126–162;

John Colmer, *Australian Autobiography: The Personal Quest* (South Melbourne, Vic.: Oxford University Press, 1989);

Chester Eagle, "George's Brother Jack," *Helix,* 11–12 (1982): 154–169;

Eagle, "Myth, Mockery and Expatriation—Love/Hate of Australia in George Johnston's *My Brother Jack*," *Commonwealth* (Paris), 6 (1984): 35–41;

Robin Gerster, "Gerrymander: The Place of Suburbia in Australian Fiction," *Meanjin,* 49 (Spring 1990): 565–575;

A. E. Goodwin, "Voyage and Kaleidoscope in George Johnston's Trilogy," *Australian Literary Studies,* 6 (1973): 143–151;

Patrick Greer, "George Johnston in Hydra," *London Magazine,* 20, nos. 8–9, (1980): 109–115;

Dirk Den Hartog, "Self-Leveling Tall Poppies: The Authorial Self in (Male) Australian Literature," in S. L. Goldberg and F. B. Smith, *Australian Cultural*

History (Melbourne: Cambridge University Press, 1988), pp. 226–241;

L. T. Hergenhan, "War in Post-1960s Fiction: Johnston, Stow, McDonald, Malouf and Les Murray," *Australian Literary Studies* (October 1985): 248–260;

Hergenhan, ed., *The Penguin New Literary History of Australia* (Melbourne, Vic.: Penguin, 1988);

Greer Johnson and Chris Tiffin, "The Evolution of George Johnston's David Meredith," *Australian Literary Studies*, 11 (October 1983): 162–170;

Dorothy Jones, "Canon to the Right of Us, Canon to the Left of Us," *New Literatures Review*, 17 (Summer 1989): 69–79;

Joseph Jones and Johanna Jones, *Australian Fiction* (Boston: Twayne, 1983), pp. 87–127;

Nicholas Jose, "Non-Chinese Characters: Translating China," *Southerly*, 52 (June 1992): 3–11;

Brian Kiernan, "The Advancing Wave: Australian Literary Biography Since 1980," in *Reconnoitres: Essays in Australian Literature in Honour of G. A. Wilkes*, edited by Margaret Harris and Elizabeth Webby (South Melbourne, Vic.: Sydney University Press/Oxford University Press, 1992), pp. 191–203;

Kiernan, *Studies in Australian Literary History* (Sydney, N.S.W.: Sydney Association for Studies in Society and Culture, University of Sydney, 1997);

Garry Kinnane, "The Reconstruction of Self: Background and Design in George Johnston's Meredith Trilogy," *Australian Literary Studies*, 11 (October 1984): 435–446;

Kinnane, "Reply to Graeme Kinross-Smith," *Westerly*, 33 (March 1988): 83;

Graeme Kinross-Smith, "Brother George Looks over Biographers' Shoulders," *Westerly*, 32 (September 1987): 75–77;

Kinross-Smith, "Coming Late into the Light–Our Brother George and the Johnston Story as Recent Australian History," *Westerly*, 32 (March 1987): 21–42;

Alan Lawson, "Where a Man Belongs," in *Studies in the Recent Australian Novel*, edited by K. G. Hamilton (St. Lucia: University of Queensland Press, 1978), pp. 168–193;

F. H. Mares, "Biography and Fiction: George Johnston's Meredith Trilogy and Garry Kinnane's Biography," *Australian Literary Studies*, 13 (May 1988): 357–364;

Mares, "A Review of *My Brother Jack*," in *Australian Postwar Novelists*, edited by Nancy Keesing (Brisbane, Qld.: Jacaranda, 1975), pp. 52–56;

David McCooey, *Artful Histories: Modern Australian Autobiography* (Melbourne, Vic.: Cambridge University Press, 1996);

Susan McKernan, "Australian Civilisation?" in her *A Question of Commitment: Australian Literature in the Twenty Years After the War* (Sydney: Allen & Unwin, 1989), pp. 209–222;

J. S. D. Mellick, "The New and the Old–Responses to Translocation," *Commonwealth* (Paris), 6 (1984): 29–34;

Patrick Morgan, "Keeping It in the Family," *Quadrant*, 18 (May/June 1974): 10–20;

John O'Hara, "The Early and the Late George Johnston," *Review*, 11–17 (March 1972): 589;

Gay Raines, "Travellers' Tales," *Australian Studies* (UK), (November 1992): 68–80;

Elizabeth Riddell, "George Johnston," *Australian Author*, 2 (1970): 43;

Hazel Rowley, "The Beautiful and the Damned: George Johnston and Auto/Biographical Fictions," *Island Magazine*, 34–35 (Autumn 1988): 148–156;

John Scheckter, "'Before It Is Too Late': George Johnston and the Doppler Effect," *Australian & New Zealand Studies in Canada*, 5 (Spring 1991): 15–130;

Peter Sekuless, "George Johnston," in his *A Handful of Hacks* (St. Leonards, N.S.W.: Allen & Unwin, 1999), pp. 85–101;

Barry Smith, "George Johnston's Anzac: The Role of Sidney Nolan and Peter Finch," *Quadrant*, 22 (June 1977): 66–69;

Geoffrey Thurley, "*My Brother Jack*: An Australian Masterpiece," *Ariel*, 5 (1974): 61–80;

Wheatley, "The Mechanics of Collaboration," *Australian Society* (December 1989): 34–35; (January 1990): 38–39.

Papers:

Collections of George Johnston's papers are included in the Angus and Robertson files at the Mitchell Library, State Library of New South Wales, Sydney; the Bobbs-Merrill MSS file at the Lilly Library, Indiana University; the Higham Archives at the Harry Ranson Humanities Research Center, University of Texas, Austin; the Johnston Estate papers at the National Library of Australia, Canberra; and the files of the Faber and Faber offices in London.

Norman Lindsay
(22 February 1879 – 21 November 1969)

James Packer
Workers Educational Association Sydney

BOOKS: *Norman Lindsay's Book,* edited by Harold Burston, illustrated by Lindsay (Sydney: N.S.W. Bookstall, 1912);

A Curate in Bohemia (Sydney: N.S.W. Bookstall, 1913);

Norman Lindsay's Book, No. II, illustrated by Lindsay (Sydney: N.S.W. Bookstall, 1915);

The Magic Pudding (Sydney: Angus & Robertson, 1918; New York: Farrar & Rinehart, 1936);

The Pen Drawings of Norman Lindsay (Sydney: Art in Australia, 1918);

Creative Effort: An Essay in Affirmation (Sydney: Privately printed, 1920; revised edition, London: Palmer, 1924);

Pen Drawings (Sydney: A. McQuitty, 1924);

The Etchings of Norman Lindsay (London: Constable, 1927);

Hyperborea: Two Fantastic Travel Essays (London: Fanfrolico, 1928);

Madame Life's Lovers: A Human Narrative Embodying the Philosophy of the Artist in Dialogue Form (London: Fanfrolico Press, 1929);

Redheap (London: Faber & Faber, 1930; Sydney: Ure Smith, 1959); republished as *Every Mother's Son* (New York: Farrar & Rinehart, 1930);

Watercolours and Etchings (Sydney: Art in Australia, 1930);

Norman Lindsay's Pen Drawings (Sydney: Art in Australia, 1931);

Mr Gresham and Olympus (New York: Farrar & Rinehart, 1932); republished as *Miracles by Arrangement* (London: Faber & Faber, 1932);

The Cautious Amorist (New York: Farrar & Rinehart, 1932; Sydney: Horwitz, 1962);

Saturdee (Sydney: Endeavour Press, 1933);

Pan in the Parlour (New York: Farrar & Rinehart, 1933);

The Flyaway Highway (Sydney: Angus & Robertson, 1936);

Age of Consent (London: Laurie; 1938; New York: Farrar & Rinehart, 1938; Sydney: Ure Smith, 1962);

Norman Lindsay, circa 1914–1923 (from John Hetherington, Norman Lindsay, *1973)*

Norman Lindsay Water Colour Book (Sydney: Springwood Press, 1939);

Paintings in Oil (Sydney: Shepherd Press, 1945);

The Cousin from Fiji (Sydney: Angus & Robertson, 1945; New York: Random House, 1946);

Halfway to Anywhere (Sydney: Angus & Robertson, 1947);

Dust or Polish? (Sydney: Angus & Robertson, 1950);

Bohemians of the Bulletin (Sydney: Angus & Robertson, 1965); republished as *Bohemians at the Bulletin* (Sydney: Angus & Robertson, 1977);

The Scribblings of an Idle Mind (London: Lansdowne Press, 1966);

Norman Lindsay's Ship Models, commentary by Lindsay, photographs by Quinton R. Davis (Sydney: Angus & Robertson, 1966);

Rooms and Houses: An Autobiographical Novel (Sydney: Ure Smith, 1968);

Selected Pen Drawings (Sydney: Angus & Robertson, 1968; New York: Bonanza, 1970?);

Pencil Drawings (Sydney: Angus & Robertson, 1969);

My Mask: For What Little I Know of the Man behind It: An Autobiography (Sydney: Angus & Robertson, 1970);

Siren and Satyr: The Personal Philosophy of Norman Lindsay (South Melbourne: Sun Books, 1976);

Puddin' Poems (London: Angus & Robertson, 1978);

Micomicana, edited by Jane Lindsay (Melbourne: Melbourne University Press, 1979);

Norman Lindsay on Life, Art and Literature, edited by Keith Wingrove (St. Lucia: University of Queensland Press, 1990);

The Complete Etchings of Norman Lindsay (Sydney: Odana, 1998).

SELECTED PERIODICAL PUBLICATIONS–UNCOLLECTED: "The Intruder," *Lone Hand* (December 1907);

"Black Bill's Friendship," *London Aphrodite* (October 1928): 99–105;

"The Master of Time," *London Aphrodite* (December 1928): 183–193.

Norman Lindsay's early reputation as a pen-and-ink artist and his notoriety as a painter of the female nude have tended to overshadow his achievements as a writer. Eight of his thirteen novels–eleven for adults, two for children–were written in the latter half of his long life. At least two of his works, the novel *Redheap* (1930) and the children's story *The Magic Pudding* (1918)–some would add his children's story for adults, *Saturdee* (1933)–are considered classics. In terms of the more general cultural life of Australia, Lindsay was central to an important period of Australian comic writing, cofounded Endeavour Press, and sponsored many writers–most notably Jack Lindsay, Kenneth Slessor, Robert D. FitzGerald, Douglas Stewart, Brian Penton, and Kenneth McKenzie–who have left a mark on Australian literary life; these accomplishments reflect the depth of his outlook and the breadth of his intellectual pursuits. Slessor's tribute to Lindsay declared that he "exercised more influence and produced more effect on this country's poets than any other single individual in Australia's history." More hostile commentators, such as Vincent Buckley and John Docker, concur in such judgments, finding Lindsay responsible for the "vitalist" strain of a distinctively Sydney tradition–and for the influential propagation of Nietzschean doctrine in a city never short of "immoralist" thinkers.

Norman Alfred William Lindsay was born on 22 February 1879, the fourth son and fifth child of Bob and Jane Lindsay, respectively, the local doctor in a small Victorian town and the daughter of a Fiji missionary. Lindsay acknowledged the Reverend Thomas Williams as a source of the peculiar single-mindedness that marked his life, while disavowing and abhorring the Wesleyanism that was the mainstay of the missionary's own single-mindedness. The Lindsays went on to have three more children, of whom Reginald, the youngest, was killed in World War I and Ruby in the influenza epidemic that followed it. Significant though these deaths proved, Lindsay was throughout his life a younger rather than an older brother, and on his own account the siblings closest to him were, in his early infancy, his sister Mary (born 1877) and in boyhood and far beyond it, his brother Lionel (born 1874). That it was the boisterous, adventurous Lionel who provided Norman with a role model in both art and life did not prevent a bitter falling-out when the role model became a rebellious teenager in Lindsay's novel *Redheap*.

A peculiarity of Lindsay's novels is his commitment in them to actual people and places, especially those of his childhood. None of the novels is set in the place of his birth, the town of Creswick, but half of them make use of the locale in some way. Redheap, the town made famous in three of the best of his novels, is nineteenth-century Creswick in pseudonym–in the same sense that "Joe Partridge" is a pseudonym for Lindsay himself in his first and last novels, for Partridge, in *Rooms and Houses: An Autobiographical Novel* (1968), is said to have grown up in Redheap. Set in the Victorian countryside near Ballarat, Creswick also served as the original of Quittagong of *Pan in the Parlour* (1933). A Creswick look-alike, Murumberee, is used in *A Curate in Bohemia* (1913) to remind readers of the horrors, even for postadolescents, of country towns. Only in *The Cousin from Fiji* (1945), set in Ballarat, does Creswick make an unmasked appearance in a Lindsay novel: in this work, all the symbolisms and frustrations of its incarnation in the other books are reduced to a neutral place-name. But Creswick was never neutral for Lindsay, and his work owes so much to it because, as he says in *My Mask: For What Little I Know of the Man behind It: An Autobiography* (1970), "[I lived] in Creswick as full a life as I was ever to live thereafter; one which had covered every experience in miniature which I was to repeat with slight variations in the years to come."

The house in Springwood, New South Wales, where Lindsay settled after returning to Australia from England in 1911

Lindsay left Creswick at the age of sixteen when his brother Lionel, already in Melbourne, hired him to ghostwrite Lionel's contributions to the weekly *The Hawklet* while Lionel was commencing work on another Melbourne publication, *The Freelance*. While in Melbourne, Lindsay met the various artists and "students" who enliven his first comic novel, *A Curate in Bohemia*, and fill out many of the pages of *Rooms and Houses*. In Melbourne, Lindsay also acquired his lifelong taste for Friedrich Nietzsche, after reading the earliest English translation—by Thomas Common of *Also sprach Zarathustra* (*Thus Spake Zarathustra*, 1883–1892). As a source of the adventures of his life Melbourne proved almost as fecund as Creswick—the reader is well into the latter two-fifths of his autobiography by the time Lindsay reaches Sydney in 1901. The climactic events of these "student days" were his marriage to Kate Parkinson on 23 May 1900, the short-order birth of their first son, Jack, and the announcement in *The Bulletin* (Sydney) in August 1900 that in regard to an exhibition of his Giovanni Boccaccio illustrations, "one might almost venture to say that, in its kind, no better work than Lindsay's best is being done anywhere."

The occasion for Lindsay's departure from Melbourne was an opportunity to work for *The Bulletin*, at which he flourished in both reputation and notoriety as a graphic artist. He was also writing. His first novel, drafted soon after his arrival in Sydney, recounts the adventures of an insecure young curate who revisits a childhood friend in the Melbourne of artists and students. Illustrated by Lindsay with a lightness of touch that marks the writing itself, the book ran through many editions after its publication in 1913. The lack of ideological "meaning" in *A Curate in Bohemia* probably resulted from the youth of an author whose work had not yet encountered the full extent of "mob" hostility that marked the rest of his life. If so, 1904 marked a turning point, for in that year Lindsay exhibited *Pollice Verso*, an emphatic rejection of the crucified Christ by a crowd of naked revelers. This work was Lindsay's version of Nietzsche's *Dere Antichrist* (The Antichrist, 1895), and it brought about the first stages of an aesthetic conflict with the editor of the "Red Page" in *The Bulletin*, A. G. Stephens (Stephens's views on Nietzsche's ethic of "self-development" nevertheless prefigured doctrines Lindsay himself espoused many years later in *Creative*

Effort: An Essay in Affirmation [1920]). "Pollice Verso," wrote the critic, "is a bad picture, a good drawing, and a magnificent piece of pen-work." As a picture, Stephens found it tainted by a moral inversion of the religion of the Reverend Williams; ever an advocate of the "tempered" Nietzsche of Havelock Ellis, he found in Lindsay's "untempered" Nietzsche the "violence [of an] excessive belittlement of the ascetic figure on the cross" and "excessive glorification of the ideals of strength and beauty in the opposing figures." It was a judgment that in outline recurred, suitably satirized, throughout Lindsay's lifetime: in Brian Penton's "stucco Hollywood temple of Lindsayism" (1937); in Bernard Smith's "pure rococo" (1945); in Robert Hughes's "make-believe world of periwigs, shipwrecks and garden gnomes" (1966).

Stephens at this stage remained sufficiently sympathetic to Lindsay's art to conclude his article with a tribute that looked to Lindsay's bringing "lasting honour to Australia that bred him." Serious feuding commenced with a Stephens article in 1912, "The Moral of Norman Lindsay." In the meantime, Lindsay's relationship with his wife deteriorated catastrophically. The union produced two more boys, Raymond and Philip, but Lindsay's relationship with one of his models, Rose Soady, soured his home life as well as created the basis for a feud with his closest friend, and Soady's current paramour, Will Dyson. Dyson–"Flack" in *Rooms and Houses*–found himself (as Flack) denouncing the up-and-coming artist in terms that Lindsay chose to dwell upon late into his eighties: "Everything's got to go your way. You put a bright-eyed front of being a generous high-minded feller, all in for the good of art, but underneath you don't give a damn for anything or anybody but your own bloody work." In *My Mask* Lindsay himself looked at the matter in a more comically immoralist way. "Rose refused to make a concession to either of us, leaving us to fight it out on our own. I can never sufficiently admire the cool assurance with which a girl may take her own decisions in an affair of that sort, without giving any hint of what she proposes to do about it. She may not formulate those decisions, but she acts upon them." Lindsay used such a situation as the plot of *The Cautious Amorist*, the book he wrote a few years later, eventually rewritten and published in 1932. In 1910 Lindsay departed for England with his sister Ruby and Dyson–the two were now married–both to escape his wife and to further his career by attempting to sell a large-scale illustration project, *The Memoirs of Casanova*. A running sore in his life until the destruction of the illustrations in an American train fire in 1940, the project was thwarted on its first outing when English and French publishers declared it fascinating but ultimately far too scandalous for publication. Lindsay returned to Sydney in 1911, where he finally broke with his wife and immediately succumbed to the severest bout of ill health of his life. After a prolonged period in the hospital he concluded his affairs in Sydney and moved to Springwood, west of Sydney in the Blue Mountains. On 14 January 1920 he married Soady, and his divorce from Kate was finalized a fortnight later. The new couple later had two daughters, Jane and Helen.

Lindsay freely relates that in ideological tenor *The Cautious Amorist* differs markedly from *A Curate in Bohemia*. In the three months of his recovery from illness Lindsay claims that he read "two to three novels a day," an occupation that brought to his attention the poor quality of the popular novel. The one exception he encountered, Louis Stone's *Jonah,* published in 1911, remained a favorite for the rest of Lindsay's life. "I had to get out of my system," he wrote in *My Mask,* "the virus of splurge of sentimentality [in the popular novel] and its rejection of all the simple realities of life censorable by puritanic taboos and interdictions, and I did that by writing [*The Cautious Amorist*]." The novel explores the amoral relationships of three men and a girl on a desert isle. This "amoralism" was probably increased when he rewrote the novel after 1927 and induced the perceived attributes of Penton into one of them "as typical of the non-moral journalistic outlook on human behaviour as so much news-value," as he claimed to Brian James in 1963. The book, centering as it does on the–not always conscious–tactical ingenuity of the girl, Sadie, is in many ways a "mystery story" in which the murder motif of the usual mystery has been replaced by the outcomes of sexuality. Like *A Curate in Bohemia, The Cautious Amorist* exhibits Lindsay's skill at comic writing, and its themes of human self-interest and the fulfillment of venal appetites prefigure in temper–if not in style–his food epics, the children's books *The Magic Pudding* and *The Flyaway Highway* (1936). *The Magic Pudding* was written, Lindsay told Nancy Kessing, as a bet on whether food provided sufficient material for a children's story. Appetite, he knew from *The Cautious Amorist,* is the ground of comedy, and his early novels and stories captured that in the plainest terms.

From 1908 to 1919 Lindsay published in *The Bulletin* vignettes of life in Creswick, featuring the adventures of twelve-year-old Peter Gimble. Brought together as chapters in his 1933 book *Saturdee,* these adventures also show similarities to *The Magic Pudding,* as the characters pursue the "moralities" of their various groups with the effect of demonstrating deeper amoralities at work. The superabundance of Nietzschean "life" is celebrated in *Saturdee,* in which Gimble steals kisses from girls–and money from his parents–and achieves from

Lindsay, circa 1914–1918, with Rose Soady, whom he married in 1920 (from John Hetherington, Norman Lindsay, *1973)*

his friends not approbation but envy and respect; in *The Magic Pudding* the pudding's desire to be eaten, and his carelessness of who the eater is, makes something of a mockery of the moral struggle by which, at the end, he is safely fenced off from the gluttonous outside world.

During World War I Lindsay was noted for the severity of his "anti-Hun" cartoons in *The Bulletin*. The profound effect of the war on his moral thinking resulted in his giving credibility to spirit communion, which in his case went further than communication with the recently departed, Reginald and Ruby, to include the souls of the great–François Rabelais, William Shakespeare, and various other cultural heroes of Lindsay's. His attempts at communication with spirits later became a source of unease within the Lindsay circle and a bone of contention with Lindsay's brother Lionel and Lindsay's son Jack, resulting in schisms that numbered among the most long-lasting and severe of Lindsay's life. Ever conscious of being made to look a fool by such infatuations, Lindsay kept ectoplasm strictly at arm's length in his public life and dropped no whisper of it in his novels. "The Skyline," written in 1918 and published as *Redheap* in 1930 in Britain–it was titled *Every Mother's Son* in the United States–continued the comic vein of the earlier books, and if it was touched at all by Lindsay's new "spiritual" preoccupations, it was only in the rather remote sense that the amoral world of the child is touched by the existential problems of adulthood. These philosophical difficulties included the blight of moral resentment, a theme of which Lindsay may have taken up freely in his letters but which none of the previous books had thoroughly investigated.

Redheap may be the name of the town in which the *Saturdee* stories are set, but the protagonists in *Redheap* belong to a different moral universe. In that novel, moralism is not thwarted by but thrives on amoralism; nineteen-year-old Robert Piper can do nothing with his life if he does not escape from the place, for its citizens have half an eye on their existential failures as they hunt down the "moral failures" of others. The mode is comic, but it is tinged by the direness behind all such depredations. Characters such as Robert's sexually thwarted sister, Hetty, are not mere busybodies but have an active moral life that in consequence of systematically evading all of the issues of selfhood equally systematically deplete their possibilities of happiness. Nor is amoralism treated with Lindsay's former leniency. Jerry Arnold, the would-be seducer of Hetty's sister Ethel, is shown in his moral deficiency to be existentially deficient. The fire he starts to secure his and Ethel's future convicts him as a destructive child unfit for the truly adult world of creativity and "effort." The analogous figure in *Redheap* is Mr. Bandparts, Robert's tutor and, as a drinker, a "free spirit." Mr. Bandparts is a child of Rabelais; and Lindsay, however he developed his philosophy of "creative effort," never dispensed with Rabelais.

Creative Effort, Lindsay's personal manifesto, was first published in Australia in 1920, and after considerable revision, republished in England in 1924. Jack Allison contends that the spiritualism induced by World War I brought about Lindsay's doctrine of "futurity"—an orientation toward the ultimate meaning of an artwork, rather than the ethics of its moment of production, a position outlined in "A Modern Malady," published in 1916 in the first issue of *Art in Australia*. As Lindsay put the matter in a letter to his sister Mary in 1951, "One had to find some feasible excuse for one's own existence and to try to derive a stable principle of continuity underlying the bedlamite foolery of existence. It drew me to write that muddled work *Creative Effort* to find out for myself whether there was any evidence to justify an act of faith in the continuity of life." The issue was further compounded when, nearly a decade after Kate's removal to Brisbane, Lindsay renewed contact with his son Jack, in 1919 a student at the University of Queensland. Jack's enthusiasm for Plato was quickly transmuted to his father, whose own enthusiasm for Nietzsche was transmuted to the son. *Creative Effort* includes declarations such as "man must strive with destiny in order to go beyond himself. He must conquer the unknown, which is not in God, but in himself." This statement may seem to include far more Nietzsche than Plato until one considers the attitude toward destiny expressed in *Saturdee:* "Take destiny by the throat and the jade will give you anything." "Effort" is a function of the fulfilled life, and the great change in Lindsay's ideological attitude at this time is in his emphasis on work—his own, and that of the people around him—as it emerges from "gaiety."

Jack Lindsay arrived in Sydney in 1920 and by 1922 had his father's support for a journal of literature, *Vision,* the only such journal at that time. It ran for four numbers throughout 1922, and an anthology of its poems, *Poetry in Australia, 1923* was published in 1923. The major contributor was Jack Lindsay, and after him, Norman Lindsay, who according to Douglas Stewart also gave the journal its name. *Vision* gave Lindsay the opportunity to develop his views on art and life, which with Jack Lindsay's departure for England in 1926 and subsequent tenure of the Lindsay-funded Fanfrolico Press in London, was extended to publishing in book form two specimens of the "NL philosophy," *Hyperborea: Two Fantastic Travel Essays* (1928) and *Madame Life's Lovers: A Human Narrative Embodying the Philosophy of the Artist in Dialogue Form* (1929). Both had been written before 1923; the first had appeared in *Vision* in 1922.

The 1920s were, in sum, Norman Lindsay's single sustained period of ideological activity, not only for the creation of so much "urgent opinion" in the early period, but also for the controversies generated by exhibitions of his artwork in London and Adelaide between 1923 and 1925 and the publication of *Redheap* in April 1930. With Jack's departure, Lindsay's sponsorship of writers had passed from poets, such as Jack and Kenneth Slessor—now in Melbourne—to novelists, such as his third son, Philip; Brian Penton—then a political reporter with the *Sydney Morning Herald;* and Godfrey Blunden. According to Lindsay, Penton "nagged" him when he sailed at the end of 1928 to take *Redheap* with him to London in order to find a publisher for it. On publication in England, *Redheap* aroused in Australia a public furor among the citizenry of Cheswick and in particular in the original for the character of "Robert Piper," Lionel Lindsay; within a month the novel was a prohibited import into Australia, which it remained until 1959. To Howard Hinton, Lindsay wrote in July 1931 of his "disgust" for the land of his birth, which "does not deserve to have a culture." He prepared to leave the country.

Norman and Rose Lindsay spent much of the latter part of 1931 in the United States. "And," to quote from the autobiography of Norman's son Philip, "it seemed that his treatment in the States had been sufficient to salve his vanity; besides, his drawing had always sold better in America than anywhere else in the world." In fact, Lindsay transmitted his sense of the business-like United States to his next novel, *Mr Gresham and Olympus* (1932), set in Sydney, which Farrar and Rinehart, according to Philip Lindsay, were anxious to publish after the success of *Every Mother's Son.* "I might have stayed [in the United States]," Norman wrote in his autobiography, "if I could have endured the racket and pace at which life is lived in America." In any event, he received a letter from Blunden alerting him to the 35 percent tariff imposed on books imported into Australia, and after failing to impress American publishers with a scheme to set up a publishing house in Australia, he decided to try the holders of Empire book rights, the English. He and Rose sailed for London.

In England the Lindsays took over Penton's flat; Penton persuaded Lindsay to change the title of the

Lindsay, circa 1918–1923 (from John Hetherington, Norman Lindsay, *1973)*

British edition of *Mr Gresham and Olympus,* also 1932, to *Miracles by Arrangement,* with an ending to suit the title. Penton's own novels were dominated by an interest in the relationship between the workings of fate ("miracle") and human will ("arrangement"), and at this stage in his relationship with Penton, as a close friend, Lindsay was prepared to believe in the commensurability of their philosophical outlooks. He later recanted, declaring the American version of the book the correct one. In pursuit of his book scheme, Lindsay met the Queenslander P. R. Stephensen, his son's former partner at the Fanfrolico Press, and when English publishers rejected all overtures for Australian representation, Lindsay and Stephensen concocted a plan for an indigenous Australian press that they would take to *The Bulletin.* In May 1932 Lindsay returned to Australia to a job as graphic artist on *The Bulletin*–his other sources of income had by then evaporated. By October, when Stephensen reached Sydney, Lindsay had persuaded Sam Prior, manager of *The Bulletin,* of the viability of the project, and Stephensen became manager of The Endeavour Press; by late January 1933 advance copies of the new publisher's first books had arrived. These included Lindsay's own *Saturdee,* and Lindsay and Stephensen quickly fell out over the details of the publication. Both Lindsay and *The Bulletin* now discovered in Stephensen a more abrasive publisher than they were prepared to tolerate, and within the year Stephensen was compelled to resign. The Endeavour Press ceased publishing by the end of 1934.

In 1932 and 1933 Lindsay published four novels, two of which were of recent vintage. Both *Mr Gresham and Olympus* and *Pan in the Parlour* are parables of adult sexuality, and the first of these is of particular interest, for its negotiating the minefield of Lindsay's middle age and continuing the "existential" themes of *Redheap* with slight resort to its resources of social comedy. On the face of it, *Mr Gresham and Olympus* is far more ideologically inflected than Lindsay's earlier novels–the *Creative Effort* motifs of "work" and "shiftlessness" are dominant–but although the conversations have a tendency to ossify into set pieces in which too much is said about "Australia" and "wowserism" (Australian puritanism), Lindsay's gift for dramatic structure is sufficiently in evidence for Gresham, his wife, Baby, his partner, Floyd, his daughter, Nina, and his son, Jerry, all to attain a respectable degree of "existential credibility." The comedy of human foibles and tics so effective in *Saturdee* fails to spark—at least, to the reader of *Saturdee*—and it is no surprise that the novel was never published in Australia, as *Saturdee,* more surprisingly, was never published in the United States. *Pan in the Parlour* was also never published in Australia, and few Australian critics, including Lindsay's usually more idolatrous biographer, John Hetherington, have treated it with much respect. Even D. R. Burns, a rare exception, fails to appreciate Lindsay's comical treatment of his own middle age as a paradigm for the sexuality of several of its characters. On the strength of this feature of both these novels of his middle age, Lindsay is generally felt to have missed the point of "mature" relationships.

The most critical year in Lindsay's marriage with Rose was 1933. In that year he set up a studio in Bridge Street, Sydney, to commence painting in oils, leaving Rose to run the Springwood property. While the thoroughly poisonous relationship that evolves between Gresham and his wife probably owes as much to Lindsay's impasse in the domain of social comedy as it does to the workings of his personal relationships, Burns's comment about his two novels of this period is probably a fair comment on Lindsay's marriage: "In both there are couples, restive under the years which have piled upon them like autumn leaves. In both the partners of the marriage burrow or attempt, in a scrabbling, furtive way, to burrow their way out of the monogamous relationship." The "scrabbling" may have been more on Norman's side than on Rose's—in *Portrait of Pa: Norman Lindsay at Springwood* (1973) Jane Lindsay recorded that with the Bridge Street arrangement her mother was "distressed and bitter" at Lindsay's "perfidious behaviour in abandoning her." Lindsay's literary response to these changed circumstances was to publish a children's book, *The Flyaway Highway,* and an adult novel, *Age of Consent* (1938), in which art and sexuality shed the larger part of their "Nietzschean" interconnection.

The Flyaway Highway, like *The Magic Pudding,* concentrates the reader's mind on the acquisition of food, but it is not food that the Highway promises in endless supply, but fiction itself. That the highway takes its Pan figure, Silvander Dan, and the children Murial-Jane and Egbert through realms of basically bad fiction provides opportunities for the sort of reflexive games that have been made respectable in adult novels only with the advent of postmodernism. Consequently, the humor is less visceral than in *The Magic Pudding,* and the story failed to make the impact on children's fiction the earlier book had made. *Age of Consent,* on the other hand, with its related theme of "escape into creativity," is a perennial favorite with adults. A landscape painter, Bradly Mudgett, with his dog, Edmund, takes an isolated shack on the south coast of New South Wales in order to create new work. He meets Cora, a young girl who lives with her grandmother in the nearby bush, turns her into his model, defies with great difficulty the efforts of the increasingly demented grandmother to portray him as her granddaughter's seducer, and on the last page of the novel avoids living happily ever after by a "dithyrambic conflict of fear and exultation." Unlike Gresham, who is tied to his art (architecture) through the joyless pursuit of a certain standard of living, Bradly paints to paint, which means, in terms of income, to barely survive. There are two Norman Lindsay alter egos in these two novels, and although Bradly is far more socially deficient and far less successful than the Sydney architect, one can gauge a certain transition in Lindsay's own life, the perverse reassertion of his "bohemianism" that results in the revitalization of his comic gift.

Seven years passed before the publication by Lindsay of any further extended literary work, but *The Cousin from Fiji* continued the trend away from ideological analysis toward fiction to be enjoyed for its purely comic element. More than in Lindsay's other two large-scale "existential" novels, *Redheap* and *Mr Gresham and Olympus,* the twists in the plot of *The Cousin from Fiji* are telegraphed by overt character analysis, but the characters are complex enough in their eccentricities to require much comment, and the denouements of the novel are effectively existential rather than, as so often in *Mr Gresham and Olympus,* experimentally psychological. Cecelia Bellairs, the prime example, has such a distinctive way of speaking and is yet so bound up with the often far-from-distinct lives around her, that the eccentricity of her speech (her "aesthetics") becomes a signature of personal value—of a capacity for commitment and freedom—that carries the plot far beyond her actual intentions. Critics are generally agreed on the quality of this novel, though Lindsay has not yet been served with the critical study that accounts fully for the relationships between his social-comic style and existential themes. Consequently, the place in Australian literature of novels such as *The Cousin from Fiji* has been little evaluated.

Lindsay's friendship with Guy Howarth, "whose incautious appreciation of *Saturdee* is mainly responsible for this investigation of his characters' later adolescence," resulted in the writing and 1947 publication of *Halfway to Anywhere.* Strictly speaking, the "investigation" is of Bill, not Peter, Gimble's later adolescence—Bill is a minor character in *Saturdee,* whose protagonist is Peter, while Peter has a minor role in *Halfway to Anywhere;* nevertheless, the book is a true sequel even if, as Hetherington points out in *Norman Lindsay: The Embattled Olympian* (1973), it has the regular structure of a novel rather than of a series of incidents. As he had done in *Saturdee*—as well as in *Redheap* and *Mr Gresham*—Lindsay took and amplified incidents from his Creswick adolescence, and although the behavior of a fifteen-year-old may be less farcical and amoral than that of a boy of ten and its author more prone to generalization, *Halfway to Anywhere* carries off its comic material with the cleverness that had come to mark Lindsay's previous late-period fiction. The same could hardly be said of *Dust or Polish?* (1950), a novel set in the Sydney of about 1950. The novel works through some unresolved material in the Lindsay corpus—the middle-aged patron of a proprietress in *Mr Gresham and Olympus* and the aged and unrelenting female despot in *Age of Consent*—but its main achievement is to work its way into the corner occupied by Raskolnikov in Fyodor Dostoevsky's *Crime and Punishment* (periodical publication, 1866; book publication, 1867) while discounting—because of Lindsay's detestation of Dostoevsky—the moral resources that novel employs to get out of it. Having worked his Dostoevskian plot to dispose of the aged despot as he did in *Age of Consent,* Lindsay allows his characters to grope around for moral justifications of a sort that reveal yet another vision of Nietzsche turned to the purposes of willful consumerism.

The literary works of Lindsay's old age—after 1950 he was in his seventies and eighties—were almost exclusively autobiographical in character. *Micomicana* (1979), a "scrapbook" fantasy, the posthumous publication of which has been recounted by Peter Ryan, and *The Scribblings of an Idle Mind* (1966), a last burst of ideological self explanation, probably escape the autobiographical tag. For the rest, *My Mask,* written in 1957, the year Lindsay relinquished the lease on Bridge Street, was published a year after his death, and *Bohemians of the Bulletin* (1965) comprises reminiscences of Lindsay's early *Bulletin* days that in some respects belong to the same project. His final novel, *Rooms and Houses*—published in 1968, but like all these works, written over many years—presents an account of Lindsay's Melbourne days, initially in a style that indicates no particular interest in doing much else.

Rooms and Houses is not merely autobiographical in the strictly limited sense of a personal history. The "Melbourne" life of the protagonist is extended to the point at which he leaves for England, and he is acquainted with Grantham, a figure who belongs to Lindsay's life only in the most abstract sense, and who, with equal abstractness, may have been used to sum up what Lindsay had always felt to be one of the central strains of his own life.

Dust jacket for Lindsay's 1950 novel, set in contemporary Sydney (Bruccoli Clark Layman Archives)

Grantham is not only Walter Gresham, Lindsay's archetypal male in a midlife crisis, he is, more importantly, Lionel Lindsay in a far more scandalous version than ever appeared in *Redheap*. Grantham inspires Partridge (Lindsay) into acts of aesthetic rebellion; he presents a philosophy that Partridge is only too anxious to publish to the world, but then he goes off the rails, becomes sexually obsessed, and comes to fear mortally the consequences of presenting to the public this same material. When Partridge, who continues undeflected in the original direction, achieves notoriety as a purveyor of "filth," Grantham derides him openly. The respectability of Creswick, supposedly pursued by Lionel, betrays the faith of their Melbourne years. The utterance is Lindsay's final existential one in a novel, and though it lacks the power of the same sort of utterance in *Redheap* or *Gresham* or *The Cousin from Fiji*, it is still the most powerful feature of *Rooms and Houses*, giving the book some small claim to distinction.

The battles of Norman Lindsay's life were fought largely around what he invariably called "funk," cowardice. He was aware of this characteristic in himself, as in the character Bradly Mudgett, but gave it no comic license when he found it in his enemies. Australia did not deserve culture because of its moral cowardice, its littleness, its intelligentsia's "funk." Each of Lindsay's great detractors was made guilty of it. A. G. Stephens "funked" facing Lindsay on *The Bulletin* stairs. Brian Penton, who had broken nastily from Lindsay in 1937, "funked" his gallbladder operation–he shortly died of cancer of the pancreas. Lionel "funked" *Redheap,* the exposure of his life as something more wanton than Creswick wanted it to be. That so fine a writer of social comedy could have found insurmountable the evils of provincialism yet made an art of that, too, indicates more than the word "funk" suggests–that Lindsay deeply resented his milieu–but in that complexity may be found an explanation for the depth and longevity of his influence on Australian literary culture. Those he influenced most immediately and significantly were the most fertile, the most easily impressed by true complexity, of their generation.

Letters:

Harry F. Chaplin, ed., *Norman Lindsay: His Books, Manuscripts, and Autograph Letters in the Library of, and Annotated by, Harry F. Chaplin* (Sydney: Wentworth Press, 1969);

"Unpublished Letters: Norman Lindsay to Lionel Lindsay," *Southerly,* 30 (1970): 289–300;

R. G. Howarth and A. W. Barker, eds., *The Letters of Norman Lindsay* (Sydney: Angus & Robertson, 1979).

Bibliographies:

Norman Lindsay on Life, Art and Literature, edited by Keith Wingrove (Brisbane: University of Queensland Press, 1990), pp. 238–241;

Martin Duwell and L. T. Hergenhan, "Norman Lindsay," *The ALS Guide to Australian Writers: A Bibliography 1963-1990* (Brisbane: University of Queensland Press, 1992), pp. 186–189.

Biographies:

Godfrey Blunden, "The Ninety Years of Norman Lindsay," in *Watercolours* (Sydney: Ure Smith, 1969), pp. 9–28;

John Hetherington, *Norman Lindsay: The Embattled Olympian* (Melbourne: Oxford University Press, 1973);

Douglas Stewart, *Norman Lindsay, A Personal Memoir* (Melbourne: Thomas Nelson, 1975).

References:

Jack Allison, "'Futurity': Norman Lindsay's Creative Stimulus," *Meanjin* (September 1970): 346–355;

Vincent Buckley, "Utopianism and Vitalism," in *Australian Literary Criticism,* edited by Grahame Johnston (Melbourne: Oxford University Press, 1962), pp. 16–29;

D. R. Burns, *The Directions of Australian Fiction, 1920-1974* (Sydney: Cassell, 1975);

Kerin Day, "A Study of the Aesthetic Theory and Creative Writings of Norman Lindsay and Their Relationship to the Work of Kenneth Slessor and R. D. Fitzgerald," dissertation, University of Sydney, 1975;

John Docker, *Australian Cultural Elites* (Sydney: Angus & Robertson, 1974);

John Hetherington, *Australian Writers and Their Work: Norman Lindsay* (Melbourne: Oxford University Press, 1969);

Robert Hughes, *Art in Australia* (Melbourne: Penguin, 1970);

Nancy Kessing, "Norman Lindsay," *Quadrant* (December 1969): 13–15;

Jane Lindsay, *Portrait of Pa: Norman Lindsay at Springwood* (Sydney: Angus & Robertson, 1973);

Philip Lindsay, *I'd Live the Same Life Over* (London: Hutchinson, 1941);

Brian Penton, "A Lindsay Family Reunion," *Daily Telegraph* (Sydney), 7 August 1937, p. 6;

Michael Pollak, *Sense and Censorship: Commentaries on Censorship Violence in Australia* (Sydney: Reed Books, 1990);

Peter Ryan, "Norman Lindsay's Scrapbook," *Quadrant* (September 2000): 87–88;

A. G. Stephens, "The Ethic of Nietzsche," *Bulletin,* 10 November 1900, pp. 2, 4;

Stephens, "Norman Lindsay's Pen Drawings," in *A. G. Stephens: Selected Writings,* edited by Leon Cantrell (Sydney: Angus & Robertson, 1977), pp. 353–357;

Douglas Stewart, "Slessor and *Vision,*" *Quadrant* (July 1975): 68–76.

Papers:

Norman Lindsay's papers and those of other prominent members of his family constitute large collections in the Mitchell Library, State Library of New South Wales, Sydney. The Rare Books collection at the University of Sydney, Fisher Library, also includes archival materials. Lindsay bequeathed a large part of his work to the University of Melbourne; he also bequeathed part of his work to the National Trust of Australia to be preserved in the house in Springwood, N.S.W., where he lived for more than fifty years.

Kenneth Mackenzie
(Seaforth Mackenzie)
(25 September 1913 - 19 January 1955)

Richard Rossiter
Edith Cowan University

BOOKS: *Our Earth* (Sydney: Angus & Robertson, 1937);

The Young Desire It: A Novel, as Seaforth Mackenzie (London: Cape, 1937; Sydney: Angus & Robertson, 1963);

Chosen People, as Seaforth Mackenzie (London: Cape, 1938);

The Moonlit Doorway: Poems (Sydney & London: Angus & Robertson, 1944);

Dead Men Rising, as Seaforth Mackenzie (London: Cape, 1951; New York: Harper, 1951; Sydney: Angus & Robertson, 1969);

The Refuge: A Confession, as Seaforth Mackenzie (London: Cape, 1954; Sydney: Angus & Robertson, 1954);

Selected Poems of Kenneth Mackenzie (Sydney: Angus & Robertson, 1961);

The Poems of Kenneth Mackenzie, edited by Evan Jones and Geoffrey Little (Sydney: Angus & Robertson, 1972);

The Model: Selected Writings of Kenneth Seaforth Mackenzie, edited by Richard Rossiter (Nedlands: University of Western Australia Press, 2000).

SELECTED PERIODICAL PUBLICATIONS—
UNCOLLECTED: "I have three people," *Westerly,* no. 3 (1966): 40-42;

"Maiden's Hill," *Westerly,* no. 3 (1966): 72-84;

"The Model," *Westerly,* no. 3 (1966): 46-71;

"The Old Adam," *Westerly,* no. 3 (1966): 43-45.

Kenneth Mackenzie is the least known but the first of the "precocious" literary talents to come out of Western Australia. Like Randolph Stow and Tim Winton, he wrote a major work at a remarkably young age: the first draft of his best-known novel *The Young Desire It: A Novel* (1937) was written when he was seventeen years old. In his comparatively short life—he frequently compared himself to John Keats and Percy Bysshe Shelley—he wrote hundreds of poems, four completed novels, radio playscripts, and many short stories.

At the insistence of his father, Mackenzie, born on 25 September 1913, was christened Kenneth Ivo Brownley Langwell Mackenzie. He was the son of parents whose families originated from Scotland: Marguerite Christine Pryde (Daisy) Paterson and Hugh Mackenzie. When Daisy later divorced Hugh, she went to the trouble to have her son's name officially changed to Kenneth Ivo Mackenzie. Much of Mackenzie's personal correspondence is signed "KIM," and he was known by this name to many of his friends. When his first novel was to be published, names were again an issue for Mackenzie. Jonathan Cape already had a Kenneth Mackenzie on their fiction list and so required a change of name. After much consideration Mackenzie settled on Seaforth Mackenzie. In a 1937 letter to his wife, Kate, he said he had chosen this name because "it's solid, and it belongs to my family: no 'Ivo' nonsense about it, no side-whiskers and silly little moustaches and liquid brown eyes about 'Seaforth.' Seaforth is a good chap." The name is that of the Scottish seat of the clan Mackenzie and was used by Cape for all Mackenzie's novels. However, when they were later republished, they appeared under the name of Kenneth Mackenzie.

Mackenzie was born in South Perth, Western Australia, and spent most of his early years in the city. In 1922 he moved with his mother—now separated from his father—and younger sister, Catherine, to "The Cottage" on the banks of the Murray River at Pinjarra, approximately sixty kilometers from Perth. Here his boyhood life was filled with experiences of nature—water, light, trees, rocks, summer breezes, and winter storms—and these images permeate his writing. Living in an environment he loved, and idolized by his mother, Kenneth found this period in many ways idyllic. In 1927, however, he was sent to board at Guildford Grammar School, and

Kenneth Mackenzie

the school proved a threatening and disturbing environment for a sensitive and protected boy unused to the hurly-burly of male adolescents.

His two years at Guildford provide the basis for his first novel, *The Young Desire It,* the first draft of which he wrote in 1930. In a letter to Jane Lindsay written in the 1940s, Mackenzie speaks of his experiences that inform the novel. He notes that he had little knowledge of a father "whose temper and behaviour were often devilish" and that he was "reared among women." He notes particularly the influence of Guildford:

> When I was at school I, being angel-faced and slim and shy, was apparently considered fair game by masters as well as certain boys. The boys were at least honestly crude in their proposals; but the masters—young men whom I thought very mature and wise—had a much better technique. They wooed the intellectual way, just at the very time I was beginning to comprehend something of literature and music, and so was most gullible. Again and again, like any simpleton, I was tricked, only to realise that what I had taken for special interest in possible intellectual promise of mine was not that at all. . . .
>
> My whole psyche was shaped by those years—first living with women only, then living entirely separated from anything womanly, and with my unfortunate appearance and the fact that I had a boy's soprano singing voice and was Chapel soloist (another cause of disgusting molestation). . . .
>
> All these long-drawn out circumstances conditioned me mentally, emotionally and—I don't doubt—sexually.

This letter provides a fair indication of the emotional territory of *The Young Desire It*. The novel depicts the experiences of Charles Fox, who suffers the shock of separation from his childhood home when sent to school, who falls in love for the first time with the elusive Margaret, and whose emotional turmoil is exacerbated by a possessive mother and a seductive male teacher. In this early work Mackenzie reveals a deft poetic sensibility in his portrayal of desire, conflict, and the ever present world of nature, which takes on a symbolic force in representing the emotional states of his characters.

In his late teens Mackenzie commenced work on his next novel, *Chosen People* (1938). It includes characters from *The Young Desire It*, Charles Fox and Richard Mawley. In this later work Mawley is the protagonist who is in love with Marjorie, a married but separated woman. He is also irresistibly attracted to Deborah Elison, a sixteen-year-old Jewish girl engaged to a Michael Levy. The Elison family is a major focus of the novel, and Mackenzie's depiction of them is drawn from his experience with a real-life family. In an interview with Diana Davis in 1965, the woman on whom the character of "Ruth Elison"–Deborah's mother–was based stated that Mackenzie was an "experimentalist [who] liked to see how people would react to things." Mackenzie appears as a young man who manipulated social circumstances for his own ends. In the same interview "Ruth" recorded that she confided in Mackenzie because even though he was "so young, you could talk about anything to him because he was so intelligent, *Chosen People* was certainly a very good picture of the way we lived. . . . " Mackenzie was drawn to the family's circumstances because he had an abiding interest in triangulated relationships, and in this family he was presented with a mother and daughter who shared the same lover. By the end of the novel the divisions are repaired; the lovers are apparently no longer divided in their feelings. However, this harmony has been achieved only by a deliberate "forgetfulness," and so the reader is left with the sense that the surface calm may be little more than illusion.

The Young Desire It was finally published in 1937 and won the Australian Literary Society Gold Medal. *Chosen People* appeared the following year, with no outcry from the family, who could have felt resentful at the airing of their private concerns. In the close-knit society of Perth in the early 1930s, the identity of the Elisons was no mystery.

In 1933, at the age of twenty, Mackenzie left Perth for Sydney, via Melbourne. By the middle of 1934 Mackenzie, with support from the poet Kenneth Slessor, had found employment in Sydney with a publisher and was also doing some movie reviews for *Smith's Weekly*. By the end of 1934 Mackenzie was married to a young widow, Kate Bartlett, whom he had met in Perth and persuaded to join him in Sydney. For the next twenty years Mackenzie eked out an existence from newspaper work, especially movie reviews; from Commonwealth Literary Fellowship grants; and from occasional royalties. His life was deeply troubled by economic struggle, wavering commitment to his marriage and family–daughter, Elisabeth, was born in 1936 and son, Hugh, in 1938–and a losing battle with alcoholism. Mackenzie nonetheless managed to keep producing work of considerable merit under these adverse conditions.

When he first arrived in Sydney, he met two men whose support and advice he highly valued–the poet Hugh McCrae and the multitalented Norman Lindsay. Thematically, Mackenzie's poetry has much in common with McCrae's–a concern with nature, love, and the passage of time. But with the possible exception of Mackenzie's first publication, *Our Earth* (1937), which was illustrated by Lindsay, the similarity ends there. Mackenzie's engagement with these themes is invariably in terms of the personal and particular. His poetry has a sense of immediacy that is lacking in McCrae's; McCrae more typically invokes the classical world of satyrs and centaurs, fauns, nymphs, and unicorns. Mackenzie's world is that espoused by Jack and Norman Lindsay in the journal *Vision*. Like much of his prose, Mackenzie's poetry is enmeshed in personal experience that is conveyed by the unpretentious speaking voice of his poems.

In the early 1940s Mackenzie became romantically involved with Jane Lindsay and frequently visited her and her father, Norman, at their family home, Springwood, at the foot of the Blue Mountains in New South Wales. Mackenzie's letters to her are full of references to the sights and sounds around him–moonlight, the call of peacocks from the nearby zoo, the barking of dogs, ambiguous doorways, and light and shadow. These references constitute the dominant iconography of his collection dedicated to Jane Lindsay, *The Moonlit Doorway*, which was published in 1944. In the same year Jane Lindsay, who was more ambivalent about their relationship than Mackenzie was, wrote to him to suggest that they go their separate ways: "I am not the woman for you. Already in too many ways I have failed to do and be just what you want . . . I am sorry."

During the war years Mackenzie seemed more concerned with the state of his personal finances than with the fortunes of nations. Although he was conscripted in 1942, he was deemed unfit for overseas service because of defective eyesight and a medical condition that caused excessive sweating. He spent most of his army service as an orderly-room corporal at Cowra in charge of Italian prisoners of war. In August 1944 he witnessed the outbreak of Japanese prisoners in Cowra.

In his 1947 application for a Commonwealth Literary Fund, Mackenzie describes the experience:

> It was a remarkable night, for most of the garrison troops were old or ageing men, unfit for any other sort

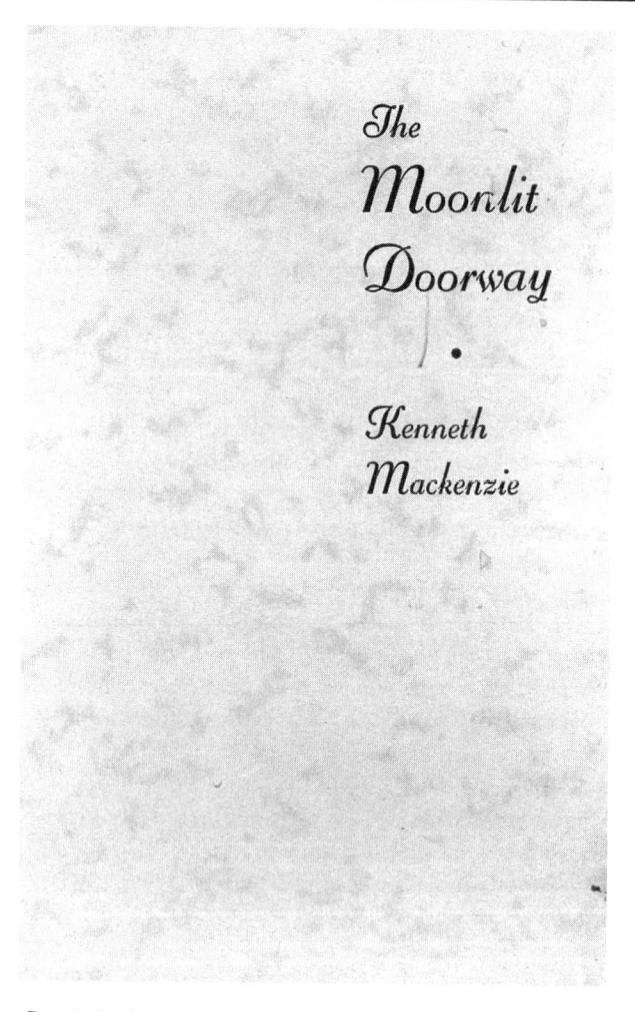

Dust jacket for Mackenzie's 1944 book, a collection of poems dedicated to Jane Lindsay, daughter of novelist Norman Lindsay (Bruccoli Clark Layman Archives)

of service, while the Japs were young and limber. They outnumbered the garrison strength by a total of 1,100 to approximately 450.

The mass outbreak formed the basis of *Dead Men Rising*, which was written in 1948, although not published by Cape in England and Harper in the United States until 1951. However, it was not published in Australia at that time because of (unspecified) concerns about libel. Many characters did bear a strong resemblance to serving army figures, but as Mackenzie observes in a letter written in 1952:

> In my first two published novels . . . several of the characters were vastly more true to life and more recognisable than any one of those in *Dead Men Rising*. In addition, they were far richer than any of my soldier semi-counterparts, and so more free to think of the costs of legal actions. There was a homosexually-inclined classics master and a silly snob of a Headmaster, both completely recognisable; there was a horrible Jewess and her former weakling lover engaged to her daughter; dear me! there were quite a few most unpleasant people carefully depicted, and I have it credibly, in the years that have passed since those publications, that the people recognised themselves easily enough, and for some god-known reason were not at all offended. . . . I don't think my wretched Army types would have minded too much.

Set against the depiction of army life in the camp in *Dead Men Rising* is the personal story of Corporal John Sergeant and his relationship with his girlfriend, Cathie. In this novel the notion of a divided self is not represented in terms of competing desires for love or recognition, but rather in Johnny's conflicted loyalties to the public, professional life of the army, and his love for Cathie. Cathie, however, sees the relationship as triangulated and implicitly Oedipal:

> If I did have a baby nothing could happen to you, Johnny. I mean, you and I would be the one person, even more than we are now. Much more. I thought of it as a triangle without a third point to sort of summarise the other two–to make a complete enclosed figure, perfect. . . . You see, Johnny? You–me–and this third point is us. It's *us* and *it*. You see?

By the end of the novel, there is still a triangle without a third point, because although Cathie is pregnant, Johnny is dead. Mackenzie does not draw explicit parallels between the private sphere and the public sphere, but it is difficult to avoid making a connection between the failure of the army to keep its promises, the failure of the prisoners to maintain their freedom, and the failure of Johnny to keep living.

In 1948 Mackenzie visited his sister and mother in Western Australia. He was in poor health, with alcohol-related illnesses. A couple of months at The Cottage did him some good. His health improved, and while there he wrote a substantial portion of *Dead Men Rising*. On his return to Sydney at the end of that year, he was unable to settle down to any regular work, and so, in a rather desperate move, the family decided they would move to a block of land that Kate owned at Kurrajong in the Blue Mountains. It was not an easy time. In a 1953 Commonwealth Literary Fellowship application Mackenzie provides some idea of their circumstances in 1949:

> With our two children, then aged thirteen and eleven years, we came to this long-neglected property to live in tents and a one-room hut which we had built with materials to hand–bark and timber growing hereabouts, discarded corrugated iron which we have not yet been able to replace, earth floors, sacking partitions, and so on. . . . We stripped and cleared wattle growth

and, whenever possible, planted trees against the sun and the west and south winds that scour the valley.... My wife found a kitchen job at a semi-private restaurant up the mountain at weekends; I worked for part of each week as a labourer; with the help of friends we made ends meet.

In spite of valiant attempts at subsistence living, the Mackenzies were desperately poor, and living conditions—with inadequate shelter and no electricity or water—extremely harsh. However, Mackenzie succeeded in gaining a fellowship of £400 for twelve months to write *The Refuge: A Confession* (1954), which he described in a letter written in 1950 as a novel concerned with "the experiences of one particular member of a group of new Australians attempting to reconcile the new life in a comparatively young country with the old habits and ways of thought in decadent Western Europe."

In Mackenzie's "Letters to the West," collected in *The Model: Selected Writings of Kenneth Seaforth Mackenzie* (2000), the literary transformation of the setting and lifestyle is apparent in the poetic-painterly description:

> Our valley is deep. The sun sets out of it soon after three o'clock p.m. in mid-winter, leaving it some hours of haunted, shadowless twilight that is slowly flooded out from below by true night; for here night does not descend upon us from the sky but rises like a dark spring welling from the velvet depths where the frogs begin early to creak and cry.
>
> During the outside world's sunset, we from our complete shadow, where lamps have been long lit since, have a view in the lowest east of brightly sunlit pasture topped by infinitely remote mountains underlining with a steady brush-stroke of Prussian blue the lemon coloured edge of the evening sky.... At these moments the valley is its own world.

Kurrajong is the basis for several of Mackenzie's narrative settings, including "Hill Farm" in *The Refuge*. In such carefully detailed descriptions, Mackenzie establishes his deep sense of belonging to natural surroundings; nature provides a sense of identity for him and his characters that is rarely evident in urban environments.

In spite of gaining a fellowship to write *The Refuge*, Mackenzie struggled to meet the deadlines. Kate had become seriously ill with pneumonia; living conditions were far from conducive to writing; Mackenzie was drinking excessively; and there was still not enough money to keep a family. Nevertheless, he completed the novel in August 1952, and it is a work of considerable power and originality. In the opening chapter, titled "The End," the reader is introduced to a crime reporter on *The Gazette* (Sydney), Lloyd Fitzherbert, and learns that Fitzherbert has just murdered his secret wife, Irma.

The following four chapters attempt to explain the events that have led to this shocking climax. The final chapter, also titled "The End," brings the reader back to events that immediately precede the opening line of the novel. Both structurally and thematically the novel exhibits modernist influences. It is described on the dust jacket as a "psychological crime-story": the psychology is once again concerned with identity constructed within triangular relationships. The most powerful and destructive triangle comprises Fitzherbert, his son Alan, and Irma. In a mirror image of the sexual triangle in *Chosen People*, Irma becomes the lover of both father and son. Fitzherbert murders her for this reason.

The intensity of the father-son relationship is evident throughout the novel, and it is most explicit in Fitzherbert's reaction to discovering Irma and Alan together in bed. He claims, "I was jealous, not of Alan but of Irma—not of my son but of my wife."

The novel is a challenge to the reader at many levels, not least because empathy is invited for a character who does not appear as a self-deluded psychopath but who nevertheless kills carefully and methodically out of uncontrollable jealousy. Contemporary readers may also be discomforted by the racist-sexist undertones of the presentation of Irma. She is seen as a mysterious, beautiful, sexual, amoral, untrustworthy woman of Lithuanian-Jewish background. She has much in common with the Elisons in *Chosen People*.

Apart from Mackenzie's novels, he wrote many short stories, none of which were published in his lifetime. The longest and most significant of these stories is "The Model" (1966). It is of particular interest because it seems to be consciously intertextual, playing off some of the issues raised in Norman Lindsay's 1938 novel, *Age of Consent*. Both works concern artists in their forties who use compliant fifteen-year-old girls as their models. Mackenzie's story concerns the fate of two models, Cora and Corrie; Lindsay's model is also named Cora. *Age of Consent* concludes with the artist, Bradley Mudgett, believing that as he has been accused of an improper sexual relationship with his model, he might as well provide the rumor with substance. Mackenzie's story is also about the relationship between artist and model. He does, however, avoid titillation while acknowledging the complexity and intensity of feelings between the older man and the young girl. The different emotional territory of child and adult is carefully delineated; the lines are not blurred as they are in Lindsay's work.

The most interesting of Mackenzie's unpublished works is an "incomplete" novel titled "Frontispiece" (excerpts of which are published in *The Model*), which bears the date 8 January 1938. Internal evidence suggests that this date may not be correct and the "incomplete" is

Dust jacket for Mackenzie's 1951 novel, based on a 1944 outbreak staged by Japanese prisoners of war at Cowra (from Bruce Bennett, ed., The Literature of Western Australia, *1979)*

qualified because the work is a highly modernist, experimental piece of writing of approximately 36,000 words, which *could* be considered to be finished in spite of its abrupt conclusion. The narrative inhabits familiar territory with Mackenzie's poetic descriptions of place and its depiction of a man whose attentions are divided between two extremely different women. Its primary focus, however, is on the nature and process of writing, especially autobiographical writing. The work raises questions about "truth," about the inadequacies of language in representing experience, and about the relationship between an author's life and his work. It possesses a high degree of self-reflexivity, with sophisticated play on its title: the story possesses a "frontispiece," but it is also about a writer who is writing a story with that title. Five thousand words into Mackenzie's manuscript his character Heron begins his task:

Taking a pencil, drawing to him the virginal block of paper, he wrote on the second sheet the title, Frontispiece, of a work destined to be left unfinished in the end; but this he could not foresee, and how, with the word written, should he hesitate now? In the selfless, unalterable innocence of the creative mind, he began to write.

In 1953 Kate, accompanied by the children, returned to Sydney to take up her former work of teaching ceramics. The family visited Mackenzie at Kurrajong either singly or together on weekends, but these visits were not always easy or relaxed for any of them. His life continued to be embattled: he had little money, almost no companionship, and drank excessively. He continued to write poems and book reviews. In 1954 Mackenzie visited Western Australia for the last time. Following a positive reception for *The Refuge,* he had expectations that Perth literary circles would provide him with recognition and endorsement of his status as a writer. His supporters were willing to do just that, but once again Mackenzie's drinking rendered him largely incapable of responding. On his return to Sydney, Mackenzie became seriously ill, and his emotional state was not improved by a letter from Kate stating she was going to divorce him for lack of support.

Mackenzie felt increasingly isolated from both his wife and his children and often experienced difficulties in meeting basic needs, such as providing himself with adequate meals. He received some heartening news in November 1954 in the form of another fellowship, to write a novel dealing with the "native problem" in Western Australia. In January 1955 Mackenzie went to visit an old friend, Len Oldershaw, at Tallong, about fifty kilometers from Goulburn. When he arrived by train at Goulburn, he was charged by the police with drunkenness. Two and a half hours later he had fallen into a creek on Oldershaw's property and drowned, although he was a good swimmer. It would seem that the "curse" of the descendants of the Earls of Seaforth–that in every generation there would be an alcoholic, an epileptic, and a half-wit–had caught up with him. The most likely explanation of his death is that he suffered an alcohol-induced epileptic seizure that resulted in his death by drowning.

Mackenzie's death was similar to descriptions in two of his poems: the title poem in *The Moonlit Doorway* begins,

"Well, this is where I go down to the river,"
the traveller with me said, and turned aside
out of the burnt road, through the black trees
spiking the slope, and went down, and never
came back into the heat from water's ease
in which he swooned, in cool joy, and died.

In the 1951 poem "Caesura," later collected in *Selected Poems of Kenneth Mackenzie* (1961), he writes,

> Blackness rises. Am I now to die
> and feel the steps no more and not see day
> break out its answering smile of hail all's well
> from east full round to east and hear the bird
> whistle all creatures that on earth do well?

The answer then was "Not now."

Kenneth Mackenzie's distinctive contribution to Australian literature is his depiction of the affective sensibilities of his characters, in both fiction and poetry, through his evocation of the natural world. From a young age he was particularly attuned to the sensory aspects of nature, and he was one of the first Australian writers to use the elements as metaphor for the emotional lives of his characters. For him the physical environment was not mere background against which narrative events were played out; rather, the sights, sounds, and feel of nature were inseparable from a sense of self.

Bibliography:

Diana Davis, "A Checklist of Kenneth Mackenzie's Works, Including Manuscript Material," *Australian Literary Studies*, 4, no. 4 (1970): 398–404.

References:

Marjorie Barnard, "The Novels of Seaforth Mackenzie," *Meanjin*, 13, no. 4 (1954): 503–511;

Donovan Clarke, "Seaforth Mackenzie: Novelist of Alienation," *Southerly*, 25, no. 2 (1965): 75–90;

Peter Cowan, "Seaforth Mackenzie's Novels," *Meanjin Quarterly*, 24 (1965): 298–307;

Diana Davis, "The Genesis of a Writer: The Early Years of Kenneth Mackenzie," *Australian Literary Studies*, 3, no. 4 (1968): 254–270;

Davis, "Kenneth Mackenzie," M.A. thesis, 1967, Melbourne University;

Davis, "Seaforth Mackenzie," *Westerly*, no. 3 (1966): 4–12;

R. G. Geering, "Seaforth Mackenzie's Fiction," *Southerly*, 26 (1966): 25–39;

Evan Jones, "A Dead Man Rising: The Poetry of Kenneth Mackenzie," *Australian Quarterly*, 36 (1964): 70–79;

Jones, "Kenneth Mackenzie's Hospital Poems," *Westerly*, no. 3 (1966): 13–38;

Jones, "Prose and Short Stories," *Westerly*, no. 3 (1966): 39–84;

Richard Rossiter, "Seaforth Mackenzie and Postmodern Facades," *Westerly*, 44, no. 1 (1999): 72–84.

Papers:

Much of Kenneth Mackenzie's family correspondence is housed in the Mitchell Library, as are manuscripts of his novels. His letters written from Sydney in 1940–1944 are in the Jane Lindsay papers at the National Library of Australia, which also holds manuscripts.

Frederic Manning

(22 July 1882 – 22 February 1935)

James Packer
Workers Educational Association Sydney

BOOKS: *The Vigil of Brunhild* (London: Murray, 1907);
Scenes and Portraits (London: Murray, 1909; revised and enlarged edition, London: Davies, 1930; New York: Scribners, 1931);
Poems (London: Murray, 1910);
Eidola (London: Murray, 1917);
The Life of Sir William White (London: Murray, 1923);
The Middle Parts of Fortune: Somme and Ancre, 1916, as F. P. (London: Davies, 1929); abridged as *Her Privates We*, as Private 19022 (London: Davies, 1930; New York & London: Putnam, 1930); republished as *Her Privates We*, as Frederick Manning (London: Davies, 1943); unabridged version republished as *The Middle Parts of Fortune: Somme and Ancre, 1916* (London: Davies, 1977; New York: St. Martin's Press, 1977; Melbourne: Text, 2000).

OTHER: *Epicurus: His Morals*, translated by Walter Charleton (1651), introduction by Manning (London: Davies, 1926).

SELECTED PERIODICAL PUBLICATIONS–UNCOLLECTED: "Three Fables," *Coterie* (London) (Easter 1920): 17–19.

Few writers have had the value of their major work accepted so readily, and yet the value of their life's achievement treated so skeptically, as the poet and fabulist Frederic Manning. Fewer still Australian writers have enjoyed more long-lasting attempts by the country of their birth to claim them when only the barest of traces of that country survive in their actual writings. Manning's most enduring work, *The Middle Parts of Fortune: Somme and Ancre, 1916* (1929), is often said to be the finest work of fiction to emerge from World War I, and while his collection of short historical works, *Scenes and Portraits* (1909), is also accorded respect, the remainder of his work, including two books of poems and a verse epic, is found to be of little merit even as "Edwardian" writing. The key to such divergent readings—and to Manning's originality as an Australian writer—lies in his talent for a certain mode of analytical thinking. A genius for the cadences of dialectic rather than those of meter did not prevent him from persevering with the latter, and his final achievement is at the last as an artist rather than as an ironist or philosopher. In this respect it is appropriate that he should have been so near a contemporary of Joseph Furphy: both, in their different ways, were poets of "the cunning of history" (Georg Wilhelm Friedrich Hegel's famous expression for the way human life constantly escapes human intentions and so ironizes them), and despite their evolution of two quite different, highly idiosyncratic styles of thought and expression, both men fictionalized their lives in equally allusive, densely metaphysical ways. Of the two, Manning is the more difficult to account for, as tragic skepticism is more demanding of readers than comic exuberance. Manning's claim to fame, unusual for an Australian writer of his period, is as a creator of prose works the value of which cannot be easily separated from their metaphysical substance. If readers do not grasp his themes, the continuity of his life's work is all but lost.

Frederic Manning was the fourth son and fifth child of a prospering and ambitious Irish Catholic accountant, William Patrick Manning, who later became mayor of Sydney and a state parliamentarian. Manning had married Honora Torpy in Sydney in 1868, and the child born in 1882 was of such frail health that despite the family's comfortable circumstances he received little institutional schooling. (His registration at Jesuit-run Riverview, the school attended by his brothers, is little more than a rumor.) Fred, however, showed himself precociously intelligent from an early age, and his education was given to the care of Arthur Howard Galton, formerly private secretary to the governor of New South Wales, Sir Robert Duff. Galton's recognition of his pupil's abilities resulted in a relationship of more or less permanent codependence that ended only with Galton's death early in 1921, more than twenty-three years after the fifteen-year-old Manning first left Australia with him, after two years of tutelage, in March 1898.

Manning's first period in London—he returned to Australia for three years in 1900—exposed him to turn-of-the-century metropolitan literary life, acquainting him with the personal circles of Max Beerbohm and William Butler Yeats. Manning was also brought into contact with Beerbohm's *The Happy Hypocrite,* a play whose Nietzschean traces can be found throughout Manning's own later work. An ironic inversion of Oscar Wilde's *The Picture of Dorian Gray* (1890), Beerbohm's "happy hypocrite" assumes the mask of goodness, and instead of plunging into self-alienation becomes the thing he assumes. Manning's only extant comment on the play, recorded in a letter to T. E. Lawrence in 1932, is of Manning's involvement, through Beerbohm, in the birth of the cult of Shavianism, but the paradoxes and duplicities of "fate" in its wrestling with "self" are the most notable characteristics of all of Manning's prose work, and became fully evident within a decade.

Manning's second period in England lasted more than twenty years, and during it the trajectory of his writing career turned entirely away from the country of his birth. Although many Australian novels—most notably Marcus Clarke's *His Natural Life* (1874) and Joseph Furphy's *Such Is Life* (1903)—showed considerable dexterity with themes of fate and self, under Galton's continuing literary guidance Manning saw no particular reason to allow himself "Australian" perturbations: after coming to rest in the Lincolnshire town of Edenham, he headed toward a reworking of that late-Victorian classicism whose chief exemplars had been Walter Pater and John Henry Newman. Manning's continuing ill health, moreover—he was an extreme example of what his age called "neurasthenic"—insulated him from interest in any literature of a "pioneering" people, even if he learned to value the independent-mindedness of such a people during World War I and proved by the forthrightness of his own attitudes toward military authority that as much as Furphy he could be "offensively Australian."

A sense of forthrightness characterizes all of Manning's prose work and is uneasily combined with the Miltonic or Tennysonian narrative versifying in his first book, *The Vigil of Brunhild,* published in 1907. Relating the career of the sixth-century queen of Austrasia and Burgundy as she herself meditates it before a priest, the poem is structured to oppose a finished life with life lived in the moment. Brunhild explains her fate through the example of her life as, in facing its extinction, it illuminates all that life can be, not simply through the medium of the story she tells:

> But the priest felt that effluence from her
> Shed a strange glory round the humid cell
> And fill him with a fearful sense of fate:
> The blind, remorseless progress of the world,
> Sombre and threatening, her figure cut
> Prow-like, and loomed through huge, tempestuous night
> Toward a doom obscure and imminent.

In stating Manning's thematic project as openly as this, *The Vigil of Brunhild* set the technique for the major work of the greater part of his life—*Scenes and Portraits,* published a little more than a year later. This series of historical pieces is, in all six "portraits" of the first edition, meditative and now dialectical. Each piece states a theme or issue upon which two or more characters meditate, willing a course of action on the basis of that theme or issue, a fate for themselves they believe fully enclosed by their own will. In each case, the theme or issue, as it develops the course of action they undertake, reveals it to be not quite the action they thought, and the life of the character is treated ironically as his will and his fate are gently but inexorably disconnected. Whereas *The Vigil of Brunhild* portrays a character whose life is distinct, because more vital, than any number of words describing it, *Scenes and Portraits* presents characters whose dialectical relationship to the words around them has made their will distinct from its outcomes.

In "The King of Uruk," Bagoas, the high priest of ancient Mesopotamian Uruk, journeys from the city and encounters two rustics, Adam and Eve. In their little kingdom of Eden, Bagoas is shown a tree that is dedicated to God, the fruit of which they are forbidden to eat. A man of some sophistication, possessing anthropological interests, Bagoas wonders aloud why a fruit so wholesome should be associated with death. "If we ate of the fruit would we not die?" inquires Eve. "If you ate of it you would know," Bagoas replies. Returning to Uruk, Bagoas relates this tale to the king, Merodach, who conceives a desire to go to Eden and experience for himself the charm of this rusticity. Doing so, he unwittingly drives out Adam and Eve, though not before Eve has eaten the fruit of the tree, apparently overcome by a desire to "know." So the story moves over two registers of knowledge: its retrospective relation to will and its prospective relation to fate.

As the first story of *Scenes and Portraits*, "The King of Uruk" sets the tone for the series as a whole. In "The House of Euripides," Euripides is shown in conversation with Socrates, Protagoras, and others; the subject is the relationship of circumstance to decision, or the possible justifications for the subversions of men's will by "the way things turn out"—the possibility of mastering fate. In the short epilogue to this story, Protagoras's own fate is related in a dialogue between two of the characters: the moment of his death is retained by the expression of knowing irony he bears on his face, a moment of realization that his life has escaped all philosophical deliberation, including his own.

Manning's own philosophical disposition was toward epicureanism—in its original sense, of restraint in pleasure, as distinct from the pure hedonism it has come to connote—and the manner of life he had even at this early age chosen was of epicurean retreat from the world of large affairs. The traces of Nietzsche so often found in his work owe mainly to Manning's refusal to resent a world in which will is apt to be frustrated by fate, or as a character puts it

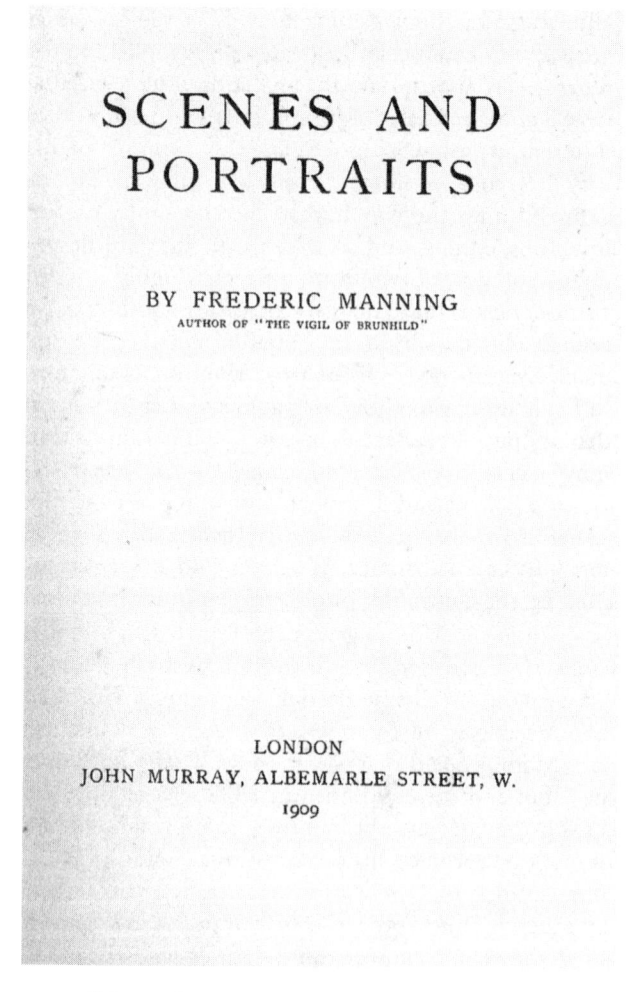

SCENES AND PORTRAITS

BY FREDERIC MANNING
AUTHOR OF "THE VIGIL OF BRUNHILD"

LONDON
JOHN MURRAY, ALBEMARLE STREET, W.
1909

Title page for Manning's second book, a collection of short historical fiction (Bruccoli Clark Layman Archives)

in the next portrait, "The Friend of Paul," a world that shows "the gods serene, into which penetrates no whisper of mortal anguish," where "no voice of prayer troubles their endless pleasure" so that "without tears or anger they gaze at once upon our sorrow and our sin, and are heedless of the hands uplifted in supplication from every corner of the earth." The middle stories of *Scenes and Portraits* illustrate some parallelism between this epicureanism and certain aspects of the world of Christianity. In the fourth story, "The Jesters of the Lord," Francis of Assisi declares of Lady Poverty, "having nothing, she possesses all things. God hath clothed her with virtues more precious than rubies; he hath given her the wide earth and all the pleasant ways thereof to be her home." But this Francis is less an idealist of Poverty than its ruthless logician: his argument for the severity of the proposed Franciscan Rule before Innocent III is that discord and dissension arise with the acquisition of property and that the fate of his proposed Order rests less with the will of its adherents than with the circumstances of their interaction with the world.

Logic, irony, and political acumen are continued into the fifth story, "At San Casciani," which details an alleged meeting of Thomas Cromwell with Niccolo Machiavelli. Machiavelli's own species of irony is well known, but Manning adds to it the touch of epicurean logic: "In all things we may observe the action of certain laws, to which man is subject, but within the limits of which he hath a certain freedom . . . ; but no man is found so prudent as to know how to adapt himself to all changes, both because he is naturally inclined to follow one course, and because having prospered in it hitherto he cannot be persuaded to change." This dialectic of fate and will results in the political paradox for which Machiavelli is famous; for example, "it happens that the people warring against their government in the cause of liberty do but increase the power they have aimed to destroy." Cromwell is persuaded to the logic of power, but not to the ironies that underlie Machiavelli's discourse, and Manning is effectively able to make Cromwell's will ironic as the fate of a political meddler lies in wait for this courtier of Henry VIII.

In the final dialogue of the 1909 edition, "The Paradise of the Disillusioned," Pope Leo XIII awakes in paradise after his death—the year is 1903. He is shortly in conversation with the author of *The Life of Jesus* (1863), Ernest Renan. There are many paradises, explains Renan. The paradise Leo has reached is the heaven of the epicureans: "We Epicureans enjoy that moment which is eternity; and every man is justified in his own eyes." This statement is immediately ironic, and a sense of comedy infuses the account. But the concern is, again, with the irony of events—the ways in which fate subverts will. For the first time, Manning puts the matter in modern, evolutionary terms:

> The spirit of progress is [says Renan] an intangible if all-pervading thing. It develops spontaneously in a thousand ways, and as it pushes towards the unknown it is impossible for us to predict with any certainty what forms it may assume. Being purely experience, and not a creed, it is liable to be extensively modified or even completely changed by some unforeseen development in any of its parts. . . . That is the reason progress seems always to be a purely destructive force. It is only after it has escaped, through imperceptible degrees, into a more or less clearly defined new phase, that we can gauge its value as a constructive force in the last.

The life of the man who wrote *Scenes and Portraits* followed to such an extent the ironies, the "subversion of intentions," woven into his first major work that those awaiting completion of his second book, a work in the same spirit, titled "The Gilded Coach," found themselves eventually disappointed. While Manning published soon after *Scenes and Portraits* a volume of poetry, *Poems* (1910), critics generally thought it showed little of the analytical incisiveness that had brought the writer the small but exclusive following he now had. That following already included Ezra Pound and in time included T. S. Eliot and T. E. Lawrence. In 1920 Pound submitted a revision of the 1913 draft of "The Gilded Coach" to the New York magazine *The Dial,* but the work was ultimately rejected because even by that stage it was too obviously incomplete—as is the draft presently in the Mitchell Library, the state of the novel at Manning's death. In his 1988 biography, *Frederic Manning: An Unfinished Life,* Jonathan Marwil reasonably suggests that the mode of writing at which Manning excelled could not be transposed upon the project of a full-scale historical novel, with its architectural demands of sustained plot and characterization. Possibly, however, a man who suffered from that crippling of the will the Greeks named *akrasia* was well placed to examine the interaction of intention and outcome that is the most marked subject of his fiction.

Set at the time of Louis XIV, "The Gilded Coach" is the tale of a certain well-regarded ecclesiastic, M. de Velay, seconded by the King for an act of diplomacy that the extant drafts of the book do not dramatize. Louis XIV is presented in the style in which Manning treated Innocent III in the earlier book; M. de Velay is a less ascetic, more accommodating Francis of Assisi. King and subject trade in ironies and are treated with irony—"Men are not governed by maxims," says the King, who then asks de Velay, "What is a political party, monsieur, but a body of men employing a set of principles to dupe their own conscience?" (To this statement Manning adds, "He did not seem aware that he had himself formulated a maxim.") Power, often cloaked but never invisible, is the most significant reality encountered in Manning's delicate prose, and no amount of irony dulls its edge. On the contrary, the epicurean temperament tests every level of the dangerous world into which it is cast—to discover the certainty of power, not its limitation. Manning, dwelling reclusively at Edenham, wrote in *Scenes and Portraits* that "people invariably suspect a man who leads a retired life, either of some shameful practices, or a guilty past." Focused upon the power he knew best, the

Buckstone Farm in Surrey, where Manning lived in 1923-1924

power of what his Renan calls "collective conscience," he produced fiction that aspired to tranquility and knew all the penalties of political delusion and social failure.

From 1909 to 1915—and after the war from December 1919 to April 1920—Manning earned a small living reviewing for the London weekly *The Spectator*. Years of frustration with progress on "The Gilded Coach" were terminated by the war, in which, after failing to attain a commission, Manning served as a private in France from August 1916 to the end of that year. Later, reapplying for a commission, he became a second lieutenant in the Royal Irish Regiment, stationed near Dublin from July 1917. Manning's war record was mixed. He was never in better health than at the Somme, a fact reflected in his promotion to lance corporal by the end of 1916; he seemed to have curbed the drinking that had lost him his first attempt at a commission, though this vice returned with duty in Ireland and remained with him as a significant source of debilitation for the rest of his life. In early 1917 Manning published *Eidola*, his second book of verse. It comprised, along with more of the bucolic poetry that had been a feature of *Poems*—by now he had come to consider these poems "mainly childish things"—many superior poems written in the trenches, on the war. These are Manning's first poems in which irony is expressed in the texture of the verse, and the sexual imagery of several of them is reminiscent of Wilfred Owen. An example is the description of Aphrodite in "Reaction":

> And we turn from the harshness of swords,
> Hungering for you . . .
> And know not that your breasts,
> Carven delicately of ivory and gold,
> The lips, red and subtile,
> Are born of the bitter sea-foam and bright blood.

Still, Manning the poet was loath to let war remake him as a modernist, and his use of the meter of the Song of Solomon, as well as its content, clearly differentiates his poetry from the most trenchant war poetry of his time. So, too, does the influence of wisdom literature, such as Job and Ecclesiastes, continue to differentiate his prose work from the literary modernism that swept Europe at the end of the war. "Three Fables," published in *Coterie* in 1920, shows Manning's unbending commitment to the prose forms that had created *Scenes and Portraits* and "The

Gilded Coach." The fables themselves are less than a page each in length, and the tone suits this brevity—moreover, they are sufficiently idiosyncratic to fulfill the editorial demands of an eclectic modernist journal such as *Coterie*—but their author makes no compromises with literary timeliness. For Manning was by now in the midst of a new period of struggle, with a messy resignation from active service in early 1918, bouts of influenza, and the deaths of Galton in February 1921 and Eva Fowler—about whom he said, "after Arthur Galton, the person to whom I owed most in England"—in July 1921. Commissioned in 1919 to write a biography of Sir William White of the Royal Navy, he was experiencing the same problems he had with "The Gilded Coach"; the biography was eventually published in 1923.

Manning remained at Edenham for two years after Galton's death, and in 1923 he left Lincolnshire for Buckstone Farm in Surrey. After spending half a year in Australia (November 1924 to May 1925), he moved to Ireland, and shortly after that began living in London, where he was commissioned by Peter Davies, just beginning his publishing career, to provide an introduction to a limited-edition republication of Walter Charlton's *Epicurus: His Morals* (1926). Between 1925 and 1927, Manning contributed several critical articles to T. S. Eliot's *Criterion* and *New Criterion*; that relationship was terminated upon Manning's displeasure with a *Criterion* review of Charleton's *Epicurus* in October 1927. Davies, also a former soldier, had been attempting to persuade Manning for years to write a memoir of the war.

The year 1929 marked the revival of the war novel, and Davies's redoubled efforts to extract one from Manning involved drastic maneuvers, including, legend has it, locking up the author in a room in a London flat. The book is dedicated "to Peter Davies who made me write it." "Peter took it from me sheet by sheet," Manning says in a letter to Lawrence (11 February 1930), "and cast it into adamantine type. But for him I might have rewritten it. What an escape!" No one knew better than its author the extent to which *The Middle Parts of Fortune* had been spared the fate of "The Gilded Coach," on which Manning spent no further efforts in the remaining years of his life.

Manning's exultation over the "escape" of his novel acknowledged more than the cause célèbre the book quickly became. *The Middle Parts of Fortune* marked the climactic moment of his peculiar career as writer and thinker. It is his most heartfelt and stylistically extended treatment of the dialectic of fortune and the struggle of men to keep a hold on their lives. "War is waged by men; not by beasts, nor by gods," he states in his Author's Prefatory Note. "It is a peculiarly human activity. To call it a crime against mankind is to miss at least half its significance; it is also the punishment." War is waged by men, and against other men—for "there is nothing in war which is not in human nature"—but, Manning insists, "the violence and passions of men become, in the aggregate, an impersonal and incalculable force, a blind and irrational movement of the collective will, which one cannot control, which one cannot understand." Manning's own experience of the war may be gauged from the poetry of *Eidola*, as in "The Trenches": "We stumble, cursing, on the slippery duckboards, / Goaded like the damned by some invisible wrath, / A will stronger than weariness, stronger than animal fear, / Implacable and monotonous," but in the 1929 novel his expression of this experience, like that so often found in those same poems, reverted to the dialectical modes and intellectual formulations of a writer who had yet to experience war firsthand.

Yet, in *The Middle Parts of Fortune* are elements that put the book beyond the abilities of a mere adept of dialectical speculation. For one thing, the central character, Bourne, is the author of all he surveys and is made to bear the existential weight of every speculative moment. This use deepens his characterization far beyond anything Manning has previously attempted—it is in fact to belittle the presentation of Bourne to call it a characterization. So when the novel reflects, "In all action a man seeks to realise himself, and the act once complete, it is no longer a part of him, it escapes from his control and has an independent objective existence," the reader does not simply see will transcending itself as the realization of itself, the transformation of itself into fate; the reader sees Bourne given over to the moment of a destiny that is far more important than its speculative residue. The speculation passes by as the reader examines the text, but Bourne continues to his very end—in the novel, he is killed—and the speculation (every speculation, in a novel that is a kaleidoscope of speculations) matters only to the extent that it is shown true of Bourne, and through Bourne, "the men."

The importance, then, of this late novel is related to its difficult metaphysical terrain, but it achieved classic status quickly through the immediacy and urgency of the life it captured—made possible, perhaps, through the metaphysics, but by no means made comprehensible through them. Bourne is comprehensible concretely, and in working on this novel Manning, for the first time in his fiction, made himself concrete. "What an escape!" reflects more than the fate of the work as a finished product; it

Manning and his mother, Honora Torpy Manning, in Rome, 1931 (from Jonathan Marwil, Frederic Manning, *1988)*

reflects the possible fate of an author who had hitherto expressed himself in the most abstract terms. Some exception may be made of the war poems, whose concrete detail delivers them from the ethereal generalities of his other verse, but the analytical spirit the war poems require to counterpoint this concreteness is less dialectical or ironical thoughtfulness than, again, ethereal generality.

The concreteness present in *The Middle Parts of Fortune* came as something of an artistic revelation to Manning, who set about preparing a novel on the lives of Lincolnshire people of the sort he had encountered in his many years spent in Edenham. No trace of this novel survives. In fact, the only significant work Manning completed in the five years remaining to him after the war novel was an additional piece in *Scenes and Portraits,* republished in a limited edition by Peter Davies in 1930. The piece, "Apologia Dei," was dedicated to T. E. Shaw–Lawrence, who claimed to have read *Scenes and Portraits* fifty times and to have identified the author of the originally pseudonymous *Middle Parts of Fortune* from that reading.

The new portrait is of Satan and, coming as a whole from the mouth of God, is no sort of dialogue. It is consequently even more abstract than any of the original portraits, and unlike *The Middle Parts of Fortune,* whose speculations on the nature of time are grounded in the circumstances of a temporal being (Bourne), the equally metaphysical speculations of "Apologia Dei" amount to the "final" philosophy Bourne philosophized against. God and Bourne do ask the same question of the human self–the definitive existential question first asked in Søren Kierkegaard's *Journals* (translated into English, 1938), of the place where a man will find himself, between recollection of past events and anticipation of events to come. This question puts time at the heart of human life, where it can never be for so abstract a being as God. "Everything flows away from [man] in dissolution," says the "Apologia Deo," "and, if he consider himself, of whom he is at first so confident, as though here, surely, were something relatively stable amid the fleeting shows of sense, at what point in his life would he fix himself?" Perhaps, despite the abstractness of the entire final portrait, readers are not to take abstractness itself too seriously–perhaps Manning's irony is now operating in the sense that the lives of "eternal" epicurean gods have no importance for men, least of all for men who define themselves in the terms of their actual existence. Thus, in the new edition of *Scenes and Portraits* Manning might be said to reflect upon ironies of discourse in *The Middle Parts of Fortune,* where, in *The Middle Parts of Fortune* itself, are only ironies of Fate.

Irony was Manning's milieu in life as in art. He published his book at a time when the fashion for war books had begun to wane; yet, it became immensely influential. He wrote it pseudonymously, yet became known for it almost immediately. An expurgated version, titled *Her Privates We* (Manning showed himself an unembarrassed retailer of unpublishable soldier-speak in the original 520-copy limited edition of 1929), was what the world saw of his books, through its various reprints, until 1977. His final residence in Australia, from 1932 to 1934, found him in a country as little bearable as at any time of his life–"it has nothing to recommend it except its climate, and the skies, which are an effect of the climate"–and he returned to the country of such a different climate and was dead within a year; he died on 22 February 1935. Australia has long claimed him as one of her writers, despite the reservations of the most influential critics of the 1930s, Nettie Palmer and P. R. Stephensen; yet, until the year 2000 no Australian publisher produced an edition of any of his books.

In *The Middle Parts of Fortune* Bourne is billeted in the house of a Frenchwoman, behind the lines. "Extraordinarily tranquil in her pessimism," the world in ruins about her, "she was perfectly clear that the Hun had to be defeated"–"justice must be done; and for her apparently justice was some divine law, working slowly and inexorably through all the confused bickerings of men. She interested [Bourne], because although she was a comparatively uneducated woman, her thought was clear, logical, and hard." For Frederic Manning too, justice was a "divine law," though one bound up with the defeat of expectations rather than of personalities. This condition produced writing whose thought was "clear, logical and hard" enough to make artistic sense of "the confused bickerings of men" and resolve the pessimism that in less metaphysical circumstances would have been entirely incompatible with tranquility.

Letters:

L. T. Hergenhan, "Some Unpublished Letters from T. E. Lawrence to Frederic Manning," *Southerly,* 23, no. 4 (1963): 242–252;

Hergenhan, "Two Expatriates: Some Correspondence from Frederic Manning to James Griffyth Fairfax," *Southerly,* 39 (1979): 59–95.

Bibliographies:

L. T. Hergenhan, "A Checklist of Recent Manning Criticism," *Australian Literary Studies,* 11 (1984): 399–400;

Verna Coleman, *The Last Exquisite: A Portrait of Frederic Manning* (Melbourne: Melbourne University Press, 1990), pp. 209–224;

Martin Duwell and Hergenhan, *The ALS Guide to Australian Writers: A Bibliography 1963–1990* (Brisbane: University of Queensland Press, 1992), pp. 209–210.

Biographies:

Kaiser Haq, "Forgotten Fred: A Portrait of Frederic Manning," *London Magazine,* new series, 23 (1983–1984): 54–78;

Jonathan Marwil, *Frederic Manning: An Unfinished Life* (Sydney: Angus & Robertson, 1988);

Verna Coleman, *The Last Exquisite: A Portrait of Frederic Manning* (Melbourne: Melbourne University Press, 1990).

Papers:

The most important collection of Manning papers, which includes the typescript of "The Gilded Coach" and the manuscript of *The Middle Parts of Fortune,* is held in the Mitchell Library (ML MSS 2594); another collection (ML MSS 2594) is also held there. The National Library of Australia holds a literary manuscript by Manning (ANL MS:1989). Collections of letters are located at the Bibliothèque Nationale, Paris; the University of Chicago; the University of Texas at Austin; Yale University; and Harvard University.

Alan Marshall
(2 May 1902 – 21 January 1984)

Joanne McPherson

BOOKS: *These Are My People* (Melbourne: Cheshire, 1944);
Tell Us About the Turkey, Jo (Sydney: Angus & Robertson, 1946);
Ourselves Writ Strange (Melbourne: Cheshire, 1948); republished as *These Were My Tribesmen* (Melbourne: Landsdowne, 1965);
Pull Down the Blind (Melbourne: Cheshire, 1949);
How Beautiful Are Thy Feet (Melbourne: Chesterhill, 1949);
Bumping into Friends (Melbourne: Cheshire, 1950);
People of the Dreamtime (Melbourne: Cheshire, 1952);
I Can Jump Puddles (Melbourne: Cheshire, 1955);
How's Andy Going? (Melbourne: Cheshire, 1956);
The Gay Provider, the Myer Story (Melbourne: Cheshire, 1961);
This Is the Grass (Melbourne: Cheshire, 1962);
In Mine Own Heart (Melbourne: Cheshire, 1963);
Whispering in the Wind (Melbourne: Nelson, 1969);
Pioneers and Painters: One Hundred Years of Eltham and Its Shire (Sydney: Nelson, 1971);
Fight for Life (Melbourne: Cassell, 1972);
Aboriginal Myths, by Marshall and Sreten Bozic (Melbourne: Gold Star Publications, 1972);
Short Stories (Melbourne: Nelson, 1973);
Hammers over the Anvil (Melbourne: Nelson, 1975);
Four Sunday Suits, and Other Stories (Nashville, Tenn.: Nelson, 1975);
The Complete Stories of Alan Marshall (Melbourne: Nelson, 1977);
Alan Marshall Talking, edited by Edward Harding (Melbourne: Longman Cheshire, 1978);
His Best Stories (Windsor, Vic.: O'Neil, 1980);
Alan Marshall's Australia (Melbourne: Hyland House, 1981);
Alan Marshall's Battlers, compiled by Gwen Hardisty (Melbourne: Hyland House, 1983).

Perhaps best known for the first book in his autobiographical trilogy, *I Can Jump Puddles* (1955), Alan Marshall was also the prolific author of many short sto-

Alan Marshall (photograph by Adrian Boddington, Melbourne; from John Hetherington, Forty-Two Faces, *1946)*

ries, children's books, novels, and newspaper advice columns. His work is vivid in its portrayal of Australian rural life and is typically concerned with the representation of courageous characters who value social solidarity and demonstrate a love of nature. As a child Marshall contracted poliomyelitis, which left his legs permanently scarred and wasted and resulted in the curvature of his spine. Despite this apparent handicap, Marshall's unrelenting determination meant that his physical inabilities rarely inhibited his active lifestyle or his desire to revisit constantly the rural and remote areas of Australia that inspired much of his work. This same determination is evident in many of the characters who populate Marshall's books, and Marshall is remembered as much for them as for the writing itself.

Born in Noorat, Victoria, on 2 May 1902, Alan William Marshall was the only son of William Bertred and Adameina Henrietta Leister Marshall and brother to Elsie, Margaret, Addie, Hilda, and Doris. William "Billy" Marshall was a stockman from Balranald, and his love of horses and the land was imparted to Alan from birth. Adameina, or Addie, was the daughter of German conductor Franz Leister and Matilda Fitzpatrick, both of whom were new immigrants to Australia. William and Adameina Marshall were married in Melbourne in May 1891 and during their honeymoon traveled by buckboard to their new home in Balranald, 272 miles from Melbourne. In Balranald, Billy established himself as a traveling salesman, and between February of 1892 and 1897 five girls were born to the growing family, with only one dying–baby Addie–of convulsions, at the age of eighteen months. However, Balranald, according to Adameina, was not a suitable home for a growing family, and, concerned for her children's education and spiritual welfare, in 1900 she convinced her husband to move to a small town in western Victoria called Noorat. There the Marshalls established an all-purpose store called "Marshall and Neale," which supplied food, furnishings, and drapery to the local community as well as chaff and oats for the livestock.

Alan, like many children in rural Australia at the turn of the century, was eager to learn to run, ride, and hunt rabbits. Until 1908 he avidly pursued these activities with family members, friends, and his favorite dog, Clyde. In that year Alan's world was dramatically altered when he contracted poliomyelitis, or infantile paralysis, during an epidemic that swept through urban and rural Victoria. As one of the few children in Noorat and the surrounding area to have contracted the disease, Alan was initially treated with fear and concern. In the first of his three autobiographical works, *I Can Jump Puddles,* Marshall explains that "For a few weeks the neighbours drove past our house, looking hurriedly, with a new interest, at the picket fence, the unbroken colts in the stockyard and my tricycle lying on its side by the chaff house. They called their children in earlier, wrapped them more warmly and gazed at them anxiously when they coughed or sneezed."

Poliomyelitis caused the muscles in Alan's legs to shrink, forcing an intolerable tightening of the sinews behind his knees until his feet were drawn up under his

Marshall in 1918, with a hat bearing a band and badge from Stott's Correspondence College in Melbourne (from Harry Marks, I Can Jump Oceans, *1976)*

body and his legs were locked into a kneeling position. These problems were exacerbated by a growing curvature in his spine. Doctors were consulted, and Alan was subjected to often torturous treatments, such as the excruciatingly painful daily straightening of his legs, none of which succeeded in alleviating his condition. Eventually, Alan's parents were forced to send him to a hospital, where he recovered much of his strength and eventually underwent an operation that, among other things, cut the sinews and tendons behind his knees. The primary effects of this operation included the straightening of his legs, the eventual abatement of pain in the limbs, and the concurrent wasting of his right leg until it was unable to bear any weight. However, his left leg, although severely scarred and wasted, was able to bear much of his weight when he used crutches, which enabled him to walk and stand unassisted. Alan spent more than eighteen months in the hospital and returned to Noorat as an oddity, a "cripple."

Olive Dixon, the year before her marriage to Marshall on 30 May 1941 (from Marks, I Can Jump Oceans, *1976)*

I Can Jump Puddles is a testament to Marshall's determination that poliomyelitis would not prevent him from behaving as other children did. He recalls being bewildered by adults who viewed him with pity and called him "courageous." Marshall spends a significant amount of time in his autobiographical works explaining why he felt that he was neither "brave" nor "crippled" by poliomyelitis but rather believed his wasted limbs to be a challenge that required both ingenuity and determination. He had these traits in abundance. With little if any assistance, he learned to move freely through the bush on crutches, where he rediscovered the joy of hunting rabbits with friends. He also learned to ride and swim, skills that were highly prized in Noorat. *I Can Jump Puddles* is essentially a collection of anecdotes that relates each "puddle," or challenge, he undertook to prove his worth not only to others but also to himself.

Marshall, however, was far from defined by his relationship with his disability. Throughout his life he held and espoused strong beliefs, many of which originated in his childhood. In this regard his father remained enormously influential throughout Marshall's life. Beginning when Alan was a child, William Marshall instilled in his son the values of human kindness, honor, and courage and the importance of social solidarity. These traits are evident in many of the characters who populate Marshall's stories, and the moral dilemmas they face are often informed by these values.

Of the other relationships that affected Marshall's work, perhaps the most influential was his relationship with his sister Elsie. As the eldest of the Marshall children, Elsie was often viewed as a mother figure, and throughout their lives Alan and Elsie Marshall remained close. She was often the first to read his plots, typically in letters, before the contents were reconstructed into short stories. Marshall was also an inspiration to Elsie, who with the encouragement of her brother and under the pseudonym Louise McConnell wrote and published in 1969 a children's book titled *Platypus Joe.*

At the age of sixteen Alan won a full scholarship for a correspondence course in accountancy from Stott's Correspondence College in Melbourne. This course offered him the chance of a secure future, and in 1920 Alan, his parents, and Doris moved to Diamond Creek, a small settlement twenty miles from Melbourne, to give Alan better access to the facilities needed for completing his course. After four years of work and study, he was prepared for the final examination in 1922 when he decided not to take it. According to Harry Marks's 1976 biographical work *I Can Jump Oceans: The World of Alan Marshall,* Marshall's refusal to take the exam was based upon a fear that accountancy represented the final blow to his dream of becoming a writer. For Marshall the consequences of this decision were enormous. Without the qualifications that the final examination offered, he had difficulty finding work and was forced to accept a variety of short-term bookkeeping positions so that he could eat while trying to make a living from his writing.

Marshall progressed through many jobs in this period as he encountered prejudice among the workforce and employers. In one instance he was employed by a haberdashery warehouse in Melbourne at half the normal wage because the owner feared that Marshall's physical disability was symptomatic of a mental one. Such ignorance followed Marshall throughout his life. Angered by the unequal relations between employers and workers and the exploitation that was common in many workplaces, Marshall often spoke out and consequently lost many jobs while trying to improve wages and work practices.

In 1924 Marshall again found himself without work, and in his search for employment was offered a job with the Trufood milk factory in Glenormiston

South, a town just outside of Noorat. Accepting the position, Marshall returned to live in Noorat with his sister Hilda and her husband. In August of that same year Marshall was also offered his first writing position, as the founding editor of the *Noorat Guild Gazette*, the local church paper. In the first issue Marshall wrote "The Ladies Page," for which he called himself Aunt Kate. Aunt Kate's column counseled its readership on the value of thrift within the household: "how carelessly we throw away odds and ends when we think they are of no value, but which, with a little care, become assets to the household. . . ." Aunt Kate then proceeded to describe the methods by which empty sardine tins could become "receptacles for toothpicks, hair pins and the like . . ." and jam tins, spittoons for visiting guests. The Aunt Kate persona of mild admonition tempered by gentle encouragement stood Marshall in good stead throughout his life, for he used the same tone when he later wrote an advice column for the magazine *Woman* under the title "Through a Man's Eyes" and then for the Melbourne *Argus* as "Alan Marshall Says."

Also appearing in the first edition of the *Noorat Guild Gazette* was the first installment of "Range Roving Robert: The Bilious Bushranger." This story was Marshall's first piece of published fiction, and it resembled his previous work, which had been rejected by publishers across Melbourne for its sensationalism and sentimentality. In the *Noorat Guild Gazette* Marshall described the story as a "pulsating, throbbing romance of the great South-East. Radiating with love, despair, hope and drink." The story itself was a short, introductory installment, which Marshall intended to make into a weekly serial in which Range Roving Robert and his hapless sidekick Arch kidnapped the beautiful Olive with "scurrilous" intentions. An overdone and farcical short piece, "Range Roving Robert" created a considerable stir in the small community of Noorat, a reaction that eventually resulted in the closure of the *Noorat Guild Gazette* after only one issue.

Restless and disappointed after sixteen months in Noorat, Alan decided to return to Melbourne, where he was again employed in a succession of auditing and bookkeeping jobs. He wrote prolifically during this period and continually submitted manuscripts to publishers and newspapers only to have them repeatedly returned. Writing under the pseudonym Marshall Kennedy, his work during this period continued to reflect his immaturity in the sensationalism of stories such as "The Madness of Mary" and "The Teeth of An Ling Foo." According to Marks, these tales were notable only for their superficiality, and he describes them as "fabrications peopled with exaggerated characters manoeuvered into melodramatic situations. . . ."

Marshall did not achieve success with his writing until 1933. In that year he wrote a story titled "A Little Son," which won the Australian Literature Society's Short Story Award. The second of his stories to achieve success was "The Little Black Bottle," which was published in *The Sun* magazine and described by John Hetherington in *Australians: Nine Profiles* (1961) as "a tense little piece of atmospheric melodrama." Marshall had many melodramatic pieces, such as "By Night," published soon thereafter, often under the pseudonym Marshall Kennedy.

In March 1935 Marshall attended his first meeting of the Writers' League, an organization that influenced him and his writing for the rest of his life. The Writers' League was one of many front groups for the Australian Communist Party and was the recipient of much fervor. At the league meetings writers gathered to share their material and debate the merits of socialism and communism. These meetings were an inspiration to Marshall, who had been raised on many of the beliefs espoused and who increasingly felt compelled to voice in his work the ideals that inspired the league.

In 1937 Marshall completed his first novel, "Factory," which was based around life within a factory. Much of the story was autobiographical, with the setting echoing the Trueform Shoe Company, a past employer of Marshall's. In a letter to Betty Roland, Marshall explains the effect he is hoping to achieve with "Factory" and its overt socialism. "I set off writing this book with the idea of a *factory* as the main character. The factory was to be presented in such a way that every other character was subordinate. I wanted to show the inevitable crash of this ponderous animal devouring and ruining as it did. I wanted all the characters in the book to be but puppets directed by the will of this creature. . . ." In the novel Marshall's writing style is clearly influenced by John dos Passos, who used short sentences to create a specific mood and effect within his work. In "Factory" the effect is somewhat grating, obscuring the strength of Marshall's descriptive discourse and discouraging the reader from empathizing with the characters. However, Marshall successfully captures the idiom of the workers, thus lending authenticity to the book and establishing one of his greatest strengths as an author, his ability to capture the tone and accent of the spoken word in written form. Despite his growing reputation as an author, Marshall was unable to get "Factory" published until 1949, when it appeared under a new title, *How Beautiful Are Thy Feet*.

By the end of the 1930s Marshall had established his reputation as a short-story writer. Much of his work resembled that of Henry Lawson with what Ken Goodwin describes as "inconsequential beginnings and end-

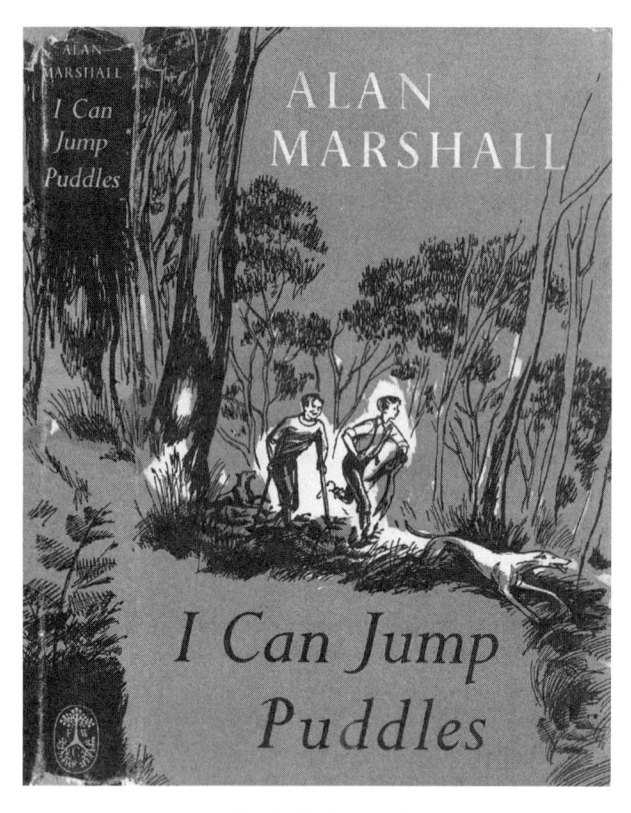

Dust jacket for Marshall's first autobiography, which focuses on his childhood struggle with poliomyelitis (Bruccoli Clark Layman Archives)

ings, but a good deal more optimism and sentimentality than Lawson." Marshall had won many of the literary competitions held throughout Australia, including two Writers' League contests, the Canberra Eisteddford Prize, the Ashton Murphy literary prize of the Queensland Authors and Artists Association, the Australian Literature Society's prize on three occasions, and the Fellowship of Australian Writers (FAW) Short Story Competition. Despite these successes, Marshall was unable to get many of his winning stories published. Similarly, his nonfictional work on the living and working conditions of the poorer classes was overlooked by many of the larger newspapers. It was, however, published by the *Worker's Voice,* a Communist Party newsletter, under the title "Proletarian Picture Book," with Marshall again writing under a pseudonym, Steve Kennedy. Eventually, the series was picked up by the English *Left Review,* which published it as the "Australian Picture Book."

In 1938 Marshall was elected president of the Writers' League in Victoria, and there began a period of increased activism among the members, who often joined the Communist Party in public demonstrations protesting the ineffective approach of the Australian government to the growth of Nazism in Europe. As a consequence, the organization was subjected to increased scrutiny from Prime Minister Joseph Aloysius Lyons's government, and the activities of the league were constantly monitored in the belief that its members were embroiled in a Communist conspiracy. In 1940 the Robert Gordon Menzies government declared the Communist Party to be an illegal organization. It quickly went underground, and the Writers' League became the focal point of increasing pressure from both Communist Party members and the Australian government. In response the Victorian chapter of the Writers' League passed a motion to disband and, under Marshall's guidance, voted itself out of existence.

When Australia joined England in declaring war against Germany and its allies in 1939, a period of increasing frustration began for Marshall. Rarely had his disability prevented him from behaving as he saw fit or attempting physically challenging endeavors, yet the chance for combat and many of the available opportunities to join in the war effort were beyond Marshall's abilities. Consequently, he sought occasions to contribute in ways that were unprecedented. Many of his short stories were published in *The Australian Imperial Forces (A. I. F.) News,* but Marshall believed he could make a more lasting contribution by seeking out the family members of those serving overseas and sending their messages and greetings to the soldiers via the Australian troops' newspaper. The journey, begun in January 1942, was undertaken by Marshall and his new bride, Olive Dixon, whom he had met at a meeting of the Writers' League and married on 30 May 1941; they traveled the rural and remote roads of Australia in search of anecdotes and messages. It ended months later with the separation of the couple and the unhappy news that many of the messages Marshall had collected and published served only to remind dispirited troops of their dead or missing comrades. These experiences formed the basis of Marshall's first published book, *These Are My People* (1944), which also marked the beginning of an important relationship between Marshall and Frank Cheshire, who published ten books by Marshall, including his autobiographical trilogy.

Tell Us About the Turkey, Jo, a collection of short stories which included some of Marshall's best-known work, was completed during the war years but remained unpublished until 1946, when restrictions on paper, caused by war shortages, were lifted. The book was enthusiastically received by readers and critics alike. Today it is often viewed as embodying some of the stylistic tensions typical of the era. Adrian Mitchell, in his essay "Fiction" for *The Oxford History of Australian Literature* (1981), edited by Leonie Kramer, explains that "A common fault [typical to much writing at this time] is that in both serious and comic stories a particular kind of sympathy is not so much generated as expected. For example, both Gavin Casey (*It's Harder for Girls*, 1942) and Alan Marshall (*Tell Us About the Turkey, Jo*, 1946) draw on aprioristic sentiments. Their fiction does not scrutinize the nature and meaning of the experiences presented; rather, they confirm values and patterns of behaviour, and their chief interest for us is in historical terms."

In October of 1945 Marshall was asked by the Royal Australian Air Force (RAAF) to travel to northern Australia as an Army Education lecturer and to write a series of articles in the process, which would be published in *The Herald* (Melbourne) and *The News* (Adelaide). This travel provided Marshall with opportunities to visit for extended periods the indigenous peoples of the Torres Strait Islands; Thursday Island; the Mapoon, Weipa, and Aurukun missions; and Arnhem Land. These experiences influenced Marshall's work, including his next novel, *Ourselves Writ Strange*, published by Cheshire in 1948, and a book of Aboriginal myths Marshall assembled, *People of the Dreamtime*, illustrated by Lesbia Thorpe and published in 1952, also by Cheshire.

Despite an acrimonious separation, Alan and Olive Marshall continued to remain married until finally, in 1957, Olive petitioned for a divorce. Marshall acquiesced, both agreeing that the marriage was irretrievable. In the years following World War II their daughters Hephzibah and Jennifer were born, but Marshall's contact with his children was often sporadic, for his work was increasingly taking him to Asia, where Cathay Pacific Airways provided him with free room, board, and flights in return for the publicity and writing that only Marshall could offer. Stationed in Hong Kong, he spent many months traveling throughout Southeast Asia—his travels leaving him with little time to devote to his wife or children. This situation was exacerbated by Olive's decision, in the hopes of improving Jennifer's health, to move to Brisbane, a location that limited Marshall's contact with his daughters to school holidays.

In 1949 and 1950 Marshall had three books published. The first, *Pull Down the Blind* (1949), was a collection of humorous articles that had originally been published in a variety of newspapers in Melbourne, Brisbane, and Adelaide. The second, *How Beautiful Are Thy Feet*, was Marshall's first novel, written in 1939 and newly rediscovered by Frank Campbell, who recommended the change of title for its publication in 1949. The novel received few reviews, and those it did receive praised it for the passionate emotions evident in the writing but questioned the structure, which suggested, according to John Morrison in *Meanjin* (Autumn 1950), "that Marshall was so excited about his raw material that he could not wait to assimilate it. . . ." Shortly thereafter, Marshall's more humorous articles were collected into a book called *Bumping into Friends* (1950). With a similar tone and many of the same themes as its predecessor, *Bumping into Friends* was received with some criticism. Kylie Tennant, for example, reviewing *Bumping into Friends* for *Meanjin* (September 1961), saw it as a collection of "slight sketches dragged from a half a dozen newspapers, too farcical to give any indication of [Marshall's] real powers as a short story writer. In these snippety bits he is writing in hobbles."

In 1953 Marshall received a £600 Commonwealth Literary Fund Fellowship to support himself while writing the story of his youth, *I Can Jump Puddles*. The book is constructed from a plethora of small incidents, each chapter an anecdote that is melded into the broader themes of the book, which primarily concern Marshall's self-concept and his relationship with his disability. Together the anecdotes form a moving, if not necessarily chronological, account of Marshall's childhood. In the Preface to *I Can Jump Puddles* he writes,

> I wanted to do much more than record the experiences of a little boy faced with the problem of his crutches; I wanted to give a picture of a period that has passed. . . .
>
> To give a picture of life at that time, I have sometimes altered scenes, made composite characters when this was necessary, changed time sequences to help the continuity and introduced dialogue. . . .
>
> A book of this nature demands a treatment that facts do not always supply; the truth it seeks to establish can only be revealed with the help of imagination.

I Can Jump Puddles was praised by many critics, including Vance Palmer, who claimed in a review for *Meanjin* (December 1955) that it was a "warm and human book" that epitomized Marshall's "mastery of his craft." Today *I Can Jump Puddles* stands as, arguably, the best of Marshall's work, for it embodies his skill in constructing landscapes, spaces, and people with a complex combination of humor, sympathy, and pathos. *I Can Jump Puddles* has sold more than three million copies and has been translated into many languages, its popularity most marked in the Eastern bloc countries of East Germany, Rumania, Czechoslovakia, and the Union of Soviet Socialist Republics (U.S.S.R.). It has been made into a successful Czechoslovakian movie (1970) by director Karel Kachyna and nine fifty-minute television episodes by the Australian Broadcasting Corporation (ABC) in 1980. Marshall's autobiographical trilogy was completed with *This Is the Grass* in 1962 and *In Mine Own Heart* in 1963. Neither of these books achieved the success of *I Can Jump Puddles*.

Marshall at Government House in Melbourne, where he received the Order of the British Empire (OBE) in 1972 (from Marks, I Can Jump Oceans, *1976)*

Between 1956 and 1963 Marshall undertook a variety of projects–including another collection of his short stories, *How's Andy Going?* (1956); his last two autobiographical works; and *The Gay Provider, the Myer Story,* published in 1961. *The Gay Provider* detailed the history of the Myer Emporium, a large store situated in central Melbourne. Despite his attempts to create a dramatic and exciting history of the store, the nature of the material almost ensured that *The Gay Provider* was dry and descriptive–a situation that was only exacerbated by an editorial committee, which, according to Marks, altered the emphasis of the book from a text concerned with "little people" to one that stressed the importance of the directors.

In 1964 Marshall was invited to visit the U.S.S.R. as a guest of the Union of Soviet Writers, and in 1965 he was offered a position on the delegation that was to attend the International Writers Meeting in the German Democratic Republic. Both occasions offered Marshall an opportunity to travel with his daughters and to enjoy the recognition that accompanied his name and works in the Communist countries. In Berlin, however, Marshall discovered that the nerves in his legs were dying, making walking–even on crutches–a difficult and painful experience. On his return to Australia, he was hospitalized, and his right leg was amputated.

In 1969 Marshall's children's book *Whispering in the Wind* was published. Written as a fantastic fairy tale with an Australian theme, the story concerns Peter's attempts to find a beautiful princess, accompanied only by his horse, Moonlight; his stockwhip, Thunderbolt; and a leather bag containing a magic leaf. On his adventures Peter encounters Greyfur, a kangaroo with a bottomless pouch, who becomes his traveling companion, and together they find Lowana and free her from her tower prison. In the story Marshall draws on Australian mythology to construct characters such as Greyfur and the bunyip. In 1972 Marshall completed another children's book, *Fight for Life,* in which Bill, lost in the bush, survives a bushfire and hunger to discover a billy (kettle) full of gold in an old mining camp.

In 1972 Marshall was awarded the Order of the British Empire (OBE) for "services to the physically handicapped," an honorary Doctor of Laws degree by the University of Melbourne, and in 1977 the Soviet Order of Friendship. Marshall continued to write and collaborate on various projects until the late 1970s, and many collections of his short stories were published from the 1970s until his death—*Short Stories* (1973), *The Complete Stories of Alan Marshall* (1977), *His Best Stories* (1980), and *Alan Marshall's Battlers* (1983). In 1972 Marshall collaborated with Sreten Bozic in the production of another book on Australian indigenous mythology, *Aboriginal Myths*, and in 1975 *Hammers over the Anvil* was published, which was later made into an Australian television series.

Alan Marshall died on 21 January 1984, and while he will probably remain best known for his autobiographical work *I Can Jump Puddles,* his achievements as an author of short stories, newspaper articles, advice columns, history books, and travelogues cannot be overlooked. He stands as an author who readily adapted to a wide breadth of literary forms and genres, constantly captured the colloquial idiom, demonstrated through word and trait a belief in social solidarity, and imparted his love of rural and remote Australia to a worldwide audience. The Victorian Premier's Literary Award for children's literature bore the name of Alan Marshall from 1988 through 1995. Ruth Park wrote of Marshall and his work in *National Times* in October 1973:

> To me, even when they work in the city, his people are country-men, basically quiet, unaffected but not guileless, with the Australian countryman's innate freedom from conditioning to authority. These people concede that Life is a bastard, but they are never bitter. The profoundly jocund spirit of the working class Australian is always there to sustain them.

Bibliography:

Martin Duwell, Marianne Ehrhardt, and Carol Hethrington, eds., *The ALS Guide to Australian Writers: A Bibliography 1963-1995* (St. Lucia: University of Queensland Press, 1997), pp. 282-284.

Biography:

Harry Marks, *I Can Jump Oceans: The World of Alan Marshall* (Melbourne: Nelson, 1976).

References:

Jack Beasley, "Gurrawilla the Song Maker: Alan Marshall: Writer Versus Cult Figure," in his *Red Letter Days: Notes from Inside an Era* (Sydney: Australasian Book Society, 1979), pp. 1-52;

John Colmer, "Alan Marshall's Autobiographical Trilogy," in his *Australian Autobiography: The Personal Quest* (Melbourne: Oxford University Press, 1989), pp. 16-31;

John Hetherington, *Australians: Nine Profiles* (Melbourne: Cheshire, 1961);

Jack Lindsay, "A Triumph Over Adversity: Comments On Alan Marshall's Writing," *Meanjin,* 28 (Summer 1969): 437-445;

John McLaren, "Discontinuous Autobiography: Some Work of Alan Marshall and Bruce Beaver," *Autobiographical and Biographical Writing in the Commonwealth,* edited by Doireann MacDermott (Sadabell, Barcelona: Editorial AUSA, 1984), pp. 147-151;

John Morrison, *The Happy Warrior* (Fairfield, Vic.: Pascoe Publishing, 1987);

John White, *Alan Marshall and the Victorian Writers' League* (Kuranda, Qld.: Rams Skull Press, 1987).

Papers:

The National Library of Australia holds Alan Marshall's papers in files MS 2741 and MS 3992.

David Martin
(22 December 1915 – 1 July 1997)

John McLaren
Victoria University

BOOKS: *Battlefields and Girls: Poems* (Glasgow: MacLellan, 1942);

Trident, by Martin, John Manifold, and Hubert Nicholson (London: Fore, 1944);

The Shepherd and the Hunter (London: Wingate, 1946);

Tiger Bay (London: Martin & Reid, 1946);

The Shoes Men Walk In (London: Pilot Press, 1946);

The Stones of Bombay (London & New York: Wingate, 1950);

From Life: Selected Poems (Sydney: Current Book Distributors, 1953);

Rob the Robber: His Life and Vindication, as Spinifex (Melbourne: Joseph Waters, 1954);

Poems of David Martin, 1938–1958 (Sydney: Edwards & Shaw, 1958);

Spiegel the Cat: A Story-Poem by David Martin Based on a Tale by Gottfried Keller (Melbourne: Cheshire, 1961; New York: Potter, 1971);

The Young Wife (London: Macmillan, 1962; Melbourne: Sun Books, 1966);

Television Tension Programmes (Melbourne: Australian Broadcasting Control Board, 1963);

The Hero of Too (Melbourne: Cassell, 1965); republished as *The Hero of the Town* (New York: Morrow, 1965);

The Gift: Poems 1959–1965 (Brisbane: Jacaranda, 1966);

The King Between (Melbourne: Cassell, 1966); republished as *The Littlest Neutral* (New York: Crown, 1966);

The Idealist (Melbourne: Jacaranda, 1968);

Where a Man Belongs (Melbourne: Cassell, 1969);

On the Road to Sydney (Melbourne: Nelson, 1970);

Hughie (Melbourne: Macmillan, 1971; New York: St. Martin's Press, 1971);

Frank and Francesca (Melbourne: Nelson, 1972);

Gary (North Melbourne, Vic.: Casssell, 1972);

The Chinese Boy (Hornsby, N.S.W.: Hodder & Stoughton, 1973);

The Cabby's Daughter (Sydney: Hodder & Stoughton, 1974);

David Martin (from John Hetherington, Forty-Two Faces, 1946)

Mister P and His Remarkable Flight (Sydney: Hodder & Stoughton, 1975);

The Devilish Mystery of the Flying Mum (West Melbourne, Vic.: Nelson, 1977);

The Mermaid Attack (Collingwood, Vic.: Outback Press, 1978);

The Man in the Red Turban (Richmond, Vic.: Hutchinson, 1978);

I Rhyme My Time (Milton, Qld.: Jacaranda, 1980);

Foreigners (Adelaide: Rigby, 1981);

Peppino Turns His Luck (Adelaide: Rigby, 1982);

Peppino (Richmond, Vic.: Hutchinson, 1983);

Armed Neutrality for Australia (Blackburn, Vic.: Dove, 1984);

The Girl Who Didn't Know Kelly (Melbourne: Hutchinson, 1985);

Fox on My Door: A Journey through My Life (Blackburn, Vic.: Collins Dove, 1987);

The Kitten Who Wouldn't Purr, by Martin and Mark Payne (South Melbourne, Vic.: Macmillan, 1987),

Clowning Sim (Blackburn, Vic.: Collins Dove, 1988);

My Strange Friend (Chippendale, N.S.W.: Pan Macmillan, 1991);

David Martin's Beechworth Book: Poems (Melbourne: Lovell, 1993);

The Young Wife: A Play (Melbourne: Privately printed, n.d.).

OTHER: *Rhyme and Reason,* edited by Martin (London: Fore, 1944);

New World, New Songs: A Selection of Poems from the Left, edited by Martin (Sydney: Current Book Distributors, 1955);

Psychological Effects of the "Western Film," in *A Study of Television Viewing,* by Martin and F. E. Emery (Melbourne: University of Melbourne, 1957);

"Apologia without Apology," *Meanjin,* 20, no. 1 (1987): 25–31.

Although generally recognized as an Australian writer, David Martin published his first work in Germany, and he was recognized in England long before he came to Australia. His work covers the whole range of literary genres and is consistently marked by an interest in the ethical, philosophical, and political issues he brought with him from his European background.

David Martin was born Ludwig Desinyi in Budapest, Hungary, on 22 December 1915. He grew up in Germany, to which his family moved at the end of World War I. His father had been an officer in the Austro-Hungarian army and came from a family of Jews with a scattering of rabbis but thoroughly assimilated into European and, particularly, German culture. Martin's mother died when he was two, and he was brought up by his stepmother, Sonia. He claimed that the formative influences on his childhood were his rivalry with his father for Sonia's affections and his bond with his twin brother, Rudoph, or Rudi. But, although his family was not formally religious, Martin was deeply affected by Judaism and, later, Zionism. Sixteen members of his family failed to escape from Europe and were driven to their deaths or slaughtered by the Nazis.

Martin was educated in schools in Germany and published his first poems in German. As German democracy began to falter in the early years of the Great Depression, and disorder and anti-Semitism spread through the country, Martin drifted through the radical groups to the left of the democratic parties, eventually joining the Communist League of Youth, selling its party publications and distributing its pamphlets. When the Communist Party was suppressed after the Reichstag fire in 1932, Martin wrote and distributed his own news sheet until the danger became too great. Martin–who declared that he loved Germany, its poets, and its songs–had his country taken from him. He fled first to Holland, where he spent a year learning practical horticulture in a Zionist training camp. He lived for a time in Hungary, then worked in kibbutzes in Palestine, and eventually joined the International Brigade in Spain. When his poor eyesight kept him out of the infantry, he was transferred to the Medical Service and worked in the front line and in the hospitals. As the republic collapsed in Spain, he made his way through France and Belgium to Britain, where he worked for a time in his father's fashion-goods business, briefly as an agricultural laborer, and even more briefly as a contracting gardener. At this time he recognized he would never return to Germany, fell in love with the idea of England, and began to write in English, although, until Britain declared war, he was in constant fear of instant deportation to almost certain death. His love affair with the English language began in 1939 when the audience at a meeting in honor of members of the International Brigade joined their voices in a folk song. Having no English past to live down, he immersed himself in traditional English verse, finding in it a bridge from German romanticism. As a political man he wanted to be heard immediately where he was. His earliest poems in English are sometimes linguistically awkward, but the best, such as "Blinded in Spain," draw on direct experience with a reticence that gives them strength. By the time he published his first collection, *Battlefields and Girls: Poems* (1942), Martin was writing poems such as "Lament for the Gordons," which uses the traditional form of a lament for the dead to make a powerful statement of revulsion at war and the politics of capitalism. This book also includes the long poem "Oranje," his meditation on his time in Holland, which culminates with the shadow of death that the Nazis have cast over this land, only to finish with the certain hope that once more "children's voices will ring in Amsterdam / For Rembrandt's children will live forever." The poem brings together the sweep of European achievement concentrated in his experience of one

Richenda Powell in 1940, the year before her marriage to Martin (from Martin, My Strange Friend, *1993)*

specific country, his revulsion at tyranny and brutality, and the trust in the human spirit that he had learned from the English romantics. The dust jacket carried a quotation by the Scots nationalist poet Hugh McDiarmid commending the collection for its "moving anti-fascist poems naturally arising from the war. . . ."

On 17 July 1941 Martin married Richenda Powell, daughter of an Anglican clergyman and descendant of the Quaker prison reformer Elizabeth Fry. His wife became his confidante, supporter, collaborator, and critic, and, despite his occasional affairs, they remained married for the rest of his life. Immediately after their marriage he joined *The Daily Express* (Glasgow) as a translator. When Hungary entered the war, the Martins became enemy aliens, but David Martin was later cleared and worked for the British Broadcasting Company (BBC), before becoming literary editor of *Reynolds News* (London). For the convenience of his readers, he had changed his name to the English David Martin. Apart from his poetry and journalism, Martin produced three major works from his time in England.

The play *The Shepherd and the Hunter* (published in 1946) was directed by Ted Willis at the Unity Theatre in April 1946. Martin recalls in *My Strange Friend* (1991) that the play was well constructed but overwritten. Set in postwar Palestine, it dramatizes the heroism of the Jewish settlers and the tragedy of the Arabs. Its subject, the idealist who is driven to a violence he abhors and that eventually destroys him as he searches for a meaning to life that cannot be found within history, became a continuing theme in Martin's work. The play received favorable reviews but was killed by lack of support from the Communist Party, which believed it was Zionist and lacked a positive message. The novel *Tiger Bay* (1946), which drew on Martin's Welsh experience, was first serialized in *Reynolds News*. It dealt with the love for a Somali sailor of a girl who had drifted from the valleys to the city. The play was later adapted for a successful movie that neither acknowledged Martin as author nor paid him any royalties. The third book, *The Shoes Men Walk In* (1946), was a collection of stories based on personal experience in prewar Europe,

Palestine, Spain, and wartime England. Several of the stories give space and shape to incidents that later reappear in his autobiography. All are marked by a sense of unmediated realism, offering no political message except for an admiration for human courage and fellowship, and an amusement at human perversity. The final story, "The Patriot," tells of an exile returning to Germany who finds himself at home by rediscovering his language.

By the end of the war Martin was again getting restless. He was tired of England, and when an opportunity came, he took a job in India as correspondent for the *Daily Express* (London), with no salary but with payment for his reports that the paper published. As he later wrote, a newspaperman who cannot find enough to report from Bombay has missed his profession. As a novelist, he found India fascinating. The writer, he frequently remarked in conversation, needs only to stand on a street corner in India to see a thousand stories go past.

The book that came from his first Indian experience was *The Stones of Bombay*, published in 1950. This novel is both realistic and political. It is set in the time immediately after the bloody partition of India and Pakistan and the assassination of the veteran independence leader, Mahatma Gandhi. The main subject of the book is Bombay [now Mumbai] itself: "There were people, people everywhere. The precincts of the station were white with them, the broad avenue that led up to the sea-front past expensive restaurants, and the square itself, which had taken on the appearance of a circus at the close of a performance when spectators invade the ring." This city is seen mainly through the eyes of Shankar, who enters it as a young refugee from Pakistan and comes to love it as he finds work and acceptance within a Communist Party whose communal practice transcends the divisions of class and of ethnic and religious communalism: "Work had made him one with his people where his sufferings had only isolated him from them. This was a ruthless and cruel town but also a passionate one that was impatient at the restraints of the past, breaking them down and plunging forward over the ruins of past lives."

From India, the Martins moved in 1949 to Australia, where for some years Martin lived in poverty, supported by Richenda's teaching, and concentrated in his writing on poetry and journalism. He joined the Communist Party—he had briefly been a member of a cell in Germany—and became associated with the Realist Writers Group. He later insisted that his poetry at this time was political but that he had always gone beyond social realism. During his first year he appears to have written an agitprop play, "Birthday of a Miner," in connection with the 1949 miners' strike. He began his long association with *The Hindu* (Madras), writing for it on both public affairs and sport—including reports on the Melbourne Olympic Games in 1956. For a time he was Sydney editor of the *Australian Jewish News,* and he contributed to *The Morning Herald* (Sydney). The Martins then moved to Putty, an isolated hamlet northwest of Sydney, where Richenda was the sole schoolteacher. Putty was a good introduction to Australia. The Martins lived in two small bare rooms but were enchanted and amazed by the bush and its birds, whose irreverence matched that of the bush children. They found the austerity of their conditions and the indifference of the parents hard to take and were glad to move to Boronia, in the foothills beyond Melbourne, at the end of 1950. The experience, however, gave Martin lasting images of Australia and its people, including the bushman who appeared as Jack Underwood of Putty Hill in *The Bulletin* (Sydney) of 23 April 1952, and in many guises in *The Hero of Too* (1965). The heat and exhausted dreaming of "Bush Christmas," from the 1958 collection *Poems of David Martin, 1938–1958,* also became a recurrent image of Martin's amused and oftentimes impatient affection for Australia, a nation, unlike Europe or India, not too enmeshed in tradition or excited by ceremony. He also completed a long narrative poem, *Spiegel the Cat: A Story-Poem by David Martin Based on a Tale by Gottfried Keller* (1961); the Swiss writer's work was a prose tale. Martin claimed that the poem was romantic, lacking the desire for change that marked his political work. But its admiration for the cheeky, rule-breaking outsider was probably closer to the source of his revolutionary politics than identity with the masses. Martin was passionate about justice but suspicious of humanity at large and drawn to the spirited individuals who appear in both his adult and his children's novels.

While India opened Martin to its stories, Australia hid them beneath an apparent emptiness. He was intrigued by its "paradox of courage that the art of the Australians was tragic but their outlook hopeful." For almost his first ten years in the country, he found its dramas hidden and wrote only poetry. Under the pen name "Spinifex" he now wrote the long satirical poem *Rob the Robber: His Life and Vindication* (1954), a fantastical version of history that mocks the then-prime minister of Australia, Robert Menzies, and his colleagues in a style of verse that echoes and anticipates *Spiegel the Cat,* but its characters lack the cat's villainous charm.

Despite his fascination with Australia, Martin was restless during his time at Boronia, spending a lot of time on Communist Party work but feeling remote from the masses who, he believed, gave his writing its strength. He traveled widely, reading his poems to workers in their workplaces, and was from the begin-

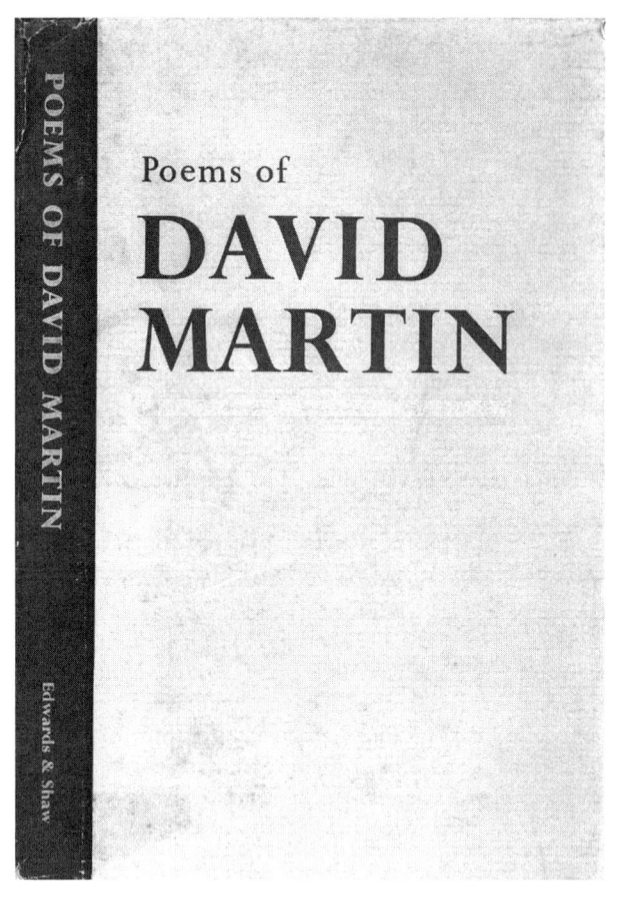

Dust jacket for Martin's 1958 book, poems written in England and Australia over two decades (Bruccoli Clark Layman Archives)

ning associated with the journals *The Realist Writer* and its successor, *Overland;* he also published stories in *Meanjin* and *Overland*. He edited a collection, *New World, New Songs: A Selection of Poems from the Left* (1955), and published *From Life: Selected Poems* (1953), a collection of his own poems, mostly written in Australia. The latter book attracted generally favorable reviews but was attacked in the 1 May 1954 edition of *The Morning Herald* (Sydney) by the critic A. D. Hope. Hope accurately identified Martin as belonging to the school that believed that the basic function of literature was "not creation but activation."

In 1955 Martin retreated from his isolation and found a home in Coburg, near Melbourne, where he enjoyed a time of creativity in both fiction and prose essays. *Poems of David Martin, 1938–1958,* published in 1958, is almost a farewell to the time he had spent hitherto as a poet in English. Of its selection, which covers the years from his arrival in England, almost half was written in Australia. Although some of the political poems make a direct intervention in such matters as the deaths of coal miners or the execution of convicted spies Julius and Ethel Rosenberg, more poems direct their attention to the outcasts of Australian history–Aborigines, convicts, and Chinese miners. Others of the collection are love poems for Richenda or others, poems of hope for a new generation, and moving elegies. In these poems Martin seems to be moving toward a humanism broader than could be contained by Marxism. He was in Europe in 1956 when his sister died in London and the Soviet Union invaded Hungary. Desolated by the knowledge that his hopes of Communism had been betrayed for years by Joseph Stalin and now by Nikita Khrushchev, Martin fought with his loyalty to the party. There was also domestic discord, as Richenda insisted that the ill reports of Communist practice were all capitalist distortions. Finally, in 1958, after his reports on a visit to Vietnam had run afoul of the Communist Party leadership, Martin resigned. But he continued to look for a party, an organization, or a leader that could take its place. As he wrote to Stephen Murray-Smith: "I am not, and never will, simply quit fighting [sic]. I am fighting now. . . . To me it appears not that I have just become tired of the struggle but that the struggle is always also a personal thing and that I have to discover again my true place in it."

Martin wrote his four most important novels during his years in Coburg. He also joined with many other poets, united only by friendship and geography, in a group that insisted that in a time of acrimony the work still mattered. They published the joint collection *Eight by Eight* in 1963. In 1968 Martin published *The Idealist,* a long narrative poem about a clergyman who confounds authority by going on a hunger strike to bring attention to the elderly. He also wrote the two essays– "Among the Bones" and "Three Realists in Search of Reality" (*Meanjin,* 18, 1959)–that established him irrevocably, and despite his later protests, among the realists and in opposition to the modernists. The first of these essays is an attack on Patrick White and those novelists who followed him in supposedly abandoning realism in search of the meaningful symbol. The second essay–on the work of Eric Lambert, Frank Hardy, and Judah Waten–uses the truthful rendering of reality as the measure of literary value. Yet, in his own fiction Martin goes beyond the depiction of reality, or even the typical example, to explore his almost metaphysical concerns with the conflicts between insider and outsider, between reason and feeling, between the destructive and creative aspects of love, and above all, with the need to belong.

During this time he began his collaboration with Cliff Green, with whom he discussed beforehand and in detail the plot of each intended novel. This plotting enabled him to anticipate the shape and balance of his novels and to know his characters before he began writing. Yet, although the strong plots enabled him to bring together the diverse strands of his novels, they sometimes lead also to a sense of rigidity, a sense that the stories and characters were being moved to preordained ends. One reason for the success of *The Young Wife* (1962) is that, during the writing, he allowed his feelings for the characters to reverse the action he believed their logic demanded.

In *The Young Wife,* the first of his major novels, the wife herself becomes the image of life in the new land breaking away from old patterns to realize new potential. This work was also the first major novel to deal with the postwar immigrant culture of Australia. Set within the Greek community of Melbourne, it has the elements of a modern Greek tragedy. Martin himself felt that it was a report from a halfway house on his journey to full assimilation in Australia. Certainly, his European background enables him to convey the cultural problems of migrants, simultaneously trying to get on with a new life and to reconstruct the old, through the institutions of the church, politics, and soccer. The characters can also be understood as projections of his own self-doubts as he moves away from the Communist Party and revolutionary socialism and at the same time struggles with his lasting obsession with the need of male and female for mutual possession. The migrant milieu also gives all of the characters the quality of outsiders observing each other from positions inside their own obsessions.

Both the outsider-insider and the migrant themes are continued in *The Hero of Too,* except that this time the narrator rather than his subjects is the outsider. The novel expresses a contentment he has found with life in Australia, but at the same time he allows himself the luxury of commenting sardonically on its ways from the point of view of the resident outsider. The novel is set in the town of Tooramit, or Too, as its inhabitants, with their Australian economy of vocalization, prefer to call it. The town is divided by class and age, but not even its marginal inhabitants, around whom the action revolves, are really outsiders. On the contrary, they hold the clues to the history that another apparent outsider, Steve Turner, is seeking. Turner may come as an outsider, but he is accepted by the generality of the town when he becomes a football hero and by the establishment when he pairs off, after many misunderstandings, with the doctor's daughter.

The book is built on an affectionate, if satirical, portrait of a bush town. Martin contrasts the town—surrounded on three sides by flat plains, but with leafy streets and spacious housing, except in its poorer quarter, and dominated by a tree-lined creek, a close-by mass of mountains, and two huge wheat silos—with the landscapes of Europe. In Tooramit there is an air of impermanence; in Europe the massive keeps and winding alleys reach back to the distant past. But these, he says, are memorials to death, while Tooramit, a town with no history, has a beauty that "derives from things that have to do with life and not with mouldering death." If, in the course of the novel, the town proves to have all the faults of society, it also has an enduring decency and tolerance that finally discovers ways of accepting those it has excluded from honor and even of starting to understand the place of the Chinese miners and the dispossessed Aborigines in its past.

The novel is also in part a satire on popular Australian legend. The eponymous hero, Dick Grogan, is a famed bushranger who turns out to have been not only a coward but also a homosexual. The strength of the novel comes from its portrayal of the bushranger, his associates and enemies, and their successors, including the night soil man and the shire president. Its weakness is in the carefully plotted romantic entanglements that bring them all together. These relationships thematically embody Martin's constant concern with the conflict between reason and romance, between the head and the heart. But although his overt message is that people should follow their feelings, the intellectual care with which he portrays passion undermines his ostensible purpose. The narrator overcomes the narrative.

His next novel, *The King Between,* published in Melbourne in 1966 and also in New York as *The Littlest Neutral* the same year, and a further collection of poems, *The Gift: Poems 1959–1965* (1966), were the products of a further trip to Southeast Asia, particularly Indochina, and of his feelings about the war in Vietnam. The hero of the novel, King Anabol, rules over the tiny state of Laodia, sandwiched between American-controlled territory and China. Just as the king's amatory desires are confused by his difficulties with his prostate, his attempts to keep his country neutral and save it from the devastation of war are undermined by his powerlessness in the midst of global politics and by his own skepticism, bordering on cynicism, about ideologues, politicians, and his own countrymen. His steady pursuit of his limited aim makes him an outsider amid the intrigues that surround him. Yet, he is, as Martin says, a true hero, and he does save his country, at least for the time. The easy tone of the book belies its seriousness, making it one of Martin's most satisfying, as well as one of the more insightful books about power politics in Asia. Its theme also anticipates the analytic and polemical study, *Armed Neutrality for Australia* (1984), and the consequent political campaign that later occupied Martin.

In 1967 the Martins went to Europe for two years, a trip that is foreshadowed in the final novel of this period, *Where a Man Belongs* (1969), which he finished revising in Malta. Although he insisted the novel was not autobiographical, it incorporates many of the crucial fragments of his life that he later revisits in *My Strange Friend*.

Where a Man Belongs tells the story of Max, a German-born writer living in Australia, and Paul, a bookkeeper he assists in the epistolary courtship of a German widow, Gudrun. Max, the narrator, accompanies Paul back to Germany to meet the widow and bring the affair to its consummation, but instead the journey brings mental turmoil and death to the lovers. The three characters are forced to confront their past and the guilt and hatred that still survive from the roles they played in two world wars and the Holocaust. Gudrun kills herself; Paul returns to Australia with Max, only to die on his arrival. Max scatters Paul's ashes in the Australian bush. The bush is the place where they both belong. The old world, apparently, has nothing to offer. The book can be read as Martin's attempt to expiate the horrors of Nazism and to come to terms with the Germany that had betrayed his ancestral culture, murdered most of his family, and made him a lifelong wanderer. In searching for a place where he belongs, Martin uses Freud rather than Marx. Max and Paul, although presented as German Jew and Australian gentile, are projections of Martin's persona and are used as an excuse for the debates over the nature of love, women, and fathers that constitute much of the text. Yet, if the novel often seems too willed, and if it fails to enlist the reader's interest in any of its characters, at its best it evokes a sense of place that transcends its intellectual problems.

The journey to Europe with Richenda was the same quest on which Martin had sent his narrator, a search for an answer to the question of where he belonged. Instead of an answer, he found himself witnessing the militarism of Germany, the silent and unrealized power of the Russian land and people, and finally the joy of the Prague spring when Aleksandr Dubček seemed to be making real the promise of Communism with a human soul. This optimism was then succeeded by the desolation of another Russian invasion and the extinction of hope. If there was one thing Martin learned from this experience, it was that "not only Germans ride uninvited into other peoples' countries." The Martins retreated to Italy, where during a perfect autumn Martin wrote his first book for children, *Hughie*, published in 1971, the story of an Aboriginal boy and his friendship across the color line. The story has no contrived happy ending, but it offers hope in the fact of friendship.

Back in Australia, Martin fell into depression. Assaulted by the emptiness and vulgarity of Australia, he at the same time believed in its people and in their country without history. He published in the Melbourne *Age* an essay on walking around Coburg, finding himself thoroughly at home, but still feeling restless. He set off from Melbourne to hitchhike to Sydney, a further journey in search of himself and of a place where he could belong. He wrote of this experience in *On the Road to Sydney* (1970), in which he describes finding himself in his affection for the eccentric characters he met along the way; he also wrote of his ambivalence about the places, particularly Canberra. Then in 1972 Martin moved to Beechworth, a country town of Victoria that in many ways resembled the Tooramit of his earlier imagination. From Beechworth he continued to contribute essays to *Meanjin* and the Sydney Jewish quarterly, *The Bridge*, and to write a regular column, "Hinterland," on literature, society, and politics for the journal *Overland*. In Beechworth also he wrote the books for children that occupied the last stage of his career.

These works have an ease that he rarely achieved in his fiction for adults. Their central characters tend to be outsiders, either by nature, as the boy in *Mister P and His Remarkable Flight* (1975), which was commended for the Australian Book Council Award; by family circumstance, as the girl in *The Cabby's Daughter* (1974); or by racial background, as the central characters of *The Chinese Boy* (1973) and *The Man in the Red Turban* (1978). Martin wrote plain tales for children, and he refused to be didactic or to engage in symbolism but instead showed his characters rising above their circumstances, if not to defeat them, at least to learn to live with them and to gain the respect of others. If his children's fiction has a theme, it is the need to enjoy difference and to extend justice to everyone.

In 1991 Martin published his autobiography, *My Strange Friend*. It gains much of its importance from the story it tells of his life, from the comfort of his early life, through the growing threat of Nazism and the restlessness that drove him from country to country, and finally to the ambivalent measure of acceptance he found for Australia, and the account of his developing beliefs and their expression in his writing. In certain ways it is the most satisfying of his works. His poetry tends toward the didactic, and can be heavy-handed. His adult fiction was always carefully plotted beforehand. His children's fiction is freer, as his characters discover themselves through action. His nonfictional prose reportage has this same freedom, as he discovers himself through writing and allows others to reveal themselves in their words spoken to him. These qualities had appeared in many of his essays and in *On the Road to Sydney*. The autobiography allowed him to develop them to the fullest. But, for all its easy narrative, it remains a haunted book—haunted by the memories of the history Martin had lived; of the Holocaust that claimed so many of his family; the evil of Stalin, who slaughtered millions and destroyed the hopes of many more; the malevolence of the lesser tyrants, such as Pol Pot; and the possibilities of a nuclear holocaust still to come.

The "friend" of the title is the self described by the writer as narrator. This alter ego emerges as cranky, inconsistent, unsociable, yet courageous in his pursuit of the single aim of writing in order to resolve the contradictions of a humanity capable of love and brutality, whose inspiring visions so easily turn to destruction. At the end of his narrative he is an atheist humble and inspired before the simple wonders of nature, and a Marxist in analysis but a pragmatist in politics, who believes that the people of Beechworth have passed nearly as far on the road to happiness as is possible. They are part of an Australia where people have learned to confront loneliness without a shudder and even the Christians are agnostics. He accepts this stoicism as a gift and looks forward to lying with Richenda in the Beechworth cemetery, near the graves of the Indian hawkers whose lives partly went into *The Man in the Red Turban*.

The autobiography was not Martin's last work. Two years later, in 1993, *David Martin's Beechworth Book: Poems* appeared, illustrated by students from Beechworth Secondary College. The author in his note tells readers "I love Beechworth" and promises that the poems in the book tell some of the strange stories of the town. The stories range from the ghosts that haunt the places where thirty pubs once stood to the lady who tends the ashes of a deceased golfer and the post-office clock that ceased to chime. They breathe the sociability and the delight in his fellows, particularly his fellow townsfolk, that his autobiography claims he lacked.

The last two years of Martin's life were difficult, as his diabetes worsened and he was forced to go into a hospital, able to communicate only with difficulty. In 1996 he was granted an Emeritus Fellowship from the Literature Board of the Australia Council. David Martin died a year later, on 1 July 1997, and was buried in the grave he and Richenda had chosen. Richenda died the following year.

Although Martin disliked being characterized as one of the social realists of Australia, he probably belongs in that category. He differs from contemporary realists such as Frank Hardy and Judah Waten by a greater skepticism about society and greater optimism about individuals, and by a cosmopolitan outlook that extended beyond the confines of any single nation. His works that will probably last best are his less didactic novels, his children's books, and his autobiographical writings.

References:

Margaret Dunkle, "David Martin: Children's Champion," *Overland*, 144 (Spring 1996): 57–58;

Alan Gardiner, "Pushed into the Bourgeois Camp: David Martin and the CPA," *Overland*, 142 (Autumn 1996): 27–30;

Nancy Keesing, "Where Does a Man Belong? David Martin and His Work," *Overland*, 63 (Autumn 1976): 10–15;

Agnes Nieuwenhuizen, *No Kidding: Top Writers for Young People Talk About Their Work* (Sydney: Macmillan, 1991), pp. 163–192;

A. A. Phillips, "The Writings of David Martin," *Meanjin*, 20, no. 1 (1987): 15–25.

Papers:

The papers of David Martin are housed in the National Library of Australia, Canberra, MS 6885.

James McAuley
(12 October 1917 – 15 October 1976)

Michael Ackland
Monash University

BOOKS: *The Darkening Ecliptic,* by McAuley and Harold Stewart as Ern Malley (Melbourne: Reed & Harris, 1944); republished as *The Poems of Ern Malley* (Melbourne: Reed & Harris, 1961);

Under Aldebaran (Melbourne: Melbourne University Press, 1946);

A Vision of Ceremony (Sydney: Angus & Robertson, 1956);

We Offer the Mass, text by McAuley, music by Richard Connolly (Sydney: Living Parish Series, 1959);

The End of Modernity: Essays on Literature, Art and Culture (Sydney: Angus & Robertson, 1959);

C. J. Brennan (Melbourne: Oxford University Press, 1963);

Hymns for the Year of Grace, text by McAuley, music by Connolly (Sydney: Living Parish Series, 1963);

The Six Days of Creation, illustrated by Leonard French (Adelaide: Australian Letters, 1963);

James McAuley (Sydney: Angus & Robertson, 1963);

Edmund Spenser and George Eliot: A Critical Excursion (Hobart: University of Tasmania, 1963);

Captain Quiros (Sydney: Angus & Robertson, 1964);

A Primer of English Versification (Sydney: Sydney University Press, 1966);

Songs of the Promise, text by McAuley, music by Connolly (Sydney: Living Parish Series, 1968);

Surprises of the Sun (Sydney: Angus & Robertson, 1969);

Generations: Poetry from Chaucer to the Present Day (Melbourne: Nelson, 1969);

The Personal Element in Australian Poetry (Sydney & London: Angus & Robertson, 1970);

Collected Poems: 1936–1970 (Sydney: Angus & Robertson, 1971);

A Map of Australian Verse: The Twentieth Century (Melbourne: Oxford University Press, 1975);

The Grammar of the Real: Selected Prose 1959–1974 (Melbourne & New York: Oxford University Press, 1975);

Music Late at Night: Poems 1970–1973 (Sydney: Angus & Robertson, 1976);

Time Given (Canberra: Brindabella Press, 1976);

James McAuley, 1970 (Mercury)

A World of Its Own, illustrated by Patricia Giles (Canberra: Australian National University Press, 1977);

The Rhetoric of Australian Poetry (Surry Hills, N.S.W.: Wentworth Press, 1978);

Collected Poems (Sydney: Angus & Robertson, 1993).

OTHER: *Song of Songs,* The Jerusalem Bible, translated by McAuley (London: Darton, Longman & Todd, 1966);

Music in the Mirabell Garden, translated from the German of Georg Trakl by McAuley (Hobart: New Albion Press, 1982).

James McAuley rose to national prominence as a poet and polemicist after his conversion to Catholicism in 1952. From the mid 1950s, when he assumed the founding editorship of *Quadrant,* the magazine of the Australian Congress for Cultural Freedom, until his death in 1976, he neither gave nor asked for quarter in the political and religious arenas. Christ and the Church Fathers who had wielded the whip against adversaries provided him with precedents, or as he remarked of one of his fictional characters in a late interview: "my choice in situations is not likely to be that of Quiros. I think it is necessary to embark on violence." Intemperance marked many of his statements during the Vietnam War. Disciplines to which he had devoted his best years were savaged as "those rickety rackety subjects which like to call themselves human or social sciences." Australian universities were pilloried for having "contributed significantly to the mental disarray of the national community," their staff charged with self-interest, cowardice, and irresponsibility that permitted "the malignant, the hysterical and the foolish" to dictate opinion and agendas. The Left responded by branding him a Catholic fascist. More moderate critics saw his attitudes as the reverse of liberal open-mindedness, and his abiding image as a Cold War warrior has impeded recognition of his important literary and intellectual achievements. Nevertheless, he has been remembered as a co-author with Harold Stewart of the most notorious literary hoax in Australia, the Ern Malley affair; as the creator of an exciting postwar collection of verse, *Under Aldebaran* (1946), as an author with epic ambitions in *Captain Quiros* (1964); and finally as a poet of great honesty, clarity, and humanity in his last collections, written after a diagnosis of cancer in 1970, as he directed his energies increasingly to creating works that would outlive him.

James Phillip McAuley was born in the burgeoning western suburbs of Sydney at Lakemba on 12 October 1917 and grew to hate their unleavened materialism and narrow-mindedness. His father, Patrick McAuley, had moved there to speculate in real estate, buying land and building houses with sufficient success to be able to retire to Homebush while James and his siblings, John and Lorna, were still small children. Patrick McAuley had abandoned his Catholic faith to marry Mary Judge in 1909 and was depicted by the poet as bigoted, unimaginative, and intensely conservative. At home, displays of emotion or faith were frowned on; outside the family's front door stretched the bleak tracks of the Western rail line, in a suburb best known before the 2000 Olympic Games for its bustling abattoir. This environment was hardly conducive to a rich cultural unfolding; nonetheless, McAuley early displayed exceptional gifts. Literacy came easily, and his rapid strides as a pianist raised the possibility of a musical career. His cautious parents chose instead to send him to Fort Street Boys' High School, the premier government school. There McAuley excelled academically, read himself out of religious belief, and captained the school with distinction. Creatively he was strong, winning prizes for poetry, prose, and as the best female impersonator.

His years at Sydney University, from 1935 to 1940, laid the basis for much of his future work. He studied English, Latin, and philosophy. The last brought him into contact with the most radical professor at the university, John Anderson, famed for bringing objective criticism to bear on a range of received opinions. Anderson placed truth above the party line and was a passionate advocate of such groundbreaking books as James Joyce's *Ulysses* (serialized in 1918, published in a single volume in 1922). McAuley, however, had reservations about Anderson's aesthetic theories. Andersonians demanded of each literary work a cogent thematic development to the exclusion of subjective or subconscious considerations. McAuley, an avowed acolyte of the early T. S. Eliot and William Blake, was moving in his own compositions away from this rational ideal, just as he distanced himself from dull English department lectures to pursue his own diverse interests, from mysticism to the writings of Rainer Maria Rilke. In 1937 McAuley won the university medal for English but finished with only Third Class Honors in philosophy. Next he wrote an ambitious master of arts thesis titled "Symbolism: An Essay in Poetics." It analyzed the evolution of symbolism in English, French, and German literature, related this development to psychoanalytic theory as well as Surrealism, and offered a "general theory of the nature of poetry." Although original in its conception and mature in its handling of major theoretical issues, the thesis failed to gain him a coveted scholarship for study in England. He therefore joined the State Department of Education after receiving a diploma in education and married fellow teacher Norma Abernathy on 20 June 1942.

McAuley's life took unforeseen directions following his call-up on 6 January 1943. After basic training and a period with the Army Education unit, he joined the Army Directorate of Civil Affairs in Melbourne, headed by a university friend, Alf Conlon. Conlon's unit reported directly to the commander in chief of the Australian army and specialized in

*McAuley with his two eldest children, Katherine and Philip
(from Michael Ackland,* Damaged Men, *2001)*

research tasks with which conventional army services were ill equipped to deal. McAuley prepared papers on the increasing wartime role of the United States, read widely in the social sciences, and pursued his literary interests with Stewart, who was assistant librarian in the Army Directorate of Civil Affairs. For the best part of a decade, Stewart's and McAuley's poetic development had run parallel, as schoolboy rivalry yielded to mutual appreciation, but their work was hardly known outside Sydney circles. Nationally they were eclipsed by a young Surrealist poet from Adelaide, Max Harris, who by 1943 had published two volumes of verse as well as a stream-of-consciousness novel, *The Vegetative Eye* (1943). Harris also edited the literary magazine *Angry Penguins,* in which he proselytized for modernism and paraded his superior judgment. Jealous of this influence and skilled since university days in parodic and impromptu compositions, the two Sydney poets McAuley and Stewart resolved to "get Maxie."

Relying on Harris's lack of critical discrimination and their own long apprenticeship in literary modernism, McAuley and Stewart wrote in a single day the sixteen-poem oeuvre of the fictive poet Ern Malley. They sent the results to Harris in the name of Ethel Malley, who to her surprise—so the hoax went—had found the manuscript among her dead brother's effects. Knowing nothing of poetry, she requested Harris's verdict. It was remarkably positive, for the hoaxers had carefully baited their trap. The series of poems, titled *The Darkening Ecliptic,* began with "Durer: Innsbruck 1495," a serious piece written by McAuley to lull Harris's suspicions.

> Now I find that once more I have shrunk
> To an interloper, robber of dead men's dream,
> I had read in books that art is not easy
> But no one warned that the mind repeats
> In its ignorance the vision of others. I am still
> The black swan of trespass on alien waters.

Describing Malley as "one of the most outstanding poets we have produced here," and asserting "the perfection and integrity of his verse," Harris devoted the June 1944 issue of *Angry Penguins* to the work of this antipodean Thomas Chatterton. The plot was exposed on 18 June by the Sydney tabloid *Fact,* which assured that the hoax reached a wide reading public. On 25 June *Fact* recounted how the poems had been rapidly written by the two Sydney poets, using free association interleaved with material drawn from random sources, to create works of patent nonsense. Their overriding aim, according to the supplement of *Fact,* the *Sunday Sun,* was to demonstrate that the Angry Penguins were "insensible of absurdity and incapable of ordinary discrimination," leading them to present as "great poetry" writing that "appeared to us to be a collection of garish images without coherent meaning and structure; as if one erected a coat of bright paint and called it a house." Harris countered that the works included much better material than its authors knew; debate on its merits continues to this day.

Ern Malley's poems are undeniably tantalizing and arresting. Often their images combine nightmarish resonance with Surrealist incongruity, as in "Baroque Exterior":

> When the hysterical vision strikes
> The facade of an era it manifests
> Its insidious relations.
> The windowed eyes gleam with terror
> The twin balconies are breasts
> And at the efflux of a period's error
> Is a carved malicious portico.
> Everyman arrests
> His motives in these anthropoid erections.

Individual poems are teasingly self-reflexive. "We are as the double almond concealed in one shell," confesses the speaker of "Colloquy with John Keats." "Palinode" highlights the Sydney tradition of literary parodies, and in "Petit Testament" the interjecting, nonsensical voice is delayed too long, so that the poem, mainly from McAuley's pen, reads from the outset like a resolution to put his past life and poetic experiments behind him:

> In the twenty fifth year of my age
> I find myself to be a dromedary
> That has run short of water between
> One oasis and the next mirage
> And having despaired of ever
> Making my obsessions intelligible
> I am content at last to be
> The sole clerk of my metamorphoses.

After years of ephemeral, scarcely known publications, it was "something to be at last speaking / Though in this No-Man's-language appropriate / Only to No-Man's Land," as Ern Malley put it, but could his co-authors create works as good or better under their own names?

McAuley answered his critics in 1946 with *Under Aldebaran,* a collection that marked a radical break with clichéd nationalist sentiment and the bush ethos. Its title referred to the pink and blue flashing star, described in Gérard de Nerval's *Sylvie* (1895), that the Australian identified with his own divided being. Aldebaran was also a fitting emblem of the epoch whose turbulence was variously captured, whether in the esoteric symbolism of "The Incarnation of Sirius," which links contemporary anarchy with the beast of Revelation, or in the opening clarion call to seize the day in "The Blue Horses," which begins:

> What loud wave-motioned hooves awaken
> Our dream-fast members from the cramp of sleep?
> The tribal images are shaken
> And crash upon their guardians. The skies
> Are shivered like a pane of glass.

McAuley's horses signal Blakean visionary change to an unwilling world, self-focused and possessive, but now threatened by "diktat, pact and gun." The volume includes works composed during the previous decade that vary considerably in content and style, from love poems written as a student to later evocations of cosmic design "Beyond the Wallace line of known delight." Contemporary influences are diverse and sometimes hidden. The celebration of the driving force behind the great Portuguese voyages of discovery in "Henry the Navigator," for example, was also a tribute to Conlon's vision and vast ambitions, while the last work of the collection, "The True Discovery of Australia," was a complex progeny of the intellectual climate of the directorate, as is acknowledged by a witty allusion to Ida Leeson, the librarian of the unit, who was the alleged custodian of Gulliver's apocryphal account of what he discovered in Australia. The same poem displays to the full McAuley's powerful satiric instinct, puncturing local pretensions—"Mentally, they're still Pliocene, / A flat terrain impermeably dense," and projecting warningly a banal, empty future for a country content with Lilliputian vistas. As a partial corrective, the collection displays a plethora of artistic ways forward but, apart from registering intense dissatisfaction, offers no substantial alternative to the present "slum culture," in which "The brutal and the vile are set / As watchers at the gate."

Years later, when McAuley oversaw a collected edition of his poetry, he retained the titles from separate volumes as section headings but changed their content. He made significant revisions to his first collection. Thus, the self-critical correlatives afforded by "The Bee-hive" and, more traumatically, "The Cavern" disappear from "Under Aldebaran," whereas retrospectively a place is found for McAuley's pithy commentary on ideological shifts during the 1930s, "Ballade of Lost Phrases," and an overtly religious note added with "Jesus," a portrait of the Messiah as bold prophet: "He thrust his speech among them like a sword. / . . . / And told them nothing that they wished to know." More importantly, the original order of the works is greatly altered. Chronology and a sense of individual evolution become his apparent criteria, so that the revised arrangement closes with "Philoctetes," an account of a legendary, self-injured archer, isolated and tormented by "pain perpetual, and my wound / Incurable, never to be healed." A veiled self-portrait, it refracted McAuley's anguished questing and a deep-seated psychological malaise that, after the war, he sought urgently to resolve.

A way forward and a redemptive credo were found in the jungles of New Guinea. Although McAuley had visited the bird-shaped northern archipelago during hostilities as an intelligence officer, his intimate acquaintance with the land, its peoples, and the work of French Catholic missionaries came afterward, while he was doing fieldwork as a lecturer in the Australian School of Pacific Administration at Sydney. In particular, he was impressed by the retired Catholic archbishop Alain de Boismenu–"the person in my experience who most completely exemplified 'greatness,'" McAuley wrote in "My New Guinea"–whose "flawless probity" made him a credible witness to the amazing life story of the recently deceased Sister Marie-Thérèse Noblet. Her spiritual dedication had called forth satanic torments, and for a decade de Boismenu, as he fought for her soul, had recognized in her suffering marks of election. McAuley, although acknowledging the profound influence of these missionaries on him, is silent about the prelate's work as an exorcist and reticent about Noblet's trials. Undoubtedly, he was apprehensive about Anglo-Saxon incredulity and derision, had he confessed to his fascination with the paranormal, and about unwelcome speculation on his own condition. His prizewinning poem at Fort Street was titled "Madness," and subsequent pieces record both unsettling mental states and that "Something–guilt, tension, or outrage– / Keeps coming in nightmare shape." Friends confirm his terrible nocturnal ordeals, claim that he feared for his sanity, and suggest that he personally identified with Noblet. Certainly, he attributed his conversion to her intercession, and a severe bout of malaria at the mission station in 1951 sealed his decision. In his notebook he recorded learning a final lesson of "absolute submission and patience" as well as attaining an inner resolve that matched his rational conviction. The following year, on 29 May, McAuley was received into the Catholic Church and braced himself for a backlash from those who remembered him as a slick apostate, roaring out sacrilegious songs. It was a modest price to pay for a faith that enabled him to make sense of his fragmented being–to see in his psychic turmoil a sign of election.

His spiritual decision unleashed a burst of creativity that produced *A Vision of Ceremony* (1956), a faith-inspired volume of poems dedicated to Noblet. In this volume, in place of shaken "tribal images," he turned to the Word and attempted to realize what he preaches in "An Art of Poetry":

Let your speech be ordered wholly
By an intellectual love;
Elucidate the carnal maze
With clear light from above.

Formal structures predominated, in part as a reaction against the enshrinement of subconscious and dream sources by Surrealism. Crucially, McAuley sought to rein in these impulses, wayward and irrational, so that poetic and personal endeavors went hand in hand to achieve a rational, coherent self-projection. In this second collection there are, however, reminders of the dark forces against which he struggled, as in "New Guinea." Dedicated to the memory of his spiritual adviser there, Archbishop de Boismenu, it depicts "Land of apocalypse, where . . . / . . . the doors of the spirit open, / And men are shaken by obscure trances." A sense of divinity is omnipresent, "But stains of blood, and evil spirits, lurk / Like cockroaches in the interstices of things." The only response adequate to this conflict between God and the devil, it concludes, is Christ's presence in the saints as exorciser to war "with demons on the outer verge." Three longer poems, which conclude the volume, project this warfare in various terms. "A Leaf of Sage," in recasting a lovers' tale from Giovanni Boccaccio's *The Decameron* (1349–1351), offers a cryptic "hieroglyph" of the speaker's youth bespoiled by evil, while the four-part "Hero and the Hydra," composed in the late 1940s, uses the sufferings of Prometheus and Heracles to project McAuley's former hopelessness before the Hydra of doubt. It closes with an image of the hero's tomb–"the end of stoic pride"–and the verdict that contemporary existence "is eaten hollow with despair."

In stark contrast, the final poem, "A Letter to John Dryden," and McAuley's contemporaneous work in *Quadrant* reflect the crusading zeal of the recent convert. In the satire he lashes out at dissenting visions and creedless, "half-way-decent simple stunted souls," appealing to Dryden's precedent:

The Modern Mind was then scarce embryonic
Which now stands forth loud, indistinct, moronic.
The great Unculture that you feared might be
"Drawn to the dregs of a democracy"
Is full upon us; here it sours and thickens
Till every work of art and honour sickens.

Liberals, in the poet's eyes fellow travelers, are his repeated target–"For ever dancing to some alien song, / And everything by turns but nothing long"; his panacea is Catholic faith: "Incarnate Word, in whom all nature lives / Cast flame upon the earth; raise up contemplatives." McAuley, however, had engagement, not contemplation, in mind, and in May 1955 he joined the CIA-funded Australian Congress for Cultural Freedom. A year later he was editing the first issue of its magazine, *Quadrant*, convinced that the Church of Rome afforded a promising alternative to the failed extremes of capitalism and communism. The latter offered only material solutions, whereas the Catholic approach to politics stressed social justice, human dignity, and the importance of an enabling metaphysical vision. His first editorial, however, stopped short of directly opposing "a resurgent Christianity" to communism's "enormous mask made of blood and lies" to conclude open-endedly: "Truly an exhilarating time!–on condition that we have relevant principles worth living and dying for."

Through such activities he expressed his commitment to the doctrine of Catholic action. This notion emphasized the need for lay participation in the church's program for winning the world back to Christ, in keeping with the activism called for by Pope Pius XI in an address headed "No longer permitted to be mediocre," which McAuley pasted in the front cover of his 1953 notebook as a source of meditation and admonition:

> The crisis we are experiencing is unique in history.... Let us thank God that he makes us live among the present problems. It is no longer permitted to anyone to be mediocre. Everyone has the imperative duty to remember that he has a mission to fulfil ... each within the limits of his activity, to bring the world back to Christ. Only by being radicals of the right will Catholics have the dynamism to withstand the radicals of the left and to conquer the world for Christ.

In 1954 McAuley aligned himself with the militant Catholic B. A. Santamaria, whose war on communist influence within the labor movement split the Australian Labor Party in the mid 1950s. McAuley played a leading role in the breakaway Democratic Labor Party and clashed bitterly with the Sydney Catholic diocese, which refused to support it. Then, as in the momentous battle against communism, ends seemed to justify

Dust jacket for McAuley's 1956 collection of poems, inspired by his conversion to Roman Catholicism in 1952 (Bruccoli Clark Layman Archives)

means, but the internecine struggle left him anxious about the judgment of posterity, as he revealed in a notebook entry of 11 March 1958: "If Australia should be saved by our efforts; or if the danger passes in other ways, making our efforts seem irrelevant, people will will [sic] later fail to understand the grim necessities, as they seemed to us, that led a handful of people to a racking struggle in the filth of politics as it is played here." Soundly defeated in New South Wales, the poet wrote darkly: "Forms vanish, kingdoms molder, / The Antirealm is here."

He put a reasoned case for his sweeping disenchantment in *The End of Modernity: Essays on Literature, Art and Culture* (1959), in which his stated goal is to analyze "the consequences for intellectual culture of the abandonment of the principle of supernatural faith as it exists in orthodox Christian life." Worked at intermittently since the beginning of the decade, the book afforded a Catholic rejoinder to Lionel Trilling's *The Liberal Imagination* (1950), arguing for "the stupendous vision and vitality which orthodoxy forever conserves," as well as a rebuttal of errors expounded by Traditionalist thinkers such as René Guénon and Ananda K. Coomaraswamy. Prior to conversion, McAuley had been drawn to their argument that the West had fallen away from traditional spiritual knowledge, leading to the catastrophes of the twentieth century. This degeneration began in earnest with the Renaissance and was confirmed by the Reformation, although its roots can be traced back to the Greek advocacy of individualism, coupled with the espousal of reason, science, and technology in place of metaphysical wisdom. Ultimately, these intellectual choices have produced a world, in McAuley's words, which echo Guénon's, "of disinherited beings, cut off from the deepest sources of human satisfaction, restless and jangled, driven by unstilled cravings through a course of life without meaning or direction." But such disintegration did not occur, according to Traditionalists, in so-called primitive societies, or those imbued with the great Oriental religions. In these communities the needs of both body and soul were catered to; objects were created as part of a sacred rite to serve the whole person; and art, unlike its modern, individualistic counterpart, existed to make primordial truth comprehensible. These views shaped McAuley's reading of Melanesian communities as well as his artistic ideal. Finally, however, he affirmed Western achievements and chose his Noblet-centered Catholicism over the abstract intricacies of Guénon's Vedanta-based metaphysic. Hence, in *The End of Modernity* Traditionalism is rejected as a form of "Oriental gnosticism" that claims "to give to the elect an exhaustive account of the universe in terms addressed to the pure intelligence." It is adjudged "strictly totalitarian" and inferior to Christian humanism.

Equally revelatory are the sections in *The End of Modernity* that deal with what he saw as the modern deviation in verse. In essence, McAuley argues that poets have wrongly attempted to fill the void of faith, to arrogate gnostic or thaumaturgic power to the poetic word. Gradually but inevitably, they have distanced themselves from the once widely understood symbolic language, substituting subjective for metaphysical knowledge and forgetting that art traditionally involved translating a divinely given idea, conceived in the mind of the artist, into his specific medium. Thus, *poesis perennis* (perennial poetry) was displaced by what he later called "the Magian heresy" and by a rash of contemporary poems that were "mere Rohrschach [*sic*] blotches encountering the reader's sensibility in a haphazardly suggestive way."

Once again, he recommends a return to the lost light shed by the West's metaphysical and theological traditions. Compellingly argued and wide-ranging, these essays display a special interest in literature as material for interpreting patterns of culture that remained a feature of his criticism.

McAuley always claimed with justice that his worldly engagements enriched his literary productions. But this symbiosis could be problematic. It left friends wondering, for example, whether his most consistent impulse was toward poetry or toward politics, while St. Peter's injunction to give reasons for his belief sometimes led to preaching or blatant proselytizing. During the 1950s he had given himself a thorough grounding in his new religion, studying works on liturgy, dogma, and scriptural interpretation; on mysteries, gnosticism, and mysticism; and on the role of a Christian intellectual in the modern world. This reading underpinned many public lectures, reviews, and editorials, as well as his poetic practice when, as he said in a notebook entry of 31 January 1954, he strove "to awaken in others through poetry that sense of what man might be, to create the dispositions necessary before the truth of doctrine can begin to pour into the heart." The resulting verse, however, often afforded statements of faith rather than tableaux that invite the reader's imagination to reenact the poet's moment of revelation. Far from being an "enabling act," conversion—as he acknowledged in an undated letter to Dorothy Green—could lead to "disorientation and deterioration" in his work, as doctrinal imperatives effaced what had been most engaging in his earlier verse, its lucid, unarmored confessional mode.

Also, his immediate political experience fed into the eighty-four-page-long poem *Captain Quiros,* written between June 1958 and January 1960. Self-consciously unfashionable, his poem portrays in formal stanzas two failed Spanish attempts to establish a God-inspired settlement in the Pacific, as well as Quiros's dying vision of the discovery and settlement of Australia. It is at once "a match against the age's mind" and a condemnation of its venality, couched in timeless terms:

> He who would rise, in deed or poetry,
> To the height of a great action, must have first
> Eaten the harsh bread of reality,
> And, schooled by blows, must with sad skill be versed
> Both in the deep corruptions of men's will
> And in their shallow weakness, which can still
> Level the best intentions to the worst.

The cumulative verdict offered by *Captain Quiros* on Western civilization and political action is damning. Irrespective of their race or noble motives, the lives of its protagonists end in disillusionment or death. Disorder, anarchy, and usurpation are recurrent motifs, as is the frustration of "Those tasks we undertake at heaven's calling." Quiros's ardent faith and self-exhausting activity recall McAuley, much as the poem draws on his knowledge of Melanesian society and of inherent evil within men "that could turn / The streams of Eden to a standing ditch." Its bickering, backstabbing Europeans could have stepped out of the local political arena, as its clerical intriguers clearly have. The head of the Sydney diocese appears as "a cold mean creature with placarded smile," who "Made baseness seem a mode of piety; / His right hand blessed the victims of his left." His ecclesiastical henchman is remembered for "dissembling double thought": "Holy detraction was his special flair, / . . . / Entangling others for the ends he sought." Defamers of true visionary endeavor, they epitomize "a failing age of drift" in which the old adage remains true: "Not ours to bring to birth / . . . / The New Jerusalem, which will never be / Christ's perfect Bride save in eternity." *Captain Quiros,* though not free of didacticism, was praised by reviewers for its sustained theme and execution and for its epic breadth and vision. But the specific context that shaped it made a sequel unlikely, as did a shift in McAuley's priorities, registered in his notebook when he rediscovered in the German Romantic Joseph von Eichendorff what he sought: "brilliant clear pictures, sweetness & gaiety. Eichendorff's poems, always a kind of perfection in my mind, have a renewed relevance to what I am trying to work towards poetically."

In 1961 the poet-polemicist escaped Sydney, scene of galling disappointment and betrayal, by accepting first a Readership in Poetry, then the vacant Chair of English at the University of Tasmania. In Hobart his commitment to Santamaria's cause remained high, and McAuley was still editor of *Quadrant,* but his professional reorientation led to more literary activity. In 1963, for instance, he published a small monograph on the Sydney symbolist poet Christopher Brennan, as well as poetic texts to *The Six Days of Creation* (1963), illustrated by Leonard French, and to *Hymns for the Year of Grace* (1963), with music composed by Richard Connolly. *A Primer of English Versification* came three years later, in 1966, together with important lectures and essays that helped establish Australian literature as an area worthy of serious criticism and scholarship. He also proposed and oversaw the foundation of a key journal in the new field, *Australian Literary Studies.* At the end of the decade, with the élan of conversion and the appeal of dogma much dissipated, he entered a new phase of his own poetry with *Surprises of the Sun* (1969). In this work, political and religious engagement yields from the outset to childhood reminiscences and confessions of fallibility,

McAuley and his wife, Norma, after their move to Tasmania in 1961 (Mercury)

thus signaling increased humility and concern with ordinary human experience, developments that were widely welcomed.

Faith, meanwhile, had become for him a source of tension as well as strength. The church was worldly in its understanding of human failings and unstinting in its forgiveness, but it also contributed to his doubts and inner tensions with the Second Vatican Council, which began in 1962. Initially, McAuley, an advocate of the Liturgical Movement, welcomed the reforms emanating from Rome, but by the late 1960s change had become, in his eyes, a mutating virus that left parishioners unsettled and threatened the authority of the church. Then came two blows that struck at the heart of his religious commitment. In 1969 he caused a permanent rupture with his friend, the archbishop of Hobart, by withdrawing his children from Catholic schools. The following year he was diagnosed as having bowel cancer and, while convalescing after a major operation, encountered Georg Trakl's verse decisively. There he found, "however terrible . . . not a nihilistic vision" but a sustaining awareness beyond the evocation of evil—"of innocence, of peace and happiness, of goodness and rightness, and of intimacy with God." This analysis is Trakl as McAuley willed him to be, as he set about wedding the clarity of Eichendorff with the somber, deep inwardness of Trakl in his final poetic testimony: *The Hazard and the Gift* (1970), *Music Late at Night: Poems 1970–1973* (1976), and *Time Given* (1976).

The imminence of death brought a subtle shift in McAuley's poetic perspective. Although only his wife was told that he had at best five years to live, McAuley knew that the number was the national average and harbored no delusions, as two poems on St. John's Park, New Town show. Prior to his 1970 diagnosis, he celebrated this local park as a repository of tradition, evoked by "solid Georgian stone" and "bronze-green oaks," only to subordinate the past unequivocally to "the raw / Instant," or current promise: "The past is not my law / . . . / Our privilege is now." A year and a colostomy later ("Better a semicolon than a fullstop," he quipped), he returned to this scene in writing "St. John's Park." The natural world, the daily cycles, and the distinct phases of human existence are now depicted with renewed physical intensity and acceptance:

> A dark-green gum bursts out in crimson flowers.
> Old people slowly rot along the wall.
> The young ones hardly notice them at all.
> Both live in the same picture-book of hours.
> Four-turreted a square tower balks the sky,
> Casting a shadow; an organ softly plays.

Human longing impinges on, but does not change, the course of nature. "The old have crept inside to meet the dark. / Loss is what nothing alters or annuls." Framing these observations is humankind's constant aspiration for transcendence, witnessed in ecclesial works or in fond projections upon the heavens, similar to those with which the poem concludes: "Faint stars prick out a sign. And Vega wakes / Liquid and trembling on the northern sky."

McAuley's final years were particularly rich in poetic compositions. Typically, in these collections existence is depicted discreetly under the aspect of eternity through simple, direct language that interweaves tokens of doubt and transience–"Mosaics of decay, dark lace, / Pale mildews cling to leaf and lath"–with desire, and the realization that mortal limitations will always deprive humankind of ultimate knowledge. As usual, his range as an essayist was broad, from Renaissance to Romantic verse, from John Milton's dilemmas to "The Moabit Sonnets of Albrecht Haushofer," with politics and poetry frequently intersecting. His sympathy was similarly comprehensive, springing in part from his own experience of evil as well as weakness, and he quoted with approval a 1972 commentary by R. F. Brissenden, which noted in his poetry a muted "outrage and bewilderment [that] . . . are intensely personal; at the same time one feels that they have been evoked through the forced contemplation of a problem that the poet reluctantly acknowledges as perennial, as inherent in the inscrutable order of the universe." Faced with an equally unknowable self and cosmos, the challenge remained for McAuley, in his life and in his verse, to show that "patience looks on beauty, / And sings beneath the knout." As his end drew near, he summed up decades of uncertainty and unquenched longing in "Parish Church":

> I bring with me my griefs, my sins, my death,
> And sink in silence as I try to pray.
> Though in this calm no impulse stirs my breath,
> At least there's nothing that I would unsay.

Publicly he tried to set a brave example of use and purpose. In 1975 his two most enduring contributions to literary scholarship appeared, *The Grammar of the Real: Selected Prose 1959–1974* and *A Map of Australian Verse*. Both bear testimony to his critical discernment and wide tastes, while *A Map of Australian Verse* afforded an innovative, well-balanced guide to Australian poetry. Intent on expanding this tradition, McAuley immersed himself in nature at Freycinet Peninsula. Everywhere he saw a land awaiting "Assimilation by the curious eye, / The experienced heart, the restless hand," as well as work ahead "for many years and lives." Unhurried and absorbed, the dying McAuley watched the movements of a wolf spider or the tides, jotting down his observations. They formed the basis for his last work, *A World of Its Own* (1977), illustrated by Patricia Giles, that testifies to the myriad life and timeless patterns studied at Coles Bay, as well as to his resolve to exercise his craft until the end. His death came on 15 October 1976; he left behind a wife and five children. Undoubtedly, McAuley, during his intense and fluctuating existence, had been "perfected at the price of pain and desolation," like de Boismenu as described in "My New Guinea." In his own case, however, the skeptic in him was less sanguine that this "law" meant entry into "the spiritual kingdom," while he hoped, with due modesty, to be "read a little now / A little when I'm dead." That much, at least, is assured by the enduring interest and readability of his work, as well as by McAuley's centrality to Australian cultural life in the crucial postwar decades when–as anthropologist, poet, and Catholic intellectual–he endeavored to lay the groundwork for realizing his vision of a society informed by genuinely humane and Christian principles.

Biographies:

Peter Coleman, *The Heart of James McAuley* (Sydney: Wildcat Press, 1980);

Cassandra Pybus, *The Devil and James McAuley* (Brisbane: University of Queensland Press, 1999);

Michael Ackland, *Damaged Men: The Precarious Lives of James McAuley and Harold Stewart* (Sydney: Allen & Unwin, 2001).

References:

Despina Balzidis, "James McAuley's Radical Ingredients," *Meanjin,* 39 (1980): 374–382;

R. F. Brissenden, "The Wounded Hero: James McAuley's *Collected Poems,*" *Southerly,* 32 (1972): 267–278;

Vincent Buckley, *Cutting Green Hay* (Ringwood: Penguin, 1983);

Richard Connolly, "Making Hymns with James McAuley: A Memoir," *Australasian Catholic Record,* 72 (1995): 387–398;

Robert Dixon, "James McAuley's New Guinea: Colonialism, Modernity, Suburbia," *Australian Literary Studies,* 18 (1998): 20–40;

Livio Dobrez, "The Three McAuleys," *Southern Review,* 9 (1976): 171–184;

Carmel Gaffney, "Music out of Decay: McAuley's Later Poetry and Georg Trakl," *Southerly,* 36 (1976): 407–419;

Michael Heyward, *The Ern Malley Affair* (Brisbane: University of Queensland Press, 1993);

Peter Kirkpatrick, "Patience and Despair: James McAuley's Pessimism," *Southerly,* 44 (1984): 191–205;

Leonie Kramer, "James McAuley's Captain Quiros: The Rational Paradise," *Southerly,* 25 (1965): 147–161;

Lynette McCreddan, *James McAuley* (Melbourne: Oxford University Press, 1992);

Susan McKernan, *A Question of Commitment: Australian Literature in the Twenty Years after the War* (Sydney: Allen & Unwin, 1989);

Quadrant, special McAuley issue, 21 (1977): 4–80;

B. A. Santamaria, *Against the Tide* (Melbourne: Oxford University Press, 1981);

Chris Wallace-Crabbe, "Beware the Past: James McAuley's Early Poetry," *Meanjin Quarterly,* 30 (1971): 323–330.

Papers:

The bulk of James McAuley's manuscripts, diaries, notebooks, and miscellaneous papers are held in the Mitchell Library, State Library of New South Wales, and diverse correspondence is held in the Australian National Library, Canberra.

Hugh McCrae

(4 October 1876 – 17 February 1958)

Justin Lucas
Victoria University

BOOKS: *Satyrs and Sunlight: Silvarum Libri* (Sydney: Sands, 1909); revised and enlarged as *Satyrs and Sunlight* (Melbourne: Lothian, 1911); revised and enlarged again as *Satyrs and Sunlight: Being the Collected Poetry of Hugh McCrae* (London: Fanfrolico Press, 1928);

Colombine (Sydney: Angus & Robertson, 1920);

The Du Poissey Anecdotes: To Which Are Joined Some Conversations with a Great Man, as Benjamin Harcourt (Sydney: Art in Australia, 1922);

Idyllia (Sydney: N.L. Press, 1922);

My Father, and My Father's Friends (Sydney: Angus & Robertson, 1935);

Poems by Hugh McCrae (Sydney: Angus & Robertson, 1939);

Forests of Pan: A Selection of Poems Not Hitherto Reprinted From Hugh McCrae's Satyrs and Sunlight, 1928 (Brisbane, Qld.: Meanjin Press, 1944);

Voice of the Forest (Sydney: Angus & Robertson, 1945);

Story-Book Only (Sydney: Angus & Robertson, 1948);

The Ship of Heaven: A Musical Fantasy in Three Acts (Sydney: Angus & Robertson, 1951).

Collections: *The Best Poems of Hugh McCrae,* edited by R. G. Howarth (Sydney: Angus & Robertson, 1961);

Hugh McCrae: Selected Poems, edited by Douglas Stewart (Sydney: Angus & Robertson, 1966).

SELECTED BROADSIDE: *The Mimshi Maiden* (Sydney: Privately printed, 1931).

RECORDING: *Hugh McCrae Reads His Own Poems,* Sydney, ABC, 1953.

OTHER: Georgiana Huntly McCrae, *Georgiana's Journal: Melbourne a Hundred Years Ago,* edited by McCrae (Sydney: Angus & Robertson, 1934).

SELECTED PERIODICAL PUBLICATION–
UNCOLLECTED: Hugh McCrae, "My Life and My Book (A Little Bit of Each)," *Southerly,* 33 (June 1973): 222–229.

Hugh McCrae (National Library of Australia)

Hugh McCrae's poetic works present current readers with something of a problem. Although McCrae's aesthetics appear detached from history, his work engaged on several levels with the problem of imagining the land that white Australians found so elusive as a source of identification and artistic sustenance. Even while being mired in thematic and formal nostalgia for European memory, McCrae's work until the 1930s included some visually striking pieces that challenged the prevailing realism of the period and led him from a disturbed pastoral to the overambitious *Vision: A*

Literary Quarterly project. Yet, having failed to find his voice after *Vision,* McCrae in his later poetry relied on early preoccupations, even while those poets around him, such as Kenneth Slessor, became icons of twentieth-century modernist innovation. However, much in McCrae's work suggests a complex and far from derivative method behind the fantasy and the dress-up pageant of *Satyrs and Sunlight: Silvarum Libri* (1909), *Colombine* (1920), and *Idyllia* (1922).

McCrae's paternal grandparents, Andrew Muirson McCrae and Georgiana Huntly McCrae, a professional portraitist of some note, had emigrated with his father from Leith, Scotland, landing at Port Phillip near the site of present-day Melbourne in 1841. Taking up the "Arthur's Seat" cattle run (tract of land for grazing) on land that had been seized in the process of the proclamation of the colony of Victoria, Andrew built a large homestead overlooking the settlement of Dromana, adjacent to the portside suburb now known as McCrae. The eldest son, George Gordon McCrae, the father of the poet, returned to Melbourne, building the property "Anchorfield" at Hawthorn and taking up a position in the Victorian government service. Hugh Raymond McCrae was born on 4 October 1876, the second son of George Gordon McCrae and Augusta Helen Brown McCrae.

Despite the explosive midcentury population growth of Melbourne, Hawthorn was then and remained until McCrae's youth a sparsely populated hamlet, "very nearly still the bush," upstream on the Yarra River, which "beside it ran sweet and clear," as McCrae recalled in a late autobiographical fragment. Scenes set in imagined preindustrial landscapes came to define McCrae's poetry for his contemporary critics, while his autobiographical pieces focus almost exclusively on the period up until his early twenties, which remained a source of poetic inspiration until the last of his work in the 1940s.

Although he remained a career public servant for thirty-four years—in contrast to his son's working life—George McCrae was, more importantly, a member of the various bohemian literary fraternities that were the bulkheads of Melbourne literary production from the mid to late nineteenth century. Playing the part of a middle-class "curate-in-bohemia," as a member of Marcus Clarke's Yorick Club, George McCrae was host to Adam Lindsay Gordon, Henry Kendall, R. H. Horne, and John Shillingsworth. Between the 1860s and the 1890s George wrote four novels on local themes, including *The Story of Balladeadro* (1867) and *Mamba ("The Bright Eyed")* (1867), purported to be a retelling of Aboriginal stories; three long poems; a memoir; and poetry for *The Bulletin* and *The Melbourne Review.* Unlike his colleague Henry Kendall, the "scholar on the tap-room floor," however, Hugh McCrae was brought up in a house that seems to have defined Victorian bourgeois respectability. Sent to the Presbyterian private secondary school Hawthorn Grammar after a variety of primary schools, Hugh failed at mathematics and excelled at classics. While at home, he read widely in the canon of seventeenth- and eighteenth-century English prose and poetry found on his father's shelves—"Marlowe, Butler, Sir Thomas Browne, Defoe, Pope, Pepys."

Under the encouragement of his father, the adolescent Hugh began to write poetry of his own. His first published work, a self-conscious attempt to offend local worthies, was submitted to the local village newspaper by the twelve-year-old, imagining "the clergyman, the chemist, the baker . . . their wives and children with its boyish rowdiness . . . thinking what a devil I was." However bohemian the reasons behind McCrae's ode "To a Pot of Beer," his response, when the local parson took his offense to George McCrae, was hardly that of a rabble-rouser; he agreed to cease writing for the paper altogether. In many ways this episode, recounted as part of a memoir of his own protobohemian identity, illustrates the kind of carefully managed persona McCrae cultivated throughout his life. Unlike his collaborators Norman and Lionel Lindsay, McCrae was remarkably shy and was unwilling to engage in critical, let alone theoretical, defense of his work, preferring to remain above conflict: "why should I philosophize? / Being happy I am wise," he later wrote.

After leaving school at seventeen, McCrae became a drafting apprentice to a Melbourne architect. His time spent at the architect's was brief, typical of his efforts at working, but it yielded two important meetings. His employer shared their building with the office of *The Champion,* one of the many magazines that encouraged aspiring authors to submit literary works. Trying to replicate the success of *The Bulletin* and *The Lone Hand,* short-lived magazines such as *The Champion* proliferated in Sydney and Melbourne at the end of the century, relying on large quantities of locally produced illustration and copy. Particularly welcome were poetic works and prose criticism, which, if they were not on local themes, gave overseas literature a local context. In many ways they carried on what George McCrae's circle had started, but whereas the Yorick Club remained aloof from the contaminating influence of "non-literary" elements, the magazines of the 1890s were the first attempts to fashion literary identities specifically mediated with a mass reading market in mind.

As McCrae's interest in architecture diminished, his own connections to the literary world grew. From contributions to *The Champion,* he began to make a living writing sketches, short stories, and poems and to

Contents page from the manuscript for McCrae's 1922 Du Poissey Anecdotes, *based on his father's stories about literary life in nineteenth-century Melbourne (from Harry F. Chaplin,* A McCrae Miscellany, *1967)*

construct an identity through the members of Melbourne bohemia who collected around such magazines. Journalists Randolf Bedford and Edward and Will Dyson encouraged McCrae to join a bohemian club, The Prehistoric Order of Cannibals, and convinced him to submit drawing work for Bernard O'Dowd's *Tocsin,* Frank Fox's *Lone Hand,* and A. G. Stephens's *Bookfellow* and *Bulletin,* as well as less enduring publications, such as *The Worker, The Trident, The Clarion,* and *The Freelance.*

In his characteristically visual manner, McCrae, for a radio program broadcast in 1938, recalled the circumstances of meeting one particular member of this group: "Across the top of my drawing board, I looked, six stories down into Collins Street. . . . One morning, in the building opposite I could see, a young man whose radiant personality was destined to influence the rest of my life. . . . I noted his dictatorian nose. . . . fringe and fez [, which] completed the effect . . . , Norman Lindsay, the artist on the *Tocsin,* from Creswick. . . . [He] had a passion for climbing on roofs." Lindsay in turn recalled McCrae as being "as handsome as a lyric poet should be with a gift of Dionysiac laughter." Upon meeting Norman Lindsay and his brother Lionel, McCrae abandoned his drafting job and moved into their Collins Street studio. For the remainder of their lives Norman Lindsay and Hugh McCrae influenced one another while each maintained his individualism as an artist–Lindsay, the aristocratic ambitious philosopher-artist; McCrae rarely committing himself to critical comment, diffident in company. The self-appointed Parnassus of an Australian artistic revival, Lindsay was instrumental in defining and directing McCrae's early poetry and provided the critical articulation and organization McCrae needed to see work through, although McCrae balked at some of Lindsay's more strident post–World War I attitudes. Judith Wright noted of the relationship: "What Lindsay did for McCrae, was, as it were, to go before him with a fiery sword of conviction and pugnacity, attacking the wowsers, [to] clear a space in which McCrae, the singer could produce his poetry."

In October 1896 Stephens, costumed in McCrae's memoir for their first meeting as "Zeus . . . eating porterhouse steak with a teaspoon," accepted a verse, "Owner Going West," for publication. A fantasy set on a farm "Twenty miles this side of Hay," the poem was a parody of a real estate advertisement for a haunted farm: "somethin' white comes stalkin' in, / White hands gropin' at its side, / Hollow face, hell's eyes, sunk chin" with "blood from fingers drippin' down." During the next six years McCrae wrote more than ninety pieces, mainly verse, the remainder short stories and sketches, for *The Bulletin.* Many of these pieces were collected in *Satyrs and Sunlight,* and most of them were lyrical fantasies. Yet, many of his works from the period between the mid 1890s until the outbreak of World War I often show a fascination for madness, moral and corporeal corruption, and savage violence, shifting between vague intimations of inevitable decay–for example, "The Fallen Statue" and "The Plain"–to a distinct fascination with malevolence and evil. In "The Murder Night," from 1901, a deluge at night is the inexorable agent of death: "The paddocks are striped with flood, / And under the barn-door creeps / A silent gutter of blood / In quiet little jerks and leaps." Lightning flashes reveal a hallucination of psychosis: "A gibbering madman stands / And sniffs his horrible fill / Of the rose in his shaking hands." In "Sixty Miles Away" the narrative persona imagines a Death's Head moth as a violator "now at her throat / Charr'd black on the silver of her skin, / I sped her spirit, scarlet to Old Charon's Wherry-boat, / And gave Corruption easy entrance in."

In May 1901 McCrae married Annie Geraldine Adams, "Nancy," daughter of a grazier who supplied the couple with some financial relief when the subsistence income of freelance writing became too slim. As soon as they had married, the McCraes moved to Sydney, encouraged by Norman Lindsay's promise of regular work at the Sydney-based *Bulletin.* For the first six months they shared a flat in Lavender Bay on the northern shore of Sydney Harbour with Lindsay and his wife, Kate, before moving into a house McCrae renamed "Kalyptos" at Chatswood in the northern commuter corridor of Sydney. While McCrae was living in Chatswood, Stephens suggested that McCrae's poetry could be produced in a collected edition by the Sydney publisher John Sands.

Of the pieces collected into the 1909 edition of *Satyrs and Sunlight,* many poems are composed using established forms, such as the Scottish folk song ("The Bairnie to the Birdie" and "The Gaberlunzie"); the ballad ("Red John of Haslingden"); the French medieval song ("Gallows Marriage"); and sonnets. This collection has commonly been read as a series of poems vivid in their visual construction and formal execution, whose exuberant tone is delivered through the ancient Greek figure of Pan–the faun, the satyr, or Silenus–beginning with the first piece, a short manifesto of intent, "I Blow My Pipes":

> I blow my pipes, the glad birds sing,
> The fat young nymphs around me spring
> I am the lord,
> I am the lord,
> I am the lord of everything!

McCrae's early poetry is dominated by satyrs, derived from ancient Greek myth, half-human, half-animal,

Title page for the 1928 third, enlarged, edition of McCrae's first book, augmented with poems such as scenes from his verse drama "Joan of Arc" (Cornell University Library)

always male. The satyr's intended purpose is to embody the poet/creator. In the upper half the poet is a human creative will, while the lower half, being animal—usually a horse—makes a connection to creative and procreative sources inaccessible to human intelligence, thus liberating it from restrictive human social behavior. Such a persona was as far from the egalitarian ethics of mateship and collective political action as an Australian poet could get at the time.

In a period in which landscape poetry dominated poetic production, moreover, McCrae's first collection is almost entirely devoid of any reference to local environment. Instead, the settings are either European—ancient Greece, medieval France, the Regency—or an imaginary Arcadian hybrid of them all. The bush becomes a "wood," a primal place of poet-gods, as in "The Deathless Gods." It is also a stage for sexual desire, often violent, as in "Ambuscade," but as Wright has noted, this wood is not a place where real women are permitted, rather women who in this landscape become as objectified and artificial as the landscape itself. "The End of Desire" demonstrates this characteristic:

> A flooded bowl of sarcenet
> Against her slender body sank,
> Death-black, and bearded all with jet
> Across the pleasures of her flank
> . . . .
> I took her closely, but while yet
> I trembled, vassal to my lust,
> Lo!– Nothing but some sarcenet
> Deep buried in a pile of dust.

In situating poetic place as a mythscape, McCrae was at odds with his contemporaries; this landscape was not concrete enough either to reap rewards, as in the works of Banjo Paterson, or to punish the foolish, as in the works of Henry Lawson. It has more in common with Christopher Brennan's alienated nonspace of silence, but unlike Brennan, McCrae feels no need to intellectualize its processes. The most enduring legacy of *Satyrs and Sunlight* was its articulation of images to which Norman Lindsay, his son Jack, and Lionel Lindsay returned after World War I in the *Vision* project, formulating images that became in the Lindsays' hands icons for the Nietzschean space of cultural regeneration of the West by Australians using the imprimatur of the ancients. Emblematic of the process is "The Deathless Gods":

> O, often I have seen in these new days
> The deathless gods,
> As some old carving, pregnant with the rays
> Of noon . . . alive singing in the woods.

While the volume sold well enough to go to several editions, McCrae's influence was only fully realized in the 1920s in the magazine *Vision*. The 1909 *Satyrs and Sunlight* was well received by *Lone Hand*, *The Sydney Morning Herald*, *The Bulletin*, and *Art in Australia*, and a second expanded version, which included more poems written from 1909 through 1911, was published by the Melbourne-based firm of Thomas Lothian in April 1911.

In May 1914, "broke and with no work" and the father of three children–Dorothea Huntly "Honey", Marjorie Francesca "Mardi", and Georgianna "Rose"–born in the previous decade, the McCraes left Australia for New York, where McCrae hoped to begin an acting career. Characteristically, McCrae had planned poorly this attempt at a career outside of writing, and for a man of his semipastoral sensibilities, New York was a disaster. He ran out of money almost at once, and, apart from some commercial illustration work, he only managed to land bit parts on Broadway in Granville-Parker productions of *Androcles and the Lion*, *The Garden of Paradise*, and *He Married a Dumb Wife*. McCrae was quick to judge and disliked virtually everything about New York and its populace: "They are typically a dime people, with dime minds and dime aspirations." After returning to Melbourne in March 1915, living first in Black Rock near Dromana, then in his childhood home "Anchorfield" in Hawthorn, McCrae played the lead role in a 1916 silent movie, *The Life of Adam Lindsay Gordon*, and became a cast member of Gregan MacMahon's Repertory Theatre, for which he played Shakespearean roles under Ian McLaren. McCrae spent the last two years of World War I working as a decoder in the wartime censor's office among men he characterized as "too inefficient for any service except government."

Not being a poet who kept to any larger program than finishing the poem at hand, McCrae had no plans for his next book. Once again the catalyst for publication was Norman Lindsay, who in a conversation outside *The Bulletin* office had casually asked McCrae what he had been working on. Bringing out a handful of loose manuscript papers, McCrae offered them for publication with the words "Do what you like with them." In 1920 the second of McCrae's poetic works, *Colombine*, was published in Sydney by Angus and Robertson.

Despite the disproportionate losses suffered by Australian troops, poetry about World War I was rare, but at the historical juncture at which McCrae's poetry of creation and violence could have been given full voice, his work became lighter and more domestic. Published in 1920, *Colombine* is a collection that is remarkable for what is not said of the war. Verses of nature and costumed drama represent McCrae's withdrawing entirely from social dynamic just as his isolation from society became more pronounced, as in the title poem:

> Here I will lie
>   Under the sky,
> Green trees above me
> All birds to love me . . .
>   Nature and I.
> Wish me good den
>   And leave me then.
> This sweet forest wind
> Is more to my mind
>   Than cities or men.

"Colombine" is as blithely and abstractly musical as "I Blow My Pipes" is vigorously declarative:

> Faint through the fluttering
>   Fall of a flute divine
> Softly the cellos sing:
>   "Colombine, Colombine"
> Softly the cellos sing
>   "Colombine" . . .
>   "Colombine" . . .

McCrae's next work, *Idyllia*, was published by Norman Lindsay on his own presses in Springwood, to which Lindsay had moved sometime earlier. The work was more a statement in Lindsay's design style, which drew heavily from English Decadence, than a publication of McCrae's poems. McCrae's poetry was not breaking into any new territory, something that became clear through the *Vision* episode. Under the pseudonym Benjamin Harcourt, McCrae also wrote and illustrated a series of prose and verse fancies, *The Du Poissey Anecdotes: To Which Are Joined Some Conversations with a Great Man* (1922), which retold stories George McCrae had told his son about nineteenth-century Melbourne and the Yorick Club, but which were set in London and used character names from London literary life of the late eighteenth century. The book, published by Art in Australia, was successful enough, but its audience was restricted to those who understood its lengthy, bookish, period in-jokes.

McCrae's substantial contribution to the period of the 1920s again came about through the aegis of the Lindsays, and almost as an accident. *Vision* magazine grew out of Norman Lindsay's *Creative Effort,* a book-length critique of western culture written during World War I and published soon afterward. Dissatisfied by the scale of critique offered by current periodicals such as *The Bulletin* and *Art in Australia,* Norman Lindsay's son Jack began to publish his own magazine, *Vision: A Literary Quarterly.* Through *Vision* Jack Lindsay espoused a cultural redemption through twin theories of antimodernism—referred to as "Primativism"—and neo-Platonism. *Vision* relied for its arguments on Norman Lindsay's theories but found in the figure of the satyr in Arcadia a more than apt analogy for Platonic form. If similar efforts in Europe were to result in modernist cultural experiments from Surrealism to fascism, an Australian equivalent was located in the space McCrae had cleared for the Lindsays. As Peter Kirkpatrick argues in a May 1992 article in *Australian Literary Studies,* "To the Australian vitalists, for whom the Nietszchean will to power was transposed into an Aestheticism where the font of creativity became centred in the individual artist's sexual life force, Arcadia was an obvious symbol of voluptuous freedom."

Through the four issues of *Vision,* between March 1923 and February 1924, the Lindsays threw themselves into a shrill yet vague evaluation of how modernism was failing art and "beauty." McCrae's influence was obvious from Jack Lindsay's foreword to the first issue:

> It is the sense of Vision that is lacking in all modernism which sets its criterion in a mass of primitive sensibility. And since Vision must always have its roots in life and sensation, the Faun, symbol of desire and poetry, who cries the songs of Olympos amid the woods of earth, is the saviour who must sound his pipes to call man to his high task.

McCrae allowed his *Satyrs and Sunlight* poetry to be used through the course of the magazine and continued to contribute poetry—along with Leon Gellert, Robert D. Fitzgerald, and Kenneth Slessor, whose own early efforts in pieces such as "Earth Visitors" and "Pan at Lane Cove" relied heavily on McCrae's imagery and phrasing: "This garden by the dark Lane Cove / Shall spark before thy music dies / With silver sandals; all thy gods / Be conjured from Ionian skies." Jack Lindsay included McCrae along with the other *Vision* poets in his 1923 anthology, *Poetry in Australia,* but the critical responses to the anthology were galvanized between McCrae and the younger poets; the reviewer in *The Bulletin* described the volume as "dirtied with the paws of the primitive beast," while the reviewer for *The Sydney Morning Herald* saw in McCrae's contribution an impression of "abounding vitality and vigour, a passion for life and beauty and colour." Already the departures between McCrae and the younger poets were beginning to show.

After *Vision* dissolved in March 1923, Jack Lindsay, while awaiting a planned expansion, which failed to eventuate, moved to London to set up a fine press, Fanfrolico, and a companion magazine, *The London Aphrodite,* which between 1926 and 1929 continued to espouse the precepts of *Vision. The London Aphrodite* published McCrae's work, but without any substantial Australian context, McCrae's poetry now seemed thoroughly outdated and drew little response from European critics. Another fine press production of McCrae's work, the 1928 edition of *Satyrs and Sunlight,* was published by the Fanfrolico Press. It included three scenes from "Joan of Arc," the manuscript of a verse drama that McCrae had been working on since 1922 and that he hoped would establish him as a dramatic poet. An impossibly complex drama, for which only an introduction and two soliloquies had been written, along with minimal stage directions—"Enter the mad King, carrying the bleeding hand of Orleans. He knocks up on the door with the Duke's hand"—the play was fragmented and discursively overwrought, and it was never performed.

McCrae received a Commonwealth Literary Fund pension of £52 per annum from 1926, having many years earlier, in a letter to A. G. Stephens, dismissed plans—inspired by Australian dramatist Louis Esson's conversations with William Butler Yeats—for state sponsorship of writers: "It never occurs to us that the real reason of failure is often dependence on others (such as Esson would like), consequent apathy and laziness, too good climate and fairly easy money and so on." During 1928 he co-edited *The New Triad* with Ernest Watt, but the publication died after the Wall Street crash. For the rest of his life McCrae survived by freelancing theater criticism, prose sketches, drawings, and cartoons to the *Melbourne Punch, The Bulletin, Art in Australia, Home,* and *The Sydney Morning Herald.* In 1929 McCrae submitted to *The Bulletin* a series of sketches on the Yorick Club of the 1870s. These essays were subsequently expanded and published by Angus and Robertson as *My Father, and My Father's Friends* in 1935. McCrae drew on his family history again when he edited his grandmother Georgiana Huntly McCrae's journal for publication along with reproductions of several of Georgiana's portraits.

By 1933 McCrae had completed a second verse drama, *The Ship of Heaven: A Musical Fantasy in Three Acts*–although his letters to Norman Lindsay have him working toward a finished version as early as 1922–which was published in 1951 by Angus and Robertson. Written in the midst of the Great Depression, the "plotless fairytale written for authentic children" concerns a tryst between Pierrot and Colombine, and again depends on unconventional staging (one character flies an airplane onto the stage) and plot development (the main character returns to life after the curtain has come down). *The Ship of Heaven* is at pains not to appear at all allegorical: in an "unspoken prologue" McCrae writes, "Obscurantists find no rebus here: play-field, only, for butterfly nonsense dreamed by Jeremy Jessamy, below a haycock *en Espagne,* 'all on a sommers dae.'" Sections of *The Ship of Heaven* were included in anthologies, but the work was staged only once–including a musical score by Dorris Fitton, a children's theater producer at the Independent Theatre of Sydney–in October 1933. Again, McCrae's hopes had been denied by overambitious dramatic construction.

The Mimshi Maiden, privately printed in 1931 and reprinted by the Halstead Press in 1938, showed that McCrae was not making thematic or formal strides in any direction. Part fairy-tale orientalism, punctuated by moments of savage violence, the title poem, again published in an art-book format by Halstead Press, is set "Round the island of Zinpangu," where the princess Mimshi is kidnapped by a tiger, which first dismembers a rickshaw driver: "Then he turned him to the coolie; / Struck him in the rearward haulers, / Showed his teeth, said 'Pully-Pully!' / Took the front ones in his maulers"; afterward the tiger takes Mimshi to his own land, where they settle: "Mimshi felt she must adore him, / (Such things sometimes do grow fixtures), / Loved the tiger; and she bore him / Little Mimshi-tiger mixtures."

The McCraes moved in 1931 from the Sydney suburb of Darling Point to the village of Camden, sixty kilometers southwest of Sydney. While describing the Anglophilic Camden as "a nice place made of roly-poly hills, with English trees among the pioneer ironbarks who had blackfellow friends even before James Ruse, at Parramatta, had 'sowed the first graines.' . . . Before that . . . before 1788," McCrae's poetry on the area in the 1939 collection was that of a domestic and satisfied man who could parody his past fascinations, as in "Reassurance":

McCrae in Camden during the late 1940s, beside a bust commissioned by the Art Gallery of New South Wales in Sydney (from Graeme Kinross-Smith, Australia's Writers, *1980)*

That was a hare (no Satyr as you thought)
That leaped behind us when we crossed the stile;
How pale your face is by the March moon caught–
And paler for your smile!

He does the same for city life in "Spring":

Pan on a tram! in a crooked horn blowing
Wicked old tunes that set the heart going,
And change, in our eyes, preademite ladies
From obvious frumps to Zoes and Sadies–
Wicked old tunes. The ticket collector
Fancies he's Paris, Achilles or Hector!
Sydney is Hellas, I drop in a coppice
Two blocks and a half past the *Bulletin* office.

World War II had poetically barely touched McCrae. Although he was not a player in the Ern Malley hoax, as an antimodernist almost by default, this battle of the books was fought to McCrae's advantage. He became for the ascendant conservative literary critics the poet who had grown out of the ferment of the 1890s but who had transcended parochial themes and issues by situating his dramas in the universal context of mythology. "Physically Hugh McCrae lives among us. . . . Mentally he inhabits the whole world in all its phases since the beginning of time," wrote R. G. Howarth in a 1957 *Southerly* special edition on McCrae's eightieth birthday, while Norman Lindsay in the same issue stuck by the *Vision* philosophy: "Some day the rest of the world will discover that the civilizing principle has elected Australian poets to revive the third big renaissance in English poetry, and Hugh McCrae will be hailed as the poet who fathered it into being." As critical reevaluation gained momentum through the 1940s and 1950s, two further anthologies—*Forests of Pan: A Selection of Poems Not Hitherto Reprinted From Hugh McCrae's Satyrs and Sunlight, 1928,* edited in 1944 by Howarth, and works selected by McCrae, *Voice of the Forest* (1945)—were published, while McCrae's work was found in school and university curricula. In 1953 McCrae was awarded an Order of the British Empire (OBE). Throughout the last ten years of his life, his shyness, compounded by the death of his wife, Nancy, in 1943, other health problems, and despair at his financial stress became increasingly debilitating. McCrae maintained contact by letters, often illustrated with macabre cartoons. They were collected in 1970 by Robert D. FitzGerald. McCrae died in Wahroonga, Sydney, on 17 February 1958.

Hugh McCrae has remained a somewhat unfashionable poet—there are no biographies of any substance on him—since the 1970s because of his problematic generalization of female figures and a disturbing, although by the standards of his times, fairly low level, racism. Even so, McCrae's poetry of the early years of the century challenged the fascination with realism, local color, and local themes to experiment with a mythologized visual landscape and an abstraction of the creative process itself. His inability to theorize, or even to debate the processes he was articulating, rendered these pieces static. Unable to move away from his achievement, and to some extent the victim of being championed in the Lindsays' almost puritan aesthetics of cultural regeneration, McCrae produced work that was formally repetitive in a period of experiment and innovation.

Letters:
Robert D. FitzGerald, ed., *The Letters of Hugh McCrae* (Sydney: Angus & Robertson, 1970);
A. W. Barker, *Dear Robertson: Letters to an Australian Publisher* (St. Lucia: University of Queensland Press, 1993).

Bibliographies:
George Mackaness, "Collecting Hugh McCrae," in his *Bibliomania: An Australian Book Collector's Essays* (Sydney: Angus & Robertson, 1965);

Harry F. Chaplin, *A McCrae Miscellany: The Books, Manuscripts, Letters and Drawings in the Library of Harry F. Chaplin* (Sydney: Wentworth Press, 1967).

Biography:
Norman Lindsay, "What Hugh McCrae Means to Me," *Southerly,* 17, no. 3 (1957): 123–127.

References:
O. N. Burgess, "Hugh McCrae and Robert Frost," *Southerly,* 17, no. 3 (1957): 152–157;
H. M. Green, "Hugh McCrae," in his *Fourteen Minutes: Short Sketches of Australian Poets and Their Work from Harpur to the Present Day* (Sydney: Angus & Robertson, 1950), pp. 86–92;
Tom Ingliss-Moore, "Hugh McCrae," in *Six Australian Poets* (Melbourne: Robertson & Mullens, 1942), pp. 38–61;
Alec King, "Australian Poet and Settler—Tough or Sentimental," *Westerly,* nos. 2–3 (October 1962): 93–96;
Peter Kirkpatrick, "Satyrs in the Top Paddock: Metaphysical Pastoral in Australian Poetry," *Australian Literary Studies,* 15 (May 1992): 141–154;
Kirkpatrick, *The Sea Coast of Bohemia: Literary Life in Sydney's Roaring Twenties* (St. Lucia: University of Queensland Press, 1993);
Jack Lindsay, "*Vision* and *The London Aphrodite,*" in *Cross Currents: Magazines and Newspapers in Australian Literature,* edited by Bruce Bennett (Melbourne: Longman Cheshire, 1981), pp. 91–101;
Noel Macainsh, "Hugh McRae [sic] and the Centaurs," *Quadrant,* 23 (October 1979): 19–26;
Kenneth Slessor, "Australian Poetry and Hugh McCrae," *Southerly,* 17, no. 3 (1957): 128–137;
Douglas Stewart, "An Introduction to McCrae: From 'A Proposed Selected Poems,'" *Southerly,* 22, no. 1 (1962): 2–11;
Stewart, "McCrae and Music," *Southerly,* 17, no. 3 (1957): 138–142;
John Webb, "The 'Dark' Element in Hugh McCrae," *Australian Literary Studies,* 6 (October 1973): 97–202;
Judith Wright, "The Affirmation of McCrae," in her *Preoccupation in Australian Poetry* (Melbourne: Oxford University Press, 1965), pp. 98–110.

Papers:
Hugh McCrae's correspondence and papers are held at the Mitchell Library, State Library of New South Wales, Sydney.

John Morrison
(29 January 1904 – 11 May 1998)

C. A. Cranston
University of Tasmania

BOOKS: *Sailors Belong Ships* (Kensington, Vic.: Dolphin, 1947);
The Creeping City (Melbourne: Cassell, 1949);
Port of Call (Melbourne: Cassell, 1950);
Black Cargo and Other Stories (Sydney: Australasian Book Society, 1955);
Twenty-Three: Stories (Sydney: Australasian Book Society, 1962);
Selected Stories (Adelaide: Rigby, 1972);
Australian by Choice (Adelaide: Rigby, 1973);
North Wind (Ringwood, Vic.: Penguin, 1982); revised and enlarged as *The Best Stories of John Morrison* (Ringwood, Vic.: Penguin, 1988; New York: Penguin, 1988);
Stories of the Waterfront (Ringwood, Vic.: Penguin, 1984);
This Freedom (Ringwood, Vic.: Penguin, 1985; New York: Penguin, 1985);
The Happy Warrior: Literary Essays on the Giants of Australian Literature (Fairfield, N.S.W.: Pascoe, 1987).

SELECTED PERIODICAL PUBLICATIONS—
UNCOLLECTED: "Something to Say," *Overland*, 7 (1956): 34–35;
"Come Back," *Meanjin*, 18 (1959): 291–298;
"Chekhov," *Overland*, 21 (1961): 53–54;
"Jim Healy," *Overland*, 21 (1961): 46;
"About the Bush and a Book," *Overland*, 22 (1961): 42;
"Literature in the Soviet Union," *Realist Writer*, 8 (1962): 14–15;
"Our Own Standard Library," *Age*, 20 June 1970, p. 15;
"Montacute. To Robert and Dorothy Clark," *Southerly*, 34 (1974): 379;
"World of Night," *Canberra Times*, 6 April 1991, p. 86.

A short-story writer, novelist, and essayist, John Morrison placed his art firmly in the realist tradition. In his autobiographical collection of essays, *The Happy Warrior: Literary Essays on the Giants of Australian Literature* (1987), Morrison maintains that to write on any subject one must have "experienced it, seen it, been involved, moved by it." Early in his career he wrote under the

John Morrison (Brendon Studios, Mount Waverly; from John Hetherington, Forty-Two Faces, *1946)*

pseudonym "Gordon" for the *Communist Review*. He was a founding member of the Realist Writers Group, a Communist literary organization of the Labor movement that included writers Frank Hardy, Bill Wannan, Walter Kaufmann, Stephen Murray-Smith, Ian Turner, Eric Lambert, Robert Close, and Nellie Stewart. His concern for decency and dignity in life and labor is revealed through multicultural working-class characters who experience the double bind of material necessity and industrial struggle, and whose occupations often reflect Morrison's own working history: dockside workers, or "wharfies," socially marooned sailors, itinerant station hands (workers on a sheep or cattle ranch), and gardeners. For the most part, the world reflected in Morrison's work is a white male Australia dating primarily from the 1920s to the 1960s; this characteristic, along with the outmoded occupations of some of his characters, who are often positioned within and defined by actual historical events, has led some critics to suggest his work is dated. As a social realist, however, Morrison is frequently concerned in his stories with the effects of social and economic change, and the fast-disappearing livelihoods reflect the dynamic relationship between what humans value and their Marxist use-value in an ever changing labor system.

Art and ideology entwine as Morrison's characters—the outsider, the anachronist, and the expatriate—reveal chilling psychological insights arising from moral dilemmas concerning idealism and material reality. To be a victim of a fixed idea is the characteristic fatal flaw, while drama often occurs within a restricted arena, such as a tram or train compartment, and the setting is primarily the Melbourne district and dockside. The sailor-character frequently represents life in transit. Another recurring character is the gardener, who occupies the marginal territory that separates the domestic (and feminine) from the outback (and masculine), allowing a narrative position from which to observe and comment on aberrant behavior, as in "The Battle of Flowers." In his introduction to *The Best Stories of John Morrison* (1988), the critic Stephen Murray-Smith cites "Pioneers" as "the finest story written in this country since Lawson." Similarly, John McLaren, who wrote the introduction to Morrison's 1987 collection *The Happy Warrior*, refers in an article for *The Australian* (1998) to Morrison's "proletarian vernacular," and says that the Henry Lawson tradition is in evidence in "The Compound," in which mateship is the trade unionist's religion.

John Gordon Morrison, the second of four children of John (a telegraph construction foreman) and Mary Turnbull Morrison, was born on 29 January 1904. He grew up in a Presbyterian family in Sunderland, in the northeast of England. The young Morrison recognized the distinction between illusion and reality early: although his father lost an eye working as a sapper in the Royal Engineers on the Western Front during World War I, and although the family experienced zeppelin raids, war became a reality for the twelve-year-old only on his seeing wounded soldiers from Flanders disembarking from a Red Cross train. The experience bore little resemblance to the heroics depicted in books he was then reading. The young boy frequented the Hendon Branch of the Andrew Carnegie Public Library, reading books on travel and natural history, including stories by G. A. Henty, H. Rider Haggard, and Robert Louis Stevenson. Morrison subscribed to *John O'London's Weekly,* a periodical that introduced him to French and Russian writers, such as Honoré de Balzac, Guy de Maupassant, Anton Chekhov, and Leo Tolstoy. However, the Polish writer Joseph Conrad and his sea novel *Lord Jim* (1900) exerted the most influence. Morrison began frequenting the docks that served as the chief port for the coalfields of County Durham. For him the sea promised masculine adventure, the possibility of a livelihood—the major industry in the area was shipbuilding—and the grey North Sea at nearby Grangetown provided Sunday morning swimming activity for the males of the family.

Morrison left Valley Road School at the age of fourteen, not an unusual move for a working-class boy in post–World War I Britain. He began work, in what was to become a checkered employment history, as a boy assistant to the deputy curator of the museum at the Sunderland Central Public Library, Museum, and Art Gallery in Mowbray Park. Morrison emphasizes the importance of this part of his life in preparing him for the practical craft of writing: he taught himself to type and write "fetching" letters that earned him interview opportunities. The museum also enabled him to further his interest in wildflowers and butterflies, and his concern for the environment was probably fostered there. When the family moved from Grangetown to Ryhope, Morrison and his lifelong friend and correspondent, Walter McLachlan, continued to explore the cliffs and the sea life. Morrison stayed at the museum for two years, postponing an apprenticeship at North Eastern Marine Engineering arranged by his father. At sixteen—now too old to be a boy assistant—he worked as an apprentice gardener to a ship owner at Cleadon House, near East Bolden. He set his sights on London and applied for a position at the Royal Botanical Gardens in Kew. Impatience and a rising desire to be near the London docks resulted in the eighteen-year-old's running away to work as a gardener at Parkside, Wimbledon, a position secured solely on the strength of his application letter. Morrison lasted a week, leaving in what was the first of many employment-related altercations.

Morrison's urge to travel, fueled by cabin-boy images in Daniel Defoe's *Robinson Crusoe* (1719) and Stevenson's *Treasure Island* (1883), resulted in his sailing to Australia as a government-assisted migrant at age nineteen. Freed from the personal and national constraints of home and oblivious to the new rules in operation in Australia, he set about entering into his vision of the Australian legend. In 1923 Morrison's youthful

"Australia" was bound up with his own entry into manhood. He rejoiced in the abundance and variety of occupations in Australia and saw labor as a means to self-sufficiency and implied economic stability. This view was later tempered by his experiences working for exploitative employers.

The Immigration Office found him work as a gardener at Zara Station, in the Riverina, New South Wales. He learned to be a "bush-head"–to handle horses, mark lambs, milk, and kill. He worked at Zara Station for ten months, writing descriptive letters to England about boundary riders and outback living. In 1924 he was living at the Federal Coffee Palace in Collins Street, queuing outside Excell's, O'Reilly's, Campbell's, and Hanson's (employment agencies) in Bourke and King Streets in Melbourne. He presented himself for an unscheduled, and brief, interview with the National Museum in Swanston Street on the basis of his Sunderland Museum experience. This period in Morrison's life was marked by an itinerancy fueled by youthful arrogance and a refusal to be exploited. Ideology and a sharp tongue ended one job at Sale, where he was milking cows and digging postholes. Similarly, a gardening job at Gisborne lasted one day; then a few days later Morrison took employment at Meelah Station, near Cressy, in the Western District. At Meelah Station, working at the wool press in a depot shed, he learned about trade unionism and was put on full wages, an experience recorded in "The Ticket" (*Overland*, 1957). He finished the season as a union wool presser at Mingawallah Station and returned to Melbourne with the intention of writing fiction. The idea foundered when he lost his wages playing cards in Fitzroy Gardens. He took work at the Berwick Hotel on the Warragul line, but since this job was also exploitative, Morrison quit and, penniless, took to the road. He ended up sewing chaff bags for food at a family farm. The Banjo Patterson image he had formed at Zara Station turned Lawsonian once he realized the disjunction between the image and the experience of the open road, and the young man began to see value in a place of his own.

At the end of the season Morrison returned yet again to the Federal Coffee Palace. He was hired as a gardener-handyman at Grendon Guest-House at Sherbrooke, in the Dandenong Ranges. The Dandenongs, says Morrison, were his first experience of hills and Australian tall timber. In them he found a sense of belonging, friendship, a library, and a place to write the draft of "The Prophet of Pandaloop." Morrison, an aspiring and self-critical writer, read Tolstoy's *Anna Karenina* (1873–1877) and became so discouraged over his own work that he left the Grendon Guest-House, sailed in the *Levuka* to Queensland, drifted for a month, then returned to the guest-house, declaring that the Dandenongs were home.

In 1925 Morrison worked as a pick-and-shovel laborer on the Mernda Road, supplementing his income by working odd jobs in exchange for accommodation in a hut owned by an Englishwoman. Morrison began a manuscript, typed on a Monarch typewriter carried from Sherbrooke on the back of his horse. It was a sight that caught the interest of J. C. V. Behan, Warden of Trinity College, Melbourne University, then living at Hackett's Hill. Behan sent the manuscript to a London publisher. The manuscript was never published, but Morrison received the encouragement he needed to continue writing.

He bought an acre of land at Kallista for £100, but the land was repossessed after he injured his leg and was unable to work for two months. He viewed this loss philosophically, saying that continued ownership of this prime real estate in the Dandenongs might have been his moral downfall. In 1927 Morrison, as did many migrants, returned to England–earning the fare back by uprooting blackberries–to see what it was he had left behind and also to try to find a publisher for his manuscript. A little more than a month later penury led him to the Salvation Army hostel in London. Morrison worked his passage back to Australia as a steward and on board met his first wife, Frances Rosina Jones, an Irish Catholic. They married on 1 September 1928 and had two children, John and Marie.

During the Great Depression, Morrison found work as a jobbing gardener, but he witnessed the struggle of others less fortunate, though he maintained that "The rich were still rich during the Depression." His sense of social justice was intensified when he was introduced by a neighbor to waterfront work. Morrison worked as a wharfie on the Melbourne docks during World War II.

Once admitted into the Waterside Workers' Federation (WWF) he became politically active. He joined the Communist Party of Australia (CPA) and began writing for the trade union press. Although the CPA was declared illegal during the war, Communist Party numbers in Australia peaked in 1944. This was the year when Morrison published "The Compound" in *New Writing*. War conditions resonate in the title, which openly criticizes the Waterside Workers' Labour Bureau in West Melbourne: he called it a "pig-pen," containing caged men, locked into a desperate competitive struggle for work. The story demonstrates Morrison's thematic concerns–the dilemma of remaining a decent and productive human in a world of Haves and Have-Nots, in which money or its absence has the power to debase and divide. The narrator of "The Compound" is by no means blind to the hierarchical

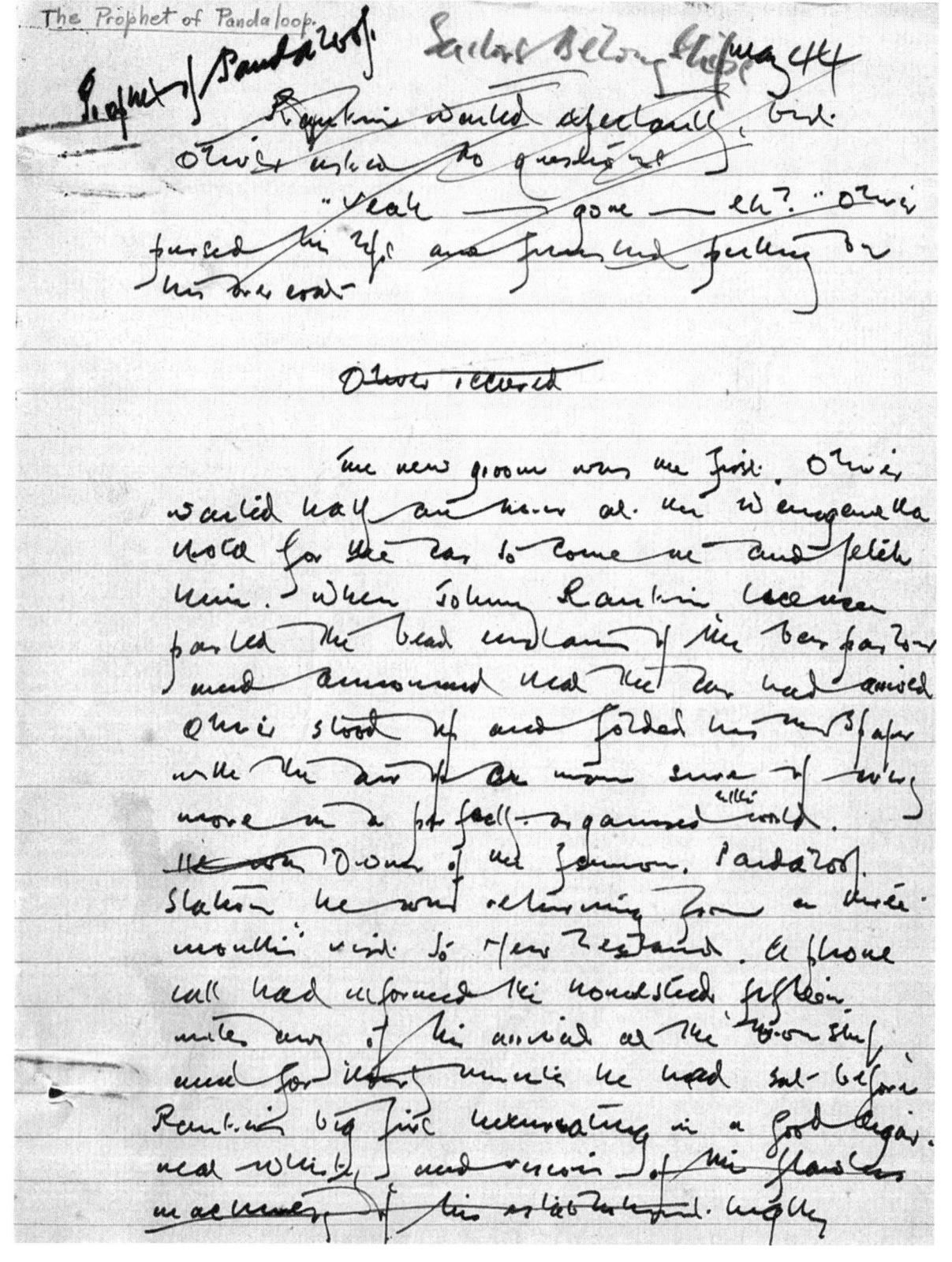

Page from an early draft of Morrison's short story "The Prophet of Pandaloop"
(National Library of Australia, MS4615)

nature of the Waterside Workers Federation—with its classification of members as Blanks, Firsts, Seconds, or Jacks—who are paid and valued according to their place within the structure. The workers themselves are distinct from management, and the parodic "The Judge and the Shipowner," published in *Australian New Writing* (1946) dispels any notion of wage equity between wharfies and parliamentarians.

While working as a wharfie—he was known as "Jack" to his wharfie friends, "John" to his writer friends—Morrison wrote thirteen stories for the *Communist Review* (Sydney) under the pseudonym "Gordon," a name assumed in consideration of his wife's religious faith. The difficulties inherent in the divided allegiances between Communism and Catholicism are amusingly transmuted into the conflicting ideologies of an atheist married to an Anglican in "Christ, the Devil and the Lunatic." Set during the Great Depression, the central character faces a moral dilemma, since stealing from a squandering lunatic in order to feed his family places him in opposition to his wife's beliefs.

The story was first published in *Sailors Belong Ships* (1947), a collection concerned with class division, racism, working conditions, and the isolation that resonates in the eponymous story, previously published in *Argus* (Melbourne). The collection was brought out by Dolphin Publications, established by the Communist writer Judah Waten and artist Vic O'Connor, to politicize an Australian realist literary tradition by giving precedence to everyday experiences. Frank Dalby Davison wrote the foreword, in which he singles out two stories published in *Australian New Writing* as representing Morrison's narrative gift: "Nightshift" (1944) and "All Through the Night" (1945). "Nightshift," which chronicles the death of a fellow wharfie, is nothing less than a performative narrative, since it was directly responsible for the erection of a landing platform at Yarraville dock. The collection includes "Tons of Work," in which the "Waterside Slave Market is open"; the dark "No Blood on Deck," in which "maiden" ships exact a toll; "The Prophet of Pandaloop," in which the prophet of socialism reorganizes a squatter's homestead; and "North Wind."

The year 1947 was important for Morrison's exposure as a writer. His stories were being published in *The Bulletin* and anthologized in the annual *Coast to Coast*. *Meanjin* published "A Coat for a Sailor," and the *Tribune* published "The Welcome," based on the docking of the *Ville de Nice* in South Melbourne. Her cargo, immigrants arriving from war-ravaged Europe, was often met with prejudice. Morrison's story illustrates a triumph over racial prejudice and union rules: the wharfies pass around the hat and treat the penniless and dispossessed population of children to ice-cream.

After encouragement from Davison, Morrison asked for and received a Commonwealth Literary Fund Grant in 1947. The novel *The Creeping City,* published in 1949, was identified by David Martin, in a 1959 article in *Meanjin*, as "one of the most Gallic novels ever written in Australia." Set in 1924 in the Dandenong Ranges, it reflects much of what Morrison experienced when he moved there in the 1920s. Melbourne is the Creeping City, and, like change, is unstoppable. The novel presents a communist utopia as three male characters are given an equal start, having purchased ten acres of bush at £1 an acre from the Victorian government. The material and intangible values placed on the environment provide the tension. Locals sell out to tourists, who are catered to by people such as Mrs. Terry, who runs a guest house for gentlefolk seeking a weekend pastoral experience. The shift in economics means that the original settlers become outcasts in the new social order. Though the novel did not sell well, it is seminal to Morrison's later fiction and received the attention of writer Gavin Casey, who reviewed it in *Meanjin* (Summer 1949). That same year, *Meanjin* editor C. B. Christesen published "The Pick-up," an industrial term made ambiguously sexual in its reference to trading human flesh, as wharfies became unemployed once a ship was unloaded. *Meanjin* also published a story in the Lawson tradition, "Going Through" (1951), a term heavy with ambiguity in its reference both to induction into the Waterside Workers' Federation and to an "unmitigated bastard."

Morrison left the dockside permanently in 1949 after being awarded a second Commonwealth Literary Fund Fellowship. This same year, the Australian Security Intelligence Organisation (ASIO) was established to continue monitoring Communist activities and to attempt blackballing Communist writers. Freed from the constraints of manual labor to write full time, Morrison produced his second novel, *Port of Call* (1950), in which "The Compound" appears as chapter 25. Possibly because of Morrison's migrant background and his experience of having his property at Kallista repossessed, *Port of Call* sensitively recognizes aspects of property ownership that are motivated by a wish to belong to something enduring in an increasingly unstable world, not by avarice. James ("Jim") Boyd embodies this social anomie: he is a Canadian sailor, constantly mistaken for an American, when he jumps ship in Melbourne. People and events from Morrison's past begin to emerge in his fiction. "Jim" is based on Morrison's hut mate, Frank, from Zara Station in New South Wales. Zara also provided the setting "Kulpinka" in the novel. "Miss Taft," self-sufficient and self-destructive, is based on Morrison's landlady during his time as a laborer on the Mernda Road. The major character finds communality and mateship at the home of a fellow wharfie, "Bo Abbott," modeled after a Tasmanian who was Morrison's fellow wharfie. In the novel Jim runs foul of the Waterside Workers' Federation. Faced with the difficulties in navigating relationships based on labor and on love, and with the complex rules and rituals associated with both, Jim returns to his ship, his illusions regarding shore life and the sea dispelled. In "The Economics of Realism: John Morrison" (*Meanjin*, no. 4, 1987) the critic Ivor Indyk writes about the economics of realism in both of Morrison's novels, saying, "the question of value is heightened because the subject in each case is in transit between two competing economies." David Martin, however, in his comments on the novels in "Three Realists in Search of Reality" (*Meanjin*, 1959), states that Morrison's "concept of total human responsibility and commitment seems closer to Sartre than to Marx" in that it "demonstrates a link between Marxism and Existentialism of which Morrison is not consciously aware."

In 1950 Prime Minister Robert Menzies's government brought in the Communist Party Dissolution Bill, declaring the Communist Party illegal, and Communists "unlawful." Although the bill was declared unconstitutional, one of Menzies's reasons for wanting the bill passed was that the government-funded Australia Council was financing known Communists, such as Morrison, to engage in subversive literature, since so-called realist writers were ostensibly holding up Australian culture for scrutiny. A literary witch-hunt followed, as the National Security Services (NSS) pursued suspected Communist sympathizers within the Fellowship of Australian Writers (FAW) and elsewhere. Morrison and his friend and fellow writer, Alan Marshall, were profiled by the NSS as Communist sympathizers, largely as a result of their activities in the Realist Writers group, a known Communist literary group, founded by Morrison and Frank Hardy. That year, when Hardy, author of *Power Without Glory* (1950), was charged with criminal libel, Morrison, Marshall, and Christesen formed the Melbourne chapter of the Frank Hardy Defense Committee. Hardy was acquitted the following year.

Morrison and Marshall were acquainted before ASIO investigations. Morrison had reviewed Marshall's novel *How Beautiful Are Thy Feet* (1949) for *Meanjin*, and his essay "Alan Marshall" (*Walkabout*, 1950; reprinted in *The Happy Warrior*, 1987) is testament to their friendship. By this time Morrison was working as chief gardener at Caulfield Grammar School in Ripponlea, traveling to work by bicycle. When the Australasian Book Society was launched in 1952, Morrison occasionally accompanied Marshall on tours through the Murray Valley, sometimes to share their love of nature, sometimes to market the books published by the Australasian Book Society. The society published Morrison's collection *Black Cargo and Other Stories* (1955), which came out the same year as Marshall's autobiographical *I Can Jump Puddles*.

Predominantly waterside stories, *Black Cargo* continues the association between the black slave trade and industrial working conditions. Australian seamen demonstrate solidarity for their Canadian counterparts over a nonunion labor ship. Slaves to the clock, management and wharfside labor signal their differences in the way time is interpreted in "Nine O'Clock Finish" (*Overland*, 1954). By contrast, in "Easy Money" (*Meanjin*, 1953) a young wharfie expresses guilt at being paid for doing nothing while the untold human cost is exemplified by the crippling of an Indian seaman. "The Fugitive" (*Meanjin*, 1953) demonstrates underclass resistance to authority in a recluse's refusal to answer "The old familiar, ominous sentence, falling on ears of the humble, generation by generation, all the way down through the ages. Slave–peasant–worker–which way did he go?" "The Sleeping Doll" (*Coast to Coast*, 1948) includes a bizarre twist because a swagman (a tramp carrying his belongings in a bag on his back) follows the boss's orders exactly. "The Door" is a study in the power of the gaze and includes hostility as railway passengers communicate mood levels through banging the carriage door.

A realist imperative forms the basis for a child's preference for the milkman over Santa Claus in "Man in the Night"; similarly, illusions regarding the notion of freedom are dispelled in "The Incense-Burner" (*Meanjin*, 1954), which echoes Morrison's experiences with the Salvation Army in London during the 1920s. A problematic notion of freedom as a moral imperative is portrayed in "The Busting of Rory O'Mahony," in which a former sailor, now gardener, resentful of his employer and his wife of twenty-six years, "busts out," assaulting his employer and deserting his wife. Few of Morrison's stories include women as central characters; the classic "The Battle of Flowers" is an exception. It records the escalating conflict between two middle-aged sisters, reduced to paupers in a biological war that turns their award-winning gardens into deserts. The gardener profits temporarily from these competing economies, confident of his own worth in the marketplace, in contrast to the eponymous Lena, in "Lena" (*Meanjin*, 1952), whose nonunion status, although she is honest and productive, opens her to exploitation. Morag Loh in "John Morrison: Writers at Work" (*Meanjin*, no. 4, 1987) has explored the criticism that Morrison's portrayal of women is shallow. Having spent his working life predominantly in the community of men, Morrison states that "It's only in the latter years of my life that women have asserted themselves and caused me to look at them as social animals."

Morrison was by now considered a "role model" by the Realist Writers (*Overland,* 156). His work, in translation, was reaching a Communist audience overseas. In Warsaw "The Compound" (1944) was translated as "Targ Niewolnikow" (1955); in Bucharest "The Prophet of Pandaloop" (1945) was translated as "Profetul Din Pandaloop" (1957); and in Budapest "The Busting of Rory O'Mahony" (1955) was translated as "O'Mahony Daridoi" (1959). Coincidentally, during this time Morrison, along with other members of the CPA, experienced disillusionment with the Party after the 1956 publication of Nikita Khrushchev's secret speech. Morrison still held to the principles of communism, however, traveling to the U.S.S.R. in 1961 and 1964 as a delegate of the Fellowship of Australian Writers. It was a time for reflection, and Morrison published "Judah Waten" (*Overland,* 1958), a personal portrayal of a fellow Communist, writer, and the man he went into battle with as a member of the Frank Hardy Defence Committee in 1950.

Morrison returned to his beloved Dandenong Ranges, moving to a shack on Mount Evelyn. Marshall also owned property in the district, as did fellow writer and friend Leonard Mann. The greater distance meant Morrison had to travel to his gardening job by train, and the setting of a railway compartment presented material for his next collection, *Twenty-Three: Stories* (1962). Temporary communities and lives in transit are portrayed in "The Hold-up," in which passengers swelter in isolated and petty sufferance as their train is held up because of a death on the track. The nihilism of the moment captures what Martin sees as an existentialist undercurrent in Morrison's work, which includes several instances of casual death. An anodyne of sorts appears in "Dog Box" (*Overland,* 1960), which is a tribute to small moments and a mother's love. Loh's comment regarding Morrison's portrayal of women as shallow finds credence in "The Last Three Years," which portrays a woman on a beach, metaphorically burying her head in the sand, while her lover struggles with the serious business of war. Women are a source of misery in "The Lonely One," though Old Sam's fear of women is a fear of loss, an idea repeated in the loneliness expressed by the chronic eccentric of "Goyai." With the death of his wife, followed by a bushfire that destroys their house, Joe Abbs's "losses" represent a reentry into the world of men in "This Freedom" (*Meanjin,* 1957). On the other hand, a win at Tattslotto provides Ernie Caslaw an escape from matrimonial bondage in "Sydney or the Bush."

A more sympathetic portrayal of women occurs in "To Kill a Snake," a story that favors Mrs. Mason's

Morrison camping on a friend's bush retreat at South Lyndhurst, Victoria, 1953 (from Graeme Kinross-Smith, Australia's Writers, *1980)*

pragmatism over Cayley's pontification; an alliance forms between the worker and women against the master of a despotic household in "To Margaret," in which a barrister, whose word is law, confronts a willful gardener; and in "Black Night in Collingwood" the wife of a Collingwood supporter breaks free from the tyranny of her husband's enslavement to a national obsession, football. Morrison himself singles out "Ward Four"–based on his experience in the Alfred hospital after a wharf accident–as a narrative that recognizes the existence of a community of working women capable of strength and dignity in a work environment that includes its own peculiar hazards.

The collection includes two other dockside stories, "The Drunk" and "The Judge and the Shipowner." In "All I Ask," set in the Dandenongs, seaman Nelson has few needs and revels in the simple domestic pleasures of mixed human companionship, good food, and a place to sleep. His sleep is interrupted by the news that the owner's son has run away to sea. The situation repeats the Realist Writers' dictum that one must live the experience in order to see through the illusion.

Morrison is master of the double bind, or as Martin says, "He writes as a compassionate man who can bear the contradictions of life." Morrison crafts situations and ethical dilemmas that provide the impetus for stories such as "A Man's World" (*Bulletin*, 1957) and "It Opens Your Eyes," in which a relationship is irreparably damaged because of a Tattslotto win. The national obsession with Tattslotto pales beside the reality of funds collected for an injured wharfie in "Bo Abbott" (*Realist Writer*, 1962), a character also in *Port of Call*. Mateship has its limits in "The Drunk" (*Meanjin*, 1960), as wharfies take on extra work to cover for a mate. Because the story tells of a drunk on the dock, it was rejected for publication by the secretary of the Waterside Workers Federation, Jim Healy. The following year Morrison published the essay "Jim Healy" (*Overland*, 1961).

Workplace solidarity is more justifiable than loyalty to one's family in the utilitarian double bind in "The Children," in which a father places the safety of his children before that of twenty schoolchildren during a bushfire. Human insignificance is explored in "Morning Glory," in which a chicken farmer justifies his right to defend property with the killing of a chicken thief; and human use-value continues as a concern in "The Man on the 'Bidgee'" (*Meanjin*, 1955), in which an aged and destitute swagman, described as a "real Australian" in a changed Australia, refuses to work for low wages. This form of dignified self-destruction stems from the swaggie's enduring sense of self-worth, as articulated in "The Ticket" (*Overland*, 1957): "The big moment for a youth is not, as we are so often told, when he first does a man's work. It is when he first receives a man's wages and finds other men standing beside him as equals." In this collection characters struggle with the burden of their choices, for there are no absolute guidelines for achieving justice. A. A. Phillips, in "The Short Stories of John Morrison" (*Overland*, 1974), sees this collection as existing "in a no-man's land lying somewhere between documentary and fiction." The comment foreshadows Morrison's gradual shift into the essay form.

Twenty-Three won the Gold Medal of the Australian Literature Society in 1963. That same year Morrison suffered a heart attack. Poor health meant an end to manual labor, but Morrison was well enough to accompany Marshall and nine other delegates to the International Conference of Writers for Peace, in Weimar, East Germany. Earlier, in "Judah Waten," in 1958, Morrison had written that now is "an age when we need lovers of men far more urgently than we need lovers of nature." The idea informed Morrison's previous work, with its concern for industrial safety, wage equity, and human dignity; but now, retired from heavy labor, Morrison revealed more clearly in his work his continuing interest in nature, formed during childhood and evident in his first novel, *The Creeping City*. As with human nature, the double aspect of nature is recalled in "Bushfire" (*Overland*, 1963; *This Freedom*, 1985), which records the dangers inherent in bush life as experienced during the bushfires of 1926 and 1939. Another change is the emphasis on the belles-lettres or essay form, as in "The Big Drink" (*The Age*, 1964; *Australian by Choice*, 1973), which celebrates a trip with Marshall to see the rising waters of Chalka Creek, which feeds the Kulkyne Forest in northern New South Wales. Graeme Kinross-Smith, in *Australia's Writers: An Illustrated Guide to Their Lives and Their Work* (1980) calls this essay "one of Morrison's greatest pieces of writing." A nature essay, it is also an elegy for the Barmah swamps and the Drowned Forest at the bottom of Lake Mulwala. Similarly, cicadas, frogs, and a multitude of birds are celebrated in "Singing-Night Christmas" (*The Age*, 1964; *Australian by Choice*, 1973).

On 9 January 1967 Morrison's wife, Frances, died after time in the Alfred Hospital. In 1968 his friend and fellow writer Bernard Cronin died. His thoughts turning to the past, Morrison wrote of the time Marshall took him to Eltham to visit bushland he had once owned but which was now farmland. Morrison records the transitory nature of humans and their environment in "The Writer and the Swagman" (*Overland*, 1969; *Australian by Choice*, 1973), reflecting on "how completely a man and his associations can be wiped from the face of the earth."

Morrison continued to write essays concerned with criticism, biography, autobiography, and the environment. "English Is Good Enough" (*Overland*, 1967; *The Happy Warrior*, 1987) is a guide to writing. "The Diamond 88" (*The Realist*, 1968; *The Happy Warrior*, 1987) is a critical examination of a chapter from Ernestine Hill's *The Territory* (1951) of the same name. "Blue and Yellow Macaw" (*Overland*, 1968; *Australian by Choice*, 1973) is an autobiographical account of the impact of the exotic on the young Morrison at the Sunderland Museum. "Pommy in Wonderland" (*Meanjin*, 1971; *Australian by Choice*, 1973) recalls the checkered employment history of Morrison, experiencing his idea of the exotic. "The Moving Waters" (*Overland*, 1971; *Australian by Choice*, 1973) recalls the beaches and marine life of Morrison's youth lost to oil spills from a shipping industry that once provided him with a living, a memory that prompts him to lament, uncharacteristically, that it "makes one despair of man and god." "Pastoral" (*Overland*, 1971; *The Happy Warrior*, 1987) observes the ecological interplay between swifts and winged ants.

Morrison dedicated his *Selected Stories* (1972) to his second wife, Rachel Gordon, a Jewish woman he married on 24 March 1969 after he returned to Melbourne. It includes reprints–"The Prophet of Pandaloop," "The Lonely One," "The Battle of Flowers," "The Nightshift," "To Margaret," "The Hold-up," "The Sleeping Doll," "This Freedom," "Goyai," "Christ, the Devil and the Lunatic," "The Children," "The Incense-Burner," "The Drunk," "It Opens Your Eyes," "The Judge and the Shipowner," and "Morning Glory"—many of which are in *Twenty-Three*. Ian Reid, in the introduction to *Selected Stories*, singles out "Goyai," "The Children," and "The Incense-Burner" as reflections of the predominant theme of loneliness "in its varieties." "Pioneers," cited by Murray-Smith as superior to anything since the work of Henry Lawson, challenges the pioneering myth: the major character, the most monstrous of Morrison's dominating males, engineers his isolation. Opinionated, a victim of fixed ideas and anachronistic ways, he causes his wife to suffer economic and emotional deprivation partly as punishment for giving birth only to girls.

The following year, 1973, *Australian by Choice*, a collection of "partly memoirs and partly reflections," was published. In his introduction Morrison stresses the value of the everyday over the imagination or high adventure in providing narrative material. Again, the collection includes reprints—"Bo Abbott," "Man on the 'Bidgee,'" "The Writer and the Swagman," "The Moving Waters," "Blue and Yellow Macaw," "Singing-Night Christmas," "Pommy in Wonderland," "The Big Drink," "Pastoral," and "English is Good Enough." New to the collection are "Murder on the One-Thirty" (*Meanjin*, 1966); "The Trinket Box" (*Meanjin*, 1967), a tale of craftsmanship and chivalry; "The Blind Man's Story" (*Overland*, 1966), in which a husband's disability ensures his complete dependence on his wife and therefore his compliance; and an essay, "How True Is That Story?" (*Overland*, 1973), in which Morrison discusses the sources for many of his stories, supporting his belief that "stories are right there under the nose."

Morrison, having taken up residence in Brighton Road, Elwood, continued to involve himself in the literary community, judging literary competitions and writing reviews and essays. "Frank Davison" (*Overland*, 1976; *The Happy Warrior*, 1987) is Morrison's personal perspective of his friend and mentor who had died in 1970. "The Books That Drove Me On" (*Educational Magazine (Vic)*, 1978; *The Happy Warrior*, 1987) examines the literature that influenced the young Morrison. One such work was the periodical *John O'London's Weekly*, which a quarter of a century later, in 1951, reviewed Morrison's *Port of Call*. "Some Thanks Delayed" (*Overland*, 1983; *The Happy Warrior*, 1987) was written as a companion piece, with its emphasis on the importance of words of encouragement; "John Morrison" (*Australian Literary Studies*, 1981; *The Happy Warrior*, 1987) is the author's statement and an analysis of the short-story form; the autobiographical "Escape" (*Overland*, 1982; *The Happy Warrior*, 1987) spans three generations of "running away"—the young Morrison's father, taking flight from a "difficult" wife; Morrison himself, eighteen years old and eager to enter the illusion of adventure and independence; and years later in Australia, his own son.

North Wind, Morrison's collection published in 1982, is dedicated to his grandson Malcolm, who was killed in 1978. The collection, with an introduction by Murray-Smith, gets its title from the story of the same name published earlier, concerning the hypochondriac Mother Lil, a victim of a fixed idea, in a story that exploits mother-in-law stereotypes. The collection also includes the earlier stories "To Margaret," "Easy Money," "The Battle of Flowers," "Ward Four," "Pioneers," "The Sleeping Doll," "The Nightshift," "Goyai," "Dog Box," "Morning Glory," and "The Incense-Burner." Morrison was now in his late seventies and to some extent the collection addresses the process of aging. In "Tinkle, Tinkle, Little Bell" (*Meanjin*, 1965) Mr. Carnation—Morrison regularly employs aptronyms—feels the sting of youth's disdain for age and seeks puerile revenge. His sourness toward lovers is in marked contrast to the relationship tenderly explored in "Transit Passenger," in which a widow and widower meet in a cafeteria and become lovers the same day. The moment celebrates a rare thing in Morrison's work—the end of loneliness and the promise of stability as two bereaved people, in transit, make permanent contact. "Perhaps You've Got It" refers to the elusive quality of happiness, as a couple in their seventies do not realize that happiness is already theirs until they win Tattslotto, and discord sets in. The theme of economics and avarice continues in "The Haunting of Hungry Jimmy." Jimmy's voracious appetite for work and money brings him success in purchasing his former employer's home.

In 1984 Marshall, probably Morrison's closest friend, died. The obituary, "The Happy Warrior" (*Overland*, 1984), applauds Marshall's "abiding conviction that only in a socialist form of society lay any prospect of mankind continuing to inhabit the planet Earth." Morrison demonstrates a greater awareness of the interrelationship between humans and the environment than was demonstrated in "Judah Waten."

Stories of the Waterfront (1984) includes dockside stories printed in earlier collections—"The Compound," "Tons of Work," "Bo Abbott," "Going Through," "All Through the Night," "The Welcome," "Nine O'Clock Finish," "A Man's World," "The Pick-Up," "The Drunk," "The Nightshift," "Black Cargo," "The Judge and the Shipowner," "No Blood on Deck," and "Easy Money"—and is recognized as an important literary history of wartime Melbourne dock-

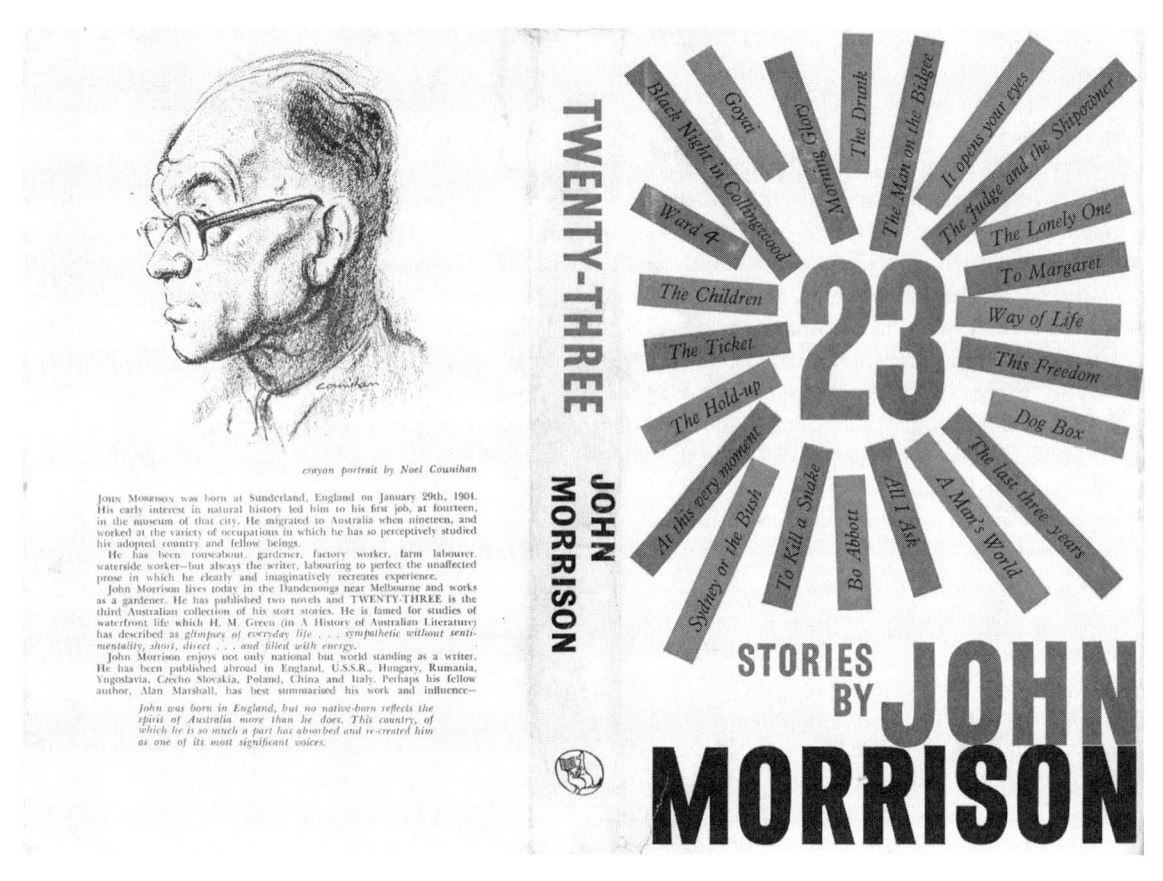

Dust jacket for Morrison's 1962 collection of short stories, which won the Gold Medal of the Australian Literature Society in 1963 (Bruccoli Clark Layman Archives)

yards. Critic Bev Roberts in the essay "Writing about Reality: John Morrison, Amanda Lohrey, Conal Fitzpatrick" for *Meanjin* (1984) notes that while "many of the stories are weakened by sentimental and polemical tendencies," they are "a valuable corrective to the biased and limited representation of both workers and unions in Australia."

This Freedom (1985), a title taken from a story published in *Twenty-Three,* includes two uncollected reprints–"Bushfire" (*Overland,* 1963), in which a community unites against a common threat, and "Appointment at Princess Gate," which provides a stark contrast through the calculated cruelty of a daughter towards her father. The other stories are "The Busting of Rory O'Mahony," "Sailors Belong Ships," "The Children," "Lena," "The Blind Man's Story," "Man in the Night," "Christ, the Devil and the Lunatic," "The Ticket," "The Man on the 'Bidgee,'" "Black Night in Collingwood," "The Fugitive," "It Opens Your Eyes," and "The Prophet of Pandaloop."

In 1986 Morrison won the Patrick White Award for Writers of Distinction. The award ($18,000), set up by White from the proceeds of the Nobel Prize for literature, is awarded to an older Australian writer who has received less critical attention than is appropriate. Morrison, then in his eighties, with a weak heart, had been a working man writing about working people; but unlike many of his Tattslotto scenarios his material windfall sowed no discord. The Morrisons continued to live in an apartment at 4/10 Maryville Street, Ripponlea, and Morrison's short stories remained in print.

The Best Stories of John Morrison (1988), originally published as *North Wind,* includes some minor revisions with the addition of a reprint of "All I Ask" and "Quiet Night in Station Street," previously uncollected. The latter humorously demonstrates Morrison's belief that "stories are right there under the nose" as Mrs. Dobbs is interrupted from her television viewing with news of her son's car accident, the invasion of two police officers, and the public acknowledgment of the girlfriend's pregnancy.

Morrison's final publication, *The Happy Warrior,* is a collection of previously published autobiographical and biographical essays on Marshall–to whom Morrison intended the title to refer–Davison, and Waten. It is a tribute to times past, friends gone, and a gently remembered childhood, a collection that "contains my heart," as Morrison describes it. In his introduction McLaren recognizes the shift in focus that accompanied Morrison's shift in form; McLaren writes, "The robust sense of egalitarian democracy, the sympathy for the vulnerable, and the anger at destruction and cruelty are what we might expect from the stories. But these prose pieces also reveal behind his apparent detachment a passionate identification with the world around him." *The Happy Warrior* completes the literary circle of the full life of an observer and participant. Morrison's works are still being read. *Stories of the Waterfront* and *This Freedom* have appeared in various high school curricula; in 1991 playwright John Romeril staged *Black Cargo* in Melbourne; and "Nine O'Clock Finish" was published in *Overland* during the last week of Morrison's life to celebrate its 150th issue. Until well into his nineties, Morrison continued to give interviews and reply to correspondence using a manual typewriter, until arthritis prevented even that. The Morrisons moved to Caulfield House Rooms until Rachel went to a special nursing home, where she died on 7 January 1997. John Morrison died 11 May 1998. In *The Australian* (14 May 1998) McLaren wrote that Morrison will be remembered "for his understanding of the rhythms of work and nature, and for his steadfast loyalty to the principles of working-class solidarity." In "John Morrison 1904–1998: Further Fragments Recalled" (*Overland*, 1998) Vane Lindesay wrote of Morrison's frustration at being unable to write about the poorly paid nurses in the hospital, and that "Among the last words I was to hear John say concerned his belief, indeed fear, of the planet's destruction, not by nuclear war, but by man-made pollution."

Interview:

"*John Morrison: Videos on Australian Writers: Archival Writers Series II*," interviewed by James Murdoch, video, Australian Council for the Arts, 1988.

References:

John Hetherington, "John Morrison: Flowers and Fiction," in his *Forty-Two Faces* (Melbourne: F. W. Cheshire, 1962), pp. 78–83;

Ivor Indyk, "The Economics of Realism: John Morrison," *Meanjin*, 66, no. 4 (1987): 502–512;

Graeme Kinross-Smith, *Australia's Writers: An Illustrated Guide to Their Lives and Their Work* (West Melbourne: Thomas Nelson, 1980), pp. 224–228;

Vane Lindesay, "John Morrison 1904–1998: Further Fragments Recalled," *Overland*, 151 (1998): 30;

Morag Loh, "John Morrison: Writers at Work," *Meanjin*, 66, no. 4 (1987): 496–501;

David Martin, "Three Realists in Search of Reality," *Meanjin*, 57, no. 3 (1959): 305–322;

Deirdre Moore, "The Realist Writers," *Overland*, 156 (1999): 24–29;

A. A. Phillips, "The Short Stories of John Morrison," *Overland*, 58 (1974): 31–35;

Bev Roberts, "Writing about Reality: John Morrison, Amanda Lohrey, Conal Fitzpatrick," *Meanjin*, 63, no. 4 (1984): 408–413.

Papers:

Collections of John Morrison's manuscripts are in the National Library of Australia; collections of his papers are held at the University of Melbourne archives.

Nettie Palmer
(18 August 1885 – 19 October 1964)

Deborah Jordan
University of Melbourne

BOOKS: *The South Wind* (London: Wilson, 1914);

Shadowy Paths (London: Euston Press, 1915);

Modern Australian Literature (1900–1923) (Melbourne: Lothian, 1924);

Henry Bournes Higgins: A Memoir (London: Harrap, 1931);

Talking It Over (Sydney: Angus & Robertson, 1932);

Spanish Struggle (Melbourne: Spanish Relief Committee, 1936);

Australians in Spain, by Palmer and Len Fox (Sydney: Forward Press, 1937; enlarged edition, Sydney: Current Books, 1948);

Fourteen Years: Extracts from a Private Journal 1925–1939 (Melbourne: Meanjin Press, 1948);

Henry Handel Richardson: A Study (Sydney: Angus & Robertson, 1950);

The Dandenongs (Melbourne: National Press, 1952);

Bernard O'Dowd, by Palmer and Victor Kennedy (Melbourne: Melbourne University Press, 1954).

Collection: *Nettie Palmer: Her Private Journal "Fourteen Years," Poems, Reviews and Literary Essays,* edited by Vivian Smith (St. Lucia: University of Queensland Press, 1988).

OTHER: Leon Joseph Villiers, *The War on the Workers,* selected by Palmer and Christian Jollie Smith (Melbourne: Workers' Press, 1918);

An Australian Story-Book, edited by Palmer (Sydney: Angus & Robertson, 1928);

C. Hartley Grattan, *Australian Literature,* preface by Palmer (Seattle: University of Washington Book Store, 1929);

Tom Petrie's Reminiscences of Early Queensland (Dating from 1837) Recorded by His Daughter [Constance Campbell Petrie], introduction by Palmer (Sydney: Angus & Robertson; Brisbane: Queensland Book Depot, 1932);

The Centenary Gift Book, edited by Palmer and Frances Fraser (Melbourne: Robertson & Mullens, 1934);

A. F. Howells, *We Went to Spain,* foreword by Palmer (Melbourne: Spanish Relief Committee, 1938);

Nettie Palmer (National Library of Australia)

Lesbia Harford, *The Poems of Lesbia Harford,* edited by Palmer (Melbourne: Melbourne University Press, 1941);

Ada Jackson, *Behold the Jew,* foreword by Palmer (Melbourne: Jewish Council to Combat Fascism and Anti-Semitism, Stewart Taylor, 1943);

Alice Henry, *Memoirs of Alice Henry,* with postscript by Palmer (Melbourne: Privately printed, 1944);

Coast to Coast 1949–1950, edited by Palmer (Sydney: Angus & Robertson, 1950).

TRANSLATION: Irma Schnierer, *Liesal Asks Why-y-y-y? A Book about Children for Grown Ups* (Sydney: Angus & Robertson, 1940).

SELECTED PERIODICAL PUBLICATIONS– UNCOLLECTED: "Literature and Otherwise," *Australia,* 7 November 1917, p. 24;
"Shaw Neilson," *Bulletin,* 22 December 1923;
"Post Mortems on Anatole France," *Bulletin,* 31 May 1925;
"The Showing Up of Walt Whitman," *Bulletin,* 25 November 1926;
"The Novel in Australia," *Courier* (Brisbane), 15 October 1927, p. 22;
"Lovely Brisbane: And a Few Indignations," *Sunday Mail* (Brisbane), 20 November 1927, p. 22;
"John Galsworthy: Artist or Mechanic?" *Courier,* 26 November 1927, p. 22;
"Readers and Writers," *Illustrated Tasmanian Mail,* 11 January 1928, p. 4;
"Novelists of Russia: Their Effect Abroad," *Courier,* 14 January 1928, p. 20;
"Edward Garnett: England's Surest Critic," *Courier,* 4 May 1929, p. 4;
"The Vanished Tribes," *Courier,* 18 May 1929, p. 25;
"Pure Literature: Poetry or Handbooks," *Courier,* 29 March 1930, p. 20;
"Is Australia Modern?" *Telegraph* (Brisbane), 19 December 1931;
"'A Nation of Charwomen' Does Housework Get Us Down?" *Australian Women's Mirror,* 28 June 1932, pp. 10, 31;
"Some Pacifists' Protests: Books Which Are Changing the World," *All About Books,* 14 October 1933, p. 162;
"The Pioneer Woman—Conscious and Unconscious Builders in a New Land," *Argus,* 16 October 1934, p. 40;
"The Discovery of Christopher Brennan," *Manuscripts,* no. 13 (1934): 1–6;
"Ruth Pitter," *Bulletin,* 20 March 1935;
"Young Literatures," *Bulletin,* 4 December 1935;
"Notes by the Way: Are Women Bored by Emancipation?" *Australian Woman's World* (March 1936): 12–13;
"Radio in War-Time: Hearing the Enemy Think," *Tomorrow,* 16 March 1938, pp. 310–312;
"Australia–an International Unit," *Meanjin Papers,* 3, no. 1 (1944): 6–11;
"The Australian Language," *Meanjin Papers,* 4, no. 3 (1945): 186–189;
"The Growth of Literature in Latin America as an Australian Sees It," *Meanjin,* 6, no. 2 (1947): 115–119.

Nettie Palmer was the most important nonacademic critic in Australia from the mid 1920s through the 1930s. Essayist, biographer, diarist, linguist, and poet, she was one of the most humane and sensitively perceptive writers of her time. At ease with the whole European tradition, she played a central part in the increasing recognition of literature in Australia and was a tireless worker for Australian readers and writers. Her involvement in Australian cultural life spans five decades. Manning Clark in *A History of Australia,* volume one (1987) described her as "the great life-affirmer, the giver of the waters of life," and Marjorie Barnard, on 16 May 1938, wrote to Palmer of her "marvellous intellectual energy that is light and joy to all of us."

Palmer received much praise during her lifetime. A. D. Hope lauded her intellectual toughness and ability to get at the essence of things; even Henry Handel Richardson in a private letter of 18 June 1929 wrote of Palmer's ease of expression and journalistic talents. Many commentators concur regarding her personal generosity, capacity to inspire others, and the significance of her voluminous correspondence and networking. Hers was a courageous attempt not only to sustain broad political and spiritual ideals but also to embody them in everyday life for the community. The great bulk of Palmer's journalism never appeared in book form.

Scholars dispute the nature of her achievement. Vivian Smith in *Vance and Nettie Palmer* (1975) argues that through interpreting others' works and trying to find an audience for their creations she found her real fulfillment; others contend she sacrificed her talents to her life with Vance Palmer and their children and consequently never fully developed as a poet or linguist. Drusilla Modjeska in *Exiles at Home. Australian Women Writers 1925–1945* (1981) presents Palmer as arbiter and patron of a socially left group of writers, despite the constraints she worked under as a woman. Modjeska believes Palmer was informed by a misconceived understanding of national culture. In the debate over the emergence and development of a radical nationalist literature, Palmer's collaboration with Vance Palmer has mitigated against a separate reading of her independent work, especially on foreign literatures. The extent of her feminist challenge to the construction of the white "Australian Legend" has been underestimated.

Janet Gertrude (Nettie) Higgins was born on 18 August 1885 at Sandhurst (Bendigo), Victoria, where her father, John Higgins, Irish-born, was an accountant. Her mother, Catharine MacDonald Higgins, was born in Australia of Scottish origin. In 1888 the family

Vance and Nettie Palmer with her brother, Esmonde Higgins (standing); and (seated) her mother, Catharine Higgins; the Palmers' elder daughter, Aileen; Nettie Palmer's father, John Higgins; and the Palmers' younger daughter, Helen (from Drusilla Modjeska, Exiles at Home, 1981)

moved to Armadale, a suburb of Melbourne, where a second daughter died in infancy. Nettie Higgins's only brother to survive childhood, Esmonde, was not born until 1897. The children's Baptist upbringing was austere, typified by their grandmother's insistence that the Higginses "aren't handsome, but we all have high principles," as Palmer recalled in a letter to Hugh McCrae in July 1948. Higgins's education began at home with her mother and continued at Miss Rudd's Seminary at Malvern. Higgins began writing early; at twelve she told her father she was a poetess, "a freak of nature" that "can't be cured / must be endured."

Between 1900 and 1904 she attended Presbyterian Ladies College (PLC), a prestigious institution with a reputation for academic excellence. An environment of warm friendships and expert teachers nurtured her scholastic and literary talents and fostered expectations about a significant future. Her prose and poetry appeared regularly in the school magazine. In "Australia" she depicted the emigrants' vision of the resolution of old-world dilemmas in the new colonies: "For greatly has the world, guilt heated sinned / So young, young, country, break and bring fresh rain." In 1903 she matriculated with honors in French, History, and English–for her English examination she gained the highest marks of all students in the state of Victoria.

In 1905 Higgins enrolled at the University of Melbourne, where she received a B.A. in 1909, a Dip. of Ed. in 1910, and an M.A. in 1912. She was awarded the exhibition and first-class honors in first-year English and gained honors in modern languages. She participated in the Literature Society of Melbourne, in which Bernard O'Dowd, with whom she shared an almost mystical appreciation of the bush, shaped her commitment to utopian socialism and cultural nationalism. She continued to publish, always using pseudonyms, such as Owen Roe O'Neill, Lalage, or Shalott. A notable example was her translation of Paul Verlaine's "Ars Poetica," used as a centerpiece representing the symbolist philosophy of the journal *The Heart of the Rose*. Higgins's evolving cultural nationalism was related to the spiritual search for knowledge and wholeness, as in her poem "The Familiar Place [Melbourne]":

City, little world of wonder,
Only realms I ever knew,
Hell may gape, or Heaven may open,
I'll know all, through knowing you.

Active in socialist, feminist, and literary circles–founding member of the Fabian Society in Melbourne and the Ex-Rays, a reading group of Old Collegians–and forming intense relationships, when faced with formal academic study Palmer writes that she "took liberties and tried to show my liberty," as she explained her creative efforts in her journal in 1909. Her results suffered. In 1907 she gained only second-class honors for Greek and Latin and finally passed mathematics. While studying for her final examinations in classical philology in January 1909, for which she gained a third class, she met Vance Palmer.

After a year's study to qualify as a teacher, Higgins traveled overseas in 1910–1911 and studied for the diploma of the International Phonetics Association in Germany, France, and England. On the margins of the suffrage movement and mixing with a group of Australian writers exploring guild socialism, she was familiar with the French ideal of nation equated with culture and the maturity and finish of German culture. Returning to Melbourne in 1912, at the completion of her diploma, Higgins taught modern languages at PLC.

Intellectually and morally rigorous, she questioned her relationship to Christianity and became involved in the Free Religious Fellowship. She continued to strive for the cosmic–writing poetry in an attempt to transcend the oppositions of gender. Taking to heart the project of the socialist intellectual to make the concept of freedom concrete, she wrote cultural criticism for the socialist press in her own name. Her main contributions were translations of overseas ideas and events in European socialism, which made them accessible for Australian readers, but she also published some of her own "proletarian songs," a definition she evolved in her review of European working-class poetry in the *Socialist* (1 August 1913).

In 1914 Higgins revisited London and married Vance Palmer on 23 May. So began one of the great intimate partnerships in Australian literary affairs. Vance Palmer became the foremost man of letters of his day. While Nettie Palmer was living in Brittany, a selection of her poems, *The South Wind,* was published in 1914, just before World War I. Culled from earlier notebooks, many poems dealt with love before love, as in "I dreamed of Love and Lover long ago"; Nature as a portent of one's lover; love poems for a woman; the separation of lovers; and loneliness and the difficulties of maintaining love when apart. Some poems celebrate the bush and the power of Nature as a transcendent force; others use metaphors of the natural world:

> Australia, you our own,
> Your last leaf shaken from Igdrasil
> To bear us forward by good or ill
> As the winds of fate have blown.

Some poems–"Visitant," "The Window," "The Escape" suggest, yet never reveal, the existence of the source of Being in homes and factories. Her poems received favorable reviews; *The Bulletin* (25 February 1915) noted their "excellent simplicity and created effect, burdened with scents that, analyzed, are not entirely to be traced to the mere words." Another review agreed: "Not less in things said, but in the mastery of the word unspoken lies Mrs Palmer's sincerity."

With France at war and the mail services disrupted, the Palmers were forced to return to London. After the birth of their daughter Aileen in 1915, Palmer's second volume of poetry, *Shadowy Paths* (1915), was published. Included in this volume were additional lyrics about motherhood, gentle songs for Palmer's young child, and antiwar poems.

> In the sorrow and the terror of the nations,
> In a world shaken through by lamentations,
>   Shall I dare know happiness
>   That I stitch a baby's dress?

Since wartime was not a propitious time to publish, there were few reviews. Later in "Nettie Palmer and her Message," published in *The Illustrated Tasmanian Mail* (25 January 1925), Gladys Hain claimed, "I do not think that any poetess has succeeded in putting that eternal hope and courage (the necessity for love and happiness) which is part of the maternal dower better than this Australian poetess of ours."

The Palmers returned to Melbourne in 1915 and moved to the nearby mountains, the Dandenongs. Palmer began her first regular journalism for a daily newspaper, *The Argus* (Melbourne), in July 1916. In spirited and provocative essays that mostly reviewed several books around a broad theme, she chose diverse subjects, from the importance of publishing poetry in cheap editions to the way cinema had permeated American society and affected current writing. Touching on a range of authors–notably James Francis Dwyer, Rebecca West, Nathaniel Hawthorne, Lord Edward Dunsany, H. G. Wells, and Hilaire Belloc–she drew with equal ease on past and contemporary writers from Britain, France, Germany, the United States, and Australia. The war, the Irish literary revival, Australian women writers, and early modernists all came under Palmer's incisive gaze.

The Palmers' second daughter, Helen, was born in 1917, but the birth was difficult, and Palmer was hospitalized with puerperal fever. Initially the Palmers had opposed the involvement of Australia in the war and were outspoken against censorship and conscription. Palmer wrote occasionally for *The Socialist, Fellowship,* and *Australia,* but she wrote no regular journalism (or poetry) for the next five years while her children were young.

In the final year of the war, disillusioned with literary and radical initiatives, Vance Palmer joined the Australian Imperial Force. Nettie Palmer lived then in Melbourne with her aunt, Ina Higgins, who was a member of the Women's Peace Army. Palmer had many private pupils and classes in language and literature. In 1919 she and Christian Jollie Smith, a radical lawyer, edited a collection of essays and poetry by the socialist and trade unionist E. J. Villiers. Palmer believed his was a rare voice–that of a proletarian poet. In 1919 she also edited *Birth,* an ultra-literary Melbourne journal; in her editorial comments for the magazine, she was at her most astringent.

On Vance Palmer's return from service, the family again lived at Emerald, where Nettie Palmer taught her daughters at home. She believed life in the bush was important for considered work and for cherishing an attachment to place. Rejecting despair and disillusionment in the aftermath of World War I and taking instead a different route from that of the European poets, she focused on the core values of creation, honor, love, nature, and what was at hand–the social, intellectual, and aesthetic life in Australia. Meanwhile, some of her friends and her brother had joined the Communist Party.

In "The Beginnings of Australian Literature," written for *Hassell's Australian Miscellany* (1922), Palmer integrates her former classical and literary studies with the utopian project of a national literature–with its need to evoke and display–to find a new view. She argues that culture, constructed as an intertextual domain, builds on earlier texts and gradually reveals a landscape in poetry. Australians inherit Geoffrey Chaucer's tradition, therefore, though not his subject matter. While differences in the natural world are most suggestive of the distinctive national life displayed–as in the works of Homer–the scenes to be expressed include "the laws, institutions, works and ways of men and women, their speeches and their quarrels, buildings and wars."

In 1924 Palmer won the Lothian Book Publishing Company prize for the best critical essay on Australian literature since 1900. In publicity prepared for *Modern Australian Literature (1900-1923)* (1924) Palmer argued that the booklet showed the existence of a distinctive literature: "Australian literature is not a nebulous something that may appear on the skyline a hundred years hence." Her rapid and vital sketches of the novels, books of short stories, belles lettres, reminiscences, travel books, and poetry had been difficult to compile because there was practically no record except the scattered books themselves. Also included were works of history, biography, drama, and children's literature.

Palmer defines the "colonial attitude" of most writers prior to the turn of the century as a preoccupation in showing off to an overseas audience and a "self-consciousness about externals that is against any deep revelation of life and character." A different tradition emerged in the 1890s with short stories of the "intimate and natural type" and with the federation of the colonies in 1901. With the "peeping glories of her opening page," writers were challenged to discover what "Australia, henceforth Australia," was to mean, through repeated and varied utterance.

For Palmer, literature showed a "more or less intense and imaginative view of the world," and she believed a personal relationship between the writer's style and matter would show this vitality. At the core of literature was a paradox–the need for an individual voice, yet the individual dependent for power on possessing, more or less, harmony and purpose with the life about one. This belief was not related to any "conscious school of writers."

Modern Australian Literature (1900-1923) was a landmark in Australian criticism, as Modjeska notes in *Exiles at Home,* the first critical survey of twentieth-century Australian writing. Most contemporary reviews were favorable, and the book sold well into the 1930s. Commentators disputed, however, the treatment of individual writers, and the Melbourne–as distinct from Sydney–bias. A. G. Stephens in *The Bulletin* decried the lack of space–all writers were foregrounded and lacked perspective. In contrast, cultural historian H. M. Green, in *A History of Australian Literature* (1961), argues that "her wide reading enabled her to regard her subject in perspective." Vivian Smith, in *Vance and Nettie Palmer,* concurs, finding Palmer's crisply formulated opinions enlivened by an alertness in the writing and a sense of discovery.

In 1925 the Palmers visited Brisbane, Queensland, where Vance Palmer's large family lived. The Palmers settled at Caloundra, a small seaside township, and the girls attended the local primary school. Palmer was extremely productive during these years. Her extensive freelance journalism in most Australian daily newspapers (primarily *The Illustrated Tasmanian Mail* and the Brisbane *Courier*), magazines, and women's press formed the basis of her formidable power as a cultural critic. In 1929 alone, for instance, she wrote more than 110 articles, averaging two thousand words each. The fees for freelance work were never high, but she contributed nearly half the family income.

The nature and content of her work encompassed four main areas–the classics, modern books and writers, general discussions, and commentary on Australian writers and writing. She dealt with a wide range of authors and overlooked no important English, American, or Australian writer. Full-column articles were devoted to such established writers as George Sand, Johann Wolfgang von Goethe, Charles Dickens, and Henrik Ibsen, and to those writers whose works had become modern classics, such as William Butler Yeats, Thomas Hardy, Marcel Proust, D. H. Lawrence, Virginia Woolf, Joseph Conrad, Emily Dickinson, and Alice Meynell. Palmer read in French and German and was receptive to developments in American writing and postcolonial literature in New Zealand, Canada, and South America. She wrote on language, linguistics, and accents; landscape and ecology; multicultural questions; cultural and built heritage; and historical and political issues.

For the women's press, especially *The Australian Women's Mirror,* significant articles addressed women's work and housework, such as "The Curse of Eve," and men were gathering in the calle, looking across the bay to the city and listening to the faint rattle of machine-guns. There was uneasiness in their faces, but it was no use asking them what the trouble was; they were emphatic that no one could know anything. Soon cars with determined-looking men in them came tearing out from town; barricades were hastily thrown up along the road and preparations made to blow up the little stone bridge between here and the station.

It was terribly hard to grasp what was happening. Everything echoed with vagueness, nothingness – nada, nada... Yet into the bright morning some evil seemed to have suddenly entered, violently shattering the quiet, threatening all the future. The big, empty houses up toward Tiana appeared in league with it, as if they had been waiting all summer for the attack, harbouring conspirators behind their handsome stone walls. I found myself thinking: "This feeling of liberation here was an illusion. The dark forces have struck back; there'll be war all over the world."

But what affected me most was the thought of A. in Barcelona among the fighting. She had stopped in town to act as interpreter for a group of French athletes coming in at midnight and was to meet us at the station this afternoon. We tried to get in to Barcelona by walking along the railway-line, but were stopped by young men with rifles. All afternoon there were awed groups in the calle, listening to the firing across the water. The loudspeakers on every window-sills gave no real news, merely buzzing like cicadas: "Tranquilo, Spaniards, tranquilo: we are winning."

After tea this evening we sat on the stone coping near the church, watching the cars being searched for arms as they came in from the Costa Brava, and wondering what was happening across the water. Suddenly the lights came out on Barcelona city (everywhere but on Montjuich) and things seemed more hopeful.

July 21st 1936

NO WAY of getting news of A. yet. Maria came in yesterday with the most bloodcurdling stories: 'The dead are lying in heaps along the Ramblas.' She was half-hysterical because her mother is living in a little street off the Ramblas, yet she seemed

Page from the revised typescript for Fourteen Years, *a compilation of Palmer's journal entries published in 1948 (National Library of Australia, MS1174/17/1)*

women's place in the past and present, as in "The Advanced Woman–Has She Disappeared?" from the *Courier* (3 January 1929). Many other articles reviewed feminist treatises, books by and about women, and polemical essays. Many pieces were portraits of individual women and their work. Others were concerned with the diversity of Australian life–in part to combat "Mrs Grundy," who "bustles about with her umbrella, measuring Queensland manners by the notch she made in her umbrella-handle in Melbourne" (*The Australian Women's Mirror*, 25 August 1925).

Green finds Palmer's work "in the best sense of the word popular," although also "critical and appreciative," and her style "without whose informal and direct simplicity some of her subjects and her attitudes towards them may have seemed scarcely suited to the pages of newspapers." Lacking more suitable outlets, as a freelancer Palmer was forced to compete for cultural legitimacy in the widest possible domain and to choose subjects familiar to her readers.

Some of Palmer's articles calling for the advancement of Australian literary and cultural life were manifestos. Palmer developed and expanded her underlying ideas on literature and its relationship to place, nationality, idiom, and language. Literature interpreted a country over and over again, confirming that both individual and social worth give a combined and cumulative power. Long before Arthur Phillips coined the phrase "the cultural cringe" in *The Australian Tradition* (1958), Palmer warned of the "inferiority complex" and how despite "strange offings of unbelief we are building up a culture that will take its place as part of the world store" in the *Illustrated Tasmanian Mail* (17 August 1927). For a literature in transition, she developed standards of absolute and relative value.

Palmer's attack on colonial-provincial attitudes was extensive and consistent. Aware of the ways social access to culture is mediated by class, her primary concern was with the way national literatures were suppressed by the process of cultural imperialism. She wrote of the paradigmatic nature of American literature, for by the 1930s she believed Australian literature was probably where American literature had stood a century before; but whatever strengths America was gaining at the time were not the result of "a spirit of colonialism." She tackled the socioeconomic aspects of cultural production, the publishing industry, censorship, and expatriatism. Her articles have an inner coherence, and she continually reassessed her views.

In *Modern Australian Literature (1900-1923)* Palmer claims that most of the best Australian prose work had been shown in the short story. She reiterated in 1928 that it was virtually impossible for readers to find these stories–nothing had been published in book form since 1901. She approached George Robertson, a publisher, then made a selection culled from back copies of *The Bulletin, Aldelphi, The Worker*, and from authors themselves. According to the preface, the stories, all from the twentieth century, are arranged to give "a unity and harmony."

The collection opens with the now famous K. S. Prichard story "The Cooboo" and ends with Henry Lawson's "A Double Buggy at Lahey's Creek." Most contemporary reviews, such as in the *Sun* (3 December 1928), found the collection surprisingly refreshing and including short stories of high quality "strong in reality," "sincerity of treatment," and "terseness and vividness of style." *The Times Literary Supplement (TLS)* (London) reviewer three years later, however, believed the only men who could describe the bush were too busy living it–"and that is the real Australia." Later scholars describe *An Australian Story-Book* (1928) as influential. It put into permanent circulation stories by Lance Skulthorpe, Nina Lowe, Myra Morris, and Lillian Goode never before published in book form.

When Palmer read, in August 1928, an American *Bookman* essay, "Australian Literature," which was scathing of English economic and social domination, she wrote to the author. Such an action was typical of her method of work. In this case, C. Hartley Grattan replied, and so began a long friendship of critical support and exchange of information, mostly by mail. Palmer reviewed and then contacted many writers of quality, such as Shaw Neilson, Dowell O'Reilly (then his wife in the publication of his letters), Eileen Duggan in New Zealand, Marjorie Barnard, Flora Eldershaw, and Frank Dalby Davison. In 1929 Palmer wrote the foreword for Grattan's book on *Australian Literature*, finding "he rightly seeks whatever is self-dependent and creative, the point of view of those native to the soil."

From 1929 to 1938 Palmer's personal column, "A Reader's Notebook," designed "to snare any Australian book of importance," appeared in *All About Books*, a semipopular literary journal. The need of the moment was sound appreciation, she believed. Palmer, moreover, took risks in her aesthetic judgements. The furor about Katharine Susannah Pritchard's *Coonardoo* (1929) was just one example of her willingness to risk her reputation in support of the quality of a novel portraying black/white sexual relationships. She also attacked when she felt it necessary–for instance, in 1929, Professor Cowling's dismissal of Australian literature as a fit subject for university courses.

In 1930 the Palmers returned to Melbourne, and their two daughters attended secondary school. Palmer's father had died, as had her uncle, Henry Bournes Higgins, and she was commissioned to write his biography, *Henry Bournes Higgins: A Memoir* (1931). It traces Higgins's Irish childhood and emigration from Ireland to Melbourne, his early career as a lawyer, his role in the Federal Convention, his membership in the first Labour Party cabinet, his work as a judge on the High Court, and his presidency of the Arbitration Court. While the character of Higgins emerges clearly, and the legal issues he dealt with as a colonial Liberal are unraveled, the context of the history of Victoria is laced with Palmer's considerable understanding of the development of colonial and national life.

The biography was widely acclaimed—in reviews in New Zealand, Ireland, and the United States as well as in London and Australia—in legal and political journals as well as newspapers. On 28 May 1931 the *TLS* found "as a whole it was worth high praise" with a well-depicted and often delightful background; on 1 August 1931 *Desiderata* (Adelaide) claimed it was one of the most significant and enduring works produced in Australia. W. K. Hancock, in the *Morpeth Review* (August 1932), called it a necessary book for all students of the development of Australia; others thought constitutional lawyers would find the pages on the movement for Federation of particular interest.

The book raised highly contentious issues; in the 1930s the Arbitration Court and the basic wage were again under threat as they had been in Higgins's time; Robert G. Menzies, later long-term prime minister of Australia, used his review of Palmer's "excellent book" in *The Australian Quarterly* (14 September 1931) to argue that Higgins's understanding of economics was flawed and the basic wage was so high that the industrial efficiency of Australia had been compromised. The left-wing *Labour Call* (15 January 1931) believed Higgins could not be blamed for any deficiency in benefits to the workers from the Arbitration Court, although it had been used to their detriment since his retirement. Sir John Quick in *All About Books* (13 July 1931) praised Palmer's thorough, careful, and thoughtful manner, which made no attempt to eulogize or apologize, leaving the readers to form their own opinions. The book was one of the few scholarly biographies of political figures in Australia at the time.

Always maintaining her steady stream of journalism and correspondence, Palmer began her association that year with the Australian Broadcasting Commission (ABC) with a regular literary talk. By the late 1930s her weekly feature, *Readers and Writers,* was broadcast during the Women's Session of the 3L0 radio program. She continued to broadcast intermittently until the 1950s.

In 1932 Palmer's belief in "the importance of myth filling out landscape to enrich memories and overtones" and preserve the legends that are the springs of poetry prompted the republication of *Tom Petrie's Reminiscences of Early Queensland (Dating from 1837) Recorded by His Daughter* (1932), as she wrote in her preface. Tom Petrie had grown up among, and had had a long association with, the Turrbal people; Palmer had delved into local histories while living in Caloundra and been befriended by the Petries.

At the height of the Great Depression, in 1932, the Palmers camped alone for eight months on Green Island, a coral cay in Queensland. Palmer revised twenty-eight essays for a selection titled *Talking It Over* (1932). The dedication read "To Vance Palmer from N. P., who perhaps talked some of it over with him." In her selection Palmer hones her postcolonial criticism with essays on "Colonial Wares" and "The Right to Orioles"; discusses "Austral English," colloquialisms, and Australian words and their derivations; and covers "Misprints" and punctuation. "On Suburbia" compares Melbourne and European cities; one essay attacks utilitarian education; others rely on ecological attunement. "The Tempestuous Petticoat" chronicles women's fashions—"the warfare between dress-makers and mere human beings."

Reviews were few during the Depression. On 24 December 1932 a reviewer from *The Telegraph* (Brisbane) found Palmer an enthusiastic visionary: "Literature is her passion, and even when she sits down to reflect upon such a subject as trains and the machine age, there is an ingenious twist back to the beloved subject of letters." In *The News* (Perth) John K. Ewers wished the essays were longer, and found the themes never trivial (18 February 1935). P. I. O'Leary wrote perceptively in the *Advocate* (11 April 1929) of the "personality" of the essay—its sharp hostility toward anything approaching sentimentality, its evident common sense, and its whimsy and wit.

In 1934, after the Palmers had returned to Victoria and settled in the Dandenong ranges, Nettie Palmer co-edited *The Centenary Gift Book,* an extremely successful venture commemorating the contributions of white women to the first one hundred years of settlement; it was written entirely by women of Victoria. The volume includes a fine balance of factual and creative material with a broad view of past and present; recognition is given to different levels of achievement, women's entry into professions and trades, suffrage victories, the struggle for educational opportunities, and different women's groups and pioneers. The book was produced in deluxe, hardback, and paperback editions. In "The Pioneer Woman—Conscious and Unconscious Builders in a New Land" (*The Argus,* 16 October 1934) Palmer made explicit her interest in women who became active public figures and those whose contribution through childbearing and child rearing was "embedded in the

Title page for Palmer's contribution to the debates about the Australian nation and its character (Yale University Libraries)

characters of their descendants and woven into the textures of our life today."

In 1933 Palmer had sounded a warning against Adolf Hitler's violent and anti-Semitic policies; in the latter half of the 1930s the fight against fascism became her main focus. A member of the Kisch Reception Committee in 1934, formed when Egon Kisch was banned but illegally visited Australia, she addressed the Writers' League on his work. In 1935, at the completion of Helen Palmer's schooling, the family traveled to Europe, living in the Bloomsbury section of London, where Palmer continued to write for the Australian press, *The Christian Science Monitor,* and the *TLS* and to give radio broadcasts through the British Broadcasting Corporation (BBC). In 1935 she attended the first International Congress of Writers for the Defence of Culture in Paris. Living in Spain, Palmer learned Spanish to pursue her interest in South American literatures.

After the attempted Falangist coup and after Aileen Palmer had joined the British Medical Aid Unit, Palmer returned to Melbourne to speak about the new people's Spain, the Second Republic, formed in 1931.

President of the Spanish Relief Committee and an executive of the Spanish Relief Council, she wrote with Len Fox the pamphlet *Australians in Spain* (1937). Also in 1937 she became the Melbourne editor of the Sydney-based *Woman Today,* a journal attempting to combine conventional women's concerns such as recipes with articles on feminist and left-wing politics—for example, the World Peace Movement. She wrote the foreword of *We Went to Spain,* published in 1938. Her series "An Australian Notebook," for the New Zealand journal *Tomorrow,* was the most direct expression of her political and intellectual views from 1937 to 1939. She endorsed the call to the antifascist struggle on the home front, "not to be undertaken without awareness of overseas dangers."

Palmer was devastated by World War II—"the blotting out of the symphonies and sonatas" she called it in a letter to her husband on 18 August 1940. A member of the Victorian International Refugees' Emergency Committee, she earned the label "Angel of the refugees," teaching them about Australian culture, showing awareness of the violence in their homelands. In 1940 she translated from German a child psychology text by Irma Schnierer, a refugee from Austria. In her foreword to Ada Jackson's *Behold the Jew* (1943), she strongly protested the "foul disease," "Anti-Semitism." During the war years she had increased family responsibilities—care for her aged mother and two aunts—and she herself suffered a series of strokes.

Throughout the late 1940s and 1950s Palmer's self-professed role was "mostly" that of "liaison officer" in literary life, as she told Clem Christesen on 16 November 1942. Her particular provenance was the crossroads between her two interests—foreign languages and literature in Australia. After her illness, she focused more on preparing her books than on widespread reviewing but still maintained professional chores—reading manuscripts, encouraging younger writers, and lecturing. With her husband she was active in the Fellowship of Australian Authors and the Council for Civil Liberties.

Palmer recorded in her diary on 24 May 1921 her admiration for the "astonishing" poems of Lesbia Harford on their first appearance and had drawn attention to them when reviewing *An Australian Anthology,* published in 1927. After Harford's death in 1927, Palmer had arranged the tribute and selection of poems for *The Illustrated Tasmanian Mail.* At the height of stringent wartime publishing, M. Dufaur Clark asked Palmer to write a foreword for the selection of Harford's poetry, which was mostly fragments. Including some biographical details in the 1941 collection *The Poems of Lesbia Harford,* Palmer also praised Harford's poetry: "without fear, and with great hope, Lesbia Harford set down in her own words glimpses of a new reality." The volume was virtually overlooked by reviewers; Hope in *Southerly* (1942) derided the poems as "feminine namby pamby." A later generation of feminists, however, rediscovered Harford.

In 1944, as Alice Henry's literary executrix, Palmer revised, duplicated, and bound copies of the *Memoirs of Alice Henry* with her own postscript. Chronicling Henry's life from 1925, Palmer, with characteristic discretion, brought out aspects of Henry's career in the Women's Trade Union Movement, her involvement in "progressive and creative" activities, her capacity to empathize with the dispossessed, and her "instinct to honour what had beauty and meaning." The memoirs were circulated among universities and libraries and in the United States by Hartley Grattan and Mary Beard, who was "frankly pleased with the book, glad of its existence."

Fourteen Years: Extracts from a Private Journal 1925–1939 (1948) is seen as Palmer's most important work. It is a skillful collation of encounters, incidents, and places drawn from a range of sources; only some of her vignettes are expanded from the brief, straightforward private diaries. Her selection echoes her premises and assumptions about what is significant. She reflects on her intentions as a critic and her aesthetic standards. Part of Palmer's intention was also to create objective debates about the Australian nation and the Australian character. Palmer outlines, too, a range of feminist beliefs and makes clear her aesthetic differences from prominent social feminists. In varying circumstances both men and women–Ruth Pitter, Christina Stead, Edmund Wilson, Havelock Ellis, and Will Dyson, for example–are depicted struggling with different aspects of the vagaries of cultural production.

Fourteen Years appeared in a limited edition of five hundred copies only. Hugh McCrae's belief that it was an immediate classic was quoted by the publisher in the promotional material. Jack Lindsay in *Life and Letters Today* (July 1949) found "a full picture" of Palmer's literary generation–their restlessness, desire for new roots, spiritual thirst, and an unsentimental nostalgia for the home earth: "we see here the Australian version of the exiles and lost generation of the US in the same period." Late-twentieth-century feminist scholarship emphasizes the resourceful self in the work that plays an active role in society–"a strong alternative self-consciousness to the phallic I," writes B. Brooks in *Women's Studies International Forum* (1990). K. Gallagher–in "Shadows and Silences: Australian Women Poets in the Twenties and Thirties," in *Poetry and Gender: Statements and Essays in Australian Women's Poetry and Poetics* (1989), edited by D. Brooks and B. Walker–finds Palmer's writing in *Fourteen Years* "erudite, urbane, immediate, and surprisingly modern in tone, with a sensuous evocativeness and visual exactness."

Part of Palmer's reputation as a critic stems from her early recognition and espousal of the significance of Richardson, the great tragic writer. Palmer's 1950 work *Henry Handel Richardson: A Study* was the first full-length critical study of an Australian woman novelist to be published by an Australian woman. Richardson was hardly known when Palmer first reviewed her work in 1925. Richardson and Palmer began a correspondence after the review, and Palmer followed up many of Richardson's requests, such as a reply to St. John Irvine in 1927 and, later, a recommendation for Richardson for the Nobel Prize. Invariably, Palmer mentioned Richardson in any of her brief surveys of Australian literature; for example, in her column in *All About Books* (19 April) she found Richardson's trilogy had "carried us right into the broad stream of European literature." Over the years Palmer wrote at least forty-five articles about Richardson, which were crucial in establishing Richardson's importance, especially in Australia.

Palmer begins *Henry Handel Richardson* with a biographical chapter and then discusses each of Richardson's novels. She compares *The Getting of Wisdom* (1910) with *The Adventures of Huckleberry Finn* (1884) by Mark Twain. She sees Richardson's *Maurice Guest* (1908) as "a study of love, in all its overwhelming intensities and erotic vagaries;" *The Fortunes of Richard Mahony* (1917) as the story of the spiritual failure to adapt to the new country, redeemed in the final volume by the emergence of Mary as a woman of initiative and courage; and *The Young Cosima* (1939) as the story of a woman's intelligent and unswerving devotion to the cause of music. A final chapter focuses on Richardson's methods of work.

The response to *Henry Handel Richardson* was mixed. On 16 March 1951 the *TLS* found Palmer had succeeded admirably in her two objectives–to uncover the gritty irritants around which the pearl of art formed in life and to analyze the novels: Palmer "knows her subject, she nearly always has something interesting or penetrating to say, and her style is clear and free of fussiness." *The Bulletin* (20 September 1950) praised the book highly as an enduring standard reference. G. A. Wilkes in *Southerly* (1951) was dismissive: he said that as a work written from personal knowledge, it was a popular book rather than a scholarly monograph. Dorothy Green, whose own study, *Ulysses Bound: Henry Handel Richardson and her Fiction* (1973), superseded Palmer's work twenty-three years later, believed Palmer's study

Palmer in Melbourne during the 1940s (from Modjeska, Exiles at Home, *1981)*

was in some essential points more accurate than those of many critics who came after her.

Although several chapters of *Henry Handel Richardson* may have been written by Vance Palmer, attribution of specific chapters to one author or the other is difficult. "We never said Nettie *and* Vance, we always said Nettie'n'Vance" recalled Arthur Phillips in 1985 in the *Fellowship of Australian Writers Newsletter*. They used the same materials, talked it over, subedited each other's work, and at times Vance Palmer reworked Nettie Palmer's material, giving it a more nationalist tone. Nettie Palmer, in turn, may have contributed several biographies to her husband's *National Portraits* (1940).

Palmer's 1950 selection of seventeen short stories for *Coast to Coast 1949–1950* was praised by Ken Levis in *Southerly* (1951) as one of the best of the series. While *The Times* found most stories in the collection relied on the tradition of anecdote and were often naive, *The Bulletin* (10 January 1951) praised its wide range of subject and locale. Palmer included a selection of then virtually unknown writers–Judith Wright, Geoffrey Dutton, and Eric Lambert.

Eighteen years after she had written a series for *The Argus* on "The Meaning of the Dandenongs," Palmer lightly revised them for publication in 1952 as *The Dandenongs*. She added a preface and postscript. Taking Rudyard Kipling's phrase about penetrating the curtain that hides the past, Palmer portrays the hill country. It is not a conventional local history of white people but an evocative account of the invasion and settlement of the Dandenongs in the context of different families, regions, and land use; various eras "like palimpsests" are superimposed upon each other. The movement through the mining period, the period of timber-getting, the days of the Swiss vignerons, and the time of berrygrowers, for instance, are counterposed with the "wild natural" setting. She offers readers a way of seeing the landscape in terms of both natural and European heritage with all the ecological damage wreaked by colonialism.

Illustrated with linocuts by Ronald G. Edwards, *The Dandenongs* was only published as a limited edition. Inexpensive, it was stocked with the main Dandenong news agents but was reviewed as far away as North Queensland. On 28 February 1953 the reviewer in *The Daily Mercury* (Mackay, Queensland) called the book a "serene little treasury of early memories, conversational, light, free from all pedantic argumentation and yet brim full of information." The book ran into a second edition the following year.

In 1954 Palmer's last major work, *Bernard O'Dowd*, appeared. Victor Kennedy, in collaboration with O'Dowd himself, had begun the study; Kennedy's wish was that Palmer complete it when he died. Her hand is clear in its systematic shaping, the wide understanding of the cultural background, the eloquent flow of the narrative, and the careful critical appraisal of O'Dowd's poetry that discusses his volumes one by one. Opening with a vivid description of O'Dowd's famous call for "Poetry Militant" in 1909 (Palmer had been in the audience), Palmer includes details about O'Dowd's origins, upbringing, and career. The focus is on his intellectual and philosophical development and affinities; Walt Whitman, for example, was a mentor. Palmer also traces O'Dowd's early involvement in the socialist movement. The biography is not straightforward. It is an account of the quest of the inner man, ever thinking upon the mysteries of life; there is a decorous lack of detail about O'Dowd's life with the poet Marie Pitt.

Contemporary reviews differed. O'Dowd was a contentious figure called variously the voice of the nation and no poet at all. *The Bulletin* (24 November 1954) reviewer, who compared O'Dowd's poetry to a steamroller, was scathing. Geoffrey Serle in *Historical Studies* (November 1955) summed up how, although O'Dowd's poetry had little appeal to the present generation of critics and over the years his stature had lessened, the historian had no doubts of his significance. As one of the few Australian literary biographies of its time written by contemporaries, the book will remain important.

Palmer continued to contribute to *Meanjin* and *Southerly* during the 1950s and was active in the Goethe Society and on the Vida Goldstein Memorial committee formed to recognize her work as a suffragette. Vance Palmer died in 1959. For a while Nettie Palmer, living with daughter Aileen, continued with a second autobiography, "The Next Fourteen Years," but she died on 19 October 1964, aged seventy-nine, before the completion of the manuscript.

Palmer's place in the literary history of Australia is assured. Her achievements were substantial—pioneering works on modern Australian literature, articulate and incisive portraits of the problems of cultural production in the interwar period, and early recognition of significant feminists and emerging postcolonial analysis. Hers was the first full-length study of an Australian novelist, and her autobiography is one of the best, if not the best, by an Australian woman. Her life, too, will always create interest—the mystique of an unfinished poetic impulse, a generous spirit, and beautifully written, intimate letters. The focus of her work on the concrete and eternal allows it to remain accessible, whatever the trend in critical theory. In 1984 the state government of Victoria established a prestigious annual literary award—the Nettie Palmer Prize for Non-Fiction.

Letters:

Letters of Henry Handel Richardson to Nettie Palmer, edited by Karl Johan Rossing (Cambridge, Mass.: Harvard University Press, 1953);

Vivian Smith, ed., *Letters of Vance and Nettie Palmer 1915–1963* (Canberra: National Library of Australia, 1977).

Interviews:

H. de Berg Collection of tape recordings, Ms 998, National Library of Australia;

Stephen Murray-Smith, "Interview with Nettie Palmer," Ms 8099, State Library of Victoria.

Bibliographies:

C. M. Hotimsky and Walter Stone, "A Bibliographical Checklist," *Meanjin,* 18, no. 2 (1959): 264–269;

Vivian Smith, "Nettie Palmer: A Checklist of Literary Journalism," *Australian Literary Studies,* 6, no. 2 (October 1973): 190–196.

References:

B. Brooks, "Nettie Palmer," *Women's Studies International Forum,* 13, no. 3 (1990): 276;

K. Gallagher, "Shadows and Silences: Australian Women Poets in the Twenties and Thirties," in *Poetry and Gender: Statements and Essays in Australian Women's Poetry and Poetics,* edited by D. Brooks and B. Walker (St. Lucia: University of Queensland Press, 1989), pp. 83–92;

Deborah Jordan, *Nettie Palmer: Search for an Aesthetic* (Melbourne: History Department, University of Melbourne, 1999);

Esther Levy, "Yours as Ever . . . NP," *Meanjin Quarterly,* 24, no. 3 (1965): 329–333;

Drusilla Modjeska, *Exiles at Home: Australian Women Writers 1925–1945* (Sydney: Angus & Robertson, 1981), pp. 43–115;

Nettie and Vance Palmer Commemorative Edition, *Meanjin,* 18 (1959);

Vance and Nettie Palmer: An Exhibition to Celebrate the Centenary of their Births, catalogue (Melbourne: Library Council of Victoria, 1986);

Vivian Smith, *Vance and Nettie Palmer* (Boston: Twayne, 1975).

Papers:

The papers of Nettie Palmer are held in the National Library of Australia, Canberra.

Vance Palmer

(28 August 1885 – 15 July 1959)

Vivian Smith
University of Sydney

BOOKS: *The Forerunners* (London: Euston Press, 1915);
The World of Men (London: Euston Press, 1915);
The Camp (Melbourne: Endacott, 1920);
The Shantykeeper's Daughter (Sydney: New South Wales Bookstall, 1920);
The Boss of Killara (Sydney: New South Wales Bookstall, 1922);
The Enchanted Island, as Rann Daly (London: Hutchinson, 1923);
The Outpost, as Daly (London: Hutchinson, 1924); revised and republished as *Hurricane,* as Palmer (Sydney: Angus & Robertson, 1935);
Cronulla: A Story of Station Life (Sydney: Cornstalk, 1924);
The Black Horse, and Other Plays (Melbourne: Endacott, 1924);
The Man Hamilton (London & Melbourne: Ward, Lock, 1928);
Men Are Human (London: Stanley Paul, 1928);
The Passage (London: Stanley Paul, 1930; Melbourne: Robertson & Mullens, 1944);
Separate Lives (London: Stanley Paul, 1931);
Daybreak (London: Stanley Paul, 1932);
Sea and Spinifex (Sydney: Shakespeare Head Press, 1934);
The Swayne Family (Sydney: Angus & Robertson, 1934);
Legend for Sanderson (Sydney: Angus & Robertson, 1937);
National Portraits (Sydney: Angus & Robertson, 1940; enlarged edition, Carlton & Melbourne: Melbourne University Press, 1954);
A. G. Stephens: His Life and Work (Melbourne: Robertson & Mullens, 1941);
Frank Wilmot (Furnley Maurice) (Melbourne: Frank Wilmot Memorial Committee, 1942);
Cyclone (Sydney: Angus & Robertson, 1947);
Hail Tomorrow, A Play in Four Acts (Sydney: Angus & Robertson, 1947);
Louis Esson and the Australian Theatre (Melbourne: Georgian House, 1948);
Golconda (Sydney: Angus & Robertson, 1948);

Vance Palmer (from Leslie Rees, The Making of Australian Drama, *1973)*

The Legend of the Nineties (Melbourne: Melbourne University Press, 1954);
Let the Birds Fly (Sydney: Angus & Robertson, 1955);
Seedtime (Sydney: Angus & Robertson, 1957);
The Rainbow Bird and Other Stories, selected by A. Edwards (Sydney: Angus & Robertson, 1957);
The Big Fellow (Sydney: Angus & Robertson, 1959).

Collection: *Intimate Portraits and Other Pieces: Essays and Articles,* selected by H. P. Heseltine (Melbourne: Cheshire, 1969).

OTHER: Tom Collins (Joseph Furphy), *Such Is Life, Being Certain Extracts from the Diary of Tom Collins (Joseph Furphy),* preface by Palmer (Melbourne: Specialty Press, 1917); abridged and edited by Palmer (London: Cape, 1937);

Ancestors, in *Best Australian One-Act Plays,* edited by William Moore and T. Inglis Moore (Sydney: Angus & Robertson, 1937);

Coast to Coast. Australian Stories, 1944, selected and edited by Palmer (Sydney: Angus & Robertson, 1945).

Vance Palmer, whose career spans the period from the Australia of the 1890s to the Australia of the 1950s, was one of the most representative figures of the literary culture of his time. The foremost man of letters of his day, he was known as a novelist, dramatist, short-story writer, poet, critic, and editor as well as a political and social commentator and interpreter. He was a man of intellectual force and integrity, and a study of his life and work exemplifies to an unusual degree the struggle that was central to the whole development of writing in his country—the struggle between an imported tradition and attitudes and the search for a viable local tradition. Though much of his enormous output is now only of historical interest, an understanding of Australia between the two world wars is greatly enhanced by a study of his writings.

Edward Vivian Palmer (always known as Vance) was born in Bundaberg, Queensland, on 28 August 1885, seventh child of Australian-born Henry Burnett Palmer, a schoolmaster with literary leanings and literary friendships, and his Irish wife, Jessie Carson Palmer. His youth was spent in a succession of country towns between Bundaberg and Stanthorpe, where his father was appointed to different schools. In 1899 he went as a boarder to Ipswich Grammar School, where he remained until December 1901. He decided against going to a university and for a while worked various jobs, such as proofreader and private secretary, meanwhile reading works by Russian and French novelists in the local library.

Palmer's literary awakening seems to have happened early. The writings of Henry Lawson, Steele Rudd, and William Ogilvie opened Palmer's eyes to the life around him. Through *The Bulletin* he also started to read the works of important Australian writers of the time—men such as Randolph Bedford, Edward Dyson, and Albert Dorrington. Barbara Baynton's stories impressed him deeply, and he became and remained a fervent admirer of Rolf Boldrewood and Price Warung.

Palmer's first significant piece of writing was an article, "An Australian National Art," which appeared in *Steele Rudd's Magazine* in January 1905. In this manifesto by a youthful writer who is clear regarding his ideals and ambitions, Palmer asserted that the artist's business is "to create interest in the life around him":

> There are some who would excuse our shortcomings in literature with the plea that our energies have so far been taken up with mercantile concerns, with building cities and laying down roads and railways. Art is really man's interpretation of the inner life of his surroundings, and until the Australian writer can attune his ear to catch the various undertones of our national life, our art must be false and unenduring. There must be no seeing through English spectacles. Our art must be original as our own fauna and flora are original.

The article ends:

> Even now the national movement is beginning. In each of our cities is arising a little band of writers, who are content to mirror with clearness the life about them. Theirs is the most glorious task ever conceived the creating of a whole literature. After all we are a very young people, and are only commencing to find out our characteristics.

This declaration from a writer of nineteen is forceful, stylish, and confident. In its essentials it remained Palmer's credo throughout his life.

Although Palmer wanted to be an Australian writer, the Australia of his time could offer him no satisfactory literary outlets. In 1905 he sailed for London, conscious of his youth and his lack of experience. He was in London for two years, engaged in menial Grub Street tasks, such as writing stories around "picture blocks" that popular magazines had used a generation before. He came back to Australia via Finland, Russia—where he attempted unsuccessfully to visit Tolstoy, for whom he felt a lifelong reverence—and Japan. Some of the incidents of these days found their way into his first important book, *The World of Men* (1915), and the volume, "From Finland to the East," which was never published. Palmer later claimed that the sight of the Russian landscape first brought home to him the value of the literary background of Australia.

Back in Australia in 1908, Palmer tried salesmanship and schoolteaching. On holiday in Sydney he met Jack London, whose influence is apparent in much of Palmer's early work. In 1909 Palmer went out west to the Maranoa to gain close experience with station (ranch) life. He was at Abbieglassie near Mitchell, first as a tutor, then as station bookkeeper, bush worker, and cattle driver. The experience of these years, and of the life of a large cattle station, provided the subject matter for five of his early novels and for many of his early stories. But Palmer was not prepared to stay indefinitely in Australia. By August 1910 he was back in London again.

This time he came in contact with writers such as Arthur Machen, Frank Harris, and Richard Middleton. Above all, Palmer found an important literary mentor and guide in A. R. Orage, the editor of *The New Age* (London). Orage's acceptance convinced Palmer that he might be able to write, as an Australian, work that would fulfill some of the ambitions he had articulated in "An Australian National Art."

In 1912 Palmer made a brief return trip to Australia, traveling through the United States and Mexico at the time of the Mexican Revolution. In London on 23 May 1914 he married Janet "Nettie" Higgins, whom he had first met in Australia in 1908. Nettie was herself an aspiring writer who had already written poetry and criticism and later made an important contribution to Australian criticism and biography. The Palmers' marriage began what was often referred to as one of the most important literary partnerships in Australia. When World War I broke out, the Palmers were in Tregastel in Brittany, where Nettie had been teaching and studying. Vance Palmer was living by writing serious stories and articles for *The New Age, The Manchester Guardian Fortnightly,* and *The British Review* and by writing commercial pulp serials. The Palmers returned to London, but their plans for the future had been largely centered in Europe. Palmer's position as a freelance writer and the difficulties of newspapers in wartime made their position extremely insecure. In September 1915 they were back in Australia. Each had published two books in England before their return. They knew they could not hope to be established as serious writers in Australia without first publishing abroad.

Palmer's *The World of Men* consists of twelve of the short nondramatic sketches he had written for *The Manchester Guardian* and *The New Age*. Their form is especially interesting. Orage favored the short sketch—he also encouraged Katherine Mansfield to concentrate on this lyrically brief way of writing—and what Orage wanted was not unlike what *The Bulletin* story of the 1890s demanded, clarity and realism, a sharp sense of the hard facts of life. Palmer was thus able to combine the two strands of his interest—his Australian background and the requirements of a sophisticated paper.

The title *The World of Men* indicates Palmer's concerns—the world of masculine will and endurance, which was seen as the world of normality. All the figures in Palmer's sketches are isolated men. Some are physically or socially isolated in bush or mulga (uninhabited areas), in foreign countries, in lighthouses or on ships, as laborers in camps, or as drovers. Others are morally isolated—a father whose half-caste son has been killed in a fall from a horse; a man who has married a native woman. Each sketch picks out and concentrates on a single moment in one of these lives to show how the individual stoically accepts his situation, to which he sees no alternative. Concerned with isolation and the creative sense of endurance through defeat, these sketches also deal with the longings of solitary men for signs of continuity and permanence.

Palmer's return to Australia in 1915 confirmed his resolve to develop as an Australian writer in Australia. But he had returned to a country that had no living literary tradition of its own: there were no publishing houses, no reviews, and no certainty of finding a body of adult readers. One of his first needs was simply to find or create an audience.

The ten years between 1915 and 1925 were an extraordinarily active time in Palmer's career—a time of aspirations and frustrations, an interrupted time of hardship and experiment. Above all, during this period Palmer was forcefully involved in the development of a form of literary nationalism. Soon after his return to Melbourne, he became acquainted with Frederick Sinclaire and his circle, which published the little journal *Fellowship,* and this periodical became the real vehicle of expression for Palmer's developing ideas and convictions. Palmer was particularly concerned with the necessity for a vital culture, attacking the local academics for their indifference to local writers—"they can never realise that most of the culture they value was hacked out of the raw, contemporary life by artists and pamphleteers of another day"—and the cultured Philistines, who were convinced, according to an article of May 1916 in *Fellowship,* "that nothing in art or life is important unless it comes out of England."

During the war years Palmer fought conscription and traveled around the country talking on the issues of imperialism and national sentiment. He published an article titled "Imperialism versus National Sentiment" in *The Worker* (1 March 1917) that is indicative of his attitudes at this time:

> We have to give up the idea of being far from town, and Imperialism will not teach us to do so. We have to learn that . . . the centre of every circle is one's own country. . . . What literature, what art, what ideas . . . ever came from a people who looked abroad for its "centre.". . . We must believe that Australia would never have come into being except for the purpose of making her own distinctive contribution to the world's life.

Palmer believed throughout his life that the proper recognition of Joseph Furphy would mark the coming of age of Australian literary culture. His article on Furphy in *Fellowship* (March 1917) was associated with another of his major tasks for that year, the republication of *Such Is Life,* originally published in 1903. The importance of Palmer's work and of his preface to the

1917 Melbourne Specialty Press edition of *Such Is Life* have tended to get less than full acknowledgment. He maintained that "*Such Is Life* will become a classic for the next generation." Palmer's preface and the republication mark the beginning of his lifelong concern with preserving what is best in the past and with establishing a canon of the important Australian writers.

Palmer's search for an audience for his ideas and convictions as an Australian writer led him in several different directions in the early 1920s. He wrote serious plays, hoping to contribute to the founding of an Australian national theater; he wrote literary criticism, especially for *The Bulletin,* in which he gave deeply considered expression to the problems facing the writer in Australia; and he even tried to establish himself as a professional novelist by writing potboilers for a paperback series that was aimed to appeal to the rural and urban masses.

The novels that Palmer wrote for the New South Wales Bookstall Company series—the main outlet for Australian pulp fiction before and after World War I—aimed, like most of the titles in the series, to exploit popular taste. What had been lived experience for Lawson and Furphy was now taking on a spurious glamour, with elements of American Western fiction being imposed on an Australian setting. Family feuds, conflicting loyalties in outback stations, the romanticized rigors of droving, the clear-cut social divisions represented by the station and the shanty (a public house, especially one unlicensed)—these are features of the series shared by Palmer's *The Shantykeeper's Daughter* (1920) and *The Boss of Killara* (1922). Both of these novels are connected with Palmer's later books, which are serious in preoccupation and theme, and they make some genuine attempt to reflect aspects of the reality of Australia. The two potboilers that followed, however, did not. Published under the pseudonym Rann Daly, *The Enchanted Island* (1923) and *The Outpost* (1924) were set in the South Seas—a favorite setting in the pulp fiction of the 1920s—and New Guinea, respectively. In 1934 Palmer rewrote *The Outpost,* based on aspects of C. A. W. Monckton's experiences as a New Guinea magistrate, and republished it in 1935 under his own name as *Hurricane.*

Among the early books, *Cronulla: A Story of Station Life* (1924) is the best. Set in 1908, it deals with the life around three homesteads owned by families of different temperaments and outlooks and the decline and restoration of one homestead, Cronulla. The novel as a whole is a pleasant pastoral idyll, marred by some of the romance elements in the part of the plot concerned with two lovers. But it is the first of Palmer's novels to be seriously preoccupied with the meaning of the spirit of place and the sense

The cottage at Emerald where Palmer wrote much of his early work

of profound attachment to an area of land and the way of life associated with it. Place is one of the main concerns of all Palmer's mature work.

Palmer's attempts to establish himself as a popular writer through the theater or through the bookstall novel proved misdirected. His feeling that he might be part of a developing national literary life centered in Melbourne was frustrated. In 1925 he and his wife decided to leave Melbourne with their two young daughters and withdraw to Caloundra in Southern Queensland to concentrate exclusively on their own writing.

In the years at Caloundra, Palmer conceived, wrote in a first form, or rewrote the small group of novels that made his reputation as a novelist—*The Man Hamilton* (1928), *Men Are Human* (1928), *The Passage* (1930), *Daybreak* (1932), and *The Swayne Family* (1934). He conceived his mining trilogy during these years, and some of his best journalism belongs to this period.

The station novel was the most popular literary form in Australia from 1909 to the early 1930s, and its popularity may be attributed partly to a nostalgia for a way of life that was slowly passing. Palmer knew as clearly as anyone that Australia was changing, but he did not welcome the change. Writing of "Australia's Transformation" in *Fellowship* (March 1921), he complained of the way Australia was breaking up into two cultures, that of the coastal cities and that of the inland, where alone the old bush ethos of the 1890s still survived. Palmer's own deepest allegiances were to the bush and to the ethos of the 1890s, and these allegiances, coupled with his inability to find deeper imaginative engagement in the developing urban Australia, held back the full development of his work. The factors that make him the representative figure of his time are those that today reveal the limitations of his creative abilities.

Palmer's mature novels fall into three main groups—the two station novels, *The Man Hamilton* and *Men Are Human;* the regional novels, *The Passage* and *Daybreak;* and the urban novel, *The Swayne Family.* The mining trilogy of the late 1940s and 1950s closely centers on some of the issues and concerns of his earlier work.

The theme of all these novels is that of finding and realizing personal identity. *The Man Hamilton,* written in 1926, is specifically concerned with the theme of the full acceptance of personal destiny. This work, originally to be called, among other titles, "Hamilton of Euroa," shows its hero associated throughout with the place with which his destiny is identified—the station Euroa. As in *Men Are Human, The Passage, Daybreak,* and *Golconda* (1948), place is conceived of and realized as both the creation and the sustenance of the individual will—that is, the will creates it but must remain rooted to it and collaborate with it, not merely exploit and abandon it.

The Man Hamilton and *Men Are Human* are closely connected books. Hamilton's relation to Lottie, his half-caste wife, and her situation when he marries her, are repeated with Boyd and Josie in the later novel. More significant are the basic differences in the working out of the situations that arise from the character of Hamilton. Hamilton is almost the only Palmer character of strong will and resolution, qualities that are expressed not in deciding his destiny but in fully accepting and realizing it: "What had happened could not be altered, but the life arising out of it could be shaped and controlled." The station Euroa is the visible expression of this process.

The plot of *The Man Hamilton* is slight, and the effect of the novel is all in its structure and point of view. Hamilton has married a half-caste woman by whom he has a son, Steve, now fourteen. Nina, a governess at a neighboring station, falls in love with Hamilton, but they decide to separate because of the son. Hamilton acts, as he earlier acted, out of a sense of necessity:

> The basis of his whole life had been fixed by something that had happened fifteen years before, or rather by the attitude he had taken towards it. Ever since, his will had been almost unconsciously employed in suppressing doubts about whether he had taken the right track, for he knew there was a subtle destruction for him in self-questioning. What had happened could not be altered, but the life arising out of it could be shaped and controlled. A sufficient task for any man, but one that he had taken simply and inevitably, realizing that it was death to go under! Death, that was, to his essential self.

The novel shows the point at which Hamilton freely chooses and freely identifies himself with his destiny and therefore gives it a new meaning. The striking of bore water symbolically reinforces this idea; new forces are released, and new possibilities open up for the future of Euroa, for which the mortgage, up to this time, has not even been paid off. Both Hamilton and Nina realize that only separation can preserve their essential personalities and integrity; and Hamilton's strength is shown to survive not merely on a series of exclusions, but also through difficult accepted decisions.

Palmer's excessive preoccupation with masculine will is a limiting factor in his work. He had great difficulty in presenting fully mature and convincing female characters: his women tend to be either witless femmes fatales, vehicles of mindless and later-regretted sexual passion, or else discontented neurotics. Nina is the strongest female character in *The Man Hamilton,* but she is not forceful enough to alter or really even to enter Hamilton's masculine world. All the other female characters are merely the opposites of Hamilton's male will.

Men Are Human, a reshaping of an earlier unpublished novel, was finished by 1928 and submitted for the first *Bulletin* novel competition of that year, in which it won third prize—first prize was shared by M. Barnard Eldershaw's *A House Is Built* (1929) and Katharine Susannah Prichard's *Coonardoo* (1929). Like *The Man Hamilton, Men Are Human* is a well-carpentered book, and the later external reshaping of earlier work clearly gave Palmer distance and detachment from his material. The novel contrasts the attitudes of Roger McCurdie, the intensely stubborn, coarse-grained station owner, with that of Duncan, his half-caste workman. Both men lose their sons in the course of the novel, and McCurdie is forced to recognize aspects of his own humanity in Duncan, for whom he has always felt something like contempt. The title is charged with overtones. Men must be fully human: the forces of life will either make them so or destroy them. Palmer intended to write a study of the different possibilities in the father-son relationship, but intentions are not realizations, and *Men Are Human* stands as a study of McCurdie's will to power, centered in Abernethy, the great station that he has built up and with which he identifies.

McCurdie, one of Palmer's strongest single character creations, is an extremely capable portrait of the wealthy, immensely vital, self-made man who perhaps more adequately than any other figure sums up the Australia of his time. He is an example of that energetic "outwardness" that D. H. Lawrence considered characteristically Australian and that Palmer tried to embody in several figures. The reader first meets McCurdie after World War I, waiting for the return of his son, whom he has not seen for more than nine years. McCurdie has been taking stock of his own career. A second marriage, political battles and intrigues, many financial adventures, and a series of exceptional public successes have made him overreach himself and lose his power. A cattleman, he hates the world of sheep, the new Australia. He now concentrates all his energies into Abernethy, the great station that is the center of his life. It is both the symbol of and the creation of his will to power, which draws others in and subordinates them. All the men who work for McCurdie–Duncan, Jeff, Larry, and Mace–have been made dependent on him: their wills have been sapped, along with the sense of their own identities. "It was because of something that went out from the old man unconsciously: you couldn't live with him without surrendering to its influence in the end." But while the source of the power may be unconscious, McCurdie is fully aware of its effects, which he foresees and enjoys.

The novel was originally titled "The Homecoming," and it opens with the arrival of McCurdie's son Boyd, who is returning after his war experiences to what he hopes will be the renewal and solace of Abernethy. A sense of the place in all its varied, sparse actuality is well conveyed throughout the novel.

Men Are Human is one of Palmer's best-written novels. Its general shaping and its total movement–from the sense of expectation at the beginning, the demonstration of Abernethy's power to hold everyone associated with it, to the end in dispersal, with McCurdie about to go, waiting "for a cloud of dust on the skyline"–has a convincing formal coherence, as opposed to mere structural symmetry. This unity is brought about through the descriptions of nature and the sense of place, and of time of day and season; moreover, beneath the surface of the novel of immediate realism with its effective imagery is a fairly dense texture of symbolism, which frequently foreshadows the action, though it is not always fully focused.

Men Are Human succeeds in suggesting the quality of station life just after World War I–its middle-class money values, its spiritual and cultural emptiness and reserve, and its types such as McCurdie and his wife, who combines lack of vitality with sterile sensuality and who longs for the town for release from the sheer inertia of station life. In her, the town-country antagonism, central in Australian writing, is well realized.

Nettie Palmer, circa 1933 (Palmer Papers, National Library of Australia, MS1174)

Although not published until 1930, when it was awarded first prize in the *Bulletin* novel competition and the Australian Literature Society Medal, *The Passage* was begun at Caloundra in 1927–1928. Apparently, Palmer planned to write about different aspects of Australian life–the out-west, the city, the orchard country, and the small fishing village–in an attempt to interpret the country imaginatively and to build up, on however small a scale, an oeuvre like that of the European realists and naturalists he admired.

An abbreviated family chronicle, *The Passage* might almost be subtitled "A study in Australian attitudes of the twenties," since Palmer sets out to dramatize and to diagnose the changes he saw happening in Australia and to show them at work in individual lives. Palmer saw two main forces acting on people–the spirit of place and the bonds of family–and he believed that Australia should resist the pull of the cities and develop its rural communities; in *The Passage* he shows the intimate connection between these forces in the character of Lew Callaway and in the various members of the Callaway family and those associated with them. Lew's development involves some attempt to assert his individuality, to break free from the constrictions of his family, and then his active acceptance of his position in his family in a particular place. This threefold pattern of resistance and rejection, negative experience, return and acceptance is found in most of Palmer's novels.

Palmer needed a clear frame in which to work, and *The Passage* is a strongly schematic book. It is divided into three sections of unequal length. The sections correspond to the development of Lavinia and the Callaways and their friends, first introduced in part 1. Part 2 shows the departure of Anna Callaway and Hughie for Brisbane. Part 3 demonstrates that the proposed development of Lavinia does not occur; it also shows that the main characters return to the Passage for the restoration of order. Lew is the central character, and the three sections relate most closely to his development. In part 1 he is burdened with family responsibilities, the pressures of which contribute to the failure of his relationship to Clem McNair, a doctor's daughter who finally decides to travel abroad to see if she can develop her artistic talent. In part 2 the reader is shown Lew's disastrous marriage with Lena Christensen, a Queensland Emma Bovary, whose unfulfilled energies turn to destruction and waste. Part 3, after the tragic death of Lew's son and the failure of his marriage, shows the reunion of Clem and Lew and the family again at the Passage.

Palmer set himself some difficult artistic problems—he was one of the most ambitious as well as one of the most conscientious novelists in Australia at the time—and the creative challenge of *The Passage* lay in the development of the central figure, Lew, an almost inarticulate fisherman. The artistic difficulty of presenting a character who is complex but not self-aware, inarticulate and unanalytical, probably needed greater formal resources than Palmer was able to command.

The Passage shows to the full Palmer's strengths and weaknesses as a novelist. It excels in sensuous evocations of the fishing village with its sense of the rhythms of nature—of the waves, the sea-life of the reef, the rainbow-birds, and the different qualities of light—and is probably his most lyrical work.

Daybreak, published in 1932, is Palmer's most dramatically conceived novel; after the epic expansion of *The Passage,* the novel *Daybreak* concentrates the action on one day in one township, with a tight use of the three unities of time, setting, and action. The central character, Bob Rossiter, a small fruit farmer in an unspecified area that can be recognized as Emerald in the Dandenongs, finds himself at the center of several conflicting demands. His wife is in the hospital for the birth of their first child, and while he is feeling the tug of anticipations, his mate Sievright, whom he first met during the war and who has been unable to adjust to postwar existence, is making increasing claims on his sense of responsibility. Sievright, on the edge of complete mental collapse because he cannot cope with the world, wants Rossiter to go off gold-seeking with him. In addition, there has been a strike at the local sawmill, and Lysaght, a left-wing political activist, is anxious for Rossiter to persuade the local orchard workers to support the mill hands in their claims. Lysaght knows that only Rossiter's support will persuade the others to join the strikers. Rossiter finds himself, then, caught between his sense of loyalty to Sievright and his intimate loyalties to his own life and future.

In writing *Daybreak* Palmer was in part using the fashion set by the American 1920s for "our town" novels. *Daybreak* inaugurates in Australian fiction of the 1930s a stream of contemporary township novels, of which the most significant are Godfrey Blunden's *No More Reality* (1935), Kylie Tennant's *Tiburon* (1935), and Patrick White's *Happy Valley* (1939).

Palmer's next novel, *The Swayne Family,* has certain affinities with *Men are Human* and *The Passage*. It too deals with a dominating parent who wants to direct, shape, and find an extension of himself through his children, but this novel is strikingly different in most respects from all of Palmer's other books. It is his only social novel and one of the first serious urban novels in Australian literature.

The unifying force in *The Swayne Family* is the family name. The family is not associated with a place or with any traditional activity connected with place—farming or fishing, for example—but it is strongly bound to a class and an attitude that may find expression in activities, whether professional or, with some reservations and suspicions as in the case of Ernest Swayne, artistic. *The Swayne Family,* unlike *The Passage* or the later mining trilogy, succeeds in dealing fully with all members of the family and developing all of its characters, even though they radiate out from Digby Swayne, whose motives and complexities of behavior are the center of the novel.

The Swayne Family is a slow-paced, closely worked book; technically, for all its muted movement and its suggestion of being a sketch for a larger saga, it is Palmer's most skillful achievement; it also seems to be the novel he worked at longest. Palmer has a good ear for dialogue; dealing with sophisticated, self-aware, and often snobbish people rather than with simpler and less articulate figures, he is able to use dialogue to reveal personality in a way he cannot do in any of his other novels. Palmer now knows how to move his novel forward, deftly weaving in background facts, establishing character through scene, and slowly and inconspicuously accumulating knowledge about his hero. The reader learns that Digby has been married twice; that he has four children by his second marriage; that his only child by his first marriage, Stephen, has been killed in World War I; and that Digby has been visiting Stephen's grave on his trip abroad.

Once again Palmer is preoccupied with the search for significant identity. This search makes him a representative figure of his time and generation and gives his work a wider human resonance than his literary nationalism might lead one to expect.

Digby hopes to find his identity reflected through his children; his children hope to find theirs by breaking free of Digby's image. The novel deals with the interacting of the two generations. Digby's obsessive need to create his own family unit is given substance by being developed against the lack of unity in his own generation, the tensions between himself and his brothers.

The Swayne Family marks the full deployment of Palmer's abilities as a novelist. Its affiliations with and debts to John Galsworthy's *The Forsyte Saga* (1922) have been often noted; the influence of *Buddenbrooks* (1901) and its author, Thomas Mann, may be felt in the scene of Digby's vision and in some aspects of the theme. The family saga was the major literary form of the time among both popular and highbrow writers, and it is characteristic of Palmer's professionalism that he should try to write an Australian parallel.

The years 1927–1934 were creatively the richest in Palmer's life. They were the years of his major novels and the years of mounting recognition for his work; they were also the years he wrote the stories of his first collection. There is a general opinion that Palmer's stories are superior to his novels, but this judgment does not survive detailed study of his work, which can best be understood if it is seen as a whole.

Separate Lives (1931) includes stories written between 1920 and 1926, when Palmer was struggling with his early novels and engaged in his work for the Pioneer Players. The stories fall into three main groups—outback and station themes, World War I themes, and character studies based on reversals of fate and destiny. The themes are all subsumed under the title *Separate Lives*. Like *The World of Men,* with which it shows continuity, *Separate Lives* is preoccupied with isolated figures, people caught at a crucial moment in their existence. Palmer set out to capture certain Australian types in his stories and novels. Some he inherited from other Australian writers, Henry Lawson and Steele Rudd as well as Randolph Bedford and Albert Dorrington; others he recorded himself for the first time.

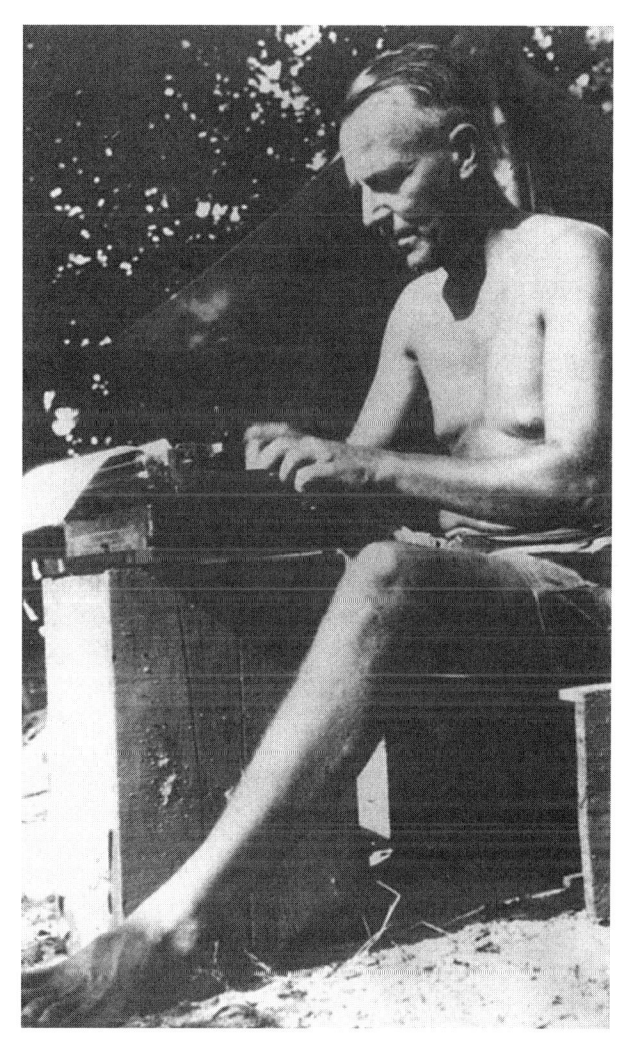

Palmer in Kalorama, Victoria, circa 1935 (Palmer Papers, National Library of Australia, MS1174)

He clearly wanted his books to present something like a microcosm of the Australia of his time.

Palmer tends to concentrate on the lives of men who work in contact with nature, such as fishermen, prospectors, shearers, and beekeepers. There are aspects of the Australian experience—those that preoccupy Martin Boyd and Patrick White, for instance—which are lacking from his work, but there is no wider range of social observation or of national types in the Australian fiction of the time. Like Anton Chekhov, Palmer wanted to show how the impassive light of art might be brought to bear on the inner life of quite ordinary people. His essential interest is in moral meanings in a world that can only be one of mateship or meanness, solitude or solidarity.

Palmer started writing stories at a time when they proved a fruitful market for a full-time author, both in Australia and overseas, and his aim was to reconcile their two potentialities—technical virtuosity, all the tricks of the trade learned from Guy de Maupassant and O. Henry; and the capacity sensitively to present a mood, "a dream, a dialogue, a study of character, a poetic reverie," a moment of vision in depth, the inheritance from Chekhov and Mansfield. The danger of the merely technical approach, apart from its commercially built-in obsolescence, is that it sacrifices experience and human reality to the fictional machine: life is tidied into a neat ending. The danger of the second aspect is that it sacrifices design and the will to form an impression with no greater support than the sincerity of its mood. Palmer does not avoid either extreme, though his greatest dangers come from the first, and the weakest stories in *Separate Lives* fail through an excess of organization.

Stories such as "The Visit" and "The Eyes of the Children," written in late 1923 or early 1924, are revealing. Both include potentially first-class fictional notions; both owe something of their conception to reversals of destiny, as well as their suggestions of a contemptuous tone, to de Maupassant. The first is an account of a meeting between two friends, one of whom is a patrol officer in New Guinea back on furlough; the other has retired from the service and is now married with children. The visit reminds the first of the world of domestic securities and joys, from which his career of adventure has separated him, while the second can only recall the memories of his youthful experiences, now shut off from him by his world of suburban responsibilities and fretfulness. One can see the deliberate process of arrangement and balance at work through the contrasting destinies of the two men, even down to the analogy touched on between being eaten alive in New Guinea and of being eaten up by suburban life. A similar overconscientious patterning can be found in much of Palmer's work. "The Eyes of the Children" fully and explicitly explores a reversal of attitude. A rather "tough" modern girl insists that the narrator tell the truth to her widowed mother about her father—a waster and a gambler—but later is herself unable to face the truth about her husband, who is not at all the ideal lover he is transformed into by her illusions. The story says something about the human capacity for self-deception and something about the nature of love; but the flow of meanings is stopped by the too-successful oppositions of expectations and roles; the mechanical ousts the moving.

The best stories in *Sea and Spinifex* (1934) show an advance on their predecessors in flexibility of movement and shape. The symmetry is more relaxed and the plotting less rigid than in many stories in the earlier volume, but these stories mark no greater technical development. The title of the book indicates its two major settings; the stories move from the coast to the inland mining areas and back, though seemingly without any schematic intention. The real advance that the book represents is thematic. Palmer now shows himself to be a sensitive observer of children; some of the stories date from the time he was writing of Peter in *The Passage,* and doubtless his observation of his own children helped him recall incidents and experiences from his own childhood. He is also an accurate observer of mob psychology and the fluctuations of group feeling—as in "The Mob" and the semidocumentary "Stowaways." But above all, he is an observer acutely aware of the role of fantasy and illusions in individual lives.

Nine of the eighteen stories in *Sea and Spinifex* are concerned with children and adolescents, and their emotional reactions to situations over which they have no control. "The Rainbow-Bird," which has become Palmer's best-known story, is concerned with the destruction of a young girl's vision of beauty when the honey-man shoots the rainbow-bird that has become the center of her imaginative life. At the end she dreams that the honey-man is dead in the place of the bird he has killed. The story is closely paralleled by "Monday Morning," in which a sensitive boy who is constantly persecuted at school because his father is a policeman hears that his tormentor has accidentally been shot; the world will never again be the same for him.

The stories dealing with youthful illusions are among the best. "The Branscombe Sisters" takes a common theme—the discovery that the idealized girl of one's imagination is not at all as one had thought—and fully registers not only the disillusionment but also the vitality of the youthful imagination and curiosity—"if only—yes, if only I'd happened to meet the darker one"—while "Young Girl's Fancy" traces the vagaries and fluctuations of emotion in a young girl when the boy she loves does not appear.

The range of Palmer's subjects and settings is varied. Two studies are of Aborigines, "Johnny" and "Home." "The Little Duck" explores the idea of a man, once half crazed and on the verge of death, who is impelled to return to the bush where he suffered so much. "Travelling" is a vignette of a loud-mouthed cook who chatters on about his experiences while those who have really endured the hardships say nothing at all. Palmer's achievement in these pieces cannot be overestimated. The balancing of situation, image, and symbol, which can easily fall into mechanical regularity or over-symmetry, brings a certain completeness of poetic resonance. In "Travelling," restraint, which in some parts of the novels can become self-defeating, becomes an achievement of artistic tact. The last words of the sketch, "that land of silence," take on a rich suggestiveness of the stoic endurance and the almost wordless courage of the men it presents.

Page from an early draft for Palmer's Golconda, *the first in a trilogy of mining novels (National Library of Australia, MS1174/3/7)*

Palmer's next novel, *Legend for Sanderson* (1937), was published upon his return to Australia after nearly eighteen months abroad, during which he lived in London and Barcelona until the outbreak of the Spanish Civil War. This book takes up his familiar theme of the search for meaningful identity through the fruitful directing of the will, and it treats the father-son relationship from the point of view of the son. But it is a curiously irresolute work, suggesting that Palmer had already resolved in his previous novels the themes—especially those of mateship and the demands of self-fulfilment of the will—that in this novel are treated so perfunctorily.

After publication of *Legend for Sanderson* Palmer felt that he was exhausted as a novelist for the time being, and for the next ten years he devoted himself almost exclusively to the writing of critical works, historical studies, and interpretative books in an attempt to come to terms with the meaning of the Australian experience. *National Portraits* (1940), *A. G. Stephens: His Life and Work* (1941), *Frank Wilmot (Furnley Maurice)* (1942), *Louis Esson and the Australian Theatre* (1948), and *The Legend of the Nineties* (1954), as well as many uncollected essays, comments, and papers were the fruits of these years. They are important stages in the search for an Australian literary identity and key works in the understanding of the Australia that was taking shape from the 1890s to World War II. While such pioneer studies came to be superseded as more-detailed historical and theoretical investigations emerged, these works are essential documents in the literary culture of their time. Sections of them, as well as parts of the posthumous *Intimate Portraits* (1969), have by virtue of personality and style a permanent aesthetic and moral value that transcends their historical importance.

The work on which Palmer placed his greatest hopes as a novelist in the last years of his life was the mining trilogy, which consists of *Golconda* (1948), *Seedtime* (1957), and *The Big Fellow* (1959). Palmer had thought of writing a novel about Mt. Isa since his visit there in 1924, and in a trilogy centered on Mt. Isa he saw his chance to sum up what he felt to be the truth about the Australia of his time.

In concentrating on the life of Macy Donovan, Palmer was partly inspired by the careers of such political figures as E. G. Theodore and W. A. Holman. Important in Palmer's imaginative world was the need to project an image of the typical Australian hero—a man of some achievement, not marked by the colonial gentility that characterizes Digby Swayne but an example of what in Australian political typology has been called "the larrikin leader."

Golconda is in some respects a panoramic documentary novel, presenting the development of a place from its discovery through its growth from a camp into a town. But the novel is concerned not only with a place in its physical aspect but also with the sense that Golconda inspires in all those involved with it, of opportunity and of test of integrity. The significant relationships and tensions in *Golconda* are between character and place rather than between character and character. This difference is seen in Christy Baughan, the eccentric gouger (miner) who was with Lane in Paraguay; in Keighley, the mining engineer; in Neda Varnek, the creative artist; and in Donovan, a "small-town big boy" who is the central and most complex character of the trilogy. His relationship to Golconda, which parallels the development of the place at least in the early stages, is presented with some subtlety. As union representative, Donovan stands for the third group of interests on the field, neither the extreme idealism of Baughan's "free community" nor the personally unearned exploitation by the big companies, but the wage earners with their human and practical concerns. The gougers and the company backers are materialistic; Baughan and Keighley are in some sense idealistic; Donovan is neither. He is driven throughout by a personal will to power and a compelling need to exercise his gift for leadership and organization.

At first Donovan is completely committed to Golconda and seems destined to become an efficient union organizer and nothing more; but developments in his private life—his affair with Carita Keighley, his feeling for Neda, his changing attitude toward Mahony—reveal possibilities of a new self-image that begins to direct his political interests. When Neda, whom Donovan loves, rejects him, he decides to stand for Parliament. The last part of the novel deals with his successful election campaign, the growing attraction of the city, and his developing confidence in his own increasing power.

Seedtime picks up the story four years later. It shows Donovan in a different world, the Brisbane of the late 1920s, and in a different focus—largely seen through the eyes of others. It traces the next stage of his political career, from failure through crisis to new success, and it develops two new relationships in his life, those with Judy and Kitty Hegarty.

Seedtime is a serious attempt to show a political figure trying to bridge the gap between the labor world of the 1890s and the modern developing Australia of the late 1920s. Donovan represents at first the labor forces of Golconda, but the bush worker belongs to another day, and Donovan's background is proving inadequate to the Australia of his time. Part of the inconclusiveness of the novel stems from Palmer's inability to detach himself from Donovan and his situation: "The city or the bush" alternative that faces Donovan is the one that Palmer himself was only intermittently able to transcend. *Seedtime* is designed to show Donovan's awkward move into the world of money, property, and Australian families with a past; and above all, it shows his experiences in Parliament.

The Big Fellow is set in Brisbane just after the mid 1940s, when Donovan has won fame as the Big Fellow of the title. His parliamentary career has been packed with experience; he has been Minister of Mines; now he is Premier of Queensland. He has two children—a daughter, Sheila, to whom he is devoted, and a son, Kevin, in whom he is deeply disappointed. Kitty and Donovan are starting to drift apart as Donovan feels a constant sense of nagging dissatisfaction at the center of his life. The novel shows Donovan's last attempt to find personal fulfillment and to inform his life with some sense of significance. He has not had an impeccable past. In *The Big Fellow* the integrity of his public image is threatened by the revival of the Mount Clutha affair, an old mining scandal with roots that go deeper into his family life than Donovan yet realizes.

At this point in his career, and with his former vitality at an ebb, Donovan must face a series of personal and public crises, some major and some minor. Peter Mahony, whom Donovan adopted after Mahony's death and who has been working as his secretary, wants to leave to study medicine; the relationship between Peter and Donovan's daughter, Sheila, has failed to develop in the way Donovan had hoped; while the return of Neda (now Madame Brouyer) from abroad, after a career of hard work and growing fame as a sculptor, plunges him into the world of jealousies and erotic tension that she has always provoked in him.

The working out of the Neda-Donovan relationship is the most important single strand in the book and is Palmer's most complete statement on the theme of romantic love. Neda has a delinquent illegitimate son, Leo, at present in a reformatory, and she enlists Donovan's aid to secure Leo's release. Donovan's renewed contact with Neda precipitates his restless longings to break free of the world of politics and family which now so oppressively encloses him. But Neda refuses to abandon her art for him; and Leo nearly kills Donovan when the latter catches him breaking into a cinema. Romantic longings and the pressures of the irrational are always punished in Palmer's world; Donovan is forced to face a series of sharp defeats.

The *Golconda* trilogy will continue to be read for historical reasons, for the way it catches the movement from the 1890s idealism of Baughan to the major labor split of the late 1940s, when new forces and patterns emerged in Australian society. The trilogy traces an important phase of Australian development and communicates it in *The Big Fellow* on the only level that can matter in a novel—through the felt sense of a human visage, marked by the various pressures of life.

Dust jacket for Palmer's 1957 novel, the second volume of his mining trilogy (Bruccoli Clark Layman Archives)

In 1955 Palmer published his first collection of stories in twenty-one years, *Let the Birds Fly,* which includes all fifteen stories Palmer wrote during this time. *Let the Birds Fly* was his last collection of stories, and with the Golconda trilogy it provides a fitting conclusion to his life's work. It is Palmer's most consistently accomplished volume of stories. The best stories in this volume are longer, more leisurely, and more closely textured than most of their predecessors and illustrate their themes through incident.

Once more the title is significant. Most of the stories are concerned with aspects of freedom, with the desire to escape from a constricting reality, or with the discovery that one's exceptional moments of freedom and transcendence are closed off and lead back to the reality from which one had hoped to escape. The pattern of release and return, acceptance and rejection is discernible in much of Palmer's work.

As in *Sea and Spinifex,* some of the best stories in *Let the Birds Fly* are written from the point of view of a child, a youth, or a person looking back to early experiences. The theme of childhood's disappointment at the behavior of adults and of youth's awakening to the world of adult relationships preoccupied Palmer and in some senses is his dominant theme. One of the earliest sketches in *The World of Men,* "The Hermit," is concerned with this central experience, as is one of his last stories, "The Catch," which dates from the early 1950s. In this story Palmer deals with a boy's happiness on holiday when he catches a grouper and with his attempt to impress his mother, who is preoccupied with a love affair. What quotation or recounting cannot convey is the meaning of the adult relationships that emerge from the whole. Again, presentation of the child's point of view enables the story to convey, with the fine economy of understatement and a significant reticence, much more than the boy knows or understands and to suggest a complex network of adult relationships and betrayals.

As with the lyric, the effectiveness of the short story lies just as much in the use of its formal resources as in its themes. The delicate sketches "Josie" (circa 1940) and "The Foal" (circa 1945) belong with early stories such as "The Rainbow-Bird" and "Monday Morning": both stories are sensitive accounts of childhood experiences. "Josie" conveys the feelings of a group of young children when they hear of the death of a half-caste girl in their class, while "The Foal" is a lyrical evocation of a child's happiness in the birth of a foal and her apprehension and fears for the life of such a frail creature. Other remarkable pieces, such as "The Search," set during the Spanish Civil War, and "Greta" suggest something of Palmer's range.

Vance Palmer died suddenly of a heart attack on 15 July 1959, just before the appearance of a commemorative issue of *Meanjin* designed to pay homage to the contribution he and Nettie Palmer had made to the development of a national literary culture. Plans were also in progress for the award of an honorary doctorate to Vance Palmer from the University of Melbourne. The Palmers were held in great esteem in the last years of their lives. Vance Palmer's broadcasts and reviews were popular and influential, and he was prominent in most of the cultural activities of the time. His work on behalf of Australian writers, especially through the Commonwealth Literary Fund, of which he was a member from 1942 to 1953, was an important service to the development of culture in Australia.

Although Palmer took himself seriously as a novelist, he is most highly regarded now for his short stories and for his literary journalism, studies, and essays. But a writer's work can suddenly become interesting in new ways, and his novels might well enjoy a revival. Whatever the future holds for his fiction, he remains one of the few authors who made a highly distinctive contribution to the formative phase of modern Australian writing.

Letters:
Vivian Smith, ed., *Letters of Vance and Nettie Palmer, 1915–1963* (Canberra: National Library of Australia, 1977).

References:
J. Barnes, "Vance Palmer: The Man of Letters," *Meanjin*, 18 (1959): 193–205;

H. P. Heseltine, *Vance Palmer* (St. Lucia: University of Queensland Press, 1970);

Ivor Indyk, "Vance Palmer and the Social Function of Literature," *Southerly* (September 1990): 346–358;

Vivian Smith, *Vance and Nettie Palmer* (Boston: Twayne, 1975);

Smith, *Vance Palmer* (Melbourne: Oxford University Press, 1971);

D. Walker, *Dream and Disillusion: A Search for Australian Cultural Identity* (Canberra: Australian National Press, 1976), pp. 31–61, 168–194.

Papers:
The papers of Vance Palmer are held at the National Library of Australia, Canberra.

Ruth Park
(1923? -)

Paul Genoni
Curtin University of Technology

BOOKS: *The Harp in the South* (Sydney: Angus & Robertson, 1948; London: Joseph, 1948; Boston: Houghton Mifflin, 1948);

The Uninvited Guest (Sydney: Angus & Robertson, 1948);

Poor Man's Orange (Sydney: Angus & Robertson, 1949); republished as *12 1/2 Plymouth Street* (Boston: Houghton Mifflin, 1951);

The Witch's Thorn (Sydney: Angus & Robertson, 1951; Boston: Houghton Mifflin, 1952);

A Power of Roses (Sydney: Angus & Robertson, 1953; London: Joseph, 1953);

Pink Flannel, illustrated by Phil Taylor (Sydney: Angus & Robertson, 1955); republished as *Dear Hearts and Gentle People* (Ringwood, Vic.: Penguin, 1981; Harmondsworth, U.K. & New York: Penguin, 1981);

Der Goldene Bumerang: Australien, die Alteste und die Nueste (Bremen: Carl Schunemann, 1955);

The Drums Go Bang! by Park and D'Arcy Niland (Sydney: Angus & Robertson, 1956);

One-a-Pecker, Two-a-Pecker (Sydney: Angus & Robertson, 1957); republished as *The Frost and the Fire* (Boston: Houghton Mifflin, 1958);

The Hole in the Hill (Sydney: Ure Smith, 1961); republished as *Secret of the Maori Cave* (Garden City, N.Y.: Doubleday, 1964);

The Ship's Cat (New York: St. Martin's Press, 1961; London: Macmillan, 1961);

Tales of the South (London: Macmillan, 1961);

The Good Looking Women (Sydney: Angus & Robertson, 1961); republished as *Serpent's Delight* (Garden City, N.Y.: Doubleday, 1962);

The Muddle-Headed Wombat (Sydney: Educational Press, 1962);

Uncle Matt's Mountain (New York: St. Martin's Press, 1962; London: Macmillan, 1962);

The Road to Christmas (New York: St. Martin's Press, 1962; London: Macmillan, 1962);

The Road under the Sea (Sydney: Ure Smith, 1962; Garden City, N.Y.: Doubleday, 1966);

Ruth Park (from Joy Hooton, Ruth Park, *1996)*

The Shaky Island (New York: McKay, 1962; London: Constable, 1962);

Airlift for Grandee (New York: St. Martin's Press, 1964; London: Macmillan, 1964; Melbourne: Macmillan, 1967);

The Muddle-Headed Wombat on Holiday (Sydney: Educational Press, 1964);

The Muddle-Headed Wombat in the Treetops (Sydney: Educational Press, 1965);

The Muddle-Headed Wombat at School (Sydney: Educational Press, 1966);

The Muddle-Headed Wombat in the Snow (Sydney: Educational Press, 1966);

Ring for the Sorcerer (Sydney: Horwitz-Martin, 1967; London: Constable, 1967);

The Sixpenny Island (Sydney: Ure Smith, 1968); republished as *Ten-Cent Island* (Garden City, N.Y.: Doubleday, 1968);

The Muddle-Headed Wombat on a Rainy Day (Sydney: Educational Press, 1969);

Nuki and the Sea Serpent: A Maori Story (London: Longman, 1969);

The Runaway Bus (Sydney: Hodder & Stoughton, 1969);

The Muddle-Headed Wombat in the Springtime (Sydney: Educational Press, 1970);

The Muddle-Headed Wombat on the River (Sydney: Educational Press, 1970);

The Companion Guide to Sydney (Sydney: Collins, 1973); revised and enlarged as *Ruth Park's Sydney*, by Park and Rafe Champion (Potts Point, N.S.W.: Duffy & Snellgrove, 1999);

The Muddle-Headed Wombat and the Bush Band (Sydney: Angus & Robertson, 1973);

Callie's Castle (Sydney: Angus & Robertson, 1974);

The Gigantic Balloon (Sydney: Collins, 1975; New York: Parents Magazine Press, 1976);

Merchant Campbell (Sydney: Collins, 1976);

The Muddle-Headed Wombat on Clean-Up Day (Sydney: Angus & Robertson, 1976);

The Muddle-Headed Wombat and the Invention (Sydney: Angus & Robertson, 1976);

Roger Bandy (Adelaide: Rigby, 1977);

Swords and Crowns and Rings (West Melbourne: Thomas Nelson, 1977; New York: St. Martin's Press, 1978);

Come Danger, Come Darkness (Sydney: Hodder & Stoughton, 1978);

Playing Beatie Bow (Melbourne: Thomas Nelson, 1980; New York: Atheneum, 1982);

When the Wind Changed (Sydney: Collins, 1980; New York: Coward, McCann & Geoghegan, 1981);

The Muddle-Headed Wombat is Very Bad (Sydney: Angus & Robertson, 1981);

The Muddle-Headed Wombat Stays at Home (Sydney: Angus & Robertson, 1982);

Norfolk Island and Lord Howe Island (Dover Heights, N.S.W.: Serendip, 1982);

The Big Brass Key (Sydney: Hodder & Stoughton, 1983);

The Sydney We Love, by Park and Cedric Emmanuel (Sydney: Thomas Nelson, 1983);

Missus (West Melbourne: Nelson, 1985; London: Joseph, 1985; New York: St. Martin's Press, 1987);

My Sister Sif (Ringwood, Vic.: Viking Kestrel, 1986; New York: Viking, 1991);

The Harp in the South, by Park and Leslie Rees (Montmorency, Vic.: Yackandandah Playscripts, 1987);

The Tasmania We Love, by Park and Cedric Emmanuel (Sydney: Thomas Nelson, 1987);

Callie's Family (Sydney: Angus & Robertson, 1988);

James (Ringwood, Vic.: Viking, 1988);

Things in Corners (Melbourne: Viking Kestrel, 1988; New York: Viking, 1989);

A Fence around the Cuckoo (Ringwood, Vic.: Viking, 1992);

Fishing in the Styx (Ringwood, Vic.: Viking, 1993; New York: Viking, 1993);

Home Before Dark: The Story of Les Darcy, a Great Australian Hero, by Park and Rafe Champion (Ringwood, Vic.: Penguin, 1995).

Collections: *The Adventures of the Muddle-Headed Wombat* (Sydney: Angus & Robertson, 1979);

Ruth Park's Harp in the South Novels (Ringwood, Vic.: Penguin, 1987).

PLAY PRODUCTION: *The Harp in the South*, by Park and Leslie Rees, Sydney, Independent Theatre, 3 March 1949.

PRODUCED SCRIPTS: *The Muddle-Headed Wombat*, ABC radio series, 1951–1972;

"No Decision," television, by Park and D'Arcy Niland, 1961.

OTHER: "Regatta Day" and "The Exile," in *Coast to Coast: Australian Stories 1944*, selected by Vance Palmer (Sydney: Angus & Robertson, 1944), pp. 41–55;

"Researching the Novel," in *Australian Author*, 3, no. 4 (1971): 27–30;

"Solace," in *Great Short Stories of Australia and New Zealand* (Sydney: Reader's Digest Services, 1980);

D'Arcy Niland, *The Penguin Best Stories of D'Arcy Niland*, selected and with an introduction by Park (Ringwood, Vic.: Penguin, 1987);

"The House to Themselves," in *Eclipsed: Two Centuries of Australian Women's Fiction*, selected by Connie Burns and Marygai McNamara (Sydney: Collins, 1989), pp. 366–370;

"The Travellers," in *Feeling Restless: Australian Women's Short Stories 1940–1969*, selected by Burns and McNamara (Sydney: Collins, 1989), pp. 252–257;

Anne Summers, *Ducks on the Pond: An Autobiography 1945–1976*, foreword by Park (Ringwood, Vic.: Viking, 1999).

Ruth Park occupies an ambivalent place in Australian literature. Her output, in a career that extends more than half a century, has been prodigious. She has written with considerable commercial success for adults, young adults, and children; her output encompasses fiction, autobiography, biography, travel guides,

Park interviewing a resident of Surry Hills, where she set her first novel,
The Harp in the South *(from Hooton,* Ruth Park, *1996)*

drama, and radio plays. The most successful of her work has been consistently in print and even translated into thirty-two languages.

Despite Park's extraordinary productivity, commercial success, and frequent acknowledgment by way of various literary prizes awarded for both her adult and her children's writings, she has received little serious critical attention. This neglect seems to result from the style of her adult fiction, which is resolutely out of favor with modern critical taste. Park's virtues as a writer are traditional, and her writing is best remembered for its graphic storytelling, lively characterization, and vivid dialogue, rather than for stylistic innovation. Nevertheless, her lengthy career as a professional writer, the multiple audiences for which she has written, and the extraordinary and ongoing popularity of her first two novels mean that she is among the most widely read and best known Australian authors of the past fifty years.

Rosina Ruth Lucia Park was born in Auckland, New Zealand, in 1923 (the year reported varies from 1917 to 1924, but 1923 is the most commonly cited), the eldest child of Melville Park and Christina Patterson Park. Ruth Park's forebears were Scottish and Irish on her father's side of the family and Swedish and Irish on her mother's. She also had an early Australian connection: her paternal grandmother had been born in Hobart.

Park's upbringing was deeply affected by the Great Depression. Her father was employed in a series of jobs in the road-building, trucking, and timber industries, which took him and his family to remote rural areas of the North Island of New Zealand. The difficult working conditions and the economic hardship endured by the family eventually led to Melville Park's loss of health and subsequent financial ruin. Not surprisingly, considering the troubled times that her family faced, childhood insecurity became a common theme in Park's fiction.

The young Park was keenly aware of her father's trauma and also the suffering the hardworking life caused for her mother, whom Park describes in the autobiographical *A Fence Around the Cuckoo* (1992) as a "delicate, slender city girl," possessed of an "ardent, speculative and romantic temperament." Park's lifelong interest in women's issues was undoubtedly formed in part by witnessing her mother's troubled life in the masculine rural communities of Depression-bound New Zealand.

Another outcome of Park's unusual childhood in the small towns and work camps was that for long periods she was denied the company of other children. Companionship was, however, not something she missed. By her own account she was a self-sufficient child who compensated for the lack of playmates by developing a rich imaginative life. She writes, "I cannot emphasise sufficiently the importance of my early life as a forest creature," and recognizes that these early years spent playing alone have been "of inestimable value to me as a writer."

Park's family was also an influence on her decision early in life to make a career as a writer. Park describes her father as "a storyteller, which is all I have ever wanted to be." Since writing paper was in short supply, she began writing on any available surface, and she later declares in *A Fence Around the Cuckoo* that "From my earliest days I was a kind of writer." A further family influence on Park was the four aunts from her mother's family. Their own families were more financially secure than Park's, and they seem to have been a boisterous and encouraging link to other worlds. The figures of aunts have been important in many of Park's novels.

Other factors that had an impact on Park's upbringing were her relationship with Maori people and her education by Catholic nuns. Park was introduced to the Maoris and their culture by her father, who had a great fondness for them. Most of her childhood friends and playmates were from Maori families. She was able to observe aspects of Maori culture firsthand and to learn something of the language; her experiences left her sympathetically disposed toward Aboriginal Australians.

Park's education commenced with the St. Joseph's nuns in the convent in the township of Te Kuiti in the King Country. As a result of her father's illness, however, the family moved to Auckland. In Auckland they were forced to live with relatives because of their own strained financial circumstances, and Park had her first exposure to the inner-city working-class suburbs that became a feature of her Australian novels.

The young Park realized that continued education was important to her fulfilling her literary ambitions, and she was seemingly provided with an important opportunity when she received a scholarship that provided for three years of secondary schooling. She was disappointed, however, when she learned that the family's dire financial position meant they were unable to continue her education even with this measure of assistance. Such was their economic hardship that Park was sent to stay with relatives on a sheep-farming property on the Hauraki Gulf. She was reluctant to leave her family, but this period allowed her to renew her affinity with the natural wonders of the island and to receive some schooling from her uncle, who was able to tutor her in Latin and French.

After two years out of the school system, Park returned to Auckland and resumed her education with the St. Joseph's nuns, this time at St. Benedict's Convent. These selfless, independent, and hardworking women were positive role models for the young Park, and she records in *A Fence Around the Cuckoo* that she always remembered them with "gratitude and affection for ever." Many of the St. Josephine's nuns working in New Zealand were Australian women, and they left Park with a favorable attitude toward Australia and Australians.

Throughout these teenage years Park held fast to her ambition to earn a living from writing. She had a taste of publication when she began sending contributions to the children's pages of *The New Zealand Herald* (Auckland) and later *The Auckland Star*.

The Auckland Star eventually gave Park her first job upon completing school, employing her as a proofreader. She saw working in journalism as a start toward her chosen career as a writer. At the same time, she continued to place stories in other papers, using various pseudonyms since employees of *The Star* were not permitted to write for rival publications. She even published her stories in overseas papers, such as *The San Francisco Chronicle* and *The San Francisco Examiner*.

An important link to Australia that developed for Park at this time was her friendship with writer Eve Langley, who was then living in Auckland. The two met in August 1940 at the offices of *The Star*. According to Langley's biographer, Joy Thwaite, Park was attracted to the older woman's "flagrant romantic bohemianism." Some of Langley's "bohemianism" may have been a manifestation of an ongoing personality disorder, but Park and Langley remained close over some years, with Thwaite describing Park as "a staunch, compassionate and helpful friend" to the ailing Langley.

Park developed an even more significant Australian connection when in the late 1930s she agreed to, at the instigation of some of the nuns from St. Benedict's, a correspondence with an aspiring young Australian writer, D'Arcy Niland. Park's correspondence with Niland eventually led to her traveling briefly to Sydney during 1940. In Sydney she encountered for the first time what she describes in *A Fence Around the Cuckoo* as "the ancient, indifferent, nonpareil continent that was to become the love of my life." Park also formed a strong personal relationship with Niland during her Sydney visit. She eventually returned to Australia in 1942, and the couple were married shortly thereafter.

In the early period of their marriage Park and Niland lived in several inner-city suburbs, including King's Cross. Niland was restricted to civilian occupations during World War II because of health problems, and he was soon "manpowered" on to the shearing circuit in rural Australia. This assignment gave Park the opportunity to increase her knowledge of Australia, and she took a variety of jobs in the remote towns in which the couple found themselves temporarily residing. On returning to Sydney in 1943 they took accommodation in the run-down Surry Hills, which Park immortalized in her early novels. The couple also became parents during the war years, with daughter Anne born in 1943 and son Rory in 1945.

Park and Niland continued to write throughout the war and postwar period. Both were determined to earn a living from their writing, something that in Australia at the time was rare outside of journalism. Park was also beginning to demonstrate her versatility as a writer. Two of her short stories were selected by Vance Palmer for inclusion in the 1944 edition of *Coast to Coast*, and a play, "The Uninvited Guest," was published in the Australian Youth Plays series in 1948.

Park's major break came when she entered a *Sydney Morning Herald* literary competition, which included a prize of £2000 for a novel. She submitted a manuscript of *The Harp in the South* (book publication, 1948), for which she won the first prize; the prize included serialization in the paper in January 1947.

The Harp in the South follows the fortunes of three generations of the Irish-Catholic Darcy family, who live together in the cramped and leaky terrace house at 12 1/2 Plymouth Street, Surry Hills. In the heavily populated novel the emotional focus eventually falls on Roie Darcy. Roie is a teenage factory worker of fragile and romantic temperament whose failed relationship with a young Jewish boy, Tommy Mendel, leaves her pregnant. She contemplates an abortion before eventually losing the baby when she is caught up in a drunken street fight.

Roie's second relationship is with Charlie Rothe, who is part Aboriginal. She eventually marries Charlie, and by the conclusion of the novel they have a daughter. This relationship is notable in that it is one of the earliest portrayals in Australian fiction of a sexual relationship between a white woman and an indigenous man. The novel also traces the lives of Roie's extended family, who live in the house, including her spirited and combative "Grandma," her feckless and alcoholic father Hughie, and her long-suffering mother, "Mumma."

Dust jacket for the U.S. edition of Park's 1948 novel, tracing three generations of an Irish family living in the slums of Sydney (Richland County Public Library)

The Harp in the South highlights the hard realities of life in Surry Hills, giving a vivid portrayal of the outcomes of unremitting poverty–domestic violence, street thuggery, drunkenness, death in childbirth, suicide, child prostitution, rape, and abortion. The reader is left, however, with a strong sense of Park's affection for the inhabitants of this rough and unsettling neighborhood, and a sense of her admiration for their capacity to endure and to find some consolation in their difficult lives. The novel features many of the hallmarks of Park's fiction–a large cast in a working-class setting; a central character who is vulnerable, teenaged, and female; an episodic and rambling structure; and a core of realism that is undercut by a streak of romanticism.

The serialization of *The Harp in the South* in *The Sydney Morning Herald* aroused a substantial controversy that was largely conducted through the letters page of the paper. Many Sydney residents were shocked by the vivid portrayal of the slums of Surry Hills and refused to believe that publication of the novel could be good for either the city or Australian literature. Indeed, such was the impact of the shocked reception of the novel that it played an important part in the slum-clearance programs that began in Surry Hills in the early 1950s. The controversy surrounding the serialization surprised and hurt Park, however, and she later attributed the outcry to her being a woman.

When *The Harp in the South* was published in its complete form in 1948, it was a major commercial success in Australia and received publication and considerable positive notice by reviewers in the United States. She minimally assisted playwright Leslie Rees to bring a stage version to production in 1949, and in the same year she published *Poor Man's Orange,* a sequel to the first novel.

Poor Man's Orange continues the story of Roie and Charlie and the other inhabitants of the Plymouth Street House. Roie dies soon after the novel opens, and the story then traces the gradual disintegration of the two men of the house, Hughie and Charlie, until Charlie's life is turned around after he forms a relationship with Roie's younger sister, Dolour. By the conclusion of the novel the two are on the verge of marriage. Dolour emerges at this time as the stable emotional center in a cast of characters who are otherwise in various states of personal disarray.

Poor Man's Orange was another critical success, receiving rave reviews in several American journals. Despite their continued financial struggles, Park and Niland were firmly established in their chosen careers, although Niland's real success came later than Park's. In the meantime they continued to support themselves by writing for the ABC. In addition to her steady stream of children's scripts Park wrote many episodes of the adult dramas *Stumpy* and *The Night Tales of the Bagman,* plus many other occasional pieces. With a growing family–she by now had a second son, Patrick–Park continued an extraordinarily demanding pace of work throughout her adult life.

In 1950 Park and Niland set out for Europe with the intention of stopping in New Zealand en route. While in Auckland, Park discovered she was pregnant again, a circumstance that required a lengthy and difficult stay with her family while she awaited the birth, this time of twin girls, Deborah and Kilmeny.

Park chose New Zealand as the location for her third novel, *The Witch's Thorn* (1951). The setting is the North Island town of Te Kano, and the period is the Great Depression of the late 1920s. The central character in another densely populated novel is again a young woman, Bethell Jury, who is twelve and thirteen during the period covered. *The Witch's Thorn* is the first of several novels in which Park focuses on a character who is "orphaned." Bethell is the illegitimate daughter of the shiftless and violent Johnny Gow and the irresponsible Queenie Jury, who deserts her child soon after the opening of the novel.

As a result of her abandonment Bethell is handed around among several families, each of which fails to provide a satisfactory home for the young girl. She is denied such security until she is united with the large and gregarious Maori family of Georgie Wi, who eventually attempts to claim her as his own illegitimate child. In a violent conclusion, Bethell is beaten and nearly killed by Johnny Gow, who is in turn swallowed by one of the town geysers.

The Witch's Thorn is the first of several novels in which Park draws distinctions between the attitudes of the more financially secure and respected members of a community and those who exist at its fringes. Bethell is let down by several of the supposedly upright families of Te Kano, while those who provide the girl with genuine support are the "outcasts," Georgie Wi and the prostitute Gracie Hush. Indeed, the eventual adoption of Bethell by the Wi family can be read as a reversal of the Australian Aboriginal "stolen generation" narratives, in which native children are removed from their families by the settler society. In *The Witch's Thorn* the indigenous family adopts the young white girl, who has been neglected by her own family.

The Witch's Thorn is also noteworthy in that it includes Park's most malevolent character, Johnny Gow. In one particularly chilling scene, he rapes his wife in the hope that she will become pregnant and thereby die either in childbirth or as the result of the strain induced by raising yet another child. Although Park has sometimes been dismissed as being overly sentimental, such judgments do little to account for Gow and the retinue of similar characters Park has created and the misery they consciously visit upon the lives of others.

Also of note in *The Witch's Thorn* is the account of the emerging sexuality of the pubescent Bethell. Park has frequently written quite frankly of female sexual desire, and in another representation of a relationship between a white female and an indigenous male, the twelve-year-old Bethell engages in an increasingly intense relationship with the young Maori, Hoot Gibson Wi:

> He pulled her into the shadow of the bushes beside the stream, where the smoky berries trembled ceaselessly in the spray. The minutes passed and Bethell did not notice them go. . . . Bethell scarcely dared to breathe. She looked at the crisp, curly hair of her companion, that was not black but a brown as dark as the darkest

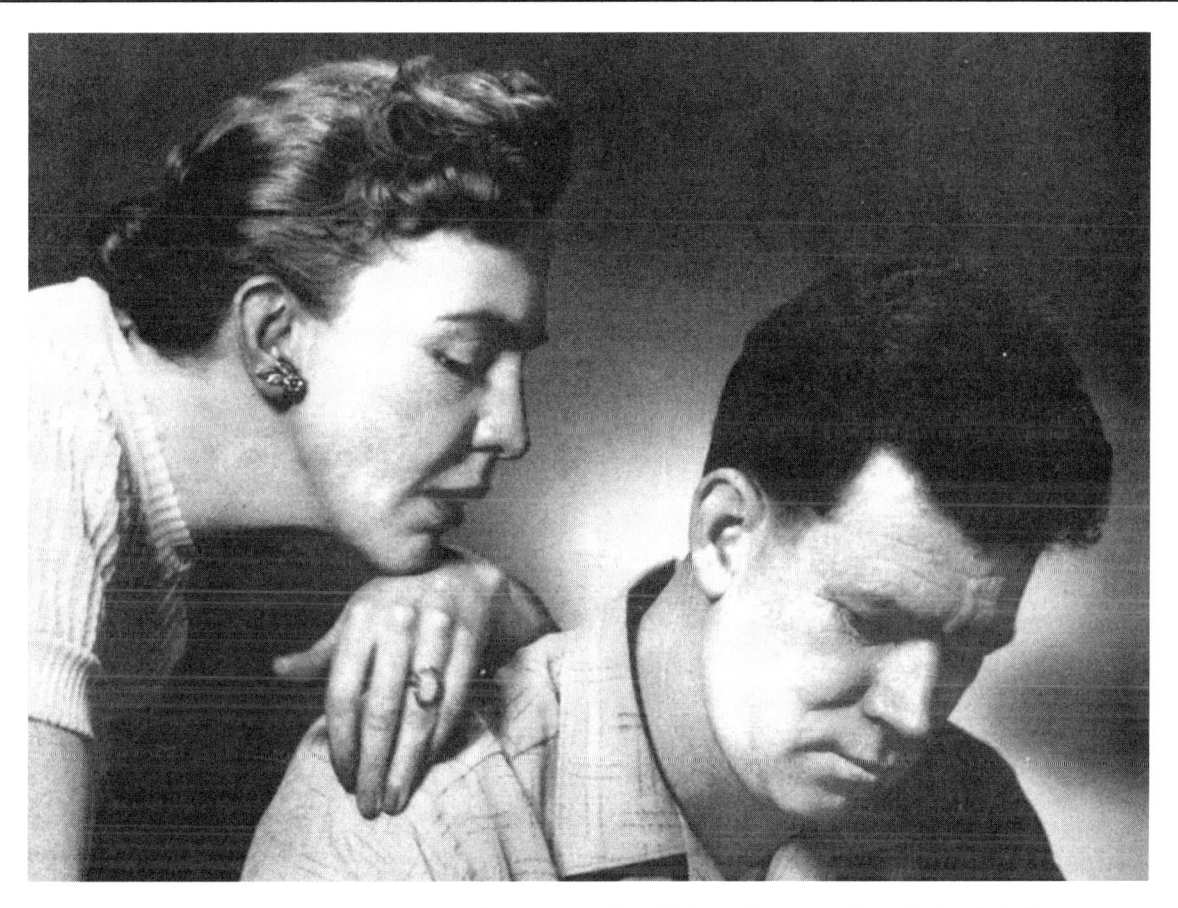

Park with her husband, D'Arcy Niland (photograph by Kara Feldman, Montgomery Dunn Studios, Sydney)

timber. She saw the pure line of his brown cheek, and the outline of his lips that was raised ever so slightly in relief, like a sculpture. All the beauty of his race was in his profile, and the girl, her mind untrammelled by comparisons, accepted that beauty with wonder and pleasure.

After returning from the enforced stay in New Zealand, Park and her expanded family settled in Neutral Bay, Sydney. When not writing for radio, Park continued to produce adult fiction. With *A Power of Roses* (1953) she returned to industrial inner-city Sydney for her setting. The central character, Miriam McKillop, is another sympathetically portrayed teenage orphan, who in this case is being raised by her Uncle Puss. The novel is set amid the same disadvantaged social and economic circumstances as those described in *The Harp in the South* and *Poor Man's Orange*. *A Power of Roses* also features a similar episodic structure and an even larger cast of characters, most of whom live in the Jerusalem, a former hotel converted into apartments for the poor.

What distinguishes *A Power of Roses* from Park's earlier Sydney novels and provides it with an additional resonance is the integration of the wider city into the action. Park reveals her fine descriptive talent in passages dealing with the harbor, the quay, and the Harbor Bridge. The bridge in particular, viewed by Miriam through a spyglass, becomes a symbol of the forces of modernism that are enveloping the city and of the opportunity for change and a life beyond the world of the urban poor. Unlike the Darcy sisters, Miriam—initially because she is under the spell of the "big palpitating rubies and zircons and tourmalines of the city lights" and eventually because Uncle Puss's sister, the worldly Constance, intervenes—comes to see that her life need not be constrained by the poverty she has known in the Jerusalem:

> Her life with Uncle Puss, which had seemed to be unique, wonderful, as cosy as a child's game in a cave, an existence as secret as an ant's in the antheap of the Jerusalem—this life, she knew now, was nothing but an existence, a beating into a harsh wind that parched the spirit and callused the sensibilities, and all for nothing. . . . The grey goose blood within Miriam, the wild and undisciplined discontent that had impelled her kin to burst from the furrow of their peasant lives, made her spirit hammer against the confines of her own body.

For her subsequent novel, *Pink Flannel* (1955), Park once more uses the setting of the New Zealand town of Te Kano in the 1920s. *Pink Flannel* is one of Park's slightest novels, which she describes as "a piece of light music." It is also the first novel in which she employs first-person narrative, a point of view that is fitting because the family circumstances it relates and the setting it invokes bear similarities to Park's own life. Also published the same year, *Der Goldene Bumerang: Australien, die Alteste und die Nueste* (The Golden Boomerang: Australians, the Oldest and the Newest) is a large factual book on Australia. The book was written to enlighten European audiences about Australia for the 1956 Melbourne Olympic Games, and it was subsequently translated into seven languages.

The narrator is the adult Jenny Hood, recalling her life as a nine-year-old orphan from Australia who has been sent to Te Kano to live with the "Radiant Aunts," the four sisters of her deceased mother. Despite the lightness of tone, Park manages to include her usual array of harsh details—a handicapped child (Cocky Cuskelly), a malevolent adult (Jenny's grandfather Syver Admiral), and a grotesque incident (a flood washing the bones and skulls of deceased Maoris through the street of the town).

A strength of the novel is its re-creation of childhood as seen through the eyes of the young Jenny, and in particular her relationships with her aunts as she learns something of the adult arts of dissembling and social contrivance. The weakness of the novel, however, is that Park bypasses other opportunities to extend its range. She touches upon issues related to encroaching modernism as the middle-class aunts join the world of commerce and encounter issues relating to their evolving dress style, but these details are unfortunately passed over all too quickly. Ultimately, the novel is concerned with the domestic affairs of the household; even the presence of the darker figure, Syver, is unsatisfactorily diminished in the concluding pages as Park contrives a conventionally happy ending.

With the success of Niland's first novel, *The Shiralee* (1955), Park and Niland became established as a recognizable literary couple. The result was the jointly written *The Drums Go Bang!*, published in 1956. In this lighthearted work Park and Niland describe the vagaries of establishing their careers as they struggle to cope with the demands of an expanding family.

Park again used New Zealand as the setting for her next novel, *One-a-Pecker, Two-a-Pecker* (1957), released in the United States as *The Frost and the Fire* (1958). The story in this historical novel begins in Australia on the Bendigo goldfields in the early 1860s, but it soon moves to the Otago gold rush of 1863 and to the fictitious Calico Town, a setting based on Queenstown, Australia. The setting in the goldfields enables Park to bring together her usual large and multicultural cast—in this case, Scottish, Irish, Italian, French, Chinese, and American characters and the young Australian woman, Currency MacQueen. Currency is another of Park's "orphans." When a young girl, she is sold by her mother to the itinerant washerwoman Mother Jerusalem MacQueen for "three sovereigns and a green linsey bodice."

Arriving at the Otago goldfields in her late teens, Currency is left to make her own way following the sudden death of Mother Jerusalem. She eventually falls in with the extended Swan family, including Tatty (Henrietta) Law, a young woman of about Currency's age. Tatty as a middle-aged woman narrates the story.

One-a-Pecker, Two-a-Pecker is one of Park's least successful novels. The plot, which features a series of unrequited and unfulfilled loves, has a melodramatic quality that Park usually manages to avoid. In addition, many of the central characters of the novel—including Currency; Tatty; Currency's love, the shadowy American known as Shannadore; and the man she eventually marries, the Italian Guiseppe Pigallo (Little Pig)—are not substantial enough to carry the story. Indeed, the fiery Currency, who fights her way to the diggings in order to claim her share of Mother Jerusalem's business in the early sections of the novel, is difficult to reconcile with the rather innocuous figure who emerges thereafter. As is evident elsewhere in her fiction, Park appears to be more at ease with the creation of minor characters. In *One-a-Pecker, Two-a-Pecker*, the peripheral figures—Uncle Alick, Grandda, and the Holy Morsel—emerge as the most memorable.

While Catholicism had been a peripheral concern in many of Park's previous novels, it takes center stage in her next novel, *The Good Looking Women* (1961), which was released in the United States as *Serpent's Delight* (1962). The story is centered on the Pond family, and the setting on this occasion is 1950s Sydney. The life of each of the four sisters of the middle-class family is affected to some degree by her devout upbringing. Elva seems destined to have more children than she can cope with because of the view of the Catholic Church on contraception; Carrie's marriage to her Catholic husband disintegrates after she admits to him that she has had an abortion rather than risk her independence by having a second child; and Ivy becomes a nun. Most significantly, the youngest, Geraldine, claims to be having visions of the Virgin. The novel chiefly deals with the strife created by these claims in what is otherwise a close family.

The other important characters are the sisters' parents—Mrs. Pond, who is keen to support Geraldine's

Dust jacket for Park's 1951 novel, about an abandoned white girl who finds a home with a Maori family (Bruccoli Clark Layman Archives)

claims to having visions, and "Pa," who is afflicted by doubts about Geraldine's claims but is hesitant about aligning himself with any of the factions that emerge in his family—and Carrie's daughter Ann, who as a teenager only several years younger than her Aunt Geraldine has the clearest understanding of her motives and actions but has great trouble making her voice heard amid the turmoil surrounding the "visions." Ann emerges as the pivotal character—another of Park's teenage female heroines—and her story, rather than Geraldine's, becomes the focus of the novel.

The success of the novel rests on its representation of the disastrous impact of Geraldine's spurious claims upon the family and its individual members. Park writes with her usual lightness of tone, but there is no denying the power of the conclusion as the impact of Geraldine's deception, which has gradually eaten away at the cohesion of the family, finally and unwittingly strikes a blow to its heart. The novel amounts to one of Park's most astute observations of character and a clear-eyed study of how innocent but misleading actions can have disastrous consequences.

The Good Looking Women was Park's final adult novel for a period of sixteen years, as she turned her attention to writing for young adults and children. Her novels for young adults began with *The Hole in the Hill*, published in 1961. The series of novels for young adults she wrote after that were well received both critically and commercially. They frequently feature many of the same characteristics as her adult novels, including teenage heroines in difficult family circumstances, a willingness to explore the particular fears that trouble many teenage years, and locations set in Australia, New Zealand, or Pacific islands.

Park's output for younger children was dominated by the Muddle-Headed Wombat character, which had already had a decade as the lead in a radio series before the first book appeared featuring the well-intentioned but bumbling wombat. Commencing with *The Muddle-Headed Wombat* in 1962, Park wrote thirteen titles in the series over the next two decades, all of which were illustrated by Noela Young.

In 1961 Park and Niland finally undertook the journey to Europe that they had abandoned a decade earlier. With their eldest daughter, Anne, they journeyed to Rome and London, spent time tracing ancestors in Ireland, and then went on to the United States. One of the significant events of this trip was that Park gave up her Catholic faith after a visit to St. Peter's in Rome. As she explains in *Fishing in the Styx* (1993), "I hadn't given Catholicism away, it had given me away."

Park suffered an upheaval in her personal life when Niland died in 1967 after experiencing several years of severe heart problems. Stricken with grief, Park entered what she called "that dark, roadless country." As always, however, she continued to write, including all editorial work on the manuscript of Niland's final novel, *Dead Men Running* (1969). Other work included preparing treatments of novels for movie scripts, writing copy for the *Reader's Digest,* and continuing to write children's material for the ABC. Park also continued writing books for younger readers during this period. She worked with many illustrators on these books, but beginning with *Callie's Castle* in 1974, she used her daughter Kilmeny Niland as illustrator, and on later books she also worked with Kilmeny's twin sister, Deborah.

Further change occurred for Park with the cessation of ABC's *Children's Session* in 1972. The program had been the backbone of her income for more than twenty-five years. Other opportunities arose, however, including the writing of *The Companion Guide to Sydney* (1973). One of a series of discursive historical travel guides published by Collins, it gave Park the opportunity to record her abiding affection for her adopted city. She also took the opportunity, however, to criticize elements of the rapid transformation of Sydney created by the prolonged postwar building boom.

The changes in Park's life continued when in 1973 she moved to Norfolk Island, where she lived for the next decade before returning to Sydney. Having forsaken Catholicism, she found other avenues of spiritual inquiry, and she eventually embraced Zen Buddhism, an interest that led to further travel and study in Japan and the United States.

Park returned to writing for adults with the publication in 1977 of one of her most successful novels, *Swords and Crowns and Rings.* The novel covers the period between 1907 and 1932, and it tells the story of a dwarf, Jackie Hanna, his struggle to find acceptance in the world, and his undying love for his childhood sweetheart, Cushie Moy. Jackie and Cushie survive a series of severe setbacks in their relationship—including the obvious disparity in their physical stature, differences in their social standing, prolonged separation, and a marriage for Jackie that ends in tragedy—before they are finally reunited at the conclusion of the novel.

Swords and Crowns and Rings demonstrates again Park's fascination with the figure of the outsider, and the culmination of the novel in the early years of the Great Depression is the setting that Park had used for some of her most successful writing. The real strength of the novel, however, comes from the success of the characters of Jackie Hanna and Cushie Moy, two of Park's most attractive heroes, and a series of excellent descriptive sections that wonderfully evoke both rural and urban settings.

Notwithstanding her prolonged break from writing adult fiction, the quality of *Swords and Crowns and Rings* was recognized by both reviewers and the reading public. The novel won the Miles Franklin Award in 1978.

Despite the success of *Swords and Crowns and Rings,* Park did not write for adults again for some years. In the interim she turned once more to material for younger readers, enjoying perhaps her greatest success in this market with *Playing Beatie Bow,* published in 1980. The novel features troubled young heroine Abigail Kirk, who finds herself in a difficult family situation. Abigail manages to travel backward in time to 1870s Sydney, where she meets Beatie Bow, a girl of similar age living amid the poverty and squalor of the area known as the Rocks. Not unexpectedly, Abigail learns many lessons from Beatie and other members of the Bow family. *Playing Beatie Bow* received the 1981 Book of the Year Award from the Australian Children's Book Council and the 1982 *Boston Globe-Horn Book* Award.

With her next adult novel, *Missus* (1985), Park produced a prequel to *The Harp in the South* and *Poor Man's Orange.* The plot covers the period from the closing years of the nineteenth century until the early years of the Depression and focuses on the hesitant romance between Hugh Darcy and Margaret Kilker (Mumma) up to the point at which they eventually wed. Their relationship develops against the backdrop of rural New South Wales, but at the close of the novel there are portents of the troubles—in the shape of the encroaching Depression and Hugh's inability to overcome his love of drink—which will eventually lead them to the postwar slums of Surry Hills.

The reception of *Missus* came as a disappointment after the success of *Swords and Crowns and Rings.* The central problem was again Park's inability to make the central characters sufficiently substantial. Hugh and Mumma may have been capable of sustaining their roles as characters in the earlier novels when their daughters were at the emotional center of the stories, but in this case where Hugh and Mumma carry the burden of the story, neither of them is capable of retaining the reader's interest.

Park does something to mask this shortcoming by employing the usual large and lively cast who suffer various romantic troubles of their own. There are successes in Margaret's protofeminist sister Josie and Hugh's crippled brother Jer, and there is also a haunting reality in the description of the several tragically doomed relationships that highlight the consequences when relationships fall upon hard times in hard places. These strengths of the novel, however, fail to mitigate the lack of a sufficiently engaging central character in the story.

In 1992 Park's *A Fence Around the Cuckoo*, the first of two autobiographical volumes, was published. It was followed in 1993 by *Fishing in the Styx*. Together, these two volumes cover her life from childhood in New Zealand to the 1990s. Although they are sometimes evasive on aspects of her personal and emotional life, the books do provide a mature and beautifully crafted reflection on the development of Park's career as a writer. *A Fence Around the Cuckoo* won several awards, including the *Melbourne Age* Book of the Year for nonfiction in 1992. *Fishing in the Styx* received the 1993 Fellowship of Australian Writers Herb Thomas Literary Award.

During this period Park also continued to undertake occasional work associated with Niland. In 1987 she selected and wrote an introduction for a collection of his short stories, and in 1995 she and Rafe Champion completed *Home Before Dark: The Story of Les Darcy, a Great Australian Hero*, a biography of an Australian boxer, which Niland had been working on in the years before his death. The book incorporates material derived from interviews Niland conducted with associates of Darcy three decades earlier in Australia and the United States. *Home Before Dark* was awarded the Christina Stead Award for nonfiction.

In latter years Park has also received several awards that celebrate her career achievements and the substantial contribution she has made to Australian literature. These honors include being made a member of the Order of Australia in 1987, being awarded the *Magpie* Award in 1993 for services to the Australian book industry, and receipt of honorary doctorates from the University of New South Wales in 1994 and Griffith University in 1999.

In all likelihood, Park's ongoing reputation will be fashioned by the ability of publishers to keep her material in print and by the vagaries of critical interest. F. C. Molloy, in "'Hearts of Gold and a Happy Ending': The Appeal of *The Harp in the South*" (*Australian Literary Studies*, 1990), has puzzled at the continuing critical neglect of Park, pointing out that "in recent years scholarly attention has been focused on Australia's women writers."

The virtues of Ruth Park's best novels are enduring, and her lifelong engagement with issues related to class, gender, and ethnicity should eventually attract scholarly interest. Although she has not approached these issues with the reforming fervor of others, she has nonetheless been an acute observer of Australian manners and mores. Park's vivid portraits of Sydney, the premier city of Australia, as it was in the middle years of the twentieth century, should also attract increasing interest and insure her recognition as one of the foremost literary archivists of the city.

Interviews:

Kate Veitch, "Ruth Park," *Australian Book Review*, 156 (November 1993): 21–22;

Veitch, "Ruth Park: A Life," *24 Hours* (December 1993): 114–118.

Biography:

Joy Hooton, ed., *Ruth Park: A Celebration* (Canberra: Friends of the National Library of Australia, 1996).

References:

Toss Gascoigne, "Know the Author: Ruth Park," *Magpies*, 3, no. 1 (1988): 14–15;

Paul Genoni, "Ruth Park and Frank Hardy: Catholic Realists," *Tirra Lirra*, 10 (Autumn/Winter 2000): 26–31;

Jill Greaves, "'The Craft so Long to Learn': Ruth Park's Story of Ruth Park," *Australian Literary Studies*, 17, no. 3 (1996): 244–253;

F. C. Molloy, "'Hearts of Gold and a Happy Ending': The Appeal of *The Harp in the South*," *Australian Literary Studies*, 14, no. 3 (1990): 316–324;

Anne M. O'Sullivan, "Structures and Narrative Point of View in *Playing Beatie Bow*," *Literature Base*, 2, no. 1 (1991): 14–16;

Joy L. Thwaite, *The Importance of Being Eve Langley* (North Ryde: Angus & Robertson, 1989).

Papers:

A collection of Ruth Park's papers, including correspondence and manuscripts, is held at the Mitchell Library, State Library of New South Wales. Unpublished scripts of many of Park's radio plays are located in the National Archives of Australia, Sydney.

Brian Penton
(4 August 1904 - 24 August 1951)

James Packer
Workers' Educational Association Sydney

BOOKS: *Landtakers: The Story of an Epoch* (Sydney: Endeavour Press, 1934; New York: Farrar & Rinehart, 1935);

Inheritors (Sydney: Angus & Robertson, 1936); republished as *Giant's Stride* (London & Melbourne: Cassell, 1936);

Think—or Be Damned: A Subversive Note on National Pride, Patriotism and Other Forms of Respectable Ostrichism Practised in Australia (Sydney: Angus & Robertson, 1941);

Advance Australia—Where? (London & Sydney: Cassell, 1943);

Censored! Being a True Account of a Notable Fight for Your Right to Read and Know, with Some Comment upon the Plague of Censorship in General (Sydney: Shakespeare Head, 1947);

A Guide for Cadets on Joining the Staff of Consolidated Press (Sydney: Consolidated Press, 1948).

OTHER: Herondas, *The Mimiambs of Herondas*, translated by Jack Lindsay, introduction by Penton (London: Fanfrolico Press, 1929);

Friedrich Nietzsche, *Thus Spake Zarathustra*, translated by Penton (New York: McKee, 1930);

"What Is Behind the Magic Phrase, Majority Rule?" in *Prospects of Democracy*, edited by W. H. C. Eddy (Sydney: Australian Consolidated Press, 1945);

The Art of William Dobell, edited by Sydney Ure Smith, introduction by Penton (Sydney: Ure Smith, 1946);

"It's Too Hard to Be Free [1938?]," first published in *The Oxford Book of Australian Essays*, edited by Imre Salusinszky (Melbourne: Oxford, 1997), pp. 118-120.

SELECTED PERIODICAL PUBLICATIONS—UNCOLLECTED:
POETRY
"Moonstruck," *New Triad* (Sydney), 1 February 1928, p. 46; revised in *London Aphrodite* (July 1929): 463.

Brian Penton, 1923 (from Patrick Buckridge, The Scandalous Penton, *1994)*

FICTION
"Interview," *London Aphrodite* (February 1929): 289-297;
"Talk," *London Aphrodite* (April 1929): 346-352.
NONFICTION
"Means and the Ideal," *Galmahra* (May 1924): 22-23;
"A Theory of the Artificial," *Galmahra* (August 1924): 26-27;
"Hardy and Realism," *Bulletin* (Sydney), 29 February 1928, p. 2;

"Hardy and Life," *Bulletin,* 18 April 1928, p. 5;

"England Today," *Bulletin,* 24 April 1929, pp. 2, 5;

"A Flight into Order," *Bulletin,* 31 July 1929, p. 2;

"Note on the Form of the Novel," *London Aphrodite* (July 1929): 434–444; revised and enlarged as "A Note on Form in the Novel," in *Scrutinies II,* edited by Edgell Rickword (London: Wishart, 1931), pp. 235–262;

"For the Love of the Fight," *Bulletin,* 30 April 1930, pp. 2, 5;

"Epstein at Home," *Bulletin,* 11 March 1931, pp. 2, 5;

"The Grey Ones," *Bulletin,* 4 November 1931, pp. 2, 5;

"The Day We Celebrate–and the Men," *Telegraph* (Sydney), 26 January 1934, p. 6;

"Why Not Be Hot and Happy?" *Telegraph,* 13 March 1934, p. 6;

"Australia–England–Which Is Home?" *Telegraph,* 20 March 1934, p. 10;

"Safety First–The Motto of the Masses," *Telegraph,* 26 April 1934, p. 8;

"Would Will Be a Bore Round Here?" *Telegraph,* 10 May 1934, p. 12;

"Climates and Our Minds," *Telegraph,* 20 July 1934, p. 8;

"Cold Shoulder for Vulgar Colonials," *Telegraph,* 3 October 1934, p. 9;

"Through the Muddle to 'Half-Death,'" as Conn Bennett, *Bulletin,* 10 October 1934, pp. 2, 5;

"This Freedom That Denies Freedom," *Telegraph,* 13 November 1934, p. 10;

"Lo! The Poor Abo Is on Our Conscience!" *Telegraph,* 16 November 1934, p. 5;

"Who Wants to Be a Suburb of London?" *Telegraph,* 28 November 1934, p. 11;

"Books, Authors–and the Public," *Telegraph,* 20 March 1935, p. 4;

"Why a Good Book's Rare," *Telegraph,* 8 April 1935, p. 6;

"'Sunstroke' Better than Brain Fog," *Telegraph,* 10 April 1935, p. 9;

"Homage to Lawson," *Daily Telegraph,* 15 May 1937, p. 6;

"For Your Dustbin: A Lindsay Family Reunion," *Daily Telegraph,* 7 August 1937, p. 6;

"Editor of the *Daily Telegraph* Says: I Think This Reader Knew Something," *Daily Telegraph,* 23 May 1941, p. 5;

"Problem: The Expert," *New York Times Magazine,* 10 December 1944, p. 13;

"Henry Handel Richardson–Great and Lonely," *Daily Telegraph,* 30 March 1946, pp. 16–17; republished in *Australian Literary Studies,* Henry Handel Richardson Special Issue (May 1998): 250–262.

In 1935 the English critic V. S. Pritchett wrote two reviews of an Australian novel recently released in London and New York. The novel was titled *Landtakers: The Story of an Epoch* (1934); its author, Brian Penton, was a feature writer for *The Daily Telegraph* (Sydney). Pritchett wrote in *The Spectator* (London) for 8 March 1935:

> Why is it that this novel stands head and shoulders above any others of its type? The answer lies, of course, primarily in the soundness of its writing, its richness in incident, character and emotional material, its power to present the historical scene with biting vividness. The real merit of Mr Penton is that he subordinates the nevertheless important element of the building of a nation to the building of a man who may epitomise the essence of the nation's spiritual struggle, but whose spiritual sources are in the country he has left. . . .

Landtakers was the first part of a trilogy, the final part of which remained unpublished as its author pursued a rather different career to become, as he is generally recognized, one of the three or four outstanding newspaper editors of any period of Australian journalism. Although he published no further novels, Penton continued the work eulogized by Pritchett in other ways. In no less than five completed monographs and a variety of journalistic forays, Penton continued to theorize about the problems of "being Australian" in terms identical to the "dramatisation of moral fear" expounded in the trilogy.

Born to Reginald and Sarah Bennett Penton, both of whom had found their separate ways from England to the colony of Queensland in the 1880s, Brian Con Penton grew up in various suburbs of Brisbane, subject to his father's straitening circumstances. As Reginald Penton progressed from traveling salesman to failed retailer to tire packer, the family moved from affluent Wooloowin to down-at-heel Fortitude Valley and New Farm, where Penton started school. A high-school dropout from Brisbane Grammar, he was at sixteen cadet reporter at *The Brisbane Courier* and attended the University of Queensland, studying for the Diploma of Journalism in 1924. On 4 January 1924, Penton married Olga Moss. His first published works–poems and articles–appeared in the university magazine, *Galmahra,* and included a precocious piece titled "A Theory of the Artificial" (1924), prefiguring his later, somewhat relentlessly analytic treatments of social mores. This article was his first from a standpoint including elements of the culture-critique of Friedrich Nietzsche and the sociology of Georg Simmel.

Infatuated like so many of his contemporaries with the idea of the great British metropolis, Penton left

Norman Lindsay. In Sydney, Penton became acquainted with Norman Lindsay himself, who by 1927 was writing to his friends that the young journalist was a writer of promise. In his writing for *The Herald,* Penton also showed promise, producing for the paper an extroverted column that could still be celebrated in 1981 when Gavin Souter's story of the first one hundred and fifty years of *The Herald,* titled *Company of Heralds,* was published. "The *Herald* had never had a writer like Penton before, and it was not too sure what to make of this 'Special Representative' whose intellect and mordant wit shone brightly through the paper's anonymity." When the Federal Parliament was established in 1927, Penton moved to Canberra, where his increasing determination to produce what he protested to be "meaningful" work seriously compromised his journalistic career. Disdain for journalism was a hallmark of the Lindsay circle, and Penton's literary ambitions overflowed into his journalism, even to the extent of making "characters" of his political subjects, as one of them loudly complained. Upon the death of Sir James Fairfax, Penton's patron at *The Herald,* Penton was removed to Sydney, and by the end of 1928 he had his sights set, once again, on London. The opportunity came as Penton ghosted the autobiography of the former prime minister, William Morris Hughes, a man whose social genius Penton had loudly applauded in his "Gallery" column and whose role as a "destructive element" in the theater of politics became the role Penton later assigned for himself in the theater of the tabloid newspaper. Penton was dispatched to London with the manuscript for *The Splendid Adventure,* which was published in May 1929. He also took Norman Lindsay's *Redheap* (1930), which was also published, relaunching Lindsay's career as a novelist.

Lindsay's eldest son, Jack, had set up the Fanfrolico Press in London in 1926, and the first year of Penton's four-and-a-half-year stay in London was marked by his absorption into the Australian contingent that collaborated with Jack Lindsay's efforts to introduce his classicist antimodernism into British culture. Through 1929 Penton wrote many miscellaneous items for the Fanfrolico offshoot, *The London Aphrodite;* an introduction to Jack Lindsay's translation of *The Mimiambs of Herondas* (1929); and some politically oriented articles for the Sydney *Bulletin.* He also completed a translation of Nietzsche's *Thus Spake Zarathustra,* which, though reportedly published in New York in 1930, has been lost. Replacing the Fanfrolico manager P. R. Stephensen in April 1929, Penton showed sufficient organizational talent to "restore order"—as Jack Lindsay wrote to his father Norman—amid the "puddle" of confusion that had marked the former manager's business

The author's mother, Sarah Penton, circa 1886 (from Buckridge, The Scandalous Penton, 1994)

Brisbane in 1925, first for Sydney, then for London, which he reached by working his passage, he later claimed, on cargo boats. London, however, was a shock. The poverty and bleakness Penton encountered in the fabled center of the imperial universe was later graphically recorded in a novel he began to draft–but never completed–in 1931 and in various newspaper articles in 1934 and 1935. With no means of supporting himself, the twenty-year-old Penton returned to Australia in June 1925 and in Sydney quickly secured a job as political journalist at *The Sydney Morning Herald.*

While working on *The Brisbane Courier,* Penton had met Ray Lindsay, the middle son of the artist style. After this time, Penton and Stephensen clashed at every opportunity.

Penton's most considered analysis of the novel is included in "Note on the Form of the Novel," published in *The London Aphrodite* in July 1929 and republished in Edgell Rickword's *Scrutinies II* in 1931. This long and detailed article sets down the terms of style by which the "self-overcoming" theorized by Nietzsche is possible in a work of fiction and gives some first indications of the personal authenticity that Penton stridently demanded in his later journalism—and which he set out to dramatize in his novels. The general point of the article coincided with what Norman Lindsay called, speaking of these novels ten years after Penton's death, their "Dostoievskian psychology." Fyodor Dostoevsky, as Penton saw him, was a novelist concerned not with the imposition of psychological categories on his characters but with the emergence of those categories as the characters developed—"form must grow out of the idea, organically develop with each development of that idea."

The practical effect of this thinking is seen in the surviving draft of "Outrageous Fortune," the earliest extant version of a Penton novel, dating to the end of 1930. This comic novel clearly shows a character whose mentality depends not upon the development of the plot of the novel—loosely identified as "fortune"—or abstract behavioral requirements, such as "virtue" or "vice," but upon the character's own condition, his being situated in a set of circumstances to which he always supplies a contingent, but entirely effective and even irrevocable, response. Dionysos Blink is one of the "insulted and injured" of life; Penton makes no effort to lift him out of the accidents in which he becomes enmeshed. The streak of Dostoevskian nastiness throughout the book is present also in the fifty or so draft pages of the 1931 novel set in London and to an extreme degree in Penton's *London Aphrodite* (April 1929) story, "Talk."

The true heir of "Outrageous Fortune," however, is the novel Penton began in 1932 under the influence of Henry Handel Richardson's *The Fortunes of Richard Mahony*—a trilogy first published under this title in 1930. Penton first read Richardson's work when Norman Lindsay came to London with a commission to "write something" on the hitherto obscure Richardson. Penton had been visibly struggling with his own fortunes throughout 1931 and by November of that year had entered what can only be taken as a crisis of self-regard when a novel by Norman Lindsay's youngest son, Phil, a former friend of Penton's who had come to resent him deeply, was accepted for publication. Now Penton conceived the large novel on Australian land settlement, ultimately titled *Landtakers,* which, along with a commissioned translation of Ludwig von Mises's *Against Socialism,* he proceeded to draft over the next eighteen months. In *Richard Mahony* "fortune" is bound up with the struggle to exist on the Australian soil and the consequences of failure. In *Landtakers* "fortune" is organized in terms of a similar struggle, but the consequences are those of success; in overcoming the Australian environment Cabell "overcomes" (that is, insidiously destroys) part of himself. Whereas Dionysos Blink in Penton's unpublished book develops his life through the contingent application of his will upon his circumstances but never overcomes his circumstances, Derek Cabell overcomes his circumstances at the risk of what he would like to preserve of his own life.

Penton returned to Sydney in September 1933 to a job on *The Telegraph* and in January 1934 began a daily column called "The Sydney Spy." In July *Landtakers* became his first published novel. Both *Landtakers* and the "Spy" journalism—while representing two paradigmatically different sorts of writing—bear the marks of a common impulse. In "The Sydney Spy" Penton's journalism achieves many of the stylistic qualities—including a kind of stream of consciousness and an overtly self-conscious presentation of his own moral failings—he had aimed for in his earlier parliamentary journalism. The column provided him with a far broader canvas. Conversely, Penton the novelist addressed large factual questions and frequently allowed the dramatization of his material to be subordinated to its historical meaning. Indeed, as Laurie Hergenhan says in "Brian Penton's 1930s Novels: 'The Roots of the New Psyche,'" published in *Unnatural Lives: Studies in Australian Convict Fiction* (1983), Penton "embarked on what must have been one of the earliest large scale, radical revaluations of Australia's past, either in fiction or in historical studies." As was typical of Penton, in both enterprises the fictional was permeated with the historical, the historical with the fictional.

While Penton made no particular claims for journalism as a "literary form," as a novelist of national and ideological formations his journalistic formulation of these issues contributed directly to the peculiar quality of his fictional work. In the four hundred or more thousand-word articles of "The Sydney Spy," the interrogative and self-investigative modes of journalistic expression are taken far beyond their usual journalistic employment. This characteristic can be clearly observed if the often-quoted passage about Australia from the second chapter of *Landtakers* is contrasted with its corresponding ideological moment in the 26 January 1934 "The Sydney Spy":

Dust jacket for the 1963 edition of Penton's 1934 novel, about pioneer life in mid-nineteenth-century Queensland (Bruccoli Clark Layman Archives)

Growing up in a period when Australians had begun to feel in themselves the germ of a new people and to fumble for words to express themselves, I often wondered what roots that new psyche was coming from. Then it struck me that the answer was somewhere in the life of this old man and his generation....

Nowadays it is difficult to see as they saw. Our eyes have grown used to the grey trees with their thin metallic foliage, the forests of a prehistoric time that stood, just as they are now, long, long before men began to crawl about the earth. The vast emptiness of the western plains, scarred by drought and flood and bushfire, today as desolate as the Sahara, to-morrow as lush as an English meadow, the dry gullies, forty feet deep, that became torrential rivers overnight, the sad silence of the bush, and the subhuman people who inhabit it—these things are commonplace to us, even beautiful; but a hundred years ago, to eyes fresh from the soft countryside of England . . . the new continent was fantastically alien. (From *Landtakers*)

On January 26, 1788, [Arthur Phillip] set foot on this pleasant land. I invite you to imagine how pleasant it looked with its grey-green trees, its current heat wave, its sharks' fins sticking up out of the beautiful harbour, its still, empty, expectant, sad silence.

You ought to try to imagine it, because what those ship-cramped emigres felt, coming across its harsh, primal color for the first time with the image of England's lush fields still in their minds, is even yet a part of your psyche, the reason why, I hazard, Australians are the most restless, inferiority-complexed people in the world, always yearning for change, for a jaunt to England, Home, and Beauty. (From "The Sydney Spy")

Throughout "The Sydney Spy" the ideologically and dramatically inflected "I" and "you" of the text coincide with the "I" and "you" of *Landtakers*—not merely in the sense that Penton in both contexts assumes the role of historian, but also in the sense that his fiction, as much as his journalism, reinvents the self at the same moment it reinvents the nation. The peculiar art of Penton's journalism may be found in the presentation of a story that through the medium of fact enlarges the self in the same way that the medium of fiction enlarges the self. The paradoxical effect of the development of this "art" is that the most lasting aspects of the drama in Penton's novels lie in the exploration of the development of Australia, reflected in the continuing interest in Penton's work as it defines the Australian "national psyche."

Landtakers tells of the immigration to Australia in the 1840s of a young Englishman, Derek Cabell. Its epigraph comprises the surviving vestige of Penton's own 1930 translation of Nietzsche's *Thus Spake Zarathustra*: "A perilous crossing, a perilous journeying, a perilous looking back, a perilous trembling and hestitating," and the novel has as a theme, through Cabell's perilous "crossing," the "destructive" coming into being of the Australian "self." The narrative follows Cabell from his first encounter with the colony at Moreton Bay, through his confrontation with the brutal McGovern, overseer of convicts on the property where he briefly works, to his rise as landowner in his own right. Deliverer of the golden fleece and killer of Aboriginals, Cabell "crosses" to a life that represents the destruction of his former life and "journeys" the distance that makes returning impossible; yet, he is always "looking back" to England, Home. This discordance between "wanting" and "being"—between action and fate—leads to a treatment of Australian history that is part metaphysical, part investigative, and it qualifies Penton as both theorist and historian of settler postcolonialism. His fellow theorist—and now bitter rival—P. R. Stephensen was quick to point out in the November 1936 issue of his journal, *The Publicist,* that Penton was "a specialist in the presentation of fictional hate." This "hate," where it is more than sheer antisentimentalism—

one of Penton's journalistic signatures—is not authorial malice so much as the product of Penton's attempt to do the utmost justice to his subject matter. The theme of "hate" that runs though *Landtakers* is at one with the energy the author invests in characterizing Australia as a land of "moral fear"—a phrase he uses in the 1941 *Think—or Be Damned: A Subversive Note on National Pride, Patriotism and Other Forms of Respectable Ostrichism Practised in Australia*—a land whose highly moraled pioneer myths obliterate the actual fact (and means) of "landtaking" and are ultimately destructive, or "corrosive," of the lives of the settlers and their descendants. One supremely disturbing aspect of this colonization is reflected in the publication of the novel in Denmark at the time of Nazi occupation under the title *Det Land er Mit* (The Land is Mine).

Stephensen had reasons of his own for ascribing "hate" to Penton's brand of fiction. Shortly after *Landtakers* was published, Penton published a vitriolic review of Vivien Crockett's *Mezzomorto* (1934), a book published by P. R. Stephensen and Company and one whose sales potential Stephensen claimed was important to the success of his company. Two court cases resulted, and Stephensen, though he financially benefited from both, was not the sort of litigant to be easily pacified. In his *Foundations of Australian Literature* (1936) he opined that Australian fiction, and the Australian image in general, could do without "the sensationalism of convictism and flogging" as represented in the works of "journalists" such as "B. Penton." Miles Franklin, in the Stephensen camp, wrote in a letter (15 February 1935) to the critic Nettie Palmer that *Landtakers* "is as harsh and flat, as arid as a police report of brutalities."

Adverse criticism was not restricted to interested parties. C. Hartley Grattan responded to the release of the American edition with an article in *The New York Times Review of Books* (16 June 1935) stating that Penton had written a "coarse, brutal and powerful novel that reveals cold intellectual force and honesty of purpose even while it betrays from chapter to chapter that the author entirely lacks that sense of awe and pity that alone would give adequate dignity and meaning to the story he has to tell." Penton's overtly "destructive" type of writing was evidently out of tune with one significant strain of the critical temper of his time. Even so, his journalistic directness had produced a novel that in quickly dispensing with humanistic formulae, rules of national sanitation, and "fine writing," found favor with critics, such as Norman Lindsay, for whom—according to an undated, unsent letter to Penton, May 1932—"destructive analysis" was, at worst, a necessary evil. Lindsay had previously written to Penton in 1929:

> It depresses me to think that work so good and vital should have to face man's rejection of any knowledge of the process under which he exists. Work like yours is up against the basic terror of his being.

Lindsay found himself even more impressed by the 1936 sequel to *Landtakers*, released in Australia under the title *Inheritors*. The second book takes up the latter part of Derek Cabell's career as a successful squatter, viewing that career and its consequences through the eyes of three of the Cabell children—Larry, James, and Harriet. While *Landtakers* had followed the course of a hatred for, but ultimate reconciliation with, the Australian landscape and Australian values, *Inheritors* traces the hatred in the landtaker's offspring for their father and the impositions of his will on them. *Inheritors*, then, is a novel that deals with the vicissitudes of social life, since the three instances of hatred are identified with differing social norms. Larry's is the hatred of the worker of the late nineteenth century for "the boss"; James's is the hatred of the conformist for his tormentor—the father who ceaselessly tells him how small a man he is; Harriet's is for the "wild man" Cabell may easily become and the unreasoning despot he usually is. These social norms are recognizable stereotypes, but in Penton's hands they are ideologically and existentially striking. Ideologically, "The Sydney Spy" provides abundant clues to the ideological inflection on the attitudes Penton fictionalizes in the novel—including reflections on generational differences, moral humbug, and social decay. Existentially, the ultimate direction of the characters in the novel is toward what remains—to quote the epigraph of *Inheritors*—"beneath their finery." James, the son who allows respectability the final say in whatever he does, is the "inheritor" reduced to the deepest self-injury. The greatest beneficiary of the Cabell fortune becomes a creature of reflex, a comic automaton.

This "existential" character reaches its climax in the remaining work of the trilogy, an untitled and barely half-completed draft of some 110,000 words—called by Penton's biographer, Patrick Buckridge, the "Third Novel"—set in twentieth-century Sydney. Textual evidence dates the typescript no later than 1943, and it seems to belong to the period immediately following *Inheritors* (1936-1937). The novel, as it stands, presents in raw form the existential problems of Australian life as represented in the lives of three of Derek Cabell's grandchildren: Derek, an army volunteer turned dilettante and businessman; Bob, a larrikin turned composer; and Pompey, a writer—ostensibly but inconsistently the narrator of the first Cabell novel, *Landtakers*. The draft is marked by a structural tendency that had been less obvious in Penton's earlier work, what may be called the "hanging denouement." As if to accord with Søren Kierkegaard's "life is understood backwards but it is lived forwards"—a statement that Penton had quoted with approval on two separate occasions in "The Sydney Spy"—Derek and Bob Cash move toward the denouements the novel is trying to provide, but so "conscious" are they, so prone to self-deferral, that they can grasp nothing concrete—except, in Bob's case, the still-elusive vocation of musician. Penton's depictions of Derek are memorably grotesque:

> He asked himself, looking at her, "Is that what I've been waiting to come up over the horizon," and had an impulse to gather her in his arms and say tender, loving words. "Christ no." He closed his eyes again, seeing the long chain of bothering consequences—the divorce, marriage, and more important the sharing of life, the demands of love, the responsibility to another person, the giving of oneself, the opening of one's secret heart, the loss of privacy, self-containment, and ease. Also, and this was worst of all, the admission, if only to oneself, of dependence upon another, the baring of the breast to the other's unpredictable power to hurt. Love her and he was done for.

The satisfactions of denouement offered by more-conventional fiction are replaced by moments of pathos in which the weight of the novel rests not so much on any structure of events as on the sheer existential residue of the characters' actions and thoughts. Whereas in "Outrageous Fortune" and *Landtakers* "action" is contingent on the plot but effective, the "Third Novel" locates plot *in* the action of the characters, so that Penton's Nietzschean reveling in the contingent becomes a spiral into reflexivity. Penton's prolonged examination of the moral becomes existential through the mode of reflexivity that makes an issue out of authorship, or the distance between writer and text—exemplified in the "Third Novel" by Penton's attempt to portray the narrator of *Landtakers*, Pompey Cash. But the result is that the "historical" project of the earlier Cabell novels—as Norman Lindsay noted in an undated letter to Penton—was brought to the point at which the social interest was overtaken by the purely existential. Rather than "symbolise a collective state of mind," Penton, according to Lindsay, had apparently chosen to write a novel "of an idiosyncratic conflict of personality."

Ten years after Penton's death, Lindsay remarked to his biographer, John Hetherington, that Penton's adherence to the project of importing "Dostoievskian psychology" into the Australian novel had "done for him" as a writer. It is tempting to find in Penton's possible reaction to Lindsay's notions of "personal idiosyncrasy" the origins of many articles he wrote for *The Daily Telegraph* in 1937 assailing Lindsay and his sons, Jack and Phil, for the want of existential content in their art and writing. These attacks marked a dramatic and debilitating break between Penton and Lindsay and were followed by the supposed replacement of Penton's literary enthusiasms with the wholehearted embrace of his journalistic career at Frank Packer's *Daily Telegraph*. Various myths exist about Penton the literary sellout—myths that are wittily retreaded in Donald Horne's *Confessions of a New Boy* (1985)—but in his journalism Penton continued his reflexive assault on the self, turning from fiction to autobiography. His most graphic display of existential drivenness is found in an unpublished piece of 1938—published finally in 1997 in *The Oxford Book of Australian Essays*, edited by Imre Salusinszky—titled "It's Too Hard to Be Free." As in the "Third Novel" Penton's stream-of-consciousness technique is directed toward moral meaning rather than sensuous display:

> A hell of a thing this civilization that liberals like Thomas Mann and Bertrand Russell exalt—I'm the first to admit it. They demand that you should be realistic, rational, free, tolerant, detached. What a business. It requires such an effort. . . . And freedom—oh that's all right, if only it was something you were born with, and kept till you died, like your liver. But damn it, as Goethe says, you've got to win the thing afresh every day. And tolerance, detachment, rationality—more bugbears. What does Bertrand Russell say about them—that they depend upon your ability to dominate your reflexes. Really now, who could be bothered.

Later still, in pieces such as "Editor of the *Daily Telegraph* Says: I Think This Reader Knew Something" (*Daily Telegraph*, 23 May 1941), Penton extended the reflexive possibilities of newspaper writing, as if rather than abandoning literary writing he actually felt compelled to reveal what was valuable in literary work in the writing forms of his own choice—the newspaper column, the review, and the editorial. The literary theme of the contingency of self Penton turned upon himself, and the Penton self was made forever ephemeral in *The Telegraph* of the 1930s and 1940s.

In accordance with the same logic, Penton continued systematically to reflect on the existential problems of Australian identity. His two books on the Australian cultural/national predicament, *Think—or Be Damned* (1941) and *Advance Australia—Where?* (1943), moved from considerations of the "Australian Oedipus Complex" to the problems for Australia in its engagement with the world order and the war. In a further, unpublished, monograph of 1948 the "international" issues became his basic concern.

Penton did not pretend that his approach to the Australian psyche was wholly original. As he wrote in

Penton as editor of The Daily Telegraph *(Sydney), 1942 (from Buckridge,* The Scandalous Penton, *1994)*

Think—or Be Damned, "There is something in [D.H.] Lawrence's Oedipus Complex theory. Deep in the unconscious of the Australian rises a sense of guilt and uneasiness when we press too hard our claim to stand on our own feet and break the ties with the Motherland." Like Stephensen, Penton claimed a considerable debt to Lawrence in his conception of the Australian predicament, but just as *Landtakers* is a more morally difficult book than Lawrence's *Kangaroo* (1923), so Penton makes more explicit, and tougher, demands on Australians in facing themselves and the world. Inescapable routines of change and destruction mark the destinies of individuals and nations; Australians, whether in the postcolonial, the war, or the postwar context, must come to terms with the realities of power that these routines reflect.

Penton's editorship of *The Daily Telegraph* (1941–1951) produced what has been called one of the "three golden ages" of Australian journalism, and his intense intellectual commitment to the issues that mark his fictional and nonfictional work was instrumental to this golden age throughout the ten years of his editorship of *The Telegraph*. The evidence for his commitment and a statement of Penton's journalistic imperatives are found in his *Guide for Cadets on Joining the Staff of Consolidated Press,* a pamphlet written in 1948. More than merely a style guide for journalistic practice at *The Daily Telegraph,* the pamphlet includes Penton's stipulations for the life of a journalist and includes a rare outburst against the "bohemianism"—code for Lindsayism—of his early years.

In the last years of his life, Penton became much like the figure he had drawn in the character of the old Derek Cabell in *Inheritors*. Ruthless, prickly, unforgiving, yet ever the cultural entrepreneur, highly aware of his effect on the staff of his newspaper, his ambiguities and staged encounters have been recorded in Horne's *Confessions of a New Boy* and by Dymphna Cusack in her accounts of "a novel contest" sponsored by *The Telegraph* and won by the novel she wrote with Florence James, *Come In Spinner* (1951).

Penton died of cancer on 24 August 1951. With his death, the puzzling aspects of his multifaceted career remained unresolved. Norman Lindsay had written to his son Phillip two years previously, "Penton is the most hated editor here, and that means a lot, where all Daily Paper executives are the basest type of cheap megalomaniacs the loathsome profession of the newspaper world has infected the world with." The "hated editor" now dead, Lindsay submitted to *The Daily Telegraph* an obituary of Penton, which appeared on 25 August 1951, in which he found himself able to declare, "Brian was the most brilliant man we have ever had in daily journalism in Australia. He was just as brilliant as an author. He wrote a remarkable novel in *Landtakers*. I think that if he had given himself to social satire in the manner of the great American novelist [H. L.] Mencken he would have earned a world-wide reputation."

So compromised a tribute was not merely a fitting finale to the Penton-Lindsay relationship; it appropriately marked the "destructive analyst's" moment of truth in the eye of the "national psyche." If Brian Penton's historical legacy is the national recognition of the foundation of Australia in destructive acts, then profound compromise necessarily characterizes the Australian appreciation of his life and art. Just as problematically, does a man who so effectively dramatized human mutability warrant the "immutable" status bestowed on literary worthies? That issues of this sort should be raised at the close of a writer's retrospective might indicate something of significance about that writer. For Penton their presence should indicate something far more important—about writing itself, as a practice and a result.

Interview:
"We Introduce . . . ," *Opinion* (June/July 1935): 18.

Bibliographies:
Ross Smith and Cheryl Taylor, "Brian Con Penton (1904-1951): A Bibliography," *Literature in Northern Queensland,* 15, no. 1 (1987): 122-128;
Martin Duwell and Laurie Hergenhan, *The ALS Guide to Australian Writers: A Bibliography 1963-1990* (St. Lucia: University of Queensland Press, 1992).

Biography:
Patrick Buckridge, *The Scandalous Penton* (St. Lucia: University of Queensland Press, 1994).

References:
Patrick Buckridge, "Biography as Social Knowledge: An Anthropological Perspective," *Southern Review,* 22, no. 1 (March 1989);
Dymphna Cusack, "Mystery of a Novel Contest," *Meanjin,* 10 (1950): 57-60;
L. F. Fitzhardinge, "The Destructive Analyst," in *The Little Digger, 1914-1952: William Morris Hughes, A Political Biography,* volume 2 (Sydney: Angus & Robertson, 1979);
Bridget Griffen-Foley, *The House of Packer: The Making of a Media Empire* (Sydney: Allen & Unwin, 1999);
Laurie Hergenhan, "Brian Penton's 1930s Novels: 'The Roots of the New Psyche,'" in her *Unnatural Lives: Studies in Australian Convict Fiction* (St. Lucia: Queensland University Press, 1983);
Donald Horne, *Confessions of a New Boy* (Melbourne: Penguin, 1985);
Jack Lindsay, *Fanfrolico and After* (London: Bodley Head, 1962);
Obituary of Brian Con Penton, *Daily Telegraph* (Sydney), 25 August 1951;
James Packer, "The Destructive Element: Determinacy, Anxiety and *Unheimlichkeit* in the Life and Fiction of Brian Penton," dissertation, University of Western Sydney, 1998;
A. A. Phillips, "The Cultural Cringe," in *The Australian Tradition* (Melbourne: Cheshire, 1958), pp. 112-117;
Gavin Souter, *Company of Heralds: A Century and a Half of Australian Publishing* (Melbourne: Melbourne University Press, 1981), p. 132;
P. R. Stephensen, "A Continent Our Theme," *Publicist* (Sydney) (November-December 1936): 11-12;
Stephensen, *The Foundations of Culture in Australia* (Sydney: Miles, 1936), p. 65.

Papers:
The University of Queensland Fryer Library holds Brian Penton's unpublished typescripts, including "Outrageous Fortune," the "Third Novel," and the untitled monograph on international power relations. Small collections of letters by and about Penton are held in the National Library of Australia in Canberra, and the Sydney University Rare Books Collection at the Fisher Library; several larger collections of his letters are held in the Mitchell Library in Sydney.

Hal Porter

(16 February 1911 – 29 September 1984)

David McCooey
Deakin University

BOOKS: *Short Stories* (Adelaide: Privately printed, 1942);

The Hexagon (Sydney: Angus & Robertson, 1956);

A Handful of Pennies (Sydney: Angus & Robertson, 1958);

The Tilted Cross (London: Faber & Faber, 1961);

A Bachelor's Children: Short Stories (Sydney: Angus & Robertson, 1962);

The Watcher on the Cast-Iron Balcony: An Australian Autobiography (London: Faber & Faber, 1963);

Stars of Australian Stage and Screen (Adelaide: Rigby, 1965);

The Cats of Venice (Sydney: Angus & Robertson, 1965);

The Paper Chase (Sydney: Angus & Robertson, 1966);

The Professor: A Play in Three Acts (London: Faber & Faber, 1966);

Elijah's Ravens: Poems (Sydney: Angus & Robertson, 1968);

The Actors: An Image of the New Japan (Sydney: Angus & Robertson, 1968);

Eden House: A Play in Three Acts (Sydney: Angus & Robertson, 1969);

Mr. Butterfry and Other Tales of New Japan (Sydney: Angus & Robertson, 1970);

The Right Thing (Adelaide: Rigby, 1971);

Selected Stories, edited by Leonie Kramer (Sydney: Angus & Robertson, 1971);

Fredo Fuss Love Life: Short Stories (Sydney: Angus & Robertson, 1974);

In an Australian Country Graveyard and Other Poems (Melbourne: Nelson, 1974);

The Extra (West Melbourne, Vic.: Nelson, 1975);

Bairnsdale: Portrait of an Australian Country Town (St. Ives, N.S.W.: Ferguson, 1977);

The Clairvoyant Goat and Other Stories (Melbourne: Nelson, 1981).

Collection: *Hal Porter*—includes revised edition of *A Handful of Pennies*, Portable Australian Authors Series, edited by Mary Lord (St. Lucia: University of Queensland Press, 1980).

PLAY PRODUCTIONS: *The Tower,* London, 1964; Melbourne, St. Martin's Theatre, 1964;

Hal Porter, 1982 (Standard Photo Service, Ballarat)

Toda-San, Adelaide, 1965; revised as *The Professor,* London, Royal Court Theatre, 25 August 1965;

Eden House, Melbourne, St. Martin's Theatre, 26 March 1969; produced again as *Home on a Pig's Back,* London, Richmond Theatre, 28 February 1972;

Parker, Ballarat, theatre unknown, 25 February 1972.

PRODUCED SCRIPT: "The Child" in *Libido,* motion picture, Producers' and Directors' Guild of Victoria, 1973.

OTHER: *Australian Poetry, 1957,* selected by Porter (Sydney: Angus & Robertson, 1957);

Coast to Coast: Australian Stories 1961-1962, edited by Porter (Sydney: Angus & Robertson, 1962);

The Tower, in *Three Australian Plays* (Melbourne: Penguin, 1963);

"Post-War Japan," in *Australians Abroad,* edited by Charles Higham and Michael Wilding (Melbourne: Chesire, 1967), pp. 170-179;

It Could Be You, edited by Porter (Adelaide: Rigby, 1972);

"Martin Boyd," "Thomas Keneally," "Hal Porter," and "Patrick White," in *Contemporary Novelists,* edited by James Vinson (London: St. James, 1972), pp. 152-154; 710-711; 996-997; 1346-1348;

"Hobart: A Big-Dipper Little City," in *Seven Cities of Australia* (Sydney: Ferguson, 1978), pp. 31-58.

SELECTED PERIODICAL PUBLICATIONS—
UNCOLLECTED: "Reputation's Blowflies: Or Read Any Good Books Lately," *Bulletin,* 6 January 1962, pp. 21-22;

"Hal Porter's Australia: South Gippsland and Its Towns," *Australian Letters,* 6 September 1964, pp. 22-50, reprinted in *The Vital Decade,* edited by Geoffrey Dutton and Max Harris (Melbourne: Sun, 1968), pp. 162-191;

"Melbourne in the Thirties," *London Magazine* (September 1965): 31-47;

"Autobiographer's Freak Show," *Age Weekend Magazine,* 24 October 1981, p. 23.

Hal Porter's *The Watcher on the Cast-Iron Balcony: An Australian Autobiography* (1963) is a key work in Australian autobiography and an undisputed masterpiece of Australian literature. Porter wrote in all genres and, after a slow start, published many books. But his autobiography and short stories are his major works. Porter was a prose stylist of a kind rarely seen in Australia. His writings are both highly mannered and documentary-like in their ability to represent Australia.

Harold Edward Porter, the eldest of six children, was born in Albert Park, Melbourne. His parents were Harold Owen Porter and Ida Violet Ruff Porter. From 1917 to 1949 his father drove the Melbourne-Bairnsdale train, though Porter described his father as an engineer. The family lived at 36 (now 86) Bellair Street, Kensington, a working-class suburb of Melbourne, until 1917, when they moved to Bairnsdale, the principal town of East Gippsland. There Porter attended State School 754.

In 1921 he attended Bairnsdale High School, where he was the youngest student. His first story was published in a school magazine in 1922. In 1924 Porter won the first of many literary competitions—the junior section of a story competition run by the *Bairnsdale Advertiser.* In 1926 he left school, having failed his Leaving Certificate by one subject. In January 1927 he became a cadet reporter for the *Bairnsdale Advertiser,* writing routine news stories and a pseudonymous column, "Around the Town." This was not the work the young aspiring writer wanted. Unable to find work with a Melbourne paper, in October he became a Junior Teacher, Third Class, of State School 1409 in North Williamstown. Only sixteen years old, he lived with his aunt and uncle in Williamstown. Apart from briefly teaching in Bairnsdale in 1931, he taught at North Williamstown for the next ten years.

On 21 March 1929 Porter's mother died. This event is central to his autobiography and several stories—especially "Act One, Scene One." At the time it led to his leaving his aunt and uncle's house and to a cooling of relations with his father. Porter began many years of living in boardinghouses, hotels, and rental properties. He was a good, if not entirely committed, teacher. Aware of his luck to be employed during the Great Depression, Porter was not ambitious enough to seek promotion. He writes in *The Paper Chase* (1966) that he acquired "the notoriety of being—surely—the oldest Junior Teacher in the Victorian Education Department if not the most elderly one south of the Tropic of Capricorn." He resigned from the Education Department in May 1937 to concentrate on writing. Living in Melbourne, he wrote little, took art classes at the National Gallery, acted with the Gregan McMahon Players, lived a bohemian lifestyle, and briefly worked as an assistant for a window-dressing firm. Also in 1937 his short story "Holiday" was published in the premier magazine of Australia, *The Bulletin*—an occurrence not repeated until 1954. In March 1938 his story "And from Madame's" won the Australian Sesquicentenary Literary Competition.

In 1938 he returned to Bairnsdale, unemployed, and lived with his father. In June 1939 he met Olivia Parnham—the Ardath cigarette girl—and a week later they married. On 1 September 1939, two days before war was declared, Porter was hit by a car. He was discharged from the hospital in late October with a permanent limp and no hope of being active in the war, about which Porter writes, "As a writer more than as a man, but also as a man, I regret losing the opportunity to experience war directly. Maybe, to lose in this manner is to win. For me it does not seem so. A slice of the century is missing from my total. I shall remain incomplete while others are fulfilled."

In 1940, seriously needing work, he applied for a position at Queen's College, a private Methodist boys' school in Adelaide. Because of the wartime shortage of teachers, Porter was successful in his application, and in the last term of 1940, as a stopgap, he taught at a one-teacher school in Balook in the Strezlecki ranges, South Gippsland. In 1941, separated from his wife, he became a resident master at Queen's College, where he had an affair with a male student. In 1942, encouraged by the student, Porter self-published *Short Stories* (250 copies). In that year he moved to Prince Alfred College, another Adelaide Methodist School. In 1943 he was divorced, and in 1946 he taught at Hutchins School in Tasmania. He was again embroiled in scandal when he supported a strike by students over the headmaster's decision to cancel the King's Birthday holiday. Porter lost his position, ostensibly because he lacked a university qualification. He remained in Hobart, involved in the theater.

In 1947 he taught at Knox Grammar, a Presbyterian school in Sydney, where he was required to teach divinity—Porter's reason for his short stay there. His next, less prestigious, appointment was assistant master at Ballarat College. In 1948 he won the *Sydney Morning Herald* literary competition with his story "The Daughter of the Late Bishop." In 1949 he managed the George Hotel in St. Kilda, Melbourne. After six months he returned to Tasmania, again working in theater. In 1950 he became a teacher for the Army Education Unit in occupied Japan, at Kure. His stay in Japan provided material for his first novel. In the following year he returned to Hobart, where he produced amateur theatricals and helped save the Theatre Royal, Australia's oldest theater.

In 1953 he taught briefly in Melbourne, worked as a cook for a sheep station (ranch), and returned to Bairnsdale, where in 1954 he became City Librarian. In 1956, when he was forty-five, his first mainstream book, *The Hexagon*, was published, and he received a Commonwealth Literary Fund (CLF) grant to write *A Handful of Pennies*, published in 1958. In 1957 his father died, and in the following year Porter became City Librarian in Shepparton, north of Melbourne. In 1960 he undertook research in London for his second novel, *The Tilted Cross* (1961). In 1961, at the age of fifty, Porter became a full-time writer. *The Tilted Cross* was accepted by Faber and Faber, and his first play, *The Tower* (1960), was co-winner of the Sydney Journalists' Club drama award.

In the 1950s, the taste for social-realist fiction no longer so dominant, Porter's stories appeared regularly in journals, especially *The Bulletin*. In 1962 his short-story reputation was cemented with *A Bachelor's Children: Short Stories*. *The Tilted Cross* won the literary prize sponsored by *The Advertiser* (Adelaide), and in April, Porter was an Australian representative at the International Novelists' Convention in Edinburgh. In

Dust jacket for Porter's first novel, set in postwar Japan (Bruccoli Clark Layman Archives)

late 1962 there was a threat regarding the possible banning of his autobiography, *The Watcher on the Cast-Iron Balcony*. The work was not banned and appeared in Australia the following September. A notice of the book in the Hobart *Mercury* (7 November 1963) imputed that, for publicity purposes, Porter encouraged talk of banning the book. Porter sued for defamation of character, winning £1,000 in damages.

In 1964 Porter's play *The Tower* was produced in England and Australia, and his second play, *Toda-San* (first performed in 1965), received second prize in the Sydney Journalists' Club competition. By the mid 1960s Porter was busy with commissioned work, including a book on Australian actors, a book on Japan, and an unwritten work, *Hal Porter's Sydney*. In 1965 *Toda-San* was produced in Australia and England as *The Professor* (published under this title in 1966). Books appeared yearly, including short stories, *The Cats of Venice* (1965), and the autobiographical *The Paper Chase* (1966). In 1967 Porter returned to Japan to lecture and undertake research. In the same year he won, with Randolph Stow, the $20,000 Encyclopaedia Britannica Award. In 1968 Porter was awarded another CLF grant to write *The Right Thing* (1971), which in manuscript won the Adelaide *Advertiser* literary competition in 1970 and second prize in the Captain Cook Bi-Centenary Literary Competition in 1971.

In 1972 Porter's third play, *Eden House,* was produced as *Home on a Pig's Back* in England. It was not a success. In the following year he received $8,000 from the CLF to complete his autobiography, and in 1974 he was awarded a three-year grant of $6,000 per annum. Books continued to be published in the 1970s, but at a slower rate, and in 1981 Porter's last work, *The Clairvoyant Goat and Other Stories,* was published. By this time Porter had bought a house in Ballarat, the first one he had ever owned, and—as detailed by his biographer—begun a relationship with a married man thirty years his junior. In 1982 he was made a member of the Order of Australia and also prosecuted for shoplifting.

On 24 July 1983 Porter was knocked down by a car in Ballarat. He received a serious head injury and remained in a coma for fourteen months. The driver, who failed to stop, was over the alcohol limit and when tried in July 1984 was fined. On 29 September 1984, Porter, age seventy-three, died.

Ten years later, in 1993, Mary Lord's biography *Hal Porter: Man of Many Parts* appeared. It began with a "Declaration of Bias," in which Lord revealed not only that Porter was a pedophile, but also that her son had been one of his victims—as reported on the front page of the national newspaper of Australia, *The Australian.* Considering this history, many reviewers wondered if Lord should not have abandoned her biography. Certainly, Lord interprets Porter's character in a generally negative way. *Hal Porter: Man of Many Parts* discloses facts about Porter's sexual life, hard drinking, use of friends, and fictionalizing of his family background—though it is odd that Porter should be filmed in front of 36 Bellair Street in the Australia Arts Council video if, as Lord argues, he was ashamed of its obvious working-class status. Lord presents Porter as essentially split, two fundamentally opposite characters, "Writer" and "Person": "Writer was amoral and Person was his saintly dupe, yet Person was a pedophile and Writer found that repugnant." Without the biography, Porter's writings and interviews show that he was deeply conservative and anti-intellectual; his nonfiction—much more than his stories—makes misogynistic and racist statements. On the other hand, Porter is relatively open about his own pathologies—even briefly admitting in *The Watcher on the Cast-Iron Balcony* to experience in pederasty.

To call Porter's writing "artificial" is to draw attention to obvious mannerisms—its syntactical dexterity, its catalogues, its wide lexis, its adjectives and adverbs, and its factitious characters and outré events. But this description ignores an important, if contradictory, aspect of Porter's writing. Like other antirealist writers—not least of them, Katherine Mansfield, one of Porter's influences—Porter's antirealist style is in service to a realist project. In *Contemporary Novelists* (1972) he writes of a "wish to record clearly an extraordinary country and . . . unique enough inhabitants." More importantly, Porter repeatedly stated that he had no imagination. In "Answers to the Funny, Kind Man" (1969) he writes,

> No character or landscape or sailors' dive or rococo event has not been put down as such, or not been winkled from its original place in the jigsaw of time and space to be refitted, *slightly* trimmed, into its new pozzie in a book-sized book, a short-story-sized short story, or a poem-shaped poem. Because one has to (I, imaginationless, *have* to) pick up a Whole Idea which needs only to be written down, most of the time extraordinarily little change is made. . . . Here, a strange and maddening thing occurs. Apparently not accepting, as I with my imperfections must accept, that undiluted fact is far more *outré* than unalloyed fiction, reviewers and thesis-writers, infallibly impercipient, castigate as fictional and contrived what is tantamount to reportage. . . .

However, in an interview with Lord, Porter admits that—unlike life—"I usually work towards a punch-line" and that his narrators are technical constructions:

> Even the times where there's a sort of Hal Pal air you usually find if I put an "I" in, it obviously isn't me—I make him pretty invisible, even if he's got to be cynical and *dégagé.* . . . In some there will be tiny bits of me, you can't avoid that, but they'd be *very* tiny bits. The "I" is usually the sort of person I want for a special reason. . . . as a technical device.

Porter, then, is a contradictory writer: outrageous in the extreme, he calls on the authority of the real for his fictions; baroque in style, he claims to have no imagination; intensely moved by the past, his detached narrative style produces something that could be called antisentimental nostalgia.

Porter is also a self-conscious regionalist. Most of his work, he writes in *Contemporary Novelists,* is "based on characters and landscapes of southernmost Australia, the less distraught, arid and intractable part, the greener, colder, well-combed terrain with its nineteenth-century provincial cities and country towns, its seaside resorts on a littoral touched by Antarctic winds." His description of himself as a "simple country boy" links several key elements: his interest in his regional background, the relationship between self and past experience, and his constant use of the theme of innocence and its loss.

Porter's first commercial publication, *The Hexagon,* includes heavily stylized poems. Despite taking the writing of poetry more seriously than that of plays, Porter's poetry is not highly regarded. His poetry is stanzaic, uses complicated rhyme scheme and dense syntax, and shows a Hopkinsian liking for portmanteau words. These elements can be seen in "Gippsland Town," which also shows how variously Porter returned to childhood for literary effect: "When I sped, morning boy, dying and dying, / Lear-the-child leaping through boxthorny town, / cabbage-rose-peopled and red-gum-smoke-flying, / sunrise's Stromboli shone like God's gown." Porter presents such pastoral baroque more successfully in his prose. As he says in the interview with Lord, "Much of the poetry goes into the short stories . . . in the mood, in the arrangement of words." *Elijah's Ravens* (1968) includes many of the poems from *The Hexagon* and only a handful of new poems.

As with all his "Japanese" work up to *The Professor*, Porter's first novel, *A Handful of Pennies*, deals with the clash between two opposing cultures, showing sympathy for the Japanese in the face of barbaric Westerners. *A Handful of Pennies* is a remarkably assured first novel. Episodic in structure, however, it reads as a series of related shorter works. The five main characters—the "handful of pennies"—are linked more by place than by plot. All returning to Australia—dead or alive—on the same flight, they represent a failure of relations between Australians and Japanese.

Interaction between "victor and vanquished" is almost always tragic in consequence, if sometimes farcical in execution. The Tasmanian schoolteacher, Paula Groot, has an affair with her house girl's brother, contracting syphilis, while the house girl goes mad. Major Evered-Hopkins, who admires the Japanese, dies because he cannot bring himself to ask for a doctor. Captain Truscott has an affair with a country girl who dishonors her family when she leaves home just before her marriage. Despite moments of comedy, the novel is somber about humanity's ability to be humane: "If it is not being cruel, humanity is deaf or blind." Despite the florid prose, documentary aspects can be seen in descriptions of the postwar landscape and Japanese festivals.

The Tilted Cross, though more baroque, is Porter's most coherent novel and one of his most important works. It is based on the life of Thomas Griffiths Wainewright—artist, writer, dandy, friend of Charles Lamb and Charles Dickens, and supposed murderer—who was convicted of fraud and transported to Van Diemen's Land, where he painted portraits. Unlike others attracted to writing about Wainewright—Dickens, Edward Bulwer-Lytton, and Marcus Clarke—Porter sets him in the Antipodes. Van Diemen's Land is a hellish land of inversions and crossings. As Giovanna Capone writes in *Incandescent Verities: The Fiction of Hal*

Dust jacket for Porter's 1961 novel, based on the life of nineteenth-century writer, painter, and convict Thomas Griffiths Wainewright (Bruccoli Clark Layman Archives)

Porter (1990): "The cross theme and crossed connections dominate the whole novel . . . the novel is structured on the chiasmus, a rhetorical figure shaped like the Greek letter *chi*." The eponymous cross is the constellation of the Southern Cross, which figures apocalyptically during the main characters' deaths.

Porter's Wainewright becomes Judas Griffin Vaneleigh, who is befriended by the Christ-like Queely Sheill. As Porter points out in "Answers to the Funny, Kind Man," the outrageous names of his characters, including Asnetha Sleep, come from life, as do some of the characters and events. *The Tilted Cross* is highly theatrical in organization and style, with vignettes and highly mannered dialogue, though the plot is quite simple: Vaneleigh, accompanied by Queely, is commissioned to paint a portrait of Lady Rose Knight of Cindermead. Also living in Cindermead is the cousin of Lady Knight's husband, Asnetha Sleep, an heiress, who is affected in dress and manner and badly deformed. Sleep draws Queely, who is intensely compassionate, into a sexual liaison. Purely through malice, Lady Knight uses this liaison to engineer Queely's downfall in order to hurt Asnetha. Queely's, like Vaneleigh's, conviction of theft is based on another's perjury.

Queely and Vaneleigh are doomed, and Queely's death is the tragic climax of the novel. Badly injured while attempting to escape jail, Queely has to have his leg amputated, and he dies of gangrene. These events are described in frightening detail, as when Queely "heard the pus from the stump of his amputated leg detaching itself in rich globules and plunging into the brimming tray set below the gangrenous fag-end of his body." But the real power of the novel comes from the use of symbol, leitmotiv, and ironic contiguity. The taproom Queely's father runs, for example, is called "The Shades," and its door is the mouth of hell. While employing Christian topoi–Judas and Christ, the crowing cock, the figures of the Apocalypse–the allegory and reversals are not simplistic. Vaneleigh and Queely are both victims, and the beau monde and demimonde interconnect through them. The people of both worlds are "shades," and at the end of a strikingly materialist and corporeal novel, Vaneleigh wonders if matter is "nothing but an idea."

A Bachelor's Children, the fruition of many years of short-story writing, showed Porter to be without equal in that form at that time. As Lord says in *Hal Porter* (1974), "He is foremost among Australian writers in his ability to re-create time and place, to evoke and sustain an atmosphere, to depict a background in meticulous detail, to record the essential nuances of conversation." The stories employ Porter's characteristic themes–the difference between appearance and reality, dreams and disillusion, impermanence, and loss of innocence. Their tone is nostalgic, though many stories rely on melodramatic or sensational plots. "Miss Rodda's," "The Daughter of the Late Bishop," and "On the Ridge" involve suicide, madness, and murder. Other stories lyrically evoke Porter's lost Eden–a country childhood. In such stories, the narrative impetus is the loss of innocence, but the use of detail, tone, and metaphor avoids sentimentality. "Act One, Scene One" begins,

> Main street. Water tower. Hitching posts. Advertisements for pills and polishes on post-and-rail fences. Boer War memorial. Cattle-yards. Livery and baiting stables. Shire Hall. Emporiums (1894). Mechanics' Institute. Rechabite Hall. Railway station: afternoon train snuffles among milk cans, cabs grind gravel. Painted weatherboards. Muscle-coloured brick. Veils are lifted for unpainted women to sip in the Crystal Tea Rooms where the tulip soda-fountain adores itself in the Spider-advertising looking-glass.

Such a milieu and such evocation constitute *The Watcher on the Cast-Iron Balcony*. Since Porter's great theme is loss of Eden, not surprisingly, his autobiography of childhood is his masterpiece. Autobiography of childhood is, for Porter, an account of first things. The importance of the first home is attested to in the title of the work. The balcony provides the controlling image of the man watching the watching boy, producing a double perspective that Porter uses to brilliant effect. Porter's temporal effects in his autobiographies are justifiably famous.

The opening four paragraphs of *The Watcher on the Cast-Iron Balcony* make up one of the most original openings in autobiography. The image of the author's dead parents–"two corpses" who were once "young, agile and lustful enough to mortise themselves together to make me"–illustrates how Porter can look at his life both artfully and dispassionately. It also shows Porter's autobiography to be the biography of his mother as well. In addition, Porter acutely recreates a post-Edwardian Australian childhood, reviving a lost world. Porter's use of catalogue–like Barry Humphries's–makes manifest the assumptions, aesthetics, and aspirations of a whole class. The long lists are never merely random but arranged through association, syntax, and resonance.

The Watcher on the Cast-Iron Balcony recounts with preternatural clarity early childhood, the psychological wrench of leaving one's first home, a country childhood, schooling, sexual initiations, and the death of a mother. These events are knitted together thematically and structurally with exceptional tonal control. For instance, the theatrical and elegiac nature of Porter's subjectivity is illustrated when the ten-year-old Porter writes a play, "Briar Rosebud." This play begins a long elegiac sequence, with the narrator figuring the ultimate deaths of members of the cast and audience. "The Queen with her gold-paper crown, *diamanté* bracelets on her freckled arms, and alive with idiotic rippling giggles, commits suicide twenty years later. War swipes out of sight the King, the Court Jester . . . and some of the audience," while the Bad Fairy contracts cancer. The children's pantomime becomes a morality play, and the emphasis on mortality refers to Porter's mother.

To emphasize fully the importance of his mother's death, Porter places its description at the end of the work, drawing attention to last things. His mother's last kiss reverses the polarity of the autobiography that has hitherto been an autobiography of beginnings. In this way the end of *The Watcher on the Cast-Iron Balcony* prefigures the later two volumes of Porter's autobiography, which also emphasize last events. "She kisses me. That, *that,* is the last of her supply of kisses. It is a dry kiss, light as the touch of a passing flame." This last kiss is a kiss of betrayal, the betrayal of death. The emotional climax of the work, the structural artfulness of the scene, and its detailed evocation of a lost world make *The Watcher on the Cast-Iron Balcony* one of the most read and influential autobiographies in Australian literature.

Less significant—though long in print and popular with amateur theatrical companies—is *The Tower,* a costume melodrama set in Van Diemen's Land, which uses material from *The Tilted Cross.* (Porter also wrote a radio play about Wainewright called *I Am Nothing.*) *The Tower* uses tight form, stock characters, and theatrical machinery to present a story that makes few claims to profundity. As Peter Fitzpatrick notes in *After the Doll: Australian Drama Since 1955* (1979), Porter is so "of the theater" in an old-fashioned sense that he could be described as "stagestruck." Like nineteenth-century melodrama, *The Tower* centers on identity, parentage, and property. Sir Rodney Haviland—brutish, hypocritical, and ambitious—has returned from England with his new (and third) bride. His stepdaughter, Amy, resents the new mistress of the house (one year her junior). Sir Rodney's adopted son, Edwin, is the son of a convict—Marcus Knight, the "real" knight of the play—employed by Sir Rodney so the secret will not be discovered. From her affair with Knight, Amy becomes pregnant. In the climax of the second act Amy rejects a more suitable suitor and confronts her stepfather, who murders her by throwing her from the tower. Edwin, the audience knows, is the only witness. The symbol of the tower suggests that the play is more than a mere resurrection of melodrama. Unseen, the tower lends the play metaphorical weight, and the hammering of the builders, combined with the image of the tower as a "tower of lies," gives full weight to Edwin's emotional destruction of his stepfather in the climax of the play.

Porter's second volume of stories, *The Cats of Venice,* shows a widening of setting and includes two of Porter's best comic stories, "Party Forty-two and Mrs Brewer" and "Say to Me Ronald!" As these stories show, melodrama in this collection gives way to satire and comedy. Others, such as "Little Old Lady Passing By" and the eponymous story, show Australians abroad, where the "foreigners" tend to come off second best. Porter's interest in disillusion and nostalgia, however, remains in stories such as "Young Woman in a Wimple," one of many stories to feature train travel, and "Francis Silver."

Porter's second volume of autobiography, *The Paper Chase,* covers events from the death of Porter's mother to his teaching in Japan. Lacking the careful structuring of his first volume, *The Paper Chase* caused some disappointment among critics. It includes, nevertheless, fascinating vignettes and centers on Porter's desire to become a writer. Given the imaginative importance of place for Porter, *The Paper Chase* details Porter's moving from one job and place to another when they have provided material to him as a writer.

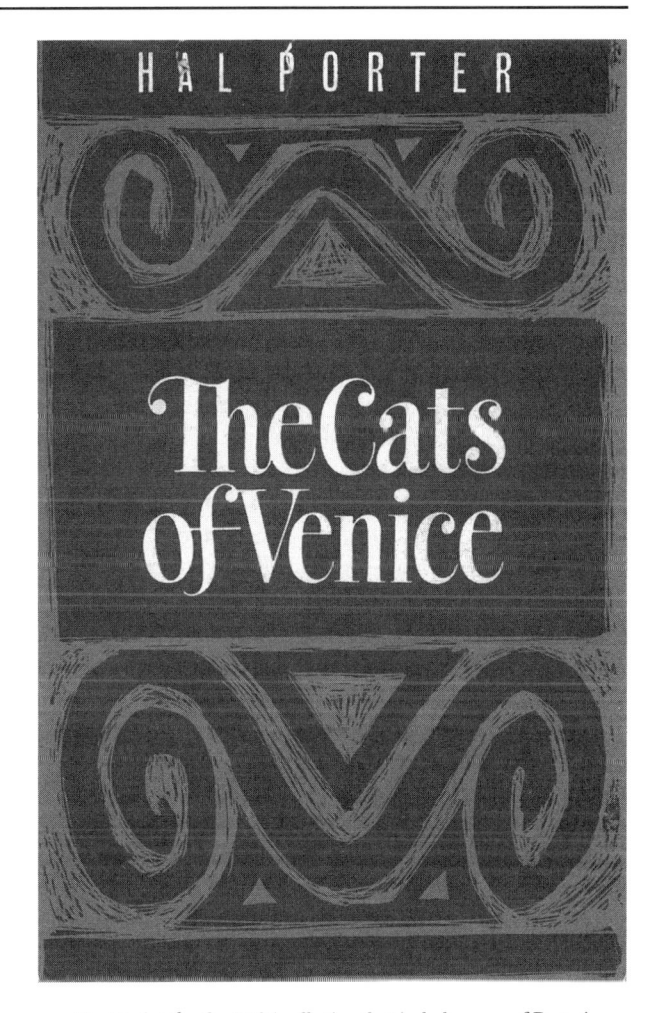

Dust jacket for the 1965 collection that includes some of Porter's best comic pieces (Bruccoli Clark Layman Archives)

The Watcher on the Cast-Iron Balcony is also concerned with otherness—the alien "uninnocent" boy that is Porter's lost self and Porter's lost mother. *The Paper Chase* is deeply involved in establishing the connections between the detached autobiographical self and others. It opens with a revelation concerning the relationship between the living and the dead. It is

> impossible to kill the dead. Indeed, it is only the dead, salted down for ever, pickled in the vat of time, who illustrate how immortal mortals are, and how unavoidable is resurrection, how immediate and permanent, with no three days required, and no hope necessary—hope, the last and most terrible of all the evils let out of Pandora's box. No need at all for hope: although as dead as mutton, Mother has come upon the earth, a very Tmu from the Book of the Dead, and with her two feet has taken possession of it.

Such phraseology as "dead as mutton" shows how dualistic Porter is in his attention to lost people and things: lovingly—or obsessively—given textual life,

Porter's ineluctable materialism does not allow them easy sentimentality.

The Paper Chase is an autobiography of education. It ends with a self-realization. Porter's house girl in Japan gives back his identity—lost because of his mother—by waking him from his moral sleep. Porter, who treats Ikuko Sakamoto with indifference and contempt, is shocked into knowledge through her farewell, which he does not deserve. When Porter is leaving Japan, Ikuko-san gives him her going-out sash and two letters expressing thanks from her father and brother. The brother calls Porter a great teacher; teacher was the position that Porter had taken in Williamstown at the beginning of the work. Porter reacts, "Teacher! I have taught nothing except that I have to be taught." Even for Porter, the watcher, the writer, the teacher, oneself is not essential, sufficient unto itself. *The Paper Chase* is less lacking in a theme than critics have usually argued. In centering on the trope of education, it works within a classic subgenre while artfully reworking its tropes—maturation, self-knowledge, and the relationship between self and others.

Porter's second play, *Toda-San* (published as *The Professor*), returns to Japanese themes. The professor, Gilbert Medlin, is another self-obsessed character whose "uninnocence" causes destruction around him. He and his sister, Gretel Medlin, a former actress, run a boardinghouse in Kyoto in which many Australians are staying. Medlin expects fanatical devotion from his students and shares his room with one of them, Toda Inagaki. Toda's sister Fusehime Ishimoto prostitutes herself so that he might buy the fine woodcuts that the professor covets. When Medlin discovers the source of the money for these gifts, he accuses his student of lying. Fusehime tries to kill herself, and her brother—in the bizarre closing moments of the play—presents his severed tongue in a box to the professor, indicating that he will never lie again.

Included in *The Professor* is a play-within-the-play supposedly based on an ancient Japanese source. The text states that the performance of the inner play should be "orientally formal and ritualistic in movement and posture." The themes of the perfectionist artist and the masks that people wear (from necessity and vanity) comment on the action of the main play and lead to the conclusion of the work. As in *A Handful of Pennies* the Australian characters come off second best, with their callousness and self-obsession contrasting with the selflessness of the Japanese characters. *The Professor* is Porter's most ambitious play, in terms of both script and production, but its apparent blindness to the relationship between Medlin and Toda—as well as the danger that the final scene will overwhelm the rest of the play—means that it is not an unqualified success.

The Actors: An Image of the New Japan (1968), a work of travel writing, briefly provoked debate in the press for its attack on Japan, but its currency quickly died out. Today it reads as the work of a man who returned to Japan seventeen years after having lived there to be inevitably disillusioned. The "New Japan" is squalid and plastic, experiencing an affluence that masks spiritual hunger. Worst of all, Japan has become Americanized: "Outside America there is no city on earth which so reproduces all the worst aspects of American civilization, or more grotesquely burlesques them. Devoid of originality, lacking the explorer nature, uncreative, the Japanese have paraphrased the West, now blowing hot, now blowing cold, on and off since the sixteenth century." Such statements have the ring of a spurned lover, a right-wing nostalgist. The levity of the young, the bustle of the city, is hysterical: Japan has become a series of symptoms. This work is classic Porteresque territory: the inner emptiness caused by experience is covered by the histrionic, theatrical display of self, about which the display is the most important feature of subjectivity.

Porter claimed to have written his third play, *Eden House*, in a fortnight. Like *The Tower*, it is an entertainment. It centers on Maxine Charlesworth, whose dominating part is clearly a vehicle for a strong character actress. Maxine, a former actress, owns Eden House, a large Victorian house that her relatives want to develop. The characters—Maxine's daughter, her unfaithful lover, and her friend—are stock characters, and the betrayals that make up the plot are contrived to produce good curtains and an entertaining evening. Some characteristic concerns are discernible—the lost paradise of childhood, the brittle and witty dialogue of overtly theatrical characters, and the loss of the glorious past for the squalid present.

Mr. Butterfry and Other Tales of New Japan (1970) is a fictional response to Porter's disillusionment with Japan. The stories are longer than those of earlier collections, and each deals with a central character. These stories are developed through time, rather than through detailing a lost static past or an individual moment of insight. The main theme of the work concerns the effects of opposing cultures. The title story is about an expatriate Australian who has married a Japanese house girl. It becomes apparent to the narrator that Mr. Butterfry's moral shortcomings and repugnant personality result from his error of judgment; other characters in the stories suffer from similar errors or flaws in personality. As the couple argue in front of the narrator, he comes to realize that "Mr Butterfry's misfortunes have not been caused by his own moral or mental debility nor by a fateful mis-mating of Japanese stars but by a gluttonously ambitious Japanese mother, the former oh-so-sweet-and-cute housegirl bred on rice slops and pickled radish in a penurious and primitive village." Porter's satire has become two-pronged, and his disillusionment with Japan makes these Japanese characters extremely different from his earlier fictional writing.

The Right Thing, Porter's last novel, again shows his problems with the novel as a form. It is his least successful novel and, like *A Handful of Pennies*, more a collection of related stories than a novel in the conventional sense. The work returns to provincial Australia and centers on the landed Ogilvies of "Erradale" in Victoria's Western District. It shows the emptiness of the social code of doing "the right thing" and how such a code can victimize innocent people. The novel is weakly structured and his least subtle work.

Fredo Fuss Love Life: Short Stories (1974) shows Porter's continued mastery of the short story. It includes familiar Porter fare—a satire of Adelaide Writers' Week; a Professor's return to his "Home Town"; and the trick ending of "The Other Woman." In "Brett," Porter's trademarks are everywhere—a first-person narrator who views and reports on a short episode, a train journey, Australians abroad, skillful use of dialogue, the difference between appearance and reality, and a punch line. In "I Wonder Who's Kissing Her Now" the narrator is an actor who is attending a ball in rural Australia in 1939. The interior monologue brilliantly creates the contradictions between the outer world and the narrator's subjective world, slowly revealing his anxiety to be a kind of madness.

Porter's last book of verse, *In an Australian Country Graveyard and Other Poems* (1974), includes his best poetry. A slim volume, illustrated—like *The Actors*—by Porter, its eponymous poem is a sequence that uses a single place and history to consider certain types of Australians. The title of the book evokes Thomas Gray's famous poem, and Gray is mentioned in the second line: "The landscape plays at Constable and Gray." The sequence is predominantly elegiac in tone, but not wholly. In the second section, "The First-comers," Porter uses uncharacteristically long lines and artful half-rhymes to give a sense of the strange familiarity and familiar strangeness of the past.

The Extra (1975) closes Porter's autobiographical trilogy. No longer finding a world in the place, but seeking—if only temporarily—a place in the world, Porter stays at his sister's farm in Western Victoria. There, he tells his readers, he writes *The Extra*. The opening descriptions of the property are as excessive and exuberant as the descriptions of his childhood place, but significantly altered to convey maturity and redolent with symbols of aging and change. The past makes the present ever recede, for here there is "not a hippie in the haystacks" and never a jetliner passes over. Porter is trying to re-create, albeit with a different emphasis, a new paradise. The work turns in on itself and is emblematic of Porter's life, as he ends by describing his return to the farm and admits that to return home is to reenter time. However, time is beaten as it becomes meaningless in such a world.

Porter in the mid 1970s (Melbourne Herald*)*

In *The Extra* Porter makes explicit the necessity of others in autobiography. Interpreting the context in which one finds oneself rather than "the self" is the primary focus in autobiography, he claims, particularly of writers:

> A writer's composed of others, can only be a thread on which, like a barbaric necklace, are strung a number of experiences. Self, as one ages, becomes decreasingly interesting to a writer. That's why this autobiography, despite my intrusion as thread, is really less about me than about events I slip into as into the wrong room at the wrong time, and . . . oops! . . . quickly out of.

The Extra is about last things. Last scenes and last words become a series of related, but distinct, tableaux, with Porter as the observer—onstage as an extra. The critical reception of *The Extra* at the time of publication was not good, perhaps not surprisingly, considering the general negativity of Porter's tone. However, *The Extra* is not merely a "book of literary reminiscences," as John Colmer describes it in the essay "Autobiography as an Art: Hal Porter" for *Australian Autobiography: The Personal Quest* (1989), but a logical end to Porter's autobiographical aesthetic—a complex melding of the different aspects of his life. The narrative of the work, while disrupted, is not dissolved by recollections of others. Memoirs of other writers—such as Kenneth Slessor, Christina Stead, and Eve Langley—along with references to Porter's present at the time of writing, are woven into the account of a "gregarious wanderer," his real-life wandering making his textual wandering appropriate. Chronology is not as important as it was in the previous volumes because, for Porter, "Self, as one ages, becomes decreasingly interesting to a writer." The reminiscences of writers, as Slessor's demonstrates, are not simply "memoir" but endings—last things figured in the lives of others.

In 1976 Porter returned to his hometown to undertake research for *Bairnsdale: Portrait of an Australian Country Town* (1977), something of a companion piece to *The Watcher on the Cast-Iron Balcony*. Part social history, part biography, part autobiography, the book begins with the 1920s—Porter's decade—and then moves through the history of the town from colonial times to the 1970s, noting everything from local worthies, council acts, institutions, agricultural and architectural history, and details such as "Ambulances in country towns." Mixing memory with historical research is not easy, and *Bairnsdale* is an endearing book, though the 1960s and 1970s are inevitably looked upon with a cold eye, another excuse for Porter to display his prejudices. In the end this work is nostalgic: "Oriental poppies and apple trees and Frau Karl Druschki roses? Too late; gone years ago."

Hal Porter—as both Writer and Person—was undeniably difficult and also charming. His oeuvre is wildly uneven, but his best writing shows him to be one of Australia's best prose stylists. Eclipsed at the time by the reputation of Patrick White (Australia's only Nobel laureate in literature), Porter, despite some superficial similarities, is quite different from White. Porter's representation of regional and suburban Australians lacks the elitist stance of White's, and Porter, whose imagination is deeply sociological and materialist, is not interested in the metaphysical realm that occupied White. As a watcher, Porter calls into being a new kind of Australia. Rich in detail, subtle and multiplex in meaning, it is a factitious world that—at its best—reverberates with the ring of truth.

Interview:

Mary Lord, "Interview with Hal Porter," *Australian Literary Studies,* 8 (1978): 269–279; revised version in *Hal Porter,* edited by Lord (Melbourne & London: Oxford University Press, 1974), pp. 395–404.

Bibliographies:

Janette Finch, *Bibliography of Hal Porter* (Adelaide: Library of Board of South Australia, 1966);

Michael Wilding, "Two Bibliographies: Hal Porter and Patrick White," *Australian Literary Studies,* 3 (1967): 142–148;

Mary Lord, "A Contribution to the Bibliography of Hal Porter," *Australian Literary Studies,* 4 (1970): 405–409.

Biographies:

John Hetherington, "Hal Porter: Country Boy At Large," in his *Forty-Two Faces* (Melbourne: Cheshire, 1962), pp. 171–176;

Graeme Kinross-Smith, "Hal Porter 1911– ," in *Australia's Writers* (Melbourne: Nelson, 1980), pp. 322–327;

Mary Lord, *Hal Porter: Man of Many Parts* (Sydney: Random House, 1993).

References:

Don Anderson, "Portraits of the Artist as a Young Man," *Meanjin,* 42, no. 3 (1983): 339–348;

John Barnes, "New Tracks to Travel: The Stories of White, Porter and Cowan," *Meanjin,* 25 (1966): 154–170;

Bruce Bennett, "Australian Perspectives on the Near North: Hal Porter and Randolph Stow," in *South Pacific Images,* edited by Chris Tiffin (Queensland: South Pacific Association for Commonwealth Literature & Language Studies, 1978), pp. 124–144;

Bennett, "Literary Constructions of the Near North," in *An Australian Compass: Essays on Place and Direction in Australian Literature* (Fremantle, W.A.: Fremantle Arts Centre Press, 1991), pp. 186–210;

Alison Broinowski, *The Yellow Lady: Australian Impressions of Asia* (Melbourne: Oxford University Press, 1992);

David Robert Burns, "A Sort of Triumph over Time: Hal Porter's Prose Narratives," *Meanjin,* 28 (1969): 19–28;

Burns, "*The Watcher on the Cast-Iron Balcony:* Hal Porter's Triumph of Creative Contradiction," *Australian Literary Studies,* 12, no. 3 (1986): 359–366;

Tim Burstall, "Comments on 'The Jetty,'" *Overland*, 71 (1978): 9–10;

Giovanna Capone, "Hal Porter, 'The Tower' and the Quintessence of Porterism," in *European Perspectives: Contemporary Essays on Australian Literature*, edited by Capone, Bruce Clunies Ross and Werner Senn (St. Lucia: University of Queensland Press, 1991), pp. 162–172;

Capone, *Incandescent Verities: The Fiction of Hal Porter* (Rome: Bulzoni, 1990);

Clunies Ross, "Some Developments in Short Fiction, 1969–1980," *Australian Literary Studies*, 10, no. 2 (1981): 165–180;

Richard N. Coe, "Portrait of an Artist as a Young Australian: Childhood, Literature and Myth," *Southerly*, 41, no. 2 (1981): 126–162;

John Colmer, "The Autobiographic Self and Other Worlds in Australian Writing," in *Perceiving Other Worlds*, edited by Edwin Thumboo (Singapore: Times Academic Press, 1991), pp. 105–114;

Colmer, "Autobiography as an Art: Hal Porter," in *Australian Autobiography: The Personal Quest* (Melbourne: Oxford University Press, 1989), pp. 50–70;

Colmer, "Hal Porter: *The Watcher on the Cast-Iron Balcony*," in *Autobiographical and Biographical Writing in the Commonwealth*—Papers from EACLALS Conference, Sitqes, Spain, 1984, edited by Doireann MacDermott (Barcelona, Spain: Editorial AUSA, 1984), pp. 57–62;

Kerry Jane Cotter, "Seers and Makers: The Child as Narrative Strategy in Some Postwar Australian Fiction," M.A. thesis, University of New England, 1988;

R. A. Duncan, "Hal Porter's Writing and the Impact of the Absurd," *Meanjin*, 29 (1970): 468–473;

Chester Eagle, "'I Had to Use a Dictionary to Write It': A Memoir of Hal," *Victorian Historical Journal*, 61, no. 1 (March 1990): 52–58;

Peter Fitzpatrick, *After the Doll: Australian Drama Since 1955* (Melbourne: Arnold, 1979), pp. 80–82;

Thelma Forshaw, "Some Remarks on the Late Great Hal Porter," *Australian Literary Studies*, 12, no. 1 (1985): 89–91;

Ronald G. Geering, "Hal Porter: The Control of Melodrama," *Southerly*, 33 (1973): 18–33;

Geering, "Hal Porter, the Watcher," *Southerly*, 24 (1964): 92–103;

Geering, "Hal Porter's Autobiography," *Southerly*, 36 (1976): 123–133;

Robin Gerster, "Gerrymander: The Place of Suburbia in Australian Fiction," *Meanjin*, 49, no. 3 (1990): 565–575;

Kerryn Goldsworthy, "Short Fiction," in *The Penguin New Literary History of Australia*, edited by L. T. Hergenhan (Melbourne: Penguin, 1988), pp. 535–546;

Reba Gostand, "Repetition and Menace in Hal Porter's *The Tower*," *Australian Literary Studies*, 6 (1973): 36–45;

Don Grant, "Seeking the Self: Imagination and Autobiography in Some Recent Australian Writing," in *Crisis and Creativity in the New Literature in English*, edited by Geoffrey V. Davis and Hena Maes-Jelinek (Amsterdam: Rodopi, 1990), pp. 309–322;

Jean Hawley-Crowcroft, "Hal Porter's Asian Stories: The Writer as Watcher," *Quadrant*, 28, no. 7 (1984): 202–203; no. 8 (1984): 41–45;

Hergenhan, "*The Tilted Cross*: The 'Duties of Innocence,'" *Southerly*, 34 (1974): 157–167;

Harry Heseltine, "Australian Fiction Since 1920," in *The Literature of Australia*, edited by Geoffrey Dutton (Ringwood, Vic.: Penguin, 1964), pp. 181–223;

Heseltine, "The Emotional Structure of *The Watcher on the Cast-Iron Balcony*," in *The Uncertain Self: Essays in Australian Literature and Criticism* (Melbourne: Oxford University Press, 1986), pp. 131–146;

Lee Jobling, "Trick Chinese Boxes: Hal Porter's Art of Autobiography," *Southerly*, 40, no. 2 (1980): 159–173;

Joseph Jones, "Postwar: The Moderns," in *Australian Fiction*, by Joseph Jones and Johanna Jones (Boston: Twayne, 1983), pp. 87–127;

Megumi Kato, "Australian Literary Images of Japan: A Japanese Perspective," in *Crossing Cultures: Essays on Literature and Culture of the Asia-Pacific*, edited by Bennett (London: Skoob, in association with University College, Australian Defence Force Academy, Canberra, and the Centre for Studies in Australian Literature, University of Western Australia, 1996), pp. 195–203;

Thomas Keneally, "A Novelist Looks at Prose Writing," *Opinion*, 11, no. 2 (1967): 34–40;

Brian Kiernan, "Short Story Chronicle," *Meanjin Quarterly*, 34, no. 1 (1975): 34–39;

Graeme Kinross-Smith, "Hal Porter: A Profile," *Australian Literary Studies*, 7 (1975): 208–212;

Christopher Koch, "In Memoriam: Hal Porter," *Quadrant*, 28, no. 11 (1984): 7–8;

Leonie Kramer, "Modern Australian Prose," *Hemisphere*, 8, no. 2 (1964): 14–17;

Alan Lawson, "'Where a Man Belongs': Hal Porter's *The Paper Chase* and George Johnston's *Clean Straw for Nothing*," in *Studies in the Recent Australian Novel*, edited by Kenneth Gordon Hamilton (St. Lucia:

University of Queensland Press, 1978), pp. 168–193;

Peter Loiterton, "The Australian Short Story: From Federation to Modern Times," *Redoubt,* 18 (1994): 129–133;

Mary Lord, *Hal Porter* (Melbourne & London: Oxford University Press, 1974);

Lord, "Hal Porter's Comic Mode," *Australian Literary Studies,* 4, no. 4 (1970): 371–382;

Brian Matthews, "Ruminating Among Ruins," in his *Romantics and Mavericks: The Australian Short Story* (Townsville, Qld.: James Cook University of North Queensland, Foundation for Australian Literary Studies, 1987), pp. 34–48;

David McCooey, *Artful Histories: Modern Australian Autobiography* (Cambridge: Cambridge University Press, 1996);

McCooey, "Australian Autobiographies of Childhood: Beginning and Myth," *Southerly,* 55, no. 1 (1995): 132–145;

Susan McKernan, "Australian Civilisation?" in *A Question of Commitment: Australian Literature in the Twenty Years After the War* (Sydney: Allen & Unwin, 1989), pp. 209–229;

Patrick Morgan, "Keeping It in the Family," *Quadrant,* 18, no. 3 (1974): 10–20;

David A. Myers, "Perspectives of Contemporary Australian Literature on Culture-Clash Between Australian and the Asia/Pacific Region," in *Australian Literature Today,* edited by R. K. Dhawan & David Kerr (New Delhi: Indian Society for Commonwealth Studies, 1993), pp. 9–39;

Shirley Neuman, "The Observer Observed: Distancing the Self in Autobiography," *Prose Studies,* 4, no. 3 (December 1981): 317–336;

Joan Newman, "The Self Observed: Hal Porter's Australian Autobiography, *The Watcher on the Cast-Iron Balcony,*" *a/b: Auto/Biography Studies,* 8, no. 1 (1993): 91–101;

Annette Onslow, "Hal Porter Revisited," *Aspect,* 5, no. 4 (1981): 83–86;

Porter, "Hal Porter: Introduction," in *Hal Porter,* edited by Lord (St. Lucia: University of Queensland Press, 1980), pp. xiii–xxix;

Vaughan Prain, "Forging Selves and Salvaging Forms: Reading Australian Autobiographical Fiction," *Meridian,* 13, no. 1 (1994): 39–48;

John Martin Douglas Pringle, "Australian Writers in London," *Bulletin,* 29 September 1962, pp. 20, 22;

Leslie Rees, *A History of Australian Drama* (Sydney: Angus & Robertson, 1987);

B. E. Richardson, "Autobiography as a Source of Social History," *Armidale & District Historical Society Journal & Proceedings,* 16 (1973): 42–47;

Patricia Rolfe, "The Middle Age of Innocence," *Bulletin,* 85, 14 December 1963, pp. 35, 37;

Anna Rutherford, "The Cross Tilted to Fall: Hal Porter's *The Tilted Cross,*" in *Commonwealth Literature and the Modern World,* edited by Maes-Jelinek (Brussels: Didier, 1975), pp. 127–135;

Vivian Smith, "A Bit Off the Map," *Island,* 65 (1995/1996): 120–124;

Alrene Sykes, "Three Australian Plays: Introduction," in *Three Australian Plays* (Ringwood, Vic.: Penguin, 1994), pp. 9–23;

Keith Thomas, "Hal Porter's 'Eden,'" *Nation,* 9 August 1969, p. 17;

Chris Wallace-Crabbe, "Ending," in *Falling into Language* (Melbourne: Oxford University Press, 1990), pp. 24–31;

Peter Ward, "The Craft of Hal Porter," *Australian Letters,* 5, no. 2 (1963): 19–25;

Linda Warley, "Locating the Subject of Post-Colonial Autobiography," *Kunapipi,* 15, no. 1 (1993): 23–31;

Gillian Lea Whitlock, "Recent Australian Autobiography: A Review Essay," *Australian Literary Studies,* 15, no. 4 (1992): 261–269;

Richard B. J. Wilson, "Short Story Chronicle: June, 1972," *Meanjin Quarterly,* 31, no. 2 (1972): 220–225;

Fay Zwicky, "The Mother of Narcissus: Autobiographical Reflections in the Work of H. H. Richardson, Hal Porter, Donald Horne and Clive James," *Island,* 18–19 (1984): 66–72.

Papers:

The Mitchell Library in Sydney, New South Wales, holds the most extensive collection of material on and by Hal Porter; the National Library of Australia holds Porter's correspondence with Alan Marshall in their Alan Marshall collection; some material is also held in the State Library of Victoria; some early correspondence by Porter is held in the library of La Trobe University, Melbourne.

Katharine Susannah Prichard
(4 December 1883 – 2 October 1969)

Delys Bird
University of Western Australia

BOOKS: *Cloveily Verses* (London: McAllan, 1913);

The Pioneers (London: Hodder & Stoughton, 1915; New York: Doran, 1915; revised edition, Adelaide: Rigby, 1963);

Windlestraws (London: Holden & Hardingham, 1917);

The New Order (Perth, W.A.: People's Printing and Publishing, 1919);

Black Opal (London: Heinemann, 1921; Sydney: Caslon, 1946);

Working Bullocks (London: Cape, 1926; New York: Viking, 1927; Sydney: Angus & Robertson, 1956);

Brumby Innes (Perth, W.A.: Patersons, 1927?);

The Wild Oats of Han (Sydney: Angus & Robertson, 1928; revised edition, Melbourne: Landsdowne, 1968; New York: Macmillan, 1973);

Coonardoo: The Well in the Shadow (London: Cape, 1929; New York: Norton, 1930; Sydney: Angus & Robertson, 1956);

Haxby's Circus: The Lightest, Brightest Little Show on Earth (London: Cape, 1930); republished as *Fay's Circus* (New York: Norton, 1931); published again as *Haxby's Circus* (Sydney: Angus & Robertson, 1945);

The Earth Lover and Other Verses (Sydney: Sunnybrook, 1932);

Kiss on the Lips and Other Stories (London: Cape, 1932);

The Real Russia (Sydney: Modern, 1934);

War: What For? (Sydney: National Movement against War, ca. 1934);

Who Wants War? (Perth, W.A.: Franklin Press, 1935);

Intimate Strangers (London: Cape, 1937);

The Materialist Conception of History: Address to the Labor Study Circle (Perth, W.A.: Labor Study Circle, 193-?);

Marx, the Man and His Work (Perth, W.A.: Labor Study Circle, 193-?);

Moon of Desire (London: Cape, 1941);

Potch and Colour (Sydney: Angus & Robertson, 1944);

The Roaring Nineties (London: Cape, 1946; Sydney: Australasian, 1946);

Katharine Susannah Prichard
(National Library of Australia)

Golden Miles (London: Cape, 1948; Sydney: Australasian, 1948);

Winged Seeds (London: Cape, 1950; Sydney: Australasian, 1950);

Why I Am a Communist (Sydney: Current Books Distributors, 1950);

N'Goola and Other Stories (Melbourne: Australasian Book Society, 1959);

Child of the Hurricane: An Autobiography (Sydney: Angus & Robertson, 1963);

Happiness: Selected Short Stories (Sydney: Angus & Robertson, 1967);

Moggie and Her Circus Pony (Melbourne: Cheshire, 1967);

Subtle Flame (Sydney: Australasian Book Society, 1967);

Brumby Innes and Bid Me to Love, edited by Katherine Brisbane (Sydney: Currency Methuen Drama, 1974);

Straight Left: Articles and Addresses on Politics, Literature, and Women's Affairs over Almost 60 Years, from 1910–1968, edited by Ric Throssell (Sydney: Wild & Woolley, 1982).

Collections: *On Strenuous Wings: A Half-Century of Selected Writings from the Works of Katharine Susannah Prichard,* edited by Joan Williams (Berlin: Seven Seas Books, 1965);

Tribute: Selected Stories of Katharine Susannah Prichard, edited by Ric Throssell (St. Lucia: University of Queensland Press, 1988);

Katharine Susannah Prichard: Stories, Journalism and Essays, Portable Australian Authors Series, edited by Delys Bird (St. Lucia: University of Queensland Press, 2000).

OTHER: *Pioneers,* in *Best Australian One-Act Plays,* edited by William Moore and T. Inglis Moore (Sydney: Angus & Robertson, 1937);

Australian Writers Speak (Sydney: Angus & Robertson, 1942);

Australian New Writing: Short Stories, Poetry, Criticism, 4 volumes, edited by Prichard, George Farwell, and Bernard Smith (Sydney: Current Book Distributors, 1943–1946);

Thomas S. Wright, *New Deal for the Aborigines,* foreword by Prichard (Sydney: Current Book Distributors, 1944).

Well-known in her lifetime in a range of areas—as a journalist, novelist, short-story writer, and playwright as well as a socialist activist and later as a peace activist—Katharine Susannah Prichard had a reputation in the literary and the political life of Australia. She occupied a prominent place among a group of Australian writers—including Frank Hardy, Dorothy Hewett, and Jean Devanny—who were members of the Communist Party of Australia (CPA). A founding member of the CPA when it was established in 1920, Prichard wrote speeches, statements, pamphlets, and articles on behalf of the party. During her long and active writing life, she became one of the outstanding literary figures of her time, and her contribution to Australian literature is now recognized as a major one. She remained true to the CPA during the Cold War era when many other Australian socialist intellectuals denounced communism, and her work was widely translated, especially in what was then the Soviet Union and the Eastern European bloc countries.

Prichard's passionately held beliefs are all evident in her writing, which is strongly marked by her love of Australia and its landscapes. She remained confident for most of her life that Australia would move toward a socialist future, and much of her fiction is predicated on this kind of utopian nationalism. Prichard was vehemently opposed to racism, war, and all forms of social injustice. Her recognition and denunciation of the effects of colonization on Aboriginal cultures, and her interest in issues to do with women's lives, also inform her work and life. Prichard's journalism was her earliest literary achievement and had a major effect on her fiction, evident in her stress on writing from personal observation and experience, her insistence on realism, and her capacity to capture and reproduce the drama of a moment, a mood, or a character. Her critical and polemical writing illustrates most clearly her view of herself as a Marxist Australian writer and her place in a political history of Australian literature, while her short fiction displays her talents and concerns at their sharpest and finest. Her poetry is slight, and she regarded it as occasional, but she was extremely interested in the literary function and potential of drama as a vehicle for education as well as entertainment and wrote many plays, nearly all of which remain unpublished.

Prichard was born in Levuka, Fiji, on 4 December 1883. She was the oldest of four children of Edith Isabel Fraser and Tom Henry Prichard, a journalist who, at the time of Katharine's birth, was editor of the *Fiji Times.* The title of Prichard's autobiography, *Child of the Hurricane* (1963), reflects her adoption of the local people's belief that she would have a marvelous life since she had survived the great storm that accompanied her birth. The family, which by then included two boys, Alan and Nigel, returned to Melbourne when she was three, and both her Fijian nurse, N'Gardo, and the child felt bereft at this separation. Prichard speculates that there was a causal relationship between the empathy she claimed with Aboriginal people in her adult life and her early upbringing by her devoted black nurse: "maybe N'Gardo is responsible for the instinctive sympathy I've always had for people of the native races. It is, I think, a tribute to that dark, protective presence in my early life." That early life is one Prichard later recalled in idyllic terms.

Tom Prichard became editor of *The Sun,* a weekly Melbourne newspaper, when Katharine was eight, and she began school in Brighton, the Melbourne suburb where the family finally settled. By then her sister, Beatrice, had been born. Subsequently, the family moved to Launceston, Tasmania, where Tom Prichard was editor of *The Daily Telegraph;* some time later he lost his job, and the impoverished family returned to Melbourne. Prichard's fictional account of her childhood,

Prichard and her son, Ric, 1922 (from Marilla North, ed., Yarn Spinners, *2001)*

The Wild Oats of Han (1928), is set in the Launceston landscape, where she and her brothers roamed. Tom Prichard's frequently long periods out of work and his worsening depressive illness had profound economic and emotional effects on his family. However, as a child, Prichard adored and sought to emulate her journalist father, and her early ambition to be a writer seems to have been motivated by her father's writing. She admired him enormously—her later habit of referring to herself as KSP stems from his use of his initials THP in a similar way. Yet, it was her mother who gave her books and encouraged her reading and writing, while her father was merely amused by her first two literary successes—a story written while the family lived in Tasmania, published on the children's page of a Melbourne newspaper, and "That Brown Boy," written after the family returned to Melbourne, which won a guinea in a children's story competition. Not until he was too ill to work and Prichard began writing his weekly political article for *The Mercury* (Hobart) for him did her father recognize her aptitude as a writer.

Prichard's education was erratic: as the eldest child and a daughter, she was expected to stay at home when necessary to help her mother. At fourteen she sat for an entrance examination to South Melbourne College and was offered a half scholarship. The school offered her intellectual stimulation, but before she could sit for her matriculation examination, her mother's illness required Prichard's nursing, and she was unable to qualify for a university scholarship. Prichard subsequently gained her matriculation, but there was no money for a university education for her. While she was encouraged in her intellectual goals, the family's financial circumstances meant that not all the children could be supported at university, and according to the conventions of the time, her brothers were given any available assistance for their education ahead of their sisters.

Prichard nevertheless read widely in philosophy and in English, German, and French classical literature in the original languages and discussed current ideas with her closest friends—Hilda Bull, who married Louis Esson; Nettie Higgins, who married Vance Palmer; and Christian Jollie-Smith—all studying at Melbourne University. In 1903 Prichard won a love-story competition for *The New Idea* (West Melbourne) with "Bush Fires," and this success reinforced her ambition to be a writer. At this time Prichard was employed as a governess, first in South Gippsland, then on a sheep station (ranch) in the far west of New South Wales. She wrote a series of six sketches based on the latter experience, and these were published monthly by *The New Idea* as "Letters from Back o' Beyond" under the general heading of "A City Girl in Central Australia." Each episode consists of a monthly letter from the narrator, "Kit," a young governess on an outback station, to her mother. This early writing and publishing experience had both negative and positive effects for Prichard. The family for whom she worked was offended by her fictionalizing of its experiences, and Prichard later repudiated what she called the sentimental tone of the series. On the other hand, she admired in retrospect what she referred to in *Child of the Hurricane* as her "vivid and realistic" descriptions of station life and the bush. Her view that fiction should always be true to its sources was perhaps initiated through this writing.

Returning to Melbourne, Prichard attended night lectures at Melbourne University. She also joined the Melbourne Literary Society and at one of its meetings was inspired by poet Bernard O'Dowd's address, "Poetry Militant." She wrote later, in "A Stormy Petrel of Australian Poetry" (an undated typescript reprinted in *Straight Left: Articles and Addresses on Politics, Literature, and Women's Affairs over Almost 60 Years, from 1910–1968,* edited by Ric Throssell and published in 1982), that those who heard this lecture "did not realise at the time that this was a statement of historical importance in the development of Australian literature." In this exploration of O'Dowd's talk and his poetry, Prichard moves toward her final statement, that the poet must always "identify himself [sic] with the needs of the people." This concept became one of the ruling principles of her own writing. In another of her several responses to this definitive moment in the establishment of her writer's stance, "A Tribute to the Memory of O'Dowd" (*Meanjin,* 1953), Prichard writes, "I felt my eyes had been opened to what I could do, as a writer, to help relieve the woes of the world." Another major influence at this time came from her meeting a visiting Austrian socialist, journalist, editor, and scholar, Rudolph Broda, who encouraged Prichard to write and published some of her articles in his journal. In 1907 Tom Prichard committed suicide, overwhelming the family with sorrow. Around this time, Prichard wrote her first novel, *The Wild Oats of Han,* an autobiographical work that was not published for another twenty years. It concerns a young girl, Han, her love of the natural world, and her observation of intricate and what are, to her, often puzzling family and social relations.

In 1908 Prichard traveled to London with letters of introduction from Alfred Deakin, the premier of Victoria and a friend of Prichard's family, and a commission from *The Herald* (Melbourne) newspaper to report on the Franco-British Exhibition. During her stay of two years she interviewed major literary figures, including George Meredith, and women in public life, such as Sarah Bernhardt. Already interested in socialism, Prichard was shocked by the sight of the poor of London. Visiting Broda's home in Paris, she met a group of young Russian revolutionaries who inspired her with their communist ideals. On her return to Australia, Prichard was appointed editor of "Women's World," the women's section of *The Herald,* at that time the highest-paid position for a woman journalist on the paper. Between 1912 and 1915 she traveled again, first to Canada and through the United States, where she tried unsuccessfully to place her stories, then to London, where she struggled to gain a reputation and a living from freelance journalism. She joined Mrs. Pankhurst's Women's Social and Political Union and marched for votes for women but withdrew from the Union because she believed in the wider cause of universal adult suffrage. Motivated by the announcement of the Hodder and Stoughton All Empire Novel Competition, she wrote *The Pioneers* (1915). It won the Australian section of the contest and was published by Hodder and Stoughton to some critical acclaim in Britain and Australia. In London she met her future husband, Captain Hugo "Jim" Throssell, a war hero whom she interviewed for one of her newspaper articles.

Prichard was feted by the literary community on her return to Melbourne, where she became involved with Guido Baracchi, a socialist intellectual whom she met on the ship to Australia, and with the work of the Victorian Labour College, inaugurated to educate militant workers. Baracchi joined the group of left-wing intellectuals and writers–including Vance and Nettie Palmer, Frank Wilmot, Hugh McCrae, Henry Tate, Hilda and Louis Esson, and Marie Pitt–who were Prichard's friends. Many of them shared her conviction that Australia would become the first socialist state. Prichard had been actively campaigning against conscription, risking imprisonment and shocking her mother; the death of her brother Alan in the Allied trenches in France in 1917 confirmed her pacifism, and she began speaking in public against war. Her particular understanding of socialism was growing throughout her early adult life. Her first play, "The Burglar," written in 1910, presents socialism as a means of helping the poor and the weak; it was a kind of radical version of late-nineteenth-century female philanthropy. Prichard's socialist politics were always similarly romantic.

The Pioneers presents an equally romanticized version of the life of the pioneers who are its subject. Its indomitable hero overcomes great adversities to establish a family dynasty that exemplifies the spirit of the young nation. Quoted by Sandra Burchill in *The Time to Write: Australian Women Writers 1890–1930* (1993), Prichard acknowledged both the novel's romanticism and its function as a materialist history, a model for the contemporary generation: "I have tried to crystallise my impressions in narrative form, humanising the story with an element of love and romance, and at the same time endeavouring to make young Australia realise

Chapter X.

Heavy timber had accumulated among the back hills where men had been working before Red Burke joined the Six Mile. Red reckoned he needed the big whim and another team of bullocks to shift some of the logs.

"Tell y' what, Red," Peter Moody said when Red told him, "there's Billy Williams and Ern Collins got a nice team and spares, workin' the other side of the mills. But they aren't doin' much. I'll send word they're to go over to you for orders shiftin' timber at the Six Mile."

Billy Williams, the bullocky, and Ern Collins who was swamping for him, turned their team into the yards on the following Monday.

When the team had spelled a day, Red brought the big whim into action. The Marloo, she was called and considered the biggest whim in the southwest. Her wheels stood ten feet high and the tallest man in the country could not touch her arch, standing with arms upstretched beneath it. Red was going to work the Marloo on a tree which had stood two hundred feet to the first branch, and lay awkwardly on a steep hillside. The log would go ninety loads or more, he reckoned and had requisitioned forty bullocks for the job, ten pairs of picked beasts for his own and Billy Williams' teams.

The teams and whim had to break their way through the bush and between trees to where the log had fallen, just over the brow, and sloping down the hill.

While the bullocks spelled out from the whim, Billy Hicks and Ern Collins dug under the log on either side, looking like queer busy beetles beside the great tree, whose crest of sear leaves and broken branches lay scattered for hundreds of yards about them. Billy passed a wire rope under the butt where he had been digging and across the brand of 'Orey Smirke's and Bolshey's initials. Red hooked the bullocks he was going to move the log with into position at the other end of the rope. Ern Collins, winding another wire rope round the butt, threw it out on the opposite side; Billy Williams caught it and hooked on his team.

Page from the revised typescript for Prichard's 1926 novel, Working Bullocks *(National Library of Australia, MS6201/3/2)* how much it owes to the patient, self-denying toil and industry of our pioneers." Written in a mode common to popular novels of the late nineteenth century, in which the often disastrous events of the narrative proceed to a triumphant conclusion, *The Pioneers* celebrates an idealized version of the Australian pioneering spirit, calling on an organicist myth of the natural growth of the new nation as a community of workers, bound together by their stoic pioneering past. This founding myth is the one also celebrated in artist Frederick McCubbin's famous nationalist triptych, also called *The Pioneers*. "The blood of pioneers" that the last sentence of Prichard's novel refers to invigorates not only their grandchildren but also the nation as a whole.

In this novel the narrative movement toward a realization of the ambitions of the pioneers through a new generation, freed from its parents' "birthstain" to create a better society, is contradicted by a nostalgic harking back to the values of the pioneering past. This tension between the desirable, natural values of the pioneers and the potential for their corruption by the commercial values of the emerging industrial society becomes familiar in Prichard's mature work. In *The Pioneers* the conflict is centered on one character and resolved by his removal, so that the ethical and political issues raised by the conflicting ideologies of conservatism and social change are deflected by a literary device. What remains, however, is only an illusion of a socialist version of historical progress.

Windlestraws, a slight, romantic novel, was published in 1917 but had only minor recognition. While Prichard had hoped that writing in a popular romance form would gain the attention of English publishers, she was later embarrassed by *Windlestraws* and largely disowned it. Living at Emerald, in the hills outside Melbourne, in a cottage given to her by her mother from money left by her brother Alan, Prichard began writing *Black Opal* (1921). Based on a small, isolated opal-mining community, the Ridge, in the far west of New South Wales, inspired initially by a visit to just such a community when she was a governess in that area, the novel sets up an opposition similar to the one central to *The Pioneers*. Into a traditional mining community where the workers' harmony is expressed through their manual toil and democratic mateship (male camaraderie) comes an American, John Armitage, who represents the economic values of the new industrialism. These values conflict not only with the traditions of the miners but also with the "Utopian dream" proposed by Michael Brady, a former member of the community who has returned to it to revivify himself and who opposes what he sees as Armitage's alien vision. Again, the forces of industrial progress are pitted against the organicist values of a community of workers in tune with their natural environment. Through the struggle, Prichard is able to articulate the desirability of a static, nature-centered world in which human beings are in accord with one another and to reject the modern, progressive forces of capitalist industrialism. When Armitage is removed from the text, that social system is implicitly dismissed. Those who accepted his ideas face ruin, while those who remained true to the values of the Ridge find a stronger ideological commitment to its way of life.

Prichard sent her massive manuscript to Hodder and Stoughton, who asked for fifty thousand words to be cut and alterations made to the two main characters. Upset with Hodder and Stoughton's demands, Prichard eventually sent the manuscript to Heinemann, who published *Black Opal* in 1921. In 1919 Prichard married Hugo Throssell, who had returned to Australia, and the couple settled in a small cottage at Greenmount, a semirural area on the escarpment some distance outside Perth in Western Australia. Throssell leased land to farm, and Prichard continued to write. She was also politically active. Writing for the communist journal *The Worker,* addressing striking Fremantle wharf laborers, and talking to Anglican synod meetings to discuss workers' grievances made her feel she was "a new champion of the people." According to CPA instructions, Prichard formed labor study circles based on Marxist philosophy for party workers in Perth. Later, she addressed striking timber workers in the southwest of the state. In 1922 Ric, a son and her only child, was born. Prichard's health suffered because of all these demands as well as those of her domestic work, but she felt she had found a "tranquil backwater" in her new environment, which she later referred to as her spiritual home, a place where she could achieve stability and happiness while living an altruistic life.

During those early years in the west, Prichard often traveled with her husband to the eastern wheat belt and the timber country of the lower southwest to gather material for her major novels and stories that she published during the next decade. Later the couple joined the Larkinville gold rush and took up a mining lease, which Throssell worked for awhile. These trips stimulated Prichard, and she described herself as "gorged with stuff to write." From late 1924 Prichard turned from her party activities to concentrate on her fiction writing, and the next decade was a period of intense creative activity, her most prolific. In 1924 "The Grey Horse" won a short-story competition held by the journal *Art in Australia*. It was later included in a 1947 anthology, *World's Greatest Short Stories*. With the publication of *Working Bullocks* (1926), the first of the major works of this period, critics and friends recognized that Prichard's writing had entered a new phase. Nettie Palmer wrote in her notebook: "*Working Bullocks* seems to me different not only in quality but in kind. No one else has written with quite that rhythm, or seen the world in quite that way. The creative lyricism of the style impresses me more than either the theme or the characters." For Palmer it represented a breakthrough that would be "as important for other writers as for KSP herself"–a shift in the national literature. Thirty years later, in his introduction to *N'Goola and Other Stories* (1959), Vance Palmer refers to "the flood of new life Katharine Prichard poured into our writing" and to *Working Bullocks* and *Coonardoo: The Well in the Shadow* (1929) as "a revelation."

Set in the tall timber country of the southwest of Western Australia, *Working Bullocks* opens with a scene Prichard had recorded in her notebook when she visited the karri forests and a timber mill. Bullocks maneuvering the huge logs impressed her as the "most tragic thing in the bush . . . the working bullocks." The novel, which Prichard began writing in 1924, follows the life of one family among a community of timber workers, with Mary Ann Colburn, who "worked like a bullock herself," established as the first of a line of strong, naturally wise, and asexual heroines in Prichard's work. The mother of eighteen children of an improvident father, Mary Colburn lives and voices the values the novel espouses. The family is presented as an ideal, natural community, and commitment to the principles of hard work and the life of the workers based on mutual support is central to it. Deb, the eldest daughter of the family, falls in love with Red Burke, a leading bullock teamster and a type of many of Prichard's male heroes–courageous, lusty, and vital, not always ethical or sober, but irresistibly attractive. Although Deb is for a time drawn to Mark Smith, an experienced political agitator who comes into the community, alerts the timber workers to their rights, and calls a strike, his sexuality is no match for Red's. As the strike collapses, so does Smith's appeal, and at the end of the novel, Deb and Red journey with their bullock team to establish their own life in the forest, breeding and working as the bullocks do.

Jack Lindsay's major Marxist reading of Prichard's work points to what he calls the "dialectical triad of people, work, nature" that emerges in *Working Bullocks* and is central to all of Prichard's mature writing. The encroaching capitalist economy with its alienating work structures threatens this dialectic; yet, paradoxically the rhetoric and ideals of the political activists who encourage the workers to act on behalf of their rights–Michael in *Black Opal,* then Mark in *Working Bullocks*–are not effective in reproducing that threefold process. Other critics found the style of the novel similar to D. H. Lawrence's. Prichard had read Lawrence's *Sons and Lovers* when it was published in 1913, and it

Dust jacket for Prichard's novel about a family of timber workers in Western Australia (from Bruce Bennett, ed., The Literature of Western Australia, *1979)*

was a revelation to her. She was later disappointed by *Kangaroo* (1923) and denied that Lawrence influenced her work. However, in much of her important early but mature work there are suggestive stylistic comparisons between the two. Throughout *Working Bullocks* the natural world is used to represent human emotions and desires: women and men labor like animals; Deb's sexuality is rendered in descriptions of aspects of nature– for example, storms and wind in huge trees–and Red's masculinity is linked to the strength of the bullocks; the communities of family and workers are represented as organic structures.

Until the mid 1930s, Prichard's fiction gained much of its narrative power from the tension achieved as she wrote within a realist tradition and at the same time drew on a romantic, poetic tradition. Undercurrents of sexual and emotional life run through many of the stories and are conveyed in descriptions of the natural and animal world, most strikingly in "The Cow" (*New Triad,* 1928) and "The Grey Horse" (*Art in Austra-*

lia, 1924). The latter story uses a modernist style and is Lawrentian in many of its aspects. "The Curse," published in 1926, is deliberately experimental. Prichard's reading, in 1924, of Carl Jung's *Psychology of the Unconscious* (1912) was significant for her, and its effects are evident in the work of this period. She called it an "extraordinary illuminating contribution to the vexed question," which is always, however, subjected to narrative exploration at the same time through a realist, materialist base.

Late in 1926, intrigued by a story she had heard of an Aboriginal woman working as a drover, Prichard spent more than two months at Turee Station in the northwest of Western Australia. There she gained firsthand knowledge of station life and of the Aboriginal people of the area. This experience generated some of her most important work, all written shortly after her return. The novella *Coonardoo* is the best known of these works and the last to be written. Prichard took only three months in early 1928 to finish the manuscript for *The Bulletin* (Sydney) novel competition of that year. It offered a prize of £100 and subsequent publication for the best novel manuscript submitted. *Coonardoo* shared first prize out of around 540 entries with *A House Is Built* (1929) by Barnard Eldershaw, the pen name of writers Marjorie Barnard and Flora Eldershaw. That this prize was shared among three women indicates the emerging importance of women's writing during this period. When the winners were announced, the chairman of the judging panel, T. B. Clegg, commented in *The Bulletin* (1928): "A notable feature in the competition was the great number of women who contributed novels, particularly upon sex questions." In her study of women writers of the 1930s and 1940s, *Exiles at Home: Australian Women Writers 1925-1945* (1981), Drusilla Modjeska recognizes that women "were writing and publishing in large numbers in the thirties and they were able to give each other comfort and support. They were politically active, they were often angry and they made sure their presence was felt as writers and as women." Australian publishers could not be found for either *Coonardoo* or *A House Is Built* in spite of the prize, but both novels were published in England the following year. Their difficulty typifies a pattern of the period: the writers most concerned to establish and consolidate a serious national literature were precisely those who had the most trouble getting their work published at home.

In particular, the topic of *Coonardoo*, the story of an Aboriginal woman of that name—one of a group of indigenous people living in close proximity to the station homestead of Bessie Watt and her son Hugh—and of the relationship between Hugh and Coonardoo, was not acceptable to Australian publishers. When *The Bulletin* declined to serialize Vance Palmer's novel, *Some Men Are Human* (1930), which was awarded third prize in *The Bulletin* competition the year *Coonardoo* and *A House Is Built* won and which treats the subject of interracial sexual relations, he was advised by *The Bulletin* that race was the problem: "the disastrous experience with *Coonardoo* shows us that the Australian public will not stand stories based on a white man's relations with an Aborigine." Although the contemporary reception of *Coonardoo* was often hostile as well as admiring, and the critical commentary on the novel since its publication has been divided about its representation of issues of race and gender, it was among the earliest Australian fiction works to raise debate on race relations. Prichard was both scrupulous and respectful in her depiction of Aboriginal life and culture and progressive in her attempt to represent that life in her fiction from the perspective of the people themselves. She sought advice on indigenous issues from Ernest Mitchell, who had been the so-called Protector of the Aborigines in Western Australia, read anthropological texts, and learned Aboriginal languages; moreover, *Coonardoo* is published with a glossary of Aboriginal words used in the text. As Susan Sheridan argues in "*Coonardoo*: A 1988 Reading of a 1928 Novel," published in *Blast* (1988): "What distinguishes this novel in literary terms is Prichard's attempt to represent Coonardoo's point of view from time to time, and to present it as specifically Aboriginal, by inscribing the culture's language and practices as a valid and coherent perspective." But she also argues that Coonardoo is constructed and her fate determined by white male desire.

The narrative structure of *Coonardoo* is tragic; it begins with the child living an idyllic life with her people on the Watt station, Wytaliba, growing up with Hugh Watt and encouraged by his mother to think of herself as his natural protector and companion but always in the relation of master and servant. Coonardoo gives birth to their son, Winni, but Hugh is unable to acknowledge his feeling for her and marries a white woman. The relationship between Hugh and Coonardoo is brought under increasing stress; the prosperity of the station decreases; and the Aboriginal community is fractured. Raped by Sam Geary, a neighbor, then terribly abused by Hugh Watt, Coonardoo—the "well in the shadows" whose life inspirits the land—becomes an outcast; the station land falls into disrepair; and the Aboriginal people are dispersed. She returns, tragically ill and alone, to die, and the final image of the novel is of Coonardoo: "Her arms and legs, falling apart, looked like those blackened and broken sticks beside the fire." This romanticism undercuts the depiction in the novel of colonial dispossession of the indigenous people and despoliation of their land, and its attempt to

*Prichard's cottage at Greenmount, Western Australia
(from Marilla North, ed.,* Yarn Spinners, *2001)*

uncover the politics of miscegenation. Typically, the union of Phyllis Watt, Hugh's daughter, and Bill Gale, a drover who will inherit Sam Geary's station, promises a different, optimistic future, but this future is white.

Two stories written and published in *The Bulletin* in 1927, "Happiness" and "The Cooboo," are significant in Prichard's output and part of the work generated by the trip to Turee. Aboriginal women in the stories are presented, as Coonardoo is, as figures of the essential woman, silent and strong with an instinctive understanding of the connections between human and natural life. "The Cooboo" has become one of Prichard's best-known stories and is based on Prichard's hearing of the Aboriginal woman mustering (counting cattle) with her baby, her cooboo, tied around her body. The spare prose style and use of suggestion rather than statement to convey situation and character in "The Cooboo" indicate Prichard's strengths as a short-story writer. "Happiness" sets up the situation later explored more deeply in *Coonardoo,* and the story is narrated through the perspective of Nardadu, expressed in the rhythms of her language and thought.

Prichard's play *Brumby Innes,* also written at this time, won the 1927 national Triad three-act-play competition, which promised a full professional production of the winning play. However, *Brumby Innes* was not performed until 1972, after Prichard's death. Margaret Williams, in "Natural Sexuality: Katharine Susannah Prichard's *Brumby Innes,*" published in *Meanjin Quarterly* (1973), calls it the "unperformed 'classic' of the outback drama of the first half of this century" and speculates that its "ruthlessly honest depiction of the white man's callousness and sexual exploitation of the Aboriginals was too dangerous for a commercial management to touch." The play begins with a corroboree and, like *Coonardoo,* attempts to engage with a portrayal of Aboriginal life. Its central character, Brumby Innes, is a swaggering drunk who exploits the black workers on his station and abuses the women; he bears a close resemblance to Sam Geary in *Coonardoo.* Yet, Brumby Innes provides the central energy of the drama, and the celebration of that energy in the play conflicts with the dramatic critique of his sexism and racism. Brumby Innes's character exemplifies the ambivalent attitude in Prichard's work toward this type of male hero. Portrayed as stereotypically masculine, such characters are admired for their energetic, vital sexuality; yet, the extreme limitations of such maleness are also acknowledged.

When Prichard sent her next novel, *Haxby's Circus: The Lightest, Brightest Little Show on Earth* (1930; published in the United States as *Fay's Circus*) to Jonathan Cape in 1929, the publisher hoped it would counteract their lack of success with *Coonardoo*: "The book has some staunch admirers, but generally we find that the public are shy of it because of its subject." *Haxby's Circus* was prompted by an incident in which a circus rider with a broken back was brought to Prichard's brother Nigel's country surgery in Victoria for treatment. Years later, when a circus came to Perth, Prichard traveled with it through the country for some weeks. This experience gave her the background for the novel, which remains something of an anomaly in her work, lacking the political dimension so central to her other novels. In it, the central character, Gina Haxby, falls during her bareback act and breaks her back. Gina's painful determination to rebuild her life becomes a metaphor for the struggle of all disenfranchised workers, and her final adoption of an identity as the clown whose act saves the circus teaches the bitter necessity of adaptation to circumstances.

The years of the Great Depression had a major effect on Prichard's family. Hugo Throssell was out of work, deeply in debt, and depressed. Prichard was "worn to frazzles," she wrote to Nettie Palmer in 1931, by domestic work and trying to make money from her writing, while she was also involved in organizing the unemployed. In a letter to Hilda Esson, Prichard commented, "I begin to feel pot-bound in this damned bourgeois environment. There isn't anything worth working for except communism, I'm sure." This was the context in which she wrote her next major novel, *Intimate Strangers* (1937). It takes up the modernist techniques of symbolic prose, indirect narration, and the depiction of the inner life of characters that Prichard had been developing, especially in *Coonardoo* and the short stories. Writing to Nettie Palmer in 1931, Prichard said, "my next novel, started about two years ago, & set on the coast here, is in the freer 'modern' method too. 'Intimate Strangers' to be called." For the first time, Prichard wrote from her life situation, and although she always denied the novel was autobiographical, its setting, characters, and incidents are close to her own. A domestic drama, its central focus is the middle-class marriage of Greg and Elodie Blackwood during the Depression. Elodie's career as a pianist has been diminished to giving music lessons and playing for small evening events, and Greg, a returned soldier and an accountant, loses his job. The couple also have two young children. The breakdown of the marriage is explored against this background, charting the couple's gradual disaffection. Each is in love with someone else. Elodie is seduced by Jerome, a wanderer who wants her to sail away with him, and Greg lusts after Dirk, a beautiful young woman who repulses his passion. The exploration in the novel of the complexities of emotional life as well as the industrial, class, and social issues raised by the Depression—exemplified both by Greg's situation and that of the unemployed wharf laborers and their families—is compelling. As always, the intersections between the social, the political, and the personal are central to the narrative, and Tony Maretti, a fisherman who questions the injustices of the capitalist system and preaches the necessity for socialist change, is a powerful voice in this novel. Although its critical history has been overshadowed by the controversy of its publishing history, *Intimate Strangers* should be accorded as significant a place in Prichard's oeuvre as *Coonardoo* has.

In mid 1933 Prichard left Perth to travel overseas with her sister, who paid her fare to London, Paris, and the Soviet Union, where she was feted as an important socialist writer. She left a draft of *Intimate Strangers* in her Greenmount workroom. Before she returned, her husband committed suicide, and she was always haunted by the possibility that he had read the manuscript of the novel, in which in that early version the failed husband takes his own life. After her husband's death, Prichard devoted herself to CPA work and to activities on behalf of world peace; she was one of the founders of the Movement against War and Fascism and in 1934 traveled to Melbourne with her young son to take part in a national Anti-War Congress. When the Spanish Civil War began in 1936, she was in the forefront of action on behalf of a Spanish Republic. She struggled over these years to clear her husband's debts, living on his meager war pension and making a little money from publishing short stories. Like those of many contemporary Australian writers, Prichard's royalties were pitifully small, and her income from her writing was rarely above a subsistence level. These years form a kind of hiatus in Prichard's writing history, during which she had no major piece of work on hand. When she returned to *Intimate Strangers* in 1938, she rewrote the ending so that Greg and Elodie find new happiness by dedicating themselves to a higher good—working for a socialist future. "We'll have something bigger than ourselves to work for," Elodie tells Greg. Despite this unconvincing, but for Prichard typically apocalyptic ending, her publisher, Jonathan Cape, was pleased with the novel. Prichard, however, always regarded it as a failure.

An outcome of her trip to Russia was her book *The Real Russia* (1934), a series of essays describing her experiences there, her meetings with Soviet writers and officials as well as with ordinary working people, and her sometimes naive admiration for everything she claimed Russian culture represented. Prichard was impressed with the close relationship between workers and writers in the Soviet Union and the ways literature informed the life of the people. She accepted wholeheartedly the emergent Soviet theory of socialist realism. The tension between a kind of materialist realism and a kind of romantic utopianism that had characterized her work until that time now disappeared, and her fiction from that time on adhered to the theory and practice of socialist realism. She began writing her most ambitious work, the "goldfields trilogy," from this standpoint. Before beginning the trilogy, Prichard wrote a slight romantic fiction, *Moon of Desire* (1941). A much earlier trip to Broome, which she found exotic, had given her the background for this novel. Hoping it would sell well—it did not—and relieve her financial worries, Prichard later described it as a rotten book. In order to support the vast undertaking of the trilogy, Prichard applied for and won a Commonwealth Grant in 1941 and for the first time enjoyed government support for her writing.

Set in Kalgoorlie in Western Australia, the goldfields trilogy deals with the discovery of gold in the area and the establishment and development of a gold-mining industry. *The Roaring Nineties* (1946) concerns the prospecting that pioneered the goldfields; *Golden Miles* (1948) deals with the consolidation of the mines with the introduction of large-scale capital and the shift for workers from the independence of prospecting to the restrictions of waged work, and *Winged Seeds* (1950) delineates the triumph of capital over labor in the industry. *Golden Miles* and *Winged Seeds* are punctuated by the incursion into this community of the events of World War I and World War II. This fictional working-class Australian history follows the fortunes of the Gough family. Sally Gough is the female pioneer who provides narrative continuity throughout the three novels, while her husband, her sons, and their wives, then their children experience the class and industrial struggles, the greed for gold, and the dignity of work that characterize life on the goldfields in Prichard's works. Sally's character provides a moral as well as domestic center for the trilogy, and through her the themes of the work are explored. Her struggle for an independent working life is that of the miners; her passion, which is not satisfied in her marriage and is diverted to working-class politics, is one that the generations of miners use to resist the power of national and international industrial capital in the mining industry. An Aboriginal woman, Kalgoorla, has a primary symbolic importance in the trilogy. The first novel of the trilogy opens with a kind of prologue, Kalgoorla's memory of the coming of white men seeking gold, their violence, and the resulting dispossession

Advertisement for the 1972 premiere of the play for which Prichard won the 1927 national Triad three-act-play competition; it was never produced in her lifetime (Australian Performing Group Collection, University of Melbourne Archives)

of her people; the novel closes with her death, but there is no attempt in this work, as there was in *Coonardoo,* to give Aboriginal people a voice.

Dinny Quinn, close friend of the Goughs and one of the original prospectors who likes nothing better than yarning about the old days, initiates the narrative, and it often calls on his yarns for explanation of and background to the action of the narrative. Together with Sally Gough's reminiscences, which act in the same way, these stories celebrate the achievements of the prospectors who pioneered the goldfields and the communal aspirations of the working miners who followed them. This retrospective narration allows for a sense of history and recognizes the complex perspectives that might be brought to it as well as the notion of a shift to a new order hostile to the values of the past—one that has to be dealt with in the present, not through sentimental harking back to those values. *Golden Miles* takes up the story of *The Roaring Nineties*. Again, events are related retrospectively, but there is a sense in this novel of the inexorable power of organized capital and of the oppressive nature of the miners' work under the demands of that capital. Tom Gough undertakes his decision to fight the system both in relation to his experience of that oppression and as a nostalgic apprehension of a better way of life in the past. However, the value of yarning and reminiscing, which still take place on the Goughs' veranda in this novel, seems increasingly irrelevant to the contemporary class struggle, which demands a scientific—that is, a theoretical—understanding of capitalism. In *Winged Seeds,* the final volume in the trilogy, Bill Gough takes up the fight for workers' rights. The political issues in this novel are international ones and contemporary to the debates about fascism before the outbreak of the war and the need for revolutionary action against the politics of the Cold War. The values of the past represented by Quinn and his mates are marginalized, but the disregard of the wisdom of the past is not necessarily viewed as positive. In many ways the narrative brings present and past into a relation in which their differences are questioned, and the values of the past formed in the struggles for survival endured by the pioneers are seen as more real. There is a splitting of the next generation between capital and labor. Tom's son, Dick, eventually aligns himself with the wealth and power of the mine owners, while his daughter, Daphne, after some wavering, declares her commitment to the workers' cause.

Although many critics read the trilogy as an unwieldy mass of historical detail peppered with socialist dictums, marking a stage in Prichard's declining career, others regarded it as she did, as her most important work, with *Winged Seeds* as its culmination. On 11 November 1946 Prichard wrote to American critic Hartley Grattan: it "more nearly accomplishes what I have wanted to do than anything else I have written." Prichard's last novel, *Subtle Flame* (1967) is overlong, preachily didactic, and turgidly romantic; she had trouble finding a publisher for it. It was, however, written when she was suffering extreme ill health, only a few years before her death. During the 1940s and 1950s, as Cold War politics were adopted in Australia, Prichard was often subjected to government harassment as a communist. She never wavered in her commitment to her political ideals, however, publicly endorsing, for example, the invasion of Czechoslovakia by Russia, and while the invasion of Hungary caused her some doubt, this initial reaction was quickly dispelled. As most of her friends and political colleagues left the Communist Party during the 1950s, she wrote to Stephen Murray Smith, then editor of *Overland,* in 1958 of her anger and disappointment at what she saw as defections: "Needless to say I am deeply grieved. . . . I can't believe that it is right to let anything interfere with allegiance to Party principles . . . the future of the world depends on the effective implementation of that theory and practice." Prichard's work often earned her more in foreign royalties than in local ones, and she was widely known and respected among Soviet writers and readers.

Prichard always believed in the political function of art and its capacity to become a center of struggle. All of her major fiction is engaged in that struggle. Her literary mentors—such as Henry Lawson, Joseph Furphy, Bernard O'Dowd, Furnley Maurice in Australia; principally Maksim Gorky, among international writers, as well as Guy de Maupassant, Anatole France, Honoré de Balzac, Victor Hugo, and later, Anton Chekov—were also for her engaged in just such a struggle. Although Prichard's zealous adoption of the philosophy of socialist realism perhaps delimited the possibilities of her adoption of the "freer, 'modern' method" that marked *Intimate Strangers* and the work leading up to it, her writing—novels, short stories, essays, and plays—represents a major contribution to Australian literature and to the construction of an Australian literary tradition. Prichard devoted herself to her ideal of an Australian literary nationalism, which she identified according to the Furphy/Lawson mode as realist and democratic. She wished in her fiction, she said, "to glean the living speech of our people": she was also impelled by a desire to "bring the colour into our work" in contrast to what she saw as the monochromatic writing of Lawson and others. Her recognition, late in her life, that the literary values and the nationalist ideals she cherished and believed would build the socialist future she envisaged for Australia were no longer dominant, was poignant. In a eulogy, "Excess of Love" (*Overland,* 1969–70), Dorothy Hewett, a close friend and a younger communist writer, remembers Prichard in 1964 standing on the loggia of her Greenmount home, holding a new book of contemporary Australian short fiction in her hand, and saying "My Australia is gone forever now." Katharine Susannah Prichard died in Perth, Western Australia, on 2 October 1969. Her Australia remains in her writing.

Letters:

Carole Ferrier, ed., *As Good as a Yarn with You: Letters Between Miles Franklin, Katharine Susannah Prichard, Jean Devanney, Marjorie Barnard, Flora Eldershaw and Eleanor Dark* (Oakleigh, Vic.: Cambridge University Press, 1992).

Biography:

Ric Throssell, *Wild Weeds and Wind Flowers: The Life and Letters of Katharine Susannah Prichard* (Sydney: Angus & Robertson, 1975).

References:

Marjorie Barnard and Flora Eldershaw, *Essays in Australian Fiction* (Melbourne: Melbourne University Press/Oxford University Press, 1938);

Jack Beasley, "My Unilateral Debate: Katharine Susannah Prichard. Rebel Heroes and Matters Pertaining," *Australian Literary Studies*, 11 (1983): 146–155;

Beasley, *The Rage for Life: The Work of Katharine Susannah Prichard* (Sydney: Current Book Distributors, 1964);

Bruce Bennett, "The Mask beyond the Mask: Katharine Susannah Prichard," *Meanjin Quarterly*, 3 (1976): 325–329;

Delys Bird, *Katharine Susannah Prichard: Stories, Journalism and Essays* (St. Lucia: University of Queensland Press, 2000);

Veronica Brady, "Katherine [sic] Susannah Prichard and the Tyranny of History: *Intimate Strangers*," *Westerly*, 26 (1981): 65–71;

Pat Buckridge, "Katharine Susannah Prichard and the Literary Dynamics of Political Commitment," in *Gender, Politics and Fiction*, edited by Carole Ferrier (St. Lucia: University of Queensland Press, 1985), pp. 85–100;

Sandra Burchill, "The Early Years of Katharine Susannah Prichard: The Growth of her Political Conscience," *Westerly*, 33 (1988): 89–100;

Burchill, "Katharine Susannah Prichard: She Did What She Could," in *The Time to Write: Australian Women Writers 1890–1930*, edited by Kay Ferres (Ringwood, Vic.: Penguin, 1993), pp. 139–161;

Leigh Dale, "*Coonardoo* and Truth," in *Tilting at Matilda: Literature, Aborigines, Women and the Church in Contemporary Australia*, edited by Dennis Haskell (Fremantle: Fremantle Arts Centre Press, 1994), pp. 129–140;

Brenton Doecke, "Australian Historical Fiction and the Popular Front: Katharine Susannah Prichard's Goldfields Trilogy," *Westerly*, 39 (1994): 25–36;

H. Drake-Brockman, *Katharine Susannah Prichard* (Melbourne: Oxford University Press, 1967);

Ferrier, "Jean Devanny, Katharine Susannah Prichard and the 'Really Proletarian Novel,'" in *Gender, Politics and Fiction*, pp. 101–117;

Van Ikin, "The Political Novels of Katharine Susannah Prichard 1: The Metaphysical Perspective: *The [sic] Black Opal* and *Working Bullocks*," *Southerly*, 43, no. 1 (1983): 80–102;

Ikin, "The Political Novels of Katharine Susannah Prichard 2: The Nature of Man: *Coonardoo* and *Intimate Strangers*," *Southerly*, 43, no. 2 (1983): 203–226;

Ikin, "The Political Novels of Katharine Susannah Prichard 3: The Surrender to Ideology: The Goldfields Trilogy and *Subtle Flame*," *Southerly*, 43, no. 3 (1983): 296–312;

Kay Iseman [Schaffer], "Katharine Susannah Prichard: Of an End a New Beginning," *Arena*, 54 (1979): 70–96;

Susan Lever, "Aboriginal Subjectivity and Western Conventions: A Reading of *Coonardoo*," *Australian and New Zealand Studies in Canada*, 10 (1993): 23–29;

Jack Lindsay, "The Novels of Katharine Susannah Prichard," *Meanjin Quarterly*, 20 (1961): 366–387;

Drusilla Modjeska, "The Platform and the Writer's Desk," in her *Exiles at Home: Australian Women Writers 1925–1945* (Sydney: Sirius Books, 1981), pp. 117–155;

Ruth Morse, "Impossible Dreams: Miscegenation and Building Nations," *Southerly*, 48 (1988): 80–96;

Overland, special Prichard issue, 12 (1958);

Kay Schaffer, "Critical Dilemmas: Looking for Katharine Susannah Prichard," *Hecate*, 10 (1984): 45–52;

Susan Sheridan, "*Coonardoo*. A 1988 Reading of a 1928 Novel," *Blast*, 6–7 (1988): 3–6;

Joan Williams, "Rage That Engenders: The Last Decade of Katharine Susannah Prichard," *Southerly*, 31 (1972): 17–29;

Margaret Williams, "Natural Sexuality: Katharine Susannah Prichard's *Brumby Innes*," *Meanjin Quarterly*, 32 (1973): 91–93.

Papers:

The major collection of Katharine Susannah Prichard's papers is held at the National Library of Australia, Canberra. Some letters are held in the Miles Franklin Papers in the Mitchell Library, Sydney; the Dorothy Hewett Papers in the National Library of Australia, Canberra; and the Nettie and Vance Palmer Papers in the National Library of Australia, Canberra.

Kenneth Slessor

(27 March 1901 – 30 June 1971)

Adrian Caesar
University College of New South Wales
Australian Defence Force Academy

BOOKS: *Thief of the Moon* (Sydney: Kirtley, 1924);

Earth Visitors (London: Fanfrolico Press, 1926);

Trio, by Slessor, Harley Matthews, and Colin Simpson (Sydney: Sunnybrook, 1931);

Surf: All About It (Sydney: Mortons, 1931?);

Cuckooz Contrey (Sydney: Frank Johnson, 1932);

Darlinghurst Nights and Morning Glories: Being 47 Strange Sights Observed from Eleventh Storeys, in a Land of Cream Puffs and Crime, by a Flat-Roof Professor (Sydney: Frank Johnson, 1933);

Funny Farmyard (Sydney: Frank Johnson, 1933);

Five Bells: XX Poems (Sydney: Frank Johnson, 1939);

One Hundred Poems, 1919–1939 (Sydney & London: Angus & Robertson, 1944); revised and enlarged as *Poems* (Sydney: Angus & Robertson, 1957);

Portrait of Sydney, edited by Gwen Morton Spencer and Sam Ure Smith (Sydney: Ure Smith, 1950);

Australian Profile (Canberra: Department of Trade, 1960);

The Grapes Are Growing: The Story of Australian Wine (Sydney: Australian Wine Board, 1963; revised, 1965);

Life at the Cross (Adelaide: Rigby, 1965);

Sydney Harbour (Sydney: Angus & Robertson, 1966);

Canberra (Adelaide: Rigby, 1966);

Bread and Wine: Selected Prose (Sydney: Angus & Robertson, 1970);

Selected Poems (London & Sydney: Angus & Robertson, 1975);

Backless Betty from Bondi, edited by Julian Croft (Sydney: Angus & Robertson, 1983);

The War Diaries of Kenneth Slessor, Official Australian Correspondent, 1940–1944, edited by Clement Semmler (St. Lucia: University of Queensland Press, 1985);

The War Despatches of Kenneth Slessor, Official Australian Correspondent, 1940–1944, edited by Semmler (St. Lucia: University of Queensland Press, 1987);

Kenneth Slessor: Poetry, Essays, War Despatches, War Diaries, Journalism, Autobiographical Material, and Letters,

Kenneth Slessor, 1940 (from Clement Semmler, ed., The War Diaries of Kenneth Slessor, *1985)*

edited by Dennis Haskell (St. Lucia: University of Queensland Press, 1991);

Collected Poems, edited by Haskell and Geoffrey Dutton (Sydney: Angus & Robertson, 1994).

OTHER: *Poetry in Australia 1923,* edited by Slessor and J. Lindsay (Sydney: Vision, 1923);

Australian Poetry 1945, edited by Slessor (Sydney: Angus & Robertson, 1945);

Penguin Book of Australian Verse, edited by Slessor, John Thomson, and R. G. Howarth (Ringwood, Vic.: Penguin, 1958).

PERIODICALS EDITED: *Vision: A Literary Quarterly,* nos. 1–4, edited with J. Lindsay and Frank Johnson (May 1923–February 1924);
Australian Outline, nos. 1 and 2 (1933, 1934);
Southerly, no. 2 (1956) – no. 4 (1961).

Despite his relatively small oeuvre, Kenneth Slessor is one of the most celebrated of Australian poets. Until the posthumous publication of *Collected Poems* in 1994, Slessor's reputation rested upon the 103 poems that constitute the much reprinted *Selected Poems* (1975), of which 100 were written by 1939. Sometimes credited with introducing modernism into Australian verse, Slessor continues to be lauded by both experimentalists and traditionalists alike. If Slessor may be said to have a relationship to modernism, it is through the temper of his work rather than its form, for his formal experimentation did not extend far, and certainly Slessor was no believer in aesthetic revolution.

Slessor was born Kenneth Adolphe Schloesser on 27 March 1901 in the small country town of Orange in New South Wales. His father, Robert, was a mining engineer who was born in London, educated in Europe, and immigrated to Australia in 1888. Robert Schloesser met and married Margaret McInnes, the daughter of a storekeeper, when he was working on the Lucknow mines near Orange. At the time, Margaret was working as a teacher at the local school. Perhaps some shared intellectual interests brought the couple together, for otherwise they seem an unlikely match. Robert came from German Jewish stock, and his immediate forebears were distinguished musicians and intellectuals of the European tradition, whereas Margaret's background was Scottish Presbyterian and could boast little, as far as is known, of distinction. Her parents came from the Hebridean Isle of Uist, where most livelihoods were gained from crofting and fishing. Margaret's father had, however, entered the respectable middle classes in Orange through his business activities and his prominent role in local affairs; he was an alderman and, later, mayor of the district. Perhaps the most influential aspects of this diverse inheritance for Slessor were his father's intensely serious philosophical speculations and intellectual polymathy together with his mother's strict and rather forbidding Presbyterianism.

Slessor's early childhood was peripatetic. The family moved to Melbourne in 1903 and spent a year in England in 1908. They then went to Sydney, first to the suburb of Kogarah and later, in 1910, to Chatswood. Slessor attended Kogarah Public School followed by a prep school that later became Mowbray House School. At this latter establishment, an enthusiastic and talented master, F. G. Phillips, introduced him to the Romantic poets—William Wordsworth; Samuel Taylor Coleridge; George Gordon, Lord Byron; John Keats; and Percy Bysshe Shelley. On the outbreak of World War I in 1914, the Schloessers changed their surname to Slessor in order to avoid the opprobrium unfairly meted out to anyone or anything with German connections. This time must have been difficult for the thirteen-year-old Kenneth. Having been brought up in a household in which French was sometimes spoken at the table and European traditions were clearly extolled, suddenly a forceful induction into Anglo-Australian mores was implied. Around this time Slessor's identity and interests began to suffer a schism that lasted a lifetime. His life and work reveal a conflict between an allegiance to aristocratic ideas of art derived from the Romantic and symbolist traditions of Europe and more conservative, populist affiliations in keeping with Australian modes and manners.

From 1915 to 1918 Slessor attended Sydney Church of England Grammar School (Shore); while attending this school he composed his first two published poems, "Goin'" (*The Bulletin,* 1917) and "France" (*The Bulletin,* 1918); a third, "Jerusalem Set Free," won a Commonwealth prize for schoolboy poetry. All three of these poems were conventional exercises in patriotic war poetry that drew on the burgeoning myth of Anzac for their inspiration. He employed a sentimental masculine vernacular learned from Rudyard Kipling and C. J. Dennis to celebrate heroic Australian manhood. Slessor later came to despise Dennis in particular and vernacular poetry in general, but he continued to write popular light verse for much of his life, and he vigorously supported the myth of the "Digger" in his later journalism.

Slessor left school in 1918 to pursue a career as a journalist. He spent 1919 learning shorthand at a business college before joining the staff of *The Sun* (Sydney) newspaper in 1920. At the same time Slessor continued to write and publish poetry in such magazines and papers as *The Bulletin* (Sydney), *The Triad,* and *Smith's Weekly* (Sydney). Already in some of these poems, which might be thought of as juvenilia, Slessor writes about the great conflicts between Nature and Art and between Beauty and Time, and he attempts to apply these concerns inherited from the European Romantic-symbolist tradition to specifically Australian circumstances and locations. Poems such as "The Uncharted" (1919), "In Tyrell's Bookshop" (1920), and "To a Forgotten Portrait" (1919) thus prefigure his more mature "serious" work—as opposed to his "light" verse—and the themes and concerns to which he obsessively returned throughout his works. In these early poems he already

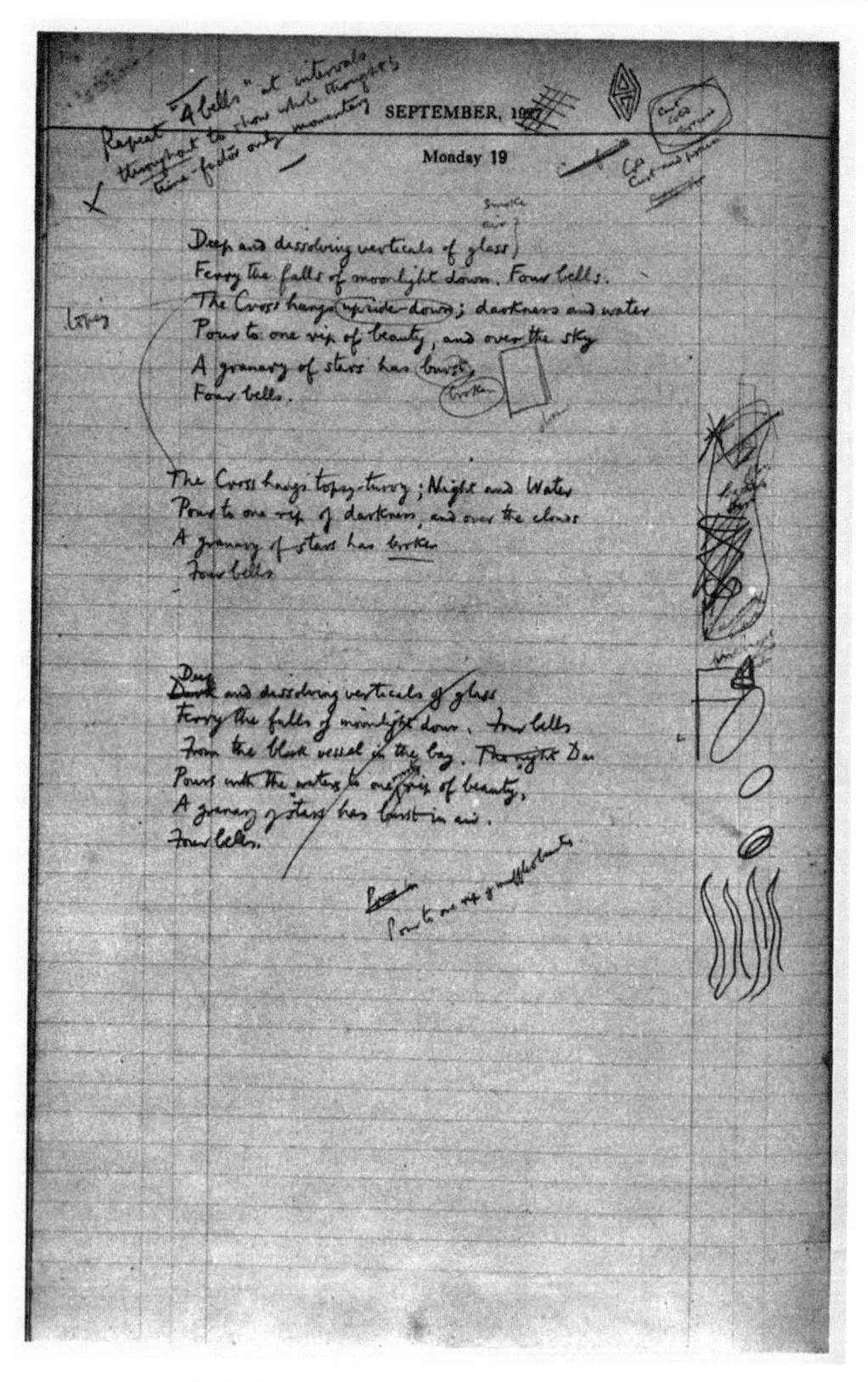

Notes for Slessor's best-known poem, "Five Bells" (National Library of Australia)

reveals a taste for the exotic and ornamental, a delight in shimmering surfaces, and a verbal exuberance that sees itself pitted against Time and Nature. Death, the dark shadow that haunts all Slessor's poetry, is already found in the young poet's lines.

Between 1920 and 1926 Slessor developed his career as a journalist–first with *The Sun,* then between 1924 and the end of 1925 with the Melbourne *Punch.* When the latter closed down, Slessor worked on the *Herald* (Melbourne) for a time before returning to Sydney and *The Sun.* In 1920, to his mother's dismay, Slessor moved out of the family home and into a flat. He caused further consternation two years later when at the age of twenty-one he married Noela Senior, who was only sixteen at the time. Noela was young, Roman Catholic, and had a family connection with a lurid past–her mother's first husband had committed a grisly murder in Orange while Slessor's mother was still living there. Margaret Slessor declared to her son that she would never acknowledge his wife. A breach began in the relations between Slessor and his family that lasted until 1927. Margaret Slessor was never entirely reconciled to Slessor's choice of a bride.

At the same time, Slessor continued to write the poems that appeared in his first two volumes, *Thief of the Moon* (1924) and *Earth Visitors* (1926). The contrast between his journalistic work and his serious poetry is striking. The newspapers he worked for were popular and kept discussion of major issues to a minimum; they were designed to entertain as much as to enlighten. Slessor's poetry and poetics, on the other hand, became increasingly aristocratic in orientation. The influences on his poetry were many, but all were related to the Romantic-symbolist heritage. From the English tradition were Coleridge, Alfred Tennyson, A. C. Swinburne, and James Elroy Flecker. Although Slessor never spoke of the French poets who had an impact on him, it is likely that both the *Symbolistes* and their immediate predecessors, the Parnassians, exerted some influence. Of the latter, Charles-Marie René Leconte de Lisle has several features in common with Slessor's early work–a belief in art for art's sake, a concern for technical perfection, an unwillingness to divulge personal feeling, and a Romanticized Hellenism. Paul Verlaine and Charles Baudelaire may also have contributed to Slessor's development. Certainly Slessor would have read Flecker's translations of Baudelaire. Hugh McCrae was a mentor closer to home. This idiosyncratic Australian poet, in the early years of the twentieth century, turned away from the prevailing radical and nationalist schools to write opalescent lyrics that owed a great deal to the French and English poets of the Decadent movement. In them Slessor found romanticized Hellenism and that interest in chivalry that characterized so much late-Victorian English poetry.

Arguably the most important and lasting influence upon Slessor, however, came through his friendship with Norman Lindsay and Lindsay's son Jack. Slessor met Jack in 1922 and through him became a friend of Norman. All three men were involved in the production of the magazine *Vision,* which lasted for only four issues–the first published in May 1923. There has been some critical debate about the extent of Norman Lindsay's influence upon Slessor, not least because Slessor himself latterly sought to downplay it and his connection with *Vision.* But such critics as T. L. Sturm, John Docker, and, more recently, Dennis Haskell all confirm that Norman Lindsay's ideas about art were extremely important to Slessor.

The cornerstone of Lindsay's Olympian aesthetic, as articulated in his book *Creative Effort* (1920), is provided by a distinction between Existence and Life, in which Existence is said to constitute the body and all the mechanisms that serve its needs–political, commercial, and scientific endeavors. Life, on the other hand, is everything beyond the corporeal. Art serves Life by transmuting the physical into the spiritual and transcendent; the means by which this transformation is achieved is "the concrete image." Lindsay's ideas were resolutely aristocratic. Much in his writings denigrates "the mob" and the "mob mind." "Beauty, gaiety and uprightness" were the products of Art through the artist's power. Although the obvious influence of such ideas upon Slessor is most evident in the early poems of *Thief of the Moon* and *Earth Visitors,* arguably the concrete image and the idea of Art inhabiting a realm that transcends the social and political are legacies from Lindsay that inform all of Slessor's work.

Thief of the Moon was published in a limited edition of 150 copies by J. T. Kirtley in 1924. It was followed by *Earth Visitors* two years later in an edition of 450 copies by the Fanfrolico Press. The second book included twenty-four of the thirty-four poems that had appeared in the first; there was not a great deal of stylistic or thematic development between the two books. Both volumes included illustrations by Norman Lindsay.

These early poems foreground artifice everywhere; for the most part, they are characterized by highly decorative surfaces, and exotic imagery and locations. These poems are exceedingly literary: some imitate the poetry of the Renaissance; others evoke a Romanticized version of an eighteenth-century world peopled by highwaymen and periwigged gallants; China provides material for Slessor's version of Orientalism while the myths of Classical Greece invite Pan to dance at Lane Cove. What all this subject matter has in common is its deliberate and emphatic distance from the social, political, and commercial world in which Slessor made a living through his journalism. Poetry was clearly operating as an escape from the mundane into a realm of magical transcendence. Even the love poems dedicated to Noela have this quality. The poems never evoke a living, breathing human being; rather, they somewhat chillingly transmute Noela into the realms of Art.

Characteristic of this early period of Slessor's work are the following lines from "Realities" (*Earth Visitors*, 1926), a poem dedicated "to the etchings of Norman Lindsay." Slessor in this poem gives the escape from existence into Life clear expression:

> The statues dance, and the old gardener is asleep,
> And golden bodies tread the paths–O, happy shapes,
> O, shining ones! Could I for ever keep
> Within your radiance, made absolute at last,
> No more amongst earth's phantoms to be cast,
> No more in the shadowy race of the world exist,
> But born into reality, remember Life
> As men see ghosts at midnight–so with me
> Might all those aery textures, the world's mist,
> Melt into beauty's actuality!

Much of Slessor's habitual and recurrent imagery has to do with the relationship between material realities and aesthetics. Jewels, stone, and precious metals are used to transform the flux of existence into art, while moonlight, sunlight, bubbles, smoke, and other vapors suggest a world that escapes the hard material of daily existence. There is so much haze in Slessor's early work that the reader gets the impression that Slessor does not want to look too closely at the world as it is. His habitual stance, looking through windows, suggests as much; there is a sense of willed separation from the everyday world of political event and struggle.

In those poems in which Slessor does locate himself in a world recognizably that of the country or the city, he finds there a terrible emptiness–a void that threatens to engulf and overwhelm him. For instance, "Winter Dawn" and "The Night Ride," both from *Earth Visitors*, are poems that not only anticipate later stylistic refinements but also suggest the intellectual impasse toward which Slessor was inexorably heading. "Winter Dawn" begins with the poet contemplating Sydney Harbor at a moment of changing light. Metaphors of transformation dominate the opening. But the attempt through "smoking panes" to make the harbor into "plated stone" is defeated by Slessor's sense that "The city, dissolves to a shell of bricks and paper, / Empty without purpose, a thing not comprehended." Similarly, in "Night Ride," one of the most celebrated of Slessor's early poems, the poet stares through a train window at the bustle of life on a station platform. Though the illuminated scene is attractive, the poet is cut off from it and

*Slessor's first wife, Noela, 1942
(National Library of Australia)*

sees there only "sinister travellers" and "unknown faces." Then the ride "into nothing but blackness resumes." And so metaphorically the reader moves from life toward death. There is no comfort in either, just a chilling sense of emptiness and alienation. The poet makes his wish to sleep seem the best of all options.

Appropriately enough, following the publication of *Earth Visitors*, 1927 proved to be a year of new beginnings for Slessor. He joined the staff of *Smith's Weekly*–the famous paper for which he worked until 1939 and that he edited from 1935 to 1939. At the same time, he began to write the poems that appeared in *Cuckooz Contrey* (1932), a volume including some of his most celebrated work–for instance, "Captain Dobbin" and "Five Visions of Captain Cook." Slessor later asserted that his time working for *Smith's Weekly* was "the happiest chapter" of his existence; certainly, it was the time of his greatest productivity as a poet. Not only did he compose 44 of the 103 poems that make up the *Selected Poems*, but between 1928 and 1933 he also wrote a further 75 pieces of "light verse," originally published in *Smith's Weekly* and later collected in *Darlinghurst Nights and Morning Glories: Being 47 Strange Sights Observed from Eleventh Storeys, in a Land of Cream Puffs and Crime, by a Flat-Roof Professor* (1933) and *Backless Betty from Bondi* (1983).

Smith's Weekly seems to have been a perfect berth for Slessor. The journalists and artists who worked for the paper had a raffish air of Bohemia about them, and their drinking sessions in the Assembly Hotel, at which Slessor partook freely, have passed into legend. While cultivating wit, eccentricity, verve, and panache, the paper also managed to be the purveyor of masculine conservative values, including an almost reverential respect for the figure of the Australian soldier, the archetypal Anzac. Clearly such values did not trouble Slessor, but they existed in a realm that he did not equate with poetry. Rather, the tension between his professional journalism and his artistic aspirations continued unabated. Possibly Slessor's relationship with Noela also exacerbated this conflict. Rumor suggests that Slessor's relationship with his wife was not altogether harmonious, and they both may have indulged in extramarital affairs. In a letter of 1931 Slessor says that he has left his wife. But for how long and under what circumstances this separation took place no ones knows. Suffice it to say that the retrospective "happiness" that Slessor located in this period was not unalloyed.

The poems in *Cuckooz Contrey* make this statement clear. The development of style in these poems, whereby the decorative excesses and verbal flummery of the earlier work is excised and a new refinement of phrasing emerges, intensifies the expression of the conflicts between Art and Nature, Life and Existence, and Time and Timelessness that are at the heart of all Slessor's work. Characteristically, he does not attempt to deal with the darkening political situation both in Australia and abroad. The Wall Street crash, the Great Depression, and their consequences, including the rise of fascism in Europe, are not dealt with at all in these poems. Indeed, the twentieth century is evident as subject matter in only a few of them. Rather, Slessor tries to fend off his sense of despair and nothingness in the face of time, mutability, and death by exploring both literally and metaphorically other exotic historical and geographical locations.

In this context he explores the sea voyage as a metaphor of both quest and escape. The city is more often than not imaged as a desert, a "decomposed metropolis"; this nicely chosen adjective suggests both deliquescence and the chaotic as against the creativity and order of Art. The Australian bush offers no comfortable alternative. "Crow Country" describes a wasteland where both physical nature and the mind are imaged as sterile, while "Talbingo" moves through a hard and stony "aching valley" to register the following conclusion: "That's what we're like out here / Beds of dried up passions." No wonder, then, that the idea of the sea beckons to Slessor's imagination, allowing him to embark with his mythologized mariners, Captain Dobbin and Captain Cook, on voyages of memory and imagination into an idealized and romanticized past. But Time and Nature always threaten to undo such gorgeous traveling.

In "Captain Dobbin" the eponymous hero of the poem has now retired to a "suburban villa" from which he observes the sea from behind glass panes. He records the movement of ships in his gazette while dreaming of his past voyages. Slessor draws the reader into the captain's inward journey, where the focus is upon the past, the ways in which it is recorded, and the stimulus to imagination that such mementos provide. A dialectic is then set up between a lost past with all its romance and adventure and a diminished present wherein the solitary Dobbin lives with and by his keepsakes. The sea is close to the captain:

Closer to him than a dead, lovely woman,
For he keeps bits of it, like old letters,
Salt tied up in bundles
Or pressed flat,
What you might call a lock of the sea's hair,
So Captain Dobbin keeps his dwarfed memento,
His urn-burial, a chest of mummied waves.

The poem reveals a deep sense that the past is lost forever and that the means of retrieving the past somehow partakes of death. Both the wonderful potential and the limitations of memory and imagination are powerfully registered. "Five Visions of Captain Cook" follows a similar trajectory; Cook is simultaneously mythologized while the processes of that mythology are subtly questioned and undermined. The dominant tone of the poem is one of nostalgia and loss.

More acidic tones of disappointment may be heard elsewhere in *Cuckooz Contrey*, not least in "Gulliver," another poem that takes its imagery from the sea and voyaging. In the poem, Gulliver is ensnared and unable to escape. Significantly, what binds him down are aspects of his own body; he is held by a "tyranny of sinews," "lashed with a hundred ropes of nerve and bone." Gulliver's efforts to free himself are in vain:

One hair I break, ten thousand hairs entwine me.
Love, hunger, drunkenness, neuralgia, debt,
Cold weather, hot weather, sleep and age—
If I could unloose their spongy fingers,
I'd have a chance yet, slip through the cage.
But who ever heard of a cage of hairs?
You can't scrape tunnels in a net.

Slessor (center) as a war correspondent in New Guinea, 19 September 1943 (Australian War Museum)

This passage may describe Slessor's sense of his own position as an artist—the body trapped in a daily existence from which he cannot escape. The poem, describing the position of Gulliver, concludes, "For God's sake call the hang-man."

Much of Slessor's "serious" poetry is concerned with masculine figures from the past, as if the poet is in search of lost heroic values. Equally significant is that his "light" verse is almost exclusively concerned with "girls"; Slessor clearly had the middle-class male audience for *Smith's Weekly* in mind as he composed these verses, which were accompanied in the paper by Virgil Reilly's drawings. "Girls" with hourglass figures, diaphanous drapes, and regular features were placed in a variety of urban and suburban settings to be admired or laughed at, celebrated or mourned, as the ambivalent verses dictated. In these verses, unlike in the serious poetry, the burgeoning consumer culture of the times is writ large. Cars, airplanes, telephones, wirelesses, advertising, fashion, jazz, posh hotels, and seedy streets are the properties and locations invoked in poem after poem. In some of these poems the reader is privy to a world in which social class divides society, in which some are exploited and some are exploiters, in which poverty, unemployment, violence, and drug addiction are real issues. But these are not poems that embody a radical politics. On the contrary, the tone of the poems and the direction of their moral censure do nothing to undermine Slessor's conservatism.

Slessor's affection for the two-dimensional "girls" of his fantasies is often juxtaposed with a discernible undertow of unpleasantness in his descriptions. The poet's unease with women is a constant subtext. "Kimono Cora," "Mannequins," "Evolution," "Country Eyes," and "The Tiger in the Rose" plainly reveal such conflicted views. Kimono Cora is dazzling in public, turning heads wherever she goes. But beneath this facade is a flat-dweller who privately lives in squalor. Slessor's attitude seems to be one of fascinated disgust. In "Evolution" the poet reminds the "barbarous, beautiful girl who thinks that she's 'frightfully slinky'" that once we were monkeys and frogs. And the mannequins belonging to the poem of that title are described in all their flounces and finery only to be exposed in the last two stanzas. Slessor has Clarice denuded of her glamour, returning to "Poverty and Squalor" in the "fourth-floor back"; she is "Lady creme de Woolworth's / frightened of the sack." In all of these poems and many others, Slessor contrasts romantic ideals with what he takes to be a sordid or at least less attractive "reality"; the "fairies" of his imagination are turned into their unflattering opposite, ensuring that always the women are either on pedestals or in the gutter.

These poems demonstrate Slessor's extraordinary technical gift; written in a wide variety of metrical and stanzaic forms, they delight in both end and internal rhymes, the more whimsical the better. Everywhere a deft lightness of touch is apparent, and that Slessor used a rhyming dictionary to concoct these confections should not detract from their panache. But as A. G. Stephens noted of *Darlinghurst Nights,* writing in his *Bulletin* diary (31 December 1931), despite the "very smart

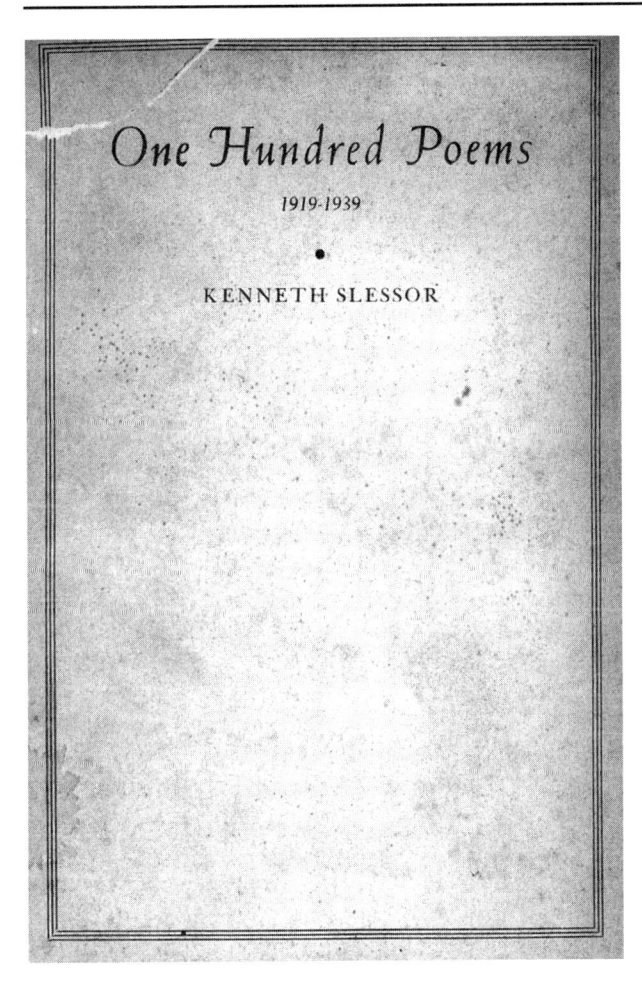

Dust jacket for Slessor's 1944 book, dedicated to Noela Slessor (Bruccoli Clark Layman Archives)

rhyming" and "fertility of ideas," the poems "have a sombre effect in sum" with "no heart shown." The book, Stephens argues, is "a bright and clever production" but "too hard and electric lit" to sell well. Most significantly, Stephens detected an undercurrent of the "disapproving Jeremiah" in Slessor's work.

After the publication of *Cuckooz Contrey* in 1932, *Darlinghurst Nights* in 1933, and the verses for children, *Funny Farmyard,* in 1933, Slessor's poetic productivity declined markedly. His next volume did not appear until 1939 and, as its title makes clear, only included twenty poems. He also continued to write light verse, but only occasionally. The prolific production of the previous years was over for good. The reasons for this change are not clear. Slessor was still working for *Smith's Weekly* and was still married, not altogether happily, to Noela. Nothing in his circumstances seems to have altered. This stagnation may be the point. That little was changing in his life may have led to a certain entropy with respect to his creative energy. Slessor's continued adherence to the poetics with which he had begun his career also militated against renewed vigor. *Five Bells: XX Poems* (1939) obsessively returns to the same issues that are the concerns of his whole oeuvre. The poems show further technical advances but no intellectual leaps.

The sonnet sequence "Out of Time" returns to the tensions between flux and stasis and between Time and Timelessness that inform so much of his writing. The sequence reaches for, but characteristically never quite attains, faith in Lindsay's notion that time can only affect things of the body, not the immortal aspects of the "Mind." The desire to escape from the exigencies of existence is also rearticulated in the remarkable poem "Sleep." Slessor deploys what he described as "narcotic" sound patterns, in which Sleep is personified as a woman inviting the persona to give himself up utterly, "Body and No-body, Flesh and no flesh," to a dissolution that has distinctly sexual overtones. But the personified and sexualized mother is also responsible for the persona's awakening into life—a terrible "riving" and "driving forth" as he suffers the "Pangs and betrayal of harsh birth." The maternal figure is, then, both desired and despised. The persona is a child both dominated and betrayed; the female figure seems to promise a timeless ecstasy but instead gives up the persona to the exigencies of himself and existence.

Other themes familiar from his earlier writings receive further treatment in the 1939 volume. "North Country" and "South Country" trace their lineage back to poems such as "Crow Country" and "Talbingo," while "Last Trams" takes up issues raised earlier in poems such as "City Nightfall" and "Winter Dawn." Both "North Country" and "South Country" are characterized by a wonderful fertility of visual imagery that precisely describes the coastal landscapes north and south of Sydney. But the poems include more than mere description. Both poems carry an atmosphere of foreboding and violence, as if Slessor cannot look at nature without somehow recoiling.

The growing bitterness that is evident in some poems from *Cuckooz Contrey* further increases in these later poems. "Cannibal Street" vents Slessor's spleen upon the appetitive nature of the human condition, while other poems—such as "Lesbia's Daughter," "The Knife," "Full Orchestra," and "To the Poetry of Hugh McCrae"—express his dwindling faith in the powers of language and intellect to redeem life.

The consummate expression of Slessor's major themes, however, is found in his finest achievement, "Five Bells." All of the poet's previous work seems to have been a prelude to the magnificently sustained 128 lines of this elegy for the artist Joe Lynch, who was lost overboard from a Sydney Harbor ferry and presumed drowned. The progress of the poem is straightforward.

A prologue introduces the concept of the relativity of time: there is time as it is measured in mechanical ways, by "little fidget wheels" or by the five bells of the title of the poem, and then there is time as "the flood that does not flow," of which memory is at least a part. The idea of the poem is that the poet can reexperience all he knows of the life of Joe Lynch within the three seconds that it takes to ring five bells. The poem describes a process from first thinking about Joe, through a re-creation of the memories of Joe, to a final meditation upon the meaning or nonmeaning of Joe's life.

From early in the poem there is a questioning not only of the status and meaning of Joe but also of the status and meaning of art and elegy. Slessor interrogates his own writing thus: "why thieve / These profitless lodgings from the flukes of thought / Anchored in time." The fragility of memory and mind in its attempts to apprehend another person's life is given expression. Joe's voice cannot be heard, and his writings are seen to be devoid of significance. Slessor then turns to Joe's artistic father, who plays the fiddle and has spent his life as a stonemason producing gravestones–"Those funereal cakes of sweet and sculptured stone." The implication is that all art is funereal insofar as it may deal with death but cannot save humans from mortality. The dead lie under the stones "Staked bone by bone, in quiet astonishment / At cargoes they never thought to bear."

As Slessor moves to the final meditation of the poem, the reader becomes aware that neither written nor spoken language will give access either to Joe or to his "meaning"; the absolute barrier that separates the living from the dead is articulated:

> If I could find an answer, could only find
> Your meaning, or could say why you were here
> Who now are gone, what purpose gave you breath
> Or seized it back, might I not hear your voice?

But all Slessor hears are sounds from the harbor, the sounds of existence proceeding in time measured by "Five bells coldly ringing out."

Some critics have attempted to find consolation in this poem by suggesting that Joe lives on by being taken up into an eternal Mind that finds expression through Slessor's memory and his poem. While one cannot and should not ignore such optimistic possibilities, the weight of negativity within the poem as a whole makes such a reading sound like clutching at straws. Failure registers strongly on several levels within the poem. Language fails to re-create Joe. Not only are Joe's words without significance, but also the words of Slessor's poem fail either to resurrect Joe as a whole person or to find the meaning of his life. Art and memory are no match for death. Not only does Slessor's art fail to immortalize its subject, but also the poem fails to mention Joe's occupation as an artist who works in black and white. Slessor does not turn to Joe's art to give his life meaning, because he does not believe it can. The paradox, then, of Slessor's greatest poem is that it has for its burden the theme of failure.

After 1939 Slessor added only three "serious" poems to the body of his work, two of which arose out of his service as a war correspondent. "An Inscription for Dog River" (*Southerly*, 1948) satirizes the vainglory of the Australian commander, Sir Thomas Blamey, while "Beach Burial" (*Southerly*, 1944) more characteristically moves back to the elegiac to provide an interesting coda to "Five Bells." In beautiful cadences the poem describes the burial of dead sailors washed ashore. The anonymity of the dead is an explicit concern, as is the inability of language to encompass adequately the mystery of their lives and deaths or the heavy task of memorializing them. The burial party write "with such perplexity, such bewildered pity" words that begin to disappear even as they are written:

> "Unknown Seamen"–the ghostly pencil
> Wavers and fades, the purple drips,
> The breath of the wet season has washed their inscriptions
> As blue as drowned men's lips . . .

As in "Five Bells," Slessor registers the inability of language to resurrect the dead or even to identify them adequately. Some critics have sought and found consolation in the final lines of the poem, where all of the dead, whether "ours" or the enemy's, are said to be "enlisted" together "on the other front." This conclusion is so vague as to be capable of many interpretations, but the most obvious front on which the dead now fight is that of time; they are engaged in the fight to be remembered. The poem suggests that this will be a losing battle.

In 1940 Slessor answered an advertisement for a job as an official war correspondent. He served in this capacity in both the Middle East and in New Guinea before his acrimonious resignation from the post in 1944. In this rift it is likely there was fault on both sides. The army accused Slessor of giving false information in an interview for *The Sun* in October 1943. For his part, Slessor accused the army of trying to censor him. No doubt the published articles based on *The Sun* interview included errors of fact, but Slessor–frustrated by his years of dealing with the army bureaucracy, by his role as war correspondent never having been adequately defined, and by his despatches regularly being savaged by home-based editors–took umbrage and returned to his job with the Sydney *Sun*.

The turbulence in Slessor's marriage continued through the war years. Noela joined Slessor in the Middle East, but this decision proved deeply unhappy for

Slessor's second wife, Pauline, with their son, Paul, circa 1956 (from Geoffrey Dutton, Kenneth Slessor: A Biography, *1991)*

both parties. Slessor apparently spent more time with his mates (male friends) than with Noela, and she is rumored to have had an affair with another journalist. Slessor was then recalled to Australia, leaving Noela on her own for many months before her eventual repatriation. In December 1944, Noela collapsed in a Sydney street, an occurrence heralding the diagnosis of cervical cancer from which she died in October 1945. A year later Slessor was still speaking of the "emotional devastation" caused by this event.

By Christmas 1946, however, he was involved with another woman, Kath McShine, about whom he wrote his post-1939 poem "Polarities." As the title suggests, this poem registers in a personalized way Slessor's ambivalence toward his beloved. The poem, though it celebrates various characteristics of his lover, ends with thumping bathos, "Sometimes I don't like her at all." Unsurprisingly, the relationship did not last. Slessor, however, remarried in December 1950. His bride was Pauline Bowe, a young woman nineteen years younger than he. Their son, Paul, was born eight months later, in August 1951. But as with his previous relationships, the second marriage was not a success. Slessor was much away from home and spent a great deal of time drinking with his friends at the Journalists' Club. The couple had rows, and Pauline started drinking heavily. She eventually left in the late 1950s, and they were divorced in 1961.

Meanwhile Slessor's professional life continued as a leading writer with *The Sun* until 1957, when he moved to *The Daily Telegraph* (Sydney), for which he worked until he died from heart disease on 30 June 1971. As well as writing hundreds of leading articles for these papers, Slessor also accepted commissions to write the texts for several guidebooks and trade journals. His involvement with literature continued through his appointment in 1953 as a member of the Advisory Board of the Commonwealth Literary Fund, his lectures on Australian poetry delivered at Sydney University in 1954, his somewhat dilatory editorship of the literary magazine *Southerly* from 1952 to 1962, and his co-editing of the *Penguin Book of Australian Verse,* published in 1958.

Various theories have been advanced for Slessor's long silence as a poet following the undeniably great "Five Bells" and "Beach Burial." It has been suggested that with the death of Noela, Slessor lost his muse and that his confidence was undermined. Lack of recognition for his work has also been cited as a possible factor. Neither of these arguments is particularly convincing. Slessor's output began to dwindle well before Noela's death, and she certainly did not disrupt his confidence through the first fifteen years of their marriage. It is true that his first volumes received little positive response from the public and that *Thief of the Moon* and *Earth Visitors* were harshly treated by the *Times Literary Supplement* (*TLS*). But Slessor's silence followed upon the first hints of genuine recognition of his stature as a poet, which came in Ronald McCuaig's lengthy essay on Slessor published in *The Bulletin* on 9 August 1939 and Douglas Stewart's enthusiastic review of *Five Bells: XX Poems,* which immediately followed. A more likely answer is that in "Five Bells" and "Beach Burial" Slessor had articulated an aesthetic and intellectual position from which he could not move forward without revising his aesthetic or in some way remaking himself. Why he found such a reinvention impossible must remain conjecture, and doubtless there are many contributing factors. What can be said with certainty is that the poems he left remain a substantial legacy.

Biography:

Geoffrey Dutton, *Kenneth Slessor: A Biography* (Ringwood, Vic.: Viking/Penguin, 1991).

References:

Vincent Buckley, "Kenneth Slessor: Realist or Romantic," in his *Essays in Poetry: Mainly Australian* (Carlton, Vic.: Melbourne University Press, 1957), pp. 111-121;

Graham Burns, *Kenneth Slessor*, second edition (Melbourne: Oxford University Press, 1975);

Adrian Caesar, *Kenneth Slessor* (Melbourne: Oxford University Press, 1995);

Julian Croft, "Notes on Slessor's 'Five Visions,'" *Australian Literary Studies*, 4, no. 4 (1969-1970): 172-174;

Croft, "Responses to Modernism," in *The Penguin New Literary History of Australia*, edited by L. Hergenhan (Ringwood, Vic.: Penguin, 1988), pp. 409-429;

Croft, "Slessor's Five Visions of Captain Cook," *Australian Literary Studies*, 4, no. 1 (1969-1970): 3-17;

Croft, "The World Outside Time: Slessor's 'Five Bells,'" *Australian Literary Studies*, 5, no. 2 (1971-1972): 121-132;

L. Dobrez, "Portrait of a Man of Sentiment," *Southerly*, no. 1 (1977): 16-32;

John Docker, "Norman Lindsay, Kenneth Slessor and the Artist Aristocracy," in *Australian Cultural Elites* (Sydney: Angus & Robertson, 1974), pp. 22-41;

Geoffrey Dutton, *Kenneth Slessor* (Gosford: Ashton Scholastic, 1987);

Robert D. FitzGerald, "Kenneth Slessor," *Australian Literary Studies*, 5, no. 2 (1971-1972): 115-120;

H. M. Green, *An Outline of Australian Literature*, revised by Dorothy Green, volume 2 (Sydney: Angus & Robertson, 1985), pp. 941-954;

Max Harris, *Kenneth Slessor* (Melbourne: Lansdowne Press, 1963);

K. Hart, "'Different Curioes,'" *Southerly*, no. 2 (1989): 182-196;

Dennis Haskell, "'On water stranger and less clear': Conceptions of Time and Death in the Work of Kenneth Slessor," *Voices* (Autumn 1991): 5-22;

Haskell, "Sheer Voice and Fidget Wheels: A Study of 'Five Bells,'" *Australian Literary Studies* (May 1988): 253-265;

H. Heseltine, "'Wherefore I Think': Notes on the Poetry of Kenneth Slessor," in *The Uncertain Self* (Melbourne: Oxford University Press, 1986), pp. 72-82;

Charles Higham, "The Poetry of Kenneth Slessor," *Quadrant*, no. 13 (Summer 1959-1960): 65-73;

R. G. Howarth, "Sound in Slessor's Poetry," *Southerly*, 16, no. 4 (1955): 189-196;

Herbert C. Jaffa, *Kenneth Slessor* (New York: Twayne, 1971);

B. Kiernan, ed., *Considerations: New Essays on Kenneth Slessor, Judith Wright, and Douglas Stewart* (Sydney: Angus & Robertson, 1977), pp. ix-xxi, 1-68;

P. Kirkpatrick, "Satyrs in the Top Paddock: Metaphysical Pastoral in Australian Poetry," *Australian Literary Studies*, 15, no. 3 (1992): 141-154;

L. Kramer, "The Landscapes of Slessor's Poetry," *Southerly*, no. 1 (1977): 3-14;

Noel Macainsh, "Aestheticism and Reality in the Poetry of Kenneth Slessor," *Westerly*, no. 1 (1982): 31-41;

Macainsh, "Kenneth Slessor and the 'Image of Actual Experience,'" *Southerly*, no. 4 (1980): 439-449;

F. T. Macartney, "The Poetry of Kenneth Slessor," *Meanjin*, 16, no. 3 (1957): 265-272;

A. Macdonald, *The Ukelele Player under the Red Lamp* (Sydney: Angus & Robertson, 1972), pp. 250-265;

D. Malouf, "Where in the World Was Kenneth Slessor? A Personal View of the Slessor Tribute at the Adelaide Writer's Week, 1974," *Southerly*, no. 2 (1974): 202-206;

James McAuley, "On Some of Slessor's Discarded Poems," *Southerly*, no. 2 (1973): 118-128;

Philip Mead, ed., *Kenneth Slessor: Critical Readings* (St. Lucia: University of Queensland Press, 1997);

H. Porter, *The Extra* (Melbourne: Thomas Nelson, 1975), pp. 93-108, 115-117;

Clement Semmler, *Kenneth Slessor* (London: Longmans, 1966);

Semmler, "War Correspondents in Australian Literature: An Outline," *Australian Literary Studies* (October 1985): 194-206;

Semmler, "What Kenneth Slessor Was Writing During His 30 Silent Years," *National Times*, 27 September 1976 - 2 October 1976, pp. 26-27;

Southerly, special Slessor issue, no. 4 (1971);

Douglas Stewart, *A Man of Sydney: An Appreciation of Kenneth Slessor* (Melbourne: Thomas Nelson, 1977);

A. Taylor, *Reading Australian Poetry* (St. Lucia: University of Queensland Press, 1987), pp. 53-69;

John Thompson, "Poetry in Australia. Kenneth Slessor," *Southerly*, 26, no. 3 (1966): 190-198;

A. K. Thomson, ed., *Critical Essays on Kenneth Slessor* (Brisbane: Jacaranda Press, 1968);

Chris Wallace-Crabbe, "Kenneth Slessor and the Powers of Language," in *The Literature of Australia*, edited by Dutton (Ringwood, Vic.: Penguin, 1964), pp. 342-352;

G. A. Wilkes, *Australian Literature: A Conspectus* (Sydney: Angus & Robertson, 1969), pp. 73-78;

Judith Wright, *Preoccupations in Australian Poetry* (Melbourne: Oxford University Press, 1965), pp. 140-153.

Papers:

The papers of Kenneth Slessor are held at the National Library of Australia, Canberra.

Christina Stead
(17 July 1902 – 31 March 1983)

Brigid Rooney
University of Sydney

BOOKS: *The Salzburg Tales* (London: Davies, 1934; New York & London: Appleton-Century, 1934; Melbourne: Sun, 1966);

Seven Poor Men of Sydney (London: Davies, 1934; New York: Appleton-Century, 1935; Sydney: Angus & Robertson, 1965);

The Beauties and Furies (London: Davies, 1936; New York: Appleton-Century, 1936);

House of All Nations (New York: Simon & Schuster, 1938; London: Davies, 1938; Sydney: Angus & Robertson, 1974);

The Man Who Loved Children (New York: Simon & Schuster, 1940; London: Davies, 1941; Sydney: Angus & Robertson, 1978);

For Love Alone (New York: Harcourt, Brace, 1944; London: Davies, 1945; Sydney: Angus & Robertson, 1966);

Letty Fox: Her Luck (New York: Harcourt, Brace, 1946; London: Davies, 1947; Sydney: Angus & Robertson, 1974);

A Little Tea, A Little Chat (New York: Harcourt, Brace, 1948);

The People with the Dogs (Boston: Little, Brown, 1952);

Dark Places of the Heart (New York: Holt, Rinehart & Winston, 1966); republished as *Cotters' England* (London: Secker & Warburg, 1967; Sydney: Angus & Robertson, 1974);

The Puzzleheaded Girl: Four Novellas comprises "The Puzzleheaded Girl," "The Dianas," "The Right-Angled Creek," and "Girl from the Beach" (New York: Holt, Rinehart & Winston, 1967; London: Secker & Warburg, 1968);

The Little Hotel (London & Sydney: Angus & Robertson, 1973; New York: Holt, Rinehart & Winston, 1975);

Miss Herbert (The Suburban Wife) (New York: Random House, 1976);

Ocean of Story: The Uncollected Stories of Christina Stead, edited by Ron G. Geering (Ringwood, Vic.: Viking, 1985; New York: Viking, 1985);

Christina Stead, circa 1937 (photograph by Stuart Munro, London; from Hazel Rowley, Christina Stead, *1993)*

I'm Dying Laughing: The Humourist, edited by Geering (London: Virago Press, 1986; New York: Holt, 1987);

The Palace with Several Sides: A Sort of Love Story, edited by Geering (Canberra: Officina Brindabella, 1986).

OTHER: *Modern Women in Love: Twentieth-Century Masterpieces of Fiction*, edited by Stead and William Blake (New York: Dryden, 1945);

Fernand Gigon, *Colour of Asia,* translated by Stead (London: Muller, 1955);

Great Stories of the South Sea Islands, edited by Stead (London: Miller, 1955);

Auguste Piccard, *In Balloon and Baththyscaphe,* translated by Stead (London: Cassell, 1956);

"What Goal in Mind?" in *We Took Their Orders and Are Dead: An Anti-war Anthology,* edited by Shirley Cass, Ros Cheney, David Malouf, and Michael Wilding (Sydney: Ure Smith, 1971), pp. 119-130;

Christina Stead: Selected Fiction and Nonfiction, edited by R. G. Geering and A. Segerberg (St. Lucia: University of Queensland Press, 1994).

SELECTED PERIODICAL PUBLICATIONS–
UNCOLLECTED: "The Writers Take Sides," in *Left Review,* 1, no. 11 (August 1935): 453-463; 469-475;

"Man's Hope," Review of Andre Malraux, *Man's Hope,* in *New Masses* (15 November 1938): 22-23;

"Wandering Workers," Review of Kylie Tennant, *Battlers,* in *New Masses* (30 September 1941): 25-26;

"Pro and Con on Aragon," by Stead and Hannah Josephson, in *New Masses* (17 February 1942): 23-24;

"Hamlet in 'The Troubles,'" Review of Boris Pasternak, *Dr. Zhivago,* in *Friendship* (May/June 1959): 8-9;

"Portrait of a Genius," Review of *Einstein: Notes of a Film Director,* in *Friendship* (August 1959): 10, 11;

"On the Women's Movement," in *Partisan Review,* 46, no. 2 (1979): 271-274;

"Some Deep Spell: A View of Stanley Burnshaw," in *Agenda,* 21, nos. 4 & 22, no. 1 (1983-1984): 1;

"'It is all a scramble for boodle': Christina Stead Sums up America," in *Australian Book Review,* 141 (June 1992): 22-24;

"Why I Left," *Independent Monthly* (December 1994/January 1995): 42-43.

Cosmopolitan and politically oriented Australian writer Christina Stead produced fourteen major works of fiction, mostly written when she was an expatriate in Britain, Europe, and the United States, between 1930 and 1960. Stead's fiction promiscuously traverses these times and places—deploying genres as diverse as the epic, romance, *künstlerroman* (novel dealing with the development of an artist), picaresque, and social and political satire—ultimately in quest of an imaginative project that has been likened in its ambition to Honoré de Balzac's *Human Comedy* (1827-1847). Stead's experimental approach to the novel and to the treatment of character is not only influenced by key nineteenth- and twentieth-century practitioners—including in addition to Balzac, Gustave Flaubert, Charles Dickens, George Eliot, James Joyce, Fyodor Dostoevsky, Henry David Thoreau, Herman Melville, and Theodore Dreiser—but is also shaped by her encounters with modernist culture and writing, radical political thought, and the theories of Charles Darwin and other scientific naturalists. Stead's fiction, while self-consciously engaging with this European and transatlantic cultural heritage, is also conditioned by the somewhat marginal, postcolonial position of an expatriate Australian white woman of her generation. Stead's novels are perhaps most remarkable for the way in which they dramatize, often satirically, the clashing perspectives of a multitude of characters who appear as epiphenomena of their societies. The most memorable of these—for example, Samuel Clemens Pollit, Jonathan Crow, Nellie Cotter, and Emily Wilkes-Howard—are obsessive and dominating talkers whose overwhelming performances simultaneously fascinate and repel their listeners.

Aiming for what she once termed (in a letter to her father's third wife, Thistle Harris [6 April 1942]) an "intelligent ferocity," Stead has attracted with her prose style both admiration and criticism—its abundance, raw energy, heterogeneity, and obscurities forestalling easy consumption by the reader. The lyrical exuberance of Stead's early prose is overtaken in her later writing—as Angela Carter puts it in her appraisal of Stead's achievement in *London Review of Books* (1982)—by a tendency "to hew her material more and more roughly." Although in significance Stead is often said to rival Patrick White, her status in the Australian literary canon remains ambiguous, since her fiction does not—beyond one and a half novels and some shorter pieces—primarily depict Australian settings or characters. Nor is Stead's fiction easily encompassed by any single national literary tradition. Rather, it is oriented toward an international context, refracting and commenting on the experience of her generation of Western intellectuals. From the 1970s onward, Stead's vivid depictions of a range of female characters have resulted in her appropriation for the feminist canon, a maneuver not undertaken without some difficulty, since in many interviews Stead herself explicitly rejected any feminist agenda. In recent years, however, new poststructuralist literary theories, such as those of Roland Barthes and Julia Kristeva, have provided commentators with relevant approaches and greater scope for responding to the contradictions, the heterogeneity, and the social and political force of Stead's writing.

Stead once claimed—in an interview with Giulia Giuffré in 1983—to have written her biography into her fictional characters, and indeed a recurring set of themes and concerns integrates her disparately located stories. Stead's biographers, Chris Williams and Hazel

Rowley, have drawn upon Stead's novels to inform their reconstruction of her early life in Australia and her complex relationship with her father. In the absence of any fixed national location, Stead's life story has functioned as a unifying text against which her books may be read. Susan Sheridan argues in her 1988 study, however, that the tendency to focus on the autobiographical dimension of Stead's fiction has "obscured both the continuities and differences" among her novels, leading critics to "ignore the prodigious variety of the narrative experiments she set herself."

Christina Ellen Stead was born in Rockdale, Sydney, Australia, on 17 July 1902, daughter of Ellen Butters Stead and David George Stead. Ellen Stead died when Christina was just two years old, and for several years afterward Christina was primarily cared for by her father. David Stead's formative influence on his daughter's view of the world was profound, evidently causing her anguish as well as joy. From this father-daughter relationship sprang Stead's devastating portrait of Samuel Clemens Pollit in her 1940 novel, *The Man Who Loved Children,* generally regarded as her best. A middle-ranking public servant with the New South Wales Department of Fisheries, David Stead was a socialist and a freethinking atheist, a self-taught naturalist involved in the Linnean Society of New South Wales, and a founding member of the Australian Conservation Foundation. Stead imparted his passion for the Australian continent, its evolutionary prehistory, and its ecology to his young daughter. In later life Christina Stead acknowledged her father's significance in nurturing her love of story: in her essay "A Waker and a Dreamer," she offers readers an alternative portrait that, while continuing to depict him as a self-absorbed idealist, adopts a gentler tone.

In 1907 David Stead married again, this time to Ada Gibbins, whose propertied father, Frederick Gibbins, offered the couple rent-free the use of Lydham Hall, a capacious sandstone house situated on a rise at Bexley, commanding a sweeping view of the Pacific Ocean and of Cape Banks and Cape Solander, through which Captain James Cook had sailed in 1770. Six children were born to this union, and for a time the family appeared to prosper. After Frederick Gibbins's death in 1917, however, Lydham Hall was sold to satisfy his debts, and Stead's family relocated to a large but rather dilapidated house at Watson's Bay. These days an exclusive harborside suburb of Sydney, Watson's Bay was then a fishing village. The bay recurs, in different guises, in several of Stead's novels. In *The Man Who Loved Children* it becomes the American locale of the Chesapeake Bay. *The Man Who Loved Children* casts this period in Stead's life as a time during which, as she

Stead in 1928 (photograph by Gilbert Stead)

wrote to Harris (7 July 1939), her family made "an etching" of her.

Stead's earliest idea for a novel came to her while she was still at school. The title of this imagined work, "The Lives of Obscure Men," conveys Stead's early interest in a theme she pursued in her first novel, *Seven Poor Men of Sydney* (1934). On completing her secondary schooling at Sydney Girls' High, where she had edited the school magazine, Stead attended Sydney Teachers' College, co-editing and contributing to the college magazine, *The Kookaburra*. Stead also undertook a psychology course at Sydney University as a nonmatriculation student. Obliged in 1923 to begin a five-year bonded period of teaching, and plagued by pharyngitis and nervous anxiety, Stead was unable to manage classroom teaching, for which she felt herself to be profoundly ill suited. Provision was made for her to tutor small groups of children with special needs and to lecture in psychology at Sydney Teachers' College. After protracted ill health and unhappiness, however, Stead managed to enlist the support of sympathetic officials and was mercifully released in 1925 from her bond to the New South Wales Education Department without incurring the usual financial penalty. In this same year, David Stead submitted his daughter's collection of children's stories to Angus and Robertson, the fledgling Sydney-based publisher of Australian literature. The rejection was kindly couched, but the incident probably did little to mitigate the resolve Stead was forming to leave Australia for England and Europe. Having attended evening classes in stenography, Stead obtained a secretarial position in the firm of an architect and subsequently in a Sydney hat factory. In the course of two more years, during which time she corresponded regularly with Keith Duncan, a lecturer she admired from Sydney University who had departed for the London School of Economics in 1926, Stead managed to accumulate sufficient funds to purchase for herself a one-way, steerage-class fare to London. In electing to leave Australia she was not alone, but following in the wake of many other Australian writers, such as Barbara Baynton, Henry Handel Richardson, Miles Franklin, and Jack Lindsay.

In March 1928, at age twenty-five, Stead arrived in London malnourished and exhausted from the rigors of the last few years. Still in poor health, she found employment at a grain firm, Strauss and Company, where she met Wilhelm Blech, the temporary associate manager, who also held the position of investments manager for the Travelers' Bank, a small private bank based in Paris. Lifelong companion, husband, and loyal supporter of Stead, Blech—who anglicized his name to William Blake—was a cosmopolitan intellectual, an American of Jewish background, and a Marxist economist. Blake shared Stead's literary enthusiasms, successfully turning his hand to writing historical novels, including *The World Is Mine* (1938) and *The Copperheads* (1941), and also producing a lively and influential text, *Elements of Marxian Economic Theory and Its Criticism* (1939). Blake not only introduced Stead to leftist and literary circles in Britain, Europe, and the United States, where the couple lived, worked, and traveled for the next forty years, but also helped to establish and manage Stead's publishing career. After some earlier attempts to interest publishers failed, Blake sent the manuscript of *Seven Poor Men of Sydney* to Sylvia Beach, the distinguished Paris bookshop owner who published Joyce's *Ulysses* (1918). This contact led to Stead's association—her longest with any single publisher—with the London-based Peter Davies, who, though recognizing Stead's idiosyncratic genius, was wary enough to ask first to see something else that she had written. Undaunted by having nothing prepared, Stead immediately began composing, with remarkable speed and efficiency, *The Salzburg Tales* (1934), drawing on her recollection of earlier stories left behind in Australia and inventing much new material for the purpose. Davies, admiring the result, agreed to publish both books, which appeared in quick succession.

The major features of Stead's mature writing are manifest in these two early publications. The reviews in England and Australia, favorable on the whole, greeted Stead as a dazzling and precocious new talent. Although a collection of short stories, the mise-en-scène of *The Salzburg Tales* harks back to the fourteenth-century origins of the novel, and many critics have noted its rewriting of Giovanni Boccaccio's *The Decameron* (1349–1351), Geoffrey Chaucer's *Canterbury Tales* (circa 1400), and the *Arabian Nights Entertainment, or The Thousand and One Nights* (translated into English in the eighteenth century). Set during the Mozart Festival at Salzburg, the stories feature a cross-section of personages, more than thirty of whom are sketched with precision, wit, and economy in the prologue, who assemble in the Capuchin Wood at the end of each of seven days to exchange their tales. The scope and variety of Stead's storytelling and her verbal dexterity are demonstrated in these tales that, as noted by Ian Reid and others, incorporate the same elements Stead herself identified, in her essay "Ocean of Story" (originally published under the title "The Short Story" in *Kenyon Review*, 1968) as generic to the short story—"the sketch, anecdote, jokes cunning, philosophical, and biting, legends and fragments." The collection is cleverly connected by the tales told at the end of each day by the Centenarist, an orchestrator of ceremonial occasions who "knew many thousand themes from the master musicians and many peasant songs and single strains picked up here and there on the earth" and who embodies the dual creativity of the Mozart Festival and the feast of stories in the collection: "He was as full of tales as the poets of Persia: he unwound endlessly his fabrics, as from a spool the silks of Arabia."

Written first but published second, *Seven Poor Men of Sydney* more dramatically signals the direction of Stead's subsequent writing. The sole Stead novel set entirely in Australia, it takes place in and around Sydney during the first three decades of the twentieth century. *Seven Poor Men of Sydney* presents a network of perspectives, voices, and experiences, its energies clustering particularly around three members of the younger generation of the Baguenault family—Michael, Catherine, and Joseph (brother, sister, and cousin). Collectively representative of a generation, class, and nation, Catherine, Michael, and Joseph dramatize three modes of perceiving reality.

The febrile and neurasthenic Michael, whose viewpoint directs the early chapters of the novel, struggles passionately within and against the conventions of family, church, and provincial society. True to his name as a "ne'er-do-well," Michael achieves little of outward

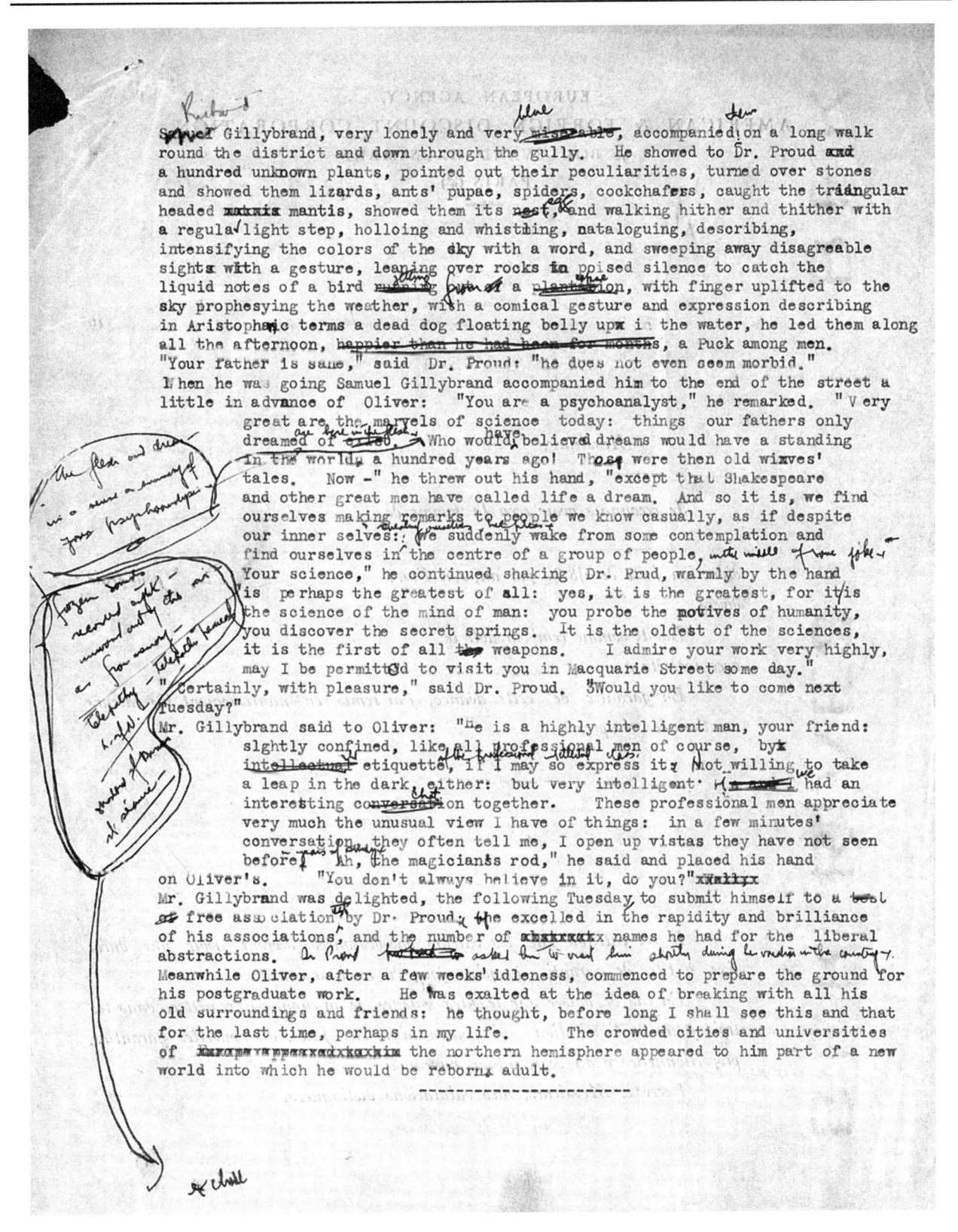

Page from an early draft of Stead's 1936 novel, The Beauties and Furies
(National Library of Australia, MS4967)

social consequence, forever paralyzed and haunted by the perceived gap between his heightened sensory experience and the unfathomable passage of time and change. His question, "How will we ever refine our eyes to see atoms and our ears to hear the messages of ants?" correlates with the impulses of the narrative. The presentation, later in the novel, of Michael's suicidal dementia is one of the most powerful and moving sequences in the novel.

Michael's sister and kindred spirit, Catherine Baguenault, is strikingly excluded from the cast list of seven poor men in the novel, an omission that signals her disruptive marginality as a vagabond woman. She is the person who, after Michael's death, discloses the story of incestuous love between herself and Michael. Catherine's wayward desire to escape conventional gender roles is partly channeled by her political agitation, and she is sympathetically observed by the kindly American Marxist of Jewish background modeled on Blake, Baruch Mendelssohn, who works at the Tank Stream printery among other key characters. There Baruch befriends Catherine's cousin—the humble, ordinary, and obscure Joseph Baguenault.

Carried along in life unquestioning, Joseph finally garners the self-knowledge to depict himself as a "letter of ordinary script" over whom "hierarchies and hierarchies" have dominion: "I am a machine. I am the end of my race." Humble Joseph emerges on the last page of the novel as the narrator of the tale of seven poor men. The unusual combination of realist themes and modernist techniques in Stead's first novel won startled praise from critics and reviewers at the time, and this favorable reception has continued in recent years. In writing *Seven Poor Men of Sydney,* Stead's contribution to the Australian novel was a pioneering one. Her Australian contemporaries in the 1930s—such as Katharine Susannah Prichard, Jean Devanny, and Dymphna Cusack—wrote within an established tradition of social realism. Although just as politically engaged as the works of these writers, *Seven Poor Men of Sydney,* differing radically in form and approach, was a forerunner of the modernist novel in Australia.

Stead's dramatic assembly and deployment in these first two books of an unusually large cast of characters—whose voices interact competitively, democratically, and energetically—were a recurring feature and strategy of her writing that she later articulated in her notes on "The Uses of the Many-Charactered Novel" (circa 1939): "the many-charactered novel is the novel of the metropolitan today . . . it is a novel of strife." This approach continued to develop in Stead's next novels, which also capitalize on observation of the strife of the 1920s and 1930s and which record the foibles and energies of businessmen, politicians, activists, and literary luminaries encountered in London, Paris, and New York. The First International Congress of Writers for the Defence of Culture, convened in Paris in 1935, was an event of some cultural and historical significance; Stead attended in the capacity of secretary to the English delegation. In company with such fellow writer-activists as Ralph Fox and Michael Gold, Stead also met with Australian writer and critic Nettie Palmer, whose diary entries record her impressions of Stead at the time. "The Writers Take Sides" (1935), Stead's own report on this problematic congress, in which a broad spectrum of leftist writers and artists combined on an anti-Fascist platform with the backing of the Comintern, is an overtly polemical essay that conveys the enthusiasms of the era along with her own sympathetic yet critical observation of would-be revolutionaries on the world stage. Stead's next novels, *The Beauties and Furies* (1936) and *House of All Nations* (1938), both set in Paris, capture the heady excitement of this period with its confluence of radical aesthetic and political movements.

Mixed reviews greeted publication of *The Beauties and Furies,* a novel exploring unfulfilled sensuality and desire in the Parisian story of lovers Oliver Fenton and Elvira Western and their encounter with the enigmatic Marpurgo. The narrative, with its linguistic excursions into surrealist discourse and its savoring of the sensualities of Paris in the 1930s, also retains an ironic perspective on romantic excess. Jennifer Gribble comments in her 1994 monograph that the romantic quest in this novel "becomes analogy for, and displacement of, political quest." Elvira, the Sleeping Beauty or unawakened Venus of the narrative, having abandoned her husband and her provincial life in an English village, escapes to bohemian Paris to rendezvous with her lover, Oliver, a student enamored of revolutionary politics. The notion of sleepwalking, or somnambulism, recurs, suggesting conjunctions between love and politics in the notion of awakening to a fully realized existence. In her 1987 monograph, Diana Brydon identifies this theme of the call to "Cythera" as the central metaphor of Stead's life and writing, arguing that a character's value may be gauged by the nature of his or her response to this call. In one of Stead's favorite paintings by Antoine Watteau, "Cythera" is the island of love in Greek mythology, emblematic of the ideal community. In *The Beauties and Furies,* the response of the lovers remains shallow and self-serving rather than profound or transforming: Oliver "plays" at revolution just as Elvira "plays" at love. The discontented Elvira is contrasted with the free-spirited Coromandel, daughter of the antique-dealer Paindebled. In a surreal scene Coromandel and Oliver make love under a fallen map of the world, under the secret eye of Coromandel's mother. Tension gathers, particularly around Marpurgo, whose voyeuristic and Prospero-like relation to the young couple is primarily narcissistic and whose conspiracies finally rebound on him. A sexual predator, puppet master, and monologuist, Marpurgo's female counterpart emerges later in Nellie Cotter, in *Cotter's England* (1967). The extreme blend of satire and fantasy, of politics and surrealism, in *The Beauties and Furies* was disconcerting for many readers. In Australia a significant early essay by M. Barnard Eldershaw, "Australian Writers 2: Christina Stead" (1937), ambivalently praises the "rich luxuriance" of Stead's style, finding her first two books successful but *The Beauties and Furies* disappointing: "No amount of meretricious glitter can animate these sawdust puppets." Certainly *The Beauties and Furies,* despite belated recognition of its strengths by a few readers, has continued to be less well known and regarded than some of Stead's other works.

House of All Nations, the voluminous novel Stead claimed to have drafted in six weeks while holidaying with Blake in Ronda, Spain, on the eve of the Spanish Civil War, was greeted with more enthusiasm by reviewers, especially in the United States, and with considerable admiration for its technical grasp of the operations of high finance. Response in England was muted, however, and by this time Australian interest in the fiction of an expatriate who failed to address local concerns was wavering, although reviews of Stead's books continued to appear in a few newspapers, such as *The Bulletin* (Sydney). Departing from the lyricism of the earlier fictions, *House of All Nations* is an experiment with the documentary novel, a genre enjoying support in radical circles at the time. Teeming with garrulous characters, Stead's novel anatomizes the corrupt machinations of the merchant banking brotherhood. The account of the shady dealings of the Banque Mercure in *House of All Nations* derives from Stead's own intimate encounter with the ruinous financial scandal that enveloped the Traveler's Bank, whose charismatic owner-directors—Peter, Aubrey, and George Neidecker—had in the 1930s employed both Blake and Stead within their privileged inner circle. The capitalists and bank employees who populate the novel include its problematically loyal Marxist consultant, Michel Alphendéry (modeled on Blake); the devious but lovable bank owners, Jules and William Bertillon; the womanizing wheat merchant, Henri Léon (based on Blake's business associate Alf Hurst); the cold and calculating rival to the Bertillons, Jacques Carriere; and the ill-fated customer's man, Aristide Raccamond, who becomes the neurotic nemesis of the bank. Paralleling the banking fraternity is the communist brotherhood, a small cell of Paris intellectuals and activists frequented by Alphendéry and bank teller-cum-poet Adam Constant (based on

Title page for Stead's 1938 novel, about corruption in the French banking industry (Richland County Public Library)

Ralph Fox), a group equally comprised of serious idealists and poseur revolutionaries. Although women play a subsidiary role in the story, they are no less colorful than the men, including the scheming and manipulative Marianne Raccamond, the vengeful harridan Suzanne Constant, and Sophie Haller, the murderously assiduous hostess who force-feeds the Raccamonds in a savagely funny dinner-party scene that travesties bourgeois manners and consumption. For some feminist critics the focus of the novel on the activities of men and marginalization of the few women characters presents a challenge. Yet, Stead's incisive treatment of "phallocracy," capitalism, and 1930s popular-front politics in this novel has recently been identified by Louise Yelin in her essay in *The Magic Phrase: Critical Essays on Christina Stead* (2000), edited by Margaret Harris.

From July 1937 to December 1946 Stead and Blake resided in the United States, mainly in and around New York City, where, though not without

Notes for Stead's 1940 novel, The Man Who Loved Children
(National Library of Australia, MS4967)

financial vagaries, the couple enjoyed a comparatively secure and productive phase of their lives. During this "American" period, Stead observed the workings of the American Communist Party, with which she sympathized but never joined. Stead's correspondence shows her disgust with the self-serving machinations of careerist party hacks involved in running *New Masses,* the communist organ to which she contributed occasional book reviews in the 1940s.

Once she had arrived in the United States, Stead permitted herself the difficult luxury of drawing on what proved exceedingly painful memories of her childhood, adolescence, and early adulthood. More than merely autobiographical, these novels actively rewrite the *künstlerroman* genre, recasting in mock-heroic terms the struggle of the artist-as a young woman and her emergence from familial provinciality into the wider world.

In *The Man Who Loved Children,* the triangle of Samuel Pollit, his wife, Henny, and adolescent stepdaughter, Louisa (or Louie), constitutes the author's allegorical portrait of family life, conveying its claustrophobia, cruelty, and chaos. Initially well received in England and the United States, the novel has attracted much critical discussion, most of which postdates its republication in 1965. As Yelin finds in her essay in *Contemporary Literature* (Winter 1990), the "changing reception history of the novel is paralleled by changes in the geography of its reception," from its early positioning as an American novel to its later appropriation for the Australian literary canon. Stead's choice of American settings for this seminally autobiographical story successfully reorients it toward social and political critique of the Roosevelt era, as demonstrated in a cogent reading by Jonathan Arac. Critical views about the relative importance of its three main characters—Sam, Henny, and Louie Pollit—have also shifted along with changing literary, cultural, and political views. With its crises concentrated in just a few days—although the story spans a year—the novel is richly detailed and compressed in its plotting of the marital collision between the impractical and narcissistic Sam Pollit and Henny, the disappointed and self-destructive mother of his brood of children. In and around impending disaster, the children, seemingly oblivious, participate in an unfolding drama of filial rebellion led by the awkward and imaginative Louie, who finally breaks free of the imprisoning forces of family life. Louie's genius in marshaling the resources of language against her father's verbal tyranny reaches maturity in her direction of her siblings in "Tragos Herpes Rom," a play in her own invented language, staging rebellion against the father. This story of rebellion against the patriarchal family held particular appeal for second-wave feminist readers,

a development that fostered appreciation of Stead's writing across national boundaries. Many variant readings of *The Man Who Loved Children,* however—treating its Nietzschean thematics, its novelization of Friedrich Engels's *Origin of the Family* (1884), its political critique of liberal humanism, and its inversion of the Oedipal narrative—have proliferated rather than stabilized its meanings for readers.

Increasing difficulties with American publishers seemed temporarily averted when Stead secured a three-book publishing contract with Harcourt, Brace, of which the first was *For Love Alone* (1944). Developing epic themes similar to those in *The Man Who Loved Children, For Love Alone* begins in Australia but concludes in England. Teresa Hawkins's journey from the antipodes to the Northern Hemisphere enacts a reverse odyssey, from family and national origins to the international condition of what Angela Carter, in her 1982 review, identifies as "the rootless urban intelligentsia." Having evolved from the earliest of Stead's drafts and jottings, *For Love Alone* presents a devastating critique of provincial life, of the social roles of modern women, and of conventional marital monogamy, memorably depicting the way women internalize their bondage: "There was a glass pane in the breast of each girl; there every other girl could see the rat gnawing at her, the fear of being on the shelf." For the rebellious protagonist of the novel, Teresa Hawkins, however, "life is only a passage. . . . to our secret desires . . . to Cytherea." Teresa's escape is accomplished through a succession of journeys, during the course of which she finds herself temporarily plunged into ever greater victimhood. The opening focus on the father, seminaked astride the doorway and haranguing his silent daughters, is soon displaced by the sinister and predatory figure of the misogynist, Jonathan Crow. Perversely fixing on Crow as an object of her questing desire, Teresa negotiates many physical and psychological ordeals before being initiated into full sensual awakening in her encounter with the generous and effusive American abroad, James Quick. In the final and, for some, controversial twist of the novel, Teresa's one night of passion with wanderer and kindred spirit Harry Girton prepares her to return voluntarily to her connubial life with James in the metropolis, having discovered through this experience that her thirst is after the "track-making and wandering of the man in the world, not after the man." Published to generally positive reviews in the United States and England, *For Love Alone* has appealed to both feminist and nationalist critics, and a considerable body of critical literature has developed on this novel.

Stead's next novel, *Letty Fox: Her Luck* (1946), published in New York and London, inaugurates a sequence of novels exploring American manners and

```
                                                              MS 4967. Fol. 2
           Teresa

    LOVE, DEATH AND THE DEVIL.


    The fertility of the tropics and youth: lunar passions:  combined with puritan
    upbringing:

    Day forest - pool
    Night forest - moonglade:
    Rocky terrifying coast - caves:
    Wild country, bald mountain - Endymion:
    Tropical forest - natives:
    Moon - monsters:
    Witches' sabbath:
    Breughel:
    Native customs:
    Sybarites' feast.
    Christians in lion's den:   grotto scult.   fauste sect
         in primitive Greektimes:
    Hartz night:
    Paolo and Francesca:(unsatisfactory, never a single lover):
    Bacchanalia, Saturnalia: (Carolines:
    Anatomy of Melancholy: Shakespeare: Metamorphoses:  Lincoln's Inn  epithal.(Donne)
    classic poetical play of spring night) ("tonight put on perfection and a woman's name"
    grotesques:        frescoes:       (Xtn. legend miserably bare of images except Song.)
    Susannah and the Elders:    Lot and his children:  Ruth and Boaz:
    Monsters: fables: animals: giants: prehistoric men:  sordid licence: corpses:
           (but as for individual men, ideal love - Shelley, Goethe, etc. no actors)
           (she imagined love with a single man but how ? Marriage night,
              moonlight holy attitude and nothing more).
    Modern times: (historic licence): interruptions of sexual consummations: illicit
           loves: impossible, undesirable loves: composition of all possible loves:
           Bohemia:  heaven and hell: public and private loves
    Landscapes: bodies both naked and hairy, mangy like bison in autumn, lion:
           mountains-cows and the like: the male parts because not allowed less seen
           but sometimes a rock, a cliff standing up in spume say at stormy cape.
           Clouds.
    (When she had finished this she had convassed the range of art and letters in several
    languages!)
```

Notes for Stead's 1944 novel, For Love Alone
(National Library of Australia, MS4967)

society. Focusing, as does *For Love Alone,* on a young woman's embarkation upon life, *Letty Fox: Her Luck* satirizes social mores in New York. According to Anita Segerberg in her 1989 essay in *Australian Literary Studies,* Stead had originally planned a book about two sisters, Teresa and Letitia, and had drafted sections of *Letty Fox* and *For Love Alone* in tandem. In contrast to Teresa's quixotic quest, however, Letty's feverish search for a suitable mate steers a course for social belonging and conventionality. Unlike the artistic, quasi-mystical Teresa, who follows the singular, heroic path of suffering and self-restraint, Letty is a vulgar "Everywoman" figure seeking through her generous promiscuity and serial monogamy some anchorage in life. Yet, although she is an unreliable narrator, Letty is not an entirely despicable figure, since she is occasionally capable of astute observation of self and others: "What I had in me that gave me most joy were two things: the capacity for an enormous output of work, and the ability to enjoy myself regardless of expense, regardless of others; a healthy trait, if a bit barbaric." The garrulous first-person narrative and picaresque plot combine to preclude the reader's close identification with Letty, who appears as a latter-day Moll Flanders and an exemplary instance of the advice she dishes out to would-be novelists. Pragmatic, resilient, and direct, Letty typifies the superficially modern—her shrewd grasp of the marital game enabling her ultimate conformity rather than resistance to its rules. While some reviews were positive, the reception of *Letty Fox: Her Luck* was generally either scandalized or uncomprehending. Confounded by its politics, Barbara Giles—in *New Masses,* 10 December 1946—complained that Letty Fox was "a play radical" rather than a genuine Communist. Other reviewers thought the novel merely vulgar and immoral, misconstruing its ironies. The news of this general disapprobation having reached Australia, in 1947 the Australian Literature Censorship Board placed a ban on the book that was not lifted until a decade later.

The decadent corruption of capitalist profiteering during World War II and the economy of modern sexuality are furiously satirized in *A Little Tea, A Little Chat* (1948). *A Little Tea, A Little Chat* was published in the United States when Stead was still under contract to Harcourt, Brace, but she found little support for publication of the novel in England, having parted company in 1947 with her London publisher Peter Davies, who was now gravely ill. Largely negative and dismissive reviews greeted the American publication of this book about Robbie Grant—predatory capitalist, incorrigible rogue, womanizer, and seducer—whose restless desires are chronicled in relentless detail. Robbie Grant is the last, and in some ways the most frenzied and despicable, of Stead's male monologuists. His pursuit of sexual gratification is performed with a serial zeal, and his self-aggrandizing and self-deceiving Don Juan fictions suppress his own callous exploitation of women, such as Myra Coppelius. Robbie meets his match, however, in the duplicitous and mercenary Barbara Downs, the Blondine, who fascinates, ensnares, and puzzles him until the end. Like the capitalists in *House of All Nations,* Grant is in perpetual flight from the specter of the angry masses, of coming revolution, and of death itself. Death, revolution, and apocalypse are conflated in the avenging angel, Azrael, who materializes as Hilbertson, Grant's long-anticipated nemesis. The relentless pursuit of Grant's unstoppable desire in the narrative and the spectacle of his frantic consumption also signal the direction and pace of narratives to come. The effects of an initially poor reception of this novel have been compounded by subsequent critical commentary relegating it, with others of this period, to minor status. Only recently, and with the benefit of post-structuralist perspectives, have a few commentators begun to reappraise these texts. Virginia Blain argues—in *Southerly,* December 1993—that the narrative of *A Little Tea, A Little Chat* reproduces Grant's own compulsive seriality, creating excess through its repetitions, the very boredom of which demands that the reader actively derive pleasure from the digressions of the text.

The People with the Dogs (1952), the third in this suite of American satires, revisits middle-class family life in a more temperate mood, following the desultory quest for love of an amiable bachelor, Edward Massine. Having inherited sufficient means, Edward whiles away his existence between his Manhattan apartment with its lively neighborhood community and the satirically named Whitehouse, his ancestral family home in the Catskills. The extended Massine clan retreats from the metropolis to Whitehouse to enjoy its quotidian dramas in pastoral serenity and to dote upon its many dogs. The affectionately rendered Edward is an unawakened man lacking direction and passion, in both personal and political senses. Caught within a now exhausted relationship, for much of the story he does little to resist its buffetings. Edward's futile attempt to uproot a wild hops vine rambling out of control on the family property, however, triggers a slow awakening. The description of the vine conveys the organic and complex interconnections of the family, its sleepy rootedness in history, and its vigorous and smothering stranglehold. Though the dimensions of his gesture are limited, Edward finally embraces commitment, and the narrative leaves him with the promise of some personal integrity and satisfaction. Neither as ironic as Letty's narrative nor as epic as Teresa's, Edward's story offers a gently satiric investigation of social mores and of the American dream of the utopian community. Though

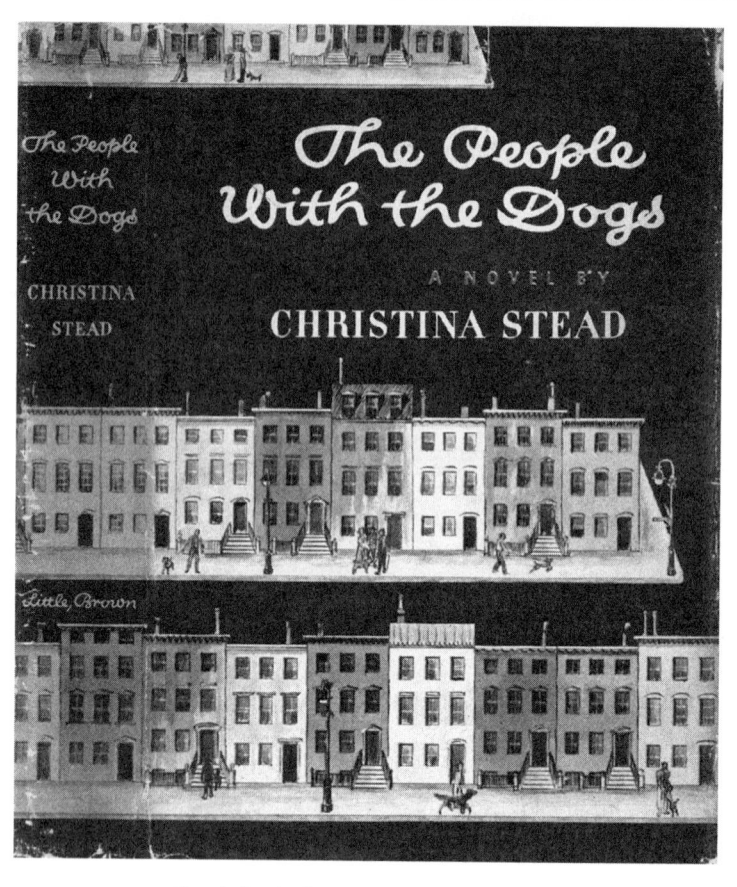

Dust jacket for Stead's 1952 novel, a satirical portrait of middle-class American family life (The Arlyn Bruccoli Collection)

Stead had sold the manuscript to Little, Brown in 1950, the novel languished for two years. The reviews of the published novel generally lacked enthusiasm. Subsequently, commentators have tended to agree that, despite its integral place within the American sequence, *The People with the Dogs* lacks Stead's usual energy and verve, even though it includes some masterful passages.

The Puzzleheaded Girl: Four Novellas, published in 1967 to favorable reviews, is a book that cannot be straightforwardly positioned in this chronology of Stead's fiction, since its elements are difficult to date. Some material from this collection likely was drafted during Stead's stay in the United States, possibly as early as 1938, while other sections were drafted much later, in the 1950s and early 1960s. The book's four novellas—"The Puzzleheaded Girl," "The Dianas," "The Right-Angled Creek," and "Girl from the Beach"—are thematically parallel, although, as Stead remarked in a letter to Stanley Burnshaw (22 July 1965), the inclusion of "The Right-Angled Creek" works to break up "the tightness of a single idea controlling the book." Collectively the novellas depict the disoriented sexuality of young American women, questioning the state of gender relations in the morally and politically conservative postwar era. As chaste Diana figures, the girls can be viewed as psychologically damaged and socially subversive. In "The Dianas" Lydia's inability to separate herself from her mother erodes her capacity to sustain a heterosexual relationship, whereas in "Girl from the Beach" Linda's similarly stunted psychology can be read as a commentary on the politics of postwar American imperialism and the lost idealism of the Left. In the title story, "The Puzzleheaded Girl," the virginal Honor Lawrence, befriended by the kindly and protective Augustus Debrett, displays what Judith Kegan Gardiner—in her essay in *World Literature Written in English* (1992)—describes as "female hysteria as a form of political rebellion." In contrast with these novellas, "The Right-Angled Creek" interrupts the hectic pace of metropolitan life to focus on the fecundity of nature. Stead's earlier lyricism returns in the exquisite description of the "spellbound" Dilley's Place, with its alien abundance and its uneasy Diana figure, the enigmatic ghost of "Poky" (after Pocahontas). Margaret Harris—in her essay in *World Literature Written in English*—says that *The Puzzleheaded Girl* "forms a kind of coda" to Stead's

American sequence, overlapping with the concerns of the posthumously published *I'm Dying Laughing: The Humourist* (1986).

The chronology of *The Puzzleheaded Girl* mirrors the obscurity of Stead's own career at a time when she was still writing prolifically. The novels written between the late 1940s and the late 1950s bear the unmistakable traces of Stead's changing fortunes and mood as a displaced, expatriate writer and articulate the anxieties of her drift into publishing marginality and political minority. Though their departure from the United States for England and Europe in 1947 was a timely one, Stead and Blake did not entirely escape the effects of McCarthyism and the attendant shift in the cultural and political climate. This time period was for the couple one of itinerancy and poverty in which they tried to derive a meager living from hack literary work. Beset by publishing obscurity and low-level harassment by the FBI, Stead witnessed with horror–and to some degree experienced–postwar European hunger. Blake's health began to deteriorate during this time, and Stead's nostalgia for Australia grew, as seen in her increased efforts to renew her Australian connections. In 1952, the year she and Blake married, Stead applied for a Commonwealth Literary Fund Fellowship but was unsuccessful. In addition, the efforts of Stead devotees in Australia–such as Douglas Stewart, Colin Roderick, Clem Christesen, Walter Stone, and Ron Geering–was gathering strength. The revitalizing of Stead's literary fortunes, however, did not occur until the republication of *The Man Who Loved Children* in 1965 by Holt, Rinehart, and Winston.

Meanwhile, Stead's fiction was becoming more intense and bleak, tending to probe reasons for the postwar malaise and the failure of the socialist ideal in the West. *The Little Hotel* (1973), *Miss Herbert (The Suburban Wife)* (1976), and *Cotters' England* all draw upon the downward spiral of personal and political fortunes during this era. None of these books–focusing on gender disorder, disillusion, decadence, and social and political anarchy–found a publisher until more than a decade later. The reasons for this fall into publishing obscurity have been attributed variously to the couple's dislocation–their lack of continuity with one publisher or with an influential literary circle–and, more insidiously, to their leftist political affiliations.

The likelihood that FBI harassment exacted a toll on Stead illuminates elements of *The Little Hotel*, the atmosphere of which reproduces a sinister sense of surveillance. Drafted by the early 1950s, *The Little Hotel* remained unpublished until 1973, although in 1952 part of the manuscript was published in Australia under the title "The Hotel-Keeper" in the literary magazine *Southerly*. In *The Little Hotel*, the apparently benign narrator,

Dust jacket for Stead's 1976 novel, a character study of a middle-class woman in postwar England (The Arlyn Bruccoli Collection)

hotelkeeper Selda Bonnard, retails the personal lives of her transient guests, feigning a warmth that belies her avid curiosity and unsavory desire for gossip. Selda's true interests lie elsewhere, detached from the individual fates of the inmates of the hotel. Unevenly sustained, Selda's narrative view vanishes during the middle of the story, supplanted by an omniscient narration that follows the guests outside the doors of the hotel. Although this haphazard approach is not atypical in Stead's novels, the unexplained shift in viewpoint affects this text in interesting ways. Paranoia is the keynote, as Selda's husband eavesdrops unashamedly and as the predatory Mr. Wilkins and Dr. Blaise devise furtive schemes to prey upon their women. Lydia Trollope's narrow personal escape from the loveless Wilkins, her mercenary partner, is a small triumph wrested from an otherwise uniformly dark picture of the relations between men and women, the oppressors and the oppressed, in fugitive-ridden Cold War Europe.

Though still unsuccessful in finding a publisher for recent work, Stead continued to be extremely productive, moving rapidly into the full drafting in 1952 of her first postwar English novel, "Cotters' England." This manuscript was not published until more than a decade later, first in the United States as *Dark Places of the Heart* in 1966 and then in 1967 in Britain as *Cotters' England*. Like *The Little Hotel*, *Cotters' England* is permeated by the horrors of surveillance and by a set of social, psychological, and political dislocations. In 1949, having sought to meet with typical English workers, Stead stayed for a brief time with friend Anne Dooley's family, the Kellys, in Newcastle. Much of the material for the novel was garnered from this encounter. The action of the novel alternates between Nellie Cotter's Lamb Street flat in London and events in the family home in Bridgehead in the industrial north. Nellie Cotter, described by her elusive husband, George, as a "Fleet Street sobsister," pretends to espouse the cause of the poor and needy, but her real mission is to prey upon them, vampire-like, with her defeatist fictions. The men in this narrative are emasculated, absent, or marginal: in London, Nellie victimizes her brother Tom, while in Bridgehead, the other sibling, Peggy, brutally unhouses Tom's counterpart, Uncle Syme. Replete with competing narratives that undermine the rational foundations of knowledge and truth, *Cotters' England* is a complex exploration of the workings of ideology that has been the subject of increasing critical attention in recent years. Although reviews were lukewarm, especially in the United States, English commentators such as Rodney Pybus—in his 1982 essay in *Stand*—have praised Stead's acute rendering of northern English dialect and culture. Critics such as Terry Sturm, seeking to identify the nature of Stead's achievement, also embraced the novel as a brilliant, if bleak, example of her fiction.

Both reviewers and critics responded with far less enthusiasm to *Miss Herbert (The Suburban Wife)*, in which Stead presents another view of postwar England, by means of the mundane life of a middle-class woman, the unsavory and disappointing Eleanor Herbert. Even so, in recent times *Miss Herbert* has been productively analyzed using feminist and queer theoretical approaches; a shrewd example of the latter is an article by Kate Lilley in *Southerly* (December 1993). Not unlike Elvira in *The Beauties and Furies*, the beautiful but shallow and relentlessly suburban Eleanor Herbert is depicted as a "Venus unknown to Venus," whose approach to life is determinedly conservative and whose blinkered views are constructed from middle-class ideologies and discourses. As Sheridan points out in her 1988 study, Eleanor's few encounters with great passion are mediated by a set of inauthentic popular discourses that effectively prohibit even as they gesture toward "authentic" desire for a fully awakened life.

Eleanor Herbert's dogged and blind optimism continues to characterize her behavior, long after opportunity has evaporated. The portrait of Eleanor and her bleak situation as a hack literary worker in postwar Britain conveys something of Stead's own experience but also imposes a moral and political distance between the author and her fictional character.

With the cultural shift after the Cold War, the revival of Stead's literary reputation was spearheaded by the 1965 republication of *The Man Who Loved Children*, which included an influential introduction by American poet and academic Randall Jarrell. Stead's reputation gathered further strength from the great wave of interest in women's writing driven by the emergence of a second wave of feminism. In Australia, Stead's reputation was most significantly shepherded by Geering, an academic whose work ensured that Stead's fiction secured a place—albeit a qualified one—in the Australian literary canon. These developments led to the eventual reprinting of Stead's earlier novels of the 1930s and 1940s as well as to the publication, long after their drafting, of the three 1950s manuscripts, a development that reinforced the erroneous perception among her readers that Stead was continuing to produce new work throughout the 1970s.

William Blake, who had been in failing health for some time, died in 1968. After his death, it would seem that Stead lost much of her will to write fiction. She had also lost her most compelling reason for remaining away from Australia any longer. Provided with a Creative Arts Fellowship to the Australian National University, Stead enjoyed a brief visit to Australia in 1969 before finally returning in 1974 to stay for the last ten years of her life. A scandal surrounding the arbitrary withdrawal of the Britannica Australia Award for Literature from Stead in 1967 on the spurious grounds that, as an expatriate, she was not sufficiently "Australian," had provoked fierce debate in Australian literary circles, prompting an outraged Patrick White to institute a prize for previously unrecognized writers of significance. Stead was the first recipient of White's prize, in 1974. Though by now much feted in Australia and elsewhere, Christina Stead produced little substantially new fiction in the years beyond 1968, although she did remain an extraordinarily prolific correspondent and as such continued to write copiously until her death on 31 March 1983. Stead's letters, selected by her literary executor, Geering, were published posthumously in two volumes in 1992.

I'm Dying Laughing was published posthumously in 1986, following substantial reconstruction by Geering. Though she had made good progress on the novel, which had been under development during the 1940s and 1950s, Stead stalled after repeated attempts

Dust jacket for Stead's posthumously published 1986 novel, edited by her literary executor, Ron G. Geering (Richland County Public Library)

to revise—following an editor's requests—to make the historical context more explicit and accessible for contemporary American readers. Increasingly unconvinced by this process, Stead finally abandoned work on the manuscript in 1974. The task of piecing the manuscript together was a considerable one that involved Geering in several years of painstaking work. Based on the lives of one-time close friends, the popular writer and social activist Ruth McKenney and her husband Richard Bransten, *I'm Dying Laughing* probes the impossibly contradictory position of leftist American writers caught up in and compromised by the Hollywood mass-cultural scene in the 1940s. Stead herself was employed as a scriptwriter in Hollywood for a brief interlude in 1942. Her novel satirizes the crassly materialist lifestyles of the party faithful, dependent on the largesse of the film industry, whose subscription to a narrow revisionism allowed American Communism to survive, if only for a time, within national and cultural boundaries. Emily Wilkes emerges as one of Stead's most compelling characters, a larger-than-life Rabelaisian figure whose boundless appetite and consumption appalls and attracts. Emily yearns to serve the revolutionary cause by writing the great proletarian novel, a goal that increasingly eludes her as she pumps out popular novels to generate the income required for her burgeoning family and hedonistic lifestyle. She and her husband, Stephen, a revolutionary scion from a wealthy American family with whom the couple self-servingly strive to remain connected, are expelled from the Hollywood-based Communist Party for their Stalinist views. They depart with their children for the Continent, where they fall further into hedonism, betraying their ideals while continuing to deceive themselves and each other. The novel ends apocalyptically in suicide and madness, with Emily last seen derelict and deranged on the steps of the Forum in Rome, clutching the disordered pages of her unfinished manuscript about her counterrevolutionary heroine, Marie Antoinette. With her tortured and seismic laughter, Emily embodies the postwar implosion of revolutionary idealism in the West. Though considered by some to be unwieldy, the critical consensus is that *I'm Dying Laughing* is an unfinished masterpiece, confirming Christina Stead's achievement as a major twentieth-century novelist.

Letters:

A Web of Friendship: Selected Letters (1928-1973), edited by R. G. Geering (Sydney: Angus & Robertson, 1992);

Talking into the Typewriter: Selected Letters (1973-1983), edited by Geering (Sydney: Angus & Robertson, 1992).

Bibliography:

Brigid Rooney, comp., "Bibliography," in *The Magic Phrase: Critical Essays on Christina Stead,* edited by Margaret Harris (St. Lucia: University of Queensland Press, 2000).

Biographies:

Chris Williams, *Christina Stead: A Life of Letters* (Fitzroy, Vic.: McPhee Gribble, 1989);

Hazel Rowley, *Christina Stead: A Biography* (Port Melbourne, Vic.: Heinemann, 1993).

References:

Jonathan Arac, "The Struggle for the Cultural Heritage: Christina Stead Refunctions Charles Dickens and Mark Twain," *Cultural Critique,* 2 (1985-1986): 171-189;

Virginia Blain, "*A Little Tea, A Little Chat:* Decadent Pleasures and the Pleasure of Decadence," *Southerly,* 53, no. 4 (December 1993): 20-35;

Diana Brydon, *Christina Stead* (London: Macmillan, 1987);

Angela Carter, "Unhappy Families—Angela Carter on the Scope of Christina Stead's Achievement," *London Review of Books,* 16 September 1982 - 6 October 1982, pp. 11-13;

M. Barnard Eldershaw, "Australian Writers 2: Christina Stead," *Bulletin,* 3 November 1937, pp. 2 and 50; revised as "Christina Stead," in *Essays in Australian Fiction* (Melbourne: Melbourne University Press, 1938), pp. 158-181; reprinted in *The Magic Phrase,* edited by Margaret Harris;

Judith Kegan Gardiner, "'Caught but not caught': Psychology and Politics in Christina Stead's *The Puzzleheaded Girl,*" *World Literature Written in English,* 32, no. 1 (1992): 26-41;

Giulia Giuffré, "Christina Stead (1902-1983)," in *A Writing Life: Interviews with Australian Women Writers,* edited by Giuffre (Sydney: Allen & Unwin, 1990), pp. 72-87;

Jennifer Gribble, *Christina Stead* (Melbourne: Oxford University Press, 1994);

Margaret Harris, "Christina Stead's Human Comedy: The American Sequence," *World Literature Written in English,* 32, no. 1 (1992): 42-51;

Harris, ed., *The Magic Phrase: Critical Essays on Christina Stead* (St. Lucia: University of Queensland Press, 2000);

Randall Jarrell, "An Unread Book," in Christina Stead, *The Man Who Loved Children* (New York: Holt, Rinehart & Winston, 1965), pp. v-xli;

Kate Lilley, "The New Curiosity Shop: Marketing Genre and Femininity in Stead's *Miss Herbert (The Suburban Wife),*" *Southerly,* 53, no. 4 (December 1993): 5-12;

Rodney Pybus, "*Cotters' England:* In Appreciation," *Stand,* 23, no. 4 (1982): 40-47;

Anita Segerberg, "A Fiction of Sisters: Christina Stead's *Letty Fox* and *For Love Alone,*" *Australian Literary Studies,* 14, no. 1 (May 1989): 15-25;

Susan Sheridan, *Christina Stead* (Brighton: Harvester, 1988);

Terry Sturm, "Christina Stead's New Realism: *The Man Who Loved Children* and *Cotters' England,*" in *Cunning Exiles,* edited by Don Anderson and Stephen Knight (Sydney: Angus & Robertson, 1974), pp. 9-35;

Chris Williams, "David Stead: The Man Who Loved Nature," *Meridian,* 8, no. 2 (1989): 101-115;

Louise Yelin, "Fifty Years of Reading: A Reception Study of *The Man Who Loved Children,*" *Contemporary Literature,* 31, no. 4 (Winter 1990): 472-498;

Yelin, "Representing the 1930s: Capitalism, Phallocracy, and the Politics of the Popular Front in *House of All Nations,*" in *The Magic Phrase,* pp. 71-88.

Papers:

The unpublished papers of Christina Stead are held in the National Library of Australia Manuscript Collection (Christina Stead Papers, MS 4967). Some of Stead's correspondence is held in the Harry Ransom Humanities Research Center, University of Texas, Austin, and smaller holdings can be found in the Berg Collection of the New York Public Library and at Yale University.

P. R. Stephensen
(20 November 1901 – 28 May 1965)

James Packer
Workers' Educational Association Sydney

BOOKS: *Policeman of the Lord: A Political Satire* (London: Sophistocles Press, 1928?);

The Bushwhackers: Sketches of Life in the Australian Outback (London: Mandrake Press, 1929);

The Well of Sleevelessness: A Tale for the Least of These Little Ones (London: Scholartis Press, 1929);

The Legend of Aleister Crowley: Being a Study of the Documentary Evidence Relating to a Campaign of Personal Vilification Unparalleled in Literary History (London: Mandrake Press, 1930; revised and enlarged edition, St. Paul: Llwellyn, 1970);

A Master of Hounds: Being the Life-Story of Harry Buckland of Ashford, anonymous (London: Faber & Faber, 1931);

Trade without Money! An Examination of the German Barter System, anonymous (Sydney: Australian Book Services, 1935);

The Foundations of Culture in Australia: An Essay Towards National Self Respect (Gordon, N.S.W.: W. J. Miles, 1936);

A Brief Survey of Australian History: Our Story in Fifteen Decades, Publicist (Sydney), special issue (January 1938);

Japan's 2,599th Anniversary: A Plea for a Better Understanding, and for More Peace, Trade & Friendship between Australia and Japan (Sydney: Publicist Publishing, 1939);

The Life and Works of A. G. Stephens ("The Bookfellow"): A Lecture Delivered to the Fellowship of Australian Writers, Sydney, 10th March 1940 (Sydney: P. R. Stephensen, 1940);

Glossary to "Bio-Politics" (Sydney: Publicist Publishing, 1941);

Fifty Points for Australia: An Exposition of a Policy for an Australia-First Party after the War (Sydney: Publicist Publishing, 1941);

William John Miles, Born at Woolloomooloo, Sydney, 27th August 1871; Died at Gordon, Sydney, 10th January 1943: Valedictory Address (Sydney, 1942);

P. R. Stephensen, 1929

Kookaburras and Satyrs: Some Recollections of the Fanfrolico Press (Cremorne: Talkarra Press, 1954);

The Viking of Van Diemen's Land: The Stormy Life of Jorgen Jorgensen, by Stephensen and Frank Clune (Sydney: Angus & Robertson, 1954);

Philip Dimmock: A Memoir of a Poet (Sydney: Talkarra Press, 1958);

Nationalism in Australian Literature: Commonwealth Literary Fund Lecture at the University of Adelaide, 30th September, 1959 (N.p., 1959);

Sydney Sails! The Story of the Royal Sydney Yacht Squadron's First 100 Years (1862–1962) (Sydney: Angus & Robertson, 1962);

The Pirates of the Brig "Cyprus," by Stephensen and Clune (London: Hart-Davis, 1962; New York: Morrow, 1963);

The History and Description of Sydney Harbour (Adelaide: Rigby, 1966; London: Angus & Robertson / Adelaide: Rigby, 1967).

Edition: *The Foundations of Culture in Australia,* edited by Craig Munro (Sydney: Allen & Unwin, 1986).

OTHER: V. I. Lenin, *Imperialism,* translated by Stephensen (London: Communist Party of Great Britain, 1925);

Lenin, *On the Road to Insurrection,* translated by Stephensen (London: Communist Party of Great Britain, 1926);

Friedrich Nietzsche, *The Antichrist of Nietzsche,* translated by Stephensen (London: Fanfrolico Press, 1928);

Beresford Egan, *The Sink of Solitude,* preface by Stephensen (London: Hermes Press, 1928);

Harry Hudson, *Flynn's Flying Doctors: An Artist's Journey through the Outback and the Story of the Flying Doctor Service in Australia,* written in collaboration with Stephensen (Melbourne: Heinemann, 1956);

William H. S. Jones, *The Cape Horn Breed: My Experiences as an Apprentice in Sail in the Full-Rigged Ship "British Isles,"* written in collaboration with Stephensen (London: Melrose, 1956; New York: Criterion, 1956);

Sir James Bisset, *Sail Ho! My Early Years at Sea,* written in collaboration with Stephensen (Sydney: Angus & Robertson, 1958; London: Hart-Davis, 1961);

Bisset, *Tramps and Ladies: My Early Years in Steamers,* written in collaboration with Stephensen (Sydney: Angus & Robertson, 1959);

Bisset, *Commodore: War, Peace and Big Ships,* written in collaboration with Stephensen (Sydney: Angus & Robertson, 1961; London: Angus & Robertson, 1961).

SELECTED PERIODICAL PUBLICATIONS–
UNCOLLECTED: "Satyrs or Kookaburras?" *Queensland University Magazine* (Brisbane) (August 1920): 16–17;

"The Fanfrolico Universe: A Rejoinder," *Biblionews* (Sydney) (February 1959): 6–9.

Since the late nineteenth century, Australian writing has been championed by many "practical idealists," among them the literary figure known variously as "P.R.S.," "Inky," or P. R. Stephensen. Writer, polemicist, publisher, and political radical, Stephensen wrote at least one book of enduring value to Australian cultural history and lived a life that earned the title bestowed on him by his biographer, Craig Munro: "Wild Man of Letters."

Percival Reginald Stephensen's father, Christian Stephensen, was the son of a Dane (family name Steffensen) who had settled in Biggenden, near Maryborough in Queensland. Christian Stephensen married Marie-Louise Tardent, daughter of a Swiss immigrant, Henry Tardent, whose organizational abilities and cultural flair were carried on by his grandson. Born in 1901, the year of the official federation of the six Australian colonies, Percival Stephensen spent his early childhood in the Queensland bush, attending Biggenden primary school before receiving a boarding scholarship to the Maryborough Boys' Grammar School in 1914. During his school years he revealed a resilient if ruthless disposition. On elevation to prefect, for example, he subjected the entire junior school at Maryborough to corporal punishment. At Maryborough he was taught by the scholar and socialist pacifist, V. Gordon Childe, who converted Stephensen to the anticonscription cause, a cause Stephensen took with him to the University of Queensland in 1919.

At the University of Queensland he took over the student magazine, even renaming it *Galmahra*–an aboriginal expression meaning "bearer of words"– perhaps a response to the title of the Sydney University arts magazine, *Hermes*. Hellenism was the dominant style at Australian universities during the early twentieth century, and Stephensen's acquaintance with Norman Lindsay's son Jack brought him in contact with the most extreme form of that style. The ensuing debate between the two young men, carried on in the pages of the *Queensland University Magazine* before Stephensen renamed it, opposed "satyrs" to "kookaburras." According to Stephensen, "what is required for endowing us with an Australian literature" precluded the importation of "fat young nymphs and pure-bred satyrs from the recognised poetical stud-farms of European libraries." In his reply, Jack Lindsay allowed that while a poet may "express his desire through a Kookaburra . . . there is no need for such contortions." Lindsay was something of a political radical, and the ensuing friendship between the two students brought Stephensen into the ambit of the Workers Education Association (WEA), for which Childe also taught. The Bolshevism Stephensen professed throughout the 1920s was owing in part to the friendship patterns he established at the University of Queensland and in the WEA.

Stephensen and his future wife, Winifred Venus Lockyer, at Oxford, 1925

After graduating from the University of Queensland in 1922, Stephensen was resident master at Ipswich Boys' Grammar School until October 1924, after which time he traveled to England as a Rhodes Scholar at Oxford. Renewing contact with Jack Lindsay in England, Stephensen combined his energetic support for workers' causes with Norman Lindsay's brand of Nietzschean philosophy, which Jack Lindsay was attempting to export to London through the Fanfrolico Press. By 1927, having translated two works by V. I. Lenin and been engaged with the 1926 General Strike—exciting the interest of the British Secret Service and risking expulsion from Oxford—Stephensen was ready to begin a career in publishing and general cultural entrepreneurship. He began to abandon his leftist activism of the early 1920s for a political aestheticism incorporating Russian anarchist Mikhail Bakunin's maxim "Live dangerously!" and the *uebermensch* (superman) of Friedrich Nietzsche, but his leftist activities were not forgotten by the Secret Service when he became involved in the "Australia First" movement during the 1940s.

In June 1927, on receipt of his second-class honors degree at Oxford, Stephensen replaced Jack Kirtley, Lindsay's original partner at the Fanfrolico Press. Stephensen also joined the advisory committee to the Workers' Theatre Movement, and during the first half of 1927 he wrote agitprop plays for the group under the name Peter Stephens. (Two of these plays—*Stanley's Pipe Dream* and *Blasting the Reds*—are extant.) Stephensen's literary energies, now turned toward general libertarianism, were largely directed to the production of limited-edition books and co-editing the Fanfrolico literary magazine, *The London Aphrodite*, "a miscellany of poems stories and essays by various hands eminent or rebellious," six issues of which were published between August 1928 and July 1929.

The ideological tenor of Stephensen's two-year association with the Fanfrolico Press may be gauged from the following lines in his prospectus for Jack Lindsay's *Dionysos*, a work on Nietzsche published by Fanfrolico late in 1928: "Issued at a moment when the schools of poetry and the abstract methodists of Art and Philosophy are almost at the bottom of their cul-de-sac, Dionysos may well be the manifesto of a new and violently human poetic effort with which an ascending generation of writers will mock the expiring snarls of outmoded *fauvistes*." In the same spirit, Stephensen translated Nietzsche's *The Antichrist* in 1928. In a 3 March 1959 letter to Harry Chaplin, Stephensen called the introduction he provided for it "the best piece of work I have ever done."

The libertarian spirit of the Fanfrolico Press was most acutely channeled through *The London Aphrodite*, for which Stephensen wrote diatribes against modernism—that is, against the evils of English devitalization—in each of the six issues. He took part in one of the most important London censorship battles of the late 1920s, pamphleteering in *The Well of Sleevelessness: A Tale for The Least of These Little Ones* (1929) against the suppression of Radclyffe Hall's lesbian novel *The Well of Loneliness* (1928). He also proposed and then produced an edition of D. H. Lawrence's paintings under the imprint of a new publishing company, Mandrake Press.

Stephensen met Lawrence late in December 1928. Though wary of Stephensen's connection with the Lindsays, whose aesthetic he glimpsed in *The London Aphrodite* and found puerile, Lawrence was eager to publish his paintings. Stephensen was therefore obliged to distance the Mandrake Press from his Fanfrolico activities, with the unintended consequence of alienating himself from Jack Lindsay. After a second meeting with Stephensen, Lawrence wrote to S. S. Koteliansky on 11 January 1929, "There will be no Lindsay—either father or son—in the Mandrake Press."

Stephensen maintained his position at the Fanfrolico Press until mid April 1929, when he was supplanted as manager by Australian Brian Penton, a protégé of Norman Lindsay. Penton was more pragmatic about the Fanfrolico Press than either Stephensen or Lindsay, and Stephensen never shared Penton's clear-eyed perception of the book trade. In fact, Lawrence feared that Stephensen's heightened sense of himself would bring his enterprises to nothing, and although the paintings were published with considerable commercial success, the other Mandrake projects, particularly Stephensen's *The Legend of Aleister Crowley: Being a Study of the Documentary Evidence Relating to a Campaign of Personal Vilification Unparalleled in Literary History* (1930), fared so poorly that by 1931 Stephensen was making his first efforts as a ghostwriter (*Pavlova* for Walford Hyden) and as an anonymous biographer (*A Master of Hounds*, 1931).

In mid 1929 Mandrake Press published Stephensen's *The Bushwhackers: Sketches of Life in the Australian Outback*, stories mostly about the Australian bush "striking back" against white intrusion. On 7 June 1929 Lawrence, whose novel *Kangaroo* (1923) is based on his 1922 visit to Australia, had written to Stephensen, "I am puzzled that you should feel you have to conquer or contradict something of me inside yourself. *Kangaroo* was only just what I felt. You may indeed know something much deeper and more vital about Australia and the Australian future. I should be the first to admit it. I should hate to think I ever said the last word, on anything. One says one's say, and leaves someone else to continue and improve on it." Stephensen took seriously Lawrence's criticism, as well as Lawrence's comment in a 17 June letter about Australian literary efforts in general: "You won't be patient enough and go deep enough into your own scene."

Though he continued to rely on Lawrence's ideological model after Lawrence's death in 1930, Stephensen gradually cast it aside. Yet, his ambitions later encompassed a Lawrencean role for himself over the "Australian scene." Lawrence's accusation that Australian writers failed to "go deep" has a curious echo in a letter Stephensen wrote to Jack Lindsay in December 1930. Lindsay had previously written to him of his current psychological impasses in a letter steeped in the earthy but peculiar psychoanalytic language with which Stephensen himself had occasionally addressed Lawrence: "We are all animals and scared to realise it," wrote Lindsay. "The dog is controlled by the knot in his penis and the bitch's mentruals which prevent him from indefinitely fornicating as man does. . . ." Stephensen replied in a manner that suggests his growing discomfort with the "dirty" experimentalism in which he and Lindsay had traded over the previous five years: "My own impression, held somewhat sceptically and for convenience, is that man has fluked a consciousness which quite transcends the abyss of animalism, where psychoanalysts still flounder and probe. 'Man is a bridge' over that abyss, not a dragnet in its depths of slime. . . ."

In 1932 Stephensen wrote Jack Lindsay a letter declaring his intention to leave England "to start Publishing in Australia." Stephensen and Norman Lindsay, who had recently been in London, had worked out a scheme with the Bulletin Company to create a new Australian publishing force in Sydney. While Jack Lindsay had become far more interested in Karl Marx than in Nietzsche, Stephensen had become more cultur-

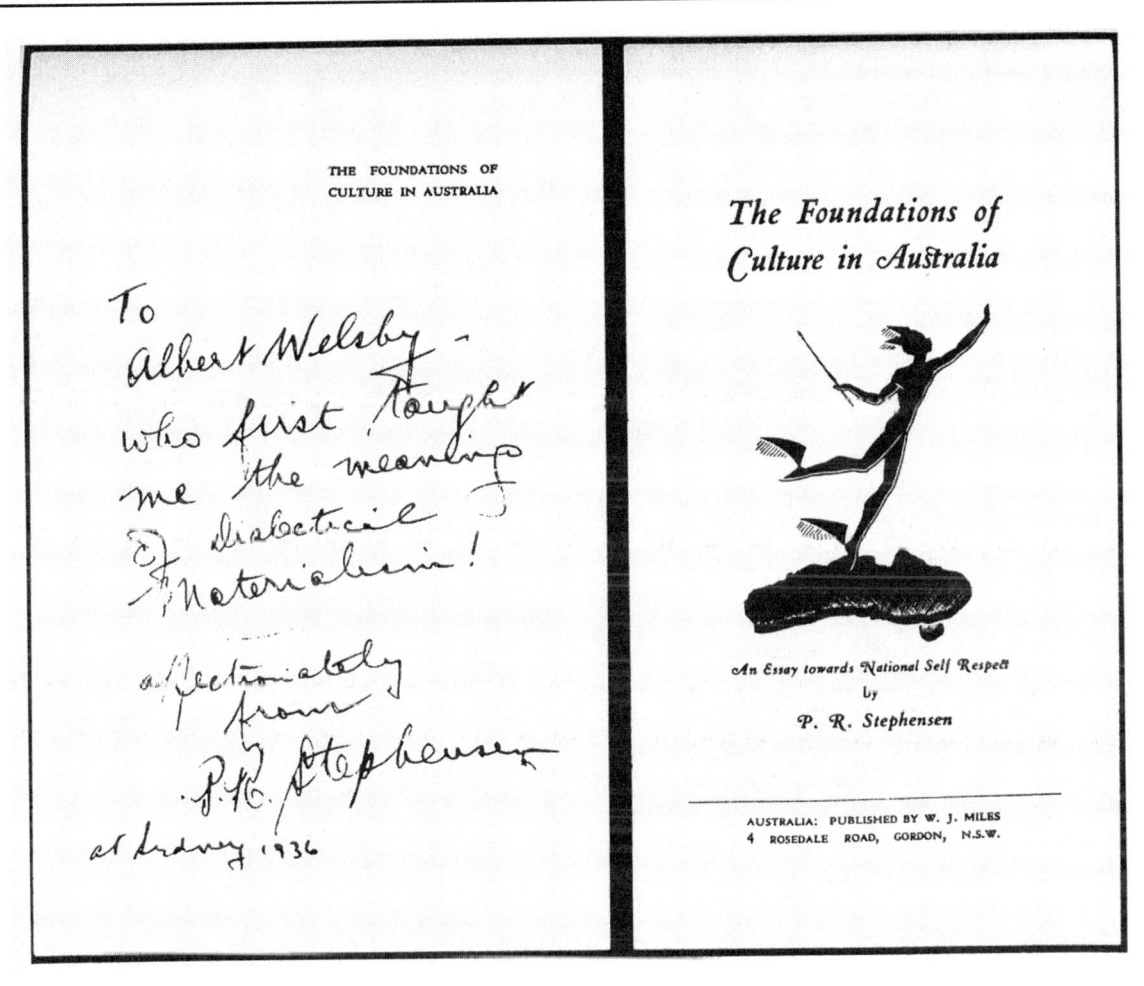

Half-title and title pages in a copy of Stephensen's 1936 essay on Australian literary and cultural identity, inscribed to a friend in the Workers' Educational Association (from Craig Munro, Wild Man of Letters, *1984)*

ally conservative than he had been as manager of the Fanfrolico Press. His cultural nationalism had reignited in the writing of *The Bushwhackers* and in his exchanges with Lawrence, even to the point of drafting the first part of a novel, "The Settlers," whose most interesting feature is the first signs of an idiosyncratic "Australian" brand of fascism. *"On the Australian plains man learned to walk upright!"* declares Stephensen's Dr Morpeth in this unfinished work. "Then he crossed to India, the home of the Aryan race. . . . *The Aryan race began in Australia.* Australia is the original home of the white man. In coming to this land we are returning home."

Stephensen's return to Australia was in the service of what became the Endeavour Press, a proprietary subsidiary of the *Bulletin*. He and Norman Lindsay quickly discovered that their project to unleash the power of the Australian literary imagination unfettered by the forces of "Overseas" was likely to bring to the surface the untutored efforts of a thousand unpublishables. Of the initial run of Endeavour publications in 1933, none was by a "new" writer. One was *Saturdee*, by Norman Lindsay; the top seller was *The Animals that Noah Forgot*, a children's book by A. B. Paterson, followed by a book on contract bridge. Most of the other Endeavour books were reprints, such as G. B. Lancaster's *Pageant* (first published in London earlier the same year) and Louis Stone's *Jonah* (first published in 1911). Sales were not good, with Miles Franklin's *Bring the Monkey* selling no more than 560 copies. By mid September 1933 Stephensen's position had become untenable. Under pressure from the directors, who had decided not to renew his contract in October, he resigned from Endeavour, taking some of his authors and founding his own press, P. R. Stephensen and Company.

During its first months, the new company survived on vanity work, including Eleanor Dark's *Prelude to Christopher* (1934), one of the most innovative Australian novels of the decade, which was published against a prepayment from Dark, to be repaid to her at two shillings a copy.

Stephensen could also claim to be the first publisher of any work by Patrick White, whom Stephensen met in pursuit of investment capital from the wealthy landowning White family. But Stephensen's most important author was Xavier Herbert, whom he had first encountered through the Endeavour Press, and in whose seminal 1930s novel *Capricornia* (eventually published by Stephensen under another imprint in 1938) he had initially felt unable to invest the necessary editorial work. For all its significance to the history of Australian literature, P. R. Stephensen and Company struggled through its short life. Stephensen's attitude (expressed in an 8 March 1934 letter to Nettie Palmer) reversed the traditional author-publisher relationship: the established writers of Australia were, he said, "too dejected to make an effort to help themselves by supporting or encouraging me." This situation was certainly the case with Patrick White, whom Stephensen asked to revise the manuscript of an early novel, "Finding Heaven." He also got little support from Herbert, who, for a period–while the manuscript for *Capricornia* was once again with an English publisher–attempted to prevent Stephensen from publishing the novel.

With financial crisis imminent, Stephensen began to find a source for his woes in acts of imputed malevolence. The greatest of these acts, he believed, was that of a former colleague, Brian Penton, who in October 1934 wrote a scathing review of Vivian Crockett's *Mezzomorto*, a book that Stephensen hoped would be his financial salvation. Stephensen sued Penton for defamation, creating a cultural cause célèbre in Sydney. The book was no *Capricornia*, nor was it as "neurotic" as Pentonian cultural criticism was apt to plead. Nothing in Penton's article, however, differed in substance from the sort of cultural criticism in which Stephensen had engaged during his days at Fanfrolico Press. Too late to save his company, Stephensen won the court case and gained some respite from his creditors.

Throughout the 1930s Stephensen involved himself with the cultural politics of national identity. In May 1935 he became chairman of the Cultural Defence Committee of the Fellowship of Australian Writers (FAW). At FAW he worked with Frank Clune, his closest associate of later years, and–in the context of "cultural defence"–he conceived his most important work, *The Foundations of Culture in Australia: An Essay Towards National Self Respect* (1936). The first part of this work appeared as a long essay in the only issue (July 1935) of *The Australian Mercury*, a periodical Stephensen attempted to establish in Sydney on the demise of P. R. Stephensen and Company. The essay was stirred into existence by a far-from-complimentary article on the standard of Australian literature by G. H. Cowling, an English-born professor of English at the University of Melbourne, which had appeared in the *Melbourne Age* on 16 February 1935. Stephensen made a point of thanking Cowling for "putting the Unteachable Englishman's point of view so succinctly on record" and went on to define the differences between Australia and Britain that made for the existence of a distinctive Australian culture. Along with Penton (whose journalistic examinations of the "National Oedipus Complex" date from 1934), Stephensen put forward a comprehensive view of an "Australian inferiority complex," deriving his psychological analysis from Lawrence and recentering "culture" on Australian soil. He went on to discuss in detail the "shouting and vigorous" energies of W. C. Wentworth's 1823 poem "Australasia," in which Australian "place" begins to emerge; the literature of the "convict stain" (Marcus Clarke, Rolf Boldrewood, Price Warung, and others) and the use to which stigmatizers of Australia were accustomed to put it; and the literature of larrikinism (youthful rowdiness) which, "if it provided an antidote to imported culture of the 'haw-haw' kind, did little more for the real development of Australia than to substitute larrikinism for convictism, as a theme, or more precisely, as an attitude, in the Australian idea." As this treatment of Australian literature left a more negative picture of the local culture than Stephensen perhaps intended, he closed the essay with a treatment of Australian art, particularly the landscape painting of Elioth Gruner, to provide "*an Australian's hypothesis of Australia.*"

Reaction to the essay was extraordinarily favorable. It is said to have galvanized the Jindyworobaks, the 1930s movement of cultural nationalism–but it did not ease Stephensen's financial difficulties. His dreams of cultural self-sufficiency coincided with his need for financial self-sufficiency in his anonymous pamphlet *Trade without Money! An Examination of the German Barter System* (1935), dealing with the economic regime in Germany.

In July 1935 Stephensen was contacted by businessman W. J. Miles, who recognized the value of "The Foundations of Culture in Australia" in terms of his own "Australia First" enthusiasms. By the end of January 1936 Miles was preparing to publish the essay, expanded to two hundred pages, in book form. In February, Miles announced plans for a political journal, *The Publicist,* for which Stephensen would receive a retainer as literary adviser. The price for this change in Stephensen's fortunes was a new emphasis on political activity, to which Stephensen acquiesced readily, although his political position, as reflected in the final parts of *The Foundations of Culture in Australia,* deeply wor-

Frank Clune and Stephensen at a book signing in the late 1940s (from Munro, Wild Man of Letters, *1984)*

ried his more liberal acquaintances. Stephensen's anti-Semitism had always been rooted in theories of a Jewish "financial international conspiracy" and it increasingly mirrored the racial nationalism of the German National Socialists.

Stephensen began to collaborate with Clune on historical fiction with *Dig* (1937), the story of the 1860–1861 expedition of Robert O'Hara Burke and William John Wills in central Australia. The collaboration continued for the rest of Stephensen's life, with Clune acknowledging Stephensen's "editorial assistance" (which was really ghostwriting) as each of more than fifty-five books was published.

Stephensen continued his literary activity by writing *A Brief Survey of Australian History: Our Story in Fifteen Decades,* a twenty-thousand-word history of Australia published as a special issue of *The Publicist* in January 1938, and by publishing a Publicist Press edition of Herbert's *Capricornia* on Australia Day (26 January) 1938. In 1940 he made several efforts to revive the literary reputation of the critic A. G. Stephens. Australia First, however, dominated Stephensen's life. When war against Germany was declared in 1939, Stephensen could no longer hide the problems of the Australia First position in respect to Germany and Japan behind his trenchantly expressed Australianism. He had frequently written in outline of a future world order in which British interests were put firmly in their place, and he had just written *Japan's 2,599th Anniversary: A Plea for a Better Understanding, and For More Peace, Trade & Friendship between Australia and Japan* (1939). Australia First had always been a target, and the war powers of the Australian federal government and its security arms made possible the suppression of the movement. Stephensen was interned in March 1942 and not released until after the war.

During the last twenty years of his life, Stephensen refused to renounce either his earlier anti-Semitism or his nationalism. On 7 November 1947 his twenty-year relationship with Winifred Venus Lockyer was formalized in marriage. He continued to work for Clune, though the relationship was never easy. Their collaboration on *The Viking of Van Dieman's Land: The Stormy Life of Jorgen Jorgensen* (1954), a biography in which Stephensen attempted a psychoanalytic treatment of his subject, is unusual because it bears his name on the title page. Clune edited it so severely for popular taste that Stephensen wrote to him complaining of "the mutilation of a work which was conceived as the most ambitious attempt at biography ever made in Australia." Also in 1954 Stephensen produced *Kookaburras and Satyrs,* a brief memoir of his Fanfrolico years, which provoked comment from Jack Lindsay, who was in the course of writing his own autobiography. The renewed acquaintance–by correspondence–found the two in as little disagreement as they had been in the 1920s.

During the 1960s Stephensen's publishing career seemed set for revival: Walter Burns, the managing director of Angus and Robertson, attempted to modernize the company and employed Stephensen to develop paperback sales. Burns's program, however, was not to the taste of the owners of the firm, and with Burns's departure, Stephensen found himself with a prospectus and no investors. It was, as a publisher, his final curtain. A few years later, on 28 May 1965, he died suddenly when he sat down after delivering a speech on book censorship to the Savage Club in Sydney.

By pursuing his course in his characteristically tempestuous and overbearing style, Stephensen found himself in a position such that, writing of Jorgen Jorgensen in *The Viking of Van Diemen's Land,* he could have been writing of himself: "His life for fifteen years had a nightmarish quality . . . had become a catastrophe. . . . his great talents were floundering in a morass of shame and disgrace." Stephensen's account of the reasons for this dilemma again seems as relevant to his own life as to Jorgensen's: "He was a poet in action–the most dangerous kind of poet, and more dangerous to himself than to others when he attempted to mould reality to conform with his capricious visions." Stephensen nonetheless professed to model his career on that of a different personality, A. G. Stephens, and in 1940 he wrote:

> Stephens lived in a world of thought in which Commerce played but a secondary part. . . . He remained, as it were, "on the outer" in Commercialist Sydney for nearly thirty years: his views conflicting with those of the money-grubbing cliques which control this City's life. He fought against the deterioration of Culture in Australia which has been such a sad feature of our national life in the past four decades; but he fought a losing battle: one man against a multitude. . . . His life is an outstanding example of the failure of Australian Democracy to provide the essentials for the fostering of a true Culture in our land. . . . His pertinacity is the amazing thing; his refusal, his stiff-backed refusal, to acknowledge defeat: his unwavering faith in Australia–and in himself.

Yet, Stephensen retrospectives started to appear in the final decade of his life. While many found it hard to take seriously a man whose anti-Jewishness went far beyond mere crankiness, his *Foundations of Culture in Australia* struck a chord with the new nationalists of the late 1950s and early 1960s. His views had anticipated the critical spirit of A. A. Philips's celebrated "The Cultural Cringe" (1950), and when P. R. Stephensen died in 1965, it had become possible to remember him as an energetic publisher and cultural warrior, as well as a pro-Aboriginal nationalist whose views feed into the prevailing sentiments of the "new Australia."

Letters:

"The D.H. Lawrence–P. R. Stephensen Letters," edited by Craig Munro, *Australian Literary Studies* (Brisbane), 11 (1984): 291–315.

Bibliography:

Craig Munro, *Wild Man of Letters: The Story of P. R. Stephensen* (Melbourne: Melbourne University Press, 1984), pp. 301–309.

Biography:

Craig Munro, *Wild Man of Letters: The Story of P. R. Stephensen* (Melbourne: Melbourne University Press, 1984).

References:

Harry F. Chaplin, ed., *The Fanfrolico Press: a Survey* (Sydney: Wentworth Press, 1976);

Ben Goldsmith, "Better Half-Dead than Read? The *Mezzomorto* Cases and their Implications for Literary Culture in the 1930s," in *Australian Literature and the Public Sphere: Refereed Proceedings of the 1998 Conference Held at the Empire Theatre and the University of Queensland, Toowoomba, 3–7 July 1998,* edited by Alison Bartlett, Robert Dixon, and Christopher Lee (Toowoomba: Association for the Study of Australian Literature, 1999);

Frances de Groen, *Xavier Herbert: A Biography* (Brisbane: University of Queensland Press, 1999);

Jack Lindsay, *Life Rarely Tells* (London: Bodley Head, 1958);

Lindsay, "Nationality and Poetry," *Queensland University Magazine* (Brisbane) (August 1920): 17–18;

Brian Penton, "The End of the Great Whoopee," *Daily Telegraph* (Sydney), 9 February 1934, p. 6.

Papers:

The largest Stephensen archive is the P. R. Stephensen Papers (MSS 1284) at the Mitchell Library in Sydney. The Fryer Library at the University of Queensland also has a collection of Stephensen papers, as well as Stephensen materials in the Walter Stone and Jack Lockyer Collections.

Douglas Stewart
(6 May 1913 – 14 February 1985)

David McCooey
Deakin University

BOOKS: *Green Lions: Poems* (Auckland: Privately printed, 1936; London: Whitcombe & Tombs, 1936);

The White Cry: Poems (London: Dent, 1939);

Elegy for an Airman, decorations by Norman Lindsay (Sydney: Johnson, 1940);

Sonnets to the Unknown Soldier (Sydney: Angus & Robertson, 1941; London: Angus & Robertson, 1941);

Ned Kelly (Sydney: Angus & Robertson, 1943; abridged edition, Sydney: Angus & Robertson, 1952);

A Girl with Red Hair (Sydney: Angus & Robertson, 1944);

The Fire on the Snow and The Golden Lover: Two Plays for Radio (Sydney: Angus & Robertson, 1944; London: Angus & Robertson, 1944);

The Dosser in Springtime (Sydney: Angus & Robertson, 1946; London: Angus & Robertson, 1946);

Shipwreck (Sydney: Shepherd, 1947);

Glencoe: A Series of Ballads (Sydney: Angus & Robertson, 1947);

The Flesh and the Spirit: An Outlook on Literature (Sydney: Angus & Robertson, 1948; Norwood, Pa.: Norwood Editions, 1978);

Sun Orchids and Other Poems, illustrated by Lindsay (Sydney: Angus & Robertson, 1952);

The Fire on the Snow, introduction by Stewart (Sydney: Angus & Robertson, 1954; London: Angus & Robertson, 1976);

The Birdsville Track and Other Poems (Sydney: Angus & Robertson, 1955);

Four Plays (Sydney: Angus & Robertson, 1958) – comprises *The Fire on the Snow, The Golden Lover, Ned Kelly,* and *Shipwreck;*

Fisher's Ghost: An Historical Comedy, illustrated by Lindsay (Sydney: Wentworth, 1960);

The Garden of Ships; A Poem, illustrated by Lindsay (Sydney: Wentworth, 1962);

Rutherford and Other Poems (Sydney: Angus & Robertson, 1962);

The Golden Lover (Sydney: Angus & Robertson, 1962);

Douglas Stewart (National Library of Australia)

Douglas Stewart (Sydney: Angus & Robertson, 1963) Australian Poets Series, selected and introduced by Stewart;

The Seven Rivers, illustrated by Margaret Coen (Sydney: Angus & Robertson, 1966); abridged edition published as *Fishing around the Monaro* (Canberra: Australian National University Press, 1978);

Collected Poems 1936–1967 (Sydney: Angus & Robertson, 1967);

Selected Poems, Modern Poets Series (Sydney: Angus & Robertson, 1973);

Brindabella, illustrated by Coen (Canberra: Brindabella, 1974);

Norman Lindsay: A Personal Memoir (Melbourne: Nelson, 1975);

The Broad Stream: Aspects of Australian Literature, Perspectives in Australian Literature (Sydney: Angus & Robertson, 1975; London: Angus & Robertson, 1975);

A Man of Sydney: An Appreciation of Kenneth Slessor (Melbourne: Nelson, 1977);

Writers of the Bulletin: 1977 Boyer Lectures (Sydney: Australian Broadcasting Commission, 1977);

Springtime in Taranaki: An Autobiography of Youth (Sydney: Hale & Iremonger, 1983);

Douglas Stewart's Garden of Friends, illustrated by Coen (Ringwood, Vic.: Viking, 1987).

PLAY PRODUCTIONS: *Ned Kelly,* Melbourne, Melbourne Union Theatre, 1943; Sydney, Elizabethan Theatre, 1956;

The Golden Lover, Melbourne, Little Theatre, 1953;

Shipwreck, Canberra, Canberra Repertory Company, June 1960;

Fisher's Ghost: An Historical Comedy, Sydney, Sydney Theatre Club, March 1961;

The Fire on the Snow, Sydney, Old Tote Theatre, 1968.

PRODUCED SCRIPTS: *The Fire on the Snow,* radio, Australian Broadcasting Commission (ABC), 6 June 1941;

Ned Kelly, radio, ABC, 1942;

The Golden Lover, radio, ABC, 24 January 1943;

The Earthquake Shakes the Land, radio, ABC, 1944;

The Back of Beyond, motion picture, script by John Heyer, verse film script by Stewart, Shell Film Unit, 1954;

Shipwreck, radio, ABC, 7 July 1973;

Douglas Stewart, video, Australian Council for the Arts, 1975;

Glencoe, radio, ABC, 29 July 1990.

RECORDING: *Poets on Record 6: Douglas Stewart,* Poets on Record Series, St. Lucia, University of Queensland Press, 1971.

OTHER: *Australian Poetry 1941,* selected by Stewart (Sydney: Angus & Robertson, 1941; London: Angus & Robertson, 1941);

Norman Lindsay and Stewart, *Paintings in Oils* (Sydney: Shepherd, 1945);

Coast to Coast: Australian Stories, 1945, selected by Stewart (Sydney: Angus & Robertson, 1946);

Australian Bush Ballads, edited by Stewart and Nancy Keesing (Sydney: Angus & Robertson, 1955);

Old Bush Songs and Rhymes of Colonial Times: Enlarged and Revised from the Collection of A. B. Paterson, edited by Stewart and Keesing (Sydney: Angus & Robertson, 1957); abridged as *The Pacific Book of Bush Ballads* (Sydney: Angus & Robertson, 1967);

Will Ogilvie, *Fair Girls and Grey Horses,* introduction by Stewart (Sydney: Angus & Robertson, 1958);

Voyager Poems, edited by Stewart (Brisbane: Jacaranda, 1960);

Kenneth Mackenzie, *Selected Poems,* selected by Stewart (Sydney: Angus & Robertson, 1961);

[Joseph Tishler], *The Book of Bellerive,* edited by Stewart (Brisbane: Jacaranda, 1961);

A. D. Hope, *A. D. Hope,* selected by Stewart, Australian Poets Series (Sydney: Angus & Robertson, 1963);

H. P. Tritton, *Time Means Tucker,* foreword by Stewart (Sydney: Shakespeare Head, 1964);

Poetry in Australia: Volume II: Modern Australian Verse, selected by Stewart (Sydney: Angus & Robertson, 1964; Berkeley: University of California Press, 1965; enlarged edition, Sydney: Angus & Robertson, 1968);

Hugh McCrae: Selected Poems, edited by Stewart, Australian Poets Series (Sydney: Angus & Robertson, 1966);

Lindsay, *Ship Models,* introduction by Stewart (Sydney: Angus & Robertson, 1966);

Short Stories of Australia: Volume I: The Lawson Tradition, compiled and introduced by Stewart (Sydney: Angus & Robertson, 1967);

Lindsay, *Selected Pen Drawings,* selected by Stewart (Sydney: Angus & Robertson, 1968);

"Comment," *Contemporary Poets of the English Language,* edited by R. Murphy (London: St. James Press, 1970), pp. 172–177, 374–376, 1007–1009;

Best Australian Short Stories, edited by Stewart and Beatrice Davis (Hawthorn, Vic.: O'Neil, 1971);

The Wide Brown Land: A New Selection of Australian Verse, chosen by Stewart (Sydney: Angus & Robertson, 1971);

Australia Fair: Poems and Paintings, selected by Stewart (Sydney: Ure Smith, 1974);

Norman Lindsay Gallery and Museum, Springwood: A National Trust Property: A Guide to the Property, edited by Stewart, text by Stewart and others (Sydney: National Trust of Australia, 1975);

Lindsay, *Norman Lindsay's Cats,* introduction by Stewart (Melbourne: Macmillan, 1975).

SELECTED PERIODICAL PUBLICATIONS–UNCOLLECTED: "On Being a Verse Playwright," *Meanjin Quarterly,* 23 (1964): 272–277;

"A Send-Off for Norman Lindsay," *Southerly,* 30 (1970): 53–54;

"Symposium," by Stewart and others, *Landfall*, 29 (1975): 294–304;

"Debts of Gratitude," *Poetry Australia*, 80 (1981): 57–61.

Douglas Stewart wrote poetry, verse drama, criticism, prose fiction, memoir, and autobiography and edited many anthologies. He held authority through his association with *The Bulletin* (as literary editor) and Angus and Robertson (as literary adviser). Many critics—including James McAuley, Nancy Keesing, and Vivian Smith—attested to his versatility, a term that attempts to cover up neither the uneven quality of his work nor the lack of critical agreement over what constitutes his most important accomplishment.

Stewart straddled two literary worlds and generations. As an editor and anthologist he was nationalist (without explicit ideology), populist, professional (interested in literary quality, but also necessarily constrained by financial considerations), and little taken with academic interests. At the same time, he was an impressive technician, had a scholarly knowledge of Australian literary history, and wrote some of his best work in a lesser-used art form—lyric poetry. In generational terms, Stewart was a late manifestation of a particular type of man of letters in Australia. He was closely connected with the two most important institutions of Australian literature of his day, *The Bulletin* and Angus and Robertson publishers, but he saw the end of the former's great, conservative (or reactionary) tradition that stretched back to the 1890s with its takeover by Consolidated Press and saw the latter lose ground (at least in terms of poetry) to newer, less mainstream ventures.

Douglas Alexander Stewart was born the second of five children, probably in Eltham, Taranaki Province, New Zealand. His father, Alexander Armstrong Stewart, was from Melbourne, and his paternal grandfather was a Presbyterian minister who had emigrated from Scotland to Australia and who became Moderator of the General Assembly of the church in Australia. Around the time of Stewart's birth, his father was the sole schoolteacher at Rawhitiroa—"pretty well nowhere," as Stewart described it—while completing his law exams. Having passed his exams, Alexander Stewart moved his family to Eltham, where he became a solicitor. According to Stewart in his autobiography of childhood, *Springtime in Taranaki: An Autobiography of Youth* (1983), his father was a brilliant youth (he was *dux* of Scotch College in Melbourne into which he matriculated at the age of thirteen), but in adulthood he lacked ambition, happy with his provincial life and partnership in a small law firm, though he was eventually admitted to the Supreme Court as a barrister. Stewart's mother, Mary FitzGerald, was the daughter of a chemist and "had considerable strength of character," though she figures less in Stewart's reminiscences than does his father.

Springtime in Taranaki attests to a materially comfortable and happy childhood. Stewart knew much of his extended family, enjoyed the beauty of Eltham and Mount Egmont, and learned one of his great passions—the art of fishing, the subject of *The Seven Rivers* (1966). At the age of four Stewart attended a private school, and from the age of eight he attended Eltham Public School, where he decided to become an author. He won a scholarship to New Plymouth Boys' High School, which he attended when he turned twelve. He describes this time in the Australia Council for the Arts video (1975) as "five years' jail (it was a boarding school)," though there were compensations—a headmaster who sometimes took Stewart fishing during school hours and an active "animal life" common to private-school boys of the time (including poaching and eating wildlife).

He began to write while at New Plymouth, his class having been directed to write poems for the school magazine. Stewart wrote a poem about trout fishing. He later sent poems to the local paper, *The Daily News* (Taranaki), but to his chagrin they were published on the children's page—the only page that printed verse. From about the age of fifteen Stewart began to send poems each week to *The Bulletin* in Sydney, although they were routinely rejected. Through this routine he came to the attention of Cecil Mann, who began to publish Stewart in a sister publication of *The Bulletin*, *The Australian Women's Mirror* (Sydney). Mann, like other *Bulletin* editors, had been sent briefly to *The Australian Women's Mirror*.

Law diverted Stewart from thoughts of a writing career. He began his law degree in the last two years of school, but at Victoria University College in Wellington he lacked interest in his subjects and failed his exams. Abandoning law for journalism, he became sole reporter for the four-page *Argus* (Eltham) and then reporter for the Taranaki *Daily News*. In 1933 he moved to Sydney for a position on *The Bulletin* as a writer of light verse. The position did not materialize, and after working briefly for *The Star* (Melbourne) and returning to Sydney to try freelancing, Stewart went back to New Zealand in 1934, where he continued as a journalist. With money from his mother he self-published his first book, *Green Lions: Poems*, in 1936.

In 1938, working his passage on the *Doric Star*, he went to England, where he met many writers, including Edmund Blunden and John Cowper Powys (both influences), and Richard Church (who published Stewart's second volume of poetry with Dent). Stewart found himself unable to write poetry and made few inroads into becoming a professional writer in England. Stewart

Dust jacket, illustrated by Norman Lindsay, for the 1946 edition of Stewart's popular play about a bushranger (Bruccoli Clark Layman Archives)

then—after asking Mann to let him run the New Zealand page of *The Bulletin,* "The Long White Cloud"—left England for Sydney, again working his passage (as third purser of the *Largs Bay*). In Sydney—where he spent the remainder of his life—he became the assistant to Mann, the editor of the "Red Page" (that is, the literary page). In 1939 Stewart published his second book of poems, *The White Cry: Poems,* and his verse play, *The Fire on the Snow* (published in book form in 1944), was published serially in *The Bulletin.*

With the outbreak of war, Stewart and Mann presented themselves for service with the Australian Imperial Forces. Stewart was found unfit for duty, while Mann, though a veteran of World War I, was taken on (briefly, as it turned out). Stewart took over Mann's position as "Red Page" editor, and when Mann returned after only three months, Stewart remained literary editor while Mann was promoted to associate editor. Stewart remained literary editor of *The Bulletin* from 1940 to 1960, and he reminisces about his days there in his 1977 book *Writers of the Bulletin: 1977 Boyer Lectures.* In 1940 and 1941 he published two small collections, *Elegy for an Airman* (1940) and *Sonnets to the Unknown Soldier* (1941), the latter beginning a long association with Angus and Robertson.

Around this time Stewart met the artist and polymath Norman Lindsay, who became an important "stimulus" (Stewart's favored term over "influence") through his enthusiasm and energy, belief in the importance of art, and productivity. Despite Stewart's association with a conservative journal and his friendship with an antimodernist artist, he was not a programmatic editor, and he sometimes had to contend with opposition from within *The Bulletin.* As Stewart related in his memoir of Lindsay, the editor of the magazine—on seeing Francis Webb's "A Drum for Ben Boyd" printed serially—told Stewart, "I hate to see great slabs of verse in the paper."

In 1941, through his professional association with Beatrice Davis of Angus and Robertson, Stewart began the yearly anthologies, *Australian Poetry* and *Coast to Coast* (short fiction). On 6 June of the same year, Stewart enjoyed his greatest success with the broadcasting on the Australian Broadcasting Commission (ABC) radio of *The Fire on the Snow,* his verse play on the ill-fated expedition to the Antarctic in 1911–1912 by Robert Falcon Scott and his team. Such was the success of the play, as Clement Semmler points out, that the ABC conducted a play competition in 1942. Stewart won the verse section with *The Golden Lover* (performed on ABC radio 24 January 1943; published, 1944). *The Fire on the Snow* was subsequently broadcast many times on the ABC and was also broadcast in Britain, Canada, and Japan. It was studied in many Australian schools, as was *Ned Kelly* (first unabridged performance, 1943; first publication, 1943), which was written for the stage but was first performed (with abbreviated text) on ABC radio in 1942. In 1944 Stewart published *The Fire and the Snow* and *The Golden Lover* in one volume; he also published his only collection of prose fiction, *A Girl with Red Hair.* In the same year a verse drama concerning the Maori wars of the 1840s, *The Earthquake Shakes the Land,* was broadcast by the ABC.

On 5 December 1946 Stewart married artist Margaret Coen, whom he had met while she was Lindsay's pupil and "acolyte" (as Stewart describes her in his book on Lindsay). Also in 1946 he published *The Dosser in Springtime,* his first "Australian" collection of poetry. In 1947 *Shipwreck,* a verse play concerning the wreck of the *Batavia,* was published, along with *Glencoe,* a series of ballads on the massacre of the MacDonalds of Glencoe in 1691.

In 1948 his only child, Margaret, "Meg," was born, and Stewart published his first book of criticism, *The Flesh and the Spirit: An Outlook on Literature*. In 1952 he published another work of verse, *Sun Orchids and Other Poems*, and in 1954 he won a United Nations Educational, Scientific, and Cultural Organization (UNESCO) traveling scholarship and traveled to Europe. Also in 1954 he was commissioned by Shell to collaborate on a motion-picture script, *The Back of Beyond*. For this project, Stewart traveled the Birdsville track and wrote the lyric sequence that appeared in the movie and in his book *The Birdsville Track and Other Poems*, published in 1955. In the same year Stewart (with Keesing) published the first of two highly popular anthologies of Australian bush poetry. Also in 1955 he became a member of the Advisory Board of the Commonwealth Literary Fund (a position he held until 1970). In the remaining years of the decade Stewart edited another anthology, and four of his plays were published in a single collection.

In 1960 Stewart received an Order of the British Empire for services to Australian literature, and he published the last of his six plays, *Fisher's Ghost: An Historical Comedy*, based on a well-known Australian legend. He also edited *Voyager Poems* (1960), a slim but historically important anthology that collected six Australian lyrical narrative poems that deal with adventurers and explorers—for example, Christopher Columbus, James Cook, and Ludwig Leichhardt. In 1960, with the change of ownership of *The Bulletin*, which was taken over by Frank Packer's Consolidated Press, Stewart moved to Angus and Robertson as literary adviser, where he stayed until 1971. In 1962 Stewart produced his last single collection of poetry, *Rutherford and Other Poems*, which showed his continuing interest in nature and exploration. In the 1960s and 1970s his verse was reproduced in selections, including his *Collected Poems 1936–1967* (1967), which won several awards, including the Sydney Myer Award and the Grace Leven Prize. In 1968 Stewart won the Britannica Australia Award in the Humanities ($10,000). He continued editing anthologies of Australian poetry and fiction until the mid 1970s. In 1979 he received the Order of Australia (AO), and had one of the categories of the New South Wales Premier's Literary Awards named after him.

After his retirement from Angus and Robertson in 1971, Stewart turned to memoir. He produced books on Lindsay and on his friend Kenneth Slessor and in 1983 his autobiography, *Springtime in Taranaki*. In 1977 he gave the ABC Boyer lectures on the writers of *The Bulletin*, evidence of his continued standing. Douglas Stewart died on 14 February 1985. In 1987 a selection from a late diary was published as *Douglas Stewart's Garden of Friends*, with illustrations by Stewart's widow, Coen.

William Butler Yeats's influence was one of the few that Stewart admitted to, and that influence is clearly discernible in Stewart's first books, *Green Lions* and *The White Cry*. The romanticism of his early poetry indicates he would later be open to Lindsay's influence. Stewart's early poems rather self-consciously evoke the New Zealand landscape as well as aspects of contemporary life and do so with the cadences of the Georgians who also influenced him—Blunden and W. H. Davies.

The early poetry—like Stewart's succeeding lyrical work—is stanzaic and centers on the relationship between the imaginary and material worlds and between historical and diurnal time; the persistence of myth; and significance of landscape. In the early poetry, however, humor is less apparent, while subjectivity is more apparent. Much of Stewart's later dramatic (and therefore less personalized) work, however, remains concerned with alienation and the strangeness of humanity in an indifferent, if beautiful, natural world.

The impact of war is felt in the two small collections published in 1940 and 1941, *Elegy for an Airman* (the first of Stewart's work with decorations or illustrations by Lindsay) and *Sonnets to the Unknown Soldier*, collections that he later admitted—in *Douglas Stewart* (1963)—"should really have been blended into a single volume." The elegy is dedicated "To the memory of Desmond Carter, a Pilot-Officer of the Royal Air Force, killed in action, 1939." Stewart and Carter had been boyhood friends, and the poem presents some of Stewart's most nostalgic work for New Zealand (it employs many proper nouns). It begins with imagery of lost bucolic innocence ("And only the blackberries stained our mouths like blood") and childhood imagination ("We lived in a castle, too, we were knights and princes"). This type of description is more than whimsy, as the occasion for the poem suggests, and there are moments bordering on the surreal, as in the seventh stanza. The poem ends on a consolatory note, but one in which imagination is the sole vehicle for consolation: "O my friend, your life goes echoing on through time / As the thrush still rings in the mind when the willows darken."

Stewart's technical assurance—something critics often observed—is present by this stage of his writing, especially in his use of half-rhyme and internal rhyme. The stress of war also produced some of Stewart's least sanguine (and perhaps more interesting) lines: "Our houses creak, / The children in bed can hear the shriek of the wind, / And the neighbors' house is a ship a long way out" (from "The Fisherman"). These early collec-

Stewart and his wife, Margaret Coen, with their cat, Fang (photograph by Michael Elton)

tions are filled with water, night, trees, winter, women, and an interest in "heritage" (the title of a poem).

In the early 1940s Stewart published three verse plays and a collection of fiction. The first of these, *The Fire on the Snow,* is Stewart's most successful and, arguably, most important work. As a radio play in verse it is an unlikely contender for popular success, but the subject matter of the play–the last days of Scott of the Antarctic–and the lofty, but accessible, verse for the theme of heroism clearly appealed to a wartime audience. Stewart began writing the work in New Zealand as a narrative poem, but given the importance of radio drama and the brief flowering of verse drama–seen simultaneously in Dylan Thomas's *Under Milk Wood* (1954)–not surprisingly, Stewart abandoned the original form. The most important enabling technical device, the Announcer, he discovered in Archibald MacLeish's *The Fall of the City* (1937).

The Fire on the Snow details the race for the South Pole, in which Scott and four companions, through bad weather and privation, reach the Pole only to find that the Norwegian team, led by Roald Amundsen, has beaten them there. Scott's team died on the return journey. Despite the heroic and desperate nature of these events, they are inherently repetitive (marching to and from the Pole), and Stewart succeeds remarkably in making them dramatic. As Leslie Rees points out in *Towards an Australian Drama* (1953), Stewart uses a form "indigenous to radio and not suitable for stage"–that is, "the continually moving single scene." The Announcer both acts as a chorus and actively sets out the themes and motifs of the play. The Announcer (unlike the other characters) generally speaks in stanzaic verse and is given the most rhetorical language. The device also allows for a self-reflexivity that furthers the aim of the drama, making heroes of Scott and his men:

> Radio hides the boards'
> Creaking and the clock's ticking
> And our words fall upon words:
> There is always someone speaking.
> But here words fall on the snow.
> . . . .
> The living thing is the word
> And the thing dead is the silence.
> These men of their own accord
> Move away into silence,
> Their skis soft on the snow.

Characterization in this play is based on profession–such as Oates the soldier and Wilson the man of science–and the themes are explicitly stated. One is the gap between desire and execution.

> Oates: Now we're here we're nowhere.
> Wilson. . . . It looks like nowhere,
>   So still and forsaken.
> Scott. . . . It must be a nightmare in winter.
>   I've dreamed of this moment for many, many years
>   But the dream was different, no footprints scarring the snow,
> No mark of men.

Despite that the "fire of human beings" in the snow must be put out, the major theme of the play is heroic endurance. Toward the end, Wilson says, "We dreamed, we so nearly triumphed, we were defeated / As every man in some great or humble way / Dreams, and nearly triumphs, and is always defeated, / And then, as we did, triumphs again in endurance." Such a statement is of a piece with a conservative nationalism common to many settler countries, in which survival itself is viewed as something worthy of celebration and something that forges a "national" character.

Not surprisingly, Stewart was drawn to one of the most fertile sites of Australian mythology–Ned Kelly, the bushranger. As H. G. Kippax says in the introduction to *Three Australian Plays* (1963), which includes

Stewart's *Ned Kelly,* "Here all the birds in the bush of the 'Australianist' legend come home to roost"—the role of the underdog, anti-authoritarianism, collision between the economies and mores of city and bush, the theme of endurance, and the hostility of the Australian landscape. Despite its almost iconic status, *Ned Kelly* has been criticized for being too long for performance, for being too static, and for lacking subtlety in its characters' speeches. But it clearly evinces a rhetorical power, and its influence on later versions of the Kelly myth—including Robert Drewe's *Our Sunshine* (1991)—can be discerned.

The play opens in 1879 with the gang "bailing up" (holding under guard) the town of Jerilderie in the style of Ben Hall, the first bushrangers to be outlawed—the play makes a great deal of the "tradition" of bushranging in Australia. Having robbed the bank, Kelly and Joe Byrne return to the pub where Steve Hart and Dan Kelly have most of the town hostage. The mise en scène highlights Kelly's opposition to institutions (the law, banks, schools, and religion), which are personified by characters in the pub. Gribble, the clergyman, foretells Kelly's end and illustrates the ambivalence about Kelly's heroic status in the play:

> What else is it, but murder? You could work, you could ride,
> Fossick for gold, explore the bush and the mountains
> And the desert beyond, discover some green island
> Useful to men in this barren and burning ocean,
> Take any way of a thousand to ease your blood
> Of Australia's restlessness or Ireland's rebellion
> Or the bitter convict memories, whatever it is
> That denies you peace and sleep. You've chosen murder.

The second, and weakest, act shows the gang in the mountain ranges in 1880, hemmed in by their pursuers and taking revenge on their betrayal by Sherritt, a friend of Byrne. The remaining action centers on the events at Glenrowan, where, having failed to derail a special police train, the gang are surrounded and—with the exception of Kelly, who is captured—killed.

Ned Kelly is partly written in prose, and the part written in poetry is more flexible than that of *The Fire on the Snow.* Stewart tends to write accentually, with most lines having five stresses without being decasyllabic. While the later play shows technical advance, in ideological terms it simply underscores much of the oxymoronic stance of *The Fire on the Snow*—triumphant failure. *Ned Kelly,* despite its ambivalence about Kelly's actions, is clearly romantic-nationalist in character: it positions the "real" Australia in the bush, and the Australian character is defined by a laconic carelessness that can lead to heroism.

Stewart's next work, also produced for radio, *The Golden Lover,* is a romantic comedy based on the Maori legend of Hinemoah and Tutanaki. In Stewart's play a young Maori wife, Tawhai, is enchanted by Whana, chief of the light-skinned "people of the mist," the Maori fairy people. Tawhai reluctantly realizes that she cannot spend her nights with her mystical lover and her days with her own people—though in returning to her own people she has the consolation of a new lover, Tiki. The play lightly deals with the way in which lovers project their imaginary beloved onto the real love object and dramatizes the common desire for both romantic passion and domestic stability. Despite being well received, the play in the early twenty-first century looks culturally naive, nostalgic, and dated.

The stories of Stewart's only work of prose fiction, *A Girl with Red Hair,* while technically assured, are similarly of the age and show the imprint of *The Bulletin* style, with its emphasis on realism, dramatic force, and the pastoral setting. *The Dosser in Springtime* shows Stewart becoming "acquainted with the Australian countryside and its creatures" and experimenting with ballad form, as he says in *Douglas Stewart.* Again, considering the shift in poetic sensibility since the 1970s, much of the personification, apostrophe, light verse, talking animals, self-consciously Australian subject matter ("The Bunyip," "The Lizards") and literary ballads seem dated. The romanticism is still present, but a lightness of tone—which defines his later lyrics—has replaced the brooding tone of the early poems. The most important poem in the collection, "The River," revisits Stewart's boyhood New Zealand. The river is both real and symbolic—a place of stones, water, and trout, and an image of an individual's development toward the "sea of life."

Stewart's next two works show his continued interest in the bloody events of history. *Shipwreck,* another verse play, deals with the wreck of the Dutch ship *Batavia* on the northwest coast of Australia in 1629 and the subsequent mutiny and slaughter that followed. Most critics disliked the play for its emphasis on violence. The work was not broadcast on the ABC until 1978. While dramatic, the historical data does not allow the kind of rich symbolic exploration that Scott and Ned Kelly allowed Stewart. Nevertheless, Stewart believed it was his best play, and Keesing reports—in *Douglas Stewart*—that he saw it as an allegory of the position of Australian soldiers (especially POWs) who fought in the war against Japan (something Susan McKernan, in *A Question of Commitment,* finds glib and inhumane). Either way, the play—as Keesing also points out—seems unbalanced by evil and lacks a hero.

Glencoe, also from 1947, deals with massacre, as well. In this play Stewart has more success with the formal requirements of his narrative. As he says in the notes to *Poets on Record 6,* after trying for six months to use the material to write another play, he "tried out a ballad," and the rest of the work appeared in five days. The sequence comprises sixteen ballads, though Stewart shows his formalist facility by using many stanzaic forms other than the classic ballad stanza. With its synthetic Scots ("Out o' your bed and awa'! / Dinna ye hear the tramp o' boots / In your father's house and ha'?"), its subject matter, and its form, the work is something of an oddity in Australian literature. The work has supporters, and Stewart's claim–in *Douglas Stewart*–that the theme of the work is "a protest against barbarity, cruelty and violence in any age" seems less tendentious than his claim for *Shipwreck*.

Sun Orchids includes some of Stewart's best short nature lyrics, as well as one of his best dramatic lyric sequences, "Worsley Enchanted," which details aspects of Sir Ernest Shackleton's voyage to the Antarctic in 1914. Frank Worsley, a New Zealander, captained the *Endurance,* which was trapped and eventually crushed by ice. After six months the crew made their way to Elephant Island, where they waited while Worsley, Tom Crean, and Shackleton rowed to South Georgia to get help for the remaining party. Despite similarities with *The Fire on the Snow,* the sequence is less abstract and more concerned with the physical and psychological experiences of such material extremity, as seen in Worsley's description of his men arriving on Elephant Island after drifting six months on ice: "But these men picked up pebbles / Wet from the sea and cold / And cradled them in their hands / As if they were coins of gold." The sequence is full of such moments, making it less concerned with heroism and endurance than with, according to *Douglas Stewart,* "the strangeness of all human experience, the mystery of our existence." It is one of Stewart's most satisfying works, linking his humor ("As morning glittered behind the window / His striped pyjamas shone like a rainbow"); his eye for detail and how details may be stylized ("Primus stove and ropes and axe / Flew through the air like startled ducks"); and his romantic interest in the relationship between the natural and the supranatural ("But bright's the sunlight and bright's the stream / And a man can walk in the midst of a dream").

Some of the short lyrics in *Sun Orchids* are among Stewart's best known ("Mahony's Mountain," "The Sunflowers" and "Helmet Orchid"), and they show a change in approach to the natural world. Stewart's balladic tendencies give way to a more imagistic approach, in which description becomes the source of significance, as in "Sun Orchids." Elsewhere, the "weird melancholy" of the Australian bush that others have noted is occasionally sounded, as in "Sunflowers." The collection also includes "Terra Australis," a kind of meta-"voyager" poem, which describes an imaginary meeting between the sixteenth-century Portuguese explorer Captain Quiros and the nineteenth-century Australian radical William Lane, both going in opposite directions looking for the new Australia.

Stewart's next collection, *The Birdsville Track,* also includes an important poetic sequence. Stewart's sequence again deals with Australian masculinity, heroism, and endurance, and again his use of stanzaic form shows his technical facility. While the sequence is rich in motif and imagery, there are effective moments of simplicity: "The sun glares down on the stones and the stones glare back."

The documentary aspect of the poem can be seen in its descriptions of animals, landmarks (a ruined house over which "Two golden butterflies" mate), and some of the Track's characters (such as Alec Scobie, "The Whipmaker," and Old Bejah, "The Afghan"). But Stewart is again concerned with the almost mystical strangeness of nature, as in "Grasshopper," in which the red grasshoppers are seen as hopping stones. The grim humor of the "The Humorists" who leave messages for each other on the skulls of their dead stock shows something of the Australian sense of the absurd, but the sequence also shows the emptiness of the place, as seen in "Place Names": "Dulkaninna, Koperamanna, / Ooroowilanie, Kilalpaninna– / Only the names / In the land remain / Like a dark well / Like the chime of a bell." In the end, humans are ineffectual, whether white or indigenous: the rainmaker "knelt down low / and the lean dogs stared / By the ratbag humpy / While no rain fell / In all the country." The sequence ends in Birdsville, which is modern ("the windsock droops / For the Flying Doctor"), small, and haunted by memories of an earlier, heroic age.

Other poems in the collection include the parodic "Cicada Song" ("Sumer is icumen in, / Loud sing cicada!") and "Crow's Nest," the wit of which shows Stewart's increasing use of humor in his late lyrics: "Never since the stringybarks stiffened to telegraph poles / And froze their flowers in porcelain has a crow been known / To nest in a tree at Crow's Nest" (Crow's Nest is a suburb of Sydney). In addition, Stewart continued his more detached, miniaturist nature poems, such as "The Brown Snake" and "Brindabella," one of Stewart's most beautifully controlled poems in terms of tone, which ends,

> The magpie lifting his beak by the frozen fern
> Sent out one ray of a carol, softened and silvery,
> Strange through the trees as sunlight's pale return,
> Then cocked his black head and listened, hunched from the cold,
> Watching that white whisper fill his green world.

Stewart fishing at Bobbin Head near Sydney (from Peter Pierce, ed., The Oxford Literary Guide to Australia, *1987)*

By the mid 1950s Stewart's main output was over. In the remaining thirty years of his life, although he wrote and edited many books, he published only one more individual collection of poetry and a light play. The latter, *Fisher's Ghost,* is based on the Australian legend of a ticket-of-leave convict who disappeared in 1826 and whose apparition pointed to where its murdered body lay. The legend had already been given considerable treatment, including an appearance in Charles Dickens's magazine *Household Words.* The work, written largely in ballad form and illustrated by Lindsay, is a pastiche of 1890s melodrama in comic mode.

In 1955 and 1957 Stewart and Keesing published their immensely successful anthologies of bush ballads and the less literary and earlier bush songs, both of which were reprinted many times over the succeeding decades. Stewart's personal preference (perhaps not surprisingly) is for the song over the ballad, partly, as he states in the introduction to *Old Bush Songs and Rhymes of Colonial Times* (1957), because of the "atmosphere" of the songs and partly because there is "no possibility of confusion of literary values," for their lack of poeticism, is unexceptional and in keeping with their form. Keesing describes the Herculean task of editing the anthologies in her autobiography *Riding the Elephant* (1988).

One of Stewart's most important anthologies is his 1960 collection of modern Australian "Voyager" poems, in which he claims that "When you begin to write about the adventurers who founded the nation you begin to approach the epic." In the eponymous poem of *Rutherford and Other Poems* Stewart redirects the "Voyager" theme away from the explorers of the past to a modern scientist, Earl Rutherford of Nelson, the New Zealand physicist who first split the atom. As Stewart writes in *Douglas Stewart,* the artist, explorer, and scientist figures are not mutually exclusive: the scientist is the "modern day equivalent of the explorer" and in his (or her) quest for truth and "his enlargement of the human mind, is the colleague, not the enemy, of the artist."

The poem, 288 lines in octaves (a favorite form for Stewart's treatment of grander themes), shows Rutherford meditating on his life and work. That his father was a wheelwright enabled Stewart to produce one of the more notable conceits of the poem: "It was as if in one swift generation / He had bridged the years from the first man to the last, / Run the whole course of human civilization." "Rutherford," as these lines suggest, is organized in terms of binary oppositions: the cosmic/the atomic; early/late; movement/stasis; savage/civilized; and human/suprahuman. Rutherford grew up, like Stewart, in Taranaki, and the interplay between bucolic memories of youth and Rutherford's scientific work means that such oppositions are seen within a human context. While Rutherford is represented as fearing the consequences of his research ("this was a dangerous toy"), he is unambiguously a modern hero: "he'd carry the load he bore, / Which was no light one, till his broad shoulders were aching." The poem could justifiably be criticized for being too sanguine on this point. *Rutherford and Other Poems* continues Stewart's interest in the bloody past in "Easter Island" and includes "The Silkworms," his most anthologized poem, one of many satires on suburbia, the more effective for being less explicit than the others—"Leopard Skin" and "Fence."

In 1967 Stewart published his *Collected Poems* (organized in reverse chronological order), which included a group of new poems under the title "The Flowering Place." The use of humor present in these new poems, such as "B Flat," demonstrates Stewart's view—presented in his notes to *Poets on Record 6*—that such poems should be considered serious poems that use humor rather than light verse. "The Flowering Place" is the last of Stewart's longer poems on an explorer, Mungo Park (again, written in octaves). In conversation with Sir Walter Scott, Park prefigures his own death by drowning and demurs to Scott's belief that writing is a "pettifogging trade." Park develops Stewart's theory of correspondence between artists, scientists, and explorers:

Each to his trade, and mine's to walk, Sir Walter;
Yet in the countries never seen by men
Who's paid the greater price, who's gone the further,
I with my travels, you with your midnight pen?

My road lies far; yet it could be, my friend,
In mile and mile we go or book and book
We take the same strange journey in the end.
What can we do but wish each other luck?

In his remaining years Stewart continued to edit anthologies and write introductions for others' books; he also turned to memoir and published a second book of literary criticism. *The Broad Stream: Aspects of Australian Literature* (1975)–like *The Flesh and the Spirit* of 1948–collects critical pieces (mostly from the "Red Page" of *The Bulletin*) from Stewart's long career in literary journalism. Both books are stridently nationalist, and Stewart sees the nationalist project as best secured through literary history. Stewart often attempts to revive earlier, forgotten writers as well as to write insightful pieces on many of the—now canonical—writers he encouraged while at *The Bulletin,* such as Judith Wright, Rosemary Dobson, David Campbell, Francis Webb, James McAuley, and Robert D. FitzGerald.

Stewart's remaining major works are autobiographical (a childhood autobiography and extracts of a diary) and biographical (memoirs of Lindsay and Slessor). All of these works include a lightness of tone, a humility on the part of the author, and a delight in anecdote. None makes large claims for biographical definitiveness. *Springtime in Taranaki*–which revisits some scenes of the earlier *Seven Rivers*–centers on education, fishing, cars, and falling in love. It is a charming work and at times funny.

Determining Stewart's place in Australian literary history is problematic. His large oeuvre presents him in opposing ways: the master of the miniature; the proponent of epic; a populist working with a "high" art ethos; and a poet suspicious of mysticism, who embraced Lindsay's vitalist, antimaterialist ethos. His view of poetry, as he puts it in *Modern Australian Verse* (1964), is that it is "an art meant to provoke not argument but pleasure," but, as McKernan argues, his large-scale works are often tendentious, especially in their use of material that is far from joyous.

In addition, there is little critical agreement about what Douglas Stewart's main achievement was. FitzGerald sees *Glencoe* as Stewart's major achievement, while Brian Elliott—in *The Landscape of Australian Poetry* (Melbourne: Chesire, 1967)—sees it as "a purely literary experiment." *The Oxford Companion to Australian Literature* claims that Stewart's "greatest contribution to Australian literature" was his work with *The Bulletin,* with Angus and Robertson, and in encouraging other writers. Critics attracted to his published work, rather than his literary advocacy and mentorship, explicitly or implicitly make claims either for his lyric or his longer work. Some see his verse plays as his greatest achievement. Oddly enough, his work is not found in recent Australian poetry anthologies, suggesting that others view his contribution as extraliterary. This absence, even if not permanent, implies that Stewart was a kind of literary man now unknown—an apolitical nationalist, intent on producing a body of work available to both popular and literary audiences. Stewart himself made few claims about his own role or the importance of his work. He is, however, unlikely to become simply a footnote to Australian literary production. Works such as *The Fire on the Snow, Ned Kelly,* "Worsley Enchanted," and the best of his nature lyrics (poems that bear comparison with the later work of poets such as Campbell and McAuley) are powerful expressions of various Australian myths and evidence of a poet who, while not stylistically "progressive," was an impressive technician. If one considers the gap between a poem such as "Mosquito Orchid," which begins

> Such infinitesimal things,
> Mosquito orchids flying
> Low where the grass tree parts
> And winter's sun lies dying
> In a flash of green and bronze
> On the dead beetle's wings
> Among the broken stones.

and the high rhetoric of *The Fire on the Snow* and *Ned Kelly,* Stewart's "versatility" clearly indicates that there is material for a wide range of critical interests. In that, the very quality that makes him critically problematic also makes him retain some vitality for those who care to read him.

Letters:
R. G. Howarth and H. W. Barker, eds., *Letters of Norman Lindsay* (Sydney: Angus & Robertson, 1970).

Interviews:
Arthur Ashworth, "From a Discussion of the Poetry of Douglas Stewart in the Presence of the Poet," *Poetry Magazine* (5 October 1966): 3–6;

John Thompson, "Poetry in Australia: Douglas Stewart," in *Considerations: New Essays on Kenneth Slessor, Judith Wright and Douglas Stewart,* edited by Brian Kiernan (Sydney: Angus & Robertson, 1977), pp. 115–126.

Bibliography:
Susan Ballyn and Jeff Doyle, *Douglas Stewart: A Bibliography* (Canberra: ADFA and the National Library of Australia, 1996).

Biographies:
Nancy Keesing, *Douglas Stewart,* Australian Writers and Their Work Series (Melbourne: Oxford University Press, 1965; revised, 1969);

Clement Semmler, *Douglas Stewart: A Critical Study* (New York: Twayne, 1974);

Graeme Kinross-Smith, "Douglas Stewart, 1913– ," in his *Australia's Writers* (Melbourne: Nelson, 1980), pp. 270–276;

Keesing, *Riding the Elephant* (Sydney: Allen & Unwin, 1988).

References:
Susan Ballyn, "Douglas Stewart's 'Glencoe,'" in *Short Fiction in the New Literatures in English: Proceedings of the Nice Conference of the European Association for Commonwealth Literature and Language Studies,* edited by J. Bardolph (Nice: Comite EACLALS, 1989), pp. 55–61;

Lawrence Bourke, "Making a Crossing: Douglas Stewart the Expatriate Patriot," *Southerly,* 53, no. 2 (1993): 40–53;

David Bradley, "Second Thoughts About Douglas Stewart," *Westerly,* 3 (1960): 23–27;

Robert D. FitzGerald, "Motif in the Work of Douglas Stewart," in his *The Elements of Poetry* (St. Lucia: University of Queensland Press, 1963), pp. 25–50;

Yasmine Gooneratne, "Douglas Stewart: The Silkworms," in *Australian Poems in Perspective,* edited by P. K. Elkin (St. Lucia: University of Queensland Press, 1978), pp. 117–140;

Paul Kavanagh, "Preternatural Mimicry: The Lyric Poetry of Douglas Stewart," *Southerly,* 43, no. 3 (1983): 265–281;

Nancy Keesing, *Douglas Stewart,* Australian Writers and Their Work Series (Melbourne: Oxford University Press, 1965; revised, 1969);

Brian Kiernan, ed., *Considerations: New Essays on Kenneth Slessor, Judith Wright and Douglas Stewart,* Perspectives in Australian Literature Series (Sydney: Angus & Robertson, 1977);

Leonie Kramer, "Two Perspectives in the Poetry of Douglas Stewart," *Southerly,* 33, no. 3 (1973): 286–299;

Igor Maver, "Mapping the Unknown: Australian Mythical Landscape in Douglas Stewart's 'Voyager' Poems," in *Australia's Changing Landscapes: Proceedings of the Second EASA Conference: Sitges, Barcelona,*

October 1993, edited by Ballyn, Doireann MacDermott, and Kathleen Firth (Barcelona: Departament de Filologia Anglesa i Alemanya, Universitat de Barcelona, 1995), pp.139–144;

James McAuley, "Douglas Stewart," in *The Literature of Australia,* edited by Geoffrey Dutton (Ringwood, Vic.: Penguin, 1964), pp. 362–376;

McAuley, "Douglas Stewart," in his *A Map of Australian Verse: The Twentieth Century* (Melbourne: Oxford University Press, 1975), pp. 219–237;

Susan McKernan, "Douglas Stewart and the *Bulletin,*" in her *A Question of Commitment: Australian Literature in the Twenty Years after the War* (Sydney: Allen & Unwin, 1989), pp. 120–140;

A. A. Phillips, "The Poetry of Douglas Stewart," *Meanjin Quarterly,* 28 (1969): 97–104;

Rodney Pybus, "Radio Drama: The Australian Experience," in *Radio Drama,* edited by Peter Lewis (London: Longman, 1981), pp. 244–259;

Leslie Rees, *Towards an Australian Drama* (Sydney: Angus & Robertson, 1953);

Dennis Robinson, "Douglas Stewart's Nature Lyrics," *Southerly,* 47, no. 1 (1987): 52–69;

Robinson, "Douglas Stewart's *Rutherford,*" *Southerly,* 47, no. 2 (1987): 150–163;

Clement Semmler, *Douglas Stewart: A Critical Study* (New York: Twayne, 1974);

Thomas W. Shapcott, "Douglas Stewart and Poetry in the 'Bulletin,' 1940 to 1960," in *Cross Currents: Magazines and Newspapers in Australian Literature,* edited by Bruce Bennett (Melbourne: Longman, 1981), pp.148–157;

Michael Sharkey, "Douglas Stewart and 'Voyager Poems,'" *Salt,* 9 (1996): 71–80;

Vivian Smith, "Douglas Stewart: Lyric Poet," *Meanjin Quarterly,* 26 (1967): 41–50.

Papers:

The Mitchell Library in Sydney, N.S.W., holds the most extensive collection of material on and by Douglas Stewart in the Stewart papers (MS 5147) and the Angus and Robertson papers (MS 3269). Angus and Robertson material is also held by HarperCollins, Sydney. The National Library of Australia has a Stewart collection (MS 4829). The bibliography by Susan Ballyn and Jeff Doyle gives an itemized description of these manuscript collections.

Harold Stewart
(14 December 1916 – 7 August 1995)

Michael Ackland
Monash University

BOOKS: *The Darkening Ecliptic,* by Stewart and James McAuley as Ern Malley (Melbourne: Reed & Harris, 1944); republished as *The Poems of Ern Malley* (Melbourne: Reed & Harris, 1961);

Phoenix Wings: Poems 1940–6 (Sydney: Angus & Robertson, 1948);

Orpheus and Other Poems (Sydney: Angus & Robertson, 1956);

A Net of Fireflies: Japanese Haiku and Haiku Paintings (Rutland, Vt. & Tokyo: Tuttle, 1960);

A Chime of Windbells: A Year of Japanese Haiku in English Verse (Rutland, Vt.: Tuttle, 1969);

The Exiled Immortal: A Song-Cycle (Canberra: Brindabella Press, 1980);

By the Old Walls of Kyoto (New York: Weatherhill, 1981);

The Ascension of the Feng Huang (Cambridge, U.K.: Willow House Press, 1998).

Harold Stewart often described himself as his country's most un-Australian, or anti-Australian, writer. In 1949 he wrote to H. M. Green: "Once, if writers mentioned dilly-bags or sick stockriders, I merely groaned—now I go berserk and commit mayhem." Six years later his complaint to A. D. Hope was directed at their entire age: "It is so long now since I gave up living in the Twentieth Century, so long since the cult of contemporaneity, the myth of modernity evaporated for me, that I find myself somewhat at a loss to know what to say about some . . . poems." Stewart's poetry supports these comments. Even in his earliest schoolboy verse and the two volumes he published in Australia in 1948 and 1956, there is nothing that links his works to their immediate context. *Phoenix Wings* (1948) consists largely of poems inspired by Stéphane Mallarmé, Paul Valéry, and Eastern legends, while *Orpheus and Other Poems* (1956) deals with a broad sweep of mythology drawn from Greece or the Asian mainland. After Stewart moved to Japan in the 1960s, he found his subject matter in those surroundings. Two books of haiku translations signaled the discovery of his Japanese vocation, while in two long poems on Eastern subjects he

Harold Stewart, 1983 (Collection of Gwen Smith)

staked strong claims to be regarded as one of the finest English-language poets of the twentieth century.

Yet, Harold Frederick Stewart owed more to his early years in the western suburbs of Sydney than he cared to acknowledge. He was born on 14 December 1916 in Drummoyne, where his father, Herbert Howard Vernon Stewart, was employed as a health inspector by the local council. Vernon Stewart had spent three decades in India, was fluent in Hindustani, and bequeathed his interest in Asian civilizations to his son. The boy's mother, Amy Muriel Stewart (née Morris), apparently passed on her remarkable memory to her son and lavished love on him and his sister, Marion, who was eight years younger than Harold.

Harold Stewart studied music at the Sydney Conservatorium High School and then transferred to Fort Street Boys' High School, where he shone academically until he discovered his homosexuality in 1933. Then his intense sense of social ostracism led to his abandonment of conventional goals, and he began to fail even subjects in which he had been a prizewinner. He dropped out of Sydney University in 1936 after two months, rejecting the conformity and career prospects the school promoted, and chose poetry as his true vocation. In "Ambition" (1934) he contrasted his lover's choice "to marry, enjoy, breed and to die," with his own ambition for "greatness":

> Instead I will surmount
> I'll overspread the years, I will span on to greatness
> by my passion in the poetry they have renounced
> as a fool's toy
> a self-sympathy, a dramatic casing for an oversensitive and sentimental soul.
> How little they all are. How much to be despised.

The following year, having just failed the leaving certificate, he let it be known that he was contemplating his own version of John Milton's *Paradise Lost* (1667).

By the outbreak of war in the Pacific during World War II, Stewart had developed self-affirming strategies and learned to use Eastern philosophies to justify his life choices. In his notebooks the outwardly feckless, rootless failure portrayed his existence as he willed it to be and identified his native land with the mediocre and nondescript, with heat and sterility. A self-proclaimed "aristocrat of the soul," he claimed to have been lifted heavenward in apotheosis and fantasized about impending deliverance: "My life has run its course, it is fulfilled & consummated. I can rise no higher than this, I have achieved the summit of human experience in the art of living.... 'God' walks with me." In other entries he expanded on his alleged immunity to social imposition, owing to a Taoist oneness with the universe: "How futile and insignificant are any efforts to confine me.... Can you conscript the wind? How would you regiment a field of grass?" This thinking, however, is Taoism shaped to answer Stewart's needs. His lack of worldly success was equated with the selfless ideal of Taoism and his indecisiveness with its call for openness to existence. He used the Taoist inversion of normal values to reinforce, rather than diminish, intellectual pride. For a time in the late 1930s Stewart found a congenial milieu among homosexual artists in the Kings Cross district of Sydney and emerged as an advocate of modern art in the student publication *Honi Soit*. He was severely constrained, however, by a lack of formal qualifications and extreme penury until he was called up for military service in September 1942.

Stewart made his first and only mark on the Australian literary scene as a collaborator in the well-known Ern Malley hoax. Its target was an opinionated avant-garde poet and literary editor, Max Harris, who was sent sixteen manuscript poems, allegedly by the deceased motor mechanic and insurance salesman Ern Malley but in fact composed by Stewart and a fellow army conscript, James McAuley, during a single day when they were on duty at Victoria Barracks. Interrupting one another and interleaving their lines with material from random sources, they sought to create portentously nonsensical works that would pass for surrealist compositions. It was a risky undertaking. Not only might Harris see through their plot, but the authors had served a long apprenticeship in modernism, and not even contrived nonsense or disjunctions could suppress their creative flair or prevent actual emotional or mental states from surfacing once their automatic writing commenced. Similarly, disparate elements—such as a pamphlet on controlling mosquitoes—tended to become part of a larger mosaic, a found object recontextualized with the playful humor of contemporary art, as in "Culture as Exhibit":

> "Swamps, marshes, borrow-pits and other
> Areas of stagnant water serve
> As breeding-grounds . . ." Now
> Have I found you, my Anopheles!
> (There is a meaning for the circumspect)
> Come, we will dance sedate quadrilles,
> A pallid polka or a yelping shimmy
> Over these sunken sodden breeding-grounds!
> We will be wraiths and wreaths of tissue-paper
> To clog the Town Council in their plans.
> Culture forsooth! Albert, get my gun.

Harris published "Malley's" work, hailing it as the work of genius. Stewart and McAuley revealed their hoax a few weeks later in the *Sunday Sun* (25 June 1944), describing their farcical method of composition and asserting that Harris's admiration for the poems demonstrated that he was "insensible of absurdity and incapable of ordinary discrimination." He not only became a public laughingstock but was also successfully prosecuted for publishing obscenity. As Stewart had anticipated, local philistines showed their usual interest in serious art only as a subject of derision.

STARRY NIGHT *by Tomoda Sōgyo, re-creating a haiku by Buson:*
What a delightful game it is to set
Fireflies loose in bed beneath the net!

A NET OF FIREFLIES

JAPANESE HAIKU AND HAIKU PAINTINGS

*with verse translations
and an essay
by*
HAROLD STEWART

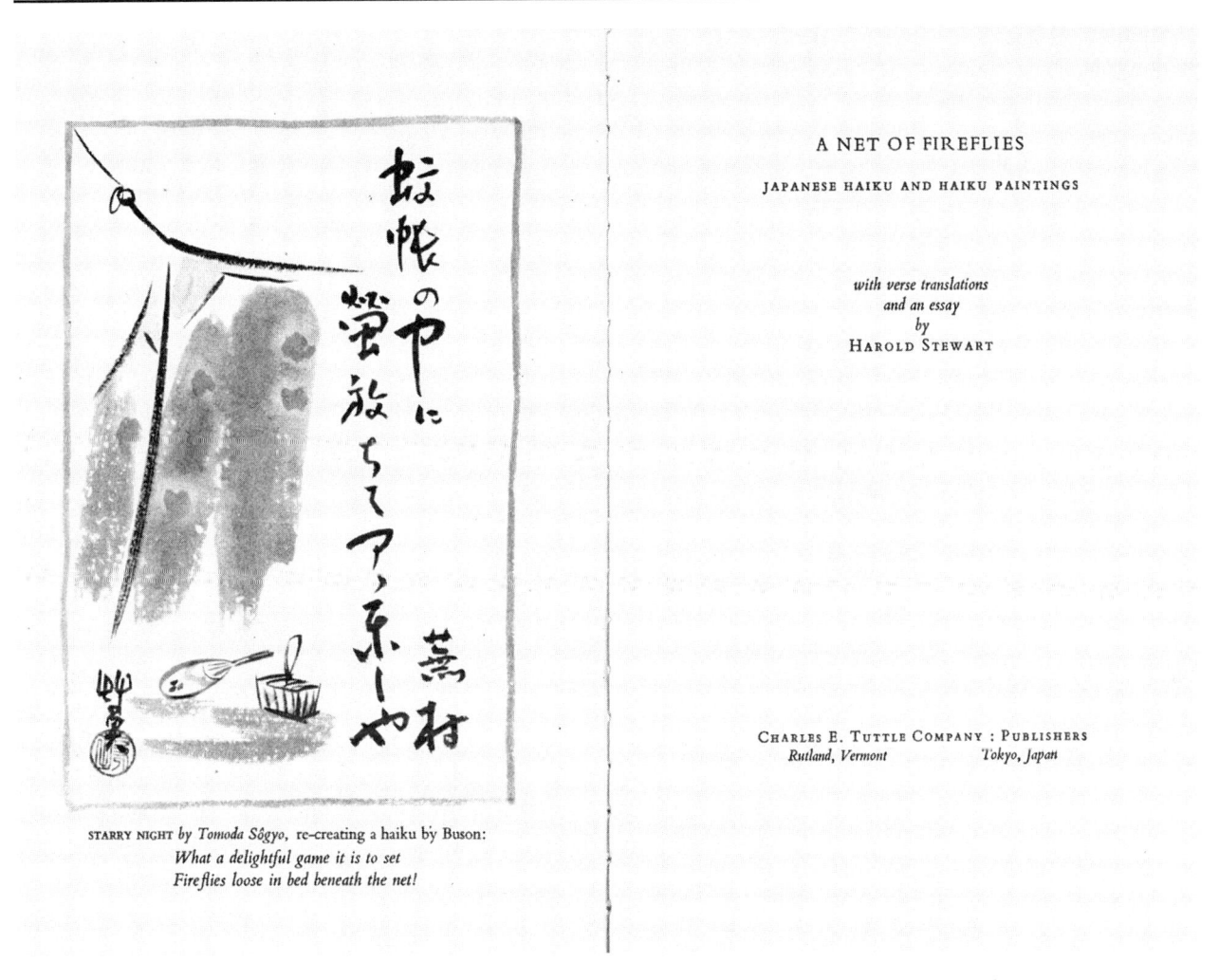

CHARLES E. TUTTLE COMPANY : PUBLISHERS
Rutland, Vermont   Tokyo, Japan

Frontispiece and title page for Stewart's 1960 book, one of three collections in which he interspersed translations and original haiku (Bruccoli Clark Layman Archives)

Stewart eventually found a theme commensurate to his epic ambition by wedding Romantic and Eastern heritages. One of Malley's poems is titled "Colloquy with John Keats"—an early favorite for Stewart, who was drawn to Keats's craftsmanship and his doctrine of "negative capability," which promised both control and anonymity in allowing the self to be subsumed completely within other objects or characters. As Stewart averred in "Dionysus ad. lib" (1942), art ideally brought "release . . . from the tyrannic license of your feelings." It also had a design with clearly defined phases, whereas "life is all tangled and unfinished and fuzzy at the edges." In April 1943 he defended his "turn towards the Chinese" to Green as a means of opening up a new poetic terrain, and of self-fulfillment:

> these are not mere fertilizing interests & agents but the very medium through which I realize myself. . . . What Greece has been, from the Renaissance on, to English

poets, Ancient China & the East in general are to me. I am most at home in their art & ideas, most myself, when effacing my self in those times & places & people. He who loses himself . . . [Stewart's ellipsis]. You see, the Western Renaissance & Medieval Christian traditions are not only worked out, but actually alien to me: they touch my experience at few points. Whereas the philosophy and art of the East coincide exactly with my way of life.

By 1946, when he left the military, Stewart had found his epic theme, and he set about making detailed notes on intellectual life in T'ang China. Excerpts of works in progress appeared during the next decade, and in 1958 his project formed the centerpiece of his application for a Saionji Memorial Scholarship to study in Japan so that he could research and write a work set during the T'ang dynasty that was to embrace its thought and arts, "especially the three great formative influences of Confucianism, Taoism and Zen Buddhism: thus summing up all that was best in the Chinese way of life." Chinese painting, he said, would provide the setting; dialogues between well-known poets, artists, and sages would give the work a flexible, dramatic structure. The trip to Japan, however, did not eventuate, and Stewart continued to eke out a precarious existence in Melbourne.

The first step toward realizing his vision came in *Phoenix Wings*, which is dominated by diverse adaptations of foreign sources. Whether in recasting French poetry or Taoist legends, Stewart chose the relative invisibility afforded by acts of translation. Only four poems have a first-person speaker who could be confounded with the author. "The Annunciation" opens the collection with an avowal of vocation; the other poems expand on the need for emancipation. In "Prelude: 'Give Me New Phoenix Wings'" the protagonist, although confronting "a wide-oncoming night" and held down by the "ballast weights of death," aspires to "his still affinity" in the starry empyrean. This theme is reiterated in "The Phoenix Palm," which, in evoking "the incandescent bird, desire," elevates Stewart's sexual dilemma to an impersonal plain: "Why must the mortal urge be born again / . . . / When will the endless round renew no more." Between these two poems falls the glittering, abstruse symbolism of "The Ascension of Feng," which at once reworks Chinese material and underlines Stewart's growing fascination with the phoenix as an ideal personal symbol. The last section of the volume comprises scenes from the proposed "Landscape Roll" that dramatize Eastern philosophies. In "The Three Tasters" Confucius, Gautama Buddha, and Lao Tzu appear as samplers of an unnamed liquid in an "earthen vessel"–or daily life. They find it bitter, whereas it is only the "inscrutable" and "yielding gentleness" of a Taoist that can reconcile itself to this fact with the same ease as it tamed "a fierce water-buffalo." Equally indicative of the poet's interests is the exchange between Chang Chih-ho and Wu Tao-tzu in "A Flight of Wild Geese." Chang, who has withdrawn from society to pursue an apparently purposeless existence in nature, sums up Stewart's position:

> Here cares and creditors no more infest
> The house of mind. Its poverty is rest.
> Possessing nothing, I am not possessed.
> The State's a monstrous and amorphous plan,
> Man's mobilized insanity, and man
> Believes it real. Afraid of being free,
> He fights to keep the cangue, and cannot flee.

Friends, understandably, were struck by the derivative, rather than the anticipatory, nature of this work—little realizing that through the great oriental traditions Stewart would eventually find himself creatively and spiritually.

During the late 1940s there occurred a crucial shift in the intellectual lens through which Stewart read and appropriated Eastern lore. During the previous decade the writings of Carl Jung had been an indispensable "bridge" between Stewart and Asian culture, introducing the poet to classics such as *The Secret of the Golden Flower* (attributed to Pinyin Lü Dongbin, one of the eight Taoist immortals) and encouraging them to be read as symbolic accounts of psychological processes long neglected by the West. By 1943 the Swiss psychiatrist's sway over Stewart was waning, although the poet preferred to attribute his insight into Jung's Procrustean approach to his later discovery of a new philosophical movement, Traditionalism. Its major theorist, René Guénon, posited a single spiritual tradition underlying all the great faiths and primitive cults from which the West, during the Renaissance and Reformation, had diverged with disastrous consequences. Guénon discerned the true teaching clearly among the metaphysical intricacies of Hinduism and granted primacy to oriental thought as well as to those initiates who, through their pursuit of Traditional knowledge, afforded the best hope of saving the West from its rampant materialism. Inspired by Guénon, Stewart studied the major Eastern faiths, regarding them in Traditionalist terms as diverse radii leading to one spiritual center, and he founded a weekly discussion group in Melbourne to propagate the French savant's ideas.

This changed source of inspiration is reflected obliquely in *Orpheus and Other Poems*. The collection opens with a twenty-seven-poem sequence reinterpreting the story of Orpheus and Eurydice to show, according to Stewart, the error of descending into the underworld beloved of psychoanalysis and the need for a superrational principle. Next come five poems grouped under the subheading "The Myths," followed by five scenes from "Landscape Roll." "Prelude: The Myths" offers a synoptic statement of contemporary attitudes toward myths, likened to "cities that have lain / Buried beneath the conscious plain" awaiting resurrection by "archeologists of mind," or Apollo's guild:

> Myths are a never-empty urn
> Of meaning: the poets thence in turn
> Pour out the symbols that presage
> The rise or ruin of their age.

The subjects of the remaining poems—drawn from Hinduism, Taoism, and Buddhism—are a testimony to Stewart's restless questing and to Traditionalist eclecticism, although much later he saw the poems as reflections of his engagement with the overarching tradition of Mahayana Buddhism.

During the late 1950s Stewart's focus began to shift toward Japanese culture when a second wave of Traditionalist theorists emerged internationally, headed by the Alsatian-born Frithjof Schuon. They emphasized the need for active involvement in a living tradition, and Schuon singled out the Japanese Jodo-Shin, or Pure Land, school of Buddhism as appropriate to the Western temperament. An enthusiastic Stewart planned to dedicate a future volume of verse to Schuon, and, in addition to taking private lessons in Japanese, he began to study haiku, which provided lessons in metaphysical resonance as well as rigorous condensation. As he states in *A Net of Fireflies: Japanese Haiku and Haiku Paintings* (1960), the outer form and inner scope of haiku are in "inverse ratio." Marker words telegraph time and season, while concrete images evoke the universal forces in which they participate. In haiku, poetry becomes ideally a form of meditation which, according to Stewart, has produced "the saints of haiku"—men aware that "the Diamond Sphere is identical with this world of dew." After researching previous haiku translations and theory by Reginald H. Blyth, Basil Hall Chamberlain, Harold Henderson, Lewis Mackenzie, Asataro Miyamori, William N. Porter, Kenneth Yasuda, and others, Stewart made the radical decision to substitute for the original structure (three lines of five, seven, and five syllables respectively) a verse form that he found congenial: the heroic couplet. It, he argued, best approximated the "poetic shock," or "moment of heightened awareness," that is "the outward sign of the active presence of Satori [enlightenment] in a haiku."

Stewart completed three books of haiku. The first, *A Net of Fireflies*, became his financial mainstay, thanks largely to American sales, the book having been reprinted twenty-five times by 1986, after which it was republished in a gift-book format. His second volume, *A Chime of Windbells: A Year of Japanese Haiku in English Verse* (1969), was reprinted ten times in less than a decade. His third, "Over the Vermilion Bridge: 350 Haiku by Ho-o in English Couplets by Harold Stewart," remains unpublished. A prefatory note on Ho-o states: "Almost nothing has so far been discovered about the life of our poet, who is known to posterity by his *go*, or studio name.... But recent research has shown that he must have been born about the end of the fifth or beginning of the sixth year of Taisho [1916 or 1917] in one of the islands of Japan. In middle life he is said to have moved to Kyoto, where he lived in obscurity and where most of his haiku were written; but the date of his death has yet to be determined." In fact, Ho-o and Stewart are one and the same person. *Ho-o* means "phoenix" and also designates the mirth aroused by the failure of scholars and laity alike to distinguish between the haiku by Stewart and those of

Stewart's long-time companion, Ueshima Masaaki, circa 1983 (Collection of Gwen Smith)

known masters, which sit easily beside one another in the two published volumes. For example, "Departure at Dawn" by Seibu, "The dawn's pink lotus-petals now expand: / Portals opening on the True Pure Land," precedes Stewart's "Divine Detachment," "The golden Buddhas pay no heed at all / To pigeon-droppings in their raftered hall," which is followed by "Perfect Purity" by Basho, "The snowy lotus-bloom: it does not spurn / Birth from the mud to which its seeds return."

Stewart journeyed to Japan in 1961, 1963, and 1966, after which he never returned to Australia, the land he dubbed "darkest Oz." The first two trips came close to being complete disasters, and in the late 1960s he had no idea that his third stay would become permanent. A major problem in 1961 was his immersion in Traditionalism. Although it corrected certain misconceptions about Asian civilizations, it also offered a typically orientalist picture of an unchanging, conceptually homogenous East, leaving Stewart ill prepared for modern actualities. As he confessed to McAuley in August 1963, he had encountered there "a ghastly irremediable mess. Japan is much further West than we are, and at first sight there is simply nothing oriental left after a hundred years of industrialization." In the National Treasures of Kyoto and Miyajima, however, he finally discovered approximations of his ideal pre-Meiji Japan. His second trip was intended to prepare him, in accordance with Schuon's admonition, to become a Pure Land Buddhist priest, but he changed his mind on the eve of ordination. During this stay he also met the love of his life, Ueshima Masaaki, in Kyoto; and the desire to be reunited with him was an important consideration in Stewart's decision to return to the Kansai region in 1966. That year they traveled extensively together, with Masaaki acting as interpreter and guide to Japanese arts and culture, before the poet settled in Kyoto, the former capital of Japan. There he spent the last twenty-nine years of his life in self-imposed exile, cultivating a compassionate religious persona that could be swept aside if his native land was mentioned in conversation. Then the deep malice that had inspired the composition of the notorious Ern Malley poems decades before resurfaced, as he dubbed the land of financial "rorts" (dishonest manipulations) and junkets the "Lurky Country" (nation of stratagems or dodges), or rebaptized a succession of its prime ministers with names such as "Goof Witless" (Gough Whitlam), "Chairman Mal" (Malcolm Fraser), "Blob Orc" (Bob Hawke), and "Poll Cheating" (Paul Keating). Stewart, the would-be Buddhist sage, could be savagely satirical, and there were aspects of his existence that sat uncomfortably with the dictates of the Dharma, but his later works conformed to his ideal self-image.

During the three decades in Kyoto, Stewart's private life remained an unhappy compromise as he pursued sexual relationships furtively and denied them publicly. Yet, artistically he blossomed, profiling himself as the acolyte of notable authorities on Pure Land Buddhism, scholars whom he assisted in translating key Buddhist texts. Stewart's faith was sincere and strong, and his arduous struggle to achieve it provided the subject of his first epic, *By the Old Walls of Kyoto* (1981). Consisting of 4,351 lines of poetry, divided into 12 cantos, and augmented by 325 pages of prose commentary, it took more than a decade to complete. According to its introduction, *By the Old Walls of Kyoto* traces "the poet's pilgrimage from the self-power methods of Zen to the Other Power teachings of Pure Land Buddhism." Furthermore, says Stewart, the poem gives "a trustworthy account of the defeats and triumphs through which he passed," and it includes a glimpse of his unreclaimed Adamic self:

> A middle-aged and moulting sensualist
> Whose cock-sure plumes have faded, I persist
> In passionate pursuits, which I disown
> After I fall a prey to senile lust.
> Revulsion turns away in self-disgust
> From stale temptations that I would resist
> And yet, despite my years, have not outgrown.

Despite Stewart's claim, however, the poem is "trustworthy" only in a general, schematic sense. He imposed an exemplary paradigm on his actual, zigzagging course to produce an ideal image of the poet-quester entirely focused on the need for inner growth.

Drawing inspiration from the Japanese adage that only perfection is good enough, Stewart took immense pains with his first epic. To ensure minute accuracy, he revisited again and again the temple sites he depicted. He composed the cantos at a rate of two per year and then revised them, he claimed, with the same care he had lavished on his haiku translations, which could be recast more than fifty times to achieve his desired effect. The verse of *By the Old Walls of Kyoto* was flexible yet sonorous, honed to read with the ease and directness of prose, as in the following passage:

> Silence awoke me, shiveringly aware
> Of even deeper cold, the whiter glare
> That dawn reflected upward from outside.
> Throwing my quilted covers off, I rose,
> And having slid my paper window wide,
> Looked out in wonder: Kyoto city lay
> Transformed by gentle snowfalls overnight
> Into a wood-block print in black and white.

Particularly impressive are the diverse moods of the poem, which, with its many resonant scenes, convey his deep learning with a deft touch. Contemplative passages are intermixed with striking imagery ("Such fools who give their future lives in pledge / For present pleasure's opiate to pain, / Are licking honey from the razor's edge"), self-mockery ("This old presumptuous fool, this foreign clown / Who tries to ape the Buddha, tumbles down!"), and blasts at contemporary Japan, where refuse and cherry blossoms float together in a temple pond. The result is a moving, personalized panorama of Kyoto, equally able to convey the conviviality of moon gazing:

> Brush-strokes of conversation, poised and placed
> Along the unspoken scroll of thought, define
> Our delicate formal friendship, meanwhile spaced
> With interludes of music, poems, wine.
> "Drink, drink the warm sweet saké!" urge my friends.
> Tonight's rare happiness that Heaven sends
> Only this once, with every moment ends.
> So drink, and give the moon your silent praise
> Till purified of self, you gaze and gaze....

or the solitary splendor of an epiphany:

> My steps, when halfway through the garden, halt.
> I stand beneath the midmost maple, spread
> Over the path, and look above my head
> Into its radiantly fretted vault
> Of foliage, pure gold and coral red,

Early draft for a poem in Stewart's "Landscape Roll" series (National Library of Australia, MS8973)

Where starry leaf on leaf is overlaid,
Filtering sunlight through translucent shade
In dazzling galaxies. Enraptured sight
Is lost in that pavilion of light.

Imperceptibly, the mundane maple expands into the "Bodhi Tree" until the viewer grasps the notion that "Now is forever. Here is everywhere." Hope, a good friend of Stewart's since the late 1930s and a critic rarely given to hyperbole, assured Stewart that, with *By the Old Walls of Kyoto*, he had written the greatest English poem of the century.

The epic was completed on 19 December 1977, and shortly thereafter Stewart began, or rather returned to, what became "Autumn Landscape Roll: A Divine Panorama." The creative act, Stewart had come to believe, was a form of meditation and spiritual asceticism that drew down conceptions already existing on a higher plain, so that the artist was not so much an originator as a medium for the Dharma. Despite this theory, the scenes he wrote in the late 1970s had pre-existed, at least in their broad outline, in his mind since the late 1940s, and he incorporated into his second epic the excerpts from "Landscape Roll" published in his first two collections of verse. The composition of "Autumn Landscape Roll" became the focus and incentive of his remaining years, filling his thoughts and dictating a daily routine that began at 5 A.M. with writing, followed by business and an afternoon nap, and then more work at night. The plot of this epic is simple and bold. It commences with a competition sponsored by the emperor between the two finest painters of the T'ang dynasty: Lu Ssu-hsun and Wu Tao-tzu. Lu relies on meticulous detail, Wu on few but suggestive brush strokes. Wu is adjudged the winner. Indeed, so realistic are Wu's creations that they blur the distinction between life and art. A scroll decorated by his brush becomes a blank when its fish swims off; a depiction of a thundering waterfall in a bedroom keeps its occupants awake. Wu is accustomed to enter imaginatively into his landscape painting, and one day never returns: "Translated out of earthly space and time / Into an autumn vision more sublime." Within his vision he encounters the seminal thinkers and faiths of that age and traverses the Buddhist cosmology from hell to paradise. The tale ends with the erasure of earthly illusion and the return of creative insight to its infinite origin beyond Western dualisms:

> Time at its terminating gyre will stop,
> And since in essence they were never two,
> The sea will slip into the shining drop,
> Whose crystal instant holds eternity.

Stewart died a fortnight after finishing the epic poem that he regarded as the summa of his life's work, leaving a manuscript of 5,356 lines, together with a brief explanatory apparatus. Its epigraph is from Wu Ching's *Pilgrimage to the West:* "I dedicate this work to the glory of the Buddha's Pure Land. . . . May it mitigate the sufferings of the lost and damned. May all who read it or hear it read . . . finally be reborn in the Realm of Uttermost Bliss; and by their common intercession may they requite me for the arduousness of my task." Stewart had traveled to the East to find the mythical Pure Land and struggled throughout his life to transform his burning animal energies into higher forms. His trials led eventually to poetry of enduring worth and to a Buddhist faith through which he attempted to resign himself to neglect and ignominy. As he wrote in *By the Old Walls of Kyoto*:

> I, who could not give up the world, go free:
> This irreligious world renounces me
> Ignored in peace and decently neglected
> Till I am safely dead, I lay no claim
> To rank, privilege, prestige, degree,
> Nor claim the flaring fraudulence of fame,
> But work unknown, my only wealth the Name.

Despite this acceptance, lack of appreciation in his homeland weighed heavily on him, especially because of the unwaning interest shown in his coproduction of the works of "Ern Malley," which became for him the "Unburiable Urn." Hoping eventually to have his mature poetic voice heard, he rewrote a selection of his earlier works to form the canonical collection "New Phoenix Wings." Like "Autumn Landscape Roll" and "Over the Vermilion Bridge," this collection remains in manuscript.

Harold Stewart died on 7 August 1995, and his bones after cremation were purest white, signifying to Buddhists a life of extraordinary merit. In Australia he was remembered in obituaries as a Buddhist recluse, and one even suggested that his finest creation was the correspondence of "Ethel Malley," the fictional sister of Ern. This judgment was further evidence that his major writing was still unknown, his work as an innovator and precursor unrecognized. This perception is changing as readers encounter the two epics that were his finest compositions, as well as his final answer to the earlier alienation and humiliation that are summed up in "Ambition" by a jeering schoolboy friend who dismissed his literary ambitions as "a fool's toy / a self-sympathy, a dramatic casing for an over- / sensitive and sentimental soul."

Interview:

R. K. Tipping, "Interview with Harold Stewart," *Westerly,* 32 (1987): 24–35.

Biography:

Michael Ackland, *Damaged Men: The Precarious Lives of James McAuley and Harold Stewart* (Sydney: Allen & Unwin, 2001).

References:

Michael Ackland, "Beyond 'Darkest Oz': The Diverse Stations of Harold Stewart's Road to Kyoto," *Southerly,* 60 (2000): 234–243;

Ronald Dunlop, "Pilgrim's Origress in Japan: Discovering Harold Stewart," *Southerly,* 43 (1983): 167–181;

Dunlop, "Some Aspects of the Poetry of Harold Stewart," *Southerly,* 23 (1963): 222–234;

Dorothy Green, "Ern Malley's Other Half: Harold Stewart's 'By the Old Walls of Kyoto,'" *Quadrant,* 21 (1977): 33–39;

Green, "Poet's Progess," *Hemisphere,* 17 (1973): 12–21;

B. J. Leckenby, "The Spiritual Journey of Harold Stewart: A Poet Inspired by Kyoto," *Kyoto Journal,* 44 (2000): 80–85.

Papers:

The bulk of Harold Stewart's correspondence, manuscripts, diaries, notebooks, and miscellaneous papers–including "Over the Vermilion Bridge" (NL MS 8973/7), "New Phoenix Wings" (NL MS 8973/10), and "Autumn Landscape Roll: A Divine Panorama" (NL MS 8973/11)–are held in the Australian National Library, Canberra. Important minor holdings are located in the Dorothy Green Papers at the Australian Defence Forces Academy in Canberra, and in the Michael Heyward Papers, La Trobe Collection, State Library of Victoria.

Dal Stivens
(31 December 1911 – 15 June 1997)

Harry Heseltine
Emeritus Professor, University of New South Wales

BOOKS: *The Tramp and Other Stories* (London: Macmillan, 1936);

The Courtship of Uncle Henry: A Collection of Tales and Stories (Melbourne: Reed & Harris, 1946);

Jimmy Brockett: Portrait of a Notable Australian (Sydney: Angus & Robertson, 1951);

The Gambling Ghost and Other Tales (Sydney: Angus & Robertson, 1953);

Ironbark Bill (Sydney: Angus & Robertson, 1955);

The Scholarly Mouse and Other Tales (Sydney: Angus & Robertson, 1957);

The Wide Arch (Sydney: Angus & Robertson, 1958);

Three Persons Make a Tiger: Translated from the Chinese of Wu Yu (Melbourne: Cheshire, 1968);

Selected Stories 1938–1968 (Sydney: Angus & Robertson, 1969);

A Horse of Air (Sydney: Angus & Robertson, 1970);

The Incredible Egg: A Billion Year Journey (New York: Weybright & Talley, 1974);

The Unicorn and Other Tales (Sydney: Wild & Woolley, 1976);

The Bushranger (Sydney: Collins, 1978);

The Demon Bowler and Other Cricket Stories (Collingwood, Vic.: Outback Press, 1979).

OTHER: *Coast to Coast: Australian Stories 1957–1958*, edited by Stivens (Sydney: Angus & Robertson, 1958).

Dal Stivens (from Graeme Kinross-Smith, Australia's Writers, 1980)

Dal Stivens's career spanned half a century, from the period of the Great Depression to the late 1970s. In that time he established a reputation as one of Australia's foremost short-story writers and as an accomplished and innovative novelist. He was especially known and admired for his refinement of the Australian "tall story," which in his hands became a genuinely original fictional form. His four novels vary markedly in subject matter, technique, and tone. All of them, like his shorter fiction, are characterized by an idiosyncratic comic sense. Among Australian writers of the middle twentieth century, none more successfully adapted the themes and attitudes that, laid down in the nineteenth century, had become the basis of a distinctively Australian tradition of prose narrative.

Dallas George Stivens was born on 31 December 1911 in Blayney, in the central west of New South Wales, the son of Francis Harold Stivens and Jane (Abbott) Stivens. J. H. M. Abbott, a relative on his mother's side of the family, was the author of several works of historical fiction and a prolific contributor to the Sydney *Bulletin* and the literary magazine *The Lone Hand*. Stivens's formative years were passed mainly in rural New South Wales, although for two years, 1927 and 1928, he attended Barker College, a private school located at Hornsby, on Sydney's far North Shore. The early bush experience, however, was what left the strongest imprint on his imagination. He found the lore of shearing sheds, itinerant workers, and bush sporting fixtures endlessly fascinating. His father, a bank manager, was an early and rich source of those tall tales, which Stivens later put to his own purposes. After leaving school he briefly followed his father's profession as a bank officer but soon abandoned a career in commerce in favor of journalism.

Stivens's first book, *The Tramp and Other Stories*, published in London in 1936 by Macmillan, was favorably reviewed by Graham Greene and H. E. Bates. The collection combines elements of the taciturn realism established in Australia by Henry Lawson with more contemporary techniques Stivens had learned from American writers such as Sherwood Anderson and Ernest Hemingway. Its best individual pieces have lost none of their original force and continue to be anthologized. "The Tramp" and "Mr Bloody Kearns," for instance, are memorable depictions of the impact of the Depression on both individual behavior and more general social attitudes.

From 1939 to 1942 Stivens was on the staff of the *Daily Telegraph* (Sydney), a morning newspaper and the principal rival of *The Sydney Morning Herald*. In 1939 he married May Burke, who died two years later. In 1945 he married Winifred Wright, from whom he was divorced in 1977. The couple had two children—a daughter, Katrin, and a son, Christopher.

Stivens's early experience as a roundsman for a large metropolitan daily gave him valuable material for his own writing, which began to appear in important local publications such as *Meanjin Papers, Southerly, The A.B.C. Weekly,* and *The Bulletin*. At the same time his life, like those of all men of his generation, was shaped by Australia's involvement in World War II. In 1943 he joined the Army Education Service, and from 1944 to 1949 he worked with the Commonwealth Government Department of Information.

Shortly after the end of the war, Stivens's second book, *The Courtship of Uncle Henry* (1946), was published by the Australian firm of Reed and Harris. Several of its thirty-four pieces continue the vein of social and psychological realism he had already mined in *The Tramp and Other Stories*. The volume is, however, more significant for its increasingly comic focus on bush material. In his preface Stivens makes the point unequivocally: "In some of the more recent tales . . . I have tried to make use of what I feel to be genuinely Australian folklore." Two of these tales, "Indians Have Special Eyesight" and "When Trumper Went for a Blob," take cricket as their subject. Stivens was a lifelong devotee of the game, but he treats it with the same combination of wryly laconic observation and elegant exaggeration that characterizes the humor of all his best writing.

In 1948 Stivens won third prize in a *Sydney Morning Herald* literary competition for a manuscript, "The Entrepreneur," published in 1951 as his first novel, *Jimmy Brockett*. The subtitle, *Portrait of a Notable Australian,* accurately represents its imaginative focus. Its dominating and vulgar eponymous hero narrates his own life story in the historic present tense, recounting some of the crucial episodes of his career. Brockett's language is vigorous, colorful, and, in its earthy imagery, always reminiscent of the working-class Sydney suburb from which he comes. His whole approach to life and to those with whom he deals is summed up in the sardonic directive he attaches to his will: "I have asked the undertaker to bury me on my face so that anyone who doesn't like this will can kiss my arse."

Brockett's first utterance is dated September 1905; his last, August 1931. In 1905 he is twenty-eight years old, has already made a trip to England, and is loosening his ties to his family and his past. His father, an immigrant from Bristol, had been in turn an unsuccessful miner and small farmer. Drifting to Sydney, he established himself in the inner-city suburb of Glebe. In such surroundings Brockett learns early to run with the pack, but, discovering his entrepreneurial talents, he soon embarks on a solo career that satisfies all his hedonistic cravings and at last brings him down.

His restless search for wealth and power leads him initially to promote wrestling and boxing matches. Soon, however, he extends his interests into real estate and horse racing. Later he adds newspaper ownership and parliamentary politics to the range of his activities. His methods, usually corrupt or illegal, depend on native cunning, blackmail, an innate shrewdness about finance, and an overweeningly forceful personality. His appetite for power and social prestige (if not respectability) is matched by his appetite for the pleasures of the flesh. He satisfies both by marrying well, but soon cruelly suppresses his wife's artistic ambitions. His wife, Sadie, dies in childbirth, leaving Brockett the legacy of a son, young Jimmy, in whom he invests whatever capacity he has for genuine love and affection as well as his hopes for establishing a dynastic line. Consequently, young Jimmy's death (caused in part by Brockett's negligence) is the one real tragedy of Brockett's life. By the time of his own death of heart failure in 1938 at the age of sixty-one, he is gross, corpulent, and still obsessed with the dreams of affluence that had served him well in his young manhood and maturity but that, as World War II looms closer and the patterns of Sydney life change with increasing rapidity, have become hopelessly old-fashioned and impossible to achieve.

Brockett's personal narrative is punctuated by several brief external comments on his personality, behavior, and values. These include snippets drawn from Sydney's urban mythology, the metropolitan press, and a scholarly essay titled "The Life and Times of Jimmy Brockett." The external narration provides a balancing commentary on his self-revelations, rounding out this fictional portrait of a representative figure from a buccaneering phase in Sydney's socioeconomic history. Brockett, with all his faults and vanities, remains one of the truly dynamic characterizations of mid-twentieth-century Australian fiction.

Between the success of "The Entrepreneur" in 1948 and the publication of *Jimmy Brockett* in 1951, Stivens left Australia for England. Following a brief appointment to the staff of the federal Labor minister Arthur Calwell, he returned to the Department of Information and in 1949 was posted to London as press officer in Australia House. In 1950 he resigned in order to devote himself to a full-time career as a writer.

Stivens remained in England until 1957, and his years in the United Kingdom were vital to the development and consolidation of his career. He contributed to a range of British publications including *Lilliput*, *John O'London's*, and *The Times Literary Supplement*, as well as having stories broadcast on the BBC. More important, he published three additional volumes of short stories, all with Angus and Robertson, a leading Australian publishing house famous since the 1890s for its fostering of local literature. In *The Gambling Ghost and Other Tales* (1953), *Ironbark Bill* (1955), and *The Scholarly Mouse and Other Tales* (1957) Stivens brought his treatment of the form to a peak of personal accomplishment.

The title piece of *The Gambling Ghost and Other Tales* and another story from the same collection, "The Hard-Working Ghost," combine two characteristic features of Stivens's short fiction—the ghost story and the outback yarn. They depend on the deadpan delivery of an Australian vernacular laced with comic metaphor. The narration of feats of strength, endurance, or native wit is so outrageous as finally to convince by the sheer impudence of the telling. By the middle 1950s Stivens had perfected a formula for loading hyperbole upon the laconic that rarely failed him thereafter.

Some of the tales of *The Gambling Ghost and Other Tales* are told in the first person—the narrator is included in the community of outback yarn spinners. Others tell of mythical figures such as Ironbark Bill, Frying-Pan Fred, or Misery-Guts Jackson. Still others work a further variation on the possibilities of short fiction. For instance, "The Helpful Pink Elephant," "The Remarkable Cockerel," and "The Big-Hearted Racehorse" draw on the tradition of instructive animal fables stretching back through Jean La Fontaine to Aesop. The

Dust jacket for the 1966 edition of Stivens's first novel, which won third prize in a 1948 Sydney Morning Herald *literary competition (Bruccoli Clark Layman Archives)*

instruction offered by Stivens's fables, however, is almost invariably sardonic in tone, unexpected in its playful deflation of conventional notions of morality and conduct.

The larger-than-life outback hero is the subject of all ten tales collected in *Ironbark Bill*. They are uniformly successful in balancing a tone of comic amusement at Bill's improbable adventures with endorsement of their value as exemplars of ingenuity and endurance. By way of contrast, many of the pieces in *The Scholarly Mouse and Other Tales* (including the title piece) belong to the mode of moral fable. They take the form of a quest in which a young animal, setting himself apart from his kind, seeks to widen the boundaries of his knowledge and experience. By the end of the tale (usually no more than a few pages long) the young dog, or basilisk, or hare, or mouse has been forced (sometimes painfully) to realize the illusory nature of the ideals that prompted his quest.

Not all the work in *The Scholarly Mouse and Other Tales* is of this kind. Several outback yarns and a cricketing story appear, together with one of Stivens's most admired pieces, "The Pepper Tree." Told in the first person, it is a touchingly nostalgic account of the narrator's boyhood love for his father, and that father's valiant but failed attempt to run a small business in the years of the Great Depression. The pepper tree of the title is a fully realized symbol of both the narrator's recalled affection and his father's dreamy and ineffectual aspirations.

After *The Scholarly Mouse and Other Tales* Stivens mainly reprinted already-published short stories or, in those few new pieces he wrote, continued the techniques he had polished during the 1950s. The novels that followed *Jimmy Brockett*, however, present a strikingly different pattern of achievement. The second of them, *The Wide Arch* (1958), draws its title from William Shakespeare's *Antony and Cleopatra* (circa 1606; published 1623): "Let Rome in Tiber melt, and the wide arch / Of the rang'd empire fall! Here is my space." The quotation distills the sacrifice of worldly ambition to obsessive personal passion, which is one of the leading themes of the novel, but the narrative also just as strongly echoes *King Lear* (performed 1606; published 1608), *Othello* (performed 1604; published 1622), and, most notably, *Hamlet* (1603).

The action, set in the affluent suburbs of Sydney, is compressed into the space of a few days over Christmas in the 1950s not long after the conclusion of the Korean War–Rod, one of the four sons of Robert Lawton, a leading Sydney barrister, has served as an army medical officer in that conflict. The elder Lawton has been unfaithful with Vicky Kemp, the widow of his best friend, whose son David in turn nurses murderous feelings toward both his mother and her lover. While the loves, hates, and jealousies of the Lawton and Kemp families are at the core of the intricate plot of *The Wide Arch*, their actions are secretly manipulated by Henry Alwyn, a contemporary of Robert Lawton whose passionate dislike of Robert is fed by a more general attraction to evil for its own sake. This Iago-like character finally takes his own life in a gesture of Nietzschean triumph of the will: "I, Henry Alwyn, leave this life because I will it so. I have dared all and won. This is my moment of supreme victory. All else would be an anticlimax."

The intertwined events of *The Wide Arch* are revealed through the voices of all its major characters; Stivens found the use of multiple points of view most apt for representing his sense of a flawed and many-faceted human reality. After *The Wide Arch*, there followed a hiatus of ten years before the appearance of his next major work. This considerable gap in his written record is in large measure to be explained by his return to Sydney in 1957 and his passionate engagement with the politics and economics of Australian writing.

Michael Wilding recorded in an obituary of Stivens (*The Australian*, 20 June 1997) that, back home and "appalled by the feudal state of the writing business here," Stivens saw a clear need for an energetic writers' organization. Together with a small group of like-minded individuals he set out to plan such an organization, and in 1963 the Australian Society of Authors was established. Stivens was the founding president, vice president in 1964 and 1965, and president again from 1967 to 1972. He was the author of the society's first book on the practicalities of publishing contracts and campaigned vigorously for the establishment of the Public Lending Right, which would guarantee authors some financial return for the borrowing of their work from public libraries.

In spite of all this practical activity, Stivens still managed to maintain his creative output, though not always through the medium of the printed word. Chronically obsessive, he set about becoming an expert in the cultivation of azaleas as well as developing a passionate interest and some skill in painting. As Barbara Jefferis, his obituarist in the Melbourne *Age* (30 July 1997), described, "He used acrylics, plastics, crayons, household oils, fabric dyes and glitter paints–anything that could be dispensed in streaks and pools through squeeze bottles and spray cans and jam jars with holes in the bottom, saying 'What I am trying to do is to create conditions where the subconscious comes through in conditions of pressure which force you to paint fast.'" Many of his canvases are distinctly reminiscent of Jackson Pollock, while others arrange masses of intense color in soft- or hard-edged compositions. Some reveal his fascination with Chinese calligraphy–his many images of birds (herons and eagles) are done with spare and economical brush strokes of black ink on white paper.

Stivens's interest in Chinese culture is clearly evident in his third major work of fiction, *Three Persons Make a Tiger: Translated from the Chinese of Wu Yu* (1968); the title, derived from a Chinese fable, means, as Stivens reveals in one of its two epigraphs, "Fiction repeated often enough will be taken for fact." The plot of the novel is a fanciful variation on the legend of the Monkey King. In Stivens's recasting of the tale, the ingenious and rebellious Monkey is sent by the Immortals on a redemptive mission to the Southern Continent, charged with the task of bringing four saints back to the Jade Emperor and the Buddha. Accompanied by the gross Pigsy, Monkey lands in what is plainly a satirical representation of 1960s Australia, to commence a series of adventures in the manner of *Gulliver's Travels*

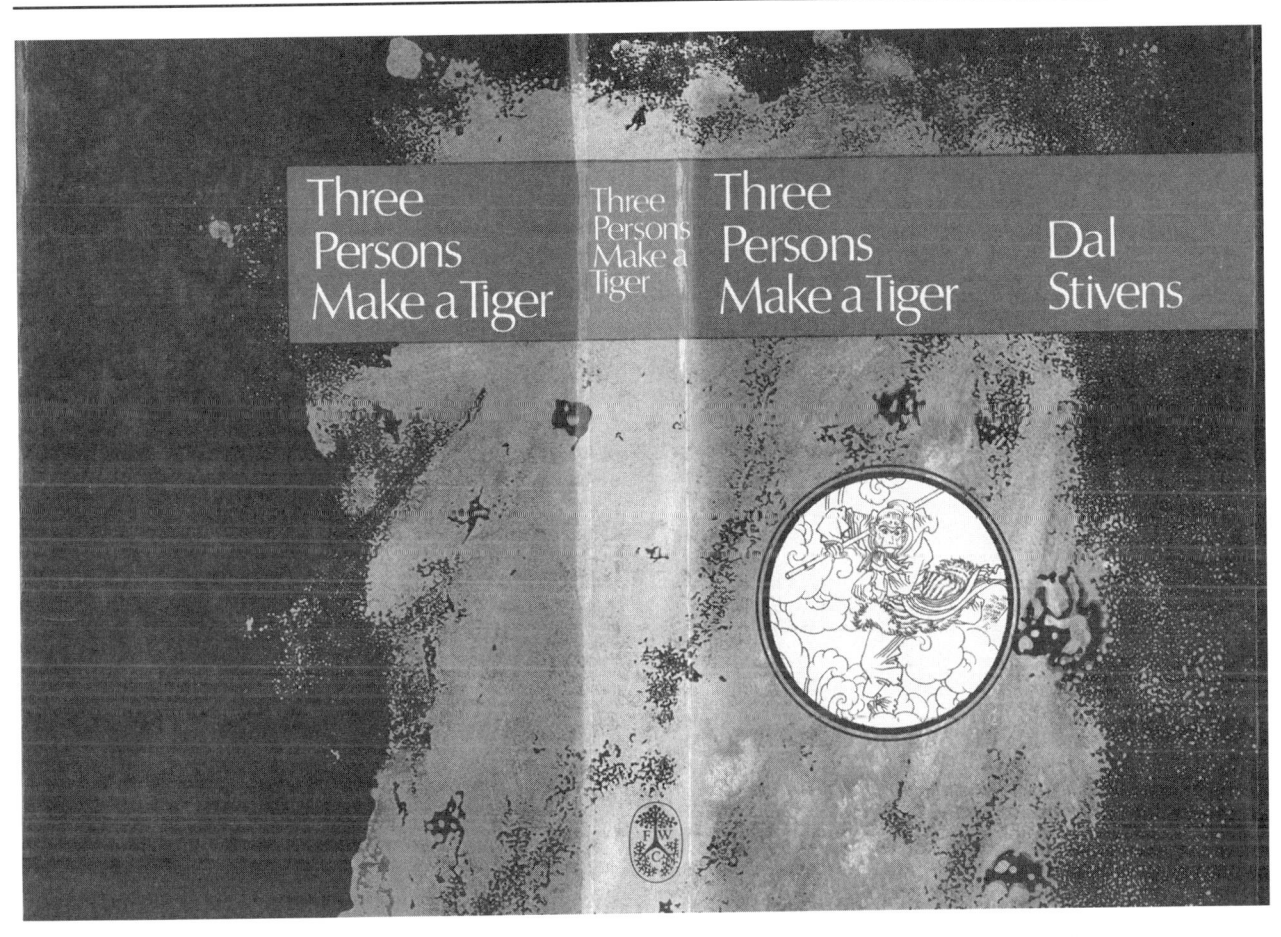

Dust jacket for Stivens's 1968 novel, whose title, Stivens said, means "Fiction repeated often enough will be taken for fact" (Bruccoli Clark Layman Archives)

(1726) or *Candide* (1759). He can find only two potential saints on the entire continent: Jed Kell Lee (a miraculous resurrection of the nineteenth-century bushranger Ned Kelly) and Gros Simonyi, a wise and humble old man recently arrived from Europe. Monkey therefore extends his search to a whole range of contemporary societies—satirical versions of nations such as the United States, Britain, and South Africa.

Applying Monkey's mordant perception and magical powers to these cultures, Stivens peels away the falsehoods and fictions by which their elites sustain themselves, demonstrating the self-interest and greed that lie beneath. Continually harassed by their enemy, the Bunyip (early encountered in Central Australia), Monkey and Pigsy finally return to the Southern Continent, where they discover a multitude of saints—followers of Simonyi, who has mounted a successful crusade based on the practice of poverty and goodwill. Reporting back to the Celestials, Monkey is told that all these holy men and women should be left on Earth, which has the greater need of them. In the course of his adventures Monkey has learned humility and is rewarded with the return of his magic powers (lost in the course of his travels) and a Heavenly Peach Banquet.

Three Persons Make a Tiger is presented as the tattered fragment of a Chinese manuscript discovered in a shop in Sydney's Chinatown. Stivens (aided by Dr. Tzu Hsu) assumes the role of translator of Wu Yu's lost work. The device gives free rein to his capacity for satiric fantasy; yet, some of his targets (for instance, the White Australia Policy) now seem a little dated. From time to time, too, the faux-naif tone of the narration becomes labored, lacking the cool incisiveness of the shorter fables. The best of these, along with a representative range of his entire short-story output up to 1969, were published as *Selected Stories 1938–1968*. The collection provides a comprehensive overview of his achievement in the genre over a thirty-year period. The last of its thirty-five stories is also one of Stivens's best in the realistic mode: "Warrigal" fuses his contempt for suburban hypocrisy, his fascination with natural history, and his superb powers of characterization.

"Warrigal" reappears as a major episode in Stivens's last novel, *A Horse of Air* (1970). The plot centers on an expedition to Central Australia by Harry Crad-

A White Heron of Okarito Complains:

It's a hell of a life really. It's all very well for those featherless ratites — Hominidae, if you must be correct — to name luxury hotels after us, make a quick buck out of our rareness and beauty, and talk nonsense about being as free as a bird. We — *Egretta alba* — know better.

It's no joke having to fish for a tenth of your weight every day. Just so you can fly. That's got to be paid for. With biting hunger to stoke a high metabolism. Body temperature 41°C. (106°F).

Who in his right mind would want to work on a night like this?

— Dal Stivens 11.9.1974.

Fair copy of a poem by Stivens and his illustration for it (from Graeme Kinross-Smith, Australia's Writers, *1980)*

dock, the wealthy son of a newspaper magnate, who goes to the desert in 1967 in search of the rare night parrot. Events are narrated primarily by Craddock himself, writing from a psychiatric hospital to which he has been voluntarily admitted. The filtering and fracturing of the action do not end with this device: Craddock's manuscript is supplemented by many entries from the diary of Joanna, his former wife, while the entire narrative is presented, following Craddock's death, by his literary executor, who supplements the text with a variety of explanatory footnotes. The whole work is preceded by half a dozen epigraphs, all of which assert both the high promise of any quest for knowledge and the disappointments and betrayals such actions almost invariably bring.

A Horse of Air realizes more fully than anything else in Stivens's canon his mature sense of the slippery, evanescent nature of reality. Frequently describing himself as a buffoon, Craddock is nevertheless a witty, intelligent, and compelling personality. Obsessive, deeply knowledgeable about animal and bird behavior, and aware of the shaping effects of his privileged background and closest personal relationships, he mocks and misleads his psychiatrist even as he writes the autobiography that is supposed to reveal his deepest secrets. In the end his expedition has been as much a journey into the recesses of his own heart as a quixotic attempt to find and study a rare bird on the edge of extinction. At another level *A Horse of Air* extends the tradition of exploration narrative, which has played an important part in the development of Australian writing. Craddock regularly judges the merits of his own endeavors against those of the expedition of Ernest Giles, who had traversed the same region as himself in 1876. Nor could Stivens have been unmindful of the impact of Patrick White's *Voss* (1957), published little more than a decade before his own encounter with the genre.

The competing voices of *A Horse of Air,* as well as its radical shifts in tone and between fantasy and actuality, required a genuine mastery of technique. The high level of achievement in this novel won for Stivens the 1970 Miles Franklin Award, Australia's premier literary prize. That was not the only recognition he received in his later years. In 1981 he received the Patrick White Literary Award for Fiction and in 1994 a Special Achievement Award in that year's New South Wales Literary Awards.

Stivens's last full-length work was *The Incredible Egg: A Billion Year Journey* (1974), which summarized his lifelong fascination with evolution, ornithology, animal behavior, and the zoological sciences in general. He followed this scientific *summa* two years later with a work of utterly different character. *The Bushranger* (1978), a novella for younger readers, encapsulates virtually all the themes and conventions of one of the great subjects of Australian colonial writing—the oppressed small settler who turns to outlawry to fight against unjust authority.

An ironic fascination with life in all its forms underlies everything Dal Stivens wrote—the most outrageous of his tall stories, the most elegant of his comic fables, the most outré of his ventures into fantasy and the unconscious. Right to the end of his life there was a freshness, an inventiveness, in his work that kindled enthusiasm in writers two and three generations his junior. While he never attempted works of grandiose proportions, his was an idiosyncratic and brilliant contribution to the literature produced in Australia in the second and third quarters of the twentieth century.

Papers:

A collection of Dal Stivens's papers is held at the National Library of Australia in Canberra.

Randolph Stow

(28 November 1935 -)

Anthony Hassall
James Cook University

BOOKS: *A Haunted Land* (London: Macdonald, 1956; New York: Macmillan, 1957);

The Bystander (London: Macdonald, 1957);

Act One: Poems (London: Macdonald, 1957);

To the Islands (London: Macdonald, 1958; Boston: Little, Brown, 1959; Melbourne: Penguin, 1962; revised edition, London & Sydney: Angus & Robertson, 1981; New York: Taplinger, 1982);

Outrider: Poems, 1956-1962 (London: Macdonald, 1962);

Poems from "The Outrider" and other Poems, Australian Artists and Poets Booklets, no. 9 (Adelaide: Australian Letters, 1963);

Tourmaline (London: Macdonald, 1963; Ringwood, Vic.: Penguin, 1965; New York: Taplinger, 1983);

The Merry-Go-Round in the Sea (London: Macdonald, 1965; New York: Morrow, 1966; Melbourne: Penguin, 1968);

Midnite: The Story of a Wild Colonial Boy (London: Macdonald, 1967; Melbourne: Cheshire, 1967; Englewood Cliffs, N.J.: Prentice-Hall, 1968);

A Counterfeit Silence: Selected Poems (Sydney: Angus & Robertson, 1969);

Eight Songs for a Mad King, music by Peter Maxwell Davies, lyrics by Stow (London: Boosey & Hawkes, 1971);

Miss Donnithorne's Maggot, music by Davies, text by Stow (London: Boosey & Hawkes, 1977);

Visitants (London: Secker & Warburg, 1979; New York: Taplinger, 1981);

The Girl Green as Elderflower (London: Secker & Warburg, 1980; New York: Viking, 1980);

The Suburbs of Hell (London: Secker & Warburg, 1984; New York: Taplinger, 1984; Richmond, Vic.: Heinemann, 1984);

Randolph Stow: Visitants, Episodes from Other Novels, Poems, Stories, Interviews, and Essays, edited by Anthony J. Hassall (St. Lucia: University of Queensland Press, 1990).

Randolph Stow, 1973 (photograph by Michael Scott)

RECORDING: *Randolph Stow Reads From His Own Work,* Poets on Record Series, no. 11 (St. Lucia: University of Queensland Press, 1974);

OTHER: *Australian Poetry 1964,* edited by Stow (Sydney: Angus & Robertson, 1964);

"Magic," in *Modern Australian Writing,* edited by Geoffrey Dutton (London: Fontana, 1966), pp. 106-119;

"Dokonikan," in *Australian Writing Today*, edited by Charles Higham (Harmondsworth, U.K.: Penguin, 1968), pp. 287–296;

"The Southland of Antichrist: The *Batavia* Disaster of 1629," in *Common Wealth*, edited by Anna Rutherford (Aarhus: Akademisk Boghandel, 1971), pp. 160–167.

SELECTED PERIODICAL PUBLICATIONS–UNCOLLECTED: "The Umbali Massacre: As told to him by Daniel Evans," *Bulletin*, 15 February 1961, pp. 45–46;

"Raw Material," *Westerly*, 6, no. 2 (1961): 3–5;

"Two Letters of 1629 on the *Batavia* Disaster," *Westerly*, 17, no. 1 (April 1972): 7–11;

"The Arrival at the Homestead: A Mind-Film," *Kunapipi*, 1, no. 1 (1979): 31–36; expanded version, *Bulletin*, 29 January 1980, pp. 164–166;

"Transfigured Histories: Recent Novels of Patrick White and Robert Drewe," *Australian Literary Studies*, 9 (1979): 26–38;

"Denmark in the Indian Ocean, 1616–1845: An Introduction," *Kunapipi*, 1, no. 1 (1979): 11–26;

"Transplantable Roots: On Being a Regional Writer in Two Countries," *BASA Magazine*, 2, no. 1 (1985): 3–8.

Randolph Stow is one of the Australian novelists of the 1950s and 1960s who abandoned the social-realist mode that had dominated Australian fiction long after the modernist novel had achieved prominence and acceptance in England and the United States. Following the lead of Patrick White–who returned from Europe to live and write in Australia in 1948, introducing the modernist novel to Australia with works such as *The Aunt's Story* (1948), *The Tree of Man* (1955), and *Riders in the Chariot* (1961) younger writers such as Stow and Christopher Koch produced novels that combined realism with a poetic response to the Australian landscape, a preoccupation with the inner lives of their characters, and a sense of the mythic qualities of the Australian experience. The initial response to these new novels from an Australian audience more accustomed to social-realist narratives was a mixture of skepticism and enthusiasm. Stow's early novels and poems won several literary prizes but were also subject to some hostile academic reviewing, as White's novels had been. In the decades that followed, however, Stow's reputation consolidated as his narrative methods became more familiar to a mainstream audience. When his semi-autobiographical *The Merry-Go-Round in the Sea* was published in 1965, it greatly enhanced his acceptance and popularity. His other works continue to evoke a mixed response, and at the beginning of the twenty-first century the critical assessment of his work remains divided between those who see him as a major figure and those who would relegate him to a more minor status as the author of a single classic work, *The Merry-Go-Round in the Sea*.

Julian Randolph Stow was born on 28 November 1935 in Geraldton, Western Australia, to Cedric Ernest and Mary (Sewell) Stow. On both sides of his family, Randolph Stow belongs to the fifth generation resident in Australia and the third generation born in Australia. The Stows came to Australia from Hadleigh in Suffolk, England, while his mother's family, the Sewells, came from the nearby Maplestead Hall in Essex, just over the county border. Randolph Stow grew up in Western Australia, and he has lived since 1966 in the East Anglia of his forebears.

One of Randolph Stow's great-great-grandfathers, the Reverend Thomas Quinton Stow (1801–1862), arrived in 1837 in the new colony of South Australia, where a church is named after him. His descendants include distinguished lawyers and judges. Randolph Stow's grandfather Frances Leslie Stow (1869–1935) and his father, Cedric Stow (1902–1959), were both lawyers in Western Australia. Randolph Stow's maternal great-grandfather George Sewell (1816–1891) arrived in Western Australia in 1836, shortly after the founding of the colony. He moved with his family to Geraldton, some five hundred kilometers north of the capital Perth, in 1866, having taken up residence at Sand Springs station in the 1850s.

Randolph Stow was educated in Geraldton, at Guildford Church of England Grammar School in Perth, and at the University of Western Australia, where he first studied law but then switched to work on a B.A. degree in French and English, graduating in 1956. A gifted linguist and student of anthropology, he later taught and studied at several universities, including Adelaide (1957), Sydney (1958), and Western Australia (1963–1964), Leeds in England (1962, 1968–1969), and Yale in the United States (1965).

Stow completed two novels, *A Haunted Land* (1956) and *The Bystander* (1957), and his first collection of poetry, *Act One* (1957), while still an undergraduate at the University of Western Australia, and all three were published in London by the time he was twenty-one, marking a precocious start to his literary career. He now regards the two novels as apprentice work and has not allowed them to be reprinted. These works begin to explore the themes that the mature Stow later made his own: a fascinated unease with the landscape of his native Western Australia, the failure to sustain love, and the alienation of the self from a feared and inescapable psychic other. *A Haunted Land* and *The Bystander* portray the country around Geraldton as harsh, alien,

383

Stow driving sheep at Sand Springs station, to which he was evacuated during World War II (from Peter Pierce, ed., The Oxford Literary Guide to Australia, *1987)*

and haunting, and the descendants of the early European settlers as tortured, restless, and bitter. There are some stylistic excesses, and the novels fail to provide a clear focus for the reader's sympathies, but the two works display a considerable command of narrative and great imaginative intensity. While their faults were noticed by reviewers, the books were widely welcomed as signaling the arrival of a gifted new writer.

Act One was awarded the Gold Medal of the Australian Literature Society, the first of many literary awards for Stow. The poems are dramatic rather than lyrical, and private rather than public. Many are nostalgic re-creations of the world of childhood—and of the "brief subtle things that a child does not realize," but which survive to haunt the adult memory. The collection also includes some brief, intense, yet dreamy narratives chronicling early, bitter experiences of love and sexuality. Stow could already portray the Western Australian landscape with a spare and resonant clarity that few other Australian writers have matched. T. S. Eliot is a continuing, though unobtrusive, influence in the poems, and there are echoes of the English ballad and lyric traditions, especially the Elizabethan lyricists and John Keats, and of the French poets Charles Baudelaire, Arthur Rimbaud, and St. John Perse.

Stow later came to regard many of the poems in *Act One* as immature, including only seventeen of the thirty-nine in the "Juvenilia" section of his *A Counterfeit Silence: Selected Poems* (1969). One early poem not included in *Act One* but later added to the "Juvenilia" section was "For One Dying," a haunting elegy for Miss Sutherland MacDonald, the woman on whom he based Rob Coram's beloved Aunt Kay in *The Merry-Go-Round in the Sea*. The elegy ends with a wish:

> I am no more the child whom you made cry
> so readily with your sad ballad-tales,
> not skilled to soothe the life that prays to die,
> not skilled to pray. But must, since all else fails,
> trust that your Lord, who owes you some amend,
> grant you a quiet night, and a perfect end.

The poem is a beautifully modulated and moving tribute to a childhood favorite dying of cancer.

In 1957 Stow worked for some months as a storeman for the Anglican mission to the Umbalgari people at Forrest River, near Wyndham in the far north of Western Australia. The harsh landscape of the region became the setting for the novel he wrote later that year. *To the Islands* (1958) was his third novel in three years, all written by the age of twenty-three. It won several prizes, including the Miles Franklin Award, the premier Australian award for fiction, and it consolidated Stow's growing reputation. The earliest of his novels that he has allowed to be reprinted, *To the Islands* was revised in 1982, modifying what Stow by then saw as marks of immaturity, but leaving the book essentially intact.

To the Islands explores some of the darker recesses of the European annexation of Australia. It tells the story of Stephen Heriot, an aging missionary in the far north of Western Australia, who has devoted his life to atoning for a massacre of Aborigines at Onmalmeri. The legend of this massacre, which is closely based on the historical Umbali massacre of 1926, serves as a focus for the conflicts explored in the book, including the friction between the European settlers and the indigenous inhabitants, the alienation of the European in a landscape claimed but not yet truly possessed (one of Stow's continuing preoccupations), and the inner alienation of Heriot, who has lost belief and love and finds himself imprisoned in a sterile ritual of atonement that has hardened into resentment and hatred. The final tableau of Heriot alone on a cliff above the Arafura Sea, confronting the strangeness of his soul and looking out toward the Aboriginal islands of the dead, is one of the unforgettable images of Australian literature. Initial criticism that Stow's mixture of "realistic" and "symbolic" fiction was somehow unsatisfactory has come to seem increasingly inappropriate as the possibilities opened up by modern and postmodern fiction have changed reader expectations. Heriot is one of Stow's most powerful and convincing portrayals of the agonized search for a home in an alien universe, and *To the Islands* remains one of Stow's most popular and successful novels.

In 1959 Stow went to Papua New Guinea, then an Australian colony, to work as a cadet patrol officer and assistant to the government anthropologist Charles Julius. He spent much of his time in the Trobriand Islands, earlier studied by the anthropologist Bronislaw Malinowski, and he learned the local Biga-Kiriwina language. After he contracted malaria, he was invalided back to Australia. Stow's experience in the Trobriand Islands was traumatic, and he explored it in some of the poems in *Outrider* (1962) and in the novels *Visitants* (1979) and *The Girl Green as Elderflower* (1980). In 1961 Stow went to England to work at Leeds University, and though he has since traveled extensively, he has made his home in England, first in London and then in East Anglia. He last visited Australia in 1974.

Outrider: Poems, 1956–1962, Stow's second collection of poetry, was illustrated with a series of paintings by Sidney Nolan and has become a collector's item. A stronger and more consistent book than *Act One*, it demonstrates how rapidly Stow's poetry had matured. All but three of the poems were republished in *A Counterfeit Silence*, indicating that Stow saw the poems in *Outrider* as mature work. Like the poems in *Act One*, many are again anguished and private, charting a journey into and out of an intense psychic crisis. "At Sandalwood" and "Jimmy Woodsers" link *Outrider* with the childhood poems of *Act One*, though their nostalgia is tempered by the now conflicting emotions aroused by "my sad-coloured country, / bitterly admired." "The Land's Meaning" explores further the poet's mystical bond with the country, which is loved but is irretrievably "other." It reveals its ultimate truths only to those who have been "bushed for forty years" in its desert wilderness. The volume also includes satirical poems, such as "The Utopia of Lord Mayor Howard," which ridicules a civic dignitary determined to replace the karri trees of Perth with "neat rose gardens," and frequently anthologized poems, such as "Ruins of the City of Hay," which mocks the utopian pretensions of Western Australia with ironic affection, and "Dust," which again humorously juxtaposes the wild generosity of the natural world and the neurotic constraints of the suburbs.

The center of *Outrider* is, however, a group of poems prompted by the psychic crisis that accompanied the malaria Stow contracted in the Trobriand Islands in 1959. These poems are dense and cryptic, recalling the later poems of Frances Webb and Bruce Beaver's *Letters to Live Poets* (1969). Stow's poet-speaker turns inward to probe, cauterize, and exorcize the anguish that accompanied his sickness. This group of poems is framed at the beginning by "The Embarkation," an enigmatic imprisonment in the "ruined cell / embattled" of a tropical beach, and at the end by "Landfall," in which the poet-speaker returns to his starting point but refuses to tell where he has been and what he has seen on his voyage. In between are poems such as "Strange Fruit" and "Sleep," which depict the torture of psychic division, the bitter internal conflict between the self and the invading "other," and the desperate need for escape. These poems are alternately lush and spare, the lines either generous or clipped, the sense of control either slipping or tightly gripped. The title poem, "Outrider," gathers together these forms and preoccupations in its haunting, strangely ballad-like depiction of the poet-speaker waking from nightmare—"that planet (ah, Christ) of black ice"—into "a dim low English room" in which his waking memories are almost as disturbing as his dreams.

After publishing four books between 1956 and 1959, Stow decided to abandon writing for a nonliterary career as an anthropologist in Papua New Guinea. There was an interval of five years between *To the Islands* and Stow's next novel, *Tourmaline* (1963), a break which he has described as his first "silence." *To the Islands* had enjoyed both critical and popular success, but *Tourmaline* won no awards, puzzling and disappointing many of its first reviewers and readers. Like *To the Islands*, *Tourmaline* is a spiritual fable, set this time in the future in an isolated Western Australian mining town after a nuclear holocaust. While *To the Islands* had contrasted missionary European Christianity with a disregarded but not unknown Aboriginal culture, *Tourmaline* juxtaposed an American style of revivalist Christianity with the Chinese philosophy of Taoism. The unfamiliarity of Taoism, which was virtually unknown in Australia at the time, contributed to the unease of many of the first readers of the novel. In 1966 Stow, irritated by their incomprehension, published "From *The Testament of Tourmaline*: Variations on Themes of the *Tao Te Ching*," a series of translations from the sacred book of Taoism. This work, which appeared first in a 1966 issue of *Poetry Australia* and later in *A Counterfeit Silence*, succeeded in alerting readers to the Taoist dimension of *Tourmaline* and led to a developing awareness of the influence of Taoism on all Stow's writing. In the years since that initial controversy, *Tourmaline* has come to be seen as a searching exploration of conflicting visions of how to live in a minimalist, survival mode after the self-immolation of Western society.

The first chapter of the novel is one of Stow's most dazzling prose poems:

> There is no stretch of land on earth more ancient than this. And so it is blunt and red and barren, littered with the fragments of broken mountains, flat, waterless. Spinifex grows here, but sere and yellow, and trees are rare, hardly to be called trees, some kind of myall with leaves starved to needles that fans out from the root and gives no shade.

Adrift in the shifting sands of this red and barren country, the town of Tourmaline exists because a man called Hart found gold there. Now that most of the gold is gone, the town exists in a coma in which life continues at a reduced, perfunctory, and undemanding level. Tourmaline comes back to a kind of life with the arrival of Michael Random, a refugee, like Heriot, struggling with his own belief. Unlike Heriot, who goes off into the desert to wrestle with his demons, Random comes in from the desert and involves the entire town in his religious struggles. A self-proclaimed "diviner," he makes it his mission to "save" the town by finding water, both literal and spiritual.

Dust jacket for Stow's first novel, published in 1956 while he was an undergraduate at the University of Western Australia (from Bruce Bennett, ed., The Literature of Western Australia, *1979)*

Random engineers a spectacular–though brief and feverish–religious revival with himself as high priest, and he divines a new seam of gold for the town. But his attempts to divine water fail, and he makes an ignominious exit back into the desert, an ending that has none of the tragic grandeur of Heriot's. Stow does not resolve the conflict between accepting and developing the country, which still troubles and divides Australians, but it is clear that he is sympathetic toward the Taoist philosophy of Tom Spring and Dave Speed, the only characters in *Tourmaline* who refuse to join Random's crusade. In contrast to Random's attempt to revive Tourmaline, their Taoist vision simply and quietly endures. To give it more prominence would be to betray its nature. The book ends with a haunting, enigmatic lament that echoes the poetry of the first chapter:

> Beware of my testament!
> (Ah, my New Holland; my gold, my darling.)
> I say we have a bitter heritage.
> That is not to run it down.

Tourmaline is Stow's most profound meditation on the spiritual malaise of white Australia. It has attracted a loyal readership, which sees the novel as a central expression of the author's abiding preoccupations, but it has never been widely popular.

In contrast, Stow's next book posed few problems for its readers, and *The Merry-Go-Round in the Sea,* published in 1965, has remained the most popular and widely read of his books. Written in New Mexico while Stow was touring the United States on a Harkness Fellowship in 1964, it has never been out of print and is widely recognized as a modern Australian classic. Another celebration of Australia and its landscape, it is set in the greener world of the coast, where most Australians live. Pitched between fiction and autobiography, the book draws heavily on the author's childhood in Geraldton during the 1940s, and the central characters Rick and Aunt Kay are based on family members Eric Sewell and Sutherland MacDonald. No mere memoir or diary, however, the book is precisely and poetically structured to contrast the secure circling of nostalgia with the remorseless linear progress of time and change.

The Merry-Go-Round in the Sea traces Rob Coram's growth from six to fourteen, from an idyllic childhood to an uncomfortable sexual awakening, and from his childhood discovery of time and mortality to his adolescent discovery that "the world and the clan and Australia had been a myth of his mind, and he had been, all the time, an individual." The book begins as a warm, nostalgic re-creation of a lost world of relative security and simplicity, "a good country to be a child in." As the boy grows older, however, and the war takes his role model, Rick, away, the emotional tone of the book is complicated by the suffering of war and the grief of growing up and out of childhood into an altogether bleaker and more restless adolescence. *The Merry-Go-Round in the Sea* captures Stow's contradictory feelings as he looks back on a golden childhood with fierce nostalgic longing. At the same time the novel presents that childhood as transient and irrevocably separate from mature experience. Left alone at the end of the book, Rob looks out toward his merry-go-round "perilously rooted in the sea," as generations of Australians looked out to an image of Great Britain beyond the sea, a fixed point and a homing beacon in the flux of antipodean existence. A powerfully engaging account of the irreconcilable nostalgias of settlers in a strange land at the other end of the world, *The Merry-Go-Round in the Sea* stands alongside Australian classics such as Henry Handel Richardson's *The Fortunes of Richard Mahony* (1917–1929) and Martin Boyd's *Lucinda Brayford* (1946).

After two eloquent celebrations of his native Western Australia, Stow wrote *Midnite: The Story of a Wild Colonial Boy* (1967), his only children's book. Like *The Merry-Go-Round in the Sea, Midnite* has remained popular with readers of all ages. Midnite is a good-natured but stupid boy bushranger with a gang of talking animals masterminded by a Siamese cat. Bushrangers such as Ned Kelly and Ben Hall are revered folk-heroes in Australia, and *Midnite* is loosely based on the Western Australian bushranger Moondyne Joe. At a more sophisticated level, the story is a literary parody that makes fun of poets and explorers such as Barcroft Boake (1866–1892) and Ludwig Leichhardt (1813–1848), both of whom died in "the Cosmic Symbolical Desert" of Australia. The literary satire is as much directed at Stow's *To the Islands,* and his poem "The Singing Bones," as it is at Patrick White's *Voss* (1957) and the desert graveyard legends of early Australian literature.

In 1969 Stow published *A Counterfeit Silence: Selected Poems. A Counterfeit Silence* includes a third of the poems from *Act One,* almost all those in *Outrider,* and nine new poems under the heading "Stations." The most striking of the new poems are the love lyric "Persephone" and the ten-part sequence "Thailand Railway," which re-creates harrowing images of the brutal life-in-death existence of Australian prisoners of war used as slave labor to build the infamous Burma-Siam railway during World War II. Like *Act One* before it, *A Counterfeit Silence* won the Grace Leven Prize for Poetry. Despite such critical recognition, however, it has long been out of print.

With the publication of *Midnite* in 1967 and *A Counterfeit Silence* in 1969, Stow completed the body of creative work that drew its major inspiration from his twenty-five years of living in Western Australia. In 1960 he went to England for the first time and, like Peter Porter and many of that generation of artistic Australians, he has continued to live there, though in the early 1960s he traveled extensively in Britain, Europe, and the United States.

The publication of *Visitants* in 1979 ended a decade of virtual silence for Stow. As the years passed with no new books, Stow's reputation went into something of a decline, from which it has still not entirely recovered, and admirers of his work feared that he might finally have given up what he called the counterfeit silence of writing for a real and permanent silence, but Stow had not abandoned writing.

The first three parts of *Visitants* were in fact completed in the latter part of 1969 and the early months of 1970. The fourth and final section was fully composed in Stow's mind before he began to write the book: "I don't start writing until I've written something through to the end, so by the time I started on *Visitants* in 1969 I had written the whole thing, in effect." But he could not bring himself to set down the final section, "Troppo," because it was too painfully close to an experience that was not yet sufficiently exorcized. The block persisted

-9-

through the patterned shade of the poinsianas and between the vincas, towards the kitchen. He thought she was pretty and strong and unhappy. Then softly he mounted to the doorway and stood there, ~~deferentially~~ with deference, in a patch of sunlight.

The eyes of Heriot, fixed on the floor, took in vaguely his broad, black, dusty feet. Then mounted to his face.

The eyes of the young man, fixed on Heriot's hand, saw it suddenly tense.

"Stephen", said Heriot.

"Yes, brother. I come back to my country."

TWO

In the eyes of Heriot the young man melted and disappeared and formed again as a bare child, a child with almond eyes and a small hawk nose betraying the ~~distant~~ and distant ~~tempest~~ legacy of an Afghan trader in the blood. But the child was a girl child, so small, so perfectly formed. In the old age black was not counted fair. But there was beauty, there was much beauty there.as hit his heart, now, when it was gone, with a blow of reverberating grief,and called his memory back along the flat years to the worst bereavement, the first and most shameful defeat, which all that morning had been feeding his despair. "Stephen", he said again. "Of course."

"You know I were coming, brother?"

"Yes, yes, I knew. I'd forgotten. I've been sick, a little bit. You came last night."

"Yes, brother. With Brother Terry."

"Where are you living?"

"With Ella. She my ~~grandmother~~ cousin. Brother."

"Well, you'll have to work, and give Ella some money to feed you. And behave yourself this time", Heriot said wearily.

"Yes, brother."

"It is no use saying: 'Yes, brother'. I've heard that before, I've heard it too often. And believed it too often, and trusted too much. You were one I thought I could believe."

searched

Stephen, in his pool of gold, shifted his feet and ~~wandered~~ with his eyes for some place in the room not accusing, not discomforting. "Yes, brother." His voice was low and very calm, beautiful in his accent.

"Why did you do that, Stephen?"

Stephen shook his head.

"Why steal when you had a job, when you were making more money than your people here have ever seen? Than I've ever seen, Stephen. Who taught you to be so much of a fool?"

"I don't know, brother."

now

"Well, you've finished with gaol, you won't go back, if you're wise."

"No, brother."

"I won't say anything more. But it was a great — a great sorrow to me, to hear what you had done. Your father was my good friend, my brother. He would have been very much ashamed."

"Yes, brother?". Stephen moved uneasily at this reference to the dead.

"And when he was dead I was your father, and — that little girl's. I was ashamed. I was ashamed", Heriot said loudly, staring with his veined eyes. "And for that little girl, Stephen. Have you forgotten that?"

murmured

"No, brother", Stephen ~~said~~, husky-voiced, tense, wishing to fly finally from this accusing and terrifying old man with his constant talk of the dead. "Brother, I go now?"

"Yes, go, go now. Have Ella and Justin given you breakfast?"

"Yes, brother."

"You will be at the work parade, I'll see you then. No, wait, walk with me to Father Way's house. I haven't had breakfast yet." Rising from his chair he appeared larger, broader, wilderhaired than before the Stephen, nervously in the doorway. "You both went everywhere with me once", Heriot said, coming beside him.

"Yes, brother."

"You grew up too quickly, Stephen. Do you know how old you are?"

"No, brother."

"Twenty-two. I remember when you were born. I was your godfather. And the little girl's. My wife, who was your godmother, thought you were more beautiful than any baby she had seen."

"Yes, brother?"

Page from the corrected typescript for To the Islands
(National Library of Australia, MS4912)

Dust jacket for Stow's 1962 book, which includes poems inspired by his experiences on the Trobriand Islands in 1959 (from Bennett, ed., The Literature of Western Australia, *1979)*

for almost a decade, while Stow researched *The Girl Green as Elderflower*, the novel that followed and complemented *Visitants*. On New Year's Day 1979 he began to write *The Girl Green as Elderflower*, completing it in a month. The writing of this sequel, a positive counterpoint to the bleakness of *Visitants*, proved therapeutic. Like Crispin Clare, the writer-protagonist of *The Girl Green as Elderflower*, Stow found the writing of this book a "rebeginning"; and in the wake of its completion he wrote the last section of *Visitants* in 1979.

Visitants—as many reviewers observed—was worth waiting for. It is Stow's most intense, most powerful, and most accomplished novel. As economical as the best short fiction of Joseph Conrad, whose work Stow admires, *Visitants* is tautly and vibrantly written, and brilliantly evocative of its Trobriand Islands setting. Its complex multivocal and multicultural structure is managed with an assurance that contains and intensifies a narrative throbbing with political violence and the terror of psychic disintegration.

Set in the Trobriand Islands off the east coast of Papua in 1959, *Visitants* depicts a tropical colonial outpost a few years away from independence. The white characters occupy a position of uneasy authority over the islanders. The failures of communication between the two cultures are heightened by the inclusion of the well-documented sightings of four human figures in a disc-shaped craft in the sky above Boianai in Papua in June 1959. The story follows the psychic disintegration of another visitant, the white patrol officer Alistair Cawdor, who loses his sense of contact with other human beings, dreaming instead of contact with the star-people in the Boianai flying saucer. The parallel story of the islanders traces an adroit political coup against the aging paramount chief, carried out under the cover of a Cargo Cult uprising. The two narratives echo one another in disturbing and haunting ways and are united by striking tropical imagery. The result is a powerful and moving study of personal and political conflict. The tortured Cawdor is Stow's most complex and convincing character, and the graphic account of his decline eclipses even the tragic intensity of Heriot in *To the Islands*.

The Girl Green as Elderflower was the first book Stow set in East Anglia, where he had lived for more than a decade. It differs from *Visitants* not only in being set as vividly in the Suffolk countryside as the early novels were set in the Geraldton district, but also in incorporating modern adaptations of local legends. It showed that Stow had gone to considerable lengths to domicile himself visually, historically, and even psychically in the country that had nurtured generations of his ancestors. If he had left one "home" in Australia, he had certainly gone "home" to another in Suffolk.

The protagonist of *The Girl Green as Elderflower*, Crispin Clare, is a novelist who finds in the Swainstead village churchyard a gravestone bearing his own name—that of an ancestor, of course. Whether Stow had precisely that experience or not, it points unmistakably to his sense of belonging in Suffolk. *The Girl Green as Elderflower* is also concerned with another kind of going away in order to come home. Clare's experience parallels Alistair Cawdor's in *Visitants*, though Clare's ends in illness, not death. In Suffolk, and within the pattern of the seasons, Clare is brought fully back to life by his newly rediscovered family and by his old and new friends. He works all these people into his translations/adaptations of twelfth-century Suffolk legends, originally recorded by Ralph of Coggeshall and William of Newburgh. In their different ways these legends address the isolation and the alienation that are part of Clare's illness, contracted while he worked as a colonial anthropologist. Clare is thus repossessing the house of his spirit—which has, in the imagery of *Visitants*, been invaded by an alien alter ego—as well as discovering a country that

Dust jacket for the U.S. edition of Stow's 1980 novel, his first set in England rather than Australia (Bruccoli Clark Layman Archives)

is in an atavistic sense already his own. Though the book is a favorite of Stow's, it has not proved as popular with his readers as the more dramatic *Visitants*.

In *The Suburbs of Hell* (1984) Stow abandoned the colonial past and wrote an entirely local East Anglian novel, set this time in Old Tornwich, the fictional counterpart of Old Harwich, to which he moved from the neighboring East Bergholt in 1981. The distance involved in moving was small–negligible by Australian standards–but the old port on the estuary of the Stour River, which Stow re-created in the novel with characteristic visual clarity, is nonetheless different from the Suffolk countryside of *The Girl Green as Elderflower*. *The Suburbs of Hell* is a meditation on the random depredations of death and a postmodern variation on the traditional murder mystery. A serial killer stalks the streets of Old Tornwich–like the Nedlands monster in Perth in 1963–and the inhabitants are terrified by a string of seemingly random and motiveless murders. There may be a copycat murderer as well, or a murderer with a definite motive who takes the opportunity to kill under the cover that the "monster" provides.

The postmodern ending of the story leaves readers with several suspects but no confirmed killer, and no end to the terror that the killer has aroused. One prime "suspect" is death itself, who looks over the shoulder of the gunman in several sequences of the book. The title and a series of epigraphs link the killings to those in *Beowulf* (circa 975–1025) and Jacobean drama, and Stow has described the book as a modern version of Chaucer's *Pardoner's Tale* (circa 1375–1400), with its parable of death. The method in *The Suburbs of Hell* is parallel to Clare's in *The Girl Green as Elderflower*, rewriting medieval legends with characters drawn from the writer's contemporary acquaintance, while preserving the basic narrative and the stark morality of the original. The country and the landscape have changed from Stow's earlier work, but his preoccupation with loneliness, alienation, terror, and death has not.

In 1990 Stow included all the poems he then wanted preserved in *Randolph Stow: Visitants, Episodes from Other Novels, Poems, Stories, Interviews, and Essays* (1990). The additional poems in the collection include a group of seven love lyrics titled "Masks" and a group of nine "Uncollected Poems." The lyrics in "Masks" are named for characters from literature and mythology, figures whose stories echo and objectify the experience of the speakers of the poems. These poems are written in two-line units—in which Stow sought to emulate what he calls "that long loose music" of Claudio Monteverdi—in sonnet-like structures of eight, fourteen, or twenty lines. The mood is predominantly elegiac, fragile moments of love remembered or anticipated, but seldom possessed. There is humor as well as pathos in "Endymion," but the anguish of loss and parting, most eloquently evoked in poems such as "Persephone," "Efire," and "Enkidu," predominates. The "Uncollected Poems" section includes spare, precise, evocative observations of landscape, such as "Frost-Parrots"; elegiac celebrations of love, such as "Simplicities of Summer" and "Orphans Betrothed"; and variations on mythological themes, such as "A Pomegranate in Winter," which is dedicated "To the Author of *A Fringe of Leaves*," Patrick White. The language in "A Pomegranate in Winter" is at once jeweled and simple:

> Bought in a frosty market, with the glaze
> of far hot gardens on them; hoarding still
> a southern flush ingrained in stubborn rinds
> they lie before me: caskets of a queen.
> The knife descends and cleaves. One cracks agape.
> Her jewels: garnets. O Proserpina.

The poet counterpoints finding a pomegranate in the market with the haunting classical myth and with the extended play of the garnet leitmotiv in White's *A Fringe of Leaves* (1976)—a story of love found and lost in two different "countries"—to create a glowing lyric of stark personal grief and of profound and resonant melancholy. Overall Stow's mature poems reveal him to be a deliberate, meticulous, and unobtrusive craftsman whose visual observations are startlingly exact, whose language is at once spare and richly evocative, and whose rhythms haunt the mind. The 1990 collection, the bulk of which is fiction, remains in print, but Stow's poetry, which is more private and more difficult of access than his novels, has been comparatively disregarded. Apart from a few anthologized pieces, it remains less widely known than it deserves.

Randolph Stow has produced an impressive body of work, and three of his novels—*To the Islands*, *The Merry-Go-Round in the Sea*, and *Visitants*—seem destined to become classics of Australian literature and indeed of modern fiction. He has written with great perception and sensitivity about the alienation of European colonists and the desperate fragility of love. No other Australian writer evokes the Australian landscape with the vivid, spare, pictorial clarity of Stow, whose only equals in this regard are painters such as William Dobell, Sidney Nolan, and Fred Williams. Stow's best work has a jewel-like clarity and finish that come from long meditation and a profound engagement with his subject.

A private rather than a social novelist, Stow is less interested in interpersonal relationships than in his characters' relationships with themselves and with God. His work portrays isolation and loneliness as the inescapable human condition. His love poems, for example, describe not the joy of union, but the "ache and waiting" between the lovers' few and infrequent meetings, and the major characters in his novels seldom sustain close relationships for any length of time. He is instead fascinated by men who are alone, adrift in the outback, the desert, or the jungle, and in search of peace with themselves and with God. But if loneliness is inescapable, it is also, paradoxically, the soil in which love may grow, as he points out in the poem "The Land's Meaning": "The love of man is a weed of the waste places. / One may think of it as the spinifex of dry souls."

Randolph Stow writes with poetic intensity in a sparse yet richly evocative manner that re-creates the sensual impact of a landscape with extraordinary vividness and imaginative power. Like his pioneering ancestors in America and Australia, he has claimed new territory, annexing his native Western Australia, charting the European experience of it, and adding it to the known literary world. His reputation is in somewhat of a decline, owing in part to his silence since *The Suburbs of Hell* and in part to his temperamental distaste for self-promotion, but the best of his work belongs at the forefront of twentieth-century Australian writing.

Interviews:

Randolph Stow: Visitants, Episodes from Other Novels, Stories, Interviews, and Essays, edited by Anthony J. Hassall (St. Lucia: University of Queensland Press, 1990).

References:

Anthony J. Hassall, *Strange Country: A Study of Randolph Stow,* revised edition (St. Lucia: University of Queensland Press, 1990);

Ray Willbanks, *Randolph Stow* (Boston: Twayne, 1978).

Papers:

Manuscripts for most of Randolph Stow's novels and some of his other works are held by the National Library of Australia.

Francis Webb
(8 February 1925 – 23 November 1973)

Bill Ashcroft
University of New South Wales

BOOKS: *A Drum for Ben Boyd* (Sydney: Angus & Robertson, 1948);
Leichhardt in Theatre (Sydney: Angus & Robertson, 1952);
Birthday (Adelaide: Advertiser Printing Office, 1953);
Socrates and Other Poems (Sydney: Angus & Robertson, 1961);
The Ghost of the Cock (Sydney: Angus & Robertson, 1964);
Collected Poems (Sydney: Angus & Robertson, 1969).

Collection: *Cap and Bells: The Poetry of Francis Webb*, edited by Michael Griffith and James A. McGlade (North Ryde, N.S.W.: Angus & Robertson, 1991).

RECORDING: *Francis Webb Reads from His Own Work*, Poets on Record, no. 13, University of Queensland Press, 1975.

Few Australian writers have experienced the particular combination of veneration and obscurity accorded to Francis Webb, a gifted thinker fondly read by other poets yet little known by ordinary readers. Webb's disrupted early life instilled in him a peripatetic nature and, by early adulthood, a full-blown case of schizophrenia. The most significant features of his life—his deep Catholic conviction and his lifelong struggle with psychological illness—are two of the more prominent impulses in his work. The technical complexity and emotional intensity of his poetry are a consequence of the interaction of all these elements.

Born in Adelaide on 8 February 1925, Francis Charles Webb-Wagg—he dropped the "Wagg" surname before high school—was the third child in a family of three girls and a boy. His father, Claude, operated a music shop, where he also taught; Webb's mother, Hazel, died of influenza in 1927. His father sent the children to live with their grandparents in North Sydney, where Francis began his education at the Sisters of Mercy in 1931. Claude never recovered from his wife's death and in 1931 had himself admitted to Callan Park

Francis Webb (from Michael J. Griffith, God's Fool, *1991)*

Mental Hospital in Sydney. Despite constant contact by letter, he refused to allow the children to see him there, and he died of peritonitis in 1945.

Webb's grandfather was a retired ferry captain, so between the influences of father and grandfather, Webb inherited a deep love of music and of the sea. His affections are best captured in the poem "For My Grandfather," first published in *The Bulletin* (3, 1946), which mentions the twenty-four-footer *Letona* raced by his grandfather on the harbor:

Webb at age four (from Griffith, God's Fool, *1991)*

Dusk over Bradley's Head: a feeble gull
Whose sinking body is the past at edge
Of form and nothing: here the beautiful
Letona gybes off the spray-shaken ledge
....
My years and yours are scrawled upon this air
Rapped by the gavel of my living breath:
Rather than time upon my wrist I wear
The dial, the four quarters, of your death.

Near the grandparents' home, at the Ball's Head promontory in Sydney Harbour, young Webb also saw an Aboriginal carving of a shark that seemed to embody the mystery of art's intervention into life. The carving represented a figure of truth, "The few innocent, infinite hours of a vision." The elements that made such an impact on his early imagination—art, place, the sea, indigenousness, and time—became enduring features of his poetic career.

Webb continued his education at Christian Brothers schools at Chatswood and Lewisham in Sydney (1938–1942), where he developed his lifelong commitment to Catholicism. Although he matriculated at the University of Sydney with First Class Honors in English in 1942, he, like so many young men of the time, saw World War II as an unquestioned national obligation, so he deferred his scholarship in order to enlist in the army. He later transferred to the air force, qualifying as a wireless gunner in Winnipeg, Manitoba, in 1944.

Webb began publishing serious poetry at seventeen under the auspices of the poet Douglas Stewart, then an editor of the "Red Page" of the Sydney *Bulletin*. Stewart remained a mentor of the young poet; and Webb, though painfully shy, struck up early friendships with Nan Macdonald, Rosemary Dobson, and Beatrice Davies at the Angus and Robertson offices in Castlereagh Street before he enlisted. When Webb republished his long poem "A Drum For Ben Boyd" in 1948 (the poem first appeared in *The Bulletin* [3 July 1946]) Stewart said of it in the "Red Page" column of *The Bulletin* (19 May 1948):

> When I first read it my opinion could be stated in two words: it was major poetry. For Webb to have written it at the age of twenty two is an extraordinary achievement; without parallel, I imagine, considering its maturity and its merits, in Australian literature.

Most of Webb's poetry is difficult, and this kind of immediate, enthusiastic response has been relatively limited. Twenty years later H. P. Heseltine claimed that "when I came face to face with the poems, they defied me," while James Tulip stated that reading Francis Webb "is like wrestling with an angel." Both, however, confirmed the claims of Webb's poetry to a distinctive place in Australian literature.

Although Webb had been writing good poetry since 1941, "A Drum for Ben Boyd" showed a burst of creative energy and poetic maturity that seems paradoxical in the light of his looming schizophrenia. A good description of Webb's career is given by one of the characters in the poem "The Canticle," first published in *Birthday* (1953): "All beauty, all joy? Yes,—and all pain and disfigurement." But while the struggle and conflict in Webb's poetry were deeply personal, they also signified a broader cultural conflict of profound importance to the poetry.

Soon after his early success Webb suffered his first nervous breakdown while in England. After returning to Australia, he held a variety of jobs and published two more books of poetry before 1953. He returned to England that year and spent the next seven years in hospitals, suffering from the effects of schizophrenia. Webb remained a bachelor all his life. He was devoted to the Catholic faith, and his search for meaning was frequently expressed through the theme of exploration in poem sequences such as "Eyre All Alone" (1961) which reflects his interpretations of major characters and events in Australia's history. The 1940s and 1950s were a time of significant nationalist reappraisal in Australia as writers and artists struggled (in part fueled by the contradictions of World War II) with the ambivalence of colonial experience.

The conflict in Webb's poetry has many clearly personal roots, but his writing consistently demonstrates the tension between a received tradition of European ideas, attitudes, and perceptions, and the growing desire to create a language and an art that could "bear the burden" of a different kind of cultural experience. The conflict out of which his work emerges is one between an aesthetic inheritance and the construction of a cultural consciousness adapted to a new place and a new society.

Webb's poetry is also deeply informed by Catholic religious tradition. In some respects his Catholicism represented a European influence upon his determinedly Australian poetry. The tradition from which Webb drew his energies is difficult to place in the context of Australian literary history. Catholicism had been the religion of the Irish working class, the rebellious and recalcitrant roots of Australian social mythology; but Webb's Catholicism was broadly European rather than "Irish." His Catholicism was not that of the Newman Society, the *Catholic Worker,* or the Catholic Labor Movement, as it might have been for almost any young Catholic intellectual of his time. His faith paid scant attention to the political tension and intrigue dominating the church in the 1950s (although his obsessive anti-communism provides an almost parodic metaphor of the times). Rather than an institutional Catholicism, Webb's was a religion of solitude, with its roots in his love of poetry, ritual, and the simple rhythms of liturgical observance. Solitude meant meditation, reflection, and studying, and his extensive reading in the Catholic poets and philosophers—Augustine, St. Francis, Pierre Teilhard de Chardin, Richard Crashaw, Robert Southwell—provided a deep fund of spiritual ideas for his work. Nowhere does his connection to this tradition seem better attested than in the succession of battered copies of *Poems of Gerard Manly Hopkins* (1918) that he kept in his coat pockets to the end of his life.

This faith provided Webb with a sense of the continuity of the sacred across cultural boundaries. It remained the "universal" core that subtly conflicted with his determination to create a peculiarly Australian poetry. But it also gave him a sense of his own place in a tradition extending beyond national roots. The marriage of passionate religious observance to a brilliant ability to evoke the uniqueness of place makes him difficult to categorize. Although it has rarely been attempted in quite this way by any other Australian writer, Webb's appropriation of elements of the European to the Australian experience is paradigmatic of the development of all postcolonial literature. The union of the mystical and the everyday, the liturgical and the cultural experience, underlies all his work and his participation in the construction of a national discourse.

Therefore, despite the density of his language and his increasingly reclusive habits, Webb's imagination was constantly drawn to the finite world of ordinary experience. In some respects Webb, like his early mentor Stewart, was concerned with examining the experience of truth through the minutest and most specific details of the physical world. Webb was concerned with experience as a bridge to an overarching spiritual order. The spiritual nature of this order is what gives the poetry its thematic cogency, and ultimately the close adherence to the traditions of Catholic thought is what sets him apart from his contemporaries.

This "theological existentialism"—the habit of illuminating a metaphysical order through each detail of experienced reality—finds its most celebrated expression in the "Natural Theology" of Thomas Aquinas, for whom the world of corporeal experience provided the clear expression of God's Being. Natural Theology is a particular way of looking at the world that Webb and many of his antecedents shared. The chief result of this perspective was a conviction of the dignity and potentiality of human life and a determination "To see in ugliness and agony a way to God."

The immortal value of man is a function of God's incarnation in mortal history, which itself signifies the perpetual accessibility of the infinite through the finite. In perhaps Webb's best-known poem, "Five Days Old," first published in *The Bulletin* (30 April 1958), readers find the purest statement of this philosophy: the idea that revelation is more often accessible through the smallest and most insignificant details of experienced reality. Objects such as the defenseless baby whom the poet holds in his hands are symbolic not only because of their obvious innocence and purity but also because that simplicity makes them bridges to the infinite in experience.

> Christmas is in the air.
> You are given into my hands
> Out of quietest, loneliest lands.
> My trembling is all my prayer.
> To blown straw was given
> All the fullness of heaven.

In some way every human birth reflects the incarnation of Christ, and such a realization is a gift as real and pre-

Webb during the early 1950s (from Griffith, God's Fool, 1991)

cious as this baby. The immensity of such a gift sets the poet trembling, which is the simplest act of prayer because it is a primal act of living. In Webb's poetry all acts are directed in some way toward what is held to be the divine center of life. The worthlessness of fly-blown straw only enhances the magnificence of the gift, and in the first lines of the second stanza the poet focuses this pure contemplative activity in philosophical statement: "The tiny, not the immense, / Will teach our groping eyes." This statement could be seen as the signature of Webb's poetry. Despite the complexity of his language, this simplicity is what he is trying to distill: the tiny is the path to the immense.

Despite his wide-ranging inheritance of European ideas and the prominence of Catholicism in his poetry, Webb was an Australian poet whose cultural orientation is nowhere more clearly demonstrated than in his explorer poems. If there is a dominant movement in Webb's poetry it is that of exploration and discovery, which becomes a subject of many poems, a metaphorical mode in many others, and a constant impetus in the language itself. This movement has its roots in Catholic thinkers, but it is also the result of his own deeply felt personal religious conviction on one hand and an historical feature of Australian culture on the other. The exploratory impetus in Australian history is itself an allegory, and the writer merely engages that allegory at its creative source. The journey inward, which such poem sequences as "Around Costessey" and "Ward Two" (published in full in *The Ghost of the Cock,* 1964) present so evocatively, is a journey that, even at its most disturbed and most personal, has clear cultural and social implications.

Between the 1940s and the 1960s, Webb was an integral part of a renaissance in Australian arts and letters, which returned to the enduring myths of Australian culture. During this period the painters Sidney Nolan, Russell Drysdale, and Arthur Boyd attempted to revivify the metaphors of Australian experience, while many Australian writers sought (for the third time since the 1890s) the mythic sources of Australian experience of the land, with its inevitable suggestions of hardship and the stereotypical qualities of toughness, resilience, and independence with which it invested its occupants.

Also during this period the poets Stewart, Robert D. FitzGerald, Kenneth Slessor, A. D. Hope, and James McAuley became drawn to the voyager theme. Webb conceived his explorer poems in similar images of space and distance, adversity and discovery. But Webb's relationship with his cultural background was more complex because of his religious vision. Religion has never had an easy relationship with secularist Australian culture, being socially and politically linked with the Establishment from the beginning and providing no indigenous forms of expression other than those of the Aboriginal people. But Webb's achievement is to reimagine, in religious terms, that mythical journey of self-discovery that is so widespread in Australian writing.

Each explorer poem presents a different theme. "A Drum for Ben Boyd" is the vehicle for a discourse on memory and being; "Leichhardt in Theatre" (first published in *The Bulletin*, 1947), a classic tragedy, dramatizes the hubris of European pretension and its apotheosis in the burning expanse of the outback. Putting the French explorer Jacques Cartier in this company, the difficult poem "A View of Montreal," which first appeared in *Leichhardt in Theatre* (1952), emphasizes the same spiritual goals as the Australian explorers—goals that pioneer Edward John Eyre seems to reach in the fourteen-part "Eyre All Alone," first published in *Socrates and Other Poems* (1961). In reconstituting the religious theme of spiritual exploration the poems establish the space of Australian landscape as the metaphor for a journey through the soul.

In his exploration of place, Webb shares with many other Australian writers a tendency to see the vast inland of Australia as a psychic region, and the actual historical explorations of that region (particularly the obsession with finding an inland sea, an essentially rich and abundantly fruitful center) as allegories of a peculiarly Australian spiritual search. His passion for discovering a spiritual center, one that could link the vastness of the Australian continent and the newness of Australian experience with the reassurance of religious tradition, makes Webb's poetry a dense metaphor of Australian cultural experience.

The explorer poems are the site of a cataclysmic confrontation in Webb's poetic world: quite simply, Time is overwhelmed by Space. European history seems to run aground in the limitlessness of Australian space. The individual is displaced and discovers, or reconstructs, a different sense of self. But this reconstruction must always occur within the immense conflict of time and space. In the early poem "The

Dust jacket for Webb's 1964 book, which includes one of his best-known works, the poem sequence "Ward Two," set in one of the psychiatric hospitals where he was a patient (Bruccoli Clark Layman Archives)

Mountains," from his first book, *A Drum for Ben Boyd* (1948), Australia is seen as the place "where Time died centuries ago, / His huge, white, rigid body broken over / The giant wheel of the sky to a flux of snow." Time is reordered in this new environment, broken over the giant wheel of the interminable landscape. History is seen later, in "Eyre All Alone," as Eyre's "decadent and wasted packhorse," because European history itself is engaged in the spiritual quest of the Australian explorers and disappearing in the process. The initial perception of the land emerges from European consciousness. In "Morgan's Country" (*The Bulletin*, 13 December 1950) readers find that "even under the sun's trajectory / This country looks grey, hunted and murderous." The European conception of the Australian environment, which lurks even now at the edges of the Australian consciousness, is nowhere better demonstrated than in the 1947 poem "Disaster Bay." Matthew

Flinders, the early explorer, misnamed the place "Green Cape," readers are told, because he tacked well offshore:

> ... he could not sense
> Violence coiled in the air, far less imagine
> A sea-whelp harbored in the groin of rock and those long
> Spiked limbs of outcropping reef that stretch well out,
> Split ships on agony like birds, pluck plumage from ribs.

This Gothic description of the coastline is perhaps drawn out of a deeper and, to Webb, more personal psychic terror than is actually suggested by history. But it is in full accord with the mythic threats of place to the early European consciousness. "Place," in this poem, can never be neutral, never simply another environment. It is the untamed monster that centuries of European civilization have served to shackle with agriculture and urbanization.

Every explorer poem in Webb's work is therefore in some sense a coming to terms with the land. Each explorer moves through his symbolic journey back into the world. The process can be seen in poems such as "Galston," first published in *Birthday;* "Vlamingh and Rottnest Island," first published in *The Bulletin* (26 March 1952); or even "Canobolas," first published in *Literary Review* (Winter 1963–1964). But the culmination in the poetry as a whole, perhaps, comes in another experience of a coastline in "The Sea," a section of "Eyre All Alone," when finally the suffering consciousness surrenders to the pure experience of beauty and unity:

> Blue is the Sound, form, essence out of nothing;
> Blue is Today harnessed, nodding at my heels;
> Blue is the grave pure language of the gulls.

This experience of the land is the polar opposite of that in "Disaster Bay." Rather than a predatory beast of destruction, the coast is finally the scene of beauty and transcendence—time has transmuted into space, spiritual essence into perceptual experience.

Although their religious and philosophic dimensions are prominent, the explorer poems also step firmly into the landscape of national mythology. As Leichhardt says:

> In the pillaged places
> Of ransacked Europe there was no passion left,
> But darkness, horizonless.
> ....
> Southward the new, the visionary!
> This is a land where man becomes a myth;
> Naked, his feet tread embers for the truth:
> Desert will claim him, mountain, precipice,
> (Larger than life's their terror, lovelier
> Than forms of mere life their forms of peril).

The country is the land of the heroic because in every way it is larger than life—the realm of myth and, most important to Webb, the realm of the spirit. The historical importance of Webb's poetry lies in the tenacious balance it maintains between religious and national mythology, which, put another way, is a balance between the past of a European tradition and the future of a "post-European" culture. In this balance, so evocatively sustained in his fallible explorers, is held a moment of becoming in Australian literature.

The dual strand of Australian consciousness, represented on the one hand by spiritual expatriates such as Henry Kingsley, Martin Boyd, and Christopher Brennan, and later Hope and McAuley, and on the other by the self-conscious nativism of nationalist writers, is finally and fully united in Webb. But while Webb's explorer poems appear to reproduce the standard mythical Australian experience, almost every metaphor includes within it an ambivalence undermining the mythic certainties of nationalism. Theological existentialism provides one driving force of Webb's poetry, but in the explorer poems he addresses himself to the fundamental myth of Australian culture: that this vast and empty landscape offers the permanent terrain of a journey of self-discovery.

Webb's poetry seems to be ambivalent toward language itself. He saw the language of words as somehow inferior to the language of painting or music in its ability to penetrate the horizon of experience, to give a voice to the silence. Like Patrick White, whose painters and musicians are always the gifted visionaries, Webb saw the writer as the inferior artist, struggling with an intractable medium. But the effect of this view was to give him an irreverence for language that allowed him to fracture its unyielding surfaces.

For Webb, however, innovation was always more than artifice. Language was the medium in which he both created the world and kept it at bay. To properly understand his writing, one must understand its most profound mystery: that his language constantly aspires to that purest language of silence. But the structural density of the language could be described as a "framework effect," an effect that bears a particular relationship to the peculiarity of schizophrenics' language. What sometimes appears to be dense and obscure, a language that inscribes space and absence to avoid the threat of enclosure, is also a taut outline of the "fullness" of the poetic experience.

Webb returned to Australia in 1960 and spent the rest of his life in psychiatric institutions, including the one in which his father died. Nevertheless, he continued to contribute poetry to journals such as *Southerly* and *Meanjin* and he published two more volumes in the 1960s. *The Ghost of the Cock* (1964) contains the sequence

Webb's grave in Catholic Lawn Cemetery, Sydney

"Ward Two," which powerfully recounts Webb's time in a Parramatta psychiatric center. Despite his frequent confinement in such centers, Webb attracted regular support from many fellow poets.

The most problematic of the labels assigned to Webb is that of schizophrenic, not only because the influence of schizophrenia upon poetic writing is uncertain but also because the idea of mental illness is still regarded as an embarrassment. Yet, studies have found that schizophrenics' special linguistic competence becomes their most distinguishing characteristic, particularly in the use of metaphor. Schizophrenics' reports of their experience always seem to be in some way metaphoric of the alienation and fragmentation of the society around them. The dividing line between "madness" and "sanity" sometimes seems to be nothing more than the line between the literal and the metaphoric. The problem lies in a disregard for the rules of the discourse in which metaphoric statements can be made. This "disregard" is caused by the fact that schizophrenics actually experience metaphor in a frightening and direct way.

In Webb's work the impulses driving the schizophrenic, the Catholic, and the Australian poet overlap. For instance, the "search for the Center" in the explorer poems, which he shares with a great deal of Australian literature, becomes at the same time the Catholic poet's search for a spiritual center and the schizophrenic's search for some focus of ontological security. The fascinating thing about this search is that whichever mode it takes, the result is always a return to the world, a rediscovery of the exceptional in the ordinary. In his last days, writing one of his most famous poem sequences–"Ward Two"–Webb looks out of his hospital window to see a girl sitting on a rock combing her hair. In this simple and beautiful image he returns to the ordinary and pitiable as the source of the sacred:

> Have the gates of death scrape open. Shall we meet
> (Beyond the platoons of rainfall) a loftier hill
> Hung with such delicate husbandries? Shall ascent
> Be a travelling homeward, past the blue frosty feet
> Of winter, past childhood, past the grey snake, the will?
> Are gestures stars in sacred dishevelment,
> The tiny, the pitiable, meaningless and rare
> As a girl beleaguered by rain, and her yellow hair?

Francis Webb died of a coronary occlusion on 23 November 1973. Torn by emotional conflicts and a peripatetic lifestyle that destroyed him at the age of forty-eight, he nevertheless produced one of the most exploratory and brilliant, if largely unsung, bodies of work in Australian poetry.

Letters:

Francis Webb, Poet & Brother: Some of His Letters and Poetry, compiled by Peter and Leonie Meere (Pomona, Qld.: P. V. Meere/Sage Old Books, 2001).

Biography:

Michael J. Griffith, *God's Fool: The Life and Poetry of Francis Webb* (North Ryde, N.S.W.: Collins/Angus & Robertson, 1991).

References:

Bill Ashcroft, *The Gimbals of Unease: The Poetry of Francis Webb* (Nedlands: Centre for Studies in Australian Literature, University of Western Australia, 1996);

Rodolpho Delmonte, *Piercing into the Psyche: The Poetry of Francis Webb* (Venice, 1979);

Rosemary Dobson, "Francis Webb," *Australian Author,* 6, no. 2 (1974): 41;

Dobson, "Francis Webb," *Australian Literary Studies,* 6 (1974): 227–229;

Patricia Excell, "Francis Webb as Mythmaker," *Australian Literary Studies,* 10 (1981), 101–105;

H. P. Heseltine, "The Very Gimbals of Unease," *Meanjin Quarterly,* 26, no. 3 (1967): 255–274;

Poetry Australia, special Webb issue, no. 56 (September 1975);

Noel Rowe, "Francis Webb and the Will of the Poem," *Southerly,* 47, no. 2 (1987): 180–197;

Andrew Taylor, "The Spilled Cruet of Innocence," in his *Reading Australian Poetry* (St. Lucia: University of Queensland Press, 1987), pp. 98–111;

James Tulip, "David Malouf, Francis Webb and Australian Religious Consciousness," in *Reconnoitres: Essays in Australian Literature in Honour of G. A. Wilkes,* edited by Margaret Harris and Elizabeth Webby (South Melbourne: Oxford University Press in association with Sydney University Press, 1992), pp. 226–237;

Tulip, "The Poetry of Francis Webb," *Southerly,* 29, no. 3 (1969), pp. 184–191;

Chris Wallace-Crabbe, "Order and Turbulence," in his *Melbourne or the Bush: Essays on Australian Literature and Society* (Sydney: Angus & Robertson, 1974), pp. 114–126.

Papers:

A collection of Francis Webb's papers, and the paintings he owned (some of which are the subjects of poems), are held at Chatswood Municipal Library, Sydney. Correspondence with Rosemary Dobson is also housed at the National Library of Australia, Canberra.

Patrick White
(28 May 1912 – 30 September 1990)

Michael Ackland
Monash University

BOOKS: *Thirteen Poems* (Sydney: Privately printed, ca. 1929);

The Ploughman and Other Poems (Sydney: Beacon Press, 1935);

Happy Valley (London: Harrap, 1939; New York: Viking, 1939);

The Living and the Dead (London: Routledge, 1941; New York: Viking, 1941);

The Aunt's Story (London: Routledge & Kegan Paul, 1948; New York: Viking, 1948);

The Tree of Man (New York: Viking, 1955; London: Eyre & Spottiswoode, 1956);

Voss (London: Eyre & Spottiswoode, 1957; New York: Viking, 1957);

Riders in the Chariot (London: Eyre & Spottiswoode, 1961; New York: Viking, 1961);

The Burnt Ones (London: Eyre & Spottiswoode, 1964; New York: Viking, 1964);

Four Plays (London: Eyre & Spottiswoode, 1965; Melbourne: Sun Books, 1965; New York: Viking, 1966); republished as *Collected Plays,* volume 1 (Sydney: Currency Press, 1985)—comprises *The Ham Funeral, The Season at Sarsaparilla, A Cheery Soul,* and *Night on Bald Mountain;*

The Solid Mandala (London: Eyre & Spottiswoode, 1966; New York: Viking, 1966);

The Vivisector (London: Cape, 1970; New York: Viking, 1970);

The Eye of the Storm (London: Cape, 1973; New York: Viking, 1974);

The Cockatoos: Shorter Novels and Stories (London: Cape, 1974; New York: Viking, 1975);

A Fringe of Leaves (London: Cape, 1976; New York: Viking, 1977);

Big Toys (Sydney: Currency Press, 1978);

The Night the Prowler: Short Story and Screenplay (London: Cape, 1978; Ringwood, Vic.: Penguin, 1978);

The Twyborn Affair (London: Cape, 1979; New York: Viking, 1980);

Flaws in the Glass: A Self-Portrait (London: Cape, 1981; New York: Viking, 1982);

Patrick White (photograph by Boris Cook, Sydney; from John Hetherington, Forty-Two Faces, *1946)*

Netherwood (Sydney: Currency Press, 1983);

Signal Driver: A Morality Play for the Times (Sydney: Currency Press, 1983);

Collected Plays, 2 volumes (Sydney: Currency Press, 1985, 1994);

Memoirs of Many in One, as Alex Xenophon Demirjian Gray, edited by White (London: Cape, 1986; New York: Viking, 1987);

Three Uneasy Pieces (Melbourne: Pascoe, 1987);

Patrick White Speaks, edited by Paul Brennan and Christine Flynn (Sydney: Primavera Press, 1989).

PLAY PRODUCTIONS: *Return to Abyssinia,* London, Boltons Theatre, 1947;

The Ham Funeral, Adelaide, Union Theatre, 15 November 1961;

The Season at Sarsaparilla, Adelaide, Union Theatre, 14 September 1962;

A Cheery Soul, Melbourne, Union Theatre, 19 November 1963;

Night on Bald Mountain, Adelaide, Union Theatre, 9 March 1964;

Big Toys, Sydney, Parade Theatre, Old Tote, 1977;

Signal Driver, Adelaide, Playhouse, State Theatre Company of South Australia, 5 March 1982;

Netherwood, Adelaide, Playhouse, State Theatre Company of South Australia, 11 June 1983;

Shepherd on the Rocks, Adelaide, Playhouse, State Theatre Company of South Australia, 9 May 1987.

Long recognized internationally as the most important writer of Australia, Patrick White is the first of his countrymen to win the Nobel Prize for literature. In addition, he has won prestigious local awards, such as the Miles Franklin Prize and the gold medal of the Australian Society. His novels have inspired many translations and an opera, his plays have aroused heated controversy, and his short stories are featured in standard Australian anthologies. Yet, neither artistic fame nor his right by birth to a place in the pastoral elite of Australia could lessen his inveterate pessimism that constituted, as he acknowledged, a deep strain of "black in White." A caustic satirist as well as a bold visionary, he discerned spiritual riches in the sun-scorched expanses of Australia but wastelands in its opulent dining rooms, cluttered with festive roasts and self-congratulatory platitudes. In these places he truly found "the Great Australian Emptiness," as he wrote memorably in "The Prodigal Son" (*Australian Letters,* April 1958), in a land where "the mind is the least of possessions . . . muscles prevail, and the march of material ugliness does not raise a quiver from the average nerves." Wary of being tainted and of self-complacency, he chose to live outside the mainstream and used alleged critical hostility as a spur to renewed creativity. The resulting fiction was at the forefront of the Australian response to modernism and to recent history. In it, the realist tradition of Australian letters is problematized and extended; taboo subjects are broached; minorities are accorded unusual prominence; and the fetid shafts of national memory are probed through narrations that, as he remarked of *A Fringe of Leaves* (1976), remind readers uncomfortably of "the reasons why we have become what we are today."

Like many of his literary forebears, Patrick White shaped his work by a dual allegiance to the colony, Australia, and to the motherland, England. By World War I the White family formed an important pastoral dynasty located on the rich upper reaches of the Hunter River, north of Sydney. Belltrees, the family seat, was one pole of his youthful experience in Australia; the other was Lulworth, a mansion in the inner East of Sydney, overlooking Rushcutters Bay, where his father, Victor Martindale White, moved to satisfy his wife, Ruth Withycombe White, in 1916. When they married in 1910, the predominantly Anglo-Saxon population of Australia still referred to the United Kingdom as "home," and their son, Patrick Victor Martindale White, born in Knightsbridge, England, on 28 May 1912, later spoke of himself as "an anachronism, something left over from that period when people were no longer English and not yet indigenous." A daughter, Suzanne, completed the family in 1917. Ruth White early had literary ambitions for her son, and because of her deference to British culture, her son was sent to England as a boarder for four years at Cheltenham College, a public (that is, private) secondary school; it was a period that drove the sensitive, sickly child in upon himself and helped shape his grim view of human nature. True to his mixed heritage, White's education was completed in the early 1930s by a prolonged period as a jackeroo, or trainee stockman-grazier, in outback New South Wales, and by studying Modern Languages at Cambridge University. This part of his education was complemented by extended vacations in Germany between 1932 and 1935, which gave him a sound grasp of German and a taste for its Romantic tradition. White, in later life, was categoric about the crucial impact of his early years. "I feel more and more, as far as creative writing is concerned, everything important happens to one before one is born," he remarked disingenuously. To childhood he attributed an unequaled clarity of vision and added in his autobiography: "One thinks to escape, but doesn't, or not wholly: the fingerprints are taken early."

One abortive attempt to escape was the attribution of seminal influence to a prenatal state, which denied, in effect, a youth and early manhood marked indelibly by his homosexuality. Even before this discovery, life had conspired to make White feel a misfit as well as set apart by suffering. Severe asthma dogged him for forty years, unsettling his comfortable childhood with unpredictable attacks. A precocious child among happy, well-to-do sensual-

White, circa 1918 (from Patrick White,
Flaws in the Glass, *1982)*

ists, he imagined himself a changeling or cuckoo in the home nest, while his privileged upbringing left him feeling a colonial in England, a toff in the antipodes. But the effect of sexual deviance was more far-reaching. It made his existence seem deformed and a sham, though it proved a significant catalyst to his artistic unfolding. By the early 1930s he had written several unpublished, naturalistic novels as well as desultory verse, selections of which were published privately by his mother in *Thirteen Poems* (circa 1929) and *The Ploughman and Other Poems* (1935). Then in 1936 he fell under the spell of James Joyce's *Ulysses* (serialized, 1918; published in book form, 1922), and his conversion to artistic modernism was clinched shortly afterward when he encountered Australian painter Roy de Maistre in London. De Maistre's abstract canvases taught him "to write from the inside out," or to make his central concern the changing theater of the individual mind. The expatriate de Maistre became White's lover, surrogate father, and artistic mentor, encouraging the young man's strong visual imagination and wrenching him

forever beyond the Victorian provincialism that held sway among art lovers in Australia.

White believed, too, that homosexuality gave him special insight into the psyches and emotions of both sexes. An inestimable boon for a novelist, it enabled him to slip in and out of his male and female characters at will, and recalled the Greek Tiresias who, according to legend, lived part of his existence as a woman, part as a man. The Western ideal of the unitary personality was displaced by the conception of himself as composed of discrete potentials or separate selves, evoked by the title of his autobiography, *Flaws in the Glass: A Self-Portrait* (1981), and related to the claim that his writing was predominantly intuitive, or conceived and executed under his feminine aspect. But transgressing sexual norms also contributed powerfully to his sense of himself as deeply flawed. He identified readily with social outcasts and recognized that there was much in common between casual, predatory homosexual coupling and prostitution—a point driven home during the London Blitz, when he "learned a lot about the whore's mentality, and . . . the whole tragi-comedy of sex."

World War II was a great caesura in his life and work. Before joining the Royal Air Force as an intelligence officer, White had led the life of a transatlantic intellectual. He was equally at home in London or New York, pursued his sexual predilection with Americans in brief affairs, and was encouraged in his vocation by excellent reviews of his initial work. Nevertheless, he was not proof against a sudden "fit of wretched patriotics." In 1941 a regulation uniform, a common enemy, and prescribed work in Egypt gave him a transitory sense of belonging in his unit but could not efface his terrible sense of otherness: "I am fond of these people. . . . But am I entitled to it? It is like reaching over into a world to which you don't belong, from oil to water, or more opposed substances." The loss of comrades completed his shift from political apathy in the 1930s to hatred of Adolf Hitler's war. Its human ravages he experienced nakedly through air attacks or as an official censor of service correspondence or, more cruelly, when required to search German corpses for military information. Egypt also afforded unexpected compensations. Although bemused by the "labelled dust" of its great archaeological museum, his heart went out to its "fierce landscape" that cleansed the soul and could make him feel like "Adam walking through the Garden." The mate he chose was Greek in origin, Manoly Lascaris, whom he met in Alexandria. By 1946 the emotion he felt for Lascaris had been transferred to Greece. White, having learned Greek and spent a year in Athens, seriously considered settling there. Shrewdly, however, he decided in favor of Australia, memories of which had been stirred in him by barren, war-torn landscapes. These memories poured into the pages of his first postwar novel, *The Aunt's Story* (1948), the final section of which was completed onboard ship before he disembarked in Sydney in October 1946.

White's published fiction can be divided into four major phases. The apprenticeship period, during which he was avowedly "drunk on the techniques of writing" and sought a distinctive theme, ended with *The Aunt's Story*. This book summarized his experience of three continents and demonstrated his mastery of the modern psychological novel. But, like its predecessors *Happy Valley* (1939) and *The Living and the Dead* (1941), it lacks an overarching, sustaining vision of existence. This vision emerged eight years later in *The Tree of Man* (1955), a novel that signaled the beginning of White's reexamination of key local preoccupations. The pioneering-farming tradition as subject matter yielded to exploration in *Voss* (1957), then to diverse forms of urban experience in *Riders in the Chariot* (1961) and *The Burnt Ones* (1964). Immensely ambitious, these books, according to "The Prodigal Son," were part of his program to reveal the limitations of the dominant realist tradition in Australian literature by discovering "the extraordinary behind the ordinary," as well as by creating "completely fresh forms out of the rocks and sticks of words" commensurate to its "mystery and poetry." This ambition resulted, however, in occasional overwriting or labored symbolism that called forth mixed reviews and A. D. Hope's notorious verdict in 1956 on *The Tree of Man*. "When so few Australian novelists can write prose at all, it is a great pity to see Mr. White, who shows on every page some touch of the born writer, deliberately chose as his medium this pretentious and illiterate verbal sludge." White never forgot this insult or the begrudging praise of local reviewers. The great character portraits in *The Solid Mandala* (1966), *The Vivisector* (1970) and *The Eye of the Storm* (1973) followed. In 1973 White received the Nobel Prize for literature. During his final phase he set his literary house in order, publishing a second collection of short stories in *The Cockatoos: Shorter Novels and Stories* (1974); a major historical novel, *A Fringe of Leaves;* and three extremely different self-portraits— *The Twyborn Affair* (1979), *Flaws in the Glass*, and *Memoirs of Many in One* (1986). Never content with any achievement and determined not to become "the waxwork so many successful Australians become," White strove for change as he tirelessly looked "for an unopened door, through which I can step and find myself rejuvenated."

His earliest published novels, *Happy Valley* and *The Living and the Dead,* reflected accurately his mixed heritage. The first is set in the high country near Cooma, where he had worked as a jackeroo; the second is set in London during the Spanish Civil War. Happy Valley is a generic country town—the more enlightened members of which long to escape—and the emotional complement of London in his next book. White's township is described as "unreal," life there likened to a hollow toy to be rattled, and suffering foregrounded in an epigraph from Mahatma Gandhi as "the indispensable condition of our being." Robbed of an informing metaphysical context, the maharishi's words teeter between nihilism and existentialism, as White's novel does. There the blindness, barrenness, and futility of human existence are recurring motifs. The town is described in the novel as little more than "a peculiarly tenacious scab on the body of the brown earth," which itself is steeped in "an underlying bitterness that had been scored deep and deep by time." In this town a human being confronted by indifferent primordial forces has no option but "to beat" his "head against the wall, substituting wall for the intangible." This belief assumes various forms. Mrs. Vic Moriarty chooses adultery with a man whose cynicism is his one sincere attribute: "Killing a sheep, or time with Vic, was the same, a bleat." The young lovers, Oliver and Alys, decide to flee, only to have their escape cut short when they run over Ernest Moriarty, who has slaughtered his wife. Yet, in comparison to the resigned, comatose lives of his neighbors, Moriarty's angry if pointless end has arguably a certain worth—"He has achieved something where we have failed"—or as the schoolteacher remarks, "'Man hasn't much to say in the matter. I know. He's a feeble creature dictated to by whatever you like, we'll call it an irrational force. But he must offer some opposition to this if he's to keep his own respect.'"

These concerns recur in *The Living and the Dead,* together with White's bitter verdict on Britain. He found life in England thin and heartless, a "blathering through cardboard," with Londoners divided into the mentally aware and the terminally apathetic. Already *Happy Valley* signaled the Australian's obsession with "so much time squandered in the face of the final issue" by characters such as the willfully blind Hilda, who "built herself a raft of superficialities and floated down the stream." *The Living and the Dead*, which focuses on two generations of the Standish family, is peopled with Hilda's metropolitan counterparts. In response to the apparent lack of

White in front of Dogwoods, the house at Castle Hill, north of Sydney, where he settled after his return to Australia in 1946 (photograph by Peggy Garlan; from David Marr, Patrick White, *1992)*

meaning of life they withdraw behind routines, exchanging one enclosure for the next. Catherine Standish, with her marriage shattered, builds a "protective cocoon inside the reduced body" of her marital home. The stockade of her son, Elyot, is made of literary studies—a sterile, shallow existence: "He had begun to arrange his life in numbered pages. He had rejected the irrational aspect of the cramped houses, the possibility of looking inward and finding a dark room." Nor does orthodox belief afford special insights, whether represented by idealistic Joe Barnett, who "was born with a faith in faith," or the more self-serving Catherine Standish: "Spiritually, she liked to believe, she managed to keep to the heights. A precious country, it was cheaply reached." Behind the trivial clutter of their daily lives, White suggests, there must be something more—though his characters, when faced with "a personal Spain . . . something destructive of the superfluous," retreat into still narrower orbits. The exception is Elyot's aptly named sister, Eden, whose departure for Spain from Victoria Station frames the main narrative, offering hope beyond stifling conformity.

The notion of opened and closed worlds is central also to *The Aunt's Story,* although in it White's emphasis falls on perception rather than action, or on the difference between pure being and a distracted life of quotidian doing. Its subject is Theodora Goodman's journey to freedom. An aged spinster who has spent her prime at the beck and call of her mother, Theodora has always been awkward, set apart as much by her strange intuitions as by signs of an unfeminine moustache. At the outset the reader is told not only that "old Mrs Goodman did die at last," but also that "Theodora had not yet learnt to dispute the apparently indisputable." Gradually she learns that she must destroy what White terms "the great monster Self" to usher in a desirable state "which resembles . . . nothing more than air or water"—an absolute openness that society dubs madness. Remarkable empathy allows her access to the secret life of people, objects, and animals in which she perceives lessons relevant to her own condition. Journeys as well as living become a series of self-encounters, and already in her childhood home so-called dream and reality are interchangeable: "She was walking in the passages of Meroe, a reflection walking through mirrors, toward the door which had always been more mirror than door, and at which she was now afraid to look." She overcomes this fear in part 2, "Jardin Exotique." The title refers to small, sun-drenched collections of succulents favored in the south of France. It is a correlative for prickly Theodora and for existence in its opaque, forbidding aspect, whereas the entrancing promise of existence is projected by a nautilus shell. As the section unfolds, characters become fluid and reality splinters, underlining how thin and permeable the membrane is that "separates experience from intuition." At crucial moments it dissolves: "The nautilus flowered and flowed, as pervasive but evasive as experience. The walls of the Hotel du Midi almost opened out." Dissolution is finally achieved through fire, foreshadowing catastrophic war in Europe and Theodora's attainment in part 3 of an emptiness that is fullness, a selflessness that is completion. The final section signals this shift with its initial portrait of her open hands and the trumpeting corn destroying "the frailer human reed." In this section "the reasonable life," described as "admirable . . . though limited," is eclipsed by disintegration or a going out of the self to identify with, and hence possess, the world at large. Beneath her physical shell, Theodora has become endless and immense, so that even when her aberrations lead to her being placed in the hands of a kindly doctor, White's conclusion affirms obliquely her enduring enlightenment: "The hat sat straight, but the doubtful rose trembled and glittered, leading a life of its own."

Underlying this espousal of vision was a recoil from the reality known by most men and women. It was as if White, during the long hiatus that separated his second and third novels, had, like Mrs. Rapallo in *The Aunt's Story*, "stood so close to the making of history that I have been suffocated by the stink." The European cast at the Hotel du Midi is spiritually dysfunctional, rootless, and overshadowed by imminent conflagration. The Australian personages fare no better. Theodora's brother-in-law, the pastoralist Frank Parrott, "was what they call a practical man, a success, but he had not survived"; her sister, Fanny, subscribes to "the comfortable narratives of wives and mothers." But the powerful emotions aroused by actual war, as well as the exemplary affection of his companion Lascaris, were already pointing the author in a different direction by his third novel when, near its conclusion, Theodora becomes or "was a world of love and compassion that she had only vaguely apprehended."

A further eight years separated the appearance of White's third and fourth novels, during which he became reacquainted with basic realities at Dogwoods, a six-acre property north of Sydney at Castle Hill. At Dogwoods he grew fruit and flowers, gathered farm produce, and bred goats as well as schnauzers. He also observed local characters who were stored away for literary resurrection as inhabitants of Sarsaparilla, within the conurbation of Barranugli. What he saw in contemporary Australia both drew and repelled him. Brought face to face again with his countrymen's cocky, physical presence, he longed, like the hero of *The Twyborn Affair*, for "the courage to stick a finger in the outraged navel and await reactions." Yet, in 1947 he also acknowledged a broadening cultural horizon to his publisher at Viking, Ben Huebsch: "The people are beginning to develop, and take an interest in books, and painting, and music, to an extent that surprises me, knowing them fourteen years ago. One gets the impression that a great deal is about to happen." Incomprehension, however, could set him fulminating: "How sick I am of the bloody word AUSTRALIAN. What a pity I am part of it; if I were not, I would get out to-morrow." Nevertheless, he recognized that underneath, he too was Australian, and that the country, unlike postwar Europe, offered people the basic necessities as well as "a reasonable expectation of justice," while the writer in him had to learn that "even the boredom and frustration presented avenues for endless exploration; even the ugliness, the bags and iron of Australian life, acquired a meaning."

Equally significant was White's return to faith in 1951. In *Flaws in the Glass* he described himself spiritually as "a lapsed Anglican egotist agnostic pantheist occultist existentialist would-be though failed Christian Australian." Enumerated here are stations of his progress, but not its culmination. The author of *The Living and the Dead* could attribute to Elyot Standish an utterly desolate view of existence: "Then it snapped. You heard the ping, ping, the glurg. You could pitch your voice, your whole soul, into the cone of darkness, to be bandied about, a ball of ineffectual down." Similarly, the war left White unable to "find any point, see any future, love my fellow men," and he confessed at the beginning of the 1950s to having gone "quite sour," as he began a novel provisionally titled "A Life Sentence on Earth." He had had, however, occasional inklings of undefined presence in barren countryside or isolated Greek monasteries. These had fed his spiritual hunger, though fittingly his search terminated mundanely at Dogwoods. There, at the height of a storm, he fell heavily in the mud, spilling the slops he carried for the schnauzers as well as the curses stored up for decades against the perceived injustice of existence. Eventually his blasphemy was staunched by an acute sense of his own ridiculousness, which, coupled with further inexplicable intimations, rekindled his faith. When Anglicanism proved irrelevant, he resolved "to evolve symbols of my own through which to worship," and these played an increasingly central role in his next creative phase.

His new novel, now titled *The Tree of Man,* proved a great labor to write after years of silence and marked a new departure. In this work the stylistic sophistication and heightened aesthetic awareness of *The Aunt's Story* are radically reduced. In Theodora's realm, reality constantly threatens to yield up another dimension ("The garden was full of music.... The fuchsias trembled like detached notes waiting to bridge the gap between bars"), whereas Stan and Amy Parker, White's pioneer couple, encounter an obdurate, intensely concrete landscape: "Then the man took an axe and struck at the side of a hairy tree . . . and the sound was cold and loud." Nevertheless, their struggle to establish a farm is imbued with archetypal resonance, so that it assumes aspects of a creation myth that Huebsch immediately recognized: "your people might be out of the Scripture. All of life and all of nature are implicit in the tale." In it White reworks such standard scenes of frontier romance as flood and bushfire, and traces with immense sympathy the long marriage of the Parkers, charting its vicissitudes as well as the irreducible solitariness and mystery of each soul. The Parkers' son, Ray, dies a minor hoodlum; their socially ambitious daughter, Thelma, develops into a prototype of shallow suburban womankind, displaying the "nastiness" inherent "in the evolution of a synthetic soul." Her restlessness apparently derives from her mother Amy's, which drives Amy into an arid affair with a traveling salesman. What elevates ordinary as well as stock events is the novelist's ability to make them portals to enlarged awareness. Both flood and fire dislocate daily habits and perceptions, allowing individuals who are possessed of sufficient humility and courage to confront ultimate questions. For Stan this revelation first occurs at the height of a storm: "The lightning, which could have opened basalt, had, it seemed, the power to open souls . . . something like this had happened, the flesh had slipped from his bones, and a light was shining in his cavernous skull." Admittedly, subsequent events confirm the power of apparent evil and the pain endemic in existence—each face in White's world will eventually have "received the fist." Yet, this negative ledger is convincingly counterbalanced by the lives of ordinary people such as the Parkers and Quigleys, in whom loving warmth prevails despite human failings, and by White's newfound conviction that even the most trivial paths chosen are part of a greater plan. Eventually, Stan's death occurs in the "boundless garden," and regeneration is confirmed by the appearance of his young grandson, an aspiring poet, who is "putting out shoots of green thought. So that, in the end, there was no end."

This endorsement of a simple, humble man was followed by a contrasting portrait of "the great monster Self" in *Voss*. Loosely based on the expeditions of Ludwig Leichhardt, the novel moved the explorer narrative into untrodden psychological and metaphysical regions. Its characters, like those in many of White's subsequent works, are broadly divisible into those who are content with accumulating material objects and those who long for more. The latter embrace figures as diverse as the saintly Palfreyman, the pragmatic Judd, seared in the furnaces of penal affliction, and Sanderson, who has combined self-mortification with pastoral success. The extremes are represented by the smug materialism of the Bonners, and Voss's intention to achieve the stature of deity, or as he puts it in terms that dismiss the Bonners' notion of possession: "in this disturbing country . . . it is possible more easily to discard the inessential and to attempt the infinite." Unexpectedly, however, these otherwise different conceptions intersect in denying the inexhaustible resonance of life and the cosmos. "If she could have turned infinity to stone," the reader is told, Mrs. Bonner would have been at peace among her comfortable furnishings, much as Voss visualizes his "Idea" rising "out of that sand . . . its granite monolith untouched." Stone-like inflexibility is the antithesis of Theodora Goodman's openness, which, for White, constitutes true possession. The key to Voss's attaining a relating openness is Laura Trevelyan, his peer in pride and imagination. She decides to save him through her example and her love, and their subsequent ability to communicate telepathically over vast distances affirms both the superrational and the German's ability to be touched by human sentiments, despite his all-devouring will.

That the author had never experienced the harsh landscape through which the expedition treks, except in written accounts or paintings, mattered little. Neither had his coast-bound readers, as Voss notes: "A pity that you huddle. . . . Your country is of great subtlety." Instead, what White depicts, as Laura expresses it, is "the country of the mind." His hostile terrain has the properties of all arid places; they are where mortification and spiritual reward may be reckoned with and where individuals can measure their own presumption against forces that surpass human energy and technology. The wilderness can also serve as a mirror of the individual soul. Laura calls Voss her desert, a metaphor for his alienation among "rocks of prejudice . . . even hatred," where "you will find your situation . . . exalted." With the distorting prism of selfhood removed, however, the desert becomes a place where "the world of semblance communicated with the world of dream." Finally, Voss, "truly humbled," realizes that he was never more than "a frail god upon a rickety throne" and dies in accordance with Aboriginal superstition. Possession, like understanding, White suggests, comes through the toil and suffering of generations ("in failure, in perpetual struggle, in becoming"), as well as through expanded perception: "The blowfly on its bed of offal is but a variation of the rainbow. Common forms are continually breaking into brilliant shapes. If we will explore them."

White's visionary potential was celebrated four years later in his most ambitious novel, *Riders in the Chariot*. Described by him as "a cantata for four voices," it plays off this capacity in four social outcasts against Australian incomprehension and its hideous byproducts. The reader is quickly warned about the first unlikely visionary, Miss Hare: "For a variety of reasons, very little of her secret, actual nature had been disclosed to other human beings." From the outset she has already achieved Voss's goal: the land "belonged to her, over and above actual rights." Whereas he strode forth proudly to possess it, she approaches her domain like a feral creature, tunneling her way through undergrowth on hands and knees, instinctively worshiping her surroundings and meekly accepting lacerations as the price of existence. Her confreres are the fertile but slatternly Mrs. Godbold, who lives with her children in a shed; Mordecai Himmelfarb, a Jew who has escaped the Nazi death camps; and Alf Dubbo, a syphilitic Aborigine with the spark of artistic greatness. Humility and an ability to witness Ezekiel's chariot in the here and now draw these four together in a calculated affront to Australian norms, while Himmelfarb's life story provides one of the earliest dramatizations of anti-Semitic madness in Germany. A former professor of English literature and a part-time Cabbalist, he is first deprived of his profession, then his wife and home, but spared for some unknown end "inside the prevailing darkness, worse because it was imposed by man—or could it have been sent by God?"

White wrote in this novel as if he wanted to explode local complacency once and for all. "I have never been one to sit and smile sweetly when there

White at Dogwoods with his cat Tom Jones and his dog Solomon (photograph by Axel Poignant; from White, Flaws in the Glass, *1982)*

was an offending eye to spit in," he confessed, adding elsewhere, "There is so much that has offended *me* over the years, and now I must give expression to my feelings." Whereas White described the Parkers as "like characters out of my childhood" seen through "a glow of morning," he saw their modern descendants as prone to superficiality. Ordinariness is raised into a secular religion and custom into a dictatorial mind-set. Opposing Miss Hare's gifts for love and revelation are the "lethal performance" of Mrs. Jolley and Mrs. Flack, who, intolerant of difference, are bent on preserving their version of normality. Swelling their hate-filled voices is Shirl Rosetree, an overcompensating migrant and apostate Jewess proud of the solid respectability she and her factory-owner husband have achieved in Paradise East. The fourth grotesque in this earthbound group is Blue. He is the epitome of blue-collar Aussie mateyness, reduced by White to a brainless physique with eyes that "filtered glimpses of an infinite squalor." Knowing instinctively that "all manner of cruelties" can be passed off as practical jokes, Blue focuses his fellow workers' distrust of the odd Jew and oversees Himmelfarb's gruesome crucifixion on a mutilated jacaranda outside their factory: "the majority were pacified by the prospect of becoming involved in some episode that would degrade them lower than they had known yet; the heights were not for them." White underscores that Nazi Germany had no monopoly on barbarity. "There is always the beast lurking, who will come up, booted, bristling, his genitals bursting from the cloth which barely contains them"—unless the voice of the angry prophet is heard, together with his redemptive message.

White's concern with expanding the nationalist canon and revealing the hidden depths missed by local realist writers assumed diverse forms in *The Burnt Ones*. It signaled the importance of Greece in his life with four stories drawn from his own or Lascaris's experience there, while the title, as White explained to Huebsch, translated a common Greek "expression of formal pity. One realizes they aren't prepared to do anything about the objects of their pity because nothing can be done." These tales are significant precursors of later migrant literature, and Greek characters or settings appear in most of his novels. In general, the stories collected in this work and in *The Cockatoos* suffer from comparison with White's longer fiction. Characterization is more shallow, and the author's habitual satire is often unleavened by a compensating perspective, though there are stories in which the clash of antithetical approaches to life is effectively dramatized. For example, "Miss Slattery and her Demon Lover" juxtaposes European experience and sexual honesty, represented by Tibby Szabo, with Miss Slattery's initial repression and subservience, in a series of comic encounters that promote her emancipation. Similarly, "Down at the Dump" defies accepted standards by affirming what the decent regard as trash. At the cemetery, which abuts the rubbish dump, the bottle-collecting Whalleys, exuding natural instinct, meet the stiff, conformist Hogbens, whose literary counterpart is safe but "dreary, dun-coloured . . . journalistic realism"—unsettled here through naturalistic details that threaten to assume a surrealistic dimension, as when "a disembowelled mattress from the dump had begun to writhe across the road. It looked like a kind of monster from out of the depth of somebody's mind, the part a decent person ignored." Also ignored locally is the spiritual dimension of life, which White insists on by conjuring up the deceased Daise Morrow beside her grave as the service intones clichés about "the risen dead." The love offered previously by this fallen woman makes her, as her name suggests, a focus of regeneration, while in the dump itself man-made waste is gradually subverted by nature's "superior resilience." Such a vision, in the words of "The Prodigal Son," could hopefully help to form "a race possessed of understanding."

The beginning of his next major creative period coincided with his last change of residence and a turn toward the theater. The death of his mother in 1963 released him from a problematic relationship and brought him further wealth that facilitated a move to a large house in the eastern suburbs of his youth, opposite Centennial Park. Self-confrontations and reckonings with his past figured prominently in his next novels. Meanwhile, his intensely theatrical imagination was finding another outlet as a playwright. Before the war he had written for the theater, and his play *Return to Abyssinia* enjoyed a brief season in London in 1947. Shortly afterward he wrote *The Ham Funeral* (1961; published, 1965). It was resurrected in 1961 for the Adelaide Festival, only to be rejected at the last minute by the governors of the Festival. This rejection launched White's career as a local dramatist, and in anger he began to write *The Season at Sarsaparilla* (performed, 1962; published, 1965). Six further plays by White were performed over the next decade and a half: *A Cheery Soul* (1963; published, 1965), *Night on Bald Mountain* (1964; published, 1965), *Big Toys* (1977; published 1978), *Signal Driver* (1982; published, 1983), *Netherwood* (1983), and *Shepherd on the Rocks* (1987).

Like his novels, his plays directly challenge naturalistic conventions. Their characteristic themes and techniques emerge in *The Ham Funeral*. A self-consciously unsettling play, it opens with a warning to the audience from the Young Man: "I'm sorry to have to announce the management won't refund any money. You must simply sit it out, and see whether you can't recognize some of the forms that will squirm before you in this mad, muddy mass of eels." The ensuing action and set hover uneasily between naturalism and symbolism. The house and its inhabitants, it is occasionally suggested, are also aspects of the Young Man's psyche. Thus, the powerful stage presences of Will and Alma Lusty are later identified with compassion and passion, and the sequestered Girl is identified with his anima, as the landlord's demise and funeral assume the dimensions of an ill-defined psychodrama. White's later plays are similarly adventurous, mixing temporal as well as mental states and drawing liberally on specifically theatrical resources. A recurring concern is the capacity of individuals to break out of ruts or through conventions to fulfill possibilities. The cumulative verdict is pessimistic. Already Will Lusty remarks, "A man only 'as to bounce like a ball to know 'ow much of 'is will is free." Similarly, *The Season at Sarsaparilla*, which vividly portrays a cross section of contemporary suburbia, demonstrates that "there's practically no end to the variations on monot-

Dust jacket for the U.S. edition of White's 1957 novel, loosely based on the Australian expeditions of German explorer Ludwig Leichhardt during the 1840s (Richland County Public Library)

ony," or on people's ability to procrastinate and compromise. Subsequent plays debunk do-gooders and idealists alike, showing humankind to be irrevocably flawed and the world to be equally destructive of love and high intentions. White's canvas of characters is predictably broad, encompassing all classes and including striking male and female leads. In no sense closet dramas, his plays were written for performance and were often rehearsed with his input. Yet, despite exploding the confines of realism and targeting current abuses or deficiencies, they lacked the massive impact of the novels and left some people regretting this dissipation of his creative energies.

The first novel to benefit, arguably, from the discipline of writing for the theater was *The Solid Mandala*, which is dominated by the complementary narratives of two brothers, Arthur and Waldo Brown. Again White's subjects are unprepossessing figures such as the world ignores, unless, as the narrator notes sardonically at the outset, "life took its cleaver to them." White takes this action instead, first in his capacity as dissecting novelist, then when the plot dictates that Waldo's corpse be ripped open at the neck by his starving dogs, much as his soul has been consumed lifelong by spite and loathing. Waldo is the first major narrator of the novel—belittling his brother, foregrounding his own authorial aspirations, and trying to create a sanitized public persona: "Mr Brown of the intellectual breathers in the Botanic Gardens must never be confused with the subfusc, almost abstract figure, living on top of a clogged grease-trap." A self-obsessed intellectual living in denial of love and fraternity, Waldo is, the author conceded, "myself at my coldest and worst." Waldo is also warped by unconfessed sexual deviance and an unresolved fixation on his mother. Both are revealed in a great, culminating scene when, prompted by compelling memories, he decks himself out in her evening finery—momentarily becoming the drag queen he has so savagely suppressed. His version of events is then corrected and subsumed within Arthur's account of his own quest for insight and completion. This mentally simple narrator is another of White's unsuspected saints, who achieves without fanfare what Waldo can only imagine. The latter, for instance, is usually "too preoccupied to notice anyone beyond the outskirts of his mind" and works in jealous secrecy on his magnum opus, "Portrait of Tiresias as a Youngish Man," whereas Arthur's empathy enables him to become the Protean Greek, to "retire behind his eyelids" and experience "that episode of the garden, first as Waldo, then as Dulcie, very intensely." Arthur is also the apostle of selfless love and of wholeness, embodied by the mandala. His preferred and suitably infantile version is four marbles. Each of these solid mandalas he assigns to an important person in his life, keeping one marble for himself and living to witness the rejection of his precious gift by Waldo, who thereby consigns himself to the torments of a lost soul. Overall, the novel at once affirms Christ's teachings and yet escapes conventional schemata, with Waldo's behavior representing a profound "blasphemy against life"; Arthur's behavior is another means by which "God reveals Himself" to those unprejudiced enough to see.

With Sarsaparilla now completed, White chose inner Sydney as the backdrop for *The Vivisector,* which affords both a portrait of the idiosyncratic painter Hurtle Duffield and an apologia for the author's lifework. Although he had known many artists, such as Francis Bacon and Sidney Nolan, White confessed that "*The Vivisector* is more about myself than any other of my unfortunate characters," and in it he explores the suffering, destructiveness, and exaltation that he associated with the artist's vocation. These traits already distinguished Alf Dubbo: "the furtive, destroying sickness, and almost as furtive, but regenerative, creative act." *The Vivisector* stresses the representative nature of this psychological profile. According to one of Hurtle's most perceptive correspondents, humans by their nature are afflicted, and creators more so because "through your art you can see further than us." Similarly, humans are cruel, but artists surpass this brutal norm through a capacity for dispassionate analysis that links them with the Godhead, conceived of as the Divine Vivisector. His action is equally evident in wars or the misshapen body of Rhoda, Hurtle's hunchback sister by adoption. Both God and painter wield the knife unsparingly, so that even Duffield's earliest work is adjudged the product of a mentally deficient person "or some kind of criminal," much as he is held personally responsible for "the ugliness and cruelties" of his later canvases. Admittedly, outraged critics of White and Duffield had grounds for complaint. The novelist acknowledged that vulgarity was a staple of his fiction, or, more accurately, what amounts to an obsession with the most sordid human functions. This belief assumes the proportions of an excremental vision in one of Hurtle's most notorious canvases, which rudely negates the notion of a benignly radiant Pantocrator by depicting "the moon in one of its destructive phases. . . . The innocent lovers are under attack. . . . The moon is *shitting* on them." The rottenness and "attempts at evil" of individuals, Duffield states, "are childlike besides the waves of enlightened evil proliferating from above."

The defense of such art is its devotion to truth. By this statement, both White and Duffield understand not only depicting existence and humankind as they really are, but also probing why they should be so. The novelist described his earliest works as lumbering clumsily after truth. Decades later in *Flaws in the Glass,* his autobiography, he asked, "Am I a destroyer? this face in the glass which has spent a lifetime searching for what it believes, but can never prove to be, the truth." The goals of Hurtle's mature art are closely related to the novelist's. First, he wishes "to arrive at the truth"–that is, "to find some formal order behind a moment of chaos and unreason" that otherwise "would have been too horrible and terrifying." The second is to project intimations of an essentially inexpressible promise beyond the knife–to paint the unattainable indigo. A less peccant individual might draw back from this hubristic endeavor. Arthur Brown, for example, was repeatedly silenced by the limitations of language, although he intuitively hit on actions that passed beyond them, whether in giving symbols of totality or in dancing the mandala, which concluded triumphantly with "his mouth . . . a silent hole, because no sound was needed to explain." White, however, makes no claims to such near perfection. Instead, just as Robert Browning does in "Andrea del Sarto," White locates in unstilled striving the hallmark of humankind, and especially creative genius:

> Only reach higher. Could. And will.
>
> Then lifting by the hairs of his scalp to brush the brushhairs bludge on the blessed blue.
>
> Before the tobbling scrawl deadwood splitting splintering the prickled stars plunge a presumptuous body crashing. Dumped.
>
> Light follows dark not usually bound by the iron feather which stroked.

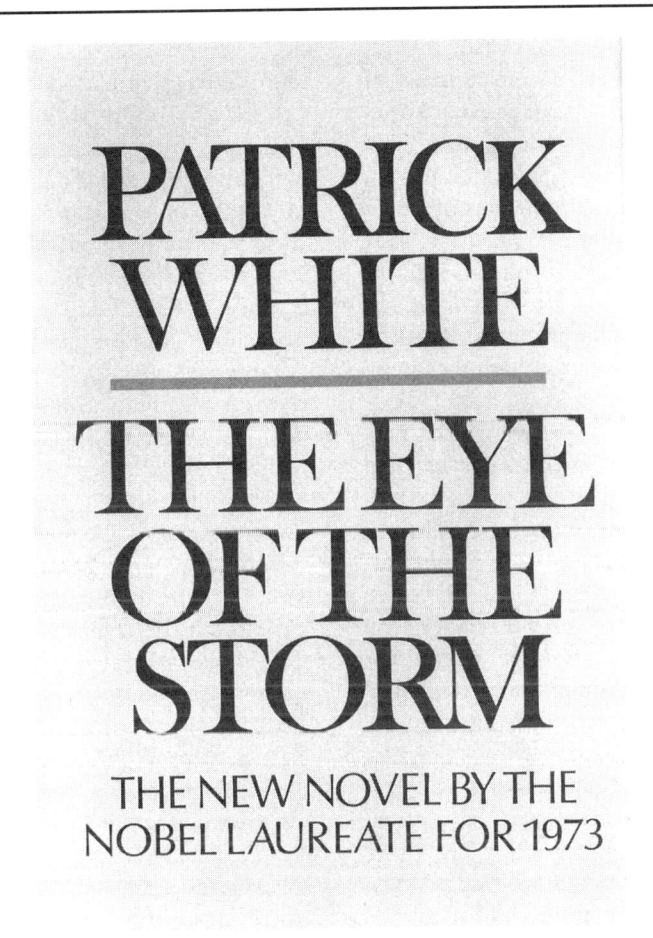

Dust jacket for the U.S. edition of White's 1973 novel, which focuses on the last days of a wealthy eighty-six-year-old woman (Richland County Public Library)

Shattering syntax points beyond normal perceptions to affirm implicitly a higher purpose as surely as did Duffield's experiences of inspiration as a momentary suffusing of his inner void by blazing, inexplicable light.

The author as vivisector is much to the fore in White's next novel, *The Eye of the Storm,* which, despite its considerable length, is one of his most intense and concentrated works. It focuses on the last days of the eighty-six-year-old Elizabeth Hunter, evoking in detail her claustrophobic sickroom and the routines and thoughts of the female staff who sustain her decaying body, as well as the mental life of her children, Dorothy de Lascabanes and Sir Basil, both of whom have returned from overseas in the hope of securing her wealth more quickly. As her mind deteriorates, so too does the present, revealing key moments in her past, while her home opposite Centennial Park evolves into a microcosm of human life, "its silence alive with clocks, suggestions of subterfuge, the blatant echoes of downright lies, together with hints of the exasperating, unknowable truth." In this novel character rivals truth in its complexity. No longer are personages divided into absolute categories of the living and the dead, nor are responses always foreseeable, so that a nihilistic view of words is attributed to the fallible but estimable family lawyer, Arnold Wyburn: "but if ever you thought they were about to help you open a door into the truth, you found, instead of a lighted room, a dark void you hadn't the courage to enter."

White's own faith in words, however, had rarely been stronger, as his portrait of the octogenarian demonstrates. Once a great beauty, Mrs. Hunter consists now only of cruelty and vanity, as "under the transparent skin, bones awaited distribution for the final game of jacks." Eventually she suffers the ultimate indignity of dying on her commode, and Dorothy underlines at the end her mother's worldliness: "could anything of a transcendental nature have illuminated a mind so sensual, mendacious, materialistic, superficial as Elizabeth Hunter's?" Nevertheless, she is granted the clearest perception of pure being in the book, and in an equally unexpected twist, the reader is invited, through Wyburn, to contemplate the possibility that "for an instant Elizabeth Hunter's image radiated all the human virtues in an unmistakably celestial aura." Unlike his earlier caricatures, no one in this work seems irremediably fallen. Rather, each person has the capacity to see "clearly right down to the root of the matter" or, as the professional actor Sir Basil said, "before his perception. . . . retired behind a legerdemain of technique and the dishonesties of living." His mother, too, might have been completely enslaved by the theatricalities of social intercourse, had not fateful interventions made her "the eternal aspirant." First, her cocooned existence is rent by news of her husband's cancer–"the charming filigree of her life had been hammered without warning into an ugly, patternless entanglement." Later she experiences directly an act of God in the form of a cyclone–a fury that harbors preternatural calm at its center: "the myth of her womanhood had been exploded" to be replaced by "this dream of glistening peace through which she moved." Occurring midway through the novel rather than at its end, this vision of a state of grace suggests the continual potential of time to reveal a "lustrous moment," or a pattern, in which cynics perceive nothing–a point clinched by Sister de Santis. The novel opens and closes with this person for whom service is a way of life. Her capacity for mundane epiphanies places her among White's riders in the chariot, and at the end she is transfigured by a faith-confirming light, too solid and intrusive to ward off.

The Nobel Prize in 1973 brought perceptible changes to White's life and work. Up until then he had successfully avoided giving interviews or taking a public stand on issues of national importance, claiming that a writer said what he had to say in his works. International recognition, coupled with unprecedented local events, weakened this resolve, and he joined a left coalition in campaigning for issues as diverse as saving Frazer Island, reinstating the sacked Labor government, and stopping conscription for the war in Vietnam. *Big Toys* expressed his disgust with Sydney power brokers, and the same privileged clique was a target as well in *The Cockatoos*, or when he mounted the podium to denounce uranium mining. "Life in this piffling British colony," he stated, "has made me a republican and driven me always farther to the Left, till I am what the conservatives describe as a 'traitor to my class.'" Less publicly, he was a munificent benefactor. His prize money from Stockholm funded a grant for Australian writers. He gave generously to causes and theaters he favored, and he made liberal art bequests to the State Gallery of New South Wales. In later life he attempted to avoid acquiring a retinue of helpers so as not to be obliged to curtail his charitable impulses.

Frazer Island also interested him as the setting for a novel that had long awaited completion, *A Fringe of Leaves*. Begun in 1961, its story of an English woman's survival among Aborigines, after shipwreck off the Queensland coast, left him ample latitude to speculate on the impact of Australia on its white settlers and on the kind of person who could have survived Eliza Frazer's ordeal. In the novel she is a simple farm girl, Ellen Gulyas, close to nature but also with undefined aspirations represented by Tintagel, a nearby site, shrouded in myth, which she never visits. Next comes induction into English social life through the Roxburgh brothers. Her mollycoddled husband, Austin, provides her with a cultivated veneer, but he is himself ill-equipped to deal with harsh realities. One aside reduces his expensive education to "a dust of dictionary words and useless knowledge"; another notes that for him death is a literary conceit, while he is excessively defensive and pessimistic. Unfulfilled passionate needs propel her into adultery with Austin's more robust brother, Garnet, who is "less her seducer than the instrument she had chosen for measuring depths she was tempted to explore." This descent is accelerated when the overlay of white acculturation, together with her clothes, is violently stripped away by the indigenous people, in a variation on White's recurring call to put aside nonessentials. Adapting to their extremely rude and savage way of life becomes for Ellen a rite of passage to self-knowledge, during which she is saved by her tough Gulyas heritage. It also provides occasions for interrogating the axioms of civilization, as when she inadvertently participates in cannibalism–described as a "sacrament" in a setting of "exquisite innocence." This scene nourishes "not only her animal body but some darker need of the hungry spirit" and strengthens rather than diminishes her stature before she is led back to a white settlement by the escaped convict Jack Chance, with whom she deepens her experience of love. How these events will affect her among so-called civilized beings is unclear. To her fellow settlers she appears an enigma, and to herself: "Mrs Roxburgh could not have explained the reason for her being there, or whether she had served a purpose, ever." The novel ends tantalizingly with an implicit warning against the human predilection to "grasp at any circumstantial straw which may indicate an ordered universe."

From the mystery of Mrs. Roxburgh, White moved daringly to mirror his own predicament in *The Twyborn Affair*. Although earlier novels had included sexually ambivalent figures, such as Elyot Standish or Waldo Brown, this work is his first overt, extended portrait of a homosexual's life. Overall it is unfulfilled and tragic, caught on the cusp between sexes. Twy-

White and Manoly Lascaris, circa 1980 (photograph by Max Dupain)

born is forced to lead a sham existence that leaves him feeling that he is a "mistake trying to correct itself" or, more sweepingly, "the stranger of all time . . . the eternal deserter in search of asylum." The novel is divided into three sections that depict his various avatars and the dilemmas they reflect. In the first he masquerades as Eudoxia, young wife of the aging Greek Angelo Valatzes on the Côte d'Azur. Their precarious idyll, however, is constantly threatened by the prying heterosexual world, as well as by jealousy and the charged emotions that draw the two men together. It ends with Angelo's death and the revelation to outsiders of the true, and hence loathsome, nature of their relationship, focused by a squalid bathroom and the grotesquely large enema it contains. Part 2 problematizes the cult of Australian masculinity. It opens with Eddie Twyborn, a decorated war hero, returning home, convinced that he has been "born without the requisites for grace." Working next as a jackeroo, he tries to come "to terms with his body . . . to live in accordance with appearances" in a milieu dominated by an aggressively masculine ethos. Sexual intercourse with the station-owner's wife, however, fails to establish his male identity; at the same time the supposedly unitary image of Australian masculinity begins to fragment. First, the conqueror of the land, Greg Lushington, is revealed on nearer acquaintance to be a frustrated poet who periodically disappears overseas "to lose—or find himself." Next the embodiment of "inviolable masculinity," his overseer, Don Prowse, displays homoerotic impulses. Though ostentatiously virile and tirelessly boasting of his conquests among the local women, he returns drunk one night and has sex with Eddie. That this incident was no isolated aberration is later confirmed when he seeks similar treatment from the jackeroo.

The matter-of-fact statement, attributed to Marcia Lushington, "that one isn't the same person every hour of the week" has massive ramifications, which the novel explores. The possibility of ambivalent or multiple identity is thereby admitted, an occurrence that has the potential to destabilize not only relationships but also gender categories and ultimately leaves Eddie/Eudoxia wondering "where civilization ended, and still more, where it began." In part 3, during his second extended disappearance from Sydney, he reemerges as Eadith Trist, madame of one of the most illustrious brothels of London. Much as twilight and the limbo between waking and dreaming are the states in which he/she feels "as much herself as a human being can afford to be," so her brothel is a natural extension of the theater of seesawing lusts that has constituted Twyborn's life. The plot is further complicated by parallels between the colonial and the homosexual struggles for acceptance and self-understanding in the face of condemnatory norms. This scene is played out against the backdrop of an impending European catastrophe that menaces individuals as well as society "with extinction by the seas of black unreason on which it floated." Beyond the theatrical roles, mirrors, and fantasies that energize both the brothel and the world at large, Eadith/Eddie/Eudoxia gropes toward final consummation through love. This time, however, the fulfillment is nonsexual. Initially he finds it with an aristocrat who, at her bidding, renounces physical coupling. His unselfish response is offered as convincing "proof" of love and, by sanguine extension, of its divine guarantor. Then, in a first in White's fiction, the protagonist is reconciled with his domineering mother. Is all ordained, including the bomb that finally cuts Twyborn down in his reassumed male guise as he hastens to a rendezvous with his mother? And if so, to what end? His parent is left in a garden reminiscent of Stan Parker's, musing "Eadith Eddie no matter which this fragment of my self which I lost is now returned where it belongs," in the company of a quizzical bird, his beak raised "towards the sun."

Memoirs dominated White's last productive years—an autobiography followed five years later by *Memoirs of Many in One,* allegedly written by Alex Xenophon Demirjian Gray and edited by White. At first sight the two works seem unrelated compositions, but they actually complement each other. The demand for information about the novelist had increased since he won the Nobel Prize and had gained further public prominence, and White decided to preempt critics "anxious to put in the warts" by trying "to show where I think the real ones are." He also thought it was time to discuss his homosexuality, his forty-year relationship with Lascaris, and the forces that had propelled his career "as truthfully and simply as I can." To Graham Greene he referred to *Flaws in the Glass* as "The Poof's Progress." Dignified, yet also lively and candid, it affords an indispensable guide to his life and work—as well as a coherent picture of his development that does not do full justice to his sense of himself as shifting, fragmented, polyphonic. In later life White maintained that his important fictional characters were latent aspects of himself, and that he was "several people in one" with "only one life between them." These diverse personae find voice in his final novel, primarily through the mental flights of demented Alex, as well as through her family and friends. These include her future editor, Patrick White—arthritic, crotchety, and "too piss-elegant by half," who shares more than unlikely blue eyes with this Greek. Her mind, like his, turns repeatedly to questions of sexuality, family relations, religion, and the theater, while to her is attributed his bawdiness and desire to scandalize. In her fantasies Alex, as a gate-crasher who suddenly metamorphoses into an apocalyptic horsewoman, is depicted confronting diverse "dinosaurs of disaster," or, as an inmate of the psychiatric hospital Bonkers Hill, having her face liberally smeared with her own excrement. Archives, as Alex asserts, "are only half the truth." The rest is provided by this coda that enables the author to reflect on the creative process, the vagaries of identity, and the public figure he has become.

White, as he once acknowledged, "had the wrong chemistry for happiness." Cynical, homosexual, and unforgiving, to the end he fired off barbs against a world in which he never felt at home, and his last slim monograph was titled *Three Uneasy Pieces* (1987). Mother's Day he dismissed as "another bit of dishonesty"; the media seemed to him bent on dragging the "supraterrestrial . . . down to ground level amongst the plastic and adulteries"; and the bicentenary of Australia celebrated "our emptiness in a great shower of bullshit." Most of all, he confessed to hating "the inner me." But from this position of rancorous outsider he succeeded in introducing "a new continent into literature," as the Nobel Prize citation underscored, and in holding up to local society daunting images of its past, present, and future potential. Admittedly, his novels are not without flaws; however, to borrow words he used to describe Christianity, these "are not sufficiently important to interfere with the goodness and rightness and immensity of the whole." Nevertheless, he located in skepticism a recipe for wisdom and, when asked for his own view of the purpose of life, he answered, "Waiting to die, really." Few writers can match White for unflinching honesty, and prolonged bouts of "torture in the country of the mind" produced the typically eclectic vision of his work, which refuses to blink the demeaning, bestial aspects of life while offering hints rather than confirmation of a higher reality.

Patrick White died after a long illness on 30 September 1990. Fiercely private and independent, he asked for his ashes to be scattered in Centennial Park, which he hoped to protect as a revenant. Similarly, his novels continue to haunt Australian intellectual life, to shock, inspire, and tantalize, reflecting and fulfilling his and Alex's credo that "words are what matter. Even when they don't communicate . . . Somebody may understand in time."

Letters:
David Marr, ed., *Patrick White: Letters* (Sydney: Random House, 1994).

Bibliographies:
Alan Lawson, *Patrick White* (Melbourne: Oxford University Press, 1974);

William J. Scheick, "A Bibliography of Writings about Patrick White, 1972–1978," *Texas Studies in Literature and Language,* 21 (1979): 296–303.

Biography:
David Marr, *Patrick White: A Life* (Sydney: Random House, 1991).

References:
May-Brit Akerhold, *Patrick White* (Amsterdam: Rodopi, 1988);

Peter Beatson, *The Eye in the Mandala. Patrick White: A Vision of Man and God* (London: Elek, 1976);

Carolyn Bliss, *Patrick White's Fiction: The Paradox of the Fortunate Fall* (London: Macmillan, 1986);

Simon During, *Patrick White* (Melbourne: Oxford University Press, 1996);

Rodney S. Edgecombe, *Vision and Style in Patrick White: A Study of Five Novels* (Tuscaloosa: University of Alabama Press, 1989);

Martin Gray, ed., *Patrick White: Life and Writings: Five Essays* (Stirling: Centre for Commonwealth Studies: University of Stirling, 1991);

Brian Kiernan, *Patrick White* (London: Macmillan, 1980);

Alan Lawson, ed., *Patrick White: Selected Writings* (St. Lucia: University of Queensland Press, 1994);

A. M. McCulloch, *A Tragic Vision: The Novels of Patrick White* (St. Lucia: University of Queensland Press, 1983);

David J. Tacey, *Patrick White: Fiction and the Unconscious* (Melbourne: Oxford University Press, 1988);

John A. Weigel, *Patrick White* (Boston: Twayne, 1983);

G. A. Wilkes, ed., *Ten Essays on Patrick White: Selections from Southerly (1964–67)* (Sydney: Angus & Robertson, 1970);

Mark Williams, *Patrick White* (London: Macmillan, 1993);

Peter Wolf, ed., *Critical Essays on Patrick White* (Boston: G. K. Hall, 1990).

Papers:
Some of Patrick White's manuscripts are collected at the Australian National Library, Canberra.

Judith Wright
(31 May 1915 – 25 June 2000)

Veronica Brady
University of Western Australia

BOOKS: *The Moving Image: Poems* (Melbourne: Meanjin Press, 1946);

Woman to Man: Poems (Sydney: Angus & Robertson, 1949);

The Gateway (Sydney: Angus & Robertson, 1953);

The Two Fires (Sydney: Angus & Robertson, 1955);

William Baylebridge and the Modern Problem [bound with *Henry Kingsley, Some Novels of Australian Life,* by Leonie J. Kramer] (Canberra: Canberra University College, 1955);

Kings of the Dingoes (Melbourne: Oxford University Press, 1958);

The Generations of Men (Melbourne: Oxford University Press, 1959; revised edition, Sydney: ETT Imprint, 1995);

The Day the Mountains Played (Milton, Qld.: Jacaranda Press, 1960);

Australian Bird Poems, Australian Artists and Poets Booklets, no. 1 (Adelaide: Australian Letters, 1961);

Birds: Poems (Sydney: Angus & Robertson, 1962);

Range the Mountains High (Melbourne: Lansdowne Press, 1962);

Charles Harpur, Australian Writers and Their Work (Melbourne: Lansdowne Press, 1963);

Country Towns (Melbourne: Oxford University Press, 1963);

Five Senses (Sydney: Angus & Robertson, 1963);

Judith Wright, Australian Poets (Sydney: Angus & Robertson, 1963);

City Sunrise (Brisbane: Shapcott Press, 1964);

Preoccupations in Australian Poetry (Melbourne: Oxford University Press, 1965);

The Nature of Love (Melbourne: Sun Books, 1966; revised edition, Watsons Bay, N.S.W.: ETT Imprint, 1997);

The Other Half (Sydney: Angus & Robertson, 1966);

The River and the Road (Melbourne: Lansdowne Press, 1966; London: Angus & Robertson, 1967; revised edition, Melbourne: Lansdowne Press, 1971);

Henry Lawson, Great Australians series (Melbourne: Oxford University Press, 1967);

Judith Wright, 1967 (from Veronica Brady, South of My Days, 1998)

Poetry from Australia, by Wright, William Hart-Smith, and Randolph Stow, selected by Howard Sergeant (Oxford & New York: Pergamon Press, 1969);

Conservation as an Emerging Concept (Melbourne: Australian Conservation Foundation, 1970);

Collected Poems, 1942–1970 (Sydney: Angus & Robertson, 1971);

Alive: Poems 1971–72 (Sydney: Angus & Robertson, 1973);

Because I Was Invited (Melbourne: Oxford University Press, 1975);
Fourth Quarter and Other Poems (Sydney: Angus & Robertson, 1976);
The Coral Battleground (West Melbourne: Thomas Nelson, 1977);
The Double Tree: Selected Poems, 1942–1976 (Boston: Houghton Mifflin, 1978);
The Cry for the Dead (Melbourne: Oxford University Press, 1981);
Phantom Dwelling (North Ryde, N.S.W.: Angus & Robertson, 1985; London: Virago, 1986);
We Call for a Treaty (Sydney: Collins/Fontana, 1985);
A Human Pattern: Selected Poems (North Ryde, N.S.W.: Angus & Robertson, 1990);
Born of the Conquerors: Selected Essays (Canberra: Aboriginal Studies Press, 1991);
Going On Talking (Springwood, N.S.W.: Butterfly Books, 1992);
Collected Poems: 1942–1985 (Pymble, N.S.W.: Angus & Robertson, 1994); republished as *Judith Wright: Collected Poems 1942–1985* (Manchester, U.K.: Carcanet, 1994);
Tales of a Great Aunt: A Memoir (Bondi Junction, N.S.W.: ETT Imprint, 1998);
Half a Lifetime, edited by Patricia Clarke (Melbourne: Text Publishing, 1999).

RECORDING: *Judith Wright Reads from Her Own Work,* Poets on Record, no. 9, St. Lucia, University of Queensland Press, 1973.

OTHER: *A Book of Australian Verse,* selected by Wright (London & Melbourne: Oxford University Press, 1956);
New Land, New Language: An Anthology of Australian Verse, compiled by Wright (Melbourne: Oxford University Press, 1957);
John Shaw Neilson, *Witnesses of Spring,* edited by Wright (Sydney: Angus & Robertson, 1970);
Journeys: Poems, by Wright, Rosemary Dobson, Gwen Harwood, Dorothy Hewett, and Fay Zwicky, edited by Zwicky (Carlton South, Vic.: Sisters, 1982).

SELECTED PERIODICAL PUBLICATION–UNCOLLECTED: "The Writer and the Crisis," *Language,* 1, no. 1 (1952): 4–6.

Judith Wright belonged to the generation who began writing and publishing in *The Bulletin* and new literary journals such as *Meanjin Papers* in the 1940s, as World War II was drawing to its end. C. B. Christesen, founder and first editor of *Meanjin Papers,* described the period as one in which it seemed as if "the old world had died at the end of the tremulous 'thirties" and that it was the task of writers and thinkers to build a new one. Wright shared these ambitions, believing, as she wrote later in *Preoccupations in Australian Poetry* (1965), that it was time to "reject outright the literature of nostalgia" and set about the task of "making Australia into our real spiritual home." Wright was also a public figure passionately involved in the environmental movement, an opponent to uranium mining and nuclear power, and a champion of Aboriginal people in their struggles for justice. But the source of all these activities lay in the conviction she articulated in her preface to *Preoccupations in Australian Poetry* that "the true function of an art and a culture is to interpret us to ourselves, and to relate us to the country and society in which we live."

Some critics have felt that in her later years especially she sacrificed her poetry to politics. But, as fellow poet A. D. Hope pointed out, there was always a consistency between the poetry and the politics. Unlike some, she did not believe in the primacy of poetry over life; rather, she saw it as the source of a larger kind of life. This belief, poet and admirer Bruce Dawe wrote in an unpublished manuscript among Wright's papers at the National Library of Australia, gave her a peculiar "gift for seeing / Not merely this, or that, but, more importantly, those: / The relatedness of things, their inter-being" and an ability, rare in contemporary poetry, to combine the lyric and the narrative, the public and the private. When she died at the age of eighty-five, she was not only arguably Australia's best-known poet but also widely regarded as the conscience of the nation—her last public act was to lead a march for Aboriginal reconciliation across the Sydney Harbor Bridge in freezing weather.

Wright's reputation became international. The Russian poet Yevgeny Yevtushenko regarded her as one of the two best women writers of her time, and even the notoriously difficult-to-please Robert Lowell admired her work. She also won many international as well as national awards, including the Encyclopaedia Britannica Award (1964), the Queen's Gold Medal for Poetry (1992), the Poetry Society of Great Britain Prize, and the Order of the Golden Ark from the Dutch government. She was nominated for the Nobel Prize and represented Australia at the World Poetry Conference, which was part of Expo '67 in Montreal. At a gathering of poets of the Pacific region at the East-West Center in Hawaii in 1974, she gave one of the earliest papers to be delivered anywhere on Aboriginal writing, having first sought permission to do so from the Aboriginal writer Jack Davis. She was also one of a distinguished group

Judith, Bruce, and Peter Wright with their mother, Ethel Bigg Wright, circa 1926 (from Brady, South of My Days, *1998)*

of writers and academics funded by the Australian government to tour India in 1970.

Judith Arundell Wright was born on 31 May 1915 at Thalgaroch Station near Armidale, New South Wales (the New England region), into a family descended from English gentry on one side and Scotch Jacobites who had fled first to France but later, changing their name from MacGregor to Wright, settled in Cornwall. She was the daughter of Phillip Arundell Wright, a pastoralist, and Ethel Mabel Bigg Wright. She was born under the shadow of the landing at Gallipoli, a crucial event in Australian history that had occurred only a month and a few days before. Her family belonged to and cherished the imperial tradition, and her mother's two brothers were serving in the Australian Imperial Force (AIF). But Wright was to question that tradition—even as a child she scandalized her father by sympathizing with Mahatma Gandhi in his struggle against the British, for example.

The great influence of her childhood, however, was the land itself. The firstborn, she felt herself something of a disappointment to her parents because she was a girl. After the birth of the second of her two brothers, her mother became a more or less permanent invalid and died when Judith was twelve. Often left to her own devices, young Judith spent much of her time outdoors. The land became for her a presence that was almost maternal and the primary source of her poetry. As she put it toward the end of her life: "As a poet you have to imitate somebody, but as I had a beautiful landscape outside that I loved so much and was in so much . . . it was my main object from the start." It also pointed her beyond the confines of the self: "Most children are brought up in the 'I' tradition . . . the ego, it's me and what I think, but when you live in very close contact with a large and splendid landscape as I did you feel yourself a good deal smaller than just I."

Wright was educated first at home, which gave her much time for reading, and then as a boarder at the New England Girls' Grammar School, where her English teacher recognized and encouraged her talent. Despite a serious riding accident that kept her in the hospital for three months during her last year at school and prevented her from matriculating at Sydney University, she nevertheless went on to the university after a year at home. There she followed her interests, studying English, history, philosophy, and anthropology, and spending time in the library reading widely to prepare herself for a writing career. In 1937, with the last of the legacy from her grandmother that had taken her to the university, she went to England, where she met some of her relatives, and then toured Europe, where she witnessed Nazism firsthand in Germany and threatening Austria and Hungary.

The riding accident, in which she had broken her pelvis, meant that she would not be a good marriage prospect because of the potential danger of pregnancy and childbirth. But from childhood, inspired by Miles Franklin's novel *My Brilliant Career* (1901), she was determined to have a career as a writer. On her return to Australia she settled in Sydney. Not long afterward, World War II broke out in Europe. In 1941 the Japanese attack on Pearl Harbor brought the threat dangerously close to home; Wright wrote in "The Moving Image" (1946), collected in *The Moving Image,* that the war, "like a bushranger," seemed as if it "held its guns on us / and forced our choice." The choice she made was to return to New England to help her father run the family properties while her two brothers were in the army.

On the train trip there she became "suddenly and sharply aware" that Australia was "my country" but now in a different, more threatened, way: "these hills and valleys were not mine, but me, the threat of Japanese invasion hung over them as over me," as she said on page 68 of the manuscript for her unpublished autobiography. Like many of her class, she had until this moment divided her loyalty and felt somehow, as she put it in "For New England," in *The Moving Image* (1946), fruit of a "double tree," part English and part Australian. But now, "whatever other blood I held," she realized that "this was the country I loved and knew." This perception changed her outlook. Putting the emphasis on place, it also challenged the modernist preoccupation with time that influenced contemporary Australian poets such as Kenneth Slessor and Robert D. FitzGerald.

The series of poems about the land and the people who pioneered it, which she published first in *The Bulletin* and *Meanjin Papers* and later collected in her first volume, *The Moving Image,* made Wright's reputation. They also transformed the bush tradition, even as she wrote about and from within it. As Douglas Stewart recognized in his review of *The Moving Image* for *The Bulletin* (16 October 1942), these were poems that marked a new beginning, promising "anything, everything, the world." The land no longer figured as an antagonist to be wrestled with and conquered but as an aspect of the self, "part of my blood's country" and a bodily, even erotic presence, as "Soldier's Farm" suggests:

This ploughland vapoured with the dust of dreams;
these delicate gatherings of dancing trees,
answered the question of his searching eyes
as his wife's body answered to his arms.

This view also helped solve the problem of finding a personal poetic voice, which Stewart identified as perhaps the crucial difficulty facing Australian poets at that time. These poems managed to capture the intonation and vocabulary of ordinary people but also to express the intensities of experience underneath their usual reticence and their deep love of the land.

Like her distant relation, Patrick White—at that time still an expatriate—Wright was determined to make Australia a mythical country. But where White wanted to create it as a "country of the mind," for Wright the heart counted as well. "South Of My Days" in *The Moving Image,* for example, expresses a sense of the land as a "bride country":

. . . high delicate outline
of bony slopes wincing under the winter,
low trees blue-leaved and olive, outcropping granite—
clean, lean, hungry country.

The New England tableland becomes the self's intimate partner, "full of old stories that still go walking in my sleep," and part of the drama being played out around her is the terror of war, as its "wild summoning cry," its "animal cry" ("The Trains") threatens to destroy them.

Perhaps this sense of vulnerability, different from the heroic notions of war and conquest that had figured so importantly in the tradition, made Wright aware of

*Wright during the 1930s (from Brady,
South of My Days, 1998)*

another set of stories from the other side of the pioneering tradition, those of its First Peoples. But her background also contributed. Her father had had an Aboriginal nurse and had shared many of her stories with his children. Poems such as "Bora Ring" and "Half-Caste Girl" recall these lost tales. But, unusual for that time, they also take some responsibility for the loss. In "Bora Ring"

> . . . the rider's heart
> halts at a sightless shadow, an unsaid word
> that fastens in the blood the ancient curse
> the fear as old as Cain.

"Nigger's Leap, New England," about a nineteenth-century massacre in which Aborigines were driven over a cliff, sounds a similar note that echoed throughout her subsequent career:

> . . . We should have known
> the night that tided up the cliffs and hid them
> had the same question on its tongue for us.
> And there they lie that were ourselves writ strange.

Wright may have begun to use "the language of ordinary men" and women. But she also brought a ferociously independent mind and heart to bear on their complacencies—though this trait was not always realized by readers at the time. "Bullocky," also in *The Moving Image,* for example, generally read as a poem in praise of the pioneering tradition, is, she herself insists, an ironic interrogation of it.

Her next collection, *Woman to Man* (1949), opened up new territory. Her elder brother had been released from the army to work the family properties, so she went north to Brisbane to work as an unpaid secretary for Christesen with his newly founded literary magazine. At one of Christesen's gatherings she met Jack Philip McKinney, a man who had survived the trenches of World War I and had decided to spend the rest of his life trying to understand the descent into barbarism it represented for him. When they met in 1945, his marriage had broken down and he was living as a recluse and self-taught philosopher, emerging from time to time to borrow books from Christesen, who had an extensive library of philosophy as well as contemporary literature.

Wright found him witty, intelligent, original, and "a joy to be with," and she was fascinated by him: "I hadn't had my mind so stretched for years," she wrote in her autobiography, *Half a Lifetime* (1999). Their discussions set her "off on new tracks of thinking," throwing a different light on the philosophy she had read at the university. She also found an integrity in him, a "certainty, passion and peace" she had not encountered before, and he became her partner—and, in 1962, her husband. He was also the first man by whom she badly wanted to have a child, and poems such as "Woman to Man" and "Woman to Child" (collected in *Women to Man,* 1949) were inspired by this desire.

With some notable exceptions, women's experiences, and particularly erotic experiences, had figured little in Australian literature and culture. But beginning with *Woman to Man,* they became a central concern of Wright's work. Even before this period, she had felt uneasy with what she saw as the "masculine or tough or glittering and self absorbed" quality of the tradition as a whole and even of predecessors such as Slessor and FitzGerald. Now, however, she had broken out of this mold into the sensuous world of the body, exploring the elemental forces of desire, conception, and birth, their terrors as well as their splendors, and linking them also to the energies of the natural world.

She was breaking new ground, and these poems had a powerful effect, gaining a new and wider audience for her poetry. Not every critic was sympathetic: for one thing, Wright depicted pregnant and birthing mothers as elemental forces, like floods, fires, and droughts—which figure as the enemy in the bush tradition. Moreover, these poems established woman as a figure of power—not always an acceptable notion to the patriarchy or the prim tradition of New Criticism then coming into vogue in academic circles. Vincent Buckley, for instance, dismissed Wright as a "highbrow Dorothy Dix" and later berated her as "a shrew." He and critics like him seemed more interested in the debate over whether she could be called a "modernist" writer and in close textual analysis of the poems, which took little account of the context.

In effect, however, Wright was moving beyond these narrow limits, driven by more-urgent and personal questions about how to survive as a woman and a poet and how to not only find a place for herself in a tradition that had hitherto largely eschewed the issues troubling her but also deal with the challenges of the postwar world. In particular the dropping of the first atomic bomb on Hiroshima in 1945 had opened a new and more dangerous world in which the meaning of "reality" had to be rethought and values redefined.

One way of doing this rethinking was to explore the possibilities of myth. She and McKinney were reading the works of Carl Gustav Jung, Ernst Cassirer, and critics such as Owen Barfield as well as attempting to come to terms with the insights of contemporary scientists such as Albert Einstein, Niels Bohr, and Werner Karl Heisenberg. But her explorations of the archetypal experiences of birth and pregnancy also introduced her to the dimension of the archaic, the nocturnal, and the oneiric, largely ignored in the Australian tradition until then. This focus enabled her to create a different image of women, who had hitherto been reduced to the types Anne Summer discusses in her *Damned Whores and God's Police* (1975). Wright, however, created images of women confronting the dangers of birth and of the descent into the underworld.

Myth also enabled her to recover the ceremonial intensities of childhood expressed in other poems in *Woman to Man*. These lines from "Child and Wattle-Tree" are typical:

> Round as the sun is the golden tree.
> Its honey dust sifts down amongst the light
> to cover me and my hot blood.

In these poems Wright was both renewing the visionary tradition of Romantics such as William Blake and creating a new "feminine" sense of reality, anticipating the work of later women writers by giving expression to the world of dreams, desires, and creativity, of the dimension within the self that exceeds rational consciousness.

The direction in which she next moved was even more contentious. The explosion of the first atomic bomb and the subsequent development of nuclear weapons appalled her, and the birth of a daughter, Meredith, in 1950, increased her sense of urgency, intensified by her sense of the body's vulnerability that had been with her since childhood. This awareness was the subject of her first memory: as a child she had wandered away from a family gathering, climbed a forbidden wood heap, and gashed her hand. As the "astoundingly red blood" flowed, she recalled in *Half a Lifetime*, a sudden self-awareness had gripped her. She was "alone, in pain and trapped in a life which I had now recognised would take me through, unstoppably, uncontrollably, until I was as old as my grandmother—and then I would die." Possessing a body, she realized (as the patriarchal Australian tradition does not), is precisely what people do and are. The crucial question was thus not how to conquer the world but—as she put it in "The Marks," a poem recalling this incident and written years later—how to "manage this trap / so ready to bleed?" to the end of her days.

It was a question underlined by several riding accidents she had suffered as a young woman and later by the experiences of pregnancy and giving birth, which remained with her and became more urgent as she grew older. The outbreak of the Korean War and the threat of a nuclear holocaust brought it before her with new intensity. Her next two collections, *The Gateway* (1953) and *The Two Fires* (1955), are filled with apprehension. "Two Songs For The World's End," in *The Gateway*, for instance, opens:

> Bombs ripen on the leafless tree
> under which the children play.
> And there my darling all alone
> dances in the spying day.

Seemingly straightforward, "The Bushfire," in *Woman to Man*, is the product of a double vision of the possibilities opened out by physics, "sub-linguistic," no longer human, which might nevertheless destroy humanity and the world of love and human feeling that she had been exploring in her earlier poems.

Wright was not always able to find images for this grim understanding, and a hortatory note began to sound, as in these lines from the title poem of *The Two Fires*:

> And now, set free by the climate of man's hate,
> that seed sets time ablaze.
> The leaves of fallen years, the forest of living days,

Dust jacket for Wright's 1949 book, poems inspired by her feelings for her future husband, Jack McKinney (Bruccoli Clark Layman Archives)

have caught like matchwood. Look, the whole world burns.

The tone is obviously declaratory, and some reviewers criticized her for sacrificing her poetry to her political concerns. Nevertheless, poetry had always been for her a way of working out where she stood, and she refused to see a poem in New Critical terms, as mere text separated from life. She felt this view would make poetry a marginal activity, and she was determined poetry should instead make a difference. She therefore believed that she had no choice but to write as she was doing: any worthwhile poetry "must come from the central core of one's living and feeling."

She was not alone in this sense of crisis. In the United States in particular, writers such as Sylvia Plath, Robert Lowell, Henry Miller, and William Faulkner were equally haunted by a sense of doom. In his Nobel Prize acceptance speech Faulkner declared, "There are no longer problems of the spirit. There is only the question: when will we be blown up?" Australia in the 1950s, however, was more complacent, and that was another reason why Wright's poems of this period generally were not so well received, though her growing reliance on Jungian thought in poems such as "Walker in Darkness" and "The Ancestor," both in *The Gateway*, may also have had something to do with it.

Living at Mount Tambourine not far from Brisbane, at a remove from public events, Wright and McKinney were exploring not only contemporary philosophy but also developments in mathematics and the sciences. As she wrote in "The Writer and the Crisis," an essay published in the short-lived magazine *Language* in 1952, "Events of vital importance are in the process of being understood and absorbed into human life-patterns." But this understanding and absorption depended to a large extent on the state of language. As she put it in the same essay: "If our world-picture is outgrown, it may be that some new and important insight is already beginning to shape itself behind the cracking shell of the old. Then language must somehow reconstellate itself to admit and express the new vision." The problem was how to carry out this reconstellation.

Wright had always been prepared to experiment and thought it important to move beyond the poems that had become popular if she were not to remain permanently at their level. There was also a political imperative, as she explained in "The Writer and the Crisis": "if language is our only tool for altering the view we hold of the world, then our world-view cannot be changed until the tool itself is altered." She was therefore giving a great deal of attention at this time to the question of language, poetic language in particular, since it alone gave access to the sources of thought and experience in the archaic and oneiric reaches of the unconscious that had become so important to her.

That focus was one of the reasons why Jung's influence was apparent. But this influence was not particularly helpful since it pushed the poetry in the direction of allegory, as in "The Lost Man" and "The Gateway." Barfield's *Poetic Diction* (1928), however, was probably more useful since it put the emphasis on the image. He argued, for instance, that "the faculty of image-making and of relation is also the faculty which brings into being any truly new insight, in whatever discipline." Wright was also becoming interested in the thought of French poet Francois Ponge, who insisted on the importance of looking closely at specific objects and through them making a "journey into the depth of things," thus "opening trapdoors in the inner self."

In this way the great question for Wright thus became not just what things are but what they mean, and many of the poems of this period, especially the poems about flowers and trees in *The Two Fires,* address themselves to this question. The first step, however, was the observation prayed for in "For Precision": "Let me be sure and economical as the rayed / suns, stars, flowers, wheels: let me fall as a gull, a hawk through the confusions of foggy talk." True, as the same poem expressed, this prayer could never be entirely answered, since it was impossible for human words to capture

> . . . the escaping wavering wandering light,
> the blur, the brilliance; forming into one chord
> what's separate and distracted, making the vague hard—
> catching the wraith.

"Nameless Flower," from *The Two Fires*, rehearses this struggle to name the unnameable, but with a lyrical delicacy:

> Three white petals float
> above the green . . .
> I'll set a word upon a word
> to be your home . . .
> . . . But before the trap is set
> the prey is gone.

Nevertheless, even though "reality" lies beyond language, so that the prey must always escape the trap, the struggle to name it must go on. This struggle in fact gives these poems their dramatic intensity since, as Barfield put it, a successful poem resembles a "ship that is wrecked on entering harbour."

But the task remained, to try to learn the language of things. If, as she put it in her essay in *Language*, "the word tree . . . is only a label" and "the tree seen, the momentous living event, slips through it as through a sieve," the attempt is still worth it, if only for the "idea which that particular sight of the tree brought to life." This idea need not always be abstruse, as the series of poems she wrote for her daughter, Meredith, published as the collection *Birds* (1962), makes clear.

At the same time Wright was becoming aware that other cultures, notably Aboriginal cultures, had been more successful in matching words to things. A camping trip through the Carnarvon ranges with McKinney and Meredith intensified this awareness. The Aboriginal languages of the place had now fallen silent. But she sensed they had been able to describe the land as English speakers cannot.

As one of "the conquerors" who had displaced them, therefore, she made a promise to continue their work to the extent that she could. In "Seven Songs for a Journey," collected in *The Two Fires*, she wrote:

> I will sing for you—
> each phrase
> the size of a stone;
> a red stone,
> a white stone,
> a grey, and a purple;
> a parrot's cry
> from a blossoming tree,
> a scale of water
> and wavering light.

True, it would, as she later told an interviewer, "take four or five hundred years for us to become indigenes." But the attempt must be made, for the sake of the people as well as the land. "At Cooloolan," a poem in the same collection, takes up this theme. The blue crane in a pool fishing at twilight "is the certain heir of lake and evening." As "a stranger, come of a conquering people," however, she feels "unloved by all my eyes delight in, / and made uneasy for an old murder's sake." The answer lies, however, in learning from "Those dark-skinned people" who once named Cooloola and who

> knew that no land is lost or won by wars,
> for earth is spirit: the invader's feet will tangle
> in nets there and his blood be thinned by fears.

From them, the poem concludes, one must come to understand that "we are justified only by love." Increasingly this love involved her in the struggles of Aboriginal people for justice, and her activism was intensified by her close friendship with Oodgeroo Noonuccal (Kath Walker), Aboriginal poet and activist, whom she met during this period.

The poems in *The Two Fires* were difficult to write. As she told a friend, "If you are writing something people can't and don't want to understand, it's a bit discouraging. Anyway I did the best I could, I suppose." But *Birds* helped to release her, as in these poems she shared a child's ability to identify with the living world and thus recovered some of the ease and trust in the world of her earlier poetry.

Perhaps as a result of this release, in the next collection, *Five Senses* (1963), human figures return. The poems are also less impersonal, expressing Wright's feeling for and delight in the earth as "a sad yet glittering star / bodied in beast and man and bird" ("A Child's Nightmare"). But there are also poems for her schoolgirl daughter, and poems about local identities such as Wright's bachelor uncle, all part of the continuing battle between "old Chaos and the shaping Word" ("A Child's Nightmare"). This battle also underlies the sequence "The Morning of the Dead," which tells of a journey north to the grave of her grandfather—another attempt to reconnect with her ancestors following her prose history *The Generations Of Men*, first published in 1959, which had its genesis in some old papers she had discovered during the time she spent in New England in 1942 and 1943. "The Morning of the Dead," however, pushes beyond historical fact into the world of myth.

Wright's husband and their daughter, Meredith, 1950 (from Brady, South of My Days, *1998)*

As she stands by his grave, meaning "travels on / into new territory past touch or sight– / is dark entreating light." The pressure this sense of mortality involved is evident in the poem that precedes this sequence, "Reading Thomas Traherne":

> Can I lose myself,
> and losing find one word
> that, in the face of what you were,
> needs to be said or heard ?

The word needs to be spoken in the face of the mortality she is exploring.

The Other Half (1966) continues in the same vein, but with a new assurance, despite the fact that her energies were increasingly taken up by the battle to save the Australian rain forest, as she and McKinney watched the developers moving into it after ravaging the Gold Coast below. She was also heavily involved, largely for financial reasons, with lectures and critical writing. These critical works, however, were never mere potboilers. Her study of Charles Harpur, which appeared in 1963, for instance, is obviously energized by the passion for justice she found in his work. Similarly, in *Preoccupations in Australian Poetry* she wrote eloquently about poets such as Christopher Brennan, who tackled the large questions of meaning and value that preoccupied her.

"Shadow," however, the final section in *Collected Poems, 1942–1970* (1971), marks a decisive break: McKinney had died in 1966. Apart from the profound sense of personal loss, his death meant the end of any dream she might still have cherished of molding the world to personal desire. As a child she had had to watch her mother moving away from her toward death, "fighting increasing pain" ("Wedding Photograph"). Many of the poems in "Shadow" watch McKinney also moving away as he grew increasingly frail; but they also celebrate the journey she and her husband had made together. In "For One Dying," despite the fact that "All human lives betray" and "all human love erodes / under time's laser ray," the poet still vows to

> Renew the central dream
> in blazing purity,
> and let my rags confirm
> and robe eternity.
> For still the angel leads.
> Ruined yet pure we go
> with all our days and deeds
> into that flame and snow.

Looking ahead, the poet determines still to put herself to the "singing school" of her art, a monument of "the spirit's significance" in a time that seemed to her increasingly barbarous. She must, however, do it alone now–"I am only I, as I was you" ("The Vision"), and for the moment poetry could not answer her deepest need: "Instruments have no song / except the living breath" ("Love Song In Absence"). Nor could it tame the savage energies of the world: "incomprehensible energy / creates us and destroys; all words are made / in the long shadow of eternity."

These destructive energies seemed to be raging also in contemporary history, with the war in Vietnam and the violent protests against it (some of which she witnessed at the International Poetry Conference in Montreal in 1967), uprisings in Eastern Europe, and the riots in Paris (which she also saw firsthand on her trip to Europe the next year with Meredith). At home, too, there was a growing sense of the threat of environmental disaster expressed in the despairing anger of poems such as "Australia 1970," which opens:

> Die, wild country, like the eaglehawk,
> dangerous till the last breath's gone,
> clawing and striking. Die
> cursing your captor through a raging eye.

Some critics found such poems excessive. But the passion that inspires them is also deeply personal, the pain of love betrayed and the desolation of loss.

More of Wright's time and energy now went into battles to save the Great Barrier Reef; to oppose the new supersonic aircraft, the Concorde (because of the threat it posed to the environment); to preserve the rain forests; and, increasingly important, to support her Aboriginal friends in their struggles. Elated by the federal election of the Labor Party under Gough Whitlam in 1972, which led to a government that seemed to be concerned about these issues, she therefore decided to leave Queensland. She moved south to Canberra, then to Braidwood, a town within driving distance, and then finally to a block of land she bought near the Shoalhaven River, where she built the house in which she hoped to spend her last years in the midst of nature.

It was difficult to settle down, however, especially when she was appointed to the Inquiry into the National Estate that the government set up. This position entailed a great deal of travel throughout Australia to compile a register. She was also appointed to the newly created Literature Board of the Australia Council, chaired by the distinguished public servant Herbert Cole "Nugget" Coombs, who became a friend. Nevertheless, she found time to write the poems that appeared in a new collection, *Alive*, published in 1973. That she was still writing poetry in the midst of all her other activities, she told a friend, was "cheering." But in a sense it was also necessary, a way of taking stock and giving shape to the shapelessness of contemporary history she felt around her.

The first poem in this new volume, a sequence titled "Habitat," makes her farewells to "Calanthe," the mountain home in which she and McKinney had lived for so long, and looks back over those years with gratitude. But it also accepts the inevitability of change. The old wooden house becomes an image to match her body, which is no longer young. The humor in this poem marks a new detachment, evident also in the self-irony of "To Mary Gilmore," in which Wright describes herself setting off to one of the many conferences she had to attend at the time:

> Having arranged for the mail and stopped the papers,
> tied loaves of bread Orlando-like to the tree,
> love-messages for birds; suitcase in hand
> I pause and regard the irony of me.
> Supposed to be fifty six, hair certainly grey,
> stepping out like sixteen on another journey.

The "intolerable wrestle with meaning," the struggle with words and things, seems in this volume to be giving way to a certain calm. In retrospect, however, it appears that the poems in this collection rather represent a kind of holding operation, seeking, as the title of one poem suggests, some "Good News" in growing older.

The poems in her next volume, *Fourth Quarter and Other Poems* (1976), are about facing and moving into the last stage of life. Nevertheless, she greets it with her former energy, as in the title poem:

> You bitter sign,
> last lemon-quarter grin,
> tell me to throw it in?
> I won't resign.

Determined to play the game to the end, she prays to the moon in "Easter Moon and Owl":

> ruler of women
> and singler out of poets
> a defiant prayer:
> . . . In my last quarter
> let me be hag, but poet.
> The lyric note may vanish from my verse,
> but you have also found acceptable
> the witch's spell–even the witch's curse.

The season she was entering was no longer spring but winter, the season of the crone. But she would "choose fire, not snow," as she wrote in "Oppositions," and live this last stage with style.

In these poems Wright also continued the struggle to express the inexpressible. The structure of the collection helped in this task: poems about a descent into a dark underworld of dream and archaic memory, such as the three "Interface" poems, are set against poems about the more immediate world, such as "The Dark Ones," about the pain of Aboriginal people and whites' fear of them, or "Cold Night," about a strangely melancholy

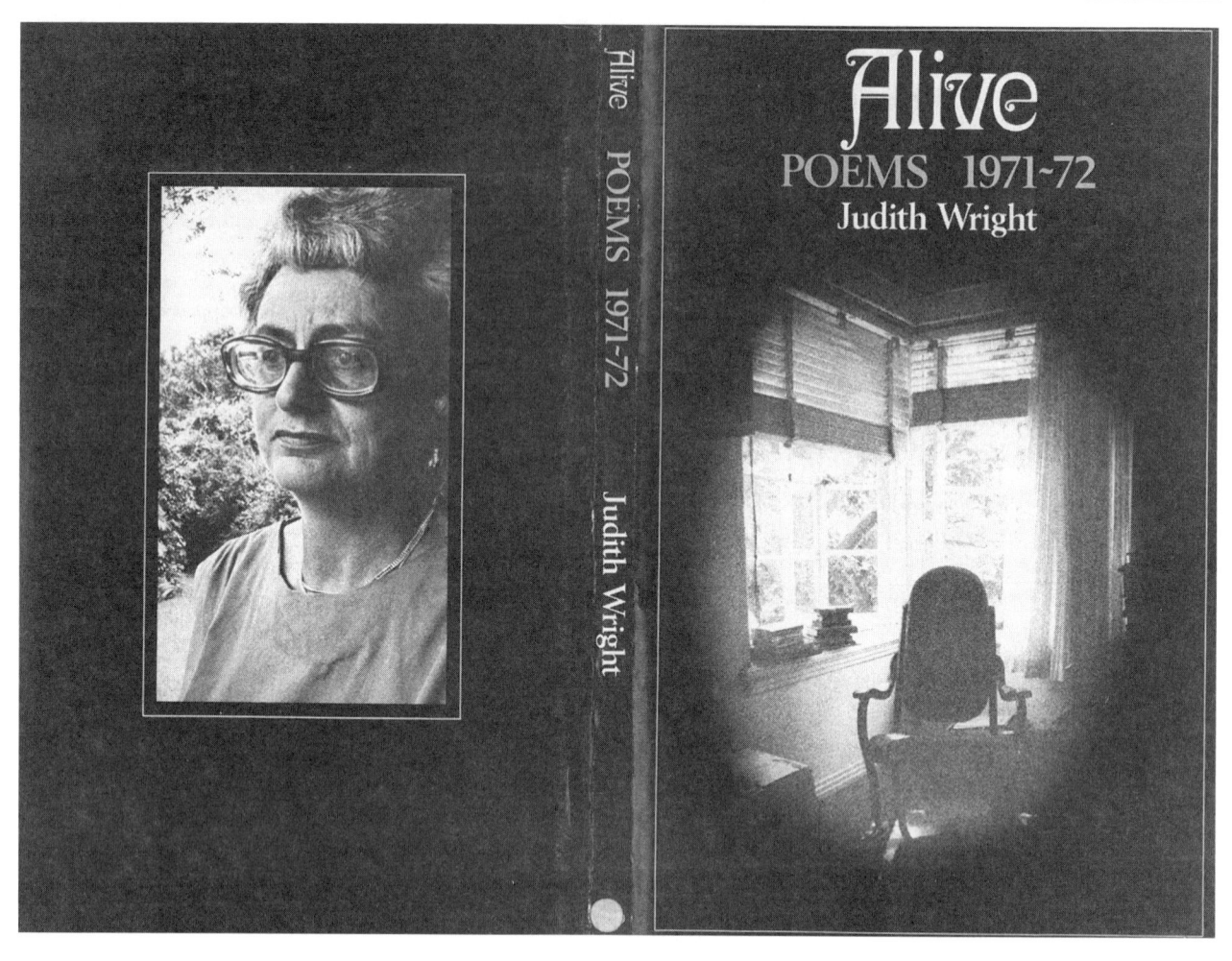

Dust jacket for Wright's 1973 book, which includes the poem sequence "Habitat," her farewell to the house in which she and McKinney lived throughout their marriage (Bruccoli Clark Layman Archives)

erotic encounter. There are poems about family and personal memory and a tribute to the recently deceased young poet Michael Dransfield that sets his tragic flamboyance against the drab rulers of the present world. Running through all these poems, however, is an austere dedication to the art of writing as well as of living, as in "For M. R.":

> When all the living's done
> it's the poems that remain.
> All that is personal, said Yeats,
> soon rots
> unless it's packed in ice and salt.

Phantom Dwelling, Wright's last volume, appeared in 1985, her seventieth year. On her birthday she announced that she would write no more poetry: she had too much to do elsewhere. She and Coombs were campaigning for a treaty with Aboriginal Australians, and she was also working for the environment, world peace, and many other causes; and her health was failing. Always hard of hearing, she had now become completely deaf, was threatened with blindness, and was growing increasingly lame–a consequence of her old riding accident. The energy that she had put into her poetry was declining, and she wanted to conserve it for the many causes and people she cared for.

Phantom Dwelling, however, was a monumental and wide-ranging conclusion to her career. It includes a sequence about a lecture tour of New Zealand, paying tribute to its beauty but pledging herself to return to her own country: "I go back to my loves, my proper winter" ("Four Poems From New Zealand," IV). A poem on family memory and history, "For A Pastoral Family" recalls the different world of the past. There is also a tribute to the poet Christopher Brennan, whom she saw as a "walker on earth's last fringes, / haunted lover / of the beckoning darkness, / last Symbolist, poor hero / lost looking for yourself."

The volume concludes with a series of poems about the natural world and its creatures around her at

"Edge," in which she sets her own life in the context of the immemorial life of the world. Experimenting with the form of the ghazal, used by ancient Persian poets such as Hafiz, whom she had long admired, she confronted the energies of creation and destruction in "Pressures," accepting yet raging still:

> Gravity's drag, time's wear, keep pressing downwards, moving loose stones downslope, sinking hills like wet meringue.
> I move more slowly this year, neck falling in folds, pulses more visible; yet there's still a thrust in the arteries.
> Blood slows, thickens, silts—yet when I saw you once again, what a joy set this pulse jumping.

"Patterns," the final poem in the volume and in her *Collected Poems: 1942–1985* (1994), ends looking out over the world into the threatening darkness.

Wright lived for another decade, battling increasing frailty but continuing to fight for the environment, for justice for Aboriginal Australians, and for an end to international violence. She died on 25 June 2000 after suffering a heart attack. Not long before her death Wright received the A. A. Phillips Award, given to writers deemed to have made an outstanding contribution to Australian literature. The citation for the award summed up her achievement: "In her writing Judith Wright has gone a long way to the creation of an Australian identity fully cognisant of the past and the present, the individual and the community, women and men, love and hate and above all the relationship between the environment and its inhabitants."

Interview:
Marion Firth, Interview with Judith Wright, *Canberra Times*, 19 March 1994.

Bibliography:
Shirley Walker, *Judith Wright*, Australian Bibliographies (Melbourne: Oxford University Press, 1981).

Biography:
Veronica Brady, *South of My Days: A Biography of Judith Wright* (Sydney: Angus & Robertson, 1998).

References:
R. F. Brissenden, "Five Senses: Judith Wright," *Australian Literary Quarterly*, 36, no. 1 (1964): 85–91;

Vincent Buckley, "The Poetry of Judith Wright," in *Essays In Poetry, Mainly Australian*, edited by A. K. Thompson (Melbourne: Melbourne University Press, 1957), pp. 158–176;

A. D. Hope, *Judith Wright*, Australian Writers and Their Work (Melbourne: Oxford University Press, 1975);

Lynne Strahan, *Just City and the Mirrors: Meanjin Quarterly and the Intellectual Front, 1940–1965* (Melbourne: Oxford University Press, 1984).

Papers:
The largest and most comprehensive collection of Judith Wright's letters and papers is held in the National Library of Australia, Canberra. The National Library also holds the oral history recorded with her in the 1980s. The *Meanjin* papers in the Baillieu Library of the University of Melbourne include correspondence between Wright and C. B. Christesen. The Fryer Library of the University of Queensland holds a collection of letters from Wright to the poet John Bligh. The archives of the Wildlife Protection Society in Brisbane include material about Wright's environmental concerns and activities from the 1950s to the 1970s.

Checklist of Further Readings

Adelaide, Debra. *Australian Women Writers: A Bibliographic Guide.* London: Pandora Press, 1988.

Beasley, Jack. *Socialism and the Novel: A Study of Australian Literature.* Sydney: Privately printed, 1957.

Bennett, Bruce, ed. *An Australian Compass: Essays on Place and Direction in Australian Literature.* South Fremantle, W.A.: Fremantle Arts Centre Press, 1991.

Bennett and Jennifer Strauss, eds. *The Oxford Literary History of Australia.* Melbourne: Oxford University Press, 1998.

Bird, Delys, Robert Dixon, and Christopher Lee, eds. *Authority and Influence: Australian Literary Criticism 1950–2000.* St. Lucia: Queensland University Press, 2001.

Brissenden, Alan, ed. *Aspects of Australian Literature.* Nedlands, W.A.: University of Western Australia Press, 1990.

Brooks, D., and B. Walker, eds. *Poetry and Gender: Statements and Essays in Australian Women's Poetry and Poetics.* St. Lucia: Queensland University Press, 1989.

Brown, Cyril. *Writing for Australia: A Nationalist Tradition in Australian Literature?* Melbourne: Hawthorn Press, 1956.

Buckley, Vincent. *Cutting Green Hay: Friendships, Movements and Cultural Conflicts in Australia's Great Decades.* Melbourne: Allen Lane/Penguin, 1983.

Burgmann, Verity, and Jenny Lee, eds. *Making a Life: A People's History of Australia Since 1788.* Ringwood, Vic.: McPhee Gribble/Penguin, 1988.

Burns, D. R. *The Directions of Australian Fiction 1920–1974.* Melbourne: Cassell, 1975.

Cantrell, Leon, ed. *Bards, Bohemians, and Bookmen: Essays in Australian Literature.* St. Lucia: Queensland University Press, 1976.

Carroll, Dennis. *Australian Contemporary Drama 1909–1982: A Critical Introduction.* New York: Peter Lang, 1985.

Carroll, John, ed. *Intruders in the Bush: The Australian Quest for Identity.* Melbourne: Oxford University Press, 1992.

Clancy, Laurie. *A Reader's Guide to Australian Fiction.* Melbourne: Oxford University Press, 1992.

Clark, Manning. *A History of Australia.* Carlton, Vic.: Melbourne University Press, 1962.

Clark. *A History of Australia,* volume 3. Carlton, Vic.: Melbourne University Press, 1973.

Clark. *A Short History of Australia.* New York: New American Library, 1963.

Colmer, John. *Australian Autobiography: The Personal Quest.* Melbourne: Oxford University Press, 1989.

Croft, Julian. *The Federal and National Impulse in Australia, 1890–1958*. Townsville, Qld.: Foundation for Australian Literary Studies, 1989.

Cromwell, Alex, ed. *From Outback to City: Changing Preoccupations in Australian Literature of the Twentieth Century*. Brooklyn, N.Y.: American Association of Australian Literary Studies, 1988.

Dever, Maryanne, ed. *Wallflowers and Witches: Women and Culture in Australia 1910–1945*. St. Lucia: Queensland University Press, 1994.

Dixon, Miriam. *The Real Matilda: Women and Identity in Australia*. Ringwood, Vic.: Penguin, 1976.

Docker, John. *Australian Cultural Elites: Intellectual Traditions in Sydney and Melbourne*. Sydney: Angus & Robertson, 1974.

Docker. *In a Critical Condition*. Ringwood, Vic.: Penguin, 1984.

Dutton, Geoffrey. *Snow on the Saltbush: The Australian Literary Experience*. Ringwood, Vic.: Viking/Penguin, 1984.

Dutton, ed. *The Literature of Australia*. Ringwood, Vic.: Penguin, 1964.

Duwell, Martin, Marianne Ehrhardt, and Carol Hetherington, eds. *The ALS Guide to Australian Writers: A Bibliography 1963–1995*. St. Lucia: Queensland University Press, 1997.

Eaden, P. R., and F. H. Mares, eds. *Mapped but Not Known: The Australian Landscape of the Imagination*. Netley, S.A.: Wakefield Press, 1986.

Edwards, Brian, and Wenche Ommundsen, eds. *Appreciating Difference: Writing Postcolonial Literary History*. Geelong, Vic.: Deakin University Press, 1998.

Eldershaw, M. Barnard. *Essays on Australian Fiction*. Melbourne: Melbourne University Press, 1938.

Ewers, John Keith. *Creative Writing in Australia*. Melbourne: Georgian House, 1962.

Ferres, Kay, ed. *The Time to Write: Australian Women Writers 1890–1930*. Ringwood, Vic.: Penguin, 1993.

Ferrier, Carole, ed. *Gender, Politics and Fiction*. St. Lucia: Queensland University Press, 1985.

Ferrier, ed. *As Good as a Yarn with You: Letters between Miles Franklin, Katharine Susannah Prichard, Jean Devanny, Marjorie Barnard, Flora Eldershaw and Eleanor Dark*. Cambridge: Cambridge University Press, 1992.

Fitzpatrick, Peter. *After "The Doll": Australian Drama Since 1955*. Melbourne: Edward Arnold Australia, 1979.

Fotheringham, Richard. *Sport in Australian Drama*. Cambridge: Cambridge University Press, 1992.

Frost, Lucy, ed. *No Place for a Nervous Lady: Voices from the Australian Bush*. Ringwood, Vic.: McPhee Gribble/Penguin, 1984.

Gerster, Robin. *Big-Noting: The Heroic Theme in Australian War Writing*. Carlton, Vic.: Melbourne University Press, 1987.

Gibson, Ross. *The Diminishing Paradise: Changing Literary Perceptions of Australia*. Sydney: Sirius Books, 1984.

Goodwin, Ken. *A History of Australian Literature*. Basingstoke, U.K.: Macmillan, 1986.

Green, H. M. *Australian Literature: 1900–1950*. Melbourne: Melbourne University Press, 1951.

Green. *A History of Australian Literature*. Sydney: Angus & Robertson, 1961.

Gunew, Sneja. *Framing Marginality: Multicultural Literary Studies*. Melbourne: Melbourne University Press, 1994.

Hadgraft, Cecil. *Australian Literature: A Critical Account to 1955*. Melbourne: Heinemann, 1960.

Harris, Margaret, and Elizabeth Webby, eds. *Reconnoitres: Essays in Australian Literature in Honour of G. A. Wilkes*. Sydney: Sydney University Press/Oxford University Press, 1992.

Head, Brian, and James Walter, eds. *Intellectual Movements and Australian Society*. Melbourne: Oxford University Press, 1988.

Healy, J. J. *Literature and the Aborigine in Australia 1770-1975*. New York: St. Martin's Press, 1979.

Hergenhan, Laurie. *Unnatural Lives: Studies in Australian Fiction about the Convicts, from James Tucker to Patrick White*. St. Lucia: Queensland University Press, 1983.

Hergenhan, ed. *The Penguin New Literary History of Australia*. Ringwood, Vic.: Penguin, 1988.

Heseltine, Harry. *The Uncertain Self: Essays in Australian Literature and Criticism*. Melbourne: Oxford University Press, 1986.

Hodge, Bob, and Vijay Mishra, eds. *The Dark Side of the Dream: Australian Literature and the Postcolonial Mind*. Sydney: Allen & Unwin, 1991.

Holloway, Peter, ed. *Contemporary Australian Drama: Perspectives Since 1955*. Sydney: Currency Press, 1981.

Hooton, Joy. *Stories of Herself When Young: Autobiographies of Childhood by Australian Women*. Melbourne: Oxford University Press, 1990.

Hope, A. D. *Australian Literature 1950-1962*. Melbourne: Melbourne University Press, 1963.

Jones, Joseph, and Johanna Jones. *Australian Fiction*. Boston: Twayne, 1983.

Kane, Paul. *Australian Poetry: Romanticism and Negativity*. Melbourne: Cambridge University Press, 1996.

Kiernan, Brian. *Images of Society and Nature: Seven Essays on Australian Novels*. Melbourne: Oxford University Press, 1971.

Kiernan. *Studies in Australian Literary History*. Sydney: Sydney Association for Studies in Society and Culture, 1997.

Kirkpatrick, Peter. *The Sea Coast of Bohemia: Literary Life in Sydney's Roaring Twenties*. St. Lucia: Queensland University Press, 1992.

Kramer, Leonie, ed. *My Country: Australian Poetry and Short Stories, Two Hundred Years*. 2 volumes. Sydney: Lansdowne Press, 1985.

Kramer, ed. *The Oxford History of Australian Literature*. Melbourne: Oxford University Press, 1981.

Lake, Marilyn. "The Politics of Respectability: Identifying the Masculinist Context," *Historical Studies*, 22, no. 86 (1986): 116-131.

Lindsay, Norman. *Bohemians of the Bulletin*. Sydney: Angus & Robertson, 1965.

Lock, Fred, and Alan Lawson. *Australian Literature–A Reference Guide*. Melbourne: Oxford University Press, 1977.

Lumb, Peter, and Anne Hazell. *Diversity and Diversion: An Annotated Bibliography of Australian Ethnic Minority Literature.* Richmond, Vic.: Hodja Educational Resources, 1983.

Macartney, Frederick T. *A Historical Outline of Australian Literature.* Sydney: Angus & Robertson, 1957.

McAuley, James. *The Personal Element in Australian Poetry.* Sydney: Angus & Robertson, 1970.

McCooey, David. *Artful Histories: Modern Australian Autobiography.* Melbourne: Cambridge University Press, 1996.

McKernan, Susan, *A Question of Commitment: Australian Literature in the Twenty Years after the War.* Sydney: Allen & Unwin, 1989.

McLaren, John. *Australian Literature: An Historical Introduction.* Melbourne: Longman Cheshire, 1989.

McLaren. *Writing in Hope and Fear: Literature as Politics in Postwar Australia.* Cambridge: Cambridge University Press, 1996.

Miller, E. Morris. *Australian Literature: A Bibliography to 1938.* Melbourne: Melbourne University Press, 1940.

Miller. *Australian Literature: A Bibliography to 1938, Extended to 1950,* revised and enlarged edition, edited by Macartney. Sydney: Angus & Robertson, 1956.

Miller. *Australian Literature from Its Beginnings to 1935.* Sydney: Sydney University Press, 1975.

Miller. *Pressmen and Governors.* Sydney: Sydney University Press, 1973.

Modjeska, Drusilla. *Exiles at Home: Australian Women Writers 1925–1945.* London & Sydney: Sirius Books, 1981.

Ommundsen, and Hazel Rowley, eds. *From a Distance: Australian Writers and Cultural Displacement.* Geelong, Vic.: Deakin University Press, 1996.

Palmer, Nettie. *Modern Australian Literature (1900–1923).* Melbourne: Lothian, 1924.

Pfisterer, Susan, and Carolyn Pickett. *Playing with Ideas: Australian Women Playwrights from the Suffragettes to the Sixties.* Sydney: Currency Press, 1999.

Pfisterer, ed. *Tremendous Worlds: Australian Women's Drama 1890–1960.* Sydney: Currency Press, 1999.

Phillips, A. A. *The Australian Tradition: Studies in a Colonial Culture.* Melbourne: Longman Cheshire, 1958.

Pierce, Peter, ed. *Oxford Literary Guide to Australia.* Melbourne: Oxford University Press, 1987.

Quartermaine, Peter, ed. *Diversity Itself: Essays in Australian Arts and Culture.* Exeter, U.K.: University of Exeter, 1986.

Ramson, W. S. *The Australian Experience: Critical Essays on Australian Novels.* Canberra: Australian National University Press, 1974.

Rees, Leslie. *A History of Australian Drama,* volume 1. Sydney: Angus & Robertson, 1978.

Rees. *Towards an Australian Drama.* Sydney: Angus & Robertson, 1953.

Reid, Ian. *Fiction and the Great Depression: Australia and New Zealand 1930–1950.* Melbourne: Edward Arnold, 1979.

Roderick, Colin. *An Introduction to Australian Fiction.* Sydney: Angus & Robertson, 1950.

Roe, Jill, ed. *My Congenials: Miles Franklin and Friends in Letters*. 2 volumes. Sydney: State Library of New South Wales/ Angus & Robertson, 1993.

Ross, Robert L. *Australian Literary Criticism 1945–1988: An Annotated Bibliography*. New York: Garland, 1989.

Schaffer, Kay. *Women and the Bush: Forces of Desire in the Australian Cultural Tradition*. Cambridge: Cambridge University Press, 1988.

Semmler, Clement, ed. *Twentieth Century Australian Literary Criticism*. Melbourne: Oxford University Press, 1967.

Sheridan, Susan. *Along the Faultlines: Sex, Race and Nation in Australian Women's Writing 1880s–1930s*. Sydney: Allen & Unwin, 1995.

Shoemaker, Adam, ed. *Black Words, White Page: Aboriginal Literature 1929–1988*. St. Lucia: Queensland University Press, 1989.

Slessor, Kenneth. *The Australian Author*. Sydney: Fellowship of Australian Writers, 1935.

Smith, Bernard W. *Australian Painting 1788–1960*. London: Oxford University Press, 1962.

Souter, Gavin. *Company of Heralds: A Century and a Half of Australian Publishing*. Melbourne: Melbourne University Press, 1981.

Spender, Dale, ed. *The Penguin Anthology of Australian Women's Writing*. Ringwood, Vic.: Penguin, 1988.

Stephensen, P. R. *The Foundations of Culture in Australia: An Essay towards National Self-Respect,* introduction by Craig Munro, revised and enlarged edition. Sydney: Allen & Unwin, 1986.

Stewart, Douglas. *The Broad Stream: Aspects of Australian Literature*. Sydney: Angus & Robertson, 1975.

Stewart. *The Flesh and the Spirit: An Outlook on Literature*. Sydney: Angus & Robertson, 1948.

Stewart. *Writers of The Bulletin: 1977 Boyer Lectures*. Sydney: Australian Broadcasting Commission, 1977.

Stewart, Ken. *The 1890s: Australian Literature and Literary Culture*. St. Lucia: Queensland University Press, 1996.

Summers, Anne. *Damned Whores and God's Police: The Colonization of Women in Australia*. Ringwood, Vic.: Penguin, 1975.

Turner, Henry Gyles, and Alexander Sutherland. *The Development of Australian Literature*. Sydney: George Robertson, 1898.

Walker, David. *Dream and Disillusion: A Search for Australian Cultural Identity*. Canberra: Australian National University Press, 1976.

Walker, Shirley, ed. *Who Is She?* St. Lucia: Queensland University Press, 1983.

Wallace-Crabbe, Chris. *Melbourne or the Bush: Essays on Australian Literature and Society*. Sydney: Angus & Robertson, 1974.

Wallace-Crabbe, ed. *The Australian Nationalists: Modern Critical Essays*. Melbourne: Oxford University Press, 1971.

Ward, Russel. *The Australian Legend*. Melbourne: Oxford University Press, 1958.

Checklist of Further Readings

Webb, Janeen, and Andrew Enstice. *Aliens and Savages: Fiction, Politics and Prejudice in Australia.* Sydney: HarperCollins, 1998.

Webby, ed. *The Cambridge Companion to Australian Literature.* Oakleigh, Vic.: Cambridge University Press, 2000.

White, Richard. *Inventing Australia: Images and Identity 1688–1980.* Sydney: Allen & Unwin, 1981.

Whitlock, Gillian, and David Carter, eds. *Images of Australia: A Reader.* St. Lucia: Queensland University Press, 1992.

Wilde, William H., Hooton, and Barry Andrews, eds. *The Oxford Companion to Australian Literature.* Melbourne: Oxford University Press, 1985.

Wilding, Michael. *Studies in Classic Australian Fiction.* Sydney: Sydney Association for Studies in Society and Culture, 1997.

Wilkes, G. A. *Australian Literature: A Conspectus.* Sydney: Angus & Robertson, 1969.

Wilkes. *The Stockyard and the Croquet Lawn: Literary Evidence for Australia's Cultural Development.* Melbourne: Edward Arnold, 1981.

Wright, Judith. *Preoccupations in Australian Poetry.* Melbourne: Oxford University Press, 1965.

Contributors

Michael Ackland	Monash University
Bill Ashcroft	University of New South Wales
Marie Louise Ayres	National Library of Australia
Bruce Bennett	University of New South Wales
Delys Bird	University of Western Australia
Veronica Brady	University of Western Australia
Barbara Brooks	Marrickville, New South Wales
Philip Butterss	University of Adelaide
Adrian Caesar	University College, University of New South Wales, Australian Defence Force Academy
C. A. Cranston	University of Tasmania
Julian Croft	University of New England, Australia
Robert Darby	Curtin, Western Australia
Maryanne Dever	Monash University
Carole Ferrier	University of Queensland
Peter Fitzpatrick	Monash University
Paul Genoni	Curtin University of Technology
Don Grant	Curtin University of Technology
Frances de Groen	University of Western Sydney
Anthony Hassall	James Cook University
Harry Heseltine	Emeritus Professor, University of New South Wales
Deborah Jordan	University of Melbourne
Josephine Jill Kinnane	West Brunswick, Victoria
Susan Lever	University College, University of New South Wales, Australian Defence Force Academy
Justin Lucas	Victoria University
David McCooey	Deakin University
John McLaren	Victoria University
Joanne McPherson	Shellharbour, New South Wales
Philip Mead	University of Tasmania
Marilla North	University of Queensland
James Packer	Workers Educational Association Sydney
Brigid Rooney	University of Sydney
Richard Rossiter	Edith Cowan University
Robert Sellick	Woollahra, New South Wales
Vivian Smith	University of Sydney
Jennifer Strauss	Monash University
Ian Syson	Victoria University
Nadia Wheatley	Hurlstone Park, New South Wales

Cumulative Index

Dictionary of Literary Biography, Volumes 1-260
Dictionary of Literary Biography Yearbook, 1980-2001
Dictionary of Literary Biography Documentary Series, Volumes 1-19
Concise Dictionary of American Literary Biography, Volumes 1-7
Concise Dictionary of British Literary Biography, Volumes 1-8
Concise Dictionary of World Literary Biography, Volumes 1-4

Cumulative Index

DLB before number: *Dictionary of Literary Biography,* Volumes 1-260
Y before number: *Dictionary of Literary Biography Yearbook,* 1980-2001
DS before number: *Dictionary of Literary Biography Documentary Series,* Volumes 1-19
CDALB before number: *Concise Dictionary of American Literary Biography,* Volumes 1-7
CDBLB before number: *Concise Dictionary of British Literary Biography,* Volumes 1-8
CDWLB before number: *Concise Dictionary of World Literary Biography,* Volumes 1-4

A

Aakjær, Jeppe 1866-1930 ....DLB-214
Abbey, Edward 1927-1989.............DLB-256
Abbey, Edwin Austin 1852-1911.......DLB-188
Abbey, Maj. J. R. 1894-1969 ....DLB-201
Abbey Press......................DLB-49
The Abbey Theatre and Irish Drama,
 1900-1945 .... DLB-10
Abbot, Willis J. 1863-1934.............DLB-29
Abbott, Jacob 1803-1879 ....DLB-1, 243
Abbott, Lee K. 1947- DLB-130
Abbott, Lyman 1835-1922.............DLB-79
Abbott, Robert S. 1868-1940 ....DLB-29, 91
Abe Kōbō 1924-1993.................DLB-182
Abelard, Peter circa 1079-1142?.....DLB-115, 208
Abelard-Schuman....................DLB-46
Abell, Arunah S. 1806-1888............DLB-43
Abell, Kjeld 1901-1961...............DLB-214
Abercrombie, Lascelles 1881-1938........DLB-19
Aberdeen University Press Limited   DLB-106
Abish, Walter 1931- DLB-130, 227
Ablesimov, Aleksandr Onisimovich
 1742-1783......................DLB-150
Abraham à Sancta Clara 1644-1709......DLB-168
Abrahams, Peter
 1919- DLB-117, 225; CDWLB-3
Abrams, M. H. 1912- DLB-67
Abramson, Jesse 1904-1979 ....DLB-241
Abrogans circa 790-800 ....DLB-148
Abschatz, Hans Aßmann von
 1646-1699......................DLB-168
Abse, Dannie 1923- DLB-27, 245
Abutsu-ni 1221-1283 ....DLB-203
Academy Chicago Publishers DLB-46
Accius circa 170 B.C.-circa 80 B.C. DLB-211
Accrocca, Elio Filippo 1923- DLB-128
Ace Books.......................DLB-46
Achebe, Chinua 1930- DLB-117; CDWLB-3
Achtenberg, Herbert 1938-...........DLB-124
Ackerman, Diane 1948- DLB-120
Ackroyd, Peter 1949- DLB-155, 231

Acorn, Milton 1923-1986...............DLB-53
Acosta, Oscar Zeta 1935?- DLB-82
Acosta Torres, José 1925- DLB-209
Actors Theatre of Louisville DLB-7
Adair, Gilbert 1944- DLB-194
Adair, James 1709?-1783?...............DLB-30
Adam, Graeme Mercer 1839-1912 ....DLB-99
Adam, Robert Borthwick II 1863-1940 ...DLB-187
Adame, Leonard 1947- DLB-82
Adameşteanu, Gabriel 1942- DLB-232
Adamic, Louis 1898-1951 ....DLB-9
Adams, Abigail 1744-1818 ....DLB-200
Adams, Alice 1926-1999 .... DLB-234; Y-86
Adams, Bertha Leith (Mrs. Leith Adams,
 Mrs. R. S. de Courcy Laffan)
 1837?-1912 ....DLB-240
Adams, Brooks 1848-1927 ....DLB-47
Adams, Charles Francis, Jr. 1835-1915 ....DLB-47
Adams, Douglas 1952- Y-83
Adams, Franklin P. 1881-1960...........DLB-29
Adams, Hannah 1755-1832 ....DLB-200
Adams, Henry 1838-1918 ...... DLB-12, 47, 189
Adams, Herbert Baxter 1850-1901 ....DLB-17
Adams, J. S. and C. [publishing house] DLB-49
Adams, James Truslow
 1878-1949 .... DLB-17; DS-17
Adams, John 1735-1826............DLB-31, 183
Adams, John 1735-1826 and
 Adams, Abigail 1744-1818............DLB-183
Adams, John Quincy 1767-1848..........DLB-37
Adams, Léonie 1899-1988..............DLB-48
Adams, Levi 1802-1832................DLB-99
Adams, Samuel 1722-1803..........DLB-31, 43
Adams, Sarah Fuller Flower
 1805-1848.....................DLB-199
Adams, Thomas 1582 or 1583-1652 .....DLB-151
Adams, William Taylor 1822-1897 ....DLB-42
Adamson, Sir John 1867-1950 ....DLB-98
Adcock, Arthur St. John 1864-1930......DLB-135
Adcock, Betty 1938- DLB-105
"Certain Gifts"....................DLB-105
Adcock, Fleur 1934- DLB-40

Addison, Joseph 1672-1719 ...DLB-101; CDBLB-2
Ade, George 1866-1944.............DLB-11, 25
Adeler, Max (see Clark, Charles Heber)
Adonias Filho 1915-1990...............DLB-145
Adorno, Theodor W. 1903-1969........DLB-242
Advance Publishing Company DLB-49
Ady, Endre 1877-1919 ...... DLB-215; CDWLB-4
AE 1867-1935 ....DLB-19; CDBLB-5
Ælfric circa 955-circa 1010.............DLB-146
Aeschines
 circa 390 B.C.-circa 320 B.C. DLB-176
Aeschylus 525-524 B.C.-456-455 B.C.
 .... DLB-176; CDWLB-1
Afro-American Literary Critics:
 An Introduction DLB-33
After Dinner Opera Company............. Y-92
Agassiz, Elizabeth Cary 1822-1907 ......DLB-189
Agassiz, Louis 1807-1873 ....DLB-1, 235
Agee, James
 1909-1955 .... DLB-2, 26, 152; CDALB-1
The Agee Legacy: A Conference at the University
 of Tennessee at Knoxville............. Y-89
Aguilera Malta, Demetrio 1909-1981 ....DLB-145
Ahlin, Lars 1915-1997 ....DLB-257
Ai 1947- DLB-120
Aichinger, Ilse 1921- DLB-85
Aidoo, Ama Ata 1942- DLB-117; CDWLB-3
Aiken, Conrad
 1889-1973 ....DLB-9, 45, 102; CDALB-5
Aiken, Joan 1924-   DLB-161
Aikin, Lucy 1781-1864.............DLB-144, 163
Ainsworth, William Harrison 1805-1882 ..DLB-21
Aistis, Jonas 1904-1973 ..... DLB-220; CDWLB-4
Aitken, George A. 1860-1917...........DLB-149
Aitken, Robert [publishing house] DLB-49
Akenside, Mark 1721-1770.............DLB-109
Akins, Zoë 1886-1958 ....DLB-26
Aksakov, Sergei Timofeevich
 1791-1859 ....DLB-198
Akutagawa, Ryūnsuke 1892-1927 ....DLB-180
Alabaster, William 1568-1640 ....DLB-132
Alain de Lille circa 1116-1202/1203......DLB-208
Alain-Fournier 1886-1914 ....DLB-65

439

Alanus de Insulis (see Alain de Lille)

Alarcón, Francisco X. 1954- DLB-122

Alarcón, Justo S. 1930- DLB-209

Alba, Nanina 1915-1968................ DLB-41

Albee, Edward 1928- DLB-7; CDALB-1

Albert the Great circa 1200-1280 .... DLB-115

Albert, Octavia 1853-ca. 1889 .... DLB-221

Alberti, Rafael 1902-1999.............. DLB-108

Albertinus, Aegidius circa 1560-1620 .... DLB-164

Alcaeus born circa 620 B.C............. DLB-176

Alcott, Bronson 1799-1888 .... DLB-1, 223

Alcott, Louisa May 1832-1888
... DLB-1, 42, 79, 223, 239; DS-14; CDALB-3

Alcott, William Andrus 1798-1859 .... DLB-1, 243

Alcuin circa 732-804 .... DLB-148

Alden, Beardsley and Company........ DLB-49

Alden, Henry Mills 1836-1919 .... DLB-79

Alden, Isabella 1841-1930............... DLB-42

Alden, John B. [publishing house]........ DLB-49

Aldington, Richard
1892-1962 .... DLB-20, 36, 100, 149

Aldis, Dorothy 1896-1966 .... DLB-22

Aldis, H. G. 1863-1919................. DLB-184

Aldiss, Brian W. 1925- DLB-14

Aldrich, Thomas Bailey
1836-1907................ DLB-42, 71, 74, 79

Alegría, Ciro 1909-1967 .... DLB-113

Alegría, Claribel 1924- DLB-145

Aleixandre, Vicente 1898-1984......... DLB-108

Aleksandravičius, Jonas (see Aistis, Jonas)

Aleksandrov, Aleksandr Andreevich
(see Durova, Nadezhda Andreevna)

Aleramo, Sibilla 1876-1960............. DLB-114

Alexander, Cecil Frances 1818-1895..... DLB-199

Alexander, Charles 1868-1923 .... DLB-91

Alexander, Charles Wesley
[publishing house] DLB-49

Alexander, James 1691-1756.......... DLB-24

Alexander, Lloyd 1924- DLB-52

Alexander, Sir William, Earl of Stirling
1577?-1640..................... DLB-121

Alexie, Sherman 1966- DLB-175, 206

Alexis, Willibald 1798-1871............. DLB-133

Alfred, King 849-899 .... DLB-146

Alger, Horatio, Jr. 1832-1899 .... DLB-42

Algonquin Books of Chapel Hill........ DLB-46

Algren, Nelson
1909-1981 ..... DLB-9; Y-81, Y-82; CDALB-1

Nelson Algren: An International
Symposium Y-00

"All the Faults of Youth and Inexperience":
A Reader's Report on
Thomas Wolfe's O Lost Y-01

Allan, Andrew 1907-1974 .... DLB-88

Allan, Ted 1916-1995................. DLB-68

Allbeury, Ted 1917- DLB-87

Alldritt, Keith 1935- DLB-14

Allen, Ethan 1738-1789................ DLB-31

Allen, Frederick Lewis 1890-1954 ...... DLB-137

Allen, Gay Wilson 1903-1995 ..... DLB-103; Y-95

Allen, George 1808-1876 .... DLB-59

Allen, George [publishing house] DLB-106

Allen, George, and Unwin Limited DLB-112

Allen, Grant 1848-1899 .... DLB-70, 92, 178

Allen, Henry W. 1912- Y-85

Allen, Hervey 1889-1949 .... DLB-9, 45

Allen, James 1739-1808................ DLB-31

Allen, James Lane 1849-1925 .... DLB-71

Allen, Jay Presson 1922- DLB-26

Allen, John, and Company............. DLB-49

Allen, Paula Gunn 1939-.............. DLB-175

Allen, Samuel W. 1917- DLB-41

Allen, Woody 1935- DLB-44

Allende, Isabel 1942- DLB-145; CDWLB-3

Alline, Henry 1748-1784............... DLB-99

Allingham, Margery 1904-1966 .... DLB-77

Allingham, William 1824-1889......... DLB-35

Allison, W. L. [publishing house] DLB-49

The Alliterative Morte Arthure and the Stanzaic
Morte Arthur circa 1350-1400 .... DLB-146

Allott, Kenneth 1912-1973 .... DLB-20

Allston, Washington 1779-1843 ...... DLB-1, 235

Almon, John [publishing house] DLB-154

Alonzo, Dámaso 1898-1990 .... DLB-108

Alsop, George 1636-post 1673 .... DLB-24

Alsop, Richard 1761-1815.............. DLB-37

Altemus, Henry, and Company DLB-49

Altenberg, Peter 1885-1919 .... DLB-81

Althusser, Louis 1918-1990 .... DLB-242

Altolaguirre, Manuel 1905-1959........ DLB-108

Aluko, T. M. 1918- DLB-117

Alurista 1947- DLB-82

Alvarez, A. 1929- DLB-14, 40

Alver, Betti 1906-1989 ..... DLB-220; CDWLB-4

Amadi, Elechi 1934- DLB-117

Amado, Jorge 1912- DLB-113

Ambler, Eric 1909-1998 .... DLB-77

American Conservatory Theatre DLB-7

American Fiction and the 1930s.......... DLB-9

American Humor: A Historical Survey
East and Northeast
South and Southwest
Midwest
West......................... DLB-11

The American Library in Paris........... Y-93

American News Company DLB-49

The American Poets' Corner: The First
Three Years (1983-1986) Y-86

American Publishing Company DLB-49

American Stationers' Company DLB-49

American Sunday-School Union DLB-49

American Temperance Union DLB-49

American Tract Society DLB-49

The American Trust for the
British Library Y-96

The American Writers Congress
(9-12 October 1981).................. Y-81

The American Writers Congress: A Report
on Continuing Business.............. Y-81

Ames, Fisher 1758-1808 .... DLB-37

Ames, Mary Clemmer 1831-1884 ...... DLB-23

Amiel, Henri-Frédéric 1821-1881........ DLB-217

Amini, Johari M. 1935- DLB-41

Amis, Kingsley 1922-1995
...... DLB-15, 27, 100, 139, Y-96; CDBLB-7

Amis, Martin 1949- DLB-194

Ammianus Marcellinus
circa A.D. 330-A.D. 395 .... DLB-211

Ammons, A. R. 1926- DLB-5, 165

Amory, Thomas 1691?-1788 .... DLB-39

Anania, Michael 1939- DLB-193

Anaya, Rudolfo A. 1937- DLB-82, 206

Ancrene Riwle circa 1200-1225 .... DLB-146

Andersch, Alfred 1914-1980............ DLB-69

Andersen, Benny 1929- DLB-214

Anderson, Alexander 1775-1870........ DLB-188

Anderson, David 1929- DLB-241

Anderson, Frederick Irving 1877-1947 ... DLB-202

Anderson, Margaret 1886-1973 .... DLB-4, 91

Anderson, Maxwell 1888-1959........DLB-7, 228

Anderson, Patrick 1915-1979 .... DLB-68

Anderson, Paul Y. 1893-1938........... DLB-29

Anderson, Poul 1926- DLB-8

Anderson, Robert 1750-1830 .... DLB-142

Anderson, Robert 1917- DLB-7

Anderson, Sherwood
1876-1941..... DLB-4, 9, 86; DS-1; CDALB-4

Andreae, Johann Valentin 1586-1654.... DLB-164

Andreas Capellanus
flourished circa 1185 .... DLB-208

Andreas-Salomé, Lou 1861-1937 .... DLB-66

Andres, Stefan 1906-1970 .... DLB-69

Andreu, Blanca 1959- DLB-134

Andrewes, Lancelot 1555-1626 ..... DLB-151, 172

Andrews, Charles M. 1863-1943 ....DLB-17

Andrews, Miles Peter ?-1814 .... DLB-89

Andrews, Stephen Pearl 1812-1886 ..... DLB-250

Andrian, Leopold von 1875-1951........ DLB-81

Andrić, Ivo 1892-1975 ...... DLB-147; CDWLB-4

Andrieux, Louis (see Aragon, Louis)

Andrus, Silas, and Son DLB-49

Andrzejewski, Jerzy 1909-1983......... DLB-215

Angell, James Burrill 1829-1916 .... DLB-64

Angell, Roger 1920- DLB-171, 185

Angelou, Maya 1928- DLB-38; CDALB-7

Anger, Jane flourished 1589 .... DLB-136

Angers, Félicité (see Conan, Laure)

Anglo-Norman Literature in the Development
of Middle English Literature DLB-146

The Anglo-Saxon Chronicle circa 890-1154 .. DLB-146

The "Angry Young Men" DLB-15
Angus and Robertson (UK) Limited DLB-112
Anhalt, Edward 1914-2000 ....DLB-26
Anners, Henry F. [publishing house] DLB-49
Annolied between 1077 and 1081.........DLB-148
Annual Awards for *Dictionary of Literary Biography* Editors
 and Contributors....... Y-98, Y-99, Y-00, Y-01
Anselm of Canterbury 1033-1109 ....DLB-115
Anstey, F. 1856-1934 .... DLB-141, 178
Anthony, Michael 1932- DLB-125
Anthony, Piers 1934- DLB-8
Anthony, Susanna 1726-1791...........DLB-200
Antin, David 1932- DLB-169
Antin, Mary 1881-1949 .... DLB-221; Y-84
Anton Ulrich, Duke of Brunswick-Lüneburg 1633-1714 ....DLB-168
Antschel, Paul (see Celan, Paul)
Anyidoho, Kofi 1947- DLB-157
Anzaldúa, Gloria 1942- DLB-122
Anzengruber, Ludwig 1839-1889 ....DLB-129
Apess, William 1798-1839 .... DLB-175, 243
Apodaca, Rudy S. 1939- DLB-82
Apollinaire, Guillaume 1880-1918......DLB-258
Apollonius Rhodius third century B.C....DLB-176
Apple, Max 1941- DLB-130
Appleton, D., and Company DLB-49
Appleton-Century-Crofts...............DLB-46
Applewhite, James 1935- DLB-105
Applewood Books DLB-46
April, Jean-Pierre 1948- DLB-251
Apuleius circa A.D. 125-post A.D. 164 .... DLB-211; CDWLB-1
Aquin, Hubert 1929-1977 ....DLB-53
Aquinas, Thomas 1224 or 1225-1274 DLB-115
Aragon, Louis 1897-1982...........DLB-72, 258
Aralica, Ivan 1930- DLB-181
Aratus of Soli circa 315 B.C.-circa 239 B.C. DLB-176
Arbasino, Alberto 1930- DLB-196
Arbor House Publishing Company.......DLB-46
Arbuthnot, John 1667-1735 ....DLB-101
Arcadia House DLB-46
Arce, Julio G. (see Ulica, Jorge)
Archer, William 1856-1924 ....DLB-10
Archilochhus mid seventh century B.C.E. DLB-176
The Archpoet circa 1130?-? DLB-148
Archpriest Avvakum (Petrovich) 1620?-1682 ....DLB-150
Arden, John 1930- DLB-13, 245
Arden of Faversham...................DLB-62
Ardis Publishers.....................Y-89
Ardizzone, Edward 1900-1979 ....DLB-160
Arellano, Juan Estevan 1947- DLB-122
The Arena Publishing Company........DLB-49

Arena Stage DLB-7
Arenas, Reinaldo 1943-1990 ....DLB-145
Arendt, Hannah 1906-1975 ....DLB-242
Arensberg, Ann 1937- Y-82
Arghezi, Tudor 1880-1967... DLB-220; CDWLB-4
Arguedas, José María 1911-1969 ....DLB-113
Argueta, Manlio 1936- DLB-145
Arias, Ron 1941- DLB-82
Arishima, Takeo 1878-1923............DLB-180
Aristophanes circa 446 B.C.-circa 386 B.C. DLB-176; CDWLB-1
Aristotle 384 B.C.-322 B.C. DLB-176; CDWLB-1
Ariyoshi Sawako 1931-1984 ....DLB-182
Arland, Marcel 1899-1986 ....DLB-72
Arlen, Michael 1895-1956 .... DLB-36, 77, 162
Armah, Ayi Kwei 1939- ... DLB-117; CDWLB-3
Armantrout, Rae 1947- DLB-193
Der arme Hartmann ?after 1150.....DLB-148
Armed Services Editions DLB-46
Armstrong, Martin Donisthorpe 1882-1974 ....DLB-197
Armstrong, Richard 1903- DLB-160
Armstrong, Terence Ian Fytton (see Gawsworth, John)
Arndt, Ernst Moritz 1769-1860 ....DLB-90
Arnim, Achim von 1781-1831 ....DLB-90
Arnim, Bettina von 1785-1859..........DLB-90
Arnim, Elizabeth von (Countess Mary Annette Beauchamp Russell) 1866-1941 ....DLB-197
Arno Press........................DLB-46
Arnold, Edward [publishing house]......DLB-112
Arnold, Edwin 1832-1904 ....DLB-35
Arnold, Edwin L. 1857-1935 ....DLB-178
Arnold, Matthew 1822-1888 .... DLB-32, 57; CDBLB-4
Preface to *Poems* (1853) DLB-32
Arnold, Thomas 1795-1842 ....DLB-55
Arnott, Peter 1962- DLB-233
Arnow, Harriette Simpson 1908-1986.......DLB-6
Arp, Bill (see Smith, Charles Henry)
Arpino, Giovanni 1927-1987 ....DLB-177
Arreola, Juan José 1918- DLB-113
Arrian circa 89-circa 155 ....DLB-176
Arrowsmith, J. W. [publishing house] DLB-106
The Art and Mystery of Publishing: Interviews Y-97
Artaud, Antonin 1896-1948............DLB-258
Arthur, Timothy Shay 1809-1885 .... DLB-3, 42, 79, 250; DS-13
The Arthurian Tradition and Its European Context DLB-138
Artmann, H. C. 1921-2000 ....DLB-85
Arvin, Newton 1900-1963 ....DLB-103
Asch, Nathan 1902-1964 ....DLB-4, 28
Ascham, Roger 1515 or 1516-1568 .....DLB-236
Ash, John 1948- DLB-40

Ashbery, John 1927- DLB-5, 165; Y-81
Ashbridge, Elizabeth 1713-1755.........DLB-200
Ashburnham, Bertram Lord 1797-1878......................DLB-184
Ashendene Press DLB-112
Asher, Sandy 1942- Y-83
Ashton, Winifred (see Dane, Clemence)
Asimov, Isaac 1920-1992........... DLB-8; Y-92
Askew, Anne circa 1521-1546 ....DLB-136
Aspazija 1865-1943 .... DLB-220; CDWLB-4
Asselin, Olivar 1874-1937 ....DLB-92
The Association of American Publishers......Y-99
The Association for Documentary Editing ... Y-00
Astell, Mary 1666-1731 ....DLB-252
Astley, William (see Warung, Price)
Asturias, Miguel Angel 1899-1974 .... DLB-113; CDWLB-3
At Home with Albert Erskine Y-00
Atheneum Publishers..................DLB-46
Atherton, Gertrude 1857-1948..... DLB-9, 78, 186
Athlone Press......................DLB-112
Atkins, Josiah circa 1755-1781 ....DLB-31
Atkins, Russell 1926- DLB-41
Atkinson, Louisa 1834-1872 ....DLB-230
The Atlantic Monthly Press.............DLB-46
Attaway, William 1911-1986 ....DLB-76
Atwood, Margaret 1939- DLB-53, 251
Aubert, Alvin 1930- DLB-41
Aubert de Gaspé, Phillipe-Ignace-François 1814-1841 ....DLB-99
Aubert de Gaspé, Phillipe Joseph 1786-1871 ....DLB-99
Aubin, Napoléon 1812-1890 ....DLB-99
Aubin, Penelope 1685-circa 1731 ....DLB-39
Preface to *The Life of Charlotta du Pont* (1723) DLB-39
Aubrey-Fletcher, Henry Lancelot (see Wade, Henry)
Auchincloss, Louis 1917- DLB-2, 244; Y-80
Auction of Jack Kerouac's *On the Road* Scroll .. Y-01
Auden, W. H. 1907-1973...DLB-10, 20; CDBLB-6
Audio Art in America: A Personal Memoir.....Y-85
Audubon, John James 1785-1851........DLB-248
Audubon, John Woodhouse 1812-1862......................DLB-183
Auerbach, Berthold 1812-1882 ....DLB-133
Auernheimer, Raoul 1876-1948 ....DLB-81
Augier, Emile 1820-1889 ....DLB-192
Augustine 354-430....................DLB-115
Responses to Ken Auletta Y-97
Aulus Cellius circa A.D. 125-circa A.D. 180? DLB-211
Austen, Jane 1775-1817 ....DLB-116; CDBLB-3
Auster, Paul 1947- DLB-227
Austin, Alfred 1835-1913...............DLB-35
Austin, Jane Goodwin 1831-1894 ....DLB-202

Cumulative Index

Austin, Mary 1868-1934......DLB-9, 78, 206, 221
Austin, William 1778-1841.............DLB-74
Australie (Emily Manning)
  1845-1890....................DLB-230
Author-Printers, 1476–1599..........DLB-167
Author Websites.......................Y-97
Authors and Newspapers Association.....DLB-46
Authors' Publishing Company..........DLB-49
Avallone, Michael 1924-1999..............Y-99
Avalon Books.......................DLB-46
Avancini, Nicolaus 1611-1686.........DLB-164
Avendaño, Fausto 1941-..............DLB-82
Averroëó 1126-1198..................DLB-115
Avery, Gillian 1926-.................DLB-161
Avicenna 980-1037...................DLB-115
Avison, Margaret 1918-................DLB-53
Avon Books.........................DLB-46
Avyžius, Jonas 1922-1999.............DLB-220
Awdry, Wilbert Vere 1911-1997........DLB-160
Awoonor, Kofi 1935-..................DLB-117
Ayckbourn, Alan 1939-..........DLB-13, 245
Aymé, Marcel 1902-1967...............DLB-72
Aytoun, Sir Robert 1570-1638.........DLB-121
Aytoun, William Edmondstoune
  1813-1865.................DLB-32, 159

B

B. V. (see Thomson, James)
Babbitt, Irving 1865-1933..............DLB-63
Babbitt, Natalie 1932-.................DLB-52
Babcock, John [publishing house]........DLB-49
Babits, Mihály 1883-1941...DLB-215; CDWLB-4
Babrius circa 150-200.................DLB-176
Baca, Jimmy Santiago 1952-...........DLB-122
Bache, Benjamin Franklin 1769-1798.....DLB-43
Bacheller, Irving 1859-1950.............DLB-202
Bachmann, Ingeborg 1926-1973...........DLB-85
Bačinskaitė-Bučienė, Salomėja (see Nėris, Salomėja)
Bacon, Delia 1811-1859............DLB-1, 243
Bacon, Francis
  1561-1626.....DLB-151, 236, 252; CDBLB-1
Bacon, Sir Nicholas circa 1510-1579.....DLB-132
Bacon, Roger circa 1214/1220-1292.....DLB-115
Bacon, Thomas circa 1700-1768.........DLB-31
Bacovia, George
  1881-1957...........DLB-220; CDWLB-4
Badger, Richard G., and Company......DLB-49
Bagaduce Music Lending Library..........Y-00
Bage, Robert 1728-1801................DLB-39
Bagehot, Walter 1826-1877..............DLB-55
Bagley, Desmond 1923-1983............DLB-87
Bagley, Sarah G. 1806-1848............DLB-239
Bagnold, Enid 1889-1981...DLB-13, 160, 191, 245
Bagryana, Elisaveta
  1893-1991.............DLB-147; CDWLB-4
Bahr, Hermann 1863-1934.........DLB-81, 118

Bailey, Abigail Abbot 1746-1815........DLB-200
Bailey, Alfred Goldsworthy 1905-......DLB-68
Bailey, Francis [publishing house].......DLB-49
Bailey, H. C. 1878-1961................DLB-77
Bailey, Jacob 1731-1808................DLB-99
Bailey, Paul 1937-....................DLB-14
Bailey, Philip James 1816-1902..........DLB-32
Baillargeon, Pierre 1916-1967............DLB-88
Baillie, Hugh 1890-1966................DLB-29
Baillie, Joanna 1762-1851...............DLB-93
Bailyn, Bernard 1922-..................DLB-17
Bainbridge, Beryl 1933-...........DLB-14, 231
Baird, Irene 1901-1981..................DLB-68
Baker, Augustine 1575-1641............DLB-151
Baker, Carlos 1909-1987...............DLB-103
Baker, David 1954-...................DLB-120
Baker, Herschel C. 1914-1990...........DLB-111
Baker, Houston A., Jr. 1943-...........DLB-67
Baker, Nicholson 1957-................DLB-227
Baker, Samuel White 1821-1893........DLB-166
Baker, Thomas 1656-1740..............DLB-213
Baker, Walter H., Company
  ("Baker's Plays")................DLB-49
The Baker and Taylor Company........DLB-49
Bakhtin, Mikhail Mikhailovich
  1895-1975....................DLB-242
Balaban, John 1943-..................DLB-120
Bald, Wambly 1902-....................DLB-4
Balde, Jacob 1604-1668................DLB-164
Balderston, John 1889-1954.............DLB-26
Baldwin, James 1924-1987
  ....DLB-2, 7, 33, 249; Y-87; CDALB-1
Baldwin, Joseph Glover
  1815-1864..............DLB-3, 11, 248
Baldwin, Louisa (Mrs. Alfred Baldwin)
  1845-1925....................DLB-240
Baldwin, Richard and Anne
  [publishing house]...............DLB-170
Baldwin, William circa 1515-1563......DLB-132
Bale, John 1495-1563.................DLB-132
Balestrini, Nanni 1935-............DLB-128, 196
Balfour, Sir Andrew 1630-1694.........DLB-213
Balfour, Arthur James 1848-1930........DLB-190
Balfour, Sir James 1600-1657...........DLB-213
Ballantine Books......................DLB-46
Ballantyne, R. M. 1825-1894............DLB-163
Ballard, J. G. 1930-...............DLB-14, 207
Ballard, Martha Moore 1735-1812......DLB-200
Ballerini, Luigi 1940-.................DLB-128
Ballou, Maturin Murray
  1820-1895.................DLB-79, 189
Ballou, Robert O. [publishing house].....DLB-46
Balzac, Honoré de 1799-1855..........DLB-119
Bambara, Toni Cade
  1939-..........DLB-38, 218; CDALB-7
Bamford, Samuel 1788-1872............DLB-190
Bancroft, A. L., and Company..........DLB-49

Bancroft, George 1800-1891...DLB-1, 30, 59, 243
Bancroft, Hubert Howe 1832-1918...DLB-47, 140
Bandelier, Adolph F. 1840-1914........DLB-186
Bangs, John Kendrick 1862-1922.....DLB-11, 79
Banim, John 1798-1842.........DLB-116, 158, 159
Banim, Michael 1796-1874........DLB-158, 159
Banks, Iain 1954-....................DLB-194
Banks, John circa 1653-1706............DLB-80
Banks, Russell 1940-..................DLB-130
Bannerman, Helen 1862-1946..........DLB-141
Bantam Books........................DLB-46
Banti, Anna 1895-1985................DLB-177
Banville, John 1945-...................DLB-14
Banville, Théodore de 1823-1891......DLB-217
Baraka, Amiri
  1934-....DLB-5, 7, 16, 38; DS-8; CDALB-1
Barańczak, Stanisław 1946-...........DLB-232
Baratynsky, Evgenii Abramovich
  1800-1844....................DLB-205
Barbauld, Anna Laetitia
  1743-1825.........DLB-107, 109, 142, 158
Barbeau, Marius 1883-1969.............DLB-92
Barber, John Warner 1798-1885.........DLB-30
Bàrberi Squarotti, Giorgio 1929-......DLB-128
Barbey d'Aurevilly, Jules-Amédée
  1808-1889....................DLB-119
Barbier, Auguste 1805-1882...........DLB-217
Barbilian, Dan (see Barbu, Ion)
Barbour, John circa 1316-1395.........DLB-146
Barbour, Ralph Henry 1870-1944.......DLB-22
Barbu, Ion 1895-1961......DLB-220; CDWLB-4
Barbusse, Henri 1873-1935.............DLB-65
Barclay, Alexander circa 1475-1552.....DLB-132
Barclay, E. E., and Company...........DLB-49
Bardeen, C. W. [publishing house].......DLB-49
Barham, Richard Harris 1788-1845.....DLB-159
Barich, Bill 1943-....................DLB-185
Baring, Maurice 1874-1945.............DLB-34
Baring-Gould, Sabine
  1834-1924................DLB-156, 190
Barker, A. L. 1918-...............DLB-14, 139
Barker, Arthur, Limited...............DLB-112
Barker, George 1913-1991..............DLB-20
Barker, Harley Granville 1877-1946......DLB-10
Barker, Howard 1946-............DLB-13, 233
Barker, James Nelson 1784-1858........DLB-37
Barker, Jane 1652-1727............DLB-39, 131
Barker, Lady Mary Anne 1831-1911....DLB-166
Barker, William circa 1520-after 1576...DLB-132
Barkov, Ivan Semenovich 1732-1768....DLB-150
Barks, Coleman 1937-..................DLB-5
Barlach, Ernst 1870-1938..........DLB-56, 118
Barlow, Joel 1754-1812................DLB-37
  The Prospect of Peace (1778).............DLB-37
Barnard, John 1681-1770...............DLB-24

442

Barnard, Marjorie 1879-1987 and Eldershaw, Flora (M. Barnard Eldershaw) 1897-1956...DLB-260
Barne, Kitty (Mary Catherine Barne) 1883-1957......DLB-160
Barnes, A. S., and Company......DLB-49
Barnes, Barnabe 1571-1609......DLB-132
Barnes, Djuna 1892-1982......DLB-4, 9, 45
Barnes, Jim 1933-......DLB-175
Barnes, Julian 1946-......DLB-194; Y-93
Julian Barnes Checklist......Y-01
Barnes, Margaret Ayer 1886-1967......DLB-9
Barnes, Peter 1931-......DLB-13, 233
Barnes, William 1801-1886......DLB-32
Barnes and Noble Books......DLB-46
Barnet, Miguel 1940-......DLB-145
Barney, Natalie 1876-1972......DLB-4
Barnfield, Richard 1574-1627......DLB-172
Baron, Richard W., Publishing Company......DLB-46
Barr, Amelia Edith Huddleston 1831-1919......DLB-202, 221
Barr, Robert 1850-1912......DLB-70, 92
Barral, Carlos 1928-1989......DLB-134
Barrax, Gerald William 1933-......DLB-41, 120
Barrès, Maurice 1862-1923......DLB-123
Barrett, Eaton Stannard 1786-1820......DLB-116
Barrie, J. M. 1860-1937......DLB-10, 141, 156; CDBLB-5
Barrie and Jenkins......DLB-112
Barrio, Raymond 1921-......DLB-82
Barrios, Gregg 1945-......DLB-122
Barry, Philip 1896-1949......DLB-7, 228
Barry, Robertine (see Françoise)
Barry, Sebastian 1955-......DLB-245
Barse and Hopkins......DLB-46
Barstow, Stan 1928-......DLB-14, 139
Barth, John 1930-......DLB-2, 227
Barthelme, Donald 1931-1989......DLB-2, 234; Y-80, Y-89
Barthelme, Frederick 1943-......DLB-244; Y-85
Bartholomew, Frank 1898-1985......DLB-127
Bartlett, John 1820-1905......DLB-1, 235
Bartol, Cyrus Augustus 1813-1900......DLB-1, 235
Barton, Bernard 1784-1849......DLB-96
Barton, John ca. 1610-1675......DLB-236
Barton, Thomas Pennant 1803-1869......DLB-140
Bartram, John 1699-1777......DLB-31
Bartram, William 1739-1823......DLB-37
Basic Books......DLB-46
Basille, Theodore (see Becon, Thomas)
Bass, Rick 1958-......DLB-212
Bass, T. J. 1932-......Y-81
Bassani, Giorgio 1916-......DLB-128, 177
Basse, William circa 1583-1653......DLB-121
Bassett, John Spencer 1867-1928......DLB-17
Bassler, Thomas Joseph (see Bass, T. J.)

Bate, Walter Jackson 1918-1999......DLB-67, 103
Bateman, Christopher [publishing house]......DLB-170
Bateman, Stephen circa 1510-1584......DLB-136
Bates, H. E. 1905-1974......DLB-162, 191
Bates, Katharine Lee 1859-1929......DLB-71
Batiushkov, Konstantin Nikolaevich 1787-1855......DLB-205
Batsford, B. T. [publishing house]......DLB-106
Battiscombe, Georgina 1905-......DLB-155
The Battle of Maldon circa 1000......DLB-146
Baudelaire, Charles 1821-1867......DLB-217
Bauer, Bruno 1809-1882......DLB-133
Bauer, Wolfgang 1941-......DLB-124
Baum, L. Frank 1856-1919......DLB-22
Baum, Vicki 1888-1960......DLB-85
Baumbach, Jonathan 1933-......Y-80
Bausch, Richard 1945-......DLB-130
Bausch, Robert 1945-......DLB-218
Bawden, Nina 1925-......DLB-14, 161, 207
Bax, Clifford 1886-1962......DLB-10, 100
Baxter, Charles 1947-......DLB-130
Bayer, Eleanor (see Perry, Eleanor)
Bayer, Konrad 1932-1964......DLB-85
Baynes, Pauline 1922-......DLB-160
Baynton, Barbara 1857-1929......DLB-230
Bazin, Hervé 1911-1996......DLB-83
Beach, Sylvia 1887-1962......DLB-4; DS-15
Beacon Press......DLB-49
Beadle and Adams......DLB-49
Beagle, Peter S. 1939-......Y-80
Beal, M. F. 1937-......Y-81
Beale, Howard K. 1899-1959......DLB-17
Beard, Charles A. 1874-1948......DLB-17
A Beat Chronology: The First Twenty-five Years, 1944-1969......DLB-16
Periodicals of the Beat Generation......DLB-16
The Beats in New York City......DLB-237
The Beats in the West......DLB-237
Beattie, Ann 1947-......DLB-218; Y-82
Beattie, James 1735-1803......DLB-109
Beatty, Chester 1875-1968......DLB-201
Beauchemin, Nérée 1850-1931......DLB-92
Beauchemin, Yves 1941-......DLB-60
Beaugrand, Honoré 1848-1906......DLB-99
Beaulieu, Victor-Lévy 1945-......DLB-53
Beaumont, Francis circa 1584-1616 and Fletcher, John 1579-1625......DLB-58; CDBLB-1
Beaumont, Sir John 1583?-1627......DLB-121
Beaumont, Joseph 1616-1699......DLB-126
Beauvoir, Simone de 1908-1986......DLB-72; Y-86
Becher, Ulrich 1910-......DLB-69
Becker, Carl 1873-1945......DLB-17
Becker, Jurek 1937-1997......DLB-75
Becker, Jurgen 1932-......DLB-75

Beckett, Samuel 1906-1989......DLB-13, 15, 233; Y-90; CDBLB-7
Beckford, William 1760-1844......DLB-39
Beckham, Barry 1944-......DLB-33
Becon, Thomas circa 1512-1567......DLB-136
Becque, Henry 1837-1899......DLB-192
Beddoes, Thomas 1760-1808......DLB-158
Beddoes, Thomas Lovell 1803-1849......DLB-96
Bede circa 673-735......DLB-146
Bedford-Jones, H. 1887-1949......DLB-251
Beecher, Catharine Esther 1800-1878......DLB-1, 243
Beecher, Henry Ward 1813-1887......DLB-3, 43, 250
Beer, George L. 1872-1920......DLB-47
Beer, Johann 1655-1700......DLB-168
Beer, Patricia 1919-1999......DLB-40
Beerbohm, Max 1872-1956......DLB-34, 100
Beer-Hofmann, Richard 1866-1945......DLB-81
Beers, Henry A. 1847-1926......DLB-71
Beeton, S. O. [publishing house]......DLB-106
Bégon, Elisabeth 1696-1755......DLB-99
Behan, Brendan 1923-1964......DLB-13, 233; CDBLB-7
Behn, Aphra 1640?-1689......DLB-39, 80, 131
Behn, Harry 1898-1973......DLB-61
Behrman, S. N. 1893-1973......DLB-7, 44
Belaney, Archibald Stansfeld (see Grey Owl)
Belasco, David 1853-1931......DLB-7
Belford, Clarke and Company......DLB-49
Belinksy, Vissarion Grigor'evich 1811-1848......DLB-198
Belitt, Ben 1911-......DLB-5
Belknap, Jeremy 1744-1798......DLB-30, 37
Bell, Adrian 1901-1980......DLB-191
Bell, Clive 1881-1964......DS-10
Bell, Daniel 1919-......DLB-246
Bell, George, and Sons......DLB-106
Bell, Gertrude Margaret Lowthian 1868-1926......DLB-174
Bell, James Madison 1826-1902......DLB-50
Bell, Madison Smartt 1957-......DLB-218
Bell, Marvin 1937-......DLB-5
Bell, Millicent 1919-......DLB-111
Bell, Quentin 1910-1996......DLB-155
Bell, Robert [publishing house]......DLB-49
Bell, Vanessa 1879-1961......DS-10
Bellamy, Edward 1850-1898......DLB-12
Bellamy, John [publishing house]......DLB-170
Bellamy, Joseph 1719-1790......DLB-31
La Belle Assemblée 1806-1837......DLB-110
Bellezza, Dario 1944-1996......DLB-128
Belloc, Hilaire 1870-1953......DLB-19, 100, 141, 174
Belloc, Madame (see Parkes, Bessie Rayner)
Bellonci, Maria 1902-1986......DLB-196
Bellow, Saul 1915-......DLB-2, 28; Y-82; DS-3; CDALB-1
Belmont Productions......DLB-46

Cumulative Index

Bels, Alberts 1938- DLB-232
Belševica, Vizma 1931- ... DLB-232; CDWLB-4
Bemelmans, Ludwig 1898-1962 .... DLB-22
Bemis, Samuel Flagg 1891-1973 .... DLB-17
Bemrose, William [publishing house] DLB-106
Ben no Naishi 1228?-1271?. DLB-203
Benchley, Robert 1889-1945. .... DLB-11
Bencúr, Matej (see Kukučín, Martin)
Benedetti, Mario 1920- DLB-113
Benedict, Pinckney 1964- DLB-244
Benedict, Ruth 1887-1948 .... DLB-246
Benedictus, David 1938- DLB-14
Benedikt, Michael 1935- DLB-5
Benediktov, Vladimir Grigor'evich
    1807-1873 .... DLB-205
Benét, Stephen Vincent
    1898-1943 .... DLB-4, 48, 102, 249
Benét, William Rose 1886-1950 .... DLB-45
Benford, Gregory 1941- Y-82
Benjamin, Park 1809-1864 .... DLB-3, 59, 73, 250
Benjamin, S. G. W. 1837-1914 .... DLB-189
Benjamin, Walter 1892-1940 .... DLB-242
Benlowes, Edward 1602-1676. .... DLB-126
Benn Brothers Limited DLB-106
Benn, Gottfried 1886-1956 .... DLB-56
Bennett, Arnold
    1867-1931.... DLB-10, 34, 98, 135; CDBLB-5
Bennett, Charles 1899-1995 .... DLB-44
Bennett, Emerson 1822-1905 .... DLB-202
Bennett, Gwendolyn 1902- DLB-51
Bennett, Hal 1930- DLB-33
Bennett, James Gordon 1795-1872 ...... DLB-43
Bennett, James Gordon, Jr. 1841-1918 .... DLB-23
Bennett, John 1865-1956 .... DLB-42
Bennett, Louise 1919- DLB-117; CDWLB-3
Benni, Stefano 1947- DLB-196
Benoit, Jacques 1941- DLB-60
Benson, A. C. 1862-1925 .... DLB-98
Benson, E. F. 1867-1940 .... DLB-135, 153
Benson, Jackson J. 1930- DLB-111
Benson, Robert Hugh 1871-1914 .... DLB-153
Benson, Stella 1892-1933 .... DLB-36, 162
Bent, James Theodore 1852-1897 ....DLB-174
Bent, Mabel Virginia Anna ?-? DLB-174
Bentham, Jeremy 1748-1832....DLB-107, 158, 252
Bentley, E. C. 1875-1956 .... DLB-70
Bentley, Phyllis 1894-1977 .... DLB-191
Bentley, Richard 1662-1742 .... DLB-252
Bentley, Richard [publishing house] DLB-106
Benton, Robert 1932- and Newman,
    David 1937- DLB-44
Benziger Brothers DLB-49
Beowulf circa 900-1000 or 790-825
    .... DLB-146; CDBLB-1
Berent, Wacław 1873-1940 .... DLB-215

Beresford, Anne 1929- DLB-40
Beresford, John Davys
    1873-1947 .... DLB-162, 178, 197
"Experiment in the Novel" (1929) DLB-36
Beresford-Howe, Constance 1922- DLB-88
Berford, R. G., Company DLB-49
Berg, Stephen 1934- DLB-5
Bergengruen, Werner 1892-1964 .... DLB-56
Berger, John 1926- DLB-14, 207
Berger, Meyer 1898-1959 .... DLB-29
Berger, Thomas 1924- DLB-2; Y-80
Bergman, Hjalmar 1883-1931. .... DLB-259
Bergman, Ingmar 1918- DLB-257
Berkeley, Anthony 1893-1971 .... DLB-77
Berkeley, George 1685-1753 .... DLB-31, 101, 252
The Berkley Publishing Corporation DLB-46
Berlin, Lucia 1936- DLB-130
Berman, Marshall 1940- DLB-246
Bernal, Vicente J. 1888-1915 .... DLB-82
Bernanos, Georges 1888-1948 .... DLB-72
Bernard, Harry 1898-1979 .... DLB-92
Bernard, John 1756-1828 .... DLB-37
Bernard of Chartres circa 1060-1124? ... DLB-115
Bernard of Clairvaux 1090-1153 .... DLB-208
The Bernard Malamud Archive at the
    Harry Ransom Humanities
    Research Center................... Y-00
Bernard Silvestris
    flourished circa 1130-1160 .... DLB-208
Bernari, Carlo 1909-1992.............DLB-177
Bernhard, Thomas
    1931-1989 ....DLB-85, 124; CDWLB-2
Bernstein, Charles 1950- DLB-169
Berriault, Gina 1926-1999 .... DLB-130
Berrigan, Daniel 1921- DLB-5
Berrigan, Ted 1934-1983 .... DLB-5, 169
Berry, Wendell 1934- DLB-5, 6, 234
Berryman, John 1914-1972 .... DLB-48; CDALB-1
Bersianik, Louky 1930- DLB-60
Berthelet, Thomas [publishing house] DLB-170
Berto, Giuseppe 1914-1978............DLB-177
Bertolucci, Attilio 1911- DLB-128
Berton, Pierre 1920- DLB-68
Bertrand, Louis "Aloysius"
    1807-1841..................... DLB-217
Besant, Sir Walter 1836-1901....... DLB-135, 190
Bessette, Gerard 1920- DLB-53
Bessie, Alvah 1904-1985 .... DLB-26
Bester, Alfred 1913-1987............... DLB-8
Besterman, Theodore 1904-1976 .... DLB-201
The Bestseller Lists: An Assessment......... Y-84
Bestuzhev, Aleksandr Aleksandrovich
    (Marlinsky) 1797-1837 .... DLB-198
Bestuzhev, Nikolai Aleksandrovich
    1791-1855..................... DLB-198
Betham-Edwards, Matilda Barbara (see Edwards,
    Matilda Barbara Betham-)

Betjeman, John
    1906-1984 .... DLB-20; Y-84; CDBLB-7
Betocchi, Carlo 1899-1986............ DLB-128
Bettarini, Mariella 1942- DLB-128
Betts, Doris 1932- DLB-218; Y-82
Beùkoviù, Matija 1939- DLB-181
Beveridge, Albert J. 1862-1927 ....DLB-17
Beverley, Robert circa 1673-1722 ..... DLB-24, 30
Bevilacqua, Alberto 1934- DLB-196
Bevington, Louisa Sarah 1845-1895..... DLB-199
Beyle, Marie-Henri (see Stendhal)
Białoszewski, Miron 1922-1983 .... DLB-232
Bianco, Margery Williams 1881-1944 ... DLB-160
Bibaud, Adèle 1854-1941 .... DLB-92
Bibaud, Michel 1782-1857 .... DLB-99
Bibliographical and Textual Scholarship
    Since World War II.................. Y-89
Bichsel, Peter 1935- DLB-75
Bickerstaff, Isaac John 1733-circa 1808.... DLB-89
Biddle, Drexel [publishing house]........ DLB-49
Bidermann, Jacob
    1577 or 1578-1639 .... DLB-164
Bidwell, Walter Hilliard 1798-1881 ...... DLB-79
Bienek, Horst 1930- DLB-75
Bierbaum, Otto Julius 1865-1910........ DLB-66
Bierce, Ambrose 1842-1914?
    .... DLB-11, 12, 23, 71, 74, 186; CDALB-3
Bigelow, William F. 1879-1966.......... DLB-91
Biggle, Lloyd, Jr. 1923- DLB-8
Bigiaretti, Libero 1905-1993............DLB-177
Bigland, Eileen 1898-1970 .... DLB-195
Biglow, Hosea (see Lowell, James Russell)
Bigongiari, Piero 1914- DLB-128
Billinger, Richard 1890-1965 .... DLB-124
Billings, Hammatt 1818-1874 .... DLB-188
Billings, John Shaw 1898-1975 ....DLB-137
Billings, Josh (see Shaw, Henry Wheeler)
Binding, Rudolf G. 1867-1938 .... DLB-66
Bingay, Malcolm 1884-1953........... DLB-241
Bingham, Caleb 1757-1817 .... DLB-42
Bingham, George Barry 1906-1988 .....DLB-127
Bingham, Sallie 1937- DLB-234
Bingley, William [publishing house]..... DLB-154
Binyon, Laurence 1869-1943 .... DLB-19
Biographia Brittanica DLB-142
Biographical Documents I Y-84
Biographical Documents II................ Y-85
Bioren, John [publishing house] DLB-49
Bioy Casares, Adolfo 1914- DLB-113
Bird, Isabella Lucy 1831-1904 .... DLB-166
Bird, Robert Montgomery 1806-1854 ... DLB-202
Bird, William 1888-1963 .... DLB-4; DS-15
Birken, Sigmund von 1626-1681 .... DLB-164
Birney, Earle 1904-1995................ DLB-88
Birrell, Augustine 1850-1933 .... DLB-98

Bisher, Furman 1918- DLB-171

Bishop, Elizabeth
  1911-1979 ....DLB-5, 169; CDALB-6

Bishop, John Peale 1892-1944 ....DLB-4, 9, 45

Bismarck, Otto von 1815-1898 ....DLB-129

Bisset, Robert 1759-1805 ....DLB-142

Bissett, Bill 1939- DLB-53

Bitzius, Albert (see Gotthelf, Jeremias)

Bjørnvig, Thorkild 1918- DLB-214

Black, David (D. M.) 1941- DLB-40

Black, Walter J. [publishing house] DLB-46

Black, Winifred 1863-1936 ....DLB-25

The Black Aesthetic: Background DS-8

Black Theaters and Theater Organizations in
  America, 1961-1982:
  A Research List DLB-38

Black Theatre: A Forum [excerpts] DLB-38

Blackamore, Arthur 1679-? DLB-24, 39

Blackburn, Alexander L. 1929- Y-85

Blackburn, Paul 1926-1971 ....DLB-16; Y-81

Blackburn, Thomas 1916-1977 ....DLB-27

Blackmore, R. D. 1825-1900 ....DLB-18

Blackmore, Sir Richard 1654-1729......DLB-131

Blackmur, R. P. 1904-1965 ....DLB-63

Blackwell, Basil, Publisher DLB-106

Blackwood, Algernon Henry
  1869-1951 ....DLB-153, 156, 178

Blackwood, Caroline 1931-1996 .....DLB-14, 207

Blackwood, William, and Sons, Ltd......DLB-154

Blackwood's Edinburgh Magazine
  1817-1980 ....DLB-110

Blades, William 1824-1890 ....DLB-184

Blaga, Lucian 1895-1961 ....DLB-220

Blagden, Isabella 1817?-1873 ....DLB-199

Blair, Eric Arthur (see Orwell, George)

Blair, Francis Preston 1791-1876 ....DLB-43

Blair, James circa 1655-1743............DLB-24

Blair, John Durburrow 1759-1823 ....DLB-37

Blais, Marie-Claire 1939- DLB-53

Blaise, Clark 1940- DLB-53

Blake, George 1893-1961...............DLB-191

Blake, Lillie Devereux 1833-1913 ...DLB-202, 221

Blake, Nicholas 1904-1972.............DLB-77
  (see Day Lewis, C.)

Blake, William
  1757-1827 ....DLB-93, 154, 163; CDBLB-3

The Blakiston Company DLB-49

Blandiana, Ana 1942- DLB-232; CDWLB-4

Blanchot, Maurice 1907- DLB-72

Blanckenburg, Christian Friedrich von
  1744-1796............................DLB-94

Blaser, Robin 1925- DLB-165

Blaumanis, Rudolfs 1863-1908 ....DLB-220

Bleasdale, Alan 1946- DLB-245

Bledsoe, Albert Taylor 1809-1877 ..DLB-3, 79, 248

Bleecker, Ann Eliza 1752-1783 ....DLB-200

Blelock and Company DLB-49

Blennerhassett, Margaret Agnew
  1773-1842 ....DLB-99

Bles, Geoffrey [publishing house] DLB-112

Blessington, Marguerite, Countess of
  1789-1849 ....DLB-166

Blew, Mary Clearman 1939- DLB-256

The Blickling Homilies circa 971 ....DLB-146

Blind, Mathilde 1841-1896 ....DLB-199

Blish, James 1921-1975................DLB-8

Bliss, E., and E. White
  [publishing house] DLB-49

Bliven, Bruce 1889-1977 ....DLB-137

Blixen, Karen 1885-1962...............DLB-214

Bloch, Robert 1917-1994 ....DLB-44

Block, Lawrence 1938- DLB-226

Block, Rudolph (see Lessing, Bruno)

Blondal, Patricia 1926-1959.............DLB-88

Bloom, Harold 1930- DLB-67

Bloomer, Amelia 1818-1894 ....DLB-79

Bloomfield, Robert 1766-1823 ....DLB-93

Bloomsbury Group DS-10

Blotner, Joseph 1923- DLB-111

Blount, Thomas 1618?-1679 ....DLB-236

Bloy, Léon 1846-1917 ....DLB-123

Blume, Judy 1938- DLB-52

Blunck, Hans Friedrich 1888-1961 ......DLB-66

Blunden, Edmund 1896-1974 ...DLB-20, 100, 155

Blundeville, Thomas 1522?-1606 ....DLB-236

Blunt, Lady Anne Isabella Noel
  1837-1917 ....DLB-174

Blunt, Wilfrid Scawen 1840-1922 ....DLB-19, 174

Bly, Nellie (see Cochrane, Elizabeth)

Bly, Robert 1926- DLB-5

Blyton, Enid 1897-1968................DLB-160

Boaden, James 1762-1839 ....DLB-89

Boas, Frederick S. 1862-1957............DLB-149

The Bobbs-Merrill Archive at the
  Lilly Library, Indiana University Y-90

Boborykin, Petr Dmitrievich 1836-1921 ..DLB-238

The Bobbs-Merrill Company DLB-46

Bobrov, Semen Sergeevich
  1763?-1810 ....DLB-150

Bobrowski, Johannes 1917-1965 ....DLB-75

The Elmer Holmes Bobst Awards in Arts
  and Letters Y-87

Bodenheim, Maxwell 1892-1954 ......DLB-9, 45

Bodenstedt, Friedrich von 1819-1892 ....DLB-129

Bodini, Vittorio 1914-1970.............DLB-128

Bodkin, M. McDonnell 1850-1933 ....DLB-70

Bodley, Sir Thomas 1545-1613 ....DLB-213

Bodley Head DLB-112

Bodmer, Johann Jakob 1698-1783 ....DLB-97

Bodmershof, Imma von 1895-1982 ......DLB-85

Bodsworth, Fred 1918- DLB-68

Boehm, Sydney 1908- DLB-44

Boer, Charles 1939- DLB-5

Boethius circa 480-circa 524 ....DLB-115

Boethius of Dacia circa 1240-? DLB-115

Bogan, Louise 1897-1970 ....DLB-45, 169

Bogarde, Dirk 1921- DLB-14

Bogdanovich, Ippolit Fedorovich
  circa 1743-1803 ....DLB-150

Bogue, David [publishing house].........DLB-106

Böhme, Jakob 1575-1624...............DLB-164

Bohn, H. G. [publishing house] DLB-106

Bohse, August 1661-1742...............DLB-168

Boie, Heinrich Christian 1744-1806.......DLB-94

Bok, Edward W. 1863-1930 ......DLB-91; DS-16

Boland, Eavan 1944- DLB-40

Boldrewood, Rolf (Thomas Alexander Browne)
  1826?-1915 ....DLB-230

Bolingbroke, Henry St John, Viscount
  1678-1751 ....DLB-101

Böll, Heinrich
  1917-1985 ....DLB-69; Y-85; CDWLB-2

Bolling, Robert 1738-1775 ....DLB-31

Bolotov, Andrei Timofeevich
  1738-1833 ....DLB-150

Bolt, Carol 1941- DLB-60

Bolt, Robert 1924-1995 ....DLB-13, 233

Bolton, Herbert E. 1870-1953 ....DLB-17

Bonaventura DLB-90

Bonaventure circa 1217-1274 ....DLB-115

Bonaviri, Giuseppe 1924- DLB-177

Bond, Edward 1934- DLB-13

Bond, Michael 1926- DLB-161

Boni, Albert and Charles
  [publishing house] DLB-46

Boni and Liveright....................DLB-46

Bonnefoy, Yves 1923- DLB-258

Bonner, Marita 1899-1971 ....DLB-228

Bonner, Paul Hyde 1893-1968............DS-17

Bonner, Sherwood (see McDowell, Katharine
  Sherwood Bonner)

Robert Bonner's Sons DLB-49

Bonnin, Gertrude Simmons (see Zitkala-Ša)

Bonsanti, Alessandro 1904-1984 ....DLB-177

Bontemps, Arna 1902-1973 ....DLB-48, 51

The Book Arts Press at the University
  of Virginia..........................Y-96

The Book League of America DLB-46

Book Publishing Accounting: Some Basic
  Concepts Y-98

Book Reviewing in America: I...........Y-87

Book Reviewing in America: II...........Y-88

Book Reviewing in America: III..........Y-89

Book Reviewing in America: IV Y-90

Book Reviewing in America: V...........Y-91

Book Reviewing in America: VI Y-92

Book Reviewing in America: VII Y-93

Book Reviewing in America: VIII.........Y-94

Book Reviewing in America and the
  Literary Scene Y-95

Book Reviewing and the
  Literary Scene Y-96, Y-97
Book Supply Company DLB-49
The Book Trade History Group Y-93
The Book Trade and the Internet Y-00
The Booker Prize Y-96
Address by Anthony Thwaite,
  Chairman of the Booker Prize Judges
  Comments from Former Booker
  Prize Winners Y-86
The Books of George V. Higgins:
  A Checklist of Editions and Printings Y-00
Boorde, Andrew circa 1490-1549 .... DLB-136
Boorstin, Daniel J. 1914- DLB-17
Booth, Franklin 1874-1948 .... DLB-188
Booth, Mary L. 1831-1889 .... DLB-79
Booth, Philip 1925- Y-82
Booth, Wayne C. 1921- DLB-67
Booth, William 1829-1912 .... DLB-190
Borchardt, Rudolf 1877-1945 .... DLB-66
Borchert, Wolfgang 1921-1947 ...... DLB-69, 124
Borel, Pétrus 1809-1859 .... DLB-119
Borges, Jorge Luis
  1899-1986 .... DLB-113; Y-86; CDWLB-3
Börne, Ludwig 1786-1837 .... DLB-90
Bornstein, Miriam 1950- DLB-209
Borowski, Tadeusz
  1922-1951 .... DLB-215; CDWLB-4
Borrow, George 1803-1881 ..... DLB-21, 55, 166
Bosch, Juan 1909- DLB-145
Bosco, Henri 1888-1976 .... DLB-72
Bosco, Monique 1927- DLB-53
Bosman, Herman Charles 1905-1951.... DLB-225
Bostic, Joe 1908-1988 .... DLB-241
Boston, Lucy M. 1892-1990 .... DLB-161
Boswell, James
  1740-1795 .... DLB-104, 142; CDBLB-2
Boswell, Robert 1953- DLB-234
Bote, Hermann
  circa 1460-circa 1520 .... DLB-179
Botev, Khristo 1847-1876 .... DLB-147
Botta, Anne C. Lynch 1815-1891 ..... DLB-3, 250
Botto, Ján (see Krasko, Ivan)
Bottome, Phyllis 1882-1963 .... DLB-197
Bottomley, Gordon 1874-1948 .... DLB-10
Bottoms, David 1949- DLB-120; Y-83
Bottrall, Ronald 1906- DLB-20
Bouchardy, Joseph 1810-1870 .... DLB-192
Boucher, Anthony 1911-1968 .... DLB-8
Boucher, Jonathan 1738-1804 .... DLB-31
Boucher de Boucherville, George
  1814-1894 .... DLB-99
Boudreau, Daniel (see Coste, Donat)
Bourassa, Napoléon 1827-1916 .... DLB-99
Bourget, Paul 1852-1935 .... DLB-123
Bourinot, John George 1837-1902 .... DLB-99
Bourjaily, Vance 1922- DLB-2, 143

Bourne, Edward Gaylord
  1860-1908 .... DLB-47
Bourne, Randolph 1886-1918 .... DLB-63
Bousoño, Carlos 1923- DLB-108
Bousquet, Joë 1897-1950 .... DLB-72
Bova, Ben 1932- Y-81
Bovard, Oliver K. 1872-1945 .... DLB-25
Bove, Emmanuel 1898-1945 .... DLB-72
Bowen, Elizabeth
  1899-1973 .... DLB-15, 162; CDBLB-7
Bowen, Francis 1811-1890 .... DLB-1, 59, 235
Bowen, John 1924- DLB-13
Bowen, Marjorie 1886-1952 .... DLB-153
Bowen-Merrill Company DLB-49
Bowering, George 1935- DLB-53
Bowers, Bathsheba 1671-1718 .... DLB-200
Bowers, Claude G. 1878-1958 .... DLB-17
Bowers, Edgar 1924-2000 .... DLB-5
Bowers, Fredson Thayer
  1905-1991 .... DLB-140; Y-80, 91
Bowles, Paul 1910-1999 ...... DLB-5, 6, 218; Y-99
Bowles, Samuel III 1826-1878 .... DLB-43
Bowles, William Lisles 1762-1850 .... DLB-93
Bowman, Louise Morey 1882-1944 ..... DLB-68
Boyd, James 1888-1944 .... DLB-9; DS-16
Boyd, John 1919- DLB-8
Boyd, Martin 1893-1972 .... DLB-260
Boyd, Thomas 1898-1935 .... DLB-9; DS-16
Boyd, William 1952- DLB-231
Boye, Karin 1900-1941 .... DLB-259
Boyesen, Hjalmar Hjorth
  1848-1895 .... DLB-12, 71; DS-13
Boyle, Kay 1902-1992 .... DLB-4, 9, 48, 86; Y-93
Boyle, Roger, Earl of Orrery 1621-1679 ... DLB-80
Boyle, T. Coraghessan 1948- DLB-218; Y-86
Božić, Mirko 1919- DLB-181
Brackenbury, Alison 1953- DLB-40
Brackenridge, Hugh Henry
  1748-1816 .... DLB-11, 37
Brackett, Charles 1892-1969 .... DLB-26
Brackett, Leigh 1915-1978 .... DLB-8, 26
Bradburn, John [publishing house] DLB-49
Bradbury, Malcolm 1932-2000 ...... DLB-14, 207
Bradbury, Ray 1920- DLB-2, 8; CDALB-6
Bradbury and Evans DLB-106
Braddon, Mary Elizabeth
  1835-1915 .... DLB-18, 70, 156
Bradford, Andrew 1686-1742 .... DLB-43, 73
Bradford, Gamaliel 1863-1932 .... DLB-17
Bradford, John 1749-1830 .... DLB-43
Bradford, Roark 1896-1948 .... DLB-86
Bradford, William 1590-1657 .... DLB-24, 30
Bradford, William III 1719-1791 ..... DLB-43, 73
Bradlaugh, Charles 1833-1891 .... DLB-57
Bradley, David 1950- DLB-33
Bradley, Ira, and Company DLB-49

Bradley, J. W., and Company DLB-49
Bradley, Katherine Harris (see Field, Michael)
Bradley, Marion Zimmer 1930-1999 .... DLB-8
Bradley, William Aspenwall 1878-1939 .... DLB-4
Bradshaw, Henry 1831-1886 .... DLB-184
Bradstreet, Anne
  1612 or 1613-1672 .... DLB-24; CDABL-2
Bradūnas, Kazys 1917- DLB-220
Bradwardine, Thomas circa
  1295-1349 .... DLB-115
Brady, Frank 1924-1986 .... DLB-111
Brady, Frederic A. [publishing house] DLB-49
Bragg, Melvyn 1939- DLB-14
Brainard, Charles H. [publishing house] .. DLB-49
Braine, John 1922-1986 . DLB-15; Y-86; CDBLB-7
Braithwait, Richard 1588-1673 .... DLB-151
Braithwaite, William Stanley
  1878-1962 .... DLB-50, 54
Braker, Ulrich 1735-1798 .... DLB-94
Bramah, Ernest 1868-1942 .... DLB-70
Branagan, Thomas 1774-1843 .... DLB-37
Branch, William Blackwell 1927- DLB-76
Brand, Max (see Faust, Frederick Schiller)
Branden Press DLB-46
Branner, H.C. 1903-1966 .... DLB-214
Brant, Sebastian 1457-1521 .... DLB-179
Brassey, Lady Annie (Allnutt)
  1839-1887 .... DLB-166
Brathwaite, Edward Kamau
  1930- DLB-125; CDWLB-3
Brault, Jacques 1933- DLB-53
Braun, Matt 1932- DLB-212
Braun, Volker 1939- DLB-75
Brautigan, Richard
  1935-1984 .... DLB-2, 5, 206; Y-80, Y-84
Braxton, Joanne M. 1950- DLB-41
Bray, Anne Eliza 1790-1883 .... DLB-116
Bray, Thomas 1656-1730 .... DLB-24
Brazdžionis, Bernardas 1907- DLB-220
Braziller, George [publishing house] DLB-46
The Bread Loaf Writers' Conference 1983 ... Y-84
Breasted, James Henry 1865-1935 .... DLB-47
Brecht, Bertolt
  1898-1956 .... DLB-56, 124; CDWLB-2
Bredel, Willi 1901-1964 .... DLB-56
Bregendahl, Marie 1867-1940 .... DLB-214
Breitinger, Johann Jakob 1701-1776 ...... DLB-97
Bremser, Bonnie 1939- DLB-16
Bremser, Ray 1934- DLB-16
Brennan, Christopher 1870-1932 .... DLB-230
Brentano, Bernard von 1901-1964 ...... DLB-56
Brentano, Clemens 1778-1842 .... DLB-90
Brentano's DLB-49
Brenton, Howard 1942- DLB-13
Breslin, Jimmy 1929-1996 .... DLB-185
Breton, André 1896-1966 .... DLB-65, 258

Breton, Nicholas circa 1555-circa 1626 ...DLB-136

The Breton Lays
 1300-early fifteenth century.........DLB-146

Brewer, Luther A. 1858-1933 ....DLB-187

Brewer, Warren and Putnam............DLB-46

Brewster, Elizabeth 1922- DLB-60

Breytenbach, Breyten 1939- DLB-225

Bridge, Ann (Lady Mary Dolling Sanders
 O'Malley) 1889-1974..............DLB-191

Bridge, Horatio 1806-1893 ....DLB-183

Bridgers, Sue Ellen 1942- DLB-52

Bridges, Robert
 1844-1930 ....DLB-19, 98; CDBLB-5

The Bridgewater Library..............DLB-213

Bridie, James 1888-1951 ....DLB-10

Brieux, Eugene 1858-1932............DLB-192

Brigadere, Anna 1861-1933...........DLB-220

Briggs, Charles Frederick
 1804-1877 ....DLB-3, 250

Brighouse, Harold 1882-1958 ....DLB-10

Bright, Mary Chavelita Dunne (see Egerton, George)

Brimmer, B. J., Company DLB-46

Brines, Francisco 1932- DLB-134

Brink, André 1935- DLB-225

Brinley, George, Jr. 1817-1875 ....DLB-140

Brinnin, John Malcolm 1916-1998.......DLB-48

Brisbane, Albert 1809-1890 ....DLB-3, 250

Brisbane, Arthur 1864-1936...........DLB-25

British Academy.....................DLB-112

The British Critic 1793-1843 ....DLB-110

The British Library and the Regular
 Readers' Group.....................Y-91

British Literary Prizes Y-98

The British Review and London Critical
 Journal 1811-1825..................DLB-110

British Travel Writing, 1940-1997.......DLB-204

Brito, Aristeo 1942- DLB-122

Brittain, Vera 1893-1970 ....DLB-191

Brizeux, Auguste 1803-1858 ....DLB-217

Broadway Publishing Company DLB-46

Broch, Hermann
 1886-1951 ....DLB-85, 124; CDWLB-2

Brochu, André 1942- DLB-53

Brock, Edwin 1927- DLB-40

Brockes, Barthold Heinrich 1680-1747....DLB-168

Brod, Max 1884-1968 ....DLB-81

Brodber, Erna 1940- DLB-157

Brodhead, John R. 1814-1873 ....DLB-30

Brodkey, Harold 1930-1996 ....DLB-130

Brodsky, Joseph 1940-1996 ....Y-87

Brodsky, Michael 1948- DLB-244

Broeg, Bob 1918- DLB-171

Brøgger, Suzanne 1944- DLB-214

Brome, Richard circa 1590-1652 ....DLB-58

Brome, Vincent 1910- DLB-155

Bromfield, Louis 1896-1956..........DLB-4, 9, 86

Bromige, David 1933- DLB-193

Broner, E. M. 1930- DLB-28

Bronk, William 1918-1999 ....DLB-165

Bronnen, Arnolt 1895-1959...........DLB-124

Brontë, Anne 1820-1849 ....DLB-21, 199

Brontë, Charlotte
 1816-1855 ......DLB-21, 159, 199; CDBLB-4

Brontë, Emily
 1818-1848 ......DLB-21, 32, 199; CDBLB-4

Brook, Stephen 1947- DLB-204

Brook Farm 1841-1847 ....DLB-223

Brooke, Frances 1724-1789 ....DLB-39, 99

Brooke, Henry 1703?-1783............DLB-39

Brooke, L. Leslie 1862-1940 ....DLB-141

Brooke, Margaret, Ranee of Sarawak
 1849-1936 ....DLB-174

Brooke, Rupert
 1887-1915 ....DLB-19, 216; CDBLB-6

Brooker, Bertram 1888-1955...........DLB-88

Brooke-Rose, Christine 1923- DLB-14, 231

Brookner, Anita 1928- DLB-194; Y-87

Brooks, Charles Timothy 1813-1883...DLB-1, 243

Brooks, Cleanth 1906-1994 ....DLB-63; Y-94

Brooks, Gwendolyn
 1917-2000 ....DLB-5, 76, 165; CDALB-1

Brooks, Jeremy 1926- DLB-14

Brooks, Mel 1926- DLB-26

Brooks, Noah 1830-1903..........DLB-42; DS-13

Brooks, Richard 1912-1992 ....DLB-44

Brooks, Van Wyck
 1886-1963 ....DLB-45, 63, 103

Brophy, Brigid 1929-1995 ....DLB-14

Brophy, John 1899-1965 ....DLB-191

Brossard, Chandler 1922-1993 ....DLB-16

Brossard, Nicole 1943- DLB-53

Broster, Dorothy Kathleen 1877-1950 ....DLB-160

Brother Antoninus (see Everson, William)

Brotherton, Lord 1856-1930 ....DLB-184

Brougham and Vaux, Henry Peter Brougham,
 Baron 1778-1868 ....DLB-110, 158

Brougham, John 1810-1880............DLB-11

Broughton, James 1913-1999............DLB-5

Broughton, Rhoda 1840-1920 ....DLB-18

Broun, Heywood 1888-1939 ......DLB-29, 171

Brown, Alice 1856-1940................DLB-78

Brown, Bob 1886-1959 ....DLB-4, 45

Brown, Cecil 1943- DLB-33

Brown, Charles Brockden
 1771-1810 ....DLB-37, 59, 73; CDALB-2

Brown, Christy 1932-1981 ....DLB-14

Brown, Dee 1908- Y-80

Brown, Frank London 1927-1962 ....DLB-76

Brown, Fredric 1906-1972 ....DLB-8

Brown, George Mackay
 1921-1996 ....DLB-14, 27, 139

Brown, Harry 1917-1986 ....DLB-26

Brown, Larry 1951- DLB-234

Brown, Marcia 1918- DLB-61

Brown, Margaret Wise 1910-1952........DLB-22

Brown, Morna Doris (see Ferrars, Elizabeth)

Brown, Oliver Madox 1855-1874 ....DLB-21

Brown, Sterling 1901-1989 ....DLB-48, 51, 63

Brown, T. E. 1830-1897 ....DLB-35

Brown, Thomas Alexander (see Boldrewood, Rolf)

Brown, Warren 1894-1978 ....DLB-241

Brown, William Hill 1765-1793 ....DLB-37

Brown, William Wells
 1815-1884 ....DLB-3, 50, 183, 248

Browne, Charles Farrar 1834-1867 ......DLB-11

Browne, Frances 1816-1879............DLB-199

Browne, Francis Fisher 1843-1913.......DLB-79

Browne, Howard 1908-1999 ....DLB-226

Browne, J. Ross 1821-1875 ....DLB-202

Browne, Michael Dennis 1940- DLB-40

Browne, Sir Thomas 1605-1682 ....DLB-151

Browne, William, of Tavistock
 1590-1645 ....DLB-121

Browne, Wynyard 1911-1964.......DLB-13, 233

Browne and Nolan...................DLB-106

Brownell, W. C. 1851-1928..............DLB-71

Browning, Elizabeth Barrett
 1806-1861 ....DLB-32, 199; CDBLB-4

Browning, Robert
 1812-1889 ....DLB-32, 163; CDBLB-4

Introductory Essay: Letters of Percy
 Bysshe Shelley (1852) DLB-32

Brownjohn, Allan 1931- DLB-40

Brownson, Orestes Augustus
 1803-1876 ....DLB-1, 59, 73, 243

Bruccoli, Matthew J. 1931- DLB-103

Bruce, Charles 1906-1971 ....DLB-68

John Edward Bruce: Three Documents....DLB-50

Bruce, Leo 1903-1979 ....DLB-77

Bruce, Mary Grant 1878-1958..........DLB-230

Bruce, Philip Alexander 1856-1933 ......DLB-47

Bruce Humphries [publishing house] DLB-46

Bruce-Novoa, Juan 1944- DLB-82

Bruckman, Clyde 1894-1955............DLB-26

Bruckner, Ferdinand 1891-1958 ....DLB-118

Brundage, John Herbert (see Herbert, John)

Brutus, Dennis
 1924- DLB-117, 225; CDWLB-3

Bryan, C. D. B. 1936- DLB-185

Bryant, Arthur 1899-1985 ....DLB-149

Bryant, William Cullen 1794-1878
 ....DLB-3, 43, 59, 189, 250; CDALB-2

Bryce Echenique, Alfredo
 1939- DLB-145; CDWLB-3

Bryce, James 1838-1922..........DLB-166, 190

Bryden, Bill 1942- DLB-233

Brydges, Sir Samuel Egerton 1762-1837 ..DLB-107

Bryskett, Lodowick 1546?-1612 ....DLB-167

Buchan, John 1875-1940 ....DLB-34, 70, 156

Buchanan, George 1506-1582 ....DLB-132

Buchanan, Robert 1841-1901 . . . . DLB-18, 35

"The Fleshly School of Poetry and Other Phenomena of the Day" (1872), by Robert Buchanan DLB-35

"The Fleshly School of Poetry: Mr. D. G. Rossetti" (1871), by Thomas Maitland (Robert Buchanan) DLB-35

Buchman, Sidney 1902-1975 . . . . DLB-26

Buchner, Augustus 1591-1661 . . . . DLB-164

Büchner, Georg 1813-1837 . . DLB-133; CDWLB-2

Bucholtz, Andreas Heinrich 1607-1671 . . . DLB-168

Buck, Pearl S. 1892-1973 . . DLB-9, 102; CDALB-7

Bucke, Charles 1781-1846 . . . . DLB-110

Bucke, Richard Maurice 1837-1902 . . . . . . DLB-99

Buckingham, Joseph Tinker 1779-1861 and Buckingham, Edwin 1810-1833 . . . . . . DLB-73

Buckler, Ernest 1908-1984 . . . . DLB-68

Buckley, William F., Jr. 1925- DLB-137; Y-80

Buckminster, Joseph Stevens 1784-1812 . . . . DLB-37

Buckner, Robert 1906- DLB-26

Budd, Thomas ?-1698 . . . . DLB-24

Budrys, A. J. 1931- DLB-8

Buechner, Frederick 1926- Y-80

Buell, John 1927- DLB-53

Bufalino, Gesualdo 1920-1996 . . . . DLB-196

Buffum, Job [publishing house] DLB-49

Bugnet, Georges 1879-1981 . . . . DLB-92

Buies, Arthur 1840-1901 . . . . DLB-99

Building the New British Library at St Pancras Y-94

Bukowski, Charles 1920-1994 . . . DLB-5, 130, 169

Bulatović, Miodrag 1930-1991 . . . . DLB-181; CDWLB-4

Bulgarin, Faddei Venediktovich 1789-1859 . . . . DLB-198

Bulger, Bozeman 1877-1932 . . . . DLB-171

Bullein, William between 1520 and 1530-1576 . . . . DLB-167

Bullins, Ed 1935- DLB-7, 38, 249

Bulwer, John 1606-1656 . . . . DLB-236

Bulwer-Lytton, Edward (also Edward Bulwer) 1803-1873 . . . . DLB-21

"On Art in Fiction "(1838) DLB-21

Bumpus, Jerry 1937- Y-81

Bunce and Brother DLB-49

Bunner, H. C. 1855-1896 . . . . DLB-78, 79

Bunting, Basil 1900-1985 . . . . DLB-20

Buntline, Ned (Edward Zane Carroll Judson) 1821-1886 . . . . DLB-186

Bunyan, John 1628-1688 . . . . . DLB-39; CDBLB-2

Burch, Robert 1925- DLB-52

Burciaga, José Antonio 1940- DLB-82

Burdekin, Katharine 1896-1963 . . . . DLB-255

Bürger, Gottfried August 1747-1794 . . . . . DLB-94

Burgess, Anthony 1917-1993 . . . . DLB-14, 194; CDBLB-8

The Anthony Burgess Archive at the Harry Ransom Humanities Research Center Y-98

Anthony Burgess's 99 Novels: An Opinion Poll Y-84

Burgess, Gelett 1866-1951 . . . . DLB-11

Burgess, John W. 1844-1931 . . . . DLB-47

Burgess, Thornton W. 1874-1965 . . . . . . DLB-22

Burgess, Stringer and Company DLB-49

Burick, Si 1909-1986 . . . . DLB-171

Burk, John Daly circa 1772-1808 . . . . DLB-37

Burk, Ronnie 1955- DLB-209

Burke, Edmund 1729?-1797 . . . . . . DLB-104, 252

Burke, James Lee 1936- DLB-226

Burke, Kenneth 1897-1993 . . . . DLB-45, 63

Burke, Thomas 1886-1945 . . . . DLB-197

Burley, Dan 1907-1962 . . . . DLB-241

Burlingame, Edward Livermore 1848-1922 . . . . DLB-79

Burman, Carina 1960- DLB-257

Burnet, Gilbert 1643-1715 . . . . DLB-101

Burnett, Frances Hodgson 1849-1924 . . . . DLB-42, 141; DS-13, 14

Burnett, W. R. 1899-1982 . . . . DLB-9, 226

Burnett, Whit 1899-1973 and Martha Foley 1897-1977 . . . . DLB-137

Burney, Fanny 1752-1840 . . . . DLB-39

Dedication, The Wanderer (1814) DLB-39

Preface to Evelina (1778) DLB-39

Burns, Alan 1929- DLB-14, 194

Burns, John Horne 1916-1953 . . . . Y-85

Burns, Robert 1759-1796 . . . . DLB-109; CDBLB-3

Burns and Oates DLB-106

Burnshaw, Stanley 1906- DLB-48

Burr, C. Chauncey 1815?-1883 . . . . DLB-79

Burr, Esther Edwards 1732-1758 . . . . . . DLB-200

Burroughs, Edgar Rice 1875-1950 . . . . DLB-8

Burroughs, John 1837-1921 . . . . DLB-64

Burroughs, Margaret T. G. 1917- DLB-41

Burroughs, William S., Jr. 1947-1981 . . . . DLB-16

Burroughs, William Seward 1914-1997 . . . . DLB-2, 8, 16, 152, 237; Y-81, Y-97

Burroway, Janet 1936- DLB-6

Burt, Maxwell Struthers 1882-1954 . . . . DLB-86; DS-16

Burt, A. L., and Company DLB-49

Burton, Hester 1913- DLB-161

Burton, Isabel Arundell 1831-1896 . . . . . DLB-166

Burton, Miles (see Rhode, John)

Burton, Richard Francis 1821-1890 . . . . DLB-55, 166, 184

Burton, Robert 1577-1640 . . . . DLB-151

Burton, Virginia Lee 1909-1968 . . . . DLB-22

Burton, William Evans 1804-1860 . . . . . . DLB-73

Burwell, Adam Hood 1790-1849 . . . . DLB-99

Bury, Lady Charlotte 1775-1861 . . . . DLB-116

Busch, Frederick 1941- DLB-6, 218

Busch, Niven 1903-1991 . . . . DLB-44

Bushnell, Horace 1802-1876 . . . . DS-13

Bussieres, Arthur de 1877-1913 . . . . DLB-92

Butler, Charles ca. 1560-1647 . . . . DLB-236

Butler, Guy 1918- DLB-225

Butler, E. H., and Company DLB-49

Butler, Joseph 1692-1752 . . . . DLB-252

Butler, Josephine Elizabeth 1828-1906 . . . DLB-190

Butler, Juan 1942-1981 . . . . DLB-53

Butler, Judith 1956- DLB-246

Butler, Octavia E. 1947- DLB-33

Butler, Pierce 1884-1953 . . . . DLB-187

Butler, Robert Olen 1945- DLB-173

Butler, Samuel 1613-1680 . . . . DLB-101, 126

Butler, Samuel 1835-1902 . . . . . . DLB-18, 57, 174

Butler, William Francis 1838-1910 . . . . . DLB-166

Butor, Michel 1926- DLB-83

Butter, Nathaniel [publishing house] DLB-170

Butterworth, Hezekiah 1839-1905 . . . . . . DLB-42

Buttitta, Ignazio 1899- DLB-114

Butts, Mary 1890-1937 . . . . DLB-240

Buzzati, Dino 1906-1972 . . . . DLB-177

Byars, Betsy 1928- DLB-52

Byatt, A. S. 1936- DLB-14, 194

Byles, Mather 1707-1788 . . . . DLB-24

Bynneman, Henry [publishing house] DLB-170

Bynner, Witter 1881-1968 . . . . DLB-54

Byrd, William circa 1543-1623 . . . . DLB-172

Byrd, William II 1674-1744 . . . . DLB-24, 140

Byrne, John Keyes (see Leonard, Hugh)

Byron, George Gordon, Lord 1788-1824 . . . . DLB-96, 110; CDBLB-3

Byron, Robert 1905-1941 . . . . DLB-195

C

Caballero Bonald, José Manuel 1926- DLB-108

Cabañero, Eladio 1930- DLB-134

Cabell, James Branch 1879-1958 . . . . . . DLB-9, 78

Cabeza de Baca, Manuel 1853-1915 . . . . DLB-122

Cabeza de Baca Gilbert, Fabiola 1898- DLB-122

Cable, George Washington 1844-1925 . . . . DLB-12, 74; DS-13

Cable, Mildred 1878-1952 . . . . DLB-195

Cabrera, Lydia 1900-1991 . . . . DLB-145

Cabrera Infante, Guillermo 1929- DLB-113; CDWLB-3

Cadell [publishing house] DLB-154

Cady, Edwin H. 1917- DLB-103

Caedmon flourished 658-680 . . . . DLB-146

Caedmon School circa 660-899 . . . . DLB-146

Cafés, Brasseries, and Bistros DS-15

Cage, John 1912-1992 . . . . DLB-193

Cahan, Abraham 1860-1951 . . . . . . DLB-9, 25, 28

Cain, George 1943- DLB-33	Campbell, William Wilfred 1858-1918 ....DLB-92	The Hero as Poet. Dante; Shakspeare (1841).................DLB-32
Cain, James M. 1892-1977.............DLB-226	Campion, Edmund 1539-1581 ....DLB-167	Carman, Bliss 1861-1929................DLB-92
Caird, Mona 1854-1932................DLB-197	Campion, Thomas 1567-1620 ....DLB-58, 172; CDBLB-1	*Carmina Burana* circa 1230 ....DLB-138
Čaks, Aleksandrs 1901-1950 ....DLB-220; CDWLB-4	Campton, David 1924- DLB-245	Carnero, Guillermo 1947- DLB-108
Caldecott, Randolph 1846-1886 ....DLB-163	Camus, Albert 1913-1960 ....DLB-72	Carossa, Hans 1878-1956 ....DLB-66
Calder, John (Publishers), Limited......DLB-112	The Canadian Publishers' Records Database Y-96	Carpenter, Humphrey 1946- DLB-155; Y-84, Y-99
Calderón de la Barca, Fanny 1804-1882................DLB-183	Canby, Henry Seidel 1878-1961 ....DLB-91	The Practice of Biography III: An Interview with Humphrey Carpenter Y-84
Caldwell, Ben 1937- DLB-38	Candelaria, Cordelia 1943- DLB-82	Carpenter, Stephen Cullen ?-1820?.......DLB-73
Caldwell, Erskine 1903-1987 ....DLB-9, 86	Candelaria, Nash 1928- DLB-82	Carpentier, Alejo 1904-1980 .... DLB-113; CDWLB-3
Caldwell, H. M., Company............DLB-49	Canetti, Elias 1905-1994 ....DLB-85, 124; CDWLB-2	Carr, Marina 1964- DLB-245
Caldwell, Taylor 1900-1985 .... DS-17	Canham, Erwin Dain 1904-1982........DLB-127	Carrier, Roch 1937- DLB-53
Calhoun, John C. 1782-1850 ... DLB-3, 248	Canitz, Friedrich Rudolph Ludwig von 1654-1699.....................DLB-168	Carrillo, Adolfo 1855-1926 ....DLB-122
Călinescu, George 1899-1965 ....DLB-220	Cankar, Ivan 1876-1918.....DLB-147; CDWLB-4	Carroll, Gladys Hasty 1904- DLB-9
Calisher, Hortense 1911- DLB-2, 218	Cannan, Gilbert 1884-1955 .... DLB-10, 197	Carroll, John 1735-1815................DLB-37
A Call to Letters and an Invitation to the Electric Chair, by Siegfried Mandel DLB-75	Cannan, Joanna 1896-1961 ....DLB-191	Carroll, John 1809-1884 ....DLB-99
Callaghan, Mary Rose 1944- DLB-207	Cannell, Kathleen 1891-1974 ....DLB-4	Carroll, Lewis 1832-1898......DLB-18, 163, 178; CDBLB-4
Callaghan, Morley 1903-1990 ....DLB-68	Cannell, Skipwith 1887-1957 ....DLB-45	The Lewis Carroll Centenary Y-98
Callahan, S. Alice 1868-1894....... DLB-175, 221	Canning, George 1770-1827............DLB-158	Carroll, Paul 1927- DLB-16
Callaloo........................ Y-87	Cannon, Jimmy 1910-1973 ....DLB-171	Carroll, Paul Vincent 1900-1968.........DLB-10
Callimachus circa 305 B.C.-240 B.C......DLB-176	Cano, Daniel 1947- DLB-209	Carroll and Graf Publishers DLB-46
Calmer, Edgar 1907- DLB-4	Cantú, Norma Elia 1947- DLB-209	Carruth, Hayden 1921- DLB-5, 165
Calverley, C. S. 1831-1884 ....DLB-35	Cantwell, Robert 1908-1978 ....DLB-9	Carryl, Charles E. 1841-1920 ....DLB-42
Calvert, George Henry 1803-1889 .... DLB-1, 64, 248	Cape, Jonathan, and Harrison Smith [publishing house]................DLB-46	Carson, Anne 1950- DLB-193
Calvino, Italo 1923-1985 ....DLB-196	Cape, Jonathan, Limited DLB-112	Carswell, Catherine 1879-1946 ....DLB-36
Cambridge, Ada 1844-1926............DLB-230	Čapek, Karel 1890-1938 ....DLB-215; CDWLB-4	Cărtărescu, Mirea 1956- DLB-232
Cambridge Press DLB-49	Capen, Joseph 1658-1725..............DLB-24	Carter, Elizabeth 1717-1806 ....DLB-109
Cambridge Songs (Carmina Cantabrigensia) circa 1050 ....DLB-148	Capes, Bernard 1854-1918.............DLB-156	Carter, Henry (see Leslie, Frank)
	Capote, Truman 1924-1984 ..... DLB-2, 185, 227; Y-80, Y-84; CDALB-1	Carter, Hodding, Jr. 1907-1972 .... DLB-127
Cambridge University Press DLB-170		Carter, John 1905-1975 ....DLB-201
Camden, William 1551-1623............DLB-172	Capps, Benjamin 1922- DLB-256	Carter, Landon 1710-1778 ....DLB-31
Camden House: An Interview with James Hardin....................Y-92	Caproni, Giorgio 1912-1990 ....DLB-128	Carter, Lin 1930- Y-81
Cameron, Eleanor 1912- DLB-52	Caragiale, Mateiu Ioan 1885-1936........DLB-220	Carter, Martin 1927-1997.... DLB-117; CDWLB-3
Cameron, George Frederick 1854-1885 ....DLB-99	Cardarelli, Vincenzo 1887-1959.........DLB-114	Carter, Robert, and Brothers............DLB-49
	Cárdenas, Reyes 1948- DLB-122	Carter and Hendee DLB-49
Cameron, Lucy Lyttelton 1781-1858.....DLB-163	Cardinal, Marie 1929- DLB-83	Cartwright, Jim 1958- DLB-245
Cameron, Peter 1959- DLB-234	Carew, Jan 1920- DLB-157	Cartwright, John 1740-1824............DLB-158
Cameron, William Bleasdell 1862-1951 ...DLB-99	Carew, Thomas 1594 or 1595-1640.....DLB-126	Cartwright, William circa 1611-1643 ....DLB-126
Camm, John 1718-1778 ....DLB-31	Carey, Henry circa 1687-1689-1743.......DLB-84	Caruthers, William Alexander 1802-1846 .... DLB-3, 248
Camon, Ferdinando 1935- DLB-196	Carey, M., and Company DLB-49	
Camp, Walter 1859-1925 ....DLB-241	Carey, Mathew 1760-1839.......... DLB-37, 73	Carver, Jonathan 1710-1780 ....DLB-31
Campana, Dino 1885-1932 ....DLB-114	Carey and Hart DLB-49	Carver, Raymond 1938-1988 .... DLB-130; Y-83, Y-88
Campbell, Bebe Moore 1950- DLB-227	Carlell, Lodowick 1602-1675............DLB-58	First Strauss "Livings" Awarded to Cynthia Ozick and Raymond Carver An Interview with Raymond Carver Y-83
Campbell, David 1915-1979............DLB-260	Carleton, William 1794-1869...........DLB-159	
Campbell, Gabrielle Margaret Vere (see Shearing, Joseph, and Bowen, Marjorie)	Carleton, G. W. [publishing house].......DLB-49	Cary, Alice 1820-1871 ....DLB-202
	Carlile, Richard 1790-1843 .... DLB-110, 158	Cary, Joyce 1888-1957....DLB-15, 100; CDBLB-6
Campbell, James Dykes 1838-1895 ......DLB-144	Carlson, Ron 1947- DLB-244	Cary, Patrick 1623?-1657 ....DLB-131
Campbell, James Edwin 1867-1896 ......DLB-50	Carlyle, Jane Welsh 1801-1866 ....DLB-55	Casey, Gavin 1907-1964 ....DLB-260
Campbell, John 1653-1728..............DLB-43	Carlyle, Thomas 1795-1881 ....DLB-55, 144; CDBLB-3	Casey, Juanita 1925- DLB-14
Campbell, John W., Jr. 1910-1971 ....DLB-8		Casey, Michael 1947- DLB-5
Campbell, Roy 1901-1957 ....DLB-20, 225	"The Hero as Man of Letters: Johnson, Rousseau, Burns" (1841) [excerpt] DLB-57	Cassady, Carolyn 1923- DLB-16
Campbell, Thomas 1777-1844 .... DLB-93, 144		

Cassady, Neal 1926-1968 . . . . DLB-16, 237
Cassell and Company DLB-106
Cassell Publishing Company DLB-49
Cassill, R. V. 1919- DLB-6, 218
Cassity, Turner 1929- DLB-105
Cassius Dio circa 155/164-post 229 . . . . . . DLB-176
Cassola, Carlo 1917-1987 . . . . DLB-177
The Castle of Perserverance circa 1400-1425 . DLB-146
Castellano, Olivia 1944- DLB-122
Castellanos, Rosario
 1925-1974 . . . . DLB-113; CDWLB-3
Castillo, Ana 1953- DLB-122, 227
Castillo, Rafael C. 1950- DLB-209
Castlemon, Harry (see Fosdick, Charles Austin)
Čašule, Kole 1921- DLB-181
Caswall, Edward 1814-1878 . . . . DLB-32
Catacalos, Rosemary 1944- DLB-122
Cather, Willa 1873-1947
 . . . . DLB-9, 54, 78, 256; DS-1; CDALB-3
Catherine II (Ekaterina Alekseevna), "The Great,"
 Empress of Russia 1729-1796 . . . . . . DLB-150
Catherwood, Mary Hartwell 1847-1902 . . . DLB-78
Catledge, Turner 1901-1983 . . . . DLB-127
Catlin, George 1796-1872 . . . . DLB-186, 189
Cato the Elder 234 B.C.-149 B.C. DLB-211
Cattafi, Bartolo 1922-1979 . . . . DLB-128
Catton, Bruce 1899-1978 . . . . DLB-17
Catullus circa 84 B.C.-54 B.C.
 . . . . DLB-211; CDWLB-1
Causley, Charles 1917- DLB-27
Caute, David 1936- DLB-14, 231
Cavendish, Duchess of Newcastle,
 Margaret Lucas 1623-1673 . . . . DLB-131, 252
Cawein, Madison 1865-1914 . . . . DLB-54
Caxton, William [publishing house] DLB-170
The Caxton Printers, Limited DLB-46
Caylor, O. P. 1849-1897 . . . . DLB-241
Cayrol, Jean 1911- DLB-83
Cecil, Lord David 1902-1986 . . . . DLB-155
Cela, Camilo José 1916- Y-89
Celan, Paul 1920-1970 . . . . . . DLB-69; CDWLB-2
Celati, Gianni 1937- DLB-196
Celaya, Gabriel 1911-1991 . . . . DLB-108
A Celebration of Literary Biography Y-98
Céline, Louis-Ferdinand 1894-1961 . . . . . . DLB-72
The Celtic Background to Medieval English
 Literature DLB-146
Celtis, Conrad 1459-1508 . . . . DLB-179
Cendrars, Blaise 1887-1961 . . . . DLB-258
Center for Bibliographical Studies and
 Research at the University of
 California, Riverside Y-91
The Center for the Book in the Library
 of Congress Y-93
Center for the Book Research Y-84
Centlivre, Susanna 1669?-1723 . . . . DLB-84

The Centre for Writing, Publishing and
 Printing History at the University
 of Reading Y-00
The Century Company DLB-49
Cernuda, Luis 1902-1963 . . . . DLB-134
Cervantes, Lorna Dee 1954- DLB-82
Ch., T. (see Marchenko, Anastasiia Iakovlevna)
Chaadaev, Petr Iakovlevich
 1794-1856 . . . . DLB-198
Chacel, Rosa 1898- DLB-134
Chacón, Eusebio 1869-1948 . . . . DLB-82
Chacón, Felipe Maximiliano 1873-? DLB-82
Chadwick, Henry 1824-1908 . . . . DLB-241
Chadwyck-Healey's Full-Text Literary Databases:
 Editing Commercial Databases of
 Primary Literary Texts Y-95
Challans, Eileen Mary (see Renault, Mary)
Chalmers, George 1742-1825 . . . . DLB-30
Chaloner, Sir Thomas 1520-1565 . . . . . . DLB-167
Chamberlain, Samuel S. 1851-1916 . . . . . DLB-25
Chamberland, Paul 1939- DLB-60
Chamberlin, William Henry 1897-1969 . . . DLB-29
Chambers, Charles Haddon 1860-1921 . . . DLB-10
Chambers, María Cristina (see Mena, María Cristina)
Chambers, Robert W. 1865-1933 . . . . . . DLB-202
Chambers, W. and R.
 [publishing house] DLB-106
Chamisso, Albert von 1781-1838 . . . . DLB-90
Champfleury 1821-1889 . . . . DLB-119
Chandler, Harry 1864-1944 . . . . DLB-29
Chandler, Norman 1899-1973 . . . . DLB-127
Chandler, Otis 1927- DLB-127
Chandler, Raymond
 1888-1959 . . . DLB-226, 253; DS-6; CDALB-5
Raymond Chandler Centenary Tributes
 from Michael Avallone, James Ellroy,
 Joe Gores, and William F. Nolan Y-88
Channing, Edward 1856-1931 . . . . DLB-17
Channing, Edward Tyrrell
 1790-1856 . . . . DLB-1, 59, 235
Channing, William Ellery
 1780-1842 . . . . DLB-1, 59, 235
Channing, William Ellery II
 1817-1901 . . . . DLB-1, 223
Channing, William Henry
 1810-1884 . . . . DLB-1, 59, 243
Chaplin, Charlie 1889-1977 . . . . DLB-44
Chapman, George
 1559 or 1560-1634 . . . . DLB-62, 121
Chapman, John DLB-106
Chapman, Olive Murray 1892-1977 . . . . . DLB-195
Chapman, R. W. 1881-1960 . . . . DLB-201
Chapman, William 1850-1917 . . . . DLB-99
Chapman and Hall DLB-106
Chappell, Fred 1936- DLB-6, 105
"A Detail in a Poem" DLB-105
Chappell, William 1582-1649 . . . . DLB-236
Char, René 1907-1988 . . . . DLB-258
Charbonneau, Jean 1875-1960 . . . . DLB-92

Charbonneau, Robert 1911-1967 . . . . DLB-68
Charles, Gerda 1914- DLB-14
Charles, William [publishing house] DLB-49
Charles d'Orléans 1394-1465 . . . . DLB-208
Charley (see Mann, Charles)
Charteris, Leslie 1907-1993 . . . . DLB-77
Chartier, Alain circa 1385-1430 . . . . DLB-208
Charyn, Jerome 1937- Y-83
Chase, Borden 1900-1971 . . . . DLB-26
Chase, Edna Woolman 1877-1957 . . . . . . DLB-91
Chase, Mary Coyle 1907-1981 . . . . DLB-228
Chase-Riboud, Barbara 1936- DLB-33
Chateaubriand, François-René de
 1768-1848 . . . . DLB-119
Chatterton, Thomas 1752-1770 . . . . DLB-109
Essay on Chatterton (1842), by
 Robert Browning DLB-32
Chatto and Windus DLB-106
Chatwin, Bruce 1940-1989 . . . . DLB-194, 204
Chaucer, Geoffrey
 1340?-1400 . . . . DLB-146; CDBLB-1
Chauncy, Charles 1705-1787 . . . . DLB-24
Chauveau, Pierre-Joseph-Olivier
 1820-1890 . . . . DLB-99
Chávez, Denise 1948- DLB-122
Chávez, Fray Angélico 1910- DLB-82
Chayefsky, Paddy 1923-1981 . . . . DLB-7, 44; Y-81
Cheesman, Evelyn 1881-1969 . . . . DLB-195
Cheever, Ezekiel 1615-1708 . . . . DLB-24
Cheever, George Barrell 1807-1890 . . . . . DLB-59
Cheever, John 1912-1982
 . . . . . . DLB-2, 102, 227; Y-80, Y-82; CDALB-1
Cheever, Susan 1943- Y-82
Cheke, Sir John 1514-1557 . . . . DLB-132
Chelsea House DLB-46
Chênedollé, Charles de 1769-1833 . . . . . . DLB-217
Cheney, Ednah Dow 1824-1904 . . . . . DLB-1, 223
Cheney, Harriet Vaughn 1796-1889 . . . . . DLB-99
Chénier, Marie-Joseph 1764-1811 . . . . . . DLB-192
Chernyshevsky, Nikolai Gavrilovich
 1828-1889 . . . . DLB-238
Cherry, Kelly 1940- Y-83
Cherryh, C. J. 1942- Y-80
Chesebro', Caroline 1825-1873 . . . . DLB-202
Chesney, Sir George Tomkyns
 1830-1895 . . . . DLB-190
Chesnut, Mary Boykin 1823-1886 . . . . . . DLB-239
Chesnutt, Charles Waddell
 1858-1932 . . . . DLB-12, 50, 78
Chesson, Mrs. Nora (see Hopper, Nora)
Chester, Alfred 1928-1971 . . . . DLB-130
Chester, George Randolph 1869-1924 . . . DLB-78
The Chester Plays circa 1505-1532;
 revisions until 1575 . . . . DLB-146
Chesterfield, Philip Dormer Stanhope,
 Fourth Earl of 1694-1773 . . . . DLB-104
Chesterton, G. K. 1874-1936
 . . . DLB-10, 19, 34, 70, 98, 149, 178; CDBLB-6

Chettle, Henry circa 1560-circa 1607.....DLB-136	Cicero 106 B.C.-43 B.C........DLB-211, CDWLB-1	Cleaver, Vera 1919- and Cleaver, Bill 1920-1981..............DLB-52
Cheuse, Alan 1940- DLB-244	Cima, Annalisa 1941- DLB-128	Cleland, John 1710-1789 ....DLB-39
Chew, Ada Nield 1870-1945 ....DLB-135	Čingo, Živko 1935-1987 ....DLB-181	Clemens, Samuel Langhorne (Mark Twain) 1835-1910..........DLB-11, 12, 23, 64, 74, 186, 189; CDALB-3
Cheyney, Edward P. 1861-1947 ....DLB-47	Cioran, E. M. 1911-1995..............DLB-220	
Chiara, Piero 1913-1986 ....DLB-177	Čipkus, Alfonsas (see Nyka-Niliūnas, Alfonsas)	Mark Twain on Perpetual Copyright Y-92
Chicano History DLB-82	Cirese, Eugenio 1884-1955 ....DLB-114	Clement, Hal 1922- DLB-8
Chicano Language....................DLB-82	Cīrulis, Jānis (see Bels, Alberts)	Clemo, Jack 1916- DLB-27
Child, Francis James 1825-1896....DLB-1, 64, 235	Cisneros, Sandra 1954- DLB-122, 152	Clephane, Elizabeth Cecilia 1830-1869....................DLB-199
Child, Lydia Maria 1802-1880 ....DLB-1, 74, 243	City Lights Books DLB-46	
Child, Philip 1898-1978 ....DLB-68	Cixous, Hélène 1937-...........DLB-83, 242	Cleveland, John 1613-1658 ....DLB-126
Childers, Erskine 1870-1922 ....DLB-70	The Claims of Business and Literature: An Undergraduate Essay by Maxwell Perkins....................Y-01	Cliff, Michelle 1946- DLB-157; CDWLB-3
Children's Book Awards and Prizes.......DLB-61		Clifford, Lady Anne 1590-1676..........DLB-151
Children's Illustrators, 1800-1880 ....DLB-163		Clifford, James L. 1901-1978............DLB-103
Childress, Alice 1916-1994 ....DLB-7, 38, 249	Clampitt, Amy 1920-1994..............DLB-105	Clifford, Lucy 1853?-1929.....DLB-135, 141, 197
Childs, George W. 1829-1894...........DLB-23	Clancy, Tom 1947- DLB-227	Clift, Charmian 1923-1969 ....DLB-260
Chilton Book Company DLB-46	Clapper, Raymond 1892-1944..........DLB-29	Clifton, Lucille 1936- DLB-5, 41
Chin, Frank 1940- DLB-206	Clare, John 1793-1864................DLB-55, 96	Clines, Francis X. 1938- DLB-185
Chinweizu 1943- DLB-157	Clarendon, Edward Hyde, Earl of 1609-1674....................DLB-101	Clive, Caroline (V) 1801-1873..........DLB-199
Chitham, Edward 1932- DLB-155		Clode, Edward J. [publishing house] DLB-46
Chittenden, Hiram Martin 1858-1917 .....DLB-47	Clark, Alfred Alexander Gordon (see Hare, Cyril)	Clough, Arthur Hugh 1819-1861 ....DLB-32
Chivers, Thomas Holley 1809-1858 ...DLB-3, 248	Clark, Ann Nolan 1896- DLB-52	Cloutier, Cécile 1930- DLB-60
Cholmondeley, Mary 1859-1925........DLB-107	Clark, C. E. Frazer, Jr. 1925- DLB-187; Y-01	Clouts, Sidney 1926-1982 ....DLB-225
Chomsky, Noam 1928- DLB-246	Clark, C. M., Publishing Company.......DLB-46	Clutton-Brock, Arthur 1868-1924......DLB-98
Chopin, Kate 1850-1904 ...DLB-12, 78; CDALB-3	Clark, Catherine Anthony 1892-1977 .....DLB-68	Coates, Robert M. 1897-1973........DLB-4, 9, 102
Chopin, Rene 1885-1953..............DLB-92	Clark, Charles Heber 1841-1915.........DLB-11	Coatsworth, Elizabeth 1893- DLB-22
Choquette, Adrienne 1915-1973 ....DLB-68	Clark, Davis Wasgatt 1812-1871 ....DLB-79	Cobb, Charles E., Jr. 1943- DLB-41
Choquette, Robert 1905- DLB-68	Clark, Eleanor 1913- DLB-6	Cobb, Frank I. 1869-1923 ....DLB-25
Choyce, Lesley 1951- DLB-251	Clark, J. P. 1935- DLB-117; CDWLB-3	Cobb, Irvin S. 1876-1944.........DLB-11, 25, 86
Chrétien de Troyes circa 1140-circa 1190..............DLB-208	Clark, Lewis Gaylord 1808-1873 ....DLB-3, 64, 73, 250	Cobbe, Frances Power 1822-1904.......DLB-190
		Cobbett, William 1763-1835 ....DLB-43, 107
Christensen, Inger 1935- DLB-214	Clark, Walter Van Tilburg 1909-1971 ....DLB-9, 206	Cobbledick, Gordon 1898-1969 ....DLB-171
The Christian Publishing Company DLB-49		Cochran, Thomas C. 1902- DLB-17
Christie, Agatha 1890-1976 ....DLB-13, 77, 245; CDBLB-6	Clark, William (see Lewis, Meriwether)	Cochrane, Elizabeth 1867-1922 .....DLB-25, 189
	Clark, William Andrews Jr. 1877-1934 ...DLB-187	Cockerell, Sir Sydney 1867-1962........DLB-201
Christine de Pizan circa 1365-circa 1431..............DLB-208	Clarke, Austin 1896-1974..............DLB-10, 20	Cockerill, John A. 1845-1896 ....DLB-23
	Clarke, Austin C. 1934- DLB-53, 125	Cocteau, Jean 1889-1963............DLB-65, 258
Christopher, John 1922- DLB-255	Clarke, Gillian 1937-..................DLB-40	Coderre, Emile (see Jean Narrache)
Christus und die Samariterin circa 950 ......DLB-148	Clarke, James Freeman 1810-1888 ....DLB-1, 59, 235	Coe, Jonathan 1961- DLB-231
Christy, Howard Chandler 1873-1952 ....DLB-188		Coetzee, J. M. 1940- DLB-225
Chulkov, Mikhail Dmitrievich 1713?-1792......................DLB-150	Clarke, Lindsay 1939- DLB-231	Coffee, Lenore J. 1900?-1984 ....DLB-44
	Clarke, Marcus 1846-1881 ....DLB-230	Coffin, Robert P. Tristram 1892-1955.....DLB-45
Church, Benjamin 1734-1778............DLB-31	Clarke, Pauline 1921- DLB-161	Coghill, Mrs. Harry (see Walker, Anna Louisa)
Church, Francis Pharcellus 1839-1906 ....DLB-79	Clarke, Rebecca Sophia 1833-1906 ......DLB-42	Cogswell, Fred 1917- DLB-60
Church, Peggy Pond 1903-1986 ....DLB-212	Clarke, Robert, and Company DLB-49	Cogswell, Mason Fitch 1761-1830........DLB-37
Church, Richard 1893-1972............DLB-191	Clarke, Samuel 1675-1729 ....DLB-252	Cohan, George M. 1878-1942 ....DLB-249
Church, William Conant 1836-1917 .....DLB-79	Clarkson, Thomas 1760-1846 ....DLB-158	Cohen, Arthur A. 1928-1986 ....DLB-28
Churchill, Caryl 1938- DLB-13	Claudel, Paul 1868-1955 ....DLB-192, 258	Cohen, Leonard 1934- DLB-53
Churchill, Charles 1731-1764...........DLB-109	Claudius, Matthias 1740-1815 ....DLB-97	Cohen, Matt 1942- DLB-53
Churchill, Winston 1871-1947.........DLB-202	Clausen, Andy 1943- DLB-16	Colbeck, Norman 1903-1987...........DLB-201
Churchill, Sir Winston 1874-1965 ....DLB-100; DS-16; CDBLB-5	Clawson, John L. 1865-1933 ....DLB-187	Colden, Cadwallader 1688-1776 .....DLB-24, 30
	Claxton, Remsen and Haffelfinger DLB-49	Colden, Jane 1724-1766 ....DLB-200
Churchyard, Thomas 1520?-1604.......DLB-132	Clay, Cassius Marcellus 1810-1903.......DLB-43	Cole, Barry 1936- DLB-14
Churton, E., and Company............DLB-106	Cleage, Pearl 1948- DLB-228	
Chute, Marchette 1909-1994...........DLB-103	Cleary, Beverly 1916- DLB-52	Cole, George Watson 1850-1939 ....DLB-140
Ciardi, John 1916-1986 ....DLB-5; Y-86	Cleary, Kate McPhelim 1863-1905 ......DLB-221	
Cibber, Colley 1671-1757...............DLB-84		

Cumulative Index

Colegate, Isabel 1931- DLB-14, 231
Coleman, Emily Holmes 1899-1974 .... DLB-4
Coleman, Wanda 1946- DLB-130
Coleridge, Hartley 1796-1849 .... DLB-96
Coleridge, Mary 1861-1907 .... DLB-19, 98
Coleridge, Samuel Taylor
 1772-1834 .... DLB-93, 107; CDBLB-3
Coleridge, Sara 1802-1852 .... DLB-199
Colet, John 1467-1519 .... DLB-132
Colette 1873-1954 .... DLB-65
Colette, Sidonie Gabrielle (see Colette)
Colinas, Antonio 1946- DLB-134
Coll, Joseph Clement 1881-1921 .... DLB-188
Collier, John 1901-1980 .... DLB-77, 255
Collier, John Payne 1789-1883 .... DLB-184
Collier, Mary 1690-1762 .... DLB-95
Collier, P. F. [publishing house] DLB-49
Collier, Robert J. 1876-1918 .... DLB-91
Collin and Small DLB-49
Collingwood, W. G. 1854-1932 .... DLB-149
Collins, An floruit circa 1653 .... DLB-131
Collins, Anthony 1676-1729 .... DLB-252
Collins, Isaac [publishing house] DLB-49
Collins, Merle 1950- DLB-157
Collins, Mortimer 1827-1876 .... DLB-21, 35
Collins, Tom (see Furphy, Joseph)
Collins, Wilkie
 1824-1889 ...... DLB-18, 70, 159; CDBLB-4
Collins, William 1721-1759 .... DLB-109
Collins, William, Sons and Company ... DLB-154
Collis, Maurice 1889-1973 .... DLB-195
Collyer, Mary 1716?-1763? DLB-39
Colman, Benjamin 1673-1747 .... DLB-24
Colman, George, the Elder 1732-1794 .... DLB-89
Colman, George, the Younger
 1762-1836 .... DLB-89
Colman, S. [publishing house] DLB-49
Colombo, John Robert 1936- DLB-53
Colquhoun, Patrick 1745-1820 .... DLB-158
Colter, Cyrus 1910- DLB-33
Colum, Padraic 1881-1972 .... DLB-19
Columella fl. first century A.D. DLB-211
Colvin, Sir Sidney 1845-1927 .... DLB-149
Colwin, Laurie 1944-1992 .... DLB-218; Y-80
Comden, Betty 1919- and
 Green, Adolph 1918- DLB-44
Come to Papa Y-99
Comi, Girolamo 1890-1968 .... DLB-114
The Comic Tradition Continued
 [in the British Novel] DLB-15
Commager, Henry Steele 1902-1998 ..... DLB-17
The Commercialization of the Image of
 Revolt, by Kenneth Rexroth DLB-16
Community and Commentators: Black
 Theatre and Its Critics DLB-38
Commynes, Philippe de
 circa 1447-1511 .... DLB-208

Compton-Burnett, Ivy 1884?-1969 .... DLB-36
Conan, Laure 1845-1924 .... DLB-99
Concord History and Life DLB-223
Concord Literary History of a Town DLB-223
Conde, Carmen 1901- DLB-108
Conference on Modern Biography Y-85
Congreve, William
 1670-1729 .... DLB-39, 84; CDBLB-2
Preface to Incognita (1692) DLB-39
Conkey, W. B., Company DLB-49
Conn, Stewart 1936- DLB-233
Connell, Evan S., Jr. 1924- DLB-2; Y-81
Connelly, Marc 1890-1980 .... DLB-7; Y-80
Connolly, Cyril 1903-1974 .... DLB-98
Connolly, James B. 1868-1957 .... DLB-78
Connor, Ralph 1860-1937 .... DLB-92
Connor, Tony 1930- DLB-40
Conquest, Robert 1917- DLB-27
Conrad, John, and Company DLB-49
Conrad, Joseph
 1857-1924 .... DLB-10, 34, 98, 156; CDBLB-5
Conroy, Jack 1899-1990 .... Y-81
Conroy, Pat 1945- DLB-6
Considine, Bob 1906-1975 .... DLB-241
The Consolidation of Opinion: Critical
 Responses to the Modernists DLB-36
Consolo, Vincenzo 1933- DLB-196
Constable, Archibald, and Company ... DLB-154
Constable, Henry 1562-1613 .... DLB-136
Constable and Company Limited DLB-112
Constant, Benjamin 1767-1830 .... DLB-119
Constant de Rebecque, Henri-Benjamin de
 (see Constant, Benjamin)
Constantine, David 1944- DLB-40
Constantin-Weyer, Maurice 1881-1964 ... DLB-92
Contempo Caravan: Kites in a Windstorm ... Y-85
A Contemporary Flourescence of Chicano
 Literature Y-84
Continental European Rhetoricians,
 1400-1600 .... DLB-236
The Continental Publishing Company DLB-49
Conversations with Editors Y-95
Conversations with Publishers I: An Interview
 with Patrick O'Connor Y-84
Conversations with Publishers II: An Interview
 with Charles Scribner III Y-94
Conversations with Publishers III: An Interview
 with Donald Lamm Y-95
Conversations with Publishers IV: An Interview
 with James Laughlin Y-96
Conversations with Rare Book Dealers I: An
 Interview with Glenn Horowitz Y-90
Conversations with Rare Book Dealers II:
 Interview with Ralph Sipper Y-94
Conversations with Rare Book Dealers
 (Publishers) III: An Interview with
 Otto Penzler Y-96
The Conversion of an Unpolitical Man,
 by W. H. Bruford DLB-66

Conway, Anne 1631-1679 .... DLB-252
Conway, Moncure Daniel
 1832-1907 .... DLB-1, 223
Cook, David C., Publishing Company ... DLB-49
Cook, Ebenezer circa 1667-circa 1732 .... DLB-24
Cook, Edward Tyas 1857-1919 .... DLB-149
Cook, Eliza 1818-1889 .... DLB-199
Cook, Michael 1933-1994 .... DLB-53
Cooke, George Willis 1848-1923 .... DLB-71
Cooke, Increase, and Company DLB-49
Cooke, John Esten 1830-1886 .... DLB-3, 248
Cooke, Philip Pendleton
 1816-1850 .... DLB-3, 59, 248
Cooke, Rose Terry 1827-1892 .... DLB-12, 74
Cook-Lynn, Elizabeth 1930- DLB-175
Coolbrith, Ina 1841-1928 .... DLB-54, 186
Cooley, Peter 1940- DLB-105
"Into the Mirror" DLB-105
Coolidge, Clark 1939- DLB-193
Coolidge, George [publishing house] DLB-49
Coolidge, Susan (see Woolsey, Sarah Chauncy)
Cooper, Anna Julia 1858-1964 .... DLB-221
Cooper, Edith Emma (see Field, Michael)
Cooper, Giles 1918-1966 .... DLB-13
Cooper, J. California 19??- DLB-212
Cooper, James Fenimore
 1789-1851 ...... DLB-3, 183, 250; CDALB-2
Cooper, Kent 1880-1965 .... DLB-29
Cooper, Susan 1935- DLB-161
Cooper, Susan Fenimore 1813-1894 ..... DLB-239
Cooper, William [publishing house] DLB-170
Coote, J. [publishing house] DLB-154
Coover, Robert 1932- DLB-2, 227; Y-81
Copeland and Day DLB-49
Ćopić, Branko 1915-1984 .... DLB-181
Copland, Robert 1470?-1548 .... DLB-136
Coppard, A. E. 1878-1957 .... DLB-162
Coppée, François 1842-1908 .... DLB-217
Coppel, Alfred 1921- Y-83
Coppola, Francis Ford 1939- DLB-44
Copway, George (Kah-ge-ga-gah-bowh)
 1818-1869 .... DLB-175, 183
Corazzini, Sergio 1886-1907 .... DLB-114
Corbett, Richard 1582-1635 .... DLB-121
Corbière, Tristan 1845-1875 .... DLB-217
Corcoran, Barbara 1911- DLB-52
Cordelli, Franco 1943- DLB-196
Corelli, Marie 1855-1924 .... DLB-34, 156
Corle, Edwin 1906-1956 .... Y-85
Corman, Cid 1924- DLB-5, 193
Cormier, Robert 1925-2000 ... DLB-52; CDALB-6
Corn, Alfred 1943- DLB-120; Y-80
Cornford, Frances 1886-1960 .... DLB-240
Cornish, Sam 1935- DLB-41
Cornish, William circa 1465-circa 1524 .. DLB-132

Cornwall, Barry (see Procter, Bryan Waller)

Cornwallis, Sir William, the Younger
circa 1579-1614 . . . . DLB-151

Cornwell, David John Moore (see le Carré, John)

Corpi, Lucha 1945- DLB-82

Corrington, John William
1932-1988 . . . . DLB-6, 244

Corriveau, Monique 1927-1976 . . . . DLB-251

Corrothers, James D. 1869-1917 . . . . DLB-50

Corso, Gregory 1930- DLB-5, 16, 237

Cortázar, Julio 1914-1984 . . . DLB-113; CDWLB-3

Cortéz, Carlos 1923- DLB-209

Cortez, Jayne 1936- DLB-41

Corvinus, Gottlieb Siegmund
1677-1746 . . . . DLB-168

Corvo, Baron (see Rolfe, Frederick William)

Cory, Annie Sophie (see Cross, Victoria)

Cory, William Johnson 1823-1892 . . . . DLB-35

Coryate, Thomas 1577?-1617 . . . . . DLB-151, 172

Ćosić, Dobrica 1921- DLB-181; CDWLB-4

Cosin, John 1595-1672 . . . . DLB-151, 213

Cosmopolitan Book Corporation DLB-46

The Cost of *The Cantos:* William Bird
to Ezra Pound Y-01

Costain, Thomas B. 1885-1965 . . . . DLB-9

Coste, Donat 1912-1957 . . . . DLB-88

Costello, Louisa Stuart 1799-1870 . . . . . . DLB-166

Cota-Cárdenas, Margarita 1941- DLB-122

Côté, Denis 1954- DLB-251

Cotten, Bruce 1873-1954 . . . . DLB-187

Cotter, Joseph Seamon, Sr. 1861-1949 . . . . DLB-50

Cotter, Joseph Seamon, Jr. 1895-1919 . . . . DLB-50

Cottle, Joseph [publishing house] DLB-154

Cotton, Charles 1630-1687 . . . . DLB-131

Cotton, John 1584-1652 . . . . DLB-24

Cotton, Sir Robert Bruce 1571-1631 . . . . . DLB-213

Coulter, John 1888-1980 . . . . DLB-68

Cournos, John 1881-1966 . . . . DLB-54

Courteline, Georges 1858-1929 . . . . DLB-192

Cousins, Margaret 1905-1996 . . . . DLB-137

Cousins, Norman 1915-1990 . . . . DLB-137

Couvreur, Jessie (see Tasma)

Coventry, Francis 1725-1754 . . . . DLB-39

Dedication, *The History of Pompey
the Little* (1751) DLB-39

Coverdale, Miles 1487 or 1488-1569 . . . . . DLB-167

Coverly, N. [publishing house] DLB-49

Covici-Friede DLB-46

Cowan, Peter 1914- DLB-260

Coward, Noel
1899-1973 . . . . DLB-10, 245; CDBLB-6

Coward, McCann and Geoghegan DLB-46

Cowles, Gardner 1861-1946 . . . . DLB-29

Cowles, Gardner "Mike" Jr.
1903-1985 . . . . DLB-127, 137

Cowley, Abraham 1618-1667 . . . . . . DLB-131, 151

Cowley, Hannah 1743-1809 . . . . DLB-89

Cowley, Malcolm
1898-1989 . . . . DLB-4, 48; Y-81, Y-89

Cowper, William 1731-1800 . . . . . . DLB-104, 109

Cox, A. B. (see Berkeley, Anthony)

Cox, James McMahon 1903-1974 . . . . . . DLB-127

Cox, James Middleton 1870-1957 . . . . . . DLB-127

Cox, Leonard ca. 1495-ca. 1550 . . . . DLB-236

Cox, Palmer 1840-1924 . . . . DLB-42

Coxe, Louis 1918-1993 . . . . DLB-5

Coxe, Tench 1755-1824 . . . . DLB-37

Cozzens, Frederick S. 1818-1869 . . . . DLB-202

Cozzens, James Gould
1903-1978 . . . . . DLB-9; Y-84; DS-2; CDALB-1

James Gould Cozzens—A View from Afar Y-97

James Gould Cozzens Case Re-opened Y-97

James Gould Cozzens: How to Read Him Y-97

Cozzens's *Michael Scarlett* Y-97

James Gould Cozzens Symposium and
Exhibition at the University of
South Carolina, Columbia Y-00

Crabbe, George 1754-1832 . . . . DLB-93

Crace, Jim 1946- DLB-231

Crackanthorpe, Hubert 1870-1896 . . . . . . DLB-135

Craddock, Charles Egbert (see Murfree, Mary N.)

Cradock, Thomas 1718-1770 . . . . DLB-31

Craig, Daniel H. 1811-1895 . . . . DLB-43

Craik, Dinah Maria 1826-1887 . . . . . DLB-35, 136

Cramer, Richard Ben 1950- DLB-185

Cranch, Christopher Pearse
1813-1892 . . . . DLB-1, 42, 243

Crane, Hart 1899-1932 . . . . . DLB-4, 48; CDALB-4

Crane, R. S. 1886-1967 . . . . DLB-63

Crane, Stephen
1871-1900 . . . . DLB-12, 54, 78; CDALB-3

Crane, Walter 1845-1915 . . . . DLB-163

Cranmer, Thomas 1489-1556 . . . . . . DLB-132, 213

Crapsey, Adelaide 1878-1914 . . . . DLB-54

Crashaw, Richard 1612 or 1613-1649 . . . . DLB-126

Craven, Avery 1885-1980 . . . . DLB-17

Crawford, Charles 1752-circa 1815 . . . . . . DLB-31

Crawford, F. Marion 1854-1909 . . . . DLB-71

Crawford, Isabel Valancy 1850-1887 . . . . . DLB-92

Crawley, Alan 1887-1975 . . . . DLB-68

Crayon, Geoffrey (see Irving, Washington)

Crayon, Porte (see Strother, David Hunter)

Creamer, Robert W. 1922- DLB-171

Creasey, John 1908-1973 . . . . DLB-77

Creative Age Press DLB-46

Creech, William [publishing house] DLB-154

Creede, Thomas [publishing house] DLB-170

Creel, George 1876-1953 . . . . DLB-25

Creeley, Robert 1926- . . . DLB-5, 16, 169; DS-17

Creelman, James 1859-1915 . . . . DLB-23

Cregan, David 1931- DLB-13

Creighton, Donald Grant 1902-1979 . . . . . DLB-88

Cremazie, Octave 1827-1879 . . . . DLB-99

Crémer, Victoriano 1909?- DLB-108

Crescas, Hasdai circa 1340-1412? DLB-115

Crespo, Angel 1926- DLB-134

Cresset Press DLB-112

Cresswell, Helen 1934- DLB-161

Crèvecoeur, Michel Guillaume Jean de
1735-1813 . . . . DLB-37

Crewe, Candida 1964- DLB-207

Crews, Harry 1935- DLB-6, 143, 185

Crichton, Michael 1942- Y-81

A Crisis of Culture: The Changing Role
of Religion in the New Republic DLB-37

Crispin, Edmund 1921-1978 . . . . DLB-87

Cristofer, Michael 1946- DLB-7

Crnjanski, Miloš
1893-1977 . . . . DLB-147; CDWLB-4

Crocker, Hannah Mather 1752-1829 . . . . DLB-200

Crockett, David (Davy)
1786-1836 . . . . DLB-3, 11, 183, 248

Croft-Cooke, Rupert (see Bruce, Leo)

Crofts, Freeman Wills 1879-1957 . . . . DLB-77

Croker, John Wilson 1780-1857 . . . . DLB-110

Croly, George 1780-1860 . . . . DLB-159

Croly, Herbert 1869-1930 . . . . DLB-91

Croly, Jane Cunningham 1829-1901 . . . . . DLB-23

Crompton, Richmal 1890-1969 . . . . DLB-160

Cronin, A. J. 1896-1981 . . . . DLB-191

Cros, Charles 1842-1888 . . . . DLB-217

Crosby, Caresse 1892-1970 . . . . DLB-48

Crosby, Caresse 1892-1970
and Crosby, Harry
1898-1929 . . . . DLB-4; DS-15

Crosby, Harry 1898-1929 . . . . DLB-48

Crosland, Camilla Toulmin
(Mrs. Newton Crosland)
1812-1895 . . . . DLB-240

Cross, Gillian 1945- DLB-161

Cross, Victoria 1868-1952 . . . . DLB-135, 197

Crossley-Holland, Kevin 1941- DLB-40, 161

Crothers, Rachel 1878-1958 . . . . DLB-7

Crowell, Thomas Y., Company DLB-49

Crowley, John 1942- Y-82

Crowley, Mart 1935- DLB-7

Crown Publishers DLB-46

Crowne, John 1641-1712 . . . . DLB-80

Crowninshield, Edward Augustus
1817-1859 . . . . DLB-140

Crowninshield, Frank 1872-1947 . . . . DLB-91

Croy, Homer 1883-1965 . . . . DLB-4

Crumley, James 1939- DLB-226; Y-84

Cruse, Mary Anne 1825?-1910 . . . . DLB-239

Cruz, Migdalia 1958- DLB-249

Cruz, Victor Hernández 1949- DLB-41

Csokor, Franz Theodor 1885-1969 . . . . . . DLB-81

Csoóri, Sándor 1930- DLB-232; CDWLB-4

Cuala Press DLB-112

Cudworth, Ralph 1617-1688..........DLB-252

Cullen, Countee 1903-1946........DLB-4, 48, 51; CDALB-4

Culler, Jonathan D. 1944-........DLB-67, 246

Cullinan, Elizabeth 1933-..........DLB-234

The Cult of Biography
Excerpts from the Second Folio Debate:
"Biographies are generally a disease of
English Literature" – Germaine Greer,
Victoria Glendinning, Auberon Waugh,
and Richard Holmes................Y-86

Culverwel, Nathaniel 1619?-1651?......DLB-252

Cumberland, Richard 1732-1811........DLB-89

Cummings, Constance Gordon 1837-1924.....................DLB-174

Cummings, E. E. 1894-1962..........DLB-4, 48; CDALB-5

Cummings, Ray 1887-1957...........DLB-8

Cummings and Hilliard..............DLB-49

Cummins, Maria Susanna 1827-1866.......................DLB-42

Cumpián, Carlos 1953-.............DLB-209

Cunard, Nancy 1896-1965............DLB-240

Cundall, Joseph [publishing house]......DLB-106

Cuney, Waring 1906-1976............DLB-51

Cuney-Hare, Maude 1874-1936.........DLB-52

Cunningham, Allan 1784-1842.....DLB-116, 144

Cunningham, J. V. 1911-.............DLB-5

Cunningham, Peter F. [publishing house]................DLB-49

Cunquiero, Alvaro 1911-1981........DLB-134

Cuomo, George 1929-..............Y-80

Cupples, Upham and Company.........DLB-49

Cupples and Leon..................DLB-46

Cuppy, Will 1884-1949.............DLB-11

Curiel, Barbara Brinson 1956-........DLB-209

Curll, Edmund [publishing house]......DLB-154

Currie, James 1756-1805............DLB-142

Currie, Mary Montgomerie Lamb Singleton,
Lady Currie (see Fane, Violet)

Cursor Mundi circa 1300..............DLB-146

Curti, Merle E. 1897-..............DLB-17

Curtis, Anthony 1926-.............DLB-155

Curtis, Cyrus H. K. 1850-1933........DLB-91

Curtis, George William 1824-1892.................DLB-1, 43, 223

Curzon, Robert 1810-1873...........DLB-166

Curzon, Sarah Anne 1833-1898........DLB-99

Cusack, Dymphna 1902-1981.........DLB-260

Cushing, Harvey 1869-1939..........DLB-187

Custance, Olive (Lady Alfred Douglas) 1874-1944.....................DLB-240

Cynewulf circa 770-840.............DLB-146

Czepko, Daniel 1605-1660...........DLB-164

Czerniawski, Adam 1934-...........DLB-232

D

Dabit, Eugène 1898-1936............DLB-65

Daborne, Robert circa 1580-1628........DLB-58

Dąbrowska, Maria 1889-1965...........DLB-215; CDWLB-4

Dacey, Philip 1939-...............DLB-105

"Eyes Across Centuries: Contemporary Poetry and 'That Vision Thing,'"...DLB-105

Dach, Simon 1605-1659.............DLB-164

Dagerman, Stig 1923-1954...........DLB-259

Daggett, Rollin M. 1831-1901.........DLB-79

D'Aguiar, Fred 1960-..............DLB-157

Dahl, Roald 1916-1990..........DLB-139, 255

Dahlberg, Edward 1900-1977.........DLB-48

Dahn, Felix 1834-1912.............DLB-129

Dal', Vladimir Ivanovich (Kazak Vladimir Lugansky) 1801-1872..............DLB-198

Dale, Peter 1938-.................DLB-40

Daley, Arthur 1904-1974............DLB-171

Dall, Caroline Healey 1822-1912......DLB-1, 235

Dallas, E. S. 1828-1879.............DLB-55

From *The Gay Science* (1866).........DLB-21

The Dallas Theater Center............DLB-7

D'Alton, Louis 1900-1951............DLB-10

Daly, Carroll John 1889-1958.........DLB-226

Daly, T. A. 1871-1948..............DLB-11

Damon, S. Foster 1893-1971..........DLB-45

Damrell, William S. [publishing house]...DLB-49

Dana, Charles A. 1819-1897......DLB-3, 23, 250

Dana, Richard Henry, Jr. 1815-1882................DLB-1, 183, 235

Dandridge, Ray Garfield.............DLB-51

Dane, Clemence 1887-1965.........DLB-10, 197

Danforth, John 1660-1730...........DLB-24

Danforth, Samuel, I 1626-1674........DLB-24

Danforth, Samuel, II 1666-1727........DLB-24

Dangerous Years: London Theater, 1939-1945.....................DLB-10

Daniel, John M. 1825-1865...........DLB-43

Daniel, Samuel 1562 or 1563-1619......DLB-62

Daniel Press.....................DLB-106

Daniells, Roy 1902-1979............DLB-68

Daniels, Jim 1956-...............DLB-120

Daniels, Jonathan 1902-1981........DLB-127

Daniels, Josephus 1862-1948........DLB-29

Daniels, Sarah 1957-..............DLB-245

Danilevsky, Grigorii Petrovich 1829-1890.....................DLB-238

Dannay, Frederic 1905-1982 and Manfred B. Lee 1905-1971.........DLB-137

Danner, Margaret Esse 1915-........DLB-41

Danter, John [publishing house]........DLB-170

Dantin, Louis 1865-1945............DLB-92

Danzig, Allison 1898-1987...........DLB-171

D'Arcy, Ella circa 1857-1937..........DLB-135

Dark, Eleanor 1901-1985............DLB-260

Darke, Nick 1948-................DLB-233

Darley, Felix Octavious Carr 1822-1888..DLB-188

Darley, George 1795-1846............DLB-96

Darmesteter, Madame James (see Robinson, A. Mary F.)

Darwin, Charles 1809-1882........DLB-57, 166

Darwin, Erasmus 1731-1802..........DLB-93

Daryush, Elizabeth 1887-1977........DLB-20

Dashkova, Ekaterina Romanovna (née Vorontsova) 1743-1810.......DLB-150

Dashwood, Edmée Elizabeth Monica de la Pasture (see Delafield, E. M.)

Daudet, Alphonse 1840-1897.........DLB-123

d'Aulaire, Edgar Parin 1898- and d'Aulaire, Ingri 1904-.............DLB-22

Davenant, Sir William 1606-1668...DLB-58, 126

Davenport, Guy 1927-.............DLB-130

Davenport, Marcia 1903-1996..........DS-17

Davenport, Robert ?-?..............DLB-58

Daves, Delmer 1904-1977............DLB-26

Davey, Frank 1940-...............DLB-53

Davidson, Avram 1923-1993..........DLB-8

Davidson, Donald 1893-1968.........DLB-45

Davidson, John 1857-1909...........DLB-19

Davidson, Lionel 1922-..............DLB-14

Davidson, Robyn 1950-.............DLB-204

Davidson, Sara 1943-..............DLB-185

Davie, Donald 1922-...............DLB-27

Davie, Elspeth 1919-..............DLB-139

Davies, Sir John 1569-1626..........DLB-172

Davies, John, of Hereford 1565?-1618...DLB-121

Davies, Peter, Limited..............DLB-112

Davies, Rhys 1901-1978..........DLB-139, 191

Davies, Robertson 1913-1995.........DLB-68

Davies, Samuel 1723-1761...........DLB-31

Davies, Thomas 1712?-1785........DLB-142, 154

Davies, W. H. 1871-1940..........DLB-19, 174

Daviot, Gordon 1896?-1952..........DLB-10
(see also Tey, Josephine)

Davis, Arthur Hoey (see Rudd, Steele)

Davis, Charles A. 1795-1867..........DLB-11

Davis, Clyde Brion 1894-1962.........DLB-9

Davis, Dick 1945-................DLB-40

Davis, Frank Marshall 1905-?........DLB-51

Davis, H. L. 1894-1960...........DLB-9, 206

Davis, John 1774-1854.............DLB-37

Davis, Lydia 1947-...............DLB-130

Davis, Margaret Thomson 1926-.....DLB-14

Davis, Ossie 1917-.............DLB-7, 38, 249

Davis, Owen 1874-1956.............DLB-249

Davis, Paxton 1925-1994............Y-89

Davis, Rebecca Harding 1831-1910...DLB-74, 239

Davis, Richard Harding 1864-1916
........DLB-12, 23, 78, 79, 189; DS-13

Davis, Samuel Cole 1764-1809........DLB-37

Davis, Samuel Post 1850-1918.........DLB-202

Davison, Frank Dalby 1893-1970.......DLB-260

Davison, Peter 1928-...............DLB-5

Davydov, Denis Vasil'evich 1784-1839 .....DLB-205	Dekker, Thomas circa 1572-1632 .....DLB-62, 172; CDBLB-1	Denton, Daniel circa 1626-1703 .....DLB-24
Davys, Mary 1674-1732 .....DLB-39	Delacorte, Jr., George T. 1894-1991 .....DLB-91	DePaola, Tomie 1934- DLB-61
Preface to *The Works of Mrs. Davys* (1725) DLB-39	Delafield, E. M. 1890-1943 .....DLB-34	Department of Library, Archives, and Institutional Research, American Bible Society Y-97
DAW Books DLB-46	Delahaye, Guy 1888-1969 .....DLB-92	De Quille, Dan 1829-1898 .....DLB-186
Dawson, Ernest 1882-1947 .....DLB-140	de la Mare, Walter 1873-1956 .....DLB-19, 153, 162, 255; CDBLB-6	De Quincey, Thomas 1785-1859 .....DLB-110, 144; CDBLB-3
Dawson, Fielding 1930- DLB-130	Deland, Margaret 1857-1945 .....DLB-78	"Rhetoric" (1828; revised, 1859) [excerpt] DLB-57
Dawson, Sarah Morgan 1842-1909 .....DLB-239	Delaney, Shelagh 1939- DLB-13; CDBLB-8	Derby, George Horatio 1823-1861 .....DLB-11
Dawson, William 1704-1752 .....DLB-31	Delano, Amasa 1763-1823 .....DLB-183	Derby, J. C., and Company DLB-49
Day, Angel flourished 1583-1599 .....DLB-167, 236	Delany, Martin Robinson 1812-1885 .....DLB-50	Derby and Miller DLB-49
Day, Benjamin Henry 1810-1889 .....DLB-43	Delany, Samuel R. 1942- DLB-8, 33	De Ricci, Seymour 1881-1942 .....DLB-201
Day, Clarence 1874-1935 .....DLB-11	de la Roche, Mazo 1879-1961 .....DLB-68	Derleth, August 1909-1971 .....DLB-9; DS-17
Day, Dorothy 1897-1980 .....DLB-29	Delavigne, Jean François Casimir 1793-1843 .....DLB-192	Derrida, Jacques 1930- DLB-242
Day, Frank Parker 1881-1950 .....DLB-92	Delbanco, Nicholas 1942- DLB-6, 234	The Derrydale Press DLB-46
Day, John circa 1574-circa 1640 .....DLB-62	Delblanc, Sven 1931-1992 .....DLB-257	Derzhavin, Gavriil Romanovich 1743-1816 .....DLB-150
Day, John [publishing house] DLB-170	Del Castillo, Ramón 1949- DLB-209	Desaulniers, Gonsalve 1863-1934 .....DLB-92
Day, The John, Company DLB-46	De León, Nephtal 1945- DLB-82	Desbordes-Valmore, Marceline 1786-1859 .....DLB-217
Day Lewis, C. 1904-1972 .....DLB-15, 20 (see also Blake, Nicholas)	Delgado, Abelardo Barrientos 1931- DLB-82	Deschamps, Emile 1791-1871 .....DLB-217
Day, Mahlon [publishing house] DLB-49	Del Giudice, Daniele 1949- DLB-196	Deschamps, Eustache 1340?-1404 .....DLB-208
Day, Thomas 1748-1789 .....DLB-39	De Libero, Libero 1906-1981 .....DLB-114	Desbiens, Jean-Paul 1927- DLB-53
Dazai Osamu 1909-1948 .....DLB-182	DeLillo, Don 1936- DLB-6, 173	des Forêts, Louis-Rene 1918- DLB-83
Deacon, William Arthur 1890-1977 .....DLB-68	de Lint, Charles 1951- DLB-251	Desiato, Luca 1941- DLB-196
Deal, Borden 1922-1985 .....DLB-6	de Lisser H. G. 1878-1944 .....DLB-117	Desnica, Vladan 1905-1967 .....DLB-181
de Angeli, Marguerite 1889-1987 .....DLB-22	Dell, Floyd 1887-1969 .....DLB-9	Desnos, Robert 1900-1945 .....DLB-258
De Angelis, Milo 1951- DLB-128	Dell Publishing Company DLB-46	DesRochers, Alfred 1901-1978 .....DLB-68
De Bow, J. D. B. 1820-1867 .....DLB-3, 79, 248	delle Grazie, Marie Eugene 1864-1931 .....DLB-81	Desrosiers, Léo-Paul 1896-1967 .....DLB-68
de Bruyn, Günter 1926- DLB-75	Deloney, Thomas died 1600 .....DLB-167	Dessì, Giuseppe 1909-1977 .....DLB-177
de Camp, L. Sprague 1907-2000 .....DLB-8	Deloria, Ella C. 1889-1971 .....DLB-175	Destouches, Louis-Ferdinand (see Céline, Louis-Ferdinand)
De Carlo, Andrea 1952- DLB-196	Deloria, Vine, Jr. 1933- DLB-175	De Tabley, Lord 1835-1895 .....DLB-35
De Casas, Celso A. 1944- DLB-209	del Rey, Lester 1915-1993 .....DLB-8	Deutsch, André, Limited DLB-112
Dechert, Robert 1895-1975 .....DLB-187	Del Vecchio, John M. 1947- DS-9	Deutsch, Babette 1895-1982 .....DLB-45
Dedications, Inscriptions, and Annotations Y-01	Del'vig, Anton Antonovich 1798-1831 .....DLB-205	Deutsch, Niklaus Manuel (see Manuel, Niklaus)
Dee, John 1527-1608 or 1609 .....DLB-136, 213	de Man, Paul 1919-1983 .....DLB-67	Devanny, Jean 1894-1962 .....DLB-260
Deeping, George Warwick 1877-1950 .....DLB-153	DeMarinis, Rick 1934- DLB-218	Deveaux, Alexis 1948- DLB-38
Defoe, Daniel 1660-1731 .....DLB-39, 95, 101; CDBLB-2	Demby, William 1922- DLB-33	The Development of the Author's Copyright in Britain DLB-154
Preface to *Colonel Jack* (1722) DLB-39	De Mille, James 1833-1880 .....DLB-251	The Development of Lighting in the Staging of Drama, 1900-1945 .....DLB-10
Preface to *The Farther Adventures of Robinson Crusoe* (1719) DLB-39	Deming, Philander 1829-1915 .....DLB-74	"The Development of Meiji Japan" DLB-180
Preface to *Moll Flanders* (1722) DLB-39	Deml, Jakub 1878-1961 .....DLB-215	De Vere, Aubrey 1814-1902 .....DLB-35
Preface to *Robinson Crusoe* (1719) DLB-39	Demorest, William Jennings 1822-1895 .....DLB-79	Devereux, second Earl of Essex, Robert 1565-1601 .....DLB-136
Preface to *Roxana* (1724) DLB-39	De Morgan, William 1839-1917 .....DLB-153	The Devin-Adair Company DLB-46
de Fontaine, Felix Gregory 1834-1896 .....DLB-43	Demosthenes 384 B.C.-322 B.C. DLB-176	De Vinne, Theodore Low 1828-1914 .....DLB-187
De Forest, John William 1826-1906 .....DLB-12, 189	Denham, Henry [publishing house] DLB-170	Devlin, Anne 1951- DLB-245
DeFrees, Madeline 1919- DLB-105	Denham, Sir John 1615-1669 .....DLB-58, 126	De Voto, Bernard 1897-1955 .....DLB-9, 256
"The Poet's Kaleidoscope: The Element of Surprise in the Making of the Poem" DLB-105	Denison, Merrill 1893-1975 .....DLB-92	De Vries, Peter 1910-1993 .....DLB-6; Y 82
DeGolyer, Everette Lee 1886-1956 .....DLB-187	Denison, T. S., and Company DLB-49	Dewdney, Christopher 1951- DLB-60
de Graff, Robert 1895-1981 .....Y-81	Dennery, Adolphe Philippe 1811-1899 .....DLB-192	Dewdney, Selwyn 1909-1979 .....DLB-68
de Graft, Joe 1924-1978 .....DLB-117	Dennie, Joseph 1768-1812 .....DLB-37, 43, 59, 73	Dewey, John 1859-1952 .....DLB-246
De Heinrico circa 980? DLB-148	Dennis, C. J. 1876-1938 .....DLB-260	Dewey, Orville 1794-1882 .....DLB-243
Deighton, Len 1929- DLB-87; CDBLB-8	Dennis, John 1658-1734 .....DLB-101	Dewey, Thomas B. 1915-1981 .....DLB-226
DeJong, Meindert 1906-1991 .....DLB-52	Dennis, Nigel 1912-1989 .....DLB-13, 15, 233	
	Denslow, W. W. 1856-1915 .....DLB-188	
	Dent, J. M., and Sons DLB-112	
	Dent, Tom 1932-1998 .....DLB-38	

Cumulative Index

DeWitt, Robert M., Publisher DLB-49
DeWolfe, Fiske and Company DLB-49
Dexter, Colin 1930- DLB-87
de Young, M. H. 1849-1925 .... DLB-25
Dhlomo, H. I. E. 1903-1956 .... DLB-157, 225
Dhuoda circa 803-after 843 .... DLB-148
The Dial 1840-1844 .... DLB-223
The Dial Press DLB-46
Diamond, I. A. L. 1920-1988 .... DLB-26
Dibble, L. Grace 1902-1998 .... DLB-204
Dibdin, Thomas Frognall 1776-1847 .... DLB-184
Di Cicco, Pier Giorgio 1949- DLB-60
Dick, Philip K. 1928-1982 .... DLB-8
Dick and Fitzgerald DLB-49
Dickens, Charles 1812-1870
 .... DLB-21, 55, 70, 159, 166; CDBLB-4
Dickey, James 1923-1997
 .... DLB-5, 193; Y-82, Y-93, Y-96;
 DS-7, DS-19; CDALB-6
James Dickey Tributes Y-97
The Life of James Dickey: A Lecture to
 the Friends of the Emory Libraries,
 by Henry Hart Y-98
Dickey, William 1928-1994 .... DLB-5
Dickinson, Emily
 1830-1886 .... DLB-1, 243; CDWLB-3
Dickinson, John 1732-1808 .... DLB-31
Dickinson, Jonathan 1688-1747 .... DLB-24
Dickinson, Patric 1914- DLB-27
Dickinson, Peter 1927- DLB-87, 161
Dicks, John [publishing house] DLB-106
Dickson, Gordon R. 1923- DLB-8
Dictionary of Literary Biography Yearbook Awards
 .... Y-92, Y-93, Y-97, Y-98, Y-99, Y-00, Y-01
The Dictionary of National Biography DLB-144
Didion, Joan 1934-
 .... DLB-2, 173, 185; Y-81, Y-86; CDALB-6
Di Donato, Pietro 1911- DLB-9
Die Fürstliche Bibliothek Corvey Y-96
Diego, Gerardo 1896-1987 .... DLB-134
Digges, Thomas circa 1546-1595 .... DLB-136
The Digital Millennium Copyright Act:
 Expanding Copyright Protection in
 Cyberspace and Beyond Y-98
Diktonius, Elmer 1896-1961 .... DLB-259
Dillard, Annie 1945- Y-80
Dillard, R. H. W. 1937- DLB-5, 244
Dillingham, Charles T., Company DLB-49
The Dillingham, G. W., Company DLB-49
Dilly, Edward and Charles
 [publishing house] DLB-154
Dilthey, Wilhelm 1833-1911 .... DLB-129
Dimitrova, Blaga 1922- DLB-181; CDWLB-4
Dimov, Dimitr 1909-1966 .... DLB-181
Dimsdale, Thomas J. 1831?-1866 .... DLB-186
Dinescu, Mircea 1950- DLB-232
Dinesen, Isak (see Blixen, Karen)
Dingelstedt, Franz von 1814-1881 .... DLB-133

Dintenfass, Mark 1941- Y-84
Diogenes, Jr. (see Brougham, John)
Diogenes Laertius circa 200 .... DLB-176
DiPrima, Diane 1934- DLB-5, 16
Disch, Thomas M. 1940- DLB-8
Disney, Walt 1901-1966 .... DLB-22
Disraeli, Benjamin 1804-1881 .... DLB-21, 55
D'Israeli, Isaac 1766-1848 .... DLB-107
Ditlevsen, Tove 1917-1976 .... DLB-214
Ditzen, Rudolf (see Fallada, Hans)
Dix, Dorothea Lynde 1802-1887 .... DLB-1, 235
Dix, Dorothy (see Gilmer, Elizabeth Meriwether)
Dix, Edwards and Company DLB-49
Dix, Gertrude circa 1874-? DLB-197
Dixie, Florence Douglas 1857-1905 .... DLB-174
Dixon, Ella Hepworth
 1855 or 1857-1932 .... DLB-197
Dixon, Paige (see Corcoran, Barbara)
Dixon, Richard Watson 1833-1900 .... DLB-19
Dixon, Stephen 1936- DLB-130
Dmitriev, Ivan Ivanovich 1760-1837 .... DLB-150
Do They Or Don't They?
 Writers Reading Book Reviews Y-01
Dobell, Bertram 1842-1914 .... DLB-184
Dobell, Sydney 1824-1874 .... DLB-32
Dobie, J. Frank 1888-1964 .... DLB-212
Döblin, Alfred 1878-1957 .... DLB-66; CDWLB-2
Dobson, Austin 1840-1921 .... DLB-35, 144
Dobson, Rosemary 1920- DLB-260
Doctorow, E. L.
 1931- DLB-2, 28, 173; Y-80; CDALB-6
Documents on Sixteenth-Century
 Literature DLB-167, 172
Dodd, Anne [publishing house] DLB-154
Dodd, Mead and Company DLB-49
Dodd, Susan M. 1946- DLB-244
Dodd, William E. 1869-1940 .... DLB-17
Doderer, Heimito von 1896-1968 .... DLB-85
Dodge, B. W., and Company DLB-46
Dodge, Mary Abigail 1833-1896 .... DLB-221
Dodge, Mary Mapes
 1831?-1905 .... DLB-42, 79; DS-13
Dodge Publishing Company DLB-49
Dodgson, Charles Lutwidge (see Carroll, Lewis)
Dodsley, R. [publishing house] DLB-154
Dodsley, Robert 1703-1764 .... DLB-95
Dodson, Owen 1914-1983 .... DLB-76
Dodwell, Christina 1951- DLB-204
Doesticks, Q. K. Philander, P. B.
 (see Thomson, Mortimer)
Doheny, Carrie Estelle 1875-1958 .... DLB-140
Doherty, John 1798?-1854 .... DLB-190
Doig, Ivan 1939- DLB-206
Doinaş, Ştefan Augustin 1922- DLB-232
Domínguez, Sylvia Maida 1935- DLB-122
Donahoe, Patrick [publishing house] DLB-49

Donald, David H. 1920- DLB-17
The Practice of Biography VI: An
 Interview with David Herbert Donald Y-87
Donaldson, Scott 1928- DLB-111
Doni, Rodolfo 1919- DLB-177
Donleavy, J. P. 1926- DLB-6, 173
Donnadieu, Marguerite (see Duras, Marguerite)
Donne, John
 1572-1631 .... DLB-121, 151; CDBLB-1
Donnelley, R. R., and Sons Company DLB-49
Donnelly, Ignatius 1831-1901 .... DLB-12
Donohue and Henneberry DLB-49
Donoso, José 1924-1996 .... DLB-113; CDWLB-3
Doolady, M. [publishing house] DLB-49
Dooley, Ebon (see Ebon)
Doolittle, Hilda 1886-1961 .... DLB-4, 45
Doplicher, Fabio 1938- DLB-128
Dor, Milo 1923- DLB-85
Doran, George H., Company DLB-46
Dorgelès, Roland 1886-1973 .... DLB-65
Dorn, Edward 1929-1999 .... DLB-5
Dorr, Rheta Childe 1866-1948 .... DLB-25
Dorris, Michael 1945-1997 .... DLB-175
Dorset and Middlesex, Charles Sackville,
 Lord Buckhurst, Earl of 1643-1706 .... DLB-131
Dorsey, Candas Jane 1952- DLB-251
Dorst, Tankred 1925- DLB-75, 124
Dos Passos, John 1896-1970
 .... DLB-4, 9; DS-1, DS-15; CDALB-5
John Dos Passos: Artist Y-99
John Dos Passos: A Centennial
 Commemoration Y-96
Dostoevsky, Fyodor 1821-1881 .... DLB-238
Doubleday and Company DLB-49
Dougall, Lily 1858-1923 .... DLB-92
Doughty, Charles M.
 1843-1926 .... DLB-19, 57, 174
Douglas, Lady Alfred (see Custance, Olive)
Douglas, Gavin 1476-1522 .... DLB-132
Douglas, Keith 1920-1944 .... DLB-27
Douglas, Norman 1868-1952 .... DLB-34, 195
Douglass, Frederick 1818-1895
 .... DLB-1, 43, 50, 79, 243; CDALB-2
Frederick Douglass Creative Arts Center Y-01
Douglass, William circa 1691-1752 .... DLB-24
Dourado, Autran 1926- DLB-145
Dove, Arthur G. 1880-1946 .... DLB-188
Dove, Rita 1952- DLB-120; CDALB-7
Dover Publications DLB-46
Doves Press DLB-112
Dowden, Edward 1843-1913 .... DLB-35, 149
Dowell, Coleman 1925-1985 .... DLB-130
Dowland, John 1563-1626 .... DLB-172
Downes, Gwladys 1915- DLB-88
Downing, J., Major (see Davis, Charles A.)
Downing, Major Jack (see Smith, Seba)

Dowriche, Anne before 1560-after 1613..............DLB-172

Dowson, Ernest 1867-1900.........DLB-19, 135

Doxey, William [publishing house].......DLB-49

Doyle, Sir Arthur Conan 1859-1930...DLB-18, 70, 156, 178; CDBLB-5

Doyle, Kirby 1932-..................DLB-16

Doyle, Roddy 1958-..................DLB-194

Drabble, Margaret 1939-.........DLB-14, 155, 231; CDBLB-8

Drach, Albert 1902-..................DLB-85

Dragojević, Danijel 1934-.............DLB-181

Drake, Samuel Gardner 1798-1875......DLB-187

The Dramatic Publishing Company......DLB-49

Dramatists Play Service...............DLB-46

Drant, Thomas early 1540s?-1578.......DLB-167

Draper, John W. 1811-1882.............DLB-30

Draper, Lyman C. 1815-1891............DLB-30

Drayton, Michael 1563-1631............DLB-121

Dreiser, Theodore 1871-1945 ....DLB-9, 12, 102, 137; DS-1; CDALB-3

Dresser, Davis 1904-1977.............DLB-226

Drewitz, Ingeborg 1923-1986...........DLB-75

Drieu La Rochelle, Pierre 1893-1945......DLB-72

Drinker, Elizabeth 1735-1807..........DLB-200

Drinkwater, John 1882-1937..............DLB-10, 19, 149

Droste-Hülshoff, Annette von 1797-1848.............DLB-133; CDWLB-2

The Drue Heinz Literature Prize Excerpt from "Excerpts from a Report of the Commission," in David Bosworth's *The Death of Descartes* An Interview with David Bosworth......Y-82

Drummond, William, of Hawthornden 1585-1649..................DLB-121, 213

Drummond, William Henry 1854-1907.....................DLB-92

Druzhinin, Aleksandr Vasil'evich 1824-1864.....................DLB-238

Dryden, Charles 1860?-1931............DLB-171

Dryden, John 1631-1700......DLB-80, 101, 131; CDBLB-2

Držić, Marin circa 1508-1567........DLB-147; CDWLB-4

Duane, William 1760-1835.............DLB-43

Dubé, Marcel 1930-..................DLB-53

Dubé, Rodolphe (see Hertel, François)

Dubie, Norman 1945-.................DLB-120

Dubois, Silvia 1788 or 1789?-1889..............DLB-239

Du Bois, W. E. B. 1868-1963....DLB-47, 50, 91, 246; CDALB-3

Du Bois, William Pène 1916-1993........DLB-61

Dubrovina, Ekaterina Oskarovna 1846-1913.....................DLB-238

Dubus, Andre 1936-1999...............DLB-130

Ducange, Victor 1783-1833............DLB-192

Du Chaillu, Paul Belloni 1831?-1903.....DLB-189

Ducharme, Réjean 1941-...............DLB-60

Dučić, Jovan 1871-1943............DLB-147; CDWLB-4

Duck, Stephen 1705?-1756.............DLB-95

Duckworth, Gerald, and Company Limited......................DLB-112

Duclaux, Madame Mary (see Robinson, A. Mary F.)

Dudek, Louis 1918-..................DLB-88

Duell, Sloan and Pearce...............DLB-46

Duerer, Albrecht 1471-1528............DLB-179

Duff Gordon, Lucie 1821-1869.........DLB-166

Dufferin, Helen Lady, Countess of Gifford 1807-1867......................DLB-199

Duffield and Green..................DLB-46

Duffy, Maureen 1933-.................DLB-14

Dufief, Nicholas Gouin 1776-1834......DLB-187

Dugan, Alan 1923-....................DLB-5

Dugard, William [publishing house].....DLB-170

Dugas, Marcel 1883-1947..............DLB-92

Dugdale, William [publishing house].....DLB-106

Duhamel, Georges 1884-1966...........DLB-65

Dujardin, Edouard 1861-1949..........DLB-123

Dukes, Ashley 1885-1959..............DLB-10

Dumas, Alexandre père 1802-1870.....DLB-119, 192

Dumas, Alexandre fils 1824-1895......................DLB-192

Dumas, Henry 1934-1968...............DLB-41

du Maurier, Daphne 1907-1989.........DLB-191

Du Maurier, George 1834-1896.................DLB-153, 178

Dunbar, Paul Laurence 1872-1906........DLB-50, 54, 78; CDALB-3

Dunbar, William circa 1460-circa 1522..........DLB-132, 146

Duncan, Dave 1933-...................DLB-251

Duncan, David James 1952-..........DLB-256

Duncan, Norman 1871-1916............DLB-92

Duncan, Quince 1940-................DLB-145

Duncan, Robert 1919-1988........DLB-5, 16, 193

Duncan, Ronald 1914-1982............DLB-13

Duncan, Sara Jeannette 1861-1922......DLB-92

Dunigan, Edward, and Brother.........DLB-49

Dunlap, John 1747-1812...............DLB-43

Dunlap, William 1766-1839.......DLB-30, 37, 59

Dunn, Douglas 1942-.................DLB-40

Dunn, Harvey Thomas 1884-1952.....DLB-188

Dunn, Stephen 1939-.................DLB-105

"The Good, The Not So Good".......DLB-105

Dunne, Finley Peter 1867-1936.......DLB-11, 23

Dunne, John Gregory 1932-...........Y-80

Dunne, Philip 1908-1992..............DLB-26

Dunning, Ralph Cheever 1878-1930......DLB-4

Dunning, William A. 1857-1922........DLB-17

Dunsany, Lord (Edward John Moreton Drax Plunkett, Baron Dunsany) 1878-1957.......DLB-10, 77, 153, 156, 255

Duns Scotus, John circa 1266-1308......DLB-115

Dunton, John [publishing house].......DLB-170

Dunton, W. Herbert 1878-1936.........DLB-188

Dupin, Amantine-Aurore-Lucile (see Sand, George)

Dupuy, Eliza Ann 1814-1880...........DLB-248

Durack, Mary 1913-1994..............DLB-260

Durand, Lucile (see Bersianik, Louky)

Duranti, Francesca 1935-.............DLB-196

Duranty, Walter 1884-1957............DLB-29

Duras, Marguerite 1914-1996..........DLB-83

Durfey, Thomas 1653-1723.............DLB-80

Durova, Nadezhda Andreevna (Aleksandr Andreevich Aleksandrov) 1783-1866..................DLB-198

Durrell, Lawrence 1912-1990 ....DLB-15, 27, 204; Y-90; CDBLB-7

Durrell, William [publishing house].....DLB-49

Dürrenmatt, Friedrich 1921-1990.........DLB-69, 124; CDWLB-2

Duston, Hannah 1657-1737............DLB-200

Dutt, Toru 1856-1877................DLB-240

Dutton, E. P., and Company...........DLB-49

Duvoisin, Roger 1904-1980............DLB-61

Duyckinck, Evert Augustus 1816-1878................DLB-3, 64, 250

Duyckinck, George L. 1823-1863.....DLB-3, 250

Duyckinck and Company..............DLB-49

Dwight, John Sullivan 1813-1893.....DLB-1, 235

Dwight, Timothy 1752-1817............DLB-37

Dybek, Stuart 1942-..................DLB-130

Dyer, Charles 1928-..................DLB-13

Dyer, Sir Edward 1543-1607...........DLB-136

Dyer, George 1755-1841...............DLB-93

Dyer, John 1699-1757.................DLB-95

Dyk, Viktor 1877-1931................DLB-215

Dylan, Bob 1941-.....................DLB-16

E

Eager, Edward 1911-1964..............DLB-22

Eagleton, Terry 1943-................DLB-242

Eames, Wilberforce 1855-1937........DLB-140

Earle, Alice Morse 1853-1911.........DLB-221

Earle, James H., and Company.........DLB-49

Earle, John 1600 or 1601-1665........DLB-151

Early American Book Illustration, by Sinclair Hamilton................DLB-49

Eastlake, William 1917-1997........DLB-6, 206

Eastman, Carol ?-....................DLB-44

Eastman, Charles A. (Ohiyesa) 1858-1939.....................DLB-175

Eastman, Max 1883-1969..............DLB-91

Eaton, Daniel Isaac 1753-1814........DLB-158

Eaton, Edith Maude 1865-1914........DLB-221

Eaton, Winnifred 1875-1954...........DLB-221

Eberhart, Richard 1904-....DLB-48; CDALB-1

Ebner, Jeannie 1918-.................DLB-85

Ebner-Eschenbach, Marie von 1830-1916.....................DLB-81

Ebon 1942-..........................DLB-41

Cumulative Index

E-Books Turn the Corner............... Y-98
Ecbasis Captivi circa 1045 .... DLB-148
Ecco Press....................... DLB-46
Eckhart, Meister circa 1260-circa 1328... DLB-115
The Eclectic Review 1805-1868........... DLB-110
Eco, Umberto 1932- DLB-196, 242
Eddison, E. R. 1882-1945.............. DLB-255
Edel, Leon 1907-1997............... DLB-103
Edelfeldt, Inger 1956- DLB-257
Edes, Benjamin 1732-1803 .... DLB-43
Edgar, David 1948- DLB-13, 233
Edgeworth, Maria
  1768-1849............. DLB-116, 159, 163
The Edinburgh Review 1802-1929 .... DLB-110
Edinburgh University Press DLB-112
The Editor Publishing Company DLB-49
Editorial Institute at Boston University Y-00
Editorial Statements DLB-137
Edmonds, Randolph 1900- DLB-51
Edmonds, Walter D. 1903-1998......... DLB-9
Edschmid, Kasimir 1890-1966 .... DLB-56
Edson, Russell 1935- DLB-244
Edwards, Amelia Anne Blandford
  1831-1892 .... DLB-174
Edwards, Dic 1953- DLB-245
Edwards, Edward 1812-1886 .... DLB-184
Edwards, James [publishing house]...... DLB-154
Edwards, Jonathan 1703-1758........ DLB-24
Edwards, Jonathan, Jr. 1745-1801....... DLB-37
Edwards, Junius 1929- DLB-33
Edwards, Matilda Barbara Betham
  1836-1919..................... DLB-174
Edwards, Richard 1524-1566 .... DLB-62
Edwards, Sarah Pierpont 1710-1758 ..... DLB-200
Effinger, George Alec 1947- DLB-8
Egerton, George 1859-1945 .... DLB-135
Eggleston, Edward 1837-1902......... DLB-12
Eggleston, Wilfred 1901-1986 .... DLB-92
Eglītis, Anšlavs 1906-1993 .... DLB-220
Ehrenreich, Barbara 1941- DLB-246
Ehrenstein, Albert 1886-1950.......... DLB-81
Ehrhart, W. D. 1948-................DS-9
Ehrlich, Gretel 1946- DLB-212
Eich, Günter 1907-1972............ DLB-69, 124
Eichendorff, Joseph Freiherr von
  1788-1857...................... DLB-90
Eifukumon'in 1271-1342............ DLB-203
1873 Publishers' Catalogues DLB-49
Eighteenth-Century Aesthetic
  Theories...................... DLB-31
Eighteenth-Century Philosophical
  Background DLB-31
Eigner, Larry 1926-1996........... DLB-5, 193
Eikon Basilike 1649..................... DLB-151
Eilhart von Oberge
  circa 1140-circa 1195 .... DLB-148

Einhard circa 770-840............... DLB-148
Eiseley, Loren 1907-1977 ....DS-17
Eisenberg, Deborah 1945- DLB-244
Eisenreich, Herbert 1925-1986.......... DLB-85
Eisner, Kurt 1867-1919............... DLB-66
Ekelöf, Gunnar 1907-1968 .... DLB-259
Eklund, Gordon 1945- Y-83
Ekman, Kerstin 1933- DLB-257
Ekwensi, Cyprian
  1921- DLB-117; CDWLB-3
Elaw, Zilpha circa 1790-? DLB-239
Eld, George [publishing house]......... DLB-170
Elder, Lonne III 1931- DLB-7, 38, 44
Elder, Paul, and Company DLB-49
The Electronic Text Center and the Electronic
  Archive of Early American Fiction at the
  University of Virginia Library.......... Y-98
Eliade, Mircea 1907-1986 ... DLB-220; CDWLB-4
Elie, Robert 1915-1973 .... DLB-88
Elin Pelin 1877-1949 ....DLB-147; CDWLB-4
Eliot, George
  1819-1880 .... DLB-21, 35, 55; CDBLB-4
Eliot, John 1604-1690 .... DLB-24
Eliot, T. S. 1888-1965
  .... DLB-7, 10, 45, 63, 245; CDALB-5
T. S. Eliot Centennial................... Y-88
Eliot's Court Press DLB-170
Elizabeth I 1533-1603 .... DLB-136
Elizabeth of Nassau-Saarbrücken
  after 1393-1456 .... DLB-179
Elizondo, Salvador 1932- DLB-145
Elizondo, Sergio 1930- DLB-82
Elkin, Stanley 1930-1995 ....DLB-2, 28, 218; Y-80
Elles, Dora Amy (see Wentworth, Patricia)
Ellet, Elizabeth F. 1818?-1877 .... DLB-30
Elliot, Ebenezer 1781-1849 .... DLB-96, 190
Elliot, Frances Minto (Dickinson)
  1820-1898 .... DLB-166
Elliott, Charlotte 1789-1871 .... DLB-199
Elliott, George 1923- DLB-68
Elliott, George P. 1918-1980........... DLB-244
Elliott, Janice 1931- DLB-14
Elliott, Sarah Barnwell 1848-1928 .... DLB-221
Elliott, Thomes and Talbot DLB-49
Elliott, William III 1788-1863........ DLB-3, 248
Ellis, Alice Thomas (Anna Margaret Haycraft)
  1932- DLB-194
Ellis, Edward S. 1840-1916.............. DLB-42
Ellis, Frederick Staridge
  [publishing house] DLB-106
The George H. Ellis Company.......... DLB-49
Ellis, Havelock 1859-1939 .... DLB-190
Ellison, Harlan 1934- DLB-8
Ellison, Ralph
  1914-1994 ...DLB-2, 76, 227; Y-94; CDALB-1
Ellmann, Richard 1918-1987 ......DLB-103; Y-87
Ellroy, James 1948- DLB-226; Y-91

Eluard, Paul 1895-1952 .... DLB-258
Elyot, Thomas 1490?-1546 .... DLB-136
Emanuel, James Andrew 1921- DLB-41
Emecheta, Buchi 1944- DLB-117; CDWLB-3
Emendations for *Look Homeward, Angel*....... Y-00
The Emergence of Black Women Writers....DS-8
Emerson, Ralph Waldo 1803-1882
  .... DLB-1, 59, 73, 183, 223; CDALB-2
Ralph Waldo Emerson in 1982 .... Y-82
Emerson, William 1769-1811 .... DLB-37
Emerson, William 1923-1997 ....Y-97
Emin, Fedor Aleksandrovich
  circa 1735-1770................ DLB-150
Emmanuel, Pierre 1916-1984 .... DLB-258
Empedocles fifth century B.C...........DLB-176
Empson, William 1906-1984 .... DLB-20
Enchi Fumiko 1905-1986 .... DLB-182
"Encounter with the West" DLB-180
The End of English Stage Censorship,
  1945-1968 .... DLB-13
Ende, Michael 1929-1995.............. DLB-75
Endō Shūsaku 1923-1996 .... DLB-182
Engel, Marian 1933-1985 .... DLB-53
Engels, Friedrich 1820-1895 .... DLB-129
Engle, Paul 1908- DLB-48
English, Thomas Dunn 1819-1902...... DLB-202
English Composition and Rhetoric (1866),
  by Alexander Bain [excerpt]......... DLB-57
The English Language: 410 to 1500..... DLB-146
Ennius 239 B.C.-169 B.C. DLB-211
Enquist, Per Olov 1934- DLB-257
Enright, D. J. 1920- DLB-27
Enright, Elizabeth 1909-1968 .... DLB-22
Epic and Beast Epic DLB-208
Epictetus circa 55-circa 125-130 ....DLB-176
Epicurus 342/341 B.C.-271/270 B.C. DLB-176
Epps, Bernard 1936- DLB-53
Epstein, Julius 1909- and
  Epstein, Philip 1909-1952 .... DLB-26
Equiano, Olaudah
  circa 1745-1797 .... DLB-37, 50; DWLB-3
Olaudah Equiano and Unfinished Journeys:
  The Slave-Narrative Tradition and
  Twentieth-Century Continuities, by
  Paul Edwards and Pauline T.
  Wangman DLB-117
The E-Researcher: Possibilities and Pitfalls ... Y-00
Eragny Press..................... DLB-112
Erasmus, Desiderius 1467-1536 .... DLB-136
Erba, Luciano 1922- DLB-128
Erdrich, Louise
  1954- DLB-152, 175, 206; CDALB-7
Erichsen-Brown, Gwethalyn Graham
  (see Graham, Gwethalyn)
Eriugena, John Scottus circa 810-877 .... DLB-115
Ernst, Paul 1866-1933 .... DLB-66, 118
Ershov, Petr Pavlovich 1815-1869 ...... DLB-205
Erskine, Albert 1911-1993 .... Y-93

Erskine, John 1879-1951 . . . . DLB-9, 102	Faber and Faber Limited DLB-112	Federal Writers' Project DLB-46
Erskine, Mrs. Steuart ?-1948 . . . . DLB-195	Faccio, Rena (see Aleramo, Sibilla)	Federman, Raymond 1928- Y-80
Ertel', Aleksandr Ivanovich 1855-1908 . . . . DLB-238	Fagundo, Ana María 1938- DLB-134	Fedorov, Innokentii Vasil'evich (see Omulevsky, Innokentii Vasil'evich)
Ervine, St. John Greer 1883-1971 . . . . DLB-10	Fair, Ronald L. 1932- DLB-33	Feiffer, Jules 1929- DLB-7, 44
Eschenburg, Johann Joachim 1743-1820 . . . DLB-97	Fairfax, Beatrice (see Manning, Marie)	Feinberg, Charles E. 1899-1988 . . . . DLB-187; Y-88
Escoto, Julio 1944- DLB-145	Fairlie, Gerard 1899-1983 . . . . DLB-77	Feind, Barthold 1678-1721 . . . . DLB-168
Esdaile, Arundell 1880-1956 . . . . DLB-201	Fallada, Hans 1893-1947 . . . . DLB-56	Feinstein, Elaine 1930- DLB-14, 40
Eshleman, Clayton 1935- DLB-5	Fancher, Betsy 1928- Y-83	Feiss, Paul Louis 1875-1952 . . . . DLB-187
Espriu, Salvador 1913-1985 . . . . DLB-134	Fane, Violet 1843-1905 . . . . DLB-35	Feldman, Irving 1928- DLB-169
Ess Ess Publishing Company DLB-49	Fanfrolico Press DLB-112	Felipe, Léon 1884-1968 . . . . DLB-108
Essex House Press DLB-112	Fanning, Katherine 1927 . . . . DLB-127	Fell, Frederick, Publishers DLB-46
Esson, Louis 1878-1943 . . . . DLB-260	Fanshawe, Sir Richard 1608-1666 . . . . . . DLB-126	Felltham, Owen 1602?-1668 . . . . . . DLB-126, 151
Essop, Ahmed 1931- DLB-225	Fantasy Press Publishers DLB-46	Felman, Soshana 1942- DLB-246
Esterházy, Péter 1950- DLB-232; CDWLB-4	Fante, John 1909-1983 . . . . DLB-130; Y-83	Fels, Ludwig 1946- DLB-75
Estes, Eleanor 1906-1988 . . . . DLB-22	Al-Farabi circa 870-950 . . . . DLB-115	Felton, Cornelius Conway 1807-1862 . . DLB-1, 235
Estes and Lauriat DLB-49	Farabough, Laura 1949- DLB-228	Fenn, Harry 1837-1911 . . . . DLB-188
Estleman, Loren D. 1952- DLB-226	Farah, Nuruddin 1945- . . . DLB-125; CDWLB-3	Fennario, David 1947- DLB-60
Eszterhas, Joe 1944- DLB-185	Farber, Norma 1909-1984 . . . . DLB-61	Fenner, Dudley 1558?-1587? DLB-236
Etherege, George 1636-circa 1692 . . . . DLB-80	Fargue, Léon-Paul 1876-1947 . . . . DLB-258	Fenno, Jenny 1765?-1803 . . . . DLB-200
Ethridge, Mark, Sr. 1896-1981 . . . . DLB-127	Farigoule, Louis (see Romains, Jules)	Fenno, John 1751-1798 . . . . DLB-43
Ets, Marie Hall 1893- DLB-22	Farjeon, Eleanor 1881-1965 . . . . DLB-160	Fenno, R. F., and Company DLB-49
Etter, David 1928- DLB-105	Farley, Harriet 1812-1907 . . . . DLB-239	Fenoglio, Beppe 1922-1963 . . . . DLB-177
Ettner, Johann Christoph 1654-1724 . . . . DLB-168	Farley, Walter 1920-1989 . . . . DLB-22	Fenton, Geoffrey 1539?-1608 . . . . DLB-136
Eugene Gant's Projected Works Y-01	Farmborough, Florence 1887-1978 . . . . . . DLB-204	Fenton, James 1949- DLB-40
Eupolemius flourished circa 1095 . . . . DLB-148	Farmer, Penelope 1939- DLB-161	Ferber, Edna 1885-1968 . . . . DLB-9, 28, 86
Euripides circa 484 B.C.-407/406 B.C. DLB-176; CDWLB-1	Farmer, Philip José 1918- DLB-8	Ferdinand, Vallery III (see Salaam, Kalamu ya)
Evans, Augusta Jane 1835-1909 . . . . DLB-239	Farnaby, Thomas 1575?-1647 . . . . DLB-236	Ferguson, Sir Samuel 1810-1886 . . . . DLB-32
Evans, Caradoc 1878-1945 . . . . DLB-162	Farningham, Marianne (see Hearn, Mary Anne)	Ferguson, William Scott 1875-1954 . . . . . . DLB-47
Evans, Charles 1850-1935 . . . . DLB-187	Farquhar, George circa 1677-1707 . . . . . . DLB-84	Fergusson, Robert 1750-1774 . . . . DLB-109
Evans, Donald 1884-1921 . . . . DLB-54	Farquharson, Martha (see Finley, Martha)	Ferland, Albert 1872-1943 . . . . DLB-92
Evans, George Henry 1805-1856 . . . . DLB-43	Farrar, Frederic William 1831-1903 . . . . . DLB-163	Ferlinghetti, Lawrence 1919- DLB-5, 16; CDALB-1
Evans, Hubert 1892-1986 . . . . DLB-92	Farrar and Rinehart DLB-46	
Evans, M., and Company DLB-46	Farrar, Straus and Giroux DLB-46	Fermor, Patrick Leigh 1915- DLB-204
Evans, Mari 1923- DLB-41	Farrell, J. G. 1935-1979 . . . . DLB-14	Fern, Fanny (see Parton, Sara Payson Willis)
Evans, Mary Ann (see Eliot, George)	Farrell, James T. 1904-1979 . . . . DLB-4, 9, 86; DS-2	Ferrars, Elizabeth 1907- DLB-87
Evans, Nathaniel 1742-1767 . . . . DLB-31	Fast, Howard 1914- DLB-9	Ferré, Rosario 1942- DLB-145
Evans, Sebastian 1830-1909 . . . . DLB-35	Faulkner, George [publishing house] DLB-154	Ferret, E., and Company DLB-49
Evaristi, Marcella 1953- DLB-233	Faulkner, William 1897-1962 . . . DLB-9, 11, 44, 102; DS-2; Y-86; CDALB-5	Ferrier, Susan 1782-1854 . . . . DLB-116
Everett, Alexander Hill 1790-1847 . . . . DLB-59	William Faulkner Centenary Y-97	Ferril, Thomas Hornsby 1896-1988 . . . . . DLB-206
Everett, Edward 1794-1865 . . . . . DLB-1, 59, 235	"Faulkner 100–Celebrating the Work," University of South Carolina, Columbia . Y-97	Ferrini, Vincent 1913- DLB-48
Everson, R. G. 1903- DLB-88	Impressions of William Faulkner Y-97	Ferron, Jacques 1921-1985 . . . . DLB-60
Everson, William 1912-1994 . . . . . DLB-5, 16, 212	Faulkner and Yoknapatawpha Conference, Oxford, Mississippi Y-97	Ferron, Madeleine 1922- DLB-53
Ewart, Gavin 1916-1995 . . . . DLB-40	Faulks, Sebastian 1953- DLB-207	Ferrucci, Franco 1936- DLB-196
Ewing, Juliana Horatia 1841-1885 . . . . DLB-21, 163	Fauset, Jessie Redmon 1882-1961 . . . . DLB-51	Fetridge and Company DLB-49
The Examiner 1808-1881 . . . . DLB-110	Faust, Frederick Schiller (Max Brand) 1892-1944 . . . . DLB-256	Feuchtersleben, Ernst Freiherr von 1806-1849 . . . . DLB-133
Exley, Frederick 1929-1992 . . . . . DLB-143; Y-81		
von Eyb, Albrecht 1420-1475 . . . . DLB-179	Faust, Irvin 1924- DLB-2, 28, 218; Y-80	Feuchtwanger, Lion 1884-1958 . . . . DLB-66
Eyre and Spottiswoode DLB-106	Fawcett, Edgar 1847-1904 . . . . DLB-202	Feuerbach, Ludwig 1804-1872 . . . . DLB-133
Ezera, Regīna 1930- DLB-232	Fawcett, Millicent Garrett 1847-1929 . . . . DLB-190	Feuillet, Octave 1821-1890 . . . . DLB-192
Ezzo ?-after 1065 . . . . DLB-148	Fawcett Books DLB-46	Feydeau, Georges 1862-1921 . . . . DLB-192
	Fay, Theodore Sedgwick 1807-1898 . . . . . DLB-202	Fichte, Johann Gottlieb 1762-1814 . . . . DLB-90
F	Fearing, Kenneth 1902-1961 . . . . DLB-9	Ficke, Arthur Davison 1883-1945 . . . . DLB-54
Faber, Frederick William 1814-1863 . . . . . DLB-32		Fiction Best-Sellers, 1910-1945 . . . . DLB-9

Cumulative Index   DLB 260

Fiction into Film, 1928-1975: A List of Movies Based on the Works of Authors in British Novelists, 1930-1959 .... DLB-15

Fiedler, Leslie A. 1917- DLB-28, 67

Field, Barron 1789-1846 .... DLB-230

Field, Edward 1924- DLB-105

Field, Joseph M. 1810-1856 .... DLB-248

Field, Michael (Katherine Harris Bradley [1846-1914] and Edith Emma Cooper [1862-1913]) DLB-240

"The Poetry File" DLB-105

Field, Eugene 1850-1895 .... DLB-23, 42, 140; DS-13

Field, John 1545?-1588 .... DLB-167

Field, Marshall, III 1893-1956 .... DLB-127

Field, Marshall, IV 1916-1965 .... DLB-127

Field, Marshall, V 1941- DLB-127

Field, Nathan 1587-1619 or 1620 ...... DLB-58

Field, Rachel 1894-1942 .... DLB-9, 22

A Field Guide to Recent Schools of American Poetry Y-86

Fielding, Helen 1958- DLB-231

Fielding, Henry 1707-1754 .... DLB-39, 84, 101; CDBLB-2

"Defense of *Amelia*" (1752) DLB-39

From *The History of the Adventures of Joseph Andrews* (1742) DLB-39

Preface to *Joseph Andrews* (1742) DLB-39

Preface to Sarah Fielding's *The Adventures of David Simple* (1744) DLB-39

Preface to Sarah Fielding's *Familiar Letters* (1747) [excerpt] DLB-39

Fielding, Sarah 1710-1768 .... DLB-39

Preface to *The Cry* (1754) DLB-39

Fields, Annie Adams 1834-1915 .... DLB-221

Fields, James T. 1817-1881 .... DLB-1, 235

Fields, Julia 1938- DLB-41

Fields, Osgood and Company DLB-49

Fields, W. C. 1880-1946 .... DLB-44

Fifty Penguin Years Y-85

Figes, Eva 1932- DLB-14

Figuera, Angela 1902-1984 .... DLB-108

Filmer, Sir Robert 1586-1653 .... DLB-151

Filson, John circa 1753-1788 .... DLB-37

Finch, Anne, Countess of Winchilsea 1661-1720 .... DLB-95

Finch, Robert 1900- DLB-88

Findley, Timothy 1930- DLB-53

Finlay, Ian Hamilton 1925- DLB-40

Finley, Martha 1828-1909 .... DLB-42

Finn, Elizabeth Anne (McCaul) 1825-1921 .... DLB-166

Finnegan, Seamus 1949- DLB-245

Finney, Jack 1911-1995 .... DLB-8

Finney, Walter Braden (see Finney, Jack)

Firbank, Ronald 1886-1926 .... DLB-36

Firmin, Giles 1615-1697 .... DLB-24

First Edition Library/Collectors' Reprints, Inc. Y-91

Fischart, Johann 1546 or 1547-1590 or 1591 .... DLB-179

Fischer, Karoline Auguste Fernandine 1764-1842 .... DLB-94

Fischer, Tibor 1959- DLB-231

Fish, Stanley 1938- DLB-67

Fishacre, Richard 1205-1248 .... DLB-115

Fisher, Clay (see Allen, Henry W.)

Fisher, Dorothy Canfield 1879-1958 ... DLB-9, 102

Fisher, Leonard Everett 1924- DLB-61

Fisher, Roy 1930- DLB-40

Fisher, Rudolph 1897-1934 .... DLB-51, 102

Fisher, Steve 1913-1980 .... DLB-226

Fisher, Sydney George 1856-1927 .... DLB-47

Fisher, Vardis 1895-1968 .... DLB-9, 206

Fiske, John 1608-1677 .... DLB-24

Fiske, John 1842-1901 .... DLB-47, 64

Fitch, Thomas circa 1700-1774 .... DLB-31

Fitch, William Clyde 1865-1909 .... DLB-7

FitzGerald, Edward 1809-1883 .... DLB-32

Fitzgerald, F. Scott 1896-1940 .... DLB-4, 9, 86, 219; Y-81, Y-92; DS-1, 15, 16; CDALB-4

F. Scott Fitzgerald Centenary Celebrations Y-96

F. Scott Fitzgerald: A Descriptive Bibliography, Supplement (2001) Y-01

F. Scott Fitzgerald Inducted into the American Poets' Corner at St. John the Divine; Ezra Pound Banned Y-99

"F. Scott Fitzgerald: St. Paul's Native Son and Distinguished American Writer": University of Minnesota Conference, 29-31 October 1982 .... Y-82

First International F. Scott Fitzgerald Conference Y-92

Fitzgerald, Penelope 1916- DLB-14, 194

Fitzgerald, Robert 1910-1985 .... Y-80

FitzGerald, Robert D. 1902-1987 .... DLB-260

Fitzgerald, Thomas 1819-1891 .... DLB-23

Fitzgerald, Zelda Sayre 1900-1948 .... Y-84

Fitzhugh, Louise 1928-1974 .... DLB-52

Fitzhugh, William circa 1651-1701 .... DLB-24

Flagg, James Montgomery 1877-1960 .... DLB-188

Flanagan, Thomas 1923- Y-80

Flanner, Hildegarde 1899-1987 .... DLB-48

Flanner, Janet 1892-1978 .... DLB-4

Flannery, Peter 1951- DLB-233

Flaubert, Gustave 1821-1880 .... DLB-119

Flavin, Martin 1883-1967 .... DLB-9

Fleck, Konrad (flourished circa 1220) DLB-138

Flecker, James Elroy 1884-1915 .... DLB-10, 19

Fleeson, Doris 1901-1970 .... DLB-29

Fleißer, Marieluise 1901-1974 .... DLB-56, 124

Fleischer, Nat 1887-1972 .... DLB-241

Fleming, Abraham 1552?-1607 .... DLB-236

Fleming, Ian 1908-1964 ... DLB-87, 201; CDBLB-7

Fleming, Paul 1609-1640 .... DLB-164

Fleming, Peter 1907-1971 .... DLB-195

Fletcher, Giles, the Elder 1546-1611 ..... DLB-136

Fletcher, Giles, the Younger 1585 or 1586-1623 .... DLB-121

Fletcher, J. S. 1863-1935 .... DLB-70

Fletcher, John (see Beaumont, Francis)

Fletcher, John Gould 1886-1950 .... DLB-4, 45

Fletcher, Phineas 1582-1650 .... DLB-121

Flieg, Helmut (see Heym, Stefan)

Flint, F. S. 1885-1960 .... DLB-19

Flint, Timothy 1780-1840 .... DLB-73, 186

Flores-Williams, Jason 1969- DLB-209

Florio, John 1553?-1625 .... DLB-172

Fo, Dario 1926- Y-97

Foix, J. V. 1893-1987 .... DLB-134

Foley, Martha (see Burnett, Whit, and Martha Foley)

Folger, Henry Clay 1857-1930 .... DLB-140

Folio Society DLB-112

Follain, Jean 1903-1971 .... DLB-258

Follen, Charles 1796-1840 .... DLB-235

Follen, Eliza Lee (Cabot) 1787-1860 ... DLB-1, 235

Follett, Ken 1949- DLB-87; Y-81

Follett Publishing Company DLB-46

Folsom, John West [publishing house] DLB-49

Folz, Hans between 1435 and 1440-1513 .... DLB-179

Fontane, Theodor 1819-1898 .... DLB-129; CDWLB-2

Fontes, Montserrat 1940- DLB-209

Fonvisin, Denis Ivanovich 1744 or 1745-1792 .... DLB-150

Foote, Horton 1916- DLB-26

Foote, Mary Hallock 1847-1938 .... DLB-186, 188, 202, 221

Foote, Samuel 1721-1777 .... DLB-89

Foote, Shelby 1916- DLB-2, 17

Forbes, Calvin 1945- DLB-41

Forbes, Ester 1891-1967 .... DLB-22

Forbes, Rosita 1893?-1967 .... DLB-195

Forbes and Company DLB-49

Force, Peter 1790-1868 .... DLB-30

Forché, Carolyn 1950- DLB-5, 193

Ford, Charles Henri 1913- DLB-4, 48

Ford, Corey 1902-1969 .... DLB-11

Ford, Ford Madox 1873-1939 .... DLB-34, 98, 162; CDBLB-6

Ford, J. B., and Company DLB-49

Ford, Jesse Hill 1928-1996 .... DLB-6

Ford, John 1586-? DLB-58; CDBLB-1

Ford, R. A. D. 1915- DLB-88

Ford, Richard 1944- DLB-227

Ford, Worthington C. 1858-1941 .... DLB-47

Fords, Howard, and Hulbert DLB-49

Foreman, Carl 1914-1984 .... DLB-26

460

Forester, C. S. 1899-1966 . . . . .DLB-191

Forester, Frank (see Herbert, Henry William)

Forman, Harry Buxton 1842-1917 . . . . . . .DLB-184

Fornés, María Irene 1930- DLB-7

Forrest, Leon 1937-1997 . . . . .DLB-33

Forster, E. M.
1879-1970 . . . . .DLB-34, 98, 162, 178, 195;
DS-10; CDBLB-6

Forster, Georg 1754-1794 . . . . .DLB-94

Forster, John 1812-1876 . . . . .DLB-144

Forster, Margaret 1938- DLB-155

Forsyth, Frederick 1938- DLB-87

Forten, Charlotte L. 1837-1914 . . . . . .DLB-50, 239

Charlotte Forten: Pages from
her Diary DLB-50

Fortini, Franco 1917- DLB-128

Fortune, Mary ca. 1833-ca. 1910 . . . . .DLB-230

Fortune, T. Thomas 1856-1928 . . . . .DLB-23

Fosdick, Charles Austin 1842-1915 . . . . . .DLB-42

Foster, Genevieve 1893-1979 . . . . .DLB-61

Foster, Hannah Webster 1758-1840 . . .DLB-37, 200

Foster, John 1648-1681 . . . . .DLB-24

Foster, Michael 1904-1956 . . . . .DLB-9

Foster, Myles Birket 1825-1899 . . . . .DLB-184

Foucault, Michel 1926-1984 . . . . .DLB-242

Foulis, Robert and Andrew / R. and A.
[publishing house] DLB-154

Fouqué, Caroline de la Motte
1774-1831 . . . . .DLB-90

Fouqué, Friedrich de la Motte
1777-1843 . . . . .DLB-90

Four Seas Company DLB-46

Four Winds Press DLB-46

Fournier, Henri Alban (see Alain-Fournier)

Fowler and Wells Company DLB-49

Fowles, John
1926- DLB-14, 139, 207; CDBLB-8

Fox, John 1939- DLB-245

Fox, John, Jr. 1862 or 1863-1919 . . . .DLB-9; DS-13

Fox, Paula 1923- DLB-52

Fox, Richard K. [publishing house] DLB-49

Fox, Richard Kyle 1846-1922 . . . . .DLB-79

Fox, William Price 1926- DLB-2; Y-81

Foxe, John 1517-1587 . . . . .DLB-132

Fraenkel, Michael 1896-1957 . . . . .DLB-4

France, Anatole 1844-1924 . . . . .DLB-123

France, Richard 1938- DLB-7

Francis, C. S. [publishing house] DLB-49

Francis, Convers 1795-1863 . . . . .DLB-1, 235

Francis, Dick 1920- DLB-87

Francis, Sir Frank 1901-1988 . . . . .DLB-201

Francis, Jeffrey, Lord 1773-1850 . . . . .DLB-107

François 1863-1910 . . . . .DLB-92

François, Louise von 1817-1893 . . . . .DLB-129

Franck, Sebastian 1499-1542 . . . . .DLB-179

Francke, Kuno 1855-1930 . . . . .DLB-71

Frank, Bruno 1887-1945 . . . . .DLB-118

Frank, Leonhard 1882-1961 . . . . .DLB-56, 118

Frank, Melvin (see Panama, Norman)

Frank, Waldo 1889-1967 . . . . .DLB-9, 63

Franken, Rose 1895?-1988 . . . . . .DLB-228, Y-84

Franklin, Benjamin
1706-1790 . . . .DLB-24, 43, 73, 183; CDALB-2

Franklin, James 1697-1735 . . . . .DLB-43

Franklin, Miles 1879-1954 . . . . .DLB-230

Franklin Library DLB-46

Frantz, Ralph Jules 1902-1979 . . . . .DLB-4

Franzos, Karl Emil 1848-1904 . . . . .DLB-129

Fraser, G. S. 1915-1980 . . . . .DLB-27

Fraser, Kathleen 1935- DLB-169

Frattini, Alberto 1922- DLB-128

Frau Ava ?-1127 . . . . .DLB-148

Fraunce, Abraham 1558?-1592 or 1593 . . .DLB-236

Frayn, Michael 1933- DLB-13, 14, 194, 245

Frederic, Harold
1856-1898 . . . . .DLB-12, 23; DS-13

Freeling, Nicolas 1927- DLB-87

Freeman, Douglas Southall
1886-1953 . . . . .DLB-17; DS-17

Freeman, Judith 1946- DLB-256

Freeman, Legh Richmond 1842-1915 . . . . .DLB-23

Freeman, Mary E. Wilkins
1852-1930 . . . . .DLB-12, 78, 221

Freeman, R. Austin 1862-1943 . . . . .DLB-70

Freidank circa 1170-circa 1233 . . . . .DLB-138

Freiligrath, Ferdinand 1810-1876 . . . . . . .DLB-133

Frémont, John Charles 1813-1890 . . . . . . .DLB-186

Frémont, John Charles 1813-1890 and
Frémont, Jessie Benton 1834-1902 . . .DLB-183

French, Alice 1850-1934 . . . . .DLB-74; DS-13

French Arthurian Literature DLB-208

French, David 1939- DLB-53

French, Evangeline 1869-1960 . . . . .DLB-195

French, Francesca 1871-1960 . . . . .DLB-195

French, James [publishing house] DLB-49

French, Samuel [publishing house] DLB-49

Samuel French, Limited DLB-106

Freneau, Philip 1752-1832 . . . . .DLB-37, 43

Freni, Melo 1934- .DLB-128

Freshfield, Douglas W. 1845-1934 . . . . . . .DLB-174

Freytag, Gustav 1816-1895 . . . . .DLB-129

Fridegård, Jan 1897-1968 . . . . .DLB-259

Fried, Erich 1921-1988 . . . . .DLB-85

Friedan, Betty 1921- DLB-246

Friedman, Bruce Jay 1930- DLB-2, 28, 244

Friedrich von Hausen circa 1171-1190 . . . .DLB-138

Friel, Brian 1929- DLB-13

Friend, Krebs 1895?-1967? DLB-4

Fries, Fritz Rudolf 1935- DLB-75

Fringe and Alternative Theater in
Great Britain DLB-13

Frisch, Max
1911-1991 . . . . .DLB-69, 124; CDWLB-2

Frischlin, Nicodemus 1547-1590 . . . . .DLB-179

Frischmuth, Barbara 1941- DLB-85

Fritz, Jean 1915- DLB-52

Froissart, Jean circa 1337-circa 1404 . . . . . .DLB-208

From John Hall Wheelock's Oral Memoir . . .Y-01

Fromentin, Eugene 1820-1876 . . . . .DLB-123

Frontinus circa A.D. 35-A.D. 103/104 . . . .DLB-211

Frost, A. B. 1851-1928 . . . . .DLB-188; DS-13

Frost, Robert
1874-1963 . . . . .DLB-54; DS-7; CDALB-4

Frostenson, Katarina 1953- DLB-257

Frothingham, Octavius Brooks
1822-1895 .DLB-1, 243

Froude, James Anthony
1818-1894 . . . . .DLB-18, 57, 144

Fruitlands 1843-1844 . . . . .DLB-223

Fry, Christopher 1907- DLB-13

Fry, Roger 1866-1934 .DS-10

Fry, Stephen 1957- .DLB-207

Frye, Northrop 1912-1991 . . . . . . .DLB-67, 68, 246

Fuchs, Daniel 1909-1993 . . . . .DLB-9, 26, 28; Y-93

Fuentes, Carlos 1928- DLB-113; CDWLB-3

Fuertes, Gloria 1918- DLB-108

Fugard, Athol 1932- DLB-225

The Fugitives and the Agrarians:
The First Exhibition Y-85

Fujiwara no Shunzei 1114-1204 . . . . .DLB-203

Fujiwara no Tameaki 1230s?-1290s? DLB-203

Fujiwara no Tameie 1198-1275 . . . . .DLB-203

Fujiwara no Teika 1162-1241 . . . . .DLB-203

Fulbecke, William 1560-1603? DLB-172

Fuller, Charles H., Jr. 1939- DLB-38

Fuller, Henry Blake 1857-1929 . . . . .DLB-12

Fuller, John 1937- .DLB-40

Fuller, Margaret (see Fuller, Sarah)

Fuller, Roy 1912-1991 . . . . .DLB-15, 20

Fuller, Samuel 1912- DLB-26

Fuller, Sarah 1810-1850
. . . . .DLB-1, 59, 73, 183, 223, 239; CDALB-2

Fuller, Thomas 1608-1661 . . . . .DLB-151

Fullerton, Hugh 1873-1945 . . . . .DLB-171

Fullwood, William flourished 1568 . . . . . .DLB-236

Fulton, Alice 1952- DLB-193

Fulton, Len 1934- Y-86

Fulton, Robin 1937- DLB-40

Furbank, P. N. 1920- DLB-155

Furman, Laura 1945- Y-86

Furness, Horace Howard
1833-1912 . . . . .DLB-64

Furness, William Henry
1802-1896 .DLB-1, 235

Furnivall, Frederick James
1825-1910 . . . . .DLB-184

Furphy, Joseph
(Tom Collins) 1843-1912 . . . . .DLB-230

461

Furthman, Jules 1888-1966............DLB-26
Furui Yoshichi 1937- DLB-182
Fushimi, Emperor 1265-1317.........DLB-203
Futabatei, Shimei
 (Hasegawa Tatsunosuke)
 1864-1909.....................DLB-180
The Future of the Novel (1899), by
 Henry James....................DLB-18
Fyleman, Rose 1877-1957............DLB-160

G

Gadallah, Leslie 1939- DLB-251
Gadda, Carlo Emilio 1893-1973........DLB-177
Gaddis, William 1922-1998........DLB-2, Y-99
Gág, Wanda 1893-1946..............DLB-22
Gagarin, Ivan Sergeevich 1814-1882....DLB-198
Gagnon, Madeleine 1938-............DLB-60
Gaine, Hugh 1726-1807..............DLB-43
Gaine, Hugh [publishing house]........DLB-49
Gaines, Ernest J.
 1933- DLB-2, 33, 152; Y-80; CDALB-6
Gaiser, Gerd 1908-1976..............DLB-69
Gaitskill, Mary 1954- DLB-244
Galarza, Ernesto 1905-1984...........DLB-122
Galaxy Science Fiction Novels DLB-46
Gale, Zona 1874-1938.........DLB-9, 228, 78
Galen of Pergamon 129-after 210........DLB-176
Gales, Winifred Marshall 1761-1839....DLB-200
Gall, Louise von 1815-1855..........DLB-133
Gallagher, Tess 1943- DLB-120, 212, 244
Gallagher, Wes 1911- DLB-127
Gallagher, William Davis 1808-1894.....DLB-73
Gallant, Mavis 1922- DLB-53
Gallegos, María Magdalena 1935- DLB-209
Gallico, Paul 1897-1976............DLB-9, 171
Gallop, Jane 1952- DLB-246
Galloway, Grace Growden 1727-1782....DLB-200
Gallup, Donald 1913- DLB-187
Galsworthy, John 1867-1933
 ......DLB-10, 34, 98, 162; DS-16; CDBLB-5
Galt, John 1779-1839.............DLB-99, 116
Galton, Sir Francis 1822-1911..........DLB-166
Galvin, Brendan 1938- DLB-5
Gambit DLB-46
Gamboa, Reymundo 1948- DLB-122
Gammer Gurton's Needle...............DLB-62
Gan, Elena Andreevna (Zeneida R-va)
 1814-1842......................DLB-198
Gannett, Frank E. 1876-1957..........DLB-29
Gao Xingjian 1940- Y-00
Gaos, Vicente 1919-1980.............DLB-134
García, Andrew 1854?-1943...........DLB-209
García, Lionel G. 1935- DLB-82
García, Richard 1941- DLB-209
García-Camarillo, Cecilio 1943- DLB-209
García Lorca, Federico 1898-1936......DLB-108

García Márquez, Gabriel
 1928- DLB-113; Y-82; CDWLB-3
Gardam, Jane 1928- DLB-14, 161, 231
Gardell, Jonas 1963- DLB-257
Garden, Alexander circa 1685-1756......DLB-31
Gardiner, John Rolfe 1936- DLB-244
Gardiner, Margaret Power Farmer
 (see Blessington, Marguerite, Countess of)
Gardner, John
 1933-1982.........DLB-2; Y-82; CDALB-7
Garfield, Leon 1921-1996............DLB-161
Garis, Howard R. 1873-1962..........DLB-22
Garland, Hamlin 1860-1940...DLB-12, 71, 78, 186
Garneau, Francis-Xavier 1809-1866......DLB-99
Garneau, Hector de Saint-Denys
 1912-1943......................DLB-88
Garneau, Michel 1939- DLB-53
Garner, Alan 1934- DLB-161
Garner, Hugh 1913-1979............DLB-68
Garnett, David 1892-1981............DLB-34
Garnett, Eve 1900-1991............DLB-160
Garnett, Richard 1835-1906...........DLB-184
Garrard, Lewis H. 1829-1887..........DLB-186
Garraty, John A. 1920- DLB-17
Garrett, George
 1929- DLB-2, 5, 130, 152; Y-83
Fellowship of Southern Writers Y-98
Garrett, John Work 1872-1942........DLB-187
Garrick, David 1717-1779.........DLB-84, 213
Garrison, William Lloyd
 1805-1879........DLB-1, 43, 235; CDALB-2
Garro, Elena 1920-1998.............DLB-145
Garth, Samuel 1661-1719............DLB-95
Garve, Andrew 1908- DLB-87
Gary, Romain 1914-1980............DLB-83
Gascoigne, George 1539?-1577........DLB-136
Gascoyne, David 1916- DLB-20
Gaskell, Elizabeth Cleghorn
 1810-1865 .....DLB-21, 144, 159; CDBLB-4
Gaspey, Thomas 1788-1871..........DLB-116
Gass, William H. 1924- DLB-2, 227
Gates, Doris 1901- DLB-22
Gates, Henry Louis, Jr. 1950- DLB-67
Gates, Lewis E. 1860-1924............DLB-71
Gatto, Alfonso 1909-1976...........DLB-114
Gault, William Campbell 1910-1995....DLB-226
Gaunt, Mary 1861-1942..........DLB-174, 230
Gautier, Théophile 1811-1872 ....DLB-119
Gauvreau, Claude 1925-1971..........DLB-88
The Gawain-Poet
 flourished circa 1350-1400..........DLB-146
Gawsworth, John (Terence Ian Fytton Armstrong)
 1912-1970......................DLB-255
Gay, Ebenezer 1696-1787............DLB-24
Gay, John 1685-1732...............DLB-84, 95
Gayarré, Charles E. A. 1805-1895........DLB-30
Gaylord, Charles [publishing house].....DLB-49

Gaylord, Edward King 1873-1974......DLB-127
Gaylord, Edward Lewis 1919- DLB-127
Geda, Sigitas 1943- DLB-232
Geddes, Gary 1940- DLB-60
Geddes, Virgil 1897- DLB-4
Gedeon (Georgii Andreevich Krinovsky)
 circa 1730-1763.................DLB-150
Gee, Maggie 1948- DLB-207
Gee, Shirley 1932- DLB-245
Geßner, Salomon 1730-1788..........DLB-97
Geibel, Emanuel 1815-1884..........DLB-129
Geiogamah, Hanay 1945- DLB-175
Geis, Bernard, Associates.............DLB-46
Geisel, Theodor Seuss 1904-1991...DLB-61; Y-91
Gelb, Arthur 1924- DLB-103
Gelb, Barbara 1926- DLB-103
Gelber, Jack 1932- DLB-7, 228
Gelinas, Gratien 1909- DLB-88
Gellert, Christian Fürchtegott
 1715-1769......................DLB-97
Gellhorn, Martha 1908-1998.........Y-82, Y-98
Gems, Pam 1925- DLB-13
Genet, Jean 1910-1986............DLB-72; Y-86
Genette, Gérard 1930- DLB-242
Genevoix, Maurice 1890-1980..........DLB-65
Genovese, Eugene D. 1930- DLB-17
Gent, Peter 1942- Y-82
Geoffrey of Monmouth
 circa 1100-1155..................DLB-146
George, Henry 1839-1897............DLB-23
George, Jean Craighead 1919- DLB-52
George, W. L. 1882-1926............DLB-197
George III, King of Great Britain and Ireland
 1738-1820......................DLB-213
George V. Higgins to Julian Symons Y-99
Georgslied 896?...................DLB-148
Gerber, Merrill Joan 1938- DLB-218
Gerhardie, William 1895-1977..........DLB-36
Gerhardt, Paul 1607-1676...........DLB-164
Gérin, Winifred 1901-1981...........DLB-155
Gérin-Lajoie, Antoine 1824-1882........DLB-99
German Drama 800-1280............DLB-138
German Drama from Naturalism
 to Fascism: 1889-1933............DLB-118
German Literature and Culture from Charlemagne
 to the Early Courtly Period
 ....DLB-148; CDWLB-2
German Radio Play, The.............DLB-124
German Transformation from the Baroque
 to the Enlightenment, The..........DLB-97
The Germanic Epic and Old English
 Heroic Poetry: Widsith, Waldere,
 and The Fight at Finnsburg..........DLB-146
Germanophilism, by Hans Kohn........DLB-66
Gernsback, Hugo 1884-1967........DLB-8, 137
Gerould, Katharine Fullerton
 1879-1944......................DLB-78
Gerrish, Samuel [publishing house]......DLB-49

Gerrold, David 1944- DLB-8	Gilmore, Mary 1865-1962............DLB-260	Godey and McMichael DLB-49
The Ira Gershwin Centenary............. Y-96	Gilroy, Frank D. 1925- DLB-7	Godfrey, Dave 1938- DLB-60
Gerson, Jean 1363-1429..............DLB-208	Gimferrer, Pere (Pedro) 1945- DLB-134	Godfrey, Thomas 1736-1763 ....DLB-31
Gersonides 1288-1344................DLB-115	Gingrich, Arnold 1903-1976 ....DLB-137	Godine, David R., Publisher DLB-46
Gerstäcker, Friedrich 1816-1872 ....DLB-129	Ginsberg, Allen 1926-1997 ....DLB-5, 16, 169, 237; CDALB-1	Godkin, E. L. 1831-1902.............DLB-79
Gerstenberg, Heinrich Wilhelm von 1737-1823......................DLB-97	Ginzburg, Natalia 1916-1991..........DLB-177	Godolphin, Sidney 1610-1643 ....DLB-126
Gervinus, Georg Gottfried 1805-1871 ....DLB-133	Ginzkey, Franz Karl 1871-1963 ....DLB-81	Godwin, Gail 1937- DLB-6, 234
Geston, Mark S. 1946- DLB-8	Gioia, Dana 1950- DLB-120	Godwin, M. J., and Company DLB-154
Al-Ghazali 1058-1111................DLB-115	Giono, Jean 1895-1970...............DLB-72	Godwin, Mary Jane Clairmont 1766-1841 ....DLB-163
Gibbings, Robert 1889-1958 ....DLB-195	Giotti, Virgilio 1885-1957 ....DLB-114	Godwin, Parke 1816-1904........DLB-3, 64, 250
Gibbon, Edward 1737-1794 ....DLB-104	Giovanni, Nikki 1943- DLB-5, 41; CDALB-7	Godwin, William 1756-1836 ......DLB-39, 104, 142, 158, 163; CDBLB-3
Gibbon, John Murray 1875-1952........DLB-92	Gipson, Lawrence Henry 1880-1971......DLB-17	Preface to *St. Leon* (1799) DLB-39
Gibbon, Lewis Grassic (see Mitchell, James Leslie)	Girard, Rodolphe 1879-1956 ....DLB-92	Goering, Reinhard 1887-1936 ....DLB-118
Gibbons, Floyd 1887-1939 ....DLB-25	Giraudoux, Jean 1882-1944............DLB-65	Goes, Albrecht 1908- DLB-69
Gibbons, Reginald 1947- DLB-120	Gissing, George 1857-1903 .....DLB-18, 135, 184	Goethe, Johann Wolfgang von 1749-1832 ....DLB-94; CDWLB-2
Gibbons, William ?-? DLB-73	The Place of Realism in Fiction (1895) DLB-18	Goetz, Curt 1888-1960 ....DLB-124
Gibson, Charles Dana 1867-1944 ....DLB-188; DS-13	Giudici, Giovanni 1924- DLB-128	Goffe, Thomas circa 1592-1629..........DLB-58
Gibson, Graeme 1934- DLB-53	Giuliani, Alfredo 1924- DLB-128	Goffstein, M. B. 1940- DLB-61
Gibson, Margaret 1944- DLB-120	Glackens, William J. 1870-1938.........DLB-188	Gogarty, Oliver St. John 1878-1957....DLB-15, 19
Gibson, Margaret Dunlop 1843-1920 ....DLB-174	Gladstone, William Ewart 1809-1898 ....DLB-57, 184	Gogol, Nikolai Vasil'evich 1809-1852 ....DLB-198
Gibson, Wilfrid 1878-1962............DLB-19	Glaeser, Ernst 1902-1963.............DLB-69	Goines, Donald 1937-1974 ....DLB-33
Gibson, William 1914- DLB-7	Glancy, Diane 1941- DLB-175	Gold, Herbert 1924- DLB-2; Y-81
Gibson, William 1948- DLB-251	Glanvill, Joseph 1636-1680 ....DLB-252	Gold, Michael 1893-1967.............DLB-9, 28
Gide, André 1869-1951 ....DLB-65	Glanville, Brian 1931- DLB-15, 139	Goldbarth, Albert 1948- DLB-120
Giguère, Diane 1937- DLB-53	Glapthorne, Henry 1610-1643?..........DLB-58	Goldberg, Dick 1947- DLB-7
Giguère, Roland 1929- DLB-60	Glasgow, Ellen 1873-1945 ....DLB-9, 12	Golden Cockerel Press DLB-112
Gil de Biedma, Jaime 1929-1990 ....DLB-108	Glasier, Katharine Bruce 1867-1950......DLB-190	Golding, Arthur 1536-1606............DLB-136
Gil-Albert, Juan 1906- DLB-134	Glaspell, Susan 1876-1948 ......DLB-7, 9, 78, 228	Golding, Louis 1895-1958.............DLB-195
Gilbert, Anthony 1899-1973 ....DLB-77	Glass, Montague 1877-1934............DLB-11	Golding, William 1911-1993 ....DLB-15, 100, 255; Y-83; CDBLB-7
Gilbert, Sir Humphrey 1537-1583 ....DLB-136	Glassco, John 1909-1981 ....DLB-68	Goldman, Emma 1869-1940 ....DLB-221
Gilbert, Michael 1912- DLB-87	Glauser, Friedrich 1896-1938...........DLB-56	Goldman, William 1931- DLB-44
Gilbert, Sandra M. 1936 ....DLB 120, 246	F. Gleason's Publishing Hall DLB-49	Goldring, Douglas 1887-1960 ....DLB-197
Gilchrist, Alexander 1828-1861 ....DLB-144	Gleim, Johann Wilhelm Ludwig 1719-1803 ....DLB-97	Goldsmith, Oliver 1730?-1774 ......DLB-39, 89, 104, 109, 142; CDBLB-2
Gilchrist, Ellen 1935- DLB-130	Glendinning, Victoria 1937- DLB-155	Goldsmith, Oliver 1794-1861..........DLB-99
Gilder, Jeannette L. 1849-1916 ....DLB-79	The Cult of Biography Excerpts from the Second Folio Debate: "Biographies are generally a disease of English Literature" Y-86	Goldsmith Publishing Company DLB-46
Gilder, Richard Watson 1844-1909 ....DLB-64, 79		Goldstein, Richard 1944- DLB-185
Gildersleeve, Basil 1831-1924 ....DLB-71		Gollancz, Sir Israel 1864-1930 ....DLB-201
Giles of Rome circa 1243-1316 ....DLB-115	Glidden, Frederick Dilley (Luke Short) 1908-1975 ....DLB-256	Gollancz, Victor, Limited DLB-112
Giles, Henry 1809-1882...............DLB-64	Glinka, Fedor Nikolaevich 1786-1880 ....DLB-205	Gombrowicz, Witold 1904-1969..........DLB-215; CDWLB-4
Gilfillan, George 1813-1878 ....DLB-144	Glover, Keith 1966- DLB-249	Gómez-Quiñones, Juan 1942- DLB-122
Gill, Eric 1882-1940.................DLB-98	Glover, Richard 1712-1785 ....DLB-95	Gomme, Laurence James [publishing house] DLB-46
Gill, Sarah Prince 1728-1771 ....DLB-200	Glück, Louise 1943- DLB-5	
Gill, William F., Company..............DLB-49	Glyn, Elinor 1864-1943 ....DLB-153	Goncharov, Ivan Aleksandrovich 1812-1891 ....DLB-238
Gillespie, A. Lincoln, Jr. 1895-1950........DLB-4	Gnedich, Nikolai Ivanovich 1784-1833 ...DLB-205	
Gilliam, Florence ?-? DLB-4	Gobineau, Joseph-Arthur de 1816-1882 ....DLB-123	Goncourt, Edmond de 1822-1896.......DLB-123
Gilliatt, Penelope 1932-1993 ....DLB-14		Goncourt, Jules de 1830-1870 ....DLB-123
Gillott, Jacky 1939-1980..............DLB-14	Godber, John 1956- DLB-233	Gonzales, Rodolfo "Corky" 1928- DLB-122
Gilman, Caroline H. 1794-1888........DLB-3, 73	Godbout, Jacques 1933- DLB-53	González, Angel 1925- DLB-108
Gilman, Charlotte Perkins 1860-1935 ....DLB-221	Goddard, Morrill 1865-1937 ....DLB-25	Gonzalez, Genaro 1949- DLB-122
Gilman, W. and J. [publishing house] DLB-49	Goddard, William 1740-1817..........DLB-43	Gonzalez, Ray 1952- DLB-122
Gilmer, Elizabeth Meriwether 1861-1951 ..DLB-29	Godden, Rumer 1907-1998 ....DLB-161	Gonzales-Berry, Erlinda 1942- DLB-209
Gilmer, Francis Walker 1790-1826 ....DLB-37	Godey, Louis A. 1804-1878 ....DLB-73	

"Chicano Language" DLB-82
González de Mireles, Jovita
 1899-1983 . . . . DLB-122
González-T., César A. 1931- DLB-82
Goodbye, Gutenberg? A Lecture at the
 New York Public Library,
 18 April 1995, by Donald Lamm Y-95
Goodis, David 1917-1967 . . . . DLB-226
Goodison, Lorna 1947- DLB-157
Goodman, Allegra 1967- DLB-244
Goodman, Paul 1911-1972 . . . . DLB-130, 246
The Goodman Theatre DLB-7
Goodrich, Frances 1891-1984 and
 Hackett, Albert 1900-1995 . . . . DLB-26
Goodrich, Samuel Griswold
 1793-1860 . . . . DLB-1, 42, 73, 243
Goodrich, S. G. [publishing house] DLB-49
Goodspeed, C. E., and Company DLB-49
Goodwin, Stephen 1943- Y-82
Googe, Barnabe 1540-1594 . . . . DLB-132
Gookin, Daniel 1612-1687 . . . . DLB-24
Goran, Lester 1928- DLB-244
Gordimer, Nadine 1923- DLB-225; Y-91
Gordon, Adam Lindsay 1833-1870 . . . . . . DLB-230
Gordon, Caroline
 1895-1981 . . . . DLB-4, 9, 102; DS-17; Y-81
Gordon, Giles 1940- DLB-14, 139, 207
Gordon, Helen Cameron, Lady Russell
 1867-1949 . . . . DLB-195
Gordon, Lyndall 1941- DLB-155
Gordon, Mary 1949- DLB-6; Y-81
Gordone, Charles 1925-1995 . . . . DLB-7
Gore, Catherine 1800-1861 . . . . DLB-116
Gore-Booth, Eva 1870-1926 . . . . DLB-240
Gores, Joe 1931- DLB-226
Gorey, Edward 1925-2000 . . . . DLB-61
Gorgias of Leontini
 circa 485 B.C.-376 B.C. DLB-176
Görres, Joseph 1776-1848 . . . . DLB-90
Gosse, Edmund 1849-1928 . . . . . DLB-57, 144, 184
Gosson, Stephen 1554-1624 . . . . DLB-172
 The Schoole of Abuse (1579) DLB-172
Gotlieb, Phyllis 1926- DLB-88, 251
Go-Toba 1180-1239 . . . . DLB-203
Gottfried von Straßburg
 died before 1230 . . . . . . DLB-138; CDWLB-2
Gotthelf, Jeremias 1797-1854 . . . . DLB-133
Gottschalk circa 804/808-869 . . . . DLB-148
Gottsched, Johann Christoph
 1700-1766 . . . . DLB-97
Götz, Johann Nikolaus 1721-1781 . . . . DLB-97
Goudge, Elizabeth 1900-1984 . . . . DLB-191
Gough, John B. 1817-1886 . . . . DLB-243
Gould, Wallace 1882-1940 . . . . DLB-54
Govoni, Corrado 1884-1965 . . . . DLB-114
Gower, John circa 1330-1408 . . . . DLB-146
Goyen, William 1915-1983 . . . . . . DLB-2, 218; Y-83

Goytisolo, José Augustín 1928- DLB-134
Gozzano, Guido 1883-1916 . . . . DLB-114
Grabbe, Christian Dietrich 1801-1836 . . . DLB-133
Gracq, Julien 1910- DLB-83
Grady, Henry W. 1850-1889 . . . . DLB-23
Graf, Oskar Maria 1894-1967 . . . . DLB-56
Graf Rudolf
 between circa 1170 and circa 1185 . . . DLB-148
Graff, Gerald 1937- DLB-246
Grafton, Richard [publishing house] DLB-170
Grafton, Sue 1940- DLB-226
Graham, Frank 1893-1965 . . . . DLB-241
Graham, George Rex 1813-1894 . . . . DLB-73
Graham, Gwethalyn 1913-1965 . . . . DLB-88
Graham, Jorie 1951- DLB-120
Graham, Katharine 1917- DLB-127
Graham, Lorenz 1902-1989 . . . . DLB-76
Graham, Philip 1915-1963 . . . . DLB-127
Graham, R. B. Cunninghame
 1852-1936 . . . . DLB-98, 135, 174
Graham, Shirley 1896-1977 . . . . DLB-76
Graham, Stephen 1884-1975 . . . . DLB-195
Graham, W. S. 1918- DLB-20
Graham, William H. [publishing house] . . . DLB-49
Graham, Winston 1910- DLB-77
Grahame, Kenneth
 1859-1932 . . . . DLB-34, 141, 178
Grainger, Martin Allerdale 1874-1941 . . . . DLB-92
Gramatky, Hardie 1907-1979 . . . . DLB-22
Grand, Sarah 1854-1943 . . . . DLB-135, 197
Grandbois, Alain 1900-1975 . . . . DLB-92
Grandson, Oton de circa 1345-1397 . . . . . DLB-208
Grange, John circa 1556-? DLB-136
Granich, Irwin (see Gold, Michael)
Granovsky, Timofei Nikolaevich
 1813-1855 . . . . DLB-198
Grant, Anne MacVicar 1755-1838 . . . . . . DLB-200
Grant, Duncan 1885-1978 . . . . DS-10
Grant, George 1918-1988 . . . . DLB-88
Grant, George Monro 1835-1902 . . . . DLB-99
Grant, Harry J. 1881-1963 . . . . DLB-29
Grant, James Edward 1905-1966 . . . . DLB-26
Grass, Günter 1927- DLB-75, 124; CDWLB-2
Grasty, Charles H. 1863-1924 . . . . DLB-25
Grau, Shirley Ann 1929- DLB-2, 218
Graves, John 1920- Y-83
Graves, Richard 1715-1804 . . . . DLB-39
Graves, Robert 1895-1985
 . . . DLB-20, 100, 191; DS-18; Y-85; CDBLB-6
Gray, Asa 1810-1888 . . . . DLB-1, 235
Gray, David 1838-1861 . . . . DLB-32
Gray, Simon 1936- DLB-13
Gray, Thomas 1716-1771 . . . . DLB-109; CDBLB-2
Grayson, Richard 1951- DLB-234
Grayson, William J. 1788-1863 . . . . DLB-3, 64, 248
The Great Bibliographers Series Y-93

The Great Modern Library Scam Y-98
The Great War and the Theater, 1914-1918
 [Great Britain] DLB-10
The Great War Exhibition and Symposium at
 the University of South Carolina Y-97
Grech, Nikolai Ivanovich 1787-1867 . . . . . DLB-198
Greeley, Horace 1811-1872 . . . DLB-3, 43, 189, 250
Green, Adolph (see Comden, Betty)
Green, Anna Katharine
 1846-1935 . . . . DLB-202, 221
Green, Duff 1791-1875 . . . . DLB-43
Green, Elizabeth Shippen 1871-1954 . . . . DLB-188
Green, Gerald 1922- DLB-28
Green, Henry 1905-1973 . . . . DLB-15
Green, Jonas 1712-1767 . . . . DLB-31
Green, Joseph 1706-1780 . . . . DLB-31
Green, Julien 1900-1998 . . . . DLB-4, 72
Green, Paul 1894-1981 . . . . DLB-7, 9, 249; Y-81
Green, T. and S. [publishing house] DLB-49
Green, Terence M. 1947- DLB-251
Green, Thomas Hill 1836-1882 . . . . DLB-190
Green, Timothy [publishing house] DLB-49
Greenaway, Kate 1846-1901 . . . . DLB-141
Greenberg: Publisher DLB-46
Green Tiger Press DLB-46
Greene, Asa 1789-1838 . . . . DLB-11
Greene, Belle da Costa 1883-1950 . . . . . . DLB-187
Greene, Benjamin H.
 [publishing house] DLB-49
Greene, Graham 1904-1991
 . . . . DLB-13, 15, 77, 100, 162, 201, 204;
 Y-85, Y-91; CDBLB-7
Greene, Robert 1558-1592 . . . . DLB-62, 167
Greene, Robert Bernard (Bob) Jr.
 1947- DLB-185
Greenfield, George 1917-2000 . . . . Y-00
Greenhow, Robert 1800-1854 . . . . DLB-30
Greenlee, William B. 1872-1953 . . . . DLB-187
Greenough, Horatio 1805-1852 . . . . . . DLB-1, 235
Greenwell, Dora 1821-1882 . . . . DLB-35, 199
Greenwillow Books DLB-46
Greenwood, Grace (see Lippincott, Sara Jane Clarke)
Greenwood, Walter 1903-1974 . . . . . . DLB-10, 191
Greer, Ben 1948- DLB-6
Greflinger, Georg 1620?-1677 . . . . DLB-164
Greg, W. R. 1809-1881 . . . . DLB-55
Greg, W. W. 1875-1959 . . . . DLB-201
Gregg, Josiah 1806-1850 . . . . DLB-183, 186
Gregg Press DLB-46
Gregory, Isabella Augusta Persse, Lady
 1852-1932 . . . . DLB-10
Gregory, Horace 1898-1982 . . . . DLB-48
Gregory of Rimini circa 1300-1358 . . . . . DLB-115
Gregynog Press DLB-112
Greiffenberg, Catharina Regina von
 1633-1694 . . . . DLB-168
Greig, Noël 1944- DLB-245

Grenfell, Wilfred Thomason 1865-1940...DLB-92

Gress, Elsa 1919-1988...DLB-214

Greve, Felix Paul (see Grove, Frederick Philip)

Greville, Fulke, First Lord Brooke 1554-1628...DLB-62, 172

Grey, Sir George, K.C.B. 1812-1898...DLB-184

Grey, Lady Jane 1537-1554...DLB-132

Grey Owl 1888-1938...DLB-92; DS-17

Grey, Zane 1872-1939...DLB-9, 212

Grey Walls Press...DLB-112

Griboedov, Aleksandr Sergeevich 1795?-1829...DLB-205

Grier, Eldon 1917-...DLB-88

Grieve, C. M. (see MacDiarmid, Hugh)

Griffin, Bartholomew flourished 1596...DLB-172

Griffin, Gerald 1803-1840...DLB-159

The Griffin Poetry Prize...Y-00

Griffith, Elizabeth 1727?-1793...DLB-39, 89

Preface to *The Delicate Distress* (1769)...DLB-39

Griffith, George 1857-1906...DLB-178

Griffiths, Ralph [publishing house]...DLB-154

Griffiths, Trevor 1935-...DLB-13, 245

Griggs, S. C., and Company...DLB-49

Griggs, Sutton Elbert 1872-1930...DLB-50

Grignon, Claude-Henri 1894-1976...DLB-68

Grigorovich, Dmitrii Vasil'evich 1822-1899...DLB-238

Grigson, Geoffrey 1905-...DLB-27

Grillparzer, Franz 1791-1872...DLB-133; CDWLB-2

Grimald, Nicholas circa 1519-circa 1562...DLB-136

Grimké, Angelina Weld 1880-1958...DLB-50, 54

Grimké, Sarah Moore 1792-1873...DLB-239

Grimm, Hans 1875-1959...DLB-66

Grimm, Jacob 1785-1863...DLB-90

Grimm, Wilhelm 1786-1859...DLB-90; CDWLB-2

Grimmelshausen, Johann Jacob Christoffel von 1621 or 1622-1676...DLB-168; CDWLB-2

Grimshaw, Beatrice Ethel 1871-1953...DLB-174

Grindal, Edmund 1519 or 1520-1583...DLB-132

Gripe, Maria (Kristina) 1923-...DLB-257

Griswold, Rufus Wilmot 1815-1857...DLB-3, 59, 250

Grosart, Alexander Balloch 1827-1899...DLB-184

Gross, Milt 1895-1953...DLB-11

Grosset and Dunlap...DLB-49

Grossman, Allen 1932-...DLB-193

Grossman Publishers...DLB-46

Grosseteste, Robert circa 1160-1253...DLB-115

Grosvenor, Gilbert H. 1875-1966...DLB-91

Groth, Klaus 1819-1899...DLB-129

Groulx, Lionel 1878-1967...DLB-68

Grove, Frederick Philip 1879-1949...DLB-92

Grove Press...DLB-46

Grubb, Davis 1919-1980...DLB-6

Gruelle, Johnny 1880-1938...DLB-22

von Grumbach, Argula 1492-after 1563?...DLB-179

Grymeston, Elizabeth before 1563-before 1604...DLB-136

Gryphius, Andreas 1616-1664...DLB-164; CDWLB-2

Gryphius, Christian 1649-1706...DLB-168

Guare, John 1938-...DLB-7, 249

Guerra, Tonino 1920-...DLB-128

Guest, Barbara 1920-...DLB-5, 193

Guèvremont, Germaine 1893-1968...DLB-68

Guidacci, Margherita 1921-1992...DLB-128

Guide to the Archives of Publishers, Journals, and Literary Agents in North American Libraries...Y-93

Guillén, Jorge 1893-1984...DLB-108

Guilloux, Louis 1899-1980...DLB-72

Guilpin, Everard circa 1572-after 1608?...DLB-136

Guiney, Louise Imogen 1861-1920...DLB-54

Guiterman, Arthur 1871-1943...DLB-11

Günderrode, Caroline von 1780-1806...DLB-90

Gundulić, Ivan 1589-1638...DLB-147; CDWLB-4

Gunn, Bill 1934-1989...DLB-38

Gunn, James E. 1923-...DLB-8

Gunn, Neil M. 1891-1973...DLB-15

Gunn, Thom 1929-...DLB-27; CDBLB-8

Gunnars, Kristjana 1948-...DLB-60

Günther, Johann Christian 1695-1723...DLB-168

Gurik, Robert 1932-...DLB-60

Gustafson, Ralph 1909-1995...DLB-88

Gustafsson, Lars 1936-...DLB-257

Gütersloh, Albert Paris 1887-1973...DLB-81

Guthrie, A. B., Jr. 1901-1991...DLB-6, 212

Guthrie, Ramon 1896-1973...DLB-4

The Guthrie Theater...DLB-7

Guthrie, Thomas Anstey (see Anstey, FC)

Gutzkow, Karl 1811-1878...DLB-133

Guy, Ray 1939-...DLB-60

Guy, Rosa 1925-...DLB-33

Guyot, Arnold 1807-1884...DS-13

Gwynne, Erskine 1898-1948...DLB-4

Gyles, John 1680-1755...DLB-99

Gyllensten, Lars 1921-...DLB-257

Gysin, Brion 1916-...DLB-16

H

H.D. (see Doolittle, Hilda)

Habermas, Jürgen 1929-...DLB-242

Habington, William 1605-1654...DLB-126

Hacker, Marilyn 1942-...DLB-120

Hackett, Albert (see Goodrich, Frances)

Hacks, Peter 1928-...DLB-124

Hadas, Rachel 1948-...DLB-120

Hadden, Briton 1898-1929...DLB-91

Hagedorn, Friedrich von 1708-1754...DLB-168

Hagelstange, Rudolf 1912-1984...DLB-69

Haggard, H. Rider 1856-1925...DLB-70, 156, 174, 178

Haggard, William 1907-1993...Y-93

Hagy, Alyson 1960-...DLB-244

Hahn-Hahn, Ida Gräfin von 1805-1880...DLB-133

Haig-Brown, Roderick 1908-1976...DLB-88

Haight, Gordon S. 1901-1985...DLB-103

Hailey, Arthur 1920-...DLB-88; Y-82

Haines, John 1924-...DLB-5, 212

Hake, Edward flourished 1566-1604...DLB-136

Hake, Thomas Gordon 1809-1895...DLB-32

Hakluyt, Richard 1552?-1616...DLB-136

Halas, František 1901-1949...DLB-215

Halbe, Max 1865-1944...DLB-118

Halberstam, David 1934-...DLB-241

Haldane, J. B. S. 1892-1964...DLB-160

Haldeman, Joe 1943-...DLB-8

Haldeman-Julius Company...DLB-46

Haldone, Charlotte 1894-1969...DLB-191

Hale, E. J., and Son...DLB-49

Hale, Edward Everett 1822-1909...DLB-1, 42, 74, 235

Hale, Janet Campbell 1946-...DLB-175

Hale, Kathleen 1898-...DLB-160

Hale, Leo Thomas (see Ebon)

Hale, Lucretia Peabody 1820-1900...DLB-42

Hale, Nancy 1908-1988...DLB-86; DS-17; Y-80, Y-88

Hale, Sarah Josepha (Buell) 1788-1879...DLB-1, 42, 73, 243

Hale, Susan 1833-1910...DLB-221

Hales, John 1584-1656...DLB-151

Halévy, Ludovic 1834-1908...DLB-192

Haley, Alex 1921-1992...DLB-38; CDALB-7

Haliburton, Thomas Chandler 1796-1865...DLB-11, 99

Hall, Anna Maria 1800-1881...DLB-159

Hall, Donald 1928-...DLB-5

Hall, Edward 1497-1547...DLB-132

Hall, Halsey 1898-1977...DLB-241

Hall, James 1793-1868...DLB-73, 74

Hall, Joseph 1574-1656...DLB-121, 151

Hall, Radclyffe 1880-1943...DLB-191

Hall, Samuel [publishing house]...DLB-49

Hall, Sarah Ewing 1761-1830...DLB-200

Hall, Stuart 1932-...DLB-242

Hallam, Arthur Henry 1811-1833...DLB-32

On Some of the Characteristics of Modern Poetry and On the Lyrical Poems of Alfred Tennyson (1831)...DLB-32

Halleck, Fitz-Greene 1790-1867...DLB-3, 250

Cumulative Index

Haller, Albrecht von 1708-1777........ DLB-168
Halliday, Brett (see Dresser, Davis)
Halliwell-Phillipps, James Orchard
    1820-1889 .... DLB-184
Hallmann, Johann Christian
    1640-1704 or 1716?.............. DLB-168
Hallmark Editions DLB-46
Halper, Albert 1904-1984............. DLB-9
Halperin, John William 1941- DLB-111
Halstead, Murat 1829-1908 .... DLB-23
Hamann, Johann Georg 1730-1788....... DLB-97
Hamburger, Michael 1924- DLB-27
Hamilton, Alexander 1712-1756 .... DLB-31
Hamilton, Alexander 1755?-1804 ...... DLB-37
Hamilton, Cicely 1872-1952.........DLB-10, 197
Hamilton, Edmond 1904-1977 .... DLB-8
Hamilton, Elizabeth 1758-1816..... DLB-116, 158
Hamilton, Gail (see Corcoran, Barbara)
Hamilton, Gail (see Dodge, Mary Abigail)
Hamilton, Hamish, Limited DLB-112
Hamilton, Ian 1938- DLB-40, 155
Hamilton, Janet 1795-1873 .... DLB-199
Hamilton, Mary Agnes 1884-1962 ...... DLB-197
Hamilton, Patrick 1904-1962 .... DLB-10, 191
Hamilton, Virginia 1936- DLB-33, 52
Hammett, Dashiell
    1894-1961 ...... DLB-226; DS-6; CDALB-5
The Glass Key and Other Dashiell Hammett
    Mysteries........................ Y-96
Dashiell Hammett: An Appeal in *TAC*...... Y-91
Hammon, Jupiter 1711-died between
    1790 and 1806 .... DLB-31, 50
Hammond, John ?-1663 .... DLB-24
Hamner, Earl 1923- DLB-6
Hampson, John 1901-1955............. DLB-191
Hampton, Christopher 1946- DLB-13
Handel-Mazzetti, Enrica von 1871-1955... DLB-81
Handke, Peter 1942- DLB-85, 124
Handlin, Oscar 1915- DLB-17
Hankin, St. John 1869-1909 .... DLB-10
Hanley, Clifford 1922- DLB-14
Hanley, James 1901-1985............. DLB-191
Hannah, Barry 1942- DLB-6, 234
Hannay, James 1827-1873 .... DLB-21
Hano, Arnold 1922- DLB-241
Hansberry, Lorraine
    1930-1965 .... DLB-7, 38; CDALB-1
Hansen, Martin A. 1909-1955......... DLB-214
Hansen, Thorkild 1927-1989 .... DLB-214
Hanson, Elizabeth 1684-1737 .... DLB-200
Hapgood, Norman 1868-1937 .... DLB-91
Happel, Eberhard Werner 1647-1690.... DLB-168
The Harbinger 1845-1849 .... DLB-223
Harcourt Brace Jovanovich DLB-46
Hardenberg, Friedrich von (see Novalis)
Harding, Walter 1917- DLB-111

Hardwick, Elizabeth 1916- DLB-6
Hardy, Frank 1917-1994.............. DLB-260
Hardy, Thomas
    1840-1928 ...... DLB-18, 19, 135; CDBLB-5
"Candour in English Fiction" (1890) DLB-18
Hare, Cyril 1900-1958 .... DLB-77
Hare, David 1947- DLB-13
Hargrove, Marion 1919- DLB-11
Häring, Georg Wilhelm Heinrich
    (see Alexis, Willibald)
Harington, Donald 1935- DLB-152
Harington, Sir John 1560-1612........ DLB-136
Harjo, Joy 1951- DLB-120, 175
Harkness, Margaret (John Law)
    1854-1923 .... DLB-197
Harley, Edward, second Earl of Oxford
    1689-1741..................... DLB-213
Harley, Robert, first Earl of Oxford
    1661-1724..................... DLB-213
Harlow, Robert 1923- DLB-60
Harman, Thomas flourished 1566-1573.. DLB-136
Harness, Charles L. 1915- DLB-8
Harnett, Cynthia 1893-1981........... DLB-161
Harper, Edith Alice Mary (see Wickham, Anna)
Harper, Fletcher 1806-1877 .... DLB-79
Harper, Frances Ellen Watkins
    1825-1911 .... DLB-50, 221
Harper, Michael S. 1938- DLB-41
Harper and Brothers................. DLB-49
Harpur, Charles 1813-1868 .... DLB-230
Harraden, Beatrice 1864-1943 .... DLB-153
Harrap, George G., and Company
    Limited....................... DLB-112
Harriot, Thomas 1560-1621........... DLB-136
Harris, Alexander 1805-1874 .... DLB-230
Harris, Benjamin ?-circa 1720........ DLB-42, 43
Harris, Christie 1907- DLB-88
Harris, Frank 1856-1931 ....DLB-156, 197
Harris, George Washington
    1814-1869 .... DLB-3, 11, 248
Harris, Joel Chandler
    1848-1908 ....DLB-11, 23, 42, 78, 91
Harris, Mark 1922- DLB-2; Y-80
Harris, Wilson 1921- DLB-117; CDWLB-3
Harrison, Mrs. Burton
    (see Harrison, Constance Cary)
Harrison, Charles Yale 1898-1954 ..... DLB-68
Harrison, Constance Cary 1843-1920 ... DLB-221
Harrison, Frederic 1831-1923........DLB-57, 190
"On Style in English Prose" (1898) DLB-57
Harrison, Harry 1925- DLB-8
Harrison, James P., Company DLB-49
Harrison, Jim 1937- Y-82
Harrison, Mary St. Leger Kingsley
    (see Malet, Lucas)
Harrison, Paul Carter 1936- DLB-38
Harrison, Susan Frances 1859-1935 ..... DLB-99
Harrison, Tony 1937- DLB-40, 245

Harrison, William 1535-1593.......... DLB-136
Harrison, William 1933- DLB-234
Harrisse, Henry 1829-1910 .... DLB-47
The Harry Ransom Humanities
    Research Center at the University
    of Texas at Austin Y-00
Harryman, Carla 1952- DLB-193
Harsdörffer, Georg Philipp 1607-1658 ... DLB-164
Harsent, David 1942- DLB-40
Hart, Albert Bushnell 1854-1943 ....DLB-17
Hart, Anne 1768-1834 .... DLB-200
Hart, Elizabeth 1771-1833............ DLB-200
Hart, Julia Catherine 1796-1867 .... DLB-99
The Lorenz Hart Centenary............ Y-95
Hart, Moss 1904-1961 .... DLB-7
Hart, Oliver 1723-1795............... DLB-31
Hart-Davis, Rupert, Limited........... DLB-112
Harte, Bret 1836-1902
    ....DLB-12, 64, 74, 79, 186; CDALB-3
Harte, Edward Holmead 1922- DLB-127
Harte, Houston Harriman 1927- DLB-127
Hartlaub, Felix 1913-1945 .... DLB-56
Hartleben, Otto Erich 1864-1905....... DLB-118
Hartley, David 1705-1757 .... DLB-252
Hartley, L. P. 1895-1972............ DLB-15, 139
Hartley, Marsden 1877-1943.......... DLB-54
Hartling, Peter 1933- DLB-75
Hartman, Geoffrey H. 1929- DLB-67
Hartmann, Sadakichi 1867-1944......... DLB-54
Hartmann von Aue
    circa 1160-circa 1205 ....DLB-138; CDWLB-2
Harvey, Gabriel 1550?-1631 ...DLB-167, 213, 236
Harvey, Jean-Charles 1891-1967 .... DLB-88
Harvill Press Limited DLB-112
Harwood, Lee 1939- DLB-40
Harwood, Ronald 1934- DLB-13
Hašek, Jaroslav 1883-1923 ...DLB-215; CDWLB-4
Haskins, Charles Homer 1870-1937...... DLB-47
Haslam, Gerald 1937- DLB-212
Hass, Robert 1941- DLB-105, 206
Hasselstrom, Linda M. 1943- DLB-256
Hastings, Michael 1938- DLB-233
Hatar, Győző 1914- DLB-215
The Hatch-Billops Collection DLB-76
Hathaway, William 1944- DLB-120
Hauff, Wilhelm 1802-1827............. DLB-90
A Haughty and Proud Generation (1922),
    by Ford Madox Hueffer............. DLB-36
Haugwitz, August Adolph von
    1647-1706..................... DLB-168
Hauptmann, Carl 1858-1921 .... DLB-66, 118
Hauptmann, Gerhart
    1862-1946 ....DLB-66, 118; CDWLB-2
Hauser, Marianne 1910- Y-83
Havel, Václav 1936- DLB-232; CDWLB-4
Haven, Alice B. Neal 1827-1863 .... DLB-260

Havergal, Frances Ridley 1836-1879 . . . . . DLB-199

Hawes, Stephen 1475?-before 1529 . . . . . . DLB-132

Hawker, Robert Stephen 1803-1875 . . . . . . DLB-32

Hawkes, John
1925-1998 . . . . DLB-2, 7, 227; Y-80, Y-98

John Hawkes: A Tribute Y-98

Hawkesworth, John 1720-1773 . . . . DLB-142

Hawkins, Sir Anthony Hope (see Hope, Anthony)

Hawkins, Sir John 1719-1789 . . . . DLB-104, 142

Hawkins, Walter Everette 1883-? DLB-50

Hawthorne, Nathaniel
1804-1864 . . . . DLB-1, 74, 183, 223; CDALB-2

Hawthorne, Nathaniel 1804-1864 and
Hawthorne, Sophia Peabody
1809-1871 . . . . DLB-183

Hawthorne, Sophia Peabody
1809-1871 . . . . DLB-183, 239

Hay, John 1835-1905 . . . . DLB-12, 47, 189

Hayashi, Fumiko 1903-1951 . . . . DLB-180

Haycox, Ernest 1899-1950 . . . . DLB-206

Haycraft, Anna Margaret (see Ellis, Alice Thomas)

Hayden, Robert
1913-1980 . . . . DLB-5, 76; CDALB-1

Haydon, Benjamin Robert
1786-1846 . . . . DLB-110

Hayes, John Michael 1919- DLB-26

Hayley, William 1745-1820 . . . . DLB-93, 142

Haym, Rudolf 1821-1901 . . . . DLB-129

Hayman, Robert 1575-1629 . . . . DLB-99

Hayman, Ronald 1932- DLB-155

Hayne, Paul Hamilton
1830-1886 . . . . DLB-3, 64, 79, 248

Hays, Mary 1760-1843 . . . . DLB-142, 158

Hayward, John 1905-1965 . . . . DLB-201

Haywood, Eliza 1693?-1756 . . . . DLB-39

From the Dedication, *Lasselia* (1723) DLB-39

From *The Tea-Table* DLB-39

From the Preface to *The Disguis'd
Prince* (1723) DLB-39

Hazard, Willis P. [publishing house] DLB-49

Hazlitt, William 1778-1830 . . . . DLB-110, 158

Hazzard, Shirley 1931- Y-82

Head, Bessie
1937-1986 . . . . DLB-117, 225; CDWLB-3

Headley, Joel T. 1813-1897 . . . DLB-30, 183; DS-13

Heaney, Seamus
1939- DLB-40; Y-95; CDBLB-8

Heard, Nathan C. 1936- DLB-33

Hearn, Lafcadio 1850-1904 . . . . . . DLB-12, 78, 189

Hearn, Mary Anne (Marianne Farningham,
Eva Hope) 1834-1909 . . . . DLB-240

Hearne, John 1926- DLB-117

Hearne, Samuel 1745-1792 . . . . DLB-99

Hearne, Thomas 1678?-1735 . . . . DLB-213

Hearst, William Randolph 1863-1951 . . . . . DLB-25

Hearst, William Randolph, Jr.
1908-1993 . . . . DLB-127

Heartman, Charles Frederick
1883-1953 . . . . DLB-187

Heath, Catherine 1924- DLB-14

Heath, James Ewell 1792-1862 . . . . DLB-248

Heath, Roy A. K. 1926- DLB-117

Heath-Stubbs, John 1918- DLB-27

Heavysege, Charles 1816-1876 . . . . DLB-99

Hebbel, Friedrich
1813-1863 . . . . DLB-129; CDWLB-2

Hebel, Johann Peter 1760-1826 . . . . DLB-90

Heber, Richard 1774-1833 . . . . DLB-184

Hébert, Anne 1916-2000 . . . . DLB-68

Hébert, Jacques 1923- DLB-53

Hecht, Anthony 1923- DLB-5, 169

Hecht, Ben 1894-1964 . . . DLB-7, 9, 25, 26, 28, 86

Hecker, Isaac Thomas 1819-1888 . . . . . DLB-1, 243

Hedge, Frederic Henry
1805-1890 . . . . DLB-1, 59, 243

Hefner, Hugh M. 1926- DLB-137

Hegel, Georg Wilhelm Friedrich
1770-1831 . . . . DLB-90

Heide, Robert 1939- DLB-249

Heidish, Marcy 1947- Y-82

Heißenbüttel, Helmut 1921-1996 . . . . DLB-75

Heike monogatari DLB-203

Hein, Christoph 1944- DLB-124; CDWLB-2

Hein, Piet 1905-1996 . . . . DLB-214

Heine, Heinrich 1797-1856 . . . . DLB-90; CDWLB-2

Heinemann, Larry 1944- DS-9

Heinemann, William, Limited DLB-112

Heinesen, William 1900-1991 . . . . DLB-214

Heinlein, Robert A. 1907-1988 . . . . DLB-8

Heinrich Julius of Brunswick
1564-1613 . . . . DLB-164

Heinrich von dem Türlin
flourished circa 1230 . . . . DLB-138

Heinrich von Melk
flourished after 1160 . . . . DLB-148

Heinrich von Veldeke
circa 1145-circa 1190 . . . . DLB-138

Heinrich, Willi 1920- DLB-75

Heinse, Wilhelm 1746-1803 . . . . DLB-94

Heinz, W. C. 1915- DLB-171

Heiskell, John 1872-1972 . . . . DLB-127

Hejinian, Lyn 1941- DLB-165

Heliand circa 850 . . . . DLB-148

Heller, Joseph
1923-1999 . . . . . . DLB-2, 28, 227; Y-80, Y-99

Heller, Michael 1937- DLB-165

Hellman, Lillian 1906-1984 . . . . . DLB-7, 228; Y-84

Hellwig, Johann 1609-1674 . . . . DLB-164

Helprin, Mark 1947- Y-85; CDALB-7

Helwig, David 1938- DLB-60

Hemans, Felicia 1793-1835 . . . . DLB-96

Hemenway, Abby Maria 1828-1890 . . . . . DLB-243

Hemingway, Ernest 1899-1961
. . . . . DLB-4, 9, 102, 210; Y-81, Y-87, Y-99;
DS-1, DS-15, DS-16; CDALB-4

The Hemingway Centenary Celebration at the
JFK Library Y-99

Ernest Hemingway: A Centennial
Celebration Y-99

The Ernest Hemingway Collection at the
John F. Kennedy Library Y-99

Ernest Hemingway Declines to Introduce
War and Peace Y-01

Ernest Hemingway's Reaction to James Gould
Cozzens Y-98

Ernest Hemingway's Toronto Journalism
Revisited: With Three Previously
Unrecorded Stories Y-92

Falsifying Hemingway Y-96

Hemingway: Twenty-Five Years Later Y-85

Not Immediately Discernible . . . but Eventually
Quite Clear: The *First Light* and *Final Years*
of Hemingway's Centenary Y-99

Hemingway Salesmen's Dummies Y-00

Second International Hemingway Colloquium:
Cuba Y-98

Hémon, Louis 1880-1913 . . . . DLB-92

Hempel, Amy 1951- DLB-218

Hemphill, Paul 1936- Y-87

Hénault, Gilles 1920- DLB-88

Henchman, Daniel 1689-1761 . . . . DLB-24

Henderson, Alice Corbin 1881-1949 . . . . . . DLB-54

Henderson, Archibald 1877-1963 . . . . DLB-103

Henderson, David 1942- DLB-41

Henderson, George Wylie 1904- DLB-51

Henderson, Zenna 1917-1983 . . . . DLB-8

Henighan, Tom 1934- DLB-251

Henisch, Peter 1943- DLB-85

Henley, Beth 1952- Y-86

Henley, William Ernest 1849-1903 . . . . DLB-19

Henning, Rachel 1826-1914 . . . . DLB-230

Henningsen, Agnes 1868-1962 . . . . DLB-214

Henniker, Florence 1855-1923 . . . . DLB-135

Henry, Alexander 1739-1824 . . . . DLB-99

Henry, Buck 1930- DLB-26

Henry VIII of England 1491-1547 . . . . . . DLB-132

Henry of Ghent
circa 1217-1229 - 1293 . . . . DLB-115

Henry, Marguerite 1902-1997 . . . . DLB-22

Henry, O. (see Porter, William Sydney)

Henry, Robert Selph 1889-1970 . . . . DLB-17

Henry, Will (see Allen, Henry W.)

Henryson, Robert
1420s or 1430s-circa 1505 . . . . DLB-146

Henschke, Alfred (see Klabund)

Hensley, Sophie Almon 1866-1946 . . . . DLB-99

Henson, Lance 1944- DLB-175

Henty, G. A. 1832?-1902 . . . . DLB-18, 141

Hentz, Caroline Lee 1800-1856 . . . . . . DLB-3, 248

Heraclitus
flourished circa 500 B.C. DLB-176

Herbert, Agnes circa 1880-1960 . . . . DLB-174

Herbert, Alan Patrick 1890-1971 . . . . . DLB-10, 191

Herbert, Edward, Lord, of Cherbury
1582-1648 . . . . DLB-121, 151, 252

Cumulative Index   DLB 260

Herbert, Frank 1920-1986 ..... DLB-8; CDALB-7
Herbert, George 1593-1633 .. DLB-126; CDBLB-1
Herbert, Henry William 1807-1858 .... DLB-3, 73
Herbert, John 1926- DLB-53
Herbert, Mary Sidney, Countess of Pembroke
   (see Sidney, Mary)
Herbert, Xavier 1901-1984............ DLB-260
Herbert, Zbigniew
   1924-1998 .... DLB-232; CDWLB-4
Herbst, Josephine 1892-1969 .... DLB-9
Herburger, Gunter 1932- DLB-75, 124
Hercules, Frank E. M. 1917-1996 .... DLB-33
Herder, Johann Gottfried 1744-1803 ..... DLB-97
Herder, B., Book Company DLB-49
Heredia, José-María de 1842-1905 ...... DLB-217
Herford, Charles Harold 1853-1931 .... DLB-149
Hergesheimer, Joseph 1880-1954 ..... DLB-9, 102
Heritage Press..................... DLB-46
Hermann the Lame 1013-1054......... DLB-148
Hermes, Johann Timotheus
   1738-1821.................... DLB-97
Hermlin, Stephan 1915-1997 .... DLB-69
Hernández, Alfonso C. 1938- DLB-122
Hernández, Inés 1947- DLB-122
Hernández, Miguel 1910-1942 .... DLB-134
Hernton, Calvin C. 1932- DLB-38
Herodotus circa 484 B.C.-circa 420 B.C.
   ....DLB-176; CDWLB-1
Heron, Robert 1764-1807 .... DLB-142
Herr, Michael 1940- DLB-185
Herrera, Juan Felipe 1948- DLB-122
Herrick, E. R., and Company DLB-49
Herrick, Robert 1591-1674 .... DLB-126
Herrick, Robert 1868-1938........ DLB-9, 12, 78
Herrick, William 1915- Y-83
Herrmann, John 1900-1959 .... DLB-4
Hersey, John 1914-1993 ... DLB-6, 185; CDALB-7
Hertel, François 1905-1985............ DLB-68
Hervé-Bazin, Jean Pierre Marie (see Bazin, Hervé)
Hervey, John, Lord 1696-1743 .... DLB-101
Herwig, Georg 1817-1875 .... DLB-133
Herzog, Emile Salomon Wilhelm
   (see Maurois, André)
Hesiod eighth century B.C. DLB-176
Hesse, Hermann
   1877-1962............ DLB-66; CDWLB-2
Hessus, Helius Eobanus 1488-1540 ......DLB-179
Hewat, Alexander circa 1743-circa 1824... DLB-30
Hewitt, John 1907- DLB-27
Hewlett, Maurice 1861-1923 .... DLB-34, 156
Heyen, William 1940- DLB-5
Heyer, Georgette 1902-1974.........DLB-77, 191
Heym, Stefan 1913- DLB-69
Heyse, Paul 1830-1914 .... DLB-129
Heytesbury, William
   circa 1310-1372 or 1373 .... DLB-115

Heyward, Dorothy 1890-1961 ....DLB-7, 249
Heyward, DuBose 1885-1940 ...DLB-7, 9, 45, 249
Heywood, John 1497?-1580? DLB-136
Heywood, Thomas
   1573 or 1574-1641 .... DLB-62
Hibbs, Ben 1901-1975................ DLB-137
Hichens, Robert S. 1864-1950 .... DLB-153
Hickey, Emily 1845-1924............. DLB-199
Hickman, William Albert 1877-1957..... DLB-92
Hicks, Granville 1901-1982 .... DLB-246
Hidalgo, José Luis 1919-1947 .... DLB-108
Hiebert, Paul 1892-1987.............. DLB-68
Hieng, Andrej 1925- DLB-181
Hierro, José 1922- DLB-108
Higgins, Aidan 1927- DLB-14
Higgins, Colin 1941-1988............. DLB-26
Higgins, George V.
   1939-1999 .... DLB-2; Y-81, Y-98, Y-99
George V. Higgins to Julian Symons Y-99
Higginson, Thomas Wentworth
   1823-1911 .... DLB-1, 64, 243
Highwater, Jamake 1942?- DLB-52; Y-85
Hijuelos, Oscar 1951- DLB-145
Hildegard von Bingen 1098-1179 .... DLB-148
Das Hildesbrandslied
   circa 820............ DLB-148; CDWLB-2
Hildesheimer, Wolfgang
   1916-1991 .... DLB-69, 124
Hildreth, Richard 1807-1865 .. DLB-1, 30, 59, 235
Hill, Aaron 1685-1750 .... DLB-84
Hill, Geoffrey 1932- DLB-40; CDBLB-8
Hill, George M., Company............. DLB-49
Hill, "Sir" John 1714?-1775 .... DLB-39
Hill, Lawrence, and Company,
   Publishers..................... DLB-46
Hill, Leslie 1880-1960................ DLB-51
Hill, Susan 1942- DLB-14, 139
Hill, Walter 1942- DLB-44
Hill and Wang DLB-46
Hillberry, Conrad 1928- DLB-120
Hillerman, Tony 1925- DLB-206
Hilliard, Gray and Company DLB-49
Hills, Lee 1906- DLB-127
Hillyer, Robert 1895-1961 .... DLB-54
Hilton, James 1900-1954............ DLB-34, 77
Hilton, Walter died 1396 .... DLB-146
Hilton and Company DLB-49
Himes, Chester 1909-1984 ....DLB-2, 76, 143, 226
Hindmarsh, Joseph [publishing house]....DLB-170
Hine, Daryl 1936- DLB-60
Hingley, Ronald 1920- DLB-155
Hinojosa-Smith, Rolando 1929- DLB-82
Hinton, S. E. 1948- CDALB-7
Hippel, Theodor Gottlieb von
   1741-1796 .... DLB-97
Hippocrates of Cos flourished circa 425 B.C.
   ....DLB-176; CDWLB-1

Hirabayashi, Taiko 1905-1972 .... DLB-180
Hirsch, E. D., Jr. 1928- DLB-67
Hirsch, Edward 1950- DLB-120
Hoagland, Edward 1932- DLB-6
Hoagland, Everett H., III 1942- DLB-41
Hoban, Russell 1925- DLB-52; Y-90
Hobbes, Thomas 1588-1679....... DLB-151, 252
Hobby, Oveta 1905- DLB-127
Hobby, William 1878-1964 ....DLB-127
Hobsbaum, Philip 1932- DLB-40
Hobson, Laura Z. 1900- DLB-28
Hobson, Sarah 1947- DLB-204
Hoby, Thomas 1530-1566 .... DLB-132
Hoccleve, Thomas
   circa 1368-circa 1437 .... DLB-146
Hochhuth, Rolf 1931- DLB-124
Hochman, Sandra 1936- DLB-5
Hocken, Thomas Morland
   1836-1910 .... DLB-184
Hodder and Stoughton, Limited........ DLB-106
Hodgins, Jack 1938- DLB-60
Hodgman, Helen 1945- DLB-14
Hodgskin, Thomas 1787-1869 .... DLB-158
Hodgson, Ralph 1871-1962 .... DLB-19
Hodgson, William Hope
   1877-1918............DLB-70, 153, 156, 178
Hoe, Robert III 1839-1909............DLB-187
Hoeg, Peter 1957- DLB-214
Højholt, Per 1928- DLB-214
Hoffenstein, Samuel 1890-1947 .... DLB-11
Hoffman, Charles Fenno 1806-1884... DLB-3, 250
Hoffman, Daniel 1923- DLB-5
Hoffmann, E. T. A.
   1776-1822............ DLB-90; CDWLB-2
Hoffman, Frank B. 1888-1958 .... DLB-188
Hoffman, William 1925- DLB-234
Hoffmanswaldau, Christian Hoffman von
   1616-1679..................... DLB-168
Hofmann, Michael 1957- DLB-40
Hofmannsthal, Hugo von
   1874-1929..........DLB-81, 118; CDWLB-2
Hofstadter, Richard 1916-1970.......DLB-17, 246
Hogan, Desmond 1950- DLB-14
Hogan, Linda 1947- DLB-175
Hogan and Thompson DLB-49
Hogarth Press..................... DLB-112
Hogg, James 1770-1835........DLB-93, 116, 159
Hohberg, Wolfgang Helmhard Freiherr von
   1612-1688 .... DLB-168
von Hohenheim, Philippus Aureolus
   Theophrastus Bombastus (see Paracelsus)
Hohl, Ludwig 1904-1980 .... DLB-56
Holbrook, David 1923- DLB-14, 40
Holcroft, Thomas 1745-1809 .... DLB-39, 89, 158
Preface to *Alwyn* (1780)................ DLB-39
Holden, Jonathan 1941- DLB-105
"Contemporary Verse Story-telling" DLB-105

468

Holden, Molly 1927-1981 ....DLB-40
Hölderlin, Friedrich 1770-1843 DLB-90; CDWLB-2
Holiday House.......................DLB-46
Holinshed, Raphael died 1580.........DLB-167
Holland, J. G. 1819-1881..............DS-13
Holland, Norman N. 1927- DLB-67
Hollander, John 1929- DLB-5
Holley, Marietta 1836-1926............DLB-11
Hollinghurst, Alan 1954- DLB-207
Hollingsworth, Margaret 1940- DLB-60
Hollo, Anselm 1934- DLB-40
Holloway, Emory 1885-1977..........DLB-103
Holloway, John 1920- DLB-27
Holloway House Publishing Company....DLB-46
Holme, Constance 1880-1955..........DLB-34
Holmes, Abraham S. 1821?-1908 ....DLB-99
Holmes, John Clellon 1926-1988......DLB-16, 237
"Four Essays on the Beat Generation".....DLB-16
Holmes, Mary Jane 1825-1907......DLB-202, 221
Holmes, Oliver Wendell
    1809-1894 ....DLB-1, 189, 235; CDALB-2
Holmes, Richard 1945- DLB-155
The Cult of Biography
    Excerpts from the Second Folio Debate:
    "Biographies are generally a disease of
    English Literature" Y-86
Holmes, Thomas James 1874-1959 ......DLB-187
Holroyd, Michael 1935- DLB-155; Y-99
Holst, Hermann E. von 1841-1904 ....DLB-47
Holt, Henry, and Company.............DLB-49
Holt, John 1721-1784 ....DLB-43
Holt, Rinehart and Winston DLB-46
Holtby, Winifred 1898-1935 ....DLB-191
Holthusen, Hans Egon 1913- DLB-69
Hölty, Ludwig Christoph Heinrich
    1748-1776........................DLB-94
Holub, Miroslav
    1923-1998............DLB-232; CDWLB-4
Holz, Arno 1863-1929.................DLB-118
Home, Henry, Lord Kames
    (see Kames, Henry Home, Lord)
Home, John 1722-1808 ....DLB-84
Home, William Douglas 1912- DLB-13
Home Publishing Company DLB-49
Homer circa eighth-seventh centuries B.C.
    ....DLB-176; CDWLB-1
Homer, Winslow 1836-1910 ....DLB-188
Homes, Geoffrey (see Mainwaring, Daniel)
Honan, Park 1928- DLB-111
Hone, William 1780-1842 ....DLB-110, 158
Hongo, Garrett Kaoru 1951- DLB-120
Honig, Edwin 1919- DLB-5
Hood, Hugh 1928- DLB-53
Hood, Mary 1946- DLB-234
Hood, Thomas 1799-1845..............DLB-96
Hook, Theodore 1788-1841............DLB-116
Hooker, Jeremy 1941- DLB-40

Hooker, Richard 1554-1600 ....DLB-132
Hooker, Thomas 1586-1647 ....DLB-24
hooks, bell 1952- DLB-246
Hooper, Johnson Jones
    1815-1862 ....DLB-3, 11, 248
Hope, Anthony 1863-1933 ....DLB-153, 156
Hope, Christopher 1944- DLB-225
Hope, Eva (see Hearn, Mary Anne)
Hope, Laurence (Adela Florence
    Cory Nicolson) 1865-1904 ....DLB-240
Hopkins, Ellice 1836-1904.............DLB-190
Hopkins, Gerard Manley
    1844-1889 ....DLB-35, 57; CDBLB-5
Hopkins, John (see Sternhold, Thomas)
Hopkins, John H., and Son DLB-46
Hopkins, Lemuel 1750-1801 ....DLB-37
Hopkins, Pauline Elizabeth 1859-1930 ....DLB-50
Hopkins, Samuel 1721-1803 ....DLB-31
Hopkinson, Francis 1737-1791 ....DLB-31
Hopkinson, Nalo 1960- DLB-251
Hopper, Nora (Mrs. Nora Chesson)
    1871-1906 ....DLB-240
Hoppin, Augustus 1828-1896 ....DLB-188
Hora, Josef 1891-1945......DLB-215; CDWLB-4
Horace 65 B.C.-8 B.C.......DLB-211; CDWLB-1
Horgan, Paul 1903-1995 .....DLB-102, 212; Y-85
Horizon Press DLB-46
Hornby, C. H. St. John 1867-1946.......DLB-201
Hornby, Nick 1957- DLB-207
Horne, Frank 1899-1974 ....DLB-51
Horne, Richard Henry (Hengist)
    1802 or 1803-1884 ....DLB-32
Horney, Karen 1885-1952.............DLB-246
Hornung, E. W. 1866-1921............DLB-70
Horovitz, Israel 1939- DLB-7
Horton, George Moses 1797?-1883? DLB-50
Horváth, Ödön von 1901-1938......DLB-85, 124
Horwood, Harold 1923- DLB-60
Hosford, E. and E. [publishing house].....DLB-49
Hoskens, Jane Fenn 1693-1770? DLB-200
Hoskyns, John 1566-1638 ....DLB-121
Hosokawa Yūsai 1535-1610............DLB-203
Hostovský, Egon 1908-1973 ....DLB-215
Hotchkiss and Company...............DLB-49
Hough, Emerson 1857-1923 ....DLB-9, 212
Houghton, Stanley 1881-1913 ....DLB-10
Houghton Mifflin Company DLB-49
Household, Geoffrey 1900-1988 ....DLB-87
Housman, A. E. 1859-1936 ....DLB-19; CDBLB-5
Housman, Laurence 1865-1959..........DLB-10
Houston, Pam 1962- DLB-244
Houwald, Ernst von 1778-1845 ....DLB-90
Hovey, Richard 1864-1900 ....DLB-54
Howard, Donald R. 1927-1987 ....DLB-111
Howard, Maureen 1930- Y-83
Howard, Richard 1929- DLB-5

Howard, Roy W. 1883-1964............DLB-29
Howard, Sidney 1891-1939........DLB-7, 26, 249
Howard, Thomas, second Earl of Arundel
    1585-1646 ....DLB-213
Howe, E. W. 1853-1937 ....DLB-12, 25
Howe, Henry 1816-1893 ....DLB-30
Howe, Irving 1920-1993 ....DLB-67
Howe, Joseph 1804-1873 ....DLB-99
Howe, Julia Ward 1819-1910 ....DLB-1, 189, 235
Howe, Percival Presland 1886-1944 .....DLB-149
Howe, Susan 1937- DLB-120
Howell, Clark, Sr. 1863-1936 ....DLB-25
Howell, Evan P. 1839-1905.............DLB-23
Howell, James 1594?-1666.............DLB-151
Howell, Soskin and Company...........DLB-46
Howell, Warren Richardson
    1912-1984 ....DLB-140
Howells, William Dean 1837-1920
    ....DLB-12, 64, 74, 79, 189; CDALB-3
Introduction to Paul Laurence Dunbar,
    Lyrics of Lowly Life (1896) DLB-50
Howitt, Mary 1799-1888 ....DLB-110, 199
Howitt, William 1792-1879 and
    Howitt, Mary 1799-1888...........DLB-110
Hoyem, Andrew 1935- DLB-5
Hoyers, Anna Ovena 1584-1655........DLB-164
Hoyos, Angela de 1940- DLB-82
Hoyt, Henry [publishing house] DLB-49
Hoyt, Palmer 1897-1979...............DLB-127
Hrabal, Bohumil 1914-1997............DLB-232
Hrabanus Maurus 776?-856...........DLB-148
Hronský, Josef Cíger 1896-1960 ....DLB-215
Hrotsvit of Gandersheim
    circa 935-circa 1000................DLB-148
Hubbard, Elbert 1856-1915.............DLB-91
Hubbard, Kin 1868-1930..............DLB-11
Hubbard, William circa 1621-1704 ......DLB-24
Huber, Therese 1764-1829 ....DLB-90
Huch, Friedrich 1873-1913 ....DLB-66
Huch, Ricarda 1864-1947 ....DLB-66
Huck at 100: How Old Is
    Huckleberry Finn? Y-85
Huddle, David 1942- DLB-130
Hudgins, Andrew 1951- DLB-120
Hudson, Henry Norman 1814-1886 .....DLB-64
Hudson, Stephen 1868?-1944 ....DLB-197
Hudson, W. H. 1841-1922 .....DLB-98, 153, 174
Hudson and Goodwin.................DLB-49
Huebsch, B. W. [publishing house]........DLB-46
Oral History: B. W. Huebsch Y-99
Hueffer, Oliver Madox 1876-1931.......DLB-197
Hugh of St. Victor circa 1096-1141 ......DLB-208
Hughes, David 1930- DLB-14
Hughes, Dusty 1947- DLB-233
Hughes, Hatcher 1881-1945 ....DLB-249
Hughes, John 1677-1720..............DLB-84

469

Cumulative Index

Hughes, Langston 1902-1967 ....DLB-4, 7, 48, 51, 86, 228; CDALB-5

Hughes, Richard 1900-1976 .... DLB-15, 161

Hughes, Ted 1930-1998 .... DLB-40, 161

Hughes, Thomas 1822-1896 .... DLB-18, 163

Hugo, Richard 1923-1982 .... DLB-5, 206

Hugo, Victor 1802-1885 .... DLB-119, 192, 217

Hugo Awards and Nebula Awards DLB-8

Hull, Richard 1896-1973 .... DLB-77

Hulme, T. E. 1883-1917 .... DLB-19

Hulton, Anne ?-1779? DLB-200

Humboldt, Alexander von 1769-1859 .... DLB-90

Humboldt, Wilhelm von 1767-1835 ...... DLB-90

Hume, David 1711-1776 .... DLB-104, 252

Hume, Fergus 1859-1932 .... DLB-70

Hume, Sophia 1702-1774 .... DLB-200

Hume-Rothery, Mary Catherine 1824-1885 .... DLB-240

Humishuma (see Mourning Dove)

Hummer, T. R. 1950- DLB-120

Humorous Book Illustration DLB-11

Humphrey, Duke of Gloucester 1391-1447 .... DLB-213

Humphrey, William 1924-1997 .. DLB-6, 212, 234

Humphreys, David 1752-1818 .... DLB-37

Humphreys, Emyr 1919- DLB-15

Huncke, Herbert 1915-1996 .... DLB-16

Huneker, James Gibbons 1857-1921 ...... DLB-71

Hunold, Christian Friedrich 1681-1721 .. DLB-168

Hunt, Irene 1907- DLB-52

Hunt, Leigh 1784-1859 ....DLB-96, 110, 144

Hunt, Violet 1862-1942 ....DLB-162, 197

Hunt, William Gibbes 1791-1833 .... DLB-73

Hunter, Evan 1926- Y-82

Hunter, Jim 1939- DLB-14

Hunter, Kristin 1931- DLB-33

Hunter, Mollie 1922- DLB-161

Hunter, N. C. 1908-1971 .... DLB-10

Hunter-Duvar, John 1821-1899 .... DLB-99

Huntington, Henry E. 1850-1927 ...... DLB-140

Huntington, Susan Mansfield 1791-1823 .... DLB-200

Hurd and Houghton DLB-49

Hurst, Fannie 1889-1968 .... DLB-86

Hurst and Blackett DLB-106

Hurst and Company DLB-49

Hurston, Zora Neale 1901?-1960 .... DLB-51, 86; CDALB-7

Husson, Jules-François-Félix (see Champfleury)

Huston, John 1906-1987 .... DLB-26

Hutcheson, Francis 1694-1746 ...... DLB-31, 252

Hutchinson, Ron 1947- DLB-245

Hutchinson, R. C. 1907-1975 .... DLB-191

Hutchinson, Thomas 1711-1780 .... DLB-30, 31

Hutchinson and Company (Publishers) Limited DLB-112

Hutton, Richard Holt 1826-1897 .... DLB-57

von Hutton, Ulrich 1488-1523 ....DLB-179

Huxley, Aldous 1894-1963 ...... DLB-36, 100, 162, 195, 255; CDBLB-6

Huxley, Elspeth Josceline 1907-1997 ....DLB-77, 204

Huxley, T. H. 1825-1895 .... DLB-57

Huyghue, Douglas Smith 1816-1891 ..... DLB-99

Huysmans, Joris-Karl 1848-1907 .... DLB-123

Hwang, David Henry 1957- DLB-212, 228

Hyde, Donald 1909-1966 and Hyde, Mary 1912- DLB-187

Hyman, Trina Schart 1939- DLB-61

I

Iavorsky, Stefan 1658-1722 .... DLB-150

Iazykov, Nikolai Mikhailovich 1803-1846 .... DLB-205

Ibáñez, Armando P. 1949- DLB-209

Ibn Bajja circa 1077-1138 .... DLB-115

Ibn Gabirol, Solomon circa 1021-circa 1058 .... DLB-115

Ibuse, Masuji 1898-1993 .... DLB-180

Ichijō Kanera (see Ichijō Kaneyoshi)

Ichijō Kaneyoshi (Ichijō Kanera) 1402-1481 .... DLB-203

The Iconography of Science-Fiction Art DLB-8

Iffland, August Wilhelm 1759-1814 ...... DLB-94

Ignatow, David 1914-1997 .... DLB-5

Ike, Chukwuemeka 1931- DLB-157

Ikkyū Sōjun 1394-1481 .... DLB-203

Iles, Francis (see Berkeley, Anthony)

Illich, Ivan 1926- DLB-242

The Illustration of Early German Literar Manuscripts, circa 1150-circa 1300 .. DLB-148

Illyés, Gyula 1902-1983 .... DLB-215; CDWLB-4

Imbs, Bravig 1904-1946 .... DLB-4

Imbuga, Francis D. 1947- DLB-157

Immermann, Karl 1796-1840 .... DLB-133

Inchbald, Elizabeth 1753-1821 .... DLB-39, 89

Ingamells, Rex 1913-1955 .... DLB-260

Inge, William 1913-1973 ... DLB-7, 249; CDALB-1

Ingelow, Jean 1820-1897 .... DLB-35, 163

Ingersoll, Ralph 1900-1985 .... DLB-127

The Ingersoll Prizes Y-84

Ingoldsby, Thomas (see Barham, Richard Harris)

Ingraham, Joseph Holt 1809-1860 .... DLB-3, 248

Inman, John 1805-1850 .... DLB-73

Innerhofer, Franz 1944- DLB-85

Innis, Harold Adams 1894-1952 .... DLB-88

Innis, Mary Quayle 1899-1972 .... DLB-88

Inō Sōgi 1421-1502 .... DLB-203

Inoue Yasushi 1907-1991 .... DLB-181

International Publishers Company DLB-46

Interviews:

Adoff, Arnold and Virginia Hamilton Y-01

Anastas, Benjamin Y-98

Baker, Nicholson Y-00

Bank, Melissa Y-98

Bernstein, Harriet Y-82

Betts, Doris Y-82

Bosworth, David Y-82

Bottoms, David Y-83

Bowers, Fredson Y-80

Burnshaw, Stanley Y-97

Carpenter, Humphrey Y-84, Y-99

Carr, Virginia Spencer Y-00

Carver, Raymond Y-83

Cherry, Kelly Y-83

Coppel, Alfred Y-83

Cowley, Malcolm Y-81

Davis, Paxton Y-89

De Vries, Peter Y-82

Dickey, James Y-82

Donald, David Herbert Y-87

Ellroy, James Y-91

Fancher, Betsy Y-83

Faust, Irvin Y-00

Fulton, Len Y-86

Furst, Alan Y-01

Garrett, George Y-83

Greenfield, George Y-91

Griffin, Bryan Y-81

Groom, Winston Y-01

Guilds, John Caldwell Y-92

Hardin, James Y-92

Harrison, Jim Y-82

Hazzard, Shirley Y-82

Herrick, William Y-01

Higgins, George V. Y-98

Hoban, Russell Y-90

Holroyd, Michael Y-99

Horowitz, Glen Y-90

Iggulden, John Y-01

Jakes, John Y-83

Jenkinson, Edward B. Y-82

Jenks, Tom Y-86

Kaplan, Justin Y-86

King, Florence Y-85

Klopfer, Donald S. Y-97

Krug, Judith Y-82

Lamm, Donald Y-95

Laughlin, James Y-96

Lindsay, Jack Y-84

Mailer, Norman Y-97

Manchester, William Y-85

McCormack, Thomas Y-98

McNamara, Katherine Y-97	An Interview with Phyllis Schlafly An Interview with Edward B. Jenkinson An Interview with Lamarr Mooneyham An Interview with Harriet Bernstein Y-82	James, Naomi 1949- DLB-204
Mellen, Joan Y-94		James, P. D. 1920- . . . DLB-87; DS-17; CDBLB-8
Menaher, Daniel Y-97		James VI of Scotland, I of England 1566-1625 . . . . DLB-151, 172
Mooneyham, Lamarr Y-82	Islas, Arturo 1938-1991 . . . . DLB-122	
Murray, Les Y-01		*Ane Schort Treatise Conteining Some Reulis and Cautelis to Be Obseruit and Eschewit in Scottis Poesi* (1584) DLB-172
Nosworth, David Y-82	Issit, Debbie 1966- DLB-233	
O'Connor, Patrick Y-84, Y-99	Ivanišević, Drago 1907-1981 . . . . DLB-181	
Ozick, Cynthia Y-83		James, Thomas 1572?-1629 . . . . DLB-213
Penner, Jonathan Y-83	Ivaska, Astrīde 1926- DLB-232	James, U. P. [publishing house] DLB-49
Pennington, Lee Y-82	Ivers, M. J., and Company DLB-49	James, Will 1892-1942 . . . . DS-16
Penzler, Otto Y-96	Iwaniuk, Wacław 1915- DLB-215	Jameson, Anna 1794-1860 . . . . DLB-99, 166
Plimpton, George Y-99	Iwano, Hōmei 1873-1920 . . . . DLB-180	Jameson, Fredric 1934- DLB-67
Potok, Chaim Y-84	Iwaszkiewicz, Jarosław 1894-1980 . . . . DLB-215	Jameson, J. Franklin 1859-1937 . . . . DLB-17
Powell, Padgett Y-01	Iyayi, Festus 1947- DLB-157	Jameson, Storm 1891-1986 . . . . DLB-36
Prescott, Peter S. Y-86	Izumi, Kyōka 1873-1939 . . . . DLB-180	Jančar, Drago 1948- DLB-181
Rabe, David Y-91		Janés, Clara 1940- DLB-134
Rallyson, Carl Y-97	# J	Janevski, Slavko 1920- DLB-181; CDWLB-4
Rechy, John Y-82	Jackmon, Marvin E. (see Marvin X)	Jansson, Tove 1914-2001 . . . . DLB-257
Reid, B. L. Y-83	Jacks, L. P. 1860-1955 . . . . DLB-135	Janvier, Thomas 1849-1913 . . . . DLB-202
Reynolds, Michael Y-95, Y-99	Jackson, Angela 1951- DLB-41	Jaramillo, Cleofas M. 1878-1956 . . . . DLB-122
Schlafly, Phyllis Y-82	Jackson, Charles 1903-1968 . . . . DLB-234	Jarman, Mark 1952- DLB-120
Schroeder, Patricia Y-99	Jackson, Helen Hunt 1830-1885 . . . . DLB-42, 47, 186, 189	Jarrell, Randall 1914-1965 . . DLB-48, 52; CDALB-1
Schulberg, Budd Y-81, Y-01		Jarrold and Sons DLB-106
Scribner, Charles III Y-94	Jackson, Holbrook 1874-1948 . . . . DLB-98	Jarry, Alfred 1873-1907 . . . . DLB-192, 258
Sipper, Ralph Y-94	Jackson, Laura Riding 1901-1991 . . . . DLB-48	Jarves, James Jackson 1818-1888 . . . . DLB-189
Staley, Thomas F. Y-00	Jackson, Shirley 1916-1965 . . . . DLB-6, 234, CDALB-1	Jasmin, Claude 1930- DLB-60
Styron, William Y-80		Jaunsudrabiņš, Jānis 1877-1962 . . . . DLB-220
Toth, Susan Allen Y-86	Jacob, Max 1876-1944 . . . . DLB-258	Jay, John 1745-1829 . . . . DLB-31
Tyler, Anne Y-82	Jacob, Naomi 1884?-1964 . . . . DLB-191	Jean de Garlande (see John of Garland)
Vaughan, Samuel Y-97	Jacob, Piers Anthony Dillingham (see Anthony, Piers)	Jefferies, Richard 1848-1887 . . . . DLB-98, 141
Von Ogtrop, Kristin Y-92	Jacob, Violet 1863-1946 . . . . DLB-240	Jeffers, Lance 1919-1985 . . . . DLB-41
Wallenstein, Barry Y-92	Jacobi, Friedrich Heinrich 1743-1819 . . . . . DLB-94	Jeffers, Robinson 1887-1962 . . . . DLB-45, 212; CDALB-4
Weintraub, Stanley Y-82	Jacobi, Johann Georg 1740-1814 . . . . DLB-97	
Williams, J. Chamberlain Y-84	Jacobs, George W., and Company DLB-49	Jefferson, Thomas 1743-1826 . . . . DLB-31, 183; CDALB-2
Editors, Conversations with Y-95	Jacobs, Harriet 1813-1897 . . . . DLB-239	
Interviews on E-Publishing Y-00	Jacobs, Joseph 1854-1916 . . . . DLB-141	Jégé 1866-1940 . . . . DLB-215
Into the Past: William Jovanovich's Reflections in Publishing Y-01	Jacobs, W. W. 1863-1943 . . . . DLB-135	Jelinek, Elfriede 1946- DLB-85
	Jacobsen, Jørgen-Frantz 1900-1938 . . . . . . DLB-214	Jellicoe, Ann 1927- DLB-13, 233
Irving, John 1942- DLB-6; Y-82	Jacobsen, Josephine 1908- DLB-244	Jemison, Mary circa 1742-1833 . . . . DLB-239
Irving, Washington 1783-1859 . . . . DLB-3, 11, 30, 59, 73, 74, 183, 186, 250; CDALB-2	Jacobson, Dan 1929- DLB-14, 207, 225	Jenkins, Dan 1929- DLB-241
	Jacobson, Howard 1942- DLB-207	Jenkins, Elizabeth 1905- DLB-155
	Jacques de Vitry circa 1160/1170-1240 . . . DLB-208	Jenkins, Robin 1912- DLB-14
Irwin, Grace 1907- DLB-68	Jæger, Frank 1926-1977 . . . . DLB-214	Jenkins, William Fitzgerald (see Leinster, Murray)
Irwin, Will 1873-1948 . . . . DLB-25	Jaggard, William [publishing house] DLB-170	Jenkins, Herbert, Limited DLB-112
Isaksson, Ulla 1916-2000 . . . . DLB-257	Jahier, Piero 1884-1966 . . . . DLB-114	Jennings, Elizabeth 1926- DLB-27
Iser, Wolfgang 1926- DLB-242	Jahnn, Hans Henny 1894-1959 . . . . . . DLB-56, 124	Jens, Walter 1923- DLB-69
Isherwood, Christopher 1904-1986 . . . . DLB-15, 195; Y-86	Jakes, John 1932- Y-83	Jensen, Johannes V. 1873-1950 . . . . DLB-214
	Jakobson, Roman 1896-1982 . . . . DLB-242	Jensen, Merrill 1905-1980 . . . . DLB-17
The Christopher Isherwood Archive, The Huntington Library Y-99	James, Alice 1848-1892 . . . . DLB-221	Jensen, Thit 1876-1957 . . . . DLB-214
	James, C. L. R. 1901-1989 . . . . DLB-125	Jephson, Robert 1736-1803 . . . . DLB-89
Ishiguro, Kazuo 1954- DLB-194	James, George P. R. 1801-1860 . . . . DLB-116	Jerome, Jerome K. 1859-1927 . . . . DLB-10, 34, 135
	James, Henry 1843-1916 . . . . . . DLB-12, 71, 74, 189; DS-13; CDALB-3	Jerome, Judson 1927-1991 . . . . DLB-105
Ishikawa Jun 1899-1987 . . . . DLB-182		Jerrold, Douglas 1803-1857 . . . . DLB-158, 159
		Jersild, Per Christian 1935- DLB-257
The Island Trees Case: A Symposium on School Library Censorship An Interview with Judith Krug	James, John circa 1633-1729 . . . . DLB-24	Jesse, F. Tennyson 1888-1958 . . . . DLB-77
	James, M. R. 1862-1936 . . . . DLB-156, 201	Jewel, John 1522-1571 . . . . DLB-236

Jewett, John P., and Company DLB-49	Johnson, Samuel 1696-1772 ... DLB-24; CDBLB-2	Jonson, Ben 1572?-1637 .... DLB-62, 121; CDBLB-1
Jewett, Sarah Orne 1849-1909 ....DLB-12, 74, 221	Johnson, Samuel 1709-1784 ....DLB-39, 95, 104, 142, 213	Jordan, June 1936- DLB-38
The Jewish Publication Society.......... DLB-49	Johnson, Samuel 1822-1882 .... DLB-1, 243	Joseph and George Y-99
Jewitt, John Rodgers 1783-1821 .... DLB-99	Johnson, Susanna 1730-1810 .... DLB-200	Joseph, Jenny 1932- DLB-40
Jewsbury, Geraldine 1812-1880 .... DLB-21	Johnson, Terry 1955- DLB-233	Joseph, Michael, Limited DLB-112
Jewsbury, Maria Jane 1800-1833 .... DLB-199	Johnson, Uwe 1934-1984 .....DLB-75; CDWLB-2	Josephson, Matthew 1899-1978 .... DLB-4
Jhabvala, Ruth Prawer 1927- DLB-139, 194	Johnston, Annie Fellows 1863-1931 ..... DLB-42	Josephus, Flavius 37-100 ....DLB-176
Jiménez, Juan Ramón 1881-1958 .... DLB-134	Johnston, Basil H. 1929- DLB-60	Josiah Allen's Wife (see Holley, Marietta)
Jimmy, Red, and Others: Harold Rosenthal Remembers the Stars of the Press Box.... Y-01	Johnston, David Claypole 1798?-1865 ... DLB-188	Josipovici, Gabriel 1940- DLB-14
Jin, Ha 1956- DLB-244	Johnston, Denis 1901-1984............. DLB-10	Josselyn, John ?-1675 .... DLB-24
Joans, Ted 1928- DLB-16, 41	Johnston, Ellen 1835-1873 .... DLB-199	Joudry, Patricia 1921- DLB-88
Jōha 1525-1602..................... DLB-203	Johnston, George 1912-1970 .... DLB-260	Jouve, Pierre-Jean 1887-1976........... DLB-258
Johannis de Garlandia (see John of Garland)	Johnston, George 1913- DLB-88	Jovanovich, William 1920-2001 .... Y-01
John, Errol 1924-1988 .... DLB-233	Johnston, Sir Harry 1858-1927 ....DLB-174	Into the Past: William Jovanovich's Reflections on Publishing............... Y-01
John, Eugenie (see Marlitt, E.)	Johnston, Jennifer 1930- DLB-14	Jovine, Giuseppe 1922- DLB-128
John of Dumbleton circa 1310-circa 1349 .... DLB-115	Johnston, Mary 1870-1936 .... DLB-9	Joyaux, Philippe (see Sollers, Philippe)
John of Garland (Jean de Garlande, Johannis de Garlandia) circa 1195-circa 1272 .... DLB-208	Johnston, Richard Malcolm 1822-1898 ... DLB-74	Joyce, Adrien (see Eastman, Carol)
Johns, Captain W. E. 1893-1968 .... DLB-160	Johnstone, Charles 1719?-1800? DLB-39	Joyce, James 1882-1941 ....DLB-10, 19, 36, 162, 247; CDBLB-6
Johnson, Mrs. A. E. ca. 1858-1922..... DLB-221	Johst, Hanns 1890-1978 .... DLB-124	James Joyce Centenary: Dublin, 1982 .... Y-82
Johnson, Amelia (see Johnson, Mrs. A. E.)	Jolas, Eugene 1894-1952.............. DLB-4, 45	James Joyce Conference Y-85
Johnson, B. S. 1933-1973 .... DLB-14, 40	Jones, Alice C. 1853-1933............. DLB-92	A Joyce (Con)Text: Danis Rose and the Remaking of Ulysses Y-97
Johnson, Benjamin [publishing house] DLB-49	Jones, Charles C., Jr. 1831-1893......... DLB-30	The New Ulysses Y-84
Johnson, Benjamin, Jacob, and Robert [publishing house] DLB-49	Jones, D. G. 1929- DLB-53	Jozsef, Attila 1905-1937 ....DLB-215; CDWLB-4
Johnson, Charles 1679-1748 .... DLB-84	Jones, David 1895-1974 .. DLB-20, 100; CDBLB-7	Judd, Orange, Publishing Company...... DLB-49
Johnson, Charles R. 1948- DLB-33	Jones, Diana Wynne 1934- DLB-161	Judd, Sylvester 1813-1853 .... DLB-1, 243
Johnson, Charles S. 1893-1956....... DLB-51, 91	Jones, Ebenezer 1820-1860............. DLB-32	Judith circa 930..................... DLB-146
Johnson, Denis 1949- DLB-120	Jones, Ernest 1819-1868 .... DLB-32	Julian Barnes Checklist.................... Y-01
Johnson, Diane 1934- Y-80	Jones, Gayl 1949- DLB-33	Julian of Norwich 1342-circa 1420 .... DLB-1146
Johnson, Dorothy M. 1905–1984....... DLB-206	Jones, George 1800-1870 .... DLB-183	Julius Caesar 100 B.C.-44 B.C. DLB-211; CDWLB-1
Johnson, E. Pauline (Tekahionwake) 1861-1913....................DLB-175	Jones, Glyn 1905- DLB-15	June, Jennie (see Croly, Jane Cunningham)
Johnson, Edgar 1901-1995 .... DLB-103	Jones, Gwyn 1907- DLB-15, 139	Jung, Franz 1888-1963 .... DLB-118
Johnson, Edward 1598-1672............. DLB-24	Jones, Henry Arthur 1851-1929 .... DLB-10	Jünger, Ernst 1895- DLB-56; CDWLB-2
Johnson, Eyvind 1900-1976 .... DLB-259	Jones, Hugh circa 1692-1760 .... DLB-24	Der jüngere Titurel circa 1275 .... DLB-138
Johnson, Fenton 1888-1958 .... DLB-45, 50	Jones, James 1921-1977........DLB-2, 143; DS-17	Jung-Stilling, Johann Heinrich 1740-1817........................ DLB-94
Johnson, Georgia Douglas 1877?-1966 .... DLB-51, 249	James Jones Papers in the Handy Writers' Colony Collection at the University of Illinois at Springfield Y-98	Justice, Donald 1925- Y-83
Johnson, Gerald W. 1890-1980 .... DLB-29	The James Jones Society................... Y-92	Juvenal circa A.D. 60-circa A.D. 130 ....DLB-211; CDWLB-1
Johnson, Greg 1953- DLB-234	Jones, Jenkin Lloyd 1911- DLB-127	The Juvenile Library (see Godwin, M. J., and Company)
Johnson, Helene 1907-1995............. DLB-51	Jones, John Beauchamp 1810-1866...... DLB-202	
Johnson, Jacob, and Company DLB-49	Jones, LeRoi (see Baraka, Amiri)	**K**
Johnson, James Weldon 1871-1938............. DLB-51; CDALB-4	Jones, Lewis 1897-1939 .... DLB-15	
Johnson, John H. 1918- DLB-137	Jones, Madison 1925- DLB-152	Kacew, Romain (see Gary, Romain)
Johnson, Joseph [publishing house]...... DLB-154	Jones, Major Joseph (see Thompson, William Tappan)	Kafka, Franz 1883-1924 ..... DLB-81; CDWLB-2
Johnson, Linton Kwesi 1952- DLB-157	Jones, Marie 1955- DLB-233	Kahn, Roger 1927- DLB-171
Johnson, Lionel 1867-1902 .... DLB-19	Jones, Preston 1936-1979 .... DLB-7	Kaikō Takeshi 1939-1989............. DLB-182
Johnson, Nunnally 1897-1977 .... DLB-26	Jones, Rodney 1950- DLB-120	Kaiser, Georg 1878-1945 ...DLB-124; CDWLB-2
Johnson, Owen 1878-1952 .... Y-87	Jones, Thom 1945- DLB-244	Kaiserchronik circca 1147............... DLB-148
Johnson, Pamela Hansford 1912- DLB-15	Jones, Sir William 1746-1794 .... DLB-109	Kaleb, Vjekoslav 1905- DLB-181
Johnson, Pauline 1861-1913 .... DLB-92	Jones, William Alfred 1817-1900..................... DLB-59	
Johnson, Ronald 1935-1998 .... DLB-169	Jones's Publishing House DLB-49	
	Jong, Erica 1942- DLB-2, 5, 28, 152	
	Jonke, Gert F. 1946- DLB-85	

Kalechofsky, Roberta 1931- DLB-28	Keats, Ezra Jack 1916-1983 ....DLB-61	Ker, John, third Duke of Roxburghe 1740-1804 ....DLB-213
Kaler, James Otis 1848-1912 ....DLB-12	Keats, John 1795-1821 ....DLB-96, 110; CDBLB-3	Ker, N. R. 1908-1982 ....DLB-201
Kames, Henry Home, Lord 1696-1782 ....DLB-31, 104	Keble, John 1792-1866.............DLB-32, 55	Kerlan, Irvin 1912-1963...............DLB-187
	Keckley, Elizabeth 1818?-1907..........DLB-239	Kermode, Frank 1919- DLB-242
Kamo no Chōmei (Kamo no Nagaakira) 1153 or 1155-1216 ....DLB-203	Keeble, John 1944- Y-83	Kern, Jerome 1885-1945 ....DLB-187
Kamo no Nagaakira (see Kamo no Chōmei)	Keeffe, Barrie 1945- DLB-13, 245	Kernaghan, Eileen 1939- DLB-251
Kampmann, Christian 1939-1988 ....DLB-214	Keeley, James 1867-1934 ....DLB-25	Kerner, Justinus 1776-1862 ....DLB-90
Kandel, Lenore 1932- DLB-16	W. B. Keen, Cooke and Company DLB-49	Kerouac, Jack 1922-1969...DLB-2, 16, 237; DS-3; CDALB-1
Kanin, Garson 1912-1999 ....DLB-7	Keillor, Garrison 1942- Y-87	The Jack Kerouac Revival................Y-95
Kant, Hermann 1926- DLB-75	Keith, Marian 1874?-1961 ....DLB-92	"Re-meeting of Old Friends": The Jack Kerouac Conference Y-82
Kant, Immanuel 1724-1804 ....DLB-94	Keller, Gary D. 1943- DLB-82	
Kantemir, Antiokh Dmitrievich 1708-1744.......................DLB-150	Keller, Gottfried 1819-1890 ....DLB-129; CDWLB-2	Auction of Jack Kerouac's On the Road Scroll ..Y-01
Kantor, MacKinlay 1904-1977........DLB-9, 102	Kelley, Edith Summers 1884-1956.........DLB-9	Kerouac, Jan 1952-1996................DLB-16
Kanze Kōjirō Nobumitsu 1435-1516 .....DLB-203	Kelley, Emma Dunham ?-? DLB-221	Kerr, Charles H., and Company DLB-49
Kanze Motokiyo (see Zeami)	Kelley, William Melvin 1937- DLB-33	Kerr, Orpheus C. (see Newell, Robert Henry)
Kaplan, Fred 1937- DLB-111	Kellogg, Ansel Nash 1832-1886..........DLB-23	Kersh, Gerald 1911-1968...............DLB-255
Kaplan, Johanna 1942- DLB-28	Kellogg, Steven 1941- DLB-61	Kesey, Ken 1935-2001........DLB-2, 16, 206; CDALB-6
Kaplan, Justin 1925- DLB-111; Y-86	Kelly, George E. 1887-1974 ....DLB-7, 249	Kessel, Joseph 1898-1979 ....DLB-72
The Practice of Biography V: An Interview with Justin Kaplan........Y-86	Kelly, Hugh 1739-1777.................DLB-89	Kessel, Martin 1901- DLB-56
	Kelly, Piet and Company................DLB-49	Kesten, Hermann 1900- DLB-56
Kaplinski, Jaan 1941- DLB-232	Kelly, Robert 1935- DLB-5, 130, 165	Keun, Irmgard 1905-1982 ....DLB-69
Kapnist, Vasilii Vasilevich 1758?-1823 ...DLB-150	Kelman, James 1946- DLB-194	Key, Ellen 1849-1926 ....DLB-259
Karadžić,Vuk Stefanović 1787-1864............DLB-147; CDWLB-4	Kelmscott Press.....................DLB-112	Key and Biddle DLB-49
	Kelton, Elmer 1926- DLB-256	Keynes, Sir Geoffrey 1887-1982.........DLB-201
Karamzin, Nikolai Mikhailovich 1766-1826 ....DLB-150	Kemble, E. W. 1861-1933 ....DLB-188	Keynes, John Maynard 1883-1946 ....DS-10
Karinthy, Frigyes 1887-1938 ....DLB-215	Kemble, Fanny 1809-1893..............DLB-32	Keyserling, Eduard von 1855-1918.......DLB-66
Karsch, Anna Louisa 1722-1791..........DLB-97	Kemelman, Harry 1908- DLB-28	Khan, Ismith 1925- DLB-125
Kasack, Hermann 1896-1966............DLB-69	Kempe, Margery circa 1373-1438 ....DLB-146	Khaytov, Nikolay 1919- DLB-181
Kasai, Zenzō 1887-1927 ....DLB-180	Kempner, Friederike 1836-1904 ....DLB-129	Khemnitser, Ivan Ivanovich 1745-1784 ....DLB-150
Kaschnitz, Marie Luise 1901-1974 ....DLB-69	Kempowski, Walter 1929- DLB-75	
Kassák, Lajos 1887-1967 ....DLB-215	Kendall, Claude [publishing company] DLB-46	Kheraskov, Mikhail Matveevich 1733-1807 ....DLB-150
Kaštelan, Jure 1919-1990 ....DLB-147	Kendall, Henry 1839-1882 ....DLB-230	
Kästner, Erich 1899-1974................DLB-56	Kendall, May 1861-1943 ....DLB-240	Khomiakov, Aleksei Stepanovich 1804-1860 ....DLB-205
Katenin, Pavel Aleksandrovich 1792-1853 ....DLB-205	Kendell, George 1809-1867 ....DLB-43	Khristov, Boris 1945- DLB-181
	Kenedy, P. J., and Sons................DLB-49	Khvoshchinskaia, Nadezhda Dmitrievna 1824-1889 ....DLB-238
Kattan, Naim 1928- DLB-53	Kenkō circa 1283-circa 1352 ....DLB-203	
Katz, Steve 1935- Y-83	Kennan, George 1845-1924.............DLB-189	Khvostov, Dmitrii Ivanovich 1757-1835.......................DLB-150
Kauffman, Janet 1945 ....DLB-218; Y-86	Kennedy, Adrienne 1931- DLB-38	
Kauffmann, Samuel 1898-1971 ....DLB-127	Kennedy, John Pendleton 1795-1870...DLB-3, 248	Kidd, Adam 1802?-1831 ....DLB-99
Kaufman, Bob 1925- DLB-16, 41	Kennedy, Leo 1907- DLB-88	Kidd, William [publishing house] DLB-106
Kaufman, George S. 1889-1961...........DLB-7	Kennedy, Margaret 1896-1967 ....DLB-36	Kidder, Tracy 1945- DLB-185
Kavan, Anna 1901-1968 ....DLB-255	Kennedy, Patrick 1801-1873 ....DLB-159	Kiely, Benedict 1919- DLB-15
Kavanagh, P. J. 1931- DLB-40	Kennedy, Richard S. 1920- DLB-111	Kieran, John 1892-1981................DLB-171
Kavanagh, Patrick 1904-1967 ....DLB-15, 20	Kennedy, William 1928- DLB-143; Y-85	Kiggins and Kellogg..................DLB-49
Kawabata, Yasunari 1899-1972 ....DLB-180	Kennedy, X. J. 1929- DLB-5	Kiley, Jed 1889-1962 ....DLB-4
Kay, Guy Gavriel 1954- DLB-251	Kennelly, Brendan 1936- DLB-40	Kilgore, Bernard 1908-1967.............DLB-127
Kaye-Smith, Sheila 1887-1956 ....DLB-36	Kenner, Hugh 1923- DLB-67	Kilian, Crawford 1941- DLB-251
Kazin, Alfred 1915-1998 ....DLB-67	Kennerley, Mitchell [publishing house] DLB-46	Killens, John Oliver 1916- DLB-33
Keane, John B. 1928- DLB-13	Kenny, Maurice 1929- DLB-175	Killigrew, Anne 1660-1685 ....DLB-131
Keary, Annie 1825-1879 ....DLB-163	Kent, Frank R. 1877-1958 ....DLB-29	Killigrew, Thomas 1612-1683 ....DLB-58
Keary, Eliza 1827-1918................DLB-240	Kenyon, Jane 1947-1995 ....DLB-120	Kilmer, Joyce 1886-1918 ....DLB-45
Keating, H. R. F. 1926- DLB-87	Keough, Hugh Edmund 1864-1912......DLB-171	Kilroy, Thomas 1934- DLB-233
Keatley, Charlotte 1960- DLB-245	Keppler and Schwartzmann............DLB-49	Kilwardby, Robert circa 1215-1279 ......DLB-115

Kimball, Richard Burleigh 1816-1892 ... DLB-202
Kincaid, Jamaica 1949-
 .... DLB-157, 227; CDALB-7; CDWLB-3
King, Charles 1844-1933 .... DLB-186
King, Clarence 1842-1901 .... DLB-12
King, Florence 1936 .... Y-85
King, Francis 1923- DLB-15, 139
King, Grace 1852-1932............. DLB-12, 78
King, Harriet Hamilton 1840-1920...... DLB-199
King, Henry 1592-1669 .... DLB-126
King, Solomon [publishing house] DLB-49
King, Stephen 1947- DLB-143; Y-80
King, Susan Petigru 1824-1875 .... DLB-239
King, Thomas 1943- DLB-175
King, Woodie, Jr. 1937- DLB-38
Kinglake, Alexander William
 1809-1891 .... DLB-55, 166
Kingsbury, Donald 1929- DLB-251
Kingsley, Charles
 1819-1875........DLB-21, 32, 163, 178, 190
Kingsley, Henry 1830-1876 .... DLB-21, 230
Kingsley, Mary Henrietta 1862-1900 .....DLB-174
Kingsley, Sidney 1906- DLB-7
Kingsmill, Hugh 1889-1949 .... DLB-149
Kingsolver, Barbara
 1955- DLB-206; CDALB-7
Kingston, Maxine Hong
 1940- DLB-173, 212; Y-80; CDALB-7
Kingston, William Henry Giles
 1814-1880..................... DLB-163
Kinnan, Mary Lewis 1763-1848 .... DLB-200
Kinnell, Galway 1927- DLB-5; Y-87
Kinsella, Thomas 1928- DLB-27
Kipling, Rudyard 1865-1936
 .... DLB-19, 34, 141, 156; CDBLB-5
Kipphardt, Heinar 1922-1982 .... DLB-124
Kirby, William 1817-1906............... DLB-99
Kircher, Athanasius 1602-1680......... DLB-164
Kireevsky, Ivan Vasil'evich 1806-1856... DLB-198
Kireevsky, Petr Vasil'evich 1808-1856... DLB-205
Kirk, Hans 1898-1962 .... DLB-214
Kirk, John Foster 1824-1904.......... DLB-79
Kirkconnell, Watson 1895-1977 .... DLB-68
Kirkland, Caroline M.
 1801-1864 ....DLB-3, 73, 74, 250; DS-13
Kirkland, Joseph 1830-1893 .... DLB-12
Kirkman, Francis [publishing house] DLB-170
Kirkpatrick, Clayton 1915- DLB-127
Kirkup, James 1918- DLB-27
Kirouac, Conrad (see Marie-Victorin, Frère)
Kirsch, Sarah 1935- DLB-75
Kirst, Hans Hellmut 1914-1989 .... DLB-69
Kiš, Danilo 1935-1989 ..... DLB-181; CDWLB-4
Kita Morio 1927- DLB-182
Kitcat, Mabel Greenhow 1859-1922..... DLB-135
Kitchin, C. H. B. 1895-1967 .... DLB-77
Kittredge, William 1932- DLB-212, 244

Kiukhel'beker, Vil'gel'm Karlovich
 1797-1846 .... DLB-205
Kizer, Carolyn 1925- DLB-5, 169
Klabund 1890-1928 .... DLB-66
Klaj, Johann 1616-1656 .... DLB-164
Klappert, Peter 1942- DLB-5
Klass, Philip (see Tenn, William)
Klein, A. M. 1909-1972................ DLB-68
Kleist, Ewald von 1715-1759........... DLB-97
Kleist, Heinrich von
 1777-1811 .... DLB-90; CDWLB-2
Klinger, Friedrich Maximilian
 1752-1831..................... DLB-94
Klíma, Ivan 1931- DLB-232; CDWLB-4
Kliushnikov, Viktor Petrovich
 1841-1892 .... DLB-238
Oral History Interview with Donald S.
 Klopfer........................ Y-97
Klopstock, Friedrich Gottlieb
 1724-1803..................... DLB-97
Klopstock, Meta 1728-1758............ DLB-97
Kluge, Alexander 1932- DLB-75
Knapp, Joseph Palmer 1864-1951....... DLB-91
Knapp, Samuel Lorenzo 1783-1838 ...... DLB-59
Knapton, J. J. and P.
 [publishing house] DLB-154
Kniazhnin, Iakov Borisovich
 1740-1791 .... DLB-150
Knickerbocker, Diedrich (see Irving, Washington)
Knigge, Adolph Franz Friedrich Ludwig,
 Freiherr von 1752-1796 .... DLB-94
Knight, Charles, and Company DLB-106
Knight, Damon 1922- DLB-8
Knight, Etheridge 1931-1992 .... DLB-41
Knight, John S. 1894-1981 .... DLB-29
Knight, Sarah Kemble 1666-1727 .... DLB-24, 200
Knight-Bruce, G. W. H. 1852-1896 .....DLB-174
Knister, Raymond 1899-1932........... DLB-68
Knoblock, Edward 1874-1945 .... DLB-10
Knopf, Alfred A. 1892-1984............... Y-84
Knopf, Alfred A. [publishing house]...... DLB-46
Knopf to Hammett: The Editoral
 Correspondence.................. Y-00
Knorr von Rosenroth, Christian
 1636-1689 .... DLB-168
"Knots into Webs: Some Autobiographical
 Sources," by Dabney Stuart........ DLB-105
Knowles, John 1926- DLB-6; CDALB-6
Knox, Frank 1874-1944 .... DLB-29
Knox, John circa 1514-1572 .... DLB-132
Knox, John Armoy 1850-1906.......... DLB-23
Knox, Lucy 1845-1884................ DLB-240
Knox, Ronald Arbuthnott 1888-1957..... DLB-77
Knox, Thomas Wallace 1835-1896 ..... DLB-189
Kobayashi Takiji 1903-1933 .... DLB-180
Kober, Arthur 1900-1975 .... DLB-11
Kobiakova, Aleksandra Petrovna
 1823-1892 .... DLB-238

Kocbek, Edvard 1904-1981 ...DLB-147; CDWB-4
Koch, Howard 1902- DLB-26
Koch, Kenneth 1925- DLB-5
Kōda, Rohan 1867-1947 .... DLB-180
Koenigsberg, Moses 1879-1945 .... DLB-25
Koeppen, Wolfgang 1906-1996 .... DLB-69
Koertge, Ronald 1940- DLB-105
Koestler, Arthur 1905-1983 ......Y-83; CDBLB-7
Kohn, John S. Van E. 1906-1976 and
 Papantonio, Michael 1907-1978 ......DLB-187
Kokoschka, Oskar 1886-1980 .... DLB-124
Kolb, Annette 1870-1967 .... DLB-66
Kolbenheyer, Erwin Guido
 1878-1962 .... DLB-66, 124
Kolleritsch, Alfred 1931- DLB-85
Kolodny, Annette 1941- DLB-67
Kol'tsov, Aleksei Vasil'evich
 1809-1842 .... DLB-205
Komarov, Matvei circa 1730-1812 ...... DLB-150
Komroff, Manuel 1890-1974............ DLB-4
Komunyakaa, Yusef 1947- DLB-120
Koneski, Blaže 1921-1993....DLB-181; CDWLB-4
Konigsburg, E. L. 1930- DLB-52
Konparu Zenchiku 1405-1468? DLB-203
Konrád, György 1933- DLB-232; CDWLB-4
Konrad von Würzburg
 circa 1230-1287 .... DLB-138
Konstantinov, Aleko 1863-1897 ....DLB-147
Konwicki, Tadeusz 1926- DLB-232
Kooser, Ted 1939- DLB-105
Kopit, Arthur 1937- DLB-7
Kops, Bernard 1926?- DLB-13
Kornbluth, C. M. 1923-1958 .... DLB-8
Körner, Theodor 1791-1813............ DLB-90
Kornfeld, Paul 1889-1942............. DLB-118
Kosinski, Jerzy 1933-1991 ....DLB-2; Y-82
Kosmač, Ciril 1910-1980 .... DLB-181
Kosovel, Srečko 1904-1926 ....DLB-147
Kostrov, Ermil Ivanovich 1755-1796 .... DLB-150
Kotzebue, August von 1761-1819 ...... DLB-94
Kotzwinkle, William 1938- DLB-173
Kovačić, Ante 1854-1889 ....DLB-147
Kovič, Kajetan 1931- DLB-181
Kozlov, Ivan Ivanovich 1779-1840 ...... DLB-205
Kraf, Elaine 1946- Y-81
Kramer, Jane 1938- DLB-185
Kramer, Larry 1935- DLB-249
Kramer, Mark 1944- DLB-185
Kranjčević, Silvije Strahimir
 1865-1908 ....DLB-147
Krasko, Ivan 1876-1958 .... DLB-215
Krasna, Norman 1909-1984 .... DLB-26
Kraus, Hans Peter 1907-1988 ....DLB-187
Kraus, Karl 1874-1936 .... DLB-118
Krause, Herbert 1905-1976............ DLB-256
Krauss, Ruth 1911-1993............... DLB-52

Kreisel, Henry 1922- ...DLB-88
Krestovsky V. (see Khvoshchinskaia, Nadezhda Dmitrievna)
Krestovsky, Vsevolod Vladimirovich 1839-1895 ...DLB-238
Kreuder, Ernst 1903-1972 ...DLB-69
Krėvė-Mickevičius, Vincas 1882-1954 ...DLB-220
Kreymborg, Alfred 1883-1966 ...DLB-4, 54
Krieger, Murray 1923- ...DLB-67
Krim, Seymour 1922-1989 ...DLB-16
Kristensen, Tom 1893-1974 ...DLB-214
Kristeva, Julia 1941- ...DLB-242
Krleža, Miroslav 1893-1981 ...DLB-147; CDWLB-4
Krock, Arthur 1886-1974 ...DLB-29
Kroetsch, Robert 1927- ...DLB-53
Kross, Jaan 1920- ...DLB-232
Krúdy, Gyula 1878-1933 ...DLB-215
Krutch, Joseph Wood 1893-1970 ...DLB-63, 206
Krylov, Ivan Andreevich 1769-1844 ...DLB-150
Kubin, Alfred 1877-1959 ...DLB-81
Kubrick, Stanley 1928-1999 ...DLB-26
Kudrun circa 1230-1240 ...DLB-138
Kuffstein, Hans Ludwig von 1582-1656 ...DLB-164
Kuhlmann, Quirinus 1651-1689 ...DLB-168
Kuhnau, Johann 1660-1722 ...DLB-168
Kukol'nik, Nestor Vasil'evich 1809-1868 ...DLB-205
Kukučín, Martin 1860-1928 ...DLB-215; CDWLB-4
Kumin, Maxine 1925- ...DLB-5
Kuncewicz, Maria 1895-1989 ...DLB-215
Kundera, Milan 1929- ...DLB-232; CDWLB-4
Kunene, Mazisi 1930- ...DLB-117
Kunikida, Doppo 1869-1908 ...DLB-180
Kunitz, Stanley 1905- ...DLB-48
Kunjufu, Johari M. (see Amini, Johari M.)
Kunnert, Gunter 1929- ...DLB-75
Kunze, Reiner 1933- ...DLB-75
Kupferberg, Tuli 1923- ...DLB-16
Kurahashi Yumiko 1935- ...DLB-182
Kureishi, Hanif 1954- ...DLB-194, 245
Kürnberger, Ferdinand 1821-1879 ...DLB-129
Kurz, Isolde 1853-1944 ...DLB-66
Kusenberg, Kurt 1904-1983 ...DLB-69
Kushchevsky, Ivan Afanas'evich 1847-1876 ...DLB-238
Kushner, Tony 1956- ...DLB-228
Kuttner, Henry 1915-1958 ...DLB-8
Kyd, Thomas 1558-1594 ...DLB-62
Kyffin, Maurice circa 1560?-1598 ...DLB-136
Kyger, Joanne 1934- ...DLB-16
Kyne, Peter B. 1880-1957 ...DLB-78
Kyōgoku Tamekane 1254-1332 ...DLB-203
Kyrklund, Willy 1921- ...DLB-257

L

L. E. L. (see Landon, Letitia Elizabeth)
Laberge, Albert 1871-1960 ...DLB-68
Laberge, Marie 1950- ...DLB-60
Labiche, Eugène 1815-1888 ...DLB-192
Labrunie, Gerard (see Nerval, Gerard de)
La Capria, Raffaele 1922- ...DLB-196
Lacombe, Patrice (see Trullier-Lacombe, Joseph Patrice)
Lacretelle, Jacques de 1888-1985 ...DLB-65
Lacy, Ed 1911-1968 ...DLB-226
Lacy, Sam 1903- ...DLB-171
Ladd, Joseph Brown 1764-1786 ...DLB-37
La Farge, Oliver 1901-1963 ...DLB-9
Laffan, Mrs. R. S. de Courcy (see Adams, Bertha Leith)
Lafferty, R. A. 1914- ...DLB-8
La Flesche, Francis 1857-1932 ...DLB-175
Laforge, Jules 1860-1887 ...DLB-217
Lagerkvist, Pär 1891-1974 ...DLB-259
Lagerlöf, Selma 1858-1940 ...DLB-259
Lagorio, Gina 1922- ...DLB-196
La Guma, Alex 1925-1985 ...DLB-117, 225; CDWLB-3
Lahaise, Guillaume (see Delahaye, Guy)
Lahontan, Louis-Armand de Lom d'Arce, Baron de 1666-1715? ...DLB-99
Laing, Kojo 1946- ...DLB-157
Laird, Carobeth 1895- ...Y-82
Laird and Lee ...DLB-49
Lalić, Ivan V. 1931-1996 ...DLB-181
Lalić, Mihailo 1914-1992 ...DLB-181
Lalonde, Michèle 1937- ...DLB-60
Lamantia, Philip 1927- ...DLB-16
Lamartine, Alphonse de 1790-1869 ...DLB-217
Lamb, Lady Caroline 1785-1828 ...DLB-116
Lamb, Charles 1775-1834 ...DLB-93, 107, 163; CDBLB-3
Lamb, Mary 1764-1874 ...DLB-163
Lambert, Betty 1933-1983 ...DLB-60
Lamming, George 1927- ...DLB-125; CDWLB-3
L'Amour, Louis 1908-1988 ...DLB-206; Y-80
Lampman, Archibald 1861-1899 ...DLB-92
Lamson, Wolffe and Company ...DLB-49
Lancer Books ...DLB-46
Landesman, Jay 1919- and Landesman, Fran 1927- ...DLB-16
Landolfi, Tommaso 1908-1979 ...DLB-177
Landon, Letitia Elizabeth 1802-1838 ...DLB-96
Landor, Walter Savage 1775-1864 ...DLB-93, 107
Landry, Napoléon-P. 1884-1956 ...DLB-92
Lane, Charles 1800-1870 ...DLB-1, 223
Lane, F. C. 1885-1984 ...DLB-241
Lane, John, Company ...DLB-49
Lane, Laurence W. 1890-1967 ...DLB-91

Lane, M. Travis 1934- ...DLB-60
Lane, Patrick 1939- ...DLB-53
Lane, Pinkie Gordon 1923- ...DLB-41
Laney, Al 1896-1988 ...DLB-4, 171
Lang, Andrew 1844-1912 ...DLB-98, 141, 184
Langevin, André 1927- ...DLB-60
Langgässer, Elisabeth 1899-1950 ...DLB-69
Langhorne, John 1735-1779 ...DLB-109
Langland, William circa 1330-circa 1400 ...DLB-146
Langton, Anna 1804-1893 ...DLB-99
Lanham, Edwin 1904-1979 ...DLB-4
Lanier, Sidney 1842-1881 ...DLB-64; DS-13
Lanyer, Aemilia 1569-1645 ...DLB-121
Lapointe, Gatien 1931-1983 ...DLB-88
Lapointe, Paul-Marie 1929- ...DLB-88
Larcom, Lucy 1824-1893 ...DLB-221, 243
Lardner, John 1912-1960 ...DLB-171
Lardner, Ring 1885-1933 ...DLB-11, 25, 86, 171; DS-16; CDALB-4
Lardner 100: Ring Lardner Centennial Symposium ...Y-85
Lardner, Ring, Jr. 1915-2000 ...DLB-26; Y-00
Larkin, Philip 1922-1985 ...DLB-27; CDBLB-8
La Roche, Sophie von 1730-1807 ...DLB-94
La Rocque, Gilbert 1943-1984 ...DLB-60
Laroque de Roquebrune, Robert (see Roquebrune, Robert de)
Larrick, Nancy 1910- ...DLB-61
Larsen, Nella 1893-1964 ...DLB-51
Larson, Clinton F. 1919-1994 ...DLB-256
La Sale, Antoine de circa 1386-1460/1467 ...DLB-208
Lasch, Christopher 1932-1994 ...DLB-246
Lasker-Schüler, Else 1869-1945 ...DLB-66, 124
Lasnier, Rina 1915- ...DLB-88
Lassalle, Ferdinand 1825-1864 ...DLB-129
Latham, Robert 1912-1995 ...DLB-201
Lathrop, Dorothy P. 1891-1980 ...DLB-22
Lathrop, George Parsons 1851-1898 ...DLB-71
Lathrop, John, Jr. 1772-1820 ...DLB-37
Latimer, Hugh 1492?-1555 ...DLB-136
Latimore, Jewel Christine McLawler (see Amini, Johari M.)
La Tour du Pin, Patrice de 1911-1975 ...DLB-258
Latymer, William 1498-1583 ...DLB-132
Laube, Heinrich 1806-1884 ...DLB-133
Laud, William 1573-1645 ...DLB-213
Laughlin, James 1914-1997 ...DLB-48; Y-96
James Laughlin Tributes ...Y-97
Conversations with Publishers IV: An Interview with James Laughlin ...Y-96
Laumer, Keith 1925- ...DLB-8
Lauremberg, Johann 1590-1658 ...DLB-164
Laurence, Margaret 1926-1987 ...DLB-53
Laurentius von Schnüffis 1633-1702 ...DLB-168

475

Cumulative Index

Laurents, Arthur 1918- DLB-26

Laurie, Annie (see Black, Winifred)

Laut, Agnes Christiana 1871-1936 .... DLB-92

Lauterbach, Ann 1942- DLB-193

Lautreamont, Isidore Lucien Ducasse, Comte de 1846-1870..................... DLB-217

Lavater, Johann Kaspar 1741-1801....... DLB-97

Lavin, Mary 1912-1996 .... DLB-15

Law, John (see Harkness, Margaret)

Lawes, Henry 1596-1662 .... DLB-126

Lawless, Anthony (see MacDonald, Philip)

Lawless, Emily (The Hon. Emily Lawless) 1845-1913 DLB-240

Lawrence, D. H. 1885-1930
..... DLB-10, 19, 36, 98, 162, 195; CDBLB-6

Lawrence, David 1888-1973 .... DLB-29

Lawrence, Jerome 1915- and
Lee, Robert E. 1918-1994 .... DLB-228

Lawrence, Seymour 1926-1994 .... Y-94

Lawrence, T. E. 1888-1935 .... DLB-195

Lawson, George 1598-1678 .... DLB-213

Lawson, Henry 1867-1922 .... DLB-230

Lawson, John ?-1711................ DLB-24

Lawson, John Howard 1894-1977 ...... DLB-228

Lawson, Louisa Albury 1848-1920...... DLB-230

Lawson, Robert 1892-1957............. DLB-22

Lawson, Victor F. 1850-1925 .... DLB-25

Layard, Sir Austen Henry 1817-1894..................... DLB-166

Layton, Irving 1912- DLB-88

LaZamon flourished circa 1200 ...... DLB-146

Lazarević, Laza K. 1851-1890......... DLB-147

Lazarus, George 1904-1997 .... DLB-201

Lazhechnikov, Ivan Ivanovich 1792-1869...................... DLB-198

Lea, Henry Charles 1825-1909......... DLB-47

Lea, Sydney 1942- DLB-120

Lea, Tom 1907- DLB-6

Leacock, John 1729-1802 .... DLB-31

Leacock, Stephen 1869-1944 .... DLB-92

Lead, Jane Ward 1623-1704 .... DLB-131

Leadenhall Press.................. DLB-106

Leakey, Caroline Woolmer 1827-1881... DLB-230

Leapor, Mary 1722-1746.............. DLB-109

Lear, Edward 1812-1888 ...... DLB-32, 163, 166

Leary, Timothy 1920-1996............. DLB-16

Leary, W. A., and Company DLB-49

Léautaud, Paul 1872-1956 .... DLB-65

Leavis, F. R. 1895-1978................ DLB-242

Leavitt, David 1961- DLB-130

Leavitt and Allen DLB-49

Le Blond, Mrs. Aubrey 1861-1934.......DLB-174

le Carré, John 1931- DLB-87; CDBLB-8

Lécavelé, Roland (see Dorgeles, Roland)

Lechlitner, Ruth 1901- DLB-48

Leclerc, Félix 1914- DLB-60

Le Clézio, J. M. G. 1940- DLB-83

Lectures on Rhetoric and Belles Lettres (1783), by Hugh Blair [excerpts] DLB-31

Leder, Rudolf (see Hermlin, Stephan)

Lederer, Charles 1910-1976 .... DLB-26

Ledwidge, Francis 1887-1917 .... DLB-20

Lee, Dennis 1939- DLB-53

Lee, Don L. (see Madhubuti, Haki R.)

Lee, George W. 1894-1976............. DLB-51

Lee, Harper 1926- DLB-6; CDALB-1

Lee, Harriet (1757-1851) and
Lee, Sophia (1750-1824)............ DLB-39

Lee, Laurie 1914-1997 .... DLB-27

Lee, Li-Young 1957- DLB-165

Lee, Manfred B. (see Dannay, Frederic, and Manfred B. Lee)

Lee, Nathaniel circa 1645-1692 .... DLB-80

Lee, Sir Sidney 1859-1926 .... DLB-149, 184

Lee, Sir Sidney, "Principles of Biography," in *Elizabethan and Other Essays*.......... DLB-149

Lee, Vernon 1856-1935 ....DLB-57, 153, 156, 174, 178

Lee and Shepard.................... DLB-49

Le Fanu, Joseph Sheridan 1814-1873............DLB-21, 70, 159, 178

Leffland, Ella 1931- Y-84

le Fort, Gertrud von 1876-1971........ DLB-66

Le Gallienne, Richard 1866-1947........ DLB-4

Legaré, Hugh Swinton 1797-1843...................DLB-3, 59, 73, 248

Legaré, James Mathewes 1823-1859... DLB-3, 248

The Legends of the Saints and a Medieval Christian Worldview............. DLB-148

Léger, Antoine-J. 1880-1950............ DLB-88

Leggett, William 1801-1839 .... DLB-250

Le Guin, Ursula K. 1929- DLB-8, 52, 256; CDALB-6

Lehman, Ernest 1920- DLB-44

Lehmann, John 1907- DLB-27, 100

Lehmann, John, Limited............ DLB-112

Lehmann, Rosamond 1901-1990 .... DLB-15

Lehmann, Wilhelm 1882-1968.......... DLB-56

Leiber, Fritz 1910-1992................ DLB-8

Leibniz, Gottfried Wilhelm 1646-1716 ... DLB-168

Leicester University Press DLB-112

Leigh, W. R. 1866-1955.............. DLB-188

Leinster, Murray 1896-1975........... DLB-8

Leiser, Bill 1898-1965............... DLB-241

Leisewitz, Johann Anton 1752-1806 ...... DLB-94

Leitch, Maurice 1933- DLB-14

Leithauser, Brad 1943- DLB-120

Leland, Charles G. 1824-1903 .... DLB-11

Leland, John 1503?-1552 .... DLB-136

Lemay, Pamphile 1837-1918............ DLB-99

Lemelin, Roger 1919-1992 .... DLB-88

Lemercier, Louis-Jean-Népomucène 1771-1840..................... DLB-192

Le Moine, James MacPherson 1825-1912 .... DLB-99

Lemon, Mark 1809-1870 .... DLB-163

Le Moyne, Jean 1913-1996............. DLB-88

Lemperly, Paul 1858-1939.............DLB-187

L'Engle, Madeleine 1918- DLB-52

Lennart, Isobel 1915-1971 .... DLB-44

Lennox, Charlotte 1729 or 1730-1804 .... DLB-39

Lenox, James 1800-1880................ DLB-140

Lenski, Lois 1893-1974................ DLB-22

Lentricchia, Frank 1940- DLB-246

Lenz, Hermann 1913-1998............. DLB-69

Lenz, J. M. R. 1751-1792............. DLB-94

Lenz, Siegfried 1926- DLB-75

Leonard, Elmore 1925- DLB-173, 226

Leonard, Hugh 1926- DLB-13

Leonard, William Ellery 1876-1944 ...... DLB-54

Leonowens, Anna 1834-1914........ DLB-99, 166

LePan, Douglas 1914- DLB-88

Lepik, Kalju 1920-1999 .... DLB-232

Leprohon, Rosanna Eleanor 1829-1879 ... DLB-99

Le Queux, William 1864-1927.......... DLB-70

Lermontov, Mikhail Iur'evich 1814-1841 .... DLB-205

Lerner, Max 1902-1992 .... DLB-29

Lernet-Holenia, Alexander 1897-1976..... DLB-85

Le Rossignol, James 1866-1969 .... DLB-92

Lescarbot, Marc circa 1570-1642 .... DLB-99

LeSeur, William Dawson 1840-1917 ..... DLB-92

LeSieg, Theo. (see Geisel, Theodor Seuss)

Leskov, Nikolai Semenovich 1831-1895.. DLB-238

Leslie, Doris before 1902-1982......... DLB-191

Leslie, Eliza 1787-1858 .... DLB-202

Leslie, Frank 1821-1880 ....DLB-43, 79

Leslie, Frank, Publishing House DLB-49

Leśmian, Bolesław 1878-1937.......... DLB-215

Lesperance, John 1835?-1891........... DLB-99

Lessing, Bruno 1870-1940 .... DLB-28

Lessing, Doris 1919- DLB-15, 139; Y-85; CDBLB-8

Lessing, Gotthold Ephraim 1729-1781...............DLB-97; CDWLB-2

Lettau, Reinhard 1929- DLB-75

Letter from Japan Y-94, Y-98

Letter from London Y-96

Letter to [Samuel] Richardson on *Clarissa* (1748), by Henry Fielding DLB-39

A Letter to the Editor of *The Irish Times* Y-97

Lever, Charles 1806-1872............. DLB-21

Lever, Ralph ca. 1527-1585 .... DLB-236

Leverson, Ada 1862-1933............. DLB-153

Levertov, Denise 1923-1997 .... DLB-5, 165; CDALB-7

Levi, Peter 1931- DLB-40

Levi, Primo 1919-1987 ....DLB-177

Lévi-Strauss, Claude 1908- DLB-242	Lily, William circa 1468-1522 . . . . DLB-132	Literary Research Archives III: The Lilly Library Y-84
Levien, Sonya 1888-1960. . . . . .DLB-44	Limited Editions Club DLB-46	Literary Research Archives IV: The John Carter Brown Library. Y-85
Levin, Meyer 1905-1981 . . . . DLB-9, 28; Y-81	Limón, Graciela 1938- DLB-209	
Levine, Norman 1923- DLB-88	Lincoln and Edmands DLB-49	Literary Research Archives V: Kent State Special Collections Y-86
Levine, Philip 1928- DLB-5	Lindesay, Ethel Forence (see Richardson, Henry Handel)	Literary Research Archives VI: The Modern Literary Manuscripts Collection in the Special Collections of the Washington University Libraries Y-87
Levis, Larry 1946- DLB-120	Lindgren, Astrid 1907-2002 . . . . .DLB-257	
Levy, Amy 1861-1889. . . . . .DLB-156, 240	Lindgren, Torgny 1938- DLB-257	
Levy, Benn Wolfe 1900-1973 . . . . . . DLB-13; Y-81	Lindsay, Alexander William, Twenty-fifth Earl of Crawford 1812-1880. . . . . .DLB-184	
Lewald, Fanny 1811-1889 . . . . DLB-129		Literary Research Archives VII: The University of Virginia Libraries Y-91
Lewes, George Henry 1817-1878 . . . . .DLB-55, 144	Lindsay, Sir David circa 1485-1555. . . . . .DLB-132	Literary Research Archives VIII: The Henry E. Huntington Library Y-92
"Criticism In Relation To Novels" (1863) DLB-21	Lindsay, David 1878-1945. . . . . .DLB-255	
	Lindsay, Jack 1900- Y-84	Literary Research Archives IX: Special Collections at Boston University. . Y-99
The Principles of Success in Literature (1865) [excerpt] DLB-57	Lindsay, Lady (Caroline Blanche Elizabeth Fitzroy Lindsay) 1844-1912. . . . . .DLB-199	The Literary Scene and Situation and . . . Who (Besides Oprah) Really Runs American Literature? Y-99
Lewis, Agnes Smith 1843-1926 . . . . .DLB-174	Lindsay, Norman 1879-1969 . . . . DLB-260	
Lewis, Alfred H. 1857-1914 . . . . .DLB-25, 186	Lindsay, Vachel 1879-1931 . . . .DLB-54; CDALB-3	
Lewis, Alun 1915-1944 . . . . .DLB-20, 162	Linebarger, Paul Myron Anthony (see Smith, Cordwainer)	Literary Societies Y-98, Y-99, Y-00, Y-01
Lewis, C. Day (see Day Lewis, C.)		"Literary Style" (1857), by William Forsyth [excerpt] DLB-57
Lewis, C. S. 1898-1963 . . . . DLB-15, 100, 160, 255; CDBLB-7	Link, Arthur S. 1920-1998 . . . . DLB 17	
	Linn, Ed 1922-2000 . . . . DLB-241	Literatura Chicanesca: The View From Without DLB-82
Lewis, Charles B. 1842-1924 . . . . .DLB-11	Linn, John Blair 1777-1804. . . . . .DLB-37	
Lewis, Henry Clay 1825-1850 . . . . .DLB-3, 248	Lins, Osman 1924-1978. . . . . .DLB-145	*Literature at Nurse, or Circulating Morals* (1885), by George Moore DLB-18
Lewis, Janet 1899-1999 . . . . Y-87	Linton, Eliza Lynn 1822-1898 . . . . .DLB-18	
Lewis, Matthew Gregory 1775-1818 . . . . DLB-39, 158, 178	Linton, William James 1812-1897 . . . . .DLB-32	The Literature of Boxing in England through Arthur Conan Doyle Y-01
	Lintot, Barnaby Bernard [publishing house] DLB-170	The Literature of the Modern Breakthrough DLB-259
Lewis, Meriwether 1774-1809 and Clark, William 1770-1838 . . . . . .DLB-183, 186		
Lewis, Norman 1908- DLB-204	Lion Books DLB-46	Littell, Eliakim 1797-1870 . . . . .DLB-79
Lewis, R. W. B. 1917- DLB-111	Lionni, Leo 1910-1999. . . . . .DLB-61	Littell, Robert S. 1831-1896. . . . . DLB-79
Lewis, Richard circa 1700-1734 . . . . DLB-24	Lippard, George 1822-1854 . . . . .DLB-202	Little, Brown and Company DLB-49
Lewis, Sinclair 1885-1951 . . . . . . DLB-9, 102; DS-1; CDALB-4	Lippincott, J. B., Company DLB-49	Little Magazines and Newspapers DS-15
	Lippincott, Sara Jane Clarke 1823-1904 . . . .DLB-43	*The Little Review* 1914-1929 . . . . DS-15
Sinclair Lewis Centennial Conference Y-85	Lippmann, Walter 1889-1974 . . . . .DLB-29	Littlewood, Joan 1914- DLB-13
Lewis, Wilmarth Sheldon 1895-1979 . . . . .DLB-140	Lipton, Lawrence 1898-1975 . . . . DLB-16	Lively, Penelope 1933- DLB-14, 161, 207
Lewis, Wyndham 1882-1957 . . . . .DLB-15	Liscow, Christian Ludwig 1701-1760. . . . . . .DLB-97	Liverpool University Press DLB-112
Lewisohn, Ludwig 1882-1955 . . .DLB-4, 9, 28, 102	Lish, Gordon 1934- DLB-130	*The Lives of the Poets*. DLB-142
Leyendecker, J. C. 1874-1951 . . . . .DLB-188	Lisle, Charles-Marie-René Leconte de 1818-1894 . . . . .DLB-217	Livesay, Dorothy 1909- DLB-68
Lezama Lima, José 1910-1976 . . . . .DLB-113		Livesay, Florence Randal 1874-1953 . . . . . . DLB-92
L'Heureux, John 1934- DLB-244	Lispector, Clarice 1925-1977 . . . . .DLB-113; CDWLB-3	"Living in Ruin," by Gerald Stern DLB-105
Libbey, Laura Jean 1862-1924 . . . . .DLB-221		Livings, Henry 1929-1998. . . . . DLB-13
The Library of America. . . . . DLB 16	LitCheck Website Y-01	Livingston, Anne Howe 1763-1841 . . . DLB-37, 200
Library History Group Y-01	A Literary Archaeologist Digs On: A Brief Interview with Michael Reynolds by Michael Rogers Y-99	Livingston, Myra Cohn 1926-1996 . . . . DLB-61
The Licensing Act of 1737 . . . . .DLB-84		Livingston, William 1723-1790 . . . . .DLB-31
Lichfield, Leonard I [publishing house] . . .DLB-170		Livingstone, David 1813-1873 . . . . .DLB-166
Lichtenberg, Georg Christoph 1742-1799 . .DLB-94	*The Literary Chronicle and Weekly Review* 1819-1828. . . . . .DLB-110	Livingstone, Douglas 1932-1996 . . . . .DLB-225
The Liddle Collection Y-97		Livy 59 B.C.-A.D. 17 . . . . . . .DLB-211; CDWLB-1
Lidman, Sara 1923- DLB-257	Literary Documents: William Faulkner and the People-to-People Program Y-86	Liyong, Taban lo (see Taban lo Liyong)
Lieb, Fred 1888-1980. . . . . .DLB-171		Lizárraga, Sylvia S. 1925- DLB-82
Liebling, A. J. 1904-1963 . . . . DLB-4, 171	Literary Documents II: *Library Journal* Statements and Questionnaires from First Novelists Y-87	Llewellyn, Richard 1906-1983 . . . . .DLB-15
Lieutenant Murray (see Ballou, Maturin Murray)		Lloyd, Edward [publishing house] DLB-106
Lighthall, William Douw 1857-1954 . . . . . .DLB-92		Lobel, Arnold 1933- DLB-61
Lilar, Françoise (see Mallet-Joris, Françoise)	Literary Effects of World War II [British novel] DLB-15	Lochridge, Betsy Hopkins (see Fancher, Betsy)
Lili'uokalani, Queen 1838-1917 . . . . .DLB-221	Literary Prizes Y-00	Locke, David Ross 1833-1888 . . . . DLB-11, 23
Lillo, George 1691-1739 . . . . DLB-84	Literary Prizes [British] DLB-15	Locke, John 1632-1704 . . . . DLB-31, 101, 213, 252
Lilly, J. K., Jr. 1893-1966 . . . . DLB-140	Literary Research Archives: The Humanities Research Center, University of Texas . . . Y-82	Locke, Richard Adams 1800-1871 . . . . .DLB-43
Lilly, Wait and Company DLB-49	Literary Research Archives II: Berg Collection of English and American Literature of the New York Public Library Y-83	Locker-Lampson, Frederick 1821-1895 . . . . .DLB-35, 184

Lockhart, John Gibson 1794-1854 .... DLB-110, 116 144
Lockridge, Ross, Jr. 1914-1948 ..... DLB-143; Y-80
Locrine and Selimus DLB-62
Lodge, David 1935- DLB-14, 194
Lodge, George Cabot 1873-1909 .... DLB-54
Lodge, Henry Cabot 1850-1924 .... DLB-47
Lodge, Thomas 1558-1625 .... DLB-172
From *Defence of Poetry* (1579) DLB-172
Loeb, Harold 1891-1974 .... DLB-4
Loeb, William 1905-1981 .... DLB-127
Lofting, Hugh 1886-1947 .... DLB-160
Logan, Deborah Norris 1761-1839 ...... DLB-200
Logan, James 1674-1751 .... DLB-24, 140
Logan, John 1923- DLB-5
Logan, Martha Daniell 1704?-1779 ...... DLB-200
Logan, William 1950- DLB-120
Logau, Friedrich von 1605-1655 .... DLB-164
Logue, Christopher 1926- DLB-27
Lohenstein, Daniel Casper von 1635-1683 .... DLB-168
Lo-Johansson, Ivar 1901-1990 .... DLB-259
Lomonosov, Mikhail Vasil'evich 1711-1765 .... DLB-150
London, Jack 1876-1916 ..... DLB-8, 12, 78, 212; CDALB-3
The London Magazine 1820-1829 .... DLB-110
Long, David 1948- DLB-244
Long, H., and Brother DLB-49
Long, Haniel 1888-1956 .... DLB-45
Long, Ray 1878-1935 .... DLB-137
Longfellow, Henry Wadsworth 1807-1882 .... DLB-1, 59, 235; CDALB-2
Longfellow, Samuel 1819-1892 .... DLB-1
Longford, Elizabeth 1906- DLB-155
Longinus circa first century DLB-176
Longley, Michael 1939- DLB-40
Longman, T. [publishing house] DLB-154
Longmans, Green and Company DLB-49
Longmore, George 1793?-1867 .... DLB-99
Longstreet, Augustus Baldwin 1790-1870 .... DLB-3, 11, 74, 248
Longworth, D. [publishing house] DLB-49
Lonsdale, Frederick 1881-1954 .... DLB-10
A Look at the Contemporary Black Theatre Movement DLB-38
Loos, Anita 1893-1981 ..... DLB-11, 26, 228; Y-81
Lopate, Phillip 1943- Y-80
Lopez, Barry 1945- DLB-256
López, Diana (see Isabella, Ríos)
López, Josefina 1969- DLB-209
Loranger, Jean-Aubert 1896-1942 .... DLB-92
Lorca, Federico García 1898-1936 ...... DLB-108
Lord, John Keast 1818-1872 .... DLB-99
The Lord Chamberlain's Office and Stage Censorship in England DLB-10

Lorde, Audre 1934-1992 .... DLB-41
Lorimer, George Horace 1867-1939 ...... DLB-91
Loring, A. K. [publishing house] DLB-49
Loring and Mussey DLB-46
Lorris, Guillaume de (see *Roman de la Rose*)
Lossing, Benson J. 1813-1891 .... DLB-30
Lothar, Ernst 1890-1974 .... DLB-81
Lothrop, D., and Company DLB-49
Lothrop, Harriet M. 1844-1924 .... DLB-42
Loti, Pierre 1850-1923 .... DLB-123
Lotichius Secundus, Petrus 1528-1560 ... DLB-179
Lott, Emeline ?-? DLB-166
Louisiana State University Press Y-97
The Lounger, no. 20 (1785), by Henry Mackenzie DLB-39
Lounsbury, Thomas R. 1838-1915 ...... DLB-71
Louÿs, Pierre 1870-1925 .... DLB-123
Lovelace, Earl 1935- DLB-125; CDWLB-3
Lovelace, Richard 1618-1657 .... DLB-131
Lovell, Coryell and Company DLB-49
Lovell, John W., Company DLB-49
Lover, Samuel 1797-1868 .... DLB-159, 190
Lovesey, Peter 1936- DLB-87
Lovinescu, Eugen 1881-1943 .... DLB-220; CDWLB-4
Lovingood, Sut (see Harris, George Washington)
Low, Samuel 1765-? DLB-37
Lowell, Amy 1874-1925 .... DLB-54, 140
Lowell, James Russell 1819-1891 ...... DLB-1, 11, 64, 79, 189, 235; CDALB-2
Lowell, Robert 1917-1977 .. DLB-5, 169; CDALB-7
Lowenfels, Walter 1897-1976 .... DLB-4
Lowndes, Marie Belloc 1868-1947 .... DLB-70
Lowndes, William Thomas 1798-1843 ... DLB-184
Lownes, Humphrey [publishing house] ... DLB-170
Lowry, Lois 1937- DLB-52
Lowry, Malcolm 1909-1957 ... DLB-15; CDBLB-7
Lowther, Pat 1935-1975 .... DLB-53
Loy, Mina 1882-1966 .... DLB-4, 54
Lozeau, Albert 1878-1924 .... DLB-92
Lubbock, Percy 1879-1965 .... DLB-149
Lucan A.D. 39-A.D. 65 .... DLB-211
Lucas, E. V. 1868-1938 .... DLB-98, 149, 153
Lucas, Fielding, Jr. [publishing house] DLB-49
Luce, Clare Booth 1903-1987 .... DLB-228
Luce, Henry R. 1898-1967 .... DLB-91
Luce, John W., and Company DLB-46
Lucian circa 120-180 .... DLB-176
Lucie-Smith, Edward 1933- DLB-40
Lucilius circa 180 B.C.-102/101 B.C. DLB-211
Lucini, Gian Pietro 1867-1914 .... DLB-114
Lucretius circa 94 B.C.-circa 49 B.C. DLB-211; CDWLB-1
Luder, Peter circa 1415-1472 .... DLB-179
Ludlum, Robert 1927- Y-82

Ludus de Antichristo circa 1160 .... DLB-148
Ludvigson, Susan 1942- DLB-120
Ludwig, Jack 1922- DLB-60
Ludwig, Otto 1813-1865 .... DLB-129
Ludwigslied 881 or 882 .... DLB-148
Luera, Yolanda 1953- DLB-122
Luft, Lya 1938- DLB-145
Lugansky, Kazak Vladimir (see Dal', Vladimir Ivanovich)
Lugn, Kristina 1948- DLB-257
Lukács, Georg (see Lukács, György)
Lukács, György 1885-1971 .... DLB-215, 242; CDWLB-4
Luke, Peter 1919- DLB-13
Lummis, Charles F. 1859-1928 .... DLB-186
Lundkvist, Artur 1906-1991 .... DLB-259
Lupton, F. M., Company DLB-49
Lupus of Ferrières circa 805-circa 862 .... DLB-148
Lurie, Alison 1926- DLB-2
Lustig, Arnošt 1926- DLB-232
Luther, Martin 1483-1546 ... DLB-179; CDWLB-2
Luzi, Mario 1914- DLB-128
L'vov, Nikolai Aleksandrovich 1751-1803 .. DLB-150
Lyall, Gavin 1932- DLB-87
Lydgate, John circa 1370-1450 .... DLB-146
Lyly, John circa 1554-1606 .... DLB-62, 167
Lynch, Patricia 1898-1972 .... DLB-160
Lynch, Richard flourished 1596-1601 ... DLB-172
Lynd, Robert 1879-1949 .... DLB-98
Lyon, Matthew 1749-1822 .... DLB-43
Lyotard, Jean-François 1924-1998 ..... DLB-242
Lysias circa 459 B.C.-circa 380 B.C. DLB-176
Lytle, Andrew 1902-1995 .... DLB-6; Y-95
Lytton, Edward (see Bulwer-Lytton, Edward)
Lytton, Edward Robert Bulwer 1831-1891 .... DLB-32

M

Maass, Joachim 1901-1972 .... DLB-69
Mabie, Hamilton Wright 1845-1916 ..... DLB-71
Mac A'Ghobhainn, Iain (see Smith, Iain Crichton)
MacArthur, Charles 1895-1956 ..... DLB-7, 25, 44
Macaulay, Catherine 1731-1791 .... DLB-104
Macaulay, David 1945- DLB-61
Macaulay, Rose 1881-1958 .... DLB-36
Macaulay, Thomas Babington 1800-1859 .... DLB-32, 55; CDBLB-4
Macaulay Company DLB-46
MacBeth, George 1932- DLB-40
Macbeth, Madge 1880-1965 .... DLB-92
MacCaig, Norman 1910-1996 .... DLB-27
MacDiarmid, Hugh 1892-1978 .... DLB-20; CDBLB-7
MacDonald, Cynthia 1928- DLB-105

MacDonald, George 1824-1905 ... DLB-18, 163, 178
MacDonald, John D. 1916-1986 ..... DLB-8; Y-86
MacDonald, Philip 1899?-1980 .... DLB-77
Macdonald, Ross (see Millar, Kenneth)
Macdonald, Sharman 1951- DLB-245
MacDonald, Wilson 1880-1967 .... DLB-92
Macdonald and Company (Publishers) ... DLB-112
MacEwen, Gwendolyn 1941-1987 .... DLB-53, 251
Macfadden, Bernarr 1868-1955 .... DLB-25, 91
MacGregor, John 1825-1892 .... DLB-166
MacGregor, Mary Esther (see Keith, Marian)
Machado, Antonio 1875-1939 .... DLB-108
Machado, Manuel 1874-1947 .... DLB-108
Machar, Agnes Maule 1837-1927 .... DLB-92
Machaut, Guillaume de
  circa 1300-1377 .... DLB-208
Machen, Arthur Llewelyn Jones
  1863-1947 .... DLB-36, 156, 178
MacInnes, Colin 1914-1976 .... DLB-14
MacInnes, Helen 1907-1985............. DLB-87
Mac Intyre, Tom 1931- DLB-245
Mačiulis, Jonas (see Maironis, Jonas)
Mack, Maynard 1909- DLB-111
Mackall, Leonard L. 1879-1937 .... DLB-140
MacKaye, Percy 1875-1956 .... DLB-54
Macken, Walter 1915-1967 .... DLB-13
Mackenzie, Alexander 1763-1820 .... DLB-99
Mackenzie, Alexander Slidell
  1803-1848 .... DLB-183
Mackenzie, Compton 1883-1972 .... DLB-34, 100
Mackenzie, Henry 1745-1831 .... DLB-39
Mackenzie, Kenneth (Seaforth)
  1913-1955 .... DLB-260
Mackenzie, William 1758-1828 .... DLB-187
Mackey, Nathaniel 1947- DLB-169
Mackey, Shena 1944- DLB-231
Mackey, William Wellington
  1937- DLB-38
Mackintosh, Elizabeth (see Tey, Josephine)
Mackintosh, Sir James 1765-1832 .... DLB-158
Maclaren, Ian (see Watson, John)
Macklin, Charles 1699-1797............ DLB-89
MacLean, Katherine Anne 1925- DLB-8
Maclean, Norman 1902-1990 .... DLB-206
MacLeish, Archibald 1892-1982
  .... DLB-4, 7, 45, 228; Y-82; CDALB-7
MacLennan, Hugh 1907-1990 .... DLB-68
MacLeod, Alistair 1936- DLB-60
Macleod, Fiona (see Sharp, William)
Macleod, Norman 1906-1985 .... DLB-4
Mac Low, Jackson 1922- DLB-193
Macmillan and Company DLB-106
The Macmillan Company DLB-49
Macmillan's English Men of Letters,
  First Series (1878-1892) DLB-144
MacNamara, Brinsley 1890-1963 .... DLB-10

MacNeice, Louis 1907-1963.......... DLB-10, 20
MacPhail, Andrew 1864-1938 .... DLB-92
Macpherson, James 1736-1796.......... DLB-109
Macpherson, Jay 1931- DLB-53
Macpherson, Jeanie 1884-1946 .... DLB-44
Macrae Smith Company DLB-46
MacRaye, Lucy Betty (see Webling, Lucy)
Macrone, John [publishing house] DLB-106
MacShane, Frank 1927-1999 .... DLB-111
Macy-Masius DLB-46
Madden, David 1933- DLB-6
Madden, Sir Frederic 1801-1873 .... DLB-184
Maddow, Ben 1909-1992.............. DLB-44
Maddux, Rachel 1912-1983........ DLB-234; Y-93
Madgett, Naomi Long 1923- DLB-76
Madhubuti, Haki R. 1942- DLB-5, 41; DS-8
Madison, James 1751-1836 .... DLB-37
Madsen, Svend Åge 1939- DLB-214
Maeterlinck, Maurice 1862-1949........ DLB-192
Mafūz, Najīb 1911- Y-88
Magee, David 1905-1977 .... DLB-187
Maginn, William 1794-1842 .... DLB-110, 159
Magoffin, Susan Shelby 1827-1855 ..... DLB-239
Mahan, Alfred Thayer 1840-1914......... DLB-47
Maheux-Forcier, Louise 1929- DLB-60
Mahin, John Lee 1902-1984 .... DLB-44
Mahon, Derek 1941- DLB-40
Maikov, Vasilii Ivanovich 1728-1778 ..... DLB-150
Mailer, Norman 1923-
  .... DLB-2, 16, 28, 185; Y-80, Y-83, Y-97;
                                DS-3; CDALB-6
Maillart, Ella 1903-1997............... DLB-195
Maillet, Adrienne 1885-1963 .... DLB-68
Maillet, Antonine 1929- DLB-60
Maillu, David G. 1939- DLB-157
Maimonides, Moses 1138-1204 .... DLB-115
Main Selections of the Book-of-the-Month
  Club, 1926-1945 .... DLB-9
Main Trends in Twentieth-Century Book
  Clubs............................. DLB-46
Mainwaring, Daniel 1902-1977 .... DLB-44
Mair, Charles 1838-1927 .... DLB-99
Maironis, Jonas
  1862-1932 .... DLB-220; CDWLB-4
Mais, Roger 1905-1955 ..... DLB-125; CDWLB-3
Major, Andre 1942- DLB-60
Major, Charles 1856-1913 .... DLB-202
Major, Clarence 1936 .... DLB-33
Major, Kevin 1949- DLB-60
Major Books DLB-46
Makemie, Francis circa 1658-1708....... DLB-24
The Making of Americans Contract Y-98
The Making of a People, by
  J. M. Ritchie DLB-66
Maksimović, Desanka
  1898-1993 .... DLB-147; CDWLB-4

Malamud, Bernard 1914-1986
  .... DLB-2, 28, 152; Y-80, Y-86; CDALB-1
Mălăncioiu, Ileana 1940- DLB-232
Malerba, Luigi 1927- DLB-196
Malet, Lucas 1852-1931................ DLB-153
Mallarmé, Stéphane 1842-1898 .... DLB-217
Malleson, Lucy Beatrice (see Gilbert, Anthony)
Mallet-Joris, Françoise 1930- DLB-83
Mallock, W. H. 1849-1923 .... DLB-18, 57
"Every Man His Own Poet; or,
  The Inspired Singer's Recipe
  Book" (1877) DLB-35
Malone, Dumas 1892-1986 .... DLB-17
Malone, Edmond 1741-1812 .... DLB-142
Malory, Sir Thomas
  circa 1400-1410 - 1471.... DLB-146; CDBLB-1
Malpede, Karen 1945- DLB-249
Malraux, André 1901-1976 .... DLB-72
Malthus, Thomas Robert
  1766-1834 .... DLB-107, 158
Maltz, Albert 1908-1985 .... DLB-102
Malzberg, Barry N. 1939- DLB-8
Mamet, David 1947- DLB-7
Mamin, Dmitrii Narkisovich 1852-1912 .. DLB-238
Manaka, Matsemela 1956- DLB-157
Manchester University Press........... DLB-112
Mandel, Eli 1922-1992................ DLB-53
Mandeville, Bernard 1670-1733 .... DLB-101
Mandeville, Sir John
  mid fourteenth century DLB-146
Mandiargues, André Pieyre de 1909- ... DLB-83
Manea, Norman 1936- DLB-232
Manfred, Frederick 1912-1994 ... DLB-6, 212, 227
Manfredi, Gianfranco 1948- DLB-196
Mangan, Sherry 1904-1961 .... DLB-4
Manganelli, Giorgio 1922-1990......... DLB-196
Manilius fl. first century A.D. DLB-211
Mankiewicz, Herman 1897-1953 .... DLB-26
Mankiewicz, Joseph L. 1909-1993 ...... DLB-44
Mankowitz, Wolf 1924-1998........... DLB-15
Manley, Delarivière 1672?-1724 ...... DLB-39, 80
Preface to The Secret History, of Queen Zarah,
  and the Zarazians (1705) DLB-39
Mann, Abby 1927- DLB-44
Mann, Charles 1929-1998 .... Y-98
Mann, Heinrich 1871-1950 .... DLB-66, 118
Mann, Horace 1796-1859 .... DLB-1, 235
Mann, Klaus 1906-1949 .... DLB-56
Mann, Mary Peabody 1806-1887 .... DLB-239
Mann, Thomas 1875-1955 .... DLB-66; CDWLB-2
Mann, William D'Alton 1839-1920..... DLB-137
Mannin, Ethel 1900-1984 .... DLB-191, 195
Manning, Emily (see Australie)
Manning, Frederic 1882-1935 .... DLB-260
Manning, Laurence 1899-1972 .... DLB-251
Manning, Marie 1873?-1945 .... DLB-29

Cumulative Index

Manning and Loring...................DLB-49
Mannyng, Robert
  flourished 1303-1338............DLB-146
Mano, D. Keith 1942-................DLB-6
Manor Books.........................DLB-46
Mansfield, Katherine 1888-1923......DLB-162
Manuel, Niklaus circa 1484-1530.....DLB-179
Manzini, Gianna 1896-1974...........DLB-177
Mapanje, Jack 1944-.................DLB-157
Maraini, Dacia 1936-................DLB-196
Marcel Proust at 129 and the Proust Society
  of America..........................Y-00
Marcel Proust's *Remembrance of Things Past*:
  The Rediscovered Galley Proofs......Y-00
March, William 1893-1954..........DLB-9, 86
Marchand, Leslie A. 1900-1999.......DLB-103
Marchant, Bessie 1862-1941..........DLB-160
Marchant, Tony 1959-................DLB-245
Marchenko, Anastasiia Iakovlevna
  1830-1880.........................DLB-238
Marchessault, Jovette 1938-..........DLB-60
Marcinkevičius, Justinas 1930-......DLB-232
Marcus, Frank 1928-.................DLB-13
Marcuse, Herbert 1898-1979..........DLB-242
Marden, Orison Swett 1850-1924......DLB-137
Marechera, Dambudzo 1952-1987.......DLB-157
Marek, Richard, Books...............DLB-46
Mares, E. A. 1938-..................DLB-122
Margulies, Donald 1954-..............DLB-228
Mariani, Paul 1940-.................DLB-111
Marie de France flourished 1160-1178...DLB-208
Marie-Victorin, Frère 1885-1944.....DLB-92
Marin, Biagio 1891-1985.............DLB-128
Marincovič, Ranko
  1913-..................DLB-147; CDWLB-4
Marinetti, Filippo Tommaso
  1876-1944.........................DLB-114
Marion, Frances 1886-1973............DLB-44
Marius, Richard C. 1933-1999..........Y-85
Markevich, Boleslav Mikhailovich
  1822-1884.........................DLB-238
Markfield, Wallace 1926-...........DLB-2, 28
Markham, Edwin 1852-1940..........DLB-54, 186
Markle, Fletcher 1921-1991........DLB-68; Y-91
Marlatt, Daphne 1942-................DLB-60
Marlitt, E. 1825-1887...............DLB-129
Marlowe, Christopher
  1564-1593..............DLB-62; CDBLB-1
Marlyn, John 1912-..................DLB-88
Marmion, Shakerley 1603-1639........DLB-58
Der Marner before 1230-circa 1287...DLB-138
Marnham, Patrick 1943-..............DLB-204
The *Marprelate Tracts* 1588-1589...DLB-132
Marquand, John P. 1893-1960.......DLB-9, 102
Marqués, René 1919-1979.............DLB-113
Marquis, Don 1878-1937...........DLB-11, 25
Marriott, Anne 1913-................DLB-68

Marryat, Frederick 1792-1848......DLB-21, 163
Marsh, Capen, Lyon and Webb.........DLB-49
Marsh, George Perkins
  1801-1882...................DLB-1, 64, 243
Marsh, James 1794-1842............DLB-1, 59
Marsh, Narcissus 1638-1713.........DLB-213
Marsh, Ngaio 1899-1982..............DLB-77
Marshall, Alan 1902-1984...........DLB-260
Marshall, Edison 1894-1967.........DLB-102
Marshall, Edward 1932-..............DLB-16
Marshall, Emma 1828-1899...........DLB-163
Marshall, James 1942-1992...........DLB-61
Marshall, Joyce 1913-...............DLB-88
Marshall, Paule 1929-........DLB-33, 157, 227
Marshall, Tom 1938-1993.............DLB-60
Marsilius of Padua
  circa 1275-circa 1342............DLB-115
Mars-Jones, Adam 1954-.............DLB-207
Marson, Una 1905-1965..............DLB-157
Marston, John 1576-1634.........DLB-58, 172
Marston, Philip Bourke 1850-1887....DLB-35
Martens, Kurt 1870-1945.............DLB-66
Martial circa A.D. 40-circa A.D. 103
  ....DLB-211; CDWLB-1
Martien, William S. [publishing house]...DLB-49
Martin, Abe (see Hubbard, Kin)
Martin, Catherine ca. 1847-1937....DLB-230
Martin, Charles 1942-..............DLB-120
Martin, Claire 1914-................DLB-60
Martin, David 1915-1997............DLB-260
Martin, Jay 1935-..................DLB-111
Martin, Johann (see Laurentius von Schnüffis)
Martin, Thomas 1696-1771...........DLB-213
Martin, Violet Florence (see Ross, Martin)
Martin du Gard, Roger 1881-1958.....DLB-65
Martineau, Harriet
  1802-1876......DLB-21, 55, 159, 163, 166, 190
Martínez, Demetria 1960-...........DLB-209
Martínez, Eliud 1935-..............DLB-122
Martínez, Max 1943-.................DLB-82
Martínez, Rubén 1962-..............DLB-209
Martinson, Harry 1904-1978.........DLB-259
Martinson, Moa 1890-1964...........DLB-259
Martone, Michael 1955-.............DLB-218
Martyn, Edward 1859-1923............DLB-10
Marvell, Andrew
  1621-1678..............DLB-131; CDBLB-2
Marvin X 1944-......................DLB-38
Marx, Karl 1818-1883...............DLB-129
Marzials, Theo 1850-1920............DLB-35
Masefield, John
  1878-1967...DLB-10, 19, 153, 160; CDBLB-5
Masham, Damaris Cudworth Lady
  1659-1708........................DLB-252
Mason, A. E. W. 1865-1948...........DLB-70
Mason, Bobbie Ann
  1940-..............DLB-173; Y-87; CDALB-7

Mason, William 1725-1797...........DLB-142
Mason Brothers.....................DLB-49
Massey, Gerald 1828-1907...........DLB-32
Massey, Linton R. 1900-1974........DLB-187
Massinger, Philip 1583-1640........DLB-58
Masson, David 1822-1907...........DLB-144
Masters, Edgar Lee
  1868-1950..............DLB-54; CDALB-3
Masters, Hilary 1928-..............DLB-244
Mastronardi, Lucio 1930-1979.......DLB-177
Matevski, Mateja 1929-....DLB-181; CDWLB-4
Mather, Cotton
  1663-1728........DLB-24, 30, 140; CDALB-2
Mather, Increase 1639-1723.........DLB-24
Mather, Richard 1596-1669..........DLB-24
Matheson, Annie 1853-1924..........DLB-240
Matheson, Richard 1926-..........DLB-8, 44
Matheus, John F. 1887-..............DLB-51
Mathews, Cornelius 1817?-1889..DLB-3, 64, 250
Mathews, Elkin [publishing house]..DLB-112
Mathews, John Joseph 1894-1979....DLB-175
Mathias, Roland 1915-...............DLB-27
Mathis, June 1892-1927..............DLB-44
Mathis, Sharon Bell 1937-...........DLB-33
Matković, Marijan 1915-1985........DLB-181
Matoš, Antun Gustav 1873-1914......DLB-147
Matsumoto Seichō 1909-1992.........DLB-182
The Matter of England 1240-1400....DLB-146
The Matter of Rome early twelfth to late
  fifteenth century.................DLB-146
Matthew of Vendôme
  circa 1130-circa 1200............DLB-208
Matthews, Brander
  1852-1929.............DLB-71, 78; DS-13
Matthews, Jack 1925-................DLB-6
Matthews, Victoria Earle 1861-1907...DLB-221
Matthews, William 1942-1997.........DLB-5
Matthiessen, F. O. 1902-1950........DLB-63
Matthiessen, Peter 1927-.........DLB-6, 173
Maturin, Charles Robert 1780-1824...DLB-178
Maugham, W. Somerset 1874-1965
  .....DLB-10, 36, 77, 100, 162, 195; CDBLB-6
Maupassant, Guy de 1850-1893.......DLB-123
Mauriac, Claude 1914-1996...........DLB-83
Mauriac, François 1885-1970.........DLB-65
Maurice, Frederick Denison
  1805-1872.........................DLB-55
Maurois, André 1885-1967............DLB-65
Maury, James 1718-1769..............DLB-31
Mavor, Elizabeth 1927-..............DLB-14
Mavor, Osborne Henry (see Bridie, James)
Maxwell, Gavin 1914-1969...........DLB-204
Maxwell, H. [publishing house]......DLB-49
Maxwell, John [publishing house]...DLB-106
Maxwell, William 1908-.........DLB-218; Y-80
May, Elaine 1932-...................DLB-44

May, Karl 1842-1912 . . . . DLB-129
May, Thomas 1595 or 1596-1650 . . . . DLB-58
Mayer, Bernadette 1945- DLB-165
Mayer, Mercer 1943- DLB-61
Mayer, O. B. 1818-1891 . . . . DLB-3, 248
Mayes, Herbert R. 1900-1987 . . . . DLB-137
Mayes, Wendell 1919-1992 . . . . DLB-26
Mayfield, Julian 1928-1984 . . . . DLB-33; Y-84
Mayhew, Henry 1812-1887 . . . . . . DLB-18, 55, 190
Mayhew, Jonathan 1720-1766 . . . . DLB-31
Mayne, Ethel Colburn 1865-1941 . . . . DLB-197
Mayne, Jasper 1604-1672 . . . . DLB-126
Mayne, Seymour 1944- DLB-60
Mayor, Flora Macdonald 1872-1932 . . . . . DLB-36
Mayrocker, Friederike 1924- DLB-85
Mazrui, Ali A. 1933- DLB-125
Mažuranić, Ivan 1814-1890 . . . . DLB-147
Mazursky, Paul 1930- DLB-44
McAlmon, Robert
  1896-1956 . . . . DLB-4, 45; DS-15
Robert McAlmon's "A Night at Bricktop's" . . Y-01
McArthur, Peter 1866-1924 . . . . DLB-92
McAuley, James 1917-1976 . . . . DLB-260
McBride, Robert M., and Company DLB-46
McCabe, Patrick 1955- DLB-194
McCaffrey, Anne 1926- DLB-8
McCarthy, Cormac 1933- DLB-6, 143, 256
McCarthy, Mary 1912-1989 . . . . DLB-2; Y-81
McCay, Winsor 1871-1934 . . . . DLB-22
McClane, Albert Jules 1922-1991 . . . . . . DLB-171
McClatchy, C. K. 1858-1936 . . . . DLB-25
McClellan, George Marion 1860-1934 . . . . DLB-50
McCloskey, Robert 1914- DLB-22
McClung, Nellie Letitia 1873-1951 . . . . . . DLB-92
McClure, Joanna 1930- DLB-16
McClure, Michael 1932- DLB-16
McClure, Phillips and Company DLB-46
McClure, S. S. 1857-1949 . . . . DLB-91
McClurg, A. C., and Company DLB-49
McCluskey, John A., Jr. 1944- DLB-33
McCollum, Michael A. 1946- Y-87
McConnell, William C. 1917- DLB-88
McCord, David 1897-1997 . . . . DLB-61
McCord, Louisa S. 1810-1879 . . . . DLB-248
McCorkle, Jill 1958- DLB-234; Y-87
McCorkle, Samuel Eusebius
  1746-1811 . . . . DLB-37
McCormick, Anne O'Hare 1880-1954 . . . . DLB-29
Kenneth Dale McCormick Tributes Y-97
McCormick, Robert R. 1880-1955 . . . . . . DLB-29
McCourt, Edward 1907-1972 . . . . DLB-88
McCoy, Horace 1897-1955 . . . . DLB-9
McCrae, Hugh 1876-1958 . . . . DLB-260
McCrae, John 1872-1918 . . . . DLB-92
McCullagh, Joseph B. 1842-1896 . . . . DLB-23

McCullers, Carson
  1917-1967 . . . . . DLB-2, 7, 173, 228; CDALB-1
McCulloch, Thomas 1776-1843 . . . . DLB-99
McDonald, Forrest 1927- DLB-17
McDonald, Walter 1934- DLB-105, DS-9
"Getting Started: Accepting the Regions
  You Own—or Which Own You," DLB-105
McDougall, Colin 1917-1984 . . . . DLB-68
McDowell, Katharine Sherwood Bonner
  1849-1883 . . . . DLB-202, 239
McDowell, Obolensky DLB-46
McEwan, Ian 1948- DLB-14, 194
McFadden, David 1940- DLB-60
McFall, Frances Elizabeth Clarke
  (see Grand, Sarah)
McFarlane, Leslie 1902-1977 . . . . DLB-88
McFarland, Ronald 1942- DLB-256
McFee, William 1881-1966 . . . . DLB-153
McGahern, John 1934- DLB-14, 231
McGee, Thomas D'Arcy 1825-1868 . . . . . . DLB-99
McGeehan, W. O. 1879-1933 . . . . DLB-25, 171
McGill, Ralph 1898-1969 . . . . DLB-29
McGinley, Phyllis 1905-1978 . . . . DLB-11, 48
McGinniss, Joe 1942- DLB-185
McGirt, James E. 1874-1930 . . . . DLB-50
McGlashan and Gill DLB-106
McGough, Roger 1937- DLB-40
McGrath, John 1935- DLB-233
McGrath, Patrick 1950- DLB-231
McGraw-Hill DLB-46
McGuane, Thomas 1939- DLB-2, 212; Y-80
McGuckian, Medbh 1950- DLB-40
McGuffey, William Holmes 1800-1873 . . . DLB-42
McGuinness, Frank 1953- DLB-245
McHenry, James 1785-1845 . . . . DLB-202
McIlvanney, William 1936- DLB-14, 207
McIlwraith, Jean Newton 1859-1938 . . . . . DLB-92
McIntosh, Maria Jane 1803-1878 . . . . DLB-239, 248
McIntyre, James 1827-1906 . . . . DLB-99
McIntyre, O. O. 1884-1938 . . . . DLB-25
McKay, Claude 1889-1948 . . . . DLB-4, 15, 51, 117
The David McKay Company DLB-49
McKean, William V. 1820-1903 . . . . DLB-23
McKenna, Stephen 1888-1967 . . . . DLB-197
The McKenzie Trust Y-96
McKerrow, R. B. 1872-1940 . . . . DLB-201
McKinley, Robin 1952- DLB-52
McKnight, Reginald 1956- DLB-234
McLachlan, Alexander 1818-1896 . . . . DLB-99
McLaren, Floris Clark 1904-1978 . . . . DLB-68
McLaverty, Michael 1907- DLB-15
McLean, John R. 1848-1916 . . . . DLB-23
McLean, William L. 1852-1931 . . . . DLB-25
McLennan, William 1856-1904 . . . . DLB-92
McLoughlin Brothers DLB-49

McLuhan, Marshall 1911-1980 . . . . DLB-88
McMaster, John Bach 1852-1932 . . . . DLB-47
McMurtry, Larry 1936-
  . . . . . DLB-2, 143, 256; Y-80, Y-87; CDALB-6
McNally, Terrence 1939- DLB-7, 249
McNeil, Florence 1937- DLB-60
McNeile, Herman Cyril 1888-1937 . . . . . . DLB-77
McNickle, D'Arcy 1904-1977 . . . . . . DLB-175, 212
McPhee, John 1931- DLB-185
McPherson, James Alan 1943- DLB-38, 244
McPherson, Sandra 1943- Y-86
McWhirter, George 1939- DLB-60
McWilliams, Carey 1905-1980 . . . . DLB-137
Mda, Zakes 1948- DLB-225
Mead, L. T. 1844-1914 . . . . DLB-141
Mead, Matthew 1924- DLB-40
Mead, Taylor ?- DLB-16
Meany, Tom 1903-1964 . . . . DLB-171
Mechthild von Magdeburg
  circa 1207-circa 1282 . . . . DLB-138
Medieval French Drama DLB-208
Medieval Travel Diaries DLB-203
Medill, Joseph 1823-1899 . . . . DLB-43
Medoff, Mark 1940- DLB-7
Meek, Alexander Beaufort
  1814-1865 . . . . DLB-3, 248
Meeke, Mary ?-1816? DLB-116
Meinke, Peter 1932- DLB-5
Mejia Vallejo, Manuel 1923- DLB-113
Melanchthon, Philipp 1497-1560 . . . . DLB-179
Melançon, Robert 1947- DLB-60
Mell, Max 1882-1971 . . . . DLB-81, 124
Mellow, James R. 1926-1997 . . . . DLB-111
Mel'nikov, Pavel Ivanovich 1818-1883 . . . DLB-238
Meltzer, David 1937- DLB-16
Meltzer, Milton 1915- DLB-61
Melville, Elizabeth, Lady Culross
  circa 1585-1640 . . . . DLB-172
Melville, Herman
  1819-1891 . . . . DLB-3, 74, 250; CDALB-2
Memoirs of Life and Literature (1920),
  by W. H. Mallock [excerpt] DLB-57
Mena, María Cristina 1893-1965 . . . . DLB-209, 221
Menander 342-341 B.C.-circa 292-291 B.C.
  . . . . DLB-176; CDWLB-1
Menantes (see Hunold, Christian Friedrich)
Mencke, Johann Burckhard
  1674-1732 . . . . DLB-168
Mencken, H. L. 1880-1956
  . . . . DLB-11, 29, 63, 137, 222; CDALB-4
H. L. Mencken's "Berlin, February, 1917" . . Y-00
Mencken and Nietzsche: An Unpublished
  Excerpt from H. L. Mencken's *My Life
  as Author and Editor* Y-93
Mendelssohn, Moses 1729-1786 . . . . DLB-97
Mendes, Catulle 1841-1909 . . . . DLB-217
Méndez M., Miguel 1930- DLB-82
Mens Rea (or Something) Y-97

The Mercantile Library of New York Y-96	Middle Hill Press DLB-106	Milton, John 1608-1674 . . . . DLB-131, 151; CDBLB-2
Mercer, Cecil William (see Yates, Dornford)	Middleton, Christopher 1926- DLB-40	Miłosz, Czesław 1911- DLB-215; CDWLB-4
Mercer, David 1928-1980 . . . . DLB-13	Middleton, Richard 1882-1911 . . . . DLB-156	Minakami Tsutomu 1919- DLB-182
Mercer, John 1704-1768 . . . . DLB-31	Middleton, Stanley 1919- DLB-14	Minamoto no Sanetomo 1192-1219 . . . . . DLB-203
Meredith, George 1828-1909 . . . . DLB-18, 35, 57, 159; CDBLB-4	Middleton, Thomas 1580-1627 . . . . DLB-58	The Minerva Press DLB-154
Meredith, Louisa Anne 1812-1895 . . DLB-166, 230	Miegel, Agnes 1879-1964 . . . . DLB-56	*Minnesang* circa 1150-1280 . . . . DLB-138
Meredith, Owen (see Lytton, Edward Robert Bulwer)	Mieželaitis, Eduardas 1919-1997 . . . . DLB-220	Minns, Susan 1839-1938 . . . . DLB-140
Meredith, William 1919- DLB-5	Mihailović, Dragoslav 1930- DLB-181	Minor Illustrators, 1880-1914 . . . . DLB-141
Mergerle, Johann Ulrich (see Abraham ä Sancta Clara)	Mihalić, Slavko 1928- DLB-181	Minor Poets of the Earlier Seventeenth Century DLB-121
Mérimée, Prosper 1803-1870 . . . . . . DLB-119, 192	Mikhailov, A. (see Sheller, Aleksandr Konstantinovich)	Minton, Balch and Company DLB-46
Merivale, John Herman 1779-1844 . . . . DLB-96	Mikhailov, Mikhail Larionovich 1829-1865 . . . . DLB-238	Mirbeau, Octave 1848-1917 . . . . DLB-123, 192
Meriwether, Louise 1923- DLB-33	Miles, Josephine 1911-1985 . . . . DLB-48	Mirk, John died after 1414? DLB-146
Merlin Press DLB-112	Miles, Susan (Ursula Wyllie Roberts) 1888-1975 . . . . DLB-240	Miron, Gaston 1928- DLB-60
Merriam, Eve 1916-1992 . . . . DLB-61	Miliković, Branko 1934-1961 . . . . DLB-181	*A Mirror for Magistrates* DLB-167
The Merriam Company DLB-49	Milius, John 1944- DLB-44	Mishima Yukio 1925-1970 . . . . DLB-182
Merril, Judith 1923-1997 . . . . DLB-251	Mill, James 1773-1836 . . . . DLB-107, 158	Mitchel, Jonathan 1624-1668 . . . . DLB-24
Merrill, James 1926-1995 . . . . . . DLB-5, 165; Y-85	Mill, John Stuart 1806-1873 . . . . DLB-55, 190; CDBLB-4	Mitchell, Adrian 1932- DLB-40
Merrill and Baker DLB-49	Millar, Andrew [publishing house] DLB-154	Mitchell, Donald Grant 1822-1908 . . . . DLB-1, 243; DS-13
The Mershon Company DLB-49	Millar, Kenneth 1915-1983 . . . . DLB-2, 226; Y-83; DS-6	Mitchell, Gladys 1901-1983 . . . . DLB-77
Merton, Thomas 1915-1968 . . . . . . DLB-48; Y-81	Millay, Edna St. Vincent 1892-1950 . . . . DLB-45, 249; CDALB-4	Mitchell, James Leslie 1901-1935 . . . . DLB-15
Merwin, W. S. 1927- DLB-5, 169	Millen, Sarah Gertrude 1888-1968 . . . . . . DLB-225	Mitchell, John (see Slater, Patrick)
Messner, Julian [publishing house] DLB-46	Miller, Arthur 1915- DLB-7; CDALB-1	Mitchell, John Ames 1845-1918 . . . . DLB-79
Mészöly, Miklós 1921- DLB-232	Miller, Caroline 1903-1992 . . . . DLB-9	Mitchell, Joseph 1908-1996 . . . . DLB-185; Y-96
Metcalf, J. [publishing house] DLB-49	Miller, Eugene Ethelbert 1950- DLB-41	Mitchell, Julian 1935- DLB-14
Metcalf, John 1938- DLB-60	Miller, Heather Ross 1939- DLB-120	Mitchell, Ken 1940- DLB-60
The Methodist Book Concern DLB-49	Miller, Henry 1891-1980 . . . . DLB-4, 9; Y-80; CDALB-5	Mitchell, Langdon 1862-1935 . . . . DLB-7
Methuen and Company DLB-112	Miller, Hugh 1802-1856 . . . . DLB-190	Mitchell, Loften 1919- DLB-38
Meun, Jean de (see *Roman de la Rose*)	Miller, J. Hillis 1928- DLB-67	Mitchell, Margaret 1900-1949 . . DLB-9; CDALB-7
Mew, Charlotte 1869-1928 . . . . DLB-19, 135	Miller, James [publishing house] DLB-49	Mitchell, S. Weir 1829-1914 . . . . DLB-202
Mewshaw, Michael 1943- Y-80	Miller, Jason 1939- DLB-7	Mitchell, W. J. T. 1942- DLB-246
Meyer, Conrad Ferdinand 1825-1898 . . . DLB-129	Miller, Joaquin 1839-1913 . . . . DLB-186	Mitchell, W. O. 1914- DLB-88
Meyer, E. Y. 1946- DLB-75	Miller, May 1899- DLB-41	Mitchison, Naomi Margaret (Haldane) 1897-1999 . . . . DLB-160, 191, 255
Meyer, Eugene 1875-1959 . . . . DLB-29	Miller, Paul 1906-1991 . . . . DLB-127	Mitford, Mary Russell 1787-1855 . . . . DLB-110, 116
Meyer, Michael 1921-2000 . . . . DLB-155	Miller, Perry 1905-1963 . . . . DLB-17, 63	Mitford, Nancy 1904-1973 . . . . DLB-191
Meyers, Jeffrey 1939- DLB-111	Miller, Sue 1943- DLB-143	Mittelholzer, Edgar 1909-1965 . . . . DLB-117; CDWLB-3
Meynell, Alice 1847-1922 . . . . DLB-19, 98	Miller, Vassar 1924-1998 . . . . DLB-105	Mitterer, Erika 1906- DLB-85
Meynell, Viola 1885-1956 . . . . DLB-153	Miller, Walter M., Jr. 1923- DLB-8	Mitterer, Felix 1948- DLB-124
Meyrink, Gustav 1868-1932 . . . . DLB-81	Miller, Webb 1892-1940 . . . . DLB-29	Mitternacht, Johann Sebastian 1613-1679 . . . . DLB-168
Mézières, Philipe de circa 1327-1405 . . . . DLB-208	Millett, Kate 1934- DLB-246	Miyamoto, Yuriko 1899-1951 . . . . DLB-180
Michael, Ib 1945- DLB-214	Millhauser, Steven 1943- DLB-2	Mizener, Arthur 1907-1988 . . . . DLB-103
Michaëlis, Karen 1872-1950 . . . . DLB-214	Millican, Arthenia J. Bates 1920- DLB-38	Mo, Timothy 1950- DLB-194
Michaels, Leonard 1933- DLB-130	Milligan, Alice 1866-1953 . . . . DLB-240	Moberg, Vilhelm 1898-1973 . . . . DLB-259
Michaux, Henri 1899-1984 . . . . DLB-258	Mills and Boon DLB-112	Modern Age Books DLB-46
Micheaux, Oscar 1884-1951 . . . . DLB-50	Milman, Henry Hart 1796-1868 . . . . DLB-96	"Modern English Prose" (1876), by George Saintsbury DLB-57
Michel of Northgate, Dan circa 1265-circa 1340 . . . . DLB-146	Milne, A. A. 1882-1956 . . . . DLB-10, 77, 100, 160	The Modern Language Association of America Celebrates Its Centennial Y-84
Micheline, Jack 1929-1998 . . . . DLB-16	Milner, Ron 1938- DLB-38	The Modern Library DLB-46
Michener, James A. 1907?-1997 . . . . DLB-6	Milner, William [publishing house] DLB-106	"Modern Novelists – Great and Small" (1855), by Margaret Oliphant DLB-21
Micklejohn, George circa 1717-1818 . . . . DLB-31	Milnes, Richard Monckton (Lord Houghton) 1809-1885 . . . . DLB-32, 184	
Middle English Literature: An Introduction DLB-146		
The Middle English Lyric DLB-146		

"Modern Style" (1857), by Cockburn
  Thomson [excerpt] DLB-57
The Modernists (1932),
  by Joseph Warren Beach............DLB-36
Modiano, Patrick 1945- DLB-83
Moffat, Yard and Company DLB-46
Moffet, Thomas 1553-1604...........DLB-136
Mohr, Nicholasa 1938- DLB-145
Moix, Ana María 1947- DLB-134
Molesworth, Louisa 1839-1921.......DLB-135
Möllhausen, Balduin 1825-1905......DLB-129
Molnár, Ferenc
  1878-1952 ....DLB 215; CDWLB-4
Molnár, Miklós (see Mészöly, Miklós)
Momaday, N. Scott
  1934- DLB-143, 175, 256; CDALB-7
Monkhouse, Allan 1858-1936..........DLB-10
Monro, Harold 1879-1932.............DLB 19
Monroe, Harriet 1860-1936.........DLB-54, 91
Monsarrat, Nicholas 1910-1979.......DLB-15
Montagu, Lady Mary Wortley
  1689-1762 ....DLB-95, 101
Montague, C. E. 1867-1928...........DLB-197
Montague, John 1929-................DLB-40
Montale, Eugenio 1896-1981..........DLB-114
Montalvo, José 1946-1994............DLB-209
Monterroso, Augusto 1921- DLB-145
Montesquiou, Robert de 1855-1921....DLB-217
Montgomerie, Alexander
  circa 1550?-1598.................DLB-167
Montgomery, James 1771-1854......DLB-93, 158
Montgomery, John 1919- DLB-16
Montgomery, Lucy Maud
  1874-1942 ....DLB-92; DS-14
Montgomery, Marion 1925- DLB-6
Montgomery, Robert Bruce (see Crispin, Edmund)
Montherlant, Henry de 1896-1972.....DLB-72
The Monthly Review 1749-1844........DLB-110
Montigny, Louvigny de 1876-1955.....DLB-92
Montoya, José 1932-.................DLB-122
Moodie, John Wedderburn Dunbar
  1797-1869........................DLB-99
Moodie, Susanna 1803-1885 ....DLB-99
Moody, Joshua circa 1633-1697.......DLB-24
Moody, William Vaughn 1869-1910....DLB-7, 54
Moorcock, Michael 1939- DLB-14, 231
Moore, Brian 1921-1999..............DLB 251
Moore, Catherine L. 1911- DLB-8
Moore, Clement Clarke 1779-1863.....DLB-42
Moore, Dora Mavor 1888-1979.........DLB-92
Moore, George 1852-1933....DLB-10, 18, 57, 135
Moore, Lorrie 1957- DLB-234
Moore, Marianne
  1887-1972.........DLB-45; DS-7; CDALB-5
Moore, Mavor 1919- DLB-88
Moore, Richard 1927- DLB-105
Moore, T. Sturge 1870-1944 ....DLB-19

Moore, Thomas 1779-1852 ....DLB-96, 144
Moore, Ward 1903-1978 ....DLB-8
Moore, Wilstach, Keys and Company DLB-49
Moorehead, Alan 1901-1983...........DLB-204
Moorhouse, Geoffrey 1931- DLB-204
The Moorland-Spingarn Research
  Center..........................DLB-76
Moorman, Mary C. 1905-1994 ....DLB-155
Mora, Pat 1942- DLB-209
Moraga, Cherríe 1952- DLB-82, 249
Morales, Alejandro 1944- DLB-82
Morales, Mario Roberto 1947- DLB-145
Morales, Rafael 1919 ....DLB-108
Morality Plays: *Mankind* circa 1450-1500 and
  Everyman circa 1500 ....DLB-146
Morante, Elsa 1912-1985.............DLB-177
Morata, Olympia Fulvia 1526-1555.....DLB-179
Moravia, Alberto 1907-1990 ....DLB-177
Mordaunt, Elinor 1872-1942 ....DLB-174
Mordovtsev, Daniil Lukich 1830-1905 ...DLB-238
More, Hannah
  1745-1833 ....DLB-107, 109, 116, 158
More, Henry 1614-1687 ....DLB 126, 252
More, Sir Thomas
  1477 or 1478?-1535................DLB-136
Moreno, Dorinda 1939- DLB-122
Morency, Pierre 1942- DLB-60
Moretti, Marino 1885-1979 ....DLB-114
Morgan, Berry 1919- DLB-6
Morgan, Charles 1894-1958 ....DLB-34, 100
Morgan, Edmund S. 1916- DLB-17
Morgan, Edwin 1920- DLB-27
Morgan, John Pierpont 1837-1913.....DLB-140
Morgan, John Pierpont, Jr. 1867-1943....DLB-140
Morgan, Robert 1944- DLB-120
Morgan, Sydney Owenson, Lady
  1776?-1859...................DLB-116, 158
Morgner, Irmtraud 1933- DLB-75
Morhof, Daniel Georg 1639-1691 .....DLB-164
Mori, Ōgai 1862-1922 ....DLB-180
Móricz, Zsigmond 1879-1942 ....DLB-215
Morier, James Justinian
  1782 or 1783?-1849...............DLB-116
Mörike, Eduard 1804-1875 ....DLB-133
Morin, Paul 1889-1963 ....DLB-92
Morison, Richard 1514?-1556 ....DLB-136
Morison, Samuel Eliot 1887-1976.....DLB-17
Morison, Stanley 1889-1967 ....DLB-201
Moritz, Karl Philipp 1756-1793 ......DLB-94
Moriz von Craûn circa 1220-1230 ....DLB-138
Morley, Christopher 1890-1957........DLB-9
Morley, John 1838-1923 ......DLB-57, 144, 190
Morris, George Pope 1802-1864 ....DLB-73
Morris, James Humphrey (see Morris, Jan)
Morris, Jan 1926- DLB-204
Morris, Lewis 1833-1907 ....DLB-35

Morris, Margaret 1737-1816............DLB-200
Morris, Richard B. 1904-1989..........DLB-17
Morris, William 1834-1896
  ....DLB-18, 35, 57, 156, 178, 184; CDBLB-4
Morris, Willie 1934-1999.................Y-80
Morris, Wright
  1910-1998..........DLB-2, 206, 218; Y-81
Morrison, Arthur 1863-1945....DLB-70, 135, 197
Morrison, Charles Clayton 1874-1966 ....DLB-91
Morrison, John 1904-1988..............DLB-260
Morrison, Toni 1931-
  ......DLB-6, 33, 143; Y-81, Y-93; CDALB-6
Morrow, William, and Company DLB-46
Morse, James Herbert 1841-1923 ....DLB-71
Morse, Jedidiah 1761-1826..............DLB-37
Morse, John T., Jr. 1840-1937..........DLB-47
Morselli, Guido 1912-1973.............DLB-177
Mortimer, Favell Lee 1802-1878 ....DLB-163
Mortimer, John
  1923- DLB-13, 245; CDBLB-8
Morton, Carlos 1942- DLB-122
Morton, H. V. 1892-1979 ....DLB-195
Morton, John P., and Company DLB-49
Morton, Nathaniel 1613-1685 ....DLB-24
Morton, Sarah Wentworth 1759-1846......DLB-37
Morton, Thomas circa 1579-circa 1647 ....DLB-24
Moscherosch, Johann Michael
  1601-1669......................DLB-164
Moseley, Humphrey
  [publishing house]................DLB-170
Möser, Justus 1720-1794 ....DLB-97
Mosley, Nicholas 1923- DLB-14, 207
Moss, Arthur 1889-1969 ....DLB-4
Moss, Howard 1922-1987 ....DLB-5
Moss, Thylias 1954- DLB-120
The Most Powerful Book Review
  in America
  [*New York Times Book Review*]............Y-82
Motion, Andrew 1952- DLB-40
Motley, John Lothrop
  1814-1877 ....DLB-1, 30, 59, 235
Motley, Willard 1909-1965 ....DLB-76, 143
Mott, Lucretia 1793-1880...............DLB-239
Motte, Benjamin Jr. [publishing house] ...DLB-154
Motteux, Peter Anthony 1663-1718........DLB-80
Mottram, R. H. 1883-1971...............DLB-36
Mount, Ferdinand 1939- DLB-231
Mouré, Erin 1955- DLB-60
Mourning Dove (Humishuma) between
  1882 and 1888?-1936 ....DLB-175, 221
Movies from Books, 1920-1974...........DLB-9
Mowat, Farley 1921- DLB-68
Mowbray, A. R., and Company,
  Limited.........................DLB-106
Mowrer, Edgar Ansel 1892-1977.........DLB-29
Mowrer, Paul Scott 1887-1971..........DLB-29
Moxon, Edward [publishing house]......DLB-106
Moxon, Joseph [publishing house].......DLB-170

Mphahlele, Es'kia (Ezekiel) 1919- DLB-125; CDWLB-3	Murner, Thomas 1475-1537 . . . . .DLB-179	Naipaul, V. S. 1932- DLB-125, 204, 207; Y-85, Y-01; CDBLB-8; CDWLB-3
Mrożek, Sławomir 1930- . . DLB-232; CDWLB-4	Muro, Amado 1915-1971 . . . . DLB-82	
Mtshali, Oswald Mbuyiseni 1940- DLB-125	Murphy, Arthur 1727-1805 . . . . DLB-89, 142	Nakagami Kenji 1946-1992 . . . . DLB-182
Mucedorus DLB-62	Murphy, Beatrice M. 1908- DLB-76	Nakano-in Masatada no Musume (see Nijō, Lady)
Mudford, William 1782-1848 . . . . DLB-159	Murphy, Dervla 1931- DLB-204	Nałkowska, Zofia 1884-1954 . . . . DLB-215
Mueller, Lisel 1924- DLB-105	Murphy, Emily 1868-1933 . . . . DLB-99	Nancrede, Joseph [publishing house] DLB-49
Muhajir, El (see Marvin X)	Murphy, Jack 1923-1980 . . . . DLB-241	Naranjo, Carmen 1930- DLB-145
Muhajir, Nazzam Al Fitnah (see Marvin X)	Murphy, John, and Company DLB-49	Narezhny, Vasilii Trofimovich 1780-1825 . . . . DLB-198
Mühlbach, Luise 1814-1873 . . . . DLB-133	Murphy, John H., III 1916- DLB-127	
Muir, Edwin 1887-1959 . . . . DLB-20, 100, 191	Murphy, Richard 1927-1993 . . . . DLB-40	Narrache, Jean 1893-1970 . . . . DLB-92
Muir, Helen 1937- DLB-14	Murray, Albert L. 1916- DLB-38	Nasby, Petroleum Vesuvius (see Locke, David Ross)
Muir, John 1838-1914 . . . . DLB-186	Murray, Gilbert 1866-1957 . . . . DLB-10	Nash, Eveleigh [publishing house] DLB-112
Muir, Percy 1894-1979 . . . . DLB-201	Murray, Jim 1919-1998 . . . . DLB-241	Nash, Ogden 1902-1971 . . . . DLB-11
Mujū Ichien 1226-1312 . . . . DLB-203	Murray, John [publishing house] DLB-154	Nashe, Thomas 1567-1601? DLB-167
Mukherjee, Bharati 1940- DLB-60, 218	Murry, John Middleton 1889-1957 . . . . . DLB-149	Nason, Jerry 1910-1986 . . . . DLB-241
Mulcaster, Richard 1531 or 1532-1611 . . . . DLB-167	"The Break-Up of the Novel" (1922) DLB-36	Nast, Conde 1873-1942 . . . . DLB-91
	Murray, Judith Sargent 1751-1820 . . . . DLB-37, 200	Nast, Thomas 1840-1902 . . . . DLB-188
Muldoon, Paul 1951- DLB-40		Nastasijević, Momčilo 1894-1938 . . . . .DLB-147
Müller, Friedrich (see Müller, Maler)	Murray, Pauli 1910-1985 . . . . DLB-41	Nathan, George Jean 1882-1958 . . . . .DLB-137
Müller, Heiner 1929-1995 . . . . DLB-124	Musäus, Johann Karl August 1735-1787 . . . DLB-97	Nathan, Robert 1894-1985 . . . . DLB-9
Müller, Maler 1749-1825 . . . . DLB-94	Muschg, Adolf 1934- DLB-75	National Book Critics Circle Awards . . . Y-00; Y-01
Muller, Marcia 1944- DLB-226	The Music of *Minnesang* DLB-138	The National Jewish Book Awards Y-85
Müller, Wilhelm 1794-1827 . . . . DLB-90	Musil, Robert 1880-1942 . . . . DLB-81, 124; CDWLB-2	The National Theatre and the Royal Shakespeare Company: The National Companies DLB-13
Mumford, Lewis 1895-1990 . . . . DLB-63		
Munby, A. N. L. 1913-1974 . . . . DLB-201	*Muspilli* circa 790-circa 850 . . . . DLB-148	
Munby, Arthur Joseph 1828-1910 . . . . DLB-35	Musset, Alfred de 1810-1857 . . . . . . .DLB-192, 217	Natsume, Sōseki 1867-1916 . . . . DLB-180
Munday, Anthony 1560-1633 . . . . . . .DLB-62, 172	Mussey, Benjamin B., and Company DLB-49	Naughton, Bill 1910- DLB-13
Mundt, Clara (see Mühlbach, Luise)	Mutafchieva, Vera 1929- DLB-181	Navarro, Joe 1953- DLB-209
Mundt, Theodore 1808-1861 . . . . DLB-133	Mwangi, Meja 1948- DLB-125	Naylor, Gloria 1950- DLB-173
Munford, Robert circa 1737-1783 . . . . DLB-31	My Summer Reading Orgy: Reading for Fun and Games: One Reader's Report on the Summer of 2001 . . . . Y-01	Nazor, Vladimir 1876-1949 . . . . .DLB-147
Mungoshi, Charles 1947- DLB-157		Ndebele, Njabulo 1948- DLB-157
Munk, Kaj 1898-1944 . . . . DLB-214		Neagoe, Peter 1881-1960 . . . . DLB-4
Munonye, John 1929- DLB-117	Myers, Frederic W. H. 1843-1901 . . . . . DLB-190	Neal, John 1793-1876 . . . . DLB-1, 59, 243
Munro, Alice 1931- DLB-53	Myers, Gustavus 1872-1942 . . . . DLB-47	Neal, Joseph C. 1807-1847 . . . . DLB-11
Munro, George [publishing house] DLB-49	Myers, L. H. 1881-1944 . . . . DLB-15	Neal, Larry 1937-1981 . . . . DLB-38
Munro, H. H. 1870-1916 . . . . DLB-34, 162; CDBLB-5	Myers, Walter Dean 1937- DLB-33	The Neale Publishing Company DLB-49
	Mykolaitis-Putinas, Vincas 1893-1967 . . . DLB-220	Nebel, Frederick 1903-1967 . . . . DLB-226
Munro, Neil 1864-1930 . . . . DLB-156	Myles, Eileen 1949- DLB-193	Neely, F. Tennyson [publishing house] . . . DLB-49
Munro, Norman L. [publishing house] DLB-49	Myrdal, Jan 1927- DLB-257	Negoițescu, Ion 1921-1993 . . . . DLB-220
	# N	Negri, Ada 1870-1945 . . . . DLB-114
Munroe, James, and Company DLB-49		"The Negro as a Writer," by G. M. McClellan DLB-50
Munroe, Kirk 1850-1930 . . . . DLB-42	Na Prous Boneta circa 1296-1328 . . . . . . DLB-208	
Munroe and Francis DLB-49	Nabl, Franz 1883-1974 . . . . DLB-81	"Negro Poets and Their Poetry," by Wallace Thurman DLB-50
Munsell, Joel [publishing house] DLB-49	Nabokov, Vladimir 1899-1977 . . . . .DLB-2, 244; Y-80, Y-91; DS-3; CDALB-1	
Munsey, Frank A. 1854-1925 . . . . DLB 25, 91		Neidhart von Reuental circa 1185-circa 1240 . . . . DLB-138
Munsey, Frank A., and Company DLB-49	The Vladimir Nabokov Archive in the Berg Collection Y-91	
Murakami Haruki 1949- DLB-182		Neihardt, John G. 1881-1973 . . . . . DLB-9, 54, 256
Murav'ev, Mikhail Nikitich 1757-1807 . . . . DLB-150	Nabokov Festival at Cornell Y-83	Neilson, John Shaw 1872-1942 . . . . DLB-230
	Nádaši, Ladislav (see Jégé)	Neledinsky-Meletsky, Iurii Aleksandrovich 1752-1828 . . . . DLB-150
Murdoch, Iris 1919-1999 . . . . . . DLB-14, 194, 233; CDBLB-8	Naden, Constance 1858-1889 . . . . DLB-199	
	Nadezhdin, Nikolai Ivanovich 1804-1856 . . . . DLB-198	Nelligan, Emile 1879-1941 . . . . DLB-92
Murdoch, Rupert 1931- DLB-127		Nelson, Alice Moore Dunbar 1875-1935 . . DLB-50
Murfree, Mary N. 1850-1922 . . . . DLB-12, 74	Naevius circa 265 B.C.-201 B.C. DLB-211	Nelson, Antonya 1961- DLB-244
Murger, Henry 1822-1861 . . . . DLB-119	Nafis and Cornish DLB-49	Nelson, Kent 1943- DLB-234
Murger, Louis-Henri (see Murger, Henry)	Nagai, Kafū 1879-1959 . . . . DLB-180	Nelson, Thomas, and Sons [U.K.] DLB-106
	Naipaul, Shiva 1945-1985 . . . . .DLB-157; Y-85	Nelson, Thomas, and Sons [U.S.] DLB-49

Nelson, William 1908-1978 . . . . .DLB-103
Nelson, William Rockhill 1841-1915. . . . . .DLB-23
Nemerov, Howard 1920-1991 . . . . . DLB-5, 6; Y-83
Németh, László 1901-1975. . . . . .DLB-215
Nepos circa 100 B.C.-post 27 B.C. DLB-211
Néris, Salomėja
   1904-1945 . . . . .DLB-220; CDWLB-4
Nerval, Gerard de 1808-1855 . . . . .DLB-217
Nesbit, E. 1858-1924 . . . . DLB-141, 153, 178
Ness, Evaline 1911-1986 . . . . .DLB-61
Nestroy, Johann 1801-1862 . . . . .DLB-133
Neugeboren, Jay 1938- DLB-28
Neukirch, Benjamin 1655-1729 . . . . .DLB-168
Neumann, Alfred 1895-1952 . . . . .DLB-56
Neumann, Ferenc (see Molnár, Ferenc)
Neumark, Georg 1621-1681 . . . . .DLB-164
Neumeister, Erdmann 1671-1756 . . . . .DLB-168
Nevins, Allan 1890-1971 . . . . DLB-17; DS-17
Nevinson, Henry Woodd 1856-1941 . . . .DLB-135
The New American Library DLB-46
New Approaches to Biography: Challenges
   from Critical Theory, USC Conference
   on Literary Studies, 1990 . . . . Y-90
New Directions Publishing Corporation . . .DLB-46
A New Edition of *Huck Finn*. Y-85
New Forces at Work in the American Theatre:
   1915-1925 . . . . .DLB-7
New Literary Periodicals:
   A Report for 1987 . . . . Y-87
New Literary Periodicals:
   A Report for 1988. . . . . .Y-88
New Literary Periodicals:
   A Report for 1989. . . . . .Y-89
New Literary Periodicals:
   A Report for 1990. . . . . .Y-90
New Literary Periodicals:
   A Report for 1991. . . . . .Y-91
New Literary Periodicals:
   A Report for 1992. . . . . .Y-92
New Literary Periodicals:
   A Report for 1993. . . . . .Y-93
The New Monthly Magazine
   1814-1884 . . . . .DLB-110
The New Variorum Shakespeare. Y-85
A New Voice: The Center for the Book's First
   Five Years Y-83
The New Wave [Science Fiction]. DLB-8
New York City Bookshops in the 1930s and 1940s:
   The Recollections of Walter Goldwater . . Y-93
Newbery, John [publishing house]. DLB-154
Newbolt, Henry 1862-1938 . . . . .DLB-19
Newbound, Bernard Slade (see Slade, Bernard)
Newby, Eric 1919- DLB-204
Newby, P. H. 1918- DLB-15
Newby, Thomas Cautley
   [publishing house] DLB-106
Newcomb, Charles King 1820-1894 . . .DLB-1, 223
Newell, Peter 1862-1924 . . . . .DLB-42
Newell, Robert Henry 1836-1901 . . . . .DLB-11

Newhouse, Samuel I. 1895-1979 . . . . .DLB-127
Newman, Cecil Earl 1903-1976 . . . . .DLB-127
Newman, David (see Benton, Robert)
Newman, Frances 1883-1928. . . . . Y-80
Newman, Francis William 1805-1897 . . . .DLB-190
Newman, John Henry
   1801-1890 . . . . DLB-18, 32, 55
Newman, Mark [publishing house] DLB-49
Newmarch, Rosa Harriet 1857-1940 . . . . .DLB-240
Newnes, George, Limited DLB-112
Newsome, Effie Lee 1885-1979 . . . . .DLB-76
Newspaper Syndication of American
   Humor DLB-11
Newton, A. Edward 1864-1940 . . . . .DLB-140
Newton, Sir Isaac 1642-1727 . . . . .DLB-252
Nexø, Martin Andersen 1869-1954 . . . . . .DLB-214
Nezval, Vítěslav
   1900-1958 . . . . .DLB-215; CDWLB-4
Ngugi wa Thiong'o
   1938- DLB-125; CDWLB-3
Niatum, Duane 1938- DLB-175
The *Nibelungenlied* and the *Klage*
   circa 1200 . . . . .DLB-138
Nichol, B. P. 1944-1988. . . . . .DLB-53
Nicholas of Cusa 1401-1464 . . . . .DLB-115
Nichols, Ann 1891?-1966. . . . . .DLB-249
Nichols, Beverly 1898-1983. . . . . .DLB-191
Nichols, Dudley 1895-1960 . . . . .DLB-26
Nichols, Grace 1950- DLB-157
Nichols, John 1940- Y-82
Nichols, Mary Sargeant (Neal) Gove
   1810-1884 .DLB-1, 243
Nichols, Peter 1927- DLB-13, 245
Nichols, Roy F. 1896-1973. . . . . .DLB-17
Nichols, Ruth 1948- DLB-60
Nicholson, Edward Williams Byron
   1849-1912. . . . . .DLB-184
Nicholson, Norman 1914- DLB-27
Nicholson, William 1872-1949. . . . . .DLB-141
Ní Chuilleanáin, Eiléan 1942- DLB-40
Nicol, Eric 1919- DLB-68
Nicolai, Friedrich 1733-1811 . . . . .DLB-97
Nicolas de Clamanges circa 1363-1437 . . .DLB-208
Nicolay, John G. 1832-1901 and
   Hay, John 1838-1905 . . . . .DLB-47
Nicolson, Adela Florence Cory (see Hope, Laurence)
Nicolson, Harold 1886-1968 . . . . . . .DLB-100, 149
Nicolson, Harold, "The Practice of Biography," in
   *The English Sense of Humour and
   Other Essays*. .DLB-149
Nicolson, Nigel 1917- DLB-155
Niebuhr, Reinhold 1892-1971 . . . . . DLB-17; DS-17
Niedecker, Lorine 1903-1970. . . . . .DLB-48
Nieman, Lucius W. 1857-1935. . . . . .DLB-25
Nietzsche, Friedrich
   1844-1900 . . . . DLB-129; CDWLB-2
Nievo, Stanislao 1928- DLB-196
Niggli, Josefina 1910- Y-80

Nightingale, Florence 1820-1910 . . . . .DLB-166
Nijō, Lady (Nakano-in Masatada no Musume)
   1258-after 1306. . . . . .DLB-203
Nijō Yoshimoto 1320-1388 . . . . .DLB-203
Nikolev, Nikolai Petrovich
   1758-1815 . . . . .DLB-150
Niles, Hezekiah 1777-1839 . . . . .DLB-43
Nims, John Frederick 1913-1999 . . . . .DLB-5
Nin, Anaïs 1903-1977. . . . . DLB-2, 4, 152
1985: The Year of the Mystery:
   A Symposium Y-85
The 1997 Booker Prize Y-97
The 1998 Booker Prize Y-98
Niño, Raúl 1961- DLB-209
Nissenson, Hugh 1933- DLB-28
Niven, Frederick John 1878-1944. . . . . .DLB-92
Niven, Larry 1938- .DLB-8
Nixon, Howard M. 1909-1983 . . . . .DLB-201
Nizan, Paul 1905-1940. . . . . .DLB-72
Njegoš, Petar II Petrović
   1813-1851 . . . . DLB-147; CDWLB-4
Nkosi, Lewis 1936- DLB-157
"The No Self, the Little Self, and the Poets,"
   by Richard Moore. DLB-105
Noah, Mordecai M. 1785-1851 . . . . .DLB-250
Noailles, Anna de 1876-1933 . . . . .DLB-258
Nobel Peace Prize
   The 1986 Nobel Peace Prize: Elie Wiesel Y-86
The Nobel Prize and Literary Politics Y-86
Nobel Prize in Literature
   The 1982 Nobel Prize in Literature:
      Gabriel García Márquez Y-82
   The 1983 Nobel Prize in Literature:
      William Golding Y-83
   The 1984 Nobel Prize in Literature:
      Jaroslav Seifert. Y-84
   The 1985 Nobel Prize in Literature:
      Claude Simon Y-85
   The 1986 Nobel Prize in Literature:
      Wole Soyinka Y-86
   The 1987 Nobel Prize in Literature:
      Joseph Brodsky Y-87
   The 1988 Nobel Prize in Literature:
      Najīb Mahfūz Y-88
   The 1989 Nobel Prize in Literature:
      Camilo José Cela. Y-89
   The 1990 Nobel Prize in Literature:
      Octavio Paz Y-90
   The 1991 Nobel Prize in Literature:
      Nadine Gordimer Y-91
   The 1992 Nobel Prize in Literature:
      Derek Walcott. Y-92
   The 1993 Nobel Prize in Literature:
      Toni Morrison Y-93
   The 1994 Nobel Prize in Literature:
      Kenzaburō Ōe. Y-94
   The 1995 Nobel Prize in Literature:
      Seamus Heaney. Y-95
   The 1996 Nobel Prize in Literature:
      Wisława Szymborska Y-96

The 1997 Nobel Prize in Literature: Dario Fo	Notes from the Underground of *Sister Carrie* ... Y-01	Oates, Joyce Carol 1938- ...DLB-2, 5, 130; Y-81
The 1998 Nobel Prize in Literature: José Saramago ... Y-98	Notker Balbulus circa 840-912 ... DLB-148	Ōba Minako 1930- ... DLB-182
The 1999 Nobel Prize in Literature: Günter Grass ... Y-99	Notker III of Saint Gall circa 950-1022 ... DLB-148	Ober, Frederick Albion 1849-1913 ... DLB-189
The 2000 Nobel Prize in Literature: Gao Xingjian ... Y-00	Notker von Zweifalten ?-1095 ... DLB-148	Ober, William 1920-1993 ... Y-93
The 2001 Nobel Prize in Literature: V. S. Naipaul ... Y-01	Nourse, Alan E. 1928- ... DLB-8	Oberholtzer, Ellis Paxson 1868-1936 ... DLB-47
Nodier, Charles 1780-1844 ... DLB-119	Novak, Slobodan 1924- ... DLB-181	Obradović, Dositej 1740?-1811 ... DLB-147
Noël, Marie 1883-1967 ... DLB-258	Novak, Vjenceslav 1859-1905 ... DLB-147	O'Brien, Charlotte Grace 1845-1909 ... DLB-240
Noel, Roden 1834-1894 ... DLB-35	Novakovich, Josip 1956- ... DLB-244	O'Brien, Edna 1932- ... DLB-14, 231; CDBLB-8
Nogami, Yaeko 1885-1985 ... DLB-180	Novalis 1772-1801 ... DLB-90; CDWLB-2	O'Brien, Fitz-James 1828-1862 ... DLB-74
Nogo, Rajko Petrov 1945- ... DLB-181	Novaro, Mario 1868-1944 ... DLB-114	O'Brien, Flann (see O'Nolan, Brian)
Nolan, William F. 1928- ... DLB-8	Novás Calvo, Lino 1903-1983 ... DLB-145	O'Brien, Kate 1897-1974 ... DLB-15
Noland, C. F. M. 1810?-1858 ... DLB-11	"The Novel in [Robert Browning's] 'The Ring and the Book'" (1912), by Henry James ... DLB-32	O'Brien, Tim 1946- ... DLB-152; Y-80; DS-9; CDALB-7
Noma Hiroshi 1915-1991 ... DLB-182	The Novel of Impressionism, by Jethro Bithell ... DLB-66	O'Casey, Sean 1880-1964 ... DLB-10; CDBLB-6
Nonesuch Press ... DLB-112	Novel-Reading: *The Works of Charles Dickens, The Works of W. Makepeace Thackeray* (1879), by Anthony Trollope ... DLB-21	Occom, Samson 1723-1792 ... DLB-175
Noonan, Robert Phillipe (see Tressell, Robert)		Ochs, Adolph S. 1858-1935 ... DLB-25
Noonday Press ... DLB-46		Ochs-Oakes, George Washington 1861-1931 ... DLB-137
Noone, John 1936- ... DLB-14	Novels for Grown-Ups ... Y-97	O'Connor, Flannery 1925-1964 ... DLB-2, 152; Y-80; DS-12; CDALB-1
Nora, Eugenio de 1923- ... DLB-134	The Novels of Dorothy Richardson (1918), by May Sinclair ... DLB-36	
Nordan, Lewis 1939- ... DLB-234	Novels with a Purpose (1864), by Justin M'Carthy ... DLB-21	O'Connor, Frank 1903-1966 ... DLB-162
Nordbrandt, Henrik 1945- ... DLB-214		Octopus Publishing Group ... DLB-112
Nordhoff, Charles 1887-1947 ... DLB-9	Noventa, Giacomo 1898-1960 ... DLB-114	Oda Sakunosuke 1913-1947 ... DLB-182
Norén, Lars 1944- ... DLB-257	Novikov, Nikolai Ivanovich 1744-1818 ... DLB-150	Odell, Jonathan 1737-1818 ... DLB-31, 99
Norman, Charles 1904-1996 ... DLB-111		O'Dell, Scott 1903-1989 ... DLB-52
Norman, Marsha 1947- ... Y-84	Novomeský, Laco 1904-1976 ... DLB-215	Odets, Clifford 1906-1963 ... DLB-7, 26
Norris, Charles G. 1881-1945 ... DLB-9	Nowlan, Alden 1933-1983 ... DLB-53	Odhams Press Limited ... DLB-112
Norris, Frank 1870-1902 ... DLB-12, 71, 186; CDALB-3	Noyes, Alfred 1880-1958 ... DLB-20	Odoevsky, Aleksandr Ivanovich 1802-1839 ... DLB-205
Norris, John 1657-1712 ... DLB-252	Noyes, Crosby S. 1825-1908 ... DLB-23	Odoevsky, Vladimir Fedorovich 1804 or 1803-1869 ... DLB-198
Norris, Leslie 1921- ... DLB-27, 256	Noyes, Nicholas 1647-1717 ... DLB-24	O'Donnell, Peter 1920- ... DLB-87
Norse, Harold 1916- ... DLB-16	Noyes, Theodore W. 1858-1946 ... DLB-29	O'Donovan, Michael (see O'Connor, Frank)
Norte, Marisela 1955- ... DLB-209	N-Town Plays circa 1468 to early sixteenth century ... DLB-146	O'Dowd, Bernard 1866-1953 ... DLB-230
North, Marianne 1830-1890 ... DLB-174	Nugent, Frank 1908-1965 ... DLB-44	Ōe Kenzaburō 1935- ... DLB-182; Y-94
North Point Press ... DLB-46	Nugent, Richard Bruce 1906- ... DLB-151	O'Faolain, Julia 1932- ... DLB-14, 231
Nortje, Arthur 1942-1970 ... DLB-125	Nušić, Branislav 1864-1938 ... DLB-147; CDWLB-4	O'Faolain, Sean 1900- ... DLB-15, 162
Norton, Alice Mary (see Norton, Andre)		Off Broadway and Off-Off Broadway ... DLB-7
Norton, Andre 1912- ... DLB-8, 52		Off-Loop Theatres ... DLB-7
Norton, Andrews 1786-1853 ... DLB-1, 235	Nutt, David [publishing house] ... DLB-106	Offord, Carl Ruthven 1910- ... DLB-76
Norton, Caroline 1808-1877 ... DLB-21, 159, 199	Nwapa, Flora 1931-1993 ... DLB-125; CDWLB-3	O'Flaherty, Liam 1896-1984 ... DLB-36, 162; Y-84
Norton, Charles Eliot 1827-1908 ... DLB-1, 64, 235	Nye, Bill 1850-1896 ... DLB-186	Ogilvie, J. S., and Company ... DLB-49
Norton, John 1606-1663 ... DLB-24	Nye, Edgar Wilson (Bill) 1850-1896 ... DLB-11, 23	Ogilvy, Eliza 1822-1912 ... DLB-199
Norton, Mary 1903-1992 ... DLB-160		Ogot, Grace 1930- ... DLB-125
Norton, Thomas (see Sackville, Thomas)	Nye, Naomi Shihab 1952- ... DLB-120	O'Grady, Desmond 1935- ... DLB-40
Norton, W. W., and Company ... DLB-46	Nye, Robert 1939- ... DLB-14	Ogunyemi, Wale 1939- ... DLB-157
Norwood, Robert 1874-1932 ... DLB-92	Nyka-Niliūnas, Alfonsas 1919- ... DLB-220	O'Hagan, Howard 1902-1982 ... DLB-68
Nosaka Akiyuki 1930- ... DLB-182		O'Hara, Frank 1926-1966 ... DLB-5, 16, 193
Nossack, Hans Erich 1901-1977 ... DLB-69	**O**	O'Hara, John 1905-1970 ... DLB-9, 86; DS-2; CDALB-5
Not Immediately Discernible . . . but Eventually Quite Clear: The *First Light* and *Final Years* of Hemingway's Centenary ... Y-99	Oakes Smith, Elizabeth 1806-1893 ... DLB-1, 239, 243	John O'Hara's Pottsville Journalism ... Y-88
		O'Hegarty, P. S. 1879-1955 ... DLB-201
A Note on Technique (1926), by Elizabeth A. Drew [excerpts] ... DLB-36	Oakes, Urian circa 1631-1681 ... DLB-24	Okara, Gabriel 1921- ... DLB-125; CDWLB-3
	Oakley, Violet 1874-1961 ... DLB-188	O'Keeffe, John 1747-1833 ... DLB-89
		Okes, Nicholas [publishing house] ... DLB-170

Okigbo, Christopher 1930-1967 ....DLB-125; CDWLB-3
Okot p'Bitek 1931-1982.....DLB-125; CDWLB-3
Okpewho, Isidore 1941- DLB-157
Okri, Ben 1959- DLB-157, 231
Olaudah Equiano and Unfinished Journeys: The Slave-Narrative Tradition and Twentieth-Century Continuities, by Paul Edwards and Pauline T. Wangman..............DLB-117
Old English Literature: An Introduction..............DLB-146
Old English Riddles eighth to tenth centuries DLB-146
Old Franklin Publishing House..............DLB-49
Old German Genesis and *Old German Exodus* circa 1050-circa 1130..............DLB-148
Old High German Charms and Blessings..............DLB-148; CDWLB-2
The *Old High German Isidor* circa 790-800..............DLB-148
The Old Manse..............DLB-223
Older, Fremont 1856-1935..............DLB-25
Oldham, John 1653-1683..............DLB-131
Oldman, C. B. 1894-1969..............DLB-201
Olds, Sharon 1942-..............DLB-120
Olearius, Adam 1599-1671..............DLB-164
O'Leary, Ellen 1831-1889..............DLB-240
Oliphant, Laurence 1829?-1888......DLB-18, 166
Oliphant, Margaret 1828-1897...DLB-18, 159, 190
Oliver, Chad 1928-..............DLB-8
Oliver, Mary 1935-..............DLB-5, 193
Ollier, Claude 1922-..............DLB-83
Olsen, Tillie 1912 or 1913- DLB-28, 206; Y-80; CDALB-7
Olson, Charles 1910-1970..............DLB-5, 16, 193
Olson, Elder 1909-..............DLB-48, 63
Omotoso, Kole 1943- DLB-125
Omulevsky, Innokentii Vasil'evich 1836 [or 1837]-1883..............DLB-238
On Learning to Write..............Y-88
Ondaatje, Michael 1943-..............DLB-60
O'Neill, Eugene 1888-1953 .....DLB-7; CDALB-5
Eugene O'Neill Memorial Theater Center..............DLB-7
Eugene O'Neill's Letters: A Review..............Y-88
Onetti, Juan Carlos 1909-1994..............DLB-113; CDWLB-3
Onions, George Oliver 1872-1961..............DLB-153
Onofri, Arturo 1885-1928..............DLB-114
O'Nolan, Brian 1911-1966..............DLB-231
Opie, Amelia 1769-1853..............DLB-116, 159
Opitz, Martin 1597-1639..............DLB-164
Oppen, George 1908-1984..............DLB-5, 165
Oppenheim, E. Phillips 1866-1946..............DLB-70
Oppenheim, James 1882-1932..............DLB-28
Oppenheimer, Joel 1930-1988..............DLB-5, 193
Optic, Oliver (see Adams, William Taylor)
Oral History: B. W. Huebsch..............Y-99

Oral History Interview with Donald S. Klopfer..............Y-97
Orczy, Emma, Baroness 1865-1947..............DLB-70
Oregon Shakespeare Festival..............Y-00
Origo, Iris 1902-1988..............DLB-155
Orlovitz, Gil 1918-1973..............DLB-2, 5
Orlovsky, Peter 1933-..............DLB-16
Ormond, John 1923-..............DLB-27
Ornitz, Samuel 1890-1957..............DLB-28, 44
O'Rourke, P. J. 1947-..............DLB-185
Orten, Jiří 1919-1941..............DLB-215
Ortese, Anna Maria 1914-..............DLB-177
Ortiz, Simon J. 1941-..............DLB-120, 175, 256
Ortnit and *Wolfdietrich* circa 1225-1250....DLB-138
Orton, Joe 1933-1967..............DLB-13; CDBLB-8
Orwell, George (Eric Arthur Blair) 1903-1950...DLB-15, 98, 195, 255; CDBLB-7
The Orwell Year..............Y-84
(Re-)Publishing Orwell..............Y-86
Ory, Carlos Edmundo de 1923-..............DLB-134
Osbey, Brenda Marie 1957-..............DLB-120
Osbon, B. S. 1827-1912..............DLB-43
Osborn, Sarah 1714-1796..............DLB-200
Osborne, John 1929-1994 .....DLB-13, CDBLB-7
Osgood, Frances Sargent 1811-1850..............DLB-250
Osgood, Herbert L. 1855-1918..............DLB-47
Osgood, James R., and Company..............DLB-49
Osgood, McIlvaine and Company..............DLB-112
O'Shaughnessy, Arthur 1844-1881..............DLB-35
O'Shea, Patrick [publishing house]..............DLB-49
Osipov, Nikolai Petrovich 1751-1799..............DLB-150
Oskison, John Milton 1879-1947..............DLB-175
Osler, Sir William 1849-1919..............DLB-184
Osofisan, Femi 1946-..............DLB-125; CDWLB-3
Ostenso, Martha 1900-1963..............DLB-92
Ostrauskas, Kostas 1926-..............DLB-232
Ostriker, Alicia 1937-..............DLB-120
Osundare, Niyi 1947-..............DLB-157; CDWLB-3
Oswald, Eleazer 1755-1795..............DLB-43
Oswald von Wolkenstein 1376 or 1377-1445..............DLB-179
Otero, Blas de 1916-1979..............DLB-134
Otero, Miguel Antonio 1859-1944..............DLB-82
Otero, Nina 1881-1965..............DLB-209
Otero Silva, Miguel 1908-1985..............DLB-145
Otfried von Weißenburg circa 800-circa 875?..............DLB-148
Otis, Broaders and Company..............DLB-49
Otis, James (see Kaler, James Otis)
Otis, James, Jr. 1725-1783..............DLB-31
Ottaway, James 1911-..............DLB-127
Ottendorfer, Oswald 1826-1900..............DLB-23
Ottieri, Ottiero 1924-..............DLB-177

Otto-Peters, Louise 1819-1895..............DLB-129
Otway, Thomas 1652-1685..............DLB-80
Ouellette, Fernand 1930-..............DLB-60
Ouida 1839-1908..............DLB-18, 156
Outing Publishing Company..............DLB-46
Outlaw Days, by Joyce Johnson..............DLB-16
Overbury, Sir Thomas circa 1581-1613..............DLB-151
The Overlook Press..............DLB-46
Overview of U.S. Book Publishing, 1910-1945..............DLB-9
Ovid 43 B.C.-A.D. 17......DLB-211; CDWLB-1
Owen, Guy 1925-..............DLB-5
Owen, John 1564-1622..............DLB-121
Owen, John [publishing house]..............DLB-49
Owen, Peter, Limited..............DLB-112
Owen, Robert 1771-1858..............DLB-107, 158
Owen, Wilfred 1893-1918........DLB-20; DS-18; CDBLB-6
The Owl and the Nightingale circa 1189-1199..............DLB-146
Owsley, Frank L. 1890-1956..............DLB-17
Oxford, Seventeenth Earl of, Edward de Vere 1550-1604..............DLB-172
Ozerov, Vladislav Aleksandrovich 1769-1816..............DLB-150
Ozick, Cynthia 1928-........DLB-28, 152; Y-83
First Strauss "Livings" Awarded to Cynthia Ozick and Raymond Carver An Interview with Cynthia Ozick........Y-83

P

Pace, Richard 1482?-1536..............DLB-167
Pacey, Desmond 1917-1975..............DLB-88
Pack, Robert 1929-..............DLB-5
Packaging Papa: *The Garden of Eden*.....Y-86
Padell Publishing Company..............DLB-46
Padgett, Ron 1942-..............DLB-5
Padilla, Ernesto Chávez 1944-..............DLB-122
Page, L. C., and Company..............DLB-49
Page, Louise 1955-..............DLB-233
Page, P. K. 1916-..............DLB-68
Page, Thomas Nelson 1853-1922..............DLB-12, 78; DS-13
Page, Walter Hines 1855-1918......DLB-71, 91
Paget, Francis Edward 1806-1882..............DLB-163
Paget, Violet (see Lee, Vernon)
Pagliarani, Elio 1927-..............DLB-128
Pain, Barry 1864-1928..............DLB-135, 197
Pain, Philip ?-circa 1666..............DLB-24
Paine, Robert Treat, Jr. 1773-1811..............DLB-37
Paine, Thomas 1737-1809....DLB-31, 43, 73, 158; CDALB-2
Painter, George D. 1914-..............DLB-155
Painter, William 1540?-1594..............DLB-136
Palazzeschi, Aldo 1885-1974..............DLB-114
Paley, Grace 1922-..............DLB-28, 218

Paley, William 1743-1805 .... DLB-251
Palfrey, John Gorham 1796-1881 .. DLB-1, 30, 235
Palgrave, Francis Turner 1824-1897 ...... DLB-35
Palmer, Joe H. 1904-1952 .... DLB-171
Palmer, Michael 1943- DLB-169
Palmer, Nettie 1885-1964 .... DLB-260
Palmer, Vance 1885-1959 .... DLB-260
Paltock, Robert 1697-1767 .... DLB-39
Paludan, Jacob 1896-1975 .... DLB-214
Pan Books Limited DLB-112
Panama, Norman 1914- and
   Frank, Melvin 1913-1988 .... DLB-26
Panaev, Ivan Ivanovich 1812-1862 ...... DLB-198
Panaeva, Avdot'ia Iakovlevna
   1820-1893 .... DLB-238
Pancake, Breece D'J 1952-1979 .... DLB-130
Panduro, Leif 1923-1977 .... DLB-214
Panero, Leopoldo 1909-1962 .... DLB-108
Pangborn, Edgar 1909-1976 .... DLB-8
"Panic Among the Philistines": A Postscript,
   An Interview with Bryan Griffin Y-81
Panizzi, Sir Anthony 1797-1879 .... DLB-184
Panneton, Philippe (see Ringuet)
Panshin, Alexei 1940- DLB-8
Pansy (see Alden, Isabella)
Pantheon Books DLB-46
Papadat-Bengescu, Hortensia
   1876-1955 .... DLB-220
Papantonio, Michael (see Kohn, John S. Van E.)
Paperback Library DLB-46
Paperback Science Fiction DLB-8
Paquet, Alfons 1881-1944 .... DLB-66
Paracelsus 1493-1541 .... DLB-179
Paradis, Suzanne 1936- DLB-53
Páral, Vladimír, 1932- DLB-232
Pardoe, Julia 1804-1862 .... DLB-166
Paredes, Américo 1915-1999 .... DLB-209
Pareja Diezcanseco, Alfredo 1908-1993 .. DLB-145
Parents' Magazine Press DLB-46
Parise, Goffredo 1929-1986 .... DLB-177
Parisian Theater, Fall 1984: Toward
   A New Baroque Y-85
Parizeau, Alice 1930- DLB-60
Park, Ruth 1923?- DLB-260
Parke, John 1754-1789 .... DLB-31
Parker, Dan 1893-1967 .... DLB-241
Parker, Dorothy 1893-1967 ...... DLB-11, 45, 86
Parker, Gilbert 1860-1932 .... DLB-99
Parker, J. H. [publishing house] DLB-106
Parker, James 1714-1770 .... DLB-43
Parker, John [publishing house] DLB-106
Parker, Matthew 1504-1575 .... DLB-213
Parker, Stewart 1941-1988 .... DLB-245
Parker, Theodore 1810-1860 .... DLB-1, 235
Parker, William Riley 1906-1968 .... DLB-103

Parkes, Bessie Rayner (Madame Belloc)
   1829-1925 .... DLB-240
Parkman, Francis
   1823-1893 .... DLB-1, 30, 183, 186, 235
Parks, Gordon 1912- DLB-33
Parks, Tim 1954- DLB-231
Parks, William 1698-1750 .... DLB-43
Parks, William [publishing house] DLB-49
Parley, Peter (see Goodrich, Samuel Griswold)
Parmenides
   late sixth-fifth century B.C. DLB-176
Parnell, Thomas 1679-1718 .... DLB-95
Parnicki, Teodor 1908-1988 .... DLB-215
Parr, Catherine 1513?-1548 .... DLB-136
Parrington, Vernon L. 1871-1929 ...... DLB-17, 63
Parrish, Maxfield 1870-1966 .... DLB-188
Parronchi, Alessandro 1914- DLB-128
Parton, James 1822-1891 .... DLB-30
Parton, Sara Payson Willis
   1811-1872 .... DLB-43, 74, 239
Partridge, S. W., and Company DLB-106
Parun, Vesna 1922- DLB-181; CDWLB-4
Pasinetti, Pier Maria 1913- DLB-177
Pasolini, Pier Paolo 1922- DLB-128, 177
Pastan, Linda 1932- DLB-5
Paston, George (Emily Morse Symonds)
   1860-1936 .... DLB-149, 197
The Paston Letters 1422-1509 .... DLB-146
Pastorius, Francis Daniel
   1651-circa 1720 .... DLB-24
Patchen, Kenneth 1911-1972 .... DLB-16, 48
Pater, Walter
   1839-1894 .... DLB-57, 156; CDBLB-4
Aesthetic Poetry (1873) DLB-35
Paterson, A. B. "Banjo" 1864-1941 ..... DLB-230
Paterson, Katherine 1932- DLB-52
Patmore, Coventry 1823-1896 .... DLB-35, 98
Paton, Alan 1903-1988 .... DS-17
Paton, Joseph Noel 1821-1901 .... DLB-35
Paton Walsh, Jill 1937- DLB-161
Patrick, Edwin Hill ("Ted") 1901-1964 .. DLB-137
Patrick, John 1906-1995 .... DLB-7
Pattee, Fred Lewis 1863-1950 .... DLB-71
Pattern and Paradigm: History as
   Design, by Judith Ryan DLB-75
Patterson, Alicia 1906-1963 .... DLB-127
Patterson, Eleanor Medill 1881-1948 .... DLB-29
Patterson, Eugene 1923- DLB-127
Patterson, Joseph Medill 1879-1946 ..... DLB-29
Pattillo, Henry 1726-1801 .... DLB-37
Paul, Elliot 1891-1958 .... DLB-4
Paul, Jean (see Richter, Johann Paul Friedrich)
Paul, Kegan, Trench, Trubner and
   Company Limited DLB-106
Paul, Peter, Book Company DLB-49
Paul, Stanley, and Company Limited DLB-112

Paulding, James Kirke
   1778-1860 .... DLB-3, 59, 74, 250
Paulin, Tom 1949- DLB-40
Pauper, Peter, Press DLB-46
Pavese, Cesare 1908-1950 .... DLB-128, 177
Pavić, Milorad 1929- DLB-181; CDWLB-4
Pavlov, Konstantin 1933- DLB-181
Pavlov, Nikolai Filippovich 1803-1864 .... DLB-198
Pavlova, Karolina Karlovna 1807-1893 .... DLB-205
Pavlović, Miodrag
   1928- DLB-181; CDWLB-4
Paxton, John 1911-1985 .... DLB-44
Payn, James 1830-1898 .... DLB-18
Payne, John 1842-1916 .... DLB-35
Payne, John Howard 1791-1852 .... DLB-37
Payson and Clarke DLB-46
Paz, Octavio 1914-1998 .... Y-90, Y-98
Pazzi, Roberto 1946- DLB-196
Peabody, Elizabeth Palmer 1804-1894 . DLB-1, 223
Peabody, Elizabeth Palmer
   [publishing house] DLB-49
Peabody, Josephine Preston 1874-1922 .. DLB-249
Peabody, Oliver William Bourn
   1799-1848 .... DLB-59
Peace, Roger 1899-1968 .... DLB-127
Peacham, Henry 1578-1644? DLB-151
Peacham, Henry, the Elder
   1547-1634 .... DLB-172, 236
Peachtree Publishers, Limited DLB-46
Peacock, Molly 1947- DLB-120
Peacock, Thomas Love 1785-1866 ... DLB-96, 116
Pead, Deuel ?-1727 .... DLB-24
Peake, Mervyn 1911-1968 .... DLB-15, 160, 255
Peale, Rembrandt 1778-1860 .... DLB-183
Pear Tree Press DLB-112
Pearce, Philippa 1920- DLB-161
Pearson, H. B. [publishing house] DLB-49
Pearson, Hesketh 1887-1964 .... DLB-149
Pechersky, Andrei (see Mel'nikov, Pavel Ivanovich)
Peck, George W. 1840-1916 .... DLB-23, 42
Peck, H. C., and Theo. Bliss
   [publishing house] DLB-49
Peck, Harry Thurston 1856-1914 ...... DLB-71, 91
Peden, William 1913-1999 .... DLB-234
Peele, George 1556-1596 .... DLB-62, 167
Pegler, Westbrook 1894-1969 .... DLB-171
Péguy, Charles Pierre 1873-1914 .... DLB-258
Pekić, Borislav 1930-1992 ... DLB-181; CDWLB-4
Pellegrini and Cudahy DLB-46
Pelletier, Aimé (see Vac, Bertrand)
Pelletier, Francine 1959- DLB-251
Pemberton, Sir Max 1863-1950 .... DLB-70
de la Peña, Terri 1947- DLB-209
Penfield, Edward 1866-1925 .... DLB-188
Penguin Books [U.K.] DLB-112
Penguin Books [U.S.] DLB-46

Penn Publishing Company DLB-49
Penn, William 1644-1718................DLB-24
Penna, Sandro 1906-1977..............DLB-114
Pennell, Joseph 1857-1926 ....DLB-188
Penner, Jonathan 1940- Y-83
Pennington, Lee 1939- Y-82
Penton, Brian 1904-1951 ....DLB-260
Pepys, Samuel
 1633-1703 ....DLB-101, 213; CDBLB-2
Percy, Thomas 1729-1811 ....DLB-104
Percy, Walker 1916-1990 .....DLB-2; Y-80, Y-90
Percy, William 1575-1648 ....DLB-172
Perec, Georges 1936-1982 ....DLB-83
Perelman, Bob 1947- DLB-193
Perelman, S. J. 1904-1979...........DLB-11, 44
Pérez, Raymundo "Tigre" 1946- DLB-122
Peri Rossi, Cristina 1941- DLB-145
Perkins, Eugene 1932- DLB-41
Perkoff, Stuart Z. 1930-1974 ....DLB-16
Perley, Moses Henry 1804-1862 ....DLB-99
Permabooks......................DLB-46
Perovsky, Aleksei Alekseevich
 (Antonii Pogorel'sky) 1787-1836 .....DLB-198
Perri, Henry 1561-1617 ....DLB-236
Perrin, Alice 1867-1934 ....DLB-156
Perry, Bliss 1860-1954................DLB-71
Perry, Eleanor 1915-1981 ....DLB-44
Perry, Henry (see Perri, Henry)
Perry, Matthew 1794-1858..............DLB-183
Perry, Sampson 1747-1823 ....DLB-158
Perse, Saint-John 1887-1975 ....DLB-258
Persius A.D. 34-A.D. 62 ....DLB-211
Perutz, Leo 1882-1957................DLB-81
Pesetsky, Bette 1932- DLB-130
Pestalozzi, Johann Heinrich 1746-1827.....DLB-94
Peter, Laurence J. 1919-1990 ....DLB-53
Peter of Spain circa 1205-1277 ....DLB-115
Peterkin, Julia 1880-1961...............DLB-9
Peters, Lenrie 1932- DLB-117
Peters, Robert 1924- DLB-105
"Foreword to Ludwig of Baviria" DLB-105
Petersham, Maud 1889-1971 and
 Petersham, Miska 1888-1960 ....DLB-22
Peterson, Charles Jacobs 1819-1887......DLB-79
Peterson, Len 1917- DLB-88
Peterson, Levi S. 1933- DLB-206
Peterson, Louis 1922-1998................DLB-76
Peterson, T. B., and Brothers DLB-49
Petitclair, Pierre 1813-1860 ....DLB-99
Petrescu, Camil 1894-1957 ....DLB-220
Petronius circa A.D. 20-A.D. 66
 ....DLB-211; CDWLB-1
Petrov, Aleksandar 1938- DLB-181
Petrov, Gavriil 1730-1801 ....DLB-150
Petrov, Valeri 1920- DLB-181

Petrov, Vasilii Petrovich 1736-1799......DLB-150
Petrović, Rastko
 1898-1949 ....DLB-147; CDWLB-4
Petruslied circa 854?.................DLB-148
Petry, Ann 1908-1997.................DLB-76
Pettie, George circa 1548-1589 ....DLB-136
Peyton, K. M. 1929- DLB-161
Pfaffe Konrad flourished circa 1172......DLB-148
Pfaffe Lamprecht flourished circa 1150 ...DLB-148
Pfeiffer, Emily 1827-1890...............DLB-199
Pforzheimer, Carl H. 1879-1957 ....DLB-140
Phaedrus circa 18 B.C.-circa A.D. 50.....DLB-211
Phaer, Thomas 1510?-1560............DLB-167
Phaidon Press Limited................DLB-112
Pharr, Robert Deane 1916-1992 ....DLB-33
Phelps, Elizabeth Stuart 1815-1852 .....DLB-202
Phelps, Elizabeth Stuart 1844-1911 ...DLB-74, 221
Philander von der Linde
 (see Mencke, Johann Burckhard)
Philby, H. St. John B. 1885-1960........DLB-195
Philip, Marlene Nourbese 1947- DLB-157
Philippe, Charles-Louis 1874-1909.......DLB-65
Philips, John 1676-1708 ....DLB-95
Philips, Katherine 1632-1664............DLB-131
Phillipps, Sir Thomas 1792-1872 ....DLB-184
Phillips, Caryl 1958- DLB-157
Phillips, David Graham 1867-1911 .....DLB-9, 12
Phillips, Jayne Anne 1952- Y-80
Phillips, Robert 1938- DLB-105
"Finding, Losing, Reclaiming: A Note
 on My Poems" DLB-105
Phillips, Sampson and Company.........DLB-49
Phillips, Stephen 1864-1915.............DLB-10
Phillips, Ulrich B. 1877-1934 ....DLB-17
Phillips, Wendell 1811-1884 ....DLB-235
Phillips, Willard 1784-1873 ....DLB-59
Phillips, William 1907- DLB-137
Phillpotts, Adelaide Eden (Adelaide Ross)
 1896-1993 ....DLB-191
Phillpotts, Eden 1862-1960 ..DLB-10, 70, 135, 153
Philo circa 20-15 B.C.-circa A.D. 50 .....DLB-176
Philosophical Library.................DLB-46
Phinney, Elihu [publishing house].......DLB-49
Phoenix, John (see Derby, George Horatio)
PHYLON (Fourth Quarter, 1950),
 The Negro in Literature:
 The Current Scene DLB-76
Physiologus circa 1070-circa 1150 ....DLB-148
Piccolo, Lucio 1903-1969..............DLB-114
Pickard, Tom 1946- DLB-40
Pickering, William [publishing house]....DLB-106
Pickthall, Marjorie 1883-1922 ....DLB-92
Pictorial Printing Company............DLB-49
Piercy, Marge 1936- DLB-120, 227
Pierro, Albino 1916- DLB-128
Pignotti, Lamberto 1926- DLB-128

Pike, Albert 1809-1891 ....DLB-74
Pike, Zebulon Montgomery
 1779-1813 ....DLB-183
Pillat, Ion 1891-1945..................DLB-220
Pilon, Jean-Guy 1930- DLB-60
Pinckney, Eliza Lucas 1722-1793 ....DLB-200
Pinckney, Josephine 1895-1957 ....DLB-6
Pindar circa 518 B.C.-circa 438 B.C.
 ....DLB-176; CDWLB-1
Pindar, Peter (see Wolcot, John)
Pineda, Cecile 1942- DLB-209
Pinero, Arthur Wing 1855-1934 ....DLB-10
Pinget, Robert 1919-1997 ....DLB-83
Pinkney, Edward Coote 1802-1828......DLB-248
Pinnacle Books DLB-46
Piñon, Nélida 1935- DLB-145
Pinsky, Robert 1940- Y-82
Robert Pinsky Reappointed Poet Laureate ...Y-98
Pinter, Harold 1930- DLB-13; CDBLB-8
Piontek, Heinz 1925- DLB-75
Piozzi, Hester Lynch [Thrale]
 1741-1821 ....DLB-104, 142
Piper, H. Beam 1904-1964...............DLB-8
Piper, Watty DLB-22
Pirckheimer, Caritas 1467-1532..........DLB-179
Pirckheimer, Willibald 1470-1530 ....DLB-179
Pisar, Samuel 1929- Y-83
Pisemsky, Aleksei Feofilaktovich
 1821-1881 ....DLB-238
Pitkin, Timothy 1766-1847 ....DLB-30
The Pitt Poetry Series: Poetry Publishing
 Today Y-85
Pitter, Ruth 1897- DLB-20
Pix, Mary 1666-1709 ....DLB-80
Pixerécourt, René Charles Guilbert de
 1773-1844 ....DLB-192
Plaatje, Sol T. 1876-1932 ....DLB-125, 225
Plante, David 1940- Y-83
Platen, August von 1796-1835 ....DLB-90
Plath, Sylvia
 1932-1963 ....DLB-5, 6, 152; CDALB-1
Plato circa 428 B.C.-348-347 B.C.
 ....DLB-176; CDWLB-1
Plato, Ann 1824?-? DLB-239
Platon 1737-1812 ....DLB-150
Platt and Munk Company..............DLB-46
Plautus circa 254 B.C.-184 B.C.
 ....DLB-211; CDWLB-1
Playboy Press DLB-46
Playford, John [publishing house] DLB-170
Plays, Playwrights, and Playgoers DLB-84
Playwrights on the Theater DLB-80
Der Pleier flourished circa 1250 ....DLB-138
Pleijel, Agneta 1940- DLB-257
Plenzdorf, Ulrich 1934- DLB-75
Plessen, Elizabeth 1944- DLB-75

Pletnev, Petr Aleksandrovich 1792-1865......DLB-205

Pliekšāne, Elza Rozenberga (see Aspazija)

Pliekšāns, Jānis (see Rainis, Jānis)

Plievier, Theodor 1892-1955..........DLB-69

Plimpton, George 1927-.....DLB-185, 241; Y-99

Pliny the Elder A.D. 23/24-A.D. 79.....DLB-211

Pliny the Younger circa A.D. 61-A.D. 112..........DLB-211

Plomer, William 1903-1973..........DLB-20, 162, 191, 225

Plotinus 204-270..........DLB-176; CDWLB-1

Plowright, Teresa 1952-..........DLB-251

Plume, Thomas 1630-1704..........DLB-213

Plumly, Stanley 1939-..........DLB-5, 193

Plumpp, Sterling D. 1940-..........DLB-41

Plunkett, James 1920-..........DLB-14

Plutarch circa 46-circa 120......DLB-176; CDWLB-1

Plymell, Charles 1935-..........DLB-16

Pocket Books..........DLB-46

Poe, Edgar Allan 1809-1849..........DLB-3, 59, 73, 74, 248; CDALB-2

Poe, James 1921-1980..........DLB-44

The Poet Laureate of the United States Statements from Former Consultants in Poetry..........Y-86

Pogodin, Mikhail Petrovich 1800-1875..........DLB-198

Pogorel'sky, Antonii (see Perovsky, Aleksei Alekseevich)

Pohl, Frederik 1919-..........DLB-8

Poirier, Louis (see Gracq, Julien)

Poláček, Karel 1892-1945...DLB-215; CDWLB-4

Polanyi, Michael 1891-1976..........DLB-100

Pole, Reginald 1500-1558..........DLB-132

Polevoi, Nikolai Alekseevich 1796-1846..........DLB-198

Polezhaev, Aleksandr Ivanovich 1804-1838..........DLB-205

Poliakoff, Stephen 1952-..........DLB-13

Polidori, John William 1795-1821..........DLB-116

Polite, Carlene Hatcher 1932-..........DLB-33

Pollard, Alfred W. 1859-1944..........DLB-201

Pollard, Edward A. 1832-1872..........DLB-30

Pollard, Graham 1903-1976..........DLB-201

Pollard, Percival 1869-1911..........DLB-71

Pollard and Moss..........DLB-49

Pollock, Sharon 1936-..........DLB-60

Polonsky, Abraham 1910-1999..........DLB-26

Polotsky, Simeon 1629-1680..........DLB-150

Polybius circa 200 B.C.-118 B.C..........DLB-176

Pomialovsky, Nikolai Gerasimovich 1835-1863..........DLB-238

Pomilio, Mario 1921-1990..........DLB-177

Ponce, Mary Helen 1938-..........DLB-122

Ponce-Montoya, Juanita 1949-..........DLB-122

Ponet, John 1516?-1556..........DLB-132

Ponge, Francis 1899-1988..........DLB-258

Poniatowski, Elena 1933-..........DLB-113; CDWLB-3

Ponsard, François 1814-1867..........DLB-192

Ponsonby, William [publishing house]....DLB-170

Pontiggia, Giuseppe 1934-..........DLB-196

Pony Stories..........DLB-160

Poole, Ernest 1880-1950..........DLB-9

Poole, Sophia 1804-1891..........DLB-166

Poore, Benjamin Perley 1820-1887..........DLB-23

Popa, Vasko 1922-1991....DLB-181; CDWLB-4

Pope, Abbie Hanscom 1858-1894..........DLB-140

Pope, Alexander 1688-1744......DLB-95, 101, 213; CDBLB-2

Popov, Mikhail Ivanovich 1742-circa 1790..........DLB-150

Popović, Aleksandar 1929-1996..........DLB-181

Popular Library..........DLB-46

Porete, Marguerite ?-1310..........DLB-208

Porlock, Martin (see MacDonald, Philip)

Porpoise Press..........DLB-112

Porta, Antonio 1935-1989..........DLB-128

Porter, Anna Maria 1780-1832.....DLB-116, 159

Porter, David 1780-1843..........DLB-183

Porter, Eleanor H. 1868-1920..........DLB-9

Porter, Gene Stratton (see Stratton-Porter, Gene)

Porter, Hal 1911-1984..........DLB-260

Porter, Henry ?-?..........DLB-62

Porter, Jane 1776-1850..........DLB-116, 159

Porter, Katherine Anne 1890-1980......DLB-4, 9, 102; Y-80; DS-12; CDALB-7

Porter, Peter 1929-..........DLB-40

Porter, William Sydney 1862-1910..........DLB-12, 78, 79; CDALB-3

Porter, William T. 1809-1858.....DLB-3, 43, 250

Porter and Coates..........DLB-49

Portillo Trambley, Estela 1927-1998.....DLB-209

Portis, Charles 1933-..........DLB-6

Posey, Alexander 1873-1908..........DLB-175

Postans, Marianne circa 1810-1865.....DLB-166

Postl, Carl (see Sealsfield, Carl)

Poston, Ted 1906-1974..........DLB-51

Potekhin, Aleksei Antipovich 1829-1908.....DLB-238

Potok, Chaim 1929-..........DLB-28, 152

A Conversation with Chaim Potok..........Y-84

Potter, Beatrix 1866-1943..........DLB-141

Potter, David M. 1910-1971..........DLB-17

Potter, Dennis 1935-1994..........DLB-233

The Harry Potter Phenomenon..........Y-99

Potter, John E., and Company..........DLB-49

Pottle, Frederick A. 1897-1987.....DLB-103; Y-87

Poulin, Jacques 1937-..........DLB-60

Pound, Ezra 1885-1972..........DLB-4, 45, 63; DS-15; CDALB-4

Poverman, C. E. 1944-..........DLB-234

Povich, Shirley 1905-1998..........DLB-171

Powell, Anthony 1905-2000...DLB-15; CDBLB-7

The Anthony Powell Society: Powell and the First Biennial Conference..........Y-01

Dawn Powell, Where Have You Been All Our Lives?..........Y-97

Powell, John Wesley 1834-1902..........DLB-186

Powell, Padgett 1952-..........DLB-234

Powers, J. F. 1917-1999..........DLB-130

Powers, Jimmy 1903-1995..........DLB-241

Pownall, David 1938-..........DLB-14

Powys, John Cowper 1872-1963.....DLB-15, 255

Powys, Llewelyn 1884-1939..........DLB-98

Powys, T. F. 1875-1953..........DLB-36, 162

Poynter, Nelson 1903-1978..........DLB-127

The Practice of Biography: An Interview with Stanley Weintraub..........Y-82

The Practice of Biography II: An Interview with B. L. Reid..........Y-83

The Practice of Biography III: An Interview with Humphrey Carpenter..........Y-84

The Practice of Biography IV: An Interview with William Manchester..........Y-85

The Practice of Biography VI: An Interview with David Herbert Donald..........Y-87

The Practice of Biography VII: An Interview with John Caldwell Guilds..........Y-92

The Practice of Biography VIII: An Interview with Joan Mellen..........Y-94

The Practice of Biography IX: An Interview with Michael Reynolds..........Y-95

Prados, Emilio 1899-1962..........DLB-134

Praed, Mrs. Caroline (see Praed, Rosa)

Praed, Rosa (Mrs. Caroline Praed) 1851-1935..........DLB-230

Praed, Winthrop Mackworth 1802-1839..DLB-96

Praeger Publishers..........DLB-46

Praetorius, Johannes 1630-1680..........DLB-168

Pratolini, Vasco 1913-1991..........DLB-177

Pratt, E. J. 1882-1964..........DLB-92

Pratt, Samuel Jackson 1749-1814..........DLB-39

Preciado Martin, Patricia 1939-..........DLB-209

Preface to The History of Romances (1715), by Pierre Daniel Huet [excerpts]..........DLB-39

Préfontaine, Yves 1937-..........DLB-53

Prelutsky, Jack 1940-..........DLB-61

Premisses, by Michael Hamburger..........DLB-66

Prentice, George D. 1802-1870..........DLB-43

Prentice-Hall..........DLB-46

Prescott, Orville 1906-1996..........Y-96

Prescott, William Hickling 1796-1859..........DLB-1, 30, 59, 235

The Present State of the English Novel (1892), by George Saintsbury..........DLB-18

Prešeren, France 1800-1849..........DLB-147; CDWLB-4

Preston, Margaret Junkin 1820-1897..........DLB-239, 248

Preston, May Wilson 1873-1949..........DLB-188

Preston, Thomas 1537-1598..........DLB-62

Prévert, Jacques 1900-1977 . . . . .DLB-258

Prichard, Katharine Susannah
    1883-1969 . . . . .DLB-260

Price, Reynolds 1933- DLB-2, 218

Price, Richard 1723-1791 . . . . .DLB-158

Price, Richard 1949- Y-81

Prideaux, John 1578-1650 . . . . .DLB-236

Priest, Christopher 1943- DLB-14, 207

Priestley, J. B. 1894-1984
    . . . DLB-10, 34, 77, 100, 139; Y-84; CDBLB-6

Priestley, Joseph 1733-1804 . . . . .DLB-252

Primary Bibliography: A Retrospective Y-95

Prime, Benjamin Young 1733-1791 . . . . . . .DLB-31

Primrose, Diana floruit circa 1630 . . . . . . .DLB-126

Prince, F. T. 1912- DLB-20

Prince, Nancy Gardner 1799-? DLB-239

Prince, Thomas 1687-1758 . . . . .DLB-24, 140

Pringle, Thomas 1789-1834 . . . . .DLB-225

Printz, Wolfgang Casper 1641-1717 . . . . .DLB-168

Prior, Matthew 1664-1721 . . . . .DLB-95

Prisco, Michele 1920- DLB-177

Pritchard, William H. 1932- DLB-111

Pritchett, V. S. 1900-1997 . . . . .DLB-15, 139

Probyn, May 1856 or 1857-1909 . . . . .DLB-199

Procter, Adelaide Anne 1825-1864 . . .DLB-32, 199

Procter, Bryan Waller 1787-1874 . . . . .DLB-96, 144

Proctor, Robert 1868-1903 . . . . .DLB-184

*Producing Dear Bunny, Dear Volodya: The Friendship
    and the Feud* Y-97

The Profession of Authorship:
    Scribblers for Bread. Y-89

Prokopovich, Feofan 1681?-1736 . . . . . . .DLB-150

Prokosch, Frederic 1906-1989 . . . . .DLB-48

The Proletarian Novel DLB-9

Pronzini, Bill 1943- DLB-226

Propertius circa 50 B.C.-post 16 B.C.
    . . . . DLB-211; CDWLB-1

Propper, Dan 1937- DLB-16

Prose, Francine 1947- DLB-234

Protagoras circa 490 B.C.-420 B.C. DLB-176

Proud, Robert 1728-1813 . . . . .DLB-30

Proust, Marcel 1871-1922 . . . . .DLB-65

Prynne, J. H. 1936- DLB-40

Przybyszewski, Stanislaw 1868-1927 . . . . . .DLB-66

Pseudo-Dionysius the Areopagite floruit
    circa 500 . . . . .DLB-115

Public Domain and the Violation of Texts Y-97

The Public Lending Right in America Statement by
    Sen. Charles McC. Mathias, Jr. PLR and the
    Meaning of Literary Property Statements on
    PLR by American Writers Y-83

The Public Lending Right in the United Kingdom
    Public Lending Right: The First Year in the
    United Kingdom Y-83

The Publication of English
    Renaissance Plays DLB-62

Publications and Social Movements
    [Transcendentalism] DLB-1

Publishers and Agents: The Columbia
    Connection Y-87

Publishing Fiction at LSU Press. Y-87

The Publishing Industry in 1998:
    Sturm-und-drang.com Y-98

The Publishing Industry in 1999. . . . . .Y-99

Pückler-Muskau, Hermann von
    1785-1871 . . . . .DLB-133

Pufendorf, Samuel von 1632-1694 . . . . . . .DLB-168

Pugh, Edwin William 1874-1930 . . . . .DLB-135

Pugin, A. Welby 1812-1852 . . . . .DLB-55

Puig, Manuel 1932-1990 . . . . DLB-113; CDWLB-3

Pulitzer, Joseph 1847-1911 . . . . .DLB-23

Pulitzer, Joseph, Jr. 1885-1955 . . . . .DLB-29

Pulitzer Prizes for the Novel,
    1917-1945 . . . . .DLB-9

Pulliam, Eugene 1889-1975 . . . . .DLB-127

Purchas, Samuel 1577?-1626 . . . . .DLB-151

Purdy, Al 1918-2000 . . . . .DLB-88

Purdy, James 1923- DLB-2, 218

Purdy, Ken W. 1913-1972 . . . . .DLB-137

Pusey, Edward Bouverie 1800-1882 . . . . . .DLB-55

Pushkin, Aleksandr Sergeevich
    1799-1837 . . . . .DLB-205

Pushkin, Vasilii L'vovich
    1766-1830 . . . . .DLB-205

Putnam, George Palmer
    1814-1872 . . . . DLB-3, 79, 250, 254

G. P. Putnam [publishing house] DLB-254

G. P. Putnam's Sons [U.K.] DLB-106

G. P. Putnam's Sons [U.S.] DLB-49

A Publisher's Archives: G. P. Putnam Y-92

Putnam, Samuel 1892-1950 . . . . .DLB-4

Puzo, Mario 1920-1999 . . . . .DLB-6

Pyle, Ernie 1900-1945 . . . . .DLB-29

Pyle, Howard
    1853-1911 . . . . .DLB-42, 188; DS-13

Pym, Barbara 1913-1980 . . . . . . DLB-14, 207; Y-87

Pynchon, Thomas 1937- DLB-2, 173

Pyramid Books DLB-46

Pyrnelle, Louise-Clarke 1850-1907 . . . . . . .DLB-42

Pythagoras circa 570 B.C.-? DLB-176

Q

Quad, M. (see Lewis, Charles B.)

Quaritch, Bernard 1819-1899 . . . . .DLB-184

Quarles, Francis 1592-1644 . . . . .DLB-126

The Quarterly Review 1809-1967 . . . . .DLB-110

Quasimodo, Salvatore 1901-1968 . . . . .DLB-114

Queen, Ellery (see Dannay, Frederic, and
    Manfred B. Lee)

Queen, Frank 1822-1882 . . . . .DLB-241

The Queen City Publishing House DLB-49

Queneau, Raymond 1903-1976 . . . . . .DLB-72, 258

Quennell, Sir Peter 1905-1993 . . . . . .DLB-155, 195

Quesnel, Joseph 1746-1809 . . . . .DLB-99

The Question of American Copyright
    in the Nineteenth Century
    Preface, by George Haven Putnam
    The Evolution of Copyright, by
      Brander Matthews
    Summary of Copyright Legislation in
      the United States, by R. R. Bowker
    Analysis of the Provisions of the
      Copyright Law of 1891, by
      George Haven Putnam
    The Contest for International Copyright,
      by George Haven Putnam
    Cheap Books and Good Books,
      by Brander Matthews DLB-49

Quiller-Couch, Sir Arthur Thomas
    1863-1944 . . . . .DLB-135, 153, 190

Quin, Ann 1936-1973 . . . . .DLB-14, 231

Quincy, Samuel, of Georgia ? - ? DLB-31

Quincy, Samuel, of Massachusetts
    1734-1789 . . . . .DLB-31

Quinn, Anthony 1915- DLB-122

The Quinn Draft of James Joyce's
    Circe Manuscript Y-00

Quinn, John 1870-1924 . . . . .DLB-187

Quiñónez, Naomi 1951- DLB-209

Quintana, Leroy V. 1944- DLB-82

Quintana, Miguel de 1671-1748
    A Forerunner of Chicano Literature . .DLB-122

Quintillian
    circa A.D. 40-circa A.D. 96 . . . . .DLB-211

Quintus Curtius Rufus fl. A.D. 35 . . . . . . .DLB-211

Quist, Harlin, Books DLB-46

Quoirez, Françoise (see Sagan, Françoise)

R

R-va, Zeneida (see Gan, Elena Andreevna)

Raabe, Wilhelm 1831-1910 . . . . .DLB-129

Raban, Jonathan 1942- DLB-204

Rabe, David 1940- DLB-7, 228

Raboni, Giovanni 1932- DLB-128

Rachilde 1860-1953 . . . . .DLB-123, 192

Racin, Kočo 1908-1943 . . . . .DLB-147

Rackham, Arthur 1867-1939 . . . . .DLB-141

Radauskas, Henrikas
    1910-1970 . . . . .DLB-220; CDWLB-4

Radcliffe, Ann 1764-1823 . . . . .DLB-39, 178

Raddall, Thomas 1903-1994 . . . . .DLB-68

Radford, Dollie 1858-1920 . . . . .DLB-240

Radichkov, Yordan 1929- DLB-181

Radiguet, Raymond 1903-1923 . . . . .DLB-65

Radishchev, Aleksandr Nikolaevich
    1749-1802 . . . . .DLB-150

Radnóti, Miklós
    1909-1944 . . . . .DLB-215; CDWLB-4

Radványi, Netty Reiling (see Seghers, Anna)

Rahv, Philip 1908-1973 . . . . .DLB-137

Raich, Semen Egorovich 1792-1855 . . . . . .DLB-205

Raičković, Stevan 1928- DLB-181

Raimund, Ferdinand Jakob 1790-1836 . . . . .DLB-90

Raine, Craig 1944- DLB-40

Raine, Kathleen 1908- DLB-20

Cumulative Index

Rainis, Jānis 1865-1929 ..... DLB-220; CDWLB-4
Rainolde, Richard circa 1530-1606 .... DLB-136, 236
Rakić, Milan 1876-1938 ..... DLB-147; CDWLB-4
Rakosi, Carl 1903- DLB-193
Ralegh, Sir Walter 1554?-1618 .... DLB-172; CDBLB-1
Ralin, Radoy 1923- DLB-181
Ralph, Julian 1853-1903 .... DLB-23
Ramat, Silvio 1939- DLB-128
Rambler, no. 4 (1750), by Samuel Johnson [excerpt] DLB-39
Ramée, Marie Louise de la (see Ouida)
Ramírez, Sergío 1942- DLB-145
Ramke, Bin 1947- DLB-120
Ramler, Karl Wilhelm 1725-1798 .... DLB-97
Ramon Ribeyro, Julio 1929- DLB-145
Ramos, Manuel 1948- DLB-209
Ramous, Mario 1924- DLB-128
Rampersad, Arnold 1941- DLB-111
Ramsay, Allan 1684 or 1685-1758 .... DLB-95
Ramsay, David 1749-1815 .... DLB-30
Ramsay, Martha Laurens 1759-1811 .... DLB-200
Ranck, Katherine Quintana 1942- DLB-122
Rand, Avery and Company DLB-49
Rand, Ayn 1905-1982 .... DLB-227; CDALB-7
Rand McNally and Company DLB-49
Randall, David Anton 1905-1975 .... DLB-140
Randall, Dudley 1914- DLB-41
Randall, Henry S. 1811-1876 .... DLB-30
Randall, James G. 1881-1953 .... DLB-17
The Randall Jarrell Symposium: A Small Collection of Randall Jarrells Excerpts From Papers Delivered at the Randall Jarrel Symposium Y-86
Randolph, A. Philip 1889-1979 .... DLB-91
Randolph, Anson D. F. [publishing house] DLB-49
Randolph, Thomas 1605-1635 ...... DLB-58, 126
Random House. DLB-46
Ranlet, Henry [publishing house] DLB-49
Ransom, Harry 1908-1976 .... DLB-187
Ransom, John Crowe 1888-1974 .... DLB-45, 63; CDALB-7
Ransome, Arthur 1884-1967 .... DLB-160
Raphael, Frederic 1931- DLB-14
Raphaelson, Samson 1896-1983 .... DLB-44
Rashi circa 1040-1105 .... DLB-208
Raskin, Ellen 1928-1984 .... DLB-52
Rastell, John 1475?-1536 .... DLB-136, 170
Rattigan, Terence 1911-1977 .... DLB-13; CDBLB-7
Rawlings, Marjorie Kinnan 1896-1953 .... DLB-9, 22, 102; DS-17; CDALB-7
Rawlinson, Richard 1690-1755 .... DLB-213
Rawlinson, Thomas 1681-1725 .... DLB-213
Raworth, Tom 1938- DLB-40

Ray, David 1932- DLB-5
Ray, Gordon Norton 1915-1986 ... DLB-103, 140
Ray, Henrietta Cordelia 1849-1916 ...... DLB-50
Raymond, Ernest 1888-1974 .... DLB-191
Raymond, Henry J. 1820-1869 .... DLB-43, 79
Michael M. Rea and the Rea Award for the Short Story Y-97
Reach, Angus 1821-1856 .... DLB-70
Read, Herbert 1893-1968 .... DLB-20, 149
Read, Martha Meredith DLB-200
Read, Opie 1852-1939 .... DLB-23
Read, Piers Paul 1941- DLB-14
Reade, Charles 1814-1884 .... DLB-21
Reader's Digest Condensed Books DLB-46
Readers Ulysses Symposium Y-97
Reading, Peter 1946- DLB-40
Reading Series in New York City Y-96
The Reality of One Woman's Dream: The de Grummond Children's Literature Collection Y-99
Reaney, James 1926- DLB-68
Rebhun, Paul 1500?-1546 .... DLB-179
Rèbora, Clemente 1885-1957 .... DLB-114
Rebreanu, Liviu 1885-1944 .... DLB-220
Rechy, John 1934- DLB-122; Y-82
The Recovery of Literature: Criticism in the 1990s: A Symposium Y-91
Redding, J. Saunders 1906-1988 ...... DLB-63, 76
Redfield, J. S. [publishing house] DLB-49
Redgrove, Peter 1932- DLB-40
Redmon, Anne 1943- Y-86
Redmond, Eugene B. 1937- DLB-41
Redpath, James [publishing house] DLB-49
Reed, Henry 1808-1854 .... DLB-59
Reed, Henry 1914- DLB-27
Reed, Ishmael 1938- DLB-2, 5, 33, 169, 227; DS-8
Reed, Rex 1938- DLB-185
Reed, Sampson 1800-1880 .... DLB-1, 235
Reed, Talbot Baines 1852-1893 .... DLB-141
Reedy, William Marion 1862-1920 ...... DLB-91
Reese, Lizette Woodworth 1856-1935 .... DLB-54
Reese, Thomas 1742-1796 .... DLB-37
Reeve, Clara 1729-1807 .... DLB-39
Preface to *The Old English Baron* (1778) DLB-39
The Progress of Romance (1785) [excerpt] DLB-39
Reeves, James 1909-1978 .... DLB-161
Reeves, John 1926- DLB-88
Reeves-Stevens, Garfield 1953- DLB-251
"Reflections: After a Tornado," by Judson Jerome DLB-105
Regnery, Henry, Company DLB-46
Rehberg, Hans 1901-1963 .... DLB-124
Rehfisch, Hans José 1891-1960 .... DLB-124
Reich, Ebbe Kløvedal 1940- DLB-214
Reid, Alastair 1926- DLB-27

Reid, B. L. 1918-1990 .... DLB-111; Y-83
The Practice of Biography II: An Interview with B. L. Reid Y-83
Reid, Christopher 1949- DLB-40
Reid, Forrest 1875-1947 .... DLB-153
Reid, Helen Rogers 1882-1970 .... DLB-29
Reid, James ?-? DLB-31
Reid, Mayne 1818-1883 .... DLB-21, 163
Reid, Thomas 1710-1796 .... DLB-31, 252
Reid, V. S. (Vic) 1913-1987 .... DLB-125
Reid, Whitelaw 1837-1912 .... DLB-23
Reilly and Lee Publishing Company DLB-46
Reimann, Brigitte 1933-1973 .... DLB-75
Reinmar der Alte circa 1165-circa 1205 .... DLB-138
Reinmar von Zweter circa 1200-circa 1250 .... DLB-138
Reisch, Walter 1903-1983 .... DLB-44
Reizei Family DLB-203
Remarks at the Opening of "The Biographical Part of Literature" Exhibition, by William R. Cagle Y-98
Remarque, Erich Maria 1898-1970 .... DLB-56; CDWLB-2
Remington, Frederic 1861-1909 .... DLB-12, 186, 188
Reminiscences, by Charles Scribner Jr. DS-17
Renaud, Jacques 1943- DLB-60
Renault, Mary 1905-1983 .... Y-83
Rendell, Ruth 1930- DLB-87
Rensselaer, Maria van Cortlandt van 1645-1689 .... DLB-200
Repplier, Agnes 1855-1950 .... DLB-221
Representative Men and Women: A Historical Perspective on the British Novel, 1930-1960 .... DLB-15
Research in the American Antiquarian Book Trade Y-97
Reshetnikov, Fedor Mikhailovich 1841-1871 .... DLB-238
Rettenbacher, Simon 1634-1706 .... DLB-168
Reuchlin, Johannes 1455-1522 .... DLB-179
Reuter, Christian 1665-after 1712 .... DLB-168
Revell, Fleming H., Company DLB-49
Reverdy, Pierre 1889-1960 .... DLB-258
Reuter, Fritz 1810-1874 .... DLB-129
Reuter, Gabriele 1859-1941 .... DLB-66
Reventlow, Franziska Gräfin zu 1871-1918 .... DLB-66
Review of Nicholson Baker's *Double Fold: Libraries and the Assault on Paper* Y-00
Review of Reviews Office DLB-112
Review of [Samuel Richardson's] *Clarissa* (1748), by Henry Fielding DLB-39
The Revolt (1937), by Mary Colum [excerpts] DLB-36
Rexroth, Kenneth 1905-1982 .... DLB-16, 48, 165, 212; Y-82; CDALB-1
Rey, H. A. 1898-1977 .... DLB-22
Reynal and Hitchcock DLB-46

Reynolds, G. W. M. 1814-1879 ....DLB-21
Reynolds, John Hamilton 1794-1852 ......DLB-96
Reynolds, Sir Joshua 1723-1792 ....DLB-104
Reynolds, Mack 1917- DLB-8
A Literary Archaelogist Digs On: A Brief
  Interview with Michael Reynolds by
  Michael Rogers Y-99
Reznikoff, Charles 1894-1976 ....DLB-28, 45
Rhett, Robert Barnwell 1800-1876........DLB-43
Rhode, John 1884-1964 ....DLB-77
Rhodes, Eugene Manlove 1869-1934 ....DLB-256
Rhodes, James Ford 1848-1927 ....DLB-47
Rhodes, Richard 1937- ,,,,,,,,,,,,DLB-185
Rhys, Jean 1890-1979
  .... DLB-36, 117, 162; CDBLB-7; CDWLB-3
Ricardo, David 1772-1823 .... DLB-107, 158
Ricardou, Jean 1932- DLB-83
Rice, Elmer 1892-1967................DLB-4, 7
Rice, Grantland 1880-1954 .... DLB-29, 171
Rich, Adrienne 1929- DLB-5, 67; CDALB-7
Richard de Fournival
  1201-1259 or 1260 ....DLB-208
Richard, Mark 1955- DLB-234
Richards, David Adams 1950- ...DLB-53
Richards, George circa 1760-1814 ....DLB-37
Richards, Grant [publishing house] DLB-112
Richards, I. A. 1893-1979.................DLB-27
Richards, Laura E. 1850-1943 ....DLB-42
Richards, William Carey 1818-1892 ......DLB-73
Richardson, Charles F. 1851-1913 ....DLB-71
Richardson, Dorothy M. 1873-1957 ......DLB-36
Richardson, Henry Handel
  (Ethel Florence Lindesay
  Robertson) 1870-1946 .... DLB-197, 230
Richardson, Jack 1935- DLB-7
Richardson, John 1796-1852 ....DLB-99
Richardson, Samuel
  1689-1761 ....DLB-39, 154; CDBLB-2
Introductory Letters from the Second
  Edition of Pamela (1741)..............DLB-39
Postscript to [the Third Edition of]
  Clarissa (1751) DLB-39
Preface to the First Edition of
  Pamela (1740) DLB-39
Preface to the Third Edition of
  Clarissa (1751) [excerpt] DLB-39
Preface to Volume 1 of Clarissa (1747) DLB-39
Preface to Volume 3 of Clarissa (1748) DLB-39
Richardson, Willis 1889-1977 ....DLB-51
Riche, Barnabe 1542-1617 ....DLB-136
Richepin, Jean 1849-1926 ....DLB-192
Richler, Mordecai 1931- DLB-53
Richter, Conrad 1890-1968 ....DLB-9, 212
Richter, Hans Werner 1908- DLB-69
Richter, Johann Paul Friedrich
  1763-1825 ....DLB-94; CDWLB-2
Rickerby, Joseph [publishing house] DLB-106
Rickword, Edgell 1898-1982 ....DLB-20

Riddell, Charlotte 1832-1906...........DLB-156
Riddell, John (see Ford, Corey)
Ridge, John Rollin 1827-1867..........DLB-175
Ridge, Lola 1873-1941................DLB-54
Ridge, William Pett 1859-1930 ....DLB-135
Riding, Laura (see Jackson, Laura Riding)
Ridler, Anne 1912- DLB-27
Ridruego, Dionisio 1912-1975 ....DLB-108
Riel, Louis 1844-1885 ....DLB-99
Riemer, Johannes 1648-1714 ....DLB-168
Rifbjerg, Klaus 1931- DLB-214
Riffaterre, Michael 1924- DLB-67
Riggs, Lynn 1899-1954 ....DLB-175
Riis, Jacob 1849-1914..................DLB-23
Riker, John C. [publishing house] DLB-49
Riley, James 1777-1840.................DLB-183
Riley, John 1938-1978 ....DLB-40
Rilke, Rainer Maria
  1875-1926 ....DLB-81; CDWLB-2
Rimanelli, Giose 1926- DLB-177
Rimbaud, Jean-Nicolas-Arthur
  1854-1891 ....DLB-217
Rinehart and Company................DLB-46
Ringuet 1895-1960.....................DLB-68
Ringwood, Gwen Pharis 1910-1984 ......DLB-88
Rinser, Luise 1911- DLB-69
Ríos, Alberto 1952- DLB-122
Ríos, Isabella 1948- DLB-82
Ripley, Arthur 1895-1961 ....DLB-44
Ripley, George 1802-1880..... DLB-1, 64, 73, 235
The Rising Glory of America:
  Three Poems...................DLB-37
The Rising Glory of America:
  Written in 1771 (1786),
  by Hugh Henry Brackenridge and
  Philip Freneau DLB-37
Riskin, Robert 1897-1955................DLB-26
Risse, Heinz 1898- DLB-69
Rist, Johann 1607-1667 ....DLB-164
Ristikivi, Karl 1912-1977 ....DLB-220
Ritchie, Anna Mowatt 1819-1870 .....DLB-3, 250
Ritchie, Anne Thackeray 1837-1919 ......DLB-18
Ritchie, Thomas 1778-1854 ....DLB-43
Rites of Passage [on William Saroyan] Y-83
The Ritz Paris Hemingway Award Y-85
Rivard, Adjutor 1868-1945 ....DLB-92
Rive, Richard 1931-1989..........DLB-125, 225
Rivera, José 1955- DLB-249
Rivera, Marina 1942- DLB-122
Rivera, Tomás 1935-1984 ....DLB-82
Rivers, Conrad Kent 1933-1968 ....DLB-41
Riverside Press.....................DLB-49
Rivington, Charles [publishing house]....DLB-154
Rivington, James circa 1724-1802 ....DLB-43
Rivkin, Allen 1903-1990 ....DLB-26
Roa Bastos, Augusto 1917- DLB-113

Robbe-Grillet, Alain 1922- DLB-83
Robbins, Tom 1936- Y-80
Roberts, Charles G. D. 1860-1943 ....DLB-92
Roberts, Dorothy 1906-1993............DLB-88
Roberts, Elizabeth Madox
  1881-1941 ....DLB-9, 54, 102
Roberts, James [publishing house] DLB-154
Roberts, Kenneth 1885-1957 ....DLB-9
Roberts, Michèle 1949- DLB-231
Roberts, Ursula Wyllie (see Miles, Susan)
Roberts, William 1767-1849.............DLB-142
Roberts Brothers DLB-49
Robertson, A. M., and Company DLB-49
Robertson, Ethel Florence Lindesay
  (see Richardson, Henry Handel)
Robertson, William 1721-1793..........DLB-104
Robins, Elizabeth 1862-1952 ....DLB-197
Robinson, A. Mary F. (Madame James
  Darmesteter, Madame Mary
  Duclaux) 1857-1944 ....DLB-240
Robinson, Casey 1903-1979 ....DLB-44
Robinson, Edwin Arlington
  1869-1935.............DLB-54; CDALB-3
Robinson, Henry Crabb 1775-1867 ......DLB-107
Robinson, James Harvey 1863-1936 ......DLB-47
Robinson, Lennox 1886-1958 ....DLB-10
Robinson, Mabel Louise 1874-1962.......DLB-22
Robinson, Marilynne 1943- DLB-206
Robinson, Mary 1758-1800 ....DLB-158
Robinson, Richard circa 1545-1607 .....DLB-167
Robinson, Therese 1797-1870........DLB-59, 133
Robison, Mary 1949- DLB-130
Roblès, Emmanuel 1914-1995 ....DLB-83
Roccatagliata Ceccardi, Ceccardo
  1871-1919 ....DLB-114
Roche, Billy 1949- DLB-233
Rochester, John Wilmot, Earl of
  1647-1680 ....DLB-131
Rochon, Esther 1948- DLB-251
Rock, Howard 1911-1976 ....DLB-127
Rockwell, Norman Perceval 1894-1978...DLB-188
Rodgers, Carolyn M. 1945- DLB-41
Rodgers, W. R. 1909-1969 ....DLB-20
Rodney, Lester 1911- DLB-241
Rodríguez, Claudio 1934-1999 ....DLB-134
Rodríguez, Joe D. 1943- DLB-209
Rodríguez, Luis J. 1954- DLB-209
Rodriguez, Richard 1944- DLB-82, 256
Rodríguez Julia, Edgardo 1946- DLB-145
Roe, E. P. 1838-1888 ....DLB-202
Roethke, Theodore
  1908-1963...........DLB-5, 206; CDALB-1
Rogers, Jane 1952- DLB-194
Rogers, Pattiann 1940- DLB-105
Rogers, Samuel 1763-1855..............DLB-93
Rogers, Will 1879-1935 ....DLB-11
Rohmer, Sax 1883-1959 ....DLB-70

Roiphe, Anne 1935- Y-80	Rostenberg, Leona 1908- DLB-140	Rukeyser, Muriel 1913-1980 ....DLB-48
Rojas, Arnold R. 1896-1988 ....DLB-82	Rostopchina, Evdokiia Petrovna 1811-1858 ....DLB-205	Rule, Jane 1931- DLB-60
Rolfe, Frederick William 1860-1913...................DLB-34, 156	Rostovsky, Dimitrii 1651-1709.........DLB-150	Rulfo, Juan 1918-1986 ......DLB-113; CDWLB-3
Rolland, Romain 1866-1944...........DLB-65	Rota, Bertram 1903-1966 ....DLB-201	Rumaker, Michael 1932- DLB-16
Rolle, Richard circa 1290-1300 - 1340 ...DLB-146	Bertram Rota and His Bookshop.........Y-91	Rumens, Carol 1944- DLB-40
Rölvaag, O. E. 1876-1931............DLB-9, 212	Roth, Gerhard 1942- DLB-85, 124	Rummo, Paul-Eerik 1942- DLB-232
Romains, Jules 1885-1972.............DLB-65	Roth, Henry 1906?-1995 ....DLB-28	Runyon, Damon 1880-1946......DLB-11, 86, 171
Roman, A., and Company DLB-49	Roth, Joseph 1894-1939 ....DLB-85	Ruodlieb circa 1050-1075 ....DLB-148
Roman de la Rose: Guillaume de Lorris 1200 to 1205-circa 1230, Jean de Meun 1235-1240-circa 1305............DLB-208	Roth, Philip 1933- DLB-2, 28, 173; Y-82; CDALB-6	Rush, Benjamin 1746-1813............DLB-37
	Rothenberg, Jerome 1931- DLB-5, 193	Rush, Rebecca 1779-? DLB-200
	Rothschild Family..................DLB-184	Rushdie, Salman 1947- DLB-194
Romano, Lalla 1906- DLB-177	Rotimi, Ola 1938- DLB-125	Rusk, Ralph L. 1888-1962 ....DLB-103
Romano, Octavio 1923- DLB-122	Routhier, Adolphe-Basile 1839-1920 .....DLB-99	Ruskin, John 1819-1900 ..... DLB-55, 163, 190; CDBLB-4
Romero, Leo 1950- DLB-122	Routier, Simone 1901-1987 ....DLB-88	Russ, Joanna 1937- DLB-8
Romero, Lin 1947- DLB-122	Routledge, George, and Sons DLB-106	Russell, B. B., and Company DLB-49
Romero, Orlando 1945- DLB-82	Roversi, Roberto 1923- DLB-128	Russell, Benjamin 1761-1845 ....DLB-43
Rook, Clarence 1863-1915 ....DLB-135	Rowe, Elizabeth Singer 1674-1737 ....DLB-39, 95	Russell, Bertrand 1872-1970 ....DLB-100
Roosevelt, Theodore 1858-1919......DLB-47, 186	Rowe, Nicholas 1674-1718 ....DLB-84	Russell, Charles Edward 1860-1941......DLB-25
Root, Waverley 1903-1982..............DLB-4	Rowlands, Samuel circa 1570-1630......DLB-121	Russell, Charles M. 1864-1926..........DLB-188
Root, William Pitt 1941- DLB-120	Rowlandson, Mary circa 1637-circa 1711..........DLB-24, 200	Russell, Eric Frank 1905-1978 ....DLB-255
Roquebrune, Robert de 1889-1978.......DLB-68		Russell, Fred 1906- DLB-241
Rorty, Richard 1931- DLB-246	Rowley, William circa 1585-1626........DLB-58	Russell, George William (see AE)
Rosa, João Guimarāres 1908-1967 ......DLB-113	Rowse, A. L. 1903-1997 ....DLB-155	Russell, Countess Mary Annette Beauchamp (see Arnim, Elizabeth von)
Rosales, Luis 1910-1992 ....DLB-134	Rowson, Susanna Haswell circa 1762-1824 ....DLB-37, 200	
Roscoe, William 1753-1831 ....DLB-163		Russell, R. H., and Son DLB-49
Danis Rose and the Rendering of *Ulysses* Y-97	Roy, Camille 1870-1943 ....DLB-92	Russell, Willy 1947- DLB-233
Rose, Reginald 1920- DLB-26	Roy, Gabrielle 1909-1983...............DLB-68	Rutebeuf flourished 1249-1277.........DLB-208
Rose, Wendy 1948- DLB-175	Roy, Jules 1907- DLB-83	Rutherford, Mark 1831-1913 ....DLB-18
Rosegger, Peter 1843-1918 ....DLB-129	The G. Ross Roy Scottish Poetry Collection at the University of South Carolina......Y-89	Ruxton, George Frederick 1821-1848 ....DLB-186
Rosei, Peter 1946- DLB-85	The Royal Court Theatre and the English Stage Company DLB-13	Ryan, Michael 1946- Y-82
Rosen, Norma 1925- DLB-28		Ryan, Oscar 1904- DLB-68
Rosenbach, A. S. W. 1876-1952 ....DLB-140	The Royal Court Theatre and the New Drama DLB-10	Ryder, Jack 1871-1936 ....DLB-241
Rosenbaum, Ron 1946- DLB-185	The Royal Shakespeare Company at the Swan........................Y-88	Ryga, George 1932- DLB-60
Rosenberg, Isaac 1890-1918 ....DLB-20, 216		Rylands, Enriqueta Augustina Tennant 1843-1908 ....DLB-184
Rosenfeld, Isaac 1918-1956 ....DLB-28	Royall, Anne Newport 1769-1854 ...DLB-43, 248	
Rosenthal, Harold 1914-1999..........DLB-241	The Roycroft Printing Shop DLB-49	Rylands, John 1801-1888 ....DLB-184
Jimmy, Red, and Others: Harold Rosenthal Remembers the Stars of the Press Box ...Y-01	Royde-Smith, Naomi 1875-1964........DLB-191	Ryleev, Kondratii Fedorovich 1795-1826......................DLB-205
	Royster, Vermont 1914- DLB-127	
Rosenthal, M. L. 1917-1996 ....DLB-5	Royston, Richard [publishing house] DLB-170	Rymer, Thomas 1643?-1713..........DLB-101
Rosenwald, Lessing J. 1891-1979 ....DLB-187	Różewicz, Tadeusz 1921- DLB-232	Ryskind, Morrie 1895-1985 ....DLB-26
Ross, Alexander 1591-1654 ....DLB-151	Ruark, Gibbons 1941- DLB-120	Rzhevsky, Aleksei Andreevich 1737-1804......................DLB-150
Ross, Harold 1892-1951..............DLB-137	Ruban, Vasilii Grigorevich 1742-1795 ...DLB-150	
Ross, Leonard Q. (see Rosten, Leo)	Rubens, Bernice 1928- DLB-14, 207	# S
Ross, Lillian 1927- DLB-185	Rudd and Carleton..................DLB-49	
Ross, Martin 1862-1915 ....DLB-135		The Saalfield Publishing Company DLB-46
Ross, Sinclair 1908-1996...............DLB-88	Rudd, Steele (Arthur Hoey Davis) DLB-230	Saba, Umberto 1883-1957 ....DLB-114
Ross, W. W. E. 1894-1966............DLB-88	Rudkin, David 1936- DLB-13	Sábato, Ernesto 1911- DLB-145; CDWLB-3
Rosselli, Amelia 1930-1996 ....DLB-128	Rudolf von Ems circa 1200-circa 1254...DLB-138	Saberhagen, Fred 1930- DLB-8
Rossen, Robert 1908-1966 ....DLB-26	Ruffin, Josephine St. Pierre 1842-1924 ....DLB-79	Sabin, Joseph 1821-1881..............DLB-187
Rossetti, Christina 1830-1894...DLB-35, 163, 240		Sacer, Gottfried Wilhelm 1635-1699 ....DLB-168
Rossetti, Dante Gabriel 1828-1882 ....DLB-35; CDBLB-4	Ruganda, John 1941- DLB-157	Sachs, Hans 1494-1576......DLB-179; CDWLB-2
	Ruggles, Henry Joseph 1813-1906 ......DLB-64	Sack, John 1930- DLB-185
Rossner, Judith 1935- DLB-6	Ruiz de Burton, María Amparo 1832-1895 ....DLB-209, 221	Sackler, Howard 1929-1982 ....DLB-7
Rostand, Edmond 1868-1918.........DLB-192		
Rosten, Leo 1908-1997...............DLB-11		Sackville, Lady Margaret 1881-1963 ....DLB-240

Sackville, Thomas 1536-1608 ....DLB-132
Sackville, Thomas 1536-1608
 and Norton, Thomas 1532-1584......DLB-62
Sackville-West, Edward 1901-1965 ......DLB-191
Sackville-West, V. 1892-1962 ....DLB-34, 195
Sadlier, D. and J., and Company.........DLB-49
Sadlier, Mary Anne 1820-1903 ....DLB-99
Sadoff, Ira 1945- DLB-120
Sadoveanu, Mihail 1880-1961 ....DLB-220
Sáenz, Benjamin Alire 1954- DLB-209
Saenz, Jaime 1921-1986 ....DLB-145
Safflu, John circa 1620-1710.............DLB-24
Sagan, Françoise 1935- DLB-83
Sage, Robert 1899-1962................DLB-4
Sagel, Jim 1947- DLB-82
Sagendorph, Robb Hansell 1900-1970....DLB-137
Sahagún, Carlos 1938- DLB-108
Sahkomaapii, Piitai (see Highwater, Jamake)
Sahl, Hans 1902- DLB-69
Said, Edward W. 1935- DLB-67
Saigyō 1118-1190....................DLB-203
Saiko, George 1892-1962...............DLB-85
St. Dominic's Press DLB-112
Saint-Exupéry, Antoine de 1900-1944 .....DLB-72
St. John, J. Allen 1872-1957 ....DLB-188
St. Johns, Adela Rogers 1894-1988 ....DLB-29
The St. John's College Robert Graves Trust .. Y-96
St. Martin's Press.....................DLB-46
St. Omer, Garth 1931 ....DLB-117
Saint Pierre, Michel de 1916-1987 ....DLB-83
Sainte-Beuve, Charles-Augustin
 1804-1869.....................DLB-217
Saints' Lives........................DLB-208
Saintsbury, George 1845-1933........DLB-57, 149
Saiokuken Sōchō 1448-1532 ....DLB-203
Saki (see Munro, H. H.)
Salaam, Kalamu ya 1947- DLB-38
Šalamun, Tomaž 1941- DLB-181; CDWLB-4
Salas, Floyd 1931- DLB-82
Sálaz-Marquez, Rubén 1935- DLB-122
Salemson, Harold J. 1910-1988 ....DLB-4
Salinas, Luis Omar 1937- DLB-82
Salinas, Pedro 1891-1951...............DLB-134
Salinger, J. D.
 1919- DLB-2, 102, 173; CDALB-1
Salkey, Andrew 1928- DLB-125
Sallust circa 86 B.C.-35 B.C.
 ....DLB-211; CDWLB-1
Salt, Waldo 1914- DLB-44
Salter, James 1925- DLB-130
Salter, Mary Jo 1954- DLB-120
Saltus, Edgar 1855-1921 ....DLB-202
Saltykov, Mikhail Evgrafovich
 1826-1889......................DLB-238
Salustri, Carlo Alberto (see Trilussa)

Salverson, Laura Goodman 1890-1970 ....DLB-92
Samain, Albert 1858-1900 ....DLB-217
Sampson, Richard Henry (see Hull, Richard)
Samuels, Ernest 1903-1996 ....DLB-111
Sanborn, Franklin Benjamin
 1831-1917....................DLB-1, 223
Sánchez, Luis Rafael 1936- DLB-145
Sánchez, Philomeno "Phil" 1917- DLB-122
Sánchez, Ricardo 1941-1995 ....DLB-82
Sánchez, Saúl 1943- DLB-209
Sanchez, Sonia 1934- DLB-41; DS-8
Sand, George 1804-1876 ....DLB-119, 192
Sandburg, Carl
 1878-1967 ....DLB-17, 54; CDALB-3
Sanders, Edward 1939- DLB-16, 244
Sandoz, Mari 1896-1966 ....DLB-9, 212
Sandwell, B. K. 1876-1954..............DLB-92
Sandy, Stephen 1934 ....DLB-165
Sandys, George 1578-1644............DLB-24, 121
Sangster, Charles 1822-1893 ....DLB-99
Sanguineti, Edoardo 1930- DLB-128
Sanjōnishi Sanetaka 1455-1537 ....DLB-203
Sansay, Leonora ?-after 1823..........DLB-200
Sansom, William 1912-1976.............DLB-139
Santayana, George
 1863-1952 ....DLB-54, 71, 246; DS-13
Santiago, Danny 1911-1988.............DLB-122
Santmyer, Helen Hooven 1895-1986........ Y-84
Sanvitale, Francesca 1928- DLB-196
Sapidus, Joannes 1490-1561...........DLB-179
Sapir, Edward 1884-1939 ....DLB-92
Sapper (see McNeile, Herman Cyril)
Sappho circa 620 B.C.-circa 550 B.C.
 ....DLB-176; CDWLB-1
Saramago, José 1922- Y-90
Sarban (John F. Wall) 1910-1989 .....DLB-255
Sardou, Victorien 1831-1908............DLB-192
Sarduy, Severo 1937- DLB-113
Sargent, Pamela 1948- DLB-8
Saro-Wiwa, Ken 1941- DLB-157
Saroyan, William
 1908-1981 ......DLB-7, 9, 86; Y-81; CDALB-7
Sarraute, Nathalie 1900-1999............DLB-83
Sarrazin, Albertine 1937-1967 ....DLB-83
Sarris, Greg 1952- DLB-175
Sarton, May 1912-1995 ....DLB-48; Y-81
Sartre, Jean-Paul 1905-1980............DLB-72
Sassoon, Siegfried
 1886-1967 ....DLB-20, 191; DS-18
Siegfried Loraine Sassoon:
 A Centenary Essay
 Tributes from Vivien F. Clarke and
 Michael Thorpe Y-86
Sata, Ineko 1904- DLB-180
Saturday Review Press DLB-46
Saunders, James 1925- DLB-13
Saunders, John Monk 1897-1940 ....DLB-26

Saunders, Margaret Marshall
 1861-1947.....................DLB-92
Saunders and Otley DLB-106
Saussure, Ferdinand de 1857-1913.......DLB-242
Savage, James 1784-1873 ....DLB-30
Savage, Marmion W. 1803?-1872 ....DLB-21
Savage, Richard 1697?-1743 ....DLB-95
Savard, Félix-Antoine 1896-1982.........DLB-68
Savery, Henry 1791-1842 ....DLB-230
Saville, (Leonard) Malcolm 1901-1982 ...DLB-160
Sawyer, Robert J. 1960- DLB-251
Sawyer, Ruth 1880-1970 ....DLB-22
Sayers, Dorothy L.
 1893-1957 ....DLB-10, 36, 77, 100; CDBLB-6
Sayle, Charles Edward 1864-1924 ....DLB-184
Sayles, John Thomas 1950- DLB-44
Sbarbaro, Camillo 1888-1967 ....DLB-114
Scalapino, Leslie 1947- DLB-193
Scannell, Vernon 1922- DLB-27
Scarry, Richard 1919-1994 ....DLB-61
Schaefer, Jack 1907-1991 ....DLB-212
Schaeffer, Albrecht 1885-1950...........DLB-66
Schaeffer, Susan Fromberg 1941- DLB-28
Schaff, Philip 1819-1893 ....DS-13
Schaper, Edzard 1908-1984 ....DLB-69
Scharf, J. Thomas 1843-1898............DLB-47
Schede, Paul Melissus 1539-1602 ....DLB-179
Scheffel, Joseph Viktor von 1826-1886 ...DLB-129
Scheffler, Johann 1624-1677............DLB-164
Schelling, Friedrich Wilhelm Joseph von
 1775-1854.....................DLB-90
Scherer, Wilhelm 1841-1886...........DLB-129
Scherfig, Hans 1905-1979 ....DLB-214
Schickele, René 1883-1940 ....DLB-66
Schiff, Dorothy 1903-1989..............DLB-127
Schiller, Friedrich
 1759-1805 ....DLB-94; CDWLB-2
Schirmer, David 1623-1687.............DLB-164
Schlaf, Johannes 1862-1941 ....DLB-118
Schlegel, August Wilhelm 1767-1845......DLB-94
Schlegel, Dorothea 1763-1839 ....DLB-90
Schlegel, Friedrich 1772-1829..........DLB-90
Schleiermacher, Friedrich 1768-1834......DLB-90
Schlesinger, Arthur M., Jr. 1917- DLB-17
Schlumberger, Jean 1877-1968 ....DLB-65
Schmid, Eduard Hermann Wilhelm
 (see Edschmid, Kasimir)
Schmidt, Arno 1914-1979 ....DLB-69
Schmidt, Johann Kaspar (see Stirner, Max)
Schmidt, Michael 1947- DLB-40
Schmidtbonn, Wilhelm August
 1876-1952....................DLB-118
Schmitz, James H. 1911- DLB-8
Schnabel, Johann Gottfried
 1692-1760....................DLB-168
Schnackenberg, Gjertrud 1953- DLB-120

Schnitzler, Arthur 1862-1931 .... DLB-81, 118; CDWLB-2
Schnurre, Wolfdietrich 1920-1989 .... DLB-69
Schocken Books DLB-46
Scholartis Press DLB-112
Scholderer, Victor 1880-1971 .... DLB-201
The Schomburg Center for Research in Black Culture DLB-76
Schönbeck, Virgilio (see Giotti, Virgilio)
Schönherr, Karl 1867-1943 .... DLB-118
Schoolcraft, Jane Johnston 1800-1841 .....DLB-175
School Stories, 1914-1960 .... DLB-160
Schopenhauer, Arthur 1788-1860 .... DLB-90
Schopenhauer, Johanna 1766-1838 ...... DLB-90
Schorer, Mark 1908-1977 .... DLB-103
Schottelius, Justus Georg 1612-1676 .... DLB-164
Schouler, James 1839-1920 .... DLB-47
Schoultz, Solveig von 1907-1996 .... DLB-259
Schrader, Paul 1946- DLB-44
Schreiner, Olive 1855-1920 .... DLB-18, 156, 190, 225
Schroeder, Andreas 1946- DLB-53
Schubart, Christian Friedrich Daniel 1739-1791 .... DLB-97
Schubert, Gotthilf Heinrich 1780-1860 .... DLB-90
Schücking, Levin 1814-1883 .... DLB-133
Schulberg, Budd 1914- DLB-6, 26, 28; Y-81
Schulte, F. J., and Company DLB-49
Schulz, Bruno 1892-1942 ... DLB-215; CDWLB-4
Schulze, Hans (see Praetorius, Johannes)
Schupp, Johann Balthasar 1610-1661 .... DLB-164
Schurz, Carl 1829-1906 .... DLB-23
Schuyler, George S. 1895-1977 .... DLB-29, 51
Schuyler, James 1923-1991 .... DLB-5, 169
Schwartz, Delmore 1913-1966 .... DLB-28, 48
Schwartz, Jonathan 1938- Y-82
Schwartz, Lynne Sharon 1939- DLB-218
Schwarz, Sibylle 1621-1638 .... DLB-164
Schwerner, Armand 1927-1999 .... DLB-165
Schwob, Marcel 1867-1905 .... DLB-123
Sciascia, Leonardo 1921-1989 .... DLB-177
Science Fantasy DLB-8
Science-Fiction Fandom and Conventions . . DLB-8
Science-Fiction Fanzines: The Time Binders DLB-8
Science-Fiction Films DLB-8
Science Fiction Writers of America and the Nebula Awards DLB-8
Scot, Reginald circa 1538-1599 .... DLB-136
Scotellaro, Rocco 1923-1953 .... DLB-128
Scott, Alicia Anne (Lady John Scott) 1810-1900 .... DLB-240
Scott, Catharine Amy Dawson 1865-1934 .... DLB-240
Scott, Dennis 1939-1991 .... DLB-125
Scott, Dixon 1881-1915 .... DLB-98
Scott, Duncan Campbell 1862-1947 ...... DLB-92

Scott, Evelyn 1893-1963 .... DLB-9, 48
Scott, F. R. 1899-1985 .... DLB-88
Scott, Frederick George 1861-1944 .... DLB-92
Scott, Geoffrey 1884-1929 .... DLB-149
Scott, Harvey W. 1838-1910 .... DLB-23
Scott, Lady Jane (see Scott, Alicia Anne)
Scott, Paul 1920-1978 ....DLB-14, 207
Scott, Sarah 1723-1795 .... DLB-39
Scott, Tom 1918- DLB-27
Scott, Sir Walter 1771-1832 .... DLB-93, 107, 116, 144, 159; CDBLB-3
Scott, Walter, Publishing Company Limited DLB-112
Scott, William Bell 1811-1890 .... DLB-32
Scott, William R. [publishing house] DLB-46
Scott-Heron, Gil 1949- DLB-41
Scribe, Eugene 1791-1861 .... DLB-192
Scribner, Arthur Hawley 1859-1932 ..... DS-13, 16
Scribner, Charles 1854-1930 .... DS-13, 16
Scribner, Charles, Jr. 1921-1995 .... Y-95
Reminiscences DS-17
Charles Scribner's Sons DLB-49; DS-13, 16, 17
Scripps, E. W. 1854-1926 .... DLB-25
Scudder, Horace Elisha 1838-1902 .... DLB-42, 71
Scudder, Vida Dutton 1861-1954 .... DLB-71
Scupham, Peter 1933- DLB-40
Seabrook, William 1886-1945 .... DLB-4
Seabury, Samuel 1729-1796 .... DLB-31
Seacole, Mary Jane Grant 1805-1881 .... DLB-166
The Seafarer circa 970 .... DLB-146
Sealsfield, Charles (Carl Postl) 1793-1864 .... DLB-133, 186
Sears, Edward I. 1819?-1876 .... DLB-79
Sears Publishing Company DLB-46
Seaton, George 1911-1979 .... DLB-44
Seaton, William Winston 1785-1866 ..... DLB-43
Secker, Martin [publishing house] DLB-112
Secker, Martin, and Warburg Limited . . . DLB-112
The Second Annual New York Festival of Mystery Y-00
Second-Generation Minor Poets of the Seventeenth Century DLB-126
Sedgwick, Arthur George 1844-1915 ..... DLB-64
Sedgwick, Catharine Maria 1789-1867 ....DLB-1, 74, 183, 239, 243
Sedgwick, Ellery 1872-1930 .... DLB-91
Sedgwick, Eve Kosofsky 1950- DLB-246
Sedley, Sir Charles 1639-1701 .... DLB-131
Seeberg, Peter 1925-1999 .... DLB-214
Seeger, Alan 1888-1916 .... DLB-45
Seers, Eugene (see Dantin, Louis)
Segal, Erich 1937- Y-86
Šegedin, Petar 1909- DLB-181
Seghers, Anna 1900-1983 .... DLB-69; CDWLB-2
Seid, Ruth (see Sinclair, Jo)
Seidel, Frederick Lewis 1936- Y-84

Seidel, Ina 1885-1974 .... DLB-56
Seifert, Jaroslav 1901-1986 .....DLB-215; Y-84; CDWLB-4
Seigenthaler, John 1927- DLB-127
Seizin Press DLB-112
Séjour, Victor 1817-1874 .... DLB-50
Séjour Marcou et Ferrand, Juan Victor (see Séjour, Victor)
Sekowski, Józef-Julian, Baron Brambeus (see Senkovsky, Osip Ivanovich)
Selby, Bettina 1934- DLB-204
Selby, Hubert, Jr. 1928- DLB-2, 227
Selden, George 1929-1989 .... DLB-52
Selden, John 1584-1654 .... DLB-213
Selected English-Language Little Magazines and Newspapers [France, 1920-1939] . . DLB-4
Selected Humorous Magazines (1820-1950) DLB-11
Selected Science-Fiction Magazines and Anthologies DLB-8
Selenić, Slobodan 1933-1995 .... DLB-181
Self, Edwin F. 1920- DLB-137
Self, Will 1961- DLB-207
Seligman, Edwin R. A. 1861-1939 .... DLB-47
Selimović, Meša 1910-1982 ....DLB-181; CDWLB-4
Selous, Frederick Courteney 1851-1917 .... DLB-174
Seltzer, Chester E. (see Muro, Amado)
Seltzer, Thomas [publishing house] DLB-46
Selvon, Sam 1923-1994 .....DLB-125; CDWLB-3
Semmes, Raphael 1809-1877 .... DLB-189
Senancour, Etienne de 1770-1846 .... DLB-119
Sendak, Maurice 1928- DLB-61
Seneca the Elder circa 54 B.C.-circa A.D. 40 .... DLB-211
Seneca the Younger circa 1 B.C.-A.D. 65 .....DLB-211; CDWLB-1
Senécal, Eva 1905- DLB-92
Sengstacke, John 1912- DLB-127
Senior, Olive 1941- DLB-157
Senkovsky, Osip Ivanovich (Józef-Julian Sekowski, Baron Brambeus) 1800-1858 .... DLB-198
Šenoa, August 1838-1881 ....DLB-147; CDWLB-4
"Sensation Novels" (1863), by H. L. Manse DLB-21
Sepamla, Sipho 1932- DLB-157, 225
Seredy, Kate 1899-1975 .... DLB-22
Sereni, Vittorio 1913-1983 .... DLB-128
Seres, William [publishing house] DLB-170
Serling, Rod 1924-1975 .... DLB-26
Sernine, Daniel 1955- DLB-251
Serote, Mongane Wally 1944- ... DLB-125, 225
Serraillier, Ian 1912-1994 .... DLB-161
Serrano, Nina 1934- DLB-122
Service, Robert 1874-1958 .... DLB-92
Sessler, Charles 1854-1935 ....DLB-187

Seth, Vikram 1952- DLB-120
Seton, Elizabeth Ann 1774-1821.........DLB-200
Seton, Ernest Thompson
    1860-1942..................DLB-92; DS-13
Setouchi Harumi 1922- DLB-182
Settle, Mary Lee 1918- DLB-6
Seume, Johann Gottfried 1763-1810........DLB-94
Seuse, Heinrich 1295?-1366............DLB-179
Seuss, Dr. (see Geisel, Theodor Seuss)
The Seventy-fifth Anniversary of the Armistice:
    The Wilfred Owen Centenary and
    the Great War Exhibit
    at the University of Virginia Y-93
Severin, Timothy 1940- DLB-204
Sewall, Joseph 1688-1769..............DLB-24
Sewall, Richard B. 1908- DLB-111
Sewell, Anna 1820-1878................DLB-163
Sewell, Samuel 1652-1730..............DLB-24
Sex, Class, Politics, and Religion [in the
    British Novel, 1930-1959]...........DLB-15
Sexton, Anne 1928-1974 ...DLB-5, 169; CDALB-1
Seymour-Smith, Martin 1928-1998......DLB-155
Sgorlon, Carlo 1930- DLB-196
Shaara, Michael 1929-1988..............Y-83
Shabel'skaia, Aleksandra Stanislavovna
    1845-1921.....................DLB-238
Shadwell, Thomas 1641?-1692..........DLB-80
Shaffer, Anthony 1926- DLB-13
Shaffer, Peter 1926- DLB-13, 233; CDBLB-8
Shaftesbury, Anthony Ashley Cooper,
    Third Earl of 1671-1713...........DLB-101
Shairp, Mordaunt 1887-1939............DLB-10
Shakespeare, Nicholas 1957- DLB-231
Shakespeare, William
    1564-1616.........DLB-62, 172; CDBLB-1
$6,166,000 for a *Book!* Observations on
    *The Shakespeare First Folio: The History
    of the Book*.......................Y-01
The Shakespeare Globe Trust............Y-93
Shakespeare Head Press DLB-112
Shakhovskoi, Aleksandr Aleksandrovich
    1777-1846.....................DLB-150
Shange, Ntozake 1948- DLB-38, 249
Shapiro, Karl 1913-2000...............DLB-48
Sharon Publications....................DLB-46
Sharp, Margery 1905-1991.............DLB-161
Sharp, William 1855-1905.............DLB-156
Sharpe, Tom 1928- DLB-14, 231
Shaw, Albert 1857-1947................DLB-91
Shaw, George Bernard
    1856-1950 ......DLB-10, 57, 190, CDBLB-6
Shaw, Henry Wheeler 1818-1885.........DLB-11
Shaw, Joseph T. 1874-1952............DLB-137
Shaw, Irwin
    1913-1984......DLB-6, 102; Y-84; CDALB-1
Shaw, Mary 1854-1929................DLB-228
Shaw, Robert 1927-1978............DLB-13, 14
Shaw, Robert B. 1947- DLB-120

Shawn, William 1907-1992 ....DLB-137
Shay, Frank [publishing house] DLB-46
Shchedrin, N. (see Saltykov, Mikhail Evgrafovich)
Shea, John Gilmary 1824-1892 ....DLB-30
Sheaffer, Louis 1912-1993 ....DLB-103
Shearing, Joseph 1886-1952............DLB-70
Shebbeare, John 1709-1788 ....DLB-39
Sheckley, Robert 1928- DLB-8
Shedd, William G. T. 1820-1894.........DLB-64
Sheed, Wilfred 1930- DLB-6
Sheed and Ward [U.S.] DLB-46
Sheed and Ward Limited [U.K.] DLB-112
Sheldon, Alice B. (see Tiptree, James, Jr.)
Sheldon, Edward 1886-1946 ....DLB-7
Sheldon and Company DLB-49
Sheller, Aleksandr Konstantinovich
    1838-1900.....................DLB-238
Shelley, Mary Wollstonecraft 1797-1851
    ....DLB-110, 116, 159, 178; CDBLB-3
Shelley, Percy Bysshe
    1792-1822 ......DLB-96, 110, 158; CDBLB-3
Shelnutt, Eve 1941- DLB-130
Shenstone, William 1714-1763..........DLB-95
Shepard, Clark and Brown DLB-49
Shepard, Ernest Howard 1879-1976......DLB-160
Shepard, Sam 1943- DLB-7, 212
Shepard, Thomas I, 1604 or 1605-1649 ...DLB-24
Shepard, Thomas II, 1635-1677.........DLB-24
Shepherd, Luke
    flourished 1547-1554.............DLB-136
Sherburne, Edward 1616-1702.........DLB-131
Sheridan, Frances 1724-1766 ....DLB-39, 84
Sheridan, Richard Brinsley
    1751-1816 .... DLB-89; CDBLB-2
Sherman, Francis 1871-1926 ....DLB-92
Sherman, Martin 1938- DLB-228
Sherriff, R. C. 1896-1975 .....DLB-10, 191, 233
Sherrod, Blackie 1919- DLB-241
Sherry, Norman 1935- DLB-155
Sherry, Richard 1506-1551 or 1555......DLB-236
Sherwood, Mary Martha 1775-1851 .....DLB-163
Sherwood, Robert E. 1896-1955 ... DLB-7, 26, 249
Shevyrev, Stepan Petrovich
    1806-1864.....................DLB-205
Shiel, M. P. 1865-1947................DLB-153
Shiels, George 1886-1949 ....DLB-10
Shiga, Naoya 1883-1971...............DLB-180
Shiina Rinzō 1911-1973 ....DLB-182
Shikishi Naishinnō 1153?-1201 ....DLB-203
Shillaber, Benjamin Penhallow
    1814-1890.................DLB-1, 11, 235
Shimao Toshio 1917-1986 ....DLB-182
Shimazaki, Tōson 1872-1943 ....DLB-180
Shine, Ted 1931- DLB-38
Shinkei 1406-1475 ....DLB-203
Ship, Reuben 1915-1975 ....DLB-88

Shirer, William L. 1904-1993 ....DLB-4
Shirinsky-Shikhmatov, Sergii Aleksandrovich
    1783-1837.....................DLB-150
Shirley, James 1596-1666................DLB-58
Shishkov, Aleksandr Semenovich
    1753-1841.....................DLB-150
Shockley, Ann Allen 1927- DLB-33
Shōno Junzō 1921- DLB-182
Shore, Arabella 1820?-1901 and
    Shore, Louisa 1824-1895..........DLB-199
Short, Luke (see Glidden, Frederick Dilley)
Short, Peter [publishing house] DLB-170
Shorter, Dora Sigerson 1866-1918.......DLB-240
Shorthouse, Joseph Henry 1834-1903.....DLB-18
Shōtetsu 1381-1459 ....DLB-203
Showalter, Elaine 1941- DLB-67
Shulevitz, Uri 1935- DLB-61
Shulman, Max 1919-1988 ....DLB-11
Shute, Henry A. 1856-1943..............DLB-9
Shute, Nevil 1899-1960 ....DLB-255
Shuttle, Penelope 1947- DLB-14, 40
Sibbes, Richard 1577-1635............DLB-151
Sibiriak, D. (see Mamin, Dmitrii Narkisovich)
Siddal, Elizabeth Eleanor 1829-1862.....DLB-199
Sidgwick, Ethel 1877-1970 ....DLB-197
Sidgwick and Jackson Limited..........DLB-112
Sidney, Margaret (see Lothrop, Harriet M.)
Sidney, Mary 1561-1621 ....DLB-167
Sidney, Sir Philip
    1554-1586............DLB-167; CDBLB-1
An *Apologie for Poetrie* (the Olney
    edition, 1595, of *Defence of Poesie*).....DLB-167
Sidney's Press DLB-49
Sierra, Rubén 1946- DLB-122
Sierra Club Books DLB-49
Siger of Brabant circa 1240-circa 1284 ....DLB-115
Sigourney, Lydia Huntley
    1791-1865 ......DLB-1, 42, 73, 183, 239, 243
Silkin, Jon 1930- DLB-27
Silko, Leslie Marmon 1948- DLB-143, 175, 256
Silliman, Benjamin 1779-1864 ....DLB-183
Silliman, Ron 1946- DLB-169
Silliphant, Stirling 1918- DLB-26
Sillitoe, Alan 1928- DLB-14, 139; CDBLB-8
Silman, Roberta 1934- DLB-28
Silva, Beverly 1930- DLB-122
Silverberg, Robert 1935- DLB-8
Silverman, Kaja 1947- DLB-246
Silverman, Kenneth 1936- DLB-111
Simak, Clifford D. 1904-1988 ....DLB-8
Simcoe, Elizabeth 1762-1850 ....DLB-99
Simcox, Edith Jemima 1844-1901 ....DLB-190
Simcox, George Augustus 1841-1905 .....DLB-35
Sime, Jessie Georgina 1868-1958 ....DLB-92
Simenon, Georges 1903-1989 ......DLB-72; Y-89
Simic, Charles 1938- DLB-105

497

Cumulative Index

"Images and 'Images,'" DLB-105
Simionescu, Mircea Horia 1928- DLB-232
Simmel, Johannes Mario 1924- DLB-69
Simmes, Valentine [publishing house] . . . DLB-170
Simmons, Ernest J. 1903-1972 . . . . DLB-103
Simmons, Herbert Alfred 1930- DLB-33
Simmons, James 1933- DLB-40
Simms, William Gilmore
  1806-1870. . . . . DLB-3, 30, 59, 73, 248
Simms and M'Intyre. DLB-106
Simon, Claude 1913- DLB-83; Y-85
Simon, Neil 1927- DLB-7
Simon and Schuster DLB-46
Simons, Katherine Drayton Mayrant
  1890-1969 . . . . Y-83
Simović, Ljubomir 1935- DLB-181
Simpkin and Marshall
  [publishing house] DLB-154
Simpson, Helen 1897-1940 . . . . DLB-77
Simpson, Louis 1923- DLB-5
Simpson, N. F. 1919- DLB-13
Sims, George 1923- DLB-87; Y-99
Sims, George Robert 1847-1922 . . . DLB-35, 70, 135
Sinán, Rogelio 1904- DLB-145
Sinclair, Andrew 1935- DLB-14
Sinclair, Bertrand William 1881-1972. . . . DLB-92
Sinclair, Catherine 1800-1864. . . . . DLB-163
Sinclair, Jo 1913-1995. . . . . DLB-28
Sinclair, Lister 1921- DLB-88
Sinclair, May 1863-1946. . . . . DLB-36, 135
Sinclair, Upton 1878-1968 . . . . DLB-9; CDALB-5
Sinclair, Upton [publishing house] DLB-46
Singer, Isaac Bashevis
  1904-1991 . . . DLB-6, 28, 52; Y-91; CDALB-1
Singer, Mark 1950- DLB-185
Singmaster, Elsie 1879-1958 . . . . DLB-9
Sinisgalli, Leonardo 1908-1981. . . . . DLB-114
Siodmak, Curt 1902-2000. . . . . DLB-44
Sîrbu, Ion D. 1919-1989 . . . . DLB-232
Siringo, Charles A. 1855-1928 . . . . DLB-186
Sissman, L. E. 1928-1976 . . . . DLB-5
Sisson, C. H. 1914- DLB-27
Sitwell, Edith 1887-1964 . . . . . . DLB-20; CDBLB-7
Sitwell, Osbert 1892-1969. . . . . DLB-100, 195
Skácel, Jan 1922-1989. . . . . DLB-232
Skalbe, Kārlis 1879-1945. . . . . DLB-220
Skármeta, Antonio
  1940- DLB-145; CDWLB-3
Skavronsky, A. (see Danilevsky, Grigorii Petrovich)
Skeat, Walter W. 1835-1912 . . . . DLB-184
Skeffington, William
  [publishing house] DLB-106
Skelton, John 1463-1529. . . . . DLB-136
Skelton, Robin 1925- DLB-27, 53
Škėma, Antanas 1910-1961. . . . . DLB-220

Skinner, Constance Lindsay
  1877-1939 . . . . DLB-92
Skinner, John Stuart 1788-1851 . . . . DLB-73
Skipsey, Joseph 1832-1903 . . . . DLB-35
Skou-Hansen, Tage 1925- DLB-214
Škvorecký, Josef 1924- DLB-232; CDWLB-4
Slade, Bernard 1930- DLB-53
Slamnig, Ivan 1930- DLB-181
Slančeková, Božena (see Timrava)
Slater, Patrick 1880-1951 . . . . DLB-68
Slaveykov, Pencho 1866-1912 . . . . DLB-147
Slaviček, Milivoj 1929- DLB-181
Slavitt, David 1935- DLB-5, 6
Sleigh, Burrows Willcocks Arthur
  1821-1869 . . . . DLB-99
A Slender Thread of Hope:
  The Kennedy Center Black
  Theatre Project DLB-38
Slesinger, Tess 1905-1945. . . . . DLB-102
Slessor, Kenneth 1901-1971 . . . . DLB-260
Slick, Sam (see Haliburton, Thomas Chandler)
Sloan, John 1871-1951 . . . . DLB-188
Sloane, William, Associates DLB-46
Small, Maynard and Company DLB-49
Small Presses in Great Britain and Ireland,
  1960-1985 . . . . DLB-40
Small Presses I: Jargon Society Y-84
Small Presses II: The Spirit That Moves
  Us Press. Y-85
Small Presses III: Pushcart Press Y-87
Smart, Christopher 1722-1771. . . . . DLB-109
Smart, David A. 1892-1957 . . . . DLB-137
Smart, Elizabeth 1913-1986 . . . . DLB-88
Smedley, Menella Bute 1820?-1877 . . . . DLB-199
Smellie, William [publishing house] DLB-154
Smiles, Samuel 1812-1904 . . . . DLB-55
Smiley, Jane 1949- DLB-227, 234
Smith, A. J. M. 1902-1980 . . . . DLB-88
Smith, Adam 1723-1790 . . . . DLB-104, 252
Smith, Adam (George Jerome Waldo Goodman)
  1930- DLB-185
Smith, Alexander 1829-1867. . . . . . . DLB-32, 55
"On the Writing of Essays" (1862) DLB-57
Smith, Amanda 1837-1915 . . . . DLB-221
Smith, Betty 1896-1972. . . . . Y-82
Smith, Carol Sturm 1938- Y-81
Smith, Charles Henry 1826-1903. . . . . . DLB-11
Smith, Charlotte 1749-1806 . . . . . . DLB-39, 109
Smith, Chet 1899-1973 . . . . DLB-171
Smith, Cordwainer 1913-1966 . . . . DLB-8
Smith, Dave 1942- DLB-5
Smith, Dodie 1896- DLB-10
Smith, Doris Buchanan 1934- DLB-52
Smith, E. E. 1890-1965 . . . . DLB-8
Smith, Elder and Company DLB-154
Smith, Elihu Hubbard 1771-1798 . . . . . . DLB-37

Smith, Elizabeth Oakes (Prince)
  (see Oakes Smith, Elizabeth)
Smith, Eunice 1757-1823. . . . . DLB-200
Smith, F. Hopkinson 1838-1915. . . . . DS-13
Smith, George D. 1870-1920. . . . . DLB-140
Smith, George O. 1911-1981 . . . . DLB-8
Smith, Goldwin 1823-1910. . . . . DLB-99
Smith, H. Allen 1907-1976 . . . . DLB-11, 29
Smith, Harrison, and Robert Haas
  [publishing house] DLB-46
Smith, Harry B. 1860-1936 . . . . DLB-187
Smith, Hazel Brannon 1914- DLB-127
Smith, Henry circa 1560-circa 1591 . . . . DLB-136
Smith, Horatio (Horace) 1779-1849 . . . . DLB-116
Smith, Horatio (Horace) 1779-1849 and
  James Smith 1775-1839 . . . . DLB-96
Smith, Iain Crichton 1928- DLB-40, 139
Smith, J. Allen 1860-1924 . . . . DLB-47
Smith, J. Stilman, and Company DLB-49
Smith, Jessie Willcox 1863-1935. . . . . . . DLB-188
Smith, John 1580-1631. . . . . DLB-24, 30
Smith, John 1618-1652 . . . . DLB-252
Smith, Josiah 1704-1781 . . . . DLB-24
Smith, Ken 1938- DLB-40
Smith, Lee 1944- DLB-143; Y-83
Smith, Logan Pearsall 1865-1946 . . . . . . DLB-98
Smith, Margaret Bayard 1778-1844 . . . . DLB-248
Smith, Mark 1935- Y-82
Smith, Michael 1698-circa 1771 . . . . DLB-31
Smith, Pauline 1882-1959 . . . . DLB-225
Smith, Red 1905-1982 . . . . DLB-29, 171
Smith, Roswell 1829-1892 . . . . DLB-79
Smith, Samuel Harrison 1772-1845 . . . . DLB-43
Smith, Samuel Stanhope 1751-1819 . . . . DLB-37
Smith, Sarah (see Stretton, Hesba)
Smith, Sarah Pogson 1774-1870 . . . . . . DLB-200
Smith, Seba 1792-1868 . . . . DLB-1, 11, 243
Smith, Stevie 1902-1971 . . . . DLB-20
Smith, Sydney 1771-1845 . . . . DLB-107
Smith, Sydney Goodsir 1915-1975 . . . . . DLB-27
Smith, Sir Thomas 1513-1577. . . . . DLB-132
Smith, W. B., and Company DLB-49
Smith, W. H., and Son DLB-106
Smith, Wendell 1914-1972 . . . . DLB-171
Smith, William flourished 1595-1597 . . . . DLB-136
Smith, William 1727-1803 . . . . DLB-31
A General Idea of the College of Mirania
  (1753) [excerpts] DLB-31
Smith, William 1728-1793. . . . . DLB-30
Smith, William Gardner 1927-1974 . . . . DLB-76
Smith, William Henry 1808-1872. . . . . . DLB-159
Smith, William Jay 1918- DLB-5
Smithers, Leonard [publishing house] . . . DLB-112
Smollett, Tobias
  1721-1771 . . . . DLB-39, 104; CDBLB-2

Dedication, *Ferdinand Count Fathom* (1753) DLB-39

Preface to *Ferdinand Count Fathom* (1753) DLB-39

Preface to *Roderick Random* (1748)..........DLB-39

Smythe, Francis Sydney 1900-1949......DLB-195

Snelling, William Joseph 1804-1848.....DLB-202

Snellings, Rolland (see Touré, Askia Muhammad)

Snodgrass, W. D. 1926- DLB-5

Snow, C. P. 1905-1980.....DLB-15, 77; DS-17; CDBLB-7

Snyder, Gary 1930- ...DLB-5, 16, 165, 212, 237

Sobiloff, Hy 1912-1970................DLB-48

The Society for Textual Scholarship and *TEXT* Y-87

The Society for the History of Authorship, Reading and Publishing Y-92

Söderberg, Hjalmar 1869-1941 ....DLB-259

Södergran, Edith 1892-1923 ....DLB-259

Soffici, Ardengo 1879-1964 ....DLB-114

Sofola, 'Zulu 1938- DLB-157

Solano, Solita 1888-1975 ....DLB-4

Soldati, Mario 1906-1999.............DLB-177

Šoljan, Antun 1932-1993 ....DLB-181

Sollers, Philippe 1936 ....DLB-83

Sollogub, Vladimir Aleksandrovich 1813-1882 ....DLB-198

Sollors, Werner 1943-................DBL-246

Solmi, Sergio 1899-1981 ....DLB-114

Solomon, Carl 1928- DLB-16

Solway, David 1941- DLB-53

Solzhenitsyn and America ,................Y-85

Somerville, Edith Œnone 1858-1949.....DLB-135

Somov, Orest Mikhailovich 1793-1833 ....DLB-198

Sønderby, Knud 1909-1966............DLB-214

Song, Cathy 1955- DLB-169

Sonnevi, Göran 1939- DLB-257

Sono Ayako 1931- DLB-182

Sontag, Susan 1933- DLB-2, 67

Sophocles 497/496 B.C.-406/405 B.C. DLB-176; CDWLB-1

Šopov, Aco 1923-1982................DLB-181

Sørensen, Villy 1929- DLB-214

Sorensen, Virginia 1912-1991 ....DLB-206

Sorge, Reinhard Johannes 1892-1916 ....DLB-118

Sorrentino, Gilbert 1929- DLB-5, 173; Y-80

Sotheby, James 1682-1742 ....DLB-213

Sotheby, John 1740-1807 ....DLB-213

Sotheby, Samuel 1771-1842 ....DLB-213

Sotheby, Samuel Leigh 1805-1861.......DLB-213

Sotheby, William 1757-1833.........DLB-93, 213

Soto, Gary 1952- DLB-82

Sources for the Study of Tudor and Stuart Drama......................DLB-62

Souster, Raymond 1921- DLB-88

The *South English Legendary circa thirteenth-fifteenth centuries*........................DLB-146

Southerland, Ellease 1943- DLB-33

Southern, Terry 1924-1995 ....DLB-2

Southern Illinois University Press Y-95

Southern Writers Between the Wars.......DLB-9

Southerne, Thomas 1659-1746 ....DLB-80

Southey, Caroline Anne Bowles 1786-1854 ....DLB-116

Southey, Robert 1774-1843 .....DLB-93, 107, 142

Southwell, Robert 1561?-1595..........DLB-167

Southworth, E. D. E. N. 1819-1899......DLB-239

Sowande, Bode 1948- DLB-157

Sowle, Tace [publishing house] DLB-170

Soyer, Jura 1912-1939.................DLB-124

Soyinka, Wole 1934- DLB-125; Y-86, Y-87; CDWLB-3

Spacks, Barry 1931- DLB-105

Spalding, Frances 1950- DLB-155

Spark, Muriel 1918- DLB-15, 139; CDBLB-7

Sparke, Michael [publishing house] DLB-170

Sparks, Jared 1789-1866.........DLB-1, 30, 235

Sparshott, Francis 1926- DLB-60

Späth, Gerold 1939- DLB-75

Spatola, Adriano 1941-1988............DLB-128

Spaziani, Maria Luisa 1924- DLB-128

Special Collections at the University of Colorado at Boulder......................Y-98

The Spectator 1828- DLB-110

Spedding, James 1808-1881 ....DLB-144

Spee von Langenfeld, Friedrich 1591-1635 ....DLB-164

Speght, Rachel 1597-after 1630 ....DLB-126

Speke, John Hanning 1827-1864 ....DLB-166

Spellman, A. B. 1935- DLB-41

Spence, Catherine Helen 1825-1910 .....DLB-230

Spence, Thomas 1750-1814 ....DLB-158

Spencer, Anne 1882-1975 ....DLB-51, 54

Spencer, Charles, third Earl of Sunderland 1674-1722 ....DLB-213

Spencer, Elizabeth 1921- DLB-6, 218

Spencer, George John, Second Earl Spencer 1758-1834 ....DLB-184

Spencer, Herbert 1820-1903 ....DLB-57

"The Philosophy of Style" (1852) DLB-57

Spencer, Scott 1945- Y-86

Spender, J. A. 1862-1942 ....DLB-98

Spender, Stephen 1909-1995 .. DLB-20; CDBLB-7

Spener, Philipp Jakob 1635-1705 ....DLB-164

Spenser, Edmund circa 1552-1599........DLB-167; CDBLB-1

Envoy from *The Shepheardes Calender* DLB-167

"The Generall Argument of the Whole Booke," from *The Shepheardes Calender* DLB-167

"A Letter of the Authors Expounding His Whole Intention in the Course of this Worke: Which for that It Giueth Great Light to the Reader, for the Better Vnderstanding Is Hereunto Annexed," from *The Faerie Qveene* (1590) DLB-167

"To His Booke," from *The Shepheardes Calender* (1579) DLB-167

"To the Most Excellent and Learned Both Orator and Poete, Mayster Gabriell Haruey, His Verie Special and Singular Good Frend E. K. Commendeth the Good Lyking of This His Labour, and the Patronage of the New Poete," from *The Shepheardes Calender* DLB-167

Sperr, Martin 1944- DLB-124

Spicer, Jack 1925-1965............DLB-5, 16, 193

Spielberg, Peter 1929- Y-81

Spielhagen, Friedrich 1829-1911 ....DLB-129

"*Spielmannsepen*" (circa 1152-circa 1500) ...DLB-148

Spier, Peter 1927- DLB-61

Spillane, Mickey 1918- DLB-226

Spink, J. G. Taylor 1888-1962..........DLB-241

Spinrad, Norman 1940- DLB-8

Spires, Elizabeth 1952- DLB-120

Spitteler, Carl 1845-1924 ....DLB-129

Spivak, Lawrence E. 1900- DLB-137

Spofford, Harriet Prescott 1835-1921 ....DLB-74, 221

Spring, Howard 1889-1965 ....DLB-191

Squibob (see Derby, George Horatio)

Squier, E. G. 1821-1888 ....DLB-189

Stacpoole, H. de Vere 1863-1951 ....DLB-153

Staël, Germaine de 1766-1817 ......DLB-119, 192

Staël-Holstein, Anne-Louise Germaine de (see Staël, Germaine de)

Stafford, Jean 1915-1979 ....DLB-2, 173

Stafford, William 1914-1993 ....DLB-5, 206

Stage Censorship: "The Rejected Statement" (1911), by Bernard Shaw [excerpts] ...DLB-10

Stallings, Laurence 1894-1968 ....DLB-7, 44

Stallworthy, Jon 1935- DLB-40

Stampp, Kenneth M. 1912 ....DLB-17

Stănescu, Nichita 1933-1983 ....DLB-232

Stanev, Emiliyan 1907-1979 ....DLB-181

Stanford, Ann 1916- DLB-5

Stangerup, Henrik 1937-1998 ....DLB-214

Stanitsky, N. (see Panaeva, Avdot'ia Iakovlevna)

Stankevich, Nikolai Vladimirovich 1813-1840 ....DLB-198

Stanković, Borisav ("Bora") 1876-1927 ....DLB-147; CDWLB-4

Stanley, Henry M. 1841-1904 ....DLB-189; DS-13

Stanley, Thomas 1625-1678............DLB-131

Stannard, Martin 1947- DLB-155

Stansby, William [publishing house] DLB-170

Stanton, Elizabeth Cady 1815-1902......DLB-79

Stanton, Frank L. 1857-1927 ....DLB-25

Stanton, Maura 1946- DLB-120

Stapledon, Olaf 1886-1950 ....DLB-15, 255

Star Spangled Banner Office DLB-49

Stark, Freya 1893-1993 ....DLB-195

Starkey, Thomas circa 1499-1538.......DLB-132

Starkie, Walter 1894-1976 ....DLB-195

Cumulative Index DLB 260

Starkweather, David 1935- DLB-7	Stern, Madeleine B. 1912- DLB-111, 140	Stone, Herbert S., and Company DLB-49
Starrett, Vincent 1886-1974 .... DLB-187	Stern, Richard 1928- DLB-218; Y-87	Stone, Lucy 1818-1893............DLB-79, 239
The State of Publishing..................Y-97	Stern, Stewart 1922- DLB-26	Stone, Melville 1848-1929 .... DLB-25
Statements on the Art of Poetry DLB-54	Sterne, Laurence	Stone, Robert 1937- DLB-152
Stationers' Company of London, The DLB-170	1713-1768 .... DLB-39; CDBLB-2	Stone, Ruth 1915- DLB-105
Statius circa A.D. 45-A.D. 96 .... DLB-211	Sternheim, Carl 1878-1942 .... DLB-56, 118	Stone, Samuel 1602-1663 .... DLB-24
Stead, Christina 1902-1983............ DLB-260	Sternhold, Thomas ?-1549 and John Hopkins ?-1570 .... DLB-132	Stone, William Leete 1792-1844........ DLB-202
Stead, Robert J. C. 1880-1959 .... DLB-92	Steuart, David 1747-1824 .... DLB-213	Stone and Kimball DLB-49
Steadman, Mark 1930- DLB-6	Stevens, Henry 1819-1886 .... DLB-140	Stoppard, Tom 1937- DLB-13, 233; Y-85; CDBLB-8
The Stealthy School of Criticism (1871), by Dante Gabriel Rossetti............. DLB-35	Stevens, Wallace 1879-1955 ... DLB-54; CDALB-5	Playwrights and Professors............. DLB-13
Stearns, Harold E. 1891-1943........... DLB-4	Stevenson, Anne 1933- DLB-40	Storey, Anthony 1928- DLB-14
Stebnitsky, M. (see Leskov, Nikolai Semenovich)	Stevenson, D. E. 1892-1973 .... DLB-191	Storey, David 1933- DLB-13, 14, 207, 245
Stedman, Edmund Clarence 1833-1908... DLB-64	Stevenson, Lionel 1902-1973 .... DLB-155	Storm, Theodor 1817-1888...DLB-129; CDWLB-2
Steegmuller, Francis 1906-1994 .... DLB-111	Stevenson, Robert Louis 1850-1894 ....DLB-18, 57, 141, 156, 174; DS-13; CDBLB-5	Story, Thomas circa 1670-1742.......... DLB-31
Steel, Flora Annie 1847-1929...... DLB-153, 156		Story, William Wetmore 1819-1895 .. DLB-1, 235
Steele, Max 1922- Y-80	"On Style in Literature: Its Technical Elements" (1885) DLB-57	Storytelling: A Contemporary Renaissance ... Y-84
Steele, Richard 1672-1729.......... DLB-84, 101; CDBLB-2	Stewart, Donald Ogden 1894-1980 .... DLB-4, 11, 26	Stoughton, William 1631-1701 .... DLB-24
Steele, Timothy 1948- DLB-120	Stewart, Douglas 1913-1985.......... DLB-260	Stow, John 1525-1605................ DLB-132
Steele, Wilbur Daniel 1886-1970 .... DLB-86	Stewart, Dugald 1753-1828........... DLB-31	Stow, Randolph 1935- DLB-260
Steere, Richard circa 1643-1721 .... DLB-24	Stewart, George, Jr. 1848-1906.......... DLB-99	Stowe, Harriet Beecher 1811-1896 ...DLB-1, 12, 42, 74, 189, 239, 243; CDALB-3
Stefanovski, Goran 1952- DLB-181	Stewart, George R. 1895-1980 .... DLB-8	
Stegner, Wallace 1909-1993 .....DLB-9, 206; Y-93	Stewart, Harold 1916-1995............ DLB-260	Stowe, Leland 1899- DLB-29
Stehr, Hermann 1864-1940 .... DLB-66	Stewart, Maria W. 1803?-1879 .... DLB-239	Stoyanov, Dimitr Ivanov (see Elin Pelin)
Steig, William 1907- DLB-61	Stewart, Randall 1896-1964 .... DLB-103	Strabo 64 or 63 B.C.-circa A.D. 25.......DLB-176
Stein, Gertrude 1874-1946 ...... DLB-4, 54, 86, 228; DS-15; CDALB-4	Stewart, Sean 1965- DLB-251	Strachey, Lytton 1880-1932 ..... DLB-149; DS-10
Stein, Leo 1872-1947................... DLB-4	Stewart and Kidd Company............ DLB-46	Strachey, Lytton, Preface to Eminent Victorians..................... DLB-149
Stein and Day Publishers DLB-46	Stickney, Trumbull 1874-1904 .... DLB-54	Strahan, William [publishing house]..... DLB-154
Steinbeck, John 1902-1968 ....DLB-7, 9, 212; DS-2; CDALB-5	Stieler, Caspar 1632-1707 .... DLB-164	Strahan and Company DLB-106
John Steinbeck Research Center........... Y-85	Stifter, Adalbert 1805-1868 .... DLB-133; CDWLB-2	Strand, Mark 1934- DLB-5
Steinem, Gloria 1934- DLB-246	Stiles, Ezra 1727-1795 .... DLB-31	The Strasbourg Oaths 842 .... DLB-148
Steiner, George 1929- DLB-67	Still, James 1906- DLB-9; Y01	Stratemeyer, Edward 1862-1930 .... DLB-42
Steinhoewel, Heinrich 1411/1412-1479....DLB-179	Stirling, S. M. 1954- DLB-251	Strati, Saverio 1924- DLB-177
Steloff, Ida Frances 1887-1989.......... DLB-187	Stirner, Max 1806-1856 .... DLB-129	Stratton and Barnard DLB-49
Stendhal 1783-1842................... DLB-119	Stith, William 1707-1755 .... DLB-31	Stratton-Porter, Gene 1863-1924 .... DLB-221; DS-14
Stephen Crane: A Revaluation Virginia Tech Conference, 1989 ....Y-89	Stock, Elliot [publishing house]......... DLB-106	Straub, Peter 1943- Y-84
Stephen, Leslie 1832-1904 ......DLB-57, 144, 190	Stockton, Frank R. 1834-1902 ....DLB-42, 74; DS-13	Strauß, Botho 1944- DLB-124
Stephen Vincent Benét Centenary Y-97	Stockton, J. Roy 1892-1972............ DLB-241	Strauß, David Friedrich 1808-1874...... DLB-133
Stephens, A. G. 1865-1933 .... DLB-230	Stoddard, Ashbel [publishing house] DLB-49	The Strawberry Hill Press DLB-154
Stephens, Alexander H. 1812-1883....... DLB-47	Stoddard, Charles Warren 1843-1909 .... DLB-186	Streatfeild, Noel 1895-1986 .... DLB-160
Stephens, Alice Barber 1858-1932 ...... DLB-188	Stoddard, Elizabeth 1823-1902......... DLB-202	Street, Cecil John Charles (see Rhode, John)
Stephens, Ann 1810-1886 .... DLB-3, 73, 250	Stoddard, Richard Henry 1825-1903 .... DLB-3, 64, 250; DS-13	Street, G. S. 1867-1936 .... DLB-135
Stephens, Charles Asbury 1844?-1931 .... DLB-42		Street and Smith DLB-49
Stephens, James 1882?-1950.... DLB-19, 153, 162	Stoddard, Solomon 1643-1729 .... DLB-24	Streeter, Edward 1891-1976 .... DLB-11
Stephens, John Lloyd 1805-1852 ... DLB-183, 250	Stoker, Bram 1847-1912........DLB-36, 70, 178; CDBLB-5	Streeter, Thomas Winthrop 1883-1965 .. DLB-140
Stephens, Michael 1946- DLB-234		Stretton, Hesba 1832-1911 .... DLB-163, 190
Stephensen, P. R. 1901-1965 .... DLB-260	Stokes, Frederick A., Company DLB-49	Stribling, T. S. 1881-1965............. DLB-9
Sterling, George 1869-1926 .... DLB-54	Stokes, Thomas L. 1898-1958 .... DLB-29	Der Stricker circa 1190-circa 1250 ...... DLB-138
Sterling, James 1701-1763 .... DLB-24	Stokesbury, Leon 1945- DLB-120	Strickland, Samuel 1804-1867.......... DLB-99
Sterling, John 1806-1844.............. DLB-116	Stolberg, Christian Graf zu 1748-1821 .... DLB-94	Strindberg, August 1849-1912 .... DLB-259
Stern, Gerald 1925- DLB-105	Stolberg, Friedrich Leopold Graf zu 1750-1819..................... DLB-94	Stringer, Arthur 1874-1950 .... DLB-92
Stern, Gladys B. 1890-1973............ DLB-197		Stringer and Townsend DLB-49
		Strittmatter, Erwin 1912- DLB-69

500

Strniša, Gregor 1930-1987 ....DLB-181
Strode, William 1630-1645 ....DLB-126
Strong, L. A. G. 1896-1958 ....DLB-191
Strother, David Hunter (Porte Crayon) 1816-1888 ....DLB-3, 248
Strouse, Jean 1945- DLB-111
Stuart, Dabney 1937- DLB-105
Stuart, Jesse 1906-1984 ..... DLB-9, 48, 102; Y-84
Stuart, Lyle [publishing house]..........DLB-46
Stuart, Ruth McEnery 1849?-1917......DLB-202
Stubbs, Harry Clement (see Clement, Hal)
Stubenberg, Johann Wilhelm von 1619-1663 ....DLB-164
Studebaker, William V. 1947- DLB-256
Studio.....................DLB-112
The Study of Poetry (1880), by Matthew Arnold DLB-35
Stump, Al 1916-1995 ....DLB-241
Sturgeon, Theodore 1918-1985 .... DLB-8; Y-85
Sturges, Preston 1898-1959 ....DLB-26
"Style" (1840; revised, 1859), by Thomas de Quincey [excerpt].......DLB-57
"Style" (1888), by Walter Pater DLB-57
Style (1897), by Walter Raleigh [excerpt]..................DLB-57
"Style" (1877), by T. H. Wright [excerpt]..................DLB-57
"Le Style c'est l'homme" (1892), by W. H. Mallock DLB-57
Styron, William 1925- DLB-2, 143; Y-80; CDALB-6
Suárez, Mario 1925- DLB-82
Such, Peter 1939- DLB-60
Suckling, Sir John 1609-1641?.....DLB-58, 126
Suckow, Ruth 1892-1960...........DLB-9, 102
Sudermann, Hermann 1857-1928 ...... DLB-118
Sue, Eugène 1804-1857 ....DLB-119
Sue, Marie-Joseph (see Sue, Eugène)
Suetonius circa A.D. 69-post A.D. 122 ...DLB-211
Suggs, Simon (see Hooper, Johnson Jones)
Sui Sin Far (see Eaton, Edith Maude)
Suits, Gustav 1883-1956 ....DLB-220; CDWLB-4
Sukenick, Ronald 1932- DLB-173; Y-81
Suknaski, Andrew 1942- DLB-53
Sullivan, Alan 1868-1947 ....DLB-92
Sullivan, C. Gardner 1886-1965 ....DLB-26
Sullivan, Frank 1892-1976 ....DLB-11
Sulte, Benjamin 1841-1923 ....DLB-99
Sulzberger, Arthur Hays 1891-1968 .....DLB-127
Sulzberger, Arthur Ochs 1926- DLB-127
Sulzer, Johann Georg 1720-1779.........DLB-97
Sumarokov, Aleksandr Petrovich 1717-1777 ....DLB-150
Summers, Hollis 1916- DLB-6
A Summing Up at Century's End Y-99
Sumner, Charles 1811-1874............DLB-235
Sumner, Henry A. [publishing house] DLB-49

Sundman, Per Olof 1922-1992 ....DLB-257
Supervielle, Jules 1884-1960 ....DLB-258
Surtees, Robert Smith 1803-1864 ....DLB-21
Survey of Literary Biographies Y-00
A Survey of Poetry Anthologies, 1879-1960.................DLB-54
Surveys: Japanese Literature, 1987-1995 ....DLB-182
Sutherland, Efua Theodora 1924-1996 ....DLB-117
Sutherland, John 1919-1956............DLB-68
Sutro, Alfred 1863-1933................DLB-10
Svendsen, Hanne Marie 1933 .... DLB-214
Swados, Harvey 1920-1972 ....DLB-2
Swain, Charles 1801-1874 ....DLB-32
Swallow Press DLB-46
Swan Sonnenschein Limited DLB-106
Swanberg, W. A. 1907- DLB-103
Swenson, May 1919-1989 ....DLB-5
Swerling, Jo 1897- DLB-44
Swift, Graham 1949- DLB-194
Swift, Jonathan 1667-1745........DLB-39, 95, 101; CDBLB-2
Swinburne, A. C. 1837-1909 ....DLB-35, 57; CDBLB-4
Swineshead, Richard floruit circa 1350.................DLB-115
Swinnerton, Frank 1884-1982 ....DLB-34
Swisshelm, Jane Grey 1815-1884 ....DLB-43
Swope, Herbert Bayard 1882-1958 ......DLB-25
Swords, T. and J., and Company DLB-49
Swords, Thomas 1763-1843 and Swords, James ?-1844 ....DLB-73
Sykes, Ella C. ?-1939.................DLB-174
Sylvester, Josuah 1562 or 1563-1618 .. ..DLB-121
Symonds, Emily Morse (see Paston, George)
Symonds, John Addington 1840-1893 .... DLB-57, 144
"Personal Style" (1890) DLB-57
Symons, A. J. A. 1900-1941............DLB-149
Symons, Arthur 1865-1945 .... DLB-19, 57, 149
Symons, Julian 1912-1994 ..... DLB-87, 155; Y-92
Julian Symons at Eighty..................Y-92
Symons, Scott 1933- DLB-53
A Symposium on The Columbia History of the Novel............................Y-92
Synge, John Millington 1871-1909 ....DLB-10, 19; CDBLB-5
Synge Summer School: J. M. Synge and the Irish Theater, Rathdrum, County Wicklow, Ireland......................Y-93
Syrett, Netta 1865-1943 .... DLB-135, 197
Szabó, Lőrinc 1900-1957 ....DLB-215
Szabó, Magda 1917- DLB-215
Szymborska, Wisława 1923- DLB-232, Y-96; CDWLB-4

T

Taban lo Liyong 1939?- DLB-125
Tabori, George 1914- DLB-245
Tabucchi, Antonio 1943- DLB-196
Taché, Joseph-Charles 1820-1894.........DLB-99
Tachihara Masaaki 1926-1980 ....DLB-182
Tacitus circa A.D. 55-circa A.D. 117 ....DLB-211; CDWLB-1
Tadijanović, Dragutin 1905- DLB-181
Tafdrup, Pia 1952- DLB-214
Tafolla, Carmen 1951- DLB-82
Taggard, Genevieve 1894-1948.........DLB-45
Taggart, John 1942- DLB-193
Tagger, Theodor (see Bruckner, Ferdinand)
Taiheiki late fourteenth century DLB-203
Tait, J. Selwin, and Sons DLB-49
Tait's Edinburgh Magazine 1832-1861......DLB-110
The Takarazaka Revue Company Y-91
Talander (see Bohse, August)
Talese, Gay 1932- DLB-185
Talev, Dimitr 1898-1966 ....DLB-181
Taliaferro, H. E. 1811-1875.............DLB-202
Tallent, Elizabeth 1954- DLB-130
TallMountain, Mary 1918-1994 ....DLB-193
Talvj 1797-1870 ....DLB-59, 133
Tamási, Áron 1897-1966 ....DLB-215
Tammsaare, A. H. 1878-1940 ....DLB-220; CDWLB-4
Tan, Amy 1952- DLB-173; CDALB-7
Tandori, Dezső 1938- DLB-232
Tanner, Thomas 1673/1674-1735 ....DLB-213
Tanizaki Jun'ichirō 1886-1965..........DLB-180
Tapahonso, Luci 1953- DLB-175
The Mark Taper Forum DLB-7
Taradash, Daniel 1913- DLB-44
Tarbell, Ida M. 1857-1944..............DLB-47
Tardivel, Jules-Paul 1851-1905 ....DLB-99
Targan, Barry 1932- DLB-130
Tarkington, Booth 1869-1946.........DLB-9, 102
Tashlin, Frank 1913-1972 ....DLB-44
Tasma (Jessie Couvreur) 1848-1897.....DLB-230
Tate, Allen 1899-1979 ...... DLB-4, 45, 63; DS-17
Tate, James 1943- DLB-5, 169
Tate, Nahum circa 1652-1715 ....DLB-80
Tatian circa 830 ....DLB-148
Taufer, Veno 1933- DLB-181
Tauler, Johannes circa 1300-1361 ....DLB-179
Tavčar, Ivan 1851-1923 ....DLB-147
Taverner, Richard ca. 1505-1575.........DLB-236
Taylor, Ann 1782-1866 ....DLB-163
Taylor, Bayard 1825-1878........DLB-3, 189, 250
Taylor, Bert Leston 1866-1921 ....DLB-25
Taylor, Charles H. 1846-1921..........DLB-25
Taylor, Edward circa 1642-1729 ....DLB-24

Taylor, Elizabeth 1912-1975 . . . . DLB-139	Theodulf circa 760-circa 821 . . . . DLB-148	Thomson, Edward William 1849-1924 . . . DLB-92
Taylor, Henry 1942- DLB-5	Theophrastus circa 371 B.C.-287 B.C. DLB-176	Thomson, James 1700-1748 . . . . DLB-95
Taylor, Sir Henry 1800-1886 . . . . DLB-32	Theriault, Yves 1915-1983 . . . . DLB-88	Thomson, James 1834-1882 . . . . DLB-35
Taylor, Jane 1783-1824 . . . . DLB-163	Thério, Adrien 1925- DLB-53	Thomson, Joseph 1858-1895 . . . . DLB-174
Taylor, Jeremy circa 1613-1667 . . . . DLB-151	Theroux, Paul 1941- DLB-2, 218; CDALB-7	Thomson, Mortimer 1831-1875 . . . . DLB-11
Taylor, John 1577 or 1578 - 1653 . . . . DLB-121	Thesiger, Wilfred 1910- DLB-204	Thon, Melanie Rae 1957- DLB-244
Taylor, Mildred D. ?- DLB-52	They All Came to Paris DS-16	Thoreau, Henry David
Taylor, Peter 1917-1994 . . . . . DLB-218; Y-81, Y-94	Thibaudeau, Colleen 1925- DLB-88	1817-1862 . . . . DLB-1, 183, 223; CDALB-2
Taylor, Susie King 1848-1912 . . . . DLB-221	Thielen, Benedict 1903-1965 . . . . DLB-102	The Thoreauvian Pilgrimage: The Structure of an
Taylor, William Howland 1901-1966 . . . DLB-241	Thiong'o Ngugi wa (see Ngugi wa Thiong'o)	American Cult DLB-223
Taylor, William, and Company DLB-49	Third-Generation Minor Poets of the	Thorpe, Adam 1956- DLB-231
Taylor-Made Shakespeare? Or Is "Shall I Die?" the	Seventeenth Century DLB-131	Thorpe, Thomas Bangs
Long-Lost Text of Bottom's Dream? Y-85	This Quarter 1925-1927, 1929-1932 . . . . DS-15	1815-1878 . . . . DLB-3, 11, 248
Teasdale, Sara 1884-1933 . . . . DLB-45	Thoma, Ludwig 1867-1921 . . . . DLB-66	Thorup, Kirsten 1942- DLB-214
Telles, Lygia Fagundes 1924- DLB-113	Thoma, Richard 1902- DLB-4	Thoughts on Poetry and Its Varieties (1833),
Temple, Sir William 1628-1699 . . . . DLB-101	Thomas, Audrey 1935- DLB-60	by John Stuart Mill DLB-32
Temple, William F. 1914-1989 . . . . DLB-255	Thomas, D. M. 1935- . . DLB-40, 207; CDBLB-8	Thrale, Hester Lynch
Temrizov, A. (see Marchenko, Anastasia Iakovlevna)	D. M. Thomas: The Plagiarism	(see Piozzi, Hester Lynch [Thrale])
Tench, Watkin ca. 1758-1833 . . . . DLB-230	Controversy Y-82	Thubron, Colin 1939- DLB-204, 231
Tenn, William 1919- DLB-8	Thomas, Dylan	Thucydides
Tennant, Emma 1937- DLB-14	1914-1953 . . . . . . DLB-13, 20, 139; CDBLB-7	circa 455 B.C.-circa 395 B.C. DLB-176
Tenney, Tabitha Gilman	The Dylan Thomas Celebration Y-99	Thulstrup, Thure de 1848-1930 . . . . DLB-188
1762-1837 . . . . DLB-37, 200	Thomas, Edward	Thümmel, Moritz August von
Tennyson, Alfred	1878-1917 . . . . DLB-19, 98, 156, 216	1738-1817 . . . . DLB-97
1809-1892 . . . . DLB-32; CDBLB-4	Thomas, Frederick William 1806-1866 . . DLB-202	Thurber, James
Tennyson, Frederick 1807-1898 . . . . DLB-32	Thomas, Gwyn 1913-1981 . . . . DLB-15, 245	1894-1961 . . . . DLB-4, 11, 22, 102; CDALB-5
Tenorio, Arthur 1924- DLB-209	Thomas, Isaiah 1750-1831 . . . . DLB-43, 73, 187	Thurman, Wallace 1902-1934 . . . . DLB-51
Tepliakov, Viktor Grigor'evich	Thomas, Isaiah [publishing house] DLB-49	Thwaite, Anthony 1930- DLB-40
1804-1842 . . . . DLB-205	Thomas, Johann 1624-1679 . . . . DLB-168	The Booker Prize
Terence circa 184 B.C.-159 B.C. or after	Thomas, John 1900-1932 . . . . DLB-4	Address by Anthony Thwaite,
. . . . DLB-211; CDWLB-1	Thomas, Joyce Carol 1938- DLB-33	Chairman of the Booker Prize Judges
Terhune, Albert Payson 1872-1942 . . . . . . DLB-9	Thomas, Lorenzo 1944- DLB-41	Comments from Former Booker
Terhune, Mary Virginia	Thomas, R. S. 1915-2000 . . . . . DLB-27; CDBLB-8	Prize Winners Y-86
1830-1922 . . . . DS-13, DS-16	Thomasîn von Zerclære	Thwaites, Reuben Gold 1853-1913 . . . . . . DLB-47
Terry, Megan 1932- DLB-7, 249	circa 1186-circa 1259 . . . . DLB-138	Tibullus circa 54 B.C.-circa 19 B.C. DLB-211
Terson, Peter 1932- DLB-13	Thomasius, Christian 1655-1728 . . . . DLB-168	Ticknor, George 1791-1871 . . . DLB-1, 59, 140, 235
Tesich, Steve 1943-1996 . . . . Y-83	Thompson, Daniel Pierce 1795-1868 . . . . DLB-202	Ticknor and Fields DLB-49
Tessa, Delio 1886-1939 . . . . DLB-114	Thompson, David 1770-1857 . . . . DLB-99	Ticknor and Fields (revived) DLB-46
Testori, Giovanni 1923-1993 . . . . DLB-128, 177	Thompson, Dorothy 1893-1961 . . . . DLB-29	Tieck, Ludwig 1773-1853 . . . . DLB-90; CDWLB-2
Tey, Josephine 1896?-1952 . . . . DLB-77	Thompson, E. P. 1924-1993 . . . . DLB-242	Tietjens, Eunice 1884-1944 . . . . DLB-54
Thacher, James 1754-1844 . . . . DLB-37	Thompson, Flora 1876-1947 . . . . DLB-240	Tikkanen, Märta 1935- DLB-257
Thackeray, William Makepeace	Thompson, Francis	Tilghman, Christopher circa 1948 . . . . . . DLB-244
1811-1863 . . . DLB-21, 55, 159, 163; CDBLB-4	1859-1907 . . . . DLB-19; CDBLB-5	Tilney, Edmund circa 1536-1610 . . . . DLB-136
Thames and Hudson Limited DLB-112	Thompson, George Selden (see Selden, George)	Tilt, Charles [publishing house] DLB-106
Thanet, Octave (see French, Alice)	Thompson, Henry Yates 1838-1928 . . . . DLB-184	Tilton, J. E., and Company DLB-49
Thatcher, John Boyd 1847-1909 . . . . DLB-187	Thompson, Hunter S. 1939- DLB-185	Time and Western Man (1927), by Wyndham
Thaxter, Celia Laighton 1835-1894 . . . . . DLB-239	Thompson, Jim 1906-1977 . . . . DLB-226	Lewis [excerpts] DLB-36
Thayer, Caroline Matilda Warren	Thompson, John 1938-1976 . . . . DLB-60	Time-Life Books DLB-46
1785-1844 . . . . DLB-200	Thompson, John R. 1823-1873 . . . . DLB-3, 73, 248	Times Books DLB-46
Thayer, Douglas 1929- DLB-256	Thompson, Lawrance 1906-1973 . . . . . . DLB-103	Timothy, Peter circa 1725-1782 . . . . DLB-43
The Theatre Guild DLB-7	Thompson, Maurice 1844-1901 . . . . . . DLB-71, 74	Timrava 1867-1951 . . . . DLB-215
The Theater in Shakespeare's Time DLB-62	Thompson, Ruth Plumly 1891-1976 . . . . . DLB-22	Timrod, Henry 1828-1867 . . . . DLB-3, 248
Thegan and the Astronomer	Thompson, Thomas Phillips 1843-1933 . . DLB-99	Tindal, Henrietta 1818?-1879 . . . . DLB-199
flourished circa 850 . . . . DLB-148	Thompson, William 1775-1833 . . . . DLB-158	Tinker, Chauncey Brewster 1876-1963 . . DLB-140
Thelwall, John 1764-1834 . . . . DLB-93, 158	Thompson, William Tappan	Tinsley Brothers DLB-106
Theocritus circa 300 B.C.-260 B.C. DLB-176	1812-1882 . . . . DLB-3, 11, 248	Tiptree, James, Jr. 1915-1987 . . . . DLB-8
Theodorescu, Ion N. (see Arghezi, Tudor)		Tišma, Aleksandar 1924- DLB-181
		Titus, Edward William
		1870-1952 . . . . DLB-4; DS-15

Tiutchev, Fedor Ivanovich 1803-1873 ....DLB-205

Tlali, Miriam 1933- DLB-157, 225

Todd, Barbara Euphan 1890-1976.......DLB-160

Todorov, Tzvetan 1939- DLB-242

Tofte, Robert
  1561 or 1562-1619 or 1620..........DLB-172

Toklas, Alice B. 1877-1967................DLB-4

Tokuda, Shūsei 1872-1943.............DLB-180

Toland, John 1670-1722...............DLB-252

Tolkien, J. R. R.
  1892-1973 ......DLB-15, 160, 255; CDBLB-6

Toller, Ernst 1893-1939................DLB-124

Tollet, Elizabeth 1694-1754 .. ..DLB-95

Tolson, Melvin B. 1898-1966 ....DLB-48, 76

Tolstoy, Aleksei Konstantinovich
  1817-1875.......................DLB-238

Tolstoy, Leo 1828-1910...............DLB-238

Tom Jones (1749), by Henry Fielding
  [excerpt].........................DLB-39

Tomalin, Claire 1933- DLB-155

Tomasi di Lampedusa, Giuseppe
  1896-1957 ....DLB-177

Tomlinson, Charles 1927- DLB-40

Tomlinson, H. M. 1873-1958 ...DLB-36, 100, 195

Tompkins, Abel [publishing house].......DLB-49

Tompson, Benjamin 1642-1714.........DLB-24

Tomson, Graham R.
  (see Watson, Rosamund Marriott)

Ton'a 1289-1372 ....DLB-203

Tondelli, Pier Vittorio 1955-1991 ....DLB-196

Tonks, Rosemary 1932- DLB-14, 207

Tonna, Charlotte Elizabeth 1790-1846 ...DLB-163

Tonson, Jacob the Elder
  [publishing house] DLB-170

Toole, John Kennedy 1937-1969 ....Y-81

Toomer, Jean 1894-1967 ...DLB-45, 51; CDALB-4

Tor Books DLB-46

Torberg, Friedrich 1908-1979 ....DLB-85

Torrence, Ridgely 1874-1950.......DLB-54, 249

Torres-Metzger, Joseph V. 1933- DLB-122

Toth, Susan Allen 1940 ....Y-86

Tottell, Richard [publishing house] DLB-170

"The Printer to the Reader," (1557)
  by Richard Tottell.................DLB-167

Tough-Guy Literature DLB-9

Touré, Askia Muhammad 1938- DLB-41

Tourgée, Albion W. 1838-1905..........DLB-79

Tournemir, Elizaveta Sailhas de (see Tur, Evgeniia)

Tourneur, Cyril circa 1580-1626.........DLB-58

Tournier, Michel 1924- DLB-83

Tousey, Frank [publishing house].......DLB-49

Tower Publications DLB-46

Towne, Benjamin circa 1740-1793.......DLB-43

Towne, Robert 1936- DLB-44

The Townely Plays fifteenth and sixteenth
  centuries DLB-146

Townshend, Aurelian
  by 1583-circa 1651 ....DLB-121

Toy, Barbara 1908- DLB-204

Tracy, Honor 1913- DLB-15

Traherne, Thomas 1637?-1674 ....DLB-131

Traill, Catharine Parr 1802-1899........DLB-99

Train, Arthur 1875-1945 ....DLB-86; DS-16

The Transatlantic Publishing Company ...DLB-49

The Transatlantic Review 1924-1925.........DS-15

The Transcendental Club 1836-1840 ....DLB-223

Transcendentalism....................DLB-223

Transcendentalists, American DS-5

A Transit of Poets and Others: American
  Biography in 1982.................Y-82

transition 1927-1938....................DS-15

Translators of the Twelfth Century: Literary Issues
  Raised and Impact Created.........DLB-115

Tranströmer, Tomas 1931- DLB-257

Travel Writing, 1837-1875............DLB-166

Travel Writing, 1876-1909 ....DLB-174

Travel Writing, 1910-1939 ....DLB-195

Traven, B. 1882? or 1890?-1969?......DLB-9, 56

Travers, Ben 1886-1980 ....DLB-10, 233

Travers, P. L. (Pamela Lyndon)
  1899-1996.....................DLB-160

Trediakovsky, Vasilii Kirillovich
  1703-1769 ....DLB-150

Treece, Henry 1911-1966 ....DLB-160

Trejo, Ernesto 1950- DLB-122

Trelawny, Edward John
  1792-1881 .... DLB-110, 116, 144

Tremain, Rose 1943- DLB-14

Tremblay, Michel 1942- DLB-60

Trends in Twentieth-Century
  Mass Market Publishing DLB-46

Trent, William P. 1862-1939...........DLB-47

Trescot, William Henry 1822-1898.......DLB-30

Tressell, Robert (Robert Phillipe Noonan)
  1870-1911......................DLB-197

Trevelyan, Sir George Otto
  1838-1928 ....DLB-144

Trevisa, John circa 1342-circa 1402......DLB-146

Trevor, William 1928- DLB-14, 139

Trierer Floyris circa 1170-1180..........DLB-138

Trillin, Calvin 1935- DLB-185

Trilling, Lionel 1905-1975 ....DLB-28, 63

Trilussa 1871-1950...................DLB-114

Trimmer, Sarah 1741-1810 ....DLB-158

Triolet, Elsa 1896-1970 ....DLB-72

Tripp, John 1927- DLB-40

Trocchi, Alexander 1925- DLB-15

Troisi, Dante 1920-1989 ....DLB-196

Trollope, Anthony
  1815-1882 .... DLB-21, 57, 159; CDBLB-4

Trollope, Frances 1779-1863 ....DLB-21, 166

Trollope, Joanna 1943- DLB-207

Troop, Elizabeth 1931- DLB-14

Trotter, Catharine 1679-1749........DLB-84, 252

Trotti, Lamar 1898-1952 ....DLB-44

Trottier, Pierre 1925- DLB-60

Trotzig, Birgitta 1929- DLB-257

Troubadours, *Trobaíritz,* and Trouvères ...DLB-208

Troupe, Quincy Thomas, Jr. 1943- DLB-41

Trow, John F., and Company DLB-49

Trowbridge, John Townsend 1827-1916 ..DLB-202

Trudel, Jean-Louis 1967- DLB-251

Truillier-Lacombe, Joseph-Patrice
  1807-1863 ....DLB-99

Trumbo, Dalton 1905-1976.............DLB-26

Trumbull, Benjamin 1735-1820..........DLB-30

Trumbull, John 1750-1831.............DLB-31

Trumbull, John 1756-1843.............DLB-183

Truth, Sojourner 1797?-1883...........DLB-239

Tscherning, Andreas 1611-1659 ....DLB-164

Tsubouchi, Shōyō 1859-1935 ....DLB-180

Tucholsky, Kurt 1890-1935............DLB-56

Tucker, Charlotte Maria
  1821-1893 ....DLB-163, 190

Tucker, George 1775-1861........DLB-3, 30, 248

Tucker, James 1808?-1866?............DLB-230

Tucker, Nathaniel Beverley
  1784-1851 ....DLB-3, 248

Tucker, St. George 1752-1827 ....DLB-37

Tuckerman, Frederick Goddard
  1821-1873 ....DLB-243

Tuckerman, Henry Theodore 1813-1871 ..DLB-64

Tumas, Juozas (see Vaizgantas)

Tunis, John R. 1889-1975 ....DLB-22, 171

Tunstall, Cuthbert 1474-1559 ....DLB-132

Tunström, Göran 1937-2000 ....DLB-257

Tuohy, Frank 1925- DLB-14, 139

Tupper, Martin F. 1810-1889 ....DLB-32

Tur, Evgeniia 1815-1892 ....DLB-238

Turbyfill, Mark 1896- DLB-45

Turco, Lewis 1934- Y-84

Turgenev, Aleksandr Ivanovich
  1784-1845 ....DLB-198

Turgenev, Ivan Sergeevich 1818-1883....DLB-238

Turnball, Alexander H. 1868-1918......DLB-184

Turnbull, Andrew 1921-1970 ....DLB-103

Turnbull, Gael 1928- DLB-40

Turner, Arlin 1909-1980 ....DLB-103

Turner, Charles (Tennyson)
  1808-1879 ....DLB-32

Turner, Ethel 1872-1958 ....DLB-230

Turner, Frederick 1943- DLB-40

Turner, Frederick Jackson
  1861-1932 ....DLB-17, 186

Turner, Joseph Addison 1826-1868.......DLB-79

Turpin, Waters Edward 1910-1968.......DLB-51

Turrini, Peter 1944- DLB-124

Tutuola, Amos 1920-1997 ...DLB-125; CDWLB-3

Twain, Mark (see Clemens, Samuel Langhorne)

Tweedie, Ethel Brilliana circa 1860-1940 . . DLB-174
The 'Twenties and Berlin, by Alex Natan . DLB-66
Two Hundred Years of Rare Books and
 Literary Collections at the
 University of South Carolina Y-00
Twombly, Wells 1935-1977 . . . . DLB-241
Twysden, Sir Roger 1597-1672 . . . . DLB-213
Tyler, Anne
 1941- DLB-6, 143; Y-82; CDALB-7
Tyler, Mary Palmer 1775-1866 . . . . DLB-200
Tyler, Moses Coit 1835-1900 . . . . DLB-47, 64
Tyler, Royall 1757-1826 . . . . DLB-37
Tylor, Edward Burnett 1832-1917 . . . . . . DLB-57
Tynan, Katharine 1861-1931 . . . . . . DLB-153, 240
Tyndale, William circa 1494-1536 . . . . . . DLB-132

U

Uchida, Yoshika 1921-1992 . . . . CDALB-7
Udall, Nicholas 1504-1556 . . . . DLB-62
Ugrešić, Dubravka 1949- DLB-181
Uhland, Ludwig 1787-1862 . . . . DLB-90
Uhse, Bodo 1904-1963 . . . . DLB-69
Ujević, Augustin ("Tin") 1891-1955 . . . . . DLB-147
Ulenhart, Niclas flourished circa 1600 . . . DLB-164
Ulibarrí, Sabine R. 1919- DLB-82
Ulica, Jorge 1870-1926 . . . . DLB-82
Ulivi, Ferruccio 1912- DLB-196
Ulizio, B. George 1889-1969 . . . . DLB-140
Ulrich von Liechtenstein
 circa 1200-circa 1275 . . . . DLB-138
Ulrich von Zatzikhoven
 before 1194-after 1214 . . . . DLB-138
Ulysses, Reader's Edition Y-97
Unaipon, David 1872-1967 . . . . DLB-230
Unamuno, Miguel de 1864-1936 . . . . . . DLB-108
Under, Marie 1883-1980
 . . . . DLB-220; CDWLB-4
Under the Microscope (1872), by
 A. C. Swinburne DLB-35
Underhill, Evelyn
 1875-1941 . . . . DLB-240
Ungaretti, Giuseppe 1888-1970 . . . . DLB-114
Unger, Friederike Helene 1741-1813 . . . . DLB-94
United States Book Company DLB-49
Universal Publishing and Distributing
 Corporation DLB-46
The University of Iowa
 Writers' Workshop
 Golden Jubilee Y-86
University of Missouri Press Y-01
The University of South Carolina Press Y-94
University of Wales Press DLB-112
University Press of Florida Y-00
University Press of Kansas Y-98
University Press of Mississippi Y-99
"The Unknown Public" (1858), by
 Wilkie Collins [excerpt] DLB-57
Uno, Chiyo 1897-1996 . . . . DLB-180

Unruh, Fritz von 1885-1970 . . . . DLB-56, 118
Unspeakable Practices II:
 The Festival of Vanguard
 Narrative at Brown University Y-93
Unsworth, Barry 1930- DLB-194
Unt, Mati 1944- DLB-232
The Unterberg Poetry Center of the
 92nd Street Y Y-98
Unwin, T. Fisher [publishing house] DLB-106
Upchurch, Boyd B. (see Boyd, John)
Updike, John 1932-
 . . . . DLB-2, 5, 143, 218, 227; Y-80, Y-82;
 DS-3; CDALB-6
John Updike on the Internet Y-97
Upīts, Andrejs 1877-1970 . . . . DLB-220
Upton, Bertha 1849-1912 . . . . DLB-141
Upton, Charles 1948- DLB-16
Upton, Florence K. 1873-1922 . . . . DLB-141
Upward, Allen 1863-1926 . . . . DLB-36
Urban, Milo 1904-1982 . . . . DLB-215
Urista, Alberto Baltazar (see Alurista)
Urquhart, Fred 1912- DLB-139
Urrea, Luis Alberto 1955- DLB-209
Urzidil, Johannes 1896-1976 . . . . DLB-85
The Uses of Facsimile Y-90
Usk, Thomas died 1388 . . . . DLB-146
Uslar Pietri, Arturo 1906- DLB-113
Ussher, James 1581-1656 . . . . DLB-213
Ustinov, Peter 1921- DLB-13
Uttley, Alison 1884-1976 . . . . DLB-160
Uz, Johann Peter 1720-1796 . . . . DLB-97

V

Vac, Bertrand 1914- DLB-88
Vācietis, Ojārs 1933-1983 . . . . DLB-232
Vaičiulaitis, Antanas 1906-1992 . . . . DLB-220
Vaculík, Ludvík 1926- DLB-232
Vaičiūnaite, Judita 1937- DLB-232
Vail, Laurence 1891-1968 . . . . DLB-4
Vailland, Roger 1907-1965 . . . . DLB-83
Vaižgantas 1869-1933 . . . . DLB-220
Vajda, Ernest 1887-1954 . . . . DLB-44
Valdés, Gina 1943- DLB-122
Valdez, Luis Miguel 1940- DLB-122
Valduga, Patrizia 1953- DLB-128
Valente, José Angel 1929-2000 . . . . DLB-108
Valenzuela, Luisa 1938- . . . DLB-113; CDWLB-3
Valeri, Diego 1887-1976 . . . . DLB-128
Valerius Flaccus fl. circa A.D. 92 . . . . . . DLB-211
Valerius Maximus fl. circa A.D. 31 . . . . . DLB-211
Valéry, Paul 1871-1945 . . . . DLB-258
Valesio, Paolo 1939- DLB-196
Valgardson, W. D. 1939- DLB-60
Valle, Víctor Manuel 1950- DLB-122
Valle-Inclán, Ramón del 1866-1936 . . . . DLB-134
Vallejo, Armando 1949- DLB-122

Vallès, Jules 1832-1885 . . . . DLB-123
Vallette, Marguerite Eymery (see Rachilde)
Valverde, José María 1926-1996 . . . . DLB-108
Van Allsburg, Chris 1949- DLB-61
Van Anda, Carr 1864-1945 . . . . DLB-25
van der Post, Laurens 1906-1996 . . . . DLB-204
Van Dine, S. S. (see Wright, Williard Huntington)
Van Doren, Mark 1894-1972 . . . . DLB-45
van Druten, John 1901-1957 . . . . DLB-10
Van Duyn, Mona 1921- DLB-5
Van Dyke, Henry 1852-1933 . . . . . . DLB-71; DS-13
Van Dyke, Henry 1928- DLB-33
Van Dyke, John C. 1856-1932 . . . . DLB-186
van Gulik, Robert Hans 1910-1967 . . . . . . DS-17
van Itallie, Jean-Claude 1936- DLB-7
Van Loan, Charles E. 1876-1919 . . . . DLB-171
Van Rensselaer, Mariana Griswold
 1851-1934 . . . . DLB-47
Van Rensselaer, Mrs. Schuyler
 (see Van Rensselaer, Mariana Griswold)
Van Vechten, Carl 1880-1964 . . . . DLB-4, 9
van Vogt, A. E. 1912-2000 . . . . DLB-8, 251
Vanbrugh, Sir John 1664-1726 . . . . DLB-80
Vance, Jack 1916?- DLB-8
Vančura, Vladislav
 1891-1942 . . . . DLB-215; CDWLB-4
Vane, Sutton 1888-1963 . . . . DLB-10
Vanguard Press DLB-46
Vann, Robert L. 1879-1940 . . . . DLB-29
Vargas Llosa, Mario
 1936- DLB-145; CDWLB-3
Varley, John 1947- Y-81
Varnhagen von Ense, Karl August
 1785-1858 . . . . DLB-90
Varnhagen von Ense, Rahel
 1771-1833 . . . . DLB-90
Varro 116 B.C.-27 B.C. DLB-211
Vasiliu, George (see Bacovia, George)
Vásquez, Richard 1928- DLB-209
Vásquez Montalbán, Manuel 1939- . . . DLB-134
Vassa, Gustavus (see Equiano, Olaudah)
Vassalli, Sebastiano 1941- DLB-128, 196
Vaughan, Henry 1621-1695 . . . . DLB-131
Vaughan, Thomas 1621-1666 . . . . DLB-131
Vaughn, Robert 1592?-1667 . . . . DLB-213
Vaux, Thomas, Lord 1509-1556 . . . . . . DLB-132
Vazov, Ivan 1850-1921 . . . . . . DLB-147; CDWLB-4
Véa Jr., Alfredo 1950- DLB-209
Veblen, Thorstein 1857-1929 . . . . DLB-246
Vega, Janine Pommy 1942- DLB-16
Veiller, Anthony 1903-1965 . . . . DLB-44
Velásquez-Trevino, Gloria 1949- DLB-122
Veley, Margaret 1843-1887 . . . . DLB-199
Velleius Paterculus
 circa 20 B.C.-circa A.D. 30 . . . . DLB-211
Veloz Maggiolo, Marcio 1936- DLB-145

Vel'tman, Aleksandr Fomich 1800-1870 .... DLB-198
Venegas, Daniel ?-? DLB-82
Venevitinov, Dmitrii Vladimirovich 1805-1827 .... DLB-205
Vergil, Polydore circa 1470-1555 .... DLB-132
Veríssimo, Erico 1905-1975 .... DLB-145
Verlaine, Paul 1844-1896 .... DLB-217
Verne, Jules 1828-1905 .... DLB-123
Verplanck, Gulian C. 1786-1870 .... DLB-59
Very, Jones 1813-1880 .... DLB-1, 243
Vian, Boris 1920-1959 .... DLB-72
Viazemsky, Petr Andreevich 1792-1878 .... DLB-205
Vicars, Thomas 1591-1638 .... DLB-236
Vickers, Roy 1888?-1965 .... DLB-77
Vickery, Sukey 1779-1821 .... DLB-200
Victoria 1819-1901 .... DLB-55
Victoria Press DLB-106
Vidal, Gore 1925- DLB-6, 152; CDALB-7
Vidal, Mary Theresa 1815-1873 .... DLB-230
Vidmer, Richards 1898-1978 .... DLB-241
Viebig, Clara 1860-1952 .... DLB-66
Viereck, George Sylvester 1884-1962 .... DLB-54
Viereck, Peter 1916- DLB-5
Viets, Roger 1738-1811 .... DLB-99
Viewpoint: Politics and Performance, by David Edgar DLB-13
Vigil-Piñon, Evangelina 1949- DLB-122
Vigneault, Gilles 1928- DLB-60
Vigny, Alfred de 1797-1863 .... DLB-119, 192, 217
Vigolo, Giorgio 1894-1983 .... DLB-114
The Viking Press DLB-46
Vilde, Eduard 1865-1933 .... DLB-220
Vilinskaia, Mariia Aleksandrovna (see Vovchok, Marko)
Villanueva, Alma Luz 1944- DLB-122
Villanueva, Tino 1941- DLB-82
Villard, Henry 1835-1900 .... DLB-23
Villard, Oswald Garrison 1872-1949 .... DLB-25, 91
Villarreal, Edit 1944- DLB-209
Villarreal, José Antonio 1924- DLB-82
Villaseñor, Victor 1940- DLB-209
Villegas de Magnón, Leonor 1876-1955 .... DLB-122
Villehardouin, Geoffroi de circa 1150-1215 .... DLB-208
Villemaire, Yolande 1949- DLB-60
Villena, Luis Antonio de 1951- DLB-134
Villiers, George, Second Duke of Buckingham 1628-1687 .... DLB-80
Villiers de l'Isle-Adam, Jean-Marie Mathias Philippe-Auguste, Comte de 1838-1889 .... DLB-123, 192
Villon, François 1431-circa 1463? DLB-208

Vine Press DLB-112
Viorst, Judith ?- DLB-52
Vipont, Elfrida (Elfrida Vipont Foulds, Charles Vipont) 1902-1992 .... DLB-160
Viramontes, Helena María 1954- DLB-122
Virgil 70 B.C.-19 B.C. DLB-211; CDWLB-1
Virtual Books and Enemies of Books Y-00
Vischer, Friedrich Theodor 1807-1887 ...DLB-133
Vitruvius circa 85 B.C.-circa 15 B.C. DLB-211
Vitry, Philippe de 1291-1361 .... DLB-208
Vivanco, Luis Felipe 1907-1975 .... DLB-108
Vivian, E. Charles 1882-1947 .... DLB-255
Viviani, Cesare 1947- DLB-128
Vivien, Renée 1877-1909 .... DLB-217
Vizenor, Gerald 1934- DLB-175, 227
Vizetelly and Company DLB-106
Voaden, Herman 1903- DLB-88
Voß, Johann Heinrich 1751-1826 .... DLB-90
Voigt, Ellen Bryant 1943- DLB-120
Vojnović, Ivo 1857-1929 ...... DLB-147; CDWLB-4
Volkoff, Vladimir 1932- DLB-83
Volland, P. F., Company DLB-46
Vollbehr, Otto H. F. 1872?-1945 or 1946 .... DLB-187
Vologdin (see Zasodimsky, Pavel Vladimirovich)
Volponi, Paolo 1924- DLB-177
Vonarburg, Élisabeth 1947- DLB-251
von der Grün, Max 1926- DLB-75
Vonnegut, Kurt 1922- DLB-2, 8, 152; Y-80; DS-3; CDALB-6
Voranc, Prežihov 1893-1950 .... DLB-147
Vovchok, Marko 1833-1907 .... DLB-238
Voynich, E. L. 1864-1960 .... DLB-197
Vroman, Mary Elizabeth circa 1924-1967 .... DLB-33

W

Wace, Robert ("Maistre") circa 1100-circa 1175 .... DLB-146
Wackenroder, Wilhelm Heinrich 1773-1798 .... DLB-90
Wackernagel, Wilhelm 1806-1869 .... DLB-133
Waddell, Helen 1889-1965 .... DLB-240
Waddington, Miriam 1917- DLB-68
Wade, Henry 1887-1969 .... DLB-77
Wagenknecht, Edward 1900- DLB-103
Wägner, Elin 1882-1949 .... DLB-259
Wagner, Heinrich Leopold 1747-1779 ..... DLB-94
Wagner, Henry R. 1862-1957 .... DLB-140
Wagner, Richard 1813-1883 .... DLB-129
Wagoner, David 1926- DLB-5, 256
Wah, Fred 1939- DLB-60
Waiblinger, Wilhelm 1804-1830 .... DLB-90
Wain, John 1925-1994 ... DLB-15, 27, 139, 155; CDBLB-8
Wainwright, Jeffrey 1944- DLB-40

Waite, Peirce and Company DLB-49
Wakeman, Stephen H. 1859-1924 ...... DLB-187
Wakoski, Diane 1937- DLB-5
Walahfrid Strabo circa 808-849 .... DLB-148
Walck, Henry Z. DLB-46
Walcott, Derek 1930- DLB-117; Y-81, Y-92; CDWLB-3
Waldegrave, Robert [publishing house] ...DLB-170
Waldman, Anne 1945- DLB-16
Waldrop, Rosmarie 1935- DLB-169
Walker, Alice 1900-1982 .... DLB-201
Walker, Alice 1944- DLB-6, 33, 143; CDALB-6
Walker, Annie Louisa (Mrs. Harry Coghill) circa 1836-1907 .... DLB-240
Walker, George F. 1947- DLB-60
Walker, John Brisben 1847-1931 .... DLB-79
Walker, Joseph A. 1935- DLB-38
Walker, Margaret 1915- DLB-76, 152
Walker, Ted 1934- DLB-40
Walker and Company DLB-49
Walker, Evans and Cogswell Company ... DLB-49
Wall, John F. (see Sarban)
Wallace, Alfred Russel 1823-1913 ...... DLB-190
Wallace, Dewitt 1889-1981 and Lila Acheson Wallace 1889-1984 .... DLB-137
Wallace, Edgar 1875-1932 .... DLB-70
Wallace, Lew 1827-1905 .... DLB-202
Wallace, Lila Acheson (see Wallace, Dewitt, and Lila Acheson Wallace)
Wallace, Naomi 1960- DLB-249
Wallant, Edward Lewis 1926-1962 .... DLB-2, 28, 143
Waller, Edmund 1606-1687 .... DLB-126
Walpole, Horace 1717-1797 ..... DLB-39, 104, 213
Preface to the First Edition of The Castle of Otranto (1764) DLB-39
Preface to the Second Edition of The Castle of Otranto (1765) DLB-39
Walpole, Hugh 1884-1941 .... DLB-34
Walrond, Eric 1898-1966 .... DLB-51
Walser, Martin 1927- DLB-75, 124
Walser, Robert 1878-1956 .... DLB-66
Walsh, Ernest 1895-1926 .... DLB-4, 45
Walsh, Robert 1784-1859 .... DLB-59
Walters, Henry 1848-1931 .... DLB-140
Waltharius circa 825 .... DLB-148
Walther von der Vogelweide circa 1170-circa 1230 .... DLB-138
Walton, Izaak 1593-1683 .... DLB-151, 213; CDBLB-1
Wambaugh, Joseph 1937- DLB-6; Y-83
Wand, Alfred Rudolph 1828-1891 ...... DLB-188
Waniek, Marilyn Nelson 1946- DLB-120
Wanley, Humphrey 1672-1726 .... DLB-213
Warburton, William 1698-1779 .... DLB-104
Ward, Aileen 1919- DLB-111

Cumulative Index

Ward, Artemus (see Browne, Charles Farrar)
Ward, Arthur Henry Sarsfield (see Rohmer, Sax)
Ward, Douglas Turner 1930- DLB-7, 38
Ward, Mrs. Humphry 1851-1920 .... DLB-18
Ward, Lynd 1905-1985 .... DLB-22
Ward, Lock and Company DLB-106
Ward, Nathaniel circa 1578-1652 .... DLB-24
Ward, Theodore 1902-1983............ DLB-76
Wardle, Ralph 1909-1988 .... DLB-103
Ware, Henry, Jr. 1794-1843 .... DLB-235
Ware, William 1797-1852 .... DLB-1, 235
Warfield, Catherine Ann 1816-1877 ..... DLB-248
Waring, Anna Letitia 1823-1910......... DLB-240
Warne, Frederick, and Company [U.K.]... DLB-106
Warne, Frederick, and Company [U.S.] ... DLB-49
Warner, Anne 1869-1913............. DLB-202
Warner, Charles Dudley 1829-1900...... DLB-64
Warner, Marina 1946- DLB-194
Warner, Rex 1905- DLB-15
Warner, Susan 1819-1885 ... DLB-3, 42, 239, 250
Warner, Sylvia Townsend
  1893-1978.................. DLB-34, 139
Warner, William 1558-1609............DLB-172
Warner Books DLB-46
Warr, Bertram 1917-1943.............. DLB-88
Warren, John Byrne Leicester (see De Tabley, Lord)
Warren, Lella 1899-1982 .... Y-83
Warren, Mercy Otis 1728-1814 ..... DLB-31, 200
Warren, Robert Penn 1905-1989
  ....DLB-2, 48, 152; Y-80, Y-89; CDALB-6
Warren, Samuel 1807-1877............ DLB-190
Die Wartburgkrieg circa 1230-circa 1280... DLB-138
Warton, Joseph 1722-1800 .... DLB-104, 109
Warton, Thomas 1728-1790 .... DLB-104, 109
Warung, Price (William Astley)
  1855-1911..................... DLB-230
Washington, George 1732-1799 .... DLB-31
Wassermann, Jakob 1873-1934......... DLB-66
Wasserstein, Wendy 1950- DLB-228
Wasson, David Atwood 1823-1887 ... DLB-1, 223
Watanna, Onoto (see Eaton, Winnifred)
Waterhouse, Keith 1929- DLB-13, 15
Waterman, Andrew 1940- DLB-40
Waters, Frank 1902-1995.........DLB-212; Y-86
Waters, Michael 1949- DLB-120
Watkins, Tobias 1780-1855 .... DLB-73
Watkins, Vernon 1906-1967 .... DLB-20
Watmough, David 1926- DLB-53
Watson, James Wreford (see Wreford, James)
Watson, John 1850-1907 .... DLB-156
Watson, Rosamund Marriott
  (Graham R. Tomson) 1860-1911.... DLB-240
Watson, Sheila 1909- DLB-60
Watson, Thomas 1545?-1592.......... DLB-132
Watson, Wilfred 1911- DLB-60

Watt, W. J., and Company DLB-46
Watten, Barrett 1948- DLB-193
Watterson, Henry 1840-1921.......... DLB-25
Watts, Alan 1915-1973 .... DLB-16
Watts, Franklin [publishing house]....... DLB-46
Watts, Isaac 1674-1748 .... DLB-95
Waugh, Alec 1898-1981............... DLB-191
Waugh, Auberon 1939-2000 ...DLB-14, 194; Y-00
The Cult of Biography
  Excerpts from the Second Folio Debate:
  "Biographies are generally a disease of
  English Literature".................. Y-86
Waugh, Evelyn
  1903-1966 ..... DLB-15, 162, 195; CDBLB-6
Way and Williams DLB-49
Wayman, Tom 1945- DLB-53
We See the Editor at Work Y-97
Weatherly, Tom 1942- DLB-41
Weaver, Gordon 1937- DLB-130
Weaver, Robert 1921- DLB-88
Webb, Beatrice 1858-1943 and
  Webb, Sidney 1859-1947.......... DLB-190
Webb, Francis 1925-1973 .... DLB-260
Webb, Frank J. ?-? DLB-50
Webb, James Watson 1802-1884 .... DLB-43
Webb, Mary 1881-1927 .... DLB-34
Webb, Phyllis 1927- DLB-53
Webb, Walter Prescott 1888-1963....... DLB-17
Webbe, William ?-1591 .... DLB-132
Webber, Charles Wilkins 1819-1856?... DLB-202
Webling, Lucy (Lucy Betty MacRaye)
  1877-1952 .... DLB-240
Webling, Peggy (Arthur Weston)
  1871-1949.................... DLB-240
Webster, Augusta 1837-1894 ..... DLB-35, 240
Webster, Charles L., and Company...... DLB-49
Webster, John
  1579 or 1580-1634? DLB-58; CDBLB-1
John Webster: The Melbourne
  Manuscript..................... Y-86
Webster, Noah
  1758-1843...... DLB-1, 37, 42, 43, 73, 243
Weckherlin, Georg Rodolf 1584-1653 ... DLB-164
Wedekind, Frank
  1864-1918 .... DLB-118; CDBLB-2
Weeks, Edward Augustus, Jr.
  1898-1989 .... DLB-137
Weeks, Stephen B. 1865-1918 .... DLB-187
Weems, Mason Locke 1759-1825...DLB-30, 37, 42
Weerth, Georg 1822-1856 .... DLB-129
Weidenfeld and Nicolson............. DLB-112
Weidman, Jerome 1913-1998.......... DLB-28
Weiß, Ernst 1882-1940................ DLB-81
Weigl, Bruce 1949- DLB-120
Weinbaum, Stanley Grauman 1902-1935 .. DLB-8
Weiner, Andrew 1949- DLB-251
Weintraub, Stanley 1929- DLB-111; Y82

The Practice of Biography: An Interview
  with Stanley Weintraub............... Y-82
Weise, Christian 1642-1708 .... DLB-168
Weisenborn, Gunther 1902-1969.... DLB-69, 124
Weiss, John 1818-1879 .... DLB-1, 243
Weiss, Peter 1916-1982 .... DLB-69, 124
Weiss, Theodore 1916- DLB-5
Weisse, Christian Felix 1726-1804 .... DLB-97
Weitling, Wilhelm 1808-1871.......... DLB-129
Welch, James 1940- DLB-175, 256
Welch, Lew 1926-1971?............... DLB-16
Weldon, Fay 1931- DLB-14, 194; CDBLB-8
Wellek, René 1903-1995 .... DLB-63
Wells, Carolyn 1862-1942 .... DLB-11
Wells, Charles Jeremiah circa 1800-1879 .. DLB-32
Wells, Gabriel 1862-1946............. DLB-140
Wells, H. G.
  1866-1946 ...DLB-34, 70, 156, 178; CDBLB-6
Wells, Helena 1758?-1824 .... DLB-200
Wells, Robert 1947- DLB-40
Wells-Barnett, Ida B. 1862-1931..... DLB-23, 221
Welty, Eudora 1909- DLB-2, 102, 143;
  .... Y-87, Y-01; DS-12; CDALB-1
Eudora Welty: Eye of the Storyteller Y-87
Eudora Welty Newsletter.................. Y-99
Eudora Welty's Funeral Y-01
Eudora Welty's Ninetieth Birthday Y-99
Wendell, Barrett 1855-1921 .... DLB-71
Wentworth, Patricia 1878-1961 .... DLB-77
Wentworth, William Charles
  1790-1872..................... DLB-230
Werder, Diederich von dem 1584-1657.. DLB-164
Werfel, Franz 1890-1945 .... DLB-81, 124
Werner, Zacharias 1768-1823........... DLB-94
The Werner Company................ DLB-49
Wersba, Barbara 1932- DLB-52
Wescott, Glenway 1901- DLB-4, 9, 102
Wesker, Arnold 1932- DLB-13; CDBLB-8
Wesley, Charles 1707-1788 .... DLB-95
Wesley, John 1703-1791 .... DLB-104
Wesley, Mary 1912- DLB-231
Wesley, Richard 1945- DLB-38
Wessels, A., and Company DLB-46
Wessobrunner Gebet circa 787-815 .... DLB-148
West, Anthony 1914-1988 .... DLB-15
West, Cornel 1953- DLB-246
West, Dorothy 1907-1998............. DLB-76
West, Jessamyn 1902-1984..........DLB-6; Y-84
West, Mae 1892-1980 .... DLB-44
West, Michelle Sagara 1963- DLB-251
West, Nathanael
  1903-1940 .... DLB-4, 9, 28; CDALB-5
West, Paul 1930- DLB-14
West, Rebecca 1892-1983 ....DLB-36; Y-83
West, Richard 1941- DLB-185
West and Johnson DLB-49

DLB 260   Cumulative Index

Westcott, Edward Noyes 1846-1898 .... DLB-202
The Western Messenger 1835-1841 .... DLB-223
Western Publishing Company DLB-46
Western Writers of America Y-99
The Westminster Review 1824-1914 .... DLB-110
Weston, Arthur (see Webling, Peggy)
Weston, Elizabeth Jane circa 1582-1612 .. DLB-172
Wetherald, Agnes Ethelwyn 1857-1940 ... DLB-99
Wetherell, Elizabeth (see Warner, Susan)
Wetherell, W. D. 1948- DLB-234
Wetzel, Friedrich Gottlob 1779-1819 ...... DLB-90
Weyman, Stanley J. 1855-1928 ..... DLB-141, 156
Wezel, Johann Karl 1747-1819 .... DLB-94
Whalen, Philip 1923- DLB-16
Whalley, George 1915-1983 .... DLB-88
Wharton, Edith 1862-1937
 ..... DLB-4, 9, 12, 78, 189; DS-13; CDALB-3
Wharton, William 1920s?- Y-80
"What You Lose on the Swings You Make Up
 on the Merry-Go-Round" Y-99
Whately, Mary Louisa 1824-1889 .... DLB-166
Whately, Richard 1787-1863 .... DLB-190
From *Elements of Rhetoric* (1828;
 revised, 1846) DLB-57
What's Really Wrong With Bestseller Lists .. Y-84
Wheatley, Dennis 1897-1977 .... DLB-77, 255
Wheatley, Phillis
 circa 1754-1784 .... DLB-31, 50; CDALB-2
Wheeler, Anna Doyle 1785-1848? DLB-158
Wheeler, Charles Stearns 1816-1843 ... DLB-1, 223
Wheeler, Monroe 1900-1988 .... DLB-4
Wheelock, John Hall 1886-1978 .... DLB-45
From John Hall Wheelock's Oral Memoir ... Y-01
Wheelwright, J. B. 1897-1940 .... DLB-45
Wheelwright, John circa 1592-1679 ...... DLB-24
Whetstone, George 1550-1587 .... DLB-136
Whetstone, Colonel Pete (see Noland, C. F. M.)
Whichcote, Benjamin 1609?-1683 .... DLB-252
Whicher, Stephen E. 1915-1961 .... DLB-111
Whipple, Edwin Percy 1819-1886 ...... DLB-1, 64
Whitaker, Alexander 1585-1617 .... DLB-24
Whitaker, Daniel K. 1801-1881 .... DLB-73
Whitcher, Frances Miriam
 1812-1852 .... DLB-11, 202
White, Andrew 1579-1656 .... DLB-24
White, Andrew Dickson 1832-1918 ...... DLB-47
White, E. B. 1899-1985 .... DLB-11, 22; CDALB-7
White, Edgar B. 1947- DLB-38
White, Edmund 1940- DLB-227
White, Ethel Lina 1887-1944 .... DLB-77
White, Hayden V. 1928- DLB-246
White, Henry Kirke 1785-1806 .... DLB-96
White, Horace 1834-1916 .... DLB-23
White, Patrick 1912-1990 .... DLB-260
White, Phyllis Dorothy James (see James, P. D.)
White, Richard Grant 1821-1885 .... DLB-64

White, T. H. 1906-1964 .... DLB-160, 255
White, Walter 1893-1955 .... DLB-51
White, William, and Company DLB-49
White, William Allen 1868-1944 ...... DLB-9, 25
White, William Anthony Parker
 (see Boucher, Anthony)
White, William Hale (see Rutherford, Mark)
Whitechurch, Victor L. 1868-1933 .... DLB-70
Whitehead, Alfred North 1861-1947 .... DLB-100
Whitehead, James 1936- Y-81
Whitehead, William 1715-1785 ..... DLB-84, 109
Whitfield, James Monroe 1822-1871 ..... DLB-50
Whitfield, Raoul 1898-1945 .... DLB-226
Whitgift, John circa 1533-1604 .... DLB-132
Whiting, John 1917-1963 .... DLB-13
Whiting, Samuel 1597-1679 .... DLB-24
Whitlock, Brand 1869-1934 .... DLB-12
Whitman, Albert, and Company DLB-46
Whitman, Albery Allson 1851-1901 ...... DLB-50
Whitman, Alden 1913-1990 .... Y-91
Whitman, Sarah Helen (Power)
 1803-1878 .... DLB-1, 243
Whitman, Walt
 1819-1892 .... DLB-3, 64, 224, 250; CDALB-2
Whitman Publishing Company DLB-46
Whitney, Geoffrey 1548 or 1552?-1601 .. DLB-136
Whitney, Isabella flourished 1566-1573 ... DLB-136
Whitney, John Hay 1904-1982 .... DLB-127
Whittemore, Reed 1919-1995 .... DLB-5
Whittier, John Greenleaf
 1807-1892 .... DLB-1, 243; CDALB-2
Whittlesey House DLB-46
Who Runs American Literature? Y-94
Whose *Ulysses*? The Function of Editing Y-97
Wickham, Anna (Edith Alice Mary Harper)
 1884-1947 .... DLB-240
Wicomb, Zoë 1948- DLB-225
Wideman, John Edgar 1941- DLB-33, 143
Widener, Harry Elkins 1885-1912 ...... DLB-140
Wiebe, Rudy 1934- DLB-60
Wiechert, Ernst 1887-1950 .... DLB-56
Wied, Martina 1882-1957 .... DLB-85
Wiehe, Evelyn May Clowes (see Mordaunt, Elinor)
Wieland, Christoph Martin 1733-1813 .... DLB-97
Wienbarg, Ludolf 1802-1872 .... DLB-133
Wieners, John 1934- DLB-16
Wier, Ester 1910- DLB-52
Wiesel, Elie
 1928- DLB-83; Y-86, 87; CDALB-7
Wiggin, Kate Douglas 1856-1923 .... DLB-42
Wigglesworth, Michael 1631-1705 ...... DLB-24
Wilberforce, William 1759-1833 .... DLB-158
Wilbrandt, Adolf 1837-1911 .... DLB-129
Wilbur, Richard
 1921- DLB-5, 169; CDALB-7
Wild, Peter 1940- DLB-5

Wilde, Lady Jane Francesca Elgee
 1821?-1896 .... DLB-199
Wilde, Oscar 1854-1900
 .... DLB-10, 19, 34, 57, 141, 156, 190;
 CDBLB-5
"The Critic as Artist" (1891) DLB-57
Oscar Wilde Conference at Hofstra
 University Y-00
From "The Decay of Lying" (1889) DLB-18
"The English Renaissance of
 Art" (1908) DLB-35
"L'Envoi" (1882) DLB-35
Wilde, Richard Henry 1789-1847 ...... DLB-3, 59
Wilde, W. A., Company DLB-49
Wilder, Billy 1906- DLB-26
Wilder, Laura Ingalls 1867-1957 ..... DLB-22, 256
Wilder, Thornton
 1897-1975 .... DLB-4, 7, 9, 228; CDALB-7
Thornton Wilder Centenary at Yale Y-97
Wildgans, Anton 1881-1932 .... DLB-118
Wiley, Bell Irvin 1906-1980 .... DLB-17
Wiley, John, and Sons DLB-49
Wilhelm, Kate 1928- DLB-8
Wilkes, Charles 1798-1877 .... DLB-183
Wilkes, George 1817-1885 .... DLB-79
Wilkins, John 1614-1672 .... DLB-236
Wilkinson, Anne 1910-1961 .... DLB-88
Wilkinson, Eliza Yonge
 1757-circa 1813 .... DLB-200
Wilkinson, Sylvia 1940- Y-86
Wilkinson, William Cleaver 1833-1920 ... DLB-71
Willard, Barbara 1909-1994 .... DLB-161
Willard, Emma 1787-1870 .... DLB-239
Willard, Frances E. 1839-1898 .... DLB-221
Willard, L. [publishing house] DLB-49
Willard, Nancy 1936- DLB-5, 52
Willard, Samuel 1640-1707 .... DLB-24
Willeford, Charles 1919-1988 .... DLB-226
William of Auvergne 1190-1249 .... DLB-115
William of Conches
 circa 1090-circa 1154 .... DLB-115
William of Ockham circa 1285-1347 .... DLB-115
William of Sherwood
 1200/1205-1266/1271 .... DLB-115
The William Chavrat American Fiction Collection
 at the Ohio State University Libraries Y-92
Williams, A., and Company DLB-49
Williams, Ben Ames 1889-1953 .... DLB-102
Williams, C. K. 1936- DLB-5
Williams, Chancellor 1905- DLB-76
Williams, Charles 1886-1945 ... DLB-100, 153, 255
Williams, Denis 1923-1998 .... DLB-117
Williams, Emlyn 1905-1987 .... DLB-10, 77
Williams, Garth 1912-1996 .... DLB-22
Williams, George Washington
 1849-1891 .... DLB-47
Williams, Heathcote 1941- DLB-13
Williams, Helen Maria 1761-1827 ...... DLB-158

507

Cumulative Index

Williams, Hugo 1942- DLB-40	Wilson, Mona 1872-1954 .... DLB-149	Wolfe, Reyner (Reginald) [publishing house] DLB-170
Williams, Isaac 1802-1865 .... DLB-32	Wilson, Robert Charles 1953- DLB-251	Wolfe, Thomas 1900-1938 .... DLB-9, 102, 229; Y-85; DS-2, DS-16; CDALB-5
Williams, Joan 1928- DLB-6	Wilson, Robley 1930- DLB-218	
Williams, Joe 1889-1972 .... DLB-241	Wilson, Romer 1891-1930 .... DLB-191	
Williams, John A. 1925- DLB-2, 33	Wilson, Thomas 1524-1581 .... DLB-132, 236	"All the Faults of Youth and Inexperience": A Reader's Report on Thomas Wolfe's *O Lost* Y-01
Williams, John E. 1922-1994 .... DLB-6	Wilson, Woodrow 1856-1924 .... DLB-47	
Williams, Jonathan 1929- DLB-5	Wimsatt, William K., Jr. 1907-1975 ...... DLB-63	Eugene Gant's Projected Works........... Y-01
Williams, Miller 1930- DLB-105	Winchell, Walter 1897-1972 .... DLB-29	The Thomas Wolfe Collection at the University of North Carolina at Chapel Hill Y-97
Williams, Nigel 1948- DLB-231	Winchester, J. [publishing house] DLB-49	
Williams, Raymond 1921- DLB-14, 231, 242	Winckelmann, Johann Joachim 1717-1768 .... DLB-97	Thomas Wolfe Centennial Celebration in Asheville Y-00
Williams, Roger circa 1603-1683 .... DLB-24		
Williams, Rowland 1817-1870 .... DLB-184	Winckler, Paul 1630-1686 .... DLB-164	Fire at Thomas Wolfe Memorial Y-98
Williams, Samm-Art 1946- DLB-38	Wind, Herbert Warren 1916- DLB-171	The Thomas Wolfe Society Y-97
Williams, Sherley Anne 1944-1999 ...... DLB-41	Windet, John [publishing house] DLB-170	Wolfe, Tom 1931- DLB-152, 185
Williams, T. Harry 1909-1979 .... DLB-17	Windham, Donald 1920- DLB-6	Wolfenstein, Martha 1869-1906 .... DLB-221
Williams, Tennessee 1911-1983..... DLB-7; Y-83; DS-4; CDALB-1	Wing, Donald Goddard 1904-1972 ..... DLB-187	Wolff, Helen 1906-1994 .... Y-94
	Wing, John M. 1844-1917 .... DLB-187	Wolff, Tobias 1945- DLB-130
Williams, Terry Tempest 1955- DLB-206	Wingate, Allan [publishing house] DLB-112	Wolfram von Eschenbach circa 1170-after 1220 .... DLB-138; CDWLB-2
Williams, Ursula Moray 1911- DLB-160	Winnemucca, Sarah 1844-1921 .... DLB-175	
Williams, Valentine 1883-1946 .... DLB-77	Winnifrith, Tom 1938- DLB-155	Wolfram von Eschenbach's *Parzival*: Prologue and Book 3 .... DLB-138
Williams, William Appleman 1921- DLB-17	Winning an Edgar Y-98	
Williams, William Carlos 1883-1963 ..... DLB-4, 16, 54, 86; CDALB-4	Winsloe, Christa 1888-1944 .... DLB-124	Wolker, Jiří 1900-1924 .... DLB-215
	Winslow, Anna Green 1759-1780 ...... DLB-200	Wollstonecraft, Mary 1759-1797 .... DLB-39, 104, 158, 252; CDBLB-3
Williams, Wirt 1921- DLB-6	Winsor, Justin 1831-1897 .... DLB-47	
Williams Brothers DLB-49	John C. Winston Company DLB-49	Wondratschek, Wolf 1943- DLB-75
Williamson, Henry 1895-1977 .... DLB-191	Winters, Yvor 1900-1968 .... DLB-48	Wood, Anthony à 1632-1695 .... DLB-213
Williamson, Jack 1908- DLB-8	Winthrop, John 1588-1649 .... DLB-24, 30	Wood, Benjamin 1820-1900 .... DLB-23
Willingham, Calder Baynard, Jr. 1922-1995 .... DLB-2, 44	Winthrop, John, Jr. 1606-1676 .... DLB-24	Wood, Charles 1932- DLB-13
	Winthrop, Margaret Tyndal 1591-1647 .. DLB-200	Wood, Mrs. Henry 1814-1887 .... DLB-18
Williram of Ebersberg circa 1020-1085 .. DLB-148	Winthrop, Theodore 1828-1861 .... DLB-202	Wood, Joanna E. 1867-1927 .... DLB-92
Willis, Nathaniel Parker 1806-1867 .... DLB-3, 59, 73, 74, 183, 250; DS-13	Wirt, William 1772-1834 .... DLB-37	Wood, Sally Sayward Barrell Keating 1759-1855 .... DLB-200
	Wise, John 1652-1725 .... DLB-24	
Willkomm, Ernst 1810-1886 .... DLB-133	Wise, Thomas James 1859-1937 .... DLB-184	Wood, Samuel [publishing house] DLB-49
Willumsen, Dorrit 1940- DLB-214	Wiseman, Adele 1928-1992 .... DLB-88	Wood, William ?-? DLB-24
Wills, Garry 1934- DLB-246	Wishart and Company DLB-112	The Charles Wood Affair: A Playwright Revived Y-83
Wilmer, Clive 1945- DLB-40	Wisner, George 1812-1849 .... DLB-43	
Wilson, A. N. 1950- DLB-14, 155, 194	Wister, Owen 1860-1938 .... DLB-9, 78, 186	Woodberry, George Edward 1855-1930 .... DLB-71, 103
Wilson, Angus 1913-1991 ..... DLB-15, 139, 155	Wister, Sarah 1761-1804 .... DLB-200	
Wilson, Arthur 1595-1652 .... DLB-58	Wither, George 1588-1667 .... DLB-121	Woodbridge, Benjamin 1622-1684 ...... DLB-24
Wilson, August 1945- DLB-228	Witherspoon, John 1723-1794 .... DLB-31	Woodcock, George 1912-1995 .... DLB-88
Wilson, Augusta Jane Evans 1835-1909 ... DLB-42	Withrow, William Henry 1839-1908 ..... DLB-99	Woodhull, Victoria C. 1838-1927 ...... DLB-79
Wilson, Colin 1931- DLB-14, 194	Witkacy (see Witkiewicz, Stanisław Ignacy)	Woodmason, Charles circa 1720-? DLB-31
Wilson, Edmund 1895-1972 .... DLB-63	Witkiewicz, Stanisław Ignacy 1885-1939 .... DLB-215; CDWLB-4	Woodress, Jr., James Leslie 1916- DLB-111
Wilson, Effingham [publishing house] ... DLB-154		Woods, Margaret L. 1855-1945 .... DLB-240
Wilson, Ethel 1888-1980 .... DLB-68	Wittig, Monique 1935- DLB-83	Woodson, Carter G. 1875-1950 .... DLB-17
Wilson, F. P. 1889-1963 .... DLB-201	Wodehouse, P. G. 1881-1975 .... DLB-34, 162; CDBLB-6	Woodward, C. Vann 1908-1999 .... DLB-17
Wilson, Harriet E. 1827/1828?-1863? DLB-50, 239, 243		Woodward, Stanley 1895-1965 .... DLB-171
	Wohmann, Gabriele 1932- DLB-75	Woodworth, Samuel 1785-1842 .... DLB-260
Wilson, Harry Leon 1867-1939 .... DLB-9	Woiwode, Larry 1941- DLB-6	Wooler, Thomas 1785 or 1786-1853 .... DLB-158
Wilson, John 1588-1667 .... DLB-24	Wolcot, John 1738-1819 .... DLB-109	Woolf, David (see Maddow, Ben)
Wilson, John 1785-1854 .... DLB-110	Wolcott, Roger 1679-1767 .... DLB-24	Woolf, Douglas 1922-1992 .... DLB-244
Wilson, John Dover 1881-1969 .... DLB-201	Wolf, Christa 1929- DLB-75; CDWLB-2	Woolf, Leonard 1880-1969 ......DLB-100; DS-10
Wilson, Lanford 1937- DLB-7	Wolf, Friedrich 1888-1953 .... DLB-124	Woolf, Virginia 1882-1941 .... DLB-36, 100, 162; DS-10; CDBLB-6
Wilson, Margaret 1882-1973 .... DLB-9	Wolfe, Gene 1931- DLB-8	
Wilson, Michael 1914-1978 .... DLB-44	Wolfe, John [publishing house] DLB-170	Woolf, Virginia, "The New Biography," *New York Herald Tribune*, 30 October 1927 ..... DLB-149
		Woollcott, Alexander 1887-1943 .... DLB-29

Woolman, John 1720-1772 . . . . DLB-31	Wurlitzer, Rudolph 1937- DLB-173	Yolen, Jane 1939- DLB-52
Woolner, Thomas 1825-1892 . . . . DLB-35	Wyatt, Sir Thomas circa 1503-1542 . . . . . DLB-132	Yonge, Charlotte Mary 1823-1901 . . . . DLB-18, 163
Woolrich, Cornell 1903-1968 . . . . DLB-226	Wycherley, William 1641-1715 . . . . DLB-80; CDBLB-2	The York Cycle circa 1376-circa 1569 . . . . DLB-146
Woolsey, Sarah Chauncy 1835-1905 . . . . . . DLB-42	Wyclif, John circa 1335-31 December 1384 . . . . DLB-146	*A Yorkshire Tragedy* DLB-58
Woolson, Constance Fenimore 1840-1894 . . . . DLB-12, 74, 189, 221	Wyeth, N. C. 1882-1945 . . . . DLB-188; DS-16	Yoseloff, Thomas [publishing house] DLB-46
Worcester, Joseph Emerson 1784-1865 . . . . DLB-1, 235	Wylie, Elinor 1885-1928 . . . . DLB-9, 45	Young, A. S. "Doc" 1919-1996 . . . . DLB-241
Worde, Wynkyn de [publishing house] . . . DLB-170	Wylie, Philip 1902-1971 . . . . DLB-9	Young, Al 1939- DLB-33
Wordsworth, Christopher 1807-1885 . . . . DLB-166	Wyllie, John Cook 1908-1968 . . . . DLB-140	Young, Arthur 1741-1820 . . . . DLB-158
Wordsworth, Dorothy 1771-1855 . . . . DLB-107	Wyman, Lillie Buffum Chace 1847-1929 . . . . DLB-202	Young, Dick 1917 or 1918 - 1987 . . . . DLB-171
Wordsworth, Elizabeth 1840-1932 . . . . DLB-98	Wymark, Olwen 1934- DLB-233	Young, Edward 1683-1765 . . . . DLB-95
Wordsworth, William 1770-1850 . . . . DLB-93, 107; CDBLB-3	Wyndham, John 1903-1969 . . . . DLB-255	Young, Frank A. "Fay" 1884-1957 . . . . DLB-241
Workman, Fanny Bullock 1859-1925 . . . . DLB-189	Wynne-Tyson, Esmé 1898-1972 . . . . DLB-191	Young, Francis Brett 1884-1954 . . . . DLB-191
The Works of the Rev. John Witherspoon (1800-1801) [excerpts] DLB-31	**X**	Young, Gavin 1928- DLB-204
A World Chronology of Important Science Fiction Works (1818-1979) DLB-8	Xenophon circa 430 B.C.-circa 356 B.C. . . . DLB-176	Young, Stark 1881-1963 . . . . . . DLB-9, 102; DS-16
World Literature Today: A Journal for the New Millennium Y-01	**Y**	Young, Waldeman 1880-1938 . . . . DLB-26
World Publishing Company DLB-46	Yasuoka Shōtarō 1920- DLB-182	Young, William [publishing house] DLB-49
World War II Writers Symposium at the University of South Carolina, 12-14 April 1995 . . . . Y-95	Yates, Dornford 1885-1960 . . . . DLB-77, 153	Young Bear, Ray A. 1950- DLB-175
Worthington, R., and Company DLB-49	Yates, J. Michael 1938- DLB-60	Yourcenar, Marguerite 1903-1987 . . . . DLB-72; Y-88
Wotton, Sir Henry 1568-1639 . . . . DLB-121	Yates, Richard 1926-1992 . . . . DLB-2, 234; Y-81, Y-92	"You've Never Had It So Good," Gusted by "Winds of Change": British Fiction in the 1950s, 1960s, and After DLB-14
Wouk, Herman 1915- Y-82; CDALB-7	Yau, John 1950- DLB-234	Yovkov, Yordan 1880-1937 . . DLB-147; CDWLB-4
Wreford, James 1915- DLB-88	Yavorov, Peyo 1878-1914 . . . . DLB-147	**Z**
Wren, Sir Christopher 1632-1723 . . . . DLB-213	The Year in Book Publishing Y-86	Zachariä, Friedrich Wilhelm 1726-1777 . . . . DLB-97
Wren, Percival Christopher 1885-1941 . . . . DLB-153	The Year in Book Reviewing and the Literary Situation Y-98	Zagajewski, Adam 1945- DLB-232
Wrenn, John Henry 1841-1911 . . . . DLB-140	The Year in British Drama Y-99, Y-00, Y-01	Zagoskin, Mikhail Nikolaevich 1789-1852 . . . . DLB-198
Wright, C. D. 1949- DLB-120	The Year in British Fiction Y-99, Y-00, Y-01	Zajc, Dane 1929- DLB-181
Wright, Charles 1935- . . . . DLB-165, Y 82	The Year in Children's Books Y-92-Y-96, Y-98, Y-99, Y-00, Y-01	Zālīte, Māra 1952- DLB-232
Wright, Charles Stevenson 1932- DLB-33	The Year in Children's Literature Y-97	Zamora, Bernice 1938- DLB-82
Wright, Frances 1795-1852 . . . . DLB-73	The Year in Drama . . . . Y-82-Y-85, Y-87 Y 96	Zand, Herbert 1923-1970 . . . . DLB-85
Wright, Harold Bell 1872-1944 . . . . DLB-9	The Year in Fiction . . . Y-84-Y-86, Y-89, Y-94-Y-99	Zangwill, Israel 1864-1926 . . . . . . DLB-10, 135, 197
Wright, James 1927-1980 . . . . DLB-5, 169; CDALB-7	The Year in Fiction: A Biased View Y-83	Zanzotto, Andrea 1921- DLB-128
Wright, Jay 1935- DLB-41	The Year in Literary Biography Y-83-Y-98, Y-00, Y-01	Zapata Olivella, Manuel 1920- DLB-113
Wright, Judith 1915-2000 . . . . DLB-260	The Year in Literary Theory Y-92-Y-93	Zasodimsky, Pavel Vladimirovich 1843-1912 . . . . DLB-238
Wright, Louis B. 1899-1984 . . . . DLB-17	The Year in London Theatre Y-92	Zebra Books DLB-46
Wright, Richard 1908-1960 . . . . . DLB-76, 102; DS-2; CDALB-5	The Year in the Novel Y-87, Y-88, Y-90-Y-93	Zebrowski, George 1945- DLB-8
Wright, Richard B. 1937- DLB-53	The Year in Poetry . . Y-83-Y-92, Y-94, Y-95, Y-96, Y-97, Y-98, Y-99, Y-00, Y-01	Zech, Paul 1881-1946 . . . . DLB-56
Wright, S. Fowler 1874-1965 . . . . DLB-255	The Year in Science Fiction and Fantasy Y-00, Y-01	Zeidner, Lisa 1955- DLB-120
Wright, Sarah Elizabeth 1928- DLB-33	The Year in Short Stories Y-87	Zeidonis, Imants 1933- DLB-232
Wright, Willard Huntington ("S. S. Van Dine") 1888-1939 . . . . DS-16	The Year in the Short Story Y-88, Y-90-Y-93	Zeami (Kanze Motokiyo) 1363-1443 . . . . . DLB-203
Wrigley, Robert 1951- DLB-256	The Year in Texas Literature Y-98	Zelazny, Roger 1937-1995 . . . . DLB-8
A Writer Talking: A Collage Y-00	The Year in U.S. Drama Y-00	Zenger, John Peter 1697-1746 . . . . DLB-24, 43
Writers and Politics: 1871-1918, by Ronald Gray DLB-66	The Year in U.S. Fiction Y-00, Y-01	Zepheria DLB-172
Writers and their Copyright Holders: the WATCH Project Y-94	The Year's Work in American Poetry Y-82	Zesen, Philipp von 1619-1689 . . . . DLB-164
Writers' Forum Y-85	The Year's Work in Fiction: A Survey Y-82	Zhukovsky, Vasilii Andreevich 1783-1852 . . . . DLB-205
Writing for the Theatre, by Harold Pinter DLB-13	Yearsley, Ann 1753-1806 . . . . DLB-109	Zieber, G. B., and Company DLB-49
Wroth, Lawrence C. 1884-1970 . . . . DLB-187	Yeats, William Butler 1865-1939 . . . . DLB-10, 19, 98, 156; CDBLB-5	Ziedonis, Imants 1933- CDWLB-4
Wroth, Lady Mary 1587-1653 . . . . DLB-121	Yep, Laurence 1948- DLB-52	Zieroth, Dale 1946- DLB-60
	Yerby, Frank 1916-1991 . . . . DLB-76	Zigler und Kliphausen, Heinrich Anshelm von 1663-1697 . . . . DLB-168
	Yezierska, Anzia 1880-1970 . . . . DLB-28, 221	Zimmer, Paul 1934- DLB-5
		Zinberg, Len (see Lacy, Ed)
		Zindel, Paul 1936- DLB-7, 52; CDALB-7

Cumulative Index

Zingref, Julius Wilhelm 1591-1635...... DLB-164
Zinnes, Harriet 1919- DLB-193
Zinzendorf, Nikolaus Ludwig von
 1700-1760..................... DLB-168
Zitkala-Ša 1876-1938................. DLB-175
Zīverts, Mārtiņš 1903-1990........... DLB-220
Zlatovratsky, Nikolai Nikolaevich
 1845-1911.................... DLB-238

Zola, Emile 1840-1902............... DLB-123
Zolla, Elémire 1926- DLB-196
Zolotow, Charlotte 1915- DLB-52
Zschokke, Heinrich 1771-1848......... DLB-94
Zubly, John Joachim 1724-1781 .... DLB-31
Zu-Bolton II, Ahmos 1936- DLB-41
Zuckmayer, Carl 1896-1977........ DLB-56, 124

Zukofsky, Louis 1904-1978 .... DLB-5, 165
Zupan, Vitomil 1914-1987............ DLB-181
Župančič, Oton 1878-1949...DLB-147; CDWLB-4
zur Mühlen, Hermynia 1883-1951....... DLB-56
Zweig, Arnold 1887-1968 .... DLB-66
Zweig, Stefan 1881-1942 .... DLB-81, 118

ISBN 0-7876-6004-3